SECOND EDITION

Management Accounting

Don R. Hansen
Oklahoma State University

Maryanne M. Mowen
Oklahoma State University

COLLEGE DIVISION South-Western Publishing Co.

Cincinnati Ohio

AQ61BA

Sponsoring Editor: Mark Hubble
Production Editor: Pamela Rockwell
Interior Design: Pamela Rockwell
Cover Design: Mike Fender

ISBN: 0-538-82165-5

1 2 3 4 5 6 7 AB 6 5 4 3 2 1

Printed in the United States of America

Library of Congress Cataloging-in-Publication Data

Hansen, Don R.
   Management accounting / Don R. Hansen, Maryanne M. Mowen. -- 2nd ed.
   p. cm.
   Includes index.
   ISBN 0-538-82165-5
   1. Managerial accounting.   I. Mowen, Maryanne M.   II. Title.
HF5657.4.H36 1992
658.15'11--dc20   91-39124
                                                              CIP

CONTENTS

· · · · · · · · · · · · · ·

P A R T 1 Cost Accumulation and Product Costing 27

■ **CHAPTER 4**
Process Costing 137

■ **CHAPTER 5**
Allocation: Service-Center Costs and Other Concepts 189

■ **CHAPTER 6**
Product Costing and Cost Management: The Advanced Manufacturing Environment 233

• • • • • • • • • • • • • • •

P A R T 2 Managerial Decision Making 301

■ **CHAPTER 7**
Special Pricing Decisions and Cost Behavior 303

■ **CHAPTER 8**
Cost-Volume-Profit Analysis: A Managerial Planning Tool   360

■ **CHAPTER 9**
Variable Costing: A Useful Management Tool   408

■ **CHAPTER 12**
Capital Budgeting: Additional Considerations   **551**

■ **CHAPTER 13**
Decision Making in the New Manufacturing Environment   **604**

P A R T   3   Planning and Control   661

■ CHAPTER 14
Budgeting for Planning and Control   663

■ CHAPTER 15
Standard Costing: A Managerial Control Tool   734

■ **CHAPTER 16**
Quality Costs and Productivity: Measurement and Control   **789**

■ **CHAPTER 17**
Decentralization, Performance Evaluation, and
Transfer Pricing   **851**

PREFACE

This text is designed to introduce students to the fundamentals of management accounting. It assumes that students have been introduced to the basics of financial accounting; however, extensive knowledge of financial accounting is not needed. Our emphasis is on the use of accounting information. Thus, the text should be of value to students with a variety of backgrounds. Although written to serve undergraduates, the text has also been used successfully at the graduate level. The assignment material has sufficient variety to accommodate both undergraduate and graduate students.

Many of the students in business schools who are required to take a course in management accounting are not majors in accounting. For these students, it is often difficult to appreciate the value of the concepts being taught. This text attempts to overcome this attitude by introducing each chapter with a motivational scenario. Most (but not all) of these scenarios are based on real-world experiences and involve managers who are faced with some problem that requires the use of accounting information for its resolution. Seeing that effective management requires a sound understanding of how to use accounting information should enhance the interest of nonaccounting majors in management accounting concepts. Students and instructors have responded positively to the scenarios and are supportive of the approach.

Management accounting is continuing to evolve and respond to changes in the manufacturing and service sectors. To deal with the evolution of management accounting concepts, we have four chapters that cover the new developments. Three of these chapters deal with changes that affect product costing, decision making, and planning and control. The remaining chapter deals with measuring and controlling quality and productivity. Also, we have integrated some of the new concepts into some of the traditional chapters. The four chapters on new manufacturing accounting have all been significantly revised to reflect some of the more recent developments. The extensive coverage of activity-based costing, JIT, strategic costing, activity-based responsibility accounting, quality, and productivity is one of the major strengths of the text. These new chapters are supported by a good variety of exercises, problems, and cases. The major revisions to these chapters as well as the rest of the text are listed in a separate section of this preface.

We should also mention that the text also covers all the traditional topics. Although there are a significant number of firms that are using the new procedures, the vast majority are apparently still using the traditional management accounting concepts. Thus, while the traditional management accounting procedures may be outmoded for some manufacturing firms, this is not true for all firms. In fairness to students, both the traditional and the new management accounting should be taught. This strategy provides students with the foundation they need to work in either the conventional or new manufacturing environment. Also, understanding the conventional approach and its limitations and the new approach with its advantages (as well as limitations) will help future managers to bring about change when it is merited. Perhaps understanding that management accounting is not a static discipline will itself contribute to additional innovative developments.

The coverage of ethical conduct for management accountants continues to be an area of emphasis in the text. Ethical lapses in the business world have led to a call for more classroom discussion of ethical behavior. The role of ethics is discussed in the first chapter and the code of ethics developed by the Institute of Management Accountants (formerly the NAA) is introduced. Several substantive problems on ethics have been added to Chapter 1 and each chapter in the text has one problem involving an ethical dilemma. These problems allow the instructor to introduce value judgments in managerial accounting decisions. Experience indicates that these problems can provoke some lively discussion in class.

We have tried to provide down-to-earth discussions of concepts and simple and numerous examples. The concepts are cast in a real-world context to add credibility and interest. We have also added additional exhibits and illustrations to help clarify the written material.

Changes in the Second Edition

1. In Chapter 2, we have added a few cost terms: *differential costs, and controllable* and *noncontrollable costs.* We also introduce the concept of a cost driver and relate it to cost behavior. The exhibits and graphs are now tied to the Robin Bat's example. Finally, the notion that there are two environments for management accounting—conventional and advanced—is introduced.

2. In Chapter 4, we have moved all coverage of FIFO to an appendix. We have also added three new exhibits to help students visualize the important concepts.

3. In Chapter 5, we have added three new exhibits that visually illustrate the concepts underlying service-department allocations. We have also moved the coverage of the reciprocal (algebraic) method to an appendix.

4. In Chapter 6, the following changes were made:
   a. We altered the introductory scenario to provide a more complete list of the symptoms of an outmoded cost system, and these symptoms are then summarized in a new exhibit.
   b. A more complete and in-depth discussion of the first stage of activity-based costing is provided with more detail concerning the nature of overhead cost pools.
   c. A new section on activity identification and classification describes and illustrates unit-level, batch-level, product-level, and facility-level activities.

d. A new section discusses when an activity-based cost system should be selected. This section should help students understand why many firms are still using conventional systems.
e. The exhibit comparing and contrasting JIT and conventional manufacturing has been altered to provide a better visual representation.
f. The coverage of JIT now includes discussions on automation and the effect JIT has on activity-based costing.
g. A new section briefly describes backflush costing.

5. The chapter on cost behavior and pricing has been moved from Chapter 8 to Chapter 7. In Chapter 7, we have introduced the notion of using cost estimation to identify cost formulas for both unit-based and nonunit-based cost drivers. We also have added some observations concerning the limitations and risks of short-term pricing.

6. Chapter 8 now covers CVP analysis (formerly Chapter 9).

7. Chapter 9 (formerly Chapter 7) now covers variable costing income statements.

8. In Chapter 12, the following changes were made:
a. ACRS was relabeled to MACRS and depreciation tables were altered to include three-year assets.
b. A new section on the limitations of current capital budgeting practices for the advanced manufacturing environment has been added (this section was formerly located in Chapter 13).
c. A case involving capital-budgeting issues and ethics was added. The case allows role playing and the roles are defined in the solutions manual.

9. Chapter 13 contains an expanded discussion concerning the move from EOQ to JIT inventory management. Also, extensive revisions have been made by adding new material on strategic costing. The role of activity-based costing for strategic costing analysis is emphasized. The effect of activity-costing on various managerial decision models is altered to reflect the new activity classification now described in Chapter 6.

10. In Chapter 15, we have simplified the presentation of the material by emphasizing the use of a three-pronged approach to variance analysis. The formula approach is also illustrated for the variable inputs. We have further simplified the presentation of the material by using only one method for overhead analysis. A significant reduction in acronyms also makes the material easier to follow.

11. In Chapter 16, we have added a section that describes the need for and decision utility of quality cost information. We have also expanded our coverage of productivity accounting by describing and illustrating profit-linked productivity measurement.

12. In Chapter 17, we have added material that discusses performance evaluation and transfer pricing for multinational firms.

13. In Chapter 18, we have added sections on life-cycle costing and activity-based responsibility accounting, with considerable attention to activity management.

14. For each chapter, the chapter summaries are now keyed to the learning objectives.

15. We have increased the total number of exercises and problems by 40%–50%. A number of exercises and problems have also been revised. Thus, more than 50% of the assignment material is new or revised.

Supplementary Material

Instructor's Manual   The instructor's manual contains a complete set of lecture notes for each chapter with transparency masters that illustrate key concepts. The transparency masters are in enlarged print to ensure their readability. The manual also provides a listing of all exercises and problems, their topical coverage, and the estimated difficulty and time required for solution.

Solutions Manual   This supplement contains the solutions for the end-of-chapter assignment material. Solutions have been error checked by four accounting professionals to ensure their accuracy and reliability. Transparencies for all solutions are also available. To help with the readability the size of print is larger than normal (14-point Letter Gothic was used).

Check Figures   A list of check figures for selected parts of every quantitative problem is available from the publisher.

Test Bank   This supplement offers multiple-choice problems, short problems, and essay problems. It has been updated and expanded in size (the quantity of problems has been increased significantly).

Study Guide   The study guide provides a detailed review of each chapter and allows students to check their understanding of the material through quizzes and exercises. Specifically, students are provided with a Key Terms Test, a Chapter Quiz, and Practice Exercises. Answers are provided for all assignment material.

Acknowledgements

We would like to express our appreciation for all who have provided helpful comments and suggestions. This book is a much better product because of the input received. The reviewers of the first edition helped significantly in the creation of a book that was well received. Many valuable comments from instructors and students who used the first edition helped us to make significant improvements in the second edition. In particular, we would like to thank all those who served as reviewers for the second edition. Their input was critical and much appreciated:

- Dan Elnathan
  University of Southern
  California—Los Angeles

- James R. Emore
  The University of Akron

- Timothy A. Farmer
  University of Missouri—St. Louis

- Paul Fenech
  St. Edwards' University

- Ed Fenton
  Gonzaga University

- Frederick A. Ferraro
  North Carolina State University

- Michael Haselkorn
  Bentley College

- Hal Hoverland
  California State University—
  San Bernardino

- Martha Lilly
  University of Northern Colorado

- Richard McDermott
  Weber State College

- JuliAnn Mazachek
  University of Kansas

- George N. Sanderson
  Moorehead State University

- Howard Toole
  San Diego State University

- Joe Weintrop
  SUNY—Buffalo

We also would like to thank those who served as error checkers for the second edition. Their input has helped us produce a higher quality book and a solutions manual that promises a high level of accuracy:

- Kevin Berry, Oklahoma State University

- Lawrence Gramling, University of Connecticut

- Cathy Xanthaky Larson, Middlesex Community College

- Don Lucy, Millersville University of Pennsylvania

Special thanks for the help in production of the manuscript go to Lori McLaughlin, Linda Stone, Amy Barnhart, Stacy Strait, and Neil Hansen. Also, we would like to thank Dan Edwards of Indiana University–Purdue University at Fort Wayne for his helpful assistance.

We also want to express our gratitude to the Institute of Management Accountants for their permission to use adapted problems from past CMA examinations. They have also given permission to reprint the ethical standards of conduct for management accountants. Similarly, we are grateful to Donna Ulmer for allowing us to use a case she created.

Finally, given the decision to transfer the accounting line to South-Western, it seems only appropriate to offer special thanks to all the PWS-KENT staff. They are true professionals and we have enjoyed our association with them. We wish them the very best. This second edition is possible largely due to their valued expertise.

Introduction:
The Role, History, and Direction
of Management Accounting

■ **LEARNING OBJECTIVES**

After studying Chapter 1, you should be able to

1. Explain why managers need accounting information.

2. Describe the responsibilities of managers.

3. Explain the differences between management accounting and financial accounting.

4. Describe the role of management accountants in an organization.

5. Identify and explain the trends affecting management accounting today.

6. Explain the importance of ethical behavior for managers and management accountants.

7. Define and explain the key terms appearing at the end of the chapter.

SCENARIO

Consider the following scenarios:

A. *Manager*: "I have just received a request to bid on the production of three specially constructed drill presses. Given the specifications described in the written request, I need to know what the expected manufacturing costs will be so that I can send in a bid that is competitive and that will assure us of a reasonable dollar return." (Pricing decision)

B. *Manager*: "I need to know what our current quality costs are. We then need to develop a program that will bring these costs to the level where they should be. Once we have identified what our quality costs are, what they should be, and how to bring them to their desired level, I need some way to monitor our quality improvement program. Perhaps you can develop a performance report that shows our planned quality costs and the actual quality costs. By comparing the actual with the planned costs, I have the necessary feedback to ensure that the plan is being implemented according to schedule." (Planning and control)

C. *Manager*: "This is incredible! This job was supposed to cost $100,000. Yet this final report shows a cost of $150,000. What happened? Were materials more expensive than expected? Did we use more labor than we should have? I need a report that identifies which costs overran their expected amounts, and I need someone to explain why! Even more important—why was I not informed about how the job was unfolding? It took two months to complete this job, and I received a report on final costs more than two weeks after it was completed. I need progress reports and on a timely basis. Perhaps we could have done something to correct the overruns before they became excessive." (Control)

D. *Manager*: "Our profits are being squeezed by the intense competition we are facing. My marketing vice-president argues that we can improve our financial position by reducing our airfares. She claims that if we reduce fares by 20 percent and simultaneously increase advertising expenditures by $500,000, then we can increase the number of passengers by 20 percent. I need to decide whether the price decrease coupled with an increase in advertising costs and passenger volume is profitable." (Cost-volume-profit decision)

E. *Manager*: "I am not at all pleased with the performance of the emergency room. This latest performance report seems to reveal a total disregard for cost control. The actual costs incurred for almost every category are higher than the planned costs. Additionally, the revenues are lower than they should be for the number of patients treated. I think I need to meet with the assistant administrator of that area." (Performance evaluation: a subdivision of control)

F. *Manager*: "We must soon decide whether the acquisition of the robotic manufacturing equipment is in our best interests or not. This is a critical decision involving enormous amounts of capital and carries with it some long-run implications regarding the type of labor that we employ. To help us in that decision, our controller has estimated the cost of capital and the increase in after-tax cash flow that would be expected over the life of the equipment." (Capital budgeting decision and long-range planning)

■ ACCOUNTING INFORMATION AND MANAGEMENT

The scenarios that open the chapter illustrate three important points concerning managers and accounting information.

1. Managers need accounting information and need to know how to use it.

2. Accounting information can help managers identify problems, solve problems, and evaluate performance (i.e., accounting information is needed and used in all phases of management, including planning, controlling, and decision making).

3. Accounting information is used in all organizations: manufacturing, merchandising, and service.

The Study of Accounting

It is virtually impossible for managers to function without information. Information is vital for the management process, and accounting is one of the major information systems within any organization. A sound understanding of accounting is absolutely necessary for managers to fulfill their organizational roles responsibly and competently. Accordingly, future managers should view accounting as one of the most important topics for study. They must understand basic accounting concepts and know how to use accounting information to be able to manage effectively. Considering how someone untrained in the basic concepts of accounting would fare in each of the above six scenarios should help convince you of the importance of learning how to use accounting information, especially when you consider that the six scenarios represent only a small sample of the possible applications of accounting.

Information Needs of Managers

Managers need an information system that will identify problems, such as the possibility of cost overruns (Scenario C) or a subunit's inability to implement a plan properly (Scenario E). Once problems are known, actions can be taken to identify and implement solutions. Accounting information can also be useful in identifying solutions. Examples include helping a manager decide whether to reduce prices and increase advertising to improve profitability (Scenario D) or helping a manager decide whether to automate or not (Scenario F). Finally, accounting information can help managers assess how well things are going within the organization, such as quantifying the firm's control of quality costs (Scenario B) or evaluating the efficiency of a subunit (Scenario E).

The Management Process

The management process describes the functions carried out by managers. It includes the following activities: (1) planning, (2) controlling, and (3) decision making.

planning

Planning   The detailed formulation of action to achieve a particular end is the management activity called *planning*. Planning, therefore, requires setting objectives and identifying methods to achieve those objectives. For example, a firm may have the objective of increasing its short-term and long-term profitability by improving the overall quality of its products. By improving product quality, the firm should be able to reduce scrap and rework, decrease the number of customer complaints and warranty work, reduce the resources currently assigned to inspection, and so on, thus increasing profitability. But how is this to be accomplished? The manager must develop some specific methods that, when implemented, will lead to the achievement of the desired objective. Such methods may include working with suppliers to improve the quality of incoming raw materials, establishing quality control circles, and studying defects to ascertain their cause.

controlling
feedback

Controlling   Planning is only half the battle. Once a plan is created, it must be implemented, and a manager must monitor its implementation to ensure that the plan is being carried out as intended. The managerial activity of monitoring a plan's implementation and taking corrective action as needed is referred to as *controlling*. Control is usually achieved with the use of feedback. **Feedback** is information that can be used to evaluate or correct the steps being taken to implement a plan. Based on the feedback, a manager may decide to let the implementation continue as is, take corrective action of some type to put the actions back in harmony with the original plan, or do some midstream replanning.

Feedback is a critical facet of the control function. It is here that accounting once again plays a vital role. Much of the feedback that managers receive is in the form of accounting reports. For example, by having a report on the trend in quality costs (e.g., a comparison of this quarter's costs of scrap and rework with those for the same quarter one year ago), managers can assess whether the firm is successfully implementing its quality improvement program. Accounting reports that provide feedback by comparing planned data with actual data are called *performance reports*.

performance reports

decision making

Decision Making   The process of choosing among competing alternatives is **decision making**. This pervasive managerial function is intertwined with planning and control. A manager cannot plan without making decisions. Managers must choose among competing objectives and methods to carry out the chosen objectives. Only one of numerous competing plans can be chosen. Similar comments can be made concerning the control function.

Decisions can be improved if information about the alternatives is gathered and made available to managers. One of the major roles of the accounting information system is to supply information that facilitates decision making. For example, the manager in Scenario A was faced with the prospect of submitting a bid on the production of three drill presses. A large number of possible bids could be submitted, but the manager must choose one and only one to submit to the prospective customer. The manager requested information concerning the expected manufacturing costs of the three drill presses. This cost information, along with the manager's knowledge of competitive conditions, should improve his or her ability to select a bid price. Imagine having to submit a bid without some idea of the manufacturing costs.

Organization Type

The use of accounting information by managers is not limited to manufacturing organizations. Regardless of the organizational form, managers must be proficient in using accounting information. The basic concepts taught in this text are applicable to a variety of settings. The six scenarios at the beginning of this chapter involved manufacturing, health-care, transportation, profit, and nonprofit organizations. Hospital administrators, presidents of corporations, dentists, educational administrators, and city managers all can improve their managerial skills by being well grounded in the basic concepts and use of accounting information.

■ MANAGEMENT ACCOUNTING AND FINANCIAL ACCOUNTING

The accounting information system within an organization has two major subsystems: a management accounting system and a financial accounting system. The principal distinction between the two systems is the targeted user. The management accounting system produces information for internal users, whereas the financial accounting system produces it for external users. Thus, **management accounting** could be properly called *internal accounting,* and **financial accounting** could be called *external accounting.* Specifically, management accounting identifies, collects, measures, classifies, and reports information that is useful to managers in planning, controlling, and decision making.

It should be emphasized, however, that both the management accounting information system and the financial accounting information system are part of the total accounting information system. Unfortunately, all too often the content of the management accounting system is driven by the needs of the financial accounting system. The reports of both managerial and financial accounting are frequently derived from the same data base, which was originally established to support the reporting requirements of financial account-

management accounting
financial accounting

ing. Many organizations need to expand this data base in order to satisfy more fully the needs of the internal users. For example, a firm's profitability is of interest to investors, but managers need to know the profitability of individual products. The accounting system should be designed to provide both total profits as well as profits for individual products. The key point here is flexibility—the accounting system should be able to supply different data for different purposes.

When comparing management accounting to financial accounting, several other differences emerge. Some of the more important differences are discussed below and are summarized in Exhibit 1–1.

▪ Management accounting is not subject to the requirements of generally accepted accounting principles. The Securities and Exchange Commission (SEC) and the Financial Accounting Standards Board (FASB) set the accounting procedures that must be followed for financial reporting. Unlike financial accounting, there is no official body that prescribes the format, content, and rules for preparing financial reports. Managers are free to choose whatever information they want—provided it can be justified on a cost-benefit basis.

▪ Management accounting emphasizes the use of accounting information for planning and decision making; because of this, management accounting emphasizes the future more than financial accounting. Financial accounting, on the other hand, has a historical orientation. It records and reports what has happened.

▪ Management accounting uses internal reports to evaluate the performance of entities, product lines, departments, and managers. Performance evaluation carries with it a strong behavioral connotation not present in financial accounting. Yet financial accounting also has a stewardship role—but it is more concerned with overall firm performance than individual segments.

▪ Management accounting provides more detailed information. The consequence of more detail is a greater ability to identify and solve problems. The

EXHIBIT 1–1

Comparison of Management and Financial Accounting

Management Accounting	Financial Accounting
1. Internally focused	1. Externally focused
2. No mandatory rules	2. Must follow externally imposed rules
3. Emphasis on the future	3. Historical orientation
4. Internal evaluation of segments carrying strong behavioral ramifications	4. External evaluation of firm as a whole
5. Detailed information	5. Information about the firm as a whole
6. Broad, multidisciplinary	6. More self-contained

need for greater detail arises because management accounting is concerned with the various segments of the business, whereas financial accounting is concerned with the business as a whole.

▪ Management accounting is much broader than financial accounting. It includes aspects of managerial economics, industrial engineering, and management science, as well as numerous other areas.

■ THE MANAGEMENT ACCOUNTANT

The management accountant is responsible for collecting, processing, and reporting information that will help managers in their planning, controlling, and decision-making activities. A key word in this definition of a management accountant's responsibility is *help*. The role of management accountants in an organization is one of support. They assist those individuals who are responsible for carrying out an organization's basic objectives. Positions that have direct responsibility for the basic objectives of an organization are referred to as ***line positions***. Positions that are supportive in nature and have only indirect responsibility for an organization's basic objectives are called ***staff positions.***

line positions

staff positions

For example, assume that the basic mission of an organization is to produce and sell a product. The partial organization chart shown in Exhibit 1–2 illustrates the organizational positions for production and finance. Because one of the basic objectives of the organization is to produce, those directly involved in production hold line positions. Although management accountants (located in the financial segment of the organizational chart) may wield considerable influence in the organization, they have no authority over the managers in the production area. The managers in line positions are the ones who set policy and make the decisions that impact production. However, by supplying and interpreting accounting information, management accountants can have significant input into policies and decisions.

The Controller

controller

The **controller**, the chief accounting officer, supervises all accounting departments. As the chief accounting officer, the controller has responsibility for both internal and external accounting requirements. This charge may include direct responsibility for taxes, SEC reports, maintenance of cost and other accounting records, internal controls, performance reporting, internal auditing, budgeting, financial statements, and systems accounting. A possible organization of a controller's office is also shown in Exhibit 1–2.[1]

---

[1]The controller's office varies from firm to firm. For example, in some organizations, the internal audit department may report directly to the financial vice-president; similarly, the systems department may report directly to the financial vice-president or even to another staff vice-president.

EXHIBIT 1-2
Partial Organization Chart, Manufacturing Company

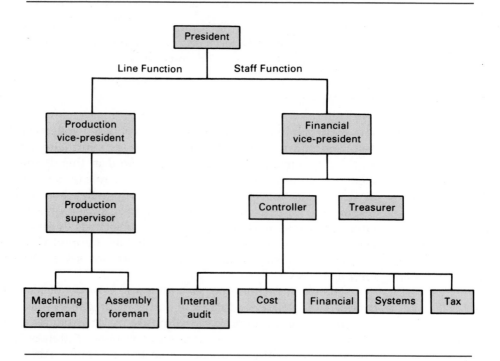

Because of the critical role that management accounting plays in the operation of an organization and because of the expertise the controller has in management accounting, the controller is often viewed as a member of the top-management team and encouraged to participate in planning, control, and decision-making activities.

■ TRENDS AFFECTING MANAGEMENT ACCOUNTING

Most of the product-costing and management accounting procedures used in the twentieth century were developed between 1880 and 1925.[2] Interestingly, many of the early developments (until about 1914) concerned managerial product costing—tracing a firm's profitability to individual products and using this information for strategic decision making. By 1925, however, most of this emphasis had been abandoned in favor of inventory costing—assigning

---

[2]The historical information in this section is taken from the following source: H. Thomas Johnson and Robert Kaplan, *Relevance Lost: The Rise and Fall of Management Accounting* (Boston: Harvard Business School Press, 1987).

manufacturing costs to products so that the cost of inventories could be reported to external users of a firm's financial statements.

Financial reporting became the driving force for the design of cost accounting systems. Managers and firms were willing to accept aggregated average cost information about individual products. Apparently, more detailed and accurate cost information about individual products was not needed. As long as a company had relatively homogeneous products that consumed resources at about the same rate, the average cost information supplied by a financially driven cost system was good enough. Furthermore, for some firms, even as product diversity increased, the need to have more accurate cost information was offset by the high cost of the information processing required to provide the information. For many firms, the cost of a more detailed cost system apparently exceeded its benefits.

Some effort to improve the managerial usefulness of conventional cost systems took place in the 1950s and 1960s. The shortcomings of information supplied by a system designed to prepare financial reports were discussed. Efforts to improve the system, however, essentially centered on making the financial accounting information more useful to users rather than producing an entirely new set of information and procedures apart from the external reporting system.

The product-costing methods and the management accounting practices that have been developed and used over the past several decades were suitable for a particular type of decision environment and for a particular type of manufacturing technology. In recent years, world-wide competitive pressures have changed the nature of our economy and have produced a response in many U.S. manufacturers that is dramatically changing the way in which they operate their businesses. These changes are creating a new environment for managerial accounting—at least for a significant number of organizations. As the environment changes, the traditional management accounting system may no longer apply. For many firms, the benefits of a more detailed, accurate cost system may now exceed its costs. Thus, new management accounting systems are emerging. The major trends that are bringing about these changes are listed below.[3]

1. Implementation of just-in-time (JIT) manufacturing

2. Increasing quality requirements

3. Increasing product diversity and complexity, coupled with shorter product life cycles

---

[3]Robert S. Kaplan, "Introduction," *Cost Accounting for the 90s* (Montvale, N.J.: National Association of Accountants, 1986). See also Robert A. Howell and Stephen R. Soucy, "The New Manufacturing Environment: Major Trends for Management Accounting," *Management Accounting* (July 1987), pp. 21–27. The article by Howell and Soucy echoes Kaplan's observations and provides a detailed analysis of the trends. It should prove interesting reading for those who wish to pursue the issue in greater depth.

4. Introduction of computer-integrated manufacturing (CIM)

5. Advances in information technology

6. Deregulation in the service industry

A brief discussion of these trends is needed to understand fully the impact on management accounting.

Just-in-Time Manufacturing

JIT manufacturing is a demand-pull system. JIT strives to produce a product only when it is needed and only in the quantities demanded by customers. Demand pulls products through the manufacturing process. Each operation produces only what is necessary to satisfy the demand of the succeeding operation. No production takes place until a signal from a succeeding process indicates the need to produce. Parts and materials arrive just in time to be used in production.

JIT manufacturing typically reduces inventories to much lower levels than found in conventional systems, increases the emphasis on quality control, and produces fundamental changes in the way production is organized and carried out. Fundamentally, JIT manufacturing focuses on continual improvement by reducing inventory costs and dealing with other economic problems. Reducing inventories frees up capital that can be used for more productive investment. Increasing quality enhances the competitive ability of the firm. Finally, changing from a traditional manufacturing setup to JIT manufacturing allows the firm to focus more on quality and productivity and, at the same time, allows a more accurate assessment of what it costs to produce its products.

Quality Emphasis

Continual improvement and elimination of waste are the two foundation principles that govern a state of manufacturing excellence. And manufacturing excellence is the key to survival in today's world-class competitive environment. Producing products with little waste and that actually perform according to specifications are the twin objectives of world-class firms. A philosophy of total quality control is replacing the conventional acceptable quality attitudes of the past.

Product Diversity and Shorter Product Life Cycles

Many firms are engaged in producing a diverse group of products—products that consume resources at vastly different rates. Additionally, the rate of technological innovation has increased for many industries, and the life of a particular product can be quite short. Managers must be able to respond quickly and decisively to changing market conditions. Information to allow them to accomplish this must be available.

JIT manufacturing

Computer-Integrated Manufacturing

Automation of the manufacturing environment allows firms to reduce inventory, increase productive capacity, improve quality and service, decrease processing time, and increase output. In other words, automation can produce a competitive advantage for a firm. The implementation of automated manufacturing typically follows JIT and is a response to the increased needs for quality and shorter response times. As more firms automate, competitive pressures will force other firms to do likewise. For many manufacturing firms, automation may be equivalent to survival.[4]

There are three possible levels of automation: the stand-alone piece of equipment, the cell, and the completely integrated factory. However, before firms attempt any level of automation, they should first do all they can to produce a more focused, simplified manufacturing process. Experience has indicated that about 80 percent of the benefits of going to a completely integrated factory can be achieved simply by implementing JIT manufacturing.[5]

If automation is justified, it may mean installation of a computer-integrated manufacturing system (CIM). CIM implies the following capabilities: (1) the products are designed through the use of a *computer-assisted design system* (CAD); (2) a *computer-assisted engineering system* (CAE) is used to test the design; (3) the product is manufactured using a *computer-assisted manufacturing system* (CAM) (CAMs use computer-controlled machines and robots); and (4) an information system connects the various automated components.

A particular type of CAM is the flexible manufacturing system. Flexible manufacturing systems are capable of producing a family of products from start to finish using robots and other automated equipment under the control of a mainframe computer. This ability to produce a variety of products with the same set of equipment is clearly advantageous.

Advances in Information Technology

Two significant advances relate to information technology. One is intimately connected with computer-integrated manufacturing. With automated manufacturing, computers are used to monitor and control operations. Because a computer is being used, a considerable amount of useful information can be collected and reported to managers about what is happening on the floor almost as it happens. It is now possible to track products continuously as they move through the factory and to report (on a real-time basis) such things as units produced, material used, scrap, and product cost. The outcome is an information system that fully integrates manufacturing with marketing and accounting data.

---

[4]For a detailed discussion of the need to automate, see Howell and Soucy, "The New Manufacturing Environment: Major Trends for Management Accounting."

[5]See Steven M. Hronec, "The Effects of Manufacturing Productivity on Cost Accounting and Management Reporting," in *Cost Accounting for the 90s*, pp. 117–25.

Automation increases both the quantity and the timeliness of information. For managers to exploit the value of the more complex information system fully, they must have access to the data of the system—they must be able to extract and analyze the data from the information system quickly and efficiently. This, in turn, implies that the tools for analysis must be powerful.

The second major advance supplies the required tools: the availability of personal computers (PCs), spreadsheet software, and graphics packages. The PC serves as a communications link to the company's information system, and spreadsheet and graphics programs supply managers with the analytical capability to use that information. The vast computing capability now available makes it possible for managers to generate their own reports and to process data in ways they deem desirable.

Deregulation in the Service Industry

Deregulation of many services (e.g., airlines and telecommunications) has increased competition in the service industry. Many service organizations are scrambling to survive. The increased competition has made managers in this industry more conscious of the need to use accounting information for planning, controlling, and decision making.

Furthermore, as the traditional smokestack industries have declined in importance, the service sector of the economy has increased in importance. The number of people employed in the service sector is significant, and many experts predict that this sector will continue to expand in size and in importance. With greater importance, the service sector will increase its demand for management accounting information.

Implications for Management Accounting

The Effect of the Service Trend   The central issue of the service-sector trend is the need for an increased awareness of management accounting's usefulness. The objective of increasing awareness can be achieved to a large extent by illustrating the applicability of management accounting concepts to service-based settings. Numerous examples, exercises, and problems with a service-based setting are offered throughout this text to help meet this objective.

The Effect of Personal Computers   PCs and software aids are available to managers in all types of organizations. PCs and user-friendly software packages allow managers to do much of their own analysis and to decrease their dependence on a centralized information systems department. If a PC also acts as a terminal and is connected to an organization's data base, managers can access information more quickly and prepare many of their own reports. The ability to enhance managerial product costing is now available. Managers are not necessarily tied to the external reporting rules for product costing. More complex product costing approaches are now possible. Greater flexibility in assessing and using information is a major consequence of PCs. Moreover, the use of PCs greatly facilitates the solution of many of the problems faced by managers. The use of PCs also carries with it the increased need for managers to have a working knowledge of the fundamental concepts of management accounting.

The Effects of a Changing Manufacturing Environment The remaining trends can be classified as changes in the manufacturing environment. These changes are dramatic and are having a correspondingly dramatic effect on management accounting. Product-costing systems, control systems, allocation, inventory management, cost structure, capital budgeting, variable costing, and many other management accounting practices are being affected because of the changing environment. The study of these changes and of their effects on management accounting practices is crucial for prospective managers and accountants. But it is also interesting! In fact, Peter Drucker has made the following observation about the revolution occurring in management accounting:[6]

The most exciting and innovative work in management today is found in accounting theory, with new concepts, new methodology—even what might be called new economic philosophy—rapidly taking shape. And while there is enormous controversy over specifics, the lineaments of the new manufacturing accounting are becoming clearer every day.

■ MANAGEMENT ACCOUNTING AND ETHICAL CONDUCT

Managers use accounting information for planning, controlling, and decision making. For what purpose? What do managers have in mind as they engage in these activities? Underlying the managerial use of accounting is the implicit assumption that it is being used to assist in achieving the basic mission of the organization, whatever that may be. According to economic theory, the primary goal and motivating force for business organizations is profit; furthermore, business organizations should attempt to make as large a profit as possible.

Virtually all the management accounting practices described in this text (and others) were developed to assist managers to maximize profits. Traditionally, the economic performance of the firm has been the overriding concern. The pursuit of high economic performance by managers who are honorable and honest usually produces significant social benefits. Unfortunately, some ways to increase profits produce undesirable social consequences. Deceptive advertising, price fixing, and manipulation of accounting data to mislead creditors, investors, and customers are all examples of socially undesirable managerial actions. For example, senior executives at General Dynamics improperly assigned $63 million of expenses to defense contracts from 1979 to

---

[6]Peter E. Drucker, ''The Emerging Theory of Manufacturing,'' *Harvard Business Review* (May-June 1990), pp. 94–102.

1982.[7] Consider also the bank overdrafts issued by managers at E. F. Hutton, which essentially gave the company interest-free use of approximately $250 million and cost the affected banks nearly $8 million.[8]

Other examples of ethical and moral lapses in the business and financial community could be given. These lapses in ethical behavior by high-level managers have created a good deal of criticism of business schools and have produced a cynical view of business among the public. A recent editorial cites polls revealing that only a third of Americans believe that businesses behave ethically and that 53 percent believe that most corporate executives are dishonest.[9]

Ethical Behavior

ethical behavior **Ethical behavior** involves choosing actions that are "right" and "proper" and "just." Our behavior can be right or wrong, it can be proper or improper, and the decisions we make can be fair or unfair. People often differ in their views of the meaning of the ethical terms cited; however, there seems to be a common principle underlying all ethical systems. This principle is expressed by the belief that each member of a group bears some responsibility for the well-being of its other members. Willingness to sacrifice one's self-interest for the well-being of the group is the heart of ethical action.[10]

Although it may seem contradictory, sacrificing one's self-interest for the collective good may not only be right and bring a sense of individual worth but may also be good business sense. Ethical behavior may pay in real economic terms. There is some empirical evidence that companies with above-average ethical standards outperform the stock market average.[11] The market may therefore reward integrity and ethical conduct.

Implications for Management Accounting

One of the major goals of management accounting is to help managers increase the profitability of their organization. Performance evaluation and rewards for managers are often linked to their unit's profit reports. Because of this profit orientation, managers often take advantage of opportunities to manipulate accounting data or to use it to justify increasing profits in an

---

[7]Roger Bennet, "Profile of Harry Crown, Founder of General Dynamics, Inc.," *New York Times,* June 16, 1985, pp. 26ff.

[8]Scott McMurray, "Battered Broker: E. F. Hutton Appears Headed for Long Siege in Bank-Draft Scheme," *The Wall Street Journal,* July 12, 1985.

[9]John S. R. Shad, "Ethics Should Be Added to the Business Curriculum," *Rocky Mountain News,* July 29, 1987, p. 49.

[10]For a detailed discussion of ethical behavior, see LaRue Tone Hosmer, *The Ethics of Management* (Homewood, Ill.: Irwin, 1987).

[11]Shad, "Ethics Should Be Added to the Business Curriculum," p. 49.

unethical or illegal way. The opportunity for the abuse of accounting information exists, as does the legitimate use of this information. Clearly, the management accounting system should not be used to justify and support unethical behavior. Futhermore, if at all possible, the evaluation and reward system should be designed to discourage unethical behavior. Essentially, the management accounting system should not be used in isolation, divorced from ethical issues. In planning, controlling, and making decisions, managers should always consider the effect of their actions on others, both within the organization and without. Answering the question "Is it right?" should always be part of the managerial process.

Managers and management accountants should not become so focused on profits that they develop a belief that the *only* goal of business is maximizing the firm's net worth. Yet in most business textbooks, including those on management accounting, the examples and problems essentially convey the message that profit maximization is the sole concern of managers and organizations. In reality, the objective of profit maximization should be constrained by the requirement that profits be achieved through legal and ethical means. While this has always been an implicit assumption of the management accounting methodology, the assumption should be made explicit. To help achieve this objective, many of the problems in this book force explicit consideration of ethical issues.

Organizations commonly establish standards of conduct for their managers and employees. Professional associations also establish ethical standards. For example, the Institute of Management Accountants has established ethical standards for management accountants. These ethical standards are presented in an appendix to this chapter. Although the standards are for management accountants, they are typical of the type of behavior that would be expected of any business professional.

To illustrate, suppose a manager's bonus is linked to reported profits, with the bonus increasing as profits increase. Thus, the manager has an incentive to find ways to increase profits, including unethical approaches. For example, a manager could increase profits by delaying promotions of deserving employees or by using cheaper parts to produce a product. In either case, if the motive is simply to increase the bonus, the behavior could be labeled as unethical. Either action is not in the best interest of the company or its employees. Yet where should the blame be assigned? After all, the reward system strongly encourages the manager to increase profits. Is the reward system at fault or is the manager who chooses to increase profits? Or both?

In reality, both probably are at fault. It is important to design the evaluation and reward system so that incentives to pursue undesirable behavior are minimized. Yet designing a perfect reward system is not a realistic expectation. Managers also have an obligation to avoid abusing the system. Standard III-3 in the Appendix makes this clear: "A management accountant should refuse any gift, favor, or hospitality that would influence their actions." Manipulating income to increase a bonus can be interpreted as a violation of this standard. Basically, the prospect of an increased bonus (e.g., a favor) should not influence a manager to engage in unethical actions.

▪ CERTIFICATION

Currently, three different forms of certification are available to management accountants: a Certificate in Public Accounting (CPA), a Certificate in Management Accounting (CMA), and a Certificate in Internal Auditing (CIA). Each certification offers peculiar advantages to a management accountant. In each case, an applicant must meet specific educational and experience requirements and pass a qualifying examination to become certified. Thus, all three certifications offer evidence that the holder has achieved a minimum level of professional competence. Furthermore, all three certifications require the holders to engage in continuing professional education in order to maintain certification. Because certification reveals a commitment to professional competency, most organizations encourage their management accountants to be certified.

The CPA

The Certificate in Public Accounting is the oldest and most well-known certification in accounting. Although the CPA does not have a management-accounting orientation, it is held by many management accountants. The purpose of the Certificate in Public Accounting is to provide minimal professional qualification for external auditors. The responsibility of external auditors is to provide assurance concerning the reliability of a firm's financial statements. Only **certified public accountants** are permitted (by law) to serve as external auditors.

certified public accountants

The CMA

Although the CPA is a prestigious accounting certification, its orientation is to external auditing. Many management accountants felt the need for a different certification—one that met the specific needs of management accountants. Accordingly, in 1974 the Institute of Management Accountants (IMA) sponsored a new certification, called the *Certificate in Management Accounting.*

As with the CPA, one of the key requirements for obtaining the CMA is passing a qualifying examination. However, the emphasis of the examination is markedly different from that of the CPA examination. Four areas are emphasized: (1) economics, finance, and management; (2) financial accounting and reporting; (3) management reporting, analysis, and behavioral issues; and (4) decision analysis and information systems. The parts to the examination reflect the needs of management accounting and underscore the earlier observation that management accounting has more of an interdisciplinary flavor than other areas of accounting. A **Certified Management Accountant (CMA)** has passed the CMA exam and has satisfied other essential requirements (e.g., experience).

Certified Management Accountant (CMA)

One of the main purposes of the CMA was to establish management accounting as a recognized, professional discipline, separate from the profession of public accounting. Since its inception, the success of the CMA program has been more than satisfactory. For many in the industrial world, the CMA has gained a reputation rivaling that of the CPA. Many firms now sponsor and pay for classes that prepare their management accountants for the qualifying examination, as well as provide other financial incentives to encourage acquisition of the CMA.

The CIA

The other certification available to internal accountants is the Certificate in Internal Auditing (CIA). The forces that led to the creation of this certification in 1974 are similar to those that resulted in the CMA. Internal auditing is different from both external auditing and management accounting, and many internal auditors felt a need for a specialized certification.

■ SUMMARY OF LEARNING OBJECTIVES

1. **Explain why managers need accounting information.** Managers need accounting information and need to know how to use it in order to be effective in their roles of planning, controlling, and decision making.

2. **Describe the responsibilities of managers.** Managers are responsible for planning, controlling, and decision making. Planning is the detailed formulation of action to achieve a particular end. Controlling is the monitoring of a plan's implementation. Decision making is choosing among competing alternatives.

3. **Explain the differences between management accounting and financial accounting.** Management accounting differs from financial accounting primarily in its targeted users. Management accounting information is intended for internal users, whereas financial accounting information is directed towards external users. Management accounting is not bound by the externally imposed rules of financial reporting. It provides more detail than financial accounting, and it tends to be broader and multidisciplinary.

4. **Describe the role of management accountants in an organization.** Management accountants are responsible for identifying, collecting, measuring, analyzing, preparing, interpreting, and communicating information used by management to achieve the basic objectives of the organization. Management accountants need to be sensitive to the information needs of managers. Management accountants serve as staff members of the organization and are responsible for providing information; they are usually intimately involved in the management process as valued members of the management team.

5. **Identify and explain the trends impacting management accounting today.** Changes in the manufacturing environment brought about by the implementation of JIT manufacturing, increasing quality requirements, product diversity, diminishing product life cycles, automation, and advances in informa-

tion technology are having a significant influence on the management accounting environment. Many traditional management accounting practices will be altered because of the revolution taking place among many manufacturing firms. Deregulation and growth in the service sector of our economy are also increasing the demand for management accounting practices.

6. Explain the importance of ethical behavior for managers and management accountants. Management accounting aids managers in their efforts to improve the economic performance of the firm. Unfortunately, some managers have overemphasized the economic dimension and have engaged in unethical and illegal actions. Many of these actions have relied on the management accounting system to bring about and even support that unethical behavior. To emphasize the importance of the ever-present constraint of ethical behavior on profit-maximizing behavior, this text presents ethical issues in many of the problems appearing at the end of each chapter.

■ KEY TERMS

Certified Public Accountant (CPA) An accountant certified to possess the professional qualifications of an external auditor. (p. 16)

Certified Management Accountant (CMA) An accountant who has satisfied the requirements to hold a certificate in management accounting. (p. 16)

Controller The chief accountant of an organization. (p. 7)

Controlling The monitoring of a plan through the use of feedback to ensure that the plan is being implemented as expected. (p. 4)

Decision making The process of choosing among a set of competing alternatives. (p. 4)

Ethical behavior Behavior that results in choices/actions that are right, proper, and just. (p. 14)

Feedback Information that can be used to evaluate or correct steps being taken to implement a plan. (p. 4)

Financial accounting The branch of accounting that is concerned with the preparation of financial reports for users external to the organization. (p. 5)

JIT manufacturing A manufacturing process in which each process produces only what is necessary to satisfy the demand of the succeeding process. (p. 10)

Line position A position in an organization filled by an individual who is directly responsible for carrying out the organization's basic objectives. (p. 7)

Management accounting The branch of accounting that is concerned with providing information for users internal to the organization. (p. 5)

Performance reports Accounting reports that provide feedback to managers by comparing planned outcomes with actual outcomes. (p. 4)

Planning Setting objectives and identifying methods to achieve those objectives. (p. 4)

Staff position A position in an organization filled by an individual who provides support for the line function; thus, a staff person is only indirectly involved with the basic objectives of an organization. (p. 7)

■ APPENDIX: STANDARDS OF ETHICAL CONDUCT FOR MANAGEMENT ACCOUNTANTS

On June 1, 1983, the Management Accounting Practices Committee of the IMA issued a statement outlining standards of ethical conduct for management accountants.[12] In this statement, management accountants are told that "they shall not commit acts contrary to these standards nor shall they condone the commission of such acts by others in their organizations." The standards and the recommended resolution of conduct are presented below.

I. Competence

Management accountants have a responsibility to

1. Maintain an appropriate level of professional competence by ongoing development of their knowledge and skills.

2. Perform their professional duties in accordance with relevant laws, regulations, and technical standards.

3. Prepare complete and clear reports and recommendations after appropriate analyses of relevant and reliable information.

II. Confidentiality

Management accountants have a responsibility to

1. Refrain from disclosing confidential information acquired in the course of their work except when authorized, unless legally obligated to do so.

2. Inform subordinates as appropriate regarding the confidentiality of information acquired in the course of their work and monitor their activities to ensure the maintenance of that confidentiality.

3. Refrain from using or appearing to use confidential information acquired in the course of their work for unethical or illegal advantage either personally or through a third party.

III. Integrity

Management accountants have a responsibility to

1. Avoid actual or apparent conflicts of interest and advise all appropriate parties of any potential conflict.

---

[12]"Standards of Ethical Conduct for Management Accountants," SMA1C, Institute of Management Accountants, 10 Paragon Drive, Montvale, N.J., 1983. The Standards of Ethical Conduct are reprinted with permission from the Institute of Management Accountants.

2. Refrain from engaging in any activity that would prejudice their abilities to carry out their duties ethically.

3. Refuse any gift, favor, or hospitality that would influence their actions.

4. Refrain from either actively or passively subverting the attainment of the organization's legitimate and ethical objectives.

5. Recognize and communicate professional limitations or other constraints that would preclude responsible judgment or successful performance of an activity.

6. Communicate unfavorable as well as favorable information and professional judgments or opinions.

7. Refrain from engaging in or supporting any activity that would discredit the profession.

IV. Objectivity

Management accountants have a responsibility to

1. Communicate information fairly and objectively.

2. Disclose fully all relevant information that could reasonably be expected to influence an intended user's understanding of the reports, comments, and recommendations presented.

In applying the standards of ethical conduct, management accountants may encounter problems in identifying unethical behavior or in resolving ethical conflict. When faced with significant ethical issues, management accountants should follow the established policies of the organization bearing on the resolution of such conflict. If these policies do not resolve the ethical conflict, management accountants should consider the following courses of action:

▪ Discuss such problems with the immediate supervisor except when it appears that the superior is involved, in which case the problem should be presented initially to the next higher management level. If satisfactory resolution cannot be achieved when the problem is initially presented, submit the issues to the next higher management level.

▪ If the immediate superior is the chief executive officer, or equivalent, the acceptable reviewing authority may be a group such as the audit committee, executive committee, board of directors, board of trustees, or owners. Contact with levels above the immediate superior should be initiated only with the superior's knowledge, assuming the superior is not involved.

▪ Clarify relevant concepts by confidential discussion with an objective advisor to obtain an understanding of possible courses of action.

- If the ethical conflict still exists after exhausting all levels of internal review, the management accountant may have no other recourse on significant matters than to resign from the organization and to submit an informative memorandum to an appropriate representative of the organization.

- Except where legally prescribed, communication of such problems to authorities or individuals not employed or engaged by the organization is not considered appropriate.

■ QUESTIONS

1. List at least four reasons that managers need to understand and use accounting information.

2. Describe the connection between planning, controlling, and feedback.

3. What role do performance reports play with respect to the control function?

4. How do management accounting and financial accounting differ?

5. What is the difference between a staff position and a line position?

6. The controller should be a member of the top management staff. Do you agree or disagree? Explain.

7. Identify the three forms of accounting certification. Which form of certification do you believe is best for a management accountant? Why?

8. Explain the role of financial reporting in the development of management accounting. Is external reporting the only reason firms choose to use inventory costs for product costing? Explain.

9. Identify and discuss the trends that are affecting the way management accounting is practiced.

10. What are the four parts to the CMA examination? What do they indicate about management accounting versus financial accounting?

11. Deregulation of service industries (e.g., airlines) has increased the demand for management accounting information. Why is this so?

12. PCs significantly increase a manager's capabilities to process and use accounting information. Do you agree? Explain.

13. What is a flexible manufacturing system?

14. What is the role of the controller in an organization? Describe some of the activities over which he or she has control.

15. What is ethical behavior? Is it possible to teach ethical behavior in a management accounting course?

16. Firms with higher ethical standards will experience a higher level of economic performance than firms with lower or poor ethical standards. Do you agree? Why or why not?

17. Review the code of ethical conduct for management accountants. Do you believe that the code will have an effect on the ethical behavior of management accountants? Explain.

PROBLEMS

P1–1   **The Managerial Process**   Each of the following scenarios requires the use of accounting information to carry out one or more of the following managerial activities: planning, control (including performance evaluation), or decision making. Identify the managerial activity or activities that are applicable for each scenario.

A. *Manager*: "A supplier approached me recently and offered to sell our company vacuum hoses for $20 each. We currently manufacture our own hoses. I need to know what costs we will avoid if we buy the vacuum hoses."

B. *Manager*: "This report indicates that we have spent 20 percent more on materials than originally planned. An investigation into the cause has revealed the problem. We were using a lower-quality material than expected and the waste has been higher than normal. By switching to the quality level originally specified, we can cut the excess cost to 10 percent."

C. *Manager*: "Our salespeople indicate that they expect to sell 15 percent more units than last year. I want a projection of the effect this increase in sales will have on profits. I also want to know our expected cash receipts and cash expenditures on a month-by-month basis. I have a feeling that some short-term borrowing may be necessary."

D. *Manager*: "Given the intensity of competition, we need to do something about increasing the efficiency of our manufacturing process. Currently, we are considering the implementation of two different automated manufacturing systems. I need to know the future cash flows associated with each system."

E. *Manager*: "At the last board meeting, we established an objective of earning a 25 percent return on sales. I need to know how many units of our product we need to sell to meet this objective. Once I have the estimated sales in units, we then need to outline a promotional campaign that will take us where we want to be. However, in order to compute the targeted sales in units, I need to know the expected unit price and a lot of cost information."

F. *Manager*: "Perhaps the Harrison Medical Clinic should not offer a full range of medical services. Some services seem to be having a difficult time showing any kind of profit. I am particularly concerned about the mental health service. It has not shown a profit since the clinic opened. I want to know what costs can be avoided if I drop the service. I also want some assessment of the impact on the other services we offer. Some of our patients may choose this clinic because we offer a full range of services."

P1–2   **The Role of Management Accountants**   Management accountants are actively involved in the process of managing the entity. This process includes making strategic, tactical, and operating decisions while helping to coordinate the efforts of the entire organization. To fulfill these objectives, the management accountant accepts certain responsibilities that can be identified as (1) planning, (2) controlling, (3) evaluating performance, (4) assuring accountability of resources, and (5) external reporting.

Required:

Describe each of these responsibilities of the management accountant and identify examples of practices and techniques.

(CMA adapted)

P1–3   **Line versus Staff**   The job responsibilities of two employees of Barney Manufacturing are described below.

Joan Dennison, cost accounting manager: Responsible for measuring and collecting costs associated with the manufacture of the garden hose product line. She is also responsible for preparing periodic reports comparing the actual costs with planned costs. These reports are provided to the production line managers and the plant manager. Joan helps explain and interpret the reports.

Steven Swasey, production manager: Responsible for the manufacture of the high-quality garden hose. He supervises the line workers, helps develop the production schedule, and is responsible for seeing that production quotas are met. He is also held accountable for controlling manufacturing costs.

Required:

Identify Joan and Steven as line or staff and explain your reasons.

P1–4   **Ethical Behavior**   Consider the following scenario:

Manager: "If I can reduce my costs by $40,000 during this last quarter, my division will show a profit 10 percent above the planned level, and I will receive a $10,000 bonus. However, given the projections for the fourth quarter, it does not look promising. I really need that $10,000. I know one way I can qualify. All I have to do is lay off my three most expensive salespeople. After all, most of the orders are in for the fourth quarter, and I can always hire new sales personnel at the beginning of the next year."

Required:

What is the right choice for the manager to make? Why did the ethical dilemma arise? Is there any way to redesign the accounting reporting system to discourage the type of behavior the manager was contemplating?

P1–5   **Ethical Issues**   Assess and comment on each of the following statements that have appeared in newspaper editorials:

1. Business students come from all segments of society. If they have not been taught ethics by their families and by their elementary and secondary schools, there is little effect a business school can have.

2. Sacrificing self-interest for the collective good won't happen unless a majority of Americans also accept this premise.

3. Competent executives manage people and resources for the good of society. Monetary benefits and titles are simply the by-products of doing a good job.

4. Unethical firms and individuals, like high rollers in Las Vegas, are eventually wiped out financially.

P1–6   **Ethical Issues**   The Alert Company is a closely held investment service group that has been very successful over the past five years, consistently providing most members of the top management group with 50 percent bonuses. In addition, both the chief financial officer and the chief executive officer have received 100 percent bonuses. Alert expects this trend to continue.

Recently, the top management group of Alert, which holds 35 percent of the outstanding shares of common stock, has learned that a major corporation is interested in acquiring Alert. Alert's management is concerned that this corporation may make an attractive offer to the other shareholders and that management would be unable to prevent the takeover. If the acquisition occurs, this executive group is uncertain about continued employment in the new corporate structure. As a consequence, the management group is considering changes to several accounting policies and practices that, although not in accordance with generally accepted accounting principles, would make the company a less attractive acquisition. Management has told Roger Deerling, Alert's controller, to implement some of these changes. Deerling has also been informed that Alert's management does not intend to disclose these changes immediately to anyone outside the immediate top management group.

Required:

Using the code of ethics for management accountants, evaluate the changes that Roger's management is considering and discuss the specific steps that he should take to resolve the situation.

(CMA adapted)

P1–7   **Ethical Behavior**   Webson Manufacturing Company produces component parts for the airline industry and has recently undergone a major computer system conversion. Michael Darwin, the controller, has established a trouble-shooting team to alleviate accounting problems that have occurred since the conversion. Michael has chosen Maureen Hughes, assistant controller, to head the team that will include Bob Randolph, cost accountant; Cynthia Wells, financial analyst; Marjorie Park, general accounting supervisor; and George Crandall, financial accountant.

      The team has been meeting weekly for the last month. Maureen insists on being part of all the team conversations in order to gather information, makes the final decision on any ideas or actions that the team develops, and prepares a weekly report for Michael. She has also used this team as a forum to discuss issues and disputes about him and other members of Webson's top management team. At last week's meeting, Maureen told the team that she thought a competitor might purchase the common stock of Webson, because she had overheard Michael talking about this on the telephone. As a result, most of Webson's employees now informally discuss the sale of Webson's common stock and how it will affect their jobs.

Required:

Is Maureen Hughes's discussion with the team about the prospective sale of Webson unethical? Discuss, citing specific standards from the code of ethical conduct to support your position.

(CMA adapted)

P1–8   **Ethical Responsibilities**   JLA Electronics is a U.S.–based high-tech company that manufactures and distributes computer and telecommunications equipment. JLA has developed a hand-held, light-weight fax system, Porto-Fax, that will allow the user total freedom in receiving and transmitting information. Marketing research studies indicate that the potential market for this item is large, and immediate action in test marketing the product is recommended.

      Despite the fact that JLA has excess capacity at its current manufacturing facility, the company has decided to build a new manufacturing plant to accommodate the Porto-Fax and is in the process of deciding where to locate the plant. The current unionized employees believe this move is being made to eliminate union involvement in the Porto-Fax manufacturing process. The management team that was formed to oversee the site selection process has already received bids from several locales, both domestic and foreign, offering a wide range of incentives to encourage the company to select particular sites.

      Some of the incentives are personal in nature such as housing at reduced cost for the selection team, reduced property taxes, open accounts at certain restaurants, and free tickets to local sporting events. Other incentives offered affect corporate profitability and include reduced tax rates, low-interest or no-interest loans, outright grants, and low-cost property. The marketing research team has reported that product price will have a major effect on the sale of Porto-Fax and recommends that the selection team pick a site that minimizes costs.

Required:

1. What is meant by the term *corporate social responsibility*?

2. Should JLA Electronics consider its social responsibility when making the final decision regarding the site selection?

3. Describe the ethical responsibilities of the individuals on the site selection team.

4. Discuss the responsibilities that the union at the current manufacturing facility may have in this situation.

(CMA adapted)

P1–9 **Ethical Behavior**   A senior majoring in accounting was hired by a small local business firm to clean up its accounting records. Initially, the student thought it was a good part-time job with an opportunity to apply some of the systems concepts he had recently learned. However, the student soon discovered (to his dismay) what the owner meant by cleaning up. The owner was preparing to apply for a badly needed loan and wanted to present the best financial statements possible. He was particularly concerned about the presence of a large note payable on the balance sheet. To correct this problem, the owner decided the note needed to be reclassified and instructed his newly hired accountant to bury the note in the contributed capital section of the balance sheet.

Required:

1. What would you do if you were the accountant? Would this be different if you were employed full time and had a family and a mortgage on a new house?

2. Apply the code of ethics for management accountants to the above situation. What is your recommendation?

PART 1

Cost Accumulation and Product Costing

Cost Concepts and Terminology

■ **LEARNING OBJECTIVES**

After studying Chapter 2, you should be able to

1. Classify costs by function and by behavior.

2. Identify product costs and period costs.

3. Explain how financial statements differ among manufacturing, service, and merchandising firms.

4. Identify the cost flow patterns for manufacturing, service, and merchandising firms.

5. Explain the difference between variable and fixed cost behavior.

6. Prepare an income statement using either the absorption-costing or contribution approach.

7. Define and explain the key terms appearing at the end of the chapter.

SCENARIO

Matt Leonard and Ruth Brown were both alumni of the local university's MBA program, having graduated at the same time. Both viewed themselves as being successful in their chosen careers. Matt was the administrator of the largest hospital in the community, and Ruth was a division manager of a company that produced medical products. The two met every Friday for lunch to discuss business (the hospital acquired a significant percentage of its supplies from Ruth's company) and exchange advice on the problems they faced in their respective organizations. This Friday Matt turned the discussion to a problem he was facing with a recently hired manager.

"Ruth, as you know, I have two assistant administrators. A month ago one of my assistants, Janice, resigned to become administrator of a small hospital in the southern part of the state. A pity, since she was by far the better of the two. Anyway, I hired an individual, Harold Capener, from a small MBA program as her replacement. This program did not have a specialization in hospital administration, but I discounted this since Harold had five years' experience as a surgical assistant in a large hospital and had earned good grades in his graduate work. However, since hiring this guy, I've uncovered what seems to be a major deficiency in his training."

"What seems to be the problem?"

"Well, I called him into my office last Monday to review some of the projects and responsibilities that I planned to assign him. First, I requested that he supply me with a budget for the coming year. I indicated that he could use last year's budget as the basis for next year's, but that I wanted him to work closely with our chief accountant to identify variable and fixed costs in the budget. I also indicated that we recently had a consultant identify the direct and indirect costs of all our surgical services as a preliminary step for evaluating the impact of the government's DRG reimbursement policies. I asked him to assess the profitability of each surgical service and to make recommendations for reducing direct and indirect surgical costs, where necessary, so that we could at least break even on each surgical service. Throughout this entire discussion I kept getting blank and puzzled looks. So before proceeding, I asked him if he had any questions or comments."

Ruth chuckled. "I'll bet I can guess his response—however, I'll let you confirm my suspicions."

"His response astonished me. He indicated that he did not know what I meant by variable or fixed costs. Nor did he understand the concept of direct and indirect surgical costs. Basically, he was totally unfamiliar with fundamental cost concepts. He also expressed surprise that he would be so strongly involved in budgeting and profitability analysis. He assumed that all of that was the responsibility of the accountants—not of managers. I spent the next forty-five minutes explaining why managers must be able to work with financial information in order to direct an organization effectively. I think he now understands that every manager should be familiar with basic cost terminology and know how financial statements are prepared."

"I can certainly sympathize. I can't imagine having a marketing manager who doesn't understand the difference between fixed and variable manufacturing costs. Many of our bids depend on understanding that difference. How are you going to deal with Harold?

Well, he's bright and works hard. I think he'll eventually be a good assistant. But he does need some good training in the basic terminology, concepts, and uses of financial information. He has agreed to take an evening course in management accounting. I need somebody who has the basic financial training and who can then become proficient in the use of financial information."

■ ORGANIZATIONAL FRAMEWORK

As the dialogue above illustrates, managers of organizations must have the capability to use and understand financial information. In order to make effective use of financial information, managers must have a basic knowledge of cost concepts and the associated terminology. Yet is it necessary for a hospital administrator to use different cost information than, say, a manager of a manufacturing division? Must training in basic cost concepts be targeted for specific organizational types? These questions can be answered by examining the major types of organizations and seeing what differences exist among them.

In general, all organizations can be classified into one of three categories: (1) manufacturing, (2) merchandising, or (3) service. Manufacturing organizations produce goods by converting raw materials into a physical product through the use of labor and capital inputs such as plant, land, and machinery. Manufacturers include companies such as Panasonic, General Motors, IBM, and General Electric, producing goods such as televisions, automobiles, computers, and appliances. Manufacturing firms usually sell their goods to merchandising firms or to other manufacturing firms.

Merchandising firms buy goods already made (by manufacturers) and then sell them to consumers or other merchandising firms. They are not involved in manufacturing. Examples include firms such as Sears, WalMart, Radio Shack, and Ace Hardware. Merchandising firms selling directly to consumers are sometimes referred to as *retailers*. Merchandising firms selling to other merchandising firms are often referred to as *wholesalers*.

Service organizations deliver or sell a service to customers. Service organizations differ from both manufacturing and merchandising firms in two ways. First, they deal with intangible products (services) rather than tangible ones. Second, many service organizations are not profit making. Examples of profit-making service organizations are Price Waterhouse (an accounting firm), American Airlines, and Prudential (an insurance company). Examples of nonprofit service organizations include the IRS and the Veterans' Administration (government agencies), the Red Cross and United Way (charitable organizations), and some hospitals.

Each of these types of organization needs cost information. The type and quantity of cost information needed by managers, however, do depend on the organization and the type of activities found within it. For example, manufacturing organizations are more complex and engage in more activities than either service or merchandising organizations; thus, managers in these firms need more cost information. While all profit-making organizations (and many nonprofit organizations) engage in marketing and administrative activities, only manufacturing firms are involved in production. Because of this, manufacturing firms have raw materials and work-in-process inventories not found in merchandising firms.[1] Similarly, they have work-in-process and finished-goods inventories not present in service organizations. As a result, manufacturing firms require a greater quantity and variety of cost information.

Since manufacturing organizations offer the richest array of cost concepts, we have chosen them as the principal setting for our study. This choice, however, does not mean that we are ignoring the other organizational types. Most of the cost concepts described here are applicable to all organizations. Furthermore, from time to time we consider examples specifically applicable to service or merchandising firms.

▪ COST AND COST CLASSIFICATION

Managerial accounting, like any discipline, has its own specialized vocabulary. Learning this vocabulary is essential to understanding the concepts and procedures discussed throughout this text. The main purpose of this chapter is to introduce the basic cost terminology used in managerial accounting.

cost

Before cost terminology can be discussed, the term *cost* itself must be defined. **Cost** is the cash or cash equivalent value sacrificed for goods and services that are expected to bring a current or future benefit to the organization. We say *cash equivalent* because noncash assets can be exchanged for the desired goods or services. For example, it may be possible to exchange land for some needed equipment.

expenses

loss

Costs are incurred to produce future benefits. In a profit-making firm, future benefits usually mean revenues. As costs are used up in the production of revenues, they are said to expire. Expired costs are called *expenses*. In each period, expenses are deducted from revenues in the income statement to determine the period's profit. A **loss** is a cost that expires without producing any revenue benefit. For example, some New York vendors purchased a large supply of "I Survived the New York Blackout" t-shirts after a major power failure. Now assume some of these t-shirts are still on hand one year after the blackout. These shirts are probably of little sales value and may literally be

---

[1]Work-in-process inventories are inventories of partially completed goods.

given away. Clearly, this produces little or no revenue, and the cost of the shirts would be shown as a loss on the income statement.

assets

Many costs do not expire in a given period. These unexpired costs are classified as **assets** and appear on the balance sheet. Equipment and the addition to a factory building are examples of assets lasting more than one period. Note that the main difference between a cost being classified as an expense or an asset is timing. This distinction is important and will be referred to in the development of other cost concepts later on in the text. An **oppor-**

opportunity cost

tunity cost is the benefit given up or sacrificed when one alternative is chosen over another. For example, choosing to attend school instead of working has an opportunity cost equal to the wages forgone. Similarly, a firm may choose to invest $100,000 in inventory for a year instead of investing the capital in a productive investment that would yield a 12 percent rate of return. The opportunity cost of having the capital tied up in inventory is $12,000 (0.12 × $100,000) and is part of the cost of carrying the inventory. While opportunity costs do not usually appear on the books or financial statements of an organization, they are often critical inputs for managerial decisions.[2] For example, the $12,000 opportunity cost of carrying inventory is equivalent to a cash outlay of $12,000. This cost is an important factor for a manager to consider when assessing different inventory policies.

differential cost

A **differential cost** is the amount by which a cost differs between two alternatives. Suppose, for example, that you are trying to decide whether to drive or fly to Padre Island over spring break. Upon investigation, you find that the cost of a round-trip plane ticket is $350. The cost of driving, including gasoline, is $200. The differential cost is computed as follows:

Flying option	$350
Driving option	200
Differential cost	$150

out-of-pocket cost
sunk cost

An **out-of-pocket cost** is a cost that involves a current cash outlay. Paying cash for office supplies is an example of an out-of-pocket cost. A **sunk cost** is a cost for which an outlay has already been made. It is a cost that has been paid and is irretrievable. Thus, sunk costs cannot be changed by any present or future decision. For example, depreciation is a sunk cost—it represents the assignment of a portion of a past cash outlay to a particular time period. Because sunk costs cannot be changed, they should have no bearing on the decision. Unfortunately, it is too often true that we attempt to consider these costs in our decisions. How often have you heard people say that they cannot afford to get rid of a car because they've sunk too much money into it (new carburetor, new tires, etc.)? Yet the outlays already made have no bearing on

---

[2]Accountants focus on recording the costs of alternatives selected rather than the costs of rejected alternatives. Consequently, the formal accounting system does not record opportunity costs.

the decision because the funds spent in the past are irretrievable regardless of whether the car is kept or not. What they need to do is compare the future costs and benefits of keeping the car with the future costs and benefits of getting rid of it.

Often managers are given responsibility for certain cost items. They are held accountable for these items and are evaluated on their ability to ensure that expenditures for the items do not exceed some predetermined level. If managers are to be held accountable for certain costs, then they must be able *controllable costs* to control these costs. **Controllable costs** are those costs heavily influenced by a manager—in effect, costs a manager is authorized to incur. For example, a maintenance manager has the ability to authorize the use of supplies in repair work. The cost of these supplies is, therefore, a controllable cost for the maintenance manager. The maintenance manager, however, is not free to set *noncontrollable cost* his own salary. His salary is an example of a **noncontrollable cost**—a cost over which he has no significant influence. Although the maintenance manager may not have control over his salary, someone does. The plant manager, for example, may be the person who has this control. All costs are controllable at some level. Controllability, therefore, depends on the point of reference.

direct costs　　**Direct costs** are those costs that are traceable to a cost object. A **cost object** *cost object* is any item or activity, such as products, departments, projects, and so on, to *indirect costs* which costs are assigned. **Indirect costs** are those costs that are common to several cost objects and, accordingly, are not directly traceable to any one particular cost object. Assume, for example, that the cost object is an assembly department. The salary of the supervisor of this department is directly traceable to the department and, therefore, is a direct cost of the department. The salary of the plant custodian, however, is common to all departments in the plant. It is an indirect cost of the assembly department. Like controllable costs, traceability depends on the point of reference. While the salary of the supervisor is a direct cost of the assembly department, it is an indirect product cost if more than one product is assembled in that department.

As can be seen, there are many different types of costs. There are different costs for different purposes. For example, some costs are used for decision making (e.g., differential costs) and other costs are used for performance evaluation (e.g., controllable costs). There are also many different ways that costs can be classified. We have chosen to classify costs into two major categories: by function and by behavior. These cost categories correspond to two different ways of organizing costs for purposes of external and internal financial reporting. The functional classification, the traditional way of viewing costs, plays a key role in the external reporting activities of a firm. Classifying costs by behavior is extremely important for the planning and control activities that take place within a firm.

▪ FUNCTIONAL CLASSIFICATION OF COSTS

In cost accounting, we try to organize costs in terms of the special purposes, or functions, they serve. In a manufacturing organization, costs are subdivided into two major functional categories: manufacturing and nonmanufac-

manufacturing costs
nonmanufacturing
costs

turing. **Manufacturing costs** are those costs associated with the production function in the plant or factory; **nonmanufacturing costs** are those costs associated with the functions of selling and administration. Manufacturing costs can be further subdivided into direct manufacturing costs and indirect manufacturing costs.

Direct Manufacturing Costs

direct manufacturing
costs

Direct manufacturing costs are those manufacturing costs that are directly traceable to the product being manufactured. In a single-product firm, all manufacturing costs belong to and are traceable to the product. In a traditional, multiple-product firm, there are two types of direct manufacturing costs: the cost of raw materials and the cost of the labor needed to convert the raw materials into a finished product.

direct materials

Raw materials are those materials that actually become part of the product. Since they are directly traceable to the product, they are commonly referred to as *direct materials*. For example, steel in an automobile, wood in furniture, alcohol in cologne, denim in jeans, and plastic in a microcomputer would all be classified as direct materials.

direct labor

The cost of labor used to convert raw materials to a finished product is defined as the straight wages paid to those employees who actually combine materials and overhead into the product (straight wages exclude overtime). This labor cost, directly traceable to the product, is usually referred to as *direct labor*. Workers on an assembly line at Chrysler and in the mixing department at Nabisco are examples of direct laborers. The activities of direct laborers can often be described with action words relating to the making of the product: mix, bake, assemble, sew, package, cut out, etc. They do the work that converts the raw materials into finished goods.

Indirect Manufacturing Costs

manufacturing
overhead

In a *traditional, multiple-product* manufacturing environment, raw materials and direct labor are the only direct product costs. All other costs associated with the manufacturing process are *indirect manufacturing costs*; these costs are common to all products being produced. In other words, indirect manufacturing costs cannot be traced to any one product. Indirect costs are lumped into one category called **manufacturing overhead**. Manufacturing overhead is also known as *factory burden* or *indirect product costs*. For simplicity, we will usually refer to manufacturing overhead as *overhead*.

indirect materials

The overhead cost category contains a wide variety of items. Many inputs other than direct labor and direct materials are needed to make a product. All factory-related indirect costs belong to the overhead category. Examples include depreciation on plant and equipment, maintenance, supplies (indirect materials), supervision, material handling and other indirect labor, utilities, property taxes, landscaping of factory grounds, and plant security. **Indirect materials** are generally those materials necessary for production that do not become part of the finished product. Lubricating oil for machinery used in production is an example of an indirect material. The oil is necessary to maintain the machinery but is not directly traceable to any one product.

Direct materials that form an insignificant part of the final product are usually lumped into the overhead category as a special kind of indirect material. This is justified on the basis of cost and convenience. The glue used in furniture or toys is an example.

indirect labor   **Indirect labor** is generally all factory labor other than those workers who actually transform the raw materials into a finished good. Examples include production-line supervisors, janitors, supply clerks, and maintenance workers.

The cost of overtime for direct laborers is usually assigned to indirect labor as well. The rationale is that typically no particular production run can be identified as the cause of the overtime. Accordingly, overtime cost is common to all production runs and is therefore an indirect manufacturing cost. Note that *only* the overtime cost itself is treated this way. If workers are paid an $8 regular rate and a $4 overtime premium, then only the $4 overtime premium is assigned to overhead. The $8 regular rate is still regarded as a direct labor cost. In certain cases, however, overtime is associated with a particular production run; for example, a special order is taken when production is at 100 percent capacity. In these special cases, it is appropriate to treat overtime premiums as a direct labor cost.

In practice, many firms also treat the cost of direct labor fringe benefits as an overhead item. This practice can be justified only on the basis of convenience since the cost of fringe benefits for direct laborers technically should be a direct labor cost. Because fringe benefits represent a significant component of the total direct labor cost, the best approach for handling this item is to assign it to the direct labor cost category. With automation of the bookkeeping function, the argument of convenience is not convincing; therefore, direct labor fringe benefits generally should be treated as a direct labor cost.

Nonmanufacturing Costs

There are two categories of nonmanufacturing costs: selling costs and administrative costs. The level of these costs can be significant (often greater than 25 percent of sales revenue), and controlling them may bring greater cost savings to a manufacturing organization than the same control exercised in the area of production costs. Furthermore, the relative importance of selling and administrative costs is greater in merchandising firms because those firms do not engage in production. Service organizations, on the other hand, do produce an intangible product so the production function is present in this type of organization. The relative importance of selling and administrative costs depends on the nature of the service being produced. Physicians and dentists, for example, do very little marketing and thus have very low selling costs.

selling costs   Those costs necessary to market and distribute a product or service are marketing or **selling costs**. They are often referred to as *order-getting* and *order-filling* costs. Examples of selling costs include such items as salaries and commissions of sales personnel, advertising, warehousing, customer service, and shipping. The first two items are examples of order-getting costs; the last three are order-filling costs.

All costs associated with the general administration of the organization that cannot be reasonably assigned to either marketing or manufacturing are **administrative costs**. General administration has the responsibility of ensuring that the various activities of the organization are properly integrated so that the overall mission of the firm is realized. The president of the firm, for example, is concerned with the efficiency of *both* marketing and manufacturing as they carry out their respective roles. Proper integration of these two functions is essential to maximize the overall profits of a firm. Examples, then, of administrative costs are top executive salaries, legal fees, printing the annual report, general accounting, and research and development.

The manufacturing and nonmanufacturing classifications give rise to some related cost concepts. The functional delineation between nonmanufacturing and manufacturing costs is essentially the basis for the concepts of period costs and product costs—at least for purposes of external reporting. Combinations of different manufacturing costs also produce the concepts of conversion costs and prime costs.

administrative costs

Related Cost Concepts

Period Costs Costs that are expensed in the period in which they are incurred are called **period costs**. Costs are incurred to produce future benefits (usually revenues) and as costs are used up, they expire and are matched against the revenues they generated.[3] Generally we can say that period costs benefit only the period in which they are incurred. This is not entirely accurate, of course. Some costs classified as period costs may actually benefit more than one period. For example, United Airlines advertises its flights to warm, sunny Florida in December. Some people will see these ads and immediately book a trip to Orlando. Others will let the idea sit quietly in the back of their minds until the following February and then buy tickets. One ad has led to sales in two different time periods. Thus, the extreme difficulty of matching advertising costs with benefitting periods justifies the expedient practice of expensing all of these costs immediately.

period costs

To illustrate the concept of period costs, we consider a sales supervisor. Her salary is incurred and expensed during the year because she is expected to produce sales during the year. The next year the same cost is incurred with the expectation that sales will be produced in *that* year. The salary is period related and should be matched with the revenues produced during that period.

---

[3]The term *incurred* is not synonymous with *paid*. *Incurred* is used to imply an accrual basis of accounting instead of a cash basis. *Incurred* means that the firm has become liable for a payment, not that a payment has been made. Under an accrual basis of accounting, expired costs of the period are matched with revenues regardless of whether an actual cash payment has been made.

All selling and administrative costs are viewed as being period related. Thus, such costs as sales commissions, depreciation on delivery trucks and warehouses, salary of the pilot for the corporate jet, legal fees, and public relations are examples of period costs. They are deducted, in total, each and every period from the revenues of the period.

Product Costs   Some costs have the potential to produce revenues beyond the current period. The costs of manufacturing a product are incurred because benefits (revenues) will be realized upon sale of the product. But products produced currently can be placed in inventory and sold in some future period. When the product is sold, the potential benefits for which the costs were incurred are realized. Then, and only then, are the costs expensed. Consequently, costs to produce a product in a current period can appear as expenses in several different future periods.

Recall that the costs of direct materials, direct labor, and overhead are incurred to produce finished goods. These costs are product related, not period related. Until the finished goods are sold, these costs appear as assets (Inventory) on the balance sheet. Therefore, for external financial reporting, product costs are defined as manufacturing costs that are first inventoried and later expensed as the goods are sold.

product costs   The unit product cost is simply the cost of producing one unit of a product. For external financial reporting, **product costs** are defined as direct materials, direct labor, and overhead. Thus, the unit product cost is the amount of direct materials, direct labor, and overhead cost assigned to a single product. For example, in producing a can of soda, Coca Cola might incur the following costs:

Direct materials (can, fructose, water, etc.)	$0.06
Direct labor	0.01
Overhead	0.08
Total unit cost	$0.15

The unit product cost just defined is driven by the requirements of external financial reporting. If a bottling company has 100,000 cans of soda on hand at the end of the year, it would be reported as a $15,000 asset ($0.15 × 100,000).

For managerial purposes, other definitions of product cost may, at times, be more suitable. For planning and decision making, managers may demand a different definition of product cost. For example, a manager may want to know the comprehensive cost of a new product—a unit cost that includes both manufacturing and nonmanufacturing costs—to have some idea of what selling price should be set to earn an acceptable return. In this case, a unit product cost might appear as follows:

Direct materials	$12
Direct labor	5
Overhead	14
Selling and administrative	6
Total unit cost	$37

The manager would then know that a proposed selling price of $36 per unit would be unacceptable. Unit selling and administrative costs must also be covered.

Other unit cost definitions based on cost behavior may also prove useful to managers. The key point to understand is that internal managerial needs should not be restricted by the formal external reporting requirements. Managerial product costing is designed to provide the information managers need and is not necessarily concerned with inventory valuation. This illustrates the maxim of "different costs for different purposes." It may also require "different systems for different purposes." One cost accounting system may be needed for inventory valuation (to satisfy external reporting requirements), another for managerial product costing, and a third for control.[4]

prime cost
conversion cost

Prime and Conversion Costs   Two other useful cost terms are *prime cost* and *conversion cost*. **Prime cost** is the sum of direct materials cost and direct labor cost. **Conversion cost** is the sum of direct labor cost and overhead cost. Conversion cost can be interpreted as the cost of converting raw materials into a final product.

■ FINANCIAL STATEMENTS AND THE FUNCTIONAL CLASSIFICATION

The functional classification is the cost classification required for *external* reporting. Regulatory bodies such as the Securities and Exchange Commission and the Financial Accounting Standards Board mandate the functional approach for financial statements prepared for external use.

The income statement based on a functional classification for a manufacturing firm is displayed in Exhibit 2–1. This income statement follows the traditional format taught in an introductory financial accounting course. Income computed by following a functional classification is frequently referred to as an **absorption-costing income** or **full-costing income** because *all* manufacturing costs are fully assigned or absorbed by the product.

absorption-costing
income
full-costing income

---

[4]Robert S. Kaplan, "One Cost System Isn't Enough," *Harvard Business Review* (January–February, 1988), pp. 61–66.

EXHIBIT 2–1

Income Statement: Functional Classification

For the Year Ended
December 31, 1993

Sales		$4,000,000
Cost of goods sold:		
Beginning finished goods inventory	$ 500,000	
Add: Cost of goods manufactured	2,400,000	
Goods available for sale	$2,900,000	
Less: Ending finished goods inventory	(300,000)	2,600,000
Gross margin		$1,400,000
Less operating expenses:		
Selling expenses	$ 600,000	
Administrative expenses	300,000	(900,000)
Income before taxes		$ 500,000

---

cost of goods sold

Under the absorption-costing approach, expenses are segregated according to function and then deducted from revenues to arrive at net income. As can be seen in Exhibit 2–1, there are two major functional categories of expense: cost of goods sold and operating expense. These categories correspond, respectively, to a firm's manufacturing and nonmanufacturing expenses. **Cost of goods sold** is the cost of direct materials, direct labor, and overhead attached to the units sold. To compute the cost of goods sold, it is first necessary to determine the cost of goods manufactured.

Cost of Goods Manufactured

cost of goods manufactured

The **cost of goods manufactured** represents the total cost of goods completed during the current period. The only costs assigned to goods completed are the manufacturing costs of direct materials, direct labor, and overhead. The details of this cost assignment are given in a supporting schedule, called the *statement of cost of goods manufactured*. An example of this supporting schedule for the income statement in Exhibit 2–1 is shown in Exhibit 2–2.

Notice in Exhibit 2–2 that the total manufacturing costs added during the period are added to the manufacturing costs found in beginning work in process, yielding total manufacturing costs to account for. The costs found in ending work in process are then deducted from total manufacturing costs to arrive at the cost of goods manufactured. If the cost of goods manufactured is for a single product, then the average unit cost can be computed by dividing the cost of goods manufactured by the units produced. For example, assume that the statement in Exhibit 2–2 was prepared for the production of bottles

EXHIBIT 2–2

Statement of Cost of Goods Manufactured		
For the Year Ended *December 31, 1993*		
Direct materials:		
Beginning inventory	$ 400,000	
Add: Purchases	900,000	
Materials available	$1,300,000	
Less: Ending inventory	(100,000)	
Direct materials used		$1,200,000
Direct labor		700,000
Manufacturing overhead:		
Indirect labor	$ 255,000	
Depreciation	345,000	
Rent	100,000	
Utilities	75,000	
Property taxes	25,000	
Maintenance	100,000	900,000
Total manufacturing costs added		$2,800,000
Add: Beginning work in process		400,000
Total manufacturing costs		$3,200,000
Less: Ending work in process		(800,000)
Cost of goods manufactured		$2,400,000

of perfume and that 480,000 bottles were completed during the period. The average unit cost is $5 per bottle ($2,400,000/480,000).

work in process   **Work in process** consists of all partially completed units found in production at a given point in time. Beginning work in process consists of the partially completed units on hand at the beginning of a period. Ending work in process consists of those on hand at the period's end. In the statement of cost of goods manufactured, the cost of these partially completed units is reported as the cost of beginning work in process and the cost of ending work in process. The cost of beginning work in process represents the manufacturing costs carried over from the prior period; the cost of ending work in process represents the manufacturing costs that will be carried over to the next period. In both cases, additional manufacturing costs must be incurred to complete the units in work in process.

Cost Flows

cost flows   Costs are accounted for from the point they are incurred to their recognition as expenses on the income statement. This process is referred to as *cost flows*.

As will be shown, the cost flows of a manufacturing firm are more complex than those of a service firm or those of a merchandising firm.

The cost flow pattern of manufacturing firms is displayed in Exhibit 2–3. For a manufacturing firm, the selling and administrative costs are expensed immediately. However, the flow of product costs is more involved. In order to produce, the firm must purchase raw materials, acquire services of direct laborers, and incur overhead costs. As raw materials are purchased, the costs are initially assigned to an inventory account. When materials are placed in production, costs flow from the Raw Materials inventory account to the Work in Process inventory account. The cost of direct labor is assigned to the Work in Process account as it is incurred. Overhead costs are accumulated in a separate account and assigned periodically to the Work in Process account (the procedures for assigning overhead are discussed in a later chapter). When the goods being worked on are completed, the costs associated with these goods are transferred to the Finished Goods inventory account. Finally, when the goods are sold, the cost of the finished goods is transferred to the Cost of Goods Sold expense account.

Comparison to Merchandising Organizations

An income statement for a merchandising firm is shown in Exhibit 2–4. Note that for a merchandising firm, the two major functional cost classifications still exist but correspond to *product costs* and *nonproduct costs*. The concept of cost of goods sold also differs. In a merchandising firm, cost of goods sold repre-

EXHIBIT 2–3
Manufacturing Firms

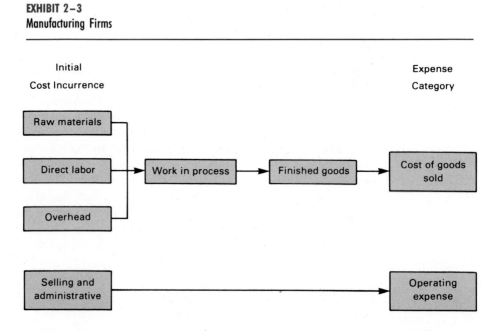

EXHIBIT 2–4
Income Statement for a Merchandising Firm

Sales		$ 5,000,000
Less cost of goods sold:		
Beginning inventory	$1,000,000	
Add: Purchases	3,000,000	
Goods available for sale	$4,000,000	
Less: Ending inventory	(850,000)	(3,150,000)
Gross margin		$ 1,850,000
Less operating expenses:		
Selling expenses	$ 500,000	
Administrative expenses	750,000	(1,250,000)
Income before taxes		$ 600,000

sents the acquisition cost of the goods, rather than the manufacturing cost. This acquisition cost is simply the amount paid for the goods being sold. This is more easily determined than is the cost of goods manufactured.

Cost Flows The cost flow pattern for a merchandising firm is shown in Exhibit 2–5. Operating costs, as incurred, are immediately expensed. Merchandise, however, is acquired, and the acquisition cost is first assigned to the Inventory account. Later, when the merchandise is sold, the costs flow, or are transferred, to an expense account.

EXHIBIT 2–5
Cost Flows: Merchandising Firm

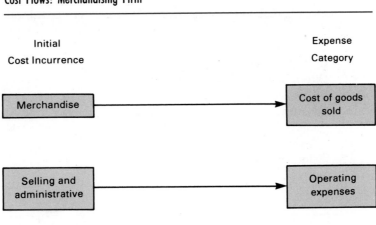

When comparing the cost flows of manufacturing and merchandising firms, we find that a manufacturing firm possesses two additional categories of inventory: raw materials and work in process. Since a merchandising firm deals only with finished goods, these production-related inventories are not required. This difference manifests itself in two ways on the financial statements of the two entities. First, manufacturing firms have a supporting schedule for the cost of goods manufactured figure appearing on the income statement. The second manifestation affects the balance sheet. A merchandising firm will show only a Merchandise inventory account in the asset section, whereas a manufacturing firm will show three inventory accounts: Finished Goods, Raw Materials, and Work in Process.

Comparison to Service Organizations

An income statement for a service organization is shown in Exhibit 2–6. For a service firm, the functional classifications correspond to service and non-service categories. The cost of services sold is computed differently from the cost of goods sold in a manufacturing firm. For example, for a dentist, the cost of services would include raw materials (e.g., amalgam for fillings), overhead (e.g., depreciation on dental equipment, utilities, and rent), and direct labor (e.g., salary of a dental assistant). But unlike a manufacturing firm, the service firm has no finished goods inventories—it is not possible to inventory services. Thus, product costs for a service firm expire in the period incurred. In a direct comparison, cost of services sold would always correspond to cost of goods manufactured.

Since all product costs are effectively period costs in a service organization, no distinction is usually made between the service and nonservice categories when preparing the income statement. However, knowing the cost of

EXHIBIT 2–6

Income Statement for a Service Organization

Sales		$ 300,000
Less expenses:		
Cost of services sold:		
Direct materials	$ 50,000	
Direct labor	100,000	
Overhead	100,000	(250,000)
Gross margin		$ 50,000
Less operating expenses:		
Selling expenses	$ 4,000	
Administrative expenses	17,500	(21,500)
Income before taxes		$ 28,500

services sold can provide valuable information for the managers or owners of service organizations. The need for a number of service organizations to cost out services has become even more critical because of the deregulatory movement that has taken place over the past five to ten years. Additionally, if a service organization wants a loan, it is helpful to present an income statement in a format familiar to bankers.

In the past, regulated service organizations were allowed to set a price that covered costs and provided a specified rate of return. Deregulation has brought stiff competition, and managers in the affected industries (e.g., airlines and telecommunications) need to know the cost of each service being marketed to make pricing decisions and profitability assessments. According to some experts, deregulation in the service industry has unleashed an enormous demand for improved cost accounting.

Understanding how income statements differ across the three different kinds of organizations provides some insight into the cost flows that occur within them. This, in turn, helps us to understand how cost accounting differs among the three types. Furthermore, studying the total cost flows for each of the three organizational categories provides a more comprehensive understanding of the cost accounting differences.

Cost Flows   The cost flow pattern for a service firm is shown in Exhibit 2–7. Raw materials, those materials directly involved in providing the service and often referred to as *supplies,* are purchased and their cost flows into the Inventory account. As materials, direct labor, and overhead are used to provide the service, these costs are immediately expensed. The cost of materials flows

EXHIBIT 2–7
Cost Flows: Service Organization

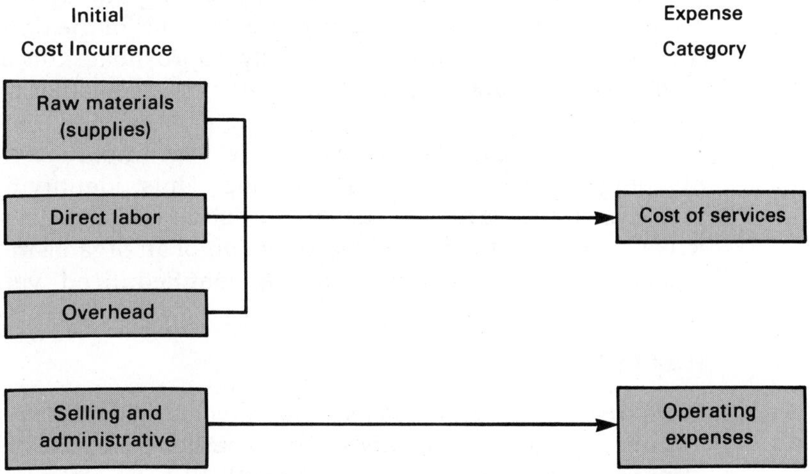

from the Inventory account to the expense account Cost of Services Sold. As with service costs, the operating costs of selling and administration are expensed as they are incurred.

Comparing the manufacturing cost flows to the cost flows of service organizations reveals some significant differences. Service organizations use direct materials, direct labor, and overhead. However, service organizations cannot build inventories of services. Consequently, there are no work-in-process or finished goods inventories.

The cost flows of all three organizations fit the functional cost classification—as did the income statements we described. Classification by cost behavior will produce a different view of both income statements and cost flows.

▪ CLASSIFICATION BY COST BEHAVIOR

Cost behavior deals with how costs change with respect to changes in activity levels. To assess cost behavior, the activity must be defined, the costs of the activity must be determined, and the changes in the activity level must be measured. The costs associated with an activity are those that are *caused* by the activity. Thus, in choosing a measure of activity-level changes, a measure must be chosen that is a *causal factor* for the activity's costs. A factor that

cost driver   causes (drives) activity costs is called a ***cost driver.*** For example, if work on the production line is the activity, then direct labor costs would be caused by the activity. Direct labor hours would then be a logical choice for a cost driver. Knowing how costs behave with respect to a relevant activity measure (cost driver) is essential for planning, control, decision making, and accurate product costing.

Assume that the cost driver is defined as the number of units produced. In general, economists assume that as the number of units produced increases, total costs will increase at a decreasing rate up to a certain point and then will increase at an increasing rate. Because of the difficulty in estimating the cost function, accountants usually approximate the underlying cost behavior by assuming a *linear relationship*. This means that total costs change at a constant rate.

Knowing how costs behave can be very important for product costing, planning, control, and decision making. Thus, identifying cost behavior is, perhaps, one of the most valuable contributions a management accountant can make to improve the overall management of an organization. Typically, three major categories of cost behavior are identified: fixed, variable, and mixed.

Fixed Costs

fixed costs   **Fixed costs** are costs that, *in total*, are constant within the relevant range as the level of the cost driver varies. To illustrate fixed cost behavior, consider a company that produces aluminum softball bats. Define the activity as producing bats and let the cost driver be the number of bats produced. The company operates one production line that can produce up to 5,000 bats per year. The production workers are supervised by a production-line manager who is paid $40,000 per year. The cost of supervision for several levels of production is given below.

Robin's Bats

| | Number of Bats | |
Supervision	Produced	Unit Cost
$40,000	1,000	$40.00
40,000	2,000	20.00
40,000	3,000	13.33
40,000	4,000	10.00
40,000	5,000	8.00

relevant range

The first step in assessing cost behavior is defining a relevant cost driver (activity measure). In this case, the cost driver is the number of bats produced. The second step is defining what is meant by **relevant range**, the range over which the assumed fixed cost relationship is valid for the normal operations of a firm. Assume that the relevant range is 1,000 to 5,000 bats. Notice that the *total* cost of supervision remains constant within this range as more bats are produced. Robin's Bats pays $40,000 for supervision regardless of whether it produces 1,000, 2,000, or 5,000 bats.

Pay particular attention to the words *in total* in the definition of fixed costs. While the total cost of supervision remains unchanged as more bats are produced, the unit cost changes as the level of the cost driver changes. As the example in the table shows, the unit cost of supervision decreases from $40 to $8. Because of the behavior of per-unit fixed costs, it is easy to get the impression that fixed costs are affected by activity level changes when in reality they are not. Unit fixed costs can often be misleading and may adversely affect some decisions. It is often safer to work with total fixed costs.

Another note of caution is needed. As more bats are produced, a second production line may be needed. This requirement, in turn, may produce the need for an additional production-line manager. Assume that this is true to produce more than 5,000 bats. The cost of supervision would then double to $80,000 as production increased above the level of 5,000 bats.

Graphical Illustration   We can gain additional insight into the nature of fixed costs by portraying them graphically. Total fixed costs can be represented by the following simple linear equation:

Total fixed cost = Dollar amount of fixed cost

$$Y_f = F$$

where Y_f = Total fixed cost
  F = Dollar amount of fixed cost

In our example for Robin's Bats, supervision cost amounted to $40,000 for any level output between 1,000 and 5,000 bats. Thus, supervision is a fixed cost, and the fixed cost equation in this case is

Total fixed cost = $40,000

To graph a simple linear equation, we need a horizontal axis to represent the cost driver (activity level) and a vertical axis to represent cost. For our example, production activity is measured in terms of units produced. The unit of measure for cost is dollars.

The graph representing fixed cost behavior is given in Exhibit 2–8. As can be seen, fixed cost behavior is described by a horizontal line. Notice that at zero bats produced, supervision cost is $40,000; at 1,000 bats produced, supervision is also $40,000. This line visually demonstrates that cost remains unchanged as the level of the cost driver varies.

Variable Costs

variable costs   **Variable costs** are defined as costs that, in total, vary in direct proportion to changes in a cost driver. To illustrate, let's expand the Robin's Bats example

EXHIBIT 2–8
Fixed Cost Behavior

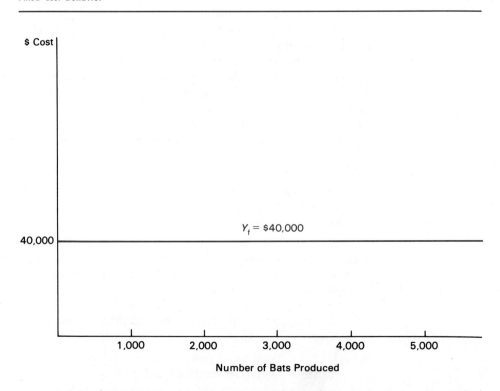

to include the cost of production-line workers. As with supervision, the activity is producing bats and the cost driver is number of bats. Each bat requires one-fourth hour of direct labor, and labor costs $12 per hour. Thus, the cost of production-line labor per bat is $3 (0.25 hour × $12 per hour). The cost of production-line labor for various levels of activity is given below:

Robin's Bats

Cost of Direct Labor	Number of Bats	Unit Cost
$ 3,000	1,000	$3
6,000	2,000	3
9,000	3,000	3
12,000	4,000	3
15,000	5,000	3

As more bats are produced, the total cost of production-line labor increases in direct proportion. For example, as production doubles from 1,000 to 2,000 units, the *total* direct-labor cost doubles from $3,000 to $6,000. Notice also that the unit cost of direct labor is constant.

Units of product, however, are not the only cost driver that can be used to describe the relationship. Direct labor hours can also be defined as the cost driver for direct labor cost. Why? Because direct labor hours also change in direct proportion to the number of units produced. The activity of producing bats can be measured in direct labor hours, using the fact that each bat requires one-fourth hour. The cost of direct labor for the Robin's Bats example, restated with direct labor hours as the cost driver, is displayed in Exhibit 2–9. As can be seen, the total variable costs predicted for each level of activity (measured by labor hours) are identical to the total variable costs predicted for each level of activity measured by units produced.

Graphical Illustration Variable costs can also be represented by a linear equation. Here total variable costs depend on the level of cost driver. This relationship can be described by the equation on p. 50.

EXHIBIT 2–9
Cost Driver: Direct Labor Hours—Robin's Bats

Cost of Direct Labor	Direct Labor Hours[a]	Cost per Hour
$ 3,000	250	$12
6,000	500	12
9,000	750	12
12,000	1,000	12
15,000	1,250	12

[a] ¼ × units produced (hours, therefore, correspond to different production levels)

$$\text{Total variable costs} = \text{Variable cost per unit} \times \text{Number of units of cost driver}$$
$$Y_v = VX$$

where Y_v = Total variable costs
        V = Variable cost per unit
        X = Number of units of cost driver

In our example for Robin's Bats, the relationship that describes the cost of direct labor is

$$\text{Total variable cost} = \$3 \times \text{Number of units produced}$$
or $$Y_v = \$3X$$

Exhibit 2–10 graphically illustrates a variable cost. Variable cost behavior is represented as a straight line coming out of the origin. Notice that at zero units produced, total variable cost is zero. However, as units produced in-

EXHIBIT 2–10
Variable Cost Behavior

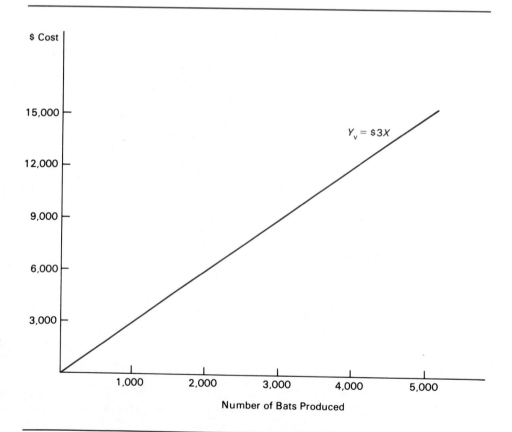

crease, the total variable cost also increases. Here it can be seen that total cost increases in direct proportion to increases in units of product (the cost driver); the rate of increase is measured by the slope of the line. At 1,000 bats produced, total direct labor cost is $3,000 (or $3 × 1,000 bats); at 2,000 bats produced, total direct labor cost is $6,000.

Mixed Costs

mixed costs   **Mixed costs** are costs that have both a fixed and a variable component. For example, a rental car often has a flat rate plus a charge per mile driven. Suppose the flat rate is $45 per day plus $0.20 per mile driven. If the car is rented for one day and driven 100 miles, the total rental is $65—the sum of the fixed charge of $45 plus the variable component of $20 ($0.20 × 100). Similarly, electricity is often billed at a flat rate per period plus a charge per kilowatt hour used. Assume that this is the case for the Robin's Bats example. Power is used to operate equipment used in the production of bats. The cost of power is $4,000 per year plus $0.50 per bat produced. The $0.50 charge per bat is based on the kilowatt hours used by each bat.

The linear equation for a mixed cost is given by

$$\text{Total cost} = \text{Fixed amount} + \text{Variable cost per unit} \times \text{Number of units}$$
$$= \text{Fixed cost} + \text{Total variable cost}$$

or $\quad\quad Y = F + VX$

where $\quad Y = \text{Total cost}$

For the Robin's Bats example, the total power cost is represented by the following equation:

$$\text{Total power cost} = \$4,000 + \$0.50 \times \text{Number of units produced}$$
$$Y = \$4,000 + \$0.50X$$

Thus, for Robin's Bats, the following shows the power cost associated with a variety of production levels:

Robin's Bats

Fixed Cost of Power	Variable Cost of Power	Total Cost	Number of Bats	Power Cost/Unit
$4,000	$ 500	$4,500	1,000	$4.50
4,000	1,000	5,000	2,000	2.50
4,000	1,500	5,500	3,000	1.83
4,000	2,000	6,000	4,000	1.50
4,000	2,500	6,500	5,000	1.30

The graph of a mixed cost for the Robin's Bat example is given in Exhibit 2–11 (the graph assumes that the relevant range is 0 to 5,000 units). Mixed

EXHIBIT 2–11
Mixed Cost Behavior

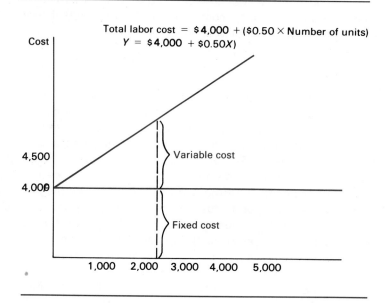

Total labor cost = $4,000 + ($0.50 × Number of units)
Y = $4,000 + $0.50X)

costs are represented by a line that intercepts the vertical axis (at $4,000 for this example). The intercept corresponds to the fixed cost component, and the slope of the line gives the variable cost per unit of cost driver (slope is $0.50 for the example portrayed).

▪ COST BEHAVIOR AND COST SYSTEMS

conventional (traditional) cost systems

activity-based cost (ABC) systems

Conventional (traditional) cost systems assume that all costs can be classified as fixed or variable with respect to changes in the *volume* of product produced. **Activity-based cost (ABC) systems,** on the other hand, assume that cost behavior is more complicated and requires additional cost drivers that are unrelated to the volume of product produced. For example, the costs of moving raw materials and partially finished goods from one point to another within a factory may be better described by the number of moves rather than the number of units produced. The net effect of an activity-based cost system is to increase the number of cost drivers that are used to describe cost behavior.

Both conventional and ABC approaches are found in practice. Conventional cost systems currently are much more widely used than ABC systems. The use of ABC systems, however, is increasing—particularly among organizations faced with increased product diversity, more product complexity, and intense competitive pressures. These organizations often adopt a just-in-time manufacturing approach (discussed in Chapters 6 and 13) and implement advanced manufacturing technology. For firms operating in this advanced manufacturing environment, the conventional cost systems may not work well. Better assessment of cost behavior and increased accuracy in product costing are both critical for the advanced manufacturing environment. The product-costing methods and the management accounting practices can differ significantly between the conventional and advanced manufacturing environments. Thus, in our study of management accounting, we will learn the methods and procedures for both conventional and advanced manufacturing environments.

Given an understanding of cost behavior, it is now possible to examine an income statement based on a cost behavioral classification. This type of income statement plays an important role in planning and control. It forms the basis for many of the conventional management accounting planning and control models.

Income Statement: Classification by Cost Behavior

The income statement based on a classification by cost behavior is displayed in Exhibit 2–12. Notice that the expenses are categorized by behavior. Variable and fixed cost behaviors are defined using units sold as the cost driver. Manufacturing and nonmanufacturing costs both appear in the same category if they have the same kind of cost behavior. Cost behavior is the emphasis—not the function.

variable cost of goods sold

variable cost of goods manufactured

Variable cost of goods sold is the total variable manufacturing costs attached to the units sold. **Variable cost of goods manufactured** is the total

EXHIBIT 2–12
Income Statement: Classification by Cost Behavior

Sales		$10,000,000
Less variable expenses:		
Variable cost of goods sold	$5,750,000	
Variable selling expenses	700,000	
Variable administrative expenses	150,000	(6,600,000)
Contribution margin		$ 3,400,000
Less fixed expenses:		
Fixed overhead	$1,000,000	
Fixed selling expenses	650,000	
Fixed administrative expenses	400,000	(2,050,000)
Income before taxes		$ 1,350,000

variable manufactured costs attached to the units produced. Variable manufacturing costs are direct materials, direct labor, and variable overhead. Examples of variable overhead items are power and supplies. Some overhead items are mixed costs and must be separated into their fixed and variable components. How this separation is done is the topic of a later chapter.

contribution margin

In computing net income, total variable expenses are first deducted from sales revenue to yield what is called *contribution margin*. Contribution margin is the amount available to cover fixed costs and provide for profit. Deducting all fixed costs from the contribution margin yields net income. This

contribution approach

income statement is often referred to as the *contribution approach.*

The contribution approach to income is consistent with a product-costing approach that treats all fixed expenses, including fixed overhead, as period expenses. Under this product-costing approach, only variable manufacturing costs are viewed as product costs. Preparation of a variable cost of goods manufactured statement parallels that of the functional cost of goods manufactured statement using, however, only variable manufacturing expenses. Similarly, the average variable cost per unit can be computed by dividing the variable cost of goods manufactured by the units produced, assuming, of course, only one type of product.

The functional approach to income, on the other hand, is consistent with the traditional absorption product-costing approach that always views fixed overhead as a product cost. The two approaches can yield different income figures. Only absorption costing is permitted for external financial reporting purposes. More importantly, the two approaches provide different kinds of information. The contribution income statement provides information that facilitates planning, control, and decision making. For example, using the contribution income statement, a manager can assess the contribution each product line is making to cover the firm's fixed costs. If a product line is making a positive contribution, then it may be a wise decision to keep the product line even though it cannot cover its *full* cost. Why? Because dropping a product line that is providing some coverage of fixed costs may actually reduce a firm's total profits. This insight is unavailable in the traditional income statement.

A comprehensive analysis of the differences between the traditional income statement and the contribution approach is covered in a later chapter. Important at this point is knowing how to prepare a contribution-approach income statement and realizing that it has potential value for improving planning, control, and decision making.

▪ SUMMARY OF LEARNING OBJECTIVES

1. **Classify costs by function and behavior.** Costs can be classified as either functional or behavioral. Functional costs are further subdivided into manufacturing and nonmanufacturing categories. Behavioral costs can be subdivided into fixed, variable, and mixed categories.

2. Identify product costs and period costs. For external reporting purposes, product costs are costs that attach to the product and are inventoried; they are expensed only when the product is sold. Direct materials, direct labor, and overhead are all classified as product costs. Period costs are costs that are related to periods of time rather than units of output. Period costs are always expensed in the period incurred. Selling and administrative costs are always classified as period costs (for external reporting purposes). For managerial purposes, definitions of product cost may differ from that required by external reporting.

3. Explain how financial statements differ among manufacturing, service, and merchandising firms. For manufacturing firms, the major functional expense classifications on the income statement are manufacturing and nonmanufacturing; for merchandising firms, the categories are product and nonproduct; for service firms, the categories are service and nonservice. For income determination in a manufacturing firm, the cost of goods manufactured must be calculated. No similar requirement exists for either a merchandising or service firm. For a service firm, the cost of services sold always corresponds to the cost of services produced. For a merchandising firm, the cost of goods acquired usually does not correspond to the cost of goods sold. The same is true for the cost of goods manufactured in a manufacturing firm.

4. Identify the cost flow patterns for manufacturing, service, and merchandising firms. Cost flow is the process of accounting for a cost from the point of incurrence to its expiration on the income statement. Of the three organizational types, manufacturing firms have the most complex cost flow; service firms have the least complex. The presence of work in process and finished goods inventories for manufacturing firms is the major cost flow difference between manufacturing and service firms. Merchandising firms have finished goods inventories, but they do not have work-in-process inventories.

5. Explain the difference between variable and fixed cost behavior. Fixed costs are costs that, in total, are constant as the cost driver (activity level) changes. Variable costs do change, in total, with changes in the cost driver (activity level). Mixed costs have both a variable and a fixed component.

6. Prepare an income statement using either the absorption-costing or variable-costing approaches. If costs are grouped according to function and then deducted from sales revenue, we have absorption-costing income statements. If, on the other hand, costs are grouped according to unit-based cost behavior and then deducted from sales revenue, we have a variable-costing income statement. For manufacturing firms, income statements, either absorption costing or variable costing, must be supported by a statement of the cost of goods manufactured.

■ KEY TERMS

Absorption-costing income Income produced by deducting costs classified according to a functional classification. Here all manufacturing costs are viewed as product costs. (p. 39)

Activity-based cost (ABC) system   A cost system that uses cost drivers in addition to units of product to describe cost behavior. (p. 52)

Administrative costs   The costs of general administration, which cannot be reasonably assigned to the marketing or manufacturing categories. (p. 37)

Asset   An unexpired cost representing a current or future benefit to the firm. (p. 33)

Contribution approach   Income produced by classifying costs by cost behavior and then deducting these costs from revenue. Here only variable manufacturing costs are viewed as product costs. (p. 54)

Contribution margin   Sales revenue less all variable expenses. It represents the amount available to cover fixed expenses and provide for profit. (p. 54)

Controllable cost   A cost that can be significantly influenced by a manager. (p. 34)

Conventional cost system   A cost system that uses only unit-based cost drivers to describe cost behavior and trace costs to products. (p. 52)

Conversion cost   The sum of direct labor cost and overhead cost. (p. 39)

Cost   The cash or cash equivalent value sacrificed for goods and services that are expected to bring a current or future benefit to the firm. (p. 32)

Cost driver   A factor that drives or causes activity costs. (p. 46)

Cost flow   The process of accounting for a cost from the point of incurrence to its expiration on the income statement. (p. 41)

Cost object   Any objective or activity to which costs are assigned. (p. 34)

Cost of goods manufactured   The cost of direct materials, direct labor, and overhead attached to the units produced in a period. (p. 40)

Cost of goods sold   The cost of direct materials, direct labor, and overhead attached to the units sold. (p. 40)

Differential cost   The amount by which cost differs between two alternatives. (p. 33)

Direct costs   Costs that are easily traceable to a cost object. (p. 34)

Direct labor   Cost of workers who transform raw materials into a finished product. (p. 35)

Direct manufacturing costs   Those manufacturing costs that can be easily traced to the product being manufactured. (p. 35)

Direct materials   Materials that become part of the product and that can be easily traced to it. (p. 35)

Expense   A cost that has expired or has been used up in the production of revenues; these appear as deductions on the income statement. (p. 32)

Fixed costs   Those costs, in total, that are constant within the relevant range as the level of the cost driver varies. (p. 46)

Full-costing income   *See* Absorption-costing income. (p. 39)

Indirect costs   Costs that are common to several cost objects and cannot be traced to any single cost object. (p. 34)

Indirect labor   Labor used in manufacturing that is not part of transforming the raw materials into the product. (p. 36)

Indirect materials All materials used in production that do not become part of the product. Insignificant direct materials are also usually assigned to this category. (p. 35)

Loss A cost that expires without producing a revenue benefit. (p. 32)

Manufacturing costs Those costs necessary to make a product. They include the costs of direct materials, direct labor, and overhead. (p. 35)

Manufacturing overhead All manufacturing costs other than direct labor and direct materials. (p. 35)

Mixed costs Those costs that have both a fixed and a variable component. (p. 51)

Noncontrollable cost A cost that cannot be significantly influenced by a manager. (p. 34)

Nonmanufacturing costs The costs associated with selling and general administration. (p. 35)

Opportunity cost The benefit sacrificed or forgone when one alternative is chosen over another. (p. 33)

Out-of-pocket cost A cost that involves a current cash outlay. (p. 33)

Period costs Costs that are related to periods of time rather than units of output; expensed each period. (p. 37)

Prime cost The sum of the cost of direct materials and direct labor. (p. 39)

Product costs Costs that attach to the product and are inventoried and expensed only when the product is sold. (p. 38)

Relevant range The range of activity over which cost behavioral relationships are valid. (p. 47)

Selling costs Those costs incurred to market and distribute a firm's products or services. (p. 36)

Sunk cost A cost for which the outlay has already been made. (p. 33)

Variable costs Those costs, in total, that vary as a cost driver (activity level) changes. (p. 48)

Variable cost of goods manufactured The cost of direct materials, direct labor, and variable overhead attached to the units produced in a period. (p. 53)

Variable cost of goods sold The total variable manufacturing costs attached to the units sold. (p. 53)

Work in process All partially completed units found in production at a given point in time. (p. 41)

■ REVIEW PROBLEM

Pop's Burger Heaven produces and sells quarter-pound hamburgers. Each burger sells for $1.50. During December, Pop's sold 10,000 burgers (the average amount sold each month). The restaurant employs cooks, servers, and one supervisor (the owner, John

Peterson). All cooks and servers are part-time employees. Pop's maintains a pool of part-time employees so that the number of employees scheduled can be adjusted to the changes in demand. Demand varies on a weekly as well as a monthly basis.

A janitor is hired to clean the building on a weekly basis. The building is leased from a local real estate company. The building has no seating capabilities. All orders are filled on a drive-through basis.

The supervisor schedules work, opens the building, counts the cash, advertises, and is responsible for hiring and firing. The following costs were incurred during December:

Hamburger meat	$1,600
Lettuce	300
Tomatoes	250
Buns	300
Other ingredients	20
Cooks' wages	2,550
Servers' wages	2,032
Supervisor's salary	2,000
Utilities	500
Depreciation:	
Cooking equipment	200
Cash register	50
Advertising	100
Rent	800
Janitorial supplies	50
Janitor's wages	120

The only mixed cost is for utilities. The fixed component is $50.

Required:

1. Classify the costs for Pop's December operations in one of the following categories: direct materials, direct labor, overhead, and selling and administrative.
2. Prepare an absorption-costing income statement for the month of December.
3. Prepare a contribution-approach income statement for December.

Solution:

1. Classification:
   a. *Direct materials*: Hamburger meat, lettuce, tomatoes, and buns
   b. *Direct labor*: Cooks' wages
   c. *Overhead*: Utilities, depreciation on the cooking equipment, rent, janitorial wages, janitorial supplies, and other ingredients
   d. *Selling and administrative*: Servers' wages, supervisor's salary, depreciation on the cash register, and advertising

Explanation of Classification:

Cooks are direct laborers because they make the hamburgers. "Other ingredients" are overhead because of cost and convenience, even though technically they are direct materials. Because the primary purpose of the building is production (cooking hamburgers), all of the rent and building-related costs are classified as indirect production costs. (An argument could be made that the building also supports the selling and administrative functions and, consequently, a portion of the rent and building-related costs should be classified as selling and administrative costs.) Servers are responsible for taking and filling orders and are, therefore, classified as sales personnel. The cash register is used to support the sales function. The supervisor is responsible for overseeing the business as a whole and coordinating the sales and production functions. Thus, his salary is an administrative cost.

2. Sales ($1.50 × 10,000) — — $15,000

Cost of goods sold:		
Direct materials	$2,450	
Direct labor	2,550	
Overhead	1,690	6,690
Gross profit		$ 8,310
Less operating expenses:		
Selling expenses	$2,182	
Administrative	2,000	(4,182)
Net income		$ 4,128

3. Sales ($1.50 × 10,000) — — $15,000

Less variable expenses:		
Variable cost of goods sold:		
Direct labor	$2,550	
Direct materials	2,450	
Variable overhead:		
Other ingredients	20	
Utilities	450	
	$5,470	
Variable selling costs	2,032	(7,502)
Contribution margin		$ 7,498
Less fixed costs:		
Fixed overhead	$1,220	
Fixed selling	150	
Fixed administrative	2,000	(3,370)
Net income		$ 4,128

■ QUESTIONS

1   Why is the manufacturing organization chosen as the framework for the study of management accounting? Do you agree with this choice?

2   Distinguish between the three types of organizations.

3   Does an organization incur a cost if it trades a building it owns for equipment? Explain.

4   What is a cost object?

5   What is a direct cost? An indirect cost?

6   What is a controllable cost?

7   Assume that the cost of buying a Honda Accord is $16,000 and the cost of buying a Mitsubishi Mirage is $11,500. What is the incremental cost of buying the Honda?

8   What is the difference between a direct manufacturing cost and an indirect manufacturing cost?

9   Explain why knowledge of cost behavior is useful information for a manager to have.

10 What is a cost driver?

11 What role does the relevant range play in the definition of a fixed cost?

12 On a per-unit basis, fixed costs are variable and variable costs are fixed. Do you agree? Explain your reasoning.

13 What is a conventional cost system? An ABC system? Which of the two is the most prevalent? Is this changing? Explain why.

14 Identify the three cost elements that determine the cost of making a product (for external reporting).

15 Product costs can be period costs, but period costs can never be product costs. Do you agree? Explain your reasoning.

16 Why are some direct materials classified as an overhead cost?

17 What is the difference between a loss and an expense?

18 What is the difference between a period cost and an expense?

19 How do the income statements of a merchandising firm and a manufacturing firm differ? How do the balance sheets differ?

20 How do the income statements of a service firm and a manufacturing firm differ? How do the balance sheets differ?

21 How does an absorption-costing income statement differ from a contribution-approach income statement? Which of the two income statements must be used for external reporting? Which of the two statements has the most value for internal purposes?

22 Explain what is meant by cost flow. How do the cost flows of the three different organizational types differ?

23 Explain why the salary of a plant manager would be classified as an overhead cost, not as an administrative cost.

24 Explain why the overtime premium paid to direct laborers is treated as an overhead cost, not as a direct labor cost.

25 Explain the difference between an opportunity cost and an out-of-pocket cost.

26 Explain why depreciation is a sunk cost.

27 A manager is considering two different production methods. Method A will have operating costs of $100,000 per year, and Method B will have operating costs of $128,000 per year. What is the differential cost?

28 A cost that is not controllable at one level may be controllable at a higher level. Explain.

29 Explain what is meant by a differential cost.

30 Explain why managerial product costing may produce a different unit cost than product costing for inventory (external reporting).

■ EXERCISES

E2–1 Cost Classification Harvey Johnson is a maintenance worker in a garden hose plant located in Stillwater, Oklahoma. Harvey is paid an annual salary of $30,000. He is responsible for maintaining and repairing a special kind of machine located in each of the two production departments (Department 1—Assembly, where plasticized tubing is cut into 75′ lengths and fitted with metal couplings at each end; and Department 2—Packaging, where the hoses are coiled and wrapped).

Harvey has a good friend, Helen Hunaker, who also works for the same company in its corporate office in Dallas, Texas. Helen is a sales representative for the firm. Her responsibilities involve creating and servicing accounts with retail outlets in the Dallas area. Helen is paid $20,000 plus a 5 percent commission on all new accounts.

Required:

1. Is Harvey's salary a manufacturing or a nonmanufacturing cost? If manufacturing, is it direct labor or indirect labor? If nonmanufacturing, is it a selling or an administrative cost?

2. Is Helen's salary a manufacturing or a nonmanufacturing cost? If manufacturing, is it direct labor or indirect labor? If nonmanufacturing, is it a selling or an administrative cost?

3. Is Harvey's salary a fixed, variable, or a mixed cost? Which is Helen's? How did you decide on your answers?

E2–2 Behavior of Overhead Costs Harrison Company manufactures 50-gallon glass aquariums. Based on past experience, Harrison has found that its total overhead costs can be represented by the following formula: Overhead = $100,000 + $25 × (Number of aquariums produced). During 1992, Harrison produced 10,000 aquariums.

Required:

1. What is the total overhead cost incurred by Harrison in 1992?

2. What is the total fixed overhead incurred by Harrison in 1992?

3. What is the total variable overhead incurred by Harrison in 1992?

4. What is the overhead cost per unit produced?

5. What is the fixed overhead cost per unit?

6. What is the variable overhead cost per unit?

7. Recalculate requirements 4, 5, and 6 for the following levels of production: (a) 20,000 units, and (b) 5,000 units. Explain this outcome.

E2–3 Cost of Goods Manufactured and Sold Sleepwell, Inc., manufactures sleeping bags. At the beginning of August, the following information was supplied by their accountant:

Raw Materials inventory	$18,500
Work in Process inventory	12,000
Finished Goods inventory	10,200

During August, direct labor cost was $40,500, raw materials' purchases were $80,000, and the total overhead cost was $105,750.

The inventories at the end of August were

Raw Materials inventory	$16,800
Work in Process inventory	23,500
Finished Goods inventory	9,100

Required:

1. Prepare a cost of goods manufactured statement for August.

2. Prepare a cost of goods sold statement for August.

E2–4   **Cost Classification**   Classify the costs below as variable, fixed, or mixed. Also identify the cost driver that allows you to define the cost behavior. (*Hint*: Cost behavior depends on the cost driver. For example, a receptionist's wages varies with the number of hours worked but is fixed with respect to units sold. Give some thought to the kind of activity associated with the cost drivers you choose.) Prepare your answer in the following format:

Cost	*Cost Behavior*	*Cost Driver*
Milk in ice cream	Variable	Units produced

1. Wages of assembly line workers

2. Circuit boards in a microcomputer

3. Advertising

4. Rental cars for sales personnel

5. Food cost of a factory cafeteria

6. Depreciation on a warehouse

7. Cost of utilities in a factory

8. Surgical gauze used in a hospital

9. The cost of all factory indirect labor

10. Amalgam used by a dentist

11. Wages of miners in a coal mine

12. The cost of leasing a building for a supermarket

13. Salary of a receptionist in a doctor's office

14. Commissions paid to sales personnel

15. The cost of forms used to file insurance claims

E2–5   **Preparation of Income Statements**   Simpson and Simpson manufacture a popular stuffed bear called Luv-Bears. Last year 50,000 bears were made and sold for $20 each. The actual unit cost for the Luv-Bear is given below.

Direct materials	$ 2.00
Direct labor	3.00
Variable overhead	2.50
Fixed overhead	4.00
Total unit cost	$11.50

The only selling expenses were a commission of $2 per unit sold and advertising totaling $100,000. Administrative expenses, all fixed, equaled $50,000. There were no beginning and ending finished goods inventories.

Required:

1. Prepare an absorption-costing income statement.
2. Prepare a contribution-approach income statement.

E2–6   **Per Unit Costs**   Refer to the data in Exercise 2–5. Calculate the following costs on a per-unit basis: prime cost, conversion cost, variable cost, full absorption cost, and variable manufacturing cost.

E2–7   **Cost Classification**   Classify the following costs as product or period costs (for external reporting purposes). For those costs that are product costs, identify the costs as direct materials, direct labor, or overhead.

   1. Legal fees paid by a corporation
   2. Depreciation on the factory building
   3. Property tax on work-in-process inventory
   4. Salary of a factory storeroom clerk
   5. Wages of a sewing machine operator in a clothes factory
   6. Lubricating oil for sewing machines
   7. Overtime wages paid to the sewing machine operators
   8. Corporate-level research and development costs
   9. Sugar in a candy bar
  10. Insurance on a warehouse and its inventory
  11. Salary of a janitor in a factory
  12. Warranty costs
  13. Depreciation on office equipment (at corporate headquarters)
  14. Pencils and paper clips for a production manager
  15. Property tax on plant and equipment

E2–8   **Cost Classification**   Refer to Exercise 2–7 and revise each cost in such a way that it will change from product to period cost, or vice versa.

Example: In 1 above, legal fees paid by a corporation are period costs. To change them into their opposites, product costs, they will have to be linked specifically to manufacturing—perhaps legal fees paid to file a patent on a new manufacturing process.

E2–9   **Cost of Goods Manufactured and Sold**   The following information comes from the accounting records of a manufacturing firm:

Direct labor cost	$12,500
Purchases of raw materials	7,500
Supplies used	675
Factory insurance	350
Commissions paid	2,000
Factory supervision	1,225
Advertising	782
Material handling	2,745
Beginning work-in-process inventory	12,500
Ending work-in-process inventory	14,250
Beginning raw materials inventory	3,475
Ending raw materials inventory	2,000
Beginning finished goods inventory	5,685
Ending finished goods inventory	3,250

Required:

1. Prepare a cost of goods manufactured statement.

2. Prepare a cost of goods sold statement.

E2–10   **Prime and Conversion Costs**   During March, Bronson, Inc., incurred the following manufacturing costs:

a. Direct laborers worked a total of 500 hours, including 100 overtime hours. The regular wage rate is $8 per hour. Overtime hours are paid at $12 per hour ($8 straight-time wage and $4 overtime premium).

b. Beginning raw materials inventory was $7,650. Purchases of raw materials were $3,350. There was no ending raw materials inventory.

c. Depreciation on plant and equipment was $10,000.

d. Insurance was $600.

e. Indirect labor was $2,000.

Required:

1. Calculate the prime cost for March.

2. Calculate the conversion cost for March.

E2–11   **Cost Assessment**   Francis, Inc., manufactures class rings. In the month of March, purchases of materials equaled $80,000, the beginning inventory of material was $47,300, and the ending inventory of material was $15,250. Payments to direct labor during the month totaled $63,000. Overhead incurred was $113,000.

Required:

1. What was the cost of materials used in production during the month of March?
2. What was prime cost for March?
3. What was conversion cost for March?
4. What was total manufacturing cost for March?
5. If ending work in process equaled $17,000 and there was no beginning work in process, what was the cost of goods manufactured?

E2–12 **Cost of Goods Manufactured and Sold**   For each of the three companies (A, B, and C) listed below, calculate the missing values.

	A	B	C
Direct materials	$15,000	$ 41,014	$10,000
Direct labor	26,000	?	7,500
Overhead	17,500	50,000	20,700
Total manufacturing cost added	$?	$125,360	$?
Beginning work in process	—	?	5,112
Ending work in process	?	12,000	7,000
Cost of goods manufactured	$44,300	$?	$?
Beginning inventory, finished goods	30,000	51,500	16,000
Ending inventory, finished goods	26,400	36,000	?
Cost of goods sold	$?	$174,110	$50,000

E2–13 **Cost Drivers**   Identify which of the following cost drivers explain changes in cost attributable to changes in the number of units produced.

a. Machine hours
b. Number of setups
c. Number of purchase orders
d. Kilowatt hours (machine-intensive production setting)
e. Number of material moves
f. Direct labor dollars
g. Direct material dollars
h. Number of inspection hours
i. Number of rework hours (rework hours are labor hours used to correct a defective or faulty product)

E2–14 **Cost Behavior and Decision Making**   Redland Paper Products is a small company that specialized in the production of paper towels until several years ago. The company had generally prospered, but five years ago, the market for towels became very competitive and profits dropped sharply. The output of the one plant owned by the company was exclusively devoted to towels. Two years ago, a decision to add a product line was made. Management determined that existing idle capacity could easily be adapted to produce paper napkins. Moreover, the variable cost of producing a package of napkins was virtually identical to that of a package of towels. Since the fixed expenses would not change, the new product was forecast to increase profits significantly.

Two years after the addition of the new product line, profits had not improved—in fact, they had actually dropped. Upon investigation, the president of the company discovered that profits had not increased as expected because the so-called fixed cost pool had increased dramatically. The president interviewed the manager of each support department. Typical responses from three of those managers are given below.

Purchasing: The new line increased the number of purchase orders. We had to use more resources to handle this increased volume.

Accounting: There were more transactions to process than before. We had to increase our staff.

Setups: There are two styles of napkins—each requiring a different setup. The increased number of setups required us to increase our expenditures.

Required:

Explain why the results of adding the new product line were not accurately projected.

▪ PROBLEMS

P2–1   **Cost Identification**   Given below is a list of cost items described in the chapter and a list of brief descriptive settings where the items are described. Match the items with the settings. There may be more than one cost classification associated with each setting; however, select the setting that seems to fit the item best.

Cost terms:

a. Loss	**i.** Variable cost
b. Sunk cost	**j.** Fixed cost
c. Opportunity cost	**k.** Prime cost
d. Controllable cost	**l.** Period cost
e. Differential cost	**m.** Product cost
f. Direct labor cost	**n.** Direct materials cost
g. Selling cost	**o.** Overhead cost
h. Conversion cost	**p.** Administrative cost

Settings:

1. Howard Mitchel, president of Kepler Insurance Company, is examining two alternative microcomputer systems. One system has a slightly higher quality printer. The difference in cost between the two systems is $1,500.

2. The design engineer estimated that the cost of raw materials, labor, and overhead for the new product would be $25 per unit produced.

3. Linda was having a hard time deciding on whether to return to school or not. She was concerned about the good salary she would have to give up for the next four years.

4. Randy Harris is chief executive officer for a medium-size firm. He is paid a salary of $90,000 per year. As he studied the financial statement prepared by the local CPA firm, he wondered how his salary was treated.

5. Maria Sanchez was disgusted. Her entire inventory of silk blouses had been ruined by a leaky roof. The inventory wasn't insured, and all she could do was write off the cost of the inventory. Well, at least some tax savings might be realized.

6. Jamie Young is in charge of the finished goods warehouse. Her salary is $35,000 per year. She reports to the vice-president of marketing.

7. All factory costs that are not classified as direct materials or direct labor.

8. Gary Sorenson was trying to reduce the cost of the material-handling activity. He discovered that material-handling costs increased in direct proportion to the number of moves made. Accordingly, he initiated a study to see whether manufacturing operations could be redesigned to reduce the number of moves.

9. Tom Wilson decided that the manager of the Cutting Department should be held responsible for the maintenance cost incurred. After all, he is the one who decides when and how frequently preventive maintenance is done.

10. The new product required machining, assembly, and painting. The design engineer requested the accounting department to estimate the labor cost of each of the three operations. The engineer supplied the estimated labor hours for each operation.

11. After obtaining the estimate of direct labor cost, the design engineer estimated the cost of the materials that would be used for the new product.

12. The design engineer totaled the costs of materials and direct labor for the new product.

13. The design engineer also estimated the cost of converting the raw materials into its final form.

14. In deciding whether to get rid of the Camaro, Bob reminded himself that it didn't really matter how much money he had spent on rebuilding the engine. The money was spent and gone! All that was important now was what it would cost him to continue owning the car.

15. The rental agreement on the company plane called for a payment of $3,000 per month, regardless of how much the plane was flown. There was no penalty for excess use. At the end of the agreement, however, ownership of the plane reverted to the lessor.

16. The auditor pointed out that sales commissions had been incorrectly assigned to Finished Goods inventory. Accordingly, the total commissions were reallocated to the income statement.

P2–2 **Cost Behavior** Benson Company is a toy manufacturer. Among the toys produced are three different models of battery-operated toy trucks: pickups, diesel cabs with trailers, and dump trucks. During the coming year, Benson expects to produce 12,000 toy dump trucks. The expected manufacturing costs for this number of trucks are given below.

Direct materials	$60,000
Direct labor	40,000
Overhead:	
Supplies	3,000
Depreciation	13,200
Indirect labor	6,000
Power	4,000
Supervision	28,000

Assume that all the individual cost items are either strictly fixed or strictly variable with respect to units produced. (Compute your answers to four decimal places.)

Required:

1. Prepare a cost formula for the following costs:
   a. Direct materials
   b. Direct labor
   c. Variable overhead
   d. Fixed overhead
   e. Total manufacturing costs

2. Assuming that 15,000 dump trucks are produced, use the cost formulas developed in requirement 1 and compute the following:
   a. Total cost of direct materials
   b. Total cost of direct labor
   c. Total cost of variable overhead
   d. Total cost of fixed overhead
   e. Total manufacturing costs

3. What is the unit cost of a toy dump truck if 12,000 units are manufactured as planned? What is the total cost if 15,000 dump trucks are manufactured? The unit cost? Why does the unit cost change?

P2–3 **Cost Classification** Classify each of the following items as (1) a direct or indirect product cost (or N/A if it is not a product cost), (2) a product or period cost, or (3) a fixed, variable, or mixed cost (assuming units of product as the cost driver).

1. Tacks in a large sofa

2. Salary of a plant security guard

3. Buttons on a shirt

4. Salary of a plant manager

5. Carpenters in a construction company

6. Salary of a warehouse clerk

7. Total overhead cost

8. Printing and postage for advertising circulars

9. Total selling costs

10. Sheetrock in a new home being built

11. Depreciation on the company's executive jet plane

12. Depletion on an existing oil well

13. Fees paid for an annual audit

14. The total cost of operating a power service center in a factory

15. Pipelines for transporting crude oil to a refinery

16. The cost of a market research study

17. Pipelines for transporting crude oil to customers

P2–4 **Income Statement: Cost of Goods Manufactured** Hannibal Company produced 2,000 leather saddles during 1993. These saddles sell for $350 each. Hannibal had 250 saddles in finished goods inventory at the beginning of the year. At the end of the year there were 350 saddles in finished goods inventory. Hannibal's accounting records provide the following information:

Purchases of raw materials	$160,000
Raw materials inventory, January 1, 1993	23,400
Raw materials inventory, December 31, 1993	33,400
Direct labor	100,000
Indirect labor	20,000
Rent, factory building	21,000
Depreciation, factory equipment	30,000
Utilities, factory	5,978
Salary, sales supervisor	55,000
Commissions, salespersons	38,000
General administration	61,000
Work-in-process inventory, January 1, 1993	6,520
Work-in-process inventory, December 31, 1993	7,498
Finished goods inventory, January 1, 1993	40,000
Finished goods inventory, December 31, 1993	57,050

Required:

1. Prepare a cost of goods manufactured statement.

2. Compute the cost of producing one unit of product in 1993.

3. Prepare an income statement on an absorption-costing basis.

P2–5   **Cost of Goods Manufactured; Cost Identification; Contribution Margin; Solving for Unknowns**   Winn Company creates, produces, and markets games of strategy. Before any employee is hired, a puzzle of some sort must be successfully solved.

You are applying for a job as an entry-level accountant. The controller of the firm wishes to test your knowledge of basic cost terms and concepts, and, at the same time, evaluate your analytical skills. To do so, he gives you the following information for 1993:

a. Total fixed overhead, $190,000.

b. Per-unit variable manufacturing cost, $25. There are no other variable costs.

c. Total current variable manufacturing costs equal 125 percent of current conversion cost.

d. Units produced, 10,000.

e. Beginning work in process is one-half the cost of ending work in process.

f. There are no beginning or ending inventories for raw materials or finished goods.

g. Cost of goods sold is $400,000.

h. Variable overhead equals 133 percent of direct labor costs.

Required:

1. Prepare a statement of cost of goods manufactured for 1993.

2. If the selling price is $50 per unit, what is the gross margin? What is the total contribution margin?

3. If you were operating below capacity and someone offered to buy 1,000 units for a price of $29 per unit, what is the change in profits (incremental profits) assuming the order is accepted? (Assume that the 1,000 units will be produced using the extra capacity available.)

P2–6 **Cost of Goods Manufactured; Cost Behavior; Unit Cost; Income Statements**   Crumbley Company produces a popular line of saltine crackers. The following data are provided for the year ended, July 31, 1992:

Units produced	20,000
Cost of goods sold	$ 70,400
Goods available for sale	$144,000
Cost of goods manufactured	$128,000
Beginning raw materials inventory	$ 20,000
Purchases, raw materials	$ 40,000
Direct labor	$ 28,000
Overhead	$ 50,000
Beginning work in process	—
Ending work in process	—

Required:

1. Prepare a statement of cost of goods manufactured. What is the full manufacturing cost per unit?

2. Assume that the total overhead can be described by the formula, $Y = \$25,600 + \$1.22X$, where X = Units produced. Prepare a statement of the *variable* cost of goods manufactured. What is the variable manufacturing cost per unit?

3. During the year, 11,000 units were sold for a price of $10 per unit. Selling and administrative costs are fixed and total $15,000. Assume that the unit cost of finished goods in beginning inventory is the same as the current cost per completed unit (for both approaches). Prepare the following:
   a. An absorption-costing income statement
   b. A contribution-approach (or behavioral) income statement

P2–7 **Cost of Goods Manufactured; Cost Behavior; Income Statements**   Lamson Company produces circuit boards that are used by manufacturers of microcomputers. For 1993, Lamson reported the following:

Inventories:	
Work in process, January 1	$ 12,500
Work in process, December 31	12,500
Finished goods, January 1 (24,000 units)	120,000
Finished goods, December 31 (12,000 units)	60,000
Raw materials, January 1	20,000
Raw materials, December 31	30,000
Costs:	
Direct materials used	$ 70,000
Direct labor	100,000
Plant depreciation	15,000
Salary, production supervisor	30,000
Indirect labor	20,000

Utilities, factory	6,000
Sales commissions	8,000
Salary, sales supervisor	20,000
Depreciation, factory equipment	5,000
Administrative costs (all fixed)	12,000
Indirect materials	4,000

Lamson produced 50,000 units during 1993 and sold 62,000 units at $12 per unit. Work-in-process and finished-goods inventories consisted of 80 percent variable costs. All costs listed above are strictly variable or strictly fixed. There are no mixed costs.

Required:

1. Prepare a statement of cost of goods manufactured. Calculate the full manufacturing cost per unit produced.

2. Prepare a statement of the cost of goods manufactured using only variable manufacturing costs. Calculate the variable manufacturing cost per unit.

3. Prepare an absorption-costing income statement.

4. Prepare an income statement using the contribution approach.

P2–8 **Cost Behavior: Multiple Cost Drivers** Anderson Company currently produces an electronic circuit board for stereo units. A manufacturing cost formula based on direct labor hours for this product is given below.

$$\text{Total manufacturing costs} = \$300,000 + \$15X$$

where X is direct labor hours. The plant is producing 10,000 units per year but has the capacity to produce 15,000. Market conditions will likely not permit any expansion of production for the stereo circuit board. The company, however, is planning to add a new product: a circuit board for small television sets. Existing equipment can be adapted to produce the product. Engineers estimate that the same direct labor hours will be used per unit. In fact, the same variable cost per direct labor hour will be incurred. The controller has argued that the fixed costs will remain at $300,000 — after all, these costs should not change as production activity increases. Thus, the manufacturing cost formula will not change for the two-product setting.

Of the fixed costs, $100,000 represents depreciation, $100,000 is the cost of operating the purchasing department, and $100,000 is the cost of operating the engineering department. Before making a final decision on the new product, a consultant was hired to assess the impact of the new product on the costs of the firm. The consultant developed the following cost formulas, using three different cost drivers:

Cost Formula	*Cost Driver*
Purchasing department cost = $40,000 + \$30X_1$	X_1 = Number of purchase orders
Engineering department cost = $50,000 + \$100X_2$	X_2 = Number of engineering orders
Remaining overhead cost = $100,000 + \$15X_3$	X_3 = Direct labor hours

The consultant also provided the following estimates of activity for each product:

	Stereo Board	*Television Board*
Units of product	10,000	5,000
Direct labor hours	20,000	10,000
Purchase orders	2,000	2,000
Engineering orders	500	1,000

Required:

1. Calculate the total cost of producing the stereo circuit boards without the new product. Do you think this cost is accurate? Explain.

2. Using only the direct-labor-hour cost formula, calculate the total cost of producing both products.

3. Using the cost formulas developed by the consultant, calculate the total cost of producing both products. Explain why the two numbers differ. Which approach do you think provides the more accurate prediction? Why?

4. Using only the variable cost portion of the unit-based formula, calculate the variable cost per unit for each product. Now calculate the cost per unit for each product using only the variable elements from each of the consultant's formulas. Which method do you think provides the more accurate product costing? Explain.

P2–9 **Cost Identification and Analysis** Melissa Scothern has decided to open a printing shop. She has secured a five-year contract to print a popular regional magazine. The contract calls for 5,000 copies each month.

Melissa has rented a building for $800 per month. Her printing equipment was purchased for $40,000 and has a life expectancy of eight years with no salvage value. Straight-line depreciation will be used.

Insurance costs for the building and equipment are $75 per month. Utilities are directly related to output and are expected to cost $250 for an output of 5,000 copies.

Materials to print the magazine will cost $0.50 per copy. Melissa will supervise the operation and will hire workers to run the presses as needed. She must pay $10 per hour. Each worker can produce 20 copies of the magazine per hour. Melissa will receive a salary of $1,200 per month.

A salesperson has been hired for $500 per month plus a 20 percent commission on all new sales. Advertising on the local radio station will cost $330 per month.

Required:

1. What is the full manufacturing cost per unit for the regional magazine?

2. How many workers will Melissa need to hire for the first month (assume 40 hours per week equals one worker; there are four weeks in a month)?

3. What is the variable manufacturing cost per unit?

4. What is the prime cost per unit? The conversion cost per unit?

5. In a single-product business, are there any indirect product costs? Explain.

6. If Melissa receives $1.80 per copy, how much will her income be for the first month of operations?

P2–10 **Cost Behavior; Unit Costs** Sandy Enterprises reported the following data for its most recent year of activity:

Production	10,000 units
Sales	10,000 units at $100 each
Inventories	No beginning or ending inventories
Costs:	
Direct materials	$500,000
Direct labor	100,000
Overhead:	
Indirect materials	25,000
Supervision	35,000
Depreciation	15,000
Utilities	12,000

Required:

1. Prepare a cost formula for manufacturing costs.

2. Compute the unit cost of production if:
   a. Production is 10,000 units.
   b. Production is 5,000 units.
   c. Production is 20,000 units.
   Why does the unit cost change?

3. What is the unit cost of direct materials at each of the three production levels given in Question 2? Of direct labor? Of overhead?

4. Compute the total cost of operating the firm if
   a. 10,000 units are produced and sold.
   b. 5,000 units are produced and sold.
   c. 20,000 units are produced and sold.

5. The president of Sandy Enterprises, as a gesture of friendship, agrees to sell 10,000 units at cost to the city in which Sandy's main plant is located. The sales commission will still be paid to the salesperson who initiated the sale (based on actual revenues received). If you were the controller, what cost would you consider using for the 10,000 units? Why?

■ MANAGERIAL DECISION CASES

C2–1 **Cost Classification, Cost Behavior, Income Statements; Service Organization** Lindley Construction Company is a family-operated business, founded in 1937 by William Lindley. In the beginning, the company consisted of Lindley and two employees laying water pipeline as subcontractors. Currently, the company employs 20 to 25 people; it is directed by John Lindley, William's son.

Lindley Construction's main line of business is installing water and sewer lines. More than 90 percent of Lindley's work comes from contracts with city and state agencies. All of the company's work is located in the state of Idaho. The company's sales volume averages $1.5 million, and profits vary between 0 and 10 percent of sales.

Sales and profits have been somewhat below average for the past three years due to a recession and intense competition. Because of this competition, John Lindley is constantly reviewing the prices that other companies bid for jobs; when a bid is lost, he makes every attempt to analyze the reasons for the differences between his bid and that of his competitors. He uses this information to increase the competitiveness of future bids.

John has become convinced that Lindley's current accounting system is deficient. Currently, all expenses are simply deducted from revenues to arrive at net income. No effort is made to distinguish among the costs of laying pipe, obtaining contracts, and administering the company. Yet all bids are based on the costs of laying pipe.

John also knows that knowledge of cost behavior is important. He is certain that the company could offer more competitive bids if he knew which costs were variable and which were fixed. For example, Lindley often has idle equipment (the company needs more equipment than is often necessary so that it can bid on larger projects). If Lindley could bid enough to cover its variable costs and use the idle equipment, equipment operators could be more productively utilized and have more job stability. In fact, if the bid covered more than variable costs, profits would increase as well, since the fixed costs remain unchanged for increased activity.

With these thoughts in mind, John began a careful review of the income statement for the previous year (see Exhibit 1). First, he noted that jobs were priced on the basis of equipment hours, with an average price of $165 per equipment hour. However, when it came to classifying costs and identifying their behavior, he decided that he needed some help. One thing that really puzzled him was how to classify his own salary of $57,000. About half of his time was spent in bidding and securing contracts, and the other half was spent in general administrative matters.

EXHIBIT 1

Lindley Construction		
Income Statement 1992		
Sales (9,100 equipment hours at $165)		$1,501,500
Less expenses:		
Utilities	$ 12,000	
Machine operators	109,000	
Rent (office building)	12,000	
CPA fees	20,000	
Other direct labor	122,850	
Administrative salaries	57,000	
Supervisor salaries	35,000	
Pipe	700,670	
Tires and fuel	209,300	
Depreciation on equipment	99,000	
Salaries of mechanics	25,000	
Advertising	7,500	
Total expenses		1,409,320
Net income		$ 92,180

Required:

1. Classify the costs as shown in Exhibit 1 as (1) costs of laying pipe (production costs); (2) costs of securing contracts (selling costs); and, (3) costs of general administration. For production costs, identify direct materials, direct labor, and overhead costs.

2. Using the functional classification developed in requirement 1, prepare a functional income statement. What is the average cost per equipment hour for laying pipe?

3. Now classify the costs as fixed or variable (assuming a unit-based cost driver). Assume that any mixed cost is 50 percent fixed and 50 percent variable.

4. Prepare a contribution-approach income statement. What is the variable cost per equipment hour? Suppose that John Lindley has idle equipment and has the opportunity to take a job at $135 per hour. Should he accept the job? Why or why not?

C2-2 **Cost Information and Ethical Behavior** Jean Erickson, manager and owner of an advertising company in Charlotte, North Carolina, had arranged a meeting with Leroy Gee, the chief accountant of a large, local competitor. Jean and Leroy were lifelong friends. They had grown up together in a small town and attended the same university.

Leroy was a competent, successful accountant but currently was experiencing some personal financial difficulties. The problems were created by some investments that had turned sour, leaving Leroy with a $15,000 personal loan to pay off—just at the time that his oldest son was scheduled to enter college.

Jean, on the other hand, was struggling to establish a successful advertising business. She had recently acquired the rights to open a branch office of a large regional advertising firm headquartered in Atlanta, Georgia. During her first two years, she had managed to build a small, profitable practice; however, the chance to gain a significant foothold in the Charlotte advertising community hinged on the success of winning a bid to represent the state of North Carolina in a major campaign to attract new industry and tourism. The meeting Jean had scheduled with Leroy concerned the bid she planned to submit.

"Leroy, I'm at a critical point in my business venture. If I can win the bid for the state's advertising dollars, I'll be set. Winning the bid will bring $600,000 to $700,000 of revenues into the firm. On top of that, I estimate that the publicity will bring another $200,000 to $300,000 of new business."

"I understand," replied Leroy. "My boss is anxious to win that business as well. It would mean a huge increase in profits for my firm. It's a competitive business, though. As new as you are, I doubt that you'll have much chance of winning."

"You may be wrong. You're forgetting two very important considerations. First, I have the backing of all the resources and talent of a regional firm. Second, I have some political connections. Last year, I was hired to run the publicity side of the governor's campaign. He was impressed with my work and would like me to have this business. I am confident that the proposals I submit will be very competitive. My only concern is to submit a bid that beats your firm. If I come in with a lower bid and with good proposals, the governor can see to it that I get the work."

"Sounds promising. If you do win, however, there will be a lot of upset people. After all, they are going to claim that the business should have been given to local advertisers, not to some out-of-state firm. Given the size of your office, you'll have to get support from Atlanta. You could take a lot of heat."

"True. But I am the owner of the branch office. That fact alone should blunt most of the criticism. Who can argue that I'm not a local? Listen, with your help, I think I can win this bid. Furthermore, if I do win it, you can reap some direct benefits. With that kind of business, I can afford to hire an accountant, and I'll make it worthwhile for you to transfer jobs. I can offer you an up-front bonus of $15,000. On top of that, I'll increase your annual salary by 20 percent. That should solve most of your financial difficulties. After all, we have been friends since day one—and what are friends for?"

"Jean, my wife would be ecstatic if I were able to improve our financial position as quickly as this opportunity affords. I certainly hope that you win the bid. What kind of help can I provide?"

"Simple. To win, all I have to do is beat the bid of your firm. Before I submit my bid, I would like you to review it. With the financial skills you have, it should be easy for you to spot any excessive costs that I may have included. Or perhaps I included the wrong kind of costs. By cutting excessive costs and eliminating costs that may not be directly related to the project, my bid should be competitive enough to meet or beat your firm's bid."

Required:

1. What would you do if you were Leroy? Fully explain the reasons for your choice.

2. What is the likely outcome if Leroy agrees to review the bid? Is there much risk to Leroy personally if he reviews the bid? Should the degree of risk have any bearing on Leroy's decision?

3. Apply the code of ethics for management accountants to the proposal given Leroy (see the Appendix to Chapter 1). What standards would be violated if Leroy agrees to review the bid? Assume that Leroy is a member of the NAA and holds a CMA.

CHAPTER 3

Job-Order Costing

■ **LEARNING OBJECTIVES**

After studying Chapter 3, you should be able to

1. Describe the differences between job-order costing and process costing and identify the types of firms that would use each method.

2. Define actual and normal costing and explain why normal costing is preferred.

3. Compute a predetermined overhead rate and use the rate to assign overhead to work in process.

4. Know the role of activity-level measurement and the choice of activity level in computing predetermined overhead rates.

5. Compute under- and overapplied overhead and know how to dispose of the overhead variance at the end of the period.

6. Identify the source documents used in job-order costing.

7. Describe the cost flows and prepare the journal entries associated with job-order costing.

8. Explain why multiple overhead rates may be preferred to a single, plant-wide overhead rate.

9. Define and explain the key terms listed at the end of the chapter.

SCENARIO

The Applegate Construction Company was established in 1957. For more than thirty years, the company specialized in building subdivisions. The company could be described as a small but successful business with a good reputation for building quality homes. Recently, Walter Applegate, the founder and owner of the company, retired and his son, Jay Applegate, assumed control of the company.

Jay decided that the company needed to expand into custom-built homes and nonresidential construction. As he began to explore these possibilities, he encountered some problems with the company's current accounting system. Accordingly, he requested a meeting with his aunt, Bonnie Barlow, the financial manager. She was responsible for bookkeeping and payroll. A local CPA firm prepared quarterly financial reports and filed all the company's tax returns.

"Bonnie, as you know, I want to see our company become one of the largest in this region. To accomplish this objective, I am convinced that we need to expand our operations so that they include custom homes and some industrial buildings. I think we can gain business in both of these areas by capitalizing on our reputation for quality. However, I am afraid that as we enter these markets, we are going to have to change our accounting system. I'm going to need your help in making the changes."

"I'm not sure why you feel that we need to change our accounting procedures. They are simple, and they've worked well for thirty years."

"In the past, our company has built homes in subdivisions that are basically the same. We've had slight variations in design so that they aren't carbon copies, but each home has required essentially the same work and materials. The cost of each home has been computed by simply accumulating the actual costs incurred over the period of time it took to build all the homes and then dividing this total by the number of units constructed. This approach will not work when we enter the market for custom-built homes or industrial units."

"I think I see the problem. Custom-built homes, for example, may require different cement work, different carpentry work, and may use more expensive materials, like a jacuzzi instead of a regular bathtub. They may also differ significantly in size from our standard units. If we divide the total construction costs of a period by the number of units produced, we don't have a very accurate representation of what it's costing to build any individual home. Additionally, the cost of our standard units could be distorted. Industrial units would cause even worse problems. It sounds like we need a different method to accumulate our construction costs."

"I agree. We need some way of tracking the labor, materials, and overhead used by each job. I don't foresee much difficulty with labor or materials, but the measurement of overhead used by each job will be difficult. I am unclear as to how much overhead should be assigned to the different jobs. It seems unfair to omit property taxes from the cost of a home built in June simply because we pay them in November. Utilities also vary from month to month."

"Jay, it seems to me that we have two issues: how to measure our construction costs, especially overhead, and how we should assign those costs to the different jobs. I have a suggestion. Let me talk to our CPA and see what advice she can give us. I am sure that she can suggest a cost system that will address both of these issues."

■ TWO ISSUES: COST ASSIGNMENT AND COST MEASUREMENT

Conceptually, computing the unit manufacturing cost is simple. The unit cost is the total manufacturing cost associated with the units produced divided by the number of units produced. For example, if Applegate Construction builds 100 subdivision homes during the year and the total cost of materials, labor, and overhead for these homes is $6 million, then the cost of each home is $60,000 ($6 million/100 homes). Although the concept is simple, the practical reality of the computation can be somewhat more complex. As the dialogue between Jay and Bonnie reveals, the straightforward approach breaks down when there are products that differ from one another or when the need for costing the product materializes before all of the actual costs associated with its production are known (or both).

cost measurement

Total manufacturing costs must be *measured*, and then these costs must be *associated* with the units produced. **Cost measurement** consists of determining the dollar amounts of direct materials, direct labor, and manufacturing overhead used in production. The dollar amounts may be the actual amounts expended for the manufacturing inputs, or they may be estimated amounts. Often, estimated amounts are used to ensure timeliness of cost information or to control costs. The process of associating the costs, once measured, with the units produced is called *cost assignment*.

cost assignment

Importance of Unit Costs

A cost accounting system has the purpose of measuring and assigning manufacturing costs so that the unit cost of a product can be determined. Unit cost is a critical piece of information for a manufacturer. Unit costs are essential for valuing inventory, determining income, and making a number of important decisions.

Disclosing the cost of inventories and determining income are financial reporting requirements that a firm faces at the end of each period. In order to report the cost of its inventories, a firm must know the number of units on hand and the unit cost. The cost of goods sold, used to determine income, also requires knowledge of the units sold and their unit cost.

Unit costs are also important for a wide variety of decisions. For example, bidding is a common requirement in the markets for custom homes and industrial buildings. It is virtually impossible to submit a meaningful bid without knowing the costs associated with the units to be produced. Product cost information is vital in a number of other areas as well. Decisions concerning product design and introduction of new products are affected by expected unit costs. Decisions to make or buy a product, accept or reject a special order, or keep or drop a product line require unit cost information.

However, whether the unit cost information should include all manufacturing costs or variable costs or only incremental costs depends on the setting and the purpose for which the information is going to be used. For financial reporting, full or absorption unit cost information is required. If a firm is operating below its production capacity, however, incremental cost information may be much more suitable as input for a decision to accept or reject a special order. Simply put, unit cost information needed for external reporting may not supply the information necessary for a number of internal decisions, especially those decisions that are short run in nature. Different costs are needed for different purposes.

It should be pointed out, however, that full cost information is useful as an input for a number of important internal decisions as well as for financial reporting. In the long run, for any product to be viable, its price must cover its full cost. Decisions to introduce a new product, continue a current product, and analyze long-run prices are examples of important internal decisions that must rely on full unit cost information.

Production of Unit Cost Information

To produce unit cost information, both cost measurement and cost assignment are required. There are a number of different ways to measure and assign costs. This chapter introduces two measurement systems and two assignment systems and discusses one of each type in detail.

The two systems for assigning costs are *job-order costing* and *process costing*. The two measurement systems introduced are *actual costing* and *normal costing*. Combinations of measurement and assignment approaches define a cost accounting system. For example, actual costing measurement with job-order cost assignment creates an actual job-order cost system. Given the two measurement systems and the two assignment systems, a total of four cost accounting systems are possible, with each system presenting a different way to compute unit costs. The four possible systems are summarized in Exhibit 3–1.

Which system should be chosen depends on the type of cost data a manager needs for controlling and directing the activities of an organization. Of the four systems, the two systems using actual costing are rarely chosen because they generally fail to supply product cost information on a timely basis. Why actual costing fails will become apparent as it is examined.

Job-Order and Process Costing:
Two Possible Assignment Systems

Manufacturing firms can be divided into two major industrial types based on different manufacturing processes: job-order manufacturing and process manufacturing. Two different cost assignment or accumulation systems have

EXHIBIT 3-1
Four Possible Cost Accounting Systems

	Cost Measurement	
Cost Assignment	Job order— Actual	Job order— Normal
	Process— Actual	Process— Normal

been developed, each corresponding to one of these systems. To understand the differences between these two cost systems, we need to understand the differences in the two manufacturing processes.

Job-Order Manufacturing and Costing   Firms operating in job-order industries produce a wide variety of products or jobs that are usually quite distinct from each other. Customized or built-to-order products fit into this category. Examples of job-order manufacturers include printing, construction, and furniture companies. A job may be a single unit such as a house, or it may be a batch of units such as eight tables. Each job is often associated with a particular customer order. However, job-order systems are also used to produce goods for inventory that are subsequently sold in the general market.

job-order costing system
For job-order manufacturing systems, manufacturing costs are accumulated by *job*. This approach to assigning costs is called a *job-order costing system*. In a job-order firm, collecting costs by job provides vital information for management. Once a job is completed, the unit cost can be obtained by dividing the total manufacturing costs by the number of units produced.

For example, if the production costs for printing 100 wedding announcements total $300, then the unit cost for this job is $3. Given the unit cost information, the manager of the printing firm can determine whether the prevailing market price provides a reasonable profit margin. If not, then this may signal to the manager that the costs are out of line with other printing firms. He or she can then take action to reduce costs, if possible, or to emphasize other types of jobs for which the firm can earn a reasonable profit margin. In fact, the profit contributions of different printing jobs offered by the firm can be computed, and this information can then be used to select the most profitable mix of printing services to offer.

Process Manufacturing and Costing   Firms in process industries mass-produce large quantities of similar or homogeneous products. Each product is essentially indistinguishable from its companion product. Examples of process manufacturers include food, cement, petroleum, and chemical firms.

Process firms accumulate manufacturing costs by *process* or by *department* for a *given period of time*. The output for the process for the same period of time is measured. Unit costs are computed by dividing the process costs for the

process costing system

given period by the output of the period. This approach to cost accumulation is known as a *process costing system*. Exhibit 3–2 summarizes and contrasts the characteristics of job-order and process costing.

Actual Costing and Normal Costing: Two Cost Measurement Approaches

actual cost system

Actual Costing   An **actual cost system** uses actual costs for direct materials, direct labor, and overhead. These actual costs are then used to determine the unit cost.

In practice, strict actual cost systems are rarely used because they cannot provide accurate unit cost information on a timely basis. Interestingly, per-unit computation of the direct materials and direct labor costs is not the source of the difficulty. Direct materials and direct labor have a definite, identifiable relationship with units produced. The main problem with using actual costs for calculation of unit cost is with manufacturing overhead. Overhead items do not have the direct relationship that direct materials and direct labor do. For example, how much of the security guard's salary should be assigned to a unit of product? Because overhead items are indirectly related to the units produced, per-unit overhead costs must be calculated by averaging. Averaging requires totaling manufacturing overhead costs for a given period and then dividing this total by the number of units produced.

If the time period chosen is relatively short (say, a month), so that cost information can be produced in a timely manner, averaging can yield per-unit overhead costs that fluctuate dramatically from month to month. This occurs for two major reasons. First, overhead costs are not incurred uniformly throughout the year. Thus, they can differ significantly from one period to the next. Second, per-unit overhead costs fluctuate dramatically because of non-uniform production.

To illustrate, consider the following example. Assume a company produces a toy gun made of plastic. Each gun requires six ounces of plastic and fifteen minutes of direct labor. For the technology used, this input-output

EXHIBIT 3–2
Comparison of Job-Order and Process Costing

Job-Order Costing	*Process Costing*
1. Wide variety of distinct products	1. Homogeneous products
2. Costs accumulated by job	2. Costs accumulated by process or department
3. Unit cost computed by dividing total job costs by units produced on that job	3. Unit cost computed by dividing process costs of the period by the units produced in the period

relationship is reasonably stable. Thus, the quantity of raw materials and the direct labor used for each toy gun are essentially the same regardless of how many toy guns are produced or when they are produced. The unit cost of these two inputs can be accurately computed.

If the cost of plastic in January is $0.30 per ounce and the price of labor is $6 per hour, then the cost of plastic per gun is $1.80 ($0.30 × 6 ounces), and the cost of direct labor per gun is $1.50 ($6 × 0.25 hours). The actual prime cost per gun, then, is $1.80 + $1.50, or $3.30. If the prices of materials and labor are reasonably stable, then the $3.30 per-unit prime cost is the same regardless of how many guns are made or when they are produced during the year.

If actual overhead costs for the manufacturer were $20,000 in April and 40,000 guns were produced, then the per-unit overhead cost is $20,000/40,000, or $0.50 per gun. Unfortunately, this averaging approach has some severe limitations as shown in the following figures:

	April	August	November
Actual overhead	$20,000	$40,000	$40,000
Actual production	40,000	40,000	160,000
Per-unit overhead[a]	$0.50	$1.00	$0.25

[a]Actual overhead/Actual production

Notice that the overhead cost per unit is different for each of the three months. April and August have the same production but different monthly overhead costs. The difference in overhead cost could be attributable to higher utility costs due to increased cooling requirements in the month of August. Thus, the toy guns produced in August have a higher per-unit overhead cost ($1.00 rather than $0.50) just because they happened to be produced when cooling was required. The difference in the per-unit overhead cost is because overhead costs were incurred nonuniformly.

Nonuniform production is the second reason for variability in per-unit overhead costs, as August and November figures show. Both months have the same total monthly overhead costs but different output levels. November's output may be much larger because of anticipation of Christmas sales. Whatever the reason, the higher output in November creates a lower per-unit overhead cost ($0.25 compared to August's $1.00).

Notice that the varying per-unit overhead costs do not signal differences in value, or even in the underlying cost structure. A toy gun produced in April is identical to one produced in August or November. The higher utility costs in August may equal August utility costs of the previous year. The problem of fluctuating per-unit overhead costs can be avoided if the firm waits until the end of the year to assign the overhead costs. For example, if April, August, and November were the only months of operation for the toy gun manufacturer, then the total overhead costs for the year are $100,000 ($20,000 + $40,000 + $40,000), and the total production is 240,000 guns

(40,000 + 40,000 + 160,000). The per-unit overhead cost is $100,000/240,000, or $0.417. By waiting until the end of the year, the firm eliminates the problems of nonuniform overhead cost incurrence and nonuniform production. The result is the same overhead cost per unit for every unit produced.

Unfortunately, waiting until the end of the year to compute an overhead rate is unacceptable. A company needs unit cost information throughout the year. This information is needed on a timely basis both for interim financial statements and to help managers make decisions such as pricing. Most decisions requiring unit cost information simply cannot wait until the end of the year. Managers must react to day-to-day conditions occurring in the marketplace in order to maintain a sound competitive position.

Another possible solution is to approximate the end-of-the-year actual overhead rate at the *beginning* of the year and then use the predetermined rate throughout the year to obtain the needed unit cost information. The end-of-the-year actual rate can be approximated by estimating the overhead costs for the coming year and dividing these estimated costs by expected actual production. Suppose, for example, that the toy manufacturer estimates on January 1 that overhead costs for the year will be $90,000 and that expected production is 225,000 units. Using this estimated data, the predetermined overhead rate is $0.40 ($90,000/225,000). (You will learn shortly that there are a number of different ways to estimate production.)

Normal Costing   Cost systems that measure overhead costs on a predetermined basis and use actual costs for direct materials and direct labor are called *normal costing systems*. The principal difficulty with normal costing is that the predetermined rate is likely to differ from the actual rate. Either actual overhead costs differ from the estimated costs or the actual level of production differs from the expected level, or both.

margin: **normal costing systems**

If the measurement error is small, however, the product cost resulting from normal costing will not differ significantly from the actual product cost determined after the fact. In the example above, the predetermined rate was $0.40, and the end-of-the-year actual rate was $0.417. Most would agree that this is not a significant difference.

Virtually all firms assign overhead to production on a predetermined basis. This fact seems to suggest that most firms successfully approximate the end-of-the-year overhead rate. Thus, the measurement problems associated with the use of actual overhead costs are solved by the use of estimated overhead costs. A job-order cost system that uses actual costs for materials and labor and estimated costs for overhead is called a *normal job-order cost system*. Similarly, in a process setting, the cost system is called a *normal process cost system*.

▪ OVERHEAD APPLICATION: A NORMAL COSTING VIEW

In normal cost systems, overhead is assigned to production through the use of a predetermined overhead rate.

Predetermined Overhead Rates

predetermined
overhead rate

The basic difference between actual costing and normal costing is the use of a predetermined overhead rate. A **predetermined overhead rate** is calculated using the following formula:

Overhead rate = Budgeted overhead/Activity level

Budgeted overhead refers simply to the estimated overhead costs for the coming year. The budgetary accountants of a firm are responsible for developing these estimates. The second input requires that the value for the activity level be specified. (Activity level is sometimes referred to as the *denominator activity level* since it appears in the denominator of the computation.) This second input has two steps: first, identify a measure of production activity; second, predict the level of this activity. (Note: A predetermined overhead rate is calculated in advance, usually at the beginning of the year. It is impossible to use actual overhead or actual activity level for the year because on January 1, we do not know what actual levels will be. Therefore, only estimated or budgeted amounts are used in calculating the predetermined overhead rate.)

Measures of Production Activity

Production activity can be measured in many different ways. In assigning overhead costs, it is important to select an activity base that is correlated with overhead consumption. This will assure that individual products receive an accurate allocation of overhead costs. While there are many choices available, five common measures are

1. Units produced
2. Direct labor hours
3. Direct labor dollars
4. Machine hours
5. Direct materials

The most obvious measure of production activity is output. If there is only one product, then overhead costs are clearly incurred to produce that product. In a single-product setting, the overhead costs of the period are directly traceable to the period's output. Clearly, for this case, units produced satisfy the cause-and-effect criterion. Unfortunately, most firms produce more than one product. Since different products typically consume different amounts of overhead, this allocation method is inaccurate. At Kraft, for example, one plant produces salad dressing, ketchup, and marshmallow creme—each in a range of sizes from personal application packs to 32-ounce jars. In a multiple-product setting, overhead costs are common to more than one product. Furthermore, different products may consume overhead at different rates.

For example, suppose a company produces fine wood furniture. One type of dining room table has very simple round legs. Another style of table has very elaborately turned and carved legs. Both types of table leg require the use of a lathe (a machine in which a piece of material is held and turned while being shaped by a tool); therefore, both types should share the cost of using this machine. Suppose that the cost of operating the lathe is $20,000, and 10,000 units of each type of leg are produced. Using units produced, the overhead cost assigned to each product would be $1 ($20,000/20,000). But one product may spend sixty minutes on the lathe, the other only fifteen. Since one product spends four times as much time on the lathe as the other, many would argue that it should receive more of the machine's cost. Using the units produced method has not given a very accurate, meaningful, or fair assignment of overhead costs. How, then, should overhead be allocated?

Some believe that the allocation of overhead is essentially arbitrary. There is no single approach to allocating overhead that will satisfy all parties concerned. It could be argued that overhead should be allocated on an ability-to-bear basis with overhead assigned in proportion to revenues generated. Using this criterion, if the product spending less time on the lathe generates more revenues than the other product, then more overhead would be allocated to it than to the other product.

The argument taken in this text is that the allocation of overhead costs should follow, as nearly as possible, a cause-and-effect relationship. Efforts should be made to identify those factors that cause the consumption of overhead. Once identified, these causal factors or *cost drivers* should be used to assign overhead to products. It seems reasonable, for example, to argue that for products using the lathe, machine hours reflect differential machine time, and, consequently, reflect the consumption of machine cost. Units produced does not necessarily reflect machine time or consumption of the machine cost; therefore, it can be argued that machine hours is a better cost driver and should be used to assign this overhead cost.

In the table leg example shown in Exhibit 3–3, the simple leg uses fifteen minutes of machine time; the ornate leg uses one hour. The total machine hours consumed by the two products is 12,500 (2,500 + 10,000). The overhead cost assigned per machine hour is $20,000/12,500, or $1.60 per MHr. Using this rate, the per-unit overhead assigned to the simple leg is $0.40 (0.25 machine hours × $1.60), and the per-unit overhead assigned to the ornate leg is $1.60 (1 machine hour × $1.60).

As the example illustrates, activity measures other than units of product are needed when a firm has multiple products. The last four measures listed earlier are all useful for multiple product settings. Some may be more useful than others, depending on how well they correlate with the actual overhead consumption. As we will discuss later, it may even be appropriate to use multiple rates.

EXHIBIT 3–3

	Simple	Ornate
Cost of operating lathe		$20,000
Total units produced		20,000
Total machine hours used		12,500
Number of legs	10,000	10,000
Time on lathe	0.25 MHrs	1 MHr
Operating cost assigned using units produced	$1	$1
Operating cost assigned using machine time	$0.40	$1.60

Activity-Level Choices

Although any reasonable level of activity could be chosen, the two leading candidates are expected actual activity and normal activity. **Expected activity level** is simply the production level the firm expects to attain for the coming year. **Normal activity level** is the average activity that a firm experiences in the long term (normal volume is computed over more than one fiscal period). Of the two choices, normal activity has the advantage of using the same activity level period after period. As a result, it produces less fluctuation from period to period in the assignment of per-unit overhead cost.

    Other activity levels used for computing predetermined overhead rates are those corresponding to the theoretical and practical levels. **Theoretical activity level** is the absolute maximum production activity of a manufacturing firm. It is the output that can be realized if everything operates perfectly. **Practical activity level** is the maximum output that can be realized if everything operates efficiently. Efficient operation allows for some imperfections such as normal breakdowns, some shortages, workers operating at less than peak capability, and so on. Normal and expected actual activities tend to reflect consumer demand while theoretical and practical activities reflect a firm's production capabilities. Exhibit 3–4 illustrates these four measures of activity.

    Given budgeted overhead, a measure of production activity, and a level of activity, a predetermined overhead rate can be computed and applied to production. Understanding exactly how overhead is applied is critical to understanding normal costing.

The Basic Concept of Overhead Application

Predetermined overhead rates are used to apply overhead costs to production as the actual production activity unfolds. The total overhead assigned to actual production at any point in time is called *applied overhead*. Applied overhead is computed using the following formula:

Applied overhead = Overhead rate × Actual production activity

(margin terms) expected activity level / normal activity level / theoretical activity level / practical activity level / applied overhead

EXHIBIT 3–4
Measures of Activity Level

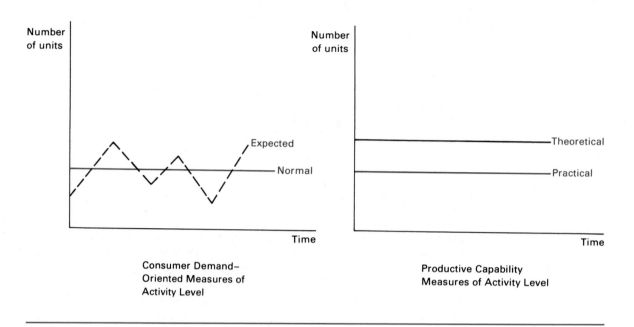

The measure of production activity used to determine the overhead rate must be the same as the measure of actual production activity. That is, if the predetermined overhead rate is calculated on the basis of direct labor hours, overhead must be applied on the basis of direct labor hours. Overhead can be applied on a daily, weekly, monthly, or any other basis as the need requires.

In attempting to understand the concept of applied overhead, there are two points that should be emphasized.

1. Applied overhead is the basis for computing per-unit overhead cost.

2. Applied overhead is rarely equal to a period's actual overhead.

These points are best illustrated with an example. Belring, Inc., produces two telephones: a cordless phone and a regular model. The company has the following estimated and actual data for 1992:

Budgeted overhead	$360,000
Normal activity (in direct labor hours)	120,000
Actual activity (in direct labor hours)	100,000
Actual overhead	$320,000

Now assume that the firm bases its predetermined overhead rate on normal activity measured in direct labor hours (*DLH*). Thus, for 1992

Predetermined overhead rate = Budgeted overhead/Normal activity
= $360,000/120,000 direct labor hours
= $3 per *DLH*

Using the overhead rate, applied overhead for 1992 is

Applied overhead = Overhead rate × Actual activity
= $3 per *DLH* × 100,000 *DLH*
= $300,000

Per-unit Overhead Cost   In a normal cost system, the predetermined overhead rate is the basis for per-unit overhead cost calculation. For example, assume that 40 percent of the actual direct labor hours worked were used to produce 80,000 units of the cordless phone, and the remaining 60 percent of direct labor time was used to produce 90,000 units of the regular model. Since the predetermined overhead rate is $3 per *DLH,* the cordless phone would be assigned a total of $120,000 of overhead ($3 × 40,000), and the regular model would be assigned $180,000 ($3 × 60,000). The per-unit overhead cost of the cordless phone is $120,000/80,000, or $1.50, and for the regular model, $180,000/90,000, or $2.

	Cordless	*Regular*
Units produced	80,000	90,000
Direct labor hours	40,000	60,000
Overhead applied to production ($3 × *DLH*)	$120,000	$180,000
Overhead per unit	$1.50	$2.00

Underapplied and Overapplied Overhead   Notice that the amount of overhead applied to production ($300,000) differs from the actual overhead ($320,000). Since the predetermined overhead rate is based on estimated data, applied overhead will rarely equal actual overhead. Since only $300,000 was applied in our example, the firm has *underapplied* overhead by $20,000. If applied overhead had been $330,000, too much overhead would have been applied to production. The firm would have *overapplied* overhead by $10,000.

overhead variance
underapplied
overhead
overapplied overhead

The difference between actual overhead and applied overhead is called an *overhead variance*. If the difference is positive (i.e., if actual overhead is greater than applied overhead) then the variance is called **underapplied overhead**. If the difference is negative (i.e., if applied overhead is greater than actual overhead) then the variance is called *overapplied overhead*.

Overhead variances occur because it is impossible to estimate perfectly future overhead costs and production activity. Their presence is virtually inevitable. A problem arises if the overhead variances are not corrected. In essence, the firm has traded off costing accuracy for convenience by applying overhead throughout the year. At year end, however, costs must be stated at actual—*not* estimated. Accordingly, at the end of a reporting period, procedures must exist to deal with the overhead variances.

Disposition of Overhead Variances

From an actual costing perspective, the overhead variance represents an error in assigning overhead costs to production. At the end of the reporting period, something must be done with the overhead variance. Usually, the variance is disposed of in one of two ways.

1. All overhead variance is allocated to cost of goods sold.

2. The overhead variance is allocated among work in process, finished goods, and cost of goods sold.

Assigned to Cost of Goods Sold   The most common practice is simply to assign the entire overhead variance to cost of goods sold. This practice is justified on the basis of materiality, the same principle used to justify expensing the entire cost of a pencil sharpener in the period acquired rather than allocating (through depreciation) its cost over the life of the sharpener. Since the overhead variance is usually relatively small, the method of disposition is not a critical matter because all production costs should appear in cost of goods sold eventually. This method works if the variance is immaterial.

Thus, the overhead variance is added to the cost of goods sold if underapplied and subtracted from cost of goods sold if overapplied. For example, assume that Belring has an ending balance in its Cost of Goods Sold account equal to $500,000. The underapplied variance of $20,000 would be added to produce a new, adjusted balance of $520,000. (This makes sense—applied overhead was $300,000 while actual was $320,000. Thus, production costs were *under*stated by $20,000, and cost of goods sold must be increased to correct the problem.) If the variance had been overapplied, it would have been subtracted from cost of goods sold to produce a new balance of $480,000.

Allocation to Production Accounts   If the overhead variance is material, it must be allocated to the period's production. Conceptually, the overhead costs of a period belong to the production of the period. Overhead costs for a period should be associated with goods started but not completed (work in process), goods finished but not sold (finished goods), and goods finished and sold (cost of goods sold). Because a period's overhead costs may flow through these three different accounts, the overhead variance should be allocated to these accounts as well.

The recommended way to achieve this allocation is to prorate the overhead variance based on the ending *applied overhead balances* in each account. Although other ending balances could be used to allocate the variance (e.g., total manufacturing costs), the applied overhead balance best reflects the additional overhead that should be assigned to each account. Using applied overhead captures the original cause-and-effect relationships used to assign overhead. Using another balance, such as total manufacturing costs, may result in an unfair assignment of the additional overhead. For example, two products, identical on all dimensions except for the cost of raw material inputs, should receive the same overhead assignment. Yet if total manufacturing costs were used to allocate an overhead variance, then the product with the more expensive materials would receive a higher overhead assignment.

To illustrate the disposition of the overhead variance using the recommended approach, assume that Belring's accounts had the following applied overhead balances for the end of 1992:

Work in Process	$ 60,000
Finished Goods	90,000
Cost of Goods Sold	150,000
Total dollar balance	$300,000

Given the above data, the percentage allocation of any overhead variance to the three accounts in 1992 is

Work in Process	20%	(60,000/300,000)
Finished Goods	30%	(90,000/300,000)
Cost of Goods Sold	50%	(150,000/300,000)

Recall that in 1992, Belring had an overhead variance that was $20,000 underapplied. Thus, Work in Process would receive 20 percent of $20,000 ($4,000), Finished Goods would receive 30 percent of $20,000 ($6,000), and Cost of Goods Sold would receive 50 percent of $20,000 ($10,000). Since underapplied means that too little overhead was assigned, these individual prorated amounts would be *added* to the ending account balances. Adding these amounts produces the following new adjusted balances of the three accounts:

	Unadjusted Balance	Prorated Underapplied Overhead	Adjusted Balance
Work in Process	$ 60,000	$ 4,000	$ 64,000
Finished Goods	90,000	6,000	96,000
Cost of Goods Sold	150,000	10,000	160,000

Of course, overapplied amounts would have been *subtracted* from the account balances because too much overhead was assigned to production.

We now have an understanding of how manufacturing costs are measured in a normal cost system. Considerable emphasis has been placed on describing how overhead costs are treated because this is the key to normal costing. Before we seriously examine any method for assigning costs, we first should know how these costs are to be measured. The way costs are measured affects the procedures followed in either job-order costing or process costing.

▪ JOB-ORDER COSTING: GENERAL DESCRIPTION

In illustrating job-order costing, we will assume a normal cost measurement approach. The actual costs of direct materials and direct labor are assigned to jobs along with a predetermined overhead rate. *How* these costs are actually assigned to the various jobs, however, is the central issue. In order to assign these costs, we must identify each job and the direct materials and direct labor associated with it. Additionally, some mechanism must exist to allocate overhead costs to each job.

job-order cost sheet

The document that identifies each job and accumulates its manufacturing costs is the **job-order cost sheet**. An example is shown in Exhibit 3–5. The cost accounting department creates such a cost sheet upon receipt of a production order. Orders are written up in response to a specific customer order or in conjunction with a production plan derived from a sales forecast. Each job-order cost sheet has a job-order number that identifies the new job.

work-in-process file

In a manual accounting system, the job-order cost sheet is a document. In today's world, however, most accounting systems are automated. The cost sheet usually corresponds to a record in a work-in-process master file. The collection of all job cost sheets define a **work-in-process file**. In a manual system, the file would be located in a filing cabinet, whereas in an automated system, it is stored electronically on magnetic tape or disk. In either system, the file of job-order cost sheets serves as a subsidiary work-in-process ledger.

Both manual and automated systems require the same kind of data in order to accumulate costs and track the progress of a job. A job cost system must have the capability to identify the quantity of direct materials, direct labor, and overhead consumed by each job. In other words, documentation and procedures are needed to associate the manufacturing inputs used by a job with the job itself. This need is satisfied through the use of materials requisitions for direct material, time tickets for direct labor, and predetermined rates for overhead.

Materials Requisitions

materials requisition form

The cost of direct materials is assigned to a job by the use of a source document known as a *materials requisition form* (see Exhibit 3–6, p. 94). Notice that the form asks for the type, quantity, and unit price of the direct materials issued and, most importantly, for the number of the job. Using this form, the

EXHIBIT 3–5
The Job-Order Cost Sheet

For	Benson Company		Job Order Number	16
Item Description	Valves		Date Ordered	April 2, 1992
Quantity Completed	100		Date Completed	April 24, 1992
			Date Shipped	April 25, 1992

Materials		Direct Labor				Overhead		
Requisition number	Amount	Ticket number	Hours	Rate	Amount	Hours	Rate	Amount
12	$300	68	8	$6	$ 48	8	10	$ 80
18	450	72	10	$7	70	10	10	100
	$750				$118			$180

Cost Summary

Direct materials	$750
Direct labor	$118
Overhead	$180
Total cost	$1048
Unit cost	$10.48

cost accounting department can enter the cost of direct materials directly onto the job-order cost sheet.

If the accounting system is automated, this posting may entail directly entering the data at a computer terminal, using the materials requisitions forms as source documents. A program then enters the cost of direct materials onto the record for each job.

In addition to providing essential information for assigning direct materials costs to jobs, the materials requisition form may also have other data items such as requisition number, date, and signature. These data items are useful for maintaining proper control over a firm's inventory of direct materials. The signature, for example, transfers responsibility for the materials from the storage area to the person receiving the materials, usually a production supervisor.

EXHIBIT 3-6
Materials Requisition Form

Material Requisition			Number 12
Date___April 8, 1992___	Department___Grinding___		Job Number___16___
Description	Quantity	Cost/Unit	Total Cost
Casing	100	3	$300
Authorized Signature___*Jim Lawson*___			

No attempt is made to trace the cost of other materials such as supplies, lubricants, and so on, to a particular job. You will recall that these indirect materials are assigned to jobs through the predetermined overhead rate.

Job Time Tickets

time ticket

Direct labor also must be associated with each particular job. The means by which direct labor costs are assigned to individual jobs is the source document known as a *time ticket* (see Exhibit 3–7). When an employee works on a particular job, he or she fills out a time ticket that identifies his or her name, wage rate, hours worked, and job number. These time tickets are collected daily and transferred to the cost accounting department, where the information is used to post the cost of direct labor to individual jobs. Again, in an automated system, posting involves entering the data onto the computer.

Time tickets are used only for direct laborers. Since indirect labor is common to all jobs, these costs belong to overhead and are allocated using the predetermined overhead rate.

EXHIBIT 3–7
Job Time Tickets

Job Time Ticket					Number 68
Employee Number___45___		Name___Ed Wilson___		Date___April 12, 1992___	
Start Time	Stop Time	Total Time	Hourly Rate	Amount	Job Number
8:00	10:00	2	6	$12	16
10:00	11:00	1	6	6	17
11:00	12:00	1	6	6	16
1:00	6:00	5	6	30	16

Approved by___*Jim Lawson*___
Department Supervisor

Overhead Application

Jobs are assigned overhead costs with the predetermined overhead rate. Typically, direct labor hours is the measure used to calculate overhead. For example, assume a firm has estimated overhead costs for the coming year of $900,000 and expected activity is 90,000 direct labor hours. The predetermined rate is

$900,000/90,000 direct labor hours = $10 per direct labor hour

Since the number of direct labor hours charged to a job is known from time tickets, the assignment of overhead costs to jobs is simple once the predetermined rate has been computed. For instance, Exhibit 3–7 reveals that Ed Wilson worked a total of eight hours on Job 16. From this time ticket, overhead totaling $80 ($10 × 8 hours) would be assigned to Job 16.

If other activity measures are used to assign overhead to jobs, then their actual values must also be collected and posted to the job cost sheets. As with direct labor costs, direct materials cost is already posted. If some other activity measure, such as machine hours, is used, then a source document that will track the machine hours used by each job must be created. A machine time ticket could easily accommodate this need.

Unit Cost Calculation

Once a job is completed, its total manufacturing cost is computed by first totaling the costs of direct materials, direct labor, and overhead, and then summing these individual totals. The grand total is divided by the number of units produced to obtain the unit cost (Exhibit 3–5 illustrates these computations).

All completed job-order cost sheets of a firm can serve as a subsidiary ledger for the finished goods inventory. In a manual accounting system, the completed sheets would be transferred from the work-in-process files to the finished goods inventory file. In an automated accounting system, an updating run would delete the finished job from the work-in-process master file and add this record to the finished goods master file. In either case, adding the totals of all completed job-order cost sheets gives the cost of finished goods inventory at any point in time. As finished goods are sold and shipped, the cost records would be pulled (or deleted) from the finished goods inventory file. These records then form the basis for calculating a period's cost of goods sold.

■ JOB-ORDER COSTING:
SPECIFIC COST FLOW DESCRIPTION

Recall that cost flow is how we account for costs from the point at which they are incurred to the point at which they are recognized as an expense on the income statement. Of principal interest in a job-order system is the flow of manufacturing costs. Accordingly, we begin with a description of exactly how we account for the three manufacturing cost elements (direct materials, direct labor, and overhead).

A simplified job shop environment is used as the framework for this description. Better Works, a company recently formed by Stan Johnson, produces customized briefcases. Stan leased a small building and bought the necessary production equipment. For the first month of operation (January), Stan has finalized two orders: one for twenty engraved briefcases for a local firm and a second for ten orange and black briefcases for the coaches of a local college. Both orders must be delivered January 31 and will be sold for manufacturing cost plus 50 percent. Stan expects to average two orders per month for the first year of operation.

Stan created two job-order cost sheets and assigned a number to each job. Job 1 is the engraved briefcases, and Job 2 the orange and black briefcases.

Accounting for Materials

Since the company is beginning business, it has no beginning inventories. To produce the thirty briefcases in January and have a supply of materials on hand at the beginning of February, Stan purchases, on account, $2,500 of raw materials. This purchase is recorded as follows:

1. Raw Materials	2,500	
Accounts Payable		2,500

Raw Materials is an inventory account. It also is the controlling account for all raw materials. When materials are purchased, the cost of these materials "flows" into the raw materials account.

Recording the Issue of Direct Materials From January 2 to January 19, the production supervisor used three requisition forms to remove $1,000 of raw materials from the storeroom. From January 20 to January 31, two additional requisition forms for $500 of raw materials were used. The first three forms revealed that the raw materials were used for Job 1; the last two requisitions were for Job 2. Thus, for January, the cost sheet for Job 1 would have a total of $1,000 in direct materials posted, and the cost sheet for Job 2 would have a total of $500 in direct materials posted. In addition, the following entry would be made:

2. Work in Process	1,500	
Raw Materials		1,500

This second entry captures the notion of raw materials flowing from the storeroom to work in process. All such flows are summarized in the Work in Process account as well as being posted individually to the respective jobs. Work in Process is a controlling account, and the job cost sheets are the subsidiary accounts. Exhibit 3–8 (p. 98) summarizes the raw materials cost flows. Notice that the source document that drives the materials cost flows is the materials requisition form.

Accounting for Direct Labor Cost

Since two jobs were in progress during January, time tickets filled out by direct laborers must be sorted by each job. Once the sorting is completed, the hours worked and the wage rate of each employee are used to assign the direct labor cost to each job. For Job 1, the time tickets showed 120 hours at an average wage rate of $5 per hour, for a total direct labor cost of $600. For Job 2, the total was $250, based on 50 hours at an average hourly wage of $5. In addition to the postings to each job's cost sheet, the following summary entry would be made:

3. Work in Process	850	
Wages Payable		850

The summary of the labor cost flows is given in Exhibit 3–9 (p. 99). Notice that the direct labor costs assigned to the two jobs exactly equal the total assigned to Work in Process. Note also that the time tickets filled out by the individual laborers are the source of information for posting the labor cost flows. Remember that the labor cost flows reflect only direct labor cost. Indirect labor is assigned as part of overhead.

EXHIBIT 3–8
Summary of Raw Materials Cost Flows

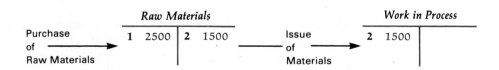

Subsidiary Accounts (Cost Sheets)

Job 1 Materials	
Req. No.	Amount
1	$ 300
2	200
3	500
	$1,000

Job 2 Materials	
Req. No.	Amount
4	$250
5	250
	$500

Source Documents: Material Requisition Forms

Accounting for Overhead

Under a normal costing approach, actual overhead costs are *never* assigned to jobs. Overhead is applied to each individual job using a predetermined overhead rate. Even with this system, however, actual overhead costs incurred must be accounted for. Thus, we will first describe how to account for applied overhead and then discuss accounting for actual overhead.

Accounting for Overhead Application Assume that Stan has estimated overhead costs for the year at $9,600. He also expects to use 4,800 direct labor hours. Accordingly, the predetermined overhead rate is

Overhead rate = $9,600/4,800 = $2 per direct labor hour

Overhead costs flow into work in process via the predetermined rate. Since direct labor hours are used to load overhead onto production, the time tickets serve as the source documents for assigning overhead to individual jobs and to the controlling Work in Process account.

For Job 1, with a total of 120 hours worked, the amount of overhead cost posted is $240 ($2 × 120). For Job 2, the overhead cost is $100 ($2 × 50). A summary entry reflects a total of $340 (i.e., all overhead applied to jobs worked on in January) in applied overhead.

EXHIBIT 3–9
Summary of Direct Labor Cost Flows

Wages Payable		Work in Process	
3 850		3 850	

Labor Cost →

WIP Subsidiary Accounts (Cost Sheets)

Job 1					Job 2			
Labor					Labor			
Ticket	*Hrs.*	*Rate*	*Amt.*		*Ticket*	*Hrs.*	*Rate*	*Amt.*
1	30	5	$150		4	25	5	$125
2	40	5	200		5	25	5	125
3	50	5	250			50		$250
	120		$600					

Source Document: Time Tickets

4. Work in Process	340	
Overhead Control		340

The credit balance in the overhead control account equals the total applied overhead at a given point in time. In normal costing, only applied overhead ever enters the Work in Process account.

Accounting for Actual Overhead Costs   To illustrate how actual overhead costs are recorded, assume that Business Works incurred the following indirect costs for January:

Lease payment	$200
Utilities	50
Equipment depreciation	100
Indirect labor	65
Total overhead costs	$415

As indicated earlier, actual overhead costs never enter the Work in Process account. The usual procedure is to record actual overhead costs on the debit side of the Overhead Control account. For example, the actual overhead costs would be recorded as follows:

5. Overhead Control	415	
Lease Payable		200
Utilities Payable		50
Accumulated Depreciation		100
Wages Payable		65

Thus, the debit balance in the Overhead Control account gives the total actual overhead costs at a given point in time. Since actual overhead costs are on the debit side of this account and applied overhead costs are on the credit side, the balance in the Overhead Control account is the overhead variance at a given point in time. For Better Works at the end of January, the actual overhead of $415 and applied overhead of $340 produce underapplied overhead of $75 (415 − 340).

The flow of overhead costs is summarized in Exhibit 3–10. To apply overhead to work in process, a company needs information from the time tickets and a predetermined overhead rate based on direct labor hours.

EXHIBIT 3–10
Summary of Overhead Cost Flows

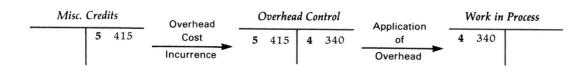

WIP Subsidiary Accounts (Cost Sheets)

Job 1		
Applied Overhead		
Hours	*Rate*	*Amount*
120	2	$240

Job 2		
Applied Overhead		
Hours	*Rate*	*Amount*
50	2	$100

Source Document: Time Ticket
Other Source: Predetermined Rate

Accounting for Finished Goods

We have already seen what takes place when a job is completed. The columns for direct materials, direct labor, and applied overhead are totaled. These totals are then transferred to another section of the cost sheet where they are summed to yield the manufacturing cost of the job. This job cost sheet is then transferred to a finished goods file. Simultaneously, the costs of the completed job are transferred from the Work in Process account to the Finished Goods account.

For example, assume that Job 1 was completed in January with the completed cost sheet shown in Exhibit 3–11. Since Job 1 is completed, the total manufacturing costs of $1,840 must be transferred from the Work in Process account to the Finished Goods account. This transfer is described by the entry on p. 102.

EXHIBIT 3–11
Completed Job-Order Cost Sheet

For:	Johnson Company			Job Order Number	1
Item Description:	Engraved Briefcases			Date Ordered	Jan. 1, 1993
Quantity Completed:	20			Date Completed	Jan. 29, 1993
				Date Shipped	Jan. 31, 1993

Materials		Direct Labor				Applied Overhead		
Requisition number	Amount	Ticket number	Hours	Rate	Amount	Hours	Rate	Amount
1	$300	1	30	5	$150	30	2	$60
2	200	2	40	5	200	40	2	80
3	500	3	50	5	250	50	2	100
	$1000				$600			$240

Cost Summary

Direct materials	$1,000
Direct labor	$600
Applied overhead	$240
Total cost	$1,840
Unit cost	$92

| 6. Finished Goods | 1,840 | |
| Work in Process | | 1,840 |

EXHIBIT 3–12
Summary of Finished Goods Cost Flow

A summary of the cost flows occurring when a job is finished is shown in Exhibit 3–12.

Completion of goods in a manufacturing process represents an important step in the flow of manufacturing costs. Because of the importance of this stage in a manufacturing operation, a schedule of the cost of goods manufactured is prepared periodically to summarize the cost flows of all production activity. This report is an important input for a firm's income statement and can be used to evaluate a firm's manufacturing effort. The cost of goods manufactured schedule was first introduced in Chapter 2. However, in a normal cost system, the report is somewhat different than the actual cost report presented in that chapter.

The schedule of the cost of goods manufactured presented in Exhibit 3–13 summarizes the production activity of Better Works for January. The key difference between this report and the one appearing in Chapter 2 is the use of applied overhead to arrive at the cost of goods manufactured. Finished goods inventories are carried at normal cost rather than actual cost.

Notice that ending work in process is $850. Where did we obtain this figure? Of the two jobs, Job 1 was finished and transferred to finished goods. Job 2 is still in process, however, and the manufacturing costs assigned thus far are direct materials, $500; direct labor, $250; and overhead applied, $100. The total of these costs gives the cost of ending work in process.

Accounting for Cost of Goods Sold

In a job-order firm, units can be produced for a particular customer or they can be produced with the expectation of selling the units as market conditions warrant. If a job is produced especially for a customer (as with Job 1), then when the job is shipped to the customer, the cost of the finished job becomes the cost of the goods sold. When Job 1 is shipped, the entries on p. 103 would be made (recall that the selling price is 150 percent of manufacturing cost).

EXHIBIT 3–13

Better Works Company

Schedule of Cost of Goods Manufactured
For the Month Ended January 31, 1993

Direct materials:			
Beginning raw materials inventory		$ 0	
Purchases of raw materials		2,500	
Total raw materials available		$2,500	
Ending raw materials		1,000	
Raw materials used			$1,500
Direct labor			850
Overhead:			
Lease	$200		
Utilities	50		
Depreciation	100		
Indirect labor	65		
Total overhead	$415		
Less: Underapplied overhead	(75)		
Overhead applied			340
Total manufacturing costs added			$2,690
Add: Beginning work in process			0
Total manufacturing costs			$2,690
Less: Ending work in process			(850)
Cost of goods manufactured			$1,840

7.	Cost of Goods Sold	1,840	
	Finished Goods		1,840
8.	Accounts Receivable	2,760	
	Sales Revenue		2,760

     In addition to these entries, a schedule of cost of goods sold usually is prepared at the end of each reporting period (e.g., monthly and quarterly). Exhibit 3–14 presents such a schedule for Better Works for January. Typically, the overhead variance is closed out to the Cost of Goods Sold account. Cost of goods sold *before* adjustment for an overhead variance is called ***normal cost of goods sold***. After adjustment for the period's overhead variance takes place, the result is called the ***adjusted cost of goods sold***. It is this latter figure that appears as an expense on the income statement.

     However, closing out the overhead variance to the Cost of Goods Sold account is not done until the end of the year. Variances are expected each month because of nonuniform production and nonuniform actual overhead

normal cost of goods sold

adjusted cost of goods sold

EXHIBIT 3–14
Schedule of Cost of Goods Sold

Beginning finished goods inventory	$ 0
Cost of goods manufactured	1,840
Goods available for sale	$1,840
Less: Ending finished goods inventory	(0)
Normal cost of goods sold	$1,840
Add: Underapplied overhead	75
Adjusted cost of goods sold	$1,915

costs. As the year unfolds, these monthly variances should, by and large, offset each other so that the year-end variance is small. Nonetheless, to illustrate how the year-end overhead variance would be treated, we will close out the overhead variance experienced by Better Works in January.

Closing the underapplied overhead to cost of goods sold requires the following entry:

9. Cost of Goods Sold	75	
Overhead Control		75

Notice that debiting Cost of Goods Sold is equivalent to adding the underapplied amount to the normal cost of goods sold figure. If the overhead variance had been overapplied, then the entry would reverse and Cost of Goods Sold would be credited.

If Job 1 had not been ordered by a customer but had been produced with the expectation that the briefcases could be sold through a subsequent marketing effort, then all twenty units may not be sold at the same time. Assume that on January 31, fifteen briefcases were sold. In this case, the cost of goods sold figure is the unit cost times the number of units sold ($92 × 15, or $1,380). The unit cost figure is found on the cost sheet in Exhibit 3–11.

Closing out the overhead variance of Cost of Goods Sold completes the description of manufacturing cost flows. To facilitate a review of these important concepts, Exhibit 3–15 shows a complete summary of the manufacturing cost flows for Better Works. Notice that these entries summarize information from the underlying job order cost sheets. Although the description in this exhibit is specific to the example, the pattern of cost flows shown would be found in any manufacturing firm that uses a normal job-order cost system.

Manufacturing cost flows, however, are not the only cost flows experienced by a firm. Nonmanufacturing costs are also incurred. A description of how we account for these costs follows.

EXHIBIT 3–15
Better Works Company
Summary of Manufacturing Cost Flows

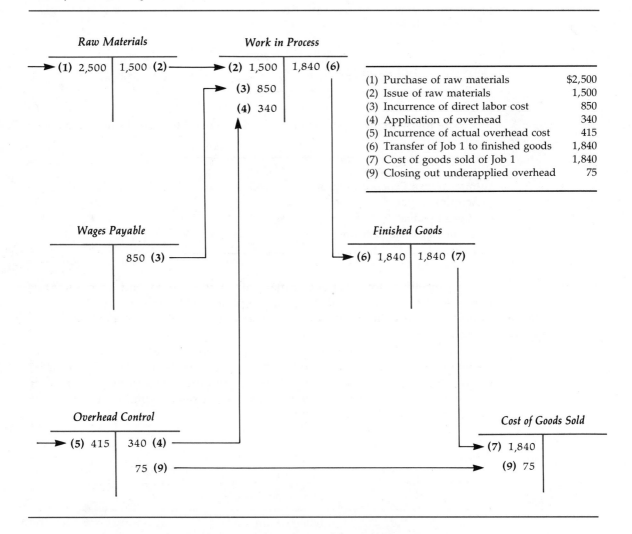

(1) Purchase of raw materials	$2,500
(2) Issue of raw materials	1,500
(3) Incurrence of direct labor cost	850
(4) Application of overhead	340
(5) Incurrence of actual overhead cost	415
(6) Transfer of Job 1 to finished goods	1,840
(7) Cost of goods sold of Job 1	1,840
(9) Closing out underapplied overhead	75

Accounting for Nonmanufacturing Costs

Recall that costs associated with selling and general administrative activities are classified as nonmanufacturing costs. These costs are period costs and are *never* assigned to the product. They are not part of the manufacturing cost flows. They do not belong to the overhead category and are treated as a totally separate category.

To illustrate how these costs are accounted for, assume Better Works had the following additional transactions in January:

Advertising circulars	$ 75
Sales commission	125
Office salaries	500
Depreciation, office equipment	50

The following compound entry could be used to record the above costs:

Selling Expense Control	200	
Administrative Expense Control	550	
Accounts Payable		75
Wages Payable		625
Accumulated Depreciation		50

Controlling accounts accumulate all of the selling and administrative expenses for a period. At the end of the period, all of these costs flow to the period's income statement. An income statement for Better Works is shown in Exhibit 3–16.

With the description of the accounting procedures for selling and administrative expenses completed, the basic essentials of a normal job-order costing system are also complete. This description has assumed that a single plant-wide overhead rate was being used. The use of a single overhead rate, however, can distort product costs.

EXHIBIT 3–16

Better Works Company		
Income Statement		
For the Month Ended January 31, 1993		
Sales		$ 2,760
Less: Cost of goods sold (from Exhibit 3–14)		(1,915)
Gross margin		$ 845
Less selling and administrative expenses:		
Selling expense	$200	
Administrative expense	550	(750)
Net income		$ 95

■ SINGLE VERSUS MULTIPLE OVERHEAD RATES

Using a single rate based on direct labor hours to assign overhead to jobs may result in unfair cost assignments (unfair in the sense that too much or too little overhead is assigned to a job). This can occur if direct labor hours do not correlate well with the consumption of overhead resources.

To illustrate, consider a company with two departments, one that is labor intensive (Department A) and the other machine intensive (Department B). The expected annual overhead costs and the expected annual usage of direct labor hours and machine hours for each department are shown in Exhibit 3–17.

Currently, the company uses a plant-wide overhead rate based on direct labor hours. Thus, the overhead rate used for product costing is $12 per direct labor hour [($60,000 + $180,000)/(15,000 + 5,000)].

Now consider two recently completed jobs, Job 23 and Job 24. Exhibit 3–18 provides production-related data concerning each job. The data reveal

EXHIBIT 3–17
Departmental Overhead Costs and Activity

	Department A	Department B	Total
Overhead costs	$60,000	$180,000	$240,000
Direct labor hours	15,000	5,000	20,000
Machine hours	5,000	15,000	20,000

EXHIBIT 3–18
Production Data for Jobs 23 and 24

	Job 23		
	Department A	Department B	Total
Prime costs	$5,000	$ 0	$5,000
Direct labor hours	500	0	500
Machine hours	1	0	1
Units produced	1,000	0	1,000
	Job 24		
	Department A	Department B	Total
Prime costs	$ 0	$5,000	$5,000
Direct labor hours	0	1	1
Machine hours	0	500	500
Units produced	0	1,000	1,000

that Job 23 spent all of its time in Department A while Job 24 spent all of its time in Department B. Using the plant-wide overhead rate, Job 23 would receive a $6,000 overhead assignment ($12 × 500 direct labor hours) and Job 24 would receive a $12 overhead assignment ($12 × 1 direct labor hour). Thus, the total manufacturing cost of Job 23 is $11,000 ($5,000 + $6,000), yielding a unit cost of $11; the total manufacturing cost of Job 24 is $5,012 ($5,000 + $12), yielding a unit cost of $5.012.

Clearly, something is wrong. Using a plant-wide rate, Job 23 received 500 times the overhead cost assignment than Job 24 received. Yet, as Exhibit 3–17 shows, Job 24 was produced in a department that is responsible for producing 75 percent of the plant's total overhead. Imagine the difficulties that this type of costing distortion can cause for a company. Some products would be overcosted while others would be undercosted, and the result could be incorrect pricing decisions that adversely affect the firm's competitive position.

The distortion in product costs is caused by the assumption that direct labor hours properly reflect the overhead consumed by the individual jobs. One cost driver for the firm as a whole does not seem to work. This type of problem can be resolved by using multiple overhead rates, where each rate uses a different cost driver. For this example, a satisfactory solution might be to develop an overhead rate for each department. In the case of the machine-intensive Department B, the rate could be based on machine hours instead of direct labor hours. It seems reasonable to believe that machine hours relate better to machine-related overhead than direct labor hours do and that direct labor hours would be a good cost driver for a labor-intensive department. If so, then more accurate product costing can be achieved by computing two departmental rates instead of one plant-wide rate.

Using data from Exhibit 3–17, the overhead rate for Department A is $4 per direct labor hour ($60,000/15,000), and the overhead rate for Department B is $12 per machine hour ($180,000/15,000). Using these rates, Job 23 would be assigned $2,000 of overhead ($4 × 500 direct labor hours) and Job 24 $6,000 of overhead ($12 × 500 machine hours). Job 24 now receives three times as much overhead cost as Job 23, which seems more sensible since Department B incurs three times as much overhead cost as Department A.

	Department A	*Department B*
Overhead cost	$60,000	$180,000
÷ Cost driver	15,000 *DLH*	15,000 MHrs
Department overhead rate	$4/*DLH*	$12/MHr
Overhead applied to:		
Job #23	$2,000	—
Job #24	—	$6,000

While moving to departmental rates may provide sufficient product-costing accuracy for some firms, even more attention on how overhead is assigned may be necessary for other firms. This chapter has focused on cost drivers that are correlated with production volume (e.g., direct labor hours and machine hours). Greater product-costing accuracy may be possible through the use of nonvolume-related cost drivers. However, discussion of further refinements of overhead assignment is left to a later chapter.

■ SUMMARY OF LEARNING OBJECTIVES

1. **Describe the differences between job-order costing and process costing and identify the types of firm that would use each method.** Job-order costing and process costing are two major cost assignment systems. Job-order systems are used for firms that produce a wide variety of heterogeneous (unique) products. Process costing is used by firms that mass-produce a homogeneous product.

2. **Define actual and normal costing and explain why normal costing is preferred.** An actual cost system requires the firm to determine the actual cost of direct materials, direct labor, and factory overhead in order to calculate unit cost. Normal cost is a mixture of actual costs for direct materials and labor and predetermined costs for overhead. Normal costing is preferred because it is capable of supplying unit cost information in a timely way. An actual cost system simply cannot supply the needed unit cost information on a timely basis.

3. **Compute a predetermined overhead rate and use the rate to assign overhead to work in process.** A predetermined overhead rate is computed by dividing the budgeted overhead for the period (typically a year) by the budgeted base for the period. Applying overhead to production is accomplished by multiplying the predetermined rate times the actual level of production activity.

4. **Know the role of activity-level measurement and the choice of activity level in the computation of predetermined overhead rates.** The base chosen to calculate the predetermined overhead rate and to apply overhead to production should bear a cause-and-effect relationship to overhead. That is, if overhead is predominantly labor oriented (e.g., supervisory labor and fringe benefits), then direct labor hours or direct labor cost may be appropriate. However, if overhead consists primarily of nonlabor costs, then a nonlabor base should be used. Other typically used bases include units produced, materials cost, and machine hours.

5. **Compute under- and overapplied overhead and know how to dispose of the overhead variance at the end of the period.** Any difference between the applied overhead and the actual overhead for a period is an overhead variance. If actual overhead is greater than applied, then overhead is said to be underapplied. If actual overhead is less than applied overhead, then overhead is overapplied. If this overhead variance is not material, it is usually

closed out to cost of goods sold. Otherwise, the variance is allocated among cost of goods sold, finished goods, and work in process.

6. **Identify the source documents used in job-order costing.** In job-order costing, the key document or record for accumulating manufacturing costs is the job-order cost sheet. Materials requisition forms (for direct materials) and time tickets (for direct labor) are the source documents needed to assign manufacturing costs to jobs.

7. **Describe the cost flows and prepare the journal entries associated with job-order costing.** In job-order costing, materials and direct labor are charged to the Work in Process account (Raw Materials and Payroll are credited, respectively). Overhead costs are assigned to work in process using a predetermined rate. The cost of completed units is credited to Work in Process and debited to Finished Goods. When goods are sold, the cost is debited to Cost of Goods Sold and credited to Finished Goods.

8. **Explain why multiple overhead rates may be preferred to a single, plant-wide overhead rate.** In order to achieve more accurate product costing, it may be necessary to use departmental overhead rates rather than a single, factory-wide rate. Departmental overhead rates provide more accurate costing by reflecting cause-and-effect relationships more accurately. By improving the accuracy of product costing, managers have better information to use in making pricing and product mix decisions.

■ KEY TERMS

Actual cost system   A cost measurement system in which actual manufacturing costs are assigned to products. (p. 82)

Adjusted cost of goods sold   Normal cost of goods sold adjusted to include overhead variance. (p. 103)

Applied overhead   The overhead assigned to production using a predetermined overhead rate. (p. 87)

Cost assignment   The process of associating manufacturing costs with the units produced. (p. 79)

Cost measurement   The process of assigning dollar values to cost items. (p. 79)

Expected activity level   The level of production activity expected for the coming period. (p. 87)

Job-order costing system   A cost accumulation method that accumulates manufacturing costs by job. (p. 81)

Job-order cost sheet   A document or record used to accumulate manufacturing costs for a job. (p. 92)

Materials requisition form   A document used to identify the cost of raw materials assigned to each job. (p. 92)

Normal activity level   The average activity level that a firm experiences over more than one fiscal period. (p. 87)

Normal costing system   A cost measurement system in which the actual costs of direct materials and direct labor are assigned to production and a predetermined rate is used to assign overhead costs to production. (p. 84)

Normal cost of goods sold   The cost of goods sold figure obtained when the per-unit normal cost is used. (p. 103)

Overapplied overhead   The overhead variance resulting when applied overhead is greater than the actual overhead cost incurred. (p. 89)

Overhead variance   The difference between the actual overhead and the applied overhead. (p. 89)

Practical activity level   The output a firm can achieve if it is operating efficiently. (p. 87)

Predetermined overhead rate   Estimated overhead divided by the estimated level of production activity. It is used to assign overhead to production. (p. 85)

Process costing system   A cost accumulation method that accumulates costs by process or department. (p. 82)

Theoretical activity level   The maximum output possible for a firm under perfect operating conditions. (p. 87)

Time ticket   A document used to identify the cost of direct labor for a job. (p. 94)

Underapplied overhead   The overhead variance resulting when the actual overhead cost incurred is greater than the applied overhead. (p. 89)

Work-in-process file   A collection of open job-order cost sheets or job-order cost records. (p. 92)

■ REVIEW PROBLEM

Timter Company uses a normal job-order costing system. The company has two departments through which most jobs pass. Selected budgeted and actual data for the past year follow:

	Department A	Department B
Budgeted overhead	$100,000	$500,000
Actual overhead	110,000	520,000
Expected activity (direct labor hours)	50,000	10,000
Expected machine hours	10,000	50,000
Actual direct labor hours	51,000	9,000
Actual machine hours	10,500	52,000

During the year, several jobs were completed. Data pertaining to one such job are as follows:

	Job 10
Direct materials	$20,000
Direct labor cost:	
Department A (5,000 hrs @ $6)	$30,000
Department B (1,000 hrs @ $6)	$ 6,000
Machine hours used:	
Department A	100
Department B	1,200
Units produced	10,000

Timter Company uses a plant-wide predetermined overhead rate to assign overhead (*OH*) to jobs. Direct labor hours (*DLH*) is used to compute the predetermined overhead rate.

Required:

1. Compute the predetermined overhead rate.

2. Using the predetermined rate, compute the per-unit manufacturing cost for Job 10.

3. Compute the overhead variance for the year and label it as over- or underapplied. Assuming that the variance is immaterial, provide the journal entry that will dispose of the variance at the end of the year.

4. Recalculate the unit manufacturing cost for Job 10 using departmental overhead rates. Use direct labor hours for Department A and machine hours for Department B. Explain why this approach provides a more accurate unit cost.

Solution:

1. Predetermined overhead rate = $600,000/60,000
   = $10 per *DLH*

Add the budgeted overhead for the two departments and divide by the total expected direct labor hours (*DLH* = 50,000 + 10,000).

2.

Direct materials	$ 20,000
Direct labor	36,000
Overhead ($10 × 6,000 *DLH*)	60,000
Total manufacturing cost	$116,000
Unit cost ($116,000/10,000)	$11.60

3. Applied overhead = Overhead rate × Total actual direct labor hours
   = $10 × (51,000 + 9,000)
   = $600,000

   Overhead variance = Total actual *OH* − Applied *OH*
   = $630,000 − $600,000
   = $30,000 underapplied

Cost of Goods Sold	30,000	
Overhead Control		30,000

4. Predetermined rate for Department A: $100,000/50,000 = $2 per *DLH*. Predetermined rate for Department B: $500,000/50,000 = $10 per machine hour.

Direct materials	$20,000
Direct labor	36,000
Overhead:	
Department A: $2 × 5,000	10,000
Department B: $10 × 1,200	12,000
Total manufacturing costs	$78,000
Unit cost ($78,000/10,000)	$ 7.80

Overhead assignment using departmental rates is more accurate because there is a higher correlation with the overhead assigned and the overhead consumed. Notice that Job 10 spends most of its time in Department A, the least overhead intensive of the two departments. Departmental rates reflect this differential time and consumption better than plant-wide rates do.

■ QUESTIONS

1 What is cost measurement? Cost accumulation? What is the difference between the two?

2 Explain why an actual overhead rate is rarely used for product costing.

3 Explain the differences between job-order costing and process costing.

4 What are some differences between a manual job-order cost system and an automated job-order cost system?

5 What is an overhead variance? Explain the difference between an underapplied and an overapplied overhead variance.

6 How are overhead variances disposed of at the end of the year? Which way of disposal is most common? Why?

7 What is the role of materials requisition forms in a job-order cost system? Time tickets? Predetermined overhead rates?

8 Explain why multiple overhead rates are often preferred to a plant-wide overhead rate.

9 Explain the role of cost drivers in assigning overhead costs to products.

10 Define the following terms: *expected actual activity, normal activity, practical activity,* and *theoretical activity.*

11 Why would some prefer normal activity to expected actual activity to compute a predetermined overhead rate?

12   When computing a predetermined overhead rate, why are units of output not commonly used as a measure of production activity?

13   Explain how overhead is assigned to production when a predetermined overhead rate is used.

14   What is the difference between applied overhead and budgeted overhead? Will they ever be the same? If so, explain how. What is the difference between applied overhead and actual overhead? Will these two ever be the same? When?

15   Wilson Company has a predetermined overhead rate of $5 per direct labor hour. The job-order cost sheet for Job 145 shows 1,000 direct labor hours costing $10,000 and materials requisitions totaling $7,500. Job 145 had 500 units completed and transferred to finished goods. What is the cost per unit for Job 145?

16   Why are the accounting requirements for job-order costing more demanding than those for process costing?

17   Explain the difference between normal cost of goods sold and adjusted cost of goods sold.

■ EXERCISES

E3–1   **Predetermined Overhead Rate; Application of Overhead; Variances; Journal Entries**
Harris Company uses a normal job-order cost system. Budgeted overhead for the coming year is $600,000. Expected actual activity is 200,000 direct labor hours. During the year, Harris worked a total of 190,000 direct labor hours and actual overhead totaled $562,000.

Required:

1. Compute the predetermined overhead rate for Harris Company.

2. How much overhead will the company assign to the Work in Process account? Prepare the journal entry that corresponds to this assignment.

3. Compute the overhead variance and label the variance as under- or overapplied overhead. Assuming the variance is not material, write the journal entry that disposes of the variance at the end of the year.

E3–2   **Predetermined Overhead Rate; Applied Overhead; Unit Cost**   Bethel Industries costs products using a normal costing system. The following data are available for 1993:

Budgeted:	
Overhead	$675,000
Machine hours	25,000
Direct labor hours	75,000
Actual:	
Overhead	$681,000
Machine hours	25,050
Direct labor hours	75,700
Prime cost	$957,000
Number of units	400,000

Overhead is applied on the basis of direct labor hours.

Required:

1. What is the predetermined overhead rate?
2. What is the applied overhead for 1993?
3. Was overhead over- or underapplied and by how much?
4. What is the normal cost per unit produced?

E3–3 **Predetermined Overhead Rate; Applied Overhead; Unit Cost**   Using the information from E3–2, above, suppose Bethel Industries applied overhead to production on the basis of machine hours instead of direct labor hours.

Required:

1. What is the predetermined overhead rate?
2. What is the applied overhead for 1993?
3. Is overhead over- or underapplied and by how much?
4. What is the normal cost per unit produced?
5. How can Bethel decide whether to use direct labor hours or machine hours as the basis for applying factory overhead?

E3–4 **Overhead Base Determination**   For each of the following independent situations, determine what cost driver would be best for charging overhead to production.

1. Caralot Cards produces specialty greeting cards sold in gift ships. Cards are cut from heavy paper stock and trimmed with ribbons, lace, etc., and then matched to an envelope and slipped into a cellophane wrapper. No machinery is used; all work is done by hand.
2. Mega Memory Computer Systems produces hard disk storage devices using state-of-the-art robotics. The storage devices move through the production cell according to directions from a series of VAX computers. The cell required significant investment in robotics, computers, and operating software. Power is a significant cost.
3. SuperTape, Inc., opened a plant in Czechoslovakia. The Czech plant receives huge rolls of masking tape from one of SuperTape's U.S. plants, then cuts it to order, wraps it, and ships it to European customers. The cutting and wrapping operations are mechanized.
4. Benson Gemsetters purchases stocks of precious and semiprecious gems as well as gold and silver. Benson's gem setters and metal workers produce rings, necklaces, earrings, and broaches for retail jewelry stores according to a standarized set of designs.
5. Anne Myers, attorney at law, has just opened her own office. Her overhead costs include rent, legal pads and forms, depreciation on office furniture and computers, and salaries for a secretary and paralegal.
6. Rob Brown runs Tree Trimmers out of his home. He employs seven people who trim and cut down trees. Overhead includes depreciation on two trucks with trailers (to haul off logs and branches), several chain saws, hedge trimmers, and a new boring device to chip out roots below ground level. Other supplies (gas, postage, brooms, shovels) and expenses (e.g., telephone answering machine) also exist.

E3–5 **Cost Flows**   For each of the following independent jobs, fill in the missing data. Factory overhead is applied in Department 1 at the rate of $6 per direct labor (*DL*) hour. Factory overhead is applied in Department 2 at the rate of $8/machine hour. Direct labor wages average $10 per hour in each department.

	213	214	217	225
Total sales revenue	?	4,375	5,600	1,150
Price/unit	12	?	14	5
Material used in production	365	?	488	207
DL payroll, Department 1	?	700	2,000	230
Machine hrs, Department 1	15	35	50	12
DL payroll, Department 2	50	100	?	0
Machine hrs, Department 2	25	50	?	?
Overhead applied, Department 1	90	?	1,200	138
Overhead applied, Department 2	?	400	160	0
Total manufacturing cost	855	3,073	?	575
Number of units	?	350	400	?
Unit cost	8.55	?	9.87	?

E3-6   **Predetermined Overhead Rate; Application of Overhead**   Alpha Company and Beta, Inc., both use predetermined overhead rates to apply factory overhead to production. Alpha's is based on direct labor hours and Beta's is based on materials cost. Budgeted production and cost data for Alpha and Beta are as follows:

	Alpha	Beta
Manufacturing overhead	$240,000	$300,000
Units	10,000	20,000
Direct labor hours	6,000	7,500
Material cost	$150,000	$400,000

At the end of the year, Alpha Company had incurred overhead of $221,000 and had produced 9,800 units using 6,100 direct labor hours and materials costing $147,000. Beta, Inc., had incurred overhead of $316,500, and had produced 20,500 units using 7,550 direct labor hours and materials costing $411,000.

Required:

1. Compute the predetermined overhead rates for Alpha and Beta.
2. Was overhead over- or underapplied for each company, and by how much?

E3-7   **Journal Entries; Account Balances**   Kaycee, Inc., manufactures brown paper grocery bags. During the month of May, the following occurred:

a. Materials were purchased on account for $23,175.

b. Materials totaling $19,000 were requisitioned for use in production.

c. Direct labor payroll for the month was $17,850 with an average wage of $8.50 per hour.

d. Actual overhead of $15,500 was incurred and paid.

e. Factory overhead is charged to production at the rate of $7 per direct labor hour.

f. Completed units costing $36,085 were transferred to finished goods.

g. Bags costing $30,000 were sold on account for $36,000.

Beginning balances as of May 1 were:

Materials	$ 5,170
Work in Process	11,200
Finished Goods	2,630

Required:

1. Prepare the journal entries for the above events.

2. Calculate the ending balances of
    a. Materials
    b. Work in Process
    c. Overhead Control
    d. Finished Goods

E3–8   **Choice of Activity Levels; Pricing Concerns**   Lomond Company is considering the use of expected actual activity for the assignment of overhead to jobs. John Simpson, Lomond's vice-president of marketing, is concerned about overhead assignment because different methods can affect the prices charged to customers. Lomond operates in an industry in which cost-plus pricing is heavily used. Firms must bid for jobs, and bids are usually expressed as full manufacturing cost plus a markup.

Simpson believes that Lomond's manufacturing costs are competitive with the rest of the firms in the industry. Since the costs of direct materials and direct labor are expected to be fairly stable over the next three years, any price changes are likely to come from changes in overhead costs. Simpson asked Beth Thompson, the controller, to estimate what the overhead rates would be for the coming three years, using expected actual activity. In response to this request, Beth prepared the following report:

	Year 1	Year 2	Year 3
Expected overhead	$341,250	$341,250	$341,250
Expected actual activity (*DLH*)	70,000	75,000	65,000
Predetermined overhead rate[a]	$4.875	$4.55	$5.25

[a]Expected overhead/Expected actual activity

Upon seeing the report, John Simpson vigorously objected to the method of overhead assignment. He argued that the company should continue to use the practical activity of 80,000 direct labor hours as it had done in the past.

Required:

1. Compute the overhead rates for each of the three years using practical activity. Why would John Simpson prefer using this measure for predetermined overhead rates? Can you think of any disadvantage that practical activity might have for this setting?

2. Suppose the controller suggests using normal activity to compute overhead rates. Recompute the overhead rates using normal activity for the next three years. Can you think of any advantage that normal activity might have over practical activity for this setting?

E3–9   **Predetermined Overhead Rate; Overhead Variances; Journal Entries**   Rayburn Company uses a predetermined overhead rate to assign overhead to jobs. Because Rayburn's production is machine dominated, overhead is applied on the basis of machine hours. The expected overhead for the year was $2.5 million, and the practical level of activity is 50,000 machine hours.

During the year, Rayburn used 48,000 machine hours and incurred actual overhead costs of $2 million. Rayburn also had the following balances of applied overhead in its accounts:

Work in Process	$ 460,000
Cost of Goods Sold	1,440,000
Finished Goods	500,000

Required:

1. Compute a predetermined overhead rate for Rayburn.

2. Compute the overhead variance and label it as under- or overapplied.

3. Assume the overhead variance is immaterial. Prepare the journal entry to dispose of the variance at the end of the year.

4. Assume the variance computed in Question 2 is material. Prepare the journal entry that appropriately disposes of the overhead variance at the end of the year.

E3–10   **Journal Entries; T-Accounts**   Porter Company uses job-order costing. During January 1992, the following data were reported:

a. Materials purchased: direct materials, $82,000; indirect materials, $10,500.

b. Materials issued: direct materials, $72,500; indirect materials, $7,000.

c. Labor cost incurred: direct labor, $52,000; indirect labor, $15,750.

d. Other manufacturing costs incurred (all payables), $49,000.

e. Overhead is applied on the basis of 125 percent of direct labor cost.

f. Work finished and transferred to finished goods cost $160,000.

g. Finished goods costing $140,000 were sold on account for 150 percent of cost.

Required:

1. Prepare journal entries to record these transactions.

2. Prepare a T-account for Manufacturing Overhead. Post all relevant information to this account. What is the ending balance in this account? What does the ending balance represent?

3. Prepare a T-account for Work in Process. Assume a beginning balance of $10,000 and post all relevant information to this account. Did you assign any actual overhead costs to Work in Process? Why or why not?

E3–11   **Applied Overhead; Cost of Goods Manufactured**   Hamblin Products, Inc., provided the following data for the year 1992:

Labor:	
Direct labor cost (25,000 hours)	$175,000
Indirect labor	35,000

Materials:
  Direct materials:
Inventory, January 1, 1992	$ 25,000
Purchases on account	200,000
Issued	190,000
Indirect materials (issued)	10,000

Other factory overhead costs:
Depreciation	55,000
Maintenance	25,000
Miscellaneous	15,500

Work in process:
Beginning inventory	110,000
Ending inventory	80,250

The company uses a predetermined overhead rate based on direct labor hours. The rate for 1992 was $5.20 per direct labor hour.

Required:

1. Compute the applied overhead for 1992. Is the overhead over- or underapplied? By how much?

2. Prepare a statement of cost of goods manufactured. Did you use actual or applied overhead when you prepared the statement of cost of goods manufactured? Explain.

E3–12   **Overhead Assignment: Actual and Normal Activity Compared**   Reynolds Printing Company specializes in wedding announcements. Reynolds uses an actual job-order cost system. An actual overhead rate is calculated at the end of each month using actual direct labor hours and overhead for the month. Once the actual cost of a job is determined, the customer is billed at actual cost plus 50 percent.

During April, Mrs. Lucky, a good friend of owner Jane Reynolds, ordered three sets of wedding announcements to be delivered May 10, June 10, and July 10, respectively. Reynolds scheduled production for each order on May 7, June 7, and July 7. The orders were assigned job numbers 115, 116, and 117, respectively.

Reynolds assured Mrs. Lucky that she would attend each of her daughters' weddings. Out of sympathy and friendship, she also offered a lower price. Instead of cost plus 50 percent, she gave her a special price of cost plus 25 percent. Additionally, she agreed to wait until the final wedding to bill for the three jobs.

On August 15, Reynolds asked her accountant to bring the completed job-order cost sheets for jobs 115, 116, and 117. She also gave instructions to lower the price as had been agreed upon. The cost sheets revealed the following information:

	Job 115	*Job 116*	*Job 117*
Cost of direct materials	$250.00	$250.00	$250.00
Cost of direct labor (5 hours)	25.00	25.00	25.00
Cost of overhead	200.00	400.00	400.00
Total cost	$475.00	$675.00	$675.00
Total price	$593.75	$843.75	$843.75
Number of announcements	500	500	500

Reynolds could not understand why the overhead costs assigned to Jobs 116 and 117 were so much higher than those for Job 115. She asked for an overhead cost summary sheet for the months of May, June, and July, which showed that actual overhead costs were $20,000 each month. She also discovered that direct labor hours worked on all jobs were 500 hours in May and 250 hours each in June and July.

Required:

1. How do you think Mrs. Lucky will feel when she receives the bill for the three sets of wedding announcements?

2. Explain how the overhead costs were assigned to each job.

3. Assume that Reynolds's average activity is 500 hours per month and that the company usually experiences overhead costs of $240,000 each year. Can you recommend a better way to assign overhead costs to jobs? Recompute the cost of each job and its price given your method of overhead cost assignment. Which method do you think is best? Why?

E3–13 **Departmental Overhead Rates**   Bryan Company uses a normal job-order cost system. Currently, a plant-wide overhead rate based on machine hours is used. Sam Perkins, the plant manager, has heard that departmental overhead rates can offer significantly better cost assignments than a plant-wide rate can. Bryan has the following data for its two departments for the coming year:

	Department A	*Department B*
Overhead costs (expected)	$50,000	$22,000
Normal activity (machine hours)	10,000	8,000

1. Compute a predetermined overhead rate for the plant as a whole based on machine hours.

2. Compute predetermined overhead rates for each department using machine hours.

3. Job 15 used 20 machine hours from Department A and 50 machine hours from Department B. Job 22 used 50 machine hours from Department A and 20 from Department B. Compute the overhead cost assigned to each job using the plant-wide rate computed in question 1. Repeat the computation using the departmental rates found in question 2. Which of the two approaches gives the fairer assignment? Why?

4. Repeat question 3 assuming the expected overhead cost for Department B is $40,000. For this company, would you recommend departmental rates over a plant-wide rate?

E3–14 **Unit Cost; Ending Work in Process; Journal Entries**   During October, Tyson Company worked on two jobs. Data relating to these two jobs follow:

	Job 68	*Job 69*
Units in each order	120	200
Units sold	120	—
Materials requisitioned	$744	$640
Direct labor hours	360	400
Direct labor cost	$1,980	$2,480

Overhead is assigned on the basis of direct labor hours at a rate of $3.75. During October, Job 68 was completed and transferred to finished goods. Job 69 was the only unfinished job at the end of the month.

Required:

1. Calculate the per-unit cost of Job 68.

2. Compute the ending balance in the Work in Process account.

3. Prepare the journal entries reflecting the completion and sale of Job 68. The selling price is 140 percent of cost. (Round your answer to the nearest dollar.)

E3–15 **Unit Cost; Journal Entries; Assignment Procedures** Hystle Furniture, Inc., received an order for ten specially designed sofas to be delivered by September 30. The order was assigned Job 237 and work began on September 1. During September, the following activity was associated with Job 237:

a. Purchased $2,000 worth of wood, $1,500 worth of fabric, and $200 worth of foam.

b. Issued $2,000 of wood, $1,500 of fabric, and $200 of foam.

c. Direct labor cost incurred: $1,360.

d. Overhead is assigned using a rate of 125 percent of direct labor cost.

e. Completed units are transferred to the warehouse.

f. Completed units are shipped to the customer. Selling price is 135 percent of cost.

Required:

1. Prepare the journal entries for the activity associated with Job 237.

2. What is the manufacturing cost per sofa?

3. Describe the procedures for identifying the materials issued to Job 237 and for identifying the cost of laborers who worked on the sofas.

E3–16 **Predetermined Overhead Rates; Variances; Cost Flows** Golding Company applies overhead based on direct labor cost. During the first quarter of 1993, the following activity took place in each of the accounts listed below.

Work in Process		Finished Goods	
Bal 20,000	230,000	Bal 40,000	200,000
DL 80,000		230,000	
OH 120,000		Bal 70,000	
DM 40,000			
Bal 30,000			

Overhead		Cost of Goods Sold	
128,500	120,000	200,000	
Bal 8,500			

Job 32 was the only job in process at the end of the first quarter. A total of 1,000 direct labor hours at $10 per hour were charged to Job 32.

Required

1. Assuming that overhead is applied on the basis of direct labor cost, what was the overhead rate used during the first quarter of 1993?

2. What was the applied overhead for the first quarter? The actual overhead? The under- or overapplied overhead?

3. What was the cost of the goods manufactured for the quarter?

4. Assume that the overhead variance is closed to the Cost of Goods Sold account. Prepare the journal entry to close out the Overhead account. What is the adjusted balance in Cost of Goods Sold?

5. For Job 32, identify the costs incurred for direct labor, direct materials, and overhead.

▪ PROBLEMS

P3–1   **Predetermined Overhead Rates; Overhead Variances; Unit Costs**   Sanderson Company uses a predetermined overhead rate to apply overhead. Overhead is applied on the basis of direct labor hours in Department 1 and on the basis of machine hours in Department 2. At the beginning of 1993, the following estimates are provided for the coming year:

	Department 1	Department 2
Direct labor hours	100,000	20,000
Machine hours	10,000	30,000
Direct labor cost	$750,000	$160,000
Overhead cost	$250,000	$162,000

Actual results reported for all jobs during 1993 are as follows:

	Department 1	Department 2
Direct labor hours	98,000	21,000
Machine hours	11,000	32,000
Direct labor cost	$748,000	$168,000
Overhead cost	$247,500	$175,000

The accounting records of the company show the following data for Job 689:

	Department 1	Department 2
Direct labor hours	125	50
Machine hours	10	205
Direct materials cost	$1,580	$2,650
Direct labor cost	$937	$400

Required:

1. Compute the predetermined overhead rate for each department.

2. Compute the applied overhead for all jobs during 1993. What is the under- or overapplied overhead for each department? For the firm?

3. Prepare the journal entry that disposes of the overhead variance, assuming it is not material in amount.

4. Compute the total cost of Job 689. If there are fifty units in Job 689, what is the unit cost?

P3–2   **Journal Entries; T-Accounts; Income Statement**   Neptune, Inc., produces customized sailboats. The company uses a normal job-order costing system. At the beginning of the year, overhead was estimated at $420,000. Normal activity, measured in direct labor hours, is 12,000 hours. Overhead is applied on the basis of direct labor hours. Beginning balances in the accounts are reported as follows:

Work in Process	$25,000
Raw Materials	30,000
Finished Goods	24,000

During the year, the company experienced the following activity:

a. Raw materials purchased, $150,000.

b. Supplies purchased, $20,000.

c. Labor cost: $200,000. Of the total labor cost, 65 percent is direct labor, 10 percent is indirect labor, 20 percent is administrative, and 5 percent is sales.

d. Actual direct labor hours were 13,000.

e. Depreciation totaled $300,000; 70 percent was factory related, 20 percent administrative, and 10 percent sales.

f. Utilities, $15,000; 90 percent was factory related, 5 percent administrative, and 5 percent sales.

g. Other overhead, $155,000 (all payables).

h. Raw materials issued, $165,000; supplies issued, $50,000.

i. Job 179, the only unfinished job at the end of the year, had the following information on its job cost sheet:

Direct materials	$1,000
Direct labor cost	900
Direct labor hours	90

j. Other selling expenses, $8,000. Other administrative expenses, $12,000.

k. Two jobs, Job 168 and Job 170, were not sold by the end of the year. The total cost of both jobs is $9,700.

l. Sales revenue for the year was $1.07 million.

m. Any over- or underapplied overhead is closed out to Cost of Goods Sold.

Required:

1. Using normal activity, compute a predetermined overhead rate.

2. Prepare journal entries for the year's activities.

3. Prepare T-accounts for Raw Materials, Overhead, Work in Process, Finished Goods, and Cost of Goods Sold. Post all relevant entries to these accounts.

4. Prepare an income statement for the year.

P3-3   **Job Cost Sheets; Journal Entries; Inventories**   On July 1, Jason Company had the following balances in its inventory accounts:

Raw Materials	$12,000
Work in Process	8,000
Finished Goods	20,000

Work in process is made up of two jobs with the following costs:

	Job 17	*Job 18*
Raw materials	$2,000	$1,410
Direct labor	1,500	1,200
Applied overhead	1,050	840

During July, Jason experienced the transactions listed below.

a. Materials purchased on account, $15,000.

b. Materials requisitioned: Job 17, $12,500; Job 18, $11,200.

c. Job tickets were collected and summarized: Job 17, 250 hours at $10 per hour; Job 18, 275 hours at $11 per hour.

d. Overhead is applied on the basis of direct labor cost.

e. Actual overhead was $4,000.

f. Job 18 was completed and transferred to the finished goods warehouse.

g. Job 18 was shipped, and the customer was billed for 160 percent of the cost.

Required:

1. Prepare job cost sheets for Jobs 17 and 18. Post the beginning inventory data and then update the cost sheets for the July activity.

2. Prepare journal entries for the July transactions.

3. Prepare a schedule of inventories on July 31.

P3-4   **Predetermined Overhead Rates; Applied Overhead; Disposition of Overhead Variances**   Velma, Inc., uses a normal job-order cost system. The company has two departments, and predetermined overhead rates are computed for each department. Estimated cost and operating data are as follows for the year 1992:

	Department A	Department B
Estimated direct labor hours	50,000	10,000
Estimated machine hours	10,000	50,000
Estimated overhead	$200,000	$400,000

At the end of 1992, Velma reported the following actual cost and operating data:

	Department A	Department B
Direct labor hours	50,000	10,000
Machine hours	10,000	50,000
Overhead	$220,000	$440,000

The company also reported ending balances in the following accounts (prior to any closing entries);

	Total	Applied Overhead
Raw Materials	$ 40,000	—
Work in Process	100,000	$ 50,000
Finished Goods	300,000	200,000
Cost of Goods Sold	600,000	350,000

Required:

1. Assume that Department A uses direct labor hours and Department B uses machine hours to apply overhead. Compute a predetermined overhead rate for each department.

2. Compute the applied overhead for each department. Prepare the journal entry that assigns applied overhead to production.

3. Compute the under- or overapplied overhead for each department. What is the total overhead variance for the firm?

4. Prepare the journal entry to dispose of the under- or overapplied overhead under the assumption that (a) the overhead variance is immaterial and (b) the overhead variance is material.

5. How much will Velma's net income change if 4(b) is the method of disposing of the overhead rather than 4(a)?

P3–5 **Journal Entries; T-Accounts; Cost of Goods Manufactured and Sold**   During February, the following transactions were completed and reported by Bixby Products, Inc.:

a. Raw materials were purchased on account, $43,500.

b. Materials issued to production to fill job order requisitions, $35,000; supplies, $12,200.

c. Payroll for the month: direct labor, $60,000; indirect labor, $20,000; administrative, $18,000; sales, $9,000.

d. Depreciation on factory plant and equipment, $8,500.

e. Property tax (on factory) accrued during the month, $450.

f. Insurance (on factory) expired with a credit to the prepaid account, $6,200.

g. Factory utilities, $6,200.

h. Advertising, $5,000.

i. Depreciation on office equipment, $1,500; on sales vehicles, $650.

j. Legal fees for preparation of lease agreements, $750.

k. Overhead is charged to production at a rate of $6 per *DLH*. Records show 8,000 direct labor hours were worked during the month.

l. Cost of jobs completed during the month, $135,000.

The company also reported the following beginning balances in its inventory accounts:

Raw Materials	$ 5,000
Work in Process	30,000
Finished Goods	60,000

Required:

1. Prepare journal entries to record the transactions occurring in February.

2. Prepare T-accounts for Raw Materials, Overhead, Work in Process, and Finished Goods. Post all relevant entries to these accounts.

3. Prepare a statement of cost of goods manufactured.

4. If the overhead variance is all allocated to Cost of Goods Sold, by how much will Cost of Goods Sold decrease or increase?

P3–6   **Journal Entries; T-Accounts; Disposition of Overhead; Income Statement**   At the beginning of the year, Polson Manufacturing Company had the following balances in its inventory accounts:

Raw Materials	$70,000
Work in Process	20,000
Finished Goods	45,000

Polson applies overhead on the basis of 150 percent of direct labor cost. During the year, Polson experienced transactions as described below.

a. Direct materials purchased, $280,000.

b. Direct materials issued, $300,000.

c. Indirect materials issued, $82,000.

d. Labor costs

Direct labor	$110,000
Indirect labor	60,000
Selling and administrative	70,000

e. Factory insurance expired, $5,000.

f. Advertising costs, $30,000.

g. Factory rent, $24,000.

h. Depreciation (office equipment); $10,000

i. Miscellaneous factory costs, $7,850.

j. Utilities (70 percent factory, 30 percent office), $10,000.

k. Overhead was applied to production.

l. Sales totaled $983,000.

Ending balances in the inventory accounts were used to prorate the overhead variance.

Raw Materials	$50,000
Work in Process	30,000
Finished Goods	20,000
Cost of Goods Sold	?

Required:

1. Prepare journal entries for the above transactions.

2. Post the journal entries relating to manufacturing costs to the appropriate T-accounts.

3. Compute the under- or overapplied overhead variance. Give the journal entry that disposes of the variance by closing it out to Cost of Goods Sold. Give the journal entry required to close out the variance if it is prorated among the appropriate accounts.

4. Prepare an income statement assuming that the variance is closed to Cost of Goods Sold. Prepare another income statement based on prorating the variance. What is the difference in income figures? Would you judge the difference to be significant?

P3–7 **Job-Order Costing: Housing Construction** Butter, Inc., is a privately held, family-founded corporation that builds single- and multiple-unit housing. Most projects Butter undertakes involve the construction of multiple units. Butter has adopted a job-order cost system for determining the cost of each unit. The costing system is fully computerized.

Each project's costs are divided into the following five categories:

1. *General conditions,* including construction site utilities, project insurance permits and licenses, architect's fees, decorating, field office salaries, and clean-up costs

2. *Hard costs,* such as subcontractors, direct materials, and direct labor

3. *Finance costs,* including title and recording fees, inspection fees, and taxes and discounts on mortgages

4. *Land costs,* which refer to the purchase price of the construction site

5. *Marketing costs,* such as advertising, sales commissions, and appraisal fees

Recently, Butter purchased land for the purpose of developing twenty new single family houses. The cost of the land was $250,000. Lot sizes vary from 1/4 to 1/2 acre. The twenty lots occupy a total of eight acres.

General condition costs for the project totaled $120,000. This $120,000 is common to all twenty units that were constructed on the building site.

Job 3, the third house built in the project, occupied a 1/4-acre lot and had the following hard costs:

Materials	$ 8,000
Direct labor	6,000
Subcontractor	14,000

For Job 3, finance costs totaled $4,765 and marketing costs, $800. General condition costs are allocated on the basis of units produced. Each unit's selling price is determined by adding 40 percent to the total of all costs.

Required:

1. Identify all production costs that are directly traceable to Job 3. Are all remaining production costs equivalent to overhead found in a manufacturing firm? Are there nonproduction costs that are directly traceable to the housing unit? Which ones?

2. Develop a job-order cost sheet for Job 3. What is the cost of building this house? Did you include finance and marketing costs in computing the unit cost? Why or why not? How did you determine the cost of land for Job 3?

3. Which of the five cost categories corresponds to overhead? Do you agree with the way in which this cost is allocated to individual housing units? Can you suggest a different allocation method?

4. Calculate the selling price of Job 3. Calculate the profit made on the sale of this unit.

P3–8   **Selection of Overhead Rates; Ethical Issues**   Tonya Martin, CMA, and controller of the Parts Division of Gunderson, Inc., was meeting with Doug Adams, manager of the division. The topic of discussion was the assignment of overhead costs to jobs and their impact on the division's pricing decisions. Their conversation is presented below.

Tonya: Doug, as you know, about 25 percent of our business is based on government contracts, with the other 75 percent based on jobs from private sources won through bidding. During the last several years, our private business has declined. We have been losing more bids than usual. After some careful investigation, I have concluded that we are overpricing some jobs because of improper assignment of overhead costs. Some jobs are also being underpriced. Unfortunately, the jobs being overpriced are coming.from our higher-volume, labor-intensive products and so we are losing business.

Doug: I think I understand. Jobs associated with our high-volume products are being assigned more overhead than they should be receiving. When we then add our standard 40 percent markup, we end up with a higher price than our competitors, who assign costs more accurately.

Tonya: Exactly. We have two producing departments, one labor intensive and the other machine intensive. The labor-intensive department generates much less overhead than the machine-intensive department. Furthermore, virtually all of our high-volume jobs are labor intensive. We have been using a plant-wide rate based on direct labor hours to assign overhead to all jobs. As a result, the high-volume, labor-intensive jobs receive a greater share of the machine-intensive department's overhead than they deserve. This problem can be greatly alleviated by switching to departmental overhead rates. For example, an average high-volume job would be assigned $100,000 of overhead using a plant-wide rate and only $70,000 using departmental rates. The change would lower our bidding price on high-volume jobs by an average of $42,000 per job. By increasing the accuracy of our product costing, we can make better pricing decisions and win back much of our private-sector business.

Doug: Sounds good. When can you implement the change in overhead rates?

Tonya: It won't take long. I can have the new system working within four to six weeks—certainly by the start of the new fiscal year.

Doug: Hold it. I just thought of a possible complication. As I recall, most of our government contract work is done in the labor-intensive department. This new overhead assignment scheme will push down the cost on the government jobs and we will lose revenues. They pay us full cost plus our standard markup. This business is not threatened by our current costing procedures, but we can't switch our rates for only the private business. Government auditors would question the lack of consistency in our costing procedures.

Tonya: You do have a point. I thought of this issue also. According to my estimates, we will gain more revenues from the private sector than we will lose from our government contracts. Besides, the costs of our government jobs are distorted; in effect, we are overcharging the government.

Doug: They don't know that and never will unless we switch our overhead assignment procedures. I think I have the solution. Officially, let's keep our plant-wide overhead rate. All of the official records will reflect this overhead costing approach for both our private and government business. Unofficially, I want you to develop a separate set of books that can be used to generate the information we need to prepare competitive bids for our private-sector business.

Required:

1. Do you believe that the solution proposed by Doug Adams is ethical? Explain.

2. Suppose that Tonya Martin decides that Adams's solution is not right. In your opinion, is Martin supported in this view by the standards of ethical conduct described in the Appendix to Chapter 1? Explain.

3. Suppose that, despite Martin's objections, Adams insists strongly on implementing the action. What should Tonya Martin do?

P3–9 **Plant-wide Overhead Rate Versus Departmental Rates; Effects on Pricing Decisions**
Alden Peterson, marketing manager for Retlief Company, was puzzled by the outcome of two recent bids. The company's policy was to bid 150 percent of the full manufacturing cost. One job (labeled Job SS) had been turned down by a prospective customer, who had indicated that the proposed price was $3 per unit higher than the winning bid. A second job (Job TT) had been accepted by a customer, who was amazed that Retlief could offer such favorable terms. This customer revealed that Retlief's price was $43 per unit lower than the next lowest bid.

Alden has been informed that the company was more than competitive in terms of cost control. Accordingly, he began to suspect that the problem was related to cost assignment procedures. Upon investigating, Alden was told that the company uses a plant-wide overhead rate based on direct labor hours. The rate is computed at the beginning of the year using budgeted data. Selected budgeted data are given below.

	Department A	Department B	Total
Overhead	$500,000	$2,000,000	$2,500,000
Direct labor hours	200,000	50,000	250,000
Machine hours	20,000	120,000	140,000

Alden also discovered that the overhead costs in Department B were higher than those in Department A because B has more equipment, higher maintenance, higher power consumption, higher depreciation, and higher setup costs. In addition to the general procedures for assigning overhead costs, Alden was supplied with the following specific manufacturing data on Job SS and Job TT:

Job SS

	Department A	Department B	Total
Direct labor hours	5,000	1,000	6,000
Machine hours	200	500	700
Prime costs	$100,000	$20,000	$120,000
Units produced	14,400	14,400	14,400

Job TT

	Department A	Department B	Total
Direct labor hours	400	600	1,000
Machine hours	200	3,000	3,200
Prime costs	$10,000	$40,000	$50,000
Units produced	1,500	1,500	1,500

Required

1. Using a plant-wide overhead rate based on direct labor hours, develop the bid prices for Job SS and Job TT (express the bid prices on a per-unit basis).

2. Using departmental overhead rates (use direct labor hours for Department A and machine hours for Department B), develop per-unit bid prices for Job SS and Job TT.

3. Compute the difference in gross profit that would have been earned had the company used departmental rates in its bids instead of the plant-wide rate.

4. Explain why the use of departmental rates in this case provides a more accurate product cost.

P3–10   **Departmental Overhead Rates; Unit Cost**   Stoney End Recordings produces cassette tapes, records, and compact discs on a job-order basis for individuals and groups who want their music recorded. In some cases, customers want one or two copies for family and friends. In others, several hundred LPs or CDs are ordered to send to radio stations across the country in hopes of getting airplay. In still other cases, several thousand records may be ordered by fledgling bands to leave with record stores on a consignment basis.

Stoney End uses a normal costing system with departmental overhead rates for the use of the recording studio (based on direct labor hours), the vinyl pressing department (based on machine hours), and the CD recording department (based on machine hours).

Budgeted amounts for 1993 were:

Overhead:	
Recording studio	$ 15,000
Vinyl pressing	$ 8,000
CD	$ 24,000
Direct labor hours:	
Recording studio	6,000
Vinyl pressing	4,000
CD	12,000
Machine hours:	
Recording studio	3,000
Vinyl pressing	1,600
CD	6,000
Average wage rates were:	
Recording studio	$12/DLH
Vinyl pressing	$ 6/DLH
CD	$25/DLH

In September, Billy Ryan and the Black Irish (a heavy metal rock band) ordered 300 LP records to distribute to radio stations and record company executives. Stoney End assigned this job the number 93-413. Job 93-413 used ten direct labor hours of recording studio time, one direct labor hour, and five machine hours in the vinyl department. Direct materials (tape, vinyl, cardboard sleeve for the record, etc.) amounted to $372.

Required:

1. Calculate overhead rates for the recording, vinyl, and CD departments.

2. Determine the total cost of Job 93-413. What is the unit cost?

P3–11 **Predetermined Overhead Rate; Departmental Overhead Rates; Job Cost** Anselmo's Kwik-Print provides a variety of photocopying and printing services. On June 5, 1993, Anselmo invested in some computer-aided photography equipment that enables customers to reproduce a picture or illustration, input it digitally into the computer, enter text into the computer, and then print out a four-color professional-quality brochure. Prior to the purchase of this equipment, Kwik-Print's overhead averaged $35,000 per year. After the installation of the new equipment, the total overhead increased to $85,000 per year. Kwik-Print has always costed jobs on the basis of actual materials and labor plus overhead assigned using a predetermined overhead rate based on direct labor hours. Budgeted direct labor hours for 1993 are 5,000, and the wage rate is $6 per hour.

Required:

1. What was the predetermined overhead rate prior to the purchase of the new equipment?

2. What was the predetermined overhead rate after the new equipment was purchased?

3. Suppose Jim Hargrove brought in several items he wanted photocopied. The job required 100 sheets of paper at $0.015 each, and twelve minutes of direct labor time. What was the cost of Jim's job on May 20, 1993? On June 20, 1993?

4. Suppose that Anselmo decides to calculate two overhead rates, one for the photocopying area based on direct labor hours as before, and one for the computer-aided printing area based on machine time. Estimated overhead applicable to the computer-aided printing area is $50,000; forecast usage of the machines is 2,000 hours. What are the two overhead rates? Which overhead rate system is better—one rate or two?

P3–12   **Departmental Overhead Rates; Job Cost**   Zorba Novelties, Inc., produces t-shirts and pottery (mugs, glassware, etc.) to customer order. The T-Shirt Department takes the design selected by the customer and hot presses it onto each shirt. The shirts are then inspected, folded, and slipped into plastic wrappers. The Pottery Department affixes a customer-selected decal onto the mug or glass and then boxes each individual item to prevent breakage.

Zorba uses a normal job order costing system. That is, each job accumulates actual direct materials and labor, and overhead is applied using a predetermined rate.

Zorba determined the following budgeted costs for the year:

	T-Shirt Department	*Pottery Department*
Overhead	$10,000	$2,100
Direct labor hours	5,000	1,500

Overhead is applied on the basis of direct labor hours.

Actual costs for one of each are as follows:

T-shirt	$3.22
Design transfer	0.46
Mug	2.50
Mug decal (each)	0.25

It takes three minutes of direct labor time to select a shirt from inventory, place the selected design transfer on it, place it on the hot press, press the design on the shirt, dispose of the paper transfer backing, and fold and wrap the shirt. In the Pottery Department, five minutes of direct labor time are required to put one decal on a mug and individually box the mug (extra decals can be affixed at the rate of one minute each). Direct labor is paid at the rate of $6.50 per hour.

Ordinarily, Zorba charges cost plus 50 percent to figure the price. However, the owner gives a quantity discount of 10 percent off price for seventy-five or more identical items offered. He also hates to be rushed and imposes a 25 percent surcharge on orders with less than seventy-two hours of lead time. (The rush surcharge is calculated on the basis of the price figured after any quantity discounts are subtracted.)

On May 17, Katie Stephens of the Campus Orientation Committee ordered 150 t-shirts to be imprinted with the campus "Welcome Frosh" design. These shirts were to be available August 1—in plenty of time for sophomore volunteers to pick one up to wear during Orientation Week.

On October 31, Leslie Adams, president of Campus Chest, raced into Zorba's to order fifty coffee mugs with the campus logo on one side and the phrase "Campus Chest Sponsor" on the other. Leslie, who was supposed to place the order in September but forgot, wanted it by noon, November 1.

Required:

1. What are the predetermined overhead rates for the two departments?
2. What is the cost of Katie's t-shirt order? Cost/unit? What price did Zorba charge Katie?
3. What is the cost of Leslie's order? What price did Zorba charge Leslie?

■ MANAGERIAL DECISION CASES

Case 3–1   **Job-Order Costing: Dental Practice**   Dr. Sherry Bird is employed by Dental Associates. Dental Associates recently installed a computerized job costing system to help monitor the cost of its services. Each patient is treated as a job and assigned a job number when he or she checks in with the receptionist. The receptionist-bookkeeper notes the time the patient enters the treatment area and when the patient leaves the area. The difference between the entry and exit times is the patient hours used and is the direct labor time assigned to the dental assistant (a dental assistant is constantly with the patient). Fifty percent of the patient hours is the direct labor time assigned to the dentist (the dentist typically splits her time between two patients).

The chart filled out by the dental assistant provides additional data that is entered into the computer. For example, the chart contains service codes that identify the nature of the treatment, such as whether the patient received a crown, a filling, or a root canal. The chart not only identifies the type of service but its level as well. For example, if a patient receives a filling, the dental assistant indicates (by a service-level code) whether the filling was one, two, three, or four surfaces. The service and service-level codes are used to determine the rate to be charged to the patient. The costs of providing different services and their levels also vary.

Costs assignable to a patient consist of materials, labor, and overhead. The type of materials used—and the quantity—are identified by the assistant and entered into the computer by the bookkeeper. Material prices are kept on file and accessed to provide the necessary cost information. Overhead is applied on the basis of patient hours. The rate used by Dental Associates is $20 per patient hour. Direct labor cost is also computed using patient hours and the wage rates of the direct laborers. Dr. Bird is paid an average of $36 per hour for her services. Dental assistants are paid an average of $6 per hour. Given the treatment time, the software program calculates and assigns the labor cost for the dentist and her assistant; overhead cost is also assigned using the treatment time and the overhead rate.

The overhead rate does not include a charge for any X rays. The X ray Department is separate from dental services; X rays are billed and costed separately. The cost of an X ray is $3.50 per film; the patient is charged $5 per film. If cleaning services are required, cleaning labor costs $9 per patient hour.

Glen Johnson, a patient (Job 267), spent thirty minutes in the treatment area and had a two-surface filling. He received two Novocain shots and used three ampules of amalgam. The cost of the shots was $1. The cost of the amalgam was $3. Other direct materials used are insignificant in amount and are included in the overhead rate. The rate charged to the patient for a two-surface filling is $45. One X ray was taken.

Required:

1. Prepare a job-cost sheet for Glen Johnson. What is the cost for providing a two-surface filling? What is the gross profit earned? Is the X ray a direct cost of the service? Why are the X rays costed separately from the overhead cost assignment?

2. Suppose that the patient time and associated patient charges are given for the following fillings:

	1 Surface	*2 Surface*	*3 Surface*	*4 Surface*
Time	20 minutes	30 minutes	40 minutes	50 minutes
Charge	$35	$45	$55	$65

Compute the cost for each filling and the gross profit for each type of filling. Assume that the cost of Novocain is $1 for all fillings. Ampules of amalgam start at two and increase by one for each additional surface. Assume also that only one X ray film is needed for all four cases. Does the increase in billing rate appear to be fair to the patient? Is it fair to the dental corporation?

Case 3–2   **Job-Order Costing and Pricing Decisions**   Nutratask, Inc., is a pharmaceutical manufacturer of amino-acid-chelated minerals and vitamin supplements. The company was founded in 1974 and is capable of performing all manufacturing functions, including packaging and laboratory functions. Currently, the company markets its products in the United States, Canada, Australia, Japan, and Belgium.

Mineral chelation enhances the mineral's availability to the body, making the mineral a more effective supplement. Most of the chelates supplied by Nutratask are in powder form, but the company has the capability to make tablets or capsules.

The production of all chelates follows a similar pattern. Upon receiving an order, the company's chemist prepares a load sheet (a bill of materials that specifies the product, the theoretical yield, and the quantities of raw materials that should be used). Once the load sheet is received by production, the materials are requisitioned and sent to the blending room. The chemicals and minerals are added in the order specified and blended together for two to eight hours, depending on the product. After blending, the mix is put on long trays and sent to the drying room, where it is allowed to dry until the moisture content is 7 to 9 percent. Drying time for most products is from one to three days.

After the product is dry, several small samples are taken and sent to a laboratory to be checked for bacterial level and to see whether the product meets customer specifications. If the product is not fit for human consumption or if it fails to meet customer specifications, additional materials are added under the direction of the chemist to bring the product up to standard. Once the product passes inspection, it is ground into a powder of different meshes (particle sizes) according to customer specifications. The powder is then placed in heavy cardboard drums and shipped to the customer (or, if requested, put in tablet or capsule form and then shipped).

Since each order is customized to meet the special needs of its customers, Nutratask uses a job-order costing system. Recently, Nutratask received a request for a 300-kilogram order of potassium aspartate. The customer offered to pay $8.80/kg. Upon receiving the request and the customer's specifications, Lanny Smith, the marketing manager, requested a load sheet from the company's chemist. The load sheet prepared showed the following material requirements:

Material	*Amount Required*
Aspartic acid	195.00 kg
Citric acid	15.00 kg
K_2CO_3 (50%)	121.50 kg
Rice	30.00 kg

The theoretical yield is 300 kg.

Lanny also reviewed past jobs that were similar to the requested order and discovered that the expected direct labor time was sixteen hours. The production workers at Nutratask earn an average of $6.50 per hour plus $6 per hour for taxes, insurance, and additional benefits.

Purchasing sent Smith a list of prices for the materials needed for the job.

Material	Price/kg
Aspartic acid	$5.75
Citric acid	2.02
K_2CO_3	4.64
Rice	0.43

Overhead is applied using a company-wide rate based on direct labor costs. The rate for the current period is 110 percent of direct labor costs.

Whenever a customer requests a bid, Nutratask usually estimates the manufacturing costs of the job and then adds a markup of 30 percent. This markup varies depending on the competition and general economic conditions. Currently, the industry is thriving, and Nutratask is operating at capacity.

Required:

1. Prepare a job cost sheet for the proposed job. What is the expected per-unit cost? Should Nutratask accept the price offered by the prospective customer? Why or why not?

2. Suppose Nutratask and the prospective customer agree on a price of cost plus 30 percent. What is the gross margin that Nutratask expects to earn on the job?

3. Suppose that the actual costs of producing 300 kg of potassium aspartate were as follows:

Direct materials:		
Aspartic acid	$1,170	
Citric acid	30	
K_2CO_3	577	
Rice	13	
Total		$1,790.00
Direct labor		225.00
Overhead		247.50

What is the actual per-unit cost? The bid price is based on expected costs. How much did Nutratask gain (or lose) because of the actual costs differing from the expected costs? Suggest some possible reasons why the actual costs differed from the projected costs. How can management use this information for dealing with future jobs?

4. Assume that the customer had agreed to pay *actual* manufacturing costs plus 30 percent. Suppose the actual costs are as described in question 3 with one addition: an underapplied overhead variance is allocated to Cost of Goods Sold and spread across all jobs sold in proportion to their total cost (unadjusted cost of goods sold).

Assume that the underapplied overhead cost added to the job in question is $30. Upon seeing the addition of the underapplied overhead in the itemized bill, the customer calls and complains about having to pay for Nutratask's inefficient use of overhead costs. If you were assigned to deal with this customer, what kind of response would you prepare? How would you explain and justify the addition of the underapplied overhead cost to the customer's bill?

Process Costing

■ **LEARNING OBJECTIVES**

After studying Chapter 4, you should be able to

1. Identify the settings for which process costing is appropriate.

2. Describe the cost flows associated with process costing.

3. Define *equivalent units* and explain their role in process costing.

4. Prepare a schedule that tracks the physical flow of units within a production department.

5. Prepare a schedule of equivalent units using the weighted average method.

6. Explain the differences between the weighted average method and the FIFO method.

7. Compute the cost per equivalent unit using the weighted average method.

8. Compute the cost of goods transferred out and the cost of the ending work in process for each production department under the weighted average method.

9. Prepare a schedule that identifies the cost each department must account for and that provides an accounting for these costs.

10. Prepare a departmental cost of production report.

11. Define and explain the key terms listed at the end of the chapter.

SCENARIO

Makenzie Gibson, owner of Healthblend Nutritional Supplements, was reviewing last year's income statement. The income reported to the IRS represented a 33 percent increase over the prior year. Makenzie was pleased with the success of the company she had founded ten years earlier. The idea for the company was the result of her recovery from some personal health problems. By working with some health-care professionals, Makenzie had learned to blend a number of different herbs into therapeutic formulas that had brought about an amazing recovery.

Convinced that the discoveries she had made should be shared with others, Makenzie began producing some of these same therapeutic formulas in the basement of her home. Now, ten years later, she is the owner of a multimillion-dollar business housed in a modern facility with more than 60 employees. The success of the business could be explained in part by two significant breakthroughs: (1) the creation of vitamin, herbal, and mineral lines that used capsules instead of tablets, and (2) the development of an improved process for the transportation and utilization of minerals.

Although pleased with the success of her business, Makenzie was convinced that she could not afford to be complacent. More than a month ago, the owner of a health food store had indicated to Makenzie that some other suppliers had dropped competing lines because they were no longer profitable. He asked Makenzie if all of her products were profitable or if she simply offered the full range as a marketing strategy. Makenzie had been forced to admit that she did not know whether all her products were profitable—in fact, she didn't even know how much it was costing to produce an individual product. All she knew was that she was earning significant profits in the aggregate.

After some reflection, she decided that knowing individual costs would be useful. Knowing product costs might have some bearing on production methods, prices, and the mix of products. With this objective in mind, she had called Jack Trench, a good friend and a partner in the local office of a large CPA firm. Jack had agreed to refer the problem to Judith Manesfield, manager of the firm's small business practice section. After several visits by some of Judith's staff, Makenzie received the following preliminary report:

Makenzie Gibson
Healthblend Nutritional Supplements
Tucson, Arizona

Dear Ms. Gibson:

As you are aware, your current accounting system makes no effort to collect the necessary data for costing out the various products that you produce. You are currently producing three major product lines: mineral, herb, and vitamin. Each product, regardless of the type, passes through three processes: picking, encapsulating, and bottling. In picking, the ingredients are measured, sifted, and blended together. In encapsulating, the powdered mix from the first process is put into two-sided capsules, then machines press the two sides together to produce the capsule. The capsules are then transferred to the bottling department where they are bottled, and the bottles are labeled and fitted with safety seals and lids.

Each bottle contains fifty capsules, and the capsules are of equal size for all three product lines. We have also noticed that the cost of materials among the three product lines differs, but that within a product line, the cost of materials for different products is not significantly different. The layout of the plant is structured so that all three product lines are produced simultaneously; thus, there are three different picking departments, one for each major product line.

Based on the nature of the manufacturing processes, our tentative recommendation is to accumulate costs of manufacturing by process for a given period of time and to measure the output for that same period. By dividing the costs accumulated for the period by the output for the period, a good measure of what each individual product is costing can be obtained.

The cost system we are recommending will require the least amount of increase in your bookkeeping activities. If you have no objections, we will proceed with the development of the cost system. As part of this development, we will conduct several training seminars so that your financial staff can operate the system once it is implemented.

■ CHOICE OF A COST ACCUMULATION METHOD

Makenzie Gibson hired the consultant in order to determine the best method for costing out Healthblend's products. The consultant responded by first studying Healthblend's methods of production. The investigation revealed a large number of similar products passing through a set of identical processes. Since each product within a product line passing through the three processes would receive similar "doses" of materials, labor, and overhead, Judith Manesfield saw no need to accumulate costs by batches (a job-costing system). Instead, she recommended accumulating costs by *process*.

Process costing works well whenever relatively homogeneous products pass through a series of processes and receive similar amounts of manufacturing costs. Job-order costing, on the other hand, works well whenever products pass through a series of processes (similar or different) that deal out different amounts of manufacturing costs. Consider a pharmacy where every prescription filled requires a different drug, different direct labor time (to select the prescribed drug, count tablets or mix and fill a bottle with liquid), and different overhead (probably charged on the basis of direct labor, it would consist of costs of the building space, computer, utilities, and so on).

Let's consider the Healthblend example in more detail. From the consultant's letter, we know that there are three departments, or processes. In the Picking Department, direct labor selects the appropriate herbs, vitamins, minerals, and inert materials (typically some binder such as corn starch) for the product to be manufactured. Then the materials are measured and combined in a mixer to blend them thoroughly in the prescribed proportions.

Only when the mix is complete is the resulting mixture sent to Encapsulation. In Encapsulation, the vitamin, mineral, or herb blend is loaded into a machine that fills one-half of a gelatin capsule. The filled half is matched to another half of the capsule and a safety seal is applied. This process is entirely mechanized. Overhead in this department consists of depreciation on machinery, maintenance of machinery, supervision, fringe benefits, light, and power. The final department is Bottling. Filled capsules are transferred to this department, loaded into a hopper, and automatically counted into bottles. Filled bottles are mechanically capped, and direct labor then manually packs the correct number of bottles into boxes to ship to retail outlets.

Now let's look at Healthblend from an accounting perspective. Suppose that Healthblend has only one picking department through which all three major product lines pass. Since the product lines differ significantly in the cost of their material inputs, accumulating material costs by process no longer makes any sense. More accurate product costing can be achieved by accumulating materials costs by batch. In this case, labor and overhead could still be accumulated by process, but raw materials would be assigned to batches using the usual job-cost approach. Note, however, that even with this change, process costing could still be used for the Encapsulating Department and the Bottling Department. In these two departments, each product receives the same amount of material, labor, and overhead.

This example illustrates that some manufacturing settings may need to use a blend of job and process costing. Using job-order procedures to assign material costs to products and a process approach to assign conversion costs is a blend known as *operation costing*. Other blends are possible as well. The example also shows that it is possible to use more than one form of costing within the same firm. This is the case if Healthblend uses operation costing for the Picking Department and process costing for the other two departments.

operation costing

The fundamental point is that the cost accounting system should be designed to fit the nature of operations. Job-order and process costing systems fit pure job and pure process manufacturing environments. There are many settings, however, in which blends of the two costing systems may be suitable. By studying the pure forms of job-order and process costing, we can develop the ability to understand and use any hybrid form.

▪ BASIC CHARACTERISTICS OF PROCESS COSTING

Process Manufacturing

Units produced in a process firm typically pass through a series of manufacturing steps or processes. Each process is responsible for one or more operations that bring a product one step closer to completion. In each process, materials, labor, and overhead inputs may be needed (typically in equal doses). Upon completion of a particular process, the partially completed goods are transferred to another process. After passing through the final process, the goods are finished and are transferred out to the warehouse.

sequential processing

parallel processing

The processes used by Healthblend Nutritional Supplements are an example of **sequential processing**. In a sequential process, units pass from one process to another in a sequential pattern with each unit processed in the same series of steps. Exhibit 4–1 shows the sequential pattern of the manufacture of Healthblend's minerals, herbs, and vitamins.

Another processing pattern is **parallel processing**, in which two or more sequential processes are required to produce a finished good. Partially completed units (e.g., two subcomponents) can be worked on simultaneously in different processes and then brought together in a final process for completion. Consider, for example, the manufacture of a mass storage (hard disk) system for personal computers. In one series of processes, read-write heads and cartridge disk drives are produced, assembled, and tested. In a second series of processes, printed circuit boards are produced and tested. These two major subcomponents then come together for assembly in the final process. Exhibit 4–2 portrays this type of process pattern. Notice that processes one and two can occur independently of (or parallel to) processes three and four.

Other forms of parallel processes also exist. Exhibit 4–3 (p. 142) shows the production process at Hillendale Dairy. The dairy produces two products, milk and cheese, in a parallel process. Both products share a common original sequential process in which cows are milked and the milk is pasteurized.

EXHIBIT 4–1
Sequential Processing Illustrated

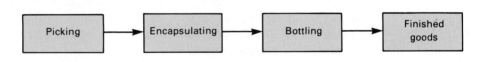

EXHIBIT 4–2
Parallel Processing Illustrated

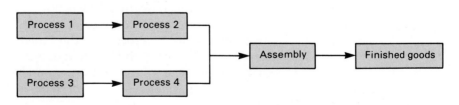

Process 1: Production and assembly of write-head and disk drive
Process 2: Testing of write-head and disk drive
Process 3: Production of circuit board
Process 4: Testing of circuit board

EXHIBIT 4–3
Alternative Form of Parallel Processing

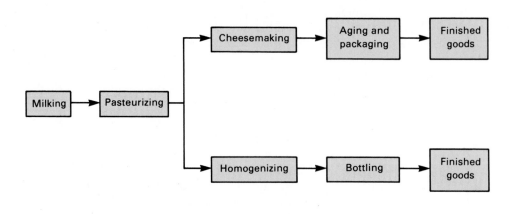

Then some of the pasteurized milk is transferred to the Cheese Department where rennin is added (to coagulate the milk), whey is drained off, and the cheese is aged and packaged. The remaining pasteurized milk is homogenized and bottled as whole milk.

Regardless of which processing pattern exists within a firm, all units produced share a common property. Since units are homogeneous and subjected to the same operations for a given process, each unit produced in a period should receive the same unit cost. Understanding how unit costs are computed requires an understanding of the manufacturing cost flows that take place in a process costing firm.

Process Costing: Cost Flows

The manufacturing cost flows for a process cost system are generally the same as those for a job-order system. As raw materials are purchased, the cost of these materials flows into a Raw Materials inventory account. Similarly, raw materials, direct labor, and applied overhead costs flow into a Work in Process account. When goods are ultimately completed, the cost of the completed goods is transferred from Work in Process to the Finished Goods account. Finally, as goods are sold, the cost of the finished goods is transferred to the Cost of Goods Sold account. The journal entries generally parallel those described in a job-order costing system (for a more detailed description of cost flows, see Chapter 3).

Although job-order and process cost flows are generally similar, some differences exist. In process costing, each processing department has its own Work in Process account. As goods are completed in a process, they are transferred to the next process. For example, if the cost of goods transferred from Encapsulating to Bottling is $10,000, then the following journal entry would occur:

Work in Process—Bottling	10,000	
Work in Process—Encapsulating		10,000

transferred-in costs

The costs transferred from a prior process (here, encapsulating) to a subsequent process (bottling) are referred to as *transferred-in costs*. These transferred-in costs are (from the viewpoint of the subsequent process) a type of raw material cost. This is true because the subsequent process receives a partially completed unit that must be subjected to additional manufacturing activity, which includes more direct labor, more overhead, and, in some cases, additional raw materials. Thus, while Encapsulating sees the capsules as a combination of raw materials, labor and overhead costs, Bottling sees only completed capsules—a raw material costing $10,000.

Cost Accumulation: The Production Report

production report

In process costing, costs are accumulated by department for a period of time. The **production report** is the document that summarizes the manufacturing activity that takes place in a process department for a given period of time. A production report contains all of the information necessary for it to function as a subsidiary Work in Process account. It is analogous to the job-order cost sheet in a job-costing system. The production report also serves as a source document for transferring costs from the Work in Process account of a prior department to the Work in Process account of a subsequent department. In the department that handles the final stage of processing, it serves as a source document for transferring costs from the Work in Process account to the Finished Goods account.

A production report provides information about the physical units processed in a department and also about the manufacturing costs associated with them. Thus, a production report is divided into a unit information section and a cost information section. The unit information section has two major subdivisions: (1) units to account for and (2) units accounted for. Similarly, the cost information section has two major subdivisions: (1) costs to account for and (2) costs accounted for. A production report then traces the flow of units through a department, identifies the costs charged to the department, shows the computation of unit costs, and reveals the disposition of the department's costs for the reporting period.

Computing the unit cost for the work performed during a period is essential to producing a production report. This unit cost is needed both to compute the cost of goods transferred out of a department and to value ending work in process. In computing the unit cost, the output of the period must be defined. A major problem of process costing is making this definition.

Output Measurement:
The Concept of Equivalent Units

To illustrate the output problem of process costing, assume that Department A had the following data for October:

Units, beginning work in process	—
Units completed	1,000
Units, ending work in process (25% complete)	600
Total manufacturing costs	$11,500

What is the output for this department? 1,000? 1,600? If we say 1,000 units, we ignore the effort expended on the units in ending work in process. Furthermore, the manufacturing costs incurred in October belong to both the units completed and to the partially completed units in ending work in process. On the other hand, if we say 1,600 units, we ignore the fact that the 600 units in ending work in process are only partially completed. Somehow output must be measured so that it reflects the effort expended on both completed and partially completed units.

equivalent units of output

The solution is to calculate equivalent units of output. **Equivalent units of output** are the complete units that could have been produced given the total amount of manufacturing effort expended for the period under consideration. Determining equivalent units of output for transferred-out units is easy; a unit would not be transferred out unless it were complete. Thus, every transferred-out unit is an equivalent unit. Units remaining in ending work-in-process inventory, however, are not complete. Thus, someone in production must "eyeball" ending work in process to estimate its degree of completion. In the example, the 600 units in ending work in process are 25 percent complete; this is equivalent to 150 fully completed units (600 × 25%). Therefore, the equivalent units for October would be the 1,000 completed units plus 150 equivalent units in ending work in process, a total of 1,150 units of output. Exhibit 4–4 illustrates the concept of equivalent units of production.

Knowing the output for a period and the manufacturing costs for the department for that period ($11,500 in this example), we can calculate a unit cost, which in this case is $10 ($11,500/1,150). The unit cost is used to assign a cost of $10,000 ($10 × 1,000) to the 1,000 units transferred out and a cost of $1,500 ($10 × 150) to the 600 units in ending work in process. This unit cost is $10 per *equivalent* unit. Thus, when valuing ending work in process, the $10 unit cost is multiplied by the equivalent units, not the actual number of partially completed units.

Exhibit 4–5 summarizes the basic characteristics of process costing. In reality, the details are more complicated than the basics just described. These complications are due to five factors.

1. The presence of beginning inventories

2. Different approaches to equivalent unit calculation

EXHIBIT 4-4
Equivalent Units of Production

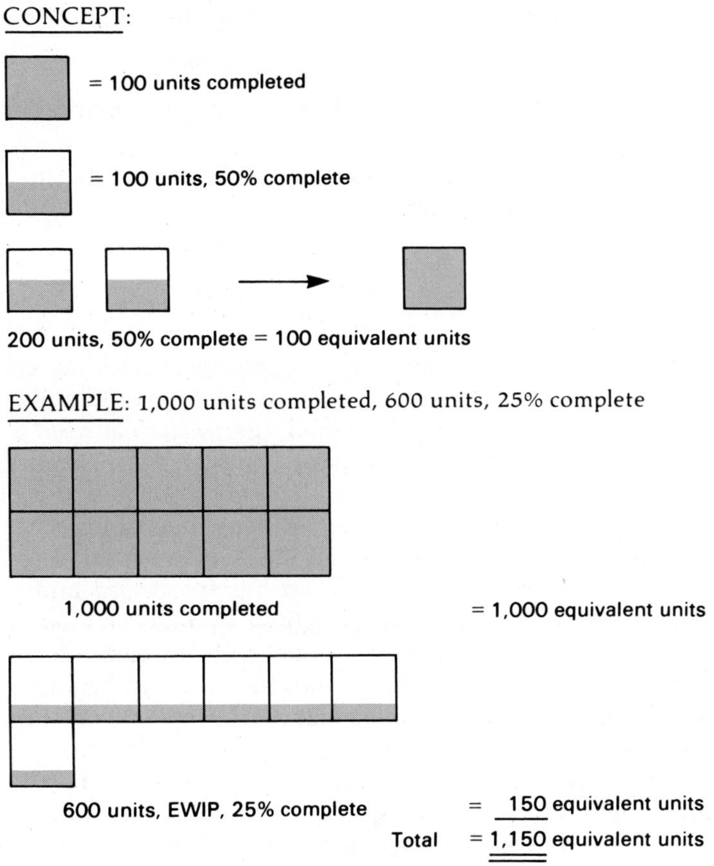

CONCEPT:

= 100 units completed

= 100 units, 50% complete

200 units, 50% complete = 100 equivalent units

EXAMPLE: 1,000 units completed, 600 units, 25% complete

1,000 units completed   = 1,000 equivalent units

600 units, EWIP, 25% complete   = __150__ equivalent units
                              Total   = 1,150 equivalent units

EXHIBIT 4-5
Basic Characteristics of Process Costing

1. Homogeneous units pass through a series of similar processes.
2. Each unit in each process receives a similar dose of manufacturing costs.
3. Manufacturing costs are accumulated by a process for a given period of time.
4. Manufacturing cost flows and the associated journal entries are generally similar to job-order costing.
5. The departmental production report is the key document for tracking manufacturing activity and costs.
6. Unit costs are computed by dividing the departmental costs of the period by the output of the period.
7. Output of a department is measured in equivalent units, not in units produced.

3. Nonuniform application of manufacturing costs (e.g., units half completed may not have half of the total manufacturing inputs needed)

4. Transferred-in goods from other processes

5. The need to gather cost and production information by department

Nonetheless, understanding these basics is essential to understanding the nature of process costing.

▪ ACCOUNTING FOR PROCESS COSTS

FIFO costing method

The presence of beginning work in process inventories complicates the computation of the unit cost. Since many firms have partially completed units in process at the beginning of a period, there is a clear need to address the issue. The work done on these partially completed units represents prior-period work, and the costs assigned to them are prior-period costs. In computing a *current period* unit cost for a department, two approaches have evolved for dealing with the prior-period output and prior-period costs found in beginning work in process: *the weighted average method* and the *first-in, first-out (FIFO) method*. Basically, the weighted average method combines beginning inventory costs with current-period costs to compute unit cost. The **FIFO costing method**, on the other hand, transfers out beginning inventory cost as a dollar amount and computes unit cost based only on current-period cost and output. If product costs do not change from period to period, the FIFO and weighted average methods yield the same results. Further discussion of the FIFO method is found in Appendix A.

Both the weighted average and FIFO approaches follow the same general pattern for costing out production. This general pattern is described by the following five steps:

1. Analysis of the flow of physical units

2. Calculation of equivalent units

3. Computation of unit cost

4. Valuation of inventories (goods transferred out and ending work in process)

5. Cost reconciliation

Knowing the physical units in beginning and ending work in process, their stage of completion, and the units completed and transferred out (Step 1) provides essential information for the computation of equivalent units (Step 2). This computation, in turn, is a prerequisite to computing unit cost (Step 3). Unit cost information and information from the equivalent unit schedule are both needed to value goods transferred out and goods in ending work in process (Step 4). Finally, the costs in beginning work in process and the costs incurred during the current period should equal the total costs assigned to goods transferred out and to goods in ending work in process (Step 5).

In the ensuing discussion, we will follow the five steps listed above. Doing so gives some structure to the method of accounting for process costs and makes it easier to learn and remember.

Weighted Average Costing

weighted average costing method

The **weighted average costing method** picks up beginning inventory costs and the accompanying equivalent output and treats them as if they belong to the current period. Prior-period output and manufacturing costs found in beginning work in process are merged with the current-period output and manufacturing costs.

The merging of beginning inventory output and current period output is accomplished by the way in which equivalent units are calculated. Under the weighted average method, equivalent units of output are computed by adding units completed to units in ending work in process times the fraction complete. Notice that the equivalent units in beginning work in process are not excluded from the computation. Consequently, these units are counted as part of the current period's equivalent units of output.

The weighted average method merges prior-period costs with current-period costs by simply adding the manufacturing costs in beginning work in process to the manufacturing costs incurred during the current period. The total cost is treated as if it were the current period's total manufacturing cost.

To illustrate the weighted average method, consider the manufacturing operation of Healthblend Nutritional Supplements. Cost and production data for the Picking Department are as follows for July (assume that units are measured in gallons):

Production:	
Units in process, July 1, 30% complete	20,000
Units completed and transferred out	50,000
Units in process, July 31, 50% complete	10,000
Costs:	
Work in process, July 1	$1,170
Costs added during July	9,830

Using the data for the Pickling Department, Exhibit 4–6 (p. 148) illustrates the use of the weighted average method to allocate manufacturing costs to units transferred out and to units remaining in ending work in process. Notice that costs from beginning work in process are pooled with costs added to production during July. These total pooled costs ($11,000) are averaged and assigned to units transferred out and to units in ending work in process. On the units side, we concentrate on the degree of completion of all units at the *end* of the period. We do not care about the percentage of completion of

EXHIBIT 4–6
Weighted Average Method

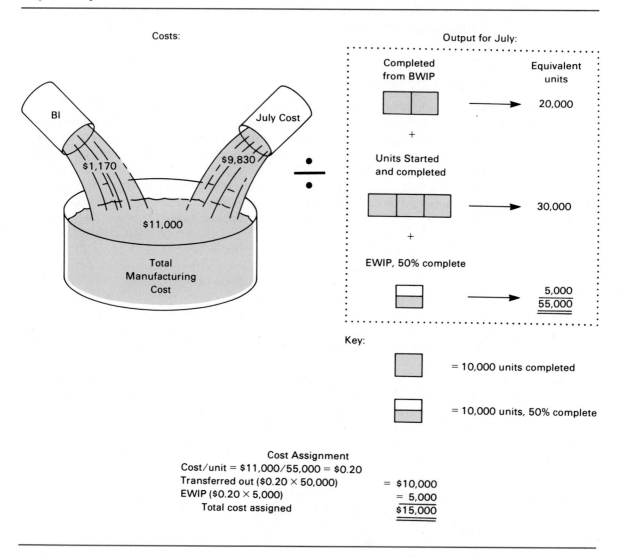

Costs:

Output for July:

Completed from BWIP — Equivalent units — 20,000

+

Units Started and completed — 30,000

+

EWIP, 50% complete — 5,000 / 55,000

BI — $1,170
July Cost — $9,830
$11,000
Total Manufacturing Cost

Key:

= 10,000 units completed

= 10,000 units, 50% complete

Cost Assignment
Cost/unit = $11,000/55,000 = $0.20
Transferred out ($0.20 × 50,000)   = $10,000
EWIP ($0.20 × 5,000)   = 5,000
Total cost assigned $15,000

beginning work in process inventory. We only care about whether these units are complete or not by the end of July. Thus, equivalent units are computed by pooling manufacturing effort from June and July.

Let's take a closer look at the July production in Healthblend's Picking Department by focusing on the five steps of the weighted average method.

physical flow
schedule

Step 1: Physical Flow Analysis The purpose of Step 1 is to trace the physical units of production. Physical units are *not* equivalent units; they are units that may be in any stage of completion. We can see in Exhibit 4–6 that there are 60,000 physical units. In this example, 20,000 are from beginning inventory. Another 40,000 were started in July. Finally, 10,000 remain in ending inventory, 50 percent complete. The analysis of physical flow of units is usually accomplished by preparing a **physical flow schedule** similar to the one shown in Exhibit 4–7.

To construct the schedule from the information given in the example, two calculations are needed. First, units started and completed in this period are obtained by subtracting the units in beginning work in process from the total units completed. Next, the units started are obtained by adding the units started and completed to the units in ending work in process. Notice that the "total units to account for" must equal the "total units accounted for." The physical flow schedule in Exhibit 4–7 is important because it contains the information needed to calculate equivalent units (Step 2).

Step 2: Calculation of Equivalent Units Given the information in the physical flow schedule, the weighted-average equivalent units for July can be calculated. This calculation is shown in Exhibit 4–8 (p. 150).

Notice that July's output is measured as 55,000 units. The 6,000 equivalent units (20,000 × 30%) found in beginning work in process are included in the 50,000 units completed. Thus, beginning inventory units are treated as if they were started and completed during the current period.

Step 3: Computation of Unit Cost In addition to the period's output, the period's manufacturing costs are needed to compute a unit cost. The weighted average method rolls back and includes the manufacturing costs associated with the units in beginning work in process. Thus, the total man-

EXHIBIT 4–7
Physical Flow Schedule

Units to account for:		
Units, beginning work in process (30% complete)		20,000
Units started during the period		40,000
Total units to account for		60,000
Units accounted for:		
Units completed and transferred out:		
Started and completed	30,000	
From beginning work in process	20,000	50,000
Units in ending work in process (50% complete)		10,000
Total units accounted for		60,000

EXHIBIT 4-8
Equivalent Units of Production: Weighted Average Method

Units completed	50,000
Add: Units, ending work in process × fraction complete	
(10,000 units × 50%)	5,000
Equivalent units of output	55,000

ufacturing cost for July is defined as $11,000 ($1,170 + $9,830). The manufacturing costs carried over from the prior period ($1,170) are treated as if they were current-period costs.

Given the manufacturing costs for July and the output for the month, the unit cost can be calculated and used to determine the cost of goods transferred out and the cost of ending work in process. For July, the weighted average method gives the following unit cost:

Unit cost = $11,000/55,000
           = $0.20 per equivalent unit

Step 4: Valuation of Inventories   Using the unit cost of $0.20, the cost of goods transferred to the Encapsulating Department is $10,000 (50,000 units × $0.20 per unit), and the cost of ending work in process is $1,000 (5,000 equivalent units × $0.20 per unit). Notice that units completed (from Step 1), equivalent units in ending work in process (from Step 2), and the unit cost (from Step 3) were all needed to value both goods transferred out and ending work in process.

Step 5: Cost Reconciliation   The total manufacturing costs assigned to inventories are as follows:

Goods transferred out	$10,000
Goods in ending work in process	1,000
Total costs accounted for	$11,000

The manufacturing costs to account for are also $11,000.

Beginning work in process	$ 1,170
Incurred during the period	9,830
Total costs to account for	$11,000

Thus, the costs to account for are exactly assigned to inventories, and we have the necessary **cost reconciliation**. Remember—the total of costs assigned to goods transferred out and to ending work in process *must agree* with the total of costs in beginning work in process and the manufacturing costs incurred during the current period.

Production Report   Steps 1 through 5 provide all of the information needed to prepare a production report for the Picking Department for July. This report is given in Exhibit 4–9.

EXHIBIT 4–9

Cost of Production Report

For July 1992
(Weighted Average Method)

Unit Information

Units to account for:

Units in beginning work in process	20,000
Units started	40,000
Total units to account for	60,000

Units accounted for:

	Physical Flow	Equivalent Units
Units completed	50,000	50,000
Units in ending work in process	10,000	5,000
Total units accounted for	60,000	55,000

Cost Information

Costs to account for:

Beginning work in process	$ 1,170
Incurred during the period	9,830
Total costs to account for	$11,000

Cost per equivalent unit $0.20

Costs accounted for:

	Transferred Out	Ending Work in Process	Total
Goods transferred out ($0.20 × 50,000)	$10,000	—	$10,000
Goods in ending work in process ($0.20 × 5,000)	—	$1,000	1,000
Total costs accounted for	$10,000	$1,000	$11,000

Evaluation of the Weighted Average Method   The weighted average method combines the cost of beginning work in process with the production cost incurred for the current period. Thus, a weighted average unit cost is formed based on the contribution of beginning work in process and current-period production. If the unit cost in a process is relatively stable from one period to the next, then this procedure has little effect on the calculation of a current-period unit cost.

The major benefit of the weighted average method is simplicity. By treating units in beginning work in process as belonging to the current period, all equivalent units belong to the same category when it comes to calculating unit costs. As a consequence, the requirements for computing unit cost are greatly simplified. The main disadvantage of this method is the sacrifice of accuracy in computing unit costs for current-period output and for units in beginning work in process. If the price of manufacturing inputs increases significantly from one period to the next, then the unit cost of current output is understated, and the unit cost of beginning work-in-process units is overstated. If greater accuracy in computing unit costs is desired, then a company should use the FIFO method to determine unit costs.

▪ SOME COMPLICATIONS OF PROCESS COSTING

The accounting for production under process costing is complicated by the presence of multiple processing departments and the nonuniform application of manufacturing costs as production unfolds. How process costing methods address these complications will now be discussed.

Nonuniform Application of Manufacturing Inputs

Up to this point, we have assumed that work in process being 60 percent complete meant that 60 percent of prime costs and overhead needed to complete the process have been used and that another 40 percent are needed to finish the units. In other words, we have assumed that manufacturing inputs are uniformly applied as the manufacturing process unfolds.

Assuming uniform application of conversion costs (direct labor and overhead) is not unreasonable. Direct labor input is usually needed throughout the process, and overhead is normally assigned on the basis of direct labor hours. Direct materials, on the other hand, are not as likely to be applied uniformly. In many instances, materials are added at either the beginning or the end of the process.

For example, look at the differences in Healthblend's three departments. In the Picking and Encapsulating departments, all materials are added at the beginning of the process. However, in the Bottling Department, materials are added both at the beginning (filled capsules and bottles) and at the end (bottle caps and boxes).

Work in process in the Picking Department that is 50 percent complete with respect to conversion inputs would be 100 percent complete with respect to the material inputs. But work in process in Bottling that is 50 percent complete with respect to conversion inputs would differ. It would be 100 percent complete with respect to bottles and transferred-in capsules, but 0 percent complete with respect to bottle caps and boxes.

Different percentage completion figures for manufacturing inputs at the same stage of completion pose a problem for the calculation of equivalent units. Fortunately, the solution is relatively simple. Equivalent unit calculations are done for *each* category of manufacturing input. Thus, there are equivalent units calculated for each category of materials and for conversion cost. The conversion cost category can be broken down into direct labor and overhead if desired. If direct labor and overhead are applied uniformly, however, this serves no useful purpose.

To illustrate, assume the Picking Department of Healthblend has the following data for September:

Production:	
Units in process, September 1, 50% complete[a]	10,000
Units completed and transferred out	60,000
Units in process, September 30, 40% complete[a]	20,000
Costs:	
Work in process, September 1:	
Materials	$ 1,600
Conversion costs	200
Total	$ 1,800
Current costs:	
Materials	$12,000
Conversion costs	3,200
Total	$15,200

[a]With respect to conversion costs

Assuming that Healthblend uses the weighted average method for process costing, the effect of nonuniform application of manufacturing inputs is easily illustrated. Exhibit 4–10 (p. 154) illustrates Step 1, creating the physical flow schedule. As the exhibit reveals, the approach to accounting for the flow of physical units is not affected by the nonuniform application of manufacturing inputs because physical units may be in any stage of completion.

Nonuniform application of inputs, however, affects the computation of equivalent units (Step 2). Exhibit 4–11 illustrates this computation. Notice that two categories of input are used to calculate equivalent units. These categories of input are needed because manufacturing inputs are applied differently. Since all materials are added at the beginning of the pro-

EXHIBIT 4–10
Physical Flow Schedule: Nonuniform Inputs

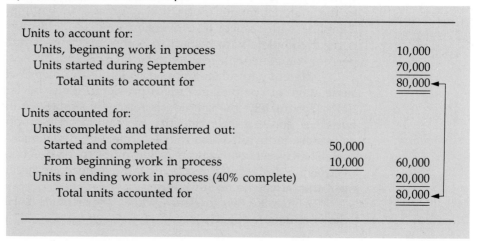

Units to account for:		
Units, beginning work in process		10,000
Units started during September		70,000
Total units to account for		80,000
Units accounted for:		
Units completed and transferred out:		
Started and completed	50,000	
From beginning work in process	10,000	60,000
Units in ending work in process (40% complete)		20,000
Total units accounted for		80,000

EXHIBIT 4–11
Calculation of Equivalent Units: Nonuniform Application

	Materials	*Conversion*
Units completed	60,000	60,000
Add: Units, ending work in process × % complete:		
20,000 × 100%	20,000	—
20,000 × 40%	—	8,000
Equivalent units of output	80,000	68,000

cess, there are 20,000 equivalent units of materials in ending work in process. However, since only 40 percent of the conversion costs have been applied, there are only 8,000 conversion equivalent units in ending work in process.

When different categories of equivalent units exist, a unit cost for each category must be computed. The cost per completed unit (Step 3) is the sum of these individual unit costs. The computations for the example are as follows:

$$\text{Unit materials cost} = (\$1,600 + 12,000)/80,000$$
$$= \$0.17$$
$$\text{Unit conversion cost} = (\$200 + 3,200)/68,000$$
$$= \$0.05$$
$$\text{Total unit cost} = \text{Unit materials cost} + \text{Unit conversion cost}$$
$$= \$0.17 + \$0.05$$
$$= \$0.22 \text{ per completed unit}$$

Valuation of goods transferred out (Step 4) is accomplished by multiplying the unit cost by the goods completed.

$$\text{Cost of goods transferred out} = \$0.22 \times 60,000$$
$$= \$13,200$$

Costing out ending work in process is done by obtaining the cost of each manufacturing input and then adding these individual input costs. For the example, this requires adding the cost of the materials in ending work in process to the conversion costs in ending work in process.

The cost of materials is the unit material cost multiplied by the material equivalent units in ending work in process. Similarly, the conversion cost in ending work in process is the unit conversion cost times the conversion equivalent units. Thus, the cost of ending work in process is as follows:

Materials: $0.17 × 20,000	$3,400
Conversion: $0.05 × 8,000	400
Total cost	$3,800

Step 5, you will recall, reconciles the costs to ensure that the computations are correct.

Costs to account for:	
Beginning work in process	$ 1,800
Incurred during the period	15,200
Total to account for	$17,000
Costs accounted for:	
Goods transferred out	$13,200
Ending work in process	3,800
Total costs accounted for	$17,000

Using the information generated from the five steps, a cost of production report can be prepared (see Exhibit 4–12, p. 156). As the example has shown, applying manufacturing inputs at different stages of a process poses no serious problems. However, the effort required to compute the costs has increased.

Multiple Departments

In process manufacturing, some departments invariably receive partially completed goods from prior departments. These transferred-in goods are a type of raw material for the subsequent process—materials that are added at the beginning of the subsequent process. For example, consider a manufacturer of denim jeans. Department 1 is the Cutting Department where the

EXHIBIT 4–12

Healthblend Company

Picking Department Cost of Production Report
For September 1992 (Weighted Average Method)

Unit Information

Units to account for:

Units, beginning work in process	10,000
Units started	70,000
Total units to account for	80,000

Units accounted for:

		Equivalent Units	
	Physical Flow	Materials	Conversion Cost
Units completed	60,000	60,000	60,000
Units in ending work in process	20,000	20,000	8,000
Total units accounted for	80,000	80,000	68,000

Cost Information

Costs to account for:

	Materials	Conversion Cost	Total
Beginning work in process	$ 1,600	$ 200	$ 1,800
Incurred during the period	12,000	3,200	15,200
Total costs to account for	$13,600	$3,400	$17,000
Cost per equivalent unit	$0.17	$0.05	$0.22

Costs accounted for:

	Transferred out	Ending Work in Process	Total
Goods transferred out (60,000 × $0.22)	$13,200	—	$13,200
Ending work in process:			
Materials (20,000 × $0.17)	—	$3,400	3,400
Conversion (8,000 × $0.05)	—	400	400
Total costs accounted for	$13,200	$3,800	$17,000

denim fabric is cut out according to pattern. Department 2 is the Assembly Department. Here denim pieces are transferred in from Cutting. Direct labor (using sewing machines and other overhead) sews thread, zippers, and rivets into the denim in the process of creating jeans. Thus, the Assembly Department has three categories of production cost: prior department cost (prepared denim pattern pieces transferred in from Cutting), direct materials (thread, zippers, etc., added in Assembly), and conversion cost (direct labor and overhead of the Assembly Department). The usual approach is to treat transferred-in goods as a separate material category when calculating equivalent units. The extension to multiple departments is straightforward and is illustrated in Appendix B.

■ SUMMARY OF LEARNING OBJECTIVES

1. **Identify the settings for which process costing is appropriate.** If a firm produces a homogeneous product that passes through a series of similar processes and receives similar amounts of manufacturing costs in each process, then process costing is probably the appropriate method for assigning costs to production. In process costing, costs are accumulated by department, and a unit cost is calculated for the output of each department.

2. **Describe the cost flows associated with process costing.** Cost flows under process costing are similar to those under job-order costing. Raw materials are purchased and debited to the materials account. Direct materials used in production, direct labor, and overhead applied are charged to the Work in Process account. In a production process with several processes, there is a Work in Process account for each department or process. Goods completed in one department are transferred out to the next department where they are treated as a type of material. When units are complete in the final department or process, their cost is credited to work in process and debited to finished goods.

3. **Define *equivalent units* and explain their role in process costing.** Equivalent units of production are the complete units that could have been produced given the total amount of manufacturing effort expended during the period being considered. That is, the number of physical units is multiplied by the percentage of completion to calculate equivalent units.

4. **Prepare a schedule that tracks the physical flow of units within a production department.** The physical flow of units within a production department consists of units to be accounted for and units accounted for. Units to be accounted for include units from beginning inventory and units started or transferred in during the period. Units accounted for consist of units completed and transferred out during the period and units on hand in ending inventory at the end of the period. Units to be accounted for must equal units accounted for.

5. **Prepare a schedule of equivalent units using the weighted average method.** Equivalent units under the weighted average method count all units as being produced during the current period. Thus, units completed and transferred out are deemed 100 percent complete. Units remaining in ending inventory are multiplied by their percentage of completion. Equivalent units must be computed for every cost category: prior department costs, direct materials, and conversion cost.

6. **Explain the differences between the weighted average method and the FIFO method.** The weighted average method treats beginning work-in-process inventory and costs as belonging to the current period. FIFO excludes prior-period work and costs, counting only current work and costs when computing unit costs. If prices are reasonably stable from one period to the next, the unit costs computed under both methods differ only slightly. In such a case, the weighted average method may be preferable because FIFO makes computations more complex.

7. **Compute the cost per equivalent unit using the weighted average method.** The cost per equivalent unit is computed by dividing the sum of beginning inventory cost and current-period cost by the number of equivalent units. If different cost categories are applied to production at different rates, then unit costs must be calculated for each cost category. The overall unit cost is the sum of the individual unit costs (i.e., unit direct materials, unit prior department, unit conversion).

8. **Compute the cost of goods transferred out and the cost of the ending work in process for each production department under the weighted average method.** The cost of goods transferred out is equal to the number of units transferred out multiplied by the unit cost. The cost of ending work in process is equal to the unit cost multiplied by the number of equivalent units in ending inventory.

9. **Prepare a schedule that identifies the cost each department must account for and that provides an accounting for these costs.** Each department is responsible for costs incurred for goods transferred in, direct materials, direct labor, and overhead. These costs are identified separately in beginning inventory and current-period costs. The sum of these costs must equal the amount of cost transferred out during the period and the cost in ending inventory.

10. **Prepare a departmental cost of production report.** The production report summarizes the manufacturing activity occurring in a department for a given period. It discloses information concerning the physical flow of units, equivalent units, unit costs, and the disposition of the manufacturing costs associated with the period. It is analogous in its role to the job-order cost sheet.

▪ KEY TERMS

Cost reconciliation Determining whether the costs assigned to units transferred out and to units in ending work in process are equal to the costs in beginning work in process plus the manufacturing costs incurred in the current period. (p. 151)

Equivalent units of output The whole units that could have been produced in a period given the amount of manufacturing inputs used. (p. 144)

FIFO costing method A unit-costing method that excludes prior-period work and costs in computing current-period unit work and costs. (p. 146)

Operation costing A costing system that uses job-order costing to assign materials costs and process costing to assign conversion costs. (p. 140)

Parallel processing A method of process manufacturing in which subunits pass through different sequential processes before being brought together in a final process. (p. 141)

Physical flow schedule A schedule that accounts for all units flowing through a department during a period. (p. 149)

Production report A report that summarizes the manufacturing activity for a department during a period and discloses physical flow, equivalent units, total costs to account for, unit cost computation, and costs assigned to goods transferred out and to units in ending work in process. (p. 143)

Sequential processing A method of process manufacturing in which units flow from one process to another in a sequential pattern. (p. 141)

Transferred-in cost The cost of goods transferred in from a prior process. (p. 143)

Weighted average method A unit-costing method that merges prior-period work and costs with current-period work and costs. (p. 147)

■ REVIEW PROBLEM

Payson Company produces a product that passes through two departments: Mixing and Cooking. In the Mixing Department, all materials are added at the beginning of the process. All other manufacturing inputs are added uniformly. The following information pertains to the Mixing Department for February:

a. Beginning work in process (BWIP), February 1: 100,000 pounds, 40 percent complete with respect to conversion costs. The costs assigned to this work are as follows:

Materials	$20,000
Labor	10,000
Overhead	30,000

b. Ending work in process (EWIP), February 28: 50,000 pounds, 60 percent complete with respect to conversion costs.

c. Units completed and transferred out: 370,000 pounds. The following costs were added during the month:

Materials	$211,000
Labor	100,000
Overhead	270,000

Required:

1. Prepare a physical flow schedule.
2. Prepare a schedule of equivalent units.
3. Compute the cost per equivalent unit.
4. Compute the cost of goods transferred out and the cost of ending work in process.
5. Prepare a cost reconciliation.

Solution:

1. Physical flow schedule:

Units to account for:		
Units, BWIP		100,000
Units started		320,000
Total units to account for		420,000
Units accounted for:		
Units completed and transferred out:		
Started and completed	270,000	
From BWIP	100,000	370,000
Units, EWIP		50,000
Total units accounted for		420,000

2. Schedule of equivalent units:

	Materials	*Conversion*
Units completed	370,000	370,000
Units EWIP × Fraction complete:		
Materials (50,000 × 100%)	50,000	—
Conversion (50,000 × 60%)	—	30,000
Equivalent units of output	420,000	400,000

3. Cost per equivalent unit:

$$\text{DM unit cost} = (\$20,000 + \$211,000)/420,000 = \$0.550$$
$$\text{CC unit cost} = (\$40,000 + \$370,000)/400,000 = \$1.025$$
$$\text{Total unit cost} = \$1.575 \text{ per equivalent unit}$$

4. Cost of goods transferred out and cost of ending work in process:

$$\text{Cost of goods transferred out} = \$1.575 \times 370,000$$
$$= \$582,750$$
$$\text{Cost of EWIP} = (\$0.55 \times 50,000) + (\$1.025 \times 30,000)$$
$$= \$58,250$$

5. Cost reconciliation:

Costs to account for:	
BWIP	$ 60,000
Costs added	581,000
Total to account for	$641,000
Costs accounted for:	
Goods transferred out	$582,750
EWIP	58,250
Total costs accounted for	$641,000

■ APPENDIX A: PRODUCTION REPORT: FIFO COSTING

Under the FIFO costing method, the equivalent units and manufacturing costs in beginning work in process are *excluded* from the current-period unit cost calculation. This method recognizes that the work and costs carried over from the prior period legitimately belong to that period.

If changes occur in the prices of the manufacturing inputs from one period to the next, then FIFO produces a more accurate unit cost than does the weighted average method. A more accurate unit cost means better cost control, better pricing decisions, and so on. Keep in mind that if the period is as short as a week or a month, however, the unit costs calculated under the two methods are not likely to differ much. In that case, the FIFO method has little, if anything, to offer over the weighted average method. Perhaps for this reason, many firms use the weighted average method.

Since FIFO excludes prior-period work and costs, we need to create two categories of completed units. FIFO assumes that units in beginning work in process are completed first, before any new units are started. Thus, one category of completed units is that of beginning work-in-process units. The second category is for those units started *and* completed during the current period.

For example, assume that a department had 20,000 units in beginning work in process and completed and transferred out a total of 50,000 units. Of the 50,000 completed units, 20,000 are the units initially found in work in process. The remaining 30,000 were started and completed during the current period.

These two categories of completed units are needed in the FIFO method so that each category can be costed correctly. For the units started and completed, the unit cost is obtained by dividing total current manufacturing costs by the current-period equivalent output. However, for the beginning work-in-process units, the total associated manufacturing costs are the sum of the prior-period costs plus the costs incurred in the current period to finish the units. Thus, the unit cost is this total cost divided by the units in beginning work in process. As can be seen in Exhibit 4–13 (p. 162), costs from the current period and from beginning inventory are not pooled. Instead,

EXHIBIT 4–13
FIFO Method

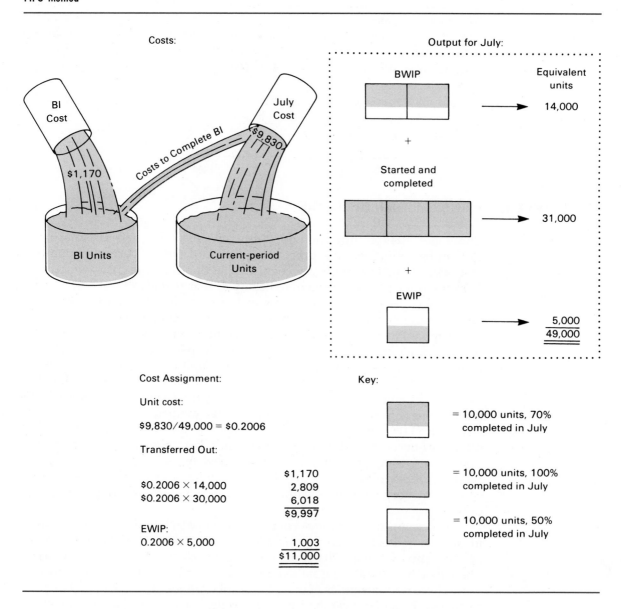

Costs:

Output for July:

BI Cost

July Cost

Costs to Complete BI

$9,830

$1,170

BI Units

Current-period Units

BWIP

Equivalent units

14,000

+

Started and completed

31,000

+

EWIP

5,000
49,000

Cost Assignment:

Unit cost:

$9,830/49,000 = $0.2006

Transferred Out:

	$1,170
$0.2006 × 14,000	2,809
$0.2006 × 30,000	6,018
	$9,997

EWIP:
0.2006 × 5,000   1,003
                      $11,000

Key:

= 10,000 units, 70% completed in July

= 10,000 units, 100% completed in July

= 10,000 units, 50% completed in July

current-period cost is added to beginning inventory cost in order to complete the units on hand at the start of the period.

The computations in Exhibit 4–13 are based on the same Healthblend data used for the weighted average method when we assumed uniform use of manufacturing inputs. Using the same data highlights the differences between the two methods. The five steps to cost out reduction are given below.

Production:	
Units in process, July 1, 30% complete	20,000
Units completed and transferred out	50,000
Units in process, July 31, 50% complete	10,000
Costs:	
Work in process, July 1	$1,170
Costs added during the month	9,830

Step 1: Physical Flow Analysis   The purpose of Step 1 is to trace the physical units of production. As with the weighted average method, in the FIFO method, a physical flow schedule is prepared. This schedule, shown in Exhibit 4–14, is identical for both methods.

Step 2: Calculation of Equivalent Units   Exhibit 4–15 (p. 164) illustrates the calculation of equivalent units under the FIFO method. From the equivalent unit computation in Exhibit 4–15, one difference between weighted average and FIFO becomes immediately apparent. The equivalent units in beginning work in process—work done in the prior period—are not counted as part of the total equivalent work. Only the equivalent work to be completed this period is counted. The equivalent work to be completed for the units from the prior period is computed by multiplying the number of units in beginning

EXHIBIT 4–14
Physical Flow Schedule

Units to account for:		
Units, beginning work in process (30% complete)		20,000
Units started during the period		40,000
Total units to account for		60,000
Units accounted for:		
Units completed:		
Started and completed	30,000	
From beginning work in process	20,000	50,000
Units in ending work in process (50% complete)		10,000
Total units accounted for		60,000

EXHIBIT 4–15
Equivalent Units of Production: FIFO Method

Units started and completed	30,000
Add: Units, beginning work in process × Fraction to complete (20,000 × 70%)	14,000
Add: Units, ending work in process × Fraction completed (10,000 × 50%)	5,000
Equivalent units of output	49,000

work in process by the percentage of work remaining. Since in this example the percentage of work done in the prior period is 30 percent, the percentage left to be completed this period is 70 percent, or an equivalent of 14,000 additional units of work.

The effect of excluding prior-period effort is to produce the current-period equivalent output. Recall that under the weighted average method, 55,000 equivalent units were computed for this month. Under FIFO, only 49,000 units are calculated for the same month. These 49,000 units represent current-period output. The difference, of course, is explained by the fact that the weighted average method rolls back and counts the 6,000 equivalent units of prior-period work (20,000 units BWIP × 30%) as belonging to this period.

Step 3: Computation of Unit Cost   The additional manufacturing costs incurred in the current period are $9,830. Thus, the current-period unit manufacturing cost is $9,830/49,000, or $0.2006. Notice that the costs of beginning inventory are excluded from this calculation. Only current-period manufacturing costs are used.

Step 4: Valuation of Inventories   The $0.2006 unit cost is used to value goods transferred out and ending work in process. Since all equivalent units in ending work in process are current-period units, the cost of ending work in process is simply $0.2006 × 5,000, or $1,003. However, when it comes to valuing goods transferred out, another difference emerges between the weighted average method and FIFO.

Under weighted average, the cost of goods transferred out is simply the unit cost times the units completed. Under FIFO, however, there are two categories of completed units. Of the 50,000 completed units, 20,000 are beginning work-in-process units and 30,000 are units started and completed in the current period. The cost of the 30,000 units that were started and completed in the current period and transferred out is $6,018 ($0.2006 × 30,000). For these units, the use of the current-period unit cost is entirely appropriate.

However, the cost of the beginning work-in-process units that were transferred out is another matter. These units started the period with $1,170 of manufacturing costs already incurred and 6,000 units of equivalent output already completed. To these beginning costs, additional costs were needed to finish the units. As we saw in Step 2, the effort expended to complete these units gives them the value of 14,000 equivalent units. These 14,000 additional units of output are part of the total current output and, therefore, cost $0.2006 per unit to complete. Thus, the total cost of finishing the units in beginning work in process is $2,809 ($0.2006 × 14,000). Adding this $2,809 to the $1,170 in cost carried over from the prior period gives a total manufacturing cost for these units of $3,979. The unit cost of these 20,000 units, then, is $0.199 ($3,979/20,000).

Step 5: Cost Reconciliation With the completion of Step 5, the cost of production report can be prepared. This report is shown in Exhibit 4–16 (p. 166). The total costs assigned to production are as follows:

Goods transferred out:	
Units, beginning work in process	$ 3,979
Units started and completed	6,018
Goods in ending work in process	1,003
Total costs accounted for	$11,000

The total manufacturing costs to account for during the period are

Beginning work in process	$ 1,170
Incurred during the period	9,830
Total costs to account for	$11,000

If the assigned manufacturing costs did not equal the $11,000 to account for, this would indicate the presence of an error; a search to find the error would then be necessary. A frequent cause of such errors is rounding. If unit costs are rounded, then the total costs assigned may not equal the total costs to account for. For example, if $0.2006 had been rounded to $0.201, cost of goods transferred out would have increased by $17 and the cost of ending work in process would have increased by $2. Total overstatement from rounding error would be $19. If you know that the difference is from rounding error, an expedient way to bring the amounts into balance is to adjust the cost of goods transferred out by simply subtracting the $19 overstatement.

■ APPENDIX B: MULTIPLE DEPARTMENT ANALYSIS

In a multiple-department setting, some departments receive partially completed goods from other departments. These partially completed goods represent a material input. In dealing with transferred-in goods, two important points should be remembered. First, the cost of this material is the cost of the

EXHIBIT 4–16

Healthblend Company

Picking Department Cost of Production Report
(FIFO method)

Unit Information

Units to account for:

Units, beginning work in process	20,000
Units started during the period	40,000
Total units to account for	60,000

Units accounted for:

	Physical Flow	Equivalent Units
Units started and completed	30,000	30,000
Units completed from beginning work in process	20,000	14,000
Units in ending work in process	10,000	5,000
Total units accounted for	60,000	49,000

Cost Information

Costs to account for:

Beginning work in process	$ 1,170
Incurred during the period	9,830
Total costs to account for	$11,000
Cost per equivalent unit	$0.2006

Costs accounted for:

	Transferred Out	Ending Work in Process	Total
Units, beginning work in process:			
From prior period	$ 1,170	—	$ 1,170
From current period (14,000 × $0.2006)	2,809	—	2,809
Units started and completed (30,000 × $0.2006)	6,018	—	6,018
Goods in ending work in process (5,000 × $0.2006)	—	$ 1,003	1,003
Total costs accounted for	$ 9,997	$ 1,003	$11,000

---

goods transferred out computed in the prior department. Second, the units started in the subsequent department correspond to the units transferred out from the prior department (assuming that there is a one-to-one relationship between the output measures of both departments).

For example, let's consider the month of September for Healthblend company and restrict our attention to the transferred-in category. Assume that the Encapsulating Department had 15,000 units in beginning inventory (with transferred-in costs of $3,000) and completed 70,000 units during the month. Further, the Picking Department completed and transferred out 60,000 units at a cost of $13,200 in September. In constructing a physical flow schedule for the Encapsulating Department, its dependence on the Picking Department must be considered:

Units to account for:	
Units, beginning work in process	15,000
Units transferred in during September	60,000
Total units to account for	75,000
Units accounted for:	
Units completed and transferred out:	
Started and completed	55,000
From beginning and work in process	15,000
Units in ending work in process	5,000
Total units accounted for	75,000

Equivalent units for the transferred-in category are calculated as follows (ignoring other input categories):

	Transferred in
Units completed	70,000
Add: Units, ending work in process × Fraction complete (5,000 × 100%)	5,000
Equivalent units of output	75,000

To compute the unit cost, we add the cost of the units transferred in from Picking in September to the transferred-in costs in beginning work in process and divide by transferred-in equivalent units:

$$\text{Unit cost (transferred-in category)} = (\$13,200 + \$3,000)/75,000$$
$$= \$16,200/75,000$$
$$= \$0.216$$

The only additional complication introduced in the analysis for a subsequent department is the presence of the transferred-in category. As has just been shown, dealing with this category is similar to handling any other category. However, it must be remembered that the current cost of this special type of raw material is the cost of the units transferred in from the prior process and that the units transferred in are the units started.

■ QUESTIONS

1   Distinguish between sequential processing and parallel processing.

2   Describe the differences between process costing and job-order costing.

3   What are equivalent units? Why are they needed in a process cost system?

4   Under the weighted average method, how are prior-period costs and output treated? How are they treated under the FIFO method?

5   Under what conditions will the weighted average and FIFO methods give essentially the same results?

6   How is the equivalent unit calculation affected when materials are added at the beginning or end of the process rather than uniformly throughout the process?

7   Explain why transferred-in costs are a special type of raw material for the receiving department.

8   What are the similarities and differences in the manufacturing cost flows for job-order firms and process firms?

9   What journal entry would be made as goods are transferred out from one department to another department? From the final department to the warehouse?

10   Describe the five steps in accounting for the manufacturing activity of a processing department and indicate how they interrelate.

11   What is a production report? What purpose does this report serve?

12   In assigning costs to goods transferred out, how do the weighted average and FIFO methods differ?

13   Describe the effect of automation on the process accounting system.

■ EXERCISES

E4–1   **Weighted Average Method; Physical Flow; Equivalent Units**   Silverado Company manufacturers a product that passes through two processes. The following information was obtained for the first department for May:

1. All materials are added at the beginning of the process.

2. Beginning work in process had 6,000 units, 33 percent complete with respect to conversion costs.

3. Ending work in process had 4,400 units, 25 percent complete with respect to conversion costs.

4. Started in process, 10,000 units.

Required:

1. Prepare a physical flow schedule.

2. Compute equivalent units.

E4–2   **Weighted Average Method; Valuation of Goods Out and Ending Work in Process**   Wise Paper Products, Inc., manufactures products that pass through two or more processes. Wise uses the weighted average method to compute unit costs. During August, equivalent units were computed as follows:

	Materials	Conversion Cost
Units completed	4,000	4,000
Units, ending work in process ×		
Fraction complete:		
2,000 × 0%	—	—
2,000 × 70%	—	1,400
Equivalent units of output	4,000	5,400

The unit cost was computed as follows:

Materials	$0.50
Conversion cost	0.25
Total	$0.75

Required:

1. Determine the cost of ending work in process and the cost of the goods transferred out.

2. If possible, prepare a physical flow schedule.

E4–3 **FIFO Method; Valuation of Goods Out and Ending Work in Process** Myerson Company uses FIFO to account for the costs of production. For the first processing department, the following equivalent unit schedule has been prepared:

	Materials	Conversion Cost
Units started and completed	22,000	22,000
Units, beginning work in process ×		
Fraction to complete:		
10,000 × 0%	—	—
10,000 × 40%	—	4,000
Units, ending work in process ×		
Fraction complete:		
8,000 × 100%	8,000	—
8,000 × 75%	—	6,000
Equivalent units of output	30,000	32,000

The cost per equivalent unit for the period was as follows:

Materials	$1.50
Conversion cost	2.50
Total	$4.00

The cost of beginning work in process was materials, $10,000; conversion costs, $20,000.

Required:

1. Determine the cost of ending work in process and the cost of goods transferred out.

2. If possible, prepare a physical flow schedule.

E4–4   **Weighted Average Method; Valuation of Goods Out and Ending Work in Process**
Refer to the data in Exercise 4–3.

Required:

Compute the cost of ending work in process and the cost of goods transferred out using the weighted average method.

E4–5   **Production Report; No Beginning Inventory**   Bander Company manufactures an industrial solvent. Department 1 mixes the chemicals required for the solvent. The following data are for 1992:

Work in process, 1/1/92	—
Gallons started	75,000
Gallons transferred out	63,000
Raw materials cost	$ 75,000
Direct labor cost	$148,800
Overhead applied	$223,200

Materials are added at the beginning of the process. Ending inventory is 95 percent complete with respect to labor and overhead.

Required:

Prepare a production report for Department 1 for 1992.

E4–6   **Physical Flow; Equivalent Units; Unit Costs, Cost Assignment**   Banray, Inc., produces nonprescription sunglasses. The sunglasses are produced in two departments. The data for Department 1 are as follows:

Beginning work in process	—
Units started	92,500
Raw materials cost	$92,500
Direct labor cost	$ 9,150
Overhead applied	$13,725
Units, ending work in process (100% materials; 80% conversion)	5,000

Required:

1. Prepare a physical flow schedule.

2. Calculate equivalent units of production for
   a. Raw materials
   b. Conversion

3. Calculate unit costs for
   a. Raw materials
   b. Conversion
   c. Total manufacturing

4. What is the total cost of units transferred out? What is the cost assigned to units in ending inventory?

E4–7 **Equivalent Units—Weighted Average Method** The following are data for four independent process-costing departments.

	A	B	C	D
Beginning inventory	3,200	1,500	—	27,000
Percent completion	33	40	—	75
Units started	19,200	20,000	48,000	33,000
Ending inventory	4,000	—	9,000	8,000
Percent completion	25	—	30	20

Required:

Compute the equivalent units of production for each of the above departments using the weighted average method.

E4–8 **Equivalent Units—FIFO Method** Using the data from Exercise 4–7, compute the equivalent units of production for each of the four departments using the FIFO method.

E4–9 **Weighted Average Method; Unit Cost; Valuation of Goods Out and Ending Work in Process** Mason Products, Inc., produces a chemical product that passes through three departments. For April, the following equivalent unit schedule was prepared for the first department:

	Materials	Conversion Cost
Units completed	5,000	5,000
Units, ending work in process × Fraction complete:		
6,000 × 100%	6,000	—
6,000 × 50%	—	3,000
Equivalent units of output	11,000	8,000

Costs assigned to beginning work in process: materials, $30,000; conversion, $5,000. Manufacturing costs incurred during April: materials, $25,000; conversion, $65,000. Mason uses the weighted average method.

Required:

1. Compute the unit cost for April.

2. Determine the cost of ending work in process and the cost of goods transferred out.

E4–10   **FIFO Method; Unit Cost; Valuation of Goods Out and Ending Work in Process**
Brown Company is a manufacturer that uses FIFO to account for its production costs.
The product Brown makes passes through two processes. During November, Brown's
controller prepared the following equivalent unit schedule:

	Materials	Conversion Cost
Units started and completed	8,000	8,000
Units, beginning work in process × Fraction to complete:		
2,000 × 0%	—	—
2,000 × 50%	—	1,000
Units, ending work in process × Fraction complete:		
4,000 × 100%	4,000	—
4,000 × 25%	—	1,000
Equivalent units of output	12,000	10,000

Costs in beginning work in process were materials, $2,000; conversion costs,
$8,000. Manufacturing costs incurred during October were materials, $24,000; conversion costs, $32,000.

Required:

1. Prepare a physical flow schedule for October.

2. Compute the cost per equivalent unit for October.

3. Determine the cost of ending work in process and the cost of goods transferred out.

E4–11   **Weighted Average Method; Equivalent Units, Unit Cost; Multiple Departments**   Kil-
ian Company has a product that passes through two processes. During December, the
first department transferred 10,000 units to the second department. The cost of the
units transferred into the second department was $20,000. Materials are added uni-
formly in the second process.

The second department had the following physical flow schedule for December:

Units to account for:	
Units, beginning work in process	2,000 (40% complete)
Units started	?
Total units to account for	?
Units accounted for:	
Units, ending work in process	4,000 (50% complete)
Units completed	?
Units accounted for	?

Costs in beginning work in process for the second department were materials,
$2,500; conversion costs, $3,000; transferred in, $4,000. Costs added during the month:
materials, $16,000; conversion costs, $25,000; transferred in, $20,000.

Required:

1. Assuming the use of the weighted average method, prepare a schedule of equivalent units.

2. Compute the unit cost for the month.

E4–12 **FIFO Method; Equivalent Units; Unit Cost; Multiple Departments** Using the same data found in Exercise 4–11, assume the company uses the FIFO method.

Required:

Prepare a schedule of equivalent units and compute the unit cost for the month of December.

E4–13 **Weighted Average Method; Unit Costs; Inventory Valuation; Cost Reconciliation** Brandy Company prepared the following schedule for the most recent month of operation:

	Beginning Work in Process	Costs Added	Total
Materials	$ 5,000	$15,000	$20,000
Conversion costs	10,000	30,000	40,000
Total	$15,000	$45,000	$60,000

The equivalent units produced are summarized in the following schedule:

	Materials	Conversion Costs
Units completed	3,000	3,000
Units, ending work in process × Fraction complete:		
2,000 × 100%	2,000	—
2,000 × 50%	—	1,000
Equivalent units of output	5,000	4,000

Required:

1. Calculate the unit costs for materials, conversion costs, and the total unit costs.

2. Compute the cost of ending work in process and the cost of goods transferred out.

3. Prepare a cost reconciliation.

E4–14 **Journal Entries; Cost of Ending Inventories** Eyrin Company has two processing departments: Assembly and Finishing. A predetermined overhead rate of $5 per *DLH* is used to assign overhead to production. The company experienced the following operating activity for September:

a. Raw materials issued to Assembly, $12,000

b. Direct labor cost: Assembly, 500 hours at $9.20 per hour; Finishing, 400 hours at $8 per hour

c. Overhead applied to production

d. Goods transferred to Finishing, $18,000

e. Goods transferred to finished goods warehouse, $20,500

f. Actual overhead incurred, $5,000

Required:

1. Prepare the required journal entries for the above transactions.

2. Assuming Assembly and Finishing have no beginning work-in-process inventories, determine the cost of each department's ending work-in-process inventories.

E4–15   **Process Costing: Food Manufacturing**   Wholesome Bread makes and supplies bread throughout the western United States. Six operations describe the production process.

a. Flour, milk, yeast, salt, butter, and so on are mixed in a large vat.

b. A conveyor belt transfers the dough to a machine that weighs it and shapes it into loaves.

c. The individual loaves are allowed to sit and rise.

d. The dough is moved to a 100-foot-long funnel oven (the dough enters the oven on racks and spends twenty minutes moving slowly through the oven).

e. The bread is removed from the oven, sucked from the pan by a vacuum, and allowed to cool.

f. The bread is sliced and wrapped.

During the week, 4,500 loaves of bread were produced. The total cost of materials (ingredients and wrapping material) was $675. The cost of direct labor and overhead totaled $1,575. There were no beginning or ending work-in-process inventories.

Required:

1. Compute the unit cost for the 4,500 loaves of bread produced during the week.

2. Would Wholesome Bread ever need to worry about using FIFO or weighted average? Why or why not? What implication does this have for the food industry in general?

3. Assume that Wholesome Bread also produces rolls and buns. Also assume that the only difference is that the machine is set to shape the dough differently. What adjustments would need to be made to cost out the three different bread products?

E4–16   **Process Costing: Automated Operations**   Sahara Soft Diapers has just opened a new plant for making its popular line of diapers. This plant is experimental in the sense that it has implemented a fully automated production process. Human hands never touch the diaper while it is in production. The production line operates as follows.

First, fluff pulp is shredded from large rolls (mechanically fed into a shredder). Next, diaper wrap is mechanically placed on a conveyor belt. The shredded pulp is sprayed onto the diaper wrap sheet as it passes underneath. As the wrap and pulp move along, another machine covers the pulp with a liner sheet. The three materials are held together by a construction adhesive. The next machine attaches a leg elastic along the sides (the product now has the appearance of a long sausage). A cutting machine then cuts the diapers into the proper length. The final machines attach the waist elastic, outer poly cover, and the release tapes. The diapers are placed in bags and then in boxes (four per box). The boxes move down the conveyor belt to a point where they are picked up by robots and cranes and carried to the finished goods storage area.

Required:

1. Describe how you would compute the unit cost of a box of diapers. Do you think that the computation of equivalent units will be needed? Explain. Also discuss the need for predetermined overhead rates.

2. Now assume that there are small, medium, and large diapers produced. Describe how you would compute unit costs for these three products.

E4–17 **FIFO Method; Physical Flow; Equivalent Units**   Johnson, Inc., manufactures a product that is processed through two departments. The following information was obtained from the first department in June:

a. All materials are added at the beginning of the process.

b. Beginning work in process had 6,000 units, which were 40 percent complete with respect to conversion costs.

c. Ending work in process consisted of 1,760 units, 25 percent complete with respect to conversion costs.

d. During the month, 13,000 units were started in process.

Required:

1. Prepare a physical flow schedule.

2. Compute equivalent units using the FIFO method.

E4–18 **Weighted Average Method; Physical Flow; Equivalent Units; Unit Costs; Cost Assignment**   Send In the Clowns, Inc., manufactures various novelty noses. Each nose is shaped from a piece of rubber in the Molding Department. The noses are then transferred to the Finishing Department where they are painted and have elastic bands attached. In April, the Molding Department reported the following data:

a. In Molding, all materials are added at the beginning of the process.

b. Beginning work in process consisted of 3,000 units, 20 percent complete with respect to direct labor and overhead. Cost in beginning inventory included direct materials, $450; and conversion costs, $138.

c. Costs added to production during the month were direct materials, $950; and conversion costs, $2,174.50.

d. At the end of the month, 9,000 units were transferred out to Finishing. Then 1,000 units remained in ending work in process, 25 percent complete.

Required:

1. Prepare a physical flow schedule.

2. Calculate equivalent units of production for direct materials and conversion cost.

3. Compute unit cost.

4. Calculate the cost of goods transferred to finishing at the end of the month. Calculate the cost of ending inventory.

E4–19 **FIFO Method; Physical Flow; Equivalent Units; Unit Costs; Cost Assignment**   Refer to the data in Exercise 4–18. Calculate the following using the FIFO method:

Required:

1. Prepare a physical flow schedule.

2. Calculate equivalent units of production for direct materials and conversion cost.

3. Compute unit cost.

4. Calculate the cost of goods transferred to Finishing at the end of the month. Calculate the cost of ending inventory.

E4–20   **Weighted Average Method; Equivalent Units; Cost per Unit; Cost of Ending Inventory; Cost of Completed Units**   Canyon Walking Tours produces maps of the Grand Canyon that outline a variety of walking tours of the north and south rim areas. In June, Canyon Walking Tours incurred costs of $66 for materials (paper, ink, etc.) and $213 for direct labor and overhead. June production consisted of 200 completed maps and 130 maps that were 100 percent complete with respect to materials but only 10 percent complete with respect to conversion cost. There was no work-in-process inventory on June 1.

Required:

1. How many units were started and completed in June?

2. Compute the cost per equivalent unit for June.

3. Determine the cost of ending work-in-process inventory and the cost of the completed maps.

▪ PROBLEMS

P4–1   **Weighted Average Method; Single Department Analysis; One Cost Category**   Littleton Company produces a product that passes through two processes: assembly and finishing. All manufacturing costs are added uniformly for both processes. The following information was obtained for the Assembly Department for December 1993:

a. Work in process, December 1, had 5,000 units (40 percent completed) and the following costs:

Direct materials	$4,000
Direct labor	6,000
Overhead	2,000

b. During the month of December, 10,000 units were completed and transferred to the Finishing Department, and the following costs were added to production:

Direct materials	$12,000
Direct labor	18,000
Overhead	6,000

c. On December 31, there were 2,500 partially completed units in process. These units were 80 percent complete.

Required:

Prepare a cost of production report for the Assembly Department for December using the weighted average method of costing. The report should disclose the physical flow of units, equivalent units, and unit costs and should track the disposition of manufacturing costs.

P4–2 **FIFO Method; Single Department Analysis; One Cost Category** Refer to the data in Problem 4–1.

Required:

Prepare a cost of production report for the Assembly Department for December using the FIFO method of costing. The report should contain the same schedules described in Problem 4–1.

P4–3 **Weighted Average Method; Single Department Analysis; Three Cost Categories** Tristar Chemicals produces an industrial chemical that passes through two processes: blending and drying. The weighted average method is used to account for the costs of production. Two chemicals, A and B, are added at the beginning of the blending process and allowed to cook for six to seven hours. After blending, the resulting product is sent to the Drying Department, where it is dried under heat lamps for twenty-four hours. The following information relates to the blending process for the month of August.

a. Work in process, August 1, 20,000 pounds, 60 percent complete with respect to conversion costs. Costs associated with partially completed units

Material A	$1,000
Material B	5,000
Direct labor	500
Overhead	1,500

b. Work in process, August 31, 30,000 pounds, 70 percent complete with respect to conversion costs.

c. Units completed and transferred out: 500,000 pounds. Costs added during the month

Material A	$ 25,500
Material B	127,500
Direct labor	12,750
Overhead	38,250

Required:

1. Prepare the following: (a) a physical flow schedule and (b) an equivalent unit schedule with cost categories for Material A, Material B, and conversion cost.

2. Calculate the unit cost for each cost category.

3. Compute the cost of ending work in process and the cost of goods transferred out.

4. Prepare a cost reconciliation.

P4–4 **Weighted Average/FIFO Method; Single Department Analysis; Two Cost Categories** Lamdin, Inc., produces a product that goes through two departments, Grinding and Polishing. Materials are added at the beginning of the grinding operation; labor and overhead are added uniformly throughout the process. The Grinding Department had work in process at the beginning and end of 1993 as follows:

	Percentage of Completion	
	Materials	*Conversion Costs*
January 1, 1993, 2,500 units	100	60
December 31, 1993, 4,000 units	100	50

The company completed 42,500 units during the year and incurred the following manufacturing costs:

Direct materials	$158,000
Direct labor	98,750
Overhead	79,000

The inventory at the beginning of the year was carried at the following costs:

Direct materials	$9,750
Direct labor	6,125
Overhead	4,950

Required:

1. Prepare a cost of production report using the weighted average method.

2. Prepare a cost of production report using the FIFO method.

P4–5   Weighted Average Method; Single Department Analysis; Transferred-in Goods   Blalack Company manufactures a product that passes through three departments. In Department B, materials are added at the end of the process. Conversion costs are incurred uniformly throughout the process. During the month of October, Department B received 30,000 units from Department A. The transferred-in cost of the 30,000 units was $69,900.

Costs added by Department B during October included the following:

Direct materials	$35,200
Direct labor	56,000
Overhead	25,600

On October 1, Department B had 5,000 units in inventory that were 30 percent complete with respect to conversion costs. On October 31, 6,000 units were in inventory, one-third complete with respect to conversion costs. The costs associated with the 5,000 units in beginning inventory were as follows:

Transferred in	$11,650
Direct labor	8,750
Overhead	4,000

Required:

Prepare a cost of production report using the weighted average method. Use the five steps outlined in the chapter to produce the information required by the report.

P4–6 **FIFO Method; Single Department Analysis with Transferred-in Goods** Hoth, Inc., manufactures a single product that passes through several processes. During the first quarter of 1993, the Mixing Department received 20,000 gallons of liquid from the Cooking Department (transferred in at $9,600). Upon receiving the liquid, the Mixing Department adds a powder and allows blending to take place for thirty minutes. The product is then passed on to the Bottling Department.

There were 4,000 gallons in process at the beginning of the quarter, 75 percent complete with respect to conversion costs. The costs attached to the beginning inventory were as follows:

Transferred in	$1,900
Powder	268
Conversion costs	600

Costs added by the Mixing Department during the first quarter were

| Powder | $1,400 |
| Conversion costs | 3,040 |

There were 3,500 gallons in ending inventory, 20 percent complete with respect to conversion costs.

Required:

Prepare a cost of production report using the FIFO method. Follow the five steps outlined in the chapter in preparing the report.

P4–7 **Weighted Average Method; Transferred-in Goods** Refer to Problem 4–6.

Required:

Prepare a cost of production report for the Mixing Department using the weighted average method.

P4–8 **Weighted Average Method; Journal Entries** Kilgorn Company uses a process costing system. The company manufactures a product that is processed in two departments, A and B. In Department A, materials are added at the beginning of the process; in

Department B, additional materials are added at the end of the process. In both departments, conversion costs are incurred uniformly throughout the process. As work is completed, it is transferred out. The following summarizes the production activity and costs for March:

	Department A	Department B
Beginning inventories:		
Physical units	10,000	8,000
Costs:		
Transferred in	—	$ 45,200
Direct materials	$ 22,000	—
Conversion costs	$ 13,800	$ 16,800
Current production:		
Units started	25,000	?
Units transferred out	30,000	35,000
Costs:		
Transferred in	—	?
Direct materials	$ 56,250	$ 39,550
Conversion costs	$103,500	$136,500
Percentage completion:		
Beginning inventory	40	50
Ending inventory	80	50

Required:

1. Using the weighted average method, prepare the following for Department A:
   a. A physical flow schedule
   b. An equivalent units calculation
   c. Calculation of unit costs
   d. Cost of ending work in process and cost of goods transferred out
   e. A cost reconciliation

2. Prepare journal entries that show the flow of manufacturing costs for Department A.

3. Repeat requirements 1 and 2 for Department B.

P4–9   **FIFO Method; Two-department Analysis**   Refer to the data in Problem 4–8.

Required:

Repeat the requirement in Problem 4–8 using the FIFO method. Note that requirement 3 requires Appendix B.

P4–10   **Weighted Average Method; Two-department Analysis**   Healthway uses a process costing system to compute the unit costs of the minerals that it produces. It has three departments: Picking, Encapsulating, and Bottling. In Picking, the ingredients for the minerals are measured, sifted, and blended together. The mix is transferred out in gallon containers. The Encapsulating Department takes the powdered mix and places it in capsules. One gallon of powdered mix converts into 1,600 capsules. After the capsules are filled and polished, they are transferred to bottling where they are placed in bottles, which are then affixed with a safety seal and a lid and labeled. Each bottle receives fifty capsules.

During July, the following results are available for the first two departments:

	Picking	*Encapsulating*
Beginning inventories:		
Physical units	5 gallons	4,000
Costs:		
Materials	$120	$ 32
Labor	$128	$ 20
Overhead	$?	$?
Transferred in	$ —	$140
Current production:		
Transferred out	125 gallons	198,000
Ending inventory	6 gallons	6,000
Costs:		
Materials	$3,144	$1,584
Transferred in	$ —	$?
Labor	$4,096	$1,944
Overhead	$?	$?
Percentage of completion:		
Beginning inventory	40	50
Ending inventory	50	40

Overhead in both departments is applied as a percentage of direct labor costs. In the Picking Department, overhead is 200 percent of direct labor. In the Encapsulating Department, the overhead rate is 150 percent of direct labor.

Required:

1. Prepare a cost of production report for the Picking Department using the weighted average method. Follow the five steps outlined in the chapter.

2. Prepare a cost of production report for the Encapsulating Department. Follow the five steps outlined in the chapter.

P4–11   **FIFO Method; Two-department Analysis**   Refer to the data in Problem 4–10.

Required:

Prepare a cost of production report for each department using the FIFO method.

P4–12   **Cost of Production Report; Ethical Behavior**   Consider the following conversation between Gary Means, manager of a division that produces industrial machinery, and his controller, Donna Simpson, a CMA and CPA:

Gary: Donna, we have a real problem. Our operating cash is too low, and we are in desperate need of a loan. As you know, our financial position is marginal, and we need to show as much income as possible—and our assets need bolstering as well.

Donna: I understand the problem, but I don't see what can be done at this point. This is the last week of the fiscal year, and it looks like we'll report income just slightly above break even.

Gary: I know all this. What we need is some creative accounting. I have an idea that might help us, and I wanted to see if you would go along with it. We have 200 partially finished machines in process, about 20 percent complete. That compares with the 1,000 units that we completed and sold during the year. When you computed the per-unit cost, you used 1,040 equivalent units, giving us a manufacturing cost of $1,500 per unit. That per-unit cost gives us cost of goods sold equal to $1.5 million and ending work in process worth $60,000. The presence of the work in process gives us a chance to improve our financial position. If we report the units in work in process as 80 percent complete, this will increase our equivalent units to 1,160. This, in turn, will decrease our unit cost to about $1,345 and cost of goods sold to $1.345 million. The value of our work in process will increase to $215,200. With those financial stats, the loan would be a cinch.

Donna: Gary, I don't know. What you're suggesting is risky. It wouldn't take much auditing skill to catch this one.

Gary: You don't have to worry about that. The auditors won't be here for at least six to eight more weeks. By that time, we can have those partially completed units completed and sold. I can bury the labor cost by having some of our more loyal workers work overtime for some bonuses. The overtime will never be reported. And, as you know, bonuses come out of the corporate budget and are assigned to overhead—next year's overhead. Donna, this will work. If we look good and get the loan to boot, corporate headquarters will treat us well. If we don't do this, we could lose our jobs.

Required:

1. Should Donna agree to Gary's proposal? Why or why not? To assist in deciding, review the standards of ethical conduct for management accountants described in the Appendix to Chapter 1. Do any apply?

2. Assume that Donna refuses to cooperate and that Gary accepts this decision and drops the matter. Does Donna have any obligation to report the divisional manager's behavior to a superior? Explain.

3. Assume that Donna refuses to cooperate; however, Gary insists that the changes be made. Now what should Donna do? What would *you* do?

4. Suppose that Donna is sixty-three and that the prospects for employment elsewhere are bleak. Assume again that Gary insists that the changes should be made. Donna also knows that Gary's superior, the owner of the company, is his father-in-law. Under these circumstances, would your recommendations for Donna differ? If you were Donna, what would you do?

P4–13 **Weighted Average Method; Multiple Department Analysis**   Strathmore, Inc., manufactures educational toys using a weighted average process costing system. Plastic is molded into the appropriate shapes in the Molding Department. Molded components are transferred to the Assembly Department where the toys are assembled and additional materials (e.g., fasteners, decals) are applied. Completed toys are then transferred to the Packaging Department where each toy is boxed.

Strathmore showed the following data on toy production for February:

	Molding	*Assembly*	*Packaging*
Beginning inventory:			
Units	500	—	150
Prior department	—	—	$ 1,959
Direct materials	$2,500	—	$ 375
Conversion cost	$1,050	—	$ 225
Started or transferred in:			
Units	1,000	?	?
February costs:			
Prior department		$14,950.00	$11,754.00

	Molding	*Assembly*	*Packaging*
Direct materials	$5,000	$ 487.60	$2,407.50
Conversion cost	$7,660	$1,166.00	$2,977.50
Ending inventory, units	200	400	—

Beginning and ending work in process for the three departments showed the following degree of completion:

	Molding	*Assembly*	*Packaging*
Degree of completion:			
BWIP, direct materials	100%	—	100%
BWIP, conversion costs	30	—	50
EWIP, direct materials	100	40%	—
EWIP, conversion costs	20	40	—

Required:

1. Prepare a physical flow schedule for February for the
   a. Molding Department
   b. Assembly Department
   c. Packaging Department

2. Compute equivalent units of production for direct materials and for conversion costs for the
   a. Molding Department
   b. Assembly Department
   c. Packaging Department

3. Complete the following unit cost chart:

	Molding	*Assembly*	*Packaging*
Unit prior department cost*			
Unit direct material cost			
Unit conversion cost	_____	_____	_____
Total Unit cost			

*Cost transferred in from prior department

4. Determine the cost of ending work in process and the cost of goods transferred out for each of the three departments.

5. Reconcile the costs for each department:

P4–14 **FIFO Method; Multiple Department Analysis** Refer to the data in Problem 4–13.

Required:

Repeat requirements 2–5 using the FIFO method.

P4–15 **Production Report** Susan Manners, cost accountant for Lean Jeans, Inc., spent the weekend completing a cost of production report for the Inspection Department for the month of December. Inspection is the final department in the production of fashion jeans. In that department, each pair of jeans is carefully inspected for quality workmanship. At the end of the inspection process, a slip of paper with "Inspected by # _____ " is slipped into a back pocket and the jeans are placed in a bin to be transferred to finished goods.

First thing Monday morning, Susan returned to work and found that someone had accidently spilled coffee on her report, partially obliterating some of the figures. Susan has only one hour to reconstruct her report—help her meet the deadline by filling in the appropriate number for each question mark.

Production Report for the Inspection Department

For the Month of December
(Weighted Average Method)

Unit Information

Units to account for:

Beginning inventory	?
Transferred in from Assembly	4,000
Total units to account for	4,700

Units accounted for:

	Equivalent Units			
	Physical Flow	*Prior Department*	*Materials*	*Conversion Cost*
Units completed	?	?	?	?
Units ending WIP	900	—	—	?
Total	4,700	?	3,800	4,250

Cost Information

Costs to account for:

	Prior Department	*Materials*	*Conversion Costs*	*Total*
Beginning WIP	$11,900	?	$ 210	$12,110
Incurred in December	?	?	4,040	72,097
Total cost	$79,900	$57	$4,250	$84,207
Unit cost	$17.00	?	$1.00	?

Costs accounted for:

	Transferred Out	*Ending WIP*	*Total*
Goods transferred out	?	—	?
Ending inventory:			
Prior department	—	?	?
Materials	—	—	—
Conversion cost	—	?	?
Total costs accounted for	$?	$15,750	$84,207

■ MANAGERIAL DECISION CASES

Case 4–1   **Process Costing versus Alternative Costing Methods; Impact on Resource Allocation Decision**   Golding Manufacturing, a division of Farnsworth Sporting, Inc., produces two different models of bows and eight models of knives. The bow-manufacturing process involves the production of two major subassemblies: the limbs and the handle. The limbs pass through four sequential processes before reaching final assembly: lay-up, molding, fabricating, and finishing. In the Lay-up Department, limbs are created by laminating layers of wood. In Molding, the limbs are heat treated, under pressure, to form a strong resilient limb. In the Fabricating Department, any protruding glue or other processing residue is removed. Finally, in Finishing, the limbs are cleaned with acetone, dried, and sprayed with the final finishes.

The handles pass through two processes before reaching final assembly: pattern and finishing. In the Pattern Department, blocks of wood are fed into a machine that is set to shape the handles. Different patterns are possible, depending on the machine's setting. After coming out of the machine, the handles are cleaned and smoothed. They then pass to the Finishing Department where they are sprayed with the final finishes. In Final Assembly, the limbs and handles are assembled into different models using purchased parts such as pulley assemblies, weight adjustment bolts, side plates, and string.

Golding, since its inception, has been using process costing to assign product costs. A predetermined overhead rate is used based on direct labor dollars (80 percent of direct labor dollars). Recently, Golding has hired a new controller, Karen Jenkins. After reviewing the product costing procedures, Karen requested a meeting with the divisional manager, Aaron Suhr. The following is a transcript of their conversation:

Karen: Aaron, I have some concerns about our cost accounting system. We make two different models of bows and are treating them as if they were the same product. Now I know that the only real difference between the models is the handle. The processing of the handles is the same, but the handles differ significantly in the amount and quality of wood used. Our current costing does not reflect this difference in material input.

Aaron: Your predecessor is responsible. He believed that tracking the difference in material cost wasn't worth the effort. He simply didn't believe that it would make much difference in the unit cost of either model.

Karen: Well, he may have been right, but I have my doubts. If there is a significant difference, it could affect our views of which model is the more important to the company. The additional bookkeeping isn't very stringent. All we have to worry about is the Pattern Department. The other departments fit what I view as a process costing pattern.

Aaron: Why don't you look into it? If there is a significant difference, go ahead and adjust the costing system.

After the meeting, Karen decided to collect cost data on the two models: the Deluxe model and the Econo model. She decided to track the costs for one week. At the end of the week, she had collected the following data from the pattern department:

a. There were a total of 2,500 bows completed: 1,000 Deluxe models and 1,500 Econo models.

b. There was no beginning work in process; however, there were 300 units in ending work in process: 200 Deluxe and 100 Econo models. Both models were 80 percent complete with respect to conversion costs and 100 percent complete with respect to materials.

c. The pattern department experienced the following costs:

Direct materials	$114,000
Direct labor	45,667

d. On an experimental basis, the requisition forms for materials were modified to identify the dollar value of the materials used by the Econo and Deluxe models:

Econo model:	$30,000
Deluxe model:	84,000

Required:

1. Compute the unit cost for the handles produced by the Pattern Department assuming that process costing is totally appropriate.

2. Compute the unit cost of each handle using the separate cost information provided on materials.

3. Compare the unit costs computed in questions 1 and 2. Is Karen justified in her belief that a pure process costing relationship is not appropriate? Describe the costing system that you would recommend.

4. In the past, the marketing manager has requested more money for advertising the Econo line. Aaron has repeatedly refused to grant any increase in this product's advertising budget because its per-unit profit (selling price less manufacturing cost) is so low. Given the results in questions 1 through 3, was Aaron justified in his position?

Case 4–2   Equivalent Units; Unit Costs; Valuation of Work-in-Process Inventories AKL Foundry manufactures metal components for different kinds of equipment used by the aerospace, commercial aircraft, medical equipment, and electronic industries. The company uses investment casting to produce the required components. Investment casting consists of creating, in wax, a replica of the final product and pouring a hard shell around it. After removing the wax, molten metal is poured into the resulting cavity. What remains after the shell is broken is the desired metal object ready to be put to its designated use.

Metal components pass through eight processes: gating, creating shell, foundry work, cut off, grinding, finishing, welding, and strengthening. Gating creates the wax mold and clusters the wax pattern around a sprue (a hole through which the molten metal will be poured through the gates into the mold in the foundry process), which is joined and supported by gates (flow channels) to form a tree of patterns. In the shell process, the wax molds are alternately dipped in a ceramic slurry and a fluidized bed of progressively coarser refractory grain until a sufficiently thick shell (or mold) completely encases the wax pattern. After drying, the mold is sent to the foundry process. Here the wax is melted out of the mold and the shell is fired, strengthened, and brought to the proper temperature. Molten metal is then poured into the dewaxed shell. Finally, the ceramic shell is removed and the finished product is sent to the cut-off process, where the parts are separated from the tree by the use of a band saw. The parts are then sent to grinding, where the gates that allowed the molten metal to flow into the ceramic cavities are ground off using large abrasive grinders. In finishing, rough edges caused by the grinders are removed by small hand-held pneumatic tools. Parts that are flawed at this point are sent to welding for corrective treatment. The last process, heat, treats the parts to bring them to the desired strength.

In 1992, the two partners who owned AKL Foundry decided to split up and divide the business. In dissolving their business relationship, they were faced with the problem of dividing the business assets equitably. Since the company had two plants—one in Arizona and one in New Mexico—a suggestion was made to split the business on the basis of geographic location—one partner would assume ownership of the plant in New Mexico and the other would assume ownership of the plant in Arizona. However, this arrangement had one major complication: the work-in-process inventory located in the Arizona plant.

The Arizona facilities had been in operation for more than a decade and were full of work in process. The New Mexico facility had been operational for only two years and had much smaller work-in-process inventories. The partner located in New Mexico argued that to disregard the unequal value of the work-in-process inventories would be grossly unfair.

Unfortunately, during the entire business history of AKL Foundry, work-in-process inventories had never been assigned any value. In computing the cost of goods sold each year, the company had followed the policy of adding depreciation to the out-of-pocket costs of direct labor, direct materials, and overhead. Accruals for the company are nearly nonexistent, and there are hardly ever any ending inventories of raw materials.

During 1992, the Arizona plant had sales of $2,028,670. The cost of goods sold is itemized as follows:

Direct materials	$378,000
Direct labor	530,300
Overhead	643,518

Upon request, the owners of AKL provided the following supplementary information (percentages are cumulative):

Costs Used by Each Process as a Percentage of Total cost		
	Materials Cost	Total Labor Cost
Gating	23%	35%
Creating shell	70	50
Foundry work	100	70
Cut off	100	72
Grinding	100	80
Finishing	100	90
Welding	100	93
Strengthening	100	100

The Gating Department had 10,000 units in beginning work in process, 60 percent complete. Assume that all materials are added at the beginning of each process. During the year, 50,000 units were completed and transferred out. The ending inventory had 11,000 unfinished units, 60 percent complete.

Required:

1. The partners of AKL want a reasonable estimate of the cost of work-in-process inventories. Using the Gating Department's inventory as an example, prepare an estimate of the cost of the ending work in process. What assumptions did you make? Did you use FIFO or weighted average? Why?

2. Assume that the creating shell process has 8,000 units in beginning work in process, 20 percent complete. During the year, 50,000 units were completed and transferred out (all 50,000 units were sold; no other units were sold). The ending work-in-process inventory had 8,000 units, 30 percent complete. Compute the value of the Creating Shell Department's ending work in process. What additional assumptions had to be made?

CHAPTER 5

Allocation: Service-Center Costs and Other Concepts

- **LEARNING OBJECTIVES**

  After studying Chapter 5, you should be able to

  1. Describe the difference between service departments and producing departments.

  2. Explain why service costs are assigned to producing departments.

  3. Explain why causal factors are used to allocate service costs.

  4. Explain why the planned or expected costs of a service center instead of the actual costs are allocated.

  5. Explain why it is desirable to allocate variable costs separately from fixed costs.

  6. Explain why fixed costs are allocated in proportion to each producing department's original service requirements.

  7. Describe the direct, sequential, and reciprocal methods of service department cost allocation.

  8. Allocate service-center costs to producing departments using the direct and sequential methods.

  9. Define and explain the key terms listed at the end of the chapter.

SCENARIO

Paula Barneck, the newly appointed director of the Lambert Medical Center (LMC), a large metropolitan hospital, was reviewing the financial report for the most recent quarter. The hospital had again shown a loss. For the past several years, it had been struggling financially. The financial problems had begun with the introduction of the federal government's new diagnostic-related group (DRG) reimbursement system. Under this system, the government mandated fixed fees for specific treatments or illnesses. The fixed fees were supposed to represent what the procedures should cost and differed from the traditional cost objective of the patient day of prior years. Although no formal assessment had been made, the general feeling of hospital management was that the DRG reimbursement was hurting LMC's financial state.

The increasing popularity of health maintenance organizations (HMOs) and physician provider organizations (PPOs) was also harming the hospital's financial well-being.[1] More and more of the hospital's potential patients were joining HMOs and PPOs, and, unfortunately, LMC was not capturing its fair share of the HMO and PPO business. HMOs and PPOs routinely asked for bids on hospital services and provided their business to the lowest bidder. In too many cases, LMC had not won that work.

Paula had accepted the position of hospital administrator knowing that she was expected to produce dramatic improvements in LMC's financial state. She was convinced that she needed more information about the hospital's product-costing methods. Only by having accurate cost information for the various procedures offered by the hospital could she evaluate the effects of DRG reimbursement and the hospital's bidding strategy.

Paula requested a meeting with Eric Rose, the hospital's controller. The following is their conversation:

Paula: Eric, as you know, we recently lost a bid on some laboratory tests that would be performed on a regular basis for a local HMO. In fact, I was told by the director of the HMO that we had the highest bid of the three submitted. I know the identity of the other two hospitals that submitted bids, and I have a hard time believing that their costs for these tests are any lower than ours. Describe exactly how we determine the cost of these lab procedures.

Eric: First, we classify all departments as either revenue-producing centers or service centers. Next, the costs of the service centers are allo-

---

[1] In both HMOs and PPOs, users pay a fixed fee for access to medical services and must use the physicians, facilities, and services provided. In HMOs, physicians, who are employed full time, are usually located in a clinic owned by the HMO, and subscribers must use these physicians. In PPOs, the health provider contracts with a group of physicians in private practice. These physicians usually serve non–PPO patients as well as PPO patients. The PPO patient can select any physician from the list of physicians under contract with the particular PPO. The PPO approach usually offers a greater selection of physicians and tends to preserve the patient's traditional freedom of choice.

cated to the revenue-producing centers. The costs directly traceable to the revenue-producing centers are then added to the allocated costs to obtain the total cost of operating the revenue-producing center. This total cost is divided by the total revenues of the revenue-producing center to obtain a cost-to-charges ratio. Finally, the cost of a particular procedure is computed by multiplying the charge for that procedure by the cost-to-charges ratio.

Paula: Let me see if I understand. The costs of laundry, housekeeping, maintenance, and other service departments are allocated to all of the revenue-producing departments. Let's assume that the lab receives $100,000 as its share of these allocated costs. The $100,000 is then added to the direct costs—let's assume these are also $100,000—to obtain total operating costs of $200,000. If the laboratory earns revenues of $250,000, the cost-to-charges ratio is 0.80 ($200,000/$250,000). Finally, if I want to know the cost of a particular lab procedure, say a blood test for which we normally charge $20, then all I do is multiply the cost-to-charges ratio of 0.8 by $20 to obtain the cost of $16. Am I right?

Eric: Absolutely. In that bid we lost, our bid was at cost, as computed using our cost-to-charges formula. Perhaps the other hospitals are bidding below their cost to capture the business.

Paula: Eric, I don't agree. The cost-to-charges ratio is a traditional approach for costing hospital products, but I'm afraid that it is no longer useful. Given the new environment in which we're operating, we need more accurate product-costing information. We need accuracy to improve our bidding, to help us assess and deal with the new DRG reimbursement system, and to evaluate the mix of services we offer. The cost-to-charges ratio approach backs into the product cost. It is indirect and inaccurate. Some procedures require more labor, more materials, and more expensive equipment than others. The cost-to-charges approach doesn't reflect these potential differences.

Eric: Well, I'm willing to change the cost accounting system so that it meets our needs. Do you have any suggestions?

Paula: Yes. I'm in favor of a more direct computation of product costs. Allocating service costs to the revenue-producing departments is only the first stage in product costing. We do need to allocate these service costs to the producing departments—but we need to be certain that we are allocating them in the right way. We also need to go a step farther and assign the costs accumulated in the revenue-producing departments to individual products. The costs directly traceable to each product should be identified and assigned directly to those products; indirect costs can be assigned through one or more overhead rates. The base for assigning the overhead costs should be associated with their incurrence. If at all possible, allocations should reflect the usage of services by the revenue-producing departments; moreover, the same criterion should govern the assignment of overhead costs to the products within the department.

Eric: Sounds like an interesting challenge. With over 30,000 products, a job-order system would be too burdensome and costly. I think some system can be developed, however, that will do essentially what you want.

Paula: Good. Listen, for our next meeting come prepared to brief me on why and how you allocate these service department costs to the revenue-producing departments. I think this is a critical step in accurate product costing. I also want to know how you propose to assign the costs accumulated in each revenue-producing department to that department's products.

■ **SERVICE DEPARTMENT COST ALLOCATION: FURTHER REFINEMENT OF OVERHEAD**

A modern hospital such as Lambert Medical Center or a manufacturing firm such as General Motors or Levi Straus is so complex that careful categorization and subdivision of cost is necessary to produce accurate product cost information. In Chapter 2, we looked at a variety of cost definitions and classifications. We saw that costs for a company could be divided into product and period costs. We further divided product cost into direct materials, direct labor, and factory overhead. In Chapter 3, overhead was assigned to units of production based on a predetermined rate. Sometimes that rate was a plant-wide rate; sometimes there were two or more departmental rates. Now, we are going to look further at the way factory overhead is assigned to products.

producing
departments

service departments

The dialogue between Paula and Eric reveals the presence of two categories of department: producing departments, and service departments. **Producing departments** are directly responsible for manufacturing or creating the products or services sold to customers. In a hospital, examples of producing departments are Emergency, Operating, Intensive Care, Obstetrics, and Respiratory Therapy. In a manufacturing setting, producing departments are those that work directly on the products being manufactured (e.g., Grinding and Assembly). **Service departments** provide essential support services for producing departments. These departments are indirectly connected with an organization's services or products. Examples include Maintenance, Grounds, Laundry, Housekeeping, and Stores.

Once the departments have been identified, the overhead costs incurred by each department can be determined. In this way, all factory costs are assigned to a department. Cafeteria, for example, would have food costs, salaries of cooks and servers, depreciation on dishwashers and stoves, and supplies (napkins, plastic forks). Overhead directly associated with a producing department such as Assembly in a furniture-making plant would include utilities measured in that department, supervisory salaries, and depreciation on equipment used in that department. Overhead that cannot be easily assigned to a producing or service department is assigned to a catchall department such as General Factory. General Factory might include depreciation on the factory building, rental of a Santa Claus suit for the factory Christmas party, the cost of restriping the parking lot, the plant manager's salary, and telephone service.

Exhibit 5–1 (p. 194) shows a factory that has been departmentalized into two producing departments (Assembly and Finishing) and four service departments (Materials Storeroom, Cafeteria, Maintenance, and General Factory). Note that each factory overhead cost must be assigned to one, and only one, department.

The dialogue between Paula and Eric also reveals the need to assign service costs to producing departments. Although service departments do not work directly on the products or services that are sold, the costs of providing these support services are part of the total product costs and must be assigned to the products. This assignment of costs consists of a two-stage allocation: (1) allocation of service-department costs to producing departments and (2) assignment of these allocated costs to individual products. The second-stage allocation, achieved through the use of overhead rates, is necessary because there are multiple products being worked on in each producing department. If there were only one product within a producing department, all the service costs allocated to that department would belong to that product. Recall that a predetermined overhead rate is computed by taking total overhead for a department and dividing it by an appropriate base. Now we see that a department's overhead consists of two parts: overhead directly associated with a producing department and overhead allocated to the producing department from the service departments. (A service department cannot have an overhead rate that assigns overhead costs to units produced because it does not make a salable product.) Both stages are important; however, since overhead rates have already been discussed extensively, the emphasis in this chapter is on the first-stage allocation.

■ OBJECTIVES OF ALLOCATION

A number of important objectives are associated with the allocation of service-department costs to producing departments and ultimately to specific products. The following major objectives have been identified by the IMA[2]:

1. To obtain a mutually agreeable price

2. To compute product-line profitability

3. To predict the economic effects of planning and control

4. To value inventory

5. To motivate managers

Of the five objectives, the first three are referred to in the introductory case. Paula, the hospital administrator, was seeking information about the

---

[2]*Statements of Management Accounting (Statement 4B), Allocation of Service and Administrative Costs* (Montvale, NJ: NAA, 1985). NAA is now known as Institute of Management Accountants.

EXHIBIT 5–1

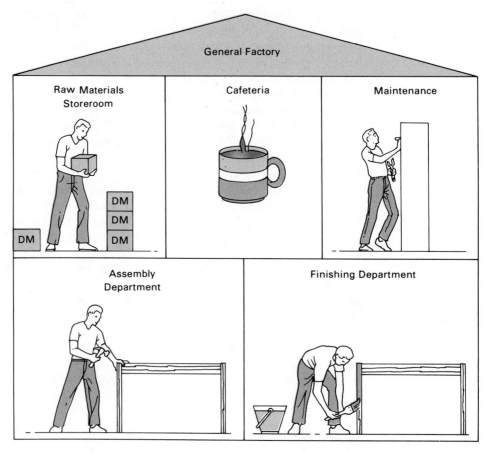

Examples of Overhead Costs Assigned to Each Department

Producing Departments

Assembly:
    Supervisory salaries
    Small tools
    Indirect materials
    Depreciation on machinery
Finishing:
    Sandpaper
    Depreciation on sanders, buffers

Service Departments

Materials Storeroom:
    Clerk's salary
    Depreciation on forklift
Cafeteria:
    Food
    Cooks' salaries
    Depreciation on stoves
Maintenance:
    Janitorial labor
    Cleaning supplies
    Machine main. labor
General Factory:
    Depreciation on building
    Security, utilities

costs of the individual services offered by the hospital. Only by knowing the costs of each service could meaningful bids be created. This is the pricing objective. If costs are not accurately allocated, the costs of some services could be overstated, resulting in bids that are too high and a loss of potential business. Alternatively, if the costs are understated, bids could be too low, producing losses on these services.

Knowing individual product costs also allows Paula to assess the profitability of those services being paid for on a DRG basis. This meets the profitability objective identified by the IMA. The current cost system apparently did not provide the information needed to assess the impact of DRG reimbursement. There was a definite belief that the new system was causing some financial damage, but how and where this was occurring was unknown. A major shortcoming of the old accounting system was its failure to accurately associate indirect costs with hospital services.

By assessing the profitability of various services, Paula is in a position to evaluate the mix of services offered by the hospital. From this evaluation, she may decide to drop some services, reallocate resources from one service to another, reprice certain services, or exercise greater cost control in some areas. These steps would meet the IMA's planning and control objective. The validity of any evaluation, however, depends to a great extent on the accuracy of the cost assignments made to individual products.

For a service organization such as a hospital, the IMA objective of inventory valuation is not relevant. For manufacturing organizations, however, this objective must be given special attention. Rules of financial reporting (GAAP) require that direct manufacturing costs and a fair share of indirect manufacturing costs be assigned to products. The procedure of allocating service costs and then assigning those costs to products is in keeping with this requirement. Inventories must be reported on a full costing basis.

Allocations also can be used to motivate managers. If the costs of service departments are not allocated to producing departments, managers may tend to overconsume these services. Consumption of a service may continue until the marginal benefit of the service equals zero. In reality, of course, the marginal cost of a service is greater than zero. By allocating the costs and holding managers of producing departments responsible for the economic performance of their units, the organization ensures that managers will use a service until the marginal benefit of the service equals its marginal cost. Thus, allocation of service costs helps each producing department select the correct level of service consumption.

There are other behavioral benefits. Allocation of service-department costs to producing departments encourages managers of those departments to monitor the performance of service departments. Since the costs of the service departments affect the economic performance of their own departments, those managers have an incentive to control service costs through means other than simple usage of the service. For instance, the managers can compare the internal costs of the service with the costs of acquiring the service externally. If a service department is not as cost effective as an outside source, perhaps the company should not continue to supply the service internally.

For example, many university libraries are moving toward the use of outside contractors for photocopying services. They have found that these contractors are more cost efficient and provide a higher level of service to library users than did the previous method of using professional librarians to make change, keep the copy machines supplied with paper, fix paper jams, etc. This possibility of comparison should result in a more efficient internal service department. Monitoring by managers of producing departments will also encourage managers of service departments to be more sensitive to the needs of the producing departments.

Clearly, then, there are good reasons for allocating service-department costs. The validity of these reasons, however, depends on the accuracy and fairness of the cost assignments made. Furthermore, it may not be possible to achieve all these objectives with a single allocation scheme; in many cases, multiple allocation schemes are needed.

▪ COST ALLOCATION: SOME BASIC GUIDELINES

Although it may not be possible to identify a method of allocation that simultaneously satisfies all of these objectives, some basic guidelines should be followed when allocating service-department costs. These guidelines are essentially compatible with the five objectives.

1. As nearly as possible, cost drivers (causal factors) should be used as the basis for cost allocation.

2. Budgeted or expected costs, not actual costs, should be allocated.

3. Costs should be allocated by behavior; fixed costs and variable costs should be allocated separately.

Selection of Cost-Allocation Bases: Causal Factors

Services exist to support activities within the producing departments. In effect, producing departments *cause* services; therefore, the costs of service departments are also caused by the activities of the producing departments. **Causal factors** are variables or activities within a producing department that provoke the incurrence of service costs. In choosing a basis for allocating service-department costs, every effort should be made to identify appropriate causal factors (cost drivers). Using causal factors results in product costs being more accurate; furthermore, if the causal factors are known, managers are more able to control the consumption of services.

To illustrate the types of cost drivers that can be used, consider the following three service departments: Power, Personnel, and Materials Handling. For Power costs, a logical allocation base is kilowatt hours, which can be measured by separate meters for each department. If separate meters do not exist, perhaps machine hours used by each department would provide a good approximation of power usage. For Personnel costs, both the number of

causal factors

employees and the labor turnover (e.g., number of new hires) are possible cost drivers. For Materials Handling, the number of material moves, the hours of material handling used, and the quantity of material moved are all possible cost drivers. When competing cost drivers exist, managers need to assess which provides the most convincing relationship.

Allocation: Budgeted Versus Actual Costs

Managers of service and producing departments usually are held accountable for the performance of their units. Their ability to control costs is an important factor in their performance evaluation. This ability is usually measured by comparing actual costs with planned or budgeted costs. If actual costs exceed budgeted costs, the department may be operating inefficiently, with the difference between the two costs the measure of that inefficiency. Similarly, if actual costs are less than budgeted costs, the unit may be operating efficiently.

A general principle of performance evaluation is that managers should not be held responsible for costs or activities over which they have no control. Since managers of producing departments have significant input regarding the level of service consumed, they should be held responsible for their share of service costs. This statement, however, has an important qualification: A department's evaluation should not be affected by the degree of efficiency achieved by another department.

This qualifying statement has an important implication for the allocation of service-department costs. *Actual* costs of a service department should not be allocated to producing departments because they include efficiencies or inefficiencies achieved by the service department. Managers of producing departments have no control over the degree of efficiency achieved by a service-department manager. By allocating *budgeted* costs instead of actual costs, no inefficiencies or efficiencies are transferred from one department to another.

Cost Behavior: Separate Allocation of
Fixed and Variable Costs

For service departments, variable costs increase as the level of service increases. For example, the cost of fuel oil for a power department increases as the kilowatt hours produced increases. Fixed costs, on the other hand, do not vary with the level of service. For example, the salary of a supervisor of a service center does not change as service output changes. Because of this difference in behavior, the cause-and-effect relationship between the producing departments and the service department also differs.

Allocation of Variable Costs   For variable costs, the cause-and-effect relationship is straightforward. Variable service costs increase in total as the quantity of service units increases. Thus, as a producing department uses more of a service, the costs of the service department increase. This suggests that the variable costs of a service department should be charged to producing departments on the basis of usage.

Whether budgeted usage or actual usage is used depends on the purpose of the allocation. For product costing, the allocation is done at the beginning of the year on the basis of budgeted usage so that a predetermined overhead rate can be computed. If the purpose is performance evaluation, however, the allocation is done at the end of the period and is based on actual usage. (Keep in mind the earlier caution about using actual *costs*. As you will see, the measure of actual usage is not the dollar cost of services but the number of service units a producing department consumes.) The use of cost information for performance evaluation is covered in more detail in the chapter on standard costing.

Both budgeted and actual usage allocations are achieved by following four steps:

1. *Determination of rate.* At the beginning of the year, the company determines what the variable cost per unit of service should be.

2. *Budgeting of usage.* Each producing department determines its expected or budgeted usage of the service for the year.

3. *Measurement of actual usage.* The actual units of service used by each producing department are measured.

4. *Allocation.* Variable service costs are allocated by multiplying the budgeted rate by the usage.

   a. For product costing, the formula is budgeted rate times budgeted usage.
   b. For performance evaluation, the allocation is found by multiplying budgeted rate by actual usage.

Consider, for example, the variable costs of a power department; these are the cost of fuel and supplies. At the beginning of the year, the manager of the Power Department, working with his supervisor and the Accounting Department, determined that the budgeted variable cost per kilowatt hour (kwh) would be $0.04. The two producing departments, Machining and Assembly, estimated usage at 800,000 and 200,000 kwh, respectively. Given these data, the cost allocated to each department at the beginning of the year would be as follows:

Machining: $0.04 × 800,000 = $32,000
Assembly: $0.04 × 200,000 = $8,000

The power costs allocated to each department would be added to other overhead costs, including those directly traceable to each department plus other service-department allocations, to compute each department's predetermined overhead rate. This rate would be used throughout the year to assign overhead costs to products passing through the departments.

During the year, each producing department would also be responsible for measuring the amount of actual power usage. Suppose, for example, that by year's end the Machining Department had used 780,000 kwh and Assembly had used 250,000 kwh. A second allocation is now made to measure the actual performance of each department against its budget. The actual power costs allocated to each department are as follows:

Machining: $0.04 × 780,000 = $31,200
Assembly: $0.04 × 250,000 = $10,000

Allocation of Fixed Costs Fixed service costs can be considered capacity costs; they are incurred to provide the capacity necessary to deliver the service units required by the producing departments. When the service department was established, its delivery capability was created based on the long-term needs of the producing departments. Since the original service needs caused the creation of the service capacity, it seems reasonable to allocate fixed service costs based on those needs.

Either the practical or the normal activity of the producing departments provide reasonable measures of original service needs.[3] Thus, budgeted fixed service costs should be allocated in proportion to practical or normal capacity of the producing departments. Budgeted fixed costs are allocated in this way regardless of whether the purpose is product costing or performance evaluation.

The allocation of fixed costs follows a three-step procedure.

1. *Determination of budgeted fixed service costs.* The fixed service costs that should be incurred for a period need to be identified.

2. *Computation of the allocation ratio.* Using the practical or normal capacity of each producing department, it is necessary to compute an allocation ratio. The allocation ratio simply gives a producing department's percentage of total capacity of all producing departments.

Allocation ratio = Producing department capacity/Total capacity

3. *Allocation.* The fixed service costs are then allocated in proportion to each producing department's original service needs.

Allocation = Allocation ratio × Budgeted fixed service costs

For example, assume that the budgeted fixed costs of the Power Department are $500,000 per year and that the practical capacities of the Machining and Assembly departments are 800,000 kwh and 200,000 kwh, respectively.

---

[3]Practical capacity is the maximum capacity if the department operates efficiently. Normal capacity is the average capacity achieved over more than one fiscal period.

The allocation ratio for the Machining Department is 0.80 (800,000/1,000,000), and the allocation ratio for the Assembly Department is 0.20 (200,000/1,000,000). Thus, the fixed service costs assigned to each department are as follows:

Machining: (0.8 × $500,000) = $400,000
Assembly: (0.2 × $500,000) = $100,000

Fixed Versus Variable Bases: A Note of Caution   Using normal or practical capacity to allocate fixed service costs provides a *fixed* base. As long as the capacities of the producing departments remain at the level originally anticipated, there is no reason to change the allocation ratios. Thus, each year the Machining Department receives 80 percent of the budgeted fixed power costs and the Assembly Department 20 percent no matter what their actual usage is. If the capacities of the departments change, the ratios should be recalculated.

In practice, some companies choose to allocate fixed costs in proportion to actual usage or expected actual usage. Since usage may vary from year to year, allocation of fixed costs would then use a variable base. Variable bases, however, have a significant drawback: they allow the actions of one department to affect the amount of cost allocated to another department.

To see how this is so, assume that Department A and Department B each work on different products. Both departments are machine intensive, so the Maintenance Department exists to serve their needs. The budgeted fixed costs of the Maintenance Department are allocated in proportion to the machine hours used by each producing department. The machine hours worked, the allocation ratios, the budgeted fixed costs, and the allocations for 1992 and 1993 are given in Exhibit 5–2.

Notice that Department A's allocation of fixed costs increased by $16,200 from 1992 to 1993 even though the machine hours it used and the total budgeted fixed costs of the Maintenance Department remained unchanged. This increase is caused by a decrease in Department B's use of machine hours. Department A is being penalized because of B's drop in productive output. Imagine the feelings of the manager of Department A when he or she is told of this large increase in allocated fixed costs! The penalty occurs because a variable base is used to allocate fixed service costs; it can be avoided by using a fixed base.

■ METHODS OF ALLOCATING SERVICE DEPARTMENT COSTS TO PRODUCING DEPARTMENTS: FIRST-STAGE ALLOCATION

So far, it has been assumed that service departments provide services only to producing departments. With this assumption, service costs can be allocated directly to the producing departments. This method of allocating service costs is known as the *direct method*.

For many companies, this assumption may not be realistic. When a company has multiple service departments, it is almost certain that they will

direct method

EXHIBIT 5–2
Variable Bases and the Allocation of Fixed Costs

	1992	1993
Machine hours worked		
Department A	30,000	30,000
Department B	50,000	20,000
Total machine hours	80,000	50,000
Allocation ratio		
Department A	0.375	0.60
Department B	0.625	0.40
Budgeted fixed costs	$72,000	$72,000
Allocation		
Department A[a]	$27,000	$43,200
Department B[b]	$45,000	$28,800

[a]0.375 × $72,000; 0.60 × $72,000
[b]0.625 × $72,000; 0.40 × $72,000

interact. For example, Personnel and Cafeteria serve each other and other service departments as well as the producing departments.

Ignoring these interactions and allocating service costs directly to producing departments may produce unfair and inaccurate cost assignments. Power, although a service department, may use 30 percent of the services of the Maintenance Department. The maintenance costs caused by the Power Department belong to that department. By not assigning these costs to the Power Department, its costs are understated. Furthermore, a producing department that is a heavy user of power and an average or below-average user of maintenance may then receive, under the direct method, a cost allocation that is also understated.

By considering service-department interactions, more accurate product costing is achieved. The result can be improved planning, control, and decision making. Two methods of allocation recognize interactions among service departments: the *sequential (or step) method* and the *reciprocal method*. These methods allocate service costs among some (or all) interacting service departments before allocating costs to the producing departments.

Exhibits 5–3 and 5–4 (pp. 202 and 203) illustrate the effect of service-department reciprocity on cost allocation using the direct and sequential methods. In Exhibit 5–3, we see that using the direct method, service department cost is allocated to producing departments only. No cost from one service department is allocated to another service department. Thus, no service department interaction is recognized.

As Exhibit 5–4 shows for the sequential method, service departments are ranked and the costs of the highest-ranking service department are allocated first—to the producing departments and to lower-ranking service de-

EXHIBIT 5–3
Allocation of Service Department Costs to Producing Department
Using the Direct Method

Service departments: Payroll (cost = **X**)
                         Power (cost = **O**)
Producing departments: Machining
                         Assembly

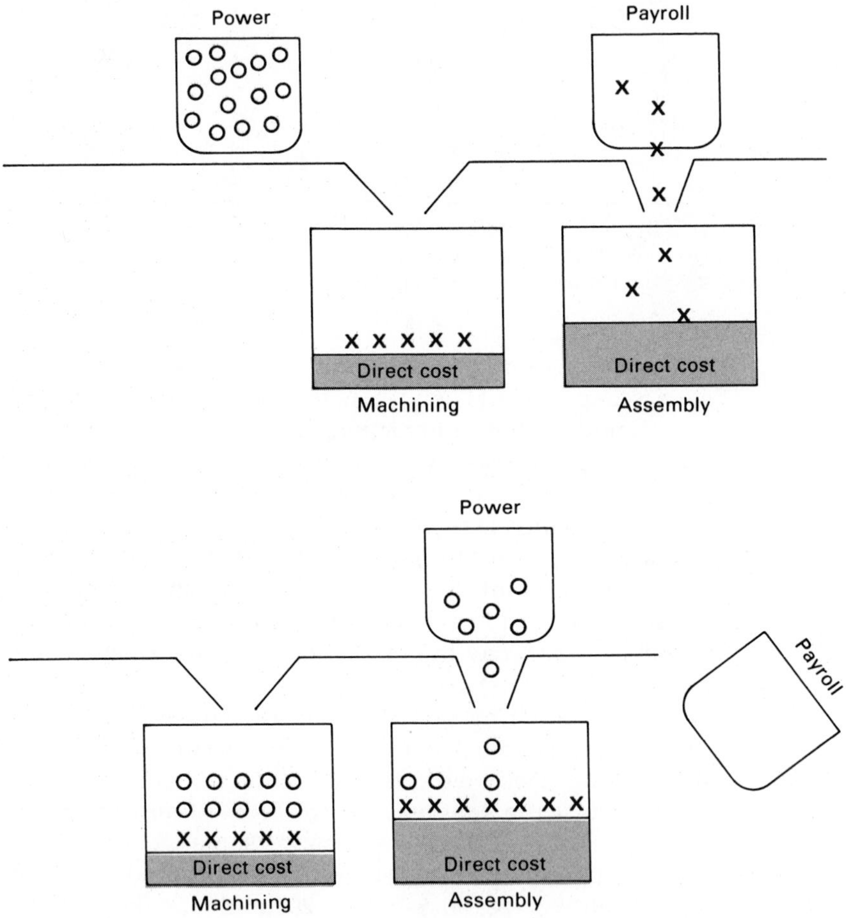

partments. Once the highest-ranking service-department's costs are allocated, the second highest-ranking service-department's costs are allocated—again, to lower-ranking service departments and producing departments. The costs of the lowest-ranked service department are allocated only to producing departments.

EXHIBIT 5–4

Allocation of Service Department Costs to Producing Department Using the Sequential Method

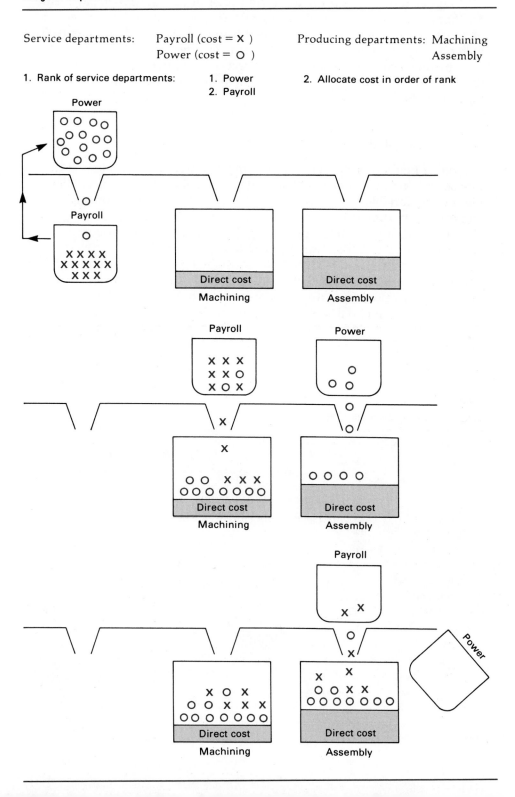

Service departments: Payroll (cost = X) Producing departments: Machining
Power (cost = O) Assembly

1. Rank of service departments: 1. Power 2. Allocate cost in order of rank
2. Payroll

Under the reciprocal method the usage of one service department by another is calculated (using simultaneous equations), and then the new total of service department costs is allocated to the producing departments. This method fully accounts for service department interaction.

In the next two sections, the direct and sequential methods are described and illustrated. The reciprocal method is described and illustrated in the Appendix.

The Direct Method of Allocation

The direct method is the simplest and most straightforward method to allocate service-department costs. It allocates them directly to the producing departments. Variable service costs are allocated directly to producing departments in proportion to each department's usage of the service. Fixed costs are also allocated directly to the producing department, but in proportion to the producing department's normal or practical capacity.

To illustrate the direct method, consider the data in Exhibit 5–5. The data show the budgeted activity and budgeted costs of two service departments and two producing departments. (Note that the same data are used to illustrate the sequential method; for the time being, ignore the allocation ratios at the bottom of Exhibit 5–5 that correspond to the sequential method.)

EXHIBIT 5–5
Data for Illustrating Allocation Methods

	Service Departments		Producing Departments	
	Power	*Maintenance*	*Grinding*	*Assembly*
Direct costs[a]:	$250,000	$160,000	$100,000	$60,000
Normal activity:				
Kilowatt hours	—	200,000	600,000	200,000
Maintenance hours	1,000	—	4,500	4,500
Allocation ratios				
Direct method:				
Kilowatt hours	—	—	0.75	0.25
Maintenance hours	—	—	0.50	0.50
Sequential method:				
Kilowatt hours	—	0.20	0.60	0.20
Maintenance hours	—	—	0.50	0.50

[a]For a producing department, direct costs refer only to overhead costs that are directly traceable to the department.

Assume that the causal factor for power costs is kilowatt hours, and the causal factor for maintenance costs is maintenance hours. These causal factors are used as the basis for allocation. In the direct method, only the kilowatt hours and the maintenance hours in the producing departments are used to compute the allocation ratios. The direct allocations based on the data given in Exhibit 5–5 are shown in Exhibit 5–6. (To simplify the illustration, no distinction is made between fixed and variable costs.)

The Sequential Method of Allocation

sequential (or step) method

The **sequential (or step) method** of allocation recognizes that interactions among the service departments occur. However, the sequential method does not fully recognize service-department interaction. Cost allocations are performed sequentially, following a predetermined ranking procedure. Usually, the sequence is defined by ranking the service departments in order of the service rendered, from the greatest to the least. Degree of service is usually measured by the direct costs of each service department; the department with the highest cost is seen as rendering the greatest service.

The costs of the service department rendering the greatest service are allocated first. They are distributed to all service departments below it in the sequence and to all producing departments. Then the costs of the service department next in sequence are similarly allocated, and so on. In the sequential method, once a service department's costs are allocated, it never receives a subsequent allocation from another service department. In other words, costs of a service department are never allocated to service departments *above* it in the sequence. Also note that the costs allocated from a service department are its direct costs *plus* any costs it receives in allocations from other service departments. The direct costs of a department, of course, are those that are directly traceable to the department.

EXHIBIT 5–6
Direct Allocation Illustrated

	Service Departments		Producing Departments	
	Power	*Maintenance*	*Grinding*	*Assembly*
Direct costs	$ 250,000	$ 160,000	$100,000	$ 60,000
Power[a]	(250,000)	—	187,500	62,500
Maintenance[b]	—	(160,000)	80,000	80,000
	$ 0	$ 0	$367,500	$202,500

[a]Allocation of power based on ratios from Exhibit 5–5: 0.75 × $250,000; 0.25 × $250,000.
[b]Allocation of maintenance based on ratios from Exhibit 5–5: 0.50 × $160,000; 0.50 × $160,000.

To illustrate the sequential method, consider the data provided in Exhibit 5–5. Using cost as a measure of service, the service department rendering more service is Power. Thus, its costs will be allocated first, followed by those for Maintenance. The allocation ratios shown in Exhibit 5–5 will be used to execute the allocation. Note that the allocation ratios for the Maintenance Department ignore the usage by the Power Department since its costs cannot be allocated to a service department above it in the allocation sequence.

The allocations obtained with the sequential method are shown in Exhibit 5–7. Notice that $50,000 of the Power Department's costs are allocated to the Maintenance Department. This reflects the fact that the Maintenance Department uses 20 percent of the Power Department's output. As a result, the cost of operating the Maintenance Department increases from $160,000 to $210,000. Also notice that when the costs of the Maintenance Department are allocated, no costs are allocated back to the Power Department, even though it uses 1,000 hours of the output of the Maintenance Department.

The sequential method is more accurate than the direct method because it recognizes some interactions among the service departments. It does not recognize all interactions, however; no maintenance costs were assigned to the Power Department even though it used 10 percent of the Maintenance Department's output. The reciprocal method corrects this deficiency (see the Appendix).

Departmental Overhead Rates and Product Costing: Second-Stage Allocation

Upon allocating all service costs to producing departments, an overhead rate can be computed for each department. This rate assigns the service costs to the products of the department. It is computed by adding the allocated service costs to the overhead costs that are directly traceable to the producing de-

EXHIBIT 5–7
Sequential Allocation Illustrated

	Service Departments		Producing Departments	
	Power	*Maintenance*	*Grinding*	*Assembly*
Direct costs	$ 250,000	$ 160,000	$100,000	$ 60,000
Power[a]	(250,000)	50,000	150,000	50,000
Maintenance[b]	—	(210,000)	105,000	105,000
	$ 0	$ 0	$355,000	$215,000

[a]Allocation of power based on ratios from Exhibit 5–5: 0.2 × $250,000; 0.6 × $250,000; 0.2 × $250,000.
[b]Allocation of maintenance costs based on ratios from Exhibit 5–5; 0.50 × $210,000; 0.50 × $210,000.

partment and dividing this total by some measure of activity, such as direct labor hours or machine hours.

For example, from Exhibit 5–7, the total overhead costs for the Grinding Department after allocation of service costs are $355,000. Assume that machine hours are the base for assigning overhead costs to products passing through the Grinding Department and that the normal level of activity is 71,000 machine hours. The overhead rate for the Grinding Department is computed as follows:

$$\text{Overhead rate} = \$355,000/71,000 \text{ machine hours}$$
$$= \$5 \text{ per machine hour}$$

Similarly, assume that the Assembly Department uses direct labor hours to assign its overhead. With a normal level of activity of 107,500 direct labor hours, the overhead rate for the Assembly Department is as follows:

$$\text{Overhead rate} = \$215,000/107,500 \text{ direct labor hours}$$
$$= \$2 \text{ per direct labor hour}$$

Using these rates, the product's unit cost can be determined. To illustrate, suppose a product requires two machine hours of grinding per unit produced and one hour of assembly. The overhead cost assigned to one unit of this product would be $12 [(2 × $5) + (1 × $2)]. If the same product uses $15 of materials and $6 of labor, then its unit cost is $33 ($12 + $15 + $6).

One might wonder, however, just how accurate this $33 cost is. Is this really what it costs to produce the product in question? Since materials and labor are directly traceable to products, the accuracy of product costs depends largely on the accuracy of the assignment of overhead costs. This, in turn, depends on the degree of correlation between the factors used to allocate service costs to departments and the factors used to allocate the department's overhead costs to the products. For example, if power costs are highly correlated with kilowatt hours and machine hours are highly correlated with a product's consumption of the Grinding Department's overhead costs, then we can have some confidence that the $5 overhead rate accurately assigns costs to individual products. However, if the allocation of service costs to the Grinding Department or the use of machine hours is faulty—or both—then product costs will be distorted. The same reasoning can be applied to the Assembly Department. To ensure accurate product costs, great care should be used in identifying and using causal factors for both stages of overhead assignment. More will be said about this in a later chapter.

■ SUMMARY OF LEARNING OBJECTIVES

1. **Describe the difference between service departments and producing departments.** Producing departments create the product(s) that the firm is in business to manufacture and sell. Service departments provide support for the producing departments but do not themselves build components of product.

2. **Explain why service costs are assigned to producing departments.** Because service departments exist to support a variety of producing departments, the costs of the service departments are common to all producing departments and must be allocated to them to satisfy a number of important objectives. These objectives include inventory valuation, product-line profitability, pricing, and planning and control. Allocation can also be used to encourage favorable managerial behavior.

3. **Explain why causal factors are used to allocate service costs.** Managers should attempt to identify those factors that cause service costs to be incurred because product costs can be more accurately determined. Furthermore, accurate identification of causal factors can help managers control costs.

4. **Explain why the planned or expected costs of a service center instead of the actual costs are allocated.** Budgeted, not actual costs, should be allocated so that the efficiencies or inefficiencies of the service departments themselves are not passed on to the producing departments.

5. **Explain why it is desirable to allocate variable costs separately from fixed costs.** Because the causal factors can differ for fixed and variable costs, these types of cost should be allocated separately. Fixed costs should be allocated on the basis of the normal or practical activity of each producing department. Variable costs should be allocated on the basis of the department's usage of the service.

6. **Explain why fixed costs are allocated in proportion to each producing department's original service requirements.** Fixed costs can be considered capacity costs. Since the original service needs caused the creation of the service capacity, it is reasonable to allocate fixed service costs based on the original requirements.

7. **Describe the direct, sequential, and reciprocal methods of service department cost allocation.** Three methods can be used to allocate service costs to producing departments: the direct method, the sequential method, and the reciprocal method. The direct method allocates all service-department direct costs to the producing departments without considering any interactions among service departments. The sequential method gives partial recognition to interactions among service departments by establishing a hierarchy based on service rendered. The service department rendering the greatest service is listed first and the department rendering the least service last. Service costs are then allocated sequentially to all user departments, service as well as producing. The reciprocal method fully considers interactions among service departments. Costs are allocated to all departments that use services.

8. **Allocate service-center costs to producing departments using the direct and sequential methods.** Under the direct method, the percentage of usage of each service center by the producing departments is calculated. Then service-center costs are allocated to producing departments according to their percentage of usage. Under the sequential method, the service department rendering the greatest service is listed first and the department rendering the least service last. Costs of the first service center are allocated to lower-ranking

service departments and to producing departments. The next highest-ranking service-department's costs are then allocated to lower-ranking service departments and to producing departments. The lowest-ranking service-department's costs are allocated only to producing departments.

■ KEY TERMS

Causal factor Activities or variables that invoke service costs. Generally, it is desirable to use causal factors as the basis for allocating service costs. (p. 196)

Direct method A method that allocates service costs directly to producing departments. This method ignores any interactions that may exist among service departments. (p. 200)

Producing department A unit within an organization responsible for producing the products or services that are sold to customers. (p. 192)

Reciprocal method A method that simultaneously allocates service costs to all user departments. It gives full consideration to interactions among service departments. (p. 211)

Sequential (or step) method A method that allocates service costs to user departments in a sequential manner. It gives partial consideration to interactions among service departments. (p. 205)

Service department A unit within an organization that provides essential support services for producing departments. (p. 192)

■ REVIEW PROBLEM

Clearfield Manufacturing produces machine parts on a job-order basis. Most business is gained through bidding. Most firms competing with Clearfield bid full cost plus a 20 percent markup. Recently, with the expectation of gaining more sales, Clearfield dropped its markup from 25 percent to 20 percent. The company operates two service departments and two producing departments. The budgeted costs and the normal activity levels for each department are given below.

	Service Departments		Producing Departments	
	A	B	C	D
Overhead costs	$100,000	$200,000	$100,000	$50,000
Number of employees	8	7	30	30
Maintenance hours	2,000	200	6,400	1,600
Machine hours	—	—	10,000	1,000
Labor hours	—	—	1,000	10,000

The direct costs of Department A are allocated on the basis of employees, those of Department B on the basis of maintenance hours. Departmental overhead rates are used to assign costs to products. Department C uses machine hours, and Department D uses labor hours.

The firm is preparing to bid on a job (Job K) that requires three machine hours per unit produced in Department C and no time in Department D. The expected prime costs per unit are $67.

Required:

1. Allocate the service costs to the producing departments using the direct method.
2. What will the bid be for Job K if the direct method of allocation is used?
3. Allocate the service costs to the producing departments using the sequential method.
4. What will the bid be for Job K if the sequential method is used?

Solution:

1.

	Service Departments		Producing Departments	
	A	B	C	D
Direct costs	$ 100,000	$ 200,000	$100,000	$ 50,000
Department A	(100,000)	—	50,000	50,000
Department B	—	(200,000)	160,000	40,000
Total	$ 0	$ 0	$310,000	$140,000

2. Department C: Overhead rate = $310,000/10,000 = $31 per machine hour. Product cost and bid price:

Overhead (3 × $31)	$ 93
Prime cost	67
Total unit cost	$160
Bid price ($160 × 1.2)	$192

3.

	Service Departments		Producing Departments	
	A	B	C	D
Direct costs	$ 100,000	$ 200,000	$100,000	$ 50,000
Department B	40,000	(200,000)	128,000	32,000
Department A	(140,000)	—	70,000	70,000
Total	$ 0	$ 0	$298,000	$152,000

4. Department C: Overhead rate = $298,000/10,000 = $29.80 per machine hour. Product cost and bid price:

Overhead (3 × 29.80)	$ 89.40
Prime cost	67.00
Total unit cost	$156.40
Bid price ($156.40 × 1.2)	$187.68

■ APPENDIX: THE RECIPROCAL METHOD OF ALLOCATION

reciprocal method   The **reciprocal method** of allocation recognizes all interactions of service departments and consists of two steps: (1) determining the total cost of each service department, where the total cost reflects interactions among the service departments, and (2) allocating each service department's costs to the producing departments.

Total Cost of Service Departments

To determine the total cost of a service department so that this total cost reflects interactions with other service departments, a system of simultaneous linear equations must be solved. Each equation, which is a cost equation for a service department, is defined as the sum of the department's direct costs plus a share of the total costs of the other service departments with which it interacts. This sum can be expressed as follows:

Total cost = Direct costs + Allocated costs

The method is best described using an example. The same data used to illustrate the direct and sequential methods will be used to illustrate the reciprocal method (see Exhibit 5–8, p. 212). The allocation ratios are interpreted as follows: Maintenance uses 20 percent of Power's output, Grinding uses 60 percent, and Assembly uses 20 percent; Power uses 10 percent of Maintenance's output, Grinding uses 45 percent, and Assembly uses 45 percent.

Now let P equal the total cost of the Power Department and M equal the total cost of the Maintenance Department. As indicated above, the total cost of a service department is the sum of its direct costs plus costs allocated to it from other service departments. Using the data and allocation ratios from Exhibit 5–8, the cost equation for each service department can be expressed as follows:

$$P = \text{Direct costs} + \text{Share of Maintenance's cost} \qquad (5.1)$$
$$= \$250,000 + 0.1M \text{ (Power's cost equation)}$$

EXHIBIT 5-8

Data for Illustrating Reciprocal Method

	Service Departments		Producing Departments	
	Power	Maintenance	Grinding	Assembly
Direct costs[a]				
Fixed	$200,000	$100,000	$ 80,000	$ 50,000
Variable	50,000	60,000	20,000	10,000
Total	$250,000	$160,000	$100,000	$ 60,000
Normal activity:				
Kilowatt hours	—	200,000	600,000	200,000
Maintenance hours	1,000	—	4,500	4,500

Allocation ratios:

	Proportion of Output Used by			
	Power	Maintenance	Grinding	Assembly
Power	—	0.20	0.60	0.20
Maintenance	0.10	—	0.45	0.45

[a]For a producing department, direct costs are defined as overhead costs that are directly traceable to the department.

$$M = \text{Direct costs} + \text{Share of Power's costs} \qquad \textbf{(5.2)}$$
$$= \$160,000 + 0.2P \text{ (Maintenance's cost equation)}$$

The direct-cost components of each equation are taken from Exhibit 5–8, as are the allocation ratios.

The Power cost equation (Equation 5.1) and the Maintenance cost equation (Equation 5.2) can be solved simultaneously to yield the total cost for each service department. Substituting Equation 5.1 into Equation 5.2 gives the following:

$$M = \$160,000 + 0.2 \ (\$250,000 + 0.1M)$$
$$M = \$160,000 + \$50,000 + 0.02M$$
$$0.98M = \$210,000$$
$$M = \$214,286$$

Substituting this value for M into Equation 5.1 yields the total cost for Power:

$$P = \$250,000 + 0.1 \ (\$214,286)$$
$$= \$250,000 + \$21,429$$
$$= \$271,429$$

EXHIBIT 5–9
Reciprocal Allocation Illustrated

	Total	Allocated to	
From	Cost	Grinding[a]	Assembly[b]
Power	$271,429	$162,857	$ 54,286
Maintenance	214,286	96,429	96,429
Total		$259,286	$150,715

[a]Power: 0.6 × $271,429; Maintenance: 0.45 × $214,286
[b]Power: 0.2 × $271,429; Maintenance: 0.45 × $214,286

After the equations are solved, the total costs of each service department are known. These total costs, unlike the direct or sequential methods, reflect all interactions between service departments.

Allocation to Producing Departments

Once the total costs of each service department are known, the allocations to the producing departments can be made. These allocations, based on the proportion of output used by each producing department, are shown in Exhibit 5–9. Notice that the total costs allocated to the producing departments equal $410,000, the total direct costs of the two service departments ($250,000 + $160,000).

■ QUESTIONS

1 Describe the two-stage allocation process for assigning service costs to products in a traditional manufacturing environment.

2 Explain how allocating service costs can be helpful in pricing decisions.

3 Why must service costs be assigned to products for purposes of inventory valuation?

4 Explain how allocation of service costs is useful for planning and control.

5 Assume that a company has decided not to allocate any service costs to producing departments. Describe the likely behavior of the managers of the producing departments. Would this be good or bad? Explain why allocation would correct this type of behavior.

6 Explain how allocating service costs will encourage service departments to operate more efficiently.

7 Why is it important to identify and use causal factors to allocate service costs?

8 Identify some possible causal factors for the following service departments:
    a. Cafeteria
    b. Custodial Services

     c. Laundry

     d. Receiving, Shipping, and Stores

     e. Maintenance

     f. Personnel

     g. Accounting

9   Explain why it is better to allocate budgeted service costs rather than actual service costs.

10   Why is it desirable to allocate variable costs and fixed costs separately?

11   Explain why either normal or practical capacity of the producing (or user) departments should be used to allocate the fixed costs of service departments.

12   Explain why variable bases should not be used to allocate fixed costs.

13   The Personnel Department has total variable costs of $20,000 and serves two producing departments, one with 100 employees and the other with 300. Using employees as the allocation base, allocate the costs of the Personnel Department to the producing departments using the direct method.

14   Explain the difference between the direct method and the sequential method.

15   The reciprocal method of allocation is more accurate than either the direct or sequential methods. Do you agree? Explain.

■ EXERCISES

E5–1   **Classifying Departments as Producing or Service** Classify each of the following departments in a factory as a producing department or a service department.

1. Assembly
2. Payroll
3. Cafeteria
4. General Factory
5. Maintenance
6. Machining
7. Inspection
8. Blending
9. Finishing
10. Personnel
11. Grounds
12. Data Processing
13. Packaging
14. Cutting
15. Engineering

E5–2   **Identifying Causal Factors** For the following service departments, identify one or more causal factors that might be useful for service-department cost allocation purposes.

1. Supervision
2. Data Processing

3. Quality Control

4. Purchasing

5. Receiving

6. Shipping

7. Vending (stocking snack machines throughout the plant)

8. Grounds

9. Building Depreciation

10. Power and Light

11. Employee Benefits

12. Housekeeping

13. Equipment Repair

14. Heating and Cooling

E5-3 **Actual versus Budgeted Costs** Bartlett Manufacturing Company evaluates managers of producing departments on their ability to control costs. In addition to the costs directly traceable to their departments, each production manager is held responsible for a share of the costs of a service center, the Maintenance Department. The total costs of the Maintenance Department are allocated on the basis of actual maintenance hours used. The total costs of maintenance and the actual hours used by each producing department are given below.

	1992	*1993*
Maintenance hours used:		
Department A	2,000	2,000
Department B	3,000	2,000
Total hours	5,000	4,000
Actual maintenance cost	$100,000	$100,000
Budgeted maintenance cost	$ 90,000[a]	$ 80,000[a]

[a]$10 per maintenance hour plus $40,000.

Required:

1. Allocate the maintenance cost to each producing department for 1992 and 1993 using the direct method with actual maintenance hours and actual maintenance costs.

2. Discuss the following statement: "The costs of maintenance increased by 25 percent for Department A and decreased by more than 16 percent for Department B. Thus, the manager of Department B is controlling maintenance costs better than the manager of Department A is."

3. Can you think of a way to allocate maintenance costs so that a more reasonable and fairer assessment of cost control can be made? Explain.

E5-4 **Fixed and Variable Cost Allocation** Refer to the data in Exercise 5-3. When the capacity of the Maintenance Department was originally established, the normal usage expected for each department was 2,000 maintenance hours. This usage is also the amount of activity planned for the two departments in 1992 and 1993.

Required:

1. Allocate the costs of the Maintenance Department using the direct method and assuming that the purpose is product costing.

2. Allocate the costs of the Maintenance Department using the direct method and assuming that the purpose is to evaluate performance.

E5–5   **Direct Method and Overhead Rates**   Finlither Company manufactures men's and women's shoes, with each type of shoe produced in separate departments. Three service departments support the production departments: Maintenance, Building and Grounds, and Food Services. Budgeted data on the five departments are as follows:

	Service Departments			Producing Departments	
	Maintenance	*Grounds*	*Food*	*Men's*	*Women's*
Overhead	$30,000	$70,000	$50,000	$20,000	$30,000
Number of employees	5	2	3	15	25
Square feet	2,000	—	3,000	5,000	10,000
Machine hours	—	—	—	2,000	3,000

The company does not break overhead into fixed and variable components.

Required:

1. Allocate the overhead costs to the producing departments using the direct method.

2. Using machine hours, compute departmental overhead rates.

E5–6   **Sequential Method**   Refer to the data in Exercise 5–5. The company has decided to use the sequential method of allocation instead of the direct method.

Required:

1. Allocate the overhead costs to the producing departments using the sequential method.

2. Using machine hours, compute departmental overhead rates.

E5–7   **Reciprocal Method**   Mycles Company has two producing departments and two service centers. The following budgeted data pertain to these four departments:

	Service Departments		Producing Departments	
	Maintenance	*Power*	*Grinding*	*Polishing*
Overhead	$72,000	$30,000	$50,000	$80,000
Maintenance hours	—	3,000	6,000	6,000
Kilowatt hours	50,000	—	100,000	150,000
Direct labor hours	—	—	20,000	30,000

Required:

1. Allocate the overhead costs of the service departments to the producing departments using the reciprocal method.

2. Using direct labor hours, compute departmental overhead rates.

E5-8   **Direct Method**   Refer to the data in Exercise 5-7. The company has decided to simplify its method of allocating service costs by switching to the direct method.

Required:

1. Allocate the costs of the service departments to the producing departments using the direct method.

2. Using direct labor hours, compute departmental overhead rates. Which rate do you consider more accurate—the one using the reciprocal method or the one using the direct method? Explain.

E5-9   **Sequential Method**   Refer to the data in Exercise 5-7.

Required:

1. Allocate the costs of the service departments using the sequential method.

2. Using direct labor hours, compute departmental overhead rates. Explain why these rates are generally more accurate than those computed using the direct method.

E5-10   **Allocation: Fixed and Variable Costs**   Thummer Temporary Employment Agency has two Texas offices, one in Dallas and one in Austin. The owner of the agency purchased a minicomputer and established a computer service center located in Dallas. Arrangements were made with the phone company so that the Austin office has access to the system. The computer service center has budgeted fixed costs of $85,000 per year and a budgeted variable rate of $20 per hour of CPU time. The normal usage of the computer is 1,500 hours per year for the Dallas office and 1,200 hours per year for the Austin office. This corresponds to the expected usage for the coming year.

Required:

1. Determine the amount of computer service costs that should be assigned to each office.

2. Since the offices produce services, not tangible products, what purpose is served by allocating the budgeted costs? Should each office compute a predetermined overhead rate? If so, how would you use this rate?

E5-11   **Allocation: Budgeted Fixed and Variable Costs**   Refer to Exercise 5-10. Assume that during the year, the computer service center incurred actual fixed costs of $90,000 and actual variable costs of $62,350; it delivered 3,000 hours of CPU time, 1,600 hours to Dallas and 1,400 to Austin.

Required:

1. Determine the amount of the service center's costs that should be allocated to each office. Explain the purposes of this allocation.

2. Did the costs allocated differ from the costs incurred by the service center? If so, explain why.

E5-12   **Fixed Cost Allocation; Variable Base**   Restum Hotels are located throughout the Southwest. The central office's fixed administrative expenses are allocated to each hotel in proportion to the unit's revenues. In 1992, the total administrative expenses were $3.5 million. In 1993, this total increased to $4 million. The hotel chain had $100 million in revenues in 1992 and 1993. The hotel with the greatest proportion of revenues was located in Phoenix, Arizona. This hotel's revenues were $10 million in 1992 and $15 million in 1993.

Required:

1. Compute the amount of fixed administrative expenses allocated to the Phoenix hotel in 1992.

2. Compute the amount of fixed administrative expenses allocated to the Phoenix hotel in 1993.

3. Compare the 1992 and 1993 allocations for the Phoenix hotel. Explain why the allocation increased.

4. Assume that you are the manager of the Phoenix hotel and that your annual bonus is a function of net income, the computation of which includes the allocated fixed administrative expenses. How would you react to Restum's allocation method? Can you recommend a better method of allocation?

E5–13   **Reciprocal Method**   Trinity Medical Clinic has two service centers and two revenue-producing departments. The controller for the clinic has decided to use the reciprocal method to allocate the costs of the service centers (A and B) to the producing departments (C and D). She has prepared the cost equations below for the two service centers. *A* equals the total cost for the first service center, and *B* equals the total costs for the second service center.

$$A = 35,000 + 0.3B$$
$$B = 40,000 + 0.2A$$

Before the controller was able to complete the allocation, she had to leave to take care of an emergency. In addition to the above equations, she left a hastily scribbled note indicating that Department C uses 20 percent of A's output and 40 percent of B's output.

Required:

Allocate the costs of the two service centers to each of the two producing departments using the reciprocal method.

E5–14   **Direct Method; Overhead Rates**   Carroll Publishing Company prints religious music. There are two producing departments (Printing and Binding), and two service departments (Cafeteria and General Factory). Budgeted data for the four departments are as follows:

	Producing Departments		Service Departments	
	Printing	*Binding*	*Cafeteria*	*General Factory*
Overhead before allocation	$40,000	$60,000	$20,000	$100,000
Employees	10	40	—	10
Square feet	1,500	4,500	2,000	—
DLH	20,000	80,000	10,000	32,000

Cafeteria costs are allocated on the basis of number of employees; general factory costs are allocated on the basis of square feet.

Required:

1. Allocate overhead costs to producing departments using the direct method.
2. Using direct labor hours, compute departmental overhead rates.

E5–15 **Sequential Method; Overhead Rates** Refer to the data in Exercise 5–14. Assume Carroll Publishing Company decides to use the sequential method.

Required:

1. Allocate overhead costs to producing departments using the sequential method.
2. Using direct labor hours, compute departmental overhead rates.

E5–16 **Reciprocal Method; Overhead Rates** Refer to the data in Exercise 5–14. Assume Carroll Publishing Company decides to use the reciprocal method.

Required:

1. Allocate overhead costs to producing departments using the reciprocal method.
2. Using direct labor hours, compute departmental overhead rates.
3. Which of the three methods do you think is best? Why?

E5–17 **Allocation: Fixed and Variable Costs** Walters Company is a medium-sized advertising firm on the West Coast. Walters has three departments that specialize in advertising and public relations services for different markets: Tangible Goods (headed by Sherri Donaldson), Nonprofit Organizations (headed by Mike Adams), and Public Relations (headed by Carla Wilson). Previously, Walters had subcontracted out necessary printing and graphics work. However, recent technological advances in desktop publishing led to the formation of a new in-house graphics department that could produce brochures, booklets, posters, etc. The Tangible Goods and Public Relations departments immediately began to use the new graphics services. Nonprofit Organizations, however, was reluctant to switch from its traditional outside supplier. Jim Walters, president and CEO of Walters Company, encouraged all departments "to get on board" with Graphics, and Paul Murphy, the head of Graphics, assured Mike Adams that Graphics could serve Mike's departmental needs by spending an additional $2,000 above total 1992 costs. So during 1993, Mike Adams decided to give Graphics a try.

Data for the Graphics Department are as follows:

	1992	1993
Actual costs	$12,000	$14,000
DLH used by:		
Tangible Goods	2,000	2,000
Public Relations	2,000	2,000
Nonprofit Organizations	—	1,000

Actual costs equaled budgeted costs in both 1992 and 1993. Graphics services are charged to user departments on the basis of actual cost per hour of graphics time used.

Required:

1. What was the graphics rate per hour charged in 1992? In 1993?

2. How much was the Nonprofit Department charged for graphics services in 1993? How do you think Mike Adams reacted to the charges?

3. How can you reconcile the difference between the rate charged Mike Adams during 1993 and the $2,000 incremental cost cited by Paul Murphy?

■ PROBLEMS

P5–1 **Direct Method, Variable versus Fixed; Costing and Performance Evaluation** Air-Borne is a small airline operating out of Boise, Idaho. Its three flights travel to Reno, Salt Lake City, and Portland. The owner of the airline wants to assess the full cost of operating each flight. As part of this assessment, the costs of two service departments (Baggage and Maintenance) must be allocated to the three flights. The two service departments that support all three flights are located in Boise (any baggage or maintenance costs at the destination airports are directly traceable to the individual flights). Budgeted and actual data for 1992 are as follows for the service departments and the three flights:

	Service Departments		Flights		
	Maintenance	*Baggage*	*Salt Lake City*	*Reno*	*Portland*
Budgeted data:					
Fixed overhead	$240,000	$150,000	$20,000	$18,000	$30,000
Variable overhead	$30,000	$64,000	$5,000	$10,000	$6,000
Number of passengers[a]	—	—	10,000	15,000	5,000
Hours of flight time[a]	—	—	2,000	4,000	2,000
Actual data:					
Fixed overhead	$235,000	$156,000	$22,000	$17,000	$29,500
Variable overhead	$80,000	$33,000	$6,200	$11,000	$5,800
Number of passengers	—	—	8,000	16,000	6,000
Hours of flight time	—	—	1,800	4,200	2,500

[a]Normal activity levels

Required:

1. Using the direct method, allocate the service costs to each flight, assuming that the objective is to determine the cost of operating each flight.

2. Using the direct method, allocate the service costs to each flight, assuming that the objective is to evaluate performance. Do any costs remain in the two service departments after the allocation? If so, how much? Explain.

P5–2 **Comparison of Methods of Allocation** Paulos Trucking is divided into two operating divisions: Perishable Foods and Household Goods. The company allocates personnel and accounting costs to each operating division. Personnel costs are allocated on the basis of employees and accounting costs on the basis of the number of transactions processed. No effort is made to separate fixed and variable costs; however, only budgeted costs are allocated. Allocations for the coming year are based on the following data:

	Service Departments		Operating Divisions	
	Personnel	Accounting	Perishable Foods	Household Goods
Overhead costs	$100,000	$205,000	$80,000	$50,000
Number of employees	20	60	60	80
Transactions processed	2,000	200	3,000	5,000

Required:

1. Allocate the service costs using the direct method.
2. Allocate the service costs using the sequential method.
3. Allocate the service costs using the reciprocal method.

P5–3 **Comparison of Methods of Allocation** Kare Foods Company specializes in the production of frozen dinners. The first of the two operating departments cooks the food. The second is responsible for packaging and freezing the dinners. The dinners are sold by the case, each case containing 25 dinners.

  Two service departments provide support for Kare's operating units: Maintenance and Power. Budgeted data for the coming quarter are given below. The company does not separate fixed and variable costs.

	Service Departments		Producing Departments	
	Maintenance	Power	Cooking	Packing and Freezing
Overhead costs	$340,000	$200,000	$75,000	$55,000
Machine hours	—	40,000	40,000	20,000
Kilowatt hours	20,000	—	100,000	80,000
Direct labor hours	—	—	5,000	30,000

  The predetermined overhead rate for Cooking is computed on the basis of machine hours; direct labor hours are used for Packing and Freezing. The prime costs for one case of standard dinners total $16. It takes two machine hours to produce a case of dinners in the Cooking Department and 0.5 direct labor hours to process a case of standard dinners in the Packing and Freezing Department.

  Recently, the Air Force has requested a bid on a three-year contract that would supply standard frozen dinners to Minuteman Missile officers and staff on duty in the field. The locations of the missile sites are remote, and the Air Force has decided that frozen dinners are the most economical means of supplying food to personnel on duty.

  The bidding policy of Kare Foods is full manufacturing cost plus 20 percent. Assume that the lowest bid of other competitors is $48.80 per case.

Required:

1. Prepare bids for Kare Foods using each of the following allocation methods:
   a. Direct method
   b. Sequential method
   c. Reciprocal method

2. Refer to requirement 1. Did all three methods produce winning bids? If not, explain why. Which method most accurately reflects the cost of producing the cases of dinners? Why?

P5–4   **Allocation; Pricing; Ethical Behavior**   Emma Hanks, manager of a division that produces valves and castings on a special order basis, was excited about an order received from a new customer. The customer, a personal friend of Bob Johnson, Emma's supervisor, had placed an order for 10,000 valves. The customer agreed to pay full manufacturing cost plus 25 percent. The order was timely since business was sluggish, and Emma had some concerns about her division's ability to meet its targeted profits. Even with the order, the division would likely fall short in meeting the target by at least $50,000. After examining the cost sheet for the order, however, Emma thought she saw a way to increase the profitability of the job. Accordingly, she called Larry Smith, CMA, the controller of the division.

Emma: Larry, this cost sheet for the new order reflects an allocation of maintenance costs to the Grinding Department based on maintenance hours used. Currently, 60 percent of our maintenance costs are allocated to Grinding on that basis. Can you tell me what the allocation ratio would be if we used machine hours instead of maintenance hours?

Larry: Sure. Based on machine hours, the allocation ratio would increase from 60 percent to 80 percent.

Emma: Excellent. Now tell me what would happen to the unit cost of this new job if we used machine hours to allocate maintenance costs.

Larry: Hold on. That'll take a few minutes. . . . The cost would increase by $10 per unit.

Emma: And with the 25 percent markup, the revenues on that job would jump by $12.50 per unit. That would increase the profitability of the division by $125,000. Larry, I want you to change the allocation base from maintenance hours worked to machine hours.

Larry: Are you sure? After all, if you recall, we spent some time assessing the causal relationships, and we found that maintenance hours reflect the consumption of maintenance cost much better than machine hours. I'm not sure that would be a fair cost assignment. We've used this base for years now.

Emma: Listen, Larry, allocations are arbitrary anyway. Changing the allocation base for this new job will increase its profitability and allow us to meet our targeted profit goals for the year. If we meet or beat those goals, we'll be more likely to get the capital we need to acquire some new equipment. Furthermore, by beating the targeted profit, we'll get our share of the bonus pool. Besides, this new customer has a prosperous business and can easily afford to pay somewhat more for this order.

Required:

1. Evaluate Emma's position. Do you agree with her reasoning? Explain. What should Emma do?

2. If you were the controller, what would you do? Do any of the standards for ethical conduct for management accountants apply to the controller (see the Appendix to Chapter 1)? Explain.

3. Suppose Larry refused to change the allocation scheme. Emma then issued the following ultimatum: "Either change the allocation or look for another job!" Larry then made an appointment with Bob Johnson and disclosed the entire affair. Bob, however, was not sympathetic. He advised Larry to do as Emma had requested, arguing that the request represented good business sense. Now what should Larry do?

4. Refer to Requirement 3. Larry decided that he cannot comply with the request to change the allocation scheme. Appeals to higher-level officials have been in vain. Angered, Larry submitted his resignation and called the new customer affected by the cost reassignment. In his phone conversation, Larry revealed Emma's plans to increase the job's costs in order to improve the division's profits. The new customer expressed her gratitude and promptly canceled her order for 10,000 valves. Evaluate Larry's actions. Should he have informed the customer about Emma's intent? Explain.

P5–5 **Predetermined Rates; Allocation for Performance Evaluation** Morsley Company operates three vehicle rental divisions: Budget, Luxury, and Trucks. The Budget Division specializes in renting compact and subcompact cars; the Luxury Division specializes in renting large luxury cars and vans; and the Truck Division rents pickups and small enclosed trucks for local moving.

Morsley has one service center, which is responsible for the service, maintenance, and cleanup of its fleet of vehicles. The costs of this service center are allocated to each operating unit on the basis of total miles driven. During the first quarter, the service center was expected to spend a total of $40,000. Of this total, $16,000 was viewed as being fixed. During the quarter, the service center incurred actual variable costs of $30,000 and actual fixed costs of $17,100.

The normal and actual miles logged for each rental unit during the first quarter are as follows:

	Budget	*Luxury*	*Truck*
Normal activity	120,000	100,000	80,000
Actual activity	150,000	110,000	100,000

Required:

1. Compute the predetermined service cost per mile driven.

2. Compute the costs that would be allocated at the end of the quarter for purposes of performance evaluation.

3. Identify the costs of the service center that were not allocated to the three rental divisions. Why were these costs not allocated to the operating units?

P5–6 **Sequential and Direct Methods** Lilly Candies has three producing departments, Mixing, Cooking, and Packaging, and five service departments. The following is the basic information on all departments (bases represent practical annual levels):

	Number of Items Processed	Number of Employees	Direct		
			Square Feet Occupied	Machine Hours	Labor Hours
Cafeteria	300	5	5,000	—	—
Personnel	1,000	10	7,000	—	—
Custodial Services	200	7	2,000	—	—
Maintenance	2,500	15	16,000	—	—
Cost Accounting	—	13	5,000	—	—
Mixing	2,800	20	40,000	4,000	30,000
Cooking	2,700	10	30,000	10,000	20,000
Packaging	3,000	20	20,000	6,000	50,000
Total	12,500	100	125,000	20,000	100,000

The budgeted overhead costs for the department are as follows for the coming year:

	Fixed	Variable	Total
Cafeteria	$ 20,000	$ 40,000	$ 60,000
Personnel	70,000	20,000	90,000
Custodial Services	80,000	—	80,000
Maintenance	100,000	100,000	200,000
Cost Accounting	130,000	16,500	146,500
Mixing	120,000	20,000	140,000
Cooking	60,000	10,000	70,000
Packaging	25,000	40,000	65,000

Required:

1. Allocate the service costs to the producing departments using the direct method.

2. Compute a predetermined fixed overhead rate and a predetermined variable overhead rate. Assume that overhead is applied using direct labor hours for Mixing and Packaging and machine hours for Cooking.

3. Allocate the service costs to the producing departments using the sequential method. (*Hint:* Allocate fixed costs in order of descending magnitude of direct fixed costs. Allocate variable costs in order of descending magnitude of direct variable costs.)

4. Compute predetermined fixed and variable overhead rates based on Requirement 3. Overhead is applied using direct labor hours for Mixing and Packaging and machine hours for Cooking.

5. Assume that the prime costs for a batch of chocolate bars total $60,000. The batch requires 1,000 direct labor hours in Mixing, 1,500 machine hours in Cooking, and 5,000 direct labor hours in Packaging. Assume that the selling price is equal to full manufacturing cost plus 30 percent. Compute the selling price of the batch assuming that costs are allocated using the direct method. Repeat using the sequential method. Comment on the implications of using different allocation methods, as-

suming that a markup of 30 percent is typical for the industry. Which allocation method do you think should be used?

P5–7 **Reciprocal Method; Cost of Operating a Service Department** Watterman Company has two producing departments (Machining and Assembly) and two service departments (Power and Maintenance). The budgeted costs and normal usage are as follows for the coming year:

	Power	Maintenance	Machining	Assembly
Overhead costs[a]	$50,000	$40,000	$120,000	$60,000
Kilowatt hours	—	100,000	300,000	100,000
Machine hours	5,000	—	10,000	5,000

[a]All overhead costs are variable.

The president of Watterman was approached by a local utility company and offered the opportunity to buy power for $0.11 per kilowatt hour. The president has asked you to determine the cost of producing the power internally so that a response to the offer can be made.

Required:

1. Compute the unit cost of kilowatts assuming no interaction exists among the two service departments. Based on this computation, how would you respond to the offer to buy the kilowatts externally?

2. Now use the reciprocal method to compute the cost of operating the Power Department. Divide this total cost by the total kilowatts produced by the Power Department to find a cost per kilowatt hour. Based on this computation, how would you respond to the offer to buy kilowatts externally?

3. Show that the decision associated with the reciprocal method (requirement 2) is correct by following two steps: (a) computing the savings realized if the Power Department is eliminated and (b) computing the cost per kilowatt saved by dividing the total savings by the kilowatts needed if the Power Department is eliminated. (*Hint:* Total savings include the direct costs of the Power Department plus any costs avoided by the Maintenance Department since it no longer needs to serve the Power Department. The total kilowatt hours consumed by the company need to be adjusted since the power needs of the Maintenance Department decrease when they decrease the amount of service they offer.)

P5–8 **Direct Method; Sequential Method; Overhead Rates** Bright, Inc., has two producing departments and four service departments. It currently uses the direct method of service-department cost allocation. Data for the company are as follows:

	Producing Departments		Service Departments			
	PD1	PD2	SD1	SD2	SD3	SD4
Overhead	$183,000	$212,400	$30,000	$35,000	$40,000	$100,000
Square feet	2,000	2,000	400	5,000	600	—
Employees	15	45	—	12	20	3
DLH	30,000	90,000	—	24,000	20,000	6,000
Machine hours	10,000	20,000	—	—	—	—

(continued on next page)

	Original
	Allocation Base
SD1	Machine hours
SD2	Number of employees
SD3	Direct labor hours
SD4	Square feet

Cara James, controller of Bright, Inc., is considering changing to a more accurate method of service department cost allocation. She has discovered the following:

1. SD1 provides its services only to the producing departments.

2. SD2 provides services to both producing and service departments based on the number of employees.

3. SD3 provides 15 percent of its service to SD1 and the remainder to PD1 and PD2 based on direct labor hours.

4. SD4 provides services to all other departments based on square footage.

Cara has decided to rank the service departments in the following order for purposes of cost allocation: SD4, SD2, SD3, SD1.

Required:

1. Allocate service department costs using the direct method and the original allocation bases.

2. Allocate service department costs using the sequential method as outlined by Cara James.

3. Calculate overhead rates for PD1 (based on machine hours) and PD2 (based on direct labor hours) using total departmental overhead costs as determined by the
   a. Direct method
   b. Sequential method

P5–9   **Fixed and Variable Cost Allocation**   Sonora Sam's is a chain of restaurants serving Sonora-style Mexican food in a family-type atmosphere. The chain has grown from one restaurant in 1987 to five restaurants located in west Texas and New Mexico. In 1993, the owner of the company decided to set up an internal accounting department to centralize control of financial information. (Previously, local CPAs handled each restaurant's bookkeeping and financial reporting.) The Accounting Department was opened in January 1993 by renting space adjacent to corporate headquarters in Albuquerque, New Mexico. All restaurants have been supplied with personal computers and modems by which to transfer information to central accounting on a weekly basis.

The Accounting Department has budgeted fixed costs of $64,000 per year. Variable costs are budgeted at $18 per hour. Actual costs in 1993 equaled budgeted costs. Further information is as follows:

| | **Actual Revenues** | | *Actual Hours of Accounting* |
	1992	*1993*	*Used in 1993*
El Paso	$337,500	$390,500	1,475
Albuquerque	450,000	456,000	400

| | Actual Revenues | | Actual Hours of Accounting |
	1992	1993	Used in 1993
Taos	$360,000	$375,000	938
Tucumcari	540,000	550,000	562
Amarillo	562,500	549,000	375

Required:

1. Suppose the total costs of the Accounting Department are allocated on the basis of 1993 sales revenue. How much will be allocated to each restaurant?

2. Suppose that Sonora Sam's views 1992 sales figures as a proxy for budgeted capacity of the restaurants. Thus, fixed accounting center costs are allocated on the basis of 1992 sales, and variable costs are allocated according to 1993 usage times the variable rate. How much Accounting Department cost will be allocated to each restaurant?

3. Comment on the two allocation schemes. Which is better? Explain.

P5–10 **Service Department Cost Allocation; Plant-wide Overhead Rate versus Departmental Rates; Effects on Pricing Decisions** (This problem is an extension of Problem 3–9. All pertinent information is repeated here.) Recall that Alden Peterson, marketing manager for Retlief Company, had been puzzled by the outcome of two recent bids. The company's policy was to bid 150 percent of the full manufacturing cost. One job (labeled Job SS) had been turned down by a prospective customer, who had indicated that the proposed price was $3 per unit higher than the winning bid. A second job (Job TT) had been accepted by a customer, who was amazed that Retlief could offer such favorable terms. This customer revealed that Retlief's price was $43 per unit lower than the next lowest bid.

Alden knew that Retlief Company was more than competitive in terms of cost control. Accordingly, he suspected that the problem was related to cost assignment procedures. Upon investigating, Alden was told that the company used a plant-wide overhead rate based on direct labor hours. The rate was computed at the beginning of the year using budgeted data. Selected budgeted data follow:

	Department A	Department B	Total
Overhead	$500,000	$2,000,000	$2,500,000
Direct labor hours	200,000	50,000	250,000
Machine hours	20,000	120,000	140,000

The above information led to a plant-wide overhead rate of $10 per direct labor hour. In addition, the following specific manufacturing data on Job SS and Job TT were given.

	Job SS		
	Department A	Department B	Total
Direct labor hours	5,000	1,000	6,000
Machine hours	200	500	700
Prime costs	$100,000	$20,000	$120,000
Units produced	14,400	14,400	14,400

	Job TT		
	Department A	*Department B*	*Total*
Direct labor hours	400	600	1,000
Machine hours	200	3,000	3,200
Prime costs	$10,000	$40,000	$50,000
Units produced	1,500	1,500	1,500

This information led to the original bid prices of $18.75 per unit for Job SS and $60 per unit for Job TT.

Then Alden discovered that the overhead costs in Department B were higher than those of Department A because B has more equipment, higher maintenance, higher power consumption, higher depreciation, and higher setup costs. So he tried reworking the two bids by using departmental overhead rates. Department A's overhead rate was $2.50 per direct labor hour; Department B's overhead rate was $16.67 per machine hour. These rates resulted in unit prices of $14.67 for Job SS and $101.01 for Job TT.

Alden still was not satisfied, however. He did some reading on overhead allocation methods and learned that proper service-department cost allocation can lead to more accurate product costs. He decided to create four service departments and recalculate departmental overhead rates. Information on departmental costs and related items follows:

	Maintenance	*Power*	*Setups*	*General Factory*	*Dept. A*	*Dept. B*
Overhead	$500,000	$225,000	$150,000	$625,000	$200,000	$800,000
Maintenance hours	—	1,500	500	—	1,000	7,000
Kilowatt hours	4,500	—	500	15,000	10,000	50,000
DLH	10,000	12,000	6,000	8,000	200,000	50,000
Number of setups	—	—	—	—	400	1600
Square feet	25,000	40,000	5,000	15,000	35,360	94,640

The following allocation bases seemed reasonable:

Service Department	*Allocation Base*
Maintenance	Maintenance hours
Power	Kilowatt hours
Setups	Number of setups
General Factory	Square feet

Required

1. Using the direct method, verify the original departmental overhead rates.
2. Using the sequential method, allocate service department costs to the producing departments. Calculate departmental overhead rates using direct labor hours for Department A and machine hours for Department B. What would the bids for Job SS and Job TT have been if these overhead rates had been in effect?

3. Which method of overhead cost assignment would you recommend to Alden? Why?

4. Suppose that the best competing bid was $4.10 lower than the original bid price (based on a plant-wide rate). Does this affect your recommendation in requirement 3? Explain.

■ MANAGERIAL DECISION CASES

C5–1 **Hospital Setting; Allocation Methods; Unit Cost Determination and Pricing Decisions** Reread the scenario at the beginning of the chapter. As Eric Rose mentally reviewed his meeting with Paula, he realized that the failure of bids could be attributable to inaccurate cost assignments. Because of this possibility, Eric decided to do some additional investigation to see whether the cost-to-charges ratio method of costing services was responsible.

Eric pulled the current year's budgeted data from his files. He found the data presented below. The number of departments and the budget have been reduced for purposes of simplification.

	Service Departments			Revenue Departments	
	Administrative	*Laundry*	*Janitorial*	*Laboratory*	*Nursing*
Overhead	$20,000	$75,000	$50,000	$43,000	$150,000
Square feet	1,000	1,200	500	5,000	20,000
Pounds of laundry	50	200	400	1,000	4,000
Employees	1	4	7	8	20

Service-department costs are allocated using the direct method.

Eric decided to compute the costs of three different lab tests using the cost-to-charges ratio and then recompute them using a more direct method, as Paula suggested. By comparing the unit costs under each approach, he could evaluate the cost-estimating ability of the cost-to-charges ratio. The three tests selected for study were the blood count test (Test B), cholesterol test (Test C), and a chemical blood analysis (Test CB).

After careful observation of the three tests, Eric concluded that the consumption of the resources of the laboratory could be associated with the relative amount of time taken by each test. Based on the amount of time needed to perform each test, Eric developed relative value units (RVUs) and associated the consumption of materials and labor with these units. The RVUs for each test and the cost per RVU for materials and labor are given below.

Test	*RVUs*	*Material per RVU*	*Labor per RVU*
B	1	$2.00	$2.00
C	2	$2.50	$2.00
CB	3	$1.00	$2.00

Eric also concluded that the pool of overhead costs collected within the laboratory should be applied using RVUs (he was convinced that RVU was a good cost driver for overhead). The laboratory's expected RVUs for the year were 22,500. The laboratory usually performs an equal number of the three tests over a year. This year was no exception.

Eric also noted that the hospital usually priced its services so that revenues exceeded costs by a specified percentage. Based on the past total costs of the laboratory, this pricing strategy had led to the following fees for the three blood tests:

	Test B	Test C	Test CB
Fees charged	$5.00	$19.33	$22.00

Required:

1. Allocate the costs of the service departments to the two revenue-producing departments using the direct method.

2. Assume that the three blood tests are the only tests performed in the laboratory. Compute the cost-to-charges ratio (total costs of the laboratory divided by the laboratory's total revenues).

3. Using the cost-to-charges ratio computed in requirement 2, estimate the cost per test for each blood test.

4. Compute the cost per test for each test using RVUs.

5. Which unit cost—the one using the cost-to-charges ratio or the one using RVUs—do you believe is the more accurate? Explain.

6. Assume that Lambert Medical Center has been requested by an HMO to bid on Test CB. Using a 5 percent markup, prepare the bid using the cost computed in requirement 3. Repeat, using the cost prepared in requirement 4. Suppose that anyone who bids $20 or less will win the bid. Discuss the implications that costing accuracy have on the hospital's problems with its bidding practices.

C5–2   **Direct Method; Settlement of a Contract Dispute**   A state government agency contracted with FlyRite Helicopters to provide helicopter services on a requirements contract. After six months, FlyRite discovered that the agency's original estimates of the number of flying hours needed were grossly overstated. FlyRite Helicopters is now making a claim against the state agency for defective specifications. The state has been advised by its legal advisors that its chances in court on this claim would not be strong, and, therefore, an out-of-court settlement is in order. As a result of the legal advice, the state agency has hired a local CPA firm to analyze the claim and prepare a recommendation for an equitable settlement.

The particulars on which the original bid was based are given below. The contract was for three different types of helicopters and had a duration of one year. Thus, the data below reflect the original annual expectations. Also, the costs and activity pertain only to the contract.

	Aircraft Type		
	Hughes 500D	206B Jet Ranger	206L-1 Long Ranger
Flying hours	1,200	1,600	900
Direct costs:			
Fixed:			
Insurance	$32,245	$28,200	$55,870

	Aircraft Type		
	Hughes 500D	*206B Jet Ranger*	*206L-1 Long Ranger*
Lease payments	$31,000	$36,000	$90,000
Pilot salaries	30,000	30,000	30,000
Variable:			
Fuel	$24,648	$30,336	$22,752
Minor servicing	6,000	8,000	4,500
Lease	—	—	72,000

In addition to the direct costs, the following indirect costs were expected:

	Fixed Costs	*Variable Costs*
Maintenance	$ 26,000	$246,667
Hanger rent	18,000	—
General administrative	110,000	—

Maintenance costs and general administrative costs are allocated to each helicopter on the basis of flying hours; hanger rent is allocated on the basis of the number of helicopters. The company has one of each type of aircraft.

During the first six months of the contract, the actual flying hours were as follows:

Type	*Flying Hours*
500D	299
206B	160
L–1	204

The state agency's revised projection of total hours for the year is given below:

Type	*Flying Hours*
500D	450
206B	600
L–1	800

Required:

1. Assume that FlyRite won the contract with a bid of cost plus 15 percent, where cost refers to cost per flying hour. Compute the original bid price per flying hour for each type of helicopter. Next, compute the original expected profit of the contract.

2. Compute the profit (or loss) earned by FlyRite for the first six months of activity. Assume that the planned costs were equal to the actual costs. Also assume that 50 percent of the fixed costs for the year have been incurred. Compute the profit that FlyRite should have earned during the first six months, assuming that 50 percent of the hours originally projected (for each aircraft type) had been flown.

3. Compute the profit (or loss) that the contract would provide FlyRite assuming the original price per flying hour and using the state agency's revised projection of hours needed.

4. Assume that the state has agreed to pay what is necessary so that FlyRite receives the profit originally expected in the contract. This will be accomplished by revising the price paid per flying hour based on the revised estimates of flying hours. What is the new price per flying hour?

CHAPTER 6

Product Costing and Cost Management: The Advanced Manufacturing Environment

■ **LEARNING OBJECTIVES**

After studying Chapter 6, you should be able to

1. Identify some of the major changes in the manufacturing environment that are affecting the practice of cost accounting.

2. Explain why using only unit-based cost drivers to assign overhead may produce distorted product costs.

3. Use unit-based and nonunit-based cost drivers to assign overhead costs to products.

4. Explain why activity-based costing produces more accurate product costs.

5. Identify and define the four major categories of activities associated with activity-based costing.

6. Explain when an activity-based cost system should be used.

7. Explain how JIT manufacturing differs from traditional manufacturing.

8. Describe how JIT manufacturing alters the fundamental cost concepts found in a conventional manufacturing environment.

9. Explain how JIT manufacturing improves product-costing accuracy.

10. Describe the effects JIT manufacturing has on allocations, process costing, and job costing.

11. Describe the accounting flows (backflush costing) for a JIT setting.

12. Define and explain the key terms listed at the end of the chapter.

SCENARIO

Ryan Chesser, president and owner of Sharp Paper, Inc., was reviewing the most recent financial reports. Profits had once again declined. The company had failed to achieve its targeted return for the third consecutive year. The inability of the company to improve its profits frustrated Ryan. After all, Sharp Paper had been a dominant factor in the industry for more than two decades. The company owns three paper mills, which produce coated and uncoated specialty printing papers. Customers have access to a variety of papers differing in finish, color, weight, and packages. More than 400 individual products were marketed by the company.[1]

To ascertain the reasons for the declining fortunes of the company, Ryan had asked his vice-presidents of production (Jeff Clark) and marketing (Jennifer Woodruff) to do some research. Ryan was particularly interested in knowing why the competition was winning bids on some major product lines in spite of aggressive pricing by Sharp. Four weeks after making the assignment, Ryan received the following report:

MEMO

To: Ryan Chesser, President
From: Jeff Clark and Jennifer Woodruff
Subject: Competitive Position of Sharp
Date: February 12, 1992

Our investigation has revealed some rather interesting information—information that we believe can benefit our company. We began by contacting some customers who have switched some of their purchases to competitors. We discovered that the switch usually involved our high-volume products. We have been losing bids on these products even when they are aggressively priced. Often the loss of business was to smaller competitors with less diverse product lines. Their prices were significantly lower than ours, and, in fact, seemed unrealistically low.

At first, we suspected that these businesses were pricing low simply to gain market penetration. However, after investigating in greater depth, it soon became apparent that our competitors were prospering and, in fact, earning a good return.

Our next effort was focused on determining whether competitors were employing a new technology that might provide significant cost advantages. Virtually all our small competitors use the same manufacturing processes that we use. A few of the full-line, larger competitors, however, are using just-in-time (JIT) manufacturing. As nearly as we can determine, this approach to manufacturing involves no new technology but does entail a significant shift in how inputs are organized and used. These JIT manufacturers have not only maintained their market share but also have managed to increase it over the past three years—at our expense.

---

[1]The setting and the issues in this introductory case are based in part on the following three articles: James P. Borden, "Review of Literature on Activity-Based Costing," *Journal of Cost Management for the Manufacturing Industry*, Vol. 4, No. 1 (Spring 1990); John K. Shank and Vijay Govindarajan, "Transaction-Based Costing for the Complex Product Line: A Field Study," *Journal of Cost Management for the Manufacturing Industry*, Vol. 2., No. 2 (Summer 1988), pp. 31–38, and Robin Cooper, "Does Your Company Need a New Cost System?" *Journal of Cost Management for the Manufacturing Industry*, Vol. 1, No. 1 (Spring 1987), pp. 45–49.

Curiously, our low-volume products appear to be the most profitable. In some cases, we are the only company that produces these specialty products. At times, we even receive referrals from some of our competitors. Furthermore, some of our operational managers have urged us to drop some of these low-volume products, arguing that they're more bother than they're worth. Yet these products are being reported as highly profitable. If this is true, why are other paper companies uninterested in competing? And why do our operational managers want to drop profitable lines?

We considered a strategy of emphasizing our low-volume products more and reducing our output of high-volume products. However, when we asked the controller's office to explain why the profit margins of the low-volume products were so much greater, which seems counterintuitive given the special processes and handling required, we did not receive any logical response given our understanding of the production processes and the market. We were even told that we could increase our margin on the low-volume products by increasing prices. Recent price increases were readily accepted by customers—without any complaints.

Given the response of the controller's office and the fact that our production technology and efficiency at least match those of our smaller competitors, we have decided that we may have a major problem with the way we compute the costs of our various products. We should be making a return equal to that of our competitors on our high-volume products. We recommend that a serious evaluation of our costing procedures be conducted.

Given the ground that some of the larger competitors have gained by using JIT manufacturing, we also recommend that we hire a consultant to explore the feasibility of implementing such a system for our company. JIT manufacturing offers some potential to enhance our ability to compete.

THE LIMITATIONS OF CONVENTIONAL PRODUCT COSTING

The two vice-presidents of Sharp Paper identified a number of symptoms that signaled problems with the company's cost system. For example, the prices of the paper company's high-volume products are significantly higher than those of smaller, prosperous competitors. Even aggressive pricing on bids is failing to win business. Yet the only difference between Sharp and these competitors seems to be the range of products produced. The company's low-volume specialty products are apparently quite profitable—in spite of the special processes and handling they require. In fact, the company apparently has a highly profitable niche all to itself—it is even receiving referrals from competitors. Also, the accounting system cannot explain the differences in profitability between the low-volume and high-volume products. Surprisingly, customers are not complaining about price increases on low-volume products. Could this be because the company is offering a deal too good to be true? Finally, operational managers want to drop seemingly profitable product lines. All these factors combine to raise questions concerning the company's costing practices. These symptoms of an outdated cost system, along with a few others not mentioned in the memo, are listed in Exhibit 6-1.[2]

The vice-presidents' report also mentioned JIT manufacturing. Other large paper manufacturers with full product lines are apparently adopting this new approach to manufacturing. Over the past ten to twenty years, a revolution has taken place in manufacturing. Innovative practices developed by the Japanese—total quality control and JIT purchasing and manufacturing—have significantly increased the competitive pressures felt by U.S. firms. Other changes, such as computer-integrated manufacturing systems, which have increased product complexity, and deregulation of service industries, have also changed the competitive environment. Thus, this new environment, referred to as the ***advanced manufacturing environment***, is characterized by firms engaged in intense competition (usually on a worldwide level), continuous improvement, total quality control, and sophisticated technology.

As firms adopt new manufacturing strategies to achieve competitive excellence, their accounting systems must also change to keep pace. Specifically, the need for more accurate product costs has forced many companies to take a serious look at their costing procedures. Cost systems that worked reasonably well in the past may no longer be acceptable. Moreover, some of the changes have also altered the nature and mix of manufacturing costs. The advanced manufacturing environment simply demands a different approach to product costing, inventory management, quality management, and so on.

advanced manufacturing environment

EXHIBIT 6-1
Symptoms of an Outdated Cost System

1. The outcome of bids is difficult to explain.
2. Competitors' prices appear unrealistically low.
3. Products that are difficult to produce show high profits.
4. Operational managers want to drop products that appear profitable.
5. Profit margins are hard to explain.
6. The company has a highly profitable niche all to itself.
7. Customers do not complain about price increases.
8. The accounting department spends a lot of time on special projects.
9. Some departments are using their own accounting system.
10. Product costs change because of changes in financial reporting regulations.

---

[2]The list of warning signals is based on the following article: Robin Cooper, "You Need a New Cost System When. . . .," *Harvard Business Review* (January-February, 1989), pp. 77–82.

Overhead Assignment: The Source of the Problem

Sharp Paper, Inc. (unfortunately, like many other companies), is trying to operate in a highly competitive environment with an outmoded cost system, one that evidently is not producing the information management needs to make sound decisions. Over time, Sharp has added product lines until it is now producing more than 400 paper products. While having a full line of products may be a sound marketing strategy, the increased complexity apparently has made it much more difficult to determine accurate unit costs. If the vice-presidents are right that products are being costed incorrectly, that could explain the problems the company is currently having in marketing its products. For example, if the unit costs of the high-volume products are overstated, this could lead to cost-plus prices or bids that are out of line with competitors. Similarly, if the low-volume products are undercosted, this could explain their apparent profitability.

If product costs are being distorted by Sharp's cost system, there must be a reason. Assuming that Sharp is using a traditional cost system such as job-order costing or process costing or some blend of the two, why would this system fail to determine product costs accurately? In all likelihood, the problem is not with assigning the costs of direct labor or direct materials. These prime costs are traceable to individual products, and most traditional cost systems are designed to ensure that this tracing takes place. Assigning overhead costs to individual products, however, is another matter. Using the conventional, unit-based methods to assign overhead costs to products can produce distorted product costs.

Overhead Costing: A Single-Product Setting

The accuracy of unit-based overhead cost assignment becomes an issue only when multiple products are manufactured in a single facility. If only a single product is produced, all overhead costs are caused by it and traceable to it. The overhead cost per unit is simply the total overhead for the year divided by the number of units produced. Accuracy is not an issue. The timing of the computation may be an issue, however; because of this, a predetermined overhead rate is usually required. The cost calculation for a single-product setting is illustrated in Exhibit 6–2.

Certainly no one would question that the cost of manufacturing the product illustrated in Exhibit 6–2 is $10 per unit. All manufacturing costs were incurred specifically to make this product. Thus, one way to ensure product-costing accuracy is to focus on producing one product. For this reason, some multiple-product firms choose to dedicate plants to the manufacture of a single product.

Such focusing may be the reason that small producers are able to compete successfully with Sharp. By focusing on only one or a few similar products, the small producers are able to calculate the cost of manufacturing their products (Sharp's high-volume products) more accurately and price them more effectively. This observation assumes that Sharp's cost system is distorting the cost of the high-volume products.

EXHIBIT 6-2
Unit Cost Computation: Single Product

	Manufacturing Costs	Units Produced	Unit Cost
Direct materials	$ 600,000	100,000	$ 6
Direct labor	100,000	100,000	1
Overhead	300,000	100,000	3
Total	$1,000,000	100,000	$10

Overhead Costing: Multiple-Product Setting with Unit-Based Cost Drivers

cost drivers

In a multiple-product setting, overhead costs are caused jointly by all products. The problem now becomes one of identifying the amount of overhead that each product consumes or causes. This is accomplished by searching for **cost drivers**, causal factors that explain the consumption of overhead.

unit-based (volume-related) cost drivers

In a conventional setting, it is normally assumed that overhead consumption is highly correlated with the number of units produced, measured in terms of direct labor hours, machine hours, or material dollars. These **unit-based (volume-related) cost drivers** assign overhead to products through the use of either plant-wide or departmental rates.

To illustrate the limitation of this conventional approach, assume that Sharp has a plant that produces two products: white and blue boxwrap. Product costing data are given in Exhibit 6-3 (p. 240). The units are three-ream rolls. Because the quantity of blue boxwrap produced is five times greater than that of white boxwrap, we can label white boxwrap a low-volume product and blue boxwrap a high-volume product.

For simplicity, only four types of overhead costs are assumed: setup, inspection, power, and fringe benefits for direct labor. These overhead costs are allocated to the two production departments using the direct method. Assume that the four service centers do not interact. Setup costs are allocated based on the number of production runs handled by each department. Since the number is identical, each department receives 50 percent of the total setup costs. Inspection costs are allocated by the number of inspection hours used by each department. Power costs are allocated in proportion to the kilowatt hours used by each department. Finally, fringe benefit costs are allocated in proportion to the direct hours used.

Plant-Wide Overhead Rate A common method to assign overhead to products is to compute a plant-wide rate using a unit-based cost driver. This approach assumes that all overhead cost variation can be explained by one cost driver. Assume that machine hours are chosen. (Direct labor hours would

EXHIBIT 6–3
Product Costing Data

	White Boxwrap	Blue Boxwrap	Total
Units produced per year	20,000	100,000	—
Prime costs	$50,000	$250,000	$300,000
Direct labor hours	20,000	100,000	120,000
Machine hours	10,000	50,000	60,000
Production runs	20	30	50
Inspection hours	800	1,200	2,000

	Departmental Data		
	Department 1	Department 2	Total
Direct labor hours:			
White boxwrap	4,000	16,000	20,000
Blue boxwrap	76,000	24,000	100,000
Total	80,000	40,000	120,000
Machine hours:			
White boxwrap	4,000	6,000	10,000
Blue boxwrap	16,000	34,000	50,000
Total	20,000	40,000	60,000
Overhead costs:			
Setup costs	$ 44,000	$ 44,000	$ 88,000
Inspection costs	37,000	37,000	74,000
Power	14,000	70,000	84,000
Direct labor fringe benefits	52,000	26,000	78,000
Total	$147,000	$177,000	$324,000

give the same allocation in this example since labor hours are used in the same proportion as machine hours.) The total overhead for the plant is $324,000, the sum of the overhead for each department ($147,000 + $177,000). Dividing the total overhead by the total machine hours yields the following overhead rate:

$$\text{Plant-wide rate} = \$324,000/60,000$$
$$= \$5.40/\text{machine hour}$$

Using this rate and other information from Exhibit 6–3, the unit cost for each product can be calculated (see Exhibit 6–4).

Departmental Rates   Based on the distribution of labor hours and machine hours in Exhibit 6–3, Department 1 is labor intensive and Department 2 machine intensive. Moreover, the overhead costs of Department 1 are less than those of Department 2. Based on these observations, it could be argued

EXHIBIT 6–4
Unit Cost Computation: Plant-Wide Rate

White Boxwrap

Prime costs ($50,000/20,000)	$2.50
Overhead costs ($5.40 × 10,000/20,000)	2.70
Unit cost	$5.20

Blue Boxwrap

Prime costs ($250,000/100,000)	$2.50
Overhead cost ($5.40 × 50,000/100,000)	2.70
Unit cost	$5.20

that departmental overhead rates would reflect the consumption of overhead better than a plant-wide rate. If true, product costs would be more accurate. This approach would yield the following departmental rates, using direct labor hours for Department 1 and machine hours for Department 2:

$$\text{Department 1 rate} = \$147,000/80,000$$
$$= \$1.84/\text{labor hour}$$
$$\text{Department 2 rate} = \$177,000/40,000$$
$$= \$4.43/\text{machine hour}$$

Using these rates and the data from Exhibit 6–3, the computation of the unit costs for each product is shown in Exhibit 6–5.

EXHIBIT 6–5
Unit Cost Computation: Departmental Rates

White Boxwrap

Prime costs ($50,000/20,000)	$2.50
Overhead costs [($1.84 × 4,000) + ($4.43 × 6,000)]/20,000	1.70
Unit cost	$4.20

Blue Boxwrap

Prime costs ($250,000/100,000)	$2.50
Overhead costs [($1.84 × 76,000) + ($4.43 × 34,000)]/100,000	2.90
Unit cost	$5.40

Problems with Costing Accuracy   The accuracy of the overhead cost assignment can be challenged regardless of whether the plant-wide or departmental rates are used. The main problem with either procedure is the assumption that machine hours or direct labor hours drive or cause all overhead costs.

From Exhibit 6–3, we know that blue boxwrap—with five times the volume of white boxwrap—uses five times the machine hours and direct labor hours. Thus, if a plant-wide rate is used, blue boxwrap will receive five times more overhead cost. But is this reasonable? Do unit-based cost drivers explain the consumption of all overhead? Does a product's consumption of overhead increase in direct proportion to the number of units produced?

Examination of the data in Exhibit 6–3 suggests that a significant portion of overhead costs is not driven or caused by the units produced. For example, setup costs are probably related to the number of production runs and inspection costs to the number of hours of inspection. Notice that blue boxwrap only has 1.5 times as many runs as the white boxwrap (30/20) and only 1.5 times as many inspection hours (1,200/800). Use of a unit-based cost driver (machine hours or labor hours) and a plant-wide rate assigns five times more overhead to the blue boxwrap than to the white. For inspection and setup costs, then, blue boxwrap is overcosted and the white is undercosted.[3]

The problem is only aggravated when departmental rates are used. Blue boxwrap consumes 19 times as many direct labor hours (76,000/4,000) as white boxwrap and 5.67 times as many machine hours (34,000/6,000). Thus, blue boxwrap receives 19 times more overhead from Department 1 and 5.67 times more overhead from Department 2. As Exhibit 6–5 shows, with departmental rates, the unit cost of the white boxwrap *decreases* to $4.20, and the unit cost of the blue boxwrap *increases* to $5.40. This change is in the wrong direction, which emphasizes the failure of unit-based cost drivers to reflect accurately each product's consumption of setup and inspection costs.

Why Unit-Based Cost Drivers Fail

At least two major factors impair the ability of a unit-based cost driver to assign overhead costs accurately: (1) the proportion of nonunit-related overhead costs to total overhead costs and (2) the degree of product diversity.[4]

Nonunit-Related Overhead Costs   In the example under discussion, there are four overhead activities: inspection, setup, fringe benefits, and power. Two,

---

[3]A more detailed discussion of the limitations of conventional product costing can be found in Robin Cooper, "The Rise of Activity-Based Costing—Part One: What Is an Activity-Based Cost System?" *Journal of Cost Management for the Manufacturing Industry*, Vol. 2, No. 2 (Summer 1988), pp. 45–54.

[4]Robin Cooper, "The Rise of Activity Costing—Part Three: How Many Cost Drivers Do You Need, and How Do You Select Them?" *Journal of Cost Management for the Manufacturing Industry*, Vol. 2, No. 4 (Winter 1989), pp. 34–46.

nonunit-based cost drivers

fringe benefits and power, are related to the number of units produced. As has already been shown, however, inspection and setup costs are not driven by the number of units produced. Setup costs, for example, are a function of the number of runs, a nonunit-based cost driver. **Nonunit-based cost drivers** are factors, other than the number of units produced, that drive costs. Thus, unit-based cost drivers cannot assign these costs accurately to products.

Using only unit-based cost drivers to assign nonunit-related overhead costs can create distorted product costs. The severity of this distortion depends on what proportion of total overhead costs these nonunit-based costs represent. For our example, setup costs and inspection costs represent a substantial share—50 percent—of total overhead ($162,000/$324,000). The percentage reflected by the simple example of Sharp Paper is representative of what can happen in real manufacturing environments. Schrader Bellows and John Deere Component Works, for example, experienced nonunit-based overhead cost ratios of about 50 percent and 40 percent, respectively.[5] This suggests that some care should be exercised in assigning nonunit-based overhead costs. If nonunit-based overhead costs are only a small percentage of total overhead costs, the distortion of product costs would be quite small. In such a case, the use of unit-based cost drivers might be acceptable.

Product Diversity When products consume overhead activities in different proportions, a firm has **product diversity**. There are several reasons that products might consume overhead in different proportions. For example, differences in product size, product complexity, setup time, and size of batches all can cause products to consume overhead at different rates. Regardless of the nature of the product diversity, product cost will be distorted whenever the quantity of unit-based input that a product consumes does not vary in direct proportion to the quantity consumed of nonunit-based inputs.[6] To illustrate, the proportion of all overhead activities consumed by both blue and white box-wrap is computed and displayed in Exhibit 6–6 (p. 244). The proportion of each activity consumed by a product is defined as the *consumption ratio*. If the quantity of the unit-based inputs consumed had varied in direct proportion to the quantity of nonunit-based inputs consumed, then the consumption ratios would have been identical. As you can see from the exhibit, the consumption ratios for these two products differ for the unit-based and nonunit-based inputs.

Since the nonunit-based overhead costs are a significant proportion of total overhead and the consumption ratios differ between unit-based and nonunit-based input categories, product costs can be distorted if a unit-based

product diversity

consumption ratio

---

[5]See Robin Cooper, "Cost Classification in Unit-Based and Activity-Based Manufacturing Cost Systems," *Journal of Cost Management for the Manufacturing Industry* (Fall 1990), pp. 4–14.

[6]Robin Cooper, "The Rise of Activity-Based Costing—Part Two: When Do I Need an Activity-Based Cost System? *Journal of Cost Management for the Manufacturing Industry*," Vol. 2, No. 3 (Fall 1988).

EXHIBIT 6-6
Product Diversity: Proportions of Consumption

Overhead Activity	White Boxwrap	Blue Boxwrap	Consumption Measure
Setups	0.40[a]	0.60[a]	Production runs
Inspection	0.40[b]	0.60[b]	Inspection hours
Power	0.17[c]	0.83[c]	Machine hours
Fringe Benefits	0.17[d]	0.83[d]	Direct labor hours

[a]20/50 (white) and 30/50 (blue)
[b]800/2,000 (white) and 1,200/2,000 (blue)
[c]10,000/60,000 (white) and 50,000/60,000 (blue)
[d]20,000/120,000 (white) and 100,000/120,000 (blue)

cost driver is used. The solution to this costing problem is to use an activity-based costing approach.

ACTIVITY-BASED PRODUCT COSTING

activity-based cost
(ABC) system

An **activity-based cost (ABC) system** is one that first traces costs to activities and then to products. Conventional product costing also involves two stages, but in the first stage, costs are traced not to activities but to an organizational unit such as the plant or departments. In both conventional and activity-based costing, the second stage consists of tracing costs to the product. The principal computational difference between the two methods is the number of cost drivers used. Activity-based costing uses a much larger number of cost drivers than the one or two unit-based cost drivers typical in a conventional system. As a result, this method has increased accuracy. From a managerial perspective, however, an ABC system offers more than just accurate product cost information. It also provides information about the cost of activities. Knowing the cost of activities allows managers to focus on those activities that might offer opportunities for cost savings—provided they are simplified, performed more efficiently, eliminated, and so on. Thus, in designing an ABC system, the first stage of product costing is an extremely important step.

First-Stage Procedure

In the first stage of activity-based costing, activities are identified and the costs of overhead activities are divided into homogeneous cost pools.[7] Activ-

---

[7]This definition of the first stage in an activity-based cost system is found in H. Thomas Johnson and Robert S. Kaplan, *Relevance Lost: The Rise and Fall of Management Accounting* (Boston: Harvard Business Press, 1987), Chapter 10. A more detailed description of both the first-stage and second-

ities are classified into categories that have an easy and clear physical interpretation and that correspond to manageable segments of the production process. Costs are associated with each of these segments. Next, homogeneous cost pools are defined. A **homogeneous cost pool** is a collection of overhead costs that are logically related to the tasks being performed and for which cost variations can be explained by a single cost driver. Thus, to be included in a homogeneous cost pool, overhead activities must be logically related and have the same consumption ratios for all products. Having the same consumption ratio implies the existence of a cost driver. The cost driver, of course, must be measurable so that overhead can be applied to products. Once a cost pool is defined, the cost per unit of the cost driver is computed for that pool. This is called the *pool rate*. Computation of the pool rate completes the first stage. Thus, the first stage produces four outcomes: (1) classification of activities, (2) association of costs with activities, (3) a set of homogeneous cost pools, and (4) a pool rate.

homogeneous cost pool

To illustrate this process, consider once again the Sharp Paper example. The four overhead activities can be classified into two categories: setup and inspection in one category and fringe benefits and power in a second category. Setup activities and inspection activities both occur each time a batch of products is produced. Thus, these two activities are logically related by the more general batch-level production activity. The costs of setup and inspection are, of course, associated with the batch-level activity. Direct labor and power activities occur each time a unit of product is produced. Thus, these two activities are logically related by the more general activity of producing a unit of product, and the costs of power and fringe benefits are associated with this unit-level activity. Finally, we can classify inspection costs and setup costs into one homogeneous cost pool, and fringe benefits and power costs into a second because the consumption ratios are the same for each set of activities (see Exhibit 6–6). For the first cost pool, the number of production runs or inspection hours could be the cost driver. Since the two cost drivers are perfectly correlated, they will assign the same amount of overhead to both products. For the second pool, machine hours or direct labor hours could be selected as the cost driver.

Assume for purposes of illustration that the number of production runs and machine hours are the cost drivers chosen. Using data from Exhibit 6–3, the first-stage outcomes are illustrated in Exhibit 6–7 (p. 246).

Second-Stage Procedure

In the second stage, the costs of each overhead pool are traced to products. This is done using the pool rate computed in the first stage and the measure of the amount of resources consumed by each product. This measure is sim-

stage procedures is found in the following three sources: Robin Cooper, "The Two-Stage Procedure in Cost Accounting: Part One," *Journal of Cost Management* (Summer 1987), pp. 43–51 and "The Two-Stage Procedure in Cost Accounting—Part Two," *Journal of Cost Management* (Fall 1987), pp. 39–45; and George J. Beaujon and Vinod R. Singhal, "Understanding the Activity Costs in an Activity-Based Cost System," *Journal of Cost Management* (Spring 1990), pp. 51–72. Most of the discussion of the two stages of activity-based costing is based on these four sources.

EXHIBIT 6–7
First-Stage Procedure: Activity-Based Costing

Pool 1:	
Setup costs	$ 88,000
Inspection costs	74,000
Total costs	$162,000
Production runs	50
Pool rate (Cost per run)	$ 3,240
Pool 2:	
Power cost	$ 84,000
Direct labor fringe benefits	78,000
Total costs	$162,000
Machine hours	60,000
Pool rate (cost per machine hour)	$2.70

ply the quantity of the cost driver used by each product. In our example, that would be the number of production runs and machine hours used by each boxwrap. Thus, the overhead assigned from each cost pool to each product is computed as follows:

Applied overhead = Pool rate × Cost driver units used

To illustrate, consider the assignment of costs from the first overhead pool to white boxwrap. From Exhibit 6–7, we know that the rate for this pool is $3,240 per production run. We also know from Exhibit 6–3 that the white wrap uses twenty production runs. Thus, the overhead assigned to white wrap from the first cost pool is $64,800 ($3,240 × 20 runs). Similar assignments would be made for the other cost pool and for the other product.

The total overhead cost per unit of product is obtained by first tracing the overhead costs from the pools to the individual products. This total is then divided by the number of units produced. The result is the unit overhead cost. Adding the per-unit overhead cost to the per-unit prime cost yields the manufacturing cost per unit. In Exhibit 6–8, the manufacturing cost per unit is computed using activity-based costing.

Comparison of Product Costs

In Exhibit 6–9, the unit cost from activity-based costing is compared with the unit costs produced by conventional costing using either a plant-wide or departmental rate. This comparison clearly illustrates the effects of using only unit-based cost drivers to assign overhead costs. The activity-based cost re-

EXHIBIT 6-8
Unit Costs: Activity-Based Costing

White Boxwrap		
Overhead:		
Pool 1: $3,240 × 20 runs	$64,800	
Pool 2: $2.70 × 10,000 mhrs	27,000	
Total overhead costs		$ 91,800
Prime costs		50,000
Total manufacturing costs		$141,800
Units produced		20,000
Unit cost		$7.09

Blue Boxwrap		
Overhead:		
Pool 1: $3,240 × 30 runs	$ 97,200	
Pool 2: $2.70 × 50,000 mhrs	135,000	
Total overhead costs		$232,200
Prime costs		250,000
Total manufacturing costs		$482,200
Units produced		100,000
Unit cost		$4.82

EXHIBIT 6-9
Comparison of Unit Costs

	White Boxwrap	Blue Boxwrap	Source
Activity-based cost	$7.09	$4.82	Exhibit 6-8
Conventional:			
Plant-wide rate	5.20	5.20	Exhibit 6-4
Departmental rate	4.20	5.40	Exhibit 6-5

flects the correct pattern of overhead consumption and is, therefore, the most accurate of the three costs shown in Exhibit 6-9. Activity-based product costing reveals that the conventional method undercosts the white boxwrap significantly and overcosts the blue boxwrap.

Using only unit-based cost drivers can lead to one product subsidizing another. This subsidy could create the appearance that one group of products is highly profitable and adversely impacts the pricing and competitiveness of another group of products. This seems to be one of the problems facing Sharp Paper. In a highly competitive environment, accurate cost information is critical for sound planning and decision making.

Activity Identification and Classification

In describing activity costing, we have mentioned that activity identification is a critical part of the process. The general nature of this process has been described in our discussion of the first stage of activity-based costing and has been illustrated with the simple Sharp Paper example. However, to avoid confusing the basic concepts, we avoided any detailed discussion of activity identification and classification. We now turn to a more complete description of this important phase in the first-stage development of ABC.

As a first step in identifying activities, broad activity categories or segments of the production process are defined and costs are associated with these broadly defined activities. Activities are classified into one of four activity categories: (1) unit-level activities, (2) batch-level activities, (3) product-level activities, and (4) facility-level activities.[8] **Unit-level activities** are those that are performed each time a unit is produced. For example, power and machine hours are used each time a unit is produced. Direct materials and direct labor activities are also unit-level activities, even though they are not overhead costs. **Batch-level activities** are those that are performed each time a batch of products is produced. The costs of batch-level activities vary with the number of batches but are fixed with respect to the number of units in each batch. Setups, inspections, production scheduling, and material handling are examples of batch-level activities. **Product-sustaining activities** are those that are performed as needed to support the various products produced by a company. These activities consume inputs that develop products or allow products to be produced and sold. Engineering changes, maintenance of equipment, and expediting are examples of product-level activities. Sharp Paper example had none of these activities, although in a more realistic setting, we would expect their presence. **Facility-level activities** are those that sustain a factory's general manufacturing process. Examples include plant management, landscaping, maintenance, security, property taxes, and plant depreciation.

unit-level activities

batch-level activities

product-sustaining activities

facility-level activities

Cost Assignment   After classifying activities into one of the four categories, the costs associated with the first three categories are assigned to products, using cost drivers that reflect the cause-and-effect relationship between ac-

---

[8]This classification and the associated definitions are taken from Robin Cooper, "Cost Classification in Unit-Based and Activity-Based Manufacturing Cost Systems."

tivity consumption and cost. Generally, this cost assignment follows the pattern illustrated by the Sharp Paper example; however, in a more complicated setting, there may be more than one cost pool for each of the general activity categories. For example, the unit-level category could have labor-related and material-related overhead pools in addition to a machine-related overhead pool.

The fourth category, facility-level activities, poses a problem for the ABC philosophy of tracing costs to products. Tracing activity costs to individual products depends on the ability to identify the amount of each activity consumed by a product. Facility-level activities (and their costs) are common to a variety of products, and it is not possible to identify individual products that consume these activities. A pure ABC system, therefore, would not assign these costs to products. They would be treated as period costs. In effect, these costs are fixed costs—costs that are not driven by any of the cost drivers found in any of the first three categories. In practice, companies adopting ABC systems usually implement a full-costing approach and allocate these facility-level costs to individual products.[9] Unit-level, batch-level, or product-sustaining cost drivers are often used for the allocation. As a practical matter, assigning these costs may not significantly distort product costs because they are likely to be small relative to the total costs that are appropriately traced to individual products.[10]

To illustrate this approach, assume that a company has two products: alternators and regulators. The overhead activities, costs, cost drivers, and pool rates are given in Exhibit 6–10 (p. 250). Using the information provided in Exhibit 6–10, the computation of the unit overhead cost for each product is shown in Exhibit 6–11 (p. 251). The facility-level costs are assigned to the products using direct labor dollars. The unit overhead cost is the sum of the unit-level, batch-level, product-level, and facility-level costs. In reporting unit overhead costs, it is recommended that the product-cost categories be reported separately, as illustrated in Exhibit 6–11. In this way, the facility-level component can be excluded if desired. Furthermore, it emphasizes the fact that only the unit-level costs vary as the number of units change. This last point is an important issue. Batch-level and product-level costs vary in proportion to factors other than changes in the number of units (they are assigned using nonunit-based cost drivers). Assigning these costs to units of product, however, does not convert them into unit-based variable costs. A diagram depicting the hierarchial approach to activity-based costing is given in Exhibit 6–12, p. 252 (for the example described in Exhibits 6–10 and 6–11).

---

[9]A study of thirty-one companies and fifty-one cost systems revealed that all companies using an ABC system allocated facility-level costs to products. See Robin Cooper, "Cost Classification in Unit-Based and Activity-Based Manufacturing Systems."

[10]At least this appears to be the experience of General Motors based on its implementation of an ABC system. See Beaujon and Singhal, "Understanding the Activity Costs in an Activity-Based Cost System," pp. 51–72.

EXHIBIT 6–10
Activity Costing Data

Overhead activities and costs:
Unit-level activities:
   Material-related overhead $300,000
   Labor-related overhead   160,000
                                 $ 460,000

Batch-level activities:
   Material handling $120,000
   Setups   180,000
                                    300,000

Product-level activities:
   Engineering   160,000
Facility-level activities:
   Supervision $ 60,000
   Depreciation   20,000
                                     80,000
     Total overhead cost $1,000,000

Cost drivers:	Regulators	Generators	Total
Units produced	100,000	200,000	—
Direct labor dollars	$250,000	$1,350,000	$1,600,000
Direct material dollars	$200,000	$1,000,000	$1,200,000
Number of material moves	600	400	1,000
Number of setups	200	200	400
Number of engineering orders	100	60	160

Pool rates:

Unit-level pools:
Material-related overhead/Direct material dollars:
  $300,000/$1,200,000 = $0.25/direct material dollar
Labor-related overhead/Direct labor dollars
  $160,000/$1,600,000 = $0.10/direct labor dollar

Batch-level pools:
Material handling overhead/Number of moves
  $120,000/1,000 = $120/move
Setup overhead/Number of setups
  $180,000/400 = $450/setup

Product-level pools:
Engineering overhead/Number of orders
  $160,000/160 = $1,000/order

Facility-level pools:
Facility overhead/Direct labor dollars
  $80,000/$1,600,000 = $0.05/direct labor dollar

EXHIBIT 6-11
Unit Overhead Computation

	Regulators	Generators
Unit-level activities:		
Material-related overhead:		
(0.25 × $200,000)/100,000	$0.50	
(0.25 × $1,000,000)/200,000		$1.25
Labor-related overhead:		
(0.10 × $250,000)/100,000	0.25	
(0.10 × $1,350,000)/200,000		0.68
Batch-level activities:		
Material-handling overhead:		
($120 × 600 moves)/100,000	0.72	
($120 × 400 moves)/200,000		0.24
Setup overhead:		
($450 × 200 setups)/100,000	0.90	
($450 × 200 setups)/200,000		0.45
Product-level activities:		
Engineering overhead:		
($1,000 × 100 orders)/100,000	1.00	
($1,000 × 60 orders)/200,000		0.30
Facility-level activities:		
General overhead:		
(0.05 × $250,000)/100,000	0.13	
(0.05 × $1,350,000)/200,000		0.34
Total unit overhead cost	$3.50	$3.26

Comparison with Conventional Costing   The hierarchial classification of activities allows us to illustrate the fundamental differences between ABC and conventional cost systems. In a conventional system, overhead is assumed to be driven only by unit-based cost drivers. Thus, in a conventional system, the costs in the batch-level, product-level, and facility-level categories are fixed costs—costs that do not vary as production volume changes. Unit-based cost systems allocate fixed overhead to individual products and then add the overhead that varies with the number of units produced (variable overhead). From the perspective of activity-based costing, the variable overhead is appropriately traced to individual products. The costs driven by unit-based cost drivers are the costs that traditionally have been labeled as variable overhead. Allocation of fixed overhead using unit-based cost drivers can be arbitrary, however, and may not reflect the activities actually being consumed by the products.

ABC systems improve product-costing accuracy by recognizing that many of the so-called fixed overhead costs vary in proportion to changes

EXHIBIT 6–12
Hierarchical Nature of Activity-Based Costing

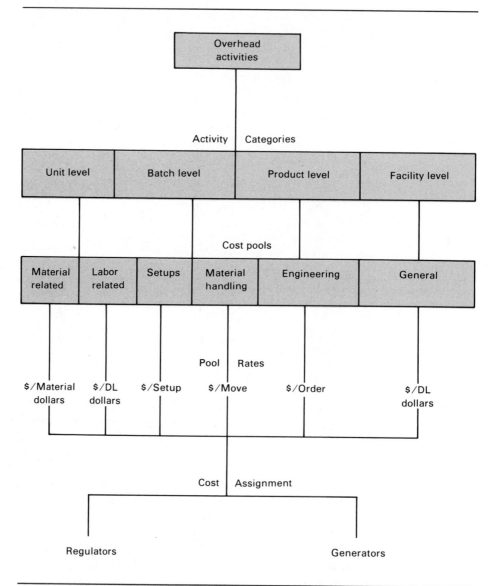

other than production volume. The result of this insight is the addition of two new categories of nonunit-based cost drivers: batch level and product level. By understanding what causes these costs, they can be traced to individual products. This cause-and-effect relationship allows managers to improve product-costing accuracy, which can significantly improve decision making. Additionally, this large pool of fixed overhead costs is no longer so mysterious. Knowing the underlying behavior of many of these costs allows managers to exert more control over the activities that cause the costs.

The Choice of Cost Drivers

At least two major factors should be considered in selecting cost drivers: (1) the cost of measurement and (2) the degree of correlation between the cost driver and the actual consumption of overhead.[11]

The Cost of Measurement In an activity-based cost system, a large number of cost drivers can be selected and used. Accordingly, where possible, it is important to select cost drivers that use information that is readily available. Information that is not available in the existing system must be produced, and this production will increase the cost of the firm's information system. A homogeneous cost pool could offer a number of possible cost drivers. For this situation, any cost driver that can be used with existing information should be chosen. This choice minimizes the costs of measurement.

In the Sharp Paper example, for instance, inspection and setup costs were placed in the same cost pool, giving the choice of using either inspection hours or number of production runs as the cost driver. If the inspection hours and runs used by the two products are already being collected by the company's information system, then which is chosen is unimportant. Assume, however, that inspection hours by product are not tracked, but data for production runs are available. In this case, production runs should be chosen as the cost driver, avoiding the need to produce any additional information.

Indirect Measures and the Degree of Correlation The existing information structure can be exploited in another way to minimize the costs of obtaining cost driver quantities. It is sometimes possible to replace a cost driver that directly measures the consumption of an activity with a cost driver that indirectly measures that consumption. For example, inspection hours could be replaced by the actual number of inspections associated with each product; this number is more likely to be known. This replacement works, of course, only if hours used per inspection are approximately equal for each product.

A list of potential cost drivers is given in Exhibit 6–13. Cost drivers that indirectly measure the consumption of an activity usually measure the number of transactions associated with that activity. Remember that it is possible to replace a cost driver that directly measures consumption with one that only indirectly measures it without loss of accuracy, provided that the quantities of activity consumed per transaction are approximately equal for each product. In such a case, the indirect cost driver has a high correlation and can be used.

---

[11]A third factor, behavioral effects, has also been mentioned by Robin Cooper. However, discussion of this factor is reserved for Chapter 18, which discusses planning and control in the new manufacturing environment. See Robin Cooper, "Activity-Based Costing—Part Three."

EXHIBIT 6–13
Potential Cost Drivers

Number of setups	Number of direct labor hours
Number of material moves	Number of vendors
Number of units reworked	Number of subassemblies
Number of orders placed	Number of labor transactions
Number of orders received	Number of units scrapped
Number of inspections	Number of parts
Number of schedule changes	Number of machine hours

When to Use an ABC System

An ABC system offers significant benefits, including the following: greater product-costing accuracy, improved decision making, enhanced strategic planning, and better ability to manage activities. These benefits, however, are not obtained without costs. An ABC system is more complex, and it requires a significant increase in measurement activity—and measurement can be costly. Although each manager will have to assess the benefits and costs associated with implementing an ABC system, there are some reasonably good guidelines that can be followed.

There are two fundamental requirements that must be met before an ABC system is even considered as a possibility. First, the nonunit-based costs should be a significant percentage of total overhead costs. If they are immaterial, then it simply doesn't matter how they are allocated to individual products. Second, the consumption ratios of unit-based and nonunit-based activities must differ. If products consume all overhead activities in roughly the same ratios, then it doesn't matter if unit-based cost drivers are used to allocate all overhead costs to individual products. The same cost assignment will be produced by either a conventional or an ABC system. Thus, firms with product homogeneity (low product diversity) may be able to use a conventional system without any problems.

Assuming that the nonunit-based costs are significant and that product diversity is high, should a manager implement an ABC system? Not necessarily. In deciding whether to implement an ABC system, a manager must assess the tradeoff between the cost of measurement and the cost of errors.[12] **measurement costs** **Measurement costs** are the costs associated with the measurements required **error costs** by the cost system. **Error costs** are the costs associated with making poor **optimal cost system** decisions based on inaccurate product costs. An **optimal cost system** is the one that minimizes the sum of measurement costs and error costs. Note,

---

[12]The discussion of these issues is based on the following article: Robin Cooper, "The Rise of Activity-Based Costing—Part Two: When Do I Need an Activity-Based Cost System?" pp. 41–48.

however, that the two costs conflict. More complex cost systems produce lower error costs but have higher measurement costs. This tradeoff is illustrated graphically in Exhibit 6–14. The message is clear. For some organizations, the optimal cost system may not be an ABC system even though it is a more accurate system. Depending on the tradeoffs, the optimal cost system may very well be a simpler, traditional, unit-based system. This could explain, in part, why most firms still maintain a conventional system.

There are, however, some changes that are taking place in the manufacturing environment that are increasing the attractiveness of more complex and accurate cost systems. New information technology, for example, is decreasing the cost of measurement. Computerized production planning systems and more powerful, less expensive computers make it easier to collect data and perform calculations. As measurement costs decrease, the cost-of-measurement curve in Exhibit 6–14 shifts downward and to the right, causing the total cost curve to shift to the right. The optimal cost system is now one that allows more accuracy.

EXHIBIT 6–14
Tradeoffs Illustrated: The Optimal Cost System

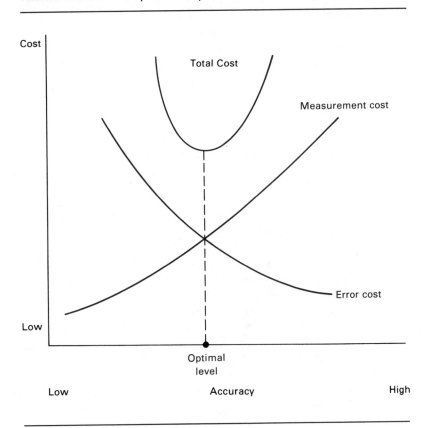

The cost of errors has also changed for many organizations. As the degree and nature of competition changes, the cost of errors can increase. Increased competition may lead a firm to drop what appear to be unprofitable products. In the opening scenario, for example, Sharp Paper was considering the possibility of dropping its high-volume products and emphasizing the low-volume lines. If the nature of the competition changes, error costs can increase as well. For example, if focused competitors emerge, then their pricing and marketing strategies will be based on more accurate cost information. The more-focused firms gain market share at the expense of the less-focused firms. Other factors such as deregulation and JIT manufacturing (which leads to a more-focused production environment) can also increase the cost of errors. As the cost of errors increases, the error-cost curve of Exhibit 6–14 shifts upward and to the right, causing the total cost curve to again shift to the right. Thus, a more accurate cost system will become optimal.

As the cost of measurement decreases and the cost of errors increases, then the existing cost system will become obsolete. A more accurate cost system is mandated. This is exactly the situation in the opening scenario that Sharp Paper was facing. The problems it was experiencing were attributable mainly to inaccurate cost information. Its cost system was no longer optimal. Furthermore, this state of affairs was being signaled. There were strong signals (symptoms) that the existing cost system was no longer useful. These symptoms of an obsolete cost system listed in Exhibit 6–1 reflect the need for a new cost system. Firms, then, should consider implementing an ABC system if they have significant nonunit-based costs and high product diversity and have experienced a decrease in measurement costs and an increase in error costs.

◼ JIT MANUFACTURING AND PRODUCT COSTING

In an activity-based cost system, costing accuracy is achieved by creating cost pools and identifying cost drivers that can be used to assign costs to each pool. Because of the large number of overhead activities that are shared by products, the effort and expense of an activity-based cost system can be considerable. As we noted previously, single-product firms and multiple-product firms that choose to dedicate entire facilities to the production of a single product have no problems with costing accuracy. All overhead activities are directly traceable to a single product.

Some of the same product-costing benefits found in a single-product environment are achieved by firms that install a JIT manufacturing system. These benefits are realized because JIT manufacturing adopts a more focused approach than that found in traditional manufacturing. Installing a JIT system affects the traceability of costs, enhances product-costing accuracy, diminishes the need for allocation of service-center costs, changes the behavior and relative importance of direct labor costs, and impacts job-order and process costing systems. To understand and appreciate these effects, we need a fundamental understanding of what JIT manufacturing is and how it differs from traditional manufacturing.

JIT Compared with Traditional Manufacturing

JIT manufacturing

JIT—or just-in-time manufacturing—is a demand-pull system. The objective of **JIT manufacturing** is to produce a product only when it is needed and only in the quantities demanded by customers. Demand pulls products through the manufacturing process. Each operation produces only what is necessary to satisfy the demand of the succeeding operation. No production takes place until a signal from a succeeding process indicates a need to produce. Parts and materials arrive just in time to be used in production.

Lower Inventories   One effect of JIT is to reduce inventories to much lower levels. Contrast this with the traditional push-through system of manufacturing. In traditional manufacturing, materials are supplied and parts produced and transferred to the succeeding process without regard to the level of demand that exists downstream. In a push-through system, inventories result when production exceeds demand. Inventories are needed as a buffer when production is less than demand. Usually, the push-through system produces significantly higher levels of inventory than a JIT system.

Manufacturing Cells and Interdisciplinary Labor   In traditional manufacturing, products are moved from one group of identical machines to another. Typically, machines with identical functions are located together in an area referred to as a *department or process*. Workers who specialize in the operation of a specific machine are located in each department. JIT replaces this traditional pattern with a pattern of manufacturing cells.

manufacturing cells

Manufacturing cells contain machines that are grouped in families, usually in a semicircle. The machines are arranged so that they can be used to perform a variety of operations in sequence. Each cell is set up to produce a particular product or product family. Products move from one machine to another from start to finish. Workers are assigned to cells and are trained to operate all machines within the cell. Thus, labor in a JIT environment is interdisciplinary, not specialized. Each manufacturing cell is essentially a minifactory; in fact, cells are often referred to as a *factory within a factory*. A comparison of the physical layout of JIT with the traditional pattern is shown in Exhibit 6–15 (p. 258).

total quality control (TQC)

acceptable quality level (AQL)

A Philosophy of Total Quality Control   JIT necessarily carries with it a much stronger emphasis on quality control. A defective part brings production to a grinding halt. Poor quality simply cannot be tolerated in a manufacturing environment that operates without inventories. Simply put, JIT cannot be implemented without a commitment to **total quality control (TQC)**. TQC is essentially a never-ending quest for perfect quality: the striving for a defect-free manufacturing process. This approach to quality is diametrically opposed to the traditional doctrine, called *acceptable quality level (AQL)*. AQL permits or allows defects to occur provided they do not exceed a predetermined level.

Decentralization of Services   JIT requires easy and quick access to support services, which means that centralized service departments must be scaled

EXHIBIT 6-15
Comparison of Physical Layout in Traditional and JIT Manufacturing

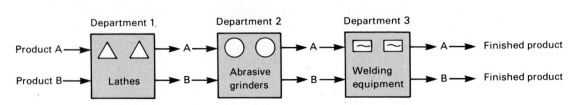

Traditional Manufacturing Layout

Each product passes through departments that specialize in one process. Departments process multiple products.

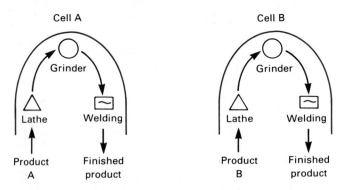

JIT Manufacturing Layout

Notice that each product passes through its own cell. All machines necessary to process each product are placed within the cell. Each cell is dedicated to the production of one product or one subassembly.

down and their personnel assigned to work directly to support production. For example, with respect to raw materials, JIT calls for multiple stock points, each one near where the material will be used. There is no need for a central stores location—in fact, such an arrangement actually hinders efficient production.

The major differences between JIT manufacturing and traditional manufacturing are summarized in Exhibit 6-16. These differences will be referred to and discussed in greater detail as the implications of JIT manufacturing for management accounting are examined.

JIT and the Traceability of Overhead Costs

In a JIT environment, many overhead activities formerly common to multiple product lines are now directly traceable to a single product. Cellular manu-

EXHIBIT 6–16
Comparison of JIT and Traditional Manufacturing

JIT	Traditional
1. Pull-through system	1. Push-through system
2. Insignificant inventories	2. Significant inventories
3. Manufacturing cells	3. Departmental structure
4. Interdisciplinary labor	4. Specialized labor
5. Total quality control	5. Acceptable quality level
6. Decentralized services	6. Centralized services

facturing, interdisciplinary labor, and decentralized service activities are the major features of JIT responsible for this change in traceability.[13]

In a departmental structure, many different products may be subjected to a process located in a single department (e.g., grinding). After completion of the process, the products are then transferred to other processes located in different departments (e.g., assembly, painting, and so on). Although a different set of processes is usually required for each product, most processes are applicable to more than one product. For example, three different products may need grinding. Because more than one product is processed in a department, the costs of that department are common to all products passing through and, therefore, indirectly traceable to any single product. In a manufacturing-cell structure, however, all processes necessary for the production of each product or major subassembly are collected in one area. Thus, the costs of operating that cell are all directly traceable to the product line it serves.

Equipment formerly located in other departments, for example, is now reassigned to cells, where it is dedicated to the production of a single product or subassembly. Because of this, depreciation is now a directly traceable product cost. Interdisciplinary workers and decentralization of services also add to the effect. Workers in the cell are trained to set up the equipment in the cell, maintain it, and operate it. Additionally, cell workers may also be used to move a partially finished part from one machine to the next. These cell workers operate directly on the product and are, therefore, direct laborers. But they also perform maintenance, setups, and material handling, support functions previously done by a different set of laborers for all product lines. Thus,

---

[13]For a more detailed discussion of the costing effects of JIT, see George Foster and Charles Horngren, "JIT: Cost Accounting and Cost Management Issues," *Management Accounting* (June 1987), pp. 19–25; Robert Howell and Stephen R. Soucy, "Cost Accounting in the New Manufacturing Environment," *Management Accounting* (August 1987), pp. 42–48; and Robert D. McIlhattan, "How Cost Management Systems Can Support the JIT Philosophy," *Management Accounting* (September 1987), pp. 20–26.

in a JIT environment, many costs formerly classified as indirect labor costs are now directly traceable to the product line. Exhibit 6–17 compares the traceability of some selected costs in traditional manufacturing with their traceability in the JIT environment.

Product-Costing Accuracy and JIT

One consequence of decreasing indirect costs and increasing direct costs is to increase the accuracy of product costing. Direct manufacturing costs are traceable to the product and can safely be said to belong to it. Indirect costs, however, are common to several products and must be assigned to these products using cost drivers and overhead rates. Because of cost and convenience, cost drivers that are less than perfectly correlated with the consumption of overhead activities may be chosen. JIT manufacturing, by reducing the pools of indirect costs and converting many of them to direct costs, diminishes the need for this difficult assessment.

For example, assume that prior to installing a JIT system, two products, a hammer and a wrench, were assigned overhead costs using an activity-based approach. One of the overhead pools contained two overhead activities: maintenance and power. The total annual costs of this pool, information concerning its cost driver (machine hours), and information pertaining to the two products are as follows:

Total maintenance and power costs	$200,000
Machine hours:	
Hammer	25,000
Wrench	25,000
Production (in units):	
Hammer	50,000
Wrench	50,000

Based on these data, the cost per unit of the cost driver is $4 ($200,000/50,000 machine hours). Using this rate, the following maintenance and overhead costs would be assigned to each product:

Hammer:	
Total cost assigned ($4 × 25,000)	$100,000
Cost per unit ($100,000/50,000)	$2
Wrench:	
Total cost assigned ($4 × 25,000)	$100,000
Cost per unit ($100,000/50,000)	$2

Now assume that the company installs JIT manufacturing and organizes a manufacturing cell for each product. Power is metered for each cell, and

EXHIBIT 6-17
Product Cost Traceability: Traditional versus JIT Manufacturing

Manufacturing Cost	Traditional Environment	JIT Environment
Direct labor	Direct	Direct
Direct materials	Direct	Direct
Material handling	Indirect	Direct
Repairs and maintenance	Indirect	Direct
Energy	Indirect	Direct
Operating supplies	Indirect	Direct
Supervision	Indirect	Direct
Insurance and taxes	Indirect	Indirect
Building depreciation	Indirect	Indirect
Equipment depreciation	Indirect	Direct
Custodial services	Indirect	Indirect
Cafeteria services	Indirect	Indirect

workers in each cell are trained to perform maintenance. The same machine hours are used for each product, and the same number of units of each product are produced. The maintenance and power costs for each cell are given below.

Cell H (produces hammers):	
Power costs	$ 50,000
Maintenance costs	30,000
Total	$ 80,000
Cell W (produces wrenches):	
Power costs	$ 60,000
Maintenance costs	60,000
Total	$120,000

Based on this information, the unit cost of each product is shown in the following table:

Hammer ($80,000/50,000)	$1.60
Wrench ($120,000/50,000)	$2.40

The unit costs under the cell structure accurately reflect the consumption of maintenance and power costs since these costs are directly traceable to each product. Focusing the manufacturing processes has increased the firm's ability to determine the costs of production. While activity-based costing offers significant improvement in product-costing accuracy, focusing offers even more potential improvement.

It should be mentioned, however, that JIT does not convert all indirect costs into direct costs. Even with JIT in place, a significant number of overhead activities remain common to the manufacturing cells. This means that activity-based costing can still be useful in tracing costs to products, but the nature of an ABC system does change. In a JIT system, the batch size is one unit of product. Thus, all batch-level activities convert into unit-level activities. Additionally, many of the batch-level activities are reduced or eliminated.[14] For example, material handling may be significantly reduced because of reorganizing from a departmental structure to a cellular structure. These changes simplify the implementation of an ABC system by significantly reducing the number of cost drivers. A pure ABC system requires the identification of cost drivers for three categories of activities: unit level, batch level, and product level. In a JIT environment, identification of cost drivers is reduced to two categories: unit level and product level. Furthermore, it is also possible that the need to use cost drivers for product-level activities may also be diminished. For example, a firm may choose to decentralize engineering activities to the cell level (and thus to the product). Engineering support, therefore, is directly traceable to the cell, and there is no need to use a cost driver to trace this cost to individual products.

cell-level activities

Also, JIT creates another category of activity: cell-level activities. **Cell-level activities** are those that sustain the cell process (e.g., supervision). These costs do not vary as the number of units increases or with product-sustaining cost drivers; however, unlike facility costs, cell-level costs are traceable to individual products. Cells also create a more logical connection with facility-level costs. It can be argued, for example, that the square footage occupied by cells drives many facility-level costs. If true, then allocation of facility-level costs to cells and, thus, to products is less arbitrary. JIT and ABC together should provide significant improvements in tracing manufacturing costs to individual products.

JIT and the Allocation of Service-Center Costs

In traditional manufacturing, centralized service centers provide support to a variety of producing departments. In a JIT environment, many services are decentralized. This is accomplished by assigning people with specialized skills (e.g., industrial engineers and production schedulers) directly to product lines and by training direct laborers within cells to perform service activities formerly done by indirect laborers (e.g., maintenance). Thus, many service costs can now be directly traced to a manufacturing cell and, consequently, to a specific product.

---

[14]See Peter B. B. Turney and James M. Reeve, "The Impact of Continuous Improvement on the Design of Activity-Based Cost Systems," *Journal of Cost Management* (Summer 1990), pp. 43–50.

By disaggregating service costs and making them directly traceable to products, JIT gives managers a much better understanding of a product's true costs. It also creates the opportunity for managers to exercise better control over service costs through better understanding and more clearly identified responsibility. Under the traditional arrangement, service and production departments were managed by at least two different managers. Technically, in such a setting, the manager of the service department was responsible for the incurrence of service costs; however, the operating managers also had a stake in the matter since service costs affected the cost of the products over which they had responsibility. Unfortunately, operating managers were able to exercise only indirect control over service costs. Because services are decentralized in JIT, operating managers receive direct responsibility for many service costs.

JIT's Effect on Direct Labor Costs

As firms implement JIT and automate, traditional direct labor costs are reduced significantly. Moreover, as direct laborers become trained in multiple functions, the level of direct labor costs tends to stabilize as production fluctuates. For example, cell workers can be used to perform preventive maintenance during a slack period in manufacturing activity. Therefore, there are two outcomes: (1) direct labor decreases as a percentage of total manufacturing costs and (2) direct labor changes from a variable to a fixed cost.

As direct labor costs decline, the emphasis on tracking and reporting direct labor costs decreases significantly. The Milwaukee plant of Harley-Davidson, for example, found after the adoption of the JIT approach that direct labor costs were less than 10 percent of the cost of manufacturing motorcycles, yet management accountants were devoting 65 percent of their administrative efforts to tracking these costs.[15] Harley-Davidson simplified the treatment of direct labor costs by combining them with overhead costs to create a conversion cost pool on a cellular level. These conversion costs are then assigned to the product as it passes through the cell.

JIT's Effect on Inventory Valuation

One of the first accounting problems eliminated by the use of JIT manufacturing is the need to determine product costs for inventory valuation. If inventories exist, they must be valued—and valued according to a certain set of rules for financial reporting purposes (GAAP). With zero inventories (or at least insignificant levels), inventory valuation is irrelevant for financial reporting purposes. GAAP guidelines for product costing are also irrelevant, freeing up the accounting system to be more responsive to managerial needs. In fact, in a JIT environment, product costing exists only to satisfy managerial

---

[15]Foster and Horngren, "JIT: Cost Accounting and Cost Management Issues."

purposes. Managers need accurate product cost information for cost-plus pricing decisions, cost trend analysis, profitability analysis by product lines, comparison to competitors' costs, make-or-buy decisions, and so on. Because JIT frees up the accounting system from the constraints of inventory valuation, managers are more likely to have the needed information.

JIT's Effect on Job-Order Costing

In implementing JIT in a job-order setting, the firm should first separate its repetitive business from its unique orders. Manufacturing cells can then be established to deal with the repetitive business. For those products where demand is insufficient to justify its own manufacturing cell, groups of dissimilar machines can be set up in a cell to make families of products or parts that require the same manufacturing sequence.[16]

With this reorganizing of the manufacturing layout, job orders are no longer needed to accumulate product costs. Instead, costs can be accumulated at the cellular level. Additionally, because lot sizes are now too small (as a result of reducing work-in-process and finished goods inventories), it is impractical to have job orders for each job. Add to this the short lead time of products occurring because of the demand-pull philosophy of JIT, and it becomes difficult to track each piece moving through the cell. In effect, the job environment has taken on the nature of a process costing system.[17]

Process Costing and JIT

In traditional process costing, manufacturing costs are accumulated by process for a period of time. Output is then measured for the same period of time. Unit cost for the period is computed by dividing the period's costs by its output. The unit cost is used to value work-in-process inventories and goods transferred out.

Although the unit-cost computation sounds simple, it is complicated by the presence of partially completed units in beginning and ending work in process and by the costs attached to the units in beginning work in process. This complication makes it necessary to define what is meant by total output and total manufacturing costs. *Output* is defined as the equivalent units for the period, where equivalent units include an accounting for the work done on the partially finished goods in work in process. Equivalent units are computed under one of two methods: weighted average or FIFO. The former counts the work done in the prior period (found in beginning work in process) as belonging to the current period; the latter excludes this work. Similar

---

[16]Walleigh, Richard C., "What's Your Excuse for Not Using JIT?" *Harvard Business Review* (March-April 1986), pp. 38–54.

[17]These points are based on experience. They are described by Henry J. Johansson, Thomas Volmann, and Vivian Wright in "The Effect of Zero Inventories on Cost (Just-in-Time)," *Cost Accounting for the 90s* (Montvale, N.J.: National Association of Accountants, 1986), pp. 141–64.

treatment is given to prior-period costs by each method. The computation of the unit cost can become quite messy, especially for FIFO.

The computation of unit cost under process costing can become complicated because of the presence of work-in-process inventories. With JIT's zero inventories, the unit-cost computation is as simple as it sounds: divide the period's costs for a process by the number of units produced. The computation of equivalent units is no longer needed, and there is no requirement to account for prior-period costs. JIT leads to significant simplification.

JIT and Automation

Once a JIT system is installed, it usually reveals where automation may be of some value. Thus, it is not uncommon for a firm adopting JIT to follow it with the acquisition of advanced manufacturing technology. Firms automate to increase productive capacity, increase efficiency, improve quality and service, decrease processing time, and increase output. There are three levels of automation: the stand-alone piece of equipment, the cell, and the completely integrated factory.

computer-numerically controlled (CNC) machines

The first level of automation is represented by **computer-numerically controlled (CNC) machines**, stand-alone machines controlled by a computer. The cell goes one step further and integrates computer-controlled machines and automated material handling equipment. A particular example of a cell is the **flexible manufacturing system (FMS).** The **FMS cell** is a system that produces a family of products from start to finish using robots and other automated equipment under the control of a mainframe computer. There may be several cells within a factory. The final step is a **computer-integrated manufacturing (CIM) system.** CIM integrates the computer-aided design, engineering, and manufacturing systems. In a CIM system, all automated components are linked by a centrally controlled information system.

flexible manufacturing system (FMS)

computer-integrated manufacturing (CIM) system

Automation increases the ability to trace costs to individual products. FMS cells, for example, are the automated counterparts of JIT manufacturing cells. Thus, many costs that were indirect in a traditional environment are now direct costs. Computer control, however, provides managers the opportunity to measure manufacturing costs more accurately and to provide managers with real-time access to cost information. This real-time access usually produces better control over the costs of production.

Backflush Costing

The JIT system also offers the opportunity to simplify the accounting for manufacturing cost flows. This simplified approach, called *backflush costing*, eliminates the Work in Process account and charges the manufacturing costs directly to Finished Goods. There are two changes relative to a conventional system: one relating to the accounting for materials and the other relating to accounting for conversion costs. JIT eliminates the need for separate accounts for raw materials and work in process. Instead, there is a single account, Raw Materials in Process (RIP). When materials are purchased in a JIT system, they are immediately placed into process. Thus, there is no need to record their purchase in a separate inventory account. As goods are finished, the cost of materials is transferred to Finished Goods. Second, labor and overhead are not treated separately. An account called Conversion Cost Control replaces the Overhead Control account. Actual conversion costs are collected on the debit side of Conversion Cost Control. Applied conversion costs are assigned to goods manufactured by debiting the Finished Goods account. The credit is to Conversion Cost Control. This transfer of costs to Finished Goods is triggered by the completion of the goods. Thus, the costs of manufacturing are "flushed" out of the system *after* the goods are completed.

To illustrate backflush costing and compare it with the conventional approach, assume that a JIT company had the following transactions during the month of March:

1. Raw materials were purchased on account for $80,000.

2. All materials as received were placed into production.

3. Actual direct labor costs, $10,000.

4. Actual overhead costs, $110,000.

5. Conversion costs applied, $110,000 (of which, $10,000 was direct labor).

6. All work was completed for the month.

The following journal entries would be made for a conventional and a JIT system:

Conventional System

1. Materials	80,000	
Accounts Payable		80,000
2. Work in Process	80,000	
Materials		80,000
3. Work in Process	10,000	
Wages Payable		10,000
4. Overhead Control	110,000	
Accounts Payable		110,000
5. Work in Process	100,000	
Overhead Control		100,000
6. Finished Goods	190,000	
Work in Process		190,000

JIT System

1. Materials in Process	80,000	
Accounts Payable		80,000
2. No entry		
3. See Entry 4 (Labor is combined with overhead.)		

4. Conversion Cost Control	120,000	
Accounts Payable		110,000
Wages Payable		10,000

5. See Entry 6 (Application is
   triggered by completion of goods.)

6. Finished Goods	190,000	
Conversion Cost Control		110,000
Materials in Process		80,000

There are other variations of backflush costing. If the system is a pure JIT system, then the goods are sold as they are produced. In this case, the debit to Finished Goods could be replaced by a debit to Cost of Goods Sold. Entry 6 would then appear as follows:

6. Cost of Goods Sold	190,000	
Conversion Cost Control		110,000
Materials in Process		80,000

An even more dramatic alteration would place the cost of materials in Cost of Goods Sold as they are purchased. The basic message is that the accounting for manufacturing cost flows can be vastly simplified. The degree of simplification, however, depends heavily on the ability of JIT to reduce inventories to significantly lower levels. If this does not happen, then the more traditional accounting approach must be used.

◼ A BROADER VIEW OF PRODUCT COSTS

In a JIT environment, work-in-process and finished goods inventories are reduced to much lower levels. Thus, the distinction between product and period costs diminishes. With little work-in-process or finished goods inventories, valuation of inventories becomes less important. Most manufacturing costs incurred are now effectively period costs. Elimination of the distinction between product and period costs has led to more attention being paid to nonmanufacturing costs.

In fact, many managers in the new environment view nonmanufacturing costs as product-related costs. They contend that a manufacturing firm is in business to produce and sell products; therefore, *all* costs are product costs. The former distinction was contrived primarily to satisfy financial reporting requirements. Attributing costs, both nonmanufacturing and manufacturing, to product lines produces a more useful view of product costing for managers and better information for control and decision making.

■ SUMMARY OF LEARNING OBJECTIVES

1. Identify some of the major changes in the manufacturing environment that are affecting the practice of cost accounting. Increased product complexity, total quality control, JIT manufacturing, service deregulation, and automation have all contributed to an increase in the competitive pressures felt by U.S. firms. The intense competition has made it more difficult for multiple-product firms to operate without accurate product cost information.

2. Explain why using only unit-based cost drivers to assign overhead may produce distorted product costs. Conventional cost systems are not able to assign the costs of nonunit-related overhead activities accurately. These overhead activities are consumed by products in different proportions than unit-based overhead activities. Because of this, assigning overhead using only unit-based drivers can distort product costs. This can be a serious matter if the nonunit-based overhead costs are a significant proportion of total overhead costs.

3. Use unit-based and nonunit-based cost drivers to assign overhead costs to products. The need for a more accurate costing system gave rise to activity-based costing. Like conventional overhead costing, activity-based costing follows a two-stage procedure. In the first stage, activities are classified and overhead costs are assigned to homogeneous cost pools defined by the activity classification rather than to production departments. *Homogeneity* means that the overhead costs assigned to a particular cost pool are logically related to the tasks being performed and are driven by the same cost driver. For this to occur, the overhead activities assigned to a cost pool must have the same consumption ratio for all products.

Once overhead costs are grouped into homogeneous cost pools, a cost driver is identified for each pool. Then an overhead rate is computed for each pool based on its driver. In the second stage, overhead costs are assigned to products by using the pools' overhead rates. This is accomplished by measuring the quantity of the cost driver consumed by each product and by multiplying this quantity by the cost per unit of the driver.

4. Explain why activity-based costing produces more accurate product costs. Overhead assignments should reflect the amount of overhead consumed by each product. Activity-based costing recognizes that all overhead does not vary with the number of units produced. By using both unit-based and nonunit-based cost drivers, overhead can be more accurately traced to individual products. This tracing is achieved by implementing the following steps: (1) identifying the major activities, (2) determining the cost of those activities, (3) identifying what causes or drives these activity costs (cost drivers), (4) assessing tthe quantities of each cost driver used by a product, and (5) calculating product costs.

5. Identify and define the four major categories of activities associated with activity-based costing. Manufacturing activities can be classified into four categories: unit level, batch level, product level, and facility level. Unit-level activities occur each time a unit of product is produced. Batch-level activities occur when batches of products are produced. Product-level activities are incurred to support production of each different type of product. Facility-level activities sustain a facility's general manufacturing processes.

6. **Explain when an activity-based costing system should be used.** An ABC system may be needed whenever nonunit-based overhead costs are a significant proportion of total overhead costs and there exists a high level of product diversity. If these two conditions are met and if a firm has experienced decreasing measurement costs or increasing error costs (or both), then the likelihood of needing the more accurate ABC system is very high.

7. **Explain how JIT manufacturing differs from traditional manufacturing.** JIT manufacturing also impacts product costing. JIT manufacturing differs from traditional manufacturing on several dimensions. JIT manufacturing is a pull-through instead of a push-through approach, reduces inventories to much lower levels, uses interdisciplinary labor instead of specialized labor, uses a focused cell structure instead of departments, and decentralizes many service functions to the cellular level. The differences affect a number of product-costing practices.

8. **Describe how JIT manufacturing alters the traditional cost concepts found in a conventional manufacturing environment.** JIT affects the traceability and behavior of costs. Because cells are dedicated to the manufacture of a single product or subassembly, many indirect product costs are converted to direct product costs. Furthermore, because of the interdisciplinary approach, many costs formerly classified as variable (e.g., direct labor and material handling) are now fixed.

9. **Explain how JIT manufacturing improves product-costing accuracy.** By creating a more focused manufacturing environment, JIT increases the number of costs that are directly traceable to products. This conversion reduces the need to use overhead cost pools and cost drivers to assign overhead costs to products, thus increasing product-costing accuracy. Although the need for cost drivers is reduced, it is not eliminated and an ABC system can be used to increase accuracy in a JIT setting.

10. **Describe the effects JIT manufacturing has on allocations, process costing, and job costing.** JIT manufacturing also decreases the need for allocation of service-center costs; many of these costs are decentralized and located within each manufacturing cell. Job-order and process-costing systems are also affected. JIT transforms job-order systems into process systems and eliminates the need to compute equivalent units for process systems.

11. **Describe the accounting flows (backflush costing) for a JIT setting.** *Backflush costing* is a simplified approach to accounting for the manufacturing cost flows. In a JIT system, the completion of the goods triggers a "flushing out" of the manufacturing costs. As materials are purchased, a Materials in Process account is debited. As materials are completed, the cost of materials is transferred to Finished Goods. At the same time, conversion costs are assigned to Finished Goods by debiting Finished Goods and crediting Conversion Cost Control.

■ KEY TERMS

Acceptable quality level (AQL)   A quality standard that allows a prespecified number of defects. (p. 257)

Activity-based cost (ABC) system   A cost system that first traces costs to activities and then traces costs from activities to products. (p. 244)

Advanced manufacturing environment   An environment characterized by intense competition (world-wide usually), sophisticated technology, total quality control, and continuous improvement. (p. 237)

Batch-level activities   Those activities that are performed each time a batch is produced. (p. 248)

Cell-level activities   Activities that sustain the cell process but that do not vary with cost drivers of other activity categories. (p. 262)

Computer-integrated manufacturing (CIM) system   A system in which all automated components—design, engineering, and manufacturing—are linked by a centrally controlled information system. (p. 265)

Computer-numerically controlled (CNC) machines   Stand-alone machines controlled by a computer. (p. 265)

Consumption ratio   The proportion of an overhead activity consumed by a product. (p. 243)

Cost drivers   Causal factors that explain the consumption of overhead. (p. 239)

Error costs   Costs incurred from making bad decisions because of inaccurate product costs. (p. 254)

Facility-level activities   Those activities that sustain a facility's general manufacturing process. (p. 248)

Flexible-manufacturing system cell (FMS)   A manufacturing cell capable of producing a family of products from start to finish using robots and other automated equipment under the control of a mainframe computer. (p. 265)

Homogeneous cost pool   A collection of overhead costs that can be explained by a single cost driver (i.e., overhead activities that have the same consumption ratio for all products). (p. 245)

JIT manufacturing   A manufacturing approach that produces only what is necessary to satisfy the demand of the succeeding process (a demand-pull system). (p. 257)

Manufacturing cells   A collection of machines dedicated to the production of a single product or subassembly. (p. 257)

Measurement costs   Costs incurred from measurements required by a cost system. (p. 254)

Nonunit-based cost drivers   Factors, other than the number of units produced, that explain the consumption of overhead. (p. 243)

Optimal cost system   A cost system that minimizes the sum of error costs and measurement costs. (p. 254)

Product diversity   The situation present when products consume overhead in different proportions. (p. 243)

Product-sustaining activities Those activities performed to support the production of each different type of product. (p. 248)

Total quality control (TQC) A quality standard that demands perfection (zero defects). (p. 257)

Unit-based (volume-related) cost drivers Factors that increase in direct proportion to the number of units produced and that explain the consumption of unit-based overhead costs. (p. 239)

Unit-level activities Activities that are performed each time a unit is produced. (p. 248)

■ REVIEW PROBLEM

Inca Pottery Company is noted for a full line of quality vases. The company operates one of its plants in Lima, Peru. That plant produces two types of vases: Indian design and contemporary. Maria Vinueza, the president of the company, recently decided to change from a volume-based costing system to an activity-based cost system. Before making the change company wide, she wanted to assess the effect on the product costs of the Lima plant. This plant was chosen because it produces only two types of vases; most other plants produce at least a dozen.

To assess the effect of the change, the following data have been gathered (for simplicity, costs are expressed in dollars rather than in Peru's *soles*):

Vase	Quantity	Prime Costs	Machine Hours	Material Moves	Setups
Indian	200,000	$700,000	50,000	700,000	100
Contemporary	50,000	150,000	12,500	100,000	50
Dollar value	—	$850,000	$250,000[a]	$300,000	$450,000

[a]The cost of maintenance

Under the current system, the costs of maintenance, material handling, and setups are assigned to the vases on the basis of machine hours.

Required:

1. Compute the unit cost of each vase using the current unit-based approach.
2. Compute the unit cost of each vase using an activity-based costing approach.
3. Assume that Maria decides to install JIT manufacturing. Two manufacturing cells are created—one for each vase (the I–cell and the C–cell). The overhead costs traceable to each cell are as follows:

Cell	Maintenance	Material Handling	Setups	Total
I–Cell	$210,000	$260,000	$300,000	$770,000
C–Cell	40,000	40,000	150,000	230,000

Assume the same level of output and prime costs as in the current system. Compute the unit cost for each vase in the JIT system. Is this cost more accurate than the activity-based cost? Explain.

Solution:

1. Total overhead is $1,000,000. The plant-wide rate is $16 per machine hour ($1,000,000/62,500). Overhead is assigned as follows:

Indian vase: $16 × 50,000 = $800,000
Contemporary vase: $16 × 12,500 = $200,000

The unit costs for the two products are as follows:

Indian vase: ($800,000 + $700,000)/200,000 = $7.50
Contemporary: ($200,000 + $150,000)/50,000 = $7.00

2. In the activity-based approach, the consumption ratios are different for all three overhead activities, so overhead pools are formed for each activity. The overhead rates for each of these pools are as follows:

Maintenance: $250,000/62,500 = $4/hour
Material handling: $300,000/800,000 = $0.375/move
Setup: $450,000/150 = $3,000/setup

Overhead is assigned as follows:

Indian vases:
$4 × 50,000	$200,000
$0.375 × 700,000	262,500
$3,000 × 100	300,000
Total	$762,500

Contemporary vases:
$4 × 12,500	$ 50,000
$0.375 × 100,000	37,500
$3,000 × 50	150,000
Total	$237,500

This produces the following unit costs:

Indian vases:
Prime costs	$ 700,000
Overhead costs	762,500
Total costs	$1,462,500

Units produced	200,000
Unit cost	$7.31
Contemporary vases:	
Prime costs	$150,000
Overhead costs	237,500
Total costs	$387,500
Units produced	50,000
Unit cost	$7.75

3. With a JIT manufacturing system, costs would be computed as follows:

Indian vases:	
Prime costs	$ 700,000
Overhead costs	770,000
Total	$1,470,000
Units produced	200,000
Unit cost	$7.35
Contemporary vases:	
Prime Costs	$ 150,000
Overhead costs	230,000
Total	$ 380,000
Units produced	50,000
Unit cost	$7.60

The unit cost here is the most accurate since all costs are directly traceable to each product. This is because of the focusing effect of JIT.

■ QUESTIONS

1 Explain how a plant-wide overhead rate, using a unit-based cost driver, can produce distorted product costs.

2 What are nonunit-related overhead activities? Nonunit-based cost drivers? Give some examples.

3 What is an overhead consumption ratio?

4 Explain how departmental overhead rates can produce product costs that are more distorted than those computed using a plant-wide rate.

5 What is meant by product diversity?

6 Overhead costs are the source of product cost distortions. Do you agree? Explain.

7 What is activity-based product costing?

8 What is a homogeneous cost pool?

9 What is the first-stage procedure in assigning overhead costs to products when using an activity-based system?

10 What is the second-stage procedure in assigning overhead costs to products when using an activity-based system?

11   What are unit-level activities? Batch-level activities? Product-level activities? Facility-level activities?

12   What role does the cost of measurement have in selecting a cost driver? What about degree of correlation with indirect measures of activity?

13   Explain why some firms may choose (correctly) to continue using conventional (unit-based) cost systems.

14   How can you tell if a cost system has become obsolete? What are some of the symptoms of an outmoded cost system?

15   Explain how low-volume products can be undercosted and high-volume products overcosted if only unit-based cost drivers are used to assign overhead costs.

16   Explain how undercosting low-volume products and overcosting high-volume products can affect the competitive position of a firm.

17   What is JIT manufacturing? List four ways in which JIT manufacturing differs from traditional manufacturing.

18   What are manufacturing cells? Explain how they differ from production departments.

19   Identify four effects that a JIT environment has on traditional costs and cost concepts.

20   Explain why some indirect manufacturing costs in traditional manufacturing become direct costs in JIT manufacturing. Give some examples of costs that change in this way.

21   In JIT manufacturing, direct labor costs are less important and largely fixed in nature. Do you agree? Explain.

22   Without inventories, there is no distinction between product and period costs. Do you agree? Explain.

23   What are flexible manufacturing system (FMS) cells? How do they differ from JIT cells?

24   How does JIT manufacturing increase product-costing accuracy?

25   Discuss the effect JIT manufacturing has on activity-based costing.

26   How is job-order costing affected in a JIT environment? Process costing?

■ EXERCISES

E6–1   **Selection of Cost Drivers and Product-Costing Accuracy**   Turtle Company produces two types of wallets. Wallet A is virtually handcrafted; Wallet B is produced through a mostly automated process. Although the handcrafted wallet is labor intensive, its production requires the use of the same equipment that Wallet B uses. Turtle Company assigns overhead using direct labor dollars. Gary Norton, sales manager, is convinced that the wallets are not being costed correctly.

To illustrate his point, he decided to focus on only the machine-related costs, which are as follows:

Depreciation	$5,000[a]
Operating costs	3,000

[a]Computed on a straight-line basis; book value at the beginning of the year was $25,000.

He also collected the expected annual prime costs for each wallet, the machine hours, and the expected production (which is the normal output for the company).

	Wallet A	Wallet B
Direct labor	$9,000	$3,000
Direct materials	$3,000	$3,000
Units	3,000	3,000
Machine hours	500	4,500

Required:

1. Compute the plant-wide rate using direct labor dollars. Use this rate to determine the machine cost per wallet produced.

2. Compute a plant-wide rate using machine hours. Use this rate to compute the machine cost per wallet produced.

3. Which rate produces the most accurate unit cost? Explain why.

E6–2 **Multiple versus Single Overhead Rates; Cost Drivers** Assume that a plant has two categories of overhead: material handling and quality inspection. The costs expected for these categories for the coming year are as follows:

Material handling	$100,000
Quality inspection	300,000

The plant currently applies overhead using direct labor hours and expected actual capacity. This figure is 50,000 direct labor hours. Charlene Wells, the plant manager, has been asked to submit a bid and has assembled the following data on the proposed job:

	Potential Job
Direct materials	$3,700
Direct labor (1,000 hours)	$7,000
Overhead	$?
Number of material moves	10
Number of inspections	5

Charlene has been told that many competitors use an activity-based approach to assign overhead to jobs. Before submitting her bid, she wants to assess the effects of this alternative approach. She estimates that the expected number of material moves for all jobs during the year is 1,000; she also expects 5,000 quality inspections to be performed.

Required:

1. Compute the total cost of the potential job using direct labor hours to assign overhead. Assuming that the bid price is full manufacturing cost plus 25 percent, what would Charlene's bid be?

2. Compute the total cost of the job using the number of material moves to allocate material handling costs and the number of inspections to allocate the quality inspection costs. Assuming a bid price of full manufacturing cost plus 25 percent, what is Charlene's bid using this approach?

3. Which approach do you think best reflects the actual cost of the job? Explain.

E6–3 **Multiple versus Single Overhead Rates: Cost Drivers** Swasey Company has identified the following overhead costs and cost drivers for the coming year:

Overhead Item	Expected Cost	Cost Driver	Expected Actual Level
Setup costs	$60,000	Number of setups	300
Ordering costs	45,000	Number of orders	4,500
Machine costs	90,000	Machine hours	18,000
Power	25,000	Kilowatt hours	50,000

The following two jobs were completed during the year:

	Job 125	Job 128
Direct materials	$750	$850
Direct labor (100 hours)	$600	$600
Units completed	100	50
Number of setups	1	1
Number of orders	4	2
Machine hours	20	30
Kilowatt hours	20	40

The company's normal activity is 4,000 direct labor hours.

Required:

1. Determine the unit cost for each job using direct labor hours to apply overhead.

2. Determine the unit cost for each job using the four cost drivers.

3. Which method produces the more accurate cost assignment? Why?

E6–4 **Activity-based Costing: Homogeneous Cost Pools; Cost Drivers** Bailey Manufacturing produces two types of thermometers: candy and weather. The overhead activities, total costs, and the other related data are as follows:

Product	Machine Hours	Setups	Receiving Orders	Packing Orders
Candy	10,000	50	100	400
Weather	10,000	25	200	200
Costs	$100,000	$7,500	$4,500	$30,000

Required:

1. Classify the overhead activities as unit level, batch level, or product sustaining.
2. Create homogeneous cost pools. Identify the activities that belong to each pool.
3. Identify the cost driver for each pool and compute the pool rate.
4. Assign the overhead costs to each product using the pool rates computed in requirement 3.

E6–5 **Conventional Costing; Activity-based Costing; Pricing** Thompson Company produces a variety of electronic equipment. One of its plants produces two dot-matrix printers: the deluxe and the regular. At the beginning of the year, the following data were prepared for this plant:

	Deluxe	Regular
Quantity	50,000	400,000
Selling price	$450	$275
Unit prime cost	$180	$110
Unit overhead cost	$15	$120

Overhead is applied using direct labor hours. Upon examining the data, the vice-president of marketing was particularly impressed with the per-unit profitability of the deluxe printer and suggested that more emphasis be placed on producing and selling this product. The plant manager objected to this strategy, arguing that the cost of the deluxe printer was understated. He argued that overhead costs could be assigned more accurately by using multiple cost drivers that reflected each product's consumption. To convince higher management that multiple rates could produce a significant difference in product costs, he obtained the following projected information from the controller for the production output given above:

Overhead Activity	Cost Driver	Pool Rate[b]	Activity Consumption[a]	
			Deluxe	Regular
Setups	Number of setups	$3,000	150	100
Machine costs	Machine hours	100	100,000	300,000
Engineering	Engineering hours	20	50,000	100,000
Packing	Packing orders	20	50,000	200,000

[a]In units of cost driver
[b]Cost per unit of cost driver

Required:

1. Using the projected data based on conventional costing, compute gross profit percentage, gross profit per unit, and total gross profit for each product.
2. Using the pool rates, compute the overhead cost per unit for each product. Using this new unit cost, compute gross profit percentage, gross profit per unit, and total gross profit for each product.

3. In view of the outcome in requirement 2, evaluate the suggestion of the vice-president of marketing to switch the emphasis to the deluxe model.

E6–6   **Two-stage Procedure: Activity-based Costing**   Yalesty Company has recently decided to convert from conventional product costing to an activity-based system. The company produces two products: hairsetters and curling irons. Information concerning these two products is given below.

	Hairsetter	Curling Iron
Quantity produced	100,000	200,000
Machine hours	50,000	50,000
Direct labor hours	100,000	100,000
Material handling (number of moves)	20,000	40,000
Engineering labor (hours)	10,000	5,000
Receiving (number of orders processed)	500	250
Setups	60	20
Maintenance (hours used)	2,000	2,000
Kilowatt hours	25,000	25,000
Packing (number of orders)	20,000	20,000

Additionally, the following overhead costs are reported:

Material handling	$120,000
Maintenance	80,000
Power	30,000
Depreciation (machines)[a]	60,000
Engineering	90,000
Receiving	40,000
Setups	96,000
Packing	30,000

[a]Depreciation is straight line. Book value at the beginning of the year is $600,000. The machine hours reported represent the normal activity level. The remaining life of the machinery is ten years or 1 million machine hours.

Required:

1. Classify the overhead activities as unit level, batch level, or product sustaining.

2. Group all overhead costs into homogeneous cost pools. Select a cost driver for each cost pool and compute a pool rate.

3. Using the pool rates calculated in requirement 2, assign all overhead costs to the two products and compute the overhead cost per unit for each.

E6–7   **Classification of Activities**   Classify the following activities as unit level, batch level, product level, or facility level. Also identify a potential cost driver for each activity.

1. Setups

2. Shipments received—raw materials

3. Direct labor support

4. Shipments made

5. Ordering supplies

6. Production order activity

7. Part administration

8. Material handling

9. Processing customer orders

10. Plant-wide supervision

11. Machining

12. Plant depreciation

13. Special product testing

14. Heating and air conditioning: plant

15. Expediting

16. Product support engineering

17. Property taxes

E6–8 **Selection of an ABC System** In 1982, Sterling Company changed its cost system. It went from using a single, plant-wide overhead rate based on direct labor hours to a system using departmental overhead rates. The departmental overhead rates used direct labor hours, machine hours, and direct material dollars to assign overhead to products.

In 1992, the president of Sterling, Pamela Jones, was mulling over the possibility of changing to an ABC system. She had heard that the life of a cost system was about ten years and was worried that the current system was no longer serving the needs of the company. She was also convinced, however, that a change to ABC simply because it was a "hot" topic was not the right approach. Any change had to be in the best economic interests of the company.

Required:

As a consultant to Pamela, identify the factors that should be considered in changing to an ABC system. In your discussion, include a definition of an outmoded or obsolete cost system.

E6–9 **Classification of Activities; Unit-Cost Computation** Blackwell Company produces two products: bicycles and tricycles. The two products are manufactured in the same plant. The following activities have been identified:

	Bicycles	*Tricycles*
Quantity produced	200,000	400,000
Machine hours	200,000	200,000
Direct labor hours	50,000	50,000
Packing (number of boxes)	200,000	400,000
Setups (number of)	500	200
Engineering support (hours)	4,000	2,000
Receiving (orders processed)	300	150
Maintenance (hours used)	4,000	4,000
Material handling (number of moves)	1,500	600
Power consumption (kilowatt hours)	25,000	25,000

In addition to the activities, the following overhead costs have been identified:

Plant supervision	$ 80,000
Material handling	168,000
Maintenance	80,000
Power	100,000
Engineering	180,000
Setups	280,000
Packing	360,000
Receiving	45,000
Depreciation (plant)	50,000
Depreciation (machines)[a]	100,000

[a]Depreciation is straight line. At the beginning of the year, book value on equipment was $600,000. The equipment is expected to last another six years or 2,400,000 machine hours.

Required:

1. Classify the above activities and costs as unit level, batch level, product level, or facility level. Identify cost drivers and calculate pool rates as needed. Assume that facility-level costs are assigned using direct labor hours.

2. Using the pool rates, calculate the overhead cost per unit for each product. In providing this calculation, prepare a report that details the cost assignment by activity category. In general terms, explain why category reporting is useful to managers.

E6–10   **Activity Classification; Cost Drivers**   Teddy Simpson was puzzled by the recent report on the company's product-cost reduction program. The Engineering Department had spent considerable effort and resources to find ways to reduce the cost per setup. The recently installed ABC system was supposed to help him understand costs of activities and product costs. Based on this information, the company believed that the unit product cost could be significantly reduced by redesigning the setup procedures. The objective was to lower the cost per die since the number of dies was the cost driver for the setup activity. Yet the reduction in cost per die was much less than expected (a 25 percent reduction in the cost per die was expected).

   In trying to understand what happened, Teddy requested a report on the activities and costs associated with setups. The accounting department provided the following information. The percentage cost breakdown is before and after the improvements were made.

Cost driver: Number of dies (number produced: 1,000 each year)
Activities and costs assigned to the setup category:

	Setup cost	
	Before	*After*
Die construction and repair	$300,000	$225,000
Maintaining die room machinery	100,000	100,000
Die design	100,000	75,000
Building maintenance	80,000	80,000
Bookkeeping for tooling-related costs	20,000	20,000

Required:

Using the information provided by the Accounting Department, explain why the expected results did not materialize.

E6–11 JIT and Traceability of Costs Assume that a company uses JIT manufacturing. Each manufacturing cell produces a single product or major subassembly. Cell workers are responsible for manufacturing the product, setting up the machinery, and maintaining the machinery. Classify the following costs as direct or indirect product costs:

1. Direct labor
2. Oil for lubricating machinery
3. Plant depreciation
4. Salary of plant supervisor
5. Salary of cell supervisor
6. Maintenance
7. Costs to set up machinery
8. Salaries of janitors
9. Power
10. Taxes on plant and equipment
11. Depreciation on machinery
12. Raw materials
13. Salary of industrial engineer
14. Parts for machinery
15. Pencils and paper clips for cell supervisor
16. Insurance on plant and equipment
17. Overtime wages for cell workers

E6–12 JIT and Product-Costing Accuracy Prior to installing a JIT system, Krumple Company used machine hours to assign maintenance costs to its three products (small, medium, and large diapers). The maintenance costs totaled $140,000 per year. The machine hours used by each product and the quantity of each product produced are as follows:

	Machine Hours	Quantity Produced
Small	30,000	7,500 boxes
Medium	30,000	7,500 boxes
Large	40,000	10,000 boxes

After installing JIT, three manufacturing cells were created, and cell workers were trained to perform maintenance. Maintenance costs for the three cells still totaled $140,000; however, these costs are now traceable to each cell as follows:

Cell, small diapers	$38,000
Cell, medium diapers	42,000
Cell, large diapers	60,000

Required:

1. Compute the pre–JIT maintenance cost per box of diapers for each type.
2. Compute maintenance cost per box of diapers for each type after installing JIT.
3. Explain why the JIT maintenance cost per box is more accurate than the pre–JIT cost.

E6–13   **JIT; Traceability of Costs; Product-Costing Accuracy**   The manufacturing costs assigned to Product A before and after installing JIT are given below.

	Before	*After*
Direct materials	$ 60,000	$ 60,000
Direct labor	40,000	50,000
Maintenance	50,000	30,000
Power	10,000	8,000
Depreciation	12,500	10,000
Material handling	8,000	4,000
Engineering	9,600	8,000
Setups	15,000	8,500
Building and grounds	11,800	12,400
Supplies	4,000	3,000
Supervision (plant)	8,200	8,200
Cell supervision	—	30,000
Departmental supervision	18,000	—
Total	$247,100	$232,100

In both the pre– and post–JIT setting, 100,000 units of Product A are manufactured. In the JIT setting, manufacturing cells are used to produce each product.

Required:

1. Compute the unit cost of the product before and after JIT. Explain why the JIT unit cost is more accurate.
2. Classify the costs in the JIT environment as direct or indirect product costs.

E6–14   **Backflush Costing**   Halley Company has installed a JIT purchasing and manufacturing system and is using backflush accounting for its cost flows. It uses the Finished Goods account, but the Work in Process account has been replaced by the Materials in Process account. During the month of March, Halley had the following transactions:

Raw materials purchased	$60,000
Direct labor cost	10,000
Overhead cost	50,000
Conversion cost applied	65,000[a]

[a]$10,000 labor and $55,000 overhead

There were no beginning or ending inventories. All goods produced were sold with a 40 percent markup.

Required:

1. Prepare the journal entries that would have been made using a traditional accounting approach for cost flows.

2. Prepare the journal entries for the month using backflush costing.

■ PROBLEMS

P6–1 **Activity-based Costing; Accuracy of Unit Costs; Multiple Overhead Rates and Cost Drivers versus Single Overhead Rates; Pricing Decisions**   Redding Equipment, Inc., manufactures custom-designed manufacturing equipment. Redding had recently received a request to manufacture twenty units of a specialized machine at a price lower than it normally accepts. Marketing manager Edith Wright indicated that if the order were accepted at that price, the company could expect additional orders from the same customer; in fact, if the company could offer this price in the market generally, she believed that sales of this machine would increase by 50 percent.

Clemont Atwood, president of Redding, was skeptical about accepting the order. The company had a policy not to accept any order that did not provide revenues at least equal to its full manufacturing cost plus 15 percent. The price offered was $2,000 per unit, compared to the normal selling price of $2,300. However, before a final decision was made, Clemont decided to request information on the estimated cost per unit. He was concerned because the company was experiencing increased competition, and the number of new orders was dropping. Also, the controller's office had recently researched the possibility of using multiple overhead rates instead of the single rate currently in use. The controller had promised more accurate product costing, and Clemont was curious about how this approach would affect the pricing of this particular machine.

Within twenty-four hours, the controller had assembled the following data:

a. The plant-wide overhead rate is based on an expected volume of 200,000 direct labor hours and the following budgeted overhead (all figures are yearly):

Depreciation, building	$ 200,000
Depreciation, equipment	100,000
Material handling	350,000
Power	180,000
Rework costs	150,000
Supervision	280,000
Cost of scrapped units	320,000
Other plant-wide overhead	220,000
Total	$1,800,000

b. Expected activity for selected cost drivers (for the year):

Material moves	5,000
Kilowatt hours	100,000
Units reworked	1,000
Units scrapped	500
Machine hours	50,000

c. Estimated data for the potential job (based on the production of 20 units):

	Potential Job
Direct labor (2,000 hours)	$10,000
Direct materials	$12,000
Number of material moves	3
Number of kilowatt hours	500
Number of units reworked	1
Number of units scrapped	1
Number of machine hours	500

Required:

1. Compute the estimated unit cost for the potential job using the current method to assign overhead on a plant-wide basis. Given this unit cost, compute the total gross profit earned by the job. Would the job be accepted under normal operating conditions?

2. Classify all overhead as unit level, batch level, product sustaining, or facility level.

3. Compute the estimated unit cost for the potential job using the cost drivers in Part *b* to assign overhead. Any facility-level overhead will be assigned using direct labor hours. Report per-unit costs by activity category. Given this cost per unit, compute the total gross profit earned by the job. Should the job be accepted?

4. Which approach—the plant-wide rate or the multiple-overhead rate with cost drivers—is the best for the company? Explain.

5. Now assume that Redding installs a JIT manufacturing system. Discuss how this change will affect the unit cost computation.

P6-2   **Cost Drivers; Overhead Pools; Accuracy of Product Costing**   Mike Carlson, president of Carlson Electronics, was convinced that his manufacturing costs had to be reduced to remain in business. The company simply had to become more efficient. During the past several years, profit margins had been squeezed by intense worldwide competition. Foreign competitors were able to produce their products at a lower cost. However, after returning from a management seminar, Mike had decided that his company's problems could be explained by two factors: how indirect manufacturing costs were assigned to products and the level of efficiency the company was achieving.

These two factors were interrelated. Based on the information he had received at the seminar, he knew that opportunities for increasing product-costing accuracy and reducing manufacturing costs rested primarily with overhead. This large group of indirect costs had been ignored and, in his judgment, had grown to unreasonable levels. In order to assign these costs accurately and control them, Mike knew that the costs of individual overhead activities had to be collected and the factors driving these costs identified. As a preliminary step, Mike requested a list of overhead activities and the expected overhead costs for the coming year. The following list was provided by the controller:

Setup costs	$ 120,000
Material handling	85,000
Costs of ordering raw materials	36,000
Costs of receiving raw materials	57,000
Quality inspections	82,000
Power	93,000
Machine depreciation	138,000
Rework	94,000
Cost of scrapped units	135,000
Plant depreciation	50,000
Maintenance	110,000
Total	$1,000,000

After receiving this information, Mike then gathered the following data for each of the three products produced by the company:

	Component 34	Component 45	Component 57
Units produced	90,000	30,000	200,000
Direct labor hours	60,000	40,000	100,000
Machine hours	18,000	12,000	30,000
Setups	40	40	40
Material moves	160	160	160
Kilowatt hours	6,000	4,000	10,000
Maintenance hours	400	200	600
Number of purchase orders	200	200	200
Number of inspections	40	40	40
Number of receiving orders	200	100	300
Number of units reworked	900	300	2,000
Number of units scrapped	225	75	500

Overhead is currently assigned to all products using a plant-wide rate based on direct labor hours. The unit prime costs for each component were also collected. They are

Component 34	$6.67
Component 45	$5.00
Component 57	$3.00

Required:

1. Using the plant-wide rate, compute the unit cost of each of the three components produced by Carlson Electronics.

2. Classify all overhead activities as unit level, batch level, product sustaining, or facility level. For each category, calculate the consumption ratios and group overhead costs into homogeneous cost pools. Compute an overhead rate for each pool.

3. Using the pool rates computed in requirement 2, compute the per-unit manufacturing cost for each of the three components. Report the unit cost by activity category.

4. Which of the two overhead costing procedures would you recommend: the plantwide rate or the multiple-rate, activity-based approach? Explain.

P6–3 **Cost Drivers and Product Costing Accuracy** Indio Company for years produced only one product: bath towels. Recently, the company decided to add a line of dinner napkins. With this addition, the need to allocate service costs to the producing departments became necessary. Surprisingly, the costs to produce the towels increased and their profitability dropped.

The marketing manager and the production manager both complained about the increase in the production cost of towels. The marketing manager was concerned because the increase in unit costs led to pressure to increase the unit price of towels. She was resisting this pressure because she was certain that the increase would harm the company's market share. The production manager was receiving pressure to cut costs also, yet he was convinced that nothing different was being done in the way the towels were produced. He was also convinced that further efficiency in the manufacture of the napkins was unlikely. After some discussion, the two managers decided that the problem had to be connected with the addition of the napkin line.

Upon investigation, they were informed that the only real change in product-costing procedures was in the way overhead costs were assigned. They were informed that a two-stage procedure was used. First, the service department costs were allocated directly to the two producing departments (Patterns and Finishing). Second, the costs accumulated in the producing departments were allocated to the two products using direct labor hours as a base. The managers were assured that great care was taken to associate overhead costs with individual products. So that they could construct their own example of cost assignment, the controller made the following information available for one of the company's service departments (the Accounting Department):

	Department		
	Accounting	*Pattern*	*Finishing*
Service cost	$220,000	—	—
Transactions processed	—	40,000	60,000
Total direct labor hours	—	20,000	40,000
Direct labor hours per napkin[a]	—	0.1	0.2
Direct labor hours per towel[a]	—	0.4	0.8

[a] Hours required to produce one set, where a set has four units

The controller remarked that the cost of operating the Accounting Department had doubled with the addition of the new product line. The increase came because of the need to process transactions, the number of which had also doubled.

During the first year of producing napkins, the company produced and sold 30,000 sets of towels and 80,000 sets of napkins. The 30,000 sets of towels matched the prior year's output for that product.

Required:

1. Compute the amount of accounting cost assigned to each set of towels and napkins, using the two-stage allocation process described by the controller.

2. Compute the amount of accounting cost assigned to a set of towels before the napkin line was added.

3. Suppose that the company decided to allocate the accounting costs directly to the product lines using the number of transactions as the allocation base. What is the accounting cost for a set of towels? For a set of napkins?

4. Which way of assigning overhead does the best job, the conventional two-stage approach or the activity-based approach using transactions processed for each product? Explain. Discuss the benefits of using cost drivers to assign overhead costs directly to individual products. Was it necessary to form manufacturing cells to carry out the cost-driver allocation?

P6–4 **Product-Costing Accuracy; Corporate Strategy; Activity-based Costing** Ogden Metal Manufacturing is engaged in the production of machine parts. One division specializes in the production of two machine parts: Part 12A and Part 18B. Historically, the profitability of the division had been tied to Part 12A. In the last two years, however, the division had been facing intense competition, and its sales of this part had dropped. Much of the competition was from foreign sources, and the divisional manager was convinced that the foreign producers were guilty of dumping. The following conversation between Ken Larson, divisional manager, and Martha Jones, marketing manager, reflects the concerns of the division's top management and some possible solutions that were being considered.

Martha: I just received a call from one of our major customers concerning Part 12A. He said that a sales representative from another firm had offered the part at $20 per unit—$11 less than what we ask.

Ken: It's costing about $21 to produce that part. I don't see how these companies can afford to sell it so cheaply. I'm not convinced that we should meet the price. Perhaps a better strategy is to emphasize producing and selling more of Part 18B. Our margin is high on this product, and we have virtually no competition for it.

Martha: You may be right. I think we can increase the price significantly and not lose business. I called a few customers to see how they would react to a 25 percent increase in price, and they all said that they would still purchase the same quantity as before.

Ken: It sounds promising. However, before we make a major commitment to Part 18B, I think we had better explore other possible explanations. I want to know how our production costs compare to our competitors. Perhaps we could be more efficient and find a way to earn a good return on Part 12A.

After his meeting with Martha, Ken requested an investigation of the production costs and comparative efficiency. The controller reported that as far as he could determine, the division's efficiency was similar to that of other competitors. To assist Ken in understanding the production activities and costs associated with the two products, the controller prepared the following data:

	Part 12A	Part 18B
Production	50,000	10,000
Selling price	$31.86	$24.00
Overhead per unit	$12.71	$6.36
Prime cost per unit	$8.53	$6.26
Number of production runs	10	20
Receiving orders	40	100
Machine hours	12,500	6,000
Direct labor hours	25,000	2,500
Engineering hours	5,000	5,000
Material moves	50	40

Upon examining the data, Ken decided that he wanted to know more about the overhead costs since they were such a high proportion of total production costs. Ken was provided the following list of overhead costs and told that they were assigned to products using direct labor hours:

Setup costs	$ 24,000
Machine costs	175,000
Receiving costs	210,000
Engineering costs	200,000
Material handling costs	90,000
Total.	$699,000

Required:

1. Verify the overhead cost per unit reported by the controller using direct labor hours to assign overhead. Compute the per-unit gross margin for each product.

2. Recompute the unit cost of each product using activity-based costing. Compute the per-unit gross margin for each product.

3. Should the company switch its emphasis from the high-volume product to the low-volume product? Comment on the validity of the divisional manager's accusation that competitors are dumping.

4. Explain the apparent lack of competition for Part 18B. Comment also on the willingness of customers to accept a 25 percent increase in price for Part 18B.

5. Assume that you are the manager of the division. Describe what actions you would take based on the information provided by the activity-based unit costs.

P6-5 **Product-Costing Accuracy; Departmental Rates; Pool Rates** Uneter Company produces two small engines for model planes (Engine A and Engine B). Both products pass through two producing departments. Engine B is by far the most popular of the two engines. The following data have been gathered for these two products:

Product-related Data

	Engine A	Engine B
Units produced per year	20,000	200,000
Prime costs	$100,000	$1,000,000
Direct labor hours	40,000	400,000
Machine hours	20,000	200,000
Production runs	40	60
Inspection hours	800	1,200

Departmental Data

	Department 1	Department 2
Direct labor hours:		
Engine A	30,000	10,000
Engine B	45,000	355,000
Total	75,000	365,000
Machine hours:		
Engine A	10,000	10,000
Engine B	160,000	40,000
Total	170,000	50,000
Overhead costs:		
Setup costs	$ 90,000	$ 90,000
Inspection costs	70,000	70,000
Power	100,000	60,000
Maintenance	80,000	100,000
Total	$340,000	$320,000

Required:

1. Compute the overhead cost per unit for each product using a plant-wide, volume-based rate.

2. Compute the overhead cost per unit for each product using departmental rates. In calculating departmental rates, use machine hours for Department 1 and direct labor hours for Department 2. Repeat using direct labor hours for Department 1 and machine hours for Department 2.

3. Compute the overhead cost per unit for each product using activity-based costing.

4. Comment on the ability of departmental rates to improve the accuracy of product costing.

P6–6 **ABC, Departmental Rates, and Pricing Decisions** (This problem is an extension of P3–9 and P5–10. All pertinent information is repeated here.) Alden Peterson, marketing manager for Retlief Company, was puzzled by the outcome of two recent bids. The company's policy was to bid 150 percent of full manufacturing cost. One job (Job SS) had been turned down by a prospective customer who had indicated that the proposed price was $3 per unit higher than the winning bid. A second job (Job TT) had been accepted by a customer who was amazed that Retlief could offer such favorable terms. This customer revealed that Retlief's price was $43 lower than the next lowest bid.

Alden knew that Retlief was competitive in terms of cost control. Accordingly, he suspected that the problem was related to cost assignment procedures. Upon investigating, he discovered that a plant-wide rate, based on direct labor hours, had been used to assign overhead to the jobs. With some help from the controller, the bids had been recalculated using departmental rates. Alden knew this could improve the accuracy of the cost assignment because one of the two producing departments was labor intensive and the other was machine-intensive. Both jobs spent time in each department although Job TT spent most of its time in the machine-intensive department. In calculating departmental rates, Alden decided to use two different methods to allocate service-department overhead to the producing departments: the direct method and the step method. He had heard that the step method would produce more accurate allocations. The unit bid price for the different approaches are summarized below.

	Job SS	Job TT
Plant-wide rate:		
Bid price	$18.75	$ 60.00
Departmental rates:		
Bid price (direct method)	14.67	101.01
Bid price (step method)	14.63	101.45

Alden had been reading about the increased accuracy of an ABC system and convinced the controller to help in obtaining the following information:

Overhead Activities	Cost	Activity Category	Cost Driver
Maintenance	$500,000	Product sustaining	Machine hours
Power	225,000	Unit level	Kilowatt hours
Setups	150,000	Batch level	Setup hours
General factory	625,000	Facility level	Machine hours[a]

[a]This is an arbitrary allocation. The controller argued that machine hours used by a job would be correlated with square footage occupied by the producing departments.

The expected levels of the cost drivers for the year are given below.

Machine hours	140,000
Kilowatt hours	100,000
Setup hours	20,000

The activity data for each job are also provided.

	Job SS	Job TT
Machine hours	700	3,200
Kilowatt hours	400	2,500
Setup hours	20	100

	Job SS	*Job TT*
Prime costs	$120,000	$50,000
Units	14,400	1,500

Required:

1. Calculate the cost of each job using activity-based costing. List the costs for each job by activity category.

2. Calculate the bid price for each job using the normal markup. How do the bid prices compare with the bids using plant-wide and departmental rates? Does this offer any real improvement? Explain.

3. Suppose that the best competing bid for Job SS was $4.20 lower than the original bid based on a plant-wide rate. Also assume that the bid on Job TT was $25 lower than the next lowest bid. Now compare the ABC bids with the bids based on departmental rates. What does this imply about the value of ABC as price competition intensifies?

4. Discuss the importance of having the facility-level costs listed separately as the job costs are detailed. Should these costs be included in the base for calculating the bid?

P6–7 **Implementing an ABC System** Jan Booth, vice-president of finance, was reviewing the responses to her suggestion that the company's cost system be replaced with an ABC system. She had sent a detailed memo to all the company's divisional managers, outlining the proposed new system and providing a brief summary of the benefits. She had also sent a copy of the memo to the divisional controllers. In her memo, she had requested a written reaction and set a meeting to discuss the issue. All the managers and controllers had responded, but she was somewhat disappointed in the reactions. Most of the responses had been negative and unsupportive of the change. Yet she knew the company was having problems.

Bids were being lost at a greater rate than ever before. The company was having a difficult time matching competitors' prices even with aggressive pricing. Furthermore, a recent study commissioned by the company revealed that the company was not out of line with others in terms of its overall efficiency. Also there was the decision by one division to drop a major product line, one that had been produced successfully for years. The traditional cost system had indicated that it was the right thing to do. Yet the profits of the division had declined dramatically the following year. Something was wrong! Based on her research, she was convinced that a major problem existed with the cost system. Her problem now was to convince these divisional types that their objections were unfounded. From the memos, she had built a list of the most common objections to the new system.[18]

1. An ABC system would be too expensive to operate.

2. An ABC system is too complicated and would be difficult to understand.

3. Improving our current system is all that's needed; for example, we can use rates based on machine hours as well as direct labor hours.

4. More accurate product costs are not needed—we know what our products cost.

5. The market sets prices—so why worry about product costs?

---

[18]This list is taken from Peter B. B. Turney, "Ten Myths about Implementing an Activity-Based Cost System," *Journal of Cost Management* (Spring 1990), pp. 24–32.

6. Cost systems aren't very important. Anyway, most of our manufacturing costs are fixed, and we cannot do much with fixed costs.

7. Only manufacturing costs are product costs—why worry about tracing nonmanufacturing costs to products?

8. Product costs are not useful for managing overhead activities. In fact, product costs are not very useful for most managerial decisions.

Required:

Prepare a memo to the divisional managers addressing each of the objections.

P6–8   **ABC Costing and Cost Behavior**   Underwood Company produces several different models of a stereo system. The company has recently adopted an ABC system. The unit cost expected for one of the models is presented below.

Model B	
Unit level costs (includes materials and labor)	$ 60
Batch-level costs	40
Product-sustaining costs	20
Facility-level costs	10
Total unit cost	$130

The unit cost is based on an expected volume of 10,000 units. These units will be produced in ten equal batches. The product-sustaining costs are all from engineering support. The product-sustaining costs are driven by engineering orders. The $20 cost assignment is based on five orders. Facility-level costs are allocated on the basis of direct labor hours (one hour per unit produced).

Required:

1. Calculate the total manufacturing cost to produce 10,000 units of Model B. Present the total cost for each activity category.

2. Now assume that the company has revised its forecast for Model B and expects to produce 15,000 units. A decision was made to handle the increased production by increasing batch size to 1,500 units. The increased production will not require an increase in engineering support. Calculate the total cost to produce the 15,000 units of Model B. Present the total cost for each activity category. Explain the outcome.

3. Assume that the revised forecast of 15,000 units is made. Now, however, the decision is made to handle the extra production by increasing the number of batches from ten to fifteen. Also, the sales of the extra 5,000 units is possible only if an engineering modification is made. This increases the expected engineering orders from five to six. Explain why the costs changed from those predicted in requirement 2.

4. Discuss the value of classifying and reporting costs by activity category.

P6–9   **JIT and Product Costing**   Wessom Company recently implemented a JIT manufacturing system. After one year of operation, the president of the company wanted to compare product cost under the JIT system with product cost under the old system. Wessom's two products are exercise springs and exercise bikes. The unit prime costs under the old system are given below.

	Springs	Bikes
Direct materials	$10	$40
Direct labor	3	20

Under the old manufacturing system, the company operated three service centers and two production departments. Overhead was applied using departmental overhead rates. The direct overhead costs associated with each department for the year preceding the installation of JIT are as follows:

Maintenance	$110,000
Material Handling	90,000
Building and Grounds	140,000
Machining	280,000
Assembly	175,000

Under the old system, the overhead costs of the service departments were allocated directly to the producing departments and then to the products passing through them (both products passed through each producing department). The overhead rate for the Machining Department was based on machine hours and for Assembly was based on direct labor hours. During the last year of operations for the old system, the Machining Department used 80,000 machine hours, and the Assembly Department 20,000 direct labor hours. Each set of exercise springs required 1 machine hour in Machining and 0.25 direct labor hours in Assembly. Each exercise bike required 2 machine hours in Machining and 0.5 hours in Assembly. Bases for allocation of the service costs are given below.

	Square Feet of Space	Number of Material Moves	Machine Hours
Machining	80,000	90,000	80,000
Assembly	40,000	60,000	20,000
Total	120,000	150,000	100,000

Upon implementing JIT, a manufacturing cell for each product was created to replace the departmental structure. Maintenance and material handling were both decentralized to the cell level. Essentially, cell workers were trained to operate the machines in each cell, assemble the components, maintain the machines, and move the partially completed units from one point to the next within the cell. During the first year of the JIT system, the company produced and sold 20,000 sets of exercise springs and 30,000 exercise bikes. This output was identical to that for the last year of operations under the old system. The following costs have been assigned to the manufacturing cells:

	Springs Cell	*Bikes Cell*
Direct materials	$180,000	$1,110,000
Direct labor	66,000	660,000
Direct overhead	99,000	350,500
Allocated overhead[a]	56,000	84,000
Total	$401,000	$2,204,500

[a]Building and grounds, allocated on the basis of square footage

Required:

1. Compute the unit cost for each product under the old manufacturing system.

2. Compute the unit cost for each product under the JIT system.

3. Which of the unit costs is the more accurate? Explain. Include in your explanation a discussion of how the computational approaches differ.

4. Explain why the total overhead costs decreased.

P6–10 **Cost Behavior; Traceability; Unit Costs; JIT and ABC** Benson Company, a manufacturer of toy trucks, has adopted JIT manufacturing. In implementing the system, three types of manufacturing cells were created, one for each type of toy truck produced. The manufacturing costs for the line of dump trucks are given below (expected production of 12,000 units).

Cell manufacturing costs:	
Direct materials	$60,000
Direct labor	40,000
Supplies	2,500
Power	3,500
Supervision	22,000
Depreciation	5,000
Other manufacturing costs:	
Share of plant depreciation	$ 7,000
Share of plant supervisor's salary	2,000
Engineering sustaining (4 orders)	12,000
Safety testing (10 samples)	8,000

Engineering sustaining costs are driven by engineering orders and safety testing costs by the number of samples.

Required:

1. Assume initially that all costs are strictly variable or strictly fixed with resepct to units produced. Prepare a cost formula for the following costs:
   a. Direct materials
   b. Direct labor
   c. All direct manufacturing costs other than labor and materials
   d. All direct manufacturing costs

    e. All indirect manufacturing costs

    f. Total manufacturing costs

2. Assuming that 12,000 dump trucks are produced, compute the following:
       a. Direct material costs
       b. Direct labor costs
       c. Direct manufacturing costs
       d. Total manufacturing costs
       e. Unit cost

3. Repeat requirement 2 for 15,000 units. Which costs changed? Why?

4. Now classify costs as unit level, batch level, product sustaining, facility level or cell level. Calculate total costs for each category for 12,000 and 15,000 units. Which costs changed? Why?

5. Refer to requirement 4. Suppose that the number of engineering orders increase from four to six and the number of samples from ten to fifteen. What happens to total costs for 12,000 units? 15,000 units? Explain.

P6–11   **Costs: Traditional versus JIT Environments**   Consider the following production costs before and after implementing a JIT system:

	Before	After
Direct labor	$ 70,000	$ 70,000
Direct materials	480,000	480,000
Material handling	100,000	20,000
Depreciation, equipment	150,000	100,000
Supplies	38,000	34,000
Rent, special equipment	10,000	10,000
Power	15,000	12,500
Salary, production supervisor	40,000	40,000
Salary, custodian	8,000	8,000
Insurance, factory	7,000	7,000
Total	$918,000	$781,500

Required:

1. Classify these costs as direct or indirect both before and after implementing JIT.

2. Explain why some indirect product costs changed to direct product costs when JIT was implemented.

3. Explain why some costs could change in amount as JIT is implemented.

4. Assume that these costs support the production of 100,000 units. Compute the unit product cost before and after implementing JIT. Which unit cost figure is more accurate? Why?

P6–12   **Cost Drivers; Product Costing; Ethical Considerations**   Consider the following conversation between Leonard Bryner, president and manager of a firm engaged in job manufacturing, and Chuck Davis, CMA, the firm's controller.

    Leonard: Chuck, as you know, our firm has been losing market share over the past three years. We have been losing more and more bids, and I don't understand why. At first I thought other firms were undercutting simply to gain business, but after examining some of the public financial reports, I believe that they are making a reasonable rate of return. I am beginning to believe that our costs and costing methods are at fault.

Chuck: I can't agree with that. We have good control over our costs. Like most firms in our industry, we use a normal job-costing system. I really don't see any significant waste in the plant.

Leonard: After talking with some other managers at a recent industrial convention, I'm not so sure that waste by itself is the issue. They talked about JIT manufacturing, conversion of overhead costs to direct manufacturing costs, and the use of something called *cost drivers* to allocate overhead. They claimed that these new procedures produce more efficiency in manufacturing, better control of overhead, and more accurate product costing. Maybe our bids are too high because these other firms have found ways to decrease their overhead and to increase the accuracy of their product costing.

Chuck: I doubt it. For one thing, I don't believe overhead costs can be made into direct manufacturing costs. That seems absurd to me. Furthermore, everyone uses some measure of production activity to assign overhead costs. I imagine that what they are calling *cost drivers* is just some new buzz word for measures of production volume. Fads in costing come and go. I wouldn't worry about it. I'll bet that our problems with decreasing sales are temporary. You might recall that we experienced a similar problem about twelve years ago—it was two years before it straightened out.

Required:

1. Do you agree with Chuck Davis and the advice that he gave Leonard Bryner? Explain.

2. Was there anything wrong or unethical in the behavior that Chuck Davis displayed? Explain your reasoning.

3. Do you think that Chuck was well informed—that he was aware of what the accounting implications of JIT were and that he knew what was meant by cost drivers? Should he have been? Review (in the Appendix of Chapter 1) the first category of the standards of ethical conduct for management accountants. Do any of these apply to Chuck's case?

P6–13 **Allocation and JIT** Folton Company produces two types of vases (A and B). Both pass through two producing departments: Molding and Painting. It also has a Maintenance Department that services and repairs the equipment used in each producing department. Budgeted data for the three departments are given below.

	Maintenance	Molding	Painting
Overhead	$100,000	$165,000	$119,000
Maintenance hours	—	15,000	5,000
Direct labor hours	—	12,000	6,000

In the Molding Department, Vase A requires 1 hour of direct labor and Vase B 2 hours. In the Painting Department, Vase A requires 0.5 hours of direct labor and Vase B 1 hour. Expected production: Vase A, 4,000 units; Vase B, 4,000 units.

Immediately after preparing the budgeted data, a consultant suggests that two manufacturing cells be created: one for the manufacture of Vase A and the other for the manufacture of Vase B. Cell workers would be trained to perform maintenance; hence, the Maintenance Department is decentralized. The total direct overhead costs esti-mated for each cell are $200,000 for Cell A and $184,000 for Cell B.

Required:

1. Allocate the service costs to each department and compute the overhead cost per unit for each vase (overhead rates use direct labor hours).

2. Compute the overhead cost per unit if manufacturing cells are created. Which unit overhead cost do you think is the more accurate—the one computed with a de-partmental structure or the one computed using a cell structure? Explain.

3. Note that the total overhead costs under each system are assumed to be the same. Would you expect the overhead costs to remain the same if the JIT manufacturing system is implemented? Explain.

P6–14   **Backflush Costing; Conversion Rate**   Flinn Company has implemented a JIT–FMS sys-tem. Annette Swasey, controller of the company, has decided to reduce the accounting requirements given the expectation of lower inventories. For one thing, she has decided to treat direct labor cost as a part of overhead and discontinue the detailed labor account-ing of the past. The company has created two manufacturing cells, Cell A and Cell B. Product-sustaining and unit-level overhead costs outside the cells are assigned to each cell using appropriate cost drivers. Facility-level costs are allocated to each cell on the basis of square footage. The budgeted labor and overhead costs are given below.

	Cell A	Cell B
Direct labor costs	$ 20,000	$10,000
Direct overhead	80,000	40,000
Product sustaining	30,000	12,000
Facility level	20,000	10,000
Total conversion cost	$150,000	$72,000

The predetermined conversion cost rate is based on available production hours in each cell. Cell A has 10,000 hours available for production, and Cell B has 6,000 hours. Conversion costs are applied to the units produced by multiplying the conversion rate by the actual time required to produce the units. Cell A produced 18,000 units, taking 0.5 hours to produce 1 unit of product (on average). Cell B produced 20,000 units, taking 0.25 hours to produce one unit of product (on average).

Other actual results for the year are given below.

Materials purchased and issued	$170,000
Labor costs	30,000
Overhead	210,000

All units produced were sold.

Required:

1. Calculate the predetermined conversion cost rates for each cell.

2. Prepare journal entries using backflush accounting. Assume that a Finished Goods account is used.

3. Repeat requirement 2, eliminating the Finished Goods account.

4. Explain why there is no need to have a Work in Process account.

■ MANAGERIAL DECISION CASE

Activity-based Costing; Consideration of Nonmanufacturing Costs Sharp Paper, Inc., has three paper mills, one of which is located in Memphis, Tennessee. The Memphis mill produces 300 different types of coated and uncoated specialty printing papers. This large variety of products was the result of a full-line marketing strategy adopted by Sharp's management. Management was convinced that the value of variety more than offset the extra costs of the increased complexity.

During 1993, the Memphis mill produced 120,000 tons of coated paper and 80,000 tons of uncoated. Of the 200,000 tons produced, 180,000 were sold. Sixty products account for 80 percent of the tons sold. Thus, 240 products are classified as low-volume products.

Lightweight lime hopsack in cartons (LLHC) is one of the low-volume products. LLHC is produced in rolls, converted into sheets of paper, and then sold in cartons. In 1993, the cost to produce and sell one ton of LLHC was as follows:

Raw materials:		
Furnish (3 different pulps)	2,225 pounds	$ 450
Additives (11 different items)	200 pounds	500
Tub size	75 pounds	10
Recycled scrap paper	(296 pounds)	(20)
Total raw materials		$ 940
Direct labor		$ 450
Overhead:		
Paper machine ($100/ton × 2,500 pounds)		$ 125
Finishing machine ($120/ton × 2,500 pounds)		150
Total overhead		$ 275
Shipping and warehousing		$ 30
Total manufacturing and selling cost		$1,695

Overhead is applied using a two-stage process. First, overhead is allocated to the paper and finishing machines using the direct method of allocation with carefully selected cost drivers. Second, the overhead assigned to each machine is divided by the budgeted tons of output. These rates are then multiplied by the number of pounds required to produce one good ton.

In 1993, LLHC sold for $2,400 per ton, making it one of the most profitable products. A similar examination of some of the other low-volume products revealed that they also had very respectable profit margins. Unfortunately, the performance of the high-volume products was less impressive, with many showing losses or very low profit margins. This situation led Ryan Chesser to call a meeting with his marketing vice-president, Jennifer Woodruff, and his controller, Jan Booth.

Ryan: The above-average profitability of our low-volume specialty products and the poor profit performance of our high-volume products make me believe that we should switch our marketing emphasis to the low-volume line. Perhaps we should drop some of our high-volume products, particularly those showing a loss.

Jennifer: I'm not convinced that the solution you are proposing is the right one. I know our high-volume products are of high quality, and I am convinced that we are as efficient in our production as other firms. I think that somehow our costs are not being assigned correctly. For example, the shipping and warehousing costs are assigned by dividing these costs by the total tons of paper sold. Yet . . .

Jan: Jennifer, I hate to disagree, but the $30 per ton charge for shipping and warehousing seems reasonable. I know that our method to assign these costs is identical to a number of other paper companies.

Jennifer: Well, that may be true, but do these other companies have the variety of products that we have? Our low-volume products require special handling and processing, but when we assign shipping and warehousing costs, we average these special costs across our entire product line. Every ton produced in our mill passes through our Mill Shipping Department and is either sent directly to the customer or to our distribution center and then eventually to customers. My records indicate quite clearly that virtually all the high-volume products are sent directly to customers whereas most of the low-volume products are sent to the distribution center. Now all the products passing through the Mill Shipping Department should receive a share of the $2,000,000 annual shipping costs. I am not convinced, however, that all products should receive a share of the receiving and shipping costs of the distribution center as currently practiced.

Ryan: Jan, is this true? Does our system allocate our shipping and warehousing costs in this way?

Jan: Yes, I'm afraid it does. Jennifer may have a point. Perhaps we need to re-evaluate our method to assign these costs to the product lines.

Ryan: Jennifer, do you have any suggestions concerning how the shipping and warehousing costs ought to be assigned?

Jennifer: It seems reasonable to make a distinction between products that spend time in the distribution center and those that do not. We should also distinguish between the receiving and shipping activities at the distribution center. All incoming shipments are packed on pallets and weigh one ton each (there are fourteen cartons of paper per pallet). In 1993, receiving processed 56,000 tons of paper. Receiving employs fifteen people at an annual cost of $600,000. Other receiving costs total about $500,000. I would recommend that these costs be assigned using tons processed. Shipping, however, is different. There are two activities associated with shipping: picking the order from inventory and loading the paper. We employ thirty people for picking and ten for loading at an annual cost of $1,200,000. Other shipping costs total $1,100,000. Picking and loading are more concerned with the number of shipping items rather than tonnage. That is, a shipping item may consist of two or three cartons instead of pallets. Accordingly, the shipping costs of the distribution center should be assigned using the number of items shipped. In 1993, for example, we handled 190,000 shipping items.

Ryan: These suggestions have merit. Jan, I would like to see what effect Jennifer's suggestions have on the per-unit assignment of shipping and warehousing for LLHC. If the effect is significant, then we will expand the analysis to include all products.

Jan: I'm willing to compute the effect, but I'd like to suggest one additional feature. Currently, we have a policy to carry about twenty-five tons of LLHC in inventory. Our current cost system totally ignores the cost of carrying this inventory. Since it costs us $1,665 to produce each ton of this product, we are tying up a lot of money in inventory, money that could be invested in other productive opportunities. In fact, the return lost is about 16 percent per year. This cost should also be assigned to the units sold.

     Ryan: Jan, this also sounds good to me. Go ahead and include the carrying cost in your computation.

     To help in the analysis, Jan gathered the following data for LLHC for 1993:

Tons sold	10
Average cartons per shipment	2
Average shipments per ton	7

Required:

1. Identify the flaws associated with the current method to assign shipping and warehousing costs to Sharp's products.

2. Compute the shipping and warehousing cost per ton of LLHC sold using the new method suggested by Jennifer and Jan.

3. Using the new costs computed in requirement 2, compute the profit per ton of LLHC. Compare this with the profit per ton computed using the old method. Do you think that this same effect would be realized for other low-volume products? Explain.

4. Comment on Ryan's proposal to drop some high-volume products and place more emphasis on low-volume products. Discuss the role of the accounting system in supporting this type of decision making.

5. After receiving the analysis of LLHC, Ryan decided to expand the analysis to all products. He also had Jan reevaluate the way in which mill overhead was assigned to products. After the restructuring was completed, Ryan took the following actions: (a) the prices of most low-volume products were increased, (b) the prices of several high-volume products were decreased, and (c) some low-volume products were dropped. Explain why Ryan's strategy changed so dramatically.

PART 2

Managerial Decision Making

Special Pricing Decisions and Cost Behavior

■ **LEARNING OBJECTIVES**

After studying Chapter 7, you should be able to

1. Describe the role of costs in pricing decisions.

2. Explain why firms may choose, on occasion, to price a product below its full cost.

3. Explain why a linear approximation of the more general non-linear cost function may represent an acceptable operational outcome.

4. Define and explain the concepts of step-variable and step-fixed costs.

5. Describe the impact of relevant range and activity-level choice on cost behavior.

6. Distinguish between committed and discretionary fixed costs.

7. Separate mixed costs into their fixed and variable components using the scatterplot method, the high-low method, or the method of least squares.

8. Discuss the use of managerial judgment in cost behavior assessment.

9. Discuss the advantages and disadvantages of each of the methods used to separate mixed costs into their fixed and variable components.

10. Define and explain the key terms listed at the end of the chapter.

SCENARIO

Joan Kapple, manager of a relatively new electronics division, is worried about her division's performance. For the third consecutive quarter, the division showed a loss. Joan believed that the reason was the loss of three major bids. In order to discuss and resolve the problem, Joan called a meeting of three key divisional executives: Bill Moyes, the divisional controller; Jim Brewer, the division's marketing manager; and Sandy Lawson, the division's senior production manager. The meeting began with Joan asking why the three bids had been lost.

Jim was the first to respond. "Joan, if you recall, at the first of the year, we decided that all jobs must be priced at a minimum of full manufacturing cost plus 50 percent. By setting this minimum target price, we are assured of covering all of our costs and earning a minimum acceptable return on our investment. In the case of those three bids, we bid full cost plus 50 percent. In two of the three bids, we were given the opportunity by the customer to match or beat a competitor's bid to win the job. In each case, however, matching the competitor's bid would have resulted in a price less than full cost plus 50 percent. In fact, matching one bid would have placed us 10 percent below full cost and matching the other bid would have returned only 20 percent above full cost. Because of this, we refused to meet either bid."

"What I don't understand," Sandy remarked, "is why it is so important for us to earn full cost plus 50 percent or more on every job when many of the costs are present whether or not a job is accepted. We certainly are not operating at capacity; a lot of our equipment is just sitting there— completely idle. It seems that what we really need to do is to utilize more of our capacity while at least recovering the additional costs caused by a job."

Jim agreed totally with Sandy's view. "If we could have met the bids as requested, and, at the same time recovered more than the incremental costs, we would have shown a profit and established relationships with customers that would have produced future sales. One problem I have, though, is that I simply don't know what these additional costs are. If I had that information I could identify whether meeting a competitor's bid would provide us with a feasible walk-away price. Perhaps Bill can help us."

"Our current accounting system is designed to provide only full cost information," Bill replied. "Corporate headquarters requires that our financial reports be on a full-costing basis. The kind of information you are requesting requires an accounting system that identifies and classifies costs by behavior. What you want is a variable-costing system. But there's no reason why our divisional accounting system can't be designed to provide both types of information."

"In that case," interjected Joan, "I want our accounting system redesigned so that it provides us the needed information. If we all want to keep our jobs, we need to move this division into a profit-making mode. Bill, tell us what needs to be done to start supplying the kind of cost information we've been discussing."

"As I said, our accounting system needs to identify and classify costs by behavior," Bill responded. "This means that every cost must be classified as fixed or variable. Once this classification is completed, I can begin supplying cost information that is more useful for making competitive bids. Given that we are facing stiff competition and have excess capacity, pricing so that we at least cover the incremental costs is a sensible short-run strategy—but in the long run our prices must cover full costs and provide an acceptable return on our investment."

"It appears that we may also want to look at our overall pricing strategy," Joan observed. "Jim, why don't you and Bill get together and prepare a report on pricing and cost behavior? I'd like to know when it is appropriate to offer prices below the minimum price we have previously identified. I also want to know just what we need to do to classify costs into fixed and variable categories. Please identify the assumptions and limitations associated with classifying all our costs into these two categories."

■ THE ROLE OF COST BEHAVIOR IN SPECIAL PRICING DECISIONS

The introductory scenario is based on actual facts and describes why a division decided to adopt a variable-costing accounting system for internal purposes. The example underscores the importance of knowing cost behavior when making pricing decisions.

With many products in well-defined markets, the selling price is established by the competitive conditions of the markets. In effect, the pricing decision is made by the markets. However, in other situations, managers have a great deal of discretion in making pricing decisions; these include custom-made products, new products, and low-volume products. The customer wanting this special work often requests bids from several competitors. A common practice of organizations faced with such a bid is to set a price equal to full manufacturing cost plus some markup. The markup is chosen to cover nonmanufacturing costs and to provide an acceptable return. The electronics division's policy of setting a minimum price of full manufacturing cost plus 50 percent is an example of this approach.

Unfortunately, the use of full cost plus markup may not provide the flexibility needed for a firm to compete successfully. For example, under certain special conditions, a firm may be able to increase profits in the short run by pricing below full cost—something not readily evident with the full-cost base for pricing. When these conditions exist, knowledge of cost behavior can play a vital role in pricing decisions. What are those conditions? When can managers, in good conscience, offer a price that is below what they normally would like to obtain?

Special Conditions and Special Prices

In the long run, most goods must be sold at a price that covers all costs and provides a reasonable return on investment; otherwise, a firm will go out of business. In the short run, however, it is often profitable to offer a price that is below the desired level. As the divisional controller indicated, price concessions are often necessary when competition is keen and when idle capacity exists. The two conditions frequently come together.

Two of the bids lost by the electronics division revealed competitors' prices that were considerably below the official cost-plus price set earlier in the year. By adamantly sticking to the original price, the division was not reacting properly to competitive pressures. For one thing, the lower price offered by the competition could signal that the division's costs are out of line. The divisional manager should find out whether competitors are operating more efficiently and, if so, determine how to make her firm more efficient.[1]

On the other hand, it may be that demand for electronic components is soft and excess capacity exists in the entire industry. The lower prices may simply reflect a scramble to obtain business that will return at least some profit, even if not at the normal level.

Incremental Costs, Cost Behavior, and Pricing

Clearly, the divisional manager needs more flexibility in pricing. But to obtain this flexibility, she needs more cost information than that supplied by a traditional full costing system. A manager needs to know what the incremental costs are. For example, a manager needs to know what additional costs will be incurred if an order or job is accepted. At the very least, these additional costs must be covered by the revenues generated by a new order. Thus, these additional costs represent the absolute minimum price that can be accepted. Only by knowing this absolute minimum price can a manager react properly in a competitive bidding environment or when excess capacity exists.

Since fixed costs are not affected by changes in activity level, the incremental costs often correspond to variable costs. Knowing which costs are fixed and which are variable is fundamental to making special pricing decisions.

As Sandy correctly pointed out, many costs would continue whether or not the bids had been won. For example, salaries of production supervisors, property taxes, depreciation, and other fixed costs are not affected by changes in production volume. On the other hand, variable costs such as raw materials, direct labor, and commissions usually result in additional expenditures. Recall that the electronics division had the opportunity to match the bids of

---

[1]Another possibility is that the division's cost accounting system is not accurately assigning costs to products, causing significant difficulties with the cost-plus pricing model. This problem is discussed in detail in Chapters 6 and 13. In this chapter, it is assumed that there is no problem with the accuracy of product costs.

competitors for two customers. If matching the bid prices would have provided revenues in excess of the variable costs, the division could have increased its profit.

To illustrate this possibility, assume that the electronics division had the following information concerning the two jobs for which the customers asked for a matching bid. (All costs and prices are expressed on a unit basis.) Both jobs could be accepted without exceeding the division's productive capacity.

	Job 1	Job 2
Units	50,000	100,000
Costs:		
Full manufacturing costs	$50	$60
Variable manufacturing costs	$30	$40
Variable selling costs	$ 1	$ 1
Full cost plus 50%	$75	$90
Full cost plus 20%	$60	n/a*
Full cost less 10%	n/a*	$54

*Not applicable since the competition did not bid this price

According to divisional policy, the minimum bid price for each job is full cost plus 50 percent; thus the actual bid prices for the two jobs were $75 and $90, respectively. The division was given the chance to match the low bids that were received by the two potential customers, which were $60 and $54, respectively.

Since the division is operating below capacity, fixed costs will not increase if either job is accepted. If the low bid is matched for the first job, the division will incur additional expenditures amounting to $31 per unit and will receive additional revenues of $60 per unit. The net effect is an additional contribution margin of $29 per unit ($60 − $31), for a total of $1.45 million. Since total fixed costs are the same regardless of whether the bid is matched or not, total profits increase by $1.45 million.

A similar analysis can be done for the second job. Matching the low bid results in additional expenditures of $41 per unit and revenues of $54 per unit. This produces a unit contribution margin of $13 ($54 − $41) and a total contribution margin of $1.3 million. Consequently, matching the low bid of the second job increases profits by $1.3 million.

Matching the low bids of both jobs increases total profits by $2.75 million ($1.45 million + $1.3 million). In the presence of excess capacity, strong competition, and the need to establish good customer relations (the division is a new venture), the division should have accepted the offer to match the two bids. Knowledge of costs and their behavior was a critical input to the correct pricing decision.

Knowledge of cost behavior is crucial for other areas of managerial responsibility as well. For example, budgeting, deciding to keep or drop a product line, and evaluating the performance of a segment all benefit from variable costing. In fact, not knowing cost behavior can lead to poor—even disastrous—decisions.

The remainder of this chapter discusses cost behavior in greater depth than we have done previously. A variable-costing system, for example, requires that all costs be classified as fixed or variable. But can all costs realistically be classified into one of these two categories? What are the assumptions and limitations associated with classifying costs in this way? Furthermore, just how good are our definitions of variable and fixed costs? Finally, what procedures can we use to break out the fixed and variable components of semivariable costs?

■ COST BEHAVIOR

cost behavior **Cost behavior** is the general term for describing whether a cost is fixed or variable in relation to changes in the level of activity. A cost that remains the same in total as activity increases or decreases is a fixed cost. A variable cost is one that increases with an increase in activity and decreases with a decrease in activity. Theoretically, separating fixed and variable costs is no problem. In fact, most economics textbooks simply assume that the cost separation has been accomplished and proceed from there. It is the management accountant who must bring cost separation from theory to reality by considering the type of decision to be made as well as the reasons for making it. In analyzing cost behavior, it helps to consider the specific concepts of time horizon and activity level measure.

Time Horizon

long run
short run

Determining whether a cost is fixed or variable depends crucially on the time horizon. We know from economics that in the **long run**, all costs are variable; in the **short run**, at least one cost is fixed. But how long is the short run? Different costs have different-length short runs. Direct materials, for example, are relatively easy to adjust. For all practical purposes, the firm may treat direct materials as strictly variable even though for the next few hours the amount of materials already purchased may be fixed. Depreciation on the plant, however, is more difficult to adjust. It could take months, or even years, to sell or expand the plant. Thus, this cost is typically seen as fixed. The length of the short-run period depends to some extent on management judgment and the purpose for which cost behavior is being estimated. In the opening scenario, the short run might consist of just a month or so—long enough to obtain the two bids and produce the order. Other types of decisions, such as product discontinuance or product mix decisions, will affect a much longer period of time. Thus, the costs that must be considered are long-run variable costs, including product design, development, market development, and market penetration. Short-run costs do not adequately reflect all the costs necessary to design, produce, market, distribute, and support a product.

Activity-Level Measures

Variable costs move in total with changes in activity level. Often the activity level is the volume of production. Tracing costs to each unit produced ranges from relatively easy (for example, direct materials) to virtually impossible (for example, janitorial services or property taxes on the factory building). For service firms, tracing costs to their units of production may be even more troublesome. Is the appropriate unit an hour of service or the performance of a particular task? Additionally, some units of service may be provided by more experienced personnel. For example, a law firm will cost (and price) an attorney's time on a case differently from a paralegal's time.

The determination of an appropriate measure of activity, or cost driver, is made easier by considering that we are trying to find out what the cost varies with. In other words, ideally the activity/cost driver relationship will be strictly variable. For example, electrical cost may be a function of machine hours, shipping expense may be a function of units sold, and hospital laundry cost may be a function of patient days. The choice of cost driver is tailored not only to the particular firm but also to the particular cost being measured.

We have defined cost drivers as causal factors that explain the consumption of activities. In general, cost drivers fall into four categories. Unit-level cost drivers increase cost every time a unit is produced. Direct materials, power to run production machinery, and direct labor can be thought of as unit-level cost drivers. Batch-level cost drivers increase cost when the number of batches increases. Examples of batch-level cost drivers include setups, scheduling, inspection, and materials moves. Product-sustaining cost drivers are associated with products. They pertain to product development, production, and sales. Product-sustaining cost drivers include engineering, maintenance, expediting, and formulating bills of materials. Finally, at the facility level, we have general overhead, which might be thought of as a capacity cost.[2]

It is important to consider carefully the question being asked in order to determine the appropriate cost driver. In the opening scenario, the costs relevant to the bids under consideration would be those at the unit and batch levels. Product-sustaining and facility-level costs would not change.

We now take a closer look at variable and fixed costs. If the cost-behavior pattern of an item is strictly variable or fixed, then that cost can be assigned to the appropriate category. However, what if the item displays a mixed cost pattern? For mixed cost items, we must break out their variable and fixed components so that each component can be assigned to the correct category. As we shall see, assigning costs to either a variable or a fixed category may not exactly correspond to how costs actually behave. What we hope is that the cost-behavior assignment approximates reality well enough to be useful. Finally, we should note that the emphasis in the remainder of the chapter on

---

[2]At the facility level, there is no cost driver in the short run because all facility costs are strictly fixed. Facility costs can vary only in the long run. We might think of the long-run situation as involving a shift in strategy, product obsolescence, or new technology. Any of these changes may require changes to be made in plant facilities.

cost behavior is on unit-level cost drivers. Thus, the analysis is primarily oriented towards conventional cost systems; however, the procedures discussed can be applied to other categories of cost driver.

Variable Costs

From Chapter 2, we know that a variable cost is a cost that, in total, varies in direct proportion to changes in a cost driver. For example, assume that Star Computers, Inc., produces personal computers. Each personal computer uses one floppy disk drive, which has a cost of $40. The total variable cost of disk drives can be expressed as

$$TVC = 40X$$

where TVC = Total variable cost of disk drives
         X = The number of personal computers produced

If 100 computers are produced, the total cost of floppy disk drives is $4,000 ($40 × 100). If 200 are produced, then the total cost is $8,000 ($40 × 200). As production doubles, the cost of floppy disk drives doubles. In other words, cost increases in direct proportion to the number of units produced.

Linearity Assumption   The definition of variable costs given above implies a *linear* relationship between the cost of floppy disk drives and the number of computers produced. This linear relationship is portrayed graphically in Exhibit 7–1. How reasonable is the assumption that costs are linear? Do costs

EXHIBIT 7–1
Linearity of Variable Costs

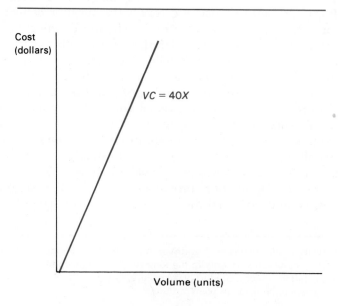

really increase in direct proportion to increases in the activity level? If not, then how well does the assumed linear cost function approximate the underlying cost function?

Economists usually assume that variable costs increase at a decreasing rate up to a certain volume, at which point they increase at an increasing rate. This type of *nonlinear* function is displayed in Exhibit 7–2. Here variable costs are assumed to increase as activity increases but not in direct proportion.

What if the nonlinear view more accurately reflects reality? What do we do then? One possibility is to determine the actual cost function—but every cost item could have a different cost function, and this approach could be very time consuming and expensive. It is much simpler to assume a linear relationship.

If the linear relationship is assumed, then the main concern is how well this assumption approximates the underlying cost function. Exhibit 7–3 gives us some idea of the consequences of assuming a linear cost function. If the operating range is between 0 and X^*, the linear function appears to approximate the actual cost function reasonably well. As defined in Chapter 2, the *relevant range* is the range of activity for which the assumed cost relationships are valid. Here *validity* refers to how closely the linear cost function approximates the underlying cost function. For volumes beyond X^*, the approximation appears to break down, and we are out of the relevant range.

Another argument can be made in favor of linear approximations. Since these approximations must be done for each cost item that displays a variable cost pattern, we can expect some approximations to overstate the actual cost and some to understate it (where actual cost is the cost predicted by the real

EXHIBIT 7–2
Nonlinearity of Variable Costs

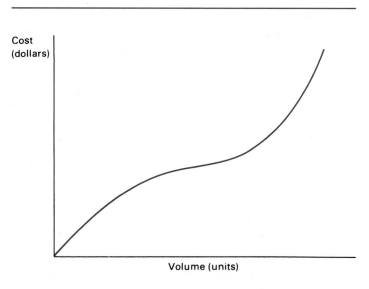

EXHIBIT 7–3
Linear Approximation

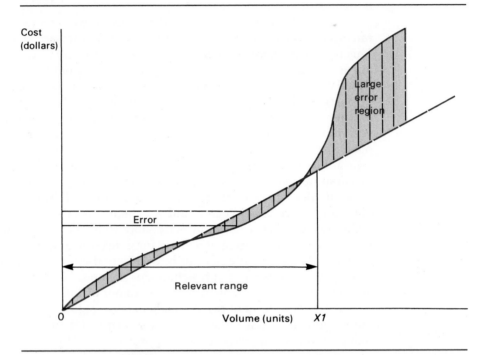

underlying cost functions). If these understatements and overstatements occur randomly, then as we aggregate the individual variable-cost items, the total error should become smaller. Since we are often interested in total variable costs (the sum of individual variable costs), the use of linear approximations should be feasible.

To illustrate this last idea, consider the following variable costs predicted for the production of 1,000 personal computers:

Cost Item	Linear Approximation	Actual Costs	Error
Motherboard	$ 50,000	$ 47,000	$ 3,000
Cabinet	10,000	11,000	(1,000)
Supplies	5,000	4,500	500
Utilities	8,000	8,700	(700)
Disk drive	40,000	41,500	(1,500)
Total	$113,000	$112,700	$ 300

The error for any one item is less than 12 percent of the actual cost. Thus, the linear approximation is close for each cost item. However, as can be seen, the total error is only $300—less than the error for any one item and representing a total error of less than 0.3 percent of the actual cost. Of course, the example is contrived—but if the errors are random, we would expect the type of behavior revealed by the example. Moreover, the more variable cost items there are, the more likely it is that the error will be negligible.

Step-Variable Costs   In our discussion of variable costs, we have assumed that the cost function (be it linear or nonlinear) is continuous. In reality, some cost functions may be discontinuous, as shown in Exhibit 7–4. This type of cost function is known as a *step function*. A **step-cost function** has the property of displaying a constant level of cost for a range of activity and then jumping to a higher level of cost at some point, where it remains for a similar range of activity.

step-cost function

 In Exhibit 7–4, the cost is $100 as long as activity is between 0 and 100 units. If the volume is between 100 and 200 units, the cost jumps to $200. For example, suppose a manufacturing firm has a number of machines, each capable of producing 100 units of output. If one machine is in operation, then lubricating oil costing $100 is needed to service the machine. If two machines are in operation, then an additional $100 of lubricating oil must be used, raising the total cost to $200.

 Items that display a step-cost behavior must be purchased in chunks. The width of the step defines the range of activity for which a quantity of the item must be acquired. The width of the step for lubricating oil is 100 units.

EXHIBIT 7–4
Step-Variable Costs

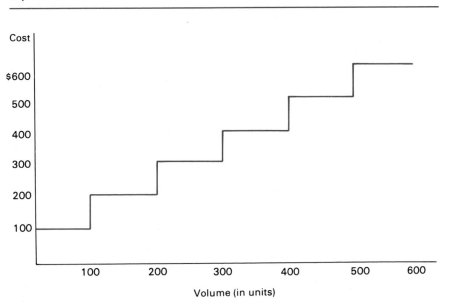

If the width of the step is narrow, the cost of the item changes in response to fairly small changes in the activity level. Costs that follow a step-cost behavior with narrow steps are defined as **step-variable costs.** Since the width of the step is narrow, we usually approximate step-variable costs with a strictly variable cost assumption.

step-variable costs

Fixed Costs

Fixed costs are costs that do not change, in total, as the activity level changes. Property taxes on a plant, for example, may be $10,000 per year. This is a facility cost; thus, total property taxes remain the same regardless of how many units, batches, or products are produced in the plant.[3] The fixed cost equation for property taxes can be expressed as:

$$FC = \$10,000$$

The graph of the fixed cost equation is shown in Exhibit 7–5.

EXHIBIT 7–5
Fixed Costs

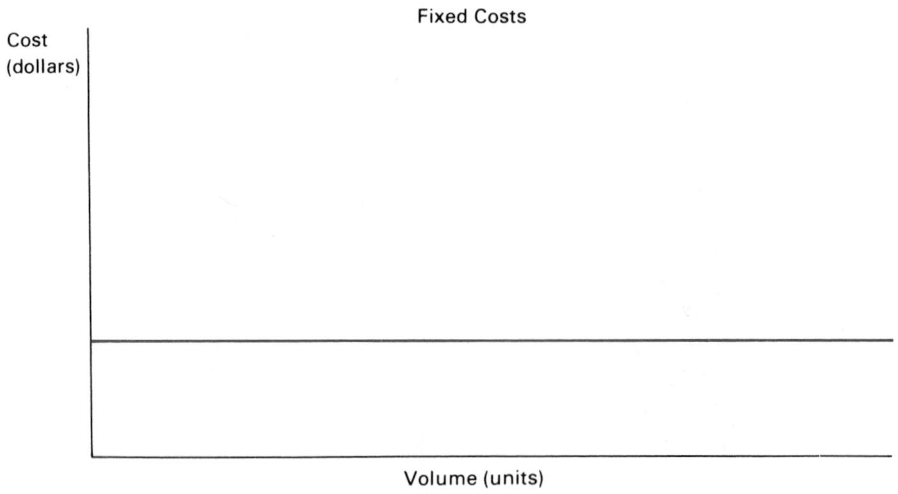

Fixed Costs

Cost
(dollars)

Volume (units)

[3]This does not mean that fixed costs cannot change. They can and do. For the property tax example, the county could raise taxes, thereby increasing the firm's total property taxes. However, the fixed nature of property taxes with respect to units, batches, or products remains unchanged. Graphically, an increase in fixed cost is seen as a parallel shift upward to the new level of cost.

Fixed costs are often viewed as providing the capacity needed to carry out the production and sales activities of a firm. This capacity can be acquired on a long-term or a short-term basis. This timing distinction serves as the basis for dividing fixed costs into two categories: committed and discretionary.

Committed Fixed Costs   Costs incurred for the acquisition of long-term capacity—such as plant, equipment, warehouses, vehicles, and salaries of top executives—are **committed fixed costs.** The firm is usually committed to these costs over a long period of time; thus, these costs are relatively difficult to change. The decision to build a plant usually means that the firm expects the plant to be in operation for many years. Similarly, hiring a chief executive officer usually reflects a commitment of several years, which is often evidenced by the signing of a contract. Committed fixed costs are vital to the delivery capacity of a firm. Without them, a firm cannot exist as a viable economic entity.

committed fixed costs

Acquisition of long-term capacity is the result of strategic planning. Underlying the strategic plan is the expectation of effectively utilizing this capacity. By comparing the actual utilization with the planned utilization, a firm exercises control over committed fixed costs.

Discretionary Fixed Costs   Costs incurred for the acquisition of short-term capacity—such as training and research and development—are **discretionary fixed costs.** These costs are planned at the beginning of each year. Unlike committed fixed costs, the level of discretionary fixed costs can be easily changed from one year to the next.

discretionary fixed costs

Discretionary fixed costs are controlled by comparing actual expenditures for the period to the budgeted or planned expenditures. For example, if a firm planned to spend $12,000 a month on advertising and $20,000 had been spent at the end of the first month, an inquiry should be made to discover why more is being spent than planned. Based on the outcome of the investigation, any necessary corrective action can be taken.

Fixed costs, whether discretionary or committed, are assumed to remain unchanged for all levels of activity. Is that realistic? What if increased demand for a product leads a firm to increase production capacity by building a new plant? What will happen then to property taxes? Obviously, in this event, property taxes would increase. Increasing production can also affect other fixed costs as well. For example, increased production could mean higher rental cost for more equipment and higher salary costs for additional production-line supervisors and stores clerks.

Step-Fixed Costs   In reality, most fixed costs probably are best described by a step-cost function. Consider the step-cost function displayed in Exhibit 7–6. Assume that the illustration describes property taxes, and each step represents the acquisition of an additional 10,000 units of productive capacity. Each chunk of productive capacity is subject to $10,000 of property taxes. Notice, however, that the step is wide, meaning that the cost of property taxes re-

EXHIBIT 7–6

Step-Fixed Costs

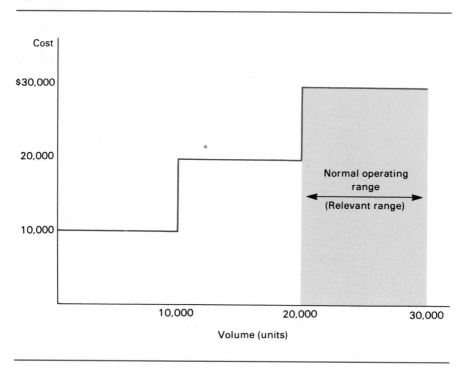

sponds only to large changes in activity level. Costs that follow a step-cost **step-fixed costs** behavior with wide steps are defined as **step-fixed costs.**

In terms of treatment, step-fixed costs are assigned to the fixed cost category. Most step-fixed costs are fixed over the normal operating range of a firm. If that range is 20,000 to 30,000 units (as shown in Exhibit 7–6), then property taxes of $30,000 would be paid. Only if activity dropped below 20,000 on a permanent basis and if a plant were sold would property taxes decrease below $30,000. Similarly, only if demand increases to the point where another plant is needed would property taxes increase above $30,000. In both cases, the change in level of expenditure would be known well in advance so that adjustments in total fixed costs could be easily made.

Now compare the step-fixed cost function in Exhibit 7–6 with the step-variable cost function in Exhibit 7–4. Notice that the principal difference between the two is the width of the steps. The width of the step in Exhibit 7–6 is 10,000 units, whereas the width of the step in Exhibit 7–4 is only 100. A step-variable cost responds to changes in activity much more rapidly than does a step-fixed cost. This explains why step-variable costs are assigned to the variable cost category and step-fixed costs to the fixed-cost category.

Mixed Costs

As we know, mixed costs have a fixed and a variable component. As an example, assume that a firm leases a photocopier. The agreement calls for a payment of $250 per month plus $0.025 per copy. The behavior of this cost is expressed by the following equation:

$$Y = \$250 + \$0.025X$$

where Y = Total cost
         X = The number of copies per month

The fixed charge of $250 makes the copying capacity available, but use of that capacity also produces a cost. In fact, for every copy produced, the company must pay an additional $0.025. The more copies made, the more the company must pay. If 1,000 copies are made during a month, then the total cost is $275 ($250 + $0.025 × 1,000). If 5,000 copies are produced, total cost is $375 ($250 + $0.025 × 5,000). Total cost increases as the activity increases, but regardless of how many copies are made, the company must pay at least $250. Exhibit 7–7 (page 318) displays the mixed cost relationship. Notice that at zero units of activity, there is some cost. As activity level increases, total cost increases.

What the Accounting Records Reveal   Sometimes, as in the photocopier example, it is easy to identify the variable and fixed components of a mixed cost. Many times, however, the only information available is the total cost and a measure of the activity level (the variables Y and X). For example, the accounting system will usually record the total cost of maintenance for a given period and the units produced during that period. How much of the total maintenance cost represents a fixed charge and how much represents a variable charge is not revealed by the accounting records. (In fact, the accounting records may not even reveal the breakdown of costs in the photocopier example.) Often, the total cost is simply recorded with no attempt to segregate the fixed and variable costs.

Need for Decomposition   Since accounting records typically reveal only the total cost and the associated activity of a mixed cost item, it is necessary to decompose the total cost into its fixed and variable components. Only through decomposition can all costs be classified into the appropriate categories.

If mixed costs are a very small percentage of total costs, however, decomposition may be more trouble than it's worth. In this case, mixed costs could be assigned to either the fixed- or variable-cost category without much concern for the classification error or its effect on decision making. Alternatively, the total mixed cost could be arbitrarily divided between the two cost categories. This option is seldom available, though. Mixed costs for many firms are of sufficient magnitude to warrant decomposition. Given the need for decomposition, how is it done?

EXHIBIT 7–7
Mixed Cost

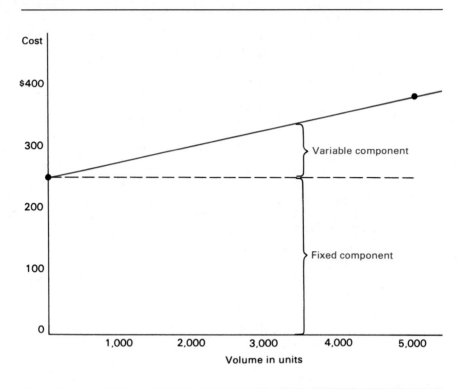

■ METHODS FOR DECOMPOSING MIXED COSTS

Mixed costs are assumed to follow a linear relationship.

$$Y = F + VX$$

where Y = Total mixed cost (the dependent variable)
        F = Fixed cost component (the intercept parameter)
        V = Variable cost per unit of activity (the slope parameter)
        X = Activity level (the independent variable)

dependent variable   The **dependent variable** is a variable whose value depends on the value of
another variable. In the above equation, total mixed cost is the dependent
independent variable   variable; it is the cost we are trying to predict. The **independent variable** is a
variable whose value does not depend on the value of another variable. In the
above equation, the activity level (e.g., units produced) is the independent
intercept parameter   variable. The **intercept parameter** corresponds to fixed cost. Graphically, the

intercept parameter is the point at which the mixed cost curve intercepts the
slope parameter vertical axis. The **slope parameter** corresponds to the variable cost per unit of
activity. Graphically, this represents the slope of the mixed cost curve.

Since the accounting records reveal only X and Y, those values must be
used to estimate the parameters F and V. With estimates of F and V, the fixed
and variable components can be estimated and the behavior of the mixed cost
can be predicted as activity changes. Four methods will be described for
estimating F and V. These methods are the high-low method, the scatterplot
method, the method of least squares, and managerial judgment.

The same data will be used with each method so that comparisons
among them can be made. Assume that the accounting records of Larson,
Inc., disclosed the following utility costs and associated production activity
for the past five months:

Month	Utilities Cost	Units Produced
June	$1,000	100
July	1,250	200
August	2,250	300
September	2,500	400
October	3,750	500

The High-Low Method

From basic geometry, we know that two points are needed to determine a
line. Once we know two points on a line, then its equation can be determined.
Recall that F, the fixed cost component, is the intercept of the total cost line,
and that V, the variable cost per unit, is the slope of the line. Given two
high-low method points, the slope and the intercept can be determined. The **high-low method**
preselects the two points that will be used to compute the parameters F and
V. Specifically, the method uses the high and low points. The high point is
defined as the point with the highest activity level. The low point is defined
as the point with the lowest activity level.

Letting (X_1, Y_1) be one point, say the low point, and (X_2, Y_2) be the
second point, the high point, the equations for determining the slope and
intercept are, respectively

$$V = \text{Change in cost/Change in activity}$$
$$= (Y_2 - Y_1)/(X_2 - X_1)$$

and

$$FC = \text{Total mixed cost} - \text{Variable cost}$$
$$= Y_2 - VX_2$$

or

$$= Y_1 - VX_1$$

Notice that the fixed cost component is computed using the total cost at either (X_1, Y_1) or (X_2, Y_2).

For Larson, the high point is $3,750 of utilities when 500 units were produced, or (500, $3,750). The low point is $1,000 of utilities cost when 100 units were produced, or (100, $1,000). Once the high and low points are defined, the values of F and V can be computed.

$$
\begin{aligned}
V &= (Y_2 - Y_1)/(X_2 - X_1) \\
&= (\$3,750 - \$1,000)/(500 - 100) \\
&= \$2,750/400 \\
&= \$6.875
\end{aligned}
$$

$$
\begin{aligned}
F &= Y_2 - VX_2 \\
&= \$3,750 - (\$6.875 \times 500) \\
&= \$312.50
\end{aligned}
$$

The cost formula using the high-low method is

$$
Y = \$312.50 + \$6.875X
$$

If production for December is expected to be 350 units, this cost formula will predict a total cost of $2,718.75, with fixed costs of $312.50 and variable costs of $2,406.25.

The high-low method has the advantage of objectivity. That is, any two people using the high-low method on a particular data set will arrive at the same answer. In addition, the high-low method allows a manager to get a quick fix on a cost relationship using only two data points. For example, a manager may have only two years of data. Sometimes this will be enough to get a crude approximation of the cost relationship.

The high-low method is usually not as good as the other methods. Why? First, the high and low points often can be what are known as *outliers*. They may represent atypical cost-activity relationships. If so, the cost formula computed using these two points will not represent what usually takes place. The scatterplot method can help a manager avoid this trap by selecting two points that appear to be representative of the general cost-activity pattern. Second, even if these points are not outliers, other pairs of points may clearly be more representative. Again, the scatterplot method allows the choice of the more representative points.

Scatterplot Method

scatterplot

The first step in applying the scatterplot method is to plot the data points so that the relationship between utility costs and activity level can be seen. This plot is referred to as a **scattergraph** and is shown in Exhibit 7–8. The vertical axis is total mixed cost and the horizontal axis is activity level or volume (utility cost and units produced, respectively, for the example).

EXHIBIT 7-8
Scattergraph for Larson, Inc.

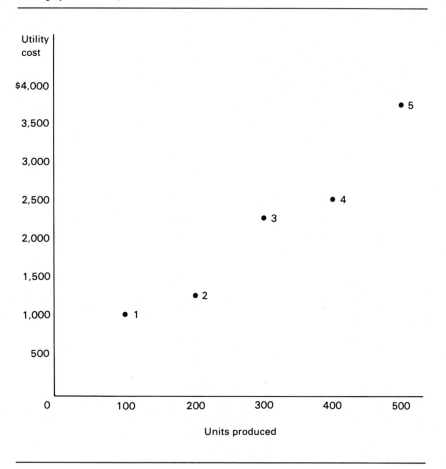

Inspecting Exhibit 7–8 gives us increased confidence that the assumption of a linear relationship between utility costs and units produced is reasonable for the indicated range of activity. Thus, one purpose of a scattergraph is to assess the validity of the assumed linear relationship. Additionally, inspecting the scattergraph may reveal several points that do not seem to fit the general pattern of behavior. Upon investigation, it may be discovered that these points (the outliers) were due to some irregular occurrences. This knowledge can provide justification for their elimination and perhaps lead to a better estimate of the underlying cost function.

A scattergraph can help a manager gain a better feel for the relationship between cost and activity. In fact, a manager can visually fit a line to the points on the scattergraph. In doing so, the manager should choose a line that he or she believes fits the points the best. In making that choice, the manager is free to use past experience with the behavior of the cost item. That is, the manager's experience may provide a good intuitive sense of how utility costs

scatterplot method

behave; the scattergraph then becomes a useful tool to quantify this intuition. Fitting a line to the points in this way is how the **scatterplot method** works.[4]

Examine Exhibit 7–8 carefully. Based only on the information contained in the graph, how would you fit a line to the points in it? Suppose that a manager decides that a line passing through points 1 and 3 provides the best fit. If so, how could this decision be used to compute the parameters F and V so that the fixed and variable cost components can be estimated?

Assuming your choice of the best-fitting line is the one passing through points 1 and 3, the variable cost per unit can be computed in the following way. First let point 1 be designated by $X_1 = 100$, $Y_1 = \$1,000$ and point 3 by $X_2 = 300$, $Y_2 = \$2,250$. (This designation is arbitrary—it really doesn't matter which point is designated (X_1, Y_1) and which one is designated (X_2, Y_2).) Next, use these two points to compute the slope:

$$
\begin{aligned}
V &= (Y_2 - Y_1)/(X_2 - X_1) \\
  &= (\$2,250 - \$1,000)/(300 - 100) \\
  &= \$1,250/200 \\
  &= \$6.25
\end{aligned}
$$

Thus, the variable cost per unit produced is \$6.25. Given the variable cost per unit, the final step is to compute the fixed-cost component using (X_2, Y_2) in the intercept equation:

$$
\begin{aligned}
F &= X_2 - VX_2 \\
  &= \$2,250 - \$6.25(300) \\
  &= \$375
\end{aligned}
$$

Of course, the fixed-cost component can also be computed using (X_1, Y_1), which produces the same result.

$$
\begin{aligned}
F &= Y_1 - VX_1 \\
  &= \$1,000 - \$6.25(100) \\
  &= \$375
\end{aligned}
$$

cost formula

The fixed and variable components of the utility cost have now been identified. The **cost formula** for utilities can be expressed as

$$
Y = \$375 + \$6.25X
$$

Using this formula, the total cost of utilities for activity levels between 100 and 500 can be predicted and then broken down into fixed and variable components. For example, assume that 350 units are planned for December.

---

[4] Keep in mind that the scattergraph and the other statistical aids are tools that can help managers improve their judgment. Using the tools does not restrict the manager from using judgment to alter any of the estimates produced by formal methods.

Using the cost formula, the predicted cost is \$2,562.50 (\$375 + \$6.25 × 350). Of this total cost, \$375 is fixed and \$2,187.50 variable.

The cost formula was obtained by fitting a line to points 1 and 3 in Exhibit 7–8. Judgment was used to select the line. Whereas one person may decide, by inspection, that the best-fitting line is the one that passes through points 1 and 3, others, using their own judgment, may decide that the line should pass through points 2 and 4 — or points 1 and 5. An unlimited number of choices exist.

A significant advantage of the scatterplot method is that it affords a manager the opportunity to inspect the data visually. Exhibit 7–9 illustrates cost behavior situations that are not appropriate for the straightforward ap-

EXHIBIT 7–9

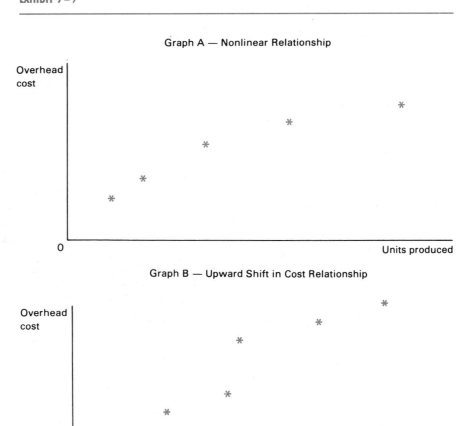

Graph A — Nonlinear Relationship

Graph B — Upward Shift in Cost Relationship

(continued)

EXHIBIT 7–9

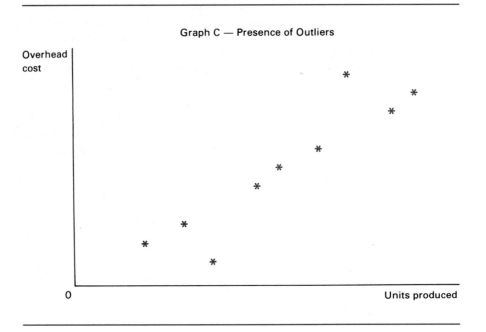

Graph C — Presence of Outliers

plication of the high-low method. Graph A shows a nonlinear relationship between overhead cost and activity level. An example of this might be a volume discount given on direct materials or evidence of learning by workers (e.g., as more hours are worked, the total cost increases at a decreasing rate due to the increased efficiency of the workers). Graph B indicates that there is an upward shift in cost after 300 units are made—perhaps this could mean that an additional supervisor must be hired or a second shift run. Graph C shows outliers that are not representative of the overall cost relationship.

The scatterplot method suffers from the lack of any objective criterion for choosing the best-fitting line. The quality of the cost formula depends on the quality of the subjective judgment of the analyst. The high-low method removes the subjectivity in the choice of the line. Regardless of who uses the method, the same line will result.

	Fixed Cost	Variable Rate	Utilities Cost at 350 Units
High-Low	$312.50	$6.875	$2,718.75
Scatterplot	375.00	6.250	2,562.50

Let's compare the results of the scatterplot method with those of the high-low method. There is a large difference between the fixed cost components and the variable rates. The predicted cost of utilities at 350 units is

$2,562.50 according to the scatterplot method and $2,718.75 according to the high-low method. Which is "right"? Since the two methods can produce vastly different cost formulas, the question of which method is the best naturally arises. Ideally, a method that is objective and, at the same time, produces the best-fitting line is needed. The method of least squares defines *best-fitting* and is objective in the sense that using the method for a given set of data will produce the same cost formula.

The Method of Least Squares

Up to this point, we have alluded to the concept of a line that best fits the points shown on a scattergraph. What is meant by a best-fitting line? Intuitively, it is the line in which the data points are closer to the line than any other line. But what is meant by closer?

Consider Exhibit 7–10. Here an arbitrary line $(Y = F + VX)$ has been drawn. The closeness of each point to the line can be measured by the vertical distance of the point from the line. This vertical distance is the difference be-

EXHIBIT 7–10
Line Deviations

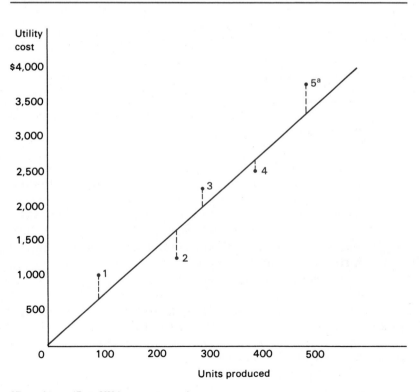

$^aE_5 = Y_5 - (F + VX_5)$

tween the actual cost and the cost predicted by the line. For point 5, this is $E_5 = Y_5 - (F + VX_5)$, where Y_5 is the actual cost, $F + VX_5$ is the predicted cost, and the deviation is represented by E_5. The **deviation** is the difference between the predicted and actual cost, which is shown by the distance from the point to the line.

deviation

The vertical distance measures the closeness of a single point to the line, but what is needed is a measure of closeness of *all* points to the line. One possibility is to add all the single measures to obtain an overall measure. However, since the single measures can have positive or negative signs, this overall measure may not be very meaningful. For example, the sum of small positive deviations could result in an overall measure greater in magnitude than the sum of large positive deviations and large negative deviations because of the canceling effect of positive and negative numbers. To correct for this problem, we could first square each single measure of closeness and then sum these squared deviations as the overall measure of closeness. Squaring the deviations avoids the cancellation problem caused by a mix of positive and negative numbers.

To illustrate this concept, a measure of closeness will be calculated for the cost formula produced by the scatterplot method.

Actual Cost	Predicted Cost[a]	Deviation[b]	Deviation Squared
$1,000	$1,000	$ —	—
1,250	1,625	− 375	140,625
2,250	2,250	—	—
2,500	2,875	− 375	140,625
3,750	3,500	250	62,500
Total measure of closeness			343,750

[a] Predicted cost = $375 + $6.25X, where X is the actual activity associated with the actual cost.
[b] Deviation = Actual cost − Predicted cost.

Since the measure of closeness is the sum of the squared deviations of the points from the line, the smaller the measure, the better the line fits the points. For example, the scatterplot method line has a closeness measure of 343,750. A similar calculation produces a closeness measure of 523,438 for the high-low line. Thus, the scatterplot line fits the points better than the high-low line. (As you can see, the scatterplot method has produced a better-fitting line than the high-low method. This outcome supports the earlier claim that the use of judgment in the scatterplot method is superior to the high-low method.)

In principle, comparing closeness measures can produce a ranking of all lines from best to worst. The line that fits the points better than any other line is called the **best-fitting line.** It is the line with the smallest (least) sum of squared deviations. The **method of least squares** identifies the best-fitting line. We rely on statistical theory to obtain the formulas that produce the best-fitting line. These formulas are given below.

best-fitting line

method of least squares

$$V = [\Sigma XY - \Sigma X \Sigma Y/n]/[\Sigma X^2 - (\Sigma X)^2/n] \tag{7.1}$$
$$F = \Sigma Y/n - v(\Sigma X/n) \tag{7.2}$$

In order to compute V and F, five inputs are needed: n, ΣX, ΣY, ΣXY, and ΣX^2. The first input, n, is the easiest to obtain— simply count the number of data points in the data set. For the Larson, Inc., example, there are five data points. The other four inputs are computed as follows:

ΣX	ΣY	ΣXY	ΣX^2
100	$ 1,000	$ 100,000	10,000
200	1,250	250,000	40,000
300	2,250	675,000	90,000
400	2,500	1,000,000	160,000
500	3,750	1,875,000	250,000
1,500	$10,750	$3,900,000	550,000

Substituting the above summations (Σ) into Equations 7.1 and 7.2, we obtain:

$$V = [3,900,000 - (1,500 \times 10,750)/5]/[550,000 - (1,500)^2/5]$$
$$= 675,000/100,000$$
$$= 6.75$$

and

$$F = \$10,750/5 - \$6.75(1,500/5)$$
$$= \$125$$

Thus, the cost formula for the method of least squares can be expressed as follows:

$$Y = 125 + 6.75X$$

Since this cost formula is the best-fitting line, it should produce better predictions of utility costs. For a production level of 350, the utility cost predicted by the least-squares line is $2,487.50 [$125 + $6.75(350)], with a fixed component of $125 plus a variable component of $2,362.50. Using this prediction as a standard, the scatterplot line most closely approximates the least-squares line.

If the least-squares line is the best-fitting line, why worry about the other two methods? Because the other two methods involve simpler computations, they can provide quick estimates of the fixed and variable components of mixed costs. The computational complexity of the least-squares method is not high, however, and calculators or software packages are available to do the computation with the simple requirement of inputting the data points. Thus, the method of least squares is generally recommended over the other two methods. Remember, however, that the use of a scattergraph may result in the detection of nonlinearity and outliers, in which case that method may produce a better cost formula.[5] Furthermore, the method of least squares requires a large number of data points for reliable estimates. In those settings where only a small number of data points are available, the scatterplot method may be more suitable.

Goodness of Fit

goodness of fit

The method of least squares has one advantage over the other two methods that has yet to be mentioned. Specifically, it is associated with a statistical measure of goodness of fit. For our cost setting, **goodness of fit** measures the degree of association between cost and activity level. The method of least squares identifies the best-fitting line, but it does not reveal how good the fit is. The best-fitting line may not be a good-fitting line. It may perform miserably when it comes to predicting costs.

To introduce the concept of a goodness-of-fit measure, consider the following list of grade point averages (GPAs) that twelve students achieved during a recent term: 4.0, 3.7, 3.5, 3.3, 3.0, 2.7, 2.3, 2.0, 1.7, 1.3, 1.0, 0.0, where 4.0 is an A and 0.0 is failing. Notice that there is large variability in GPAs. Some students did very well; some students did terribly. How would you explain this variability?

Suppose someone suggested that the variability in GPAs can be explained by the hours of study per week each student averaged during the school term. Upon further investigation, GPAs and hours of study per week were associated in the following way:

	Student											
	1	2	3	4	5	6	7	8	9	10	11	12
GPA	4.0	3.7	3.5	3.3	3.0	2.7	2.3	2.0	1.7	1.3	1.0	0.0
Hours of study	18	40	35	30	25	20	10	22	8	6	4	—

With a few exceptions, it looks as if students with higher GPAs also spent more time studying. Hours of study probably will account for a significant percentage of the variability in GPAs. Suppose that 90 percent of the total variability in GPAs is explained by hours of study—would you feel comfortable using hours of study to predict a student's GPA? Suppose, however, that only 35 percent of the total variability is explained by hours of study. While this reflects significant explanatory power, it also indicates that the predictive ability of study hours is far from perfect.[6]

To obtain better explanatory power, additional variables might be needed. For example, ability may offer an additional reason as to why GPAs vary so

---

[5] If they represent unusual events that are unlikely to reoccur, outliers should be excluded before using the method of least squares.

[6] Hours of study in this example actually explains about 71 percent of the variability in GPA.

much. Hours of study and ability together may explain most of the variation. Sometimes more than one explanatory variable is needed.

Notice that in trying to find a good independent variable to explain the variability in the dependent variable, we tried to find a variable that seems to "cause" the dependent variable. In the case of explaining GPAs, we chose hours of study and ability (perhaps as measured by ACT or SAT score). We did not choose to look at the students' heights or at their income level. While statistical methods never prove causation, our own knowledge of relationships will lead us to choose variables that act as drivers just as we looked for cost drivers in Chapter 6.

In our cost setting, we are assuming that one variable—differences in activity level—will explain variability in cost. Our experience with utility costs and activity level suggests that knowledge of activity level will give us a good indication of total utility costs. The scattergraph shown in Exhibit 7–8 confirms this belief because it reveals that utility cost and activity level seem to move together. It is quite likely that a significant percentage of the total variability in cost is explained by activity level. We can determine statistically just how much variability is explained by looking at the coefficient of determination. The percentage of variability in the dependent variable explained by an independent variable (in **coefficient of** this case, activity level) is called the *coefficient of determination.* This percentage **determination** is a goodness-of-fit measure. The higher the percentage of cost variability explained, the better the fit. Since the coefficient is the *percentage* of variability explained, it always has a value between 0 and 1.0. The coefficient of determination (R^2) is computed by the following formula:

$$R^2 = V[\Sigma XY - \Sigma X \Sigma Y/n]/[\Sigma Y^2 - (\Sigma Y)^2/n] \qquad (7.3)$$

where V is the slope computed using the method of least squares.

To compute the coefficient of determination (R^2) for the utility cost example, the required inputs are V, n, ΣX, ΣXY, ΣY, and ΣY^2. In our prior computation of V, the same inputs were required except for ΣY^2. The computation of ΣY^2 is as follows:

$$
\begin{array}{r}
\$\ 1,000,000 \\
1,562,500 \\
5,062,500 \\
6,250,000 \\
\underline{14,062,500} \\
\$27,937,500 \\
\end{array}
$$

Using the above inputs, the coefficient of determination can be calculated.

$$
\begin{aligned}
R^2 &= 6.75[3,900,000 - (1,500) \times (10,750)/5]/[27,937,500 - (10,750)^2/5] \\
&= 6.75(675,000)/4,825,000 \\
&= 0.9443
\end{aligned}
$$

Thus, 94.43 percent of the variability in utility cost is explained by activity level. This result tells us that the least-squares line is a good-fitting line.

There is no cut-off point for a good versus a bad coefficient of determination. Clearly, the closer R^2 is to one, the better. However, is 89 percent good enough? How about 73 percent? Or even 46 percent? The answer is that it depends. If your cost equation yields a coefficient of determination of 75 percent, you know that your independent variable explains three-fourths of the variability in cost. You also know that some other factor or combination of factors explains the remaining one-fourth. Depending on your tolerance for error, you may want to continue working with that equation by trying different independent variables (for example, machine hours rather than units produced) or by trying multiple regression (which is explained in a succeeding section of this chapter).

coefficient of
correlation

An alternative measure of goodness of fit is the **coefficient of correlation,** which is the square root of the coefficient of determination. Since square roots can be negative, the value of the coefficient of correlation can range between -1 and $+1$. If the coefficient of correlation is positive, then the two variables (in this example, cost and activity) move together in the same direction and positive correlation exists. Perfect positive correlation would yield a value of 1.00 for the coefficient of correlation. If, on the other hand, the coefficient of correlation is negative, then the two variables move in a predictable fashion but in opposite directions. Perfect negative correlation would yield a coefficient of correlation of -1.00. A coefficient of correlation value close to zero indicates no correlation. That is, knowledge of the movement of one variable gives us no clue as to the movement of the other variable. Exhibit 7–11 illustrates the concept of correlation.

For Larson, the coefficient of correlation (r) is computed as follows:

$$r = \sqrt{0.9443}$$
$$= 0.9718$$

The square root is positive because the correlation between X and Y is positive. In other words, as activity level (number of units produced) increases, the utility cost increases. This positive correlation is reflected by a positive value for V. If cost decreases as activity level increases, then the coefficient of correlation (and the value of V) is negative. The sign of V reveals the sign of the coefficient of correlation. The very high positive correlation between utility cost and units produced indicates that units represent a good choice for the independent variable.

Multiple Regression

In the Larson, Inc., example, more than 94 percent of the cost variability was explained by changes in activity level—units produced. Suppose that only 60 percent of the variability could be explained by this variable. In this case, a search should be made for additional explanatory variables. For example,

EXHIBIT 7–11
Concept of Correlation

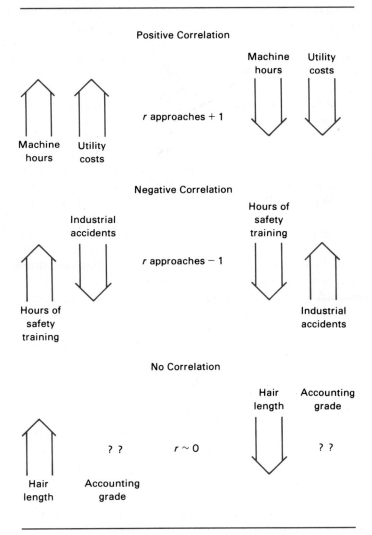

month of the year might be useful—particularly if heating and cooling are significant requirements in winter and summer months.

In the case of two explanatory variables, the linear equation is expanded to include the additional variable:

$$Y = F + VX + CZ$$

where Z is the second variable, for example, a number representing the month of the year.

With three variables (X, Y, Z), a minimum of three points is needed to compute the parameters F, V, and C. Seeing the points becomes difficult because they must be plotted in three dimensions. Using the scatterplot method and the high-low method is not practical.

However, the extension of the method of least squares is straightforward. It is relatively simple to develop a set of equations that provides values for F, V, and C that yields the best-fitting equation. Whenever least squares is used to fit an equation involving two or more explanatory variables, the method is called ***multiple regression.*** The computational complexity of multiple regression, which increases significantly, is facilitated by the computer.

multiple regression

Let's return to Larson, Inc. There is no real need to try to improve on the results of utility cost estimation. The independent variable (units produced) explains about 94 percent of the variability in utilities. Suppose that Larson decides to use regression to predict total factory overhead cost. The dependent variable, factory overhead, is a combination of many different factors. It is unlikely that just one independent variable can successfully explain the variance of overhead cost. Therefore, Larson might estimate an equation using several independent variables that are meant to capture the variability of overhead due to unit, batch, and product-sustaining activities. Since facility-level activity is fixed in the short run, we can view the intercept (or constant) term as an expression of that activity. One possible equation, estimated using multiple regression, is shown here.

$$\text{Factory overhead} = \$2{,}206.78 + \$14.73 \text{ (Units)} + \$311.08 \text{ (Setups)}$$
$$+ \$2.91 \text{ (Engineering hours)}$$
$$R^2 = 0.92$$

In this equation, there is facility-level cost of $2,206.78 per month. Unit-level activities add $14.73 for each unit produced. Batch-level activities (measured here by setups) add $311.08 to total overhead every time a setup must be done. Finally, product-sustaining level activities (measured here by engineering hours) add $2.91 to overhead for each hour worked by plant engineers. To estimate factory overhead for the next month, we must first estimate the number of units to be produced, the number of setups to be done, and the number of engineering hours to be worked.

	Regression		
	Budgeted amounts ×	*Coefficient* =	*Budgeted Overhead*
Units	225	$ 14.73	$3,314.25
Setups	10	311.08	3,110.80
Engineering hours	344	2.91	1,001.04
Fixed overhead	—	2,206.78	2,206.78
Total			$9,632.87

Given the budgeted activity levels, total overhead of $9,632.87 would be budgeted. Of this amount, $2,206.78 represents facility-related costs; $3,314.25 represents unit-level activities; $3,110.80 represents batch-level activities; and $1,001.04 represents product-sustaining level activities. Larson can also use this information to see what impact reducing or increasing certain activities would have on costs. For example, if setups could be reduced to eight, the predicted overhead cost would decrease by $622.16 (2 × $311.08).

Managerial Judgment

Managerial judgment is by far the most widely used method in practice.[7] Many managers simply use their experience and past observation of cost-volume relationships to determine fixed and variable costs. This method, however, may take a number of forms. Some managers simply assign particular costs to the fixed category and others to the variable category. They ignore the possibility of mixed costs. Thus, a chemical firm may regard materials and utilities as strictly variable and all other costs as fixed. Even labor, the textbook example of a variable cost, may be fixed for this firm. The appeal of this method is simplicity. Before opting for this course, management would do well to make sure that each cost is predominantly fixed or variable and that the decisions being made are not highly sensitive to errors in classifying costs as fixed or variable.

Management may instead identify mixed costs and divide these costs into fixed and variable components by deciding just what the fixed and variable parts are—that is, using experience to say that a certain amount of a cost is fixed and that, therefore, the rest must be variable. Our photocopier example with the fixed monthly cost of $250 and the variable rate of $0.025 per copy falls into this category. Then the variable component can be computed using one or more cost/volume data points. This has the advantage of accounting for mixed costs but is subject to a similar type of error as the strict fixed/variable dichotomy. That is, management may be wrong in its assessment.

Finally, management may use experience and judgment to refine statistical estimation results. Perhaps the experienced manager might "eyeball" the data and throw out several points as being highly unusual or might revise results of estimation to take account of projected changes in cost structure or technology. Statistical techniques are highly accurate in depicting the past—but they cannot foresee the future, which is, of course, what management really wants.

The advantage of using managerial judgment to separate fixed and variable costs is its simplicity. In situations in which the manager has a deep understanding of the firm and its cost patterns, this method can give good results. However, if the manager does not have good judgment, errors will

---

[7] Maryanne M. Mowen, *Accounting for Costs as Fixed and Variable* (Montvale, N.J.: National Association of Accountants, 1986), pp. 19–20.

occur. Therefore, it is important to consider the experience of the manager, the potential for error, and the effect that error could have on related decisions.

▪ SUMMARY OF LEARNING OBJECTIVES

1. Describe the role of costs in pricing decisions. The separation of costs into fixed and variable categories allows managers to make better, more informed decisions. This is particularly true for special pricing decisions because many costs within the firm do not vary with additional units produced and may be irrelevant to the short-run pricing decision.

2. Explain why firms may choose, on occasion, to price a product below its full cost. A product may be priced below full cost when competitive conditions and excess capacity exist. The firm may price a product below full cost but above incremental cost, recognizing that in this short-run situation many costs are fixed and will not increase because of the special order. A firm cannot price products below full cost over the long run.

3. Explain why a linear approximation of the more general nonlinear cost function may represent an acceptable operational outcome. For variable costs, the usual assumption is that costs increase in direct proportion to increases in the activity level. This assumption is strictly true if the underlying cost function is neither nonlinear nor a step function. Even if the cost function is nonlinear or the steps narrow, the assumption of linearity still may produce reasonable approximations of cost behavior. Additionally, managers may find that over the relevant range, cost behavior patterns are reasonably linear and that any error from assuming linearity is small.

4. Define and explain the concepts of step-variable and step-fixed costs. A step-variable cost is one with relatively narrow width steps. A step-function with relatively wide steps is generally considered to be step-fixed. As long as the organization expects to operate within the relevant range, the assumption of fixed costs is totally reasonable in the case of step-fixed costs.

5. Describe the impact of relevant range and activity-level choice on cost behavior. The relevant range allows the manager to assume linearity of cost. Activity-level choice is important because costs that are fixed at one activity level can be variable at another activity level. Activity-based costing suggests four levels of activity within the plant: unit-level activities, batch-level activities, product-sustaining activities, and facility-level activities.

6. Distinguish between committed and discretionary fixed costs. Discretionary fixed costs are short term in nature, and their levels can be changed from one period to the next without impairing the normal capacity of a firm. Committed fixed costs, on the other hand, are long term in nature. Changing the level of these costs usually requires more time and involves some serious strategic planning.

7. **Separate mixed costs into their fixed and variable components using the scatterplot method, the high-low method, or the method of least squares.** In order to classify mixed costs into fixed and variable categories, it is necessary to break out, or decompose, the fixed and variable components. Since the accounting records normally reveal only the total mixed cost and the associated activity level, a separate methodology must be used to accomplish this decomposition. Three such methods are the scatterplot method, the high-low method, and the method of least squares.

The scatterplot method involves inspecting a scattergraph (a plot showing total mixed cost at various activity levels) and selecting two points that seem best to represent the relationship between cost and activity. Since two points determine a line, the two selected points can be used to determine the intercept and the slope of the line on which they lie. The intercept gives an estimate of the fixed-cost component and the slope an estimate of the variable cost per unit of activity.

In the high-low method, the two points chosen from the scattergraph are the high and the low points with respect to activity level. These two points are then used to compute the intercept and the slope on the line on which they lie.

The method of least squares uses all of the data points (except outliers) on the scattergraph and produces a line that best fits all of the points. The line is best fitting in the sense that it is closest to all the points as measured by the sum of the squared deviations of the points from the line.

8. **Discuss the use of managerial judgment in cost behavior assessment.** Managerial judgment can be used alone or in conjunction with the high-low, scatterplot, or least-squares method. Managers use their experience and knowledge of cost and activity level relationships to identify outliers, understand structural shifts, and adjust parameters due to anticipated changing conditions.

9. **Discuss the advantages and disadvantages of each of the methods used to separate mixed costs into their fixed and variable components.** The high-low method is objective and easy. However, if either the high or low point is not representative of the true cost relationship, the relationship will be misestimated.

The scatterplot method is a good way to identify nonlinearity, the presence of outliers, and the presence of a shift in the cost relationship. Its disadvantage is that it is subjective.

Of the three methods, the method of least squares produces the line that best fits the data points and is, therefore, recommended over the other two methods. The method of least squares also allows the computation of a goodness-of-fit measure. This measure, the coefficient of determination, shows the percentage of the total variability in cost that is explained by the variable being analyzed. The higher the percentage, the better the fit.

■ KEY TERMS

Best-fitting line The line that fits a set of data points the best in the sense that the sum of the squared deviations of the data points from the line is the smallest. (p. 326)

Coefficient of correlation   The square root of the coefficient of determination, which is used to express not only the degree of correlation between two variables but also the direction of the relationship. (p. 330)

Coefficient of determination   The percentage of total variability in a dependent variable (e.g., cost) that is explained by an independent variable (e.g., activity level). It assumes a value between 0 and 1. (p. 329)

Committed fixed costs   Costs incurred for the acquisition of long-term capacity, usually as the result of strategic planning. (p. 315)

Cost behavior   The way in which a cost changes in relation to changes in the level of an activity. (p. 308)

Cost formula   A linear function, $Y = F + VX$, where Y = Total mixed cost, F = Fixed cost, V = Variable cost per unit of activity, and X = Activity level. (p. 322)

Dependent variable   A variable whose value depends on the value of another variable. For example, Y in the cost formula $Y = F + VX$ depends on the value of X. (p. 318)

Deviation   The difference between the cost predicted by a cost formula and the actual cost. It measures the distance of a data point from the cost line. (p. 326)

Discretionary fixed costs   Costs incurred for the acquisition of short-term capacity or services, usually as the result of yearly planning. (p. 315)

Goodness of fit   The degree of association between Y and X (cost and activity). It is measured by how much of the total variability in Y is explained by X. (p. 328)

High-low method   A method for fitting a line to a set of data points using the high and low points in the data set. For a cost formula, the high and low points represent the high and low activity levels. It is used to break out the fixed and variable components of a mixed cost. (p. 319)

Independent variable   A variable whose value does not depend on the value of another variable. For example, in the cost formula $Y = F + VX$, the variable X is an independent variable. (p. 318)

Intercept parameter   The fixed cost, representing the point where the cost formula intercepts the vertical axis. In the cost formula $Y = F + VX$, F is the intercept parameter. (p. 318)

Long run   Period of time in which all costs are variable. (p. 308)

Method of least squares   A statistical method to find a line that best fits a set of data. It is used to break out the fixed and variable components of a mixed cost. (p. 326)

Multiple regression   The use of least squares analysis to determine the parameters in a linear equation involving two or more explanatory variables. (p. 332)

Scattergraph   A plot of (X, Y) data points. For cost analysis, X is activity level and Y is the associated cost at that activity level. (p. 320)

Scatterplot method   A method to fit a line to a set of data using two points that are selected by judgment. It is used to break out the fixed and variable components of a mixed cost. (p. 322)

Short run   Period of time in which at least one cost is fixed. (p. 308)

Slope parameter   The variable cost per unit of activity, represented by V in the cost formula $Y = F + VX$. (p. 319)

Step-cost function A cost function in which cost is defined for ranges of activity rather than point values. The function has the property of displaying constant cost over a range of activity and then changing to a different cost level as a new range of activity is encountered. (p. 313)

Step-fixed cost A step-cost function in which cost remains constant over wide ranges of activity. (p. 316)

Step-variable cost A step-cost function in which cost remains constant over relatively narrow ranges of activity. (p. 314)

■ REVIEW PROBLEM

Kim Wilson, controller of Max Enterprises, has decided to estimate the fixed and variable components associated with the company's setup costs. She has collected the following data for the past six months:

Number of Setups	Total Setup Costs
10	$ 800
20	1,100
15	900
12	900
18	1,050
25	1,250

Required:

1. Estimate the fixed and variable components for setup costs using the high-low method. Using the cost formula, predict the total cost of setups if fourteen setups are planned for the coming month.

2. Estimate the fixed and variable components using the method of least squares. Using the cost formula, predict the total cost of setups if fourteen setups are planned for the coming month.

3. For the method of least squares, compute the coefficient of determination and the coefficient of correlation.

Solution:

1. The estimate of fixed and variable costs using the high-low method, where Y = total cost and X = number of setups, is as follows:

$$V = (Y_2 - Y_1)/(X_2 - X_1)$$
$$= (1,250 - 800)/(25 - 10)$$
$$= 450/15$$
$$= \$30 \text{ per setup}$$

$$F = Y_2 - VX_2$$
$$= \$1,250 - \$30(25)$$
$$= \$500$$

$$Y = \$500 + \$30X$$
$$= \$500 + \$30 \times 14$$
$$= \$920$$

2. The calculation using the method of least squares is as follows:

ΣX^2	ΣX	ΣY	ΣXY
100	10	$ 800	$ 8,000
400	20	1,100	22,000
225	15	900	13,500
144	12	900	10,800
324	18	1,050	18,900
625	25	1,250	31,250
1,818	100	$6,000	$104,450

$$V = [\Sigma XY - \Sigma X\Sigma Y/n]/[\Sigma X^2 - (\Sigma X)^2/n]$$
$$= [104,450 - (100 \times 6,000/6)]/[1,818 - (100 \times 100/6)]$$
$$= 4,450/151.33$$
$$= \$29.41 \text{ per setup}$$

$$F = \Sigma Y/n - V\Sigma X/n$$
$$= 6000/6 - 29.41(100/6)$$
$$= \$509.83$$

$$Y = 509.83 + 29.41X$$
$$= 509.83 + 29.41(14)$$
$$= \$921.57$$

3. The computation of the coefficient of determination (R^2) and the correlation coefficient (r) is as follows:

ΣY^2
$ 640,000
1,210,000
810,000
810,000
1,102,500
1,562,500
$6,135,000

$$R^2 = [v(\Sigma XY - \Sigma X\Sigma Y/n]/[\Sigma Y^2 - (\Sigma Y)^2/n]$$
$$= 29.41(4,450)/(6,135,000 - 6,000,000)$$
$$= 0.969$$
$$r = \sqrt{0.969}$$
$$= 0.985$$

■ QUESTIONS

1   Why is knowledge of cost behavior important for managerial decision making? Give an example to illustrate your answer.

2   Explain why a linear cost function is often assumed for variable costs, even though the underlying variable cost function may be nonlinear.

3   Describe the difference between a variable cost and a step-variable cost. When is it reasonable to treat step-variable costs as if they were variable costs?

4   What is the difference between a step-fixed cost and a step-variable cost?

5   What is meant by relevant range for variable costs? For fixed costs?

6   Explain the difference between committed and discretionary fixed costs. Give examples of each.

7   How does the length of the time horizon affect the classification of cost as fixed or variable? What is the meaning of short run? Long run?

8   What four levels of activity are identified in activity-based costing? Give an example of an activity at each level.

9   How do managers exercise control over committed fixed costs? Over discretionary costs?

10 Why do mixed costs pose a problem when it comes to classifying costs into fixed and variable categories?

11 Why is a scattergraph a good first step in decomposing mixed costs into their fixed and variable components?

12 Describe how the scatterplot method breaks out the fixed and variable costs from a mixed cost. Now describe how the high-low method works. How do the two methods differ?

13 What are the advantages of the scatterplot method over the high-low method? The high-low method over the scatterplot method?

14 Describe the method of least squares. Why is this method better than either the high-low method or the scatterplot method?

15 What is meant by the best-fitting line?

16 Is the best-fitting line necessarily a good-fitting line? Explain.

17 Describe what is meant by goodness of fit. Explain the meaning of the coefficient of determination.

18 What is the difference between the coefficient of determination and the coefficient of correlation? Which of the two measures of goodness of fit do you prefer? Why?

19 When is multiple regression required to explain cost behavior?

20 Some firms assign mixed costs to either the fixed or variable cost categories without any attempt to decompose them. Explain how this practice can be defended.

21 Explain what is meant by the statement that overhead costs are positively correlated with activity level.

■ EXERCISES

E7–1 **Step Costs; Relevant Range** Buster, Inc., produces large industrial machinery. A process cost system is used. Buster has a group of indirect laborers called materials handlers. Their responsibility is to deliver materials (both raw materials and partially completed units) to the various production departments. Buster also hires supervisors to oversee production. Buster's accounting and production history reveals the following relationships between units produced and the costs of materials handling and supervision (measured on an annual basis):

Units Produced	Materials Handling	Supervision
0–250	$12,000	$120,000
250–500	24,000	120,000
500–750	36,000	120,000
750–1,000	48,000	120,000
1,000–1,250	60,000	240,000
1,250–1,500	72,000	240,000
1,500–1,750	84,000	240,000
1,750–2,000	96,000	240,000

Required:

1. Prepare two graphs, one that illustrates the relationship between materials handling cost and units produced and one that illustrates the relationship between the cost of supervision and units produced. Let cost be the vertical axis and units produced the horizontal axis.

2. How would you classify each cost? Why?

3. Suppose that the normal range of activity is between 1,250 and 1,500 units. Further suppose that a special order calling for an additional 500 units is received. By how much will the cost of materials handling increase? Supervision?

E7–2 **Cost Behavior; Classification and Graphing** PLW Concrete Company owns ten ready-mix trucks. Each truck can deliver (on average) 10,000 cubic yards of concrete per year (considering the truck's capacity, weather, and distance to each job). One driver per truck is needed. The labor cost of each driver is $25,000 per year. Depreciation on each truck averages $20,000. Raw materials (cement, gravel, and so on) cost about $25 per cubic yard of concrete.

Required:

1. Prepare a graph for each of three costs: truck drivers' wages, truck depreciation, and raw materials. Use the vertical axis for cost and the horizontal axis for concrete sold per year. Assume concrete sales can range from 0 to 100,000 cubic yards.

2. How would you classify each of the three types of cost? Why? Assume that the normal operating range for the company is 80,000 to 90,000 cubic yards. Does this change your cost classification? Why?

3. Is truck depreciation a committed fixed cost or a discretionary fixed cost? Explain.

E7–3 **Mixed Costs when not a Material Part of Cost Structure** Electrico Company produces semiconductors. The president of the company has recently requested fixed and variable cost information. Upon investigation, the controller discovered that, with the exception of maintenance and utilities, all manufacturing costs easily could be classified into either category. In fact, she discovered that the vast majority of costs were fixed. The total amount in each category, excluding maintenance and utilities, was fixed, $8 million per year; variable, $2 million per year (based on last year's volume). Maintenance costs average $50,000 per year, and utilities average $30,000 per year. Both of these costs were judged to be mixed.

Required:

1. What methods could be used to break out the fixed and variable cost components of maintenance and utilities? Do you have sufficient information to break out the two components? If not, what information do you need?

2. What percentage of fixed and variable costs do the costs of maintenance and utilities represent? Would it make much difference if the costs of maintenance and utilities were arbitrarily assigned to either the fixed or variable category? What if they were divided fifty-fifty between each category? Explain.

3. Suppose that the low and high points for maintenance are 1,000 hours and $40,000, and 1,800 hours and $60,000. Assume 1,400 hours are worked. Compare the high-low division of the cost with a fifty-fifty arbitrary split. Does this have much effect on the total variable costs of the firm? Would it likely affect any decisions made by managers?

E7–4 **Scatterplot Method** Betty Yeager has been operating a dental practice for the past five years. As part of her practice, she provides a dental hygiene service. She has found that her costs for this service increase with patient load. Costs for this service over the past seven months are as follows:

Month	Patients Served	Total Cost
May	320	$2,000
June	480	2,500
July	600	3,000
August	200	1,900
September	720	4,500
October	560	2,900
November	630	3,400
December	300	2,200

Required:

1. Prepare a scattergraph based on the above data. Use cost for the vertical axis and number of patients for the horizontal. Based on an examination of the scattergraph, does there appear to be a linear relationship between the cost of dental hygiene services and patients served?

2. Fit a line to the data points that you believe best describes the relationship between costs and activity. Determine the equation of this line.

3. Assume that 450 patients are expected to receive dental hygiene services in January. Using the equation you found in requirement 2, what is the predicted cost of dental hygiene services for that month?

E7–5 **High-Low Method** Refer to the data in Exercise 7–4. (*Note:* Either do Exercise 7–4 before this exercise or exclude requirement 3.)

Required:

1. Compute the cost formula for dental hygiene services using the high-low method.

2. Calculate the predicted cost of dental hygiene services for January for 450 patients using the formula found in requirement 1.

3. Which cost formula—the one you computed using the scatterplot method or the one using the high-low method—do you think is the best? Explain.

E7–6   **Method of Least Squares**   Refer to the data in Exercise 7–4.

Required:

1. Compute the cost formula for dental hygiene services using the method of least squares.

2. Using the formula computed in requirement 1, what is the predicted cost of dental hygiene services for January for 450 patients?

3. Compute the coefficient of determination. What does this measure tell you about the cost formula computed in requirement 1?

E7–7   **Prediction of Overhead Using Cost Formula; Overhead Rates**   Simpson, Inc., has determined that its total overhead cost can be expressed by the equation $Y = F + VX$, where total overhead cost is Y, total fixed overhead is F, and total variable overhead is VX (V is variable overhead per direct labor hour and X is total direct labor hours).

Required:

1. Assume that total overhead is $250,000, variable overhead per direct labor hour is $5, and the activity level is 30,000 direct labor hours. What is the fixed overhead?

2. Assume that Simpson computes a predetermined overhead rate of $9 based on 25,000 direct labor hours. The predetermined variable overhead rate is $6 per direct labor hour. What is the budgeted fixed overhead? What is the budgeted variable overhead? What is the predetermined fixed overhead rate?

3. Given your answer in requirement 1, what is the predicted overhead for 40,000 direct labor hours?

E7–8   **Method of Least Squares; Special Pricing**   Quincy Medical Center recently began operations as a community health center. The principal objective of the medical center is to provide family-centered health services with an emphasis on preventive medicine. During the first six months of operations, the need for annual physical exams was stressed in the community. Special rates of $50 were offered for physicals, and the response was enthusiastic.

The director of QMC was not certain that it could continue to offer physicals at the same price. Some staff physicians, however, insisted that the rate be maintained for at least another six months. They believed that the low price encouraged many individuals who otherwise would not do so to have a physical. The director believed that continuance of the program might be feasible provided that QMC covered at least its variable costs. Those costs were not obvious, however; the accountant had recorded only the number of exams per month along with the total cost associated with these exams.

Month	*Number of Exams*	*Operating Costs*
February	100	$ 6,500
March	150	8,500
April	200	12,000

Month	Number of Exams	Operating Costs
May	225	13,000
June	175	10,000
July	300	16,500

Required:

1. Determine the variable cost per physical exam using the method of least squares.

2. Can the medical center continue offering the $50 price and still cover its variable costs?

3. Assume 250 physical exams are administered in August. What is the total expected cost of these physical exams? How much revenue would be needed to cover the variable costs? What is the full cost per patient in August?

E7–9 **High-Low Method; Cost Formula**   During the past year, the high and low levels of activity occurred in April and October. The total costs of three overhead items are presented below for those levels.

Item	Direct Labor Hours	Total Cost
Salaries		
Low	10,000	$130,000
High	25,000	130,000
Power		
Low	10,000	13,000
High	25,000	32,500
Janitorial services		
Low	10,000	22,000
High	25,000	37,000

Required:

1. Determine the cost behavior of each item. Use the high-low method where applicable to assess the fixed and variable components.

2. Using your knowledge of cost behavior, predict the cost of each item for an activity level of 15,000 direct labor hours.

3. Construct a cost formula that can be used to predict the total cost of the three items. Using this formula, predict the total cost if the activity level is 18,000 direct labor hours.

E7–10 **Method of Least Squares; Evaluation of Cost Equation**   The method of least squares was used to develop a cost equation to predict the cost of utilities. The following computer output was received:

Intercept	$30,500
Slope	10
Coefficient of correlation	0.85

The activity variable used was machine hours.

Required:

1. What is the cost formula?

2. Using the cost formula, predict the cost of utilities if 10,000 machine hours are used.

3. What percentage of the variability in utility cost is explained by machine hours? Do you think the equation will predict well? Why or why not?

E7–11   **Activity-Level Classification; Cost Driver**   Classify each of the following situations according to activity-based costing level: unit, batch, product sustaining, or facility. Select an appropriate cost driver for each.

1. Use of a die in a stamping machine that impresses a raised design on commemorative medals (a die must be replaced after 1,000 coins are stamped).

2. Engineering change order to correct inefficient use of a machine.

3. Power used by a drill press.

4. Salary of the plant nurse.

5. Inspection labor when a random sample of units from each batch is inspected.

6. Inspection labor when every unit is inspected.

7. Cost of setting up the assembly line to produce Taurus station wagons instead of Mustangs.

8. Installation of a new data processing system to keep track of payroll for the plant.

9. Reroofing the main building of the plant due to tornado damage.

10. Cost of adding another agent in purchasing due to an increase in the number of materials to be bought for manufacture of a new product.

11. Cost of building a level-ten clean room in which to produce a new hard disk storage device. (*Note*: A level-ten clean room is one in which there are no more than ten airborne dust particles per cubic foot.)

12. Overtime paid to direct labor to expedite production of a special order.

13. Overtime put in each autumn at a toy company to gear up production for the Christmas season.

14. Rework caused by the complex electronic design of one of the products.

E7–12   **Multiple Regression**   Anson, Inc., is interested in determining its quality control costs. It estimated the following multiple regression equation based on twenty-four months of data.

$$\text{Quality Control Cost} = 253.16 + 36.05 \text{ INSPECT} - 7.76 \text{ TRAINING HOURS}$$
$$R^2 = 0.873$$

In the above equation, INSPECT represents the number of times a batch is inspected. TRAINING HOURS is the number of hours plant employees spend in quality control seminars each month.

Required:

1. If Anson, Inc., plans eight inspections and three hours of training for five new employees next month, what are the anticipated quality control costs?

2. Is the number of inspections positively or negatively correlated with quality control costs? Are training hours positively or negatively correlated with quality control costs?

3. What does R^2 mean in this equation?

E7–13   **Coefficients of Correlation and Determination**   Seth Williams works for Audiotron-
ics as the cost accountant for the Model X–7 line of tape recorders. Seth is interested
in developing a better understanding of the behavior of various overhead cost items.
He has run four regression equations, one for each set of variables A, B, C, and D,
with the following results:

	Variable 1	*Variable 2*	*Coefficient of Correlation*
A.	Total overhead	Machine hours	0.94
B.	Indirect labor and fringe benefits	Direct labor hours	0.80
C.	Utilities cost	Units produced	−0.02
D.	Cost of plant accidents	Dollars awarded for employee safety suggestions	−0.89

Required:

1. In sets A, B, C, and D above, what is the independent variable? The dependent
variable?

2. In the regression equation run for each set, what is the expected R^2? Is each one a
good or bad result in terms of goodness of fit? What would you advise Seth to do
in each of the four cases?

E7–14   **Cost Behavior Patterns**   The following graphs represent cost behavior patterns that
might occur in a company's cost structure. The vertical axis represents total cost (not
cost per unit) and the horizontal axis represents activity level or volume.

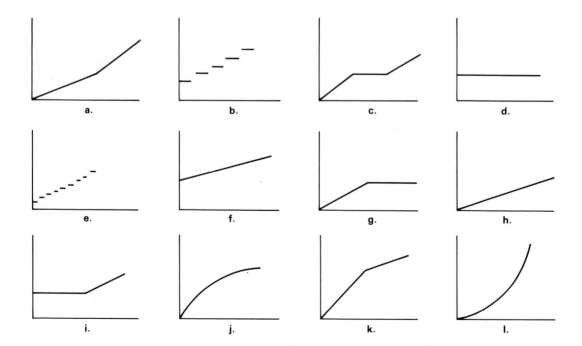

Required:

For each of the following situations, choose the graph from the group on page 345 that best illustrates the cost pattern involved.

1. The cost of photocopying when a flat fee of $200 per month is charged plus an additional charge of $0.02 per copy made.

2. Rent paid by a shoe store to the owner of the mall in which the store is located. Rent is charged at the rate of 7 percent of sales up to total annual sales of $500,000, and 4.5 percent of sales above $500,000.

3. Monthly direct labor cost of $15 per hour for the first 2,000 hours and $25 per hour for all hours worked in excess of 2,000.

4. Cost of a raw material that must be purchased in increments of 1,000 pounds.

5. The cost of tuition at a local college that charges $220 per credit hour up to fifteen credit hours. Hours taken in excess of fifteen are free.

6. The cost of tuition at another college that charges $4,500 per semester for any course load ranging from twelve to sixteen credit hours. Students taking fewer than twelve credit hours are charged $375 per credit hour. Students taking more than sixteen credit hours are charged $4,500 plus $300 per credit hour in excess of sixteen.

7. A beauty shop's purchase of soaking solution to remove artificial nails. Each jar of solution can soak off approximately fifty nails before losing effectiveness.

8. Purchase of a washer-dryer by an aerobics center to launder towels used by customers.

9. Use of claims forms by customers filing claims with an insurance company.

10. Cost of labor at a local fast-food restaurant. Three employees are always on duty during working hours; more employees can be called in during periods of heavy demand to work on an "as-needed" basis.

11. A manufacturer of farm equipment found that routine maintenance of heavy machinery was tied to the number of machine hours. However, the more often maintenance workers deal with the machinery, the more likely that mistakes are made that would require still more repairs and maintenance.

E7–15 **Scatterplot Method; Budgeted Cost**   Becker, Inc., wants to estimate factory overhead for the coming year. Becker's controller has put together the following data for the past ten years:

Factory Overhead	Direct Labor Hours
$57,000	4,400
68,900	5,200
42,000	2,400
45,000	2,800
48,000	3,200
44,475	2,730
54,000	4,000
53,250	3,900
61,500	5,000
57,750	4,500

Becker anticipates producing 18,800 units next year. Each unit requires fifteen minutes of direct labor time.

Required:

1. Prepare a scatterplot of the data on page 346. Use overhead cost for the vertical axis and direct labor hours for the horizontal axis. Based on your visual inspection of the scatterplot, draw a line that you believe best represents the cost relationship.

2. Calculate the fixed cost and variable rate based on the line you drew for requirement 1.

3. Based on the cost formula developed in requirement 2, what is Becker's budgeted overhead for next year?

E7–16 High-Low Method; Budgeted Cost Refer to the data in Exercise 7–15.

Required:

1. Calculate the annual fixed cost and variable rate for Becker's overhead using the high-low method.

2. Based on the cost formula developed in requirement 1, what is Becker's budgeted overhead for next year?

E7–17 Method of Least Squares; Budgeted Cost; Comparison of Methods Refer to the data in Exercise 7–15. (*Note:* Either do Exercises 7–15 and 7–16 before this exercise, or omit requirement 3.)

Required:

1. Calculate the annual fixed cost and variable rate for Becker's overhead using the method of least squares. (*Hint:* The sum of factory overhead is 529,875; the sum of direct labor hours is 38,130; the sum of factory overhead times direct labor hours is 2,091,546,750; the sum of direct labor hours squared is 154,152,900.)

2. Based on the cost formula developed in requirement 1, what is budgeted overhead for next year?

3. Compare the results of the scatterplot method, the high-low method, and the method of least squares. Which do you think is best? Explain.

■ PROBLEMS

P7–1 Cost Behavior; High-Low Method; Pricing Decision Hinckley Medical Clinic offers a number of specialized medical services, one of which is psychiatric care. Because of the reputation the clinic has developed over the years, demand for these services is strong. As a result, Hinckley recently opened a 100-bed psychiatric hospital near the clinic. The hospital facility itself is leased on a long-term basis. All equipment within the facility is owned by the clinic.

Since the clinic had no experience with in-patient psychiatric services, it decided to operate the hospital for two months before determining how much to charge per patient day on an ongoing basis. As a temporary measure, the clinic adopted a patient-day charge of $75, an amount equal to the charges made by a psychiatric hospital in a nearby city.

This initial per-day charge was quoted to patients entering the hospital during the first two months with assurances that if the actual operating costs of the new hospital justified it, the charge could be less. In no case would the charges be more. A temporary policy of billing after sixty days was adopted so that adjustments could be made if necessary.

The hospital opened on January 1. During January, the hospital had 2,100 patient days of activity. During February, the activity was 2,250 patient days. Costs for these two levels of activity are as follows:

	2,100 Patient Days	2,250 Patient Days
Salaries, nurses	$ 5,400	$ 5,400
Aides	1,200	1,200
Laboratory	25,000	26,500
Pharmacy	30,000	31,000
Lease	10,000	10,000
Laundry	16,800	18,000
Administration	12,000	12,000
Depreciation	30,000	30,000

Required:

1. Classify each cost as fixed, variable, or mixed.

2. Use the high-low method to separate the mixed costs into their fixed and variable components.

3. Tom Krance, the hospital's administrator, has estimated that the hospital will average 2,000 patient days per month. If the hospital is to be operated as a nonprofit organization, how much will it need to charge per patient day? How much of this charge is variable? How much is fixed?

4. Suppose the hospital averages 2,500 patient days per month. How much would need to be charged per patient day for the hospital to cover its costs? Explain why the charge per patient day decreased as the activity increased.

P7–2 **Cost Behavior; High-Low Method; Variable Costing; Income Statements** Timmons Data, Inc., offers three computer services: computer usage, software development, and systems development. Computer usage involves selling computer time to customers. Many businesses find it more convenient and less costly to satisfy their equipment needs by accessing Timmons's computer through the use of remote terminals supplied by Timmons.

Timmons also has a number of standard software packages that it sells to customers. Part of the service includes installing the software and training the client's staff to use it. Creating software from scratch is also possible. Customized software also includes installation and training.

Systems development entails analysis of a current system, design of a new system, and implementation of the new system. Most of Timmons's clients in this service segment are small businesses.

Results of operations for the third quarter 1992 are as follows:

	July	August	September
Revenues:			
Computer usage	$100,000	$120,000	$140,000
Software	50,000	40,000	40,000
Systems development	30,000	35,000	50,000
Total revenues	$180,000	$195,000	$230,000

	July	August	September
Expenses:			
Rent	$ (5,000)	$ (5,000)	$ (5,000)
Depreciation:			
Computer	(50,000)	(50,000)	(50,000)
Office Equipment	(500)	(500)	(500)
Materials	(11,000)	(11,250)	(12,500)
Utilities	(1,130)	(1,200)	(1,300)
Wages and salaries	(72,000)	(73,000)	(78,000)
Custodial services	(800)	(800)	(800)
Sales promotion	(4,000)	(4,000)	(4,000)
Total expenses	$(144,430)	$(145,750)	$(152,100)
Net income	$ 35,570	$ 49,250	$ 77,900

Required:

1. Classify all costs in the above income statement as fixed, variable, or mixed. Use the high-low method to decompose any mixed costs into their fixed and variable components.

2. Using the information from requirement 1, prepare variable-costing income statements for each month.

P7–3 **Least Squares; Correlation; Bidding Decision** Eccles, Inc., produces metal products to customer specification. Virtually all business is secured on a bid basis. The profits for Eccles had declined in recent years. One reason was Eccles's inability to compete because of the age of its plant and equipment. To reverse the decline and become more competitive, Eccles completely renovated its manufacturing facilities. The mix of manufacturing inputs changed dramatically—what had been a labor-intensive operation now was highly machine intensive. While direct labor costs declined, the costs of overhead such as indirect labor, supplies, utilities, and depreciation increased significantly.

Although the new plant had been in operation for eighteen months, profits were well below expectations. A number of reasons were offered to explain the lower-than-expected profits. First, because the plant and equipment were new, many kinks were being worked out during the first year of operations. It takes time for personnel to learn to run the equipment efficiently. Second, because the costs of production were higher, the bids were higher on average than those of competitors. This resulted in the loss of some bids that might have otherwise come to the company. Third, excess capacity in the industry was pushing prices down even further than anticipated.

To control costs better and in order to prepare bids that were more competitive, management decided that more information on the behavior of costs in the new environment was needed. In particular, management wanted to know the variable costs associated with each product. A decision had been made to allow marketing to offer bids that were lower than the usual full cost plus 30 percent guideline. In fact, marketing was allowed to offer bids as low as the variable cost of a job, resulting in the need to know variable costs.

Tracing materials and direct labor to a job posed little difficulty. Unfortunately, these costs represented less than 50 percent of the total costs of most jobs. Assessing the increase in overhead attributable to a particular job was the real problem. Thus, the key to getting a good handle on cost behavior seemed to be an analysis of the behavior of overhead costs. After some investigation, it was determined that overhead tended to vary with machine hours. Because the first twelve months of operations were spent working out problems with the new facilities, it was decided to use only the preceding six months of overhead costs. These costs and the associated activity (measured in machine hours) are as follows:

Month	Machine Hours	Overhead Costs
January	10,000	$2,000,000
February	12,000	2,300,000
March	11,000	2,000,000
April	9,000	1,800,000
May	15,000	2,700,000
June	14,000	2,500,000

Customers are charged for the number of machine hours used. There are no beginning or ending work-in-process or finished-goods inventories for any month. Variable nonmanufacturing costs are estimated at $2 per machine hour. Fixed non-manufacturing costs total $2.4 million per year; they are incurred uniformly through-out the year. For simplicity, assume that each job incurs prime costs equal to $120 per machine hour.

Required:

1. Using the method of least squares, develop an overhead cost formula.

2. Compute the coefficient of determination. Comment on the overhead cost formula.

3. Suppose that the fiscal year ended June 30. Also assume that management has decided that the overhead formula computed in requirement 1 accurately portrays overhead costs for the coming year. Using this formula, develop fixed and variable overhead rates based on an annual practical activity level of 216,000 machine hours.

4. Using the pricing guideline of full cost plus 30 percent, compute the usual bid price per machine hour.

5. Assume that Eccles expects to sell 14,500 machine hours of work in the month of July at the price computed in requirement 4. Prepare a variable-costing income statement for July. Now suppose that a customer requests a job requiring 2,500 machine hours and offers to pay $300 per machine hour (the $300 price matches the bid of a smaller, local competitor). There are no other additional sales expected for the month. Should Eccles match the bid? What effect would matching the bid have on the income for the month of July? Comment on the value of knowing variable costs.

P7–4   **Scattergraph; High-Low Method; Method of Least Squares**   Nickles Company has gathered data on its overhead costs and activity for the past ten months. Tina Paulsen, a member of the controller's department, has convinced management that overhead costs can be better estimated and controlled if the fixed and variable components are known. Tina is convinced that variation in overhead costs can be explained by vari-ation in direct labor hours. The data she collected are as follows:

Month	Direct Labor Hours	Total Overhead
1	1,000	$13,000
2	800	11,000
3	1,500	19,000
4	1,200	17,000
5	1,300	16,000
6	1,100	13,000
7	1,600	21,000
8	1,400	16,000
9	1,700	22,000
10	900	10,000

Required:

1. Prepare a scattergraph, plotting the overhead costs against direct labor hours. Use the vertical axis for costs and the horizontal for hours.

2. Select two points which make the best fit and compute a cost formula for overhead costs.

3. Using the high-low method, prepare an overhead cost formula.

4. Using the method of least squares, prepare an overhead cost formula.

5. Compare the costs predicted by each formula for the odd data points (months 1, 3, and so on). Do you believe that least squares is better than either the high-low method or the scatterplot method? Explain.

P7–5 **Cost Formulas; Single and Multiple Variables; Coefficient of Correlation** Grant Products, Inc., recently developed the following cost formula for overhead using the least squares method: $Y = 10,000 + 100X$, where $X =$ units produced and the coefficient of correlation equals 0.8. Prime costs averaged $200 per unit produced, and variable selling expenses were $10 per unit sold. There were no variable administrative costs.

Required:

1. Compute the total unit variable cost. Suppose that Grant is producing well below capacity and that an opportunity to accept an order for 20,000 units at $325 per unit exists. Should Grant accept the order? (The order would not displace any of Grant's regular orders.)

2. Explain the significance of the 0.8 coefficient of correlation. Did this have a bearing on your answer in requirement 1? Should it have a bearing? Why?

3. Suppose that a multiple regression equation is developed for overhead costs: $Y = 9,500 + 98X + 50Z$, where $X =$ units produced, $Z =$ product weight (in pounds), and the correlation coefficient is 0.95. Assume that the units in the special order weigh one pound each. Recompute the unit variable cost. Would you now accept the order at $325 per unit? Explain.

P7–6 **Scattergraph; High-Low Method; Method of Least Squares** The management of Fernelius Company has decided to adopt variable costing for internal purposes. Fernelius uses a highly automated manufacturing process, and its power costs are significant. Management has decided that power costs are mixed; thus, they must be decomposed into their fixed and variable elements to implement the variable-costing system. The following data for the past eight quarters have been collected:

Quarter	Machine Hours	Power Cost
1	20,000	$26,000
2	25,000	38,000
3	30,000	42,500
4	22,000	37,000
5	21,000	34,000
6	18,000	29,000
7	24,000	36,000
8	28,000	40,000

Required:

1. Prepare a scattergraph by plotting power costs against machine hours. Fit a line to the data set; select two points and determine the cost formula for power.

2. Using the high and low points, compute a power cost formula.

3. Use the method of least squares to compute a power cost formula. Also compute the coefficient of determination.

4. Compute the expected cost for 23,000 machine hours using each of the three formulas. Which cost formula would you recommend? Explain.

P7–7   **Method of Least Squares; High-Low Method; Cost Reimbursement**   Air Force Logistics Centers have the responsibility to keep Air Force weapon systems at minimum operational capability. The logistics centers also service other customers such as the army, the navy, the Department of Defense, and foreign governments. Each center has its own specialties; for example, Hill Air Force Base is concerned with the entire fleet of intercontinental ballistic missiles plus F–4 and F–16 fighter jets.

All depot maintenance work is financed by the Air Force Industrial Fund, established in July 1968. The fund is operated on a revolving basis with sales rates used to recover the costs of operations. As jobs are worked on, the customer is billed for their costs. Revenues return to the fund to be used again in the future in an ongoing process.

Operating capital for the fund is obtained by up-front billing. Customers are to pay in advance a fixed percentage of the estimated cost of the job. The remaining part of the bill is spread out as the job is completed. A job-order cost system is used to accumulate the costs of the maintenance work; however, because of the cash-flow requirements, most customers are billed using estimated costs rather than actual costs of the job.

Each job passes through different departments, depending on the type of maintenance needed. These departments are called *resource control centers* (RCCs). Direct labor hours and material usage are estimated for each RCC. Materials costs are charged directly to the job; direct labor hours and rates are used to assign direct labor cost, overhead, and general and administrative costs to the job.

Because customers are charged estimated costs, it is important to know the behavior of costs. For example, overhead includes such shop costs as indirect labor, depreciation, supplies, and other expenses that cannot be directly identified with a specific job order. Assume that the following total shop costs have been collected for the past twelve months, along with the total direct labor hours worked for the same period:

Month	Direct Labor Hours	Shop Costs
1	250,000	$4,100,000
2	230,000	3,900,000
3	275,000	4,500,000
4	260,000	4,150,000
5	240,000	4,200,000
6	280,000	4,600,000
7	300,000	5,000,000
8	290,000	4,700,000
9	305,000	5,100,000
10	270,000	4,300,000
11	265,000	4,250,000
12	285,000	4,700,000

Required:

1. Prepare a cost formula for shop costs using the high-low method and the method of least squares. Also compute the coefficient of correlation for the method of least squares.

2. Assume that maintenance at Hill Air Force Base expects to work 250,000 direct labor hours on jobs during July. Using the cost formula developed by the method of least squares, what per-hour charge for shop costs should be made for the jobs in July? What per-hour charge should be made if the high-low formula is used? Which formula would maintenance prefer to use? Explain.

P7–8 **Method of Least Squares; Coefficient of Determination; Pricing and Cost Recovery** A major source of revenues for many hospitals is treatment of Medicare patients. Currently, Medicare treatments are reimbursed on the basis of diagnostic related groups (DRGs). A DRG is an illness classification—a reason for going to the hospital for treatment—for which the government pays a fixed amount. If the costs of the treatment are greater than the DRG reimbursement, the hospital loses money. If, however, the costs of the treatment are less than the reimbursement, the hospital gains money. Knowing how much a treatment costs is important because it enables the hospital to estimate how much it will make or lose on each service. It may also enable hospitals to build a case for increasing a DRG rate. Thus, estimating the costs of the various services provided is essential for managerial planning.

For example, the Respiratory Therapy Department of a local community hospital offers a number of services, such as oxygen, ABG analysis, aeromed treatment, and CPT treatment. ABG analysis requires the use of supplies, technical labor, capital equipment, and maintenance. The total costs of ABG analysis for the past eight months are as follows:

Month	Number of Treatments	Total Cost
1	250	$3,250
2	260	3,400
3	280	3,600
4	300	3,700
5	270	3,400
6	230	3,200
7	240	3,250
8	255	3,400

Required:

1. Prepare a cost formula for ABG analysis using the method of least squares. Compute the coefficient of determination for the formula.

2. For the coming month, the hospital expects to supply 280 ABG analyses, 50 percent for Medicare patients. If the DRG reimbursement is $12 per analysis, how much will the hospital need to charge the remaining patients per treatment to cover all its costs for supplying ABG analyses? Suppose that the hospital charges non-Medicare patients the expected cost for each ABG analysis. How much will the hospital gain (or lose) on ABG analyses?

P7–9   **Method of Least Squares**   Dotter Company is developing an overhead cost formula. Past experience has convinced management that overhead and machine hours are highly correlated. Data for the past twenty months have been gathered and the following expressions have been computed:

$$\Sigma X = 40,000$$
$$\Sigma XY = \$1,200,000,000$$
$$\Sigma X^2 = 120,000,000$$
$$\Sigma Y = \$500,000$$

Required:

1. Using the method of least squares, determine the overhead cost formula.

2. Suppose that $\Sigma Y^2 = 13,600,000,000$. Is the management of Dotter Company justified in assuming that overhead costs and machine hours are highly correlated?

3. Predict the total overhead cost for 2,000 machine hours. How much of this total overhead cost is fixed? How much is variable?

P7–10   **High-Low Method; Scatterplot**   Gainsville Regional Hospital has collected data on all of its departments for the past seven months. Data for Radiology follow:

	Cost	Number of Procedures
September 1991	$69,500	1,700
October 1991	64,250	1,550
November 1991	52,000	1,200
December 1991	66,000	1,600
January 1992	83,000	1,800
February 1992	66,550	1,330
March 1992	79,500	1,700

Required:

1. Using the high-low method, calculate the variable rate per procedure and the fixed cost for Radiology.

2. Prepare a scatterplot for Radiology using the above data. (*Hint:* Use one symbol, perhaps an "*x*," for observations occurring in 1991, and another symbol for observations occurring in 1992.)

3. Upon looking into the events that happened in Radiology at the end of 1991, you find that the department bought a Magnetic Resonance Imaging (MRI) machine.

Monthly depreciation on the machine amounts to $10,000. Now, using the scatter-plot from requirement 2, calculate the fixed cost and variable rate applicable to October 1991; calculate the fixed cost and variable rate applicable to March 1992. Discuss your findings. Which cost formula should be used to budget radiology expense for the remainder of 1992?

P7–11 **Comparison of Regression Equations** Entwhistle Company is attempting to determine cost behavior in its Putnam City plant. The plant controller has accumulated the following data:

Month	Factory Overhead	Machine Hours	Setups
February	7,700	2,000	7
March	7,650	2,100	5
April	10,052	3,000	5
May	9,400	2,700	6
June	9,584	3,000	2
July	8,480	2,500	4
August	8,550	2,400	6
September	9,735	2,900	5
October	10,500	3,000	9

Required:

1. Estimate a regression equation with machine hours as the independent variable. If the Putnam City plant forecasts 2,600 machine hours for the next month, what will budgeted factory overhead cost be?

2. Estimate a regression equation with setups as the independent variable. If the Putnam City plant forecasts eight setups for the next month, what will budgeted factory overhead cost be?

3. Which of the two regression equations do you think does a better job of predicting factory overhead? Explain.

P7–12 **Suspicious Acquisition of Data; Ethical Issues** Bill Lewis, manager of the Thomas Electronics Division, called a meeting with his controller, Brindon Peterson, CMA, and his marketing manager, Patty Fritz. The following is a transcript of the conversation that took place during the meeting.

Bill: Brindon, the variable costing system that you developed has proved to be a big plus for our division. Our success in winning bids has increased and, as a result, our revenues have increased by 25 percent. However, if we intend to meet this year's profit targets, we are going to need something extra—am I not right, Patty?

Patty: Absolutely. While we have been able to win more bids, we still are losing too many, particularly to our major competitor, Kilborn Electronics. If I knew more about their bidding strategy, I imagine we could be more successful competing with them.

Bill: Would knowing their variable costs help?

Patty: Certainly. It would give me their minimum price. With that knowledge, I'm sure we could find a way to beat them on several jobs, particularly for those jobs where we are at least as efficient. It would also help us identify where we are not cost competitive. With this information, we might be able to find ways to increase our efficiency.

Bill: Well, I have good news. I have some data here in these handouts that reveal bids that Kilborn made on several jobs. I have also been able to obtain the direct labor hours worked for many of these jobs. But that's not all. I have monthly totals for manufacturing costs and direct labor hours for all jobs for the past ten months. Brindon, with this information, can you estimate what the variable manufacturing cost per hour is? If you can, we can compute the variable costs for each job and the markup that Kilborn is using.

Brindon: Yes, an analysis of the data you're requesting is possible. I have a question, though, before I do this. How did you manage to acquire these data? I can't imagine that Kilborn would willingly release this information.

Bill: What does it matter how the data were acquired? The fact is, we have them, and we have an opportunity to gain a tremendous competitive advantage. With that advantage, we can meet our profit targets, and we will all end the year with a big bonus.

After the meeting, in a conversation with Patty, Brindon learned that Bill was dating Jackie Wilson, a cost accountant (and CMA) who happened to work for Kilborn. Patty speculated that Jackie might be the source of the Kilborn data. Upon learning this, Brindon expressed some strong reservations to Patty about analyzing the data.

Required:

1. Assume that Bill did acquire the data from Jackie Wilson. Comment on Jackie's behavior. Which standards of ethical conduct did she violate (see the Appendix to Chapter 1)?

2. Were Brindon's instincts correct—should he have felt some reservations about analyzing the data? Would it be ethical to analyze the data? Do any of the IMA standards of ethical conduct apply (see the Appendix to Chapter 1)? What would you do if you were Brindon? Explain.

P7–13   **Classification of Costs as Fixed and Variable**   Caralot Cards manufactures high-quality greeting cards priced for the luxury end of the market. The cards are sold in department and specialty stores. Each of the six varieties of cards consists of a die-cut paper card with a scented stuffed fabric "pillow" and various trimmings. Direct laborers work in their homes and are paid on a piecework basis. The owner is the entire marketing and administrative staff. She provides a display box to each store carrying her cards. The cards are sold on a consignment basis. The sales commission is a percentage amount based on sales price and is paid to the department or specialty store.

As a first step in budgeting and break-even analysis, the accountant for Caralot Cards decided to classify costs according to behavior. The following types of costs were determined:

▪ Raw materials (cards, fabric, bows, ribbon, lace)

▪ Operating supplies (scent, glue, polyfill, thread)

▪ Packaging materials (cellophane)

▪ Direct labor (paid on a piecework basis)

▪ Sales commission

- Administrative salaries
- Payroll taxes
- Interest expense
- Telephone
- Freight postage—Out
- Samples
- Display boxes
- Travel and entertainment
- Vehicle—Repairs and maintenance
- Vehicle—Gas and parking
- Vehicle—Insurance
- Accounting and legal
- Advertising
- Rent
- Office supplies
- Janitorial
- Dues and subscriptions
- Depreciation—Office furniture
- Depreciation—Vehicle

Required:

Classify each of the above costs according to activity-based costing level of activity (unit, batch, product sustaining, or facility) if a product cost, or marketing or administrative if a nonproduct cost. Suggest a cost driver for each activity level.

■ MANAGERIAL DECISION CASE

Activity-Based Costing; Cost Estimation with Multiple Cost Drivers Bonnie Scott, president of Kranston Company, was disappointed with the latest internal financial reports. Apparently, the recent move to variable costing had not brought as many benefits as expected. The company was still losing bids on the products that had been the backbone of the company for the past two decades. Her review of the internal reports also revealed that the company had even lost some bids that provided only a slight premium over the job's variable costs. Distressed, Bonnie requested that Rick Anderson, vice-president of finance, come to her office immediately.

Bonnie: Rick, I need some additional explanation on these latest reports. When the executive committee met last quarter, everyone was optimistic that variable costing would enhance our ability to compete and win bids, especially with our traditional high-volume business. Yet the results of the latest quarter indicate that we are still losing ground with our main products. We're even losing bids that are barely covering our variable costs. This suggests one of two things to me. We are either producing less efficiently than our principal competitor or we really do not know what our manufacturing costs are. All the information I can gather seems to support my production managers' claims that we are efficient. What about the possibility of bad costing? Could it be that we really have not been successful in accurately identifying our variable costs? Maybe this new system has some flaws.

Rick: You may be right about the costing system. I've been doing some research and apparently there is a real possibility that we have not been successful in identifying our real cost behavior. If you recall, when we decided that our variable overhead was explained by direct labor hours, we computed a variable cost of $20 per direct labor hour using the method of least squares. The coefficient of correlation was 0.74. Although this means that only about 55 percent of the overhead cost variability was explained, most of us believed it was good enough for our purposes. Apparently it isn't.

Bonnie: It takes time and experience to make useful changes. I still believe that knowing cost behavior is important in making competitive bids and in accurately assigning costs to products. Do you have any proposal for solving our problem?

Rick: Yes, as a matter of fact, I do. I intend to expand the search for other variables that may explain the variability in our overhead costs. Some have suggested that costs vary with variables that are nonvolume related such as setup time.

Bonnie: Good idea. When you have finished, I would like to see the difference it makes in the projections of the variable costs for two jobs we recently bid, one that we lost and one that we won. It seems we are winning more and more jobs involving the very specialized, difficult products and losing on our main products.

After the meeting with Bonnie, Rick invested considerable time and effort to develop a better understanding of the company's overhead behavior. As a result of this effort, the following multiple regression equation was developed.

$$Y = 100,000 + 5X_1 + 50X_2 + 40X_3$$

where Y = Total overhead cost
X_1 = Direct labor hours
X_2 = Hours of setup time
X_3 = Number of material moves

The equation Rick developed explained 95 percent of the total variability in overhead costs. Pleased with the outcome, Rick gathered the following data on two jobs:

	Job 35P	Job 47P
Direct labor hours	100	50
Setup time (in hours)	5	25
Material moves	10	20
Direct labor cost	$800	$400
Direct materials cost	900	600

The costs and activities for both jobs are estimates that were used for bidding. Job 35P was for one of the main products, and the bid had been lost. Job 47P, on the other hand, was for a very specialized product, and the bid had been won. Both bids had been made using the following overhead formula based on direct labor hours:

$$Y = 700,000 + 20X_1$$

where the variables are defined as in the multiple regression formula. The bid price for each job was variable cost plus 10 percent.

Required:

1. Compute the bid price for each job assuming that direct labor hours is used to assign all the variable overhead.

2. Compute the bid price for each job assuming that direct labor hours, setup time, and material moves are used to assign variable overhead costs to jobs. Explain why this approach may solve the bidding problems of Kranston.

3. Suppose that the bid price computed in requirement 2 for Job 35P is still higher than the winning bid of a competitor. Assuming the competitor is earning a reasonable return on the job, what possible actions can Bonnie now take?

CHAPTER 8

Cost-Volume-Profit Analysis: A Managerial Planning Tool

■ **LEARNING OBJECTIVES**

After studying Chapter 8, you should be able to

1. Develop a cost-volume-profit equation from the variable-costing income statement.

2. Compute the break-even point in units and sales revenues for a single-product setting.

3. Compute the units and sales revenues required to achieve a targeted level of profit.

4. Assess the effects of changes in costs and prices on the profitability of a firm and use this assessment to aid in making decisions.

5. Compute the break-even point and targeted profit levels for a multiple-product setting.

6. Assess the effect of changes in sales mix for a multiple-product firm.

7. Prepare a profit-volume graph and a cost-volume-profit graph and explain the meaning of each.

8. Calculate the margin of safety and explain how it is used.

9. Calculate operating leverage and explain its significance.

10. Define and explain the key terms listed at the end of the chapter.

SCENARIO

During the last month of the fourth quarter, John Kapple, manager of an electronics division, called a meeting of the division's executive committee. Members include Bill Moyes, controller; Jim Brewer, marketing manager; and Sandy Lawson, senior production manager. John had just received a preliminary report on the division's profit performance for the year, and it was gloomy. From all indications, the division was going to show a loss of $3.5 million. This would be the second straight year of significant losses.

"I felt confident at the beginning of the year that our division would at least break even," John remarked.[1] "In fact, break even was the target that I agreed upon with Kent Olsen at the head office. I suppose that we simply lost too many bids this year. It is unfortunate that the variable-costing system wasn't in place at the beginning of the year. We learned too late the importance of knowing what each job's out-of-pocket costs are—at least too late to be of any benefit this year. Fortunately, the variable-costing system became operational two weeks ago, and I understand that it has already played a role in winning a major bid for next year. I think this is encouraging; however, if we expect this division to continue operating, we need at least to break even this coming year. I asked Bill to prepare a projected income statement for the coming year. Bill, what can we expect?"

"Jim and I spent a lot of time developing a sales forecast. The variable-costing system certainly has a positive effect, which we factored in when developing our forecast. Once we had a sales forecast, I calculated the sales volume needed to break even. Unfortunately, our projected sales revenue is still well below the break-even volume. As best as I can estimate, we can cut our loss from $3.5 million to $1.5 million."

"Well, given this report, I think you can all see that we have a serious problem," John said. "We cannot tolerate another operating loss of that magnitude. We must either increase revenues more or cut costs—or perhaps do both. Jim, what are the possibilities of increasing revenues beyond the projected level?"

"Not very good," Jim replied. "Our pricing strategy is to maintain full-cost plus pricing on our existing business and new small orders and to use special pricing only on new large-volume orders. The competition is especially keen on large-volume orders. Our competition recognizes, as we now do, that a small contribution per unit on a large volume can produce a sizable overall profit increase. We have already built into the forecast a significant increase in sales revenue. Only a limited amount of business is available, though, and I honestly don't believe that we can capture more of it than Bill and I have estimated."

"I was afraid that you'd say that," John admitted. "This means we must focus our attention on costs in order to lower the break-even point to our

---

[1] To *break even* means to have exactly enough sales revenues to cover all costs. *Break even* means zero profits.

projected sales volume. Somehow we must decrease costs by at least $1.5 million. Sandy, I want you to look at production and engineering. Bill, you look at accounting and administration. Jim, see what can be done with the Marketing Department. In two weeks, I want recommendations from each of you on how we can cut costs in those areas and still carry out the same level of projected sales activity. I want costs reduced by at least $1.5 million.''

■ ISSUES ADDRESSED BY COST-VOLUME-PROFIT ANALYSIS

The above case is a good example of how cost-volume-profit analysis (or CVP analysis) can be used for managerial planning. The revenues, costs, and profits for the coming year were projected with the outcome a predicted loss. Projected sales volume was compared with the sales volume needed to break even. The first question concerned the possibility of increasing sales volume in order to reach the break-even volume. Once it was clear that this was not possible, the manager was forced to consider other measures. If sales cannot be increased to achieve the break-even volume, the next choice is to lower costs so that projected revenues become the break-even volume.

Interestingly, the division successfully cut costs. In fact, fixed overhead was reduced by $2 million, resulting in a projected profit of $500,000. How was this accomplished? To explain, we note a few examples of cost reductions made by the divisional executives. Although the list is not exhaustive, it conveys the essential flavor of the approach taken.

In production and engineering, several high-priced sustaining engineers were released. Sustaining engineers were employed to sustain products that had been sold. Their basic responsibility involved redesigning products to improve them as deficiencies and limitations were reported by users. Sustaining efforts were dropped for those products that were older and diminishing in sales, products at the end of the product life cycle. By dropping sustaining for these products, less engineering time was needed, and the number of engineers employed was reduced accordingly.

In marketing, several nonproductive employees were let go. These employees poured over and analyzed masses of data that ultimately had little bearing on sales.

In accounting, it was discovered that reports were being prepared that were never being used by anyone. Many reports simply sat on desks accumulating dust, yet people were being paid to generate them. These useless reports were eliminated; as a consequence, the accounting staff was reduced by 33 percent.

A simple application of CVP analysis led to a significant increase in cost efficiency within the electronics division. In this case, CVP analysis was a valuable tool to identify the extent and magnitude of the economic trouble the division was facing and to help to pinpoint the necessary solution. CVP can address many other issues as well.

CVP analysis focuses on prices, revenues, volume, costs, profits, and sales mix. Most questions involving any of these six areas or combinations thereof can be addressed by CVP analysis. The following list is a sample of the types of questions that can be raised and answered by CVP analysis:

1. How many units must be sold (or how much sales revenue must be generated) in order to break even?

2. How many units must be sold to earn a before-tax profit equal to $60,000? A before-tax profit equal to 15 percent of revenues? An after-tax profit of $45,000?

3. Will overall profits increase if the unit price is increased by $2 and units sold decrease 15 percent?

4. What is the effect on profits if advertising expenditures increase by $8,000 and sales increase from 1,600 to 1,725 units?

5. What is the effect on profits if the selling price is decreased from $400 to $375 per unit and sales increase from 1,600 units to 1,900 units?

6. What is the effect on profits if the selling price is decreased from $400 to $375 per unit, advertising expenditures are increased by $8,000, and sales increase from 1,600 units to 2,300 units?

7. What is the effect on profits of a change in the sales mix?

This list is by no means complete, but it should provide you with some insight into the power of CVP analysis. So far we have not mentioned anything about how CVP analysis is executed. The rest of this chapter deals with the mechanics and terminology of CVP analysis. However, your objective in studying CVP analysis is more than to learn the mechanics. You should keep in mind that CVP analysis is an integral part of financial planning and decision making. Every manager should be thoroughly conversant with its concepts.

■ VARIABLE-COSTING INCOME BASIS OF CVP ANALYSIS

Since we are interested in how revenues, expenses, and profits behave as volume changes, the variable-costing (or contribution) income statement is the logical basis of CVP analysis. The first step in developing the methodology of CVP analysis is to express the variable-costing income statement as a narrative equation:

$$\text{Profit before taxes} = \text{Sales revenues} - \text{Variable expenses} - \text{Fixed expenses}$$

There are two approaches to CVP analysis: the *units-sold approach* and the *sales-revenue approach*. The **units-sold approach** measures sales activity and answers CVP questions in terms of the number of units sold; the **sales-revenue approach** measures sales activity and answers CVP questions in terms of the total revenues generated. Initially, we will explore each approach assuming a single-product analysis. Later the analysis will be extended to include multiple products.

units-sold approach

sales-revenue approach

Single-Product Analysis: Units-Sold Approach

To illustrate the units-sold approach, the narrative equation for variable-costing income must be converted to an analytical equation. We will use the following variables:

P = Selling price per unit
X = Units sold
V = Variable cost per unit sold
F = Total fixed costs
I = Net income, or profit before taxes

Using the above notation, sales revenue is expressed as PX (the unit selling price times the units sold), and total variable costs are VX (the unit variable cost times units sold). With these expressions, the units-sold form of the variable-costing income statement is expressed as

$$I = PX - VX - F \qquad \text{(8.1)}$$

Suppose you were asked how many units must be sold in order to earn a before-tax profit of I. You could answer the question by solving Equation 8.1 for X. To solve, factor out X to get

$$I = (P - V)X - F$$

Rearrange as

$$(P - V)X = F + I$$

and divide by $P - V$ to isolate X

$$X = (F + I)/(P - V) \qquad \text{(8.2)}$$

What is the meaning of $P - V$? P is the selling price per unit, and V is the variable cost per unit. Recall that the difference between revenues and variable expenses is called the *contribution margin*. Thus $P - V$, the difference between unit revenue and unit variable cost, is the *contribution margin per unit*. Knowing this, the narrative version of Equation 8.2 can be stated as follows:

$$\text{Units sold} = (\text{Fixed costs} + \text{Profits before taxes})/(\text{Unit contribution margin})$$

Sample Applications of the Units-Sold Approach

Assume that Reston Company manufactures an economy-line woodburning stove. For the coming year, the controller has prepared the following projected income statement:

Sales (1,000 units @ $400)	$ 400,000
Less: Variable expenses	(325,000)
Contribution margin	$ 75,000
Less: Fixed expenses	(45,000)
Profit before taxes	$ 30,000

A considerable amount of information can be extracted from the income statement. For example, the income statement is based on sales of 1,000 units; the selling price (P) is $400 per unit, the variable cost per unit (V) is $325 ($325,000/1,000), and total fixed expenses (F) are $45,000. The contribution margin per unit can be computed in one of two ways. One way is to divide the total contribution margin by the units sold for a result of $75 per unit ($75,000/1,000). A second way is to compute $P - V$. Doing so yields the same result, $75 per unit ($400 - $325).

break-even point **Break-even Point** For the first application, the **break-even point**, will be computed. Recall that the break-even point is where total revenues equal total costs, the point of zero profits. The units-sold approach identifies the number of units that must be sold to break even. Setting $I = 0$ in Equation 8.2, the following result is obtained for Reston Company:

$$X = (F + I)/(P - V)$$
$$= (\$45,000 + \$0)/(\$400 - \$325)$$
$$= \$45,000/\$75 \text{ per unit}$$
$$= 600 \text{ units}$$

Reston must sell exactly 600 woodburning stoves in order to break even. An income statement based on the sale of 600 stoves can be prepared to check the accuracy of this statement.

Sales (600 @ $400)	$ 240,000
Less: Variable expenses	(195,000)
Contribution margin	$ 45,000
Less: Fixed expenses	(45,000)
Profit before taxes	$ 0

Profit Targets   Consider the following three questions:

1. How many woodburning stoves must be sold to earn a before-tax profit of $60,000?

2. How many woodburning stoves must be sold to earn a before-tax profit equal to 15 percent of sales revenue?

3. How many woodburning stoves must be sold to earn an after-tax profit of $45,000 assuming that the corporate tax rate is 40 percent?

To answer the first question, set $I = \$60,000$ and solve the following equation:

$$
\begin{aligned}
X &= (F + I)/(P - V) \\
&= (\$45,000 + \$60,000)/(\$400 - \$325) \text{ per unit} \\
&= \$105,000/\$75 \text{ per unit} \\
&= 1,400 \text{ woodburning stoves}
\end{aligned}
$$

Reston must sell 1,400 stoves to earn a before-tax profit of $60,000. The following income statement verifies this outcome:

Sales (1,400 units @ $400)	$ 560,000
Less: Variable expenses	(455,000)
Contribution margin	$ 105,000
Less: Fixed expenses	(45,000)
Profit before taxes	$ 60,000

Another way to check this number of units is to use the break-even point. As was just shown, Reston must sell 1,400 stoves—800 more than the break-even volume of 600 units—to earn a profit of $60,000. The contribution margin per stove is $75. Multiplying $75 by the 800 stoves above break even produces the profit of $60,000 ($75 × 800). This outcome demonstrates that contribution margin per unit for each unit above break even is equivalent to profit per unit. Since the break-even point had already been computed, the answer to the first question in the list above could have been calculated by dividing the unit contribution margin into the target profit and adding the resulting amount to the break-even volume.

In general, assuming that fixed costs remain the same, the impact on a firm's profits resulting from a change in the number of units sold can be assessed by multiplying the unit contribution margin by the change in units sold. For example, if 1,500 stoves instead of 1,400 are sold, how much more profit will be earned? The change in units sold is an increase of 100 stoves, and the unit contribution margin is $75. Thus, profits will increase by $7,500 ($75 × 100).

The second question on page 366 requires that we determine the number of stoves that must be sold in order to earn a profit equal to 15 percent of sales revenue. Sales revenue is represented by PX. Thus, before-tax profit is 15 percent of PX (0.15 PX). Since P is $400 per unit, before-tax profit (I) can be expressed as $60X (or 0.15 × $400X). Notice that the profit target is a function of X. Whenever the profit target involves X, using Equation 8.1 $-I = PX - VX - F$—is better than using Equation 8.2 $-X = (I + F)/(P - V)$—since less algebraic manipulation is needed. Substituting $I = 60X$ into the first equation and solving for X yields the following:

$$
\begin{aligned}
I &= PX - VX - F \\
\$60X &= \$400X - \$325X - \$45{,}000 \\
\$60X &= \$75X - \$45{,}000 \\
\$15X &= \$45{,}000 \\
X &= 3{,}000 \text{ units}
\end{aligned}
$$

Does a volume of 3,000 stoves achieve a profit equal to 15 percent of sales revenue? For 3,000 stoves, the total revenue is $1.2 million ($400 × 3,000). The profit can be computed without preparing a formal income statement. Remember that above break even, the contribution margin per unit is the profit per unit. The break-even volume is 600 stoves. If 3,000 stoves are sold, then 2,400 (3,000 − 600) stoves above the break-even point are sold. The before-tax profit, therefore, is $180,000 ($75 × 2,400), which is 15 percent of sales ($180,000/$1,200,000).

Some additional development is needed to answer the third question on page 366. This question expresses the profit target in after-tax terms, but the profit target in Equations 8.1 and 8.2 is expressed in before-tax terms. Therefore, to use either equation, the after-tax profit target must first be converted to a before-tax profit target. If t represents the tax rate, then the tax paid on a before-tax profit of I is tI. The after-tax profit is computed by subtracting the tax from the before-tax profit.

$$
\begin{aligned}
\text{After-tax profit} &= \text{Before-tax profit} - \text{Taxes} \\
&= I - tI \\
&= (1 - t)I
\end{aligned}
$$

Now divide both sides of the equation by $(1 - t)$

$$
I = (\text{After-tax profit})/(1 - t)
$$

Thus, to convert the after-tax profit to before-tax profit, simply divide the after-tax profit by $(1 - t)$.

The third question gives an after-tax profit target of $45,000 and states the tax rate to be 40 percent. To convert the after-tax profit target into a before-tax profit target, divide it by 0.6 (1 − 0.4). Thus, the before-tax profit is $75,000 ($45,000/0.6). With this conversion, Equation 8.2 can now be used:

$$X = (F + I)/(P - V)$$
$$= (\$45,000 + \$75,000)/\$75$$
$$= \$120,000/\$75$$
$$= 1,600 \text{ units}$$

To verify the accuracy of the analysis, an income statement based on sales of 1,600 stoves has been prepared.

Sales (1,600 @ $400)	$ 640,000
Less: Variable expenses	(520,000)
Contribution margin	$ 120,000
Less: Fixed costs	(45,000)
Profit before taxes	$ 75,000
Less: Taxes (40% tax rate)	(30,000)
Profit after taxes	$ 45,000

Pricing Decisions   Reston Company recently conducted a market study that revealed three possible outcomes: (1) if advertising expenditures increase by $8,000, sales will increase from 1,600 units to 1,725 units; (2) a price decrease from $400 per stove to $375 per stove would increase sales from 1,600 units to 1,900 units; and (3) decreasing prices to $375 and increasing advertising expenditures by $8,000 will increase sales from 1,600 units to 2,300 units. Should Reston maintain its current price and advertising policies, or should it select one of the three alternatives described by the marketing study?

Consider the first alternative. What is the effect on profits if advertising costs increase by $8,000 and sales increase by 125 units? This question can be answered without using the equations but by employing the contribution margin per unit.

We know that the unit contribution margin is $75. Since units sold increase by 125, the incremental increase in total contribution margin is $9,375 ($75 × 125 units). However, since fixed costs increase by $8,000, the incremental increase in profits is only $1,375 ($9,375 − $8,000). Exhibit 8–1 summarizes the effects of the first alternative. Notice that we need to look only at the incremental increase in total contribution margin and fixed expenses to compute the increase in total profits.

For the second alternative, fixed expenses do not increase. Thus, it is possible to answer the question by looking only at the effect on total contribution margin. For the current price of $400, the contribution margin per unit is $75. If 1,600 units are sold, the total contribution margin is $120,000 ($75 × 1,600). If the price is dropped to $375, then the contribution margin drops to $50 per unit ($375 − $325). If 1,900 units are sold at the new price, then the new total contribution margin is $95,000 ($50 × 1,900). Dropping the price results in a profit decline of $25,000 ($120,000 − $95,000). The effects of the second alternative are summarized in Exhibit 8–2.

EXHIBIT 8–1
Summary of the Effects of the First Alternative

	Status Quo	Proposed Price Change
Units sold	1,600	1,725
Unit contribution margin	×$75	×$75
Total contribution margin	$120,000	$129,375
Less: Fixed costs	(45,000)	(53,000)
Profit	$ 75,000	$ 76,375
		Incremental Effect
Change in sales volume		125
Unit contribution margin		×$75
Change in contribution margin		$ 9,375
Less: Increase in fixed expenses		(8,000)
Increase in profits		$ 1,375

EXHIBIT 8–2
Summary of the Effects of the Second Alternative

	Status Quo	Proposed Price Change
Units sold	1,600	1,900
Unit contribution margin	×$75	×$50
Total contribution margin	$120,000	$ 95,000
Less: Fixed expenses	(45,000)	(45,000)
Profit	$ 75,000	$ 50,000
		Incremental Effect
Change in contribution margin		($ 25,000)
($95,000 − $120,000)		
Less: Change in fixed expenses		—
Change in profits		($ 25,000)

The third alternative calls for a decrease in the unit selling price and an increase in advertising costs. Like the first alternative, the profit impact can be assessed by looking at the incremental effects on contribution margin and fixed expenses. The incremental profit change can be found by (1) computing the incremental change in total contribution margin, (2) computing the incremental change in fixed expenses, and (3) adding the two results.

As shown, the current total contribution margin (for 1,600 units sold) is $120,000. Since the new unit contribution margin is $50, the new total contribution margin is $130,000 ($50 × 2,600 units). Thus, the incremental increase in total contribution margin is $10,000 ($130,000 − $120,000). However, to achieve this incremental increase in contribution margin, an incremental increase of $8,000 in fixed costs is needed. The net effect is an incremental increase in profits of $2,000. The effects of the third alternative are summarized in Exhibit 8–3.

Of the three alternatives identified by the marketing study, the one that promises the most benefit is the third. It increases total profits by $2,000. The first alternative increases profits by only $1,375, and the second actually decreases profits by $25,000.

These examples are all based on a units-sold approach. Sales volume is measured in units sold. Variable costs and contribution margin are also expressed on a units-sold basis. It is also possible to express sales volume in another way, using revenues rather than units sold. In this approach, variable costs and contribution margin are seen as a percentage of revenues. This method will be explored next.

Single-Product Analysis: Sales-Revenue Approach

In some cases when using CVP analysis, managers may prefer to use sales revenues as the measure of sales activity instead of units sold. Converting a units-sold measure to a sales-revenue measure can be done simply by multiplying the unit sales price by the units sold. For example, the break-even point for Reston Company was computed to be 600 woodburning stoves. Since the selling price for each stove is $400, the break-even volume in revenues is $240,000 ($400 × 600). Any answer expressed in units sold can be easily con-

EXHIBIT 8–3
Summary of the Effects of the Third Alternative

	Status Quo	Proposed Price Change
Units sold	1,600	2,600
Unit contribution margin	× $75	x$50
Total contribution margin	$120,000	$130,000
Less: Fixed expenses	(45,000)	(53,000)
Profit	$ 75,000	$ 77,000

	Incremental Effect
Change in contribution margin	$ 10,000
($130,000 − $120,000)	
Less: Change in fixed expenses	(8,000)
($53,000 − $45,000)	
Change in profits	$ 2,000

verted to one expressed in sales revenues, but the answer can be computed more directly by developing a separate formula for the sales-revenue case. This formula uses the following variables:

$R = PX$ (Price × Units sold)
$vr = (V/P)$ (Variable costs/Sales revenues)
$F = $ Total fixed costs
$I = $ Profit before taxes

The sales-revenue form of variable-costing income is expressed as follows:

$$I = R - F - (vr)R \qquad\qquad (8.3)$$

Some immediate differences between the sales-revenue approach and the units-sold approach should be mentioned. First, of course, sales activity is defined as sales revenues instead of units sold. Second, variable costs are defined as a percentage of sales rather than as an amount per unit sold. Logically, if costs vary in total with the units sold, then the same costs should vary in total with sales in dollars. For example, assume that variable costs are $6 per unit sold and that 100 units are sold for $10 each. Using the units-sold approach, total variable costs are $600 ($6 × 100 units sold). Alternatively, since each unit sold earns $10 of revenue, we would say that for every $10 of revenue earned, $6 of variable costs are incurred, or, equivalently, that 60 percent of each dollar of revenue earned is attributable to variable cost ($6/$10). Thus, using the sales-revenue approach, we would expect total variable costs of $600 for revenues of $1,000 (0.60 × $1,000).

variable cost ratio　　The parameter vr is called the **variable cost ratio**. It is simply the proportion of each sales dollar that must be used to cover variable costs. Alternatively, vr can be thought of as the variable cost per sales dollar. The variable cost ratio can be computed either by dividing total variable costs by total sales revenues or, in the case of a single product, by dividing the unit variable cost by unit revenue. In the latter case, $vr = V/P$, where V is the variable cost per unit sold and P is the unit selling price.

Equation 8.3 can be solved for R to determine the sales revenues needed to earn a profit target of I. First, factor out R

$$I = (1 - vr)R - F$$

rearrange as

$$(1 - vr)R = F + I$$

and divide both sides by $(1 - vr)$

$$R = (F + I)/(1 - vr)$$

What is the meaning of $(1 - vr)$? Since vr equals V/P, $1 - vr$ equals $1 - V/P$, which equals $(P - V)/P$. As you know, $(P - V)$ is the unit contri-

contribution margin
ratio

bution margin, and P is the unit selling price. Thus, $(P - V)/P$ is the **contribution margin ratio**, the proportion of each sales dollar available to cover fixed costs and provide for profit. It makes sense that the complement of the variable cost ratio, $(1 - vr)$, is the contribution margin ratio. After all, the proportion of the sales dollar left after variable costs are covered should be the contribution margin component.

The contribution margin ratio can be computed in two ways. One way is to calculate the variable cost ratio (vr) and then subtract this number from one $(1 - vr)$. The second way is to divide the contribution margin by the sales revenue (either on a total basis or on a per-unit basis).

Given the definition of $(1 - vr)$, the narrative version of 8.4 can be expressed as follows:

$$R = \text{(Fixed costs + Profit before taxes)/(Contribution margin ratio)} \qquad \textbf{(8.4)}$$

Sample Applications of the Sales-Revenue Approach

Since answers using the units-sold approach can be easily converted to sales revenues, only a couple of simple examples will be used to illustrate the direct application of the sales-revenue approach. The same data as for the earlier examples will be used. Recall that Reston Company projected the following variable-costing income for the coming year:

Sales (1,000 units @ $400)	$ 400,000
Less: Variable expenses	(325,000)
Contribution margin	$ 75,000
Less: Fixed costs	(45,000)
Profit before taxes	$ 30,000

From this income statement, the information needed to carry out CVP analysis under the sales-revenue approach can be easily extracted. The variable cost ratio is 0.8125 ($325,000/$400,000), and fixed costs are $45,000. The contribution margin ratio is 0.1875 (computed either as $1 - 0.8125$, or $75,000/$400,000).

Break-even Point   Given the information in this income statement, how much sales revenue must Reston earn to break even? Setting $I = 0$ in Equation 8.4, the following result is obtained:

$$\begin{aligned} R &= (F + I)/(1 - vr) \\ &= (\$45,000 + 0)/0.1875 \\ &= \$240,000 \end{aligned}$$

Thus, Reston must earn revenues totaling $240,000 in order to break even.

Profit Target   Consider the following question: How much sales revenue must Reston generate to earn a before-tax profit of $60,000? (This question parallels one asked for the units-sold approach but phrases the question directly in terms of sales revenue.) To answer the question, set I to equal $60,000 and solve Equation 8.4:

$$R = (F + I)/(1 - vr)$$
$$= (\$45,000 + \$60,000)/0.1875$$
$$= \$105,000/0.1875$$
$$= \$560,000$$

Reston must earn revenues equal to $560,000 to achieve a profit target of $60,000. Since break even is $240,000, additional sales of $320,000 ($560,000 − $240,000) must be earned above break even. Notice that multiplying the contribution margin ratio by revenues above break even yields the profit of $60,000 (0.1875 × $320,000). Above break even, the contribution margin ratio is a profit ratio; therefore, it represents the proportion of each sales dollar assignable to profit. For this example, every sales dollar earned above break even increases profits by $0.1875.

In general, assuming that fixed costs remain unchanged, the contribution margin ratio can be used to find the profit impact of a change in sales revenue. To obtain the total change in profits from a change in revenues, simply multiply the contribution margin ratio times the change in sales. For example, if sales revenues are $540,000 instead of $560,000, how will the expected profits be affected? A decrease in sales revenues of $20,000 will cause a decrease in profits of $3,750 (0.1875 × $20,000).

Comparison of the Two Approaches

For a single-product setting, converting the units-sold answers to sales-revenue answers is simply a matter of multiplying the unit sales price by the units sold. Why, then, bother with a separate formula for the sales revenue approach? For a single-product setting, neither approach has any real advantage over the other. Both offer essentially the same level of conceptual and computational difficulty. Each approach does supply a different view of CVP analysis, though. Because each approach supplies different insights and different concepts (the concepts of unit contribution margin and contribution margin ratio), it is worthwhile to study both approaches.

In a multiple-product setting, however, CVP analysis is more complex. In this situation, the sales-revenue approach assumes a significant computational advantage. This approach maintains essentially the same computational requirements found in the single-product setting, whereas the units-sold approach becomes more difficult. Even though the conceptual complexity of CVP analysis does increase with multiple products, the operation is reasonably straightforward.

■ MULTIPLE-PRODUCT ANALYSIS

Reston Company has decided to offer two models of woodburning stoves: an economy model to sell for $400 and a deluxe model to sell for $800. The Marketing Department is convinced that 1,200 economy models and 800 deluxe models can be sold during the coming year. The controller has prepared the following projected income statement based on the sales forecast:

	Economy Model	Deluxe Model	Total
Sales	$ 480,000	$ 640,000	$1,120,000
Less: Variable expenses	(390,000)	(480,000)	(870,000)
Contribution margin	$ 90,000	$ 160,000	$ 250,000
Less: Direct fixed expenses	(30,000)	(40,000)	(70,000)
Product margin	$ 60,000	$ 120,000	$ 180,000
Less: Common fixed expenses			(26,250)
Profit before taxes			$ 153,750

The Units-Sold Approach and Multiple Products

The owner of Reston is somewhat apprehensive about adding a new product line and wants to know how many of each model must be sold to break even. If you were given the responsibility to answer this question, how would you respond?

One possible response is to use the equation $X = (F + I)/(P - V)$ and setting $I = 0$. This equation presents some immediate problems, however. It was developed for a single-product analysis. For two products, there are *two* unit contribution margins. The economy model has a contribution margin per unit of $75 ($400 − $325), and the deluxe model has one of $200 ($800 − $600).[2]

One possible solution is to apply the analysis separately to each product line. It is possible to obtain individual break-even points when income is defined as product margin. Break even for the economy line is as follows:

$$X = (F + I)/(P - V)$$
$$= (\$30,000 + 0)/\$75$$
$$= 400 \text{ units}$$

---

[2]The variable cost per unit is derived from the income statement. For the deluxe model, total variable costs are $480,000 based on sales of 800 units. This yields a per-unit variable cost of $600 ($480,000/800). A similar computation produces the per-unit variable cost for the economy model.

Break even for the deluxe model can be computed as well.

$$X = (F + I)/(P - V)$$
$$= (\$40{,}000 + 0)/\$200$$
$$= 200 \text{ units}$$

Thus, 400 economy models and 200 deluxe models must be sold to achieve a break-even product margin. But a break-even product margin covers only direct fixed costs; the common fixed costs remain to be covered. Selling these numbers of stoves would result in a loss equal to the common fixed costs. No break-even point for the firm as a whole has yet been identified. Somehow the common fixed costs must be factored into the analysis.

Allocating the common fixed costs to each product line before computing a break-even point may resolve this difficulty. The problem with this approach is that allocation of the common fixed costs is arbitrary. Thus, no meaningful break-even volume is readily apparent.

Another possible solution is to convert the multiple-product problem into a single-product problem. If this can be done, then all of the single-product CVP methodology can be applied directly. The key to this conversion is to identify the expected sales mix of the products being marketed.

sales mix **Sales Mix**   **Sales mix** is the relative combination of products being sold by a firm. For example, if Reston plans on selling 1,200 economy models and 800 deluxe models, then the sales mix is 1,200:800. Usually the sales mix is reduced to the smallest possible relative numbers, where each number typically assumes a value greater than or equal to one and is expressed as an integer. The relative mix 1,200:800 can be reduced to 12:8 and further to 3:2. The ratio 3:2 could be reduced to 1.5:1, but doing so may result in more awkward computations. Thus, the sales mix is expressed as 3:2. For every three economy models sold, two deluxe models are sold.

A number of different sales mixes can be used to define the break-even volume. For example, a sales mix of 2:1 will define a break-even point of 550 economy models and 275 deluxe models. The total contribution margin produced by this mix is $96,250 [($75 × 550) + ($200 × 275)]. Similarly, if 350 economy models and 350 deluxe models are sold (corresponding to a 1:1 sales mix), the total contribution margin is also $96,250 [($75 × 350) + ($200 × 350)]. Since total fixed costs are $96,250, both sales mixes define break-even points. Fortunately, every sales mix need not be considered. Can Reston really expect a sales mix of 2:1 or 1:1? For every two economy models sold, does Reston expect to sell a deluxe model? Or for every economy model, can Reston really sell one deluxe model?

According to Reston's marketing study, a sales mix of 3:2 can be expected. That is the ratio that should be used; others can be ignored. The sales mix that is expected to prevail should be used for CVP analysis.

Sales Mix and CVP Analysis   Defining a particular sales mix allows us to convert a multiple-product problem to a single-product CVP format. Since

Reston expects to sell three economy models for every two deluxe models, it can define the single product it sells as a *package* containing three economy models and two deluxe models. By defining the product as a package, the multiple-product problem is converted into a single-product one. To use the units-sold approach defined by Equation 8.1, the package selling price and variable cost per package must be known. To compute these package values, the sales mix, the individual product prices, and the individual variable costs are needed. Given the individual product data found on the projected income statement on page 374, the package values can be computed as follows:

Product	*P*	*V*	*P − V*	*Mix*	*Package CM*
Economy	$400	$325	$ 75	3	$225[a]
Deluxe	$800	$600	200	2	400[b]
Package total					$625

[a]Found by multiplying the number of units in the package (3) by the unit contribution margin (*P − V* = $75)

[b]Found by multiplying the number of units in the package (2) by the unit contribution margin (*P − V* = $200)

Given the package contribution margin, the single-product CVP equation can be used to determine the number of packages that need to be sold to break even. From Reston's projected income statement, we know that the total fixed costs for the company are $96,250. Thus, the break-even point is

$$X = (F + I)/(P − V)$$
$$= (\$96,250 + 0)/\$625$$
$$= 154 \text{ packages}$$

Reston must sell 462 economy models (3 × 154) and 308 deluxe models (2 × 154) to break even. An income statement verifying this solution is presented in Exhibit 8–4.

For a given sales mix, CVP analysis can be used as if the firm were selling a single product. However, actions that change the prices of individual products can affect the sales mix. Accordingly, pricing decisions may involve a new sales mix and must reflect this possibility. Keep in mind that a new sales mix will affect the units of each product that need to be sold in order to achieve a desired profit target. If the sales mix for the coming period is uncertain, it may be necessary to look at several different mixes. In this way, a manager can gain some insight into the possible outcomes facing the firm.

The complexity of the units-sold approach for the multiple-product setting increases dramatically as the number of products increases. Imagine performing this analysis for a firm with several hundred products. This observation seems more overwhelming than it actually is. Computers can easily handle a problem with so much data. Furthermore, many firms simplify the problem by analyzing product groups rather than individual products. An-

EXHIBIT 8–4

Income Statement: Break-even Solution

	Economy Model	Deluxe Model	Total
Sales	$ 184,800	$ 246,400	$ 431,200
Less: Variable costs	(150,150)	(184,800)	(334,950)
Contribution margin	$ 34,650	$ 61,600	$ 96,250
Less: Direct fixed costs	(30,000)	(40,000)	(70,000)
Segment margin	$ 4,650	$ 21,600	$ 26,250
Less: Common fixed costs			(26,250)
Profit before taxes			$ 0

other way to handle the increased complexity is to switch from the units-sold to the sales-revenue approach. This approach can accomplish a multiple-product CVP analysis using only the summary data found in an organization's income statement. The computational requirements are much simpler.

The Sales Revenue Approach and Multiple-Product Analysis

To illustrate the sales-revenue approach, the same examples will be used. However, the only information needed is the projected income statement for the firm as a whole.

Sales	$1,120,000
Less: Variable costs	(870,000)
Contribution margin	$ 250,000
Total: Fixed costs	(96,250)
Profit before taxes	$ 153,750

Notice that this income statement corresponds to the total column of the more detailed income statement on page 374. The projected income statement rests on the assumption that 1,200 economy models and 800 deluxe models will be sold (a 3:2 sales mix). The sales-revenue approach uses the expected sales mix as the basis for CVP analysis. (As with the units-sold approach, a different sales mix will produce different results.)

With the income statement, the usual CVP questions can be addressed. For example, how much sales revenue must be earned to break even? To answer this question, the contribution margin ratio is needed. This ratio can be computed from the income statement simply by dividing total contribution margin by total sales. Doing so gives a ratio of 0.2232 ($250,000/$1,120,000). With this ratio, the break-even sales volume can be computed as follows[3]:

$$X = (F + 0)/(1 - vr)$$
$$= (\$96,250 + 0)/0.2232$$
$$= \$431,228$$

The sales-revenue approach implicitly uses the assumed sales mix but avoids the requirement of building a package contribution margin. No knowledge of individual product data is needed. The computational effort is similar to that used in the single-product setting. Moreover, the answer is still expressed in sales revenues. Unlike the units-sold approach, the answer to CVP questions using the sales-revenue approach is still expressed in a single summary measure. The sales-revenue approach, however, does sacrifice information concerning individual product performance.

If desired, the contribution margin ratio can be computed using the package data. Recall that the package's selling price was $2,800, and its contribution margin was $625. These figures also yield a ratio of 0.2232 ($625/$2,800). However, using this approach involves the same level of computational complexity as the units-sold approach.

CVP analysis can offer additional insight by graphing the relationships implied by Equation 8.2 or 8.4. A visual portrayal of concepts always seems to enrich one's understanding. Charts and graphs of CVP problems are also useful in presenting an analysis to management. For example, in the case described at the beginning of the chapter, the controller could have enhanced his report to the divisional manager by preparing a graph that portrayed the division's current CVP relationships.

▪ GRAPHICAL REPRESENTATION OF CVP RELATIONSHIPS

The Profit-Volume Graph

profit-volume graph   A **profit-volume graph** visually portrays the relationship between profits and sales volume. The profit-volume graph is the graph of the linear equation $I = PX - VX - F$, with I as the dependent variable and X as the independent variable. Usually, values of the independent variable are measured along the horizontal axis and values of the dependent variable along the vertical.

To make this discussion more concrete, a simple set of data will be used. Assume that Tyson Company produces a single product with the following cost and price data:

---

[3]Because of rounding error in the contribution margin ratio, the sales volume is slightly overstated. The correct answer is $431,200 (obtained by multiplying the package selling price by the packages needed to break even: $2,800 × 154).

Total fixed costs	$100
Variable costs per unit	5
Selling price per unit	10

Using these data, the profit-volume equation can be expressed as

$$I = \$10X - \$5X - \$100$$
$$= \$5X - \$100$$

The graph of $I = \$5X - \$100$ is the profit-volume graph for the Tyson Company example. Units sold will be plotted along the horizontal axis and profit (or loss) along the vertical axis. Two points are needed to graph a linear equation. While any two points will do, the two points often chosen are those that correspond to zero sales volume and zero profits. Setting $X = 0$ results in $I = -100$. The point corresponding to zero sales volume, therefore, is $(0, -100)$. In other words, when no sales take place, the company suffers a loss equal to its total fixed costs. Setting $I = \$0$ results in $X = 20$. The point corresponding to zero profits (break even) is $(20, \$0)$. These two points, plotted in Exhibit 8–5 (p. 380), define the profit graph shown in the same figure.

The graph in Exhibit 8–5 can be used to assess Tyson's profit (or loss) at any level of sales activity. For example, the profit associated with the sale of forty units can be read from the graph by (1) drawing a vertical line from the horizontal axis to the profit line and (2) drawing a horizontal line from the profit line to the vertical axis. As illustrated in Exhibit 8–5, the profit associated with sales of forty units is $100.

The profit-volume graph, while easy to interpret, fails to reveal how costs change as sales volume changes. An alternative approach to graphing can provide this detail.

The Cost-Volume-Profit Graph

cost-volume-profit graph

The **cost-volume-profit graph** depicts the relationships among cost, volume, and profits. To obtain the more detailed relationships, it is necessary to graph two separate lines: the total revenue line and the total cost line. These two lines are represented, respectively, by the following two equations:

$$R = PX$$
$$Y = F + VX$$

Using the Tyson Company example, the revenue and cost equations are

$$R = \$10X$$
$$Y = \$100 + \$5X$$

To portray both equations in the same graph, the vertical axis is measured in dollars and the horizontal axis in units sold.

EXHIBIT 8–5
Profit-Volume Graph

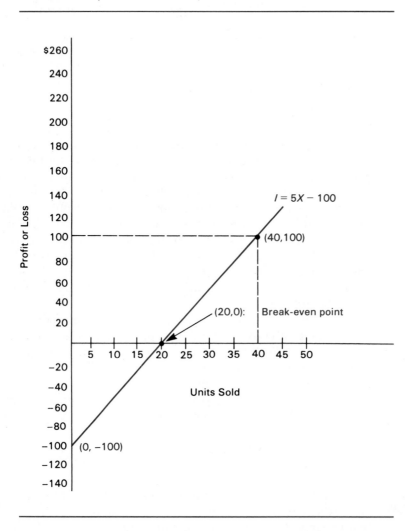

Two points are needed to graph each equation. We will use the same X-coordinates used for the profit-volume graph. For the revenue equation, setting $X = 0$ results in $R = 0$; setting $X = 20$ results in $R = \$200$. Therefore, the two points for the revenue equation are (0, \$0) and (20, \$200). For the cost equation, $X = 0$ and $X = 20$ produce the points (0, \$100) and (20, \$200). The graph of each equation appears in Exhibit 8–6.

Notice that the total revenue line begins at the origin and rises with a slope equal to the selling price per unit (a slope of 10). The total cost line intercepts the vertical axis at a point equal to total fixed costs and rises with a slope equal to the variable cost per unit (a slope of 5). When the total

Exhibit 8–6
Cost-Volume-Profit Graph

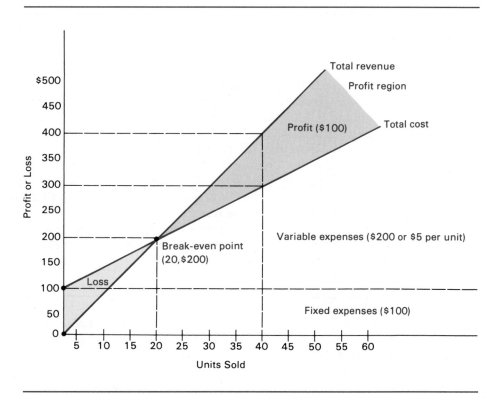

revenue line lies below the total cost line, a loss region is defined. Similarly, when the total revenue line lies above the total cost line, a profit region is defined. The point where the total revenue line and the total cost line intersect is the break-even point. To break even, Tyson Company must sell 20 units and thus receive $200 total revenues.

Now let's compare the information available from the CVP graph to that available from the profit-volume graph. To do so, consider the sale of forty units. Recall that the profit-volume graph revealed that selling forty units produced profits of $100. Examine Exhibit 8–6 again. The CVP graph also shows profits of $100, but it reveals more as well. The CVP graph discloses that total revenues of $400 and total costs of $300 are associated with the sale of forty units. Furthermore, the total costs can be broken down into fixed costs of $100 and variable costs of $200. The CVP graph provides revenue and cost information not provided by the profit-volume graph. Unlike the profit-volume graph, some computation is needed to determine the profit associated with a given sales volume. Nonetheless, because of the greater information content, managers are likely to find the CVP graph a more useful tool.

■ **ADDITIONAL CONCEPTS**

Margin of Safety

margin of safety

The **margin of safety** is the units sold or expected to be sold or the revenue earned or expected to be earned above the break-even volume. For example, if the break-even volume for a company is 200 units and the company is currently selling 500 units, the margin of safety is 300 units (500 − 200). The margin of safety can be expressed in sales revenue as well. If the break-even volume is $200,000 and current revenues are $350,000, then the margin of safety is $150,000.

The margin of safety can be viewed as a crude measure of risk. There are always events, unknown when plans are made, that can lower sales below the original expected level. If a firm's margin of safety is large given the expected sales for the coming year, the risk of suffering losses should sales take a downward turn is less than if the margin of safety is small. Managers who face a low margin of safety may wish to consider actions to increase sales or decrease costs. These steps will increase the margin of safety and lower the risk of incurring losses.

Operating Leverage

Operating leverage is concerned with the relative mix of fixed costs and variable costs in an organization. It is sometimes possible to trade off fixed costs for variable costs. As variable costs decrease, the unit contribution margin increases, making the contribution of each unit sold that much greater. In such a case, the effect of fluctuations in sales on profitability increases. Thus, firms that have bought lower variable costs by increasing the proportion of fixed costs will benefit with greater increases in profits as sales increase than will firms with a lower proportion of fixed costs. Fixed costs are being used as leverage to increase profits. Unfortunately, it is also true that firms with a higher operating leverage will also experience greater reductions in profits as

operating leverage

sales decrease. Therefore, **operating leverage** is the use of fixed costs to extract higher percentage changes in profits as sales activity changes.

The greater the degree of operating leverage, the more that changes in sales activity will affect profits. Because of this phenomenon, the mix of costs that an organization chooses can have a considerable influence on its operating risk and profit level.

degree of operating leverage (DOL)

The **degree of operating leverage (DOL)** can be measured for a given level of sales by taking the ratio of contribution margin to profit, as follows:

$$DOL = \text{Contribution margin/Profit}$$

If fixed costs are used to lower variable costs such that contribution margin increases and profit decreases, then the ratio of contribution margin to sales increases, signaling an increase in the degree of operating leverage. This measure is important because it reveals the degree of change in profits for a percentage change in sales volume. When multiplied by the percentage change in sales, the degree of operating leverage will provide the percentage change in profits:

$$\text{Percentage change in profits} = DOL \times \text{Percentage change in sales}$$

To illustrate the utility of these concepts, consider a firm that is planning to add a new product line. In adding the line, the firm can choose to rely heavily on automation or on labor. If the firm chooses to emphasize automation rather than labor, fixed costs will be higher and unit variable costs will be lower. Relevant data for a sales level of 10,000 units follow:

	Automated System	Manual System
Sales	$1,000,000	$1,000,000
Less: Variable expenses	(500,000)	(800,000)
Contribution margin	$ 500,000	$ 200,000
Less: Fixed costs	(375,000)	(100,000)
Profit before taxes	$ 125,000	$ 100,000
Unit selling price	$ 100	$ 100
Unit variable cost	50	80
Unit contribution margin	50	20

The degree of operating leverage (DOL) for the automated system is 4.0 ($500,000/$125,000). The degree of operating leverage for the manual system is 2.0 ($200,000/$100,000). We can also assess the effect on profits of a percentage change in sales volume by multiplying DOL by the percentage change. For example, if sales increase by 40 percent, profits for the automated system would increase by 160 percent (0.40 × 4.0) and for the manual system by 80 percent (0.40 x 2.0). The automated system has a greater percentage increase because it has a higher degree of operating leverage. The claimed effect on profits is verified by the following income statement reflecting a 40 percent increase in sales:

	Automated System	Manual System
Sales	$1,400,000	$ 1,400,000
Less: Variable costs	(700,000)	(1,120,000)
Contribution margin	$ 700,000	$ 280,000
Less: Fixed costs	(375,000)	(100,000)
Profit before taxes	$ 325,000	$ 180,000

Income for the automated system increases from \$125,000 to \$325,000 (160 percent), and income for the manual system increases from \$100,000 to \$180,000 (80 percent).

In choosing between the two systems, the effect of operating leverage is a valuable piece of information. As the 40 percent increase in sales illustrates, this effect can bring a significant benefit to the firm. However, the effect is a two-edged sword. As sales decrease, the automated system will also show much higher percentage decreases. Moreover, the increased operating leverage is available under the automated system because of the presence of increased fixed costs. The break-even point for the automated system is 7,500 units (\$375,000/\$50), whereas the break-even point for the manual system is 5,000 units (\$100,000/\$20). Thus, the automated system has greater operating risk. The increased risk, of course, provides a potentially higher profit level (as long as units sold exceed 9,167).[4]

In choosing between the automated and the manual systems, the manager must assess the likelihood that sales will exceed 9,167 units. If, after careful study, there is a strong belief that sales will easily exceed this level, the choice is obvious: the automated system. On the other hand, if sales are unlikely to exceed 9,167 units, the manual system is preferable.

▪ LIMITATIONS OF CVP ANALYSIS

A number of limitations are commonly mentioned with respect to CVP analysis.

1. The analysis assumes a linear revenue function and a linear cost function.

2. The analysis assumes that what is produced is sold.

3. The analysis assumes that fixed and variable costs can be accurately identified.

4. For multiple-product analysis, the sales mix is assumed to be known.

5. The selling prices and costs are assumed to be known with certainty.

Criticisms 1 through 3 pose fewer problems than do points 4 and 5. It is virtually impossible to predict with certainty the sales mix, the selling prices, and the costs for an upcoming period. However, with the capabilities of spread-sheet analysis, the sensitivity of variables to changes in predicted values can be readily assessed. Furthermore, there are formal ways of explicitly building uncertainty into the CVP model. Exploration of these issues, however, is left to a more advanced course of study.

---

[4]This benchmark is computed by equating the profit equations of the two systems and solving for X:

$$50X - 375,000 = 20X - 100,000$$
$$X = 9,167$$

■ SUMMARY OF LEARNING OBJECTIVES

1. **Develop a cost-volume-profit equation from the variable-costing income statement.** The variable-costing income statement can be expressed as follows: Profit before taxes = Sales revenues − Variable expenses − Fixed expenses. This equation can be manipulated to solve for a number of unknowns.

2. **Compute the break-even point in units and sales revenues for a single-product setting.** The break-even point in units is computed by dividing total fixed costs by the contribution margin per unit. The break-even point in sales revenues is computed by dividing total fixed costs by the contribution margin ratio.

3. **Compute the units and sales revenues required to achieve a targeted level of profit.** To compute the units and sales revenues required to achieve a targeted level of profit, simply add the targeted profit to fixed costs and apply the break-even equations.

4. **Assess the effects of changes in costs and prices on the profitability of a firm and use this assessment to aid in making decisions.** Changes in the fixed and variable cost patterns affect the profitability of a firm. The firm can use CVP analysis to see just how a particular change in price or cost would affect the break-even point.

5. **Compute the break-even point and targeted profit levels for a multiple-product setting.** Multiple-product analysis requires that an assumption be made concerning the expected sales mix. Given a particular sales mix, a multiple-product problem can be converted into a single-product analysis. However, it should be remembered that the answers change as the sales mix changes.

6. **Assess the effect of changes in sales mix for a multiple-product firm.** If the sales mix changes in a multiple-product firm, the break-even point will also change. In general, increases in the sales of high contribution margin products will decrease the break-even point, while increases in the sales of low contribution margin products will increase the break-even point.

7. **Prepare a profit-volume graph and a cost-volume-profit graph and explain the meaning of each.** The profit-volume graph portrays the relationship between profits and sales volume. Typically, profit or loss is measured on the vertical axis, and units sold are on the horizontal axis. A cost-volume-profit graph illustrates the relationships among cost, volume, and profits. In this graph, there is a total revenue line and a total cost line. The point at which the total revenue line crosses the total cost line is the break-even point.

8. **Calculate the margin of safety and explain how it is used.** The margin of safety is sales revenue minus break-even sales revenue. The margin of safety acts as a crude measure of risk.

EXHIBIT 8–7
Summary of Important Equations

1.	Variable costing net income	$I = PX - VX - F$
2.	Break-even point in units	$X = F/(P - V)$
3.	Sales revenue	$R = PX$
4.	Break-even point in sales dollars	$R = F/(1 - vr)$
5.	Variable cost ratio	$vr = V/P$
6.	Contribution margin ratio	Contribution margin ratio $= 1 - vr$
7.	Margin of safety	$MS = $ Sales $-$ Break-even sales
8.	Degree of operating leverage	$DOL = (P - V)/I$
9.	Percentage change in profits	% change profits $= DOL \times$ % change in sales
10.	Total variable cost	Total variable cost $= VX$
11.	After-tax net income	After-tax net income $= I - tI$
12.	Income taxes	Taxes $= tI$

9. **Calculate operating leverage and explain its significance.** Operating leverage is measured by dividing the contribution margin by profit. The degree of operating leverage allows the firm to assess the impact of a change in sales activity on profits.

The subject of cost-volume-profit analysis naturally lends itself to the use of numerous equations. Some of the more common equations used in this chapter are summarized in Exhibit 8–7.

▪ KEY TERMS

Break-even point   The point where total sales revenue equals total costs. The point of zero profits. (p. 365)

Contribution margin ratio   Contribution margin divided by sales revenue. It is the proportion of each sales dollar available to cover fixed costs and provide for profit. (p. 372)

Cost-volume-profit graph   A graph that depicts the relationships among costs, volume, and profits. It consists of a total revenue line and a total cost line. (p. 379)

Degree of operating leverage (DOL)   A measure of the sensitivity of profit changes to changes in sales volume. It measures the percentage change in profits resulting from a percentage change in sales. (p. 382)

Margin of safety   The units sold or expected to be sold or sales revenue earned or expected to be earned above the break-even volume. (p. 382)

Operating leverage   The use of fixed costs to extract higher percentage changes in profits as sales activity changes. Leverage is achieved by increasing fixed costs while lowering variable costs. (p. 382)

Profit-volume graph A graphical portrayal of the relationship between profits and sales activity. (p. 378)

Sales mix The relative combination of products (or services) being sold by an organization. (p. 375)

Sales-revenue approach An approach to CVP analysis that uses sales revenue to measure sales activity. Variable costs and contribution margin are expressed as percentages of sales revenue. (p. 364)

Units-sold approach An approach to CVP analysis that uses units sold to measure sales activity. Variable costs and contribution margin are expressed on a unit-sold basis. (p. 364)

Variable cost ratio Variable costs divided by sales revenues. It is the proportion of each sales dollar needed to cover variable costs. (p. 371)

■ REVIEW PROBLEM

Henders Company's projected profit for the coming year is as follows:

	Total	Per Unit
Sales	$ 200,000	$ 20
Less: Variable costs	(120,000)	(12)
Contribution margin	$ 80,000	$ 8
Less: Fixed expenses	(64,000)	
Net income	$ 16,000	

Required:

1. Compute the break-even point in units.

2. How many units must be sold to earn a profit of $30,000?

3. Compute the contribution margin ratio. Using that ratio, compute the additional profit that Henders would earn if sales were $25,000 more than expected.

4. Suppose Henders would like to earn a profit equal to 20 percent of sales revenue. How many units must be sold for this goal to be realized? Prepare an income statement to prove your answer.

5. For the projected level of sales, compute the margin of safety.

6. If sales were to increase by 30 percent, by what percentage would profits increase? Do not compute a new level of income to answer this question.

Solution:

1. The break-even point is $(F + I)/(P - V) = (\$64,000 + 0)/(\$20 - \$12) = \$64,000/\$8 = 8,000$ units.

2. The number of units that must be sold to earn a profit of $30,000 is $(F + I)/(P - V) = (\$64,000 + \$30,000)/\$8 = \$94,000/\$8 = 11,750$ units.

3. The contribution margin ratio is $\$8/\$20 = 0.40$. With additional sales of $25,000, the additional profit would be $0.40 \times \$25,000 = \$10,000$.

4. To find the number of units sold for a profit equal to 20 percent of sales, let $I = 0.20 \times PX = 0.2 \times 20X = 4X$. To solve for X

$$I = PX - VX - F$$
$$4X = 20X - 12X - 64,000$$
$$4X = 64,000$$
$$X = 16,000 \text{ units}$$

The income statement is as follows:

Sales (16,000 × $20)	$ 320,000
Less: Variable expenses (16,000 × $12)	(192,000)
Contribution margin	$ 128,000
Less: Fixed expenses	(64,000)
Net income	$ 64,000

Net income/Sales = $64,000/$320,000 = 0.20, or 20 percent.

5. The margin of safety is 10,000 − 8,000 = 2,000 units, or $40,000 in sales revenues.

6. The degree of operating leverage is $80,000/$16,000 = 5.0. If sales increased by 30 percent, profits would increase by 5.0 × 0.30 = 1.50, or 150 percent.

▪ QUESTIONS

1 Explain how CVP analysis can be used for managerial planning.

2 Describe the difference between the units-sold approach to CVP analysis and the sales-revenue approach.

3 Define the term *break-even point*.

4 Explain why contribution margin per unit becomes profit per unit above the break-even point.

5 If the contribution margin per unit is $7 and the break-even point is 10,000 units, how much profit will a firm make if 15,000 units are sold?

6 What is the variable cost ratio? The contribution margin ratio? How are the two ratios related?

7 Suppose a firm has fixed costs of $20,000 and a contribution margin ratio equal to 0.4. How much sales revenue must the firm have in order to break even?

8 Suppose a firm with a contribution margin ratio of 0.3 increased its advertising expenses by $10,000 and found that sales increased by $30,000. Was it a good decision to increase advertising expenses?

9 Define the term *sales mix* and give an example to support your definition.

10 Explain how CVP analysis developed for single products can be used in a multiple-product setting.

11   Assume that a firm has two products—Product A and Product B. Last year 2,000 units
      of A and 1,000 units of B were sold. The same sales mix is expected for the coming
      year. Total fixed expenses are $30,000, and the unit contribution margins are $10 for A
      and $5 for B. How many units of A and how many units of B must be sold to break
      even?

12   Wilson Company has a contribution margin ratio of 0.6. The break-even point is
      $100,000. During the year, Wilson earned total revenues of $200,000. What was Wilson's
      profit?

13   Explain how a change in sales mix can change a company's break-even point.

14   Define the term *margin of safety*. Explain how it can be used as a crude measure of
      operating risk.

15   Explain what is meant by the term *operating leverage*.

16   Assume that a firm has net income of $100,000 and a total contribution margin of
      $200,000. What is the firm's degree of operating leverage?

17   If a firm's degree of operating leverage is 3 and it experiences a 20 percent increase in
      sales, by what percentage will the firm's profits increase?

18   The break-even point for a firm is $1.2 million in revenues. During the past year, the
      firm earned $2 million in revenues. What is the margin of safety for this firm?

■ EXERCISES

E8–1 **Units Sold; After-Tax Profit; Margin of Safety**   Crunchy Morsels, Inc., manufactures
      and sells corn chips. Currently, Crunchy produces only one type of corn chip. The
      chips are packaged in 11-ounce bags and sold to retailers for $1.50 per bag. The
      variable costs per bag are as follows:

Corn	$0.70
Vegetable oil	0.10
Miscellaneous ingredients	0.03
Selling	0.17

Fixed manufacturing costs total $300,000 per year. Administrative costs (all fixed) total
$100,000.

Required:

1. Compute the number of bags of corn chips that must be sold for Crunchy to break
   even.

2. How many bags of corn chips must be sold for Crunchy to earn a before-tax profit
   of $150,000?

3. Assuming a tax rate of 60 percent, how many bags of corn chips must be sold to
   earn an after-tax profit of $284,000?

4. Suppose that Crunchy expects to sell 1.2 million bags of corn chips. What is the
   margin of safety?

E8–2   Contribution Margin; Unit Amounts   Information on four independent companies is given below. Calculate the correct amount for each question mark.

	A	B	C	D
Sales	$5,000	?	?	$9,000
Total variable cost	(4,000)	(11,700)	(9,750)	?
Contribution margin	1,000	3,900	?	?
Total fixed cost	?	(4,000)	?	(750)
Net income	500	?	400	2,850
Units sold	?	1,300	125	90
Price	$5	?	$130	?
Variable cost/Unit	?	$9	?	?
Contribution margin/Unit	?	$3	?	?
Contribution margin ratio	?	?	60%	?
Break-even in units	?	?	?	?

E8–3   CVP; Margin of Safety   Skyways Aviation Services had revenues of $675,000 last year, with total variable costs of $202,500 and fixed costs of $200,000.

Required:

1. What is the contribution margin ratio for Skyways based on last year's data? What is the break-even point in sales revenue?
2. What was the margin of safety for Skyways last year?
3. Skyways is considering starting a multimedia advertising campaign that is supposed to increase sales by $150,000 per year. The campaign will cost $106,000. Is the advertising campaign a good idea? Explain.

E8–4   CVP   Stevenson Company's break-even point is 1,000 units. Variable cost per unit is $150; total fixed costs are $80,000 per year. What price does Stevenson charge?

E8–5   Contribution Margin; CVP; Net Income; Margin of Safety   Sweet Sue, Inc., produces a particularly rich praline fudge. Each ten-ounce box sells for $5.50. Variable unit costs are as follows:

Pecans	$ 0.75
Sugar	0.35
Butter	1.75
Other ingredients	0.24
Box, packing material	0.76
Selling commission	0.55

Fixed overhead cost is $24,000 per year. Fixed selling and administrative costs are $9,000 per year. Sweet Sue sold 35,000 boxes last year.

Required:

1. What is the contribution margin per unit for a box of praline fudge? What is the contribution margin ratio?

2. How many boxes must be sold to break even? What is the break-even sales revenue?

3. What was Sweet Sue's net income last year?

4. What was the margin of safety?

5. Suppose that Sweet Sue, Inc., raises the price to $6 per box but that anticipated sales will drop to 31,500 boxes. What will the new break-even point in units be? Should Sweet Sue raise the price? Explain.

E8-6 **Sales-Revenue Approach; Variable-Cost Ratio; Contribution Margin Ratio; Margin of Safety** Lambert produces and sells an economy line of ski parkas. The budgeted income statement for the coming year is

Sales	$ 600,000
Less: Variable expenses	(400,000)
Contribution margin	$ 200,000
Less: Fixed expenses	(120,000)
Profit before taxes	$ 80,000
Less: Taxes	(24,000)
Profit after taxes	$ 56,000

Required:

1. What is Lambert's variable cost ratio? Its contribution margin ratio?

2. Suppose Lambert's actual revenues are $60,000 more than budgeted. By how much will before-tax profits increase? Give the answer without preparing a new income statement.

3. How much sales revenue must Lambert earn in order to break even? What is the expected margin of safety?

4. How much sales revenue must Lambert generate to earn a before-tax profit of $100,000? An after-tax profit of $84,000? Prepare a contribution income statement to verify the accuracy of your last answer.

E8-7 **CVP Analysis with Target Profits** Tom Flannery has developed a new recipe for fried chicken and plans to open a take-out restaurant in Oklahoma City. His father-in-law has agreed to invest $500,000 in the operation provided Tom can convince him that profits will be at least 20 percent of sales revenues. Tom estimated that total fixed expense would be $24,000 per year and that variable expense would be approximately 40 percent of sales revenues.

Required:

1. How much sales revenue must be earned to produce profits equal to 20 percent of sales revenue? Prepare a contribution income statement to verify your answer.

2. If Tom plans on selling 12-piece buckets of chicken for $10 each, how many buckets must he sell to earn a profit equal to 20 percent of sales? 25 percent of sales? Prepare a contribution income statement to verify the second answer.

3. Suppose Tom's father-in-law meant that the after-tax profit had to be 20 percent of sales revenue. Under this assumption, how much sales revenue must be generated by Tom's chicken business? (Assume that the tax rate is 40 percent.)

E8–8 **Operating Leverage** Income statements for two different companies in the same industry are as follows:

	Company A	Company B
Sales	$ 500,000	$ 500,000
Less: Variable costs	(350,000)	(200,000)
Contribution margin	$ 150,000	$ 300,000
Less: Fixed costs	(50,000)	(250,000)
Net income	$ 100,000	$ 50,000

Required:

1. Compute the degree of operating leverage for each company.

2. Compute the break-even point for each company. Explain why the break-even point for Company B is higher.

3. Suppose that both companies experience a 50 percent increase in revenues. Compute the percentage change in profits for each company. Explain why the percentage increase in Company B's profits is so much larger than that of Company A.

E8–9 **CVP Analysis with Multiple Products** Thompson Company produces scientific and business calculators. For the coming year, Thompson expects to sell 200,000 scientific calculators and 100,000 business calculators. A segmented income statement for the two products is given below.

	Scientific	Business	Total
Sales	$ 5,000,000	$2,000,000	$ 7,000,000
Less: Variable costs	(2,400,000)	(900,000)	(3,300,000)
Contribution margin	$ 2,600,000	$1,100,000	$ 3,700,000
Less: Direct fixed costs	($ 1,200,000)	(960,000)	(2,160,000)
Segment margin	$ 1,400,000	$ 140,000	$ 1,540,000
Less: Common fixed costs			(800,000)
Net income			$ 740,000

Required:

1. Compute the number of scientific calculators and the number of business calculators that must be sold to break even.

2. Using information from only the total column of the income statement, compute the sales revenue that must be generated for the company to break even.

E8–10 **Contribution Analysis** Fox Company produces a deluxe pen-and-pencil set. The selling price of the set is $50. The variable cost per set is $30. Total fixed costs are $2.5 million. Expected sales for the coming year are 150,000 sets. Management is unhappy with the expected profits and is trying to find ways to increase overall performance. The marketing manager has proposed two alternatives: (1) increase advertising by $100,000, which should produce additional sales of 10,000 units, or (2) decrease the selling price to $45 per set, which should boost sales from 150,000 sets to 165,000 sets.

Required:

1. Prepare an income statement that reflects expected sales for the coming year. Ignore the proposals by the marketing manager.

2. Without preparing income statements, assess the impact on profits of each of the marketing manager's proposals. Which would you recommend?

3. Prepare income statements for the two proposals to verify your analysis in requirement 2.

E8–11   **Changes in Break-even Points with Changes in Unit Prices**   The income statement for Sanders, Inc., is as follows:

Sales	$ 500,000
Less: Variable expenses	(275,000)
Contribution margin	$ 225,000
Less: Fixed expenses	(180,000)
Net income	$ 45,000

Sanders produces and sells a single product. The above income statement is based on sales of 100,000 units.

Required:

1. Compute the break-even point in units and in revenues.

2. Suppose that the selling price increases by 10 percent. Will the break-even point increase or decrease? Recompute it.

3. Suppose that the variable cost per unit increases by $0.35. Will the break-even point increase or decrease? Recompute it.

4. Can you predict whether the break-even point increases or decreases if both the selling price and the unit variable cost increase? Recompute the break-even point incorporating both of the changes in requirements 2 and 3.

5. Assume that total fixed costs increase by $50,000. (Assume no other changes from the original data.) Will the break-even point increase or decrease? Recompute it.

E8–12   **CVP and Profit-Volume Graphs**   Lotts Company produces and sells one product. The selling price is $10, and the unit variable cost is $6. Total fixed costs are $10,000.

Required:

1. Prepare a CVP graph with units sold as the horizontal axis and dollars as the vertical axis. Label the break-even point on the horizontal axis.

2. Prepare CVP graphs for each of the following scenarios:
   a. Fixed costs increase by $5,000.
   b. Unit variable cost increases to $7.
   c. Unit selling price increases to $12.
   d. Assume both a and b.

3. Prepare a profit-volume graph using the original data. Repeat, following the scenarios in requirement 2.

4. Which of the two graphs do you think provides the most information? Why?

E8–13 **Basic CVP Concepts** Auflager Company produces a single product. The projected income statement for the coming year is as follows:

Sales (50,000 units @ $40)	$ 2,000,000
Less: Variable costs	(1,100,000)
Contribution margin	$ 900,000
Less: Fixed costs	(765,000)
Net income	$ 135,000

Required:

1. Compute the unit contribution margin and the units that must be sold to break even. Suppose that 30,000 units are sold above break even. What is the profit?

2. Compute the contribution margin ratio and the break-even point in dollars. Suppose that revenues are $200,000 more than expected. What would the total profit be?

3. Compute the margin of safety.

4. Compute the operating leverage. Compute the new profit level if sales are 20 percent higher than expected.

5. How many units must be sold to earn a profit equal to 10 percent of sales?

6. Assume that the tax rate is 40 percent. How many units must be sold to earn an after-tax profit of $180,000?

E8–14 **CVP; Before and After-Tax Targeted Net Income** CF Company produces a line of peach chutney. Currently, CF charges a price of $3.50 per jar. Variable costs are $1.40 per jar and fixed costs are $50,000. The tax rate is 33 percent. In 1992, 27,300 jars were sold.

Required:

1. What is CF's net income after taxes for 1992?

2. What is CF's break-even revenue?

3. Suppose CF wants to earn before-tax net income of $13,000. How many units must be sold?

4. Suppose CF wants to earn after-tax net income of $13,000. How many units must be sold?

E8–15 **Multiproduct Break Even** Parker Pottery produces a line of vases and a line of ceramic figurines. Each line uses the same equipment and labor; hence, there are no traceable fixed costs. Common fixed costs equal $30,000. Parker's accountant has begun to assess the profitability of the two lines and has gathered the following data for 1992:

	Vases	Figurines
Price	$ 40	$ 70
Variable cost	30	42
Contribution margin	10	28
Number of units	1,000	500

Required:

1. Compute the number of vases and the number of figurines that must be sold for the company to break even.

2. Parker Pottery is considering undertaking an advertising campaign to highlight the quality of its ceramic figurines. The campaign will cost $5,000 and if it is successful, the projected sales of vases will remain at 1,000 while figurine sales will increase to 1,000 units. What is the new break-even point in units for each of the products?

■ **PROBLEMS**

P8–1   **Basic CVP Concepts**   Topper Company produces a variety of glass products. One division makes windshields for compact automobiles. The division's projected income statement for the coming year is as follows:

Sales (150,000 units @ $50)	$ 7,500,000
Less: Variable expenses	(3,500,000)
Contribution margin	$ 4,000,000
Less: Fixed expenses	(3,200,000)
Net income	$ 800,000

Required:

1. Compute the contribution margin per unit and calculate the break-even point in units. Repeat using the contribution margin ratio.

2. The divisional manager has decided to increase the advertising budget by $100,000 and cut the selling price to $45. These actions will increase sales revenues by $1 million. Will the division be better off?

3. Suppose sales revenues exceed the estimated amount on the income statement by $540,000. Without preparing a new income statement, by how much are profits underestimated?

4. Refer to the original data. How many units must be sold to earn an after-tax profit of $1.254 million? Assume a tax rate of 34 percent. Repeat the analysis assuming that the after-tax profit target is 10 percent of sales revenues.

5. Compute the safety margin based on the income statement given above.

6. Compute the operating leverage based on the income statement above. If sales revenues are 20 percent greater than expected, what is the percentage increase in profits?

P8–2   **Multiple-Product Analysis; Changes in Sales Mix**   Unicorn Enterprises produces two strategy games, Mystical Wars and Magical Dragons. The projected income for the coming year, segmented by product line, follows:

	Wars	*Dragons*	*Total*
Sales	$ 500,000	$ 800,000	$1,300,000
Less: Variable expenses	(230,000)	(460,000)	(690,000)
Contribution margin	$ 270,000	$ 340,000	$ 610,000
Less: Direct fixed expenses	(120,000)	(180,000)	(300,000)
Product margin	$ 150,000	$ 160,000	$ 310,000
Less: Common fixed expenses			(210,000)
Net income			$ 100,000

The sales prices are $10 for Mystical Wars and $20 for Magical Dragons.

Required:

1. Compute the number of games of each kind that must be sold for Unicorn Enterprises to break even.

2. Compute the revenue that must be earned to produce a net income of 10 percent of sales revenues.

3. Assume that the marketing manager changes the sales mix of the two games so that the ratio is seven Mystical War games to three Magical Dragon games. Repeat requirements 1 and 2. Will the owner of Unicorn Enterprises be pleased with the anticipated change in sales mix?

4. Refer to the original data. Suppose that Unicorn can increase the sales of Magical Dragons with increased advertising. The extra advertising would cost an additional $100,000, and some of the potential purchasers of Mystical Wars would switch to Magical Dragons. In total, sales of Magical Dragons would increase by 15,000 units and sales of Mystical Wars would decrease by 5,000 units. Would Unicorn be better off with this strategy? Prepare income statements for each product line to verify your analysis. Do you have any additional recommendations?

P8–3 **CVP Equation; Basic Concepts; Solving for Unknowns** Azucar Company produces a chocolate almond bar. Each bar sells for $0.40. The variable costs for each bar (sugar, chocolate, almonds, wrapper, labor, and so on) total $0.25. The total fixed costs are $60,000. During the most recent year, 1 million bars were sold. The president of Azucar, not fully satisfied with the profit performance of the chocolate bar, was considering the following options to increase the bar's profitability: (1) increase advertising; (2) increase the quality of the ingredients and, simultaneously, increase the selling price; (3) increase the selling price; (4) a combination of the three. (Ignore income taxes for all requirements.)

Required:

1. The sales manager is confident that an advertising campaign could double sales volume. If the company president's goal is to increase this year's profits by 50 percent over last year's, what is the maximum amount that can be spent on advertising?

2. Refer to the original data and assume that the company increases the quality of its ingredients, thus increasing variable costs to $0.30. Answer the following questions:
   a. How much must the selling price be increased to maintain the same break-even point in units?
   b. What will the new price be if the company wants to increase the old contribution margin ratio by 50 percent?

3. Refer to the original data. The company has decided to increase its selling price to $0.50. The sales volume drops from 1 million to 800,000 bars. Was the decision to increase the price a good one? Compute the sales volume that would be needed at the new price for the company to earn the same profit as last year.

4. Refer to the original data. The sales manager is convinced that by increasing the quality of the ingredients (increasing variables costs to $0.30) and by advertising the increased quality (advertising dollars would be increased by $100,000), sales volume could be doubled. He has also indicated that a price increase would not affect the ability to double sales volume as long as the price increase is not more than 20 percent of the current selling price. Compute the selling price that would be needed

to achieve the goal of increasing profits by 50 percent. Is the sales manager's plan feasible? What selling price would you choose? Why?

P8-4 **CVP Analysis with Multiple Services** We-Care Lawn Service is a lawn-care company operating in a northern metropolitan area. We-Care offers chemical fertilization, insect control, and weed and crabgrass control for a customer's lawn and foundation. Four chemical applications are given per growing period, which lasts from April through October.

Four chemicals are used in the applications: dacthal crabgrass control, trimel weed control, urea fertilizer, and dursban insecticide. In the first application, dacthal accounts for 75 percent of the chemical cost followed by 10 percent trimel, 10 percent urea, and 5 percent dursban; in the remaining three applications, dacthal is not used—it is ineffective after May 31.

We-Care offers two services: residential and commercial. The price charged per residential application is $13.50. The average residential area is 0.1 acres. Commercial applications are for any area larger than an acre and are priced at $40 per acre per application.

We-Care's variable costs consist of chemicals, direct labor, operating expenses for its truck, and operating supplies. For the first application, the cost of chemicals is $40 per acre; for the remaining applications, chemicals cost $10 per application per acre. We-Care has one employee who is classified as direct labor. He is paid $6 per hour. Residential lawns should be sprayed at a rate of three lawns per hour (including travel time). Commercial applications are sprayed at a rate of forty-five minutes per acre. Operating expenses for the truck average $13.78 per acre per residential lawn application and $5 per acre per commercial application. Operating supplies average $4.13 per acre per application, regardless of the type of service.

Fixed costs for the year follow:

Truck lease	$12,337
Depreciation, equipment	1,747
Truck insurance	1,339
Telephone	1,200
Tax and license	1,085
Advertising	10,000
Salary of supervisor	12,000
Total	$39,708

Based on last year's experience, We-Care services two acres of residential property for every acre of commercial property. The owner expects the same sales mix for the coming year.

Required:

1. Assume that every customer receives all four applications. Compute the acres of residential applications and the acres of commercial applications that must be serviced for We-Care to break even. Given the acres of residential servicing, compute the average number of residential customers.

2. Given the break-even point computed in requirement 1, determine the labor hours needed to service the break-even volume. Is one employee sufficient? Assume that the employee works eight hours hours per day and a total of 140 days during the seven-month growing season. What volume is needed before a second employee is hired? Discuss the effect on CVP analysis if additional employees are needed.

3. Assume that 60 percent of all residential customers receive only the first application, with the remaining 40 percent receiving all four. All commercial customers receive all four applications. Redo the break-even analysis. (*Hint:* There are now two types of residential customers, producing a mix of three services.)

P8-5   Basics of the Sales-Revenue Approach   Kiltop Company produces a toy dart gun. The projected income statement for the coming year follows:

Sales	$ 480,000
Less: Variable costs	(249,600)
Contribution margin	$ 230,400
Less: Fixed costs	(180,000)
Net income	$ 50,400

Required:

1. Compute the contribution margin ratio for the toy gun.

2. How much revenue must Kiltop earn in order to break even?

3. What volume of sales must be earned if Kiltop wants to earn an after-tax income equal to 8 percent of sales? Assume that the tax rate is 34 percent.

4. What is the effect on the contribution margin ratio if the unit selling price and unit variable cost each increase by 10 percent?

5. Suppose that management has decided to give a 3 percent commission on all sales. The projected income statement does not reflect this commission. Recompute the contribution margin ratio assuming that the commission will be paid. What effect does this have on the break-even point?

6. If the commission is paid as described in requirement 5, management expects sales revenues to increase by $80,000. Is it a sound decision to implement the commission? Support your answer with appropriate computations.

7. Refer to the original data. Compute the safety margin and the operating leverage. Compute the percentage change in profits if sales increase by 15 percent.

P8-6   CVP Analysis: Sales-Revenue Approach; Pricing; After-Tax Profit Target   Kline Consulting is a service organization that specializes in the design, installation, and servicing of mechanical, hydraulic, and pneumatic systems. For example, some manufacturing firms with machinery that cannot be turned off for servicing need some type of system to lubricate the machinery during use. To deal with this type of problem for a client, Kline designed a central lubricating system that pumps lubricants intermittently to bearings and other moving parts.

The operating results for the firm in 1993 are as follows:

Sales	$ 802,429
Less: Variable costs	(430,000)
Contribution margin	$ 372,429
Less: Fixed expenses	(154,750)
Net income	$ 217,679

In 1994, Kline expects variable costs to increase by 5 percent and fixed costs by 4 percent.

Required:

1. What is the contribution margin ratio for 1993?

2. Compute Kline's break-even point for 1993 in dollars.

3. Suppose that Kline would like to see a 6 percent increase in net income in 1994. By what percentage (on average) must Kline raise its bids to cover the expected cost increases and obtain the desired net income? Assume that Kline expects the same mix and volume of services in 1994 as in 1993.

4. In 1994, how much revenue must be earned for Kline to earn an after-tax profit of $175,000? Assume a tax rate of 34 percent.

P8–7 **CVP with Multiple Products; Sales Mix Changes; Changes in Fixed and Variable Costs** Artistic Woodcrafting, Inc., began in 1981 as a one-person cabinet-making operation. Business soon expanded and employees were added. By 1992, sales volume totaled $850,000. Volume for the first five months of 1993 totaled $600,000, and sales were expected to be $1.6 million for the entire year. Unfortunately, the cabinet business in the region where Artistic Woodcrafting is located is highly competitive. More than 200 cabinet shops are all competing for the same business.

  Artistic currently offers two different quality grades of cabinets: Grade I and Grade II, with Grade I being the higher quality. The average unit selling prices, unit variable costs, and direct fixed costs are as follows:

	Unit Price	*Unit Variable Cost*	*Direct Fixed*
Grade I	$3,400	$2,686	$95,000
Grade II	1,600	1,328	95,000

Common fixed costs (fixed costs not traceable to either cabinet) are $35,000. Currently, for every three Grade I cabinets sold, seven Grade II cabinets are sold.

Required:

1. Calculate the Grade I and the Grade II cabinets that are expected to be sold during 1993.

2. Calculate the number of Grade I cabinets and the number of Grade II cabinets that must be sold for the company to break even.

3. Artistic Woodwork can buy computer-controlled machines that will make doors, drawers, and frames. If the machines are purchased, the variable costs for each type of cabinet will decrease by 9 percent, but common fixed costs will increase by $44,000. Compute the effect on net income in 1993 and also calculate the new break-even point. Assume the machines are purchased at the beginning of the sixth month. Fixed costs for the company are incurred uniformly throughout the year.

4. Refer to the original data. Artistic Woodwork is considering adding a retail outlet. This will increase common fixed costs by $70,000 per year. As a result of adding the retail outlet, the additional publicity and emphasis on quality will allow the firm to change the sales mix to 1:1. The retail outlet is also expected to increase sales by 30 percent. Assume that the outlet is opened at the beginning of the sixth month. Calculate the effect on the company's expected profits for 1993 and calculate the

new break-even point. Assume that fixed costs are incurred uniformly throughout the year.

P8–8   **Ethics and a CVP Application**   Danna Lumus, the marketing manager for a division that produces a variety of paper products, was considering the divisional manager's request for a sales forecast for a new line of paper napkins. The divisional manager was gathering data so that he could choose between two different production processes. The first process would have a variable cost of $10 per case produced and fixed costs of $100,000. The second process would have a variable cost of $6 per case and fixed costs of $200,000. The selling price would be $30 per case. Danna had just completed a marketing analysis that projected annual sales of 30,000 cases.

Danna was reluctant to report the 30,000 forecast to the divisional manager. She knew that the first process was labor intensive, whereas the second was largely automated with little labor and no requirement for an additional production supervisor. If the first process were chosen, Jerry Johnson, a good friend, would be appointed as the line supervisor. If the second process were chosen, Jerry and an entire line of laborers would be laid off. After some consideration, Danna revised the projected sales downward to 22,000 cases.

She believed that the revision downward was justified. Since it would lead the divisional manager to choose the manual-oriented system, it showed a sensitivity to the needs of current employees—a sensitivity that she was afraid her divisional manager did not possess. He was too focused on quantitative factors in his decision making and usually ignored the qualitative aspects.

Required:

1. Compute the break-even point for each process.

2. Compute the sales volume for which the two processes are equally profitable. Identify the range of sales for which the manual process is more profitable than the automated process. Identify the range of sales for which the automated process is more profitable than the manual process. Why did the divisional manager want the sales forecast?

3. Discuss Danna's decision to alter the sales forecast. Do you agree with it? Did she act ethically? Was her decision justified since it helped a number of employees retain their employment? Should the impact on employees be factored into decisions? In fact, is it unethical not to consider the impact of decisions on employees?

4. Even though Danna is not a management accountant, do any of the ethical standards for management accountants listed in the Appendix to Chapter 1 apply? Explain.

P8–9   **Multiple Products; Break-even Analysis; Operating Leverage**   Naturo Food Products produces two different types of snack bars: granola and carob. Naturo sells the bars by the case to retail outlets. Granola bars sell for $30 a case, carob bars for $20. The projected income statement for the coming year follows:

Sales	$ 600,000
Less: Variable costs	(400,000)
Contribution margin	$ 200,000
Less: Fixed expenses	(150,000)
Net income	$ 50,000

The owner of Naturo estimates that 60 percent of the sales revenues will be produced by granola bars with the remaining 40 percent by carob bars. Granola bars are also responsible for 60 percent of the variable expenses. Of the fixed expenses, one-third are common to both products, and one-half are directly traceable to the granola bar product line.

Required:

1. Compute the sales revenue that must be earned for Naturo to break even.

2. Compute the number of cases of granola bars and of carob bars that must be sold for Naturo to break even.

3. Compute the degree of operating leverage for Naturo Products. Now assume that the actual revenues will be 40 percent higher than the projected revenues. By what percentage will profits increase with this change in sales volume?

P8–10 **Multiproduct Break Even** Garibaldi, Inc., manufactures two products, A and B. Fixed costs equal $146,000. Product A sells for $12 and has variable costs of $6; Product B sells for $8 and has variable costs of $5.

Required:

1. What is the contribution margin per unit and the contribution margin ratio for Product A and for Product B?

2. If Garibaldi sells 20,000 units of A and 40,000 units of B, what is the net income?

3. How many units of Product A and how many units of Product B must be sold for Garibaldi to break even?

4. Assume that Garibaldi has the opportunity to rearrange its plant to produce only Product B. If this is done, fixed costs will decrease by $35,000 and 70,000 units of B can be produced and sold. Is this a good idea? Explain.

P8–11 **CVP; Margin of Safety** Ellis Company produces a single product. Last year's income statement is as follows:

Sales (29,000 units)	$1,218,000
Less: Variable costs	(812,000)
Contribution margin	406,000
Less: Fixed costs	(300,000)
Net income	$ 106,000

Required:

1. Compute the break-even point in units and sales dollars.

2. What was the margin of safety for Ellis Company last year?

3. Suppose that Ellis Company is considering an investment in new technology that will increase fixed costs by $250,000 per year but will lower variable costs to 45 percent of sales. Units sold will remain unchanged. Prepare a budgeted income statement assuming that Ellis makes this investment. What is the new break-even point in units and sales dollars, assuming that the investment is made?

P8–12 **Multiplant Break Even** The PTO Division of the Galva Manufacturing Company produces power take-off units for the farm equipment business. The PTO Division, headquartered in Peoria, has a newly renovated plant in Peoria and an older, less automated plant in Moline. Both plants produce the same power take-off units for farm tractors that are sold to most domestic and foreign tractor manufacturers.

The PTO Division expects to produce and sell 192,000 power take-off units during the coming year. The division production manager has the following data available regarding the unit costs, unit prices, and production capacities for the two plants.

	Peoria		Moline	
Selling price		$150.00		$150.00
Variable manufacturing cost	$72.00		$88.00	
Fixed manufacturing cost	30.00		15.00	
Commission (5%)	7.50		7.50	
General and administrative expense	25.50		21.00	
Total unit cost		135.00		131.50
Unit profit		$ 15.00		$ 18.00
Production rate per day		400 units		320 units

All fixed costs are based on a normal year of 240 working days. When the number of working days exceeds 240, variable manufacturing costs increase by $3 per unit in Peoria and $8 per unit in Moline. Capacity for each plant is 300 working days.

Galva Manufacturing charges each of its plants a per-unit fee for administrative services such as payroll, general accounting, and purchasing because Galva considers these services to be a function of the work performed at the plants. For each of the plants, a fee of $6.50 represents the variable portion of the general and administrative expense.

Wishing to maximize the higher unit profit at Moline, PTO's production manager has decided to manufacture 96,000 units at each plant. This production plan results in Moline's operating at capacity and Peoria's operating at its normal volume. Galva's corporate controller is not happy with this plan; he wonders if it might be better to produce relatively more at the automated plant in Peoria.

Required:

1. Determine the annual break-even units for each of PTO's plants.
2. Calculate the operating income that would result from the division production manager's plan to produce 96,000 units at each plant.
3. Calculate the operating income that would result from sales of 192,000 power take-off units if 120,000 of them were produced at the Peoria plant and the remainder at the Moline plant.

(CMA adapted)

P8–13   **CVP Analysis and Assumptions**   Marston Corporation manufactures pharmaceutical products that are sold through a network of sales agents located in the United States and Canada. The agents are currently paid an 18 percent commission on sales, and this percentage was used when Marston prepared the following pro forma income statement for the fiscal year ending June 30, 1992.

Marston Corporation

Pro Forma Income Statement
For the Year Ending June 30, 1992
($000 omitted)

Sales		$26,000
Cost of goods sold		
Variable	$11,700	
Fixed	2,870	14,570
Gross profit		11,430
Selling and administrative costs		
Commissions	$ 4,680	
Fixed advertising cost	750	
Fixed administrative cost	1,850	7,280
Operating income		4,150
Fixed interest cost		650
Income before income taxes		3,500
Income taxes (40%)		1,400
Net income		$ 2,100

Since the completion of the above statement, Marston has learned that its agents are requiring an increase in the commission rate to 23 percent for the upcoming year. As a result, Marston's president has decided to investigate the possibility of hiring its own sales staff in place of the network of sales agents and has asked Tom Ross, Marston's controller, to gather information on the costs associated with this change.

Ross estimates that Marston will have to hire eight salespeople to cover the current market area, and the annual payroll cost of each of these employees will average $80,000, including fringe benefit expense. Travel and entertainment expense is expected to total $600,000 for the year, and the annual cost of hiring a sales manager and sales secretary will be $150,000. In addition to their salaries, the eight salespeople will each earn commissions at the rate of 10 percent on the first $2 million in sales and 15 percent on all sales over $2 million. For planning purposes, Ross expects that all eight salespeople will exceed the $2 million mark and that sales will be at the level previously projected. Ross believes that Marston should also increase its advertising budget by $500,000.

Required:

1. Calculate Marston Corporation's break-even point in sales dollars for the fiscal year ending June 30, 1992, if the company hires its own sales force and increases its advertising costs.

2. If Marston Corporation continues to sell through its network of sales agents and pays the higher commission rate, determine the estimated volume in sales dollars for the fiscal year ending June 30, 1992, that would be required to generate the same net income as that projected in the pro forma income statement presented above.

3. Describe the general assumptions underlying break-even analysis that might limit its usefulness in this case.

(CMA adapted)

▪ MANAGERIAL DECISION CASES

Case 8–1   **Service Organization; Multiple Products; Break Even; Pricing and Scheduling Decisions**   Utah Metropolitan Ballet is located in Salt Lake City. The company is housed in the Capitol Theater, one of three buildings that make up the Bicentennial Arts Center in downtown Salt Lake City. The Ballet company features five different ballets per year. For the upcoming season, the five ballets to be performed are *The Dream, Petrushka, The Nutcracker, Sleeping Beauty,* and *Bugaku.*

The president and general manager has tentatively scheduled the following number of performances for each ballet for the coming season:

Dream	5
Petrushka	5
Nutcracker	20
Sleeping Beauty	10
Bugaku	5

To produce each ballet, costs must be incurred for costumes, props, rehearsals, royalties, guest artist fees, choreography, salaries of production staff, music, and wardrobe. These costs are fixed for a particular ballet regardless of the number of performances. These direct fixed costs are given below for each ballet.

Dream	*Petrushka*	*Nutcracker*	*Sleeping Beauty*	*Bugaku*
$275,500	$145,500	$70,500	$345,000	$155,500

Other fixed costs are incurred as follows:

Advertising	$ 80,000
Insurance	15,000
Administrative salaries	222,000
Office rental, phone, and so on	84,000
Total	$401,000

For each performance of each ballet, the following costs are also incurred:

Utah Symphony	$3,800
Auditorium rental	700
Dancers' payroll	4,000
Total	$8,500

The auditorium in which the ballet is presented has 1,854 seats, which are classified as A, B, and C. The best viewing ranges from A seats to C seats. Information concerning the different types of seat is given below:

	A Seats	B Seats	C Seats
Quantity	114	756	984
Price	$35	$25	$15
Percentage sold for each performance[a]			
Nutcracker	100	100	100
All others	100	80	75

[a]Based on past experience, the same percentages are expected for the coming season.

Required:

1. Compute the expected revenues from the performances that have been tentatively scheduled. Prepare a variable costing income statement for each ballet.

2. Calculate the number of performances of each ballet required to produce the revenues needed to cover each ballet's direct fixed expenses.

3. Calculate the number of performances of each ballet required for the company as a whole to break even. If you were the president and general manager, how would you alter the tentative schedule of performances?

4. Suppose that it is possible to offer a matinee of the popular *Nutcracker*. Seats would sell for $5 less than in the evening, and the rental of the auditorium would be $200 less. The president and general manager believe that five matinee performances are feasible and that 80 percent of each type of seat can be sold. What effect will the matinee have on the company's profitability? On the overall break-even point?

5. Suppose that no additional evening performances can be offered beyond those tentatively scheduled. Assume that the company will offer five matinee performances of *The Nutcracker*. Also, the company expects to receive $60,000 in government grants and contributions from supporters of the fine arts. Will the company break even? If not, what actions would you take to bring revenues in line with costs? Assume that no additional performances of *The Nutcracker* are feasible.

Case 8–2   **Cost Behavior; Break-even Analysis; CVP Analysis for Evaluation and Decision Making**   Reinert Moving and Storage was established in 1962 by Allen Reinert in Lincoln, Nebraska. In 1978, the company achieved million-dollar booking status. The company experienced modest growth for the next two years; however, after the deregulation of the transportation industry in 1980, the company's growth accelerated significantly for several years. Unfortunately, by the end of 1989, the company actually experienced a drop in revenues. During the next two years, the revenues earned essentially matched those of 1989. The revenues reported at the end of 1992 totaled $5.493 million. An income statement for 1992 follows:

Revenues:		
Local	$1,433,500	
Intrastate	510,000	
Interstate	2,490,500	
Containers	333,000	
Packing	437,000	
Storage	289,000	
Total revenues		$ 5,493,000
Less expenses:		
Outside vehicle repair	$ 220,000	
Fuel	352,000	
Sales commissions	102,000	
Tires, oil, lube	20,500	
Wages (driver and helper)	1,584,000	
Internal maintenance	293,000	
Advertising	88,000	
Equipment rental	422,000	
Packing materials	557,000	
Salaries	821,000	
Cargo loss claims	234,000	
Utilities	16,700	
Insurance	44,000	
Fuel taxes and tariffs	132,000	
Bad debt	193,000	
Depreciation	205,000	
Total expenses		(5,284,200)
Income before taxes		$ 208,800
Less: Taxes (state and federal: 42%)		(87,696)
Net income		$ 121,104

Upon reviewing the income statement for 1992, Allen Reinert called a meeting to discuss the financial status of the company. He invited sales manager Heidi Jackson and controller Eric Bilodeau.

Allen: Our before-tax income has dropped from a high of 12 percent of sales to about 4 percent this last year. I know that both of you are aware of our problem and have some suggestions on how we can improve the situation.

Heidi: Allen, competition has become quite intense in our industry. I have two suggestions to help improve sales. First, we need to increase our advertising budget. We have a good reputation, and I think we need to capitalize on it. I suggest that we emphasize our expertise in crating electronic equipment and other sensitive instruments. Our losses in this area are minuscule. We have a much better record than any of our competitors and we need to let customers—and potential customers—know about the quality of our services.

Allen: This sounds good. How much more do you need for advertising and what kind of increase in sales would you predict?

Heidi: To do it right, I would need to double our current advertising budget. I would guess that sales would increase by 20 percent. I also have another suggestion. I think we should look at the international goods and freight-moving market. Many firms ship goods internationally, and I believe that they would switch to us if we entered that market. My preliminary analysis reveals that we could pick up $500,000 of sales during the first year.

Allen: Both suggestions seem to offer some potential for improving our profitability. Eric, would you gather the data needed to estimate the effect of each of these two alternatives on our profits?

Eric: Sure. I have a suggestion also—I plan to install a cost accounting system. At this point, we have no real idea how much each of our services is costing. I believe that there is some hope to reduce costs without affecting the quality of our services.

Allen: I'm all for reducing costs where possible. However, keep in mind that I don't want to lay off any employees yet. I like the idea of providing security to our employees. I would rather see everyone take a pay cut before we reduce our work force. So far we have been able to keep everyone even with the drop in sales we've had. I think it's a good policy. If these two ideas of Heidi's work out, no new hires may be necessary, and we have trained, loyal employees ready for the new business.

Required:

1. Classify all expenses in the 1992 income statement as either variable or fixed. Assume that each expense is strictly variable or strictly fixed with respect to sales revenue. Once the classification is completed, prepare a variable-costing income statement.

2. Using the information obtained in requirement 1, compute the revenue that Reinert Moving and Storage needs to generate to break even. Now compute the revenue that is needed to earn a profit equal to 12 percent of sales revenue.

3. What is the maximum amount that Reinert can spend on additional advertising assuming profits remain unchanged for 1993 and that sales will increase by 20 percent, as predicted by Heidi? Suppose that Heidi spends the amount she requested and that sales increase by 20 percent—what is the change in profits? Should the suggestion be adopted?

4. Suppose that the directly traceable fixed expenses associated with entry into the international market are $200,000. Assume that the variable cost ratio for this segment is the same as that computed in the 1992 income statement prepared in requirement 1. How much revenue must be generated from international shipping for this segment to break even? What is the expected margin of safety? Would you recommend entry into the international market? Why?

5. Suppose that Allen Reinert decides both to increase advertising and to enter the international market. Assume that actual sales increased by 10 percent, and that $340,000 of the increase came from international sales and the remainder from the increased advertising. Using data from the case in requirements 1 and 4, answer the following questions:
   a. How much did before-tax profits change because of these two decisions?
   b. What is the profit change attributable to the advertising campaign? The international market? What is your recommendation for the coming year? Should the company continue these two strategies? Or should it do only one or neither? Explain.
   c. Suppose that the company achieved its target profit of 12 percent of sales in spite of the less-than-expected increase in profits from the advertising campaign and the international market. The remaining increase in profits was achieved by cutting variable costs. What is the new variable cost ratio?

CHAPTER 9

Variable Costing:
A Useful Management Tool

■ **LEARNING OBJECTIVES**

After studying Chapter 9, you should be able to

1. Prepare an income statement using variable costing.

2. Prepare an income statement using absorption costing.

3. Compute the unit cost for a product using either variable costing or absorption costing.

4. Explain the differences between variable costing and absorption costing.

5. Reconcile the difference in variable-costing income and absorption-costing income.

6. Discuss the advantages of variable costing for purposes of performance evaluation of managers, segment evaluation, and planning and control.

7. Prepare a segmented income statement based on a variable-costing approach and explain why such an income statement is preferred to a segmented income statement using absorption costing.

8. Define and explain the key terms appearing at the end of the chapter.

SCENARIO

Eric Hipple, president and owner of Protzman Block and Pipe Company, had just completed a meeting with the company's divisional managers. The divisions were scattered throughout the Western states and specialized in concrete pipe and blocks. Eric had called the meeting to discuss the downturn in business the company had experienced during the past two years. He came down hard on the divisional managers, pointing out that their jobs would be on the line if some immediate improvements were not forthcoming. He spent the entire meeting reviewing financial results and proposing new marketing strategies. Since he allowed no time for discussion or rebuttal, he agreed to meet with a spokesperson for the divisional managers. Norma Richardson, manager of the division in Sacramento, had been selected as the spokesperson. The following is the conversation that took place.

Norma: Eric, I understand why you are upset with the most recent financial results; however, I believe there are some legitimate reasons for our problems. One reason for the decline in profits is the slump in residential and commercial construction. High interest rates are adversely affecting construction, and, as you know, our fate is interlinked with that of construction.

Eric: I know that the construction industry is suffering. I also know that we have gone through similar periods in the past and have done much better. Besides, how do you explain the fact that two divisions reported above-normal earnings? It appears to me that these two divisional managers are on the ball. I suspect that as times have gotten tough, they have been more aggressive in controlling costs and in soliciting new business.

Norma: Let me address both of these issues. Since the last recession in the construction industry, a number of new competitors have entered the market. Competition has intensified, and most of us are losing a lot of bids. Part of the problem is the minimum bid policy. The company policy is never to bid below full cost. Several managers—including me—have lost bids that were at full cost. Apparently, some competitors are bidding below their full cost. We would like to request a change in the minimum bid policy. We believe that the floor for bids ought to be variable cost rather than full cost. In times . . .

Eric: Hogwash! Bidding below full cost is nonsense. It's impossible to sell blocks and pipes below their full cost and stay in business. Those companies that do so will be the first ones to go bankrupt.

Norma: I agree that in the long run prices must be structured so that all costs are covered. But in times of economic distress, bids that at least cover their variable costs have the potential to make a positive contribution towards coverage of fixed costs. After all, in the short run, fixed costs will be there regardless of how much we sell and produce. Eric, my last company used variable costing, and the information it supplied definitely helped ease us through bad economic times. We were able to make more competitive bids. When times improved, we were able to return to a normal pricing policy. Variable costing offers other benefits as well. Let me re-

409

turn to the other issue you raised, one that has most of your divisional managers concerned. The two divisions that reported above-normal earnings did so by producing for inventory. Their above-normal earnings were not attributable to better sales or better control of operating costs. Variable-costing income statements would have avoided this anomaly.

Eric: Explain what you mean. How can you increase income by producing for inventory?

Norma: As you know, we use a predetermined rate to assign fixed overhead to production. Each unit we produce has fixed overhead attached to it. If production is greater than sales, some of the period's fixed overhead costs will be inventoried instead of being expensed on the income statement. The two divisions that reported higher income than the rest of us did so because they increased their inventories much more than we did. Most, if not all, of their greater profitability is the result of putting fixed costs in inventory. In comparing the performance of the different divisions, you need to recognize this difference. Financial statements that are prepared with variable and fixed costs differentiated would allow you to assess relative divisional performance more accurately. I think you need to look into variable costing.

Eric: Well, perhaps you're right. What you have said makes some sense. This company has prospered in the past because I've been willing to accept change. I want you to prepare a formal report detailing for me what variable costing is all about. I want to know how it differs from our current approach and how it can help me improve the management of this company.

■ VARIABLE COSTING AND ABSORPTION COSTING: AN ANALYSIS AND COMPARISON

In the introductory case, two methods of costing are identified: variable costing and full costing. Variable costing is the method compatible with the contribution or behavioral approach to income determination first mentioned in Chapter 2. Full costing, or absorption costing, is the costing method compatible with the functional approach to income determination also mentioned in Chapter 2.

Currently, absorption costing is required for external reporting. The FASB, the IRS, and other regulatory bodies do not accept variable costing as an acceptable product-costing method for external reporting. Yet, as the dialogue between Eric and Norma suggests, variable costing can supply vital cost information for decision making and control, information not supplied by absorption costing. For *internal* application, variable costing is an invaluable managerial tool.

EXHIBIT 9-1

Classification of Costs as Product or Period Costs
Under Absorption and Variable Costing

	Absorption Costing	*Variable Costing*
Product Costs	Direct materials	Direct materials
	Direct labor	Direct labor
	Variable overhead	Variable overhead
	Fixed overhead	
Period Costs		Fixed overhead
	Selling expense	Selling expense
	Administrative expense	Administrative expense

Variable costing stresses the difference between fixed and variable manufacturing costs. This distinction is critical for many decision and control models that are used in management accounting. Studying variable costing provides a good foundation for the application of other important management accounting topics such as cost-volume-profit analysis, relevant costing, and flexible budgeting.

variable costing

Variable costing assigns only variable manufacturing costs to the product; these costs include direct materials, direct labor, and variable overhead. Fixed overhead is excluded from the product cost. Under variable costing, fixed overhead of a period is seen as expiring that period and is charged in total against the revenues of the period.[1]

absorption costing

Absorption costing assigns *all* manufacturing costs to the product. Direct materials, direct labor, variable overhead, and fixed overhead define the cost of a product. Thus, under absorption costing, fixed overhead is viewed as a *product* cost, not a period cost. Under this method, fixed overhead is assigned to the product through the use of a predetermined fixed overhead rate and does not expire until the product is sold. In other words, fixed overhead is an inventoriable cost. Exhibit 9-1 illustrates the classification of costs as product or period cost under absorption and variable costing.

Inventory Valuation

An example is needed in order to make the inventory valuations of absorption and variable costing more concrete. During the most recent year, Fairchild Company had the following data associated with the product it makes:

---

[1]Variable costing is more commonly known as *direct costing*. Direct costing, however, is a misnomer. Not all variable manufacturing costs are direct product costs. For example, variable overhead, by definition, consists of *indirect* manufacturing costs. Clearly, the more descriptive name for this method is *variable costing*, which is the term that will be used in this text.

Units, beginning inventory	—
Units produced	10,000
Units sold ($300 per unit)	8,000
Normal volume	10,000
Variable costs per unit:	
Direct labor	$100
Direct materials	50
Variable overhead[a]	50
Variable selling and administrative	10
Fixed costs:	
Fixed overhead[a]	$250,000
Fixed selling and administrative	100,000

[a] Estimated and actual overhead are equal.

The unit cost obtained under each method differs.

	Variable Costing	Absorption Costing
Direct labor	$100	$100
Direct materials	50	50
Variable overhead	50	50
Fixed overhead ($250,000/10,000)	—	25
Total per unit cost	$200	$225

Under variable costing, each product is reported on the balance sheet at $200 per unit; under absorption costing, the unit cost is $225. The $25 difference is attributable to the way fixed overhead is treated. Under absorption costing, fixed overhead is spread over all the units produced, whereas variable costing assigns no fixed overhead to production. Exhibit 9–2 (pages 413 and 414) portrays the assignment of manufacturing, selling, and administrative costs to the income statement and the balance sheet under absorption and variable costing.

Note that none of the selling and administrative costs, either variable or fixed, are assigned to the product under either method. Both methods treat these costs as period costs.

Income Statements: Analysis and Reconciliation

Differences in the computation of product cost produce differences in income figures. Under variable costing, the total fixed manufacturing overhead of the period is deducted from the revenues of the period. Under absorption costing, fixed overhead is unitized and becomes part of the product cost. Only the fixed overhead attached to the units sold is deducted from period revenues.

EXHIBIT 9-2
Income Statement and Balance Sheet Treatment of Costs
Under Variable Costing

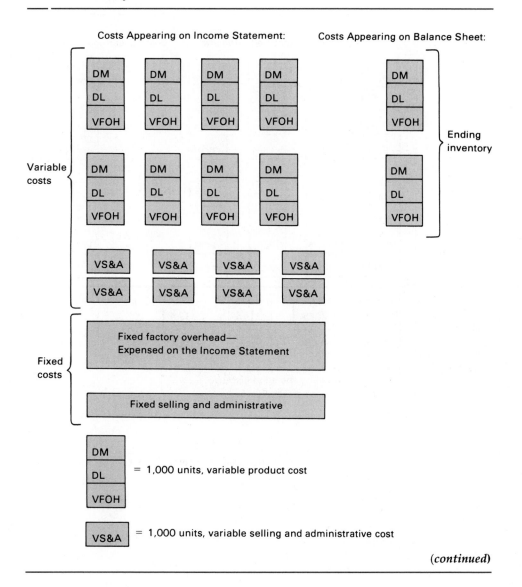

If the fixed overhead attached to the units sold is different from the total fixed overhead of the period, the two income figures will be different. The difference arises because of the amount of fixed overhead recognized as an expense under the two methods.

For example, Fairchild produced 10,000 units and sold only 8,000 units.

EXHIBIT 9–2
Income Statement and Balance Sheet Treatment of Costs
Under Variable Costing

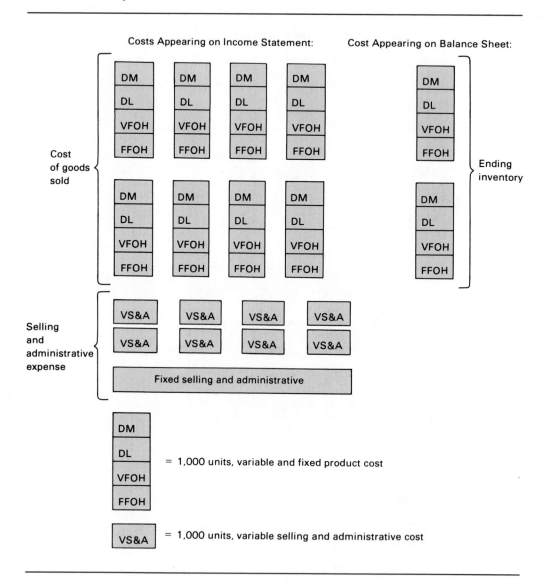

The 2,000 units not sold went into inventory. Income statements appear in Exhibits 9–3 and 9–4. These income statements reveal that absorption-costing income is $50,000 higher than variable-costing income. As the following analysis shows, this difference is due to some of the period's fixed overhead flowing into inventory when absorption costing is used.

For variable costing (Exhibit 9–3), the variable cost of goods sold is $1.6

EXHIBIT 9-3

Fairchild Company		
Variable-Costing Income Statement		
Sales		$ 2,400,000
Less variable expenses:		
Variable cost of goods sold	$1,600,000	
Variable selling and administrative	80,000	(1,680,000)
Contribution margin		$ 720,000
Less fixed expenses:		
Fixed overhead	$ 250,000	
Fixed selling and administrative	100,000	(350,000)
Net income		$ 370,000

EXHIBIT 9-4

Fairchild Company	
Absorption-Costing Income Statement	
Sales	$ 2,400,000
Less: Cost of goods sold	(1,800,000)
Gross margin	600,000
Less: Selling and administrative expenses	(180,000)
Net income	$ 420,000

million ($200 × 8,000 units sold). The fixed overhead deducted as an expense is $250,000. Thus, the total manufacturing expenses deducted are $1.85 million. The total selling and administrative expenses deducted are $180,000 ($80,000 variable + $100,000 fixed).

For absorption costing, the cost of goods sold is $1.8 million ($225 × 8,000 units sold). Of this amount, $200,000 ($25 × 8,000) represents the fixed overhead that was recognized as an expense. The total selling and administrative expenses deducted are $180,000.

Variable costing recognizes the same amount of selling and administrative expense ($180,000) but recognizes $50,000 more manufacturing expense than absorption costing. Thus, income using variable costing is $50,000 less than using absorption costing. For absorption costing, where did the other $50,000 of fixed overhead go?

Under absorption costing, each unit produced was assigned fixed overhead of $25. Recall that of the 10,000 units produced, 2,000 units were not sold. These 2,000 units went into inventory and carried with them $50,000 ($25 × 2,000) of the period's fixed overhead. Only when these 2,000 units are sold will that $50,000 of fixed overhead be recognized as an expense. Thus, under absorption costing, $50,000 of the period's fixed overhead flows into inventory, and its recognition as an expense is deferred to a future period.

Under absorption costing, fixed overhead is a product cost. Because of this, the amount of fixed overhead recognized as an expense is affected by the relationship between production and sales within a period. Since variable-costing income always recognizes fixed overhead as an expense in the period, the production and sales relationship also affects the relationship between absorption-costing and variable-costing income.

Production, Sales, and Income Relationships

Whenever production is greater than sales, income reported under absorption costing is greater than that reported under variable costing. Producing more than what is sold means creating inventory. Under absorption costing, as units flow into inventory, they carry with them some of the period's fixed overhead; therefore, not all of that overhead will be recognized as an expense. Variable costing, however, always recognizes the total fixed overhead of the period as an expense. Thus, income under absorption costing will be greater than income under variable costing by the amount of fixed overhead that flowed into inventories.

The relationship between the two incomes changes as the relationship between production and sales changes. If more is sold than was produced, variable-costing income is greater than absorption-costing income. The reason is just the opposite of that for the first outcome. Selling more than was produced means that inventory is being used. Under absorption costing, units coming out of inventory have attached to them fixed overhead from a prior period. In addition, units produced and sold have all of the current period's fixed overhead attached. Thus, the amount of fixed overhead expensed by absorption costing is greater than the current period's fixed overhead by the amount of fixed overhead flowing out of inventory. Accordingly, variable-costing income is greater than absorption-costing income by the amount of fixed overhead flowing out of inventory. Exhibit 9–5 illustrates the differences between cost going into and out of inventory under absorption and variable costing.

If production and sales are equal, of course, no difference exists between the two reported incomes. Since the units produced are all sold, absorption costing—like variable costing—will recognize the total fixed overhead of the period as an expense. No fixed overhead flows into or out of inventory.

The relationships between production, sales, and the two reported incomes are summarized in Exhibit 9–6. Note that if production is greater than

EXHIBIT 9–5
Cost Flows Into and Out of Inventory:
Absorption Versus Variable Costing

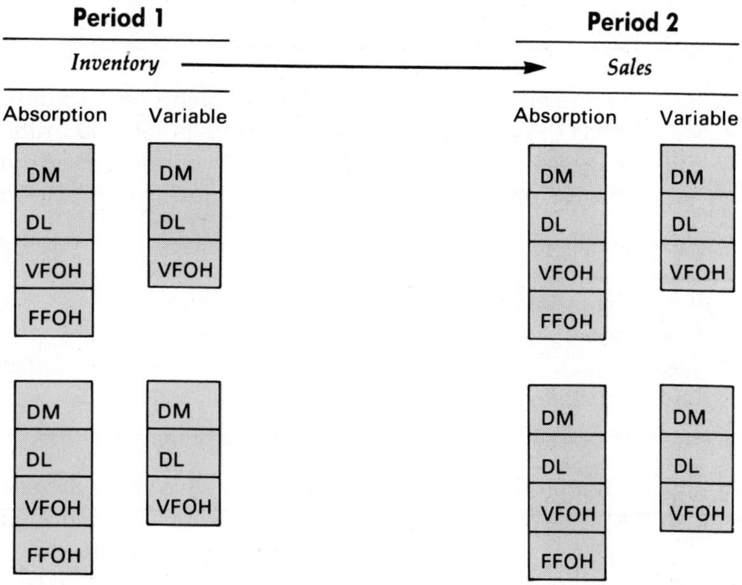

Period 1				Period 2		
Inventory ————————————→				*Sales*		
Absorption	Variable			Absorption	Variable	

DM DL VFOH FFOH (Absorption) / DM DL VFOH (Variable) — Period 1 and Period 2

EXHIBIT 9–6
Production, Sales, and Income Relationships

	If	*Then*
1.	Production > Sales	$I_A > I_v$[a]
2.	Production < Sales	$I_A < I_v$
3.	Production = Sales	$I_A = I_v$

[a]I_A = Absorption-costing income
I_v = Variable-costing income

sales, then inventory has increased. If production is less than sales, inventory must have decreased. If production is equal to sales, beginning inventory is equal to ending inventory.

To fully illustrate these relationships, consider the following example. The example is based on the operational data of Belnip, Inc., in the years 1991, 1992, and 1993.

Variable costs per unit:	
Direct materials	$4.00
Direct labor	1.50
Variable overhead (estimated and actual)	0.50
Variable selling and administrative	0.25

Estimated fixed overhead was $150,000 each year. Actual fixed overhead also was $150,000. Normal production volume is 150,000 units per year. The sales price each year was $10 per unit. Fixed selling and administrative expenses were $50,000 per year. Other operating data were as follows:

	1991	1992	1993
Beginning inventory	—	—	50,000
Production	150,000	150,000	150,000
Sales	150,000	100,000	200,000
Ending inventory	—	50,000	—

Income statements prepared under variable costing are shown in Exhibit 9–7. Exhibit 9–8 gives the income statements for absorption costing.

In 1991, the net incomes for each method are identical. We must conclude that both methods expensed the same amount of fixed overhead. Under

EXHIBIT 9–7
Variable-Costing Income Statements
(in thousands of dollars)

	1991	1992	1993
Sales	$1,500.00	$1,000.00	$ 2,000.00
Less variable expenses:			
Variable cost of goods sold[a]	(900.00)	(600.00)	(1,200.00)
Variable selling and administrative[b]	(37.50)	(25.00)	(50.00)
Contribution margin	$ 562.50	$ 375.00	$ 750.00
Less fixed expenses:			
Fixed overhead	(150.00)	(150.00)	(150.00)
Fixed selling and administrative	(50.00)	(50.00)	(50.00)
Net income	$ 362.50	$ 175.00	$ 550.00

[a]Beginning inventory	—	—	$ 300
Variable cost of goods manufactured	$900	$ 900	900
Goods available for sale	900	900	1,200
Less: Ending inventory	—	(300)	—
Variable cost of goods sold	$900	$ 600	$1,200
[b]$0.25 per unit × Units sold			

EXHIBIT 9–8
Absorption-Costing Income Statement
(in thousands of dollars)

	1991	1992	1993
Sales	$ 1,500.00	$1,000.00	$ 2,000.00
Less: Cost of goods sold[a]	(1,050.00)	(700.00)	(1,400.00)
Gross margin	450.00	300.00	600.00
Less: Selling and administrative expense	(87.50)	(75.00)	(100.00)
Net income	$ 362.50	$ 225.00	$ 500.00

	1991	1992	1993
[a]Beginning inventory	—	—	$ 350.00
Cost of goods manufactured	$1,050.00	$1,050.00	1,050.00
Goods available for sale	1,050.00	1,050.00	1,400.00
Less: Ending inventory	—	(350.00)	—
Normal cost of goods sold	$1,050.00	$ 700.00	$1,400.00

variable costing, we know that the period's fixed overhead of $150,000 was expensed. Under absorption costing, the fixed overhead is unitized and becomes part of the product cost. Estimated fixed overhead was $150,000 each year. The fixed overhead rate is $1 per unit ($150,000/150,000 units produced) for all three years. The **applied fixed overhead** is $150,000 ($1 × 150,000) for all three years. Since the actual fixed overhead in every year is also $150,000, there is no fixed overhead variance in any year. Thus, the fixed overhead expensed for any year is simply the overhead rate times the number of units sold. For 1991, the total fixed overhead expensed under absorption costing is $150,000 ($1 × 150,000 units sold). Both methods did indeed recognize the same amount of fixed overhead expense.

In 1992, however, the story is different. From Exhibits 9–7 and 9–8, we see that the absorption-costing income is $50,000 greater than the variable-costing income ($225,000 − $175,000). The difference between the two incomes exists because there is $50,000 less fixed overhead expensed under the absorption-costing method.

Under absorption costing, each unit produced is assigned $1 of fixed overhead. Since 150,000 units were produced but only 100,000 units were sold, 50,000 units were placed in inventory. These 50,000 units carried with them $1 of fixed overhead each, for a total of $50,000. This $50,000 of the current period's fixed overhead will not be recognized as an expense until the units in inventory are sold. Thus, under absorption costing, the period's $150,000 of fixed overhead can be broken down into two categories: $100,000 is expensed and $50,000 is inventoried.

Under variable costing, however, the total fixed overhead of $150,000 is expensed since it is viewed as a period cost. Since variable costing recognizes $150,000 of fixed overhead expense and absorption costing recognizes only $100,000 of fixed overhead expense, the income reported by absorption costing is $50,000 more.

applied fixed overhead

In 1993, the relationship between the two incomes reverses. The difference is now $50,000 in favor of variable costing (see Exhibits 9–7 and 9–8). The favorable difference occurs because absorption costing not only recognizes $150,000 of fixed overhead expense for units produced and sold in this period but also recognizes the $50,000 of fixed overhead attached to the units in inventory that were produced in 1992 but sold in 1993. Thus, the total fixed overhead recognized as an expense is $200,000 under absorption costing versus only $150,000 under variable costing.

The key to explaining the difference between the two incomes is an analysis of the flow of fixed overhead. Variable costing *always* recognizes the period's fixed overhead as an expense—no more, no less. Absorption costing, on the other hand, recognizes only the fixed overhead *attached* to the units sold. If production is different from sales, fixed overhead will either flow into or out of inventory. If the amount of fixed overhead in inventory increases, then absorption-costing income is greater than variable-costing income by the amount of the net increase. If the fixed overhead in inventory decreases, then variable-costing income is greater than absorption-costing income by the amount of the net decrease.

The change of fixed overhead in inventory is exactly equal to the difference between the two incomes. This change can be computed by multiplying the fixed overhead rate times the change in total units in the beginning and ending inventories (which is the difference between production and sales). The differences between the two incomes can be expressed as:

$$I_A - I_V = \text{Fixed overhead rate} \times (\text{Production} - \text{Sales})$$

Exhibit 9–9 shows how this shortcut approach can be used to provide an explanation of the differences.

The Treatment of Fixed Factory Overhead in Absorption Costing

The difference between absorption and variable costing centers on the recognition of expense associated with fixed factory overhead. Variable costing is easier to use. Actual fixed factory overhead is expensed in the period incurred. Under absorption costing, however, fixed factory overhead must be assigned to units produced. It is expensed only when the units to which it is attached are sold. This presents two problems that we have not explicitly considered. First, how do we convert factory overhead applied on the basis of direct labor hours or machine hours into factory overhead applied to units produced? Second, what is done when actual factory overhead does not equal applied factory overhead?

The first problem is solved relatively easily. Suppose that factory overhead is applied on the basis of direct labor hours. Further suppose that it takes 0.25 direct labor hours to produce one unit. If the fixed factory overhead rate is $12 per direct labor hour, then the fixed factory overhead per unit is $3 (0.25 × $12).

EXHIBIT 9–9
Reconciliation of Variable and Absorption Costing
(in thousands of dollars)

	1991	1992	1993
Net income:			
Absorption costing	$362.50	$225.00	$500.00
Variable costing	362.50	175.00	550.00
Difference	$ 0	50.00	$(50.00)
Explanation:			
Units produced	150	150	150
Units sold	(150)	(100)	(200)
Change in inventory	0	50	(50)
Fixed overhead rate	×$1	×$1	×$1
Difference explained[a]	$ 0	$ 50	$ (50)

[a]In 1991, absorption costing recognized only the period's fixed overhead as an expense. No fixed overhead flowed into or out of inventory. In 1992, $50,000 of fixed overhead flowed into inventory, and its recognition as an expense is deferred to a future period. In 1993, $50,000 of fixed overhead flowed out of inventory and was recognized as an expense.

The solution to the second problem requires more thought. First, we must calculate the applied fixed factory overhead and assign it to units produced. Then, the total applied amount is compared to actual fixed factory overhead. If the over- or underapplied amount is immaterial, it is closed to Cost of Goods Sold. Any units going into ending inventory take with them the applied fixed factory overhead. Variable factory overhead (which can also be over- or underapplied) is treated in the same fashion. Review Problem II at the end of this chapter illustrates the handling of over- and underapplied fixed and variable factory overhead.

If the over- or underapplied amount is material, then it is allocated among ending Work in Process, Finished Goods, and Cost of Goods Sold. This complication is beyond the scope of this text.

■ BENEFITS OF VARIABLE COSTING

The separation of fixed and variable costs is generally recognized as a basic need for many of the planning, control, and decision-making activities a manager faces. Income statements and inventory valuations using variable costing provide valuable insights for internal purposes. In fact, variable costing offers many advantages. In the following discussion, we focus on three: (1) the evaluation of managerial performance, (2) the evaluation of segments, and (3) planning and control.

Performance Evaluation of Managers

The evaluation of managers is often tied to the profitability of the units they control. How income changes from one period to the next and how actual income compares to planned income are frequently used as signals of managerial ability. To be meaningful signals, however, income should reflect managerial effort. For example, if a manager has worked hard and increased sales while holding costs in check, income should increase over the prior period, signaling success. In general terms, if income performance is expected to reflect managerial performance, then managers have the right to expect the following:

1. As sales revenue increases from one period to the next, all other things being equal, income should increase.

2. As sales revenue decreases from one period to the next, all other things being equal, income should decrease.

3. As sales revenue remains unchanged from one period to the next, all other things being equal, income should remain unchanged.

Interestingly, income under variable costing always follows this expected association between sales and income; under absorption costing, at times it does not. To illustrate, assume that a division of Myers, Inc., has the following operating data for its first two years. (For simplicity, we assume no selling and administrative costs.)

	1992	1993
Variable manufacturing costs per unit	$ 10	$ 10
Production (expected and actual)	10,000	5,000
Sales ($25 per unit)	5,000	10,000
Fixed overhead (estimated and actual)	$100,000	$100,000

The product cost under variable costing is $10 per unit for both years. Assuming that expected actual volume is used to compute a predetermined fixed overhead rate, the product cost under absorption costing is $20 per unit in 1992 and $30 per unit in 1993 ($10 + $100,000/10,000 for 1992; $10 + $100,000/5,000 for 1993).

The variable-costing and absorption-costing income statements are shown in Exhibit 9–10. Sales increased from 5,000 to 10,000 units. Total fixed costs, the variable manufacturing cost per unit, and the unit sales price are the same for both periods. Thus, the doubling of sales represents the only change from one period to the next. Under variable costing, income increased by $75,000 from 1992 to 1993 (from a loss of $25,000 to a profit of $50,000). However, under absorption costing, despite the increase in sales, net income decreased by $25,000 (from a profit of $25,000 to a profit of $0)!

EXHIBIT 9–10
Variable- and Absorption-Costing Income Statements

Variable-Costing Income		
	1992	*1993*
Sales	$ 125,000	$ 250,000
Less variable expenses:		
Variable cost of goods sold[a]	(50,000)	(100,000)
Contribution margin	75,000	$ 150,000
Less fixed expenses:		
Fixed overhead	(100,000)	(100,000)
Net income (loss)	$ (25,000)	$ 50,000

Absorption-Costing Income		
	1992	*1993*
Sales	$ 125,000	$ 250,000
Less cost of goods sold[b]	(100,000)	(250,000)
Net income (loss)	$ 25,000	0

[a]$10 × 5,000 in 1992 and $10 × 10,000 in 1993

[b]Beginning inventory	$ —	$100,000
Cost of goods manufactured	200,000	150,000
Goods available for sale	200,000	250,000
Less: Ending inventory	(100,000)	(—)
Cost of goods sold	$ 100,000	$250,000

The firm improved its sales performance from 1992 to 1993 (twice as many units were sold), fixed costs remained the same, and the unit variable cost was the same; yet absorption costing fails to reveal this improved performance. Variable costing, on the other hand, produces an increase in income corresponding to the improved sales performance. If you were the manager, which income approach would you prefer?

Segmented Reporting, Evaluation, and Decision Making

The utility of variable costing for performance evaluation extends beyond the evaluation of managers. Managers themselves need to evaluate the activities over which they have responsibility. For example, managers must continually evaluate the profit contributions of plants, product lines, and sales territories.

The separation of fixed and variable costs basic to variable costing is critical for making accurate evaluations. Implicit in an evaluation is an associated decision—whether to continue to operate a plant or not, or whether to keep or drop a product line. Without a distinction between fixed and variable costs, the evaluation of profit-making activities and the resulting decision may both be erroneous.

Reporting the profit contributions of activities or other units within an **segmented reporting** organization is called **segmented reporting.** Segmented reports prepared on a variable-costing basis produce better evaluations and decisions than those prepared on an absorption-costing basis. Let's take a closer look at segmentation and segmented reporting and see why this is true.

To evaluate many different activities within a firm, a manager needs more than the summary information appearing in a firm's income statement. For example, in a company with several divisions operating in different markets, the manager would certainly want to know how profitable each division has been. This knowledge may lead to greater overall profit by eliminating unprofitable divisions, giving special attention to problem divisions, allocating additional investment capital to the more profitable divisions, and so on.

Divisional income statements, however, are not all that a good managerial accounting system should supply. Even finer segmentation is needed for managers to carry out their responsibilities properly. Divisions are made up of different plants; thus, knowledge of plant profitability is needed for the same reasons that divisional profitability is necessary. Plants produce products, and information on product profitability is critical. Some products may be profitable—some may not be. Similarly, profit information on sales territories, special projects, individual salespersons, and so on, is important.

Managers need to know the profitability of various segments within a firm to be able to make evaluations and decisions concerning each segment's **segment** continued existence, level of funding, and so on. A **segment** is any profit-making entity within the organization; it may be a part of the organization or an activity within it. A segment report can provide valuable information on costs controllable by the segment manager. Controllable costs are those whose level can be influenced by a manager. Thus, a manager who has no responsibility for a cost should not be held accountable for that cost. For example, divisional managers have no power to authorize corporate-level costs such as research and development and salaries of top managers. Therefore, divisional managers should not be held accountable for the incurrence of those costs. If noncontrollable costs are included in a segment report, they should be separated from controllable costs and labeled as noncontrollable. For example, fixed costs common to two or more plants within a division would not be allocated to each plant but instead would be shown as a common cost for the division.

Segmented Reporting: Absorption-Costing Basis   Should segmented reporting be on a variable-costing basis or an absorption-costing basis? To answer this question, let's consider Elcom, Inc., a firm that manufactures stereos and video recorders in a single plant and uses absorption costing for both external and internal reporting. Exhibit 9–11 gives the absorption-costing income statements by product line and in total for 1992.

EXHIBIT 9–11

Elcom, Inc.			
Segmented Income Statement, 1992			
Absorption-Costing Basis			
	Stereos	*Video Recorders*	*Total*
Sales	$ 400,000	$ 290,000	$ 690,000
Less: Cost of goods sold	(350,000)	(300,000)	(650,000)
Gross margin	$ 50,000	$ (10,000)	$ 40,000
Less: Selling and administrative expense	(30,000)	(20,000)	(50,000)
Net income (loss)	$ 20,000	$ (30,000)	$ (10,000)

EXHIBIT 9–12

Elcom, Inc.	
Income Statement, 1993	
Absorption-Costing Basis	
Sales	$ 400,000
Less: Cost of goods sold	(430,000)
Gross margin	$ (30,000)
Less: Selling and administrative expense	(35,000)
Net income (loss)	$ (65,000)

Upon seeing the product-line performance, the president of Elcom, Devon Lauffer, decided to stop producing video recorders, reasoning that profits would increase by $30,000. A year later, however, the result was quite different. The income statement for 1993 is shown in Exhibit 9–12. Income actually decreased by $55,000. Why was the outcome so different from what Devon anticipated?

Devon simply did not have the right kind of cost information to evaluate accurately the performance of the video recorder product line. The decision to drop video recorders was based on misleading cost information. The external financial reporting system is not a good source for segment reports. Often the information needed for internal purposes differs significantly from that required for external reporting. Cost behavior and the traceability of costs may not be critical concerns for reporting results to external parties, but they can be of vital concern to managers attempting to make strategic decisions.

Upon investigation, Devon discovered that many fixed costs that had been allocated to the video recorders were not eliminated when that product line was dropped. Since both stereos and video recorders were produced in the same plant, much of the fixed manufacturing overhead was common to the two products. This includes depreciation on the plant itself, taxes, insurance, and the plant manager's salary, among other items. When the video recorders were dropped, all these common fixed overhead costs were loaded entirely on the stereo product line. Similarly, some fixed selling and administrative costs previously assigned to the video recorder line were then fully assigned to the stereo line.

Segmented Reporting: Variable-Costing Basis   A segmented income statement using variable costing, with a slight modification, provides the essential cost information for a proper assessment of the role that the video recorder line should have assumed. Exhibit 9–13 gives the segmented income statement using variable costing for 1992.

Segmented income statements using variable costing have one feature in addition to the variable-costing income statements already shown. Fixed expenses are broken down into two categories: *direct fixed expenses* and *common fixed expenses*. This additional subdivision highlights controllable versus noncontrollable costs and enhances the manager's ability to evaluate properly each segment's contribution to overall firm performance.

EXHIBIT 9–13

	Elcom, Inc.		
	Segmented Income Statement, 1992 *Variable-Costing Basis*		
	Stereos	*Video Recorders*	*Total*
Sales	$ 400,000	$ 290,000	$ 690,000
Less variable expenses:			
Variable cost of goods sold	(300,000)	(200,000)	(500,000)
Variable selling and administrative	(5,000)	(10,000)	(15,000)
Contribution margin	$ 95,000	$ 80,000	$ 175,000
Less direct fixed expenses:			
Direct fixed overhead	(30,000)	(20,000)	(50,000)
Direct selling and administrative	(10,000)	(5,000)	(15,000)
Product margin	$ 55,000	$ 55,000	$ 110,000
Less common fixed expenses:			
Common fixed overhead			(100,000)
Common selling and administrative			(20,000)
Net income (loss)			$ (10,000)

Note: Segments are defined as product lines.

direct fixed expenses

Direct fixed expenses are fixed expenses that are directly traceable to a segment (a product line in this example). These are sometimes referred to as *avoidable fixed expenses* or *traceable fixed expenses* because they vanish if the segment is eliminated. These fixed expenses are caused by the existence of the segment itself. In the Elcom example, depreciation on equipment used in producing video recorders and the salary of the production supervisor of the video recorder production line are examples of direct fixed expenses.

common fixed expenses

Common fixed expenses cannot be directly traced to a particular segment. They are caused by more than one segment. These expenses persist even if one of the segments to which they are common is eliminated. In the Elcom example, plant depreciation and the salary of the sales supervisor are common fixed expenses. Elimination of the video recorder line did not eliminate the plant and its associated depreciation. Similarly, the plant supervisor still was needed to oversee the production of the stereo product line.

Fixed costs that are direct for one segment may be indirect, or common, for another. For example, suppose that the stereo product line is segmented into two sales territories. In that case, the depreciation on the equipment used to produce stereos is common to both territories but directly traceable to the product segment itself.

Now let's examine Exhibit 9–13 to see whether this form of segmented income statement is more useful than the absorption-costing format. Notice that both stereos and video recorders have large positive contribution margins ($95,000 for stereos and $80,000 for video recorders). Both products are providing revenue above variable costs that can be used to help cover the firm's fixed costs. However, some of the firm's fixed costs are caused by the segments themselves. Thus, the real measure of the profit contribution of each segment is what is left over after these direct fixed costs are covered.

segment margin

The profit contribution each segment makes towards covering a firm's common fixed costs is called the **segment margin.** The segment margin is a meaningful measure of performance for the segment. A segment should at least be able to cover both its variable costs and its direct fixed costs. If it cannot consistently produce a positive segment margin, it is consistently dragging down the firm's total profit. It becomes time to consider dropping the product. Ignoring any effect a segment may have on the sales of other segments, the segment margin measures the change in a firm's profits that would occur if the segment were eliminated.

From Exhibit 9–13, we see that the video recorder line contributes $55,000 towards covering Elcom's common fixed costs. If the line is dropped, total profit decreases by $55,000 —exactly what happened, as shown in Exhibit 9–12. Dropping the video recorder line was a disastrous decision, and now we know why.

The correct decision is to retain both product lines. Both are making equal contributions to the firm's profitability. Dropping either product simply aggravates the problem, unless it is replaced by a product with a higher segment margin. Since both products have large, positive contribution margins, other solutions to the net loss are needed. Increasing the sales of either or both might solve the problem. Or perhaps an aggressive cost-reduction program might improve profitability. Whatever the solution, the variable-costing approach has allowed the manager to focus directly on the real issues.

The problem with using absorption costing for the type of managerial decision portrayed in the Elcom example is that the method does not make any distinction between fixed and variable costs. This distinction is basic to variable costing. While a full-costing approach may be appropriate for reporting overall firm performance to external parties, it is woefully inadequate when it comes to reporting segment performance.

Planning and Control

Financial planning requires managers to estimate future sales, future production levels, future costs, and so on. Sales forecasts determine production plans, which in turn determine the level of expenditures required for raw materials, direct labor, and manufacturing overhead.

Because sales forecasts are not certain, management may wish to look at several different levels of sales to assess the range of possibilities facing the firm. Knowledge of cost behavior is fundamental to achieve this outcome. Fixed costs do not vary with volume changes, so distinguishing between fixed and variable costs is essential to making an accurate cost assessment at the different possible sales and production volumes.

Management ultimately will decide on expected sales and production levels for the coming year. Given these levels, the costs that should occur can also be determined. The financial plan, then, consists of the expected activity levels and the associated expected costs. This plan can be used to monitor the actual performance as it unfolds.

If actual performance is different than what was expected, corrective action may be necessary. By comparing actual data (feedback) with the expected data (the standard) and taking corrective action when necessary, managers exercise control. For the control process to work, though, cost behavior must be known.

Suppose the financial plan called for 12,000 units to be produced for the year, and the utility cost planned for the year is $18,000. At the end of the first month, the company produced 3,000 units and spent $4,500 on utilities. Are utility costs being incurred as planned?

Under an absorption-costing approach, the planned utility cost per unit produced is $1.50 ($18,000/12,000). Therefore, for 3,000 units, we should spend $4,500 ($1.50 × 3,000). Since the expected utility cost for 3,000 units is $4,500, and the actual cost was $4,500, the plan appears to be unfolding as expected. Unfortunately, this calculation ignores cost behavior. It assumes that all costs are variable. In reality, the utility cost is a flat fee of $1,000 per month plus $0.50 per kilowatt hour. If it takes one kilowatt hour to produce one unit of output, the expected cost for the 3,000 units produced in one month is $2,500 ($1,000 + $0.50 × 3,000 units). The company should have spent $2,500 on utilities to produce 3,000 units, but it spent $4,500. The plan is not unfolding as it should.

The correct signal about the planned utility cost is given when cost behavior is considered. Once again, we see the importance of the distinction between fixed and variable costs. Since this distinction is basic to variable costing, we must conclude that variable costing is superior to absorption costing for internal purposes. Evidence from three different managerial applications supports this conclusion.

■ SUMMARY OF LEARNING OBJECTIVES

1. Prepare an income statement using variable costing. A variable-costing income statement divides expenses according to cost behavior. First, variable expenses of manufacturing, marketing, and administration are subtracted from sales to yield the contribution margin. Then all fixed expenses are subtracted from the contribution margin to yield variable-costing net income.

2. Prepare an income statement using absorption costing. An absorption-costing income statement divides expenses according to function. First, the cost of goods sold is subtracted from sales to yield gross profit (or gross margin). Then marketing expense and administrative expense are subtracted from gross profit to yield absorption-costing net income.

3. Compute the unit cost for a product using either variable costing or absorption costing. Unit production cost under variable costing consists of direct materials, direct labor, and variable factory overhead. Unit production cost under absorption costing consists of direct materials, direct labor, variable factory overhead, and a share of fixed factory overhead.

4. Explain the differences between variable costing and absorption costing. Absorption (or full) costing assigns all manufacturing costs to production, whereas variable (or direct) costing assigns only variable manufacturing costs to production. Under variable costing, fixed manufacturing overhead is viewed as a period cost. Under absorption costing, it is a product cost.

5. Reconcile the difference in variable-costing income and absorption-costing income. Because of the different ways to treat fixed overhead, the two methods generate differences in reported incomes. If production is greater than sales, absorption-costing income is greater than variable-costing income; the difference is the amount of fixed overhead attached to the units flowing into inventory under absorption costing. If sales exceed production, variable-costing income is greater than absorption-costing income by the amount of fixed overhead flowing out of inventory. When sales and production are equal, the two methods produce equal levels of income.

6. Discuss the advantages of variable costing for purposes of performance evaluation of managers, segment evaluation, and planning and control. Although variable costing cannot be used for external reporting, it has a number of important internal applications for management. By separating costs according to behavior, it enhances traceability and controllability of costs. As a result, performance evaluation, segment reporting, and planning and control are all made easier by the cost information produced by a variable-costing system. This suggests that both costing methods should exist within a firm. Organizations need more than one type of cost system since cost management may have different requirements than financial reporting.

7. **Prepare a segmented income statement based on a variable-costing approach and explain why such an income statement is preferred to a segmented income statement using absorption costing.** A segmented income statement takes the following form:

	Segment X	Segment Y	Company
Sales	XXX	YYY	CCC
Less variable expenses	(XX)	(YY)	(CC)
Contribution margin	XXX	YYY	CCC
Less direct fixed expenses	(XX)	(YY)	(CC)
Product margin	XX	YY	CC
Less common fixed expenses			(CC)
Net income (loss)			CC

The use of variable costing emphasizes the cost of behavior of each segment so that management can properly evaluate each segment's contribution to overall firm performance.

■ KEY TERMS

Absorption costing   A product-costing method that assigns *all* manufacturing costs to a product: direct materials, direct labor, variable overhead, and fixed overhead. (p. 411)

Applied fixed overhead   The fixed manufacturing overhead that is assigned to production using a predetermined fixed overhead rate. (p. 419)

Common fixed expenses   Fixed expenses that cannot be directly traced to individual segments and that are unaffected by the elimination of any one segment. (p. 427)

Direct fixed expenses   Fixed costs that are directly traceable to a given segment and, consequently, disappear if the segment is eliminated. (p. 427)

Segment   A subunit of a company of sufficient importance to warrant the production of performance reports. (p. 424)

Segment margin   The contribution a segment makes to cover common fixed costs and provide for profit after direct fixed costs and variable costs are deducted from the segment's sales revenue. (p. 427)

Segmented reporting The process of preparing financial performance reports for each segment of importance within a firm. (p. 424)

Variable costing A product-costing method that assigns only variable manufacturing costs to production: direct materials, direct labor, and variable overhead. Fixed overhead is treated as a period cost. (p. 411)

■ REVIEW PROBLEMS

I **Absorption and Variable Costing; Segmented Income Statement** Fine Leathers Company produces a lady's wallet and a man's wallet. Selected data for the past year are presented below.

	Lady's Wallet	Man's Wallet
Production (units)	100,000	200,000
Sales (units)	90,000	210,000
Selling price	$5.50	$4.50
Direct labor hours	50,000	80,000
Manufacturing costs:		
Direct materials	$ 75,000	$100,000
Direct labor	250,000	400,000
Variable overhead	20,000	24,000
Fixed overhead:		
Direct	50,000	40,000
Common[a]	20,000	20,000
Nonmanufacturing costs:		
Variable selling	$ 30,000	$ 60,000
Direct fixed selling	35,000	40,000
Common fixed selling[b]	25,000[b]	25,000

[a]Common overhead totals $40,000 and is divided equally between the two products.
[b]Common fixed selling totals $50,000 and is divided equally between the two products.

Budgeted fixed overhead for the year, $130,000, equaled the actual fixed overhead. Fixed overhead is assigned to products using a plant-wide rate based on expected direct labor hours, which were 130,000. The company had 10,000 man's wallets in inventory at the beginning of the year. These wallets had the same unit cost as the man's wallets produced during the year.

Required:

1. Compute the unit cost for the lady's and man's wallets using the variable-costing method. Compute the unit cost using absorption costing.
2. Prepare an income statement using absorption costing.
3. Prepare an income statement using variable costing.
4. Reconcile the difference between the two income statements.
5. Prepare a segmented income statement using products as segments.

Solution:

1. Unit cost for the lady's wallet is as follows:

Direct materials ($75,000/100,000)	$0.75
Direct labor ($250,000/100,000)	2.50
Variable overhead ($20,000/100,000)	0.20
Variable cost per unit	$3.45
Fixed overhead [(50,000 × $1.00)/100,000]	0.50
Absorption cost per unit	$3.95

The unit cost for the man's wallet is as follows:

Direct materials ($100,000/200,000)	$0.50
Direct labor ($400,000/200,000)	2.00
Variable overhead ($24,000/200,000)	0.12
Variable cost per unit	$2.62
Fixed overhead [(80,000 × $1.00)/200,000]	0.40
Absorption cost per unit	$3.02

Notice that the only difference between the two unit costs is the assignment of the fixed overhead cost. Notice also that the fixed overhead unit cost is assigned using the predetermined fixed overhead rate ($130,000/130,000 hours = $1 per hour). For example, the lady's wallets used 50,000 direct labor hours and so receive $1 × 50,000, or $50,000, of fixed overhead. This total, when divided by the units produced, gives the $0.50 per-unit fixed overhead cost. Finally, observe that variable nonmanufacturing costs are not part of the unit cost under variable costing. For both approaches, only manufacturing costs are used to compute the unit costs.

2. The income statement under absorption costing is as follows:

Sales [($5.50 × 90,000) + ($4.50 × 210,000)]	$1,440,000
Less: Cost of goods sold:	
[($3.95 × 90,000) + ($3.02 × 210,000)]	(989,700)
Gross margin	$ 450,300
Less: Selling expenses[a]	(215,000)
Net income	$ 235,300

[a]The sum of selling expenses for both products

3. The income statement under variable costing is as follows:

Sales [($5.50 × 90,000) + ($4.50 × 210,000)]	$1,440,000
Less variable expenses:	
Variable cost of goods sold [($3.45 × 90,000) + ($2.62 × 210,000)]	$ 860,700

Variable selling expenses	(90,000)
Contribution margin	$ 489,300
Less fixed expenses:	
Fixed overhead	(130,000)
Fixed selling	(125,000)
Net income	$ 234,300

4. Reconciliation is as follows:

$$I_A - I_V = \$235,300 - \$234,300 = \$1,000$$

Thus, variable-costing income is $1,000 less than absorption-costing income. This difference can be explained by the net change of fixed overhead found in inventory under absorption costing.

Lady's wallets:	
Units produced	100,000
Units sold	90,000
Increase in inventory	10,000
Unit fixed overhead	× $0.50
Increase in fixed overhead	$5,000

Man's wallets:	
Units produced	200,000
Units sold	210,000
Decrease in inventory	(10,000)
Unit fixed overhead	× $0.40
Decrease in fixed overhead	($4,000)

Net change is a $1,000 ($5,000 − $4,000) increase in fixed overhead in inventories. Thus, under absorption costing, there is a net flow of $1,000 of the current period's fixed overhead into inventory. Since variable costing recognized all of the current period's fixed overhead as an expense, variable-costing income should be $1,000 lower than absorption costing, as it is.

5. Segmented income statement:

	Lady's Wallets	Man's Wallets	Total
Sales	$ 495,000	$ 945,000	$1,440,000
Less variable expenses:			
Variable cost of goods sold	(310,500)	(550,200)	(860,700)

continued on next page

	Lady's Wallets	Man's Wallets	Total
Variable selling expenses	(30,000)	(60,000)	(90,000)
Contribution margin	$154,500	$334,800	$489,300
Less direct fixed expenses:			
Direct fixed overhead	(50,000)	(40,000)	(90,000)
Direct selling expenses	(35,000)	(40,000)	(75,000)
Product margin	$ 69,500	$254,800	$324,300
Less common fixed expenses:			
Common fixed overhead			(40,000)
Common selling expenses			(50,000)
Net income			$234,300

II   **Absorption and Variable Costing with Over- and Underapplied Overhead**   Bellingham, Inc., has just completed its first year of operations. The unit costs on a normal costing basis are as follows:

Manufacturing costs (per unit):	
Direct materials (2 lbs @ $2)	$ 4.00
Direct labor (1.5 hrs @ $9)	13.50
Variable overhead (1.5 hrs @ $2)	3.00
Fixed overhead (1.5 hrs @ $3)	4.50
Total	$25.00
Selling and administrative costs:	
Variable	$5/unit
Fixed	$190,000

During the year, the company had the following activity:

Units produced	24,000
Units sold	21,500
Unit selling price	$42
Direct labor hours worked	36,000

Actual fixed overhead was $12,000 less than budgeted fixed overhead. Budgeted variable overhead was $5,000 less than the actual variable overhead. The company used an expected actual activity level of 36,000 direct labor hours to compute the predetermined overhead rates. Any overhead variances are closed to Cost of Goods Sold.

Required:

1. Compute the unit cost using (a) absorption costing and (b) variable costing.
2. Prepare an absorption-costing income statement.
3. Prepare a variable-costing income statement.
4. Reconcile the difference between the two income statements.

Solution:

1.

Absorption Unit Cost		*Variable Unit Cost*	
Direct materials	$ 4.00	Direct materials	$ 4.00
Direct labor	13.50	Direct labor	13.50
Variable overhead	3.00	Variable overhead	3.00
Fixed overhead	4.50	Total	$20.50
Total	$25.00		

2. **Bellingham, Inc.**

Absorption Costing Income Statement

Sales (21,500 @ $42)		$ 903,000
Cost of goods sold (21,500 @ $25.00)	537,500	
Less: Overapplied overhead[a]	(7,000)	530,500
Gross margin		372,500
Less: Selling and administrative expense		(297,500)
Net income		$ 75,000

[a]The budgeted fixed overhead rate of $3 per direct labor hour was computed based on 36,000 direct labor hours. Therefore, budgeted fixed overhead must have been $108,000. Since actual fixed overhead was $12,000 less than budgeted, actual fixed overhead must be $96,000. Similarly, the variable overhead rate of $2 per direct labor hour implies budgeted variable overhead of $72,000 ($2 × 36,000 direct labor hours). Since actual variable overhead was $5,000 higher than budgeted overhead, actual variable overhead must be $77,000.

    Both variable and fixed overhead were applied on the basis of direct labor hours. Since 36,000 hours were worked, total applied overhead amounts to $180,000. Actual overhead was $173,000 (actual fixed of $96,000 plus actual variable of $77,000).

Applied overhead	$180,000
Actual overhead	(173,000)
Overapplied overhead	7,000

3. **Bellingham, Inc.**

Variable Costing Income Statement

Sales (21,500 @ $42)		$ 903,000
Variable cost of goods sold (21,500 @ $20.50)	440,750	
Add: Underapplied variable overhead	5,000	(445,750)
Variable selling expense (21,500 @ $5)		(107,500)
Contribution margin		349,750
Less:		
Fixed factory overhead	96,000	
Selling and administrative expense	190,000	(286,000)
Net income		$ 63,750

Note that the underapplied variable overhead is simply the actual variable overhead of $77,000 minus the applied variable overhead of $72,000 ($2 × 36,000 direct labor hours). Note also that actual fixed factory overhead is charged on the income statement, not applied fixed factory overhead.

4. $I_A - I_V$ = Fixed overhead rate (Production − Sales)
$75,000 − $63,750 = $4.50 (24,000 − 21,500)
$11,250 = $4.50 (2,500)
$11,250 = $11,250

■ QUESTIONS

1   What is the only difference between the way costs are assigned under variable and absorption costing?

2   The variable manufacturing costs of a company are $10 per unit, variable selling expenses are $2 per unit, and the fixed overhead rate is $5 per unit. What is the per-unit inventory cost of the product under absorption costing? Under variable costing?

3   Why is variable costing a more descriptive term for the product-costing method popularly known as *direct costing*?

4   If production is greater than sales, why is absorption-costing income greater than variable-costing income?

5   If sales are greater than production, why is variable-costing income greater than absorption-costing income?

6   Assume that a company has a fixed overhead rate of $8 per unit produced. During the year, the company produced 10,000 units and sold 8,000. What is the difference in income generated according to absorption costing and to variable costing?

7   The fixed overhead expense recognized on an income statement was $100,000. The fixed overhead for the period was $80,000. Was the income statement prepared using absorption costing or variable costing? Explain.

8   Why is variable costing better than absorption costing for the evaluation of managerial performance?

9   Why is variable costing better than absorption costing for the evaluation of segment performance?

10   Why is variable costing better than absorption costing for planning and controlling costs?

11   What is a direct fixed expense? Why is it useful for segment performance evaluation?

12   What is the difference between segment margin and contribution margin?

13   What is the difference between a direct fixed cost and a common fixed cost? Why is this difference important?

14   Explain how income under absorption costing can increase from one period to the next even though selling prices and costs have remained the same.

15   How would a segment be identified within a firm?

■ EXERCISES

E9–1 **Unit Costs; Inventory Valuation; Variable and Absorption Costing** Conway Company produced 70,000 units during its first year of operations and sold 65,000 at $8 per unit. The company chose practical activity—at 70,000 units—to compute its predetermined overhead rate. Manufacturing costs are as follows:

Expected and actual fixed overhead	$140,000
Expected and actual variable overhead	35,000
Direct labor	280,000
Direct materials	105,000

Required:

1. Calculate the unit cost and the cost of finished goods inventory under absorption costing.

2. Calculate the unit cost and the cost of finished goods inventory under variable costing.

3. What is the dollar amount that would be used to report the cost of finished goods inventory to external parties. Why?

E9–2 **Income Statements; Variable and Absorption Costing** The following information pertains to Velman, Inc., for 1992:

Beginning inventory, units	—
Units produced	10,000
Units sold	8,000
Ending inventory, units	2,000
Variable costs per unit:	
Direct materials	$5.00
Direct labor	3.00
Variable overhead	2.50
Variable selling expenses	3.50
Fixed costs per year:	
Fixed overhead	$20,000
Fixed selling and administrative	25,000

There are no work-in-process inventories. Normal activity is 10,000 units. Expected and actual overhead costs are the same.

Required:

1. Without preparing an income statement, indicate what the difference will be between variable-costing income and absorption-costing income.

2. Assume the selling price per unit is $25. Prepare an income statement (a) using variable costing and (b) using absorption costing.

E9–3 **Income Statements and Firm Performance: Variable and Absorption Costing** Handley Company had the following operating data for its first two years of operations:

Variable cost per unit:	
Direct materials	$4
Direct labor	5
Variable overhead	3
Fixed costs per year:	
Overhead	$120,000
Selling and administrative	20,000

Handley produced 20,000 units in the first year and sold 15,000. In the second year, it produced 15,000 units and sold 20,000 units. The selling price per unit each year was $21. Handley uses an actual cost system for product costing.

Required:

1. Prepare income statements for both years using absorption costing. Has firm performance, as measured by income, improved or declined from Year 1 to Year 2?

2. Prepare income statements for both years using variable costing. Has firm performance, as measured by income, improved or declined from Year 1 to Year 2?

3. Which method do you think most accurately measures firm performance? Why?

E9–4 **Absorption Costing; Variable Costing; Reconciliation with Fixed Overhead Variance** Farley Company uses a predetermined overhead rate based on normal capacity expressed in units of output. Normal capacity is 60,000 units and the expected fixed overhead cost for the year is $120,000.

During the year, Farley produced 55,000 units and sold 50,000. There was no beginning finished goods inventory. The variable-costing income statement for the year is given below.

Sales (50,000 units @ $20)	$1,000,000
Less variable costs:	
Variable cost of goods sold	(500,000)
Variable selling expenses	(250,000)
Contribution margin	$ 250,000
Less fixed costs:	
Fixed overhead	(125,000)
Fixed selling and administrative	(75,000)
Net income	$ 50,000

Any under- or overapplied overhead is closed to Cost of Goods Sold. Variable cost of goods sold is already adjusted for any variable overhead variance.

Required:

1. Farley Company needs an income statement based on absorption costing for external reporting. Using the information given above, prepare this statement.

2. Explain the difference between the income reported by variable costing and by absorption costing.

E9–5 **Segmented Income Statements; Product-Line Analysis** Byers Company produces two rifles: automatic and semiautomatic. During the past year, 5,000 automatic rifles and 10,000 semiautomatic rifles were produced and sold. Fixed costs for Byers totaled $250,000, of which $50,000 can be avoided if the automatic rifles are not produced and $75,000 can be avoided if the semiautomatic rifles are not produced. Revenue and variable cost information are

	Automatic	*Semiautomatic*
Variable expenses per rifle	$220	$190
Selling price per rifle	250	200

Required:

1. Prepare product-line income statements. Segregate direct and common fixed costs.

2. What would the effect be on Byer's profit if the semiautomatic line is dropped? The automatic line?

3. What would be the effect on firm profits if an additional 1,000 automatic rifles could be produced (using existing capacity) and sold for $230 on a special-order basis? Existing sales would be unaffected by the special order.

E9–6 **Product-Line Analysis with Complementary Effects** FunTime Company produces three lines of greeting cards: scented, musical, and regular. Segmented income statements for the past year are as follows:

	Scented	*Musical*	*Regular*	*Total*
Sales	$10,000	$ 15,000	$ 25,000	$ 50,000
Less: Variable expenses	(7,000)	(12,000)	(12,500)	(31,500)
Contribution margin	$ 3,000	$ 3,000	$ 12,500	$ 18,500
Less: Direct fixed expenses	(4,000)	(5,000)	(3,000)	(12,000)
Segment margin	$ (1,000)	$ (2,000)	$ 9,500	$ 6,500
Common fixed expenses				(7,500)
Net profit (loss)				$ (1,000)

Kathy Bunker, president of FunTime, is concerned about the financial performance of her firm and is seriously considering dropping both the scented and musical product lines. However, before making a final decision, she consults Jim Dorn, FunTime's vice-president of marketing.

Required:

1. Jim believes that by increasing advertising by $1,000 ($250 for the scented line and $750 for the musical line), sales of those two lines would increase by 30 percent. If you were Kathy, how would you react to this information?

2. Jim warns Kathy that eliminating the scented and musical lines would lower the sales of the regular line by 20 percent. Given this information, would it be profitable to eliminate the scented and musical lines?

3. Suppose that eliminating either line reduces sales of the regular cards by 10 percent. Would a combination of increased advertising (the option described in requirement 1) and eliminating one of the lines be beneficial? Identify the best combination for the firm.

E9–7   **Absorption Costing; Variable Costing; Income Statements; Inventory Valuations; Income Reconciliation**   Kerney Company produces and sells Little League baseballs. The operating costs for the past year were

Variable costs per unit:	
Direct labor	$0.50
Direct materials	1.00
Variable overhead	0.25
Variable selling	0.10
Fixed costs per year:	
Fixed overhead	$175,000
Selling and administrative	60,000

During the year, Kerney produced 350,000 baseballs and sold 325,000 at $3.50 each. Kerney had no beginning finished goods inventory. An actual cost system is used for product costing.

Required:

1. What is the per-unit inventory cost that will be reported on Kerney's balance sheet at the end of the year? What will be the reported income?

2. What would the per-unit inventory cost be under variable costing? Does this differ from the unit cost computed in requirement 1? Why? What would income be using variable costing?

3. Reconcile the difference between the variable-costing and the absorption-costing income figures.

E9–8   **Variable Costing; Absorption Costing; Income Statements; Inventory Valuation; Underapplied Fixed Overhead**   During its first year of operations, Peterson, Inc., produced 210,000 beach balls and sold 200,000. Fixed overhead was applied at $0.50 per unit produced. Fixed overhead was underapplied by $10,000. This fixed overhead variance was closed to Cost of Goods Sold. There was no variable overhead variance. The results of the year's operations are as follows (on an absorption-costing basis):

Sales (200,000 units @ $2.50)	$ 500,000
Less: Cost of goods sold	(410,000)
Gross margin	$ 90,000
Less: Selling and administrative (all fixed)	(35,000)
Net income	$ 55,000

Required:

1. Give the cost of the firm's ending inventory under absorption costing. What is the cost of the ending inventory under variable costing?

2. Prepare a variable-costing income statement. Reconcile the difference between the two income figures.

E9–9   **Segmented Income Statements; Absorption Costing; Variable Costing; Regional Analysis**   Wilson Company sells its products in the Southwest and Midwest. Major plants are located in each region. Based on a recent quarterly income statement, the president of the company expressed some concern regarding performance in the Southwest. The income statement (prepared on an absorption-costing basis) follows:

Wilson Company

Income Statement
(dollars in thousands)

	Midwest	Southwest	Total
Sales	$10,000	$ 12,000	$ 22,000
Less: Cost of goods sold	(7,000)	(10,000)	(17,000)
Gross margin	$ 3,000	$ 2,000	$ 5,000
Less: Selling and administrative	(2,000)	(2,500)	(4,500)
Net income (loss)	$ 1,000	$ (500)	$ 500

Wilson sold all of the units produced during the quarter. There were no beginning or ending finished goods inventories. Twenty percent of the cost of goods sold represents fixed costs. Of total fixed production costs, 30 percent are directly traceable to the Midwest and 20 percent to the Southwest. The remaining fixed production costs, common to both regions, are equally allocated between them. Selling and administrative costs are all fixed. Of the total, $2 million representing common costs are equally divided between the two regions. Of the remaining selling and administrative fixed costs, 40 percent are directly traceable to the Midwest and 60 percent to the Southwest.

Required:

1. Prepare a variable-costing segmented income statement for the quarter ended. Should the company consider eliminating its Southwest regional activity?

2. Express the contribution margin and the segment margin computed in requirement 1 as a percentage of sales. Now assume that each region increases its sales activity in the next quarter by 10 percent. Assuming the same cost relationships, prepare a new variable-costing segmented income statement. Recompute the contribution margin and segment margin ratios. What happened? Explain.

E9–10   **Unit Cost; Inventory Valuation; Absorption and Variable Costing; Contribution Margin**   Corbin Company manufactures yo-yos. In January 1993, Corbin began producing neon-colored yo-yos. During the month of January, 5,000 were produced and 4,500 were sold at $5.50 each. The following costs were incurred:

Materials (plastic, string, axles)	$3,750
Direct labor	4,500
Variable factory overhead	1,250
Fixed factory overhead	7,500

Selling commission of 10 percent of sales price was paid. Administrative expense, all fixed, amounted to $2,000.

Required:

1. Calculate the unit cost and cost of ending inventory under absorption costing.
2. Calculate the unit cost and cost of ending inventory under variable costing.
3. What is the contribution margin per unit?

E9–11   **Net Income; Absorption and Variable Costing**   Refer to Exercise 9–10.

Required:

1. Prepare an absorption-costing income statement for Corbin Company for January 1993.
2. Prepare a variable-costing income statement for Corbin Company for January 1993.
3. Reconcile the difference between the two net incomes.

E9–12   **Inventory Valuation under Absorption and Variable Costing; Variable-Costing Net Income**   Quillen Company manufactured 12,000 units during the year and sold 14,000. Quillen's accountant prepared the following income statement:

Sales (14,000 @ $26)		$364,000
Cost of goods sold (14,000 @ $18)		252,000
Gross profit		112,000
Marketing expense	28,000	
Administrative expense	15,000	(43,000)
Net income		$ 69,000

Marketing expense is 50 percent fixed. Administrative expense is entirely fixed. The fixed factory overhead rate is $3 per unit. Beginning inventory was 5,000 units, and there were no price changes from one year to the next.

Required:

1. Prepare a variable costing income statement for Quillen Company.
2. What was the value of ending inventory under absorption costing?
3. What was the value of ending inventory under variable costing?

E9–13   **Calculating Unit and Total Costs Under Absorption Costing**   Each of the following independent companies, Company A, Company B, and Company C, uses absorption costing. Calculate the correct amounts for every question mark below. There are no overhead variances. Prices have stayed constant for all relevant time periods.

	A	B	C
Unit information:			
Price	$22	?	?
Direct materials	4	2	6
Direct labor	3	4	1
Variable overhead	1	1	1
Fixed overhead	?	3	1

	A	B	C
Contribution margin	$ 14	?	?
Gross profit	$ 9	?	?
Units sold	2,000	7,600	?
Units produced	2,000	8,000	?
Beginning inventory, units	500	0	3,000
Total information:			
Sales	?	$114,000	$136,000
Cost of goods sold	?	?	72,000
Gross profit	?	38,000	?
Variable marketing	?	9,500	24,000
Fixed marketing	5,000	8,000	?
Fixed administrative	3,000	?	8,300
Net income	?	500	16,700
Value of ending inventory	6,500	?	9,000

E9–14 **Inventory Valuation and Net Income Under Variable Costing** Refer to Exercise 9–13.

Required:

1. What are the net incomes for companies A, B, and C using variable costing?

2. What are the values of ending inventory for companies A, B, and C using variable costing?

E9–15 **Variable and Absorption Costing** Arthur Company manufactures heavy-duty motors for industrial use. The motors are sold for $400 each. Cost of goods sold is $300; of that amount, $95 is for direct materials. Variable overhead is applied at twice the rate of direct labor. Total fixed overhead is $660,000. Production was 12,000 units for this year due to the need to increase inventory by 2,000 units. Selling and administrative costs, all fixed, amounted to $217,000.

Required:

1. What was absorption-costing net income for Arthur Company for the year? What was variable-costing net income?

2. If beginning inventory was zero, what was the value of ending inventory under absorption costing?

3. What is the contribution margin per unit for Arthur Company?

■ **PROBLEMS**

P9–1 **Variable and Absorption-Costing Income Statements** Mendoza Company manufactures backpacks. Sales for last year totaled $1,450,000. Cost of goods sold amounted to 40 percent of sales; of the total, 20 percent represented fixed manufacturing expenses. Selling expenses were equally split between fixed and variable components. Administrative expense, all fixed, totaled $89,000. Net income for last year was $491,000. Mendoza produced and sold 72,500 backpacks last year.

Required:

1. Prepare an absorption-costing income statement for Mendoza Company for last year.

2. Prepare a variable-costing income statement for Mendoza Company for last year.

3. What is the variable cost per backpack? What is the variable production cost per backpack?

P9–2   **Variable Costing and Break-even Analysis**   Cartwright Ranch Supply Company manufactures a variety of fencing materials. Cartwright's 1992 income statement is as follows:

Sales	$ 960,000
Variable cost of goods sold	(192,000)
Variable selling expense	(96,000)
Contribution margin	672,000
Fixed overhead	(300,000)
Fixed selling and administrative	(139,000)
Net income	$ 233,000

Cartwright believes it can increase the average price of its products by 6 percent during 1993. No change in quantity of products sold is forecast. Advertising will increase by $30,000, and administrative expense will increase by $9,000. Production costs will remain constant.

Required:

1. Calculate Cartwright's break-even revenue for 1992.

2. Prepare a budgeted variable-costing income statement for 1993.

3. Calculate Cartwright's break-even revenue for 1993 using the forecast changes.

P9–3   **Variable Costing; Targeted Net Income**   Madengrad Company manufactures a single electronic product called *Precisionmix*. This unit is a batch-density monitoring device attached to large industrial mixing machines used in flour, rubber, petroleum, and chemical manufacturing. Precisionmix sells for $900 per unit. The following variable costs are incurred to produce each Precisionmix device:

Direct labor	$180
Direct materials	240
Factory overhead	105
Variable product cost	525
Marketing cost	75
Total variable cost	$600

Madengrad's income tax rate is 40 percent, and annual fixed costs are $6,600,000. Except for an operating loss incurred in the year of incorporation, the firm has been profitable over the last five years. Madengrad is forecasting sales of 21,500 units for next year and has budgeted production at that level.

Required:

1. Prepare a pro forma variable-costing income statement for Madengrad Company for next year.

2. What annual sales volume in units is required for Madengrad to achieve an after-tax net income of $540,000?

3. Madengrad has just learned of a significant change in production technology that will cause a 10 percent increase in total annual fixed costs and a 20 percent unit labor cost increase as a result of higher skilled direct labor. However, this change permits the replacement of a costly imported component with a domestic component. The effect is to reduce unit material costs by 25 percent. No change in selling price is forecast.
   a. After incorporating these changes, Madengrad Company's contribution margin would be what percent of sales?
   b. What would Madengrad Company's new break-even point in units be?
   c. Should Madengrad shift to the new technology?

(CMA adapted)

P9-4 **Segment Analysis; Addition of a New Product** Trinity Company currently produces two products, A and B. The company has sufficient floor space to manufacture an additional product, with two (C and D) currently under consideration. Only one of the two products can be chosen. The expected annual sales and associated costs for each product are as follows:

	Product C	Product D
Sales	$100,000	$125,000
Variable costs as a percentage of sales:		
Production	50%	65%
Selling and administrative	10%	5%
Direct fixed expenses	$ 10,000	$ 11,250

The common fixed costs of the company are allocated to each product line on the basis of sales revenues.

The following income statement for last year's operations is also available:

	Product A	Product B	Total
Sales	$ 250,000	$ 375,000	$ 625,000
Less variable expenses:			
Production	(100,000)	(250,000)	(350,000)
Selling and administrative	(20,000)	(65,000)	(85,000)
Contribution margin	130,000	60,000	190,000
Less: Direct fixed expenses	(10,000)	(55,000)	(65,000)
Segment margin	$ 120,000	$ 5,000	$ 125,000
Less: Common fixed expenses			(75,000)
Net income			$ 50,000

Required:

1. Prepare an income statement that reflects the impact of adding Product C on the firm's profits. Repeat for Product D. Which of the two would you recommend adding?

2. Suppose that both products C and D could be added if either A or B is dropped. Would you drop one of the current products to add both C and D? If so, which would you drop? Why?

P9–5   **Income Statements; Variable Costing; Absorption Costing**   The following information pertains to the first year of operation for Young Company:

Units produced	90,000
Expected actual production	100,000
Units sold	80,000
Unit selling price	$10
Costs	
Budgeted (and actual) fixed overhead	$200,000
Budgeted (and actual) variable overhead	150,000
Total cost of direct materials used	180,000
Total cost of direct labor	225,000
Variable selling and administrative	40,000
Fixed selling and administrative	110,000

Any under- or overapplied overhead is closed to Cost of Goods Sold.

Required:

1. Without preparing formal income statements, compute the difference that will exist between absorption-costing and variable-costing income.

2. Prepare absorption-costing and variable-costing income statements.

3. Reconcile the difference between the two income figures. (Have you already done this in answering requirement 1?)

P9–6   **Sales; Income Behavior; Variable Costing; Absorption Costing**   Quincy Products Division was organized as a new division of Troy, Inc., to produce a new electronic toy called *Lazerlight*. Lazerlight consists of a gun, a breastplate, and a helmet. The gun shoots a beam of light that initiates a signal when it strikes the breastplate or helmet, allowing individuals with the complete set to engage in "combat." With the recent popularity of simulated war games, Quincy's divisional manager expected a good response to the product. In the first year of operations, Quincy reported the following net income to its stockholders:

Quincy Products

Income Statement
For the Year Ended December 31, 1992

Sales (@ $80)	$ 40,000,000
Less: Cost of goods sold (@ $60[a])	(30,000,000)
Gross margin	$ 10,000,000

Income Statement
For the Year Ended December 31, 1992

Less: Selling and administrative[b]	(5,125,000)
Net income	$4,875,000

[a]Direct materials	$24
Direct labor	12
Variable overhead	10
Fixed overhead	14
Total	$60

[b]$6.25 per unit variable; $2,000,000 fixed

In 1992, Quincy produced 100,000 units more than it sold because sales were less than expected. The divisional manager was confident that sales for the second year would be 20 percent higher; the product had been well received in spite of failing to hit the first year's sales goal. Overhead is applied on the basis of units produced using expected actual activity. Any under- or overapplied overhead is closed to Cost of Goods Sold. For the first year, there was no under- or overapplied overhead.

For 1993, fixed costs and unit variable costs remained the same; the selling price also remained unchanged. Budgeted fixed costs equaled actual fixed costs. In 1993, Quincy produced 500,000 units and sold 600,000. Production was 100,000 less than expected because of unexpected equipment problems; however, the divisional manager was not displeased because the 20 percent sales increase had been achieved, and production costs were completely in line with plans.

Required:

1. Prepare the 1993 income statement required for stockholders. Did income increase or decrease? What do you think the reaction of the parent company, Troy, Inc., would be to this income statement? What would the divisional manager's reaction be?

2. Prepare variable-costing income statements for 1992 and 1993. How do you suppose Troy, Inc., would react now?

3. Reconcile and explain the differences between variable-costing and absorption-costing income figures for 1992 and 1993.

4. Which type of income statement (variable or absorption costing) do you think the divisional manager would prefer? Why?

P9-7 **Variable Costing; Absorption Costing; Income Statements; Inventory Valuations**
Ripten Company produces and sells a single product. Cost data for the product are given below.

Unit variable costs:	
Direct materials	$4
Direct labor	2
Variable overhead	2
Variable selling	1
Total	$9

continued on next page

Fixed costs per year:[a]

Overhead	$600,000
Selling and administrative	300,000
Total	$900,000

[a] Fixed costs are incurred uniformly throughout the year.

During the first three months, the company produced and sold the following units:

	Units Produced	Units Sold
Month 1	50,000	40,000
Month 2	40,000	40,000
Month 3	40,000	30,000

The company uses an actual cost system to assign the costs of production. The selling price of the product is $12 per unit. A LIFO inventory system is used.

Required:

1. What is the unit cost for each month under absorption costing? Under variable costing?

2. Without preparing income statements, determine the difference between absorption-costing and variable-costing income for each of the three months.

3. Prepare income statements for absorption costing and variable costing for each of the three months. Reconcile the net income figures.

P9–8   **Segmented Income Statements; Analysis of Proposals to Improve Profits**   Harris, Inc., has two divisions. One produces and sells paper diapers; the other produces and sells paper napkins and towels. A segmented income statement for the most recent quarter is given below.

	Diaper Division	Paper and Towel Division	Total
Sales	$ 500,000	$ 750,000	$1,250,000
Less: Variable expenses	(425,000)	(460,000)	(885,000)
Contribution margin	$ 75,000	$ 290,000	$ 365,000
Less: Direct fixed expenses	(85,000)	(110,000)	(195,000)
Segment margin	$ (10,000)	$ 180,000	$ 170,000
Less: Common fixed expenses			(130,000)
Net income			$ 40,000

On seeing the quarterly statement, Karen Norris, president of Harris, Inc., was distressed. "The diaper division is killing us," she complained. "It's not even covering its own fixed costs. I'm beginning to believe that we should shut down that division. This is the seventh consecutive quarter it has failed to provide a positive segment margin. I was certain that Fran Simmons could turn it around. But this is her third quarter, and she hasn't done much better than the previous divisional manager."

"Well, before you get too excited about the situation, perhaps you should evaluate

Fran's most recent proposals," remarked Tom Ferguson, the company's vice-president of finance. "She wants to lease some new production equipment and at the same time increase the advertising budget by $25,000 per quarter. She made some improvements in the design of the diaper and wants to let the public know about them. According to her marketing people, sales should increase by 10 percent if the right advertising is done—and done quickly. The new production machinery will increase the rate of production, lower labor costs, and result in less waste of materials. Fran claims that variable costs will be reduced by 30 percent. The cost of the lease is $105,000 per quarter."

Upon hearing this news, Karen calmed considerably, and, in fact, was somewhat pleased. After all, she was the one who had selected Fran and had a great deal of confidence in Fran's judgment and abilities.

Required:

1. Assuming that Fran's proposals are sound, should Karen Norris be pleased with the prospects for the diaper division? Prepare a segmented income statement for the next quarter that reflects the implementation of Fran's proposals. Assume that the paper division's sales increase by 5 percent for the next quarter and that the same cost relationships hold.

2. Suppose that everything materializes as Fran projected except for the 10 percent increase in sales—no change in sales revenues took place. Are the proposals still sound? What if the variable costs are reduced by 40 percent instead of 30 percent with no change in sales?

P9–9 **Performance Evaluation; Absorption Costing Compared with Variable Costing** Kathy Wise was manager of a new medical supplies division. She had just finished her second year and had been visiting with the company's vice-president of operations. In the first year, the net income for the division had shown a substantial increase over the prior year. Her second year saw an even greater increase. The vice-president was extremely pleased and promised Kathy a $5,000 bonus if the division showed a similar increase in profits for the upcoming year. Kathy was elated. She was completely confident that the goal could be met. Sales contracts were already well ahead of last year's performance, and she knew that there would be no increases in costs.

At the end of the third year, Kathy received the following data regarding operations for the first three years:

	Year 1	Year 2	Year 3
Production	10,000	11,000	9,000
Sales (in units)	8,000	10,000	12,000
Unit selling price	$10	$10	$10
Unit costs:			
Fixed overhead[a]	$2.90	$3.00	$3.00
Variable overhead	1.00	1.00	1.00
Direct materials	1.90	2.00	2.00
Direct labor	1.00	1.00	1.00
Variable selling	0.40	0.50	0.50
Actual fixed overhead	$29,000	$30,000	$30,000
Other fixed costs	$9,000	$10,000	$10,000

[a]The predetermined fixed overhead rate is based on expected actual units of production and expected fixed overhead. Expected production each year was 10,000 units. Any under- or overapplied fixed overhead is closed to Cost of Goods Sold.

| | Yearly Income Statements | | |
	Year 1	Year 2	Year 3
Sales revenue	$80,000	$100,000	$120,000
Less: Cost of goods sold[a]	54,400	67,000	86,600
Gross margin	$25,600	$ 33,000	$ 33,400
Less: Selling and administrative	12,200	15,000	16,000
Net income	$13,400	$ 18,000	$ 17,400

[a]Assumes a LIFO inventory flow

Upon examining the operating data, Kathy was pleased. Sales had increased by 20 percent over the previous year, and costs had been kept stable. However, when she saw the yearly income statements, she was dismayed and perplexed. Instead of seeing a significant increase in income for the third year, she saw a small decrease. Surely the Accounting Department had made an error.

Required:

1. Explain to Kathy why she lost her $5,000 bonus.

2. Prepare variable-costing income statements for each of the three years. Reconcile the differences between the absorption-costing and variable-costing incomes.

3. If you were the vice-president of Kathy's company, which income statement (variable costing or absorption costing) would you prefer to use for evaluating Kathy's performance? Why?

P9–10 **Absorption Costing and Performance Evaluation** Wilmont Company's executive committee was meeting to select a new vice-president of operations. The leading candidate was Howard Kimball, manager of Wilmont's largest division. Howard had been divisional manager for three years. The president of Wilmont, Larry Olsen, was impressed with the significant improvements in the division's profits since Howard had assumed command. In the first year of operations, divisional profits had increased by 20 percent. They had shown significant improvements for the following two years as well. To bolster support for Howard, the company's president circulated the following divisional income statements (dollars in thousands):

	1992	1993	1994
Sales	$ 30,000	$ 32,000	$ 34,000
Less: Cost of goods sold[a]	(26,250)	(26,400)	(27,200)
Gross margin	$ 3,750	$ 5,600	$ 6,800
Less: Selling and administrative[b]	(3,000)	(3,600)	(3,800)
Net income	$ 750	$ 2,000	$ 3,000

[a]Assumes a LIFO inventory flow
[b]All costs are fixed.

"As you can see," Larry observed at a meeting, "Howard has increased profits by a factor of four since 1992. That's by far the most impressive performance of any divisional manager. We could certainly use someone with that kind of drive. I definitely believe that Howard should be the new vice-president."

"I'm not quite as convinced that Howard's performance is as impressive as it appears," responded Bill Peters, the vice-president of finance. "I could hardly believe that Howard's division could show the magnitude of improvement revealed by the income statements, so I asked the divisional controller to supply some additional information. As the data suggest, the profits realized by Howard's division may be attributable to a concerted effort to produce for inventory. In fact, I believe it can be shown that the division is actually showing a loss each year and that real profits have declined by as much as 15 percent since 1992." Peters then showed the following information:

	1992	1993	1994
Sales (units)	150,000	160,000	170,000
Production[a]	200,000	250,000	300,000
Actual (and budgeted) fixed overhead	$15,000,000	$15,000,000	$15,000,000
Fixed overhead rate	$75	$60	$50
Unit variable production costs	$100	$105	$110

[a]Represents both expected and actual production. Fixed overhead rates are computed using expected actual production.

Required:

1. Explain what Bill Peters meant by "producing for inventory."

2. Recast the income statements in a variable-costing format. Now how does the performance of the division appear?

3. Reconcile the differences in the income figures using the two methods for each of the three years.

4. If you were a shareholder, how could you detect income increases that are caused mainly by production for inventory?

P9–11 **Comparison of Variable and Absorption Costing; Predetermined Overhead Rates** Jackson, Inc., has just completed its first year of operations. The unit costs on a normal costing basis are as follows:

Manufacturing costs (per unit):	
Direct materials (2 lbs @ $2)	$ 4.00
Direct labor (1.5 hrs @ $7)	10.50
Variable overhead (1.5 hrs @ $2)	3.00
Fixed overhead (1.5 hrs @ $3)	4.50
Total	$22.00
Nonmanufacturing costs:	
Variable	10% of sales
Fixed	$200,000

During the year, the company had the following activity:

Units produced	25,000
Units sold	20,000
Unit selling price	$40
Direct labor hours worked	37,500

Actual fixed overhead was $10,000 greater than budgeted fixed overhead. Actual variable overhead was $5,000 greater than budgeted variable overhead. The company used an expected actual activity level of 37,500 direct labor hours to compute the predetermined overhead rates. Any overhead variances are closed to Cost of Goods Sold.

Required:

1. Compute the unit cost using (a) absorption costing and (b) variable costing.
2. Prepare an absorption-costing income statement.
3. Prepare a variable-costing income statement.
4. Reconcile the difference between the two income statements.

P9–12 **Segmented Income Statements; Adding and Dropping Product Lines**   Nancy Henderson has just been appointed manager of Palmroy's glass products division. She has two years to make the division profitable. If the division is still showing a loss after two years, it will be eliminated, and Nancy will be reassigned as an assistant divisional manager in another division. The divisional income statement for the most recent year is given below.

Sales	$ 5,350,000
Less: Variable expenses	(4,750,000)
Contribution margin	$ 600,000
Less: Direct fixed expenses	(750,000)
Divisional margin	$ (150,000)
Less: Common fixed expenses (allocated)	(200,000)
Divisional profit (loss)	$ (350,000)

Upon arriving at the division, Nancy requested the following data on the division's three products:

	Product A	Product B	Product C
Sales (units)	10,000	20,000	15,000
Unit selling price	$ 150.00	$ 140.00	$ 70.00
Unit variable cost	100.00	110.00	103.33
Direct fixed costs	100,000.00	500,000.00	150,000.00

She also gathered data on a proposed new product (Product D). If this product is added, it would displace one of the current products; the quantity that could be produced and sold would equal the quantity sold of the product it displaces, although demand limits the maximum quantity that could be sold to 20,000 units. Because of specialized production equipment, it is not possible for the new product to displace part of the production of a second product. The information on Product D is as follows:

Unit selling price	$ 70
Unit variable cost	30
Direct fixed costs	640,000

Required:

1. Prepare segmented income statements for Products A, B, and C.

2. Determine the products that Nancy should produce for the coming year. Prepare segmented income statements that prove your combination is the best for the division. By how much will profits improve given the combination that you selected? (*Hint:* Your combination may include one, two, or three products.)

P9–13 **Comprehensive Review Problem: Variable Costing, Absorption Costing, Segmented Reporting** The Clock Division of Thurmond Company produces both wall clocks and table clocks. The clocks are sold in two regions, the West and the Southwest. The table below gives the sales of the Clock Division during 1992 (in units).

	West	Southwest	Total
Wall clocks	100,000	250,000	350,000
Table clocks	250,000	520,000	770,000

Production data for 1992 are as follows (there were no beginning or ending work-in-process inventories):

	Wall Clocks	Table Clocks
Production	300,000	800,000
Direct labor hours	30,000	40,000
Manufacturing costs:		
Direct materials	$450,000	$720,000
Direct labor	210,000	200,000
Variable overhead	60,000	90,000
Fixed overhead[a]	360,000	540,000

[a]Common fixed overhead of $280,000 has been allocated to the two products on the basis of actual direct labor hours and is included in each total.

The selling prices are $4.50 for wall clocks and $3 for table clocks. Variable nonmanufacturing costs are 20 percent of the selling price for wall clocks and 30 percent of the selling price for table clocks. Total fixed nonmanufacturing costs are $300,000: one-third common to both products, and one-third directly traceable to each product. Of the fixed costs (both manufacturing and nonmanufacturing), 20 percent are common to both sales regions, 40 percent are directly traceable to the West, and 40 percent are directly traceable to the Southwest.

Overhead is applied on the basis of direct labor hours. Normal volume is 75,000 hours (300,000 wall clocks, 900,000 table clocks), and the preceding actual overhead figures correspond to the budgeted figures used to compute the predetermined overhead rate. Any under- or overapplied overhead is closed to Cost of Goods Sold. Assume that any beginning finished goods inventory has the same unit costs as current production. The company uses LIFO to value inventories.

Required:

1. Compute the unit costs for each product using (a) absorption costing and (b) variable costing.

2. Prepare absorption-costing and variable-costing income statements for 1992. Reconcile the difference between the two income figures.

3. Prepare a segmented income statement on a variable-costing basis where segments are defined as products.

4. Prepare a segmented income statement on a variable-costing basis where segments are defined as sales regions.

P9–14   **Ethical Issues; Absorption Costing; Performance Measurement**   Ruth Swazey, division controller and CMA, was upset by a recent memo she received from the divisional manager, Paul Chesser. Ruth was scheduled to present the division's financial performance at headquarters in one week. In the memo, Paul had given Ruth some instructions for this upcoming report. In particular, she had been told to emphasize the significant improvement in the division's profits over last year. Ruth, however, didn't believe that there was any real underlying improvement in the division's performance and was reluctant to say otherwise. She knew that the increase in profits was because of Paul's conscious decision to produce for inventory.

In an earlier meeting, Paul had convinced his plant managers to produce more than they knew they could sell. He argued that by deferring some of this period's fixed costs, reported profits would jump. He pointed out two significant benefits. First, by increasing profits, the division could exceed the minimum level needed so that all the managers would qualify for the annual bonus. Second, by meeting the budgeted profit level, the division would be better able to compete for much-needed capital. Ruth had objected but had been overruled. The most persuasive counterargument was that the increase in inventory could be liquidated in the coming year as the economy improved. Ruth, however, considered this event unlikely. From past experience, she knew that it would take at least two years of improved market demand before the productive capacity of the division was exceeded.

Required:

1. Discuss the behavior of Paul Chesser, the divisional manager. Was the decision to produce for inventory an ethical one?

2. What should Ruth Swazey do? Should she comply with the directive to emphasize the increase in profits? If not, what options does she have?

3. In the Appendix to Chapter 1, ethical standards for management accountants were listed. Identify any standards that apply in this situation.

■ MANAGERIAL DECISION CASE

Variable Costing versus Absorption Costing   Norma Richardson, manager of a division specializing in concrete pipe and concrete blocks, had just been rebuffed by Eric Hipple, president of the company. Eric had called a meeting of all divisional managers to discuss the downturn in business the company had been experiencing during the past two years. Eric had come down hard on the managers, pointing out that their jobs would be on the line if some immediate improvements were not forthcoming.

Norma, acting as spokesperson for the divisional managers, had tried to explain to Eric why revenues and profits were declining. In the divisional managers' view, business was suffering because residential and commercial construction was down. With the slump in the construction business, competition had intensified. Norma indicated that her division had lost several bids to competitors who were bidding below the full cost of the product. Since company policy prohibited divisional managers from accepting any jobs below full cost, these bids were lost. Norma, on behalf of the managers, requested a change in company policy concerning bids. She proposed that the floor for bids be changed to variable cost rather than full cost. In times of economic distress, bids that cover at least their variable costs would make a positive contribution towards covering fixed costs and would help maintain the divisions' profits.

Norma also proposed that divisional income statements be changed to a variable-costing basis so that a better picture of divisional performance would be available. Additionally, income statements for individual products, organized on a variable-costing basis, would provide better information concerning product performance and would facilitate bidding.

Upon hearing the request, Eric Hipple flatly turned it down. Eric was convinced that all costs must be covered or the company would go under. "It's impossible to sell a product for less than what it costs and stay in business. Those companies that do so will be the first ones to go bankrupt. Also, I want to see the income produced by your divisions when all costs are considered—not just variable costs. I don't believe in variable costing. If any of you can prove to me that variable costing is a better approach, then I would consider changing."

Upon returning home, Norma decided to prepare more formal arguments to convince Eric of the value of variable costing. To help in building her case, she had the divisional controller supply the following information concerning the concrete block line ($8 \times 8 \times 16$ blocks):

Last quarter's production (and sales)	100,000
Productive capacity	140,000
Unit manufacturing cost:	
Direct materials	$0.22
Direct labor	0.14
Variable overhead	0.09
Fixed overhead[a]	0.10
Total	$0.55

[a]Based on the productive capacity of 140,000 units

Nonmanufacturing costs:		
Selling costs:		
Fixed	$10,000	
Variable	5% of sales	
Administrative (all fixed)		$20,000

Total fixed overhead costs were $14,000 (budgeted and actual). Variable overhead was incurred as expected. Overhead variances are closed to Cost of Goods Sold. The average selling price for the 100,000 units sold was $0.90.

Required:

1. Prepare absorption-costing and variable-costing income statements for the last quarter's results. Will this information help Norma in building her case?

2. Suppose that Norma consults her marketing manager and finds that the division could have produced and sold 30,000 more concrete blocks with a unit selling price of $0.54. Compute the gross margin on the sale of these additional 30,000 blocks, assuming a price of $0.54. Now compute the total contribution margin on the 30,000 blocks. Discuss why the two figures differ.

3. Prepare absorption-costing and variable-costing income statements that reflect the sale of the additional 30,000 units at $0.54. Which figure in Requirement 2, gross margin or contribution margin, gave the best indication of the impact of the 30,000 additional units on the division's profits? Explain.

4. What approach would you take to convince Eric that variable costing is a useful managerial tool? Does he have any basis for his contention that a company must cover its full costs and that income statements should reflect all costs, not just variable costs? Explain.

Relevant Costs for Special Decisions

■ **LEARNING OBJECTIVES**

After studying Chapter 10, you should be able to

1. Define and explain the concept of relevant costs.

2. Distinguish between relevant and irrelevant costs.

3. Use a relevant-costing decision model as an aid in choosing among competing alternatives.

4. Identify business situations in which relevant costing is appropriate.

5. Choose the optimal product mix when faced with one constrained resource.

6. Define and explain the key terms listed at the end of this chapter.

SCENARIO

Tidwell Products, Inc., manufactures potentiometers. A potentiometer is a device that adjusts electrical resistance. Potentiometers are used in switches and knobs, for example, to control the volume on a radio or to raise or lower the lights using a dimmer switch. Currently, all parts necessary for the assembly of the products are produced internally. The firm, in operation for five years, has a single plant located in Wichita, Kansas. The facilities for the manufacture of potentiometers are leased, with five years remaining on the lease. All equipment is owned by the company. Because of increases in demand, production has been expanded significantly over the five years of operation, straining the capacity of the leased facilities. Currently, the company needs more warehousing and office space, as well as more space for the production of plastic moldings. The current output of these moldings, used to make potentiometers, needs to be expanded to accommodate the increased demand for the main product.

Leo Tidwell, owner and president of Tidwell Products, has asked his vice-president of marketing, John Tidwell, and his vice-president of finance, Linda Thayn, to meet and discuss the problem of limited capacity. This is the second meeting the three have had concerning the problem. In the first meeting, Leo rejected Linda's proposal to build the company's own plant. He believed it was too risky to invest the capital necessary to build a plant at this stage of the company's development. The combination of leasing a larger facility and subleasing the current plant was also considered but was rejected; subleasing would be difficult, if not impossible. At the end of the first meeting, Leo asked John to explore the possibility of leasing another facility comparable to the current one. He also assigned Linda the task of identifying other possible solutions. As the second meeting began, Leo asked John to give a report on the leasing alternative.

"After some careful research," John responded, "I'm afraid that the idea of leasing an additional plant is not a very good one. Although we have some space problems, our current level of production doesn't justify another plant. In fact, I expect it will be at least five years before we need to be concerned about expanding into another facility like the one we have now. My market studies reveal a modest growth in sales over the next five years. All this growth can be absorbed by our current production capacity. The large increases in demand that we experienced the past five years are not likely to be repeated. Leasing another plant would be an overkill solution."

"Even modest growth will aggravate our current space problems," Leo observed. "As you both know, we are already operating three production shifts. But, John, you are right—except for plastic moldings, we could expand production, particularly during the graveyard shift. Linda, I hope that you have been successful in identifying some other possible solutions. Some fairly quick action is needed."

"Fortunately," Linda replied, "I believe that I have two feasible alternatives. One is to rent an additional building to be used for warehousing. By transferring our warehousing needs to the new building, we will free up internal space for offices and for expanding the production of plastic mold-ings. I have located a building within two miles of our plant that we could use. It has the capacity to handle our current needs and the modest growth that John mentioned. The second alternative may be even more attractive. We currently produce all the parts that we use to manufacture potentiome-ters, including shafts and bushings. In the last several months, the mar-ket has been flooded with these two parts. Prices have tumbled as a result. It might be better to buy shafts and bushings instead of making them. If we stop internal production of shafts and bushings, this would free up the space we need. Well, Leo, what do you think? Are these alternatives fea-sible? Or should I continue my search for additional solutions?"

"I like both alternatives," responded Leo. "In fact, they are exactly the types of solutions we are looking for. All we have to do now is choose the one best for our company. A key factor that must be examined is the cost of each alternative. Linda, you're the financial chief—prepare a report that de-tails the costs that impact this decision."

RELEVANT COSTS DEFINED

Linda identified two alternatives: (1) make all parts internally and rent a warehouse and (2) buy shafts and bushings (metal linings used as bearings for the shafts) from external suppliers and stop internal production of these parts. Both alternatives solve the space limitation problem faced by Tidwell Products. A significant input in choosing among the two alternatives is cost. All other things being equal, the alternative with the lower cost should be chosen. But what is meant by lower cost? How do we identify and define the costs that impact the decision?

relevant costs In choosing between the two alternatives, only the costs relevant to the decision should be considered. **Relevant costs** are future costs that differ across alternatives. All decisions relate to the future; accordingly, only future costs can be relevant to decisions. However, to be relevant, a cost must not only be a future cost, but also it must differ from one alternative to another. If a future cost is the same for more than one alternative, it has no effect on the decision. Such a cost is an *irrelevant* cost. The ability to identify relevant and irrelevant costs is an important decision-making skill.

Relevant Costs Illustrated

To illustrate the concept of relevant costs, consider Tidwell's make-or-buy alternatives. Assume that the cost of direct labor used to produce shafts and bushings is $150,000 per year (based on normal volume). Should this cost be a factor in the decision? Is the direct labor cost a future cost that differs across the two alternatives? It is certainly a future cost. To produce the shafts and bushings for another year requires the services of direct laborers, who must be paid. But does it differ across the two alternatives? If shafts and bushings are purchased from an external supplier, no internal production is needed. The services of the direct laborers can be eliminated, reducing the direct labor cost for shafts and bushings under this alternative to zero. Thus, the cost of direct labor differs across alternatives ($150,000 for the make alternative and $0 for the buy alternative). It is, therefore, a relevant cost.

Implicit in this analysis is the use of a past cost to estimate a future cost. The most recent cost of direct labor for normal activity was $150,000. This past cost was used as the estimate of next year's cost. Although past costs are never relevant, they are often used to predict what future costs will be.

Illustration of an Irrelevant Past Cost

Tidwell Products uses machinery to manufacture shafts and bushings. This machinery was purchased five years ago and is being depreciated at an annual rate of $125,000. Is this $125,000 a relevant cost? In other words, is depreciation a future cost that differs across the two alternatives?

sunk cost

Depreciation, in this case, represents an allocation of a cost already incurred. It is a **sunk cost**, an allocation of a past cost. Thus, regardless of which alternative is chosen, the acquisition cost of the machinery cannot be avoided. It is the same across both alternatives. Although we allocate this sunk cost to future periods and call that allocation *depreciation*, none of the original cost is avoidable. Sunk costs are past costs. They are always the same across alternatives and are, therefore, always irrelevant.

In choosing between the two alternatives, the acquisition cost of the machinery used to produce shafts and bushings and its associated depreciation should not be a factor. What was paid for the machinery in the past has no bearing on what Tidwell Products should do now. All that matters is how the two alternatives differ in their future costs.

Illustration of an Irrelevant Future Cost

Assume that the cost to lease the plant—$120,000—is allocated to different production departments, including the department that produces shafts and bushings, which receives $12,000 of the cost. Is this $12,000 cost relevant to the make-or-buy decision facing Tidwell?

The lease payment is a future cost since it must be paid during each of the next five years. But does the cost differ across the make-and-buy alternatives? Whatever option Tidwell chooses, the lease payment must be made—it is the same across both alternatives. The amount of the payment allocated to the remaining departments may change if production of shafts and bushings is stopped, but the level of the total payment is unaffected by the decision. It is therefore an irrelevant cost.

The example illustrates the importance of identifying allocations of common fixed costs. Allocations of common fixed costs can be safely classified as irrelevant since any choice usually does not affect the level of cost. The only effect may be a reallocation of those common fixed costs to fewer cost objects or segments.

We can now look at all three cost examples for the production of shafts and bushings to see which are relevant in deciding whether or not to continue production. Of the three, only direct labor cost is relevant since it is the only one that occurs if production continues but stops if production stops.

	Cost to Make	−	Cost Not to Make	=	Relevant Cost
Direct labor	$150,000		—		$150,000
Depreciation	125,000		$125,000		—
Allocated lease	12,000		12,000		—
	$287,000		$137,000		$150,000

The same concepts apply to benefits. One alternative may produce a different amount of future benefits than another alternative (for example, differences in future revenues). If future benefits differ across alternatives, then they are relevant and should be included in the analysis.

How should managers use this information about costs and benefits in making decisions? The rest of the chapter describes a recommended decision-making approach, identifies the limitations of the approach, and offers several examples of how relevant costing is used for special decisions. Additionally, special decisions relating to how a company should utilize scarce resources are considered.

■ DECISION-MAKING APPROACH

Identifying relevant costs is only part of the overall decision process that a manager should undertake—and it is not the first step. Four steps precede this one and three steps follow it. The eight steps describing the recommended decision-making process are as follows:

1. Recognize and define the problem.

2. Identify alternatives as possible solutions to the problem.

3. Eliminate alternatives that are clearly not feasible.

4. Identify the costs and benefits associated with each feasible alternative.

5. Classify costs and benefits as relevant or irrelevant and eliminate irrelevant ones from consideration.

6. Express all relevant costs and benefits on a periodically recurring basis.

7. Total the relevant costs and benefits for each alternative.

8. Select the alternative with the greatest overall benefit.

decision model

The eight steps define a simple decision model. A **decision model** is a set of procedures that, if followed, will lead to a decision. The first step is to recognize and define a specific problem. For example, the members of Tidwell's management team all recognized the need for additional space for warehousing, offices, and the production of plastic moldings. The amount of space needed, the reasons for the need, and how the additional space would be used are all important dimensions of the problem; however, how the additional space should be acquired is the central question that must be answered.

Step 2 is to list and consider possible solutions. Tidwell Products identified the following possible solutions:

1. Build its own facility with sufficient capacity to handle current and immediately foreseeable needs.

2. Lease a larger facility and sublease its current facility.

3. Lease an additional, similar facility.

4. Lease an additional building that would be used for warehousing only, thereby freeing up space for expanded production.

5. Buy shafts and bushings externally and use the space made available (previously used for producing these parts) to solve the space problem.

The next step (Step 3) is to eliminate those alternatives that are not feasible. The first alternative was eliminated because it carried too much risk for the company. The second alternative was not considered feasible because subleasing was not a viable option. The third was eliminated because it went too far in solving the space problem, and, presumably, was too expensive. The fourth and fifth alternatives were feasible. Both were perceived as being within the cost and risk constraints as well as being able to solve the space needs of the company.

Once the feasible set of alternatives is identified, the decision model calls for a cost-benefit analysis of each one. This analysis encompasses Steps 4 through 8. In identifying the total relevant costs associated with each alternative, it is important that these costs be expressed on a periodically recurring basis. To compare the relevant costs of each alternative, the same relationships must hold period after period for the time span being considered. This allows the comparison to be meaningful.

For example, assume that Tidwell Products cannot sell the machinery used to produce shafts and bushings if these parts are purchased externally. If the total relevant cost to make shafts and bushings and lease a warehouse is $480,000 per year, and the total relevant cost to buy the two parts is $500,000 per year, the make alternative is superior to the buy alternative. But this is true only if these same relationships hold over the entire time frame being considered. Suppose the lease on the warehouse is ten years, with the following costs for the make-and-purchase options:

Year	Make Alternative	Buy Alternative
1	$480,000	$500,000
2	480,000	500,000
.	.	.
.	.	.
10	480,000	500,000

In this case, the make alternative is more desirable than the buy alternative.[1]

But what if Tidwell Products can sell the machinery it uses to make the shafts and bushings for $180,000? How do we deal with this one-time benefit? It is relevant; it will occur in the future and will occur only for the buy alternative. It could be used to reduce the total relevant cost of the buy alternative in Year 1. In this case, the total relevant cost is $320,000 ($500,000 − $180,000) for the first year and $500,000 per year thereafter. The annual total relevant costs for each alternative now appear as follows:

Year	Make Alternative	Buy Alternative
1	$480,000	$320,000
2	480,000	500,000
.	.	.
.	.	.
10	480,000	500,000

Including one-time costs or benefits can distort the analysis. Which of the two alternatives is better? In Year 1, the buy alternative is, but for subsequent years, the make alternative is superior. Is the difference from years 2 through 10 enough for the make alternative to overcome the $180,000 benefit that the buy alternative experiences in Year 1? Over ten years, the make alternative's total cost is $4.8 million; the buy alternative's total cost is $4.82 million. Does this indicate that the make alternative is superior?

Summing costs for each alternative over the ten years ignores the time value of money. Under the buy alternative, Tidwell Products will receive $180,000 at the beginning of the first year from selling the machinery. We must assume that the company will use the money productively. A reasonable assumption is that the money will be invested by the company in a ten-year project that produces a stream of equal annual payments. Assume that Tidwell Products invests the $180,000 in a project with a ten-year life that produces a recurring benefit of $30,000 per year. This recurring benefit reduces

---

[1]For the make alternative to dominate, the cost to make must be less than the cost to buy for each year of the ten-year horizon. The pattern given is only one of many that could hold. Relevant cost analysis compares the costs for only one point in time, but it assumes that the relative cost relationships will continue to hold for future periods affected by the decision.

the cost of the buy alternative to $470,000 per year ($500,000 − $30,000). Since the cost of the make alternative is $480,000 per year, the buy alternative is now superior in every year. Comparability in annual costs is reestablished by assessing the periodic effects that the one-time benefit produces. The integrity of the relevant-costing model is restored.

It should be mentioned that when the cash flow patterns become complicated for competing alternatives, it becomes difficult to produce a stream of equal cash flows for each alternative. In such a case, more sophisticated procedures can and should be used for the analysis. These procedures are discussed in later chapters, which deal with the long-run investment decisions referred to as *capital budgeting*.

Qualitative Factors

In the scenario, the buy alternative is less costly and would be chosen. However, actual decisions usually involve other factors besides cost, which receives so much emphasis in the above decision model. Even given the favorable quantitative position of buying versus making, it is still possible that the make alternative would be chosen.

Relevant cost analysis can be and probably should be viewed as only one input for the final decision. A number of qualitative factors can significantly affect a manager's decision making. For example, in the make-or-buy decision facing Tidwell Products, Leo Tidwell likely would be concerned with such qualitative considerations as the quality of the shafts and bushings purchased externally, the reliability of supply sources, the expected stability of prices over the next several years, labor relations, community image, and so on. To illustrate the possible impact of qualitative factors on the make-or-buy decision, consider the first two factors, quality and reliability of supply.

If the quality of shafts and bushings is significantly less if purchased externally than what is available internally, the quantitative advantage from purchasing may be more fictitious than real. Settling for lower-quality materials may adversely affect the quality of the potentiometers, thus harming sales. Because of this, Tidwell Products may choose to continue to produce the parts internally.

Similarly, if supply sources are not reliable, production schedules could be interrupted, and customer orders could arrive late. These factors can increase labor costs and overhead and hurt sales. Again, depending on the perceived tradeoffs, Tidwell products may decide that internal production of the parts is better than purchasing them, even if relevant cost analysis gives the initial advantage to purchasing.

While relevant cost analysis plays a key role in decision making, then, it does have its limitations. Relevant cost information is not all the information a manager should consider. Other information is often needed to make an informed decision. If the qualitative factors are essentially equal across alternatives, however, relevant costs become the deciding factor instead of being just one input among several.

■ ILLUSTRATIVE EXAMPLES OF RELEVANT COST APPLICATIONS

Make-or-Buy Decisions

make-or-buy decisions

Managers are often faced with the decision of whether to make or buy components used in manufacture. Indeed, management periodically should evaluate past decisions concerning production. Conditions upon which prior decisions were based may have changed and, as a result, a different approach may be required. Periodic evaluations, of course, are not the only source of these **make-or-buy decisions**. Frequently, as with Tidwell Products, the decision is motivated by an indirectly related, underlying problem.

To illustrate more fully the cost analysis of a make-or-buy problem, assume that Swasey Manufacturing currently produces an electronic component used in one of its printers. In one year, Swasey will switch production to another type of printer and the electronic component will not be used. However, for the coming year, Swasey must produce 10,000 of these parts to support the production requirements for the old printer. The costs associated with the production of these 10,000 parts are as follows:

	Total Cost	*Unit Cost*
Rental of equipment	$12,000	$1.20
Equipment depreciation	2,000	0.20
Direct materials	10,000	1.00
Direct labor	20,000	2.00
Variable overhead	8,000	0.80
General fixed overhead	30,000	3.00
Total	$82,000	$8.20

Most of the equipment is rented. However, one specialized piece of machinery had to be custom made and was purchased. Rental equipment can be returned at any time without penalty; the company is charged only for the time the equipment is held. The specialized machinery will not be fully depreciated at the end of the year; however, the company plans to scrap it since it cannot be sold. The company recently purchased sufficient materials for 5,000 components. There is no alternative use for the materials. Variable overhead is applied to the electronic component at $0.40 per direct labor dollar. General fixed overhead for the plant totals $1 million. General fixed overhead is assigned to products based on the space occupied by each product. The manufacturing facilities for the component under consideration occupy 6,000 of the plant's 200,000 square feet. Thus, $30,000 of the general fixed overhead is allocated to the electronic component (0.03 × $1,000,000).

Swasey has been approached by a potential supplier of the component. The supplier will build the electronic component to Swasey's specifications for $4.75 per unit. Should Swasey Manufacturing make or buy the component?

At first glance, the opportunity to buy the component seems very attractive—$4.75 per unit is considerably less than the full manufacturing cost of $8.20 per unit. However, as we already know, some of the manufacturing costs should not be considered in the decision.

The problem and the feasible alternatives are both readily identifiable. Since the horizon for the decision is only one period, there is no need to be concerned about periodically recurring costs. Relevant costing is particularly useful for short-run analysis. We simply need to identify the relevant costs, total them, and make a choice (assuming no overriding qualitative concerns).

Of the cost items listed above, depreciation can be eliminated; it is a sunk cost. Since the direct materials already purchased have no alternative use, half of the cost of total direct materials is also a sunk cost. General overhead is not relevant either. The $30,000 is an allocation of a common fixed cost that will continue even if the component is purchased externally.

All other costs are relevant. The cost of renting the equipment is relevant since it will not be needed if the part is bought externally. Similarly, direct labor, the remaining 5,000 units of direct materials, and variable overhead are all relevant; they would not be incurred if the component is bought externally. Of course, the purchase cost is also relevant. If the component is made, this cost would not be incurred. A listing of the total relevant costs for each alternative follows:

	Make Alternative	*Buy Alternative*
Rental of equipment	$12,000	$ —
Direct materials	5,000	—
Variable overhead	8,000	—
Direct labor	20,000	—
Purchase cost	—	47,500
Total relevant cost	$45,000	$47,500

The analysis shows that making the product produces a $2,500 advantage over buying it. The offer of the supplier should be rejected.

The same analysis can be done on a unit-cost basis. Once the relevant costs are identified, relevant unit costs can be compared. For this example, these costs are $4.50 ($45,000/10,000) for the make alternative and $4.75 for the buy alternative. Identifying the relevant unit cost for the make alternative permits a direct comparison with the quoted outside unit price.

Keep-or-Drop Decisions

Often a manager needs to determine whether or not a segment, such as a product line, should be kept or dropped. Segmented reports prepared on a **keep-or-drop decisions** variable-costing basis provide valuable information for these **keep-or-drop decisions**. Both the segment's contribution margin and its segment margin are useful in evaluating the performance of segments. However, while segmented reports provide useful information for keep-or-drop decisions, relevant costing describes how the information should be used to arrive at a decision.

To illustrate, consider Norton Materials, Inc., which produces concrete blocks, bricks, and roofing tile. The controller has prepared the following estimated income statement for 1992 (in thousands of dollars):

	Blocks	Bricks	Tile	Total
Sales revenue	$ 500	$ 800	$ 150	$1,450
Less: Variable expenses	(250)	(480)	(140)	(870)
Contribution margin	250	320	10	580
Less direct fixed expenses:				
Salaries	(37)	(40)	(35)	(112)
Advertising	(10)	(10)	(10)	(30)
Depreciation	(53)	(40)	(10)	(103)
Total	$(100)	$ (90)	$ (55)	$ (245)
Segment margin	$ 150	$ 230	$ (45)	$ 335
Less: Common fixed expenses				(125)
Net income				$ 210

The projected performance of the roofing tile line shows a negative segment margin. This would represent the third consecutive year of poor performance for that line. The president of Norton Materials, Tom Blackburn, concerned about this poor performance, is trying to decide whether to drop or keep the roofing tile line.

His first reaction is to take steps to increase the sales revenue of roofing tiles. He is considering an aggressive sales promotion coupled with an increase in the selling price. The marketing manager thinks that this approach would be fruitless, however; the market is saturated and the level of competition too keen to hold out any hope for increasing the firm's market share. An increase in the selling price would almost certainly result in a decrease in sales revenue.

Increasing the product line's profitability through cost cutting is not feasible either. Costs were cut the past two years to reduce the loss to its present anticipated level. Any further reductions would lower the quality of the product and adversely affect sales.

With no hope for improving the profit performance of the line beyond its projected level, Tom has decided to drop it. He reasons that the firm will lose a total of $10,000 in contribution margin but save $45,000 by dismissing the line's supervisor and eliminating its advertising budget. (The depreciation cost of $10,000 is not relevant since it represents an allocation of a sunk cost.) Thus, dropping the product line has a $35,000 advantage over keeping it. Before finalizing the decision, Tom decided to notify the marketing manager and the production supervisor. The following memo was sent to both individuals:

MEMO

TO: Karen Golding, Marketing, and Larry Olsen, Production
FROM: Tom Blackburn, President
SUBJECT: Tentative Decision Concerning the Production of Roofing Tiles
DATE: March 14, 1992

Since there is no realistic expectation of improving the profitability of the roofing tile line, I have reluctantly decided to discontinue its production. I realize that this decision will have a negative impact on the community since our work force will need to be reduced. I am also sympathetic about the disruption this may cause in the personal lives of many employees.

However, we must be prepared to take actions that are in the best interests of the firm. By eliminating the roofing tile line, we can improve the firm's cash position by $35,000 per year. To support this decision, I am including the following analysis (focusing only on the tile segment):

	Keep	Drop
Sales	$ 150	$—
Less: Variable expenses	(140)	—
Contribution margin	$ 10	$—
Less: Advertising	(10)	—
Less: Cost of supervision	(35)	—
Total relevant benefit (loss)	$ (35)	$ 0

I have included only future costs and benefits that differ across the two alternatives. Depreciation on the tile equipment is not relevant since it is simply an allocation of a sunk cost. Also, the level of common fixed costs is unchanged regardless of whether we keep or drop the tile line.

At this point, I view the decision as tentative and welcome any response. Perhaps I am overlooking something that would affect the decision. Please respond as soon as possible.

Keep or Drop with Complementary Effects   In response to the memo, the marketing manager wrote that dropping the roofing tile line would lower sales of blocks by 10 percent and bricks by 8 percent. She explained that many customers buy roofing tile at the same time they purchase blocks or bricks. Some will go elsewhere if they cannot buy both products at the same location.

Shortly after receiving this response, Tom Blackburn decided to repeat the analysis, factoring in the effect that dropping the tile line would have on the sales of the other two lines. He decided to use total firm sales and total costs for each alternative. As before, depreciation and common fixed costs were excluded from the analysis on the basis of irrelevancy.

Dropping the product line reduces total sales by $264,000: $50,000 (0.10 × $500,000) for blocks, $64,000 (0.08 × $800,000) for the bricks, and $150,000 for roofing tiles. Similarly, total variable expenses are reduced by $203,400:

$25,000 (0.10 × $250,000) for blocks, $38,400 (0.08 × $480,000) for bricks, and $140,000 for tile. Thus, total contribution margin is reduced by $60,600 ($264,000 − $203,400). Since dropping the tile line saves only $45,000 in supervision costs and advertising, the net effect is a disadvantage of $15,600 ($45,000 − $60,600). The following is a summary of the analysis using the new information (in thousands):

	Keep	Drop	Difference
Sales	$1,450.00	$1,186.00	$ 264.00
Less: Variable expenses	(870.00)	(666.60)	(203.40)
Contribution margin	$ 580.00	$ 519.40	$ 60.60
Less: Advertising	(30.00)	(20.00)	(10.00)
Less: Cost of supervision	(112.00)	(77.00)	(35.00)
Total	$ 438.00	422.40	$ 15.60

Tom was pleased to find the outcome favoring production of the roofing tile. The unpleasant task of dismissing some of his work force was no longer necessary. However, just as he was preparing to write a second memo announcing his new decision, he received Larry Olsen's written response to his first memo.

Keep or Drop with Alternative Use of Facilities The production supervisor's response was somewhat different. He agreed that roofing tile should be eliminated but suggested that it be replaced with the production of floor tile. He gave assurances that existing machinery could be converted to produce this new product with little or no cost. He had also contacted the marketing manager about the marketability of floor tile and included this assessment in his response.

The marketing manager saw the market for floor tile as stronger and less competitive than for roofing tile. However, the other two lines would still lose sales at the same rate; producing floor tile does not change that result. The following estimated financial statement for floor tile was also submitted (in thousands of dollars):

Sales	$100
Less: Variable expenses	(40)
Contribution margin	$ 60
Less: Direct fixed expenses	(55)
Segment margin	$ 5

Tom Blackburn was now faced with a third alternative: replacing the roofing tile with floor tile. Should the roofing tile line be kept or should it be dropped and replaced with the floor tile?

From his prior analysis, Tom knows that dropping the roofing tile decreases the firm's contribution margin by $60,600. Producing the floor tile will generate $60,000 more in contribution margin according to the estimate. Dropping the roofing tile line and replacing it with floor tile, then, will cause a $600 net decrease in total contribution margin ($60,600 − $60,000). The same outcome can be developed by directly comparing the relevant benefits and costs of the two alternatives (dollars expressed in thousands).

	Keep	*Drop and Replace*	*Difference*
Sales	$1,450.00	$1,286.00[a]	$ 164.00
Variable expenses	(870.00)	(706.60)[b]	(163.40)
Contribution margin	$ 580.00	$ 579.40	($ 0.60)

[a]$1,450 − $150 − $50 − $64 + $100
[b]$870 − $140 − $25 − $38.4 + $40

The Norton Materials example again illustrates the decision process underlying relevant costing. First, a problem was identified and defined (the poor performance of the roofing tile product line). Next, possible solutions were listed and those that were not feasible were eliminated. For example, increasing sales or further decreasing costs were both rejected as feasible solutions. Three feasible solutions were examined: (1) keeping the product line, (2) dropping it, and (3) dropping the product line and replacing it with another product. An analysis of the costs and benefits of the feasible alternatives led to the selection of the preferred alternative (keeping the product line).

The example provides some insights beyond the simple application of the relevant costing decision model. The initial analysis, which focused on two feasible alternatives, led to a tentative decision to drop the product line. Additional information provided by the marketing manager led to a reversal of the first decision. Before that decision could be implemented, the manager was made aware of a third feasible alternative, which required additional analysis.

Often managers do not possess all the information necessary to make the best decision. They also may not be able to identify all feasible solutions. Managers benefit from gathering all the information available before finalizing a decision. They should also attempt to identify as many feasible solutions as possible. As the example clearly illustrates, limited information can result in poor decisions. Also, if the set of feasible solutions is too narrow, the best solution may never be selected simply because the manager has not thought of it. Managers can benefit from obtaining input from others who are familiar with the problem. By so doing, both the set of information and the set of feasible solutions can be expanded. The result is improved decision making.

Special-Order Decisions

Price discrimination laws require that firms sell identical products at the same price to competing customers in the same market. These restrictions do not apply to competitive bids or to noncompeting customers. Bid prices can vary to customers in the same market, and firms often have the opportunity to consider special orders from potential customers in markets not ordinarily **special-order** served. **Special-order decisions** focus on whether a specially priced order **decisions** should be accepted or rejected. These orders often can be attractive, especially when the firm is operating below its maximum productive capacity.

Suppose, for example, that an ice-cream company is operating at 80 percent of its productive capacity. The company has a capacity of 20 million half-gallon units. The company produces only premium ice cream. The total costs associated with producing and selling 16 million units are as follows (in thousands of dollars):

	Total	Unit Cost
Variable costs:		
Dairy ingredients	$11,200	$0.70
Sugar	1,600	0.10
Flavoring	2,400	0.15
Direct labor	4,000	0.25
Packaging	3,200	0.20
Commissions	320	0.02
Distribution	480	0.03
Other	800	0.05
Total variable costs	$24,000	$1.50
Fixed costs:		
Salaries	$ 960	$0.060
Depreciation	320	0.020
Utilities	80	0.005
Taxes	32	0.002
Other	160	0.010
Total fixed costs	$ 1,552	$0.097
Total costs	$25,552	$1.597
Wholesale selling price	$32,000	$2.00

An ice-cream distributor from a geographic region not normally served by the company has offered to buy 2 million units at $1.55 per unit, provided its own label can be attached to the product. The distributor has also agreed to pay the transportation costs. Since the distributor approached the company directly, there is no sales commission. As the manager of the ice-cream company, would you accept this order or reject it?

The offer of $1.55 is well below the normal selling price of $2.00; in fact, it is even below the total unit cost. Nonetheless, accepting the order may be profitable for the company. The company does have idle capacity, and the order will not displace other units being produced to sell at the normal price. Additionally, many of the costs are not relevant; fixed costs will continue regardless of whether the order is accepted or rejected.

If the order is accepted, a benefit of $1.55 per unit will be realized that otherwise wouldn't be. However, all of the variable costs except for distribution ($0.03) and commissions ($0.02) also will be incurred, producing a cost of $1.45 per unit. Therefore, the company will see a net benefit of $0.10 ($1.55 − $1.45). For an order of 2 million half gallons, the company's profits would increase by $200,000 ($0.10 × 2,000,000). The relevant cost analysis can be summarized as follows:

	Accept	*Reject*
Revenues	$ 3,100,000	$—
Dairy ingredients	(1,400,000)	—
Sugar	(200,000)	—
Flavorings	(300,000)	—
Direct labor	(500,000)	—
Packaging	(400,000)	—
Other	(100,000)	—
Total	$ 200,000	$ 0

Decisions to Sell or Process Further

Joint products have common processes and costs of production up to a split-off point. At that point, they become distinguishable. For example, certain minerals such as copper and gold may both be found in a given ore. The ore must be mined, crushed, and treated before the copper and gold are separated. The point of separation is called the **split-off point**. The costs of mining, crushing, and treatment are common to both products.

split-off point

Often joint products are sold at the split-off point. Sometimes it is more profitable to process a joint product further, beyond the split-off point, prior to selling it. Determining whether to **sell or process further** is an important decision that a manager must make.

sell or process further

To illustrate, consider Appletime Corporation. Appletime is a large corporate farm that specializes in growing apples. Each plot produces approximately one ton of apples. The trees in each plot must be sprayed, fertilized, watered, and pruned. When the apples are ripened, workers are hired to pick them. The apples are then transported to a warehouse, where they are washed and sorted. The approximate cost of all these activities (including processing) is $300 per ton per year.

Apples are sorted into three grades (A, B, and C) determined by size and blemishes. Large apples without blemishes (bruises, cuts, wormholes, and so on) are sorted into one bin and classified as Grade A. Small apples without blemishes are sorted into a second bin and classified as Grade B. All remaining apples are placed in a third bin and classified as Grade C. Every ton of apples produces 800 pounds of Grade A, 600 pounds of Grade B, and 600 pounds of Grade C.

Grade A apples are sold to large supermarkets for $0.40 per pound. Grade B apples are packaged in five-pound bags and sold to supermarkets for

$1.30 per bag. (The cost of each bag is $0.05.) Grade C apples are processed further and made into applesauce. The sauce is sold in 16-ounce cans for $0.75 each. The cost of processing is $0.10 per pound of apples. The final output is 500 16-ounce cans. Exhibit 10–1 summarizes the process.

A large supermarket chain recently requested that Appletime supply 16-ounce cans of apple pie filling for which the chain was willing to pay $0.90 per can. Appletime determined that the Grade B apples would be suitable for this purpose and estimated that it would cost $0.20 per pound to process the apples into pie filling. The output would be 500 16-ounce cans.

In deciding whether to sell Grade B apples at split-off or to process them further and sell them as pie filling, the common costs of spraying, pruning, and so on, are not relevant. The company must pay the $300 per ton for these activities regardless of whether it sells at split-off or processes further. However, the revenues earned at split-off are likely to differ from the revenues that would be received if the Grade B apples were sold as pie filling. Therefore revenues are a relevant consideration. Similarly, the processing costs occur only if further processing takes place. Hence, processing costs are relevant.

Since there are 600 pounds of Grade B apples at split-off, Appletime sells 120 five-pound bags at a net per-unit price of $1.25 ($1.30 − $0.05). Thus the total net revenues at split-off are $150 ($1.25 × 120). If the apples are processed into pie filling, then the total revenues are $450 ($0.90 × 500). Therefore, the incremental revenues from processing further are $300 ($450 − $150). The incremental costs of processing are $120 ($0.20 × 600 pounds). Since revenues increase by $300 and costs by only $120, the net benefit of

EXHIBIT 10–1
Appletime's Joint Process

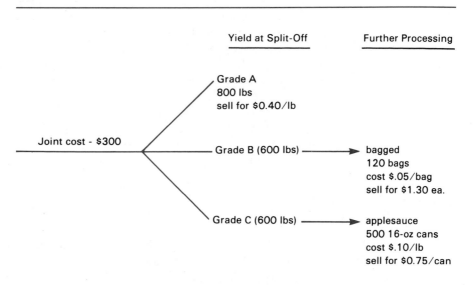

processing further is $180. Thus, Appletime should process the Grade B apples into pie filling. The analysis is summarized as follows:

	Sell	Process further	Difference
Revenues	$150	$ 450	$ 300
Processing cost	—	(120)	(120)
Total	$150	$ 330	$ 180

▪ PRODUCT MIX DECISIONS

In the example above, of every 2,000 pounds of apples harvested, 800 were Grade A, 600 were Grade B, and 600 were Grade C. Although the relative amounts of each type of apple can be influenced to some extent by the procedures followed in spraying, watering, fertilizing, and so on, the mix of apples is largely beyond Appletime's control. However, many organizations have total discretion in choosing their product mix. Moreover, decisions about product mix can have a significant impact on an organization's profitability.

Each mix represents an alternative that carries with it an associated profit level. A manager should choose the alternative that maximizes total profits. Since fixed costs do not vary with activity level, the total fixed costs of a firm would be the same for all possible mixes and, therefore, are not relevant to the decision. Thus, a manager needs to choose the alternative that maximizes total contribution margin.

Assume, for example, that Jorgenson Company produces two types of gears: X and Y, with unit contribution margins of $25 and $10, respectively. If the firm possesses unlimited resources and the demand for each product is unlimited, then the product mix decision is simple—produce an infinite number of each product. Unfortunately, every firm faces limited resources and limited demand for each product. These limitations are called **constraints**. A manager must choose the optimal mix given the constraints found within the firm.

constraints

Assuming that Jorgenson can sell all that is produced, some may argue that only Gear X should be produced and sold—it has the larger contribution margin. However, this solution is not necessarily the best. The selection of the optimal mix can be significantly affected by the relationships of the constrained resources to the individual products. These relationships affect the quantity of each product that can be produced and, consequently, the total contribution margin that can be earned. This point is most vividly illustrated with one resource constraint.

One Constrained Resource

Assume that each gear must be notched by a special machine. The firm owns eight machines that together provide 40,000 hours of machine time per year. Gear X requires two hours of machine time, and Gear Y requires one half hour of machine time. Assuming no other constraints, what is the optimal mix of gears? Since each unit of Gear X requires two hours of machine time, 20,000 units of Gear X can be produced per year (40,000/2). At $25 per unit, Jorgenson can earn a total contribution margin of $500,000. On the other hand, Gear Y requires only 0.5 hours of machine time per unit; therefore, 80,000 (40,000/0.5) gears can be produced. At $10 per unit, the total contribution margin is $800,000. Producing only Gear Y yields a higher profit level than producing only Gear X—even though the unit contribution margin for Gear X is 2.5 times larger than that for Gear Y.

The contribution margin per unit of each product is not the critical concern. The contribution margin per unit of *scarce resource* is the deciding factor. The product yielding the highest contribution margin per machine hour should be selected. Gear X earns $12.50 per machine hour ($25/2), but Gear Y earns $20 per machine hour ($10/0.5). Thus, the optimal mix is 80,000 units of Gear Y and none of Gear X.

Multiple Constrained Resources

The presence of only one constrained resource is unrealistic. All organizations face multiple constraints: limitations of raw materials, limitations of labor inputs, limited demand for each product, and so on. The solution of the product mix problem in the presence of multiple constraints is considerably more complicated and requires the use of a specialized mathematical technique known as *linear programming*, which is defined and illustrated in the Appendix to this chapter.

■ SUMMARY OF LEARNING OBJECTIVES

1. **Define and explain the concept of relevant costs.** Managers are often faced with the need to choose among competing alternatives, such as whether a component should be produced internally or purchased from an external supplier. In making this type of decision, only those costs and benefits that impact the decision should be considered. These are referred to as *relevant* costs and benefits. They are those future costs and benefits that differ across alternatives.

2. **Distinguish between relevant and irrelevant costs.** Relevant costs are those costs that can be affected by the decision and that differ across alternatives. Irrelevant costs are sunk costs (past outlays) or are costs that are incurred no matter which alternative is chosen.

3. **Use a relevant-costing decision model as an aid in choosing among competing alternatives.** The decision-making model described in this chapter consists of eight steps: problem recognition, alternative identification, elimination of unfeasible alternatives, determination of costs/benefits of each alternative, classification of costs/benefits as relevant or irrelevant, expression of all relevant costs/benefits on a periodically recurring basis, totaling relevant

costs and benefits for each alternative, and selection of the alternative with the greatest benefit.

In using cost analysis to choose among alternatives, managers should take steps to ensure that all important feasible alternatives are being considered and that all relevant costs and benefits are identified. Additionally, managers should use cost analysis as only one input. Often, qualitative factors will override the formal cost analysis.

4. **Identify business situations in which relevant costing is appropriate.** Several examples illustrating the application of the relevant costing model were given within the chapter. Applications were illustrated for make-or-buy decisions, keep-or-drop decisions, special-order decisions, and sell-or-process-further decisions. Product-mix decisions were also discussed. The list of applications is by no means exhaustive but was given to illustrate the scope and power of relevant costing analysis.

5. **Choose the optimal product mix when faced with one constrained resource.** In dealing with a resource constraint, it is important to phrase the product contribution margin in terms of contribution margin per unit of constrained resource.

▪ KEY TERMS

Constraint A mathematical expression that expresses a resource limitation. (p. 474)

Constraint set The collection of all constraints that pertain to a particular optimization problem. (p. 479)

Decision model A specific set of procedures that, when followed, produces a decision. (p. 462)

Feasible set of solutions The collection of all feasible solutions. (p. 479)

Feasible solution A product mix that satisfies all constraints. (p. 479)

Keep-or-drop decision A relevant costing analysis that focuses on keeping or dropping a segment of a business. (p. 466)

Make-or-buy decision Relevant costing analysis that focuses on whether a component should be made internally or purchased externally. (p. 465)

Objective function The function to be optimized, usually a profit function; thus, optimization usually means maximizing profits. (p. 478)

Optimal solution The feasible solution that produces the best value for the objective function (the largest value if seeking to maximize the objective function; the minimum otherwise). (p. 479)

Relevant costs Future costs that change across alternatives. (p. 459)

Sell or process further Relevant costing analysis that focuses on whether a product should be processed beyond the split-off point. (p. 472)

Simplex method An algorithm that identifies the optimal solution for a linear programming problem. (p. 480)

Special-order decision   Relevant costing analysis that focuses on whether a specially priced order should be accepted or rejected. (p. 471)

Split-off point   Point at which products become distinguishable after passing through a common process. (p. 472)

Sunk cost   A cost for which the outlay has already been made and that cannot be affected by a future decision. (p. 460)

■ REVIEW PROBLEM

Rianne Company produces a light fixture with the following unit cost:

Direct materials	$2
Direct labor	1
Variable overhead	3
Fixed overhead	2
Unit cost	$8

The production capacity is 300,000 units per year. Because of a depressed housing market, the company expects to produce only 180,000 fixtures for the coming year. The company also has fixed selling costs totaling $500,000 per year and variable selling costs of $1 per unit sold. The fixtures normally sell for $12 each.

At the beginning of the year, a customer from a geographic region outside the area normally served by the company offered to buy 100,000 fixtures for $7 each. The customer also offered to pay all transportation expenses. Since there would be no sales commissions involved, this order would not have any variable selling expenses.

Required:

Should the company accept the order? Provide both qualitative and quantitative justification for your decision. Assume that no other orders are expected beyond the regular business and the special order.

Solution:

The company is faced with a problem of idle capacity. Accepting the special order would bring production up to near capacity. There are two options: accept or reject the order. If the order is accepted, then the company could avoid laying off employees and would enhance and maintain its community image. However, the order is considerably below the normal selling price of $12. Because the price is so low, the company needs to assess the potential impact of the sale on its regular customers and on the profitability of the firm. Considering the fact that the customer is located in a region not usually served by the company, the likelihood of an adverse impact on regular business is not high. Thus, the qualitative factors seem to favor acceptance.

The only remaining consideration is the profitability of the special order. To assess profitability, the firm should identify the relevant costs and benefits of each alternative. This analysis is as follows:

	Accept	*Reject*
Revenues	$ 700,000	$—
Direct materials	(200,000)	—
Direct labor	(100,000)	—
Variable overhead	(300,000)	—
Total benefits	$ 100,000	$ 0

Accepting the order would increase profits by $100,000 (the fixed overhead and selling expenses are all irrelevant since they are the same across both alternatives). Conclusion: The order should be accepted since both qualitative and quantitative factors favor it.

▪ APPENDIX: LINEAR PROGRAMMING

Linear programming is a method that searches among possible solutions until it finds the optimal solution. The theory of linear programming permits many solutions to be ignored. In fact, all but a finite number of solutions are eliminated by the theory, with the search then limited to the resulting finite set.

To illustrate how linear programming can be used to solve a problem of multiple constrained resources, we will use the earlier example of the product mix for Jorgenson Company. Assume that there are demand constraints for both Gear X and Gear Y. For Gear X, no more than 15,000 units can be sold and for Gear Y no more than 40,000 units. As before, the objective is to maximize Jorgenson's total contribution margin subject to the constraints faced by Jorgenson.

The objective can be expressed mathematically. Let X be the number of units produced and sold of Gear X and Y stand for Gear Y. Since the unit contribution margins are $25 and $10 for X and Y, respectively, the total contribution margin (Z) can be expressed as

$$Z = \$25X + \$10Y \tag{10.1}$$

objective function   Equation 10.1 is called the *objective function*.

Jorgenson also has three constraints. One is the limited machine hours available for production, and the other two reflect the demand limitations for each product. Consider the machine-hour constraint first. Two machine hours are used for each unit of Gear X, and 0.5 machine hours are used for each unit of Gear Y. Thus, the total machine hours used can be expressed as $2X + 0.5Y$. The maximum of 40,000 machine hours available can be expressed mathematically as follows:

$$2X + 0.5Y \leq 40,000 \tag{10.2}$$

The two demand constraint limitations can also be expressed mathematically:

$$X \leq 15,000 \tag{10.3}$$

$$Y \leq 40,000 \tag{10.4}$$

Jorgenson's problem is to select the number of units of X and Y that maximize total contribution margin subject to the constraints in Equations 10.2, 10.3, and 10.4. This problem can be expressed in the following way, which is the standard formulation for a linear programming problem (often referred to as a *linear programming model*):

$$\text{Max } Z = \$25X + \$10Y$$

subject to

$$2X + 0.5Y \leq 40{,}000$$
$$X \leq 15{,}000$$
$$Y \leq 40{,}000$$
$$X \geq 0$$
$$Y \geq 0$$

The last two constraints are called *nonnegativity constraints* and simply reflect the reality that negative quantities of a product cannot be produced. All

constraint set

constraints, taken together, are referred to as the **constraint set**.

feasible solution

feasible set of
solutions

A **feasible solution** is a solution that satisfies the constraints in the linear programming model. The collection of all feasible solutions is called the *feasible set of solutions*. For example, producing and selling 10,000 units of Gear X and 20,000 units of Gear Y would be a feasible solution and a member of the feasible set. This product mix uses 30,000 machine hours [(2 × 10,000) + (0.5 × 20,000)], which is under the limit for machine hours. Additionally, the company can sell the indicated amounts since they do not exceed the demand constraints for each product. If this mix is selected, the company would earn a contribution margin totaling $450,000 [($25 × 10,000) + ($10 × 20,000)].

However, the mix of 10,000 units of X and 20,000 units of Y is not the best mix. One better solution would be to produce and sell 12,000 units of X and 30,000 units of Y. This mix uses 39,000 machine hours [(2 × 12,000) + (0.5 × 30,000)] and produces a total contribution margin of $600,000 [($25 × 12,000) + ($10 × 30,000)]. This feasible solution is better than the first because it produces $150,000 more in profits. There are, however, even better feasible solutions. The objective is to identify the best. The best feasible solution—the one that maxi-

optimal solution

mizes the total contribution margin—is called the **optimal solution**.

When there are only two products, the optimal solution can be identified by graphing. Since solving the problem by graphing provides considerable insight into the way linear programming problems are solved, the Jorgenson problem will be solved in this way.

Four steps are followed in solving the problem graphically.

1. Graph each constraint.

2. Identify the feasible set of solutions.

3. Identify all corner-point values in the feasible set.

4. Select the corner point that yields the largest value for the objective function.

The graph of each constraint for the Jorgenson problem is shown in Exhibit 10–2. The nonnegativity constraints put the graph in the first quadrant. The other constraints are graphed by assuming that equality holds. Since each constraint is a linear equation, the graph is obtained by identifying two points on the line, plotting those points, and connecting them.

A feasible area for each constraint (except for the nonnegativity constraints) is determined by everything that lies below (or to the left) of the resulting line. The *feasible set* or *region* is the intersection of each constraint's feasible area. The feasible set is shown by the figure *ABCDE*; it includes the boundary of the figure.

There are five corner points: *A, B, C, D,* and *E*. Their values, obtained directly from the graph, are (0,0) for *A,* (15,0) for *B,* (15,20) for *C,* (10,40) for *D,* and (0,40) for *E*. The impact of these values on the objective function is as follows (expressed in thousands):

Corner Point	X-value	Y-value	Z = \$25X + \$10Y
A	0	0	0
B	15	0	375
C	15	20	575
D	10	40	650[a]
E	0	40	400

[a]Optimal solution

The optimal solution calls for producing and selling 10,000 units of Gear X and 40,000 units of Gear Y. No other feasible solution will produce a larger contribution margin. It has been shown in the literature on linear programming that the optimal solution will always be one of the corner points. Thus, once the graph is drawn and the corner points identified, finding the solution is simply a matter of computing the value of each corner point and selecting the one with the greatest value.

Graphical solutions are not practical with more than two or three products. Fortunately, an algorithm called the **simplex method** can be used to solve larger linear programming problems. This algorithm has been coded and is available for use on computers to solve these larger problems.

simplex method

The linear programming model is an important tool for making product mix decisions, though it requires very little independent managerial decision making. The mix decision is made by the linear programming model itself. Assuming that the linear programming model is a reasonable representation of reality, the main role for management is to ensure that accurate data are used as input to the model. This includes the ability to recognize the irrelevancy of fixed costs and the ability to assess the accounting and technological inputs accurately (e.g., the unit selling prices, the unit costs, and the amount of resource consumed by each product as it is produced).

EXHIBIT 10-2
Graphical Solution (Coordinates represent thousands)

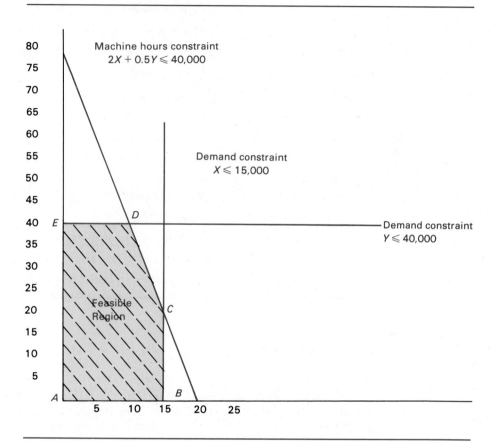

QUESTIONS

1   What is a relevant cost? A relevant revenue?

2   Explain why depreciation on an existing asset is always irrelevant.

3   Give an example of a future cost that is not relevant.

4   Explain why relevant costs need to be expressed on a periodically recurring basis.

5   Relevant costs always determine which alternative should be chosen. Do you agree? Explain.

6   Can direct materials ever be irrelevant in a make-or-buy decision? Explain.

7   Discuss the importance of complementary effects in a keep-or-drop decision.

8   What are some ways a manager can expand his or her knowledge of the feasible set of alternatives?

9   Suppose that a product can be sold at split-off for $5,000 or processed further at a cost of $1,000 and then sold for $6,400. Should the product be processed further?

10   Give an example of a fixed cost that is relevant.

11   What is the difference, if any, between a relevant cost and a differential cost?

12   Should joint costs be considered in a sell-or-process-further decision? Explain.

13   When, if ever, is depreciation a relevant cost?

14   What role do past costs play in relevant costing decisions?

15   When can a firm legally offer different prices for the same product?

16   Why would a firm ever offer a price on a product that is below its full cost?

17   Why are fixed costs never relevant in a product mix decision?

18   Suppose that a firm produces two products. Should the firm always place the most emphasis on the product with largest contribution margin per unit? Explain.

19   Discuss the purpose of linear programming.

20   What is an objective function? A constraint? A constraint set?

21   What is a feasible solution? A feasible set of solutions?

22   Explain the procedures for graphically solving a linear programming problem. What solution method is usually used when the problem includes more than two or three products?

▪ EXERCISES

E10–1   **Lease Decision; Relevance of Book Value**   The manager of a plant is trying to decide whether to lease a new forklift or continue using the one already owned. With careful maintenance, the old forklift will last another five years. The lease on the new forklift is also for five years, at the end of which it will be returned to the lessor. Information on the forklift owned by the company is given below:

Original cost	$15,000
Accumulated depreciation	7,500
Annual depreciation	1,500
Annual operating costs	2,800
Annual maintenance	1,200

Cost information for the new forklift is as follows:

Annual lease payment	$4,200
Annual operating costs	1,200
Annual maintenance	—

If the decision is to lease, the old forklift will be sold for $5,000, which will be used to pay off a five-year note that requires annual payments of $1,320.

Required:

1. What are the alternatives being considered by the plant manager?

2. Identify the relevant costs and benefits of each alternative. Should the plant manager lease the new forklift?

3. What is the most that the plant manager would be willing to pay per year for a leased forklift?

E10–2 **Keep or Buy; Sunk Costs** Shane Gasser purchased a 1972 Fiat Spider in 1985 for $1,900. Since purchasing the car, he has spent the following amounts on parts and labor:

Fuel pump	$ 30
Canvas top	165
Master cylinder	45
Disk brakes	32
Hoses, plugs	28
Labor	100
Total	$400

Shane is not totally satisfied with the Fiat. To bring the car to a condition that he feels it should be, he anticipates the following costs of restoration:

Rebuilt engine	$ 500
New paint job	500
Tires	300
New interior	300
Miscellaneous maintenance	300
Total	$1,900

In a visit to a used car dealer, Shane has found a one-year-old Yugo in mint condition for $2,850. Shane has advertised and found that he can sell the Fiat for only $1,200. If he buys the Yugo, Shane will pay cash, but he would need to sell the Fiat.

Required:

1. In trying to decide whether to restore the Fiat or buy the Yugo, Shane is distressed because he already has spent $2,300 on the Fiat. The investment seems too much to give up. How would you react to Shane's concern?

2. Assuming that Shane would be equally happy with the Fiat or the Yugo, should he buy the Yugo or should he restore the Fiat?

E10–3 **Make or Buy** Swift Company is currently manufacturing Part 6785, producing 5,000 units annually. The part is used in the production of several products made by Swift. The cost per unit for 6785 is as follows:

Direct materials	$3.00
Direct labor	2.00
Variable overhead	1.00
Fixed overhead	1.50
Total	$7.50

Of the total fixed overhead assigned to 6785, $1,500 is direct fixed overhead and the remainder is common fixed overhead. An outside supplier has offered to sell the part to Swift for $7.05. There is no alternative use for the facilities currently used to produce the part.

Required:

1. Should Swift Company make or buy Part 6785?

2. What is the most Swift would be willing to pay an outside supplier?

E10–4   **Keep or Drop; Product Substitutes**   Ernest Golding, president of Golding Corporation, had just received the following variable-costing income statement:

	Product A	*Product B*
Sales	$100,000	$ 250,000
Less: Variable expenses	(50,000)	(145,000)
Contribution margin	$ 50,000	$ 105,000
Less: Fixed expenses	(80,000)	(110,000)
Net income (loss)	$ (30,000)	$ (5,000)

Golding was distressed since this was the fifth consecutive quarter that both products had shown a loss. Upon careful review, Golding discovered that $70,000 of the total fixed costs were common to both products; the common fixed costs are allocated to the individual products on the basis of sales revenues. Golding also was told that the products were substitutes for each other. If either product is dropped, the sales of the other product will increase; Product A's by 50 percent if B is dropped and B's by 10 percent if A is dropped.

Required:

1. Prepare a segmented income statement in proper form for the past quarter.

2. Assume that Golding will choose among one of the following alternatives:
   a. Keep both products
   b. Drop both products
   c. Drop Product A
   d. Drop Product B

   Which is the best alternative? Provide computational support.

E10–5   **Special-Order Decision; Qualitative Aspects**   Cindy Burnson, the manager of Fondike Company, was agonizing over an offer for an order requesting 7,000 boxes of birthday cards. Fondike was operating at 70 percent of its capacity and could use the extra business; unfortunately, the order's offering price of $7.75 per box was below the cost to produce the cards. The controller was opposed to taking a loss on the deal. However, the personnel manager argued in favor of accepting the order even though a loss would be incurred; it would avoid the problem of layoffs and would help maintain the community image of the company. The full cost to produce a box of birthday cards is presented below:

Direct materials	$2.00
Direct labor	3.00
Variable overhead	1.50
Fixed overhead	2.50
Total	$9.00

The order is from a customer in a region not ordinarily serviced by the company. No variable selling or administrative expenses would be associated with the order.

Required:

1. Assume that the company would accept the order only if it increases total profits. Should the company accept or reject the order? Provide supporting computations.

2. Consider the personnel manager's concerns. Discuss the merits of accepting the order even if it decreases total profits.

E10–6 **Sell or Process Further; Basic Analysis** A division of Triple Products produces three products from a common input. The joint costs for a typical quarter are described below.

Direct materials	$20,000
Direct labor	30,000
Overhead	15,000

The revenues from each product are as follows: Product A, $43,000; Product B, $32,000; and Product C, $25,000.

Management is considering processing Product A beyond the split-off point, which would increase the sales value of Product A to $76,000. However, to process Product A further means that the company must rent some special equipment costing $17,500 per quarter. Additional materials and labor also needed would cost $12,650 per quarter.

Required:

1. What is the gross profit earned by the three products for one quarter?

2. Should the division process Product A further or sell Product A at split-off? What is the effect of the decision on quarterly gross profit?

E10–7 **Product Mix Decision; Single Constraint** Olsen Company produces two products that use the same material input. Product A uses two pounds of the material for every unit produced; and Product B uses five pounds. Currently, Olsen has 6,000 pounds of the material in inventory. All of the material is imported. For the coming year, Olsen plans to import 6,000 pounds to produce 1,000 units of Product A and 2,000 units of Product B. The detail of each product's unit contribution margin is given below.

	Product A	Product B
Selling price	$ 81	$139
Less variable expenses:		
Direct materials	(20)	(50)
Direct labor	(21)	(14)
Variable overhead	(10)	(15)
Contribution margin	$ 30	$ 60

Olsen Company has received word that the source of the material has been shut down by embargo. Consequently, the company will not be able to import the 6,000 pounds it planned to use in the coming year's production. There is no other source of the material.

Required:

1. Compute the total contribution margin that the company would earn if it could import the 6,000 pounds of the material.

2. Determine the optimal usage of the company's inventory of 6,000 pounds of the material. Compute the total contribution margin for the product mix that you recommend.

E10–8   **Product Mix; Multiple Constraints**   Refer to the data in Exercise 10–7. Assume that Product A uses three direct labor hours for every unit produced and that Product B uses two hours. A total of 6,000 direct labor hours are available for the coming year.

Required:

1. Formulate the linear programming problem faced by Olsen Company. To do so, you must derive mathematical expressions for the objective function and for the material and labor constraints.

2. Solve the linear programming problem using the graphical approach.

3. Compute the total contribution margin produced by the optimal mix developed in requirement 2.

E10–9   **Buy or Keep; Identification of Relevant Costs and Benefits**   Warren Company is currently using manufacturing machinery that some company officers believe is outdated. They are urging the president to acquire the latest computerized equipment, maintaining that output will increase and operating costs decrease. The company president has commissioned a report that compares costs and revenues of the existing equipment with that of the new equipment. The report is as follows:

	Old	New
Cost of acquisition	$250,000	$540,000
Accumulated depreciation[a]	100,000	—
Annual operating cost	60,000	30,000
Annual maintenance	6,000	4,000
Salvage value[b]	—	—

	Old	New
Output	100,000	120,000
Output selling price	100	100

[a]Using the straight-line method. Expected life for both machines is six years.
[b]At the end of the coming six years. Currently, the old machinery has a market value of $75,000. If the old machinery is sold, a six-year note will be paid off, saving the company annual payments of $16,222.

Required:

Identify all costs and benefits relevant to the decision to keep or buy. Ignore taxes.

E10–10 **Keep or Drop; Complementary Effects** Dutson Company manufactures running shoes and tennis shoes. The projected income statements for the two products are as follows:

	Running Shoes	*Tennis Shoes*
Sales	$ 450,000	$ 750,000
Less: Variable costs	(270,000)	(300,000)
Contribution margin	$ 180,000	$ 450,000
Less: Direct fixed expenses	(200,000)	(220,000)
Segment margin	$ (20,000)	$ 230,000
Less: Common fixed costs (allocated)	(50,000)	(75,000)
Net income (loss)	$ (70,000)	$ 155,000

The president of the company is considering dropping the running shoes. However, if the line is dropped, sales of tennis shoes will drop by 10 percent.

Required:

1. Should the company drop or keep the line of running shoes? Provide supporting computations.

2. Assume that increasing the advertising budget by $20,000 will increase sales of running shoes by 5 percent and tennis shoes by 3 percent. Prepare a segmented income statement that reflects the effect of increased advertising. Should advertising be increased?

E10–11 **Special Order** The Killian Company manufactures two skin care lotions, Liquid Skin and Silken Skin, out of a joint process. The joint (common) costs incurred are $420,000 for a standard production run that generates 180,000 gallons of Liquid Skin and 120,000 gallons of Silken Skin. Additional processing costs beyond the split-off point are $1.40 per gallon for Liquid Skin and $0.90 per gallon for Silken Skin. Liquid Skin sells for $2.40 per gallon while Silken Skin sells for $3.90 per gallon.

    The Overnight Hotel Chain has asked the Killian Company to supply it with 240,000 gallons of Silken Skin at a price of $3.65 per gallon. Overnight plans to have the Silken Skin bottled in 1.5-ounce personal-use containers that are supplied in each of its hotel rooms as part of the complimentary personal products for guest use.

    If Killian accepts the order, it will save $0.05 per gallon in packaging of Silken Skin. There is sufficient excess capacity for the order. However, the market for Liquid

Skin is saturated, and any additional sales of Liquid Skin would take place at a price of $1.60 per gallon.

Required:

1. What is the profit normally earned on one production run of Liquid Skin and Silken Skin?

2. Should Killian accept the special order? Explain.

(CMA adapted)

E10–12   **Product Mix Decision; Single Constraint**   Carstairs Company manufactures three types of floppy diskette storage units. Each of the three types requires the use of a special machine that has total operating capacity of 10,000 hours per year. Information on the three types of storage units is as follows:

	Basic	*Standard*	*Deluxe*
Selling price	$10.00	$15.00	$25.00
Variable cost	5.00	7.00	12.00
Machine hours required	0.10	0.25	0.75

Carstairs Company's marketing director has assessed demand for the three types of storage units and believes that the firm can sell as many units as it can produce.

Required:

1. How many of each type of unit should be produced and sold to maximize the company's contribution margin? What is the total contribution margin for your selection?

2. Now suppose that Carstairs Company believes that it can sell no more than 50,000 of each of the three types at the prices estimated. What product mix would you recommend and what would be the total contribution margin?

E10–13   **Effect of Opportunity Cost on Pricing Decision**   King Petroleum Company refines crude oil into a number of products (e.g., gasoline, kerosene, naphtha) using a joint production process. A by-product of the refining process is sludge. Sludge is trucked to King's asphalt plants, where it is mixed with water and other chemicals to produce an asphalt emulsion used to repair roads. One asphalt manufacturing plant is located at Hutchinson, Kansas. The Hutchinson plant faces seasonal production; two-thirds of its asphalt emulsion sales take place in the months of May through August, and the plant operates at capacity during those months.

King's Hutchinson plant has provided the following data on the emulsion:

Average price per gallon	$0.550
Materials	0.308
Conversion cost	0.070

The average price per gallon is figured as the average accepted bid price on all jobs for the previous year. Materials are direct materials. Conversion cost is a semivariable cost; it is approximately 30 percent variable.

In October 1992, the Hutchinson School District requested bids for resurfacing several school parking lots. The resurfacing job should require 2,400 gallons of asphalt emulsion.

Required:

1. What is the lowest price per gallon of asphalt emulsion that the Hutchinson plant could bid on the school district job?

2. Suppose the school district wanted to wait until school was out in June to resurface the parking lots. What price per gallon should King's Hutchinson plant bid then?

E10–14 **Make or Buy** Laughlin Company produces automatic coffee makers. Laughlin manufactures all parts necessary for the assembly of the coffee makers, including the tempered glass pots. Recently, Laughlin has received a proposal from Katz Glass Works to produce the tempered glass pots and to sell them for $2.45 each. Laughlin requires 30,000 pots per year, and Katz Glass Works has promised to supply that level of demand.

Internal data on the manufacture of glass pots are as follows:

Direct materials	$1.00
Direct labor	0.80
Factory overhead (25% variable)	2.40
Full manufacturing cost	$4.20

Required:

1. Should Laughlin accept Katz Glass Works' offer? Explain.

2. Independent of your answer to requirement 1, give two qualitative reasons that Laughlin might reject the offer. Give two qualitative reasons that Laughlin might accept it.

E10–15 **Comparison of Alternatives** Alice Kahle is the director of the Newkirk Drug Counseling Center. She and her staff design programs to assist clients to become and stay drug free. Most clients are referred to the Center through their probation officers. The Center is funded through a combination of state and federal grants. Alice anticipates that funding will last for another two to three years. After that, in all probability the Center will cease to exist.

The Center has just been informed that it will lose the lease on its office in two months. Alice is considering three other sites. Information on the sites is as follows:

▪ *Site 1*: This site is a 1,600-square-foot office in downtown Newkirk. Other lessees include an attorney, a bail bond agency, and two insurance agencies. Monthly rent is $450. The office has no interior walls, and permanent partitions cannot be installed. However, private meetings between caseworker and client are crucial. Therefore, Alice believes that she must rent moveable partitions to surround each caseworker's desk for $85 per month.

▪ *Site 2*: This site is a 2,400-square-foot office in a strip mall in a suburban area of Newkirk. It is close to caseworkers' homes but relatively farther from clients' homes.

The monthly rent is $500. The office has been subdivided into three smaller offices. One will be suitable for the reception area, one would serve as Alice's office, and the third would accommodate the caseworkers. Permanent partitions could be installed in the caseworkers' office at a cost of $1,500.

▪ Site 3: A former client's parents have heard about the Center's need for space. They have offered to donate a house that they previously used as a rental home. This site is an older house in Newkirk that is located in a rapidly commercializing district. The house provides plenty of space and privacy for all caseworkers. However, the plumbing and electrical work are not up to standard and must be repaired before the Center can move in. Additionally, federal regulations on handicapped access must be followed, so ramps and handrails must be built. Alice has received estimates on the work needed and figures the total cost will be $15,000.

Required:

1. Determine the relevant costs associated with each site. Does it matter whether the Center will exist for two or three years? Explain.

2. Write a memo to Alice summarizing the qualitative and quantitative aspects of each site.

E10–16 **Special Order**   SNL Enterprises manufactures Yard-A-Pult, a mechanical household waste disposal device that can be seen advertised on late-night weekend TV. SNL prices the Yard-A-Pult at $80 each. Manufacturing costs consist of the following:

Direct materials	$ 7.75
Direct labor	14.00
Variable overhead	14.00
Fixed overhead	21.00
Full manufacturing cost	$56.75

Productive capacity is 500,000 units; currently, SNL produces and sells 375,000 Yard-A-Pults. SNL pays a 10 percent commission to its salespeople.

Z-Mart, a national chain of discount stores, wants to buy 100,000 Yard-A-Pults at $40 each. Z-Mart wants to have its own logo imprinted on each one. SNL believes this will add $1.20 to direct materials cost and will require the purchase of a special imprinting machine costing $50,000. The imprinting machine would be used only for this order and would be scrapped (with zero salvage value) afterwards. No sales commission would be paid.

Required:

1. By how much will SNL Enterprise's net income change if the order is accepted?

2. Discuss three qualitative factors that might be considered in making the decision to accept or reject the special order.

E10–17 **Relevant Costs**   Vance Manufacturing Company produced 1,000 units in July that did not meet specifications. Vance could rework the units and sell them for their original price of $40 each. If the rework is done, additional costs will be incurred: direct materials of $0.75, direct labor of 1.25 hours at $10 per hour; and variable overhead applied at the rate of $4 per direct labor hour. Alternatively, Vance could sell the units "as is" for $15 each.

Vance lists the following original manufacturing costs for the 1,000 units:

Direct materials	$ 8
Direct labor	10
Variable overhead	4
Fixed overhead	6
Full manufacturing cost	$28

Required:

1. What are the relevant costs and revenues for each alternative?

2. Which alternative should Vance choose and why?

■ PROBLEMS

P10–1   **Make or Buy; Qualitative Considerations**   Gray Dentistry Services is part of an HMO that operates in a large metropolitan area. Currently, Gray has its own dental laboratory to produce porcelain and gold crowns. The unit costs to produce the crowns are as follows:

	Porcelain	*Gold*
Raw materials	$ 60	$ 90
Direct labor	20	20
Variable overhead	5	5
Fixed overhead	22	22
Total	$107	$137

Fixed overhead is detailed as follows:

Salary (supervisor)	$30,000
Depreciation	5,000
Rent (lab facility)	20,000

Overhead is applied on the basis of direct labor hours. The rates above were computed using 5,500 direct labor hours.

A local dental laboratory has offered to supply Gray all the crowns it needs. Its price is $100 for porcelain crowns and $132 for gold crowns; however, the offer is conditional on supplying both types of crowns—it will not supply just one type for the price indicated. If the offer is accepted, the equipment used by Gray's laboratory would be scrapped (it is old and has no market value), and the lab facility would be closed. Gray uses 1,500 porcelain crowns and 1,000 gold crowns per year.

Required:

1. Should Gray continue to make its own crowns or should they be purchased from the external supplier? What is the dollar effect of purchasing?

2. What qualitative factors should Gray consider in making this decision?

3. Suppose that the lab facility is owned rather than rented and that the $20,000 is depreciation rather than rent. What effect does this have on the analysis in requirement 1?

4. Refer to the original data. Assume that the volume of crowns is 3,000 porcelain and 2,000 gold. Should Gray make or buy the crowns? Explain the outcome.

P10–2   **Sell or Process Further** Godfrey Drug Corporation buys three chemicals that are processed to produce two popular ingredients for over-the-counter drugs. The purchased chemicals are blended for two to three hours and then heated for fifteen minutes. The results of the process are two separate chemicals, X and Y, which are sent to a drying room until their moisture content is reduced to 6 to 8 percent. For every 1,100 pounds of chemicals used, 500 pounds of each chemical are produced. After drying, X and Y are sold to companies that process them into their final form. The selling prices are $10 per pound for X and $25 per pound for Y. The costs to produce 500 pounds of each chemical are as follows:

Chemicals	$5,500
Direct labor	4,500
Overhead	3,500

The chemicals are packaged in 25-pound bags and shipped. The cost of each bag is $0.75. Shipping costs $0.10 per pound.

Godfrey Company could process X further by grinding it into a fine powder and then molding the powder into tablets. The tablets can be sold directly to retail drug stores as a generic brand. If this route is taken, the revenue received per bottle of tablets would be $3.00, with five bottles produced by every pound of X. The costs of grinding and tableting total $2.50 per pound of X. Bottles cost $0.20 each. Bottles are shipped in boxes that hold twenty-five at a shipping cost of $1.00 per box.

Required:

1. Should Godfrey sell X at split-off or should X be processed and sold as tablets?

2. If Godfrey normally sells 180,000 pounds of X per year, what will be the difference in profits if X is processed further?

P10–3   **Keep or Drop** SoundEasy is a retailer of radios, stereos, and televisions. The store carries two portable sound systems that have radios, tape players, and speakers. System A, of slightly higher quality than System B, costs $20 more. With rare exceptions, the store also sells a headset when a system is sold. The headset can be used with either system. Variable-costing income statements for the three products are shown below.

	System A	*System B*	*Headset*
Sales	$ 45,000	$ 32,500	$ 8,000
Less: Variable expenses	(20,000)	(25,500)	(3,200)
Contribution margin	$ 25,000	$ 7,000	$ 4,800
Less: Fixed costs[a]	(10,000)	(18,000)	(2,700)
Net income	$ 15,000	$(11,000)	$ 2,100

[a]Includes common fixed costs totaling $17,000, allocated to each product in proportion to its revenues.

The owner of the store is concerned about the profit performance of System B and is considering dropping it. If the product is dropped, sales of System A will increase by 30 percent and sales of headsets will drop by 25 percent.

Required:

1. Prepare segmented income statements for the three products using a better format.

2. Prepare segmented income statements for System A and the headsets assuming that System B is dropped. Should System B be dropped?

3. Suppose that a third system, System C, with a similar quality to System B, could be acquired. Assume that with System C the sales of System A would remain unchanged; however, System C would produce only 80 percent of the revenues of System B and sales of the headsets would drop by 10 percent. The contribution margin ratio of C is 50 percent, and its direct fixed costs would be identical to those of System B. Should System B be dropped and replaced with System C?

P10–4 **Accept or Reject a Special Order**   Patrick Sjoblom, manager of an electronics division, was considering an offer by Kelly Vargas, manager of a sister division. Kelly's division was operating below capacity and had just been given an opportunity to produce 10,000 units of one of its products for a customer in a market not normally served. The opportunity involves a product that uses an electrical component produced by Patrick's division. Each unit that Kelly's department produces requires two of the components. However, the price the customer is willing to pay is well below the price usually charged; to make a reasonable profit on the order, Kelly needed a price concession from Patrick's division. Kelly had offered to pay full manufacturing cost for the parts. So that Patrick would know that everything was above board, Kelly had supplied the following unit-cost and price information concerning the special order, excluding the cost of the electrical component:

Selling price	$30
Less costs:	
Direct materials	15
Direct labor	7
Variable overhead	2
Fixed overhead	3
Gross profit	$ 3

The normal selling price of the electrical component is $1.60 per unit. Its full manufacturing cost is $1.20 ($1.00 variable and $0.20 fixed). Kelly had argued that paying $1.60 per component would wipe out the gross profit and result in her division showing a loss. Patrick was interested in the offer because his division was also operating below capacity (the order would not use all the excess capacity).

Required:

1. Should Patrick accept the order at a selling price of $1.20 per unit? By how much will his division's profits be changed if the order is accepted? By how much will the profits of Kelly's division change if Patrick agrees to supply the part at full cost?

2. Suppose that Patrick offers to supply the component at $1.40. In offering the price, Patrick says that it is a firm offer not subject to negotiation. Should Kelly accept this

price and produce the special order? If Kelly accepts the price, what is the change in profits for Patrick's division?

3. Assume that Patrick's division is operating at full capacity and that Patrick refuses to supply the part for less than the full price. Should Kelly still accept the special order? Explain.

P10–5   **Keep or Drop a Division**   Lee Wright, president and general manager of Fossett Company, was concerned about the future of one of the company's largest divisions. The division's most recent quarterly income statement is as follows:

Sales	$ 3,680,000
Less: Cost of goods sold	(2,800,000)
Gross profit	$ 880,000
Less: Selling and administrative	(1,000,000)
Net profit (loss)	$ (120,000)

Lee is giving serious consideration to shutting down the division since this is the ninth consecutive quarter that it has shown a loss. To help him in his decision, the following additional information has been gathered:

▪ The division produces one product at a selling price of $100 to outside parties.

▪ The division sells 50 percent of its output to another division within the company for $84 (full manufacturing cost plus 20 percent). The internal price is set by company policy. If the division is shut down, the user division would buy the part externally for $100 per unit.

▪ The fixed overhead assigned per unit is $20.

▪ There is no alternative use for the facilities if shut down. The facilities and equipment would be sold and the proceeds invested to produce an annuity of $100,000 per year.

▪ Of the fixed selling and administrative expenses, 30 percent represent allocated expenses from corporate headquarters.

▪ Variable selling expenses are $5 per unit sold for units sold externally. These expenses are avoided for internal sales. There are no variable administrative expenses.

Required:

1. Prepare an income statement that more accurately reflects the division's profit performance.

2. Should the president shut down the division? What would be the effect on the company's profits if the division were closed?

P10–6   **Plant Shutdown or Continue to Operate; Qualitative Considerations**   GianAuto Corporation manufactures automobiles, vans, and trucks. Among the various GianAuto plants around the United States is the Denver cover plant, where vinyl covers and upholstery fabric are sewn. These are used to cover interior seating and other surfaces of GianAuto products.

Pam Vosilo is the plant manager for Denver cover. The plant was the first GianAuto plant in the region. As other area plants were opened, Vosilo, in recognition of her management ability, was given the responsibility to manage them. Vosilo functions as a regional manager although the budget for her and her staff is charged to the Denver plant.

Vosilo has just received a report indicating that GianAuto could purchase the entire annual output of Denver cover from outside suppliers for $30 million. Vosilo was astonished at the low outside price because the budget for Denver cover's operating costs was set at $52 million. Vosilo believes that Denver cover will have to close down operations in order to realize the $22 million in annual cost savings.

The budget (in thousands) for Denver cover's operating costs for the coming year follows:

Materials		$12,000
Labor:		
Direct	$13,000	
Supervision	3,000	
Indirect plant	4,000	20,000
Overhead:		
Depreciation—Equipment	$ 5,000	
Depreciation—Building	3,000	
Pension expense	4,000	
Plant manager and staff	2,000	
Corporate allocation	6,000	20,000
Total budgeted costs		$52,000

Additional facts regarding the plant's operations are as follows:

■ Due to Denver cover's commitment to use high-quality fabrics in all its products, the Purchasing Department was instructed to place blanket orders with major suppliers to ensure the receipt of sufficient materials for the coming year. If these orders are canceled as a consequence of the plant closing, termination charges would amount to 15 percent of the cost of direct materials.

■ Approximately 700 plant employees will lose their jobs if the plant is closed. This includes all direct laborers and supervisors as well as the plumbers, electricians, and other skilled workers classified as indirect plant workers. Some would be able to find new jobs, but many others would have difficulty. All employees would have difficulty matching Denver cover's base pay of $9.40 per hour, the highest in the area. A clause in Denver cover's contract with the union may help some employees; the company must provide employment assistance to its former employees for twelve months after a plant closing. The estimated cost to administer this service would be $1 million for the year.

■ Some employees would probably elect early retirement because Denver cover has an excellent pension plan. In fact, $3 million of next year's pension expense would continue whether Denver cover is open or not.

■ Vosilo and her staff would not be affected by the closing of Denver cover. They would still be responsible for administering three other area plants.

■ Denver cover considers equipment depreciation to be a variable cost and uses the units-of-production method to depreciate its equipment; Denver cover is the only

GianAuto plant to use this depreciation method. However, Denver cover uses the customary straight-line method to depreciate its building.

Required:

1. Prepare a quantitative analysis to help in deciding whether or not to close the Denver cover plant. Explain how you treated the nonrecurring relevant costs.

2. Consider the analysis in requirement 1 and add to it the qualitative factors that you believe are important to the decision. What is your decision? Would you close the plant? Explain.

(CMA adapted)

P10–7 **Product Mix Decision; Single and Multiple Constraints; Basics of Linear Programming** Paper Products, Inc., produces facial tissues and table napkins. The manufacturing process is highly mechanized; both products are produced by the same machinery by using different settings. For the coming period, 200,000 machine hours are available. Management is trying to decide on the quantities of each product to produce. The following data are available (for napkins, one unit is one package of napkins; for facial tissue, one unit is one box of tissue):

	Napkins	*Tissue*
Machine hours per unit	1.00	0.50
Unit selling price	$2.50	$3.00
Unit variable cost	$1.50	$2.25

Required:

1. Determine the units of each product that should be produced in order to maximize profits.

2. Because of market conditions, the company can sell no more than 150,000 packages of napkins and 300,000 boxes of paper tissue. Do the following:
   a. Formulate the problem as a linear programming problem.
   b. Determine the optimal mix using a graph.
   c. Compute the maximum profits given the optimal mix.

P10–8 **Keep or Drop; Product Mix** Olat Corporation produces three gauges. These gauges measure density, permeability, and thickness and are known as *D-gauges, P-gauges,* and *T-gauges.* For many years, the company has been profitable and has operated at capacity (which is 82,000 direct labor hours). In the last two years, however, prices on all gauges were reduced and selling expenses increased to meet competition and keep the plant operating at full capacity. Third-quarter results (in thousands), as shown below, are representative of recent experience.

	D-gauge	*P-gauge*	*T-gauge*	*Total*
Sales	$ 900	$ 1,600	$ 900	$ 3,400
Less: Cost of goods sold	(770)	(1,048)	(950)	(2,768)
Gross profit	$ 130	$ 552	$ (50)	$ 632
Less: Selling and administrative	(185)	(370)	(135)	(690)
Net income (loss)	$ (55)	$ 182	$(185)	$ (58)

Mel Carlo, president of Olat, is concerned about the results of the pricing, selling, and production policies. After reviewing the third-quarter results, he asked his management staff to consider the following three-point course of action:

1. Discontinue production of the T-gauge. T-gauges would not be returned to the line of products unless the problems with the gauge can be identified and resolved.
2. Increase quarterly sales promotion by $100,000 on the P-gauge to increase sales volume by 25 percent.
3. To accommodate the increased demand of P-gauges, cut production of the D-gauge by 50 percent and reduce traceable advertising and promotion costs for this line by $20,000 each quarter.

George Spears, controller, suggested that a more careful study of the financial relationships be made to determine the possible effects on the company's operating results as a consequence of these proposed actions. The president agreed, and JoAnn Brower, assistant controller, was given the assignment. She gathered the following information:

- All three gauges are manufactured with common equipment and facilities.

- The quarterly general selling and administrative expenses are allocated to the three product lines in proportion to their dollar sales volumes.

- Special selling expenses (advertising and shipping) are incurred on each gauge as follows:

	Advertising[a]	Shipping[b]
D-gauge	$100,000	$ 4
P-gauge	210,000	10
T-gauge	40,000	10

[a]Per quarter
[b]Per unit

- The unit manufacturing costs for the three products are as follows:

	D-gauge	P-gauge	T-gauge
Raw materials	$17	$ 31	$ 50
Direct labor[a]	20	40	60
Variable overhead	30	45	60
Fixed overhead	10	15	20
Total	$77	$131	$190

[a]The wage rate averages $10 per hour.

- The unit sales prices for the three products are $90 for the D-gauge, $200 for the P-gauge, and $180 for the T-gauge.

- The company is manufacturing at capacity and selling all that it produces.

Required:

1. Prepare a variable-costing segmented income statement for the three product lines. Make sure that you separate direct fixed expenses from common fixed expenses.

2. Should the T-gauge line be dropped as the president suggests? Explain.

3. Evaluate the remaining two suggestions of the president (combined with the first). Was the president correct in promoting the P-gauge rather than the D-gauge? Explain.

(CMA adapted)

P10–9   **Product Mix Decisions**   Calen Company manufactures and sells three products in a factory of three departments. Both labor and machine time are applied to the products as they pass through each department. The nature of the machine processing and of the labor skills required in each department is such that neither machines nor labor can be switched from one department to another.

Calen's management is attempting to plan its production schedule for the next several months. The planning is complicated by the fact that labor shortages exist in the community and some machines will be down several months for repairs.

Following is information regarding available machine and labor time by department and the machine hours and direct labor hours required per unit of product. These data should be valid for at least the next six months.

		Department		
Monthly Capacity		*1*	*2*	*3*
Machine hours available		3,000	3,100	2,700
Labor hours available		3,700	4,500	2,750
Product	*Input per Unit Produced*			
401	Labor hours	2	3	3
	Machine hours	1	1	2
402	Labor hours	1	2	—
	Machine hours	1	1	—
403	Labor hours	2	2	2
	Machine hours	2	2	1

Sales believes that the monthly demand for the next six months will be as follows:

Product	*Units Sold*
401	500
402	400
403	1,000

Inventory levels will not be increased or decreased during the next six months. The unit cost and price data for each product are as follows:

	Product		
	401	*402*	*403*
Unit costs:			
Direct material	$ 7	$ 13	$ 17
Direct labor	66	38	51
Variable overhead	27	20	25

	Product		
	401	*402*	*403*
Fixed overhead	15	10	32
Variable selling	3	2	4
Total unit cost	$118	$ 83	$129
Unit selling price	$196	$123	$167

Required:

1. Calculate the monthly requirement for machine hours and direct labor hours for producing Products 401, 402, and 403 to determine whether the factory can meet the monthly sales demand.

2. Determine the quantities of 401, 402, and 403 that should be produced monthly to maximize profits. Prepare a schedule that shows the contribution to profits of your product mix.

3. Assume that the machine hours available in Department 3 are 1,500 instead of 2,700. Calculate the optimal monthly product mix using the graphing approach to linear programming. Prepare a schedule that shows the contribution to profits from this optimal mix.

(CMA adapted)

P10–10   **Make or Buy**   Henderson Company produces two products, A and B. The segmented income statement for a typical quarter is given below.

	Product A	*Product B*	*Total*
Sales	$150,000	$ 80,000	$ 230,000
Less: Variable expenses	(80,000)	(46,000)	(126,000)
Contribution margin	$ 70,000	$ 34,000	$ 104,000
Less: Direct fixed expenses[a]	(20,000)	(38,000)	(58,000)
Segment margin	$ 50,000	$ (4,000)	$ 46,000
Less: Common fixed expenses			(30,000)
Net income			$ 16,000

[a]Includes depreciation.

Product A uses a subassembly that is purchased from an external supplier for $25 per unit. Each quarter, 2,000 subassemblies are purchased. All units produced are sold, and there are no ending inventories of subassemblies. Henderson is considering making the subassembly rather than buying it. Unit variable manufacturing costs are as follows:

Direct materials	$2
Direct labor	3
Variable overhead	2

Two alternatives exist to supply the productive capacity:

1. Lease the needed space and equipment at a cost of $27,000 per quarter for the space and $10,000 per quarter for a supervisor. There are no other fixed expenses.

2. Drop Product B. The equipment could be adapted with virtually no cost and the existing space utilized to produce the subassembly. The direct fixed expenses, including supervision, would be $38,000, $8,000 of which is depreciation on equipment. If Product B is dropped, there will be no effect on the sales of Product A.

Required:

1. Should Henderson Company make or buy the subassembly? If it makes the subassembly, which alternative should be chosen? Explain and provide supporting computations.

2. Suppose that dropping Product B will decrease sales of Product A by 6 percent. What effect does this have on the decision?

3. Assume that dropping Product B decreases sales of Product A by 6 percent and that 2,800 subassemblies are required per quarter. As before, assume that there are no ending inventories of subassemblies and that all units produced are sold. Assume also that the per-unit sales price and variable costs are the same as in requirement 1. Include the leasing alternative in your consideration. Now what is the correct decision?

P10–11   **Make or Buy: Ethical Considerations**   Pamela McDonald, CMA and controller for Murray Manufacturing, Inc., was having lunch with Roger Branch, manager of the company's Power Department. Over the past six months, Pamela and Roger had developed a romantic relationship and were making plans for marriage. To keep company gossip at a minimum, Pamela and Roger had kept the relationship very quiet, and no one in the company was aware of it. The topic of the luncheon conversation centered on a decision concerning the company's Power Department that Larry Johnson, president of the company, was about to make.

 Pamela: Roger, in our last executive meeting, we were told that a local utility company offered to supply power and quoted a price per kilowatt hour that they said would hold for the next three years. They even offered to enter into a contractual agreement with us.

 Roger: This is news to me. Is the bid price a threat to my area? Can they sell us power cheaper than we make it? And why wasn't I informed about this matter? I should have some input. This burns me. I think I should give Larry a call this afternoon and lodge a strong complaint.

 Pamela: Calm down, Roger. The last thing I want you to do is call Larry. Larry made us all promise to keep this whole deal quiet until a decision had been made. He did not want you involved because he wanted to make an unbiased decision. You know that the company is struggling somewhat, and they are looking for ways to save money.

 Roger: Yeah, but at my expense? And at the expense of my department's workers? At my age, I doubt that I could find a job that pays as well and has the same benefits. How much of a threat is this offer?

 Pamela: Jack Lacy, my assistant controller, prepared an analysis while I was on vacation. It showed that internal production is cheaper than buying, but not by much. Larry asked me to review the findings and submit a final recommendation for next Wednesday's meeting. I've reviewed Jack's analysis and it's faulty. He overlooked the interactions of your department with other service departments. When these are considered, the analysis is overwhelmingly in favor of purchasing the power. The savings are about $300,000 per year.

 Roger: If Larry hears that, my department's gone. Pam, you can't let this happen. I'm three years away from having a vested retirement. And my workers—they have home mortgages, kids in college, families to support. No, it's not right. Pam, just tell him that your assistant's analysis is on target. He'll never know the difference.

Pamela: Roger, what you're suggesting doesn't sound right either. Would it be ethical for me to fail to disclose this information?

Roger: Ethical? Do you think it's right to lay off employees that have been loyal, faithful workers simply to fatten the pockets of the owners of this company? The Murrays already are so rich that they don't know what to do with their money. I think that it's even more unethical to penalize me and my workers. Why should we have to bear the consequences of some bad marketing decisions? Anyway, the effects of those decisions are about gone, and the company should be back to normal within a year or so.

Pamela: You may be right. Perhaps the well-being of you and your workers is more important than saving $300,000 for the Murrays.

Required:

1. Should Pamela have told Roger about the impending decision concerning the Power Department? In revealing this information, did Pamela violate any of the ethical standards described in the Appendix of Chapter 1?

2. Should Pamela provide Larry with the correct data concerning the Power Department? Or should she protect its workers? What would you do if you were Pamela?

P10–12 **Make or Buy** Sportway, Inc., is a wholesale distributor supplying a wide range of moderately priced sporting equipment to large chain stores. About 60 percent of Sportway's products are purchased from other companies while the remainder of the products are manufactured by Sportway. The company's Plastics Department is currently manufacturing molded fishing tackle boxes. Sportway is able to manufacture and sell 8,000 tackle boxes annually, making full use of its direct labor capacity at available work stations. Presented below are the selling price and costs associated with Sportway's tackle boxes.

Selling price per box		$86.00
Costs per box		
Molded plastic	$ 8.00	
Hinges, latches, handle	9.00	
Direct labor ($15/hour)	18.75	
Manufacturing overhead	12.50	
Selling and administrative	17.00	65.25
Profit per box		$20.75

Because Sportway believes it could sell 12,000 tackle boxes if it had sufficient manufacturing capacity, the company has looked into the possibility of purchasing the tackle boxes for distribution. Maple Products, a steady supplier of quality products, would be able to provide up to 9,000 tackle boxes per year at a price of $68 per box delivered to Sportway's facility.

Bart Johnson, Sportway's product manager, has suggested that the company could make better use of its Plastics Department by manufacturing skateboards. To support his position, Johnson has a market study that indicates an expanding market for skateboards and a need for additional suppliers. Johnson believes that Sportway could expect to sell 17,500 skateboards annually at a price of $45 per skateboard. Johnson's estimate of the costs to manufacture the skateboards is presented below:

Selling price per skateboard		$45.00
Costs per skateboard		
Molded plastic	$5.50	
Wheels, hardware	7.00	
Direct labor ($15/hour)	7.50	
Manufacturing overhead	5.00	
Selling and administrative cost	9.00	34.00
Profit per skateboard		$11.00

In the Plastics Department, Sportway uses direct labor hours as the application base for manufacturing overhead. Included in the manufacturing overhead for the current year is $50,000 of factory-wide, fixed manufacturing overhead that has been allocated to the Plastics Department. For each unit of product that Sportway sells, regardless of whether the product has been purchased or is manufactured by Sportway, an allocated $6 fixed overhead cost per unit for distribution is included in the selling and administrative costs for all products. Total selling and administrative costs for the purchased tackle boxes would be $10 per unit.

Required:

1. In order to maximize the company's profitability, prepare an analysis based on the data presented that will show which product or products Sportway, Inc., should manufacture and/or purchase and that will show the associated financial impact. Support your answer with appropriate calculations.

2. Discuss some qualitative factors that might impact on Sportway's decision.

(CMA adapted)

P10–13 **Make or Buy** Sarbec Company needs a total of 125 tons of sheet steel, 50 tons of 2-inch width and 75 tons of 4-inch width, for a customer's job. Sarbec can purchase the sheet steel in these widths directly from Jensteel Corporation, a steel manufacturer, or it can purchase sheet steel from Jensteel that is twenty-four inches wide and have it slit into the desired widths by Precut, Inc. Both vendors are local and have previously supplied materials to Sarbec.

Precut specializes in slitting sheet steel that is provided by a customer into any desired width. When negotiating a contract, Precut tells its customers that there is a scrap loss in the slitting operation but that this loss has never exceeded 2.5 percent of input tons. Precut recommends that if a customer has a specific tonnage requirement, it should supply an adequate amount of steel to yield the desired quantity. Precut's charges for steel slitting are based on good output, not input handled.

The 24-inch-wide sheet steel is a regular stock item of Jensteel and can be shipped to Precut within five days after receipt of Sarbec's purchase order. If Jensteel is to do the slitting, shipment to Sarbec would be scheduled for fifteen days after receipt of the order. Precut has quoted delivery at ten days after receipt of the sheet steel. In prior dealings, Sarbec has found both Jensteel and Precut to be reliable vendors with high-quality products.

Sarbec has received the following price quotations from Jensteel and Precut:

Jensteel Corporation Rates

Size	Gauge	Quantity	Cost per ton
2''	14	50 tons	$210
4''	14	75 tons	200
24''	14	125 tons	180

Precut, Inc., Steel Slitting Rates

Size	Gauge	Quantity	Price per Ton of Output
2''	14	50 tons	$18
4''	14	75 tons	15

Freight and Handling Charges

Destination	Cost per Ton
Jensteel to Sarbec	$10.00
Jensteel to Precut	5.00
Precut to Sarbec	7.50

In addition to the above information, Precut has informed Sarbec that if it purchases 100 output tons of each width, the per-ton slitting rates would be reduced 12 percent. Sarbec knows that the same customer will be placing a new order in the near future for the same material and estimates it would have to store the additional tonnage for an average of two months at a carrying cost of $1.50 per month for each ton. There would be no change in Jensteel's prices for additional tons delivered to Precut.

Required:

1. Prepare an analysis that will show whether Sarbec Company should:
   a. Purchase the required slit steel directly from Jensteel Corporation.
   b. Purchase the 24-inch-wide sheet steel from Jensteel and have it slit by Precut, Inc., into fifty output tons two inches wide and seventy-five output tons four inches wide.
   c. Take advantage of Precut's reduced slitting rates by purchasing 100 output tons of each width.

2. Ignoring your answer to requirement 1, present three qualitative reasons why Sarbec Company may favor the purchase of the slit steel directly from Jensteel Corporation.

(CMA adapted)

■ MANAGERIAL DECISION CASE

Centralize versus Decentralize   Central University, a Midwestern university with approximately 13,000 students, was in the middle of a budget crisis. For the third consecutive year, state appropriations for higher education remained essentially unchanged (the university is currently in its 1992–93 academic year). Yet utilities, social security benefits, insurance, and other operating expenses have increased. Moreover, the faculty were becoming restless, and some members had begun to leave for other, higher-paying opportunities.

The president and the academic vice-president had announced their intention to eliminate some academic programs and to reduce others. The savings that result would be used to cover the increase in operating expenses and for raises for the remaining faculty. Needless to say, the possible dismissal of tenured faculty aroused a great deal of concern throughout the university.

With this background, the president and academic vice-president called a meeting of all department heads and deans to discuss the budget for the coming year. As the budget was presented, the academic vice-president noted that Continuing Education, a separate, centralized unit, had accumulated a deficit of $504,000 over the past several years, which must be eliminated during the coming fiscal year. The vice-president noted that allocating the deficit equally among the seven colleges would create a hardship on some of the colleges, wiping out all of their operating budget except for salaries.

After some discussion of alternative ways to allocate the deficit, the head of the Accounting Department suggested an alternative solution: decentralize Continuing Education, allowing each college to assume responsibility for its own continuing education programs. In this way, the overhead of a centralized continuing education could be avoided.

The academic vice-president responded that the suggestion would be considered, but it was received with little enthusiasm. The vice-president observed that Continuing Education was now generating more revenues than costs—and that the trend was favorable.

A week later, at a meeting of the Deans' Council, the vice-president reviewed the role of Continuing Education. He pointed out that only the dean of Continuing Education held tenure. If Continuing Education were decentralized, her salary ($50,000) would continue; however, she would return to her academic department, and the university would save $20,000 of instructional wages since fewer temporary faculty would be needed in her department. All other employees in the unit were classified as staff. Continuing Education had responsibility for all noncredit offerings. Additionally, it had nominal responsibility for credit courses offered in the evening on campus and for credit courses offered off-campus. However, all scheduling and staffing of these evening and off-campus courses were done by the heads of the academic departments. What courses were offered and who staffed them had to be approved by the head of each department. According to the vice-president, one of the main contributions of the Continuing Education Department to the evening and off-campus programs is advertising. He estimated that $30,000 per year is being spent.

After reviewing this information, the vice-president made available the following information pertaining to the department's performance for the past several years (the 1992–93 data were projections). He once again defended keeping a centralized department, emphasizing the favorable trend revealed by the accounting data. (All numbers are expressed in thousands.)

	1989–90	1990–91	1991–92	1992–93
Tuition revenues:				
Off-campus	$300	$ 400	$ 400	$ 410
Evening	—ᵃ	525	907	1,000
Noncredit	135	305	338	375
Total	$435	$1,230	$1,645	$1,785

	1989–90	*1990–91*	*1991–92*	*1992–93*
Operating costs:				
Administration	$(132)	$ (160)	$ (112)	$ (112)
Off-campus:				
Direct[b]	(230)	(270)	(270)	(260)
Indirect	(350)	(410)	(525)	(440)
Evening	(—)[a]	(220)	(420)	(525)
Noncredit	(135)	(305)	(338)	(375)
Total	$(847)	$(1,365)	$(1,665)	$(1,712)
Income (loss)	$(412)	$ (135)	$ (20)	$ 73

[a] In 1989–90, the department had no responsibility for evening courses. Beginning in 1990, it was given the responsibility to pay for any costs of instruction incurred when temporary or adjunct faculty were hired to teach evening courses. Tuition revenues earned by evening courses also began to be assigned to the department at the same time.
[b] Instructional wages.

The dean of the College of Business was unimpressed by the favorable trend identified by the academic vice-president. The dean maintained that decentralization still would be in the best interests of the university. He argued that although decentralization would not fully solve the deficit, it would provide a sizable contribution each year to the operating budgets for each of the seven colleges.

The academic vice-president disagreed vehemently. He was convinced that Continuing Education was now earning its own way and would continue to produce additional resources for the university.

Required:

You have been asked by the president of Central University to assess which alternative, centralization or decentralization, is in the best interest of the school. The president is willing to decentralize provided that significant savings can be produced and the mission of the Continuing Education Department will still be carried out. Prepare a memo to the president that details your analysis and reasoning and recommends one of the two alternatives. Provide both qualitative and quantitative reasoning in the memo.

CHAPTER 11

Capital Budgeting: Long-Run Investment Decisions

- **LEARNING OBJECTIVES**

    After studying Chapter 11, you should be able to

    1. Explain the difference between discounting and nondiscounting models.

    2. Compute the payback period for an investment.

    3. Explain the role of the payback period in capital budgeting decisions.

    4. Compute the accounting rate of return for an investment.

    5. Compute the present value of future cash flows.

    6. Use net present value analysis to determine whether an investment is acceptable.

    7. Explain why the cost of capital is used as the discount rate in the net present value model.

    8. Use the internal rate of return to assess the acceptability of an investment.

    9. Define and explain the key terms appearing at the end of the chapter.

SCENARIO

TastyFood Corporation, a large food-store chain, is considering investing in an automated deposit processing system for all of its stores. An investment of $2 million would provide the system for all 150 existing stores as well as for the 30 stores to be opened by the beginning of the following year. The president of TastyFood assigned the responsibility to assess the investment to a special capital acquisitions committee. The first act of the committee was to design a pilot study to test such a system in seven stores for a period of nine months.

At the end of the nine months, Maryanne Wise, chair of the capital acquisitions committee and vice-president of finance, scheduled a committee meeting to evaluate the outcome of the pilot study. Besides Maryanne, the committee included Stan Miller, controller; Ron Thomas, vice-president of operations; and Paula Summers, area supervisor for the seven stores where the pilot study was conducted.

"As you recall," Maryanne remarked, "we met more than nine months ago and agreed to implement a pilot study before committing ourselves to an automated deposit system. Because of her close scrutiny of the project, Paula has agreed to give us a summary of the benefits observed in the pilot study."

"I'm extremely pleased with the results of the pilot study," Paula replied, "as I think you will be. To quantify the financial impact of this project, I have classified the benefits into four categories: immediate, near term, indirect, and potential for future. Immediate benefits are those that are available in a store as soon as the equipment is operational. Near-term benefits are those that will be realized only after the local system is connected to the store computer. Indirect benefits are those that accrue from the project but are more difficult to quantify. Potential future benefits can result from the ability of the system to interface directly with the accounting system. Here is a handout that describes some of the specific benefits found in each category."

SPECIFIC BENEFITS BY CATEGORY

Immediate Benefits

1. *Bank Charge Reduction.* An automated deposit processing system reduces the charges for processing checks since it encodes the dollar amount on all checks prior to depositing them.

2. *Productivity Gains.* Automation of the system reduces the amount of additional payroll required during the busy season.

3. *Forms Cost Reduction.* Automation of the system eliminates nearly 3 million documents used per year to process deposits manually.

Near-Term Benefits

■ *Reduction of Cash Shortages.* Once the system is connected to the store computer, a cash variance analysis can be provided the next day. Currently, this analysis is performed manually at headquarters and is several weeks old by the time it arrives in the store. The ability to respond more quickly to cash shortages should reduce annual losses.

Indirect Benefits

1. *Greater Data Integrity.* By reducing manual calculations, greater data integrity will result. This will decrease time spent on making corrections to incorrect deposit information.

2. *Lower Training Costs.* Since the system is simpler and has fewer forms, new cashiers and new store openings should require less training time.

Potential for Future Benefits

Interfacing Abilities By processing data through the store computer to the host computer in headquarters, an interface program at the host can provide savings in time to both the sales audit and cash/banking calculations by eliminating manual entries and expediting bank reconciliations.

"After seeing these benefits, I'm convinced that automatic deposits are a good idea," observed Ron Thomas. "In fact, I wonder why we weren't smart enough to do this years ago. Since I'm also convinced that committees are notorious for wasting time and resources, I move that we attach Paula's handout to a recommendation to implement the automated system for the entire company. Then we can get back to more pressing matters."

"Wait a minute!" interjected Stan. "While the description of the benefits of the automated system is impressive, we shouldn't be too hasty in our decisions. After all, we are talking about investing $2 million. We need to be certain that this is a sound investment."

"But that's the whole point, Stan. The benefits make it clear that the investment is sound. Why waste any more time deliberating over an obvious conclusion? We could spend hours discussing a matter that is already clearly decided. What do you say, Maryanne? Can we vote on this matter and adjourn?"

"Well, Ron, we can—if you will first answer the following questions. How much will this investment increase the profits of the firm? What effect will it have on our overall value? Will the investment earn at least the return required by company policy? How long will it take for us to recover the investment through the savings alluded to in Paula's handout? Only when we know the answers to some of those questions can we accurately assess the soundness of the investment. The pilot study provides us with the fundamental information we need to estimate the future cash savings associated with automation. Once we have these estimates, we can use some financial models to assess the merits of the proposed investment. Stan, for our next meeting, please bring estimates of the cash flows over the life of the proposed system. I will come prepared to discuss some of the financial models that will help us assess the financial merits of the investment."

■ CAPITAL BUDGETING DECISIONS

capital budgeting

The problem of whether to invest or not invest in an automated deposit processing system is an example of a **capital budgeting** decision. Capital budgeting is concerned with the acquisition of long-term assets and usually involves a significant outlay of funds, often referred to as *capital outlays*. As the case at the opening of the chapter illustrates, estimating a project's cash flows and using them to assess the project's soundness are critical steps in a capital budgeting decision. How cash flows can be used to evaluate the merits of a proposed project is the focus of this chapter and the next. We will study some of the financial models that Maryanne was planning to discuss in her next committee meeting.

Because capital budgeting decisions place large amounts of resources at risk for long periods of time and simultaneously affect the future development of the firm, they are among the most important decisions managers make. Every organization has limited resources, which should be used to maintain or enhance its long-run profitability. Poor capital budgeting decisions can be disastrous. For example, the failure of the American steel industry to upgrade its production facilities has proved to be a mistake. Foreign competitors with more modern facilities have been able to produce more steel at lower costs. The current state of the American steel industry would be significantly better if the right capital budgeting decisions had been made years ago.

■ DESCRIPTIONS OF CAPITAL BUDGETING

independent projects

Two types of capital budgeting projects will be considered. **Independent projects** are projects that, if accepted or rejected, do not affect the cash flows of other projects. Suppose that the managers of the Marketing and the Research and Development departments jointly propose the addition of a new product line that would entail making significant outlays for working capital and equipment. If no other new product lines are being considered and the new product line is not complementary with existing product lines, the decision involving the new product line stands alone. Since it is independent of other proposals, the project can be evaluated on its own merits.

mutually exclusive projects

For the second class of capital budgeting projects, a firm must choose among several alternatives that will provide the same basic service. Acceptance of one option precludes the acceptance of another. Thus, **mutually exclusive projects** are those projects that, if accepted, preclude the acceptance of all other competing projects. For example, TastyFoods was considering replacing its existing manual deposit processing system with an automated system. Part of the company's deliberation would concern different types of automated systems. If three different automated systems were being considered, there are four alternatives in all—the current system plus the three potential new systems. Once one system is chosen, the other three are excluded; they are mutually exclusive.

Notice that one of the competing alternatives in the example is that of maintaining the status quo (the manual system). This emphasizes the fact that new investments that replace existing investments must prove to be economically superior. Of course, at times replacement of the old system is mandatory and not discretionary if the firm wishes to remain in business (e.g., equipment in the old system may be worn out, making the old system not a viable alternative). In such a situation, going out of business could be a viable alternative, especially if none of the new investment alternatives is profitable.

Typical capital investment decisions are investments in long-term capital assets. These assets depreciate over their lives, and the original investment is used up as the assets are employed. In general terms, a sound capital investment will earn back its original capital outlay over its life and, at the same time, provide a reasonable return on the original investment. Thus, one task of a manager is to decide whether or not a capital investment will earn back its original outlay and provide a reasonable return. By making this assessment, a manager can decide on the acceptability of independent projects and compare competing projects on the basis of their economic merits. But what is meant by reasonable return? It is generally agreed that any new project must cover the *opportunity cost* of the funds invested. Furthermore, it is usually assumed that managers should select projects that promise to maximize the wealth of the owners of the firm.

To make a capital budgeting decision, a manager must estimate the quantity and timing of cash flows, assess the risk of the investment, and consider the impact of the project on the firm's profits. One of the most difficult tasks is to estimate the cash flows. Projections must be made years into the future, and forecasting is far from a perfect science. Obviously, as the accuracy of cash-flow forecasts increases, the reliability of the decision improves. Although forecasting future cash flows is a critical part of the capital budgeting process, forecasting methods will not be considered here. They are best left to more advanced courses. Consequently, cash flows are assumed to be known; the focus will be on making capital budgeting decisions *given* these cash flows. However, the discussion will reveal the sensitivity of decisions to changes in the given cash flows.

Managers must set goals and priorities for capital expenditures. They also must identify some basic criteria for the acceptance or rejection of proposed investments. Another problem faced by managers is ranking acceptable investments in order of their value to the firm. In this chapter, we will study four basic methods to guide managers in accepting or rejecting potential investments. The methods include both nondiscounting and discounting decision approaches (two methods are discussed for each approach). The discussion of discounting models is restricted to independent projects; in the following chapter, the analysis of discounting models is expanded to include competing projects. Other complications—such as ranking projects, tax implications, inflation, and risk analysis—are reserved for the following chapter.

■ NONDISCOUNTING MODELS

nondiscounting
models

discounting models

The basic capital budgeting decision models can be classified into two major categories: nondiscounting models and discounting models. **Nondiscounting models** ignore the time value of money, whereas **discounting models** explicitly consider it. Although many accounting theorists disparage the nondiscounting models because they ignore the time value of money, many firms continue to use these models in making capital budgeting decisions.[1] However, the use of discounting models has increased over the years, and few firms use only one model—indeed, firms seem to use both types of models.[2] This suggests that both categories supply useful information to managers as they struggle to make a capital budgeting decision.

The Payback Period

payback period

One type of nondiscounting model is the payback period. The **payback period** is the time required for a firm to recover its original investment. For example, if the original investment is $100,000, and the firm expects the project to generate annual cash flows at $50,000, then the payback period is two years ($100,000/$50,000). When the cash flows of a project are assumed to be even, the following formula can be used to compute its payback period:

Payback period = Original investment/Annual cash inflow

If, however, the cash flows are uneven, the payback period is computed by adding the annual cash flows until such time as the original investment is recovered. If a fraction of a year is needed, it is assumed that cash flows occur evenly within each year. For example, suppose that an original investment of $100,000 has a life of five years with the following expected annual cash flows: $30,000, $30,000, $20,000, $40,000, and $50,000. The payback period for the

---

[1]The time value of money conveys the notion that a dollar now is worth more than a dollar one period from now. The reason, of course, is that a dollar now can be invested so that one period from now we get back the dollar plus some return on the investment.

[2]In the mid-1950s, Robichek and McDonald reported that only 9 percent of large firms were using discounting models; by 1975, Petry reported that 66 percent of large firms were using these techniques. Also in 1975, Petty, Scott, and Bird surveyed Fortune 500 firms and found that 63.4 percent of the respondents used discounting models as their primary evaluation technique, with most of the remaining firms using them as secondary techniques. The same study also found that more than half of the firms used nondiscounting models as either a primary or a secondary evaluation technique. For additional detail, see A. A. Robichek and J. G. McDonald, "Financial Planning in Transition, Long Range Planning Service," Report No. 268 (Menlo Park, Calif.: Stanford Research Institute, January 1966); G. H. Petry, "Effective Use of Capital Budgeting Tools," *Business Horizons*, Vol. 18, No. 5 (October 1975), pp. 57–65; J. W. Petty, D. F. Scott, and M. M. Bird, "The Capital Budgeting Decision Making Process of Large Corporations," *The Engineering Economist*, Vol. 20, No. 3 (Spring 1975), pp. 159–86.

project is 3.5 years, computed as follows: $30,000 (1 year) + $30,000 (1 year) + $20,000 (1 year) + $20,000 (0.5 year) = $100,000 (3.5 years). Notice that in the fourth year, when only $20,000 is needed and $40,000 is available, the amount of time required to earn the $20,000 is found by dividing the amount needed by the annual cash flow ($20,000/$40,000). This analysis is summarized in Exhibit 11–1.

One way to use the payback period is to set a maximum payback period for all projects and to reject any project that exceeds this level. Why would a firm use the payback period in this way? Some analysts suggest that the payback period can be used as a rough measure of risk, with the notion that the longer it takes for a project to pay for itself, the riskier it is. Also, firms with riskier cash flows could require a shorter payback period than normal. Additionally, firms with liquidity problems would be more interested in projects with quick paybacks. Another critical concern is obsolescence. In some industries, the risk of obsolescence is high; firms within these industries would be interested in recovering funds rapidly.

Another reason, less beneficial to the firm, may also be at work. Many managers in a position to make capital budgeting decisions may choose investments with quick payback periods out of self-interest. If a manager's performance is measured using such short-run criteria as annual net income, he or she may choose projects with quick paybacks to show improved net income as quickly as possible. Consider that division managers often are responsible for making capital budgeting decisions and are evaluated on divisional profit. The tenure of divisional managers, however, is typically short—three to five years would be average. Consequently, the incentive is for such managers to shy away from investments that promise healthy long-run returns but relatively meager returns in the short run.

The payback period can be used to choose among competing alternatives. Under this approach, the investment with the shortest payback period is preferred over investments with longer payback periods. However, this use

EXHIBIT 11–1
Payback Analysis: Uneven Cash Flows

Year	Unrecovered Investment (Beginning of Year)	Cash Flow (End of Year)
1	$100,000	$30,000
2	70,000	30,000
3	40,000	20,000
4	20,000[a]	40,000[a]
5	—	50,000

[a]At the beginning of Year 4, $20,000 is needed to recover the investment. Since an inflow of $40,000 is expected, only 0.5 years is needed to recover the $20,000. Thus, the payback is 3.5 years.

of the payback period is less defensible because this measure suffers from two major deficiencies: (1) it ignores the performance of the investments beyond the payback period and (2) it ignores the time value of money.

These two significant deficiencies are easily illustrated. Assume that two competing investments, A and B, both requiring an initial outlay of $100,000, have a five-year life and display the following annual cash flows:

Investment	Year 1	Year 2	Year 3	Year 4	Year 5
A	$80,000	$20,000	$20,000	$20,000	$20,000
B	20,000	80,000	5,000	5,000	5,000

Both investments have payback periods of two years. Thus, if a manager uses the payback period to choose among competing investments, the two investments would be equally desirable. In reality, however, A should be preferred over B for two reasons. First, A provides a much larger dollar return for the years beyond the payback period ($60,000 versus $15,000). Second, A returns $80,000 in the first year while B returns only $20,000. The extra $60,000 that A provides in the first year could be put to productive use, such as investing it in another project. It is better to have a dollar now than one year from now because the dollar on hand can be invested to provide a return one year from now.

In summary, the payback period provides to managers information that can be used as follows:

1. To help control the risks associated with the uncertainty of future cash flows

2. To help minimize the impact of an investment on a firm's liquidity problems

3. To help control the risk of obsolescence

4. To help control the effect of the investment on performance measures

However, the method suffers significant deficiencies: it ignores a project's total profitability and the time value of money. While the computation of the payback period may be useful to a manager, to rely on it solely for a capital budgeting decision would be foolish.

The Accounting Rate of Return

accounting rate of return

The accounting rate of return is the second commonly used nondiscounting model. The **accounting rate of return** measures the return on a project in terms of income, as opposed to using a project's cash flow. The accounting rate of return is computed by the following formula:

Accounting rate of return = Average income/Investment

The average income of a project is obtained by adding the net income for each year of the project and then dividing this total by the number of years. Average net income can be approximated by subtracting average depreciation from average cash flow. Assuming that all revenues earned in a period are collected and that depreciation is the only noncash expense, the approximation is exact.

Investment can be defined as the original investment or as the average investment. Letting I equal original investment, S equal salvage value, and assuming that investment is uniformly consumed, average investment is defined as follows[3]:

Average investment $= (I + S)/2$

To illustrate the computation of the accounting rate of return, assume that an investment requires an initial outlay of $100,000. The life of the investment is five years with the following cash flows: $30,000, $30,000, $40,000, $30,000, $50,000. Assume that the asset has no salvage value after the five years and that all revenues earned within a year are collected in that year. The total cash flow for the five years is $180,000, making the average cash flow $36,000 ($180,000/5). Average depreciation is $20,000 ($100,000/5). The average net income is the difference between these two figures: $16,000 ($36,000 − $20,000). Using the average net income and original investment, the accounting rate of return is 16 percent ($16,000/$100,000). If average investment is used instead of original investment, then the accounting rate of return would be 32 percent ($16,000/$50,000).

Often debt contracts require that a firm maintain certain financial accounting ratios, which can be affected by the income reported and by the level of long-term assets. Accordingly, the accounting rate of return may be used as a screening measure to ensure that any new investment will not adversely affect these ratios. Additionally, because bonuses to managers are often based on accounting income, they may have a personal interest in seeing that any new investment contributes significantly to net income. A manager seeking to maximize personal income will select investments that return the highest net income dollar per dollar invested.

Unlike the payback period, the accounting rate of return does consider a project's profitability; like the payback period, it ignores the time value of money. Ignoring the time value of money is a critical deficiency in this method as well; it can lead a manager to choose investments that do not maximize profits. For example, assume that two investments, A and B, each require an outlay of $100,000 and have no salvage value. Suppose they generate the following cash flows:

---

[3]The average investment formula is computed using the definition of the average value of a function and requires the use of calculus. The investment consumption function is $C(t) = I + [(S − I)/t^*]t$, where t is time and t^* is the life of the investment. By integrating $C(t)$ from 0 to t^* and dividing the result by t^*, the expression $(I + S)/2$ is obtained.

Investment	Year 1	Year 2	Year 3	Year 4	Year 5
A	$80,000	$20,000	$20,000	$20,000	$20,000
B	20,000	80,000	20,000	20,000	20,000

The average cash flow is $32,000 for each investment, the average depreciation is $20,000, and, therefore, the average net income is $12,000. Using original investment, the accounting rate of return for both projects is 12 percent ($12,000/$100,000). Using the accounting rate of return criterion, then, a manager would find both investments equally desirable. As before, however, A is preferable to B because it allows the firm to reinvest an extra $60,000 one year sooner than does B.

It is because the payback period and the accounting rate of return ignore the time value of money that they are referred to as *nondiscounting models*. Discounting models use **discounted cash flows**, which are future cash flows expressed in terms of their present value. But before discounting models can be discussed, we first need to introduce and discuss the concepts of future value and present value.

discounted cash flows

■ FUTURE VALUE AND PRESENT VALUE

Future Value

Suppose a bank advertises a 5 percent annual interest rate. If a customer invests $100, he or she would receive, after one year, the original $100 plus $5 interest [$100 + (0.05)(100) = (1 + 0.05) 100 = (1.05)(100) = $105]. This result can be expressed by the following equation, where F is the future amount, P is the initial or current outlay, and i is the interest rate:

$$F = P(1+i) \tag{11.1}$$

For the example, $F = \$100 \ (1 + 0.05) = \$100 \ (1.05) = \$105$.

Now suppose that the same bank offers a 6 percent rate if the customer leaves the original deposit, plus any interest, on deposit for a total of two years. How much will the customer receive at the end of two years? Again assume that a customer invests $100. Using Equation 11.1, the customer will earn $106 at the end of Year 1 [$F = \$100 \ (1 + 0.06) = (\$100)(1.06) = \$106$]. If this amount is left in the account for a second year, Equation 11.1 is used again with P now assumed to be $106. At the end of the second year, then, the total is $112.36 [$F = \$106 \ (1 + 0.06) = (\$106)(1.06) = \$112.36$]. In the second year, interest is earned on both the original deposit and the interest earned in the first year. The earning of interest on interest is referred to as **compounding of interest**. The value that will accumulate by the end of an investment's life, assuming a specified compound return, is the **future value**. The future value of the $100 deposit in the second example is $112.36.

compounding of interest

future value

A more direct way to compute the future value is possible. Since the first application of Equation 11.1 can be expressed as $F = \$106 = (1.06)\ \$100$, the second application can be expressed as $F = (1.06)\ \$106 = (1.06)\ (1.06)\ \$100 = (1.06)^2\ \$100 = (1 + i)^2 P$. This suggests the following formula for computing amounts for n periods into the future:

$$F = P(1 + i)^n \tag{11.2}$$

Present Value

present value

Often a manager needs to compute not the future value but the amount that must be invested *now* in order to earn some given future value. The amount that must be invested now to produce the future value is known as the *present value* of the future amount. For example, how much must be invested now in order to earn $363 two years from now, assuming that the interest rate is 10 percent? Or put another way, what is the present value of $363 to be received two years from now?

In this example, the future value, the years, and the interest rate are all known; we want to know the current outlay that will produce that future amount. In Equation 11.2, the variable representing the current outlay (the present value of F) is P. Thus, to compute the present value of a future outlay, all we need to do is solve Equation 11.2 for P:

$$P = F/(1 + i)^n \tag{11.3}$$

Using Equation 11.3, we can compute the present value of $363:

$$P = \$363/(1 + 0.1)^2$$
$$= \$363/1.21$$
$$= \$300$$

The present value, $300, is what the future amount of $363 is worth *today*. All other things being equal, having $300 today is the same as having $363 two years from now. Put another way, if a firm requires a 10 percent rate of return, the most the firm would be willing to pay today is $300 for any investment that yields $363 two years from now.

discounting

discount rate
discount factor

The process of computing the present value of future cash flows is often referred to as *discounting*; thus, we say that we have discounted the future value of $363 to its present value of $300. The interest rate used to discount the future cash flow is the **discount rate**. The expression $1/(1 + i)^n$ in Equation 11.3 is the **discount factor**. By letting the discount factor, called *df*, equal $1/(1 + i)^n$, Equation 11.3 can be expressed as $P = F(df)$. To simplify the computation of present value, a table of discount factors is given for various combinations of i and n (see Exhibit 11–7 in the Appendix (page 532)). For example, the discount factor for $i = 10$ percent and $n = 2$ is 0.826 (simply go to the 10 percent column of the table and move down to the second row). With the discount factor, the present value of $363 is computed as follows:

$$P = F(df)$$
$$= \$363 \times 0.826$$
$$= \$300$$

Present Value of an Uneven Series of Cash Flows Exhibit 11–7 can be used to compute the present value of any future cash flow or series of future cash flows. A series of future cash flows is called an ***annuity***. The present value of an annuity is found by computing the present value of each future cash flow and then summing these values. For example, suppose that an investment is expected to produce the following annual cash flows: $110, $121, and $133.10. Assuming a discount rate of 10 percent, the present value of this series of cash receipts is computed in Exhibit 11–2.

Present Value of a Uniform Series of Cash Flows If the series of cash flows is even, the computation of the annuity's present value is simplified. Assume, for example, that an investment is expected to return $100 per year for three years. Using Exhibit 11–7 and assuming a discount rate of 10 percent, the present value of the annuity is computed in Exhibit 11–3.

annuity

EXHIBIT 11–2
Present Value of an Uneven Series of Cash Flows

Year	Cash Receipt	Discount Factor	Present Value[a]
1	$110.00	0.909	$100.00
2	121.00	0.826	100.00
3	133.10	0.751	100.00
			$300.00

[a]Rounded

EXHIBIT 11–3
Present Value of Uniform Series of Cash Flows

Year	Cash Receipt	Discount Factor	Present Value
1	$100	0.909	$ 90.90
2	100	0.826	82.60
3	100	0.751	75.10
		2.486	$248.60

Note: The annual cash flow of $100 can be multiplied by the sum of the discount factors (2.486) to obtain the present value of the uniform series ($248.60).

As with the uneven series of cash flows, the present value in Exhibit 11–3 was computed by calculating the present value of each cash flow separately and then summing them. However, in the case of an annuity displaying uniform cash flows, the computations can be reduced from three to one as described in the note to the exhibit. The sum of the individual discount factors can be thought of as a discount factor for an annuity of uniform cash flows. A table of discount factors that can be used for an annuity of uniform cash flows is available in Exhibit 11–8 in the Appendix (page 533).

■ DISCOUNTING MODELS:
THE NET PRESENT VALUE METHOD

Discounting models explicitly consider the time value of money and, therefore, incorporate the concept of discounting cash inflows and outflows. Two discounting models will be considered: *net present value* (NPV) and *internal rate of return* (IRR). The net present value method will be discussed first; the internal rate of return method is discussed in the following section.

net present value   **Net present value** is the difference in the present value of the cash inflows and outflows associated with a project:

$$NPV = [\Sigma CF_t/(1 + i)^t] - I$$
$$= [\Sigma (CF_t)(df_t)] - I$$
$$= P - I \qquad\qquad \textbf{(11.4)}$$

where I = The present value of the project's cost (usually the initial outlay)
         CF_t = The cash inflow to be received in period t, with
              $t = 1 \ldots n$
         i = The required rate of return
         n = The useful life of the project
         t = The time period
         P = The present value of the project's future cash inflows

A Defining Example

A simple, one-period example will be used to develop an understanding of net present value. Assume that Nancy Wilson is approached by a friend who offers her an opportunity to invest $1,000 in a business venture. The friend assures Nancy that one year from now she will receive a payoff of $1,200. Currently, Nancy has $500 in a money market account that will earn 8 percent interest for the coming year. To raise the other $500, Nancy would need to borrow $500 from the local credit union at a cost of 12 percent per year. Both principal and interest will be repaid at the end of the year. Nancy is confident that she can afford to invest the $1,000 but is not certain that it would make her better off. Should she accept the friend's offer and make the investment?

Choice of a Discount Rate   In answering the question, first consider the rate of return that Nancy would require. If she removes the $500 from the money-

EXHIBIT 11–4
Cost of Capital Illustrated

Source	Amount of Capital	Percentage Cost	Dollar Cost
Savings	$ 500	8%	$ 40
Loan	$ 500	12	60
Total	$1,000	10%[a]	$100

[a]This weighted average can be computed in two ways:
  1. $100/$1,000 = 0.10
  2. (0.5 x 0.08) + (0.5 x 0.12) = 0.10

market account, then she will lose the 8 percent interest for the coming year, creating an opportunity cost of $40 (0.08 × $500). Also, if she borrows $500 from the credit union, she must pay interest of 12 percent, or $60 (0.12 × $500). Thus, to break even, she would need to recover the $1,000 invested and earn a return of $100 ($40 + $60). Any return above the $100 would increase her economic well-being and make the investment desirable. The $100 return itself represents Nancy's **cost of capital**, the weighted average of the costs of funds from all sources. The rate of return corresponding to the cost of capital would be 10 percent ($100/$1,000) and is defined as the **required rate of return**. It is also referred to as the *hurdle rate*. Exhibit 11–4 summarizes Nancy's capital requirements.

> cost of capital

> required rate of
> return
> hurdle rate

Exhibit 11–4 illustrates that the cost of capital is a blend of the costs of capital from all sources. In fact, it is a weighted average of the costs from the various sources, where the weight is defined by the relative amount from each source. For our example, $500 from savings and $500 from a loan represent the sources of the total $1,000 of capital. Thus, each source contributes 50 percent (500/1,000) to the total capital raised. The relative weights, then, are 0.5 for savings and 0.5 for the loan. As the note in Exhibit 11–4 shows, the weighted cost of capital can also be computed by using the relative weights and the individual rates.

Net Present Value: A Measure of Profitability For Nancy to earn a profit, her investment must return more than $1,100 one year from now (the $1,000 invested plus $100 to cover her cost of capital). Since the investment will return $1,200, Nancy will earn a profit of $100 ($1,200 − $1,100). This profit, however, is expressed in future dollars. The profit can also be expressed in *current* dollars by computing its present value. Using the discount rate of 10 percent for one year (0.909), the present value of $100 is $90.90 ($100 × 0.909). The profit of the investment, expressed in current dollars, is equivalent to the project's net present value. To see this, apply the definition of net present value, using the required rate of return of 10 percent.

Year	Cash Flow (CF)	Discount Factor (df)[a]	Present Value [CF (df)]
0	$(1,000)	1.000	$(1,000.00)
1	1,200	0.909	1,090.80[b]
	Net present value		$ 90.80

[a]From Exhibit 11–7
[b]Because of rounding error, the product will be slightly less than $1,090.80.

If the net present value is positive, it signals that (1) the initial investment has been recovered, (2) the cost of capital has been recovered, and (3) a return in excess of (1) and (2) has been received. Thus, if NPV is greater than zero, the investment is profitable and therefore is acceptable. If NPV equals zero, the decision maker will find acceptance or rejection of the investment equal. Finally, if NPV is less than zero, the investment should be rejected. In this case, it is earning less than the required rate of return.[4]

The Reinvestment Assumption   The NPV model implicitly assumes that all cash flows generated by a project are reinvested to earn the required rate of return throughout the life of the project. Assume that the investment opportunity for Nancy Wilson promises two years of returns instead of one. At the end of the first year, $550 will be received; at the end of the second year, the payoff will be $605. Assume now that Nancy has $1,000 in savings available to invest, which, if left in the account for two years, will earn a rate of 10 percent per year.

Assuming that the only source of capital for Nancy is her savings, her cost of capital is 10 percent. Using 10 percent as the discount rate, the net present value of the investment opportunity can be computed as follows:

Year	Cash Flow (CF)	Discount Factor (df)[a]	Present Value [CF (df)]
0	$(1,000)	1.000	$(1,000)
1	550	0.909	500[b]
2	605	· 0.826	500[b]
	Net present value		$ 0

[a]From Exhibit 11–7
[b] Because of rounding error in the discount factor, the product will be slightly less than $500.

According to the net present value analysis, Nancy will be no worse or better off if she invests in the project presented to her by her friend. This

---

[4]In a world in which future cash flows can be predicted with certainty, the required rate of return is the cost of capital. The market-determined cost of capital is the discount rate that should be used if the objective is to maximize profits.

conclusion, however, depends on an implicit assumption concerning reinvestment of the $550 received at the end of Year 1. If Nancy had left the $1,000 in the savings account for two years, the future value of this $1,000 is $1,210 (using Equation 11.2, $F = 1.1^2 \times \$1,000 = 1.21 \times \$1,000 = \$1,210$). For the investment opportunity, Nancy will have $1,210 at the end of Year 2 *only* *if* she reinvests the $550 she receives at the end of Year 1 at 10 percent. By doing so, she will receive $605 (1.1 × $550) at the end of Year 2 from this reinvestment. Adding that $605 to the $605 to be received at the end of Year 2 from the *original* investment produces $1,210. If the $550 is reinvested at less than 10 percent, however, Nancy will be worse off by accepting her friend's investment offer than by leaving her $1,000 in savings. On the other hand, if the $550 can be reinvested to earn more than 10 percent, she will be better off by making the investment. As the example shows, NPV analysis implicitly assumes that the cash inflows received are reinvested to earn the required rate of return throughout the life of the project.

Summary and Discussion of Net Present Value Concepts

The Nancy Wilson example was designed to be as simple as possible in order to develop the concepts pertaining to the use of the net present value method. The following important concepts were brought out by the example:

1. Net present value (NPV) measures the profitability of an investment. If the NPV is positive, it measures the increase in wealth. For a firm, this means that the size of a positive NPV measures the increase in the value of the firm resulting from an investment.

2. To use the NPV method, a discount rate must be identified. The appropriate discount rate for NPV analysis is the firm's cost of capital. The cost of capital is a weighted average of the cost of capital from all sources.

3. The NPV method assumes that each cash inflow from a project will be reinvested to earn the firm's required rate of return throughout the life of the project.

NPV and Firm Value   Although the example was based on an investment decision faced by an individual, the concepts apply equally well to organizations. Accordingly, if the firm's goal is to maximize its market value, a manager should select a portfolio of projects that promises the highest total NPV.

The Cost of Capital   For a firm, the cost of capital should reflect the returns expected by the different parties contributing funds. Essentially, the cost of capital is the opportunity cost of funds provided to the firm. Sources of funds for a firm include debt, the contributions of common stockholders, and the contributions of preferred stockholders. Thus, for a firm, the weighted average cost of capital is the after-tax cost of debt, preferred stock, and common stock. The weights are equal to the proportion of total financing that is provided by each source of capital. For example, assume that a firm used debt, common equity, and preferred stock for financing with after-tax costs of 7 percent, 14 percent, and 11 percent, respectively. The proportion of each type of financing in the firm's financial structure is 20 percent for debt, 60 percent for common equity, and 20 percent for preferred stock. Using these proportions as weights, the firm's cost of capital would be computed as follows (letting K = cost of capital):

$$K = 0.2(0.07) + 0.6(0.14) + 0.2(0.11)$$
$$= 0.12$$

How the cost of each source of capital is computed is discussed in finance texts and occasionally in advanced cost accounting texts. At this point, what should be understood is that each source of capital does not have a cost attached to it and contributes to the firm's overall cost of capital.

A More Realistic Example Using Net Present Value

Golden Toys, Inc., has developed a new toy laser gun that it believes is superior to anything on the market. The marketing manager is excited about the new toy's prospects after completing a detailed market study that revealed expected annual revenues of $150,000. The toy has a projected life of five years. Equipment to produce the toy gun would cost $160,000. After five years, that equipment can be sold for $20,000. In addition to equipment, working capital is expected to increase by $20,000 because of increases in inventories and receivables. The firm expects to recover the investment in working capital at the end of the project's life. Annual cash operating expenses are estimated at $90,000. Assuming that the required rate of return is 12 percent, should the company manufacture the new toy laser gun?

In order to answer the question, two steps must be taken: (1) the cash flows for each year must be identified and (2) the NPV must be computed using the cash flows from Step 1. The solution to the problem is given in Exhibit 11–5.

Notice that Step 2 offers two approaches for computing NPV. Step 2A computes NPV by using discount factors from Exhibit 11–7. Step 2B simplifies the computation by using a single discount factor from Exhibit 11–8 for the even cash flows occurring in Years 1–4.

■ DISCOUNTING MODELS: INTERNAL RATE OF RETURN

internal rate of return

Another discounting model is the internal rate of return (IRR) method. The **internal rate of return** is defined as the interest rate that sets the present value of a project's cash inflows equal to the present value of the project's cost. In

EXHIBIT 11-5

Cash Flows and NPV Analysis

Step 1. Cash-Flow Identification

Year	Item	Cash Flow
0	Equipment	$(160,000)
	Working capital	(20,000)
	Total	$(180,000)
1–4	Revenues	$ 150,000
	Operating expenses	(90,000)
	Total	$ 60,000
5	Revenues	$ 150,000
	Operating expenses	(90,000)
	Salvage	20,000
	Recovery of working capital	20,000
	Total	$ 100,000

Step 2A. NPV Analysis

Year	Cash Flow[a]	Discount Factor[b]	Present Value
0	$(180,000)	1.000	$(180,000)
1	$ 60,000	0.893	53,580
2	60,000	0.797	47,820
3	60,000	0.712	42,720
4	60,000	0.636	38,160
5	100,000	0.567	56,700
	Net present value		$ 58,980

[a]From Step 1
[b]From Exhibit 11–7

Step 2B. NPV Analysis

Year	Cash Flow	Discount Factor	Present Value
0	$(180,000)	1.000	$(180,000)
1–4	60,000	3.037	182,220
5	100,000	0.567	56,700
	Net present value		$ 58,920[a]

[a]Differs from computation in Step 2A because of rounding error

other words, it is the interest rate that sets the project's NPV at zero. The following equation can be used to determine a project's IRR:

$$I = \Sigma CF_t/(1 + i)^t \tag{11.5}$$

where $t = 1 \ldots n$

Once the IRR for a project is computed, it is compared with the firm's required rate of return. If the IRR is greater than the required rate, the project is deemed acceptable; if the IRR is equal to the required rate of return, acceptance or rejection of the investment is equal; if the IRR is less than the required rate of return, the project is rejected.

The internal rate of return is the most widely used of the capital budgeting techniques. One reason for its popularity may be that it is a rate of return, a concept that managers are comfortable in using. Another possibility is that managers may believe (in most cases, incorrectly) that the IRR is the true or actual compounded rate of return being earned by the initial investment. Whatever the reasons for its popularity, a basic understanding of the IRR is necessary. As with NPV, we will begin with a simple example.

Single-Period Example

Recall that Nancy Wilson has the opportunity to invest $1,000 now for a return of $1,200 one year from now. Nancy is able to acquire the necessary capital by borrowing $500 from a credit union and removing $500 from her savings account. The cost of using this capital is 10 percent. The question is whether Nancy should make the investment.

Using the IRR criterion, the investment should be accepted only if the IRR is greater than 10 percent. To compute the IRR, the interest rate that equates the present value of $1,200 to the investment of $1,000 must be identified. Using Equation 11.5, the IRR for the investment being considered by Nancy is computed as follows:

$$I = CF_t/(1+i)^t$$
$$\$1,000 = \$1,200/(1 + i)^1$$
$$\$1,000 (1 + i) = \$1,200$$
$$1 + i = \$1,200/\$1,000$$
$$1 + i = 1.20$$
$$i = 1.20 - 1$$
$$i = 0.20$$

Thus, the IRR is 0.20, or 20 percent.

Since the internal rate of return is 20 percent, the investment should be accepted. This rate is greater than the required rate of return, which is only 10 percent (remember that the required rate of return is equal to the cost of capital). In the special case of a one-period analysis, the IRR represents the actual or true rate of return being earned by the investment (the actual rate of return for the one period is ($1,200 − $1,000)/$1,000 = 0.20). This result, however, holds for the multiple-period case only if a project's cash inflows are reinvested to earn its internal rate of return. More will be said about this later.

Multiple-Period Setting: Uniform Cash Flows

To illustrate the computation of the IRR in a multiple-period setting, assume that Nancy has an opportunity to invest $1,000 in order to receive $474.83 at the end of each year for the next three years. The IRR is the interest rate that equates the present value of the three equal receipts of $474.83 to the investment of $1,000. Since the series of cash flows is uniform, a single discount factor from Exhibit 11–8 can be used to compute the present value of the annuity. Letting *df* be this discount factor and *CF* be the annual cash flow, Equation 11.5 assumes the following form:

$$I = CF(df)$$

Solving for *df*, we obtain:

$$df = I/CF$$
$$= \text{Investment/Annual cash flow}$$

Once the discount factor is computed, go to Exhibit 11–8 and find the row corresponding to the life of the project, then move across that row until the computed discount factor is found. The interest rate corresponding to this discount factor is the IRR.

For example, the discount factor for Nancy's investment is 2.106 ($1,000/$474.83). Since the life of the investment is three years, we must find the third row in Exhibit 11–8 and then move across this row until we encounter 2.106. The interest rate corresponding to 2.106 is 20 percent, which is the IRR.

Exhibit 11–8 does not provide discount factors for every possible interest rate. If a discount factor is computed for a series of uniform cash flows and it falls between two discount factors found in the table, the interest rate can be approximated by using interpolation. To illustrate, assume that the annual cash inflows expected by Nancy are $482.16 instead of $474.83. The new discount factor is 2.074 ($1,000/$482.16). Going once again to the third row in Exhibit 11–8, we find that the discount factor—and thus the IRR—lies between 20 and 22 percent.

The IRR can be approximated by defining an *interest interval* and a *discount interval* and by assuming that the IRR is the same *relative* distance into the interest interval as the discount factor is into the discount interval. This approximation of the IRR is illustrated in Exhibit 11–6. Of course, a business calculator can provide a direct assessment of the IRR and makes interpolation unnecessary.

EXHIBIT 11–6
IRR: Approximation Using Interpolation

Interest Interval	*Discount Factor Interval*
20%	2.106
22	2.042
2%	0.064

Distance of IRR into Discount Factor Interval

Discount factor, 20%	2.106
Discount factor, IRR	(2.074)
Absolute distance	0.032
Relative distance	0.032/0.064 = 0.5

Approximation of IRR

IRR ~ 0.20 + (0.5)(0.02)
      ~ 0.21

Multiple-Period Setting: Uneven Cash Flows

If the cash flows are not uniform, then Equation 11.5 must be used. For a multiple-period setting, Equation 11.5 can be solved by trial and error or by using a business calculator. To illustrate solution by trial and error, assume that a $1,000 investment produces cash flows of $600 and $720 for each of two years. The IRR is the interest rate that sets the present value of these two cash inflows equal to $1,000:

$$P = [\$600/(1 + i)] + [\$720/(1 + i)^2]$$
$$= \$1,000$$

To solve the above equation by trial and error, start by selecting a possible value for i. Given this first guess, the present value of the future cash flows is computed and then compared to the initial investment. If the present value is greater than the initial investment, the interest rate is too low; if the present value is less than the initial investment, the interest rate is too high. The next guess is adjusted accordingly.

Assume the first guess to be 14 percent. Using i equal to 0.14, Exhibit 11–7 yields the following discount factors: 0.877 and 0.769. These discount factors produce the following present value for the two cash inflows:

$$P = (0.877 \times \$600) + (0.769 \times \$720)$$
$$= \$1,079.88$$

Since P is greater than $1,000, the interest rate selected is too low. A higher guess is needed. If the next guess is 24 percent, we obtain the following:

$$P = (0.806 \times \$600) + (0.650 \times \$720)$$
$$= \$951.60$$

Since P is less than $1,000, the interest rate is too high. We now know that the IRR is between 14 and 24 percent. Once a present value above and below the investment is found, interpolation can be used to approximate the IRR, using a present value interval and an interest interval. The present value interval is ($1,079.88, $951.60) with a length of 128.28. The interest interval is (0.14, 0.24) with a length of 0.10. For the IRR, we know that P equals $1,000. The actual distance into the present value interval for the present value corresponding to the IRR is 79.88 ($1,079.88 $-$ $1,000). The relative distance is 0.62 (79.88/128.28). Thus, IRR is approximately 20.2 percent (0.14 + 0.62 x 0.10). Since the closest value to 20.2 percent in Exhibit 11–7 is 20 percent, this value becomes our next guess:

$$P = (0.833 \times \$600) + (0.694 \times \$720)$$
$$= \$999.48$$

Since this value is reasonably close to $1,000, we can say that the IRR is 20 percent. (The IRR is, in fact, exactly 20 percent; the present value is slightly less than the investment because of rounding error in the discount factors found in Exhibit 11–7.)

The Reinvestment Assumption

The IRR represents the actual compounded rate of return on the entire original investment if and only if the cash inflows are reinvested to earn a rate of return equal to the IRR throughout the life of the project. For example, if a return of 20 percent is to be earned on $1,000 over two years, then the future value of the $1,000 at the end of two years would be $1,440 ($1,000 $\times$ $(1.2)^2$ = $1,440).

From an earlier example, we know that an investment of $1,000 producing a cash inflow of $600 at the end of Year 1 and a cash inflow of $720 at the end of Year 2 yields an IRR of 20 percent. We also know that the actual return is 20 percent only if the original investment yields a future value of $1,440. Thus, we can say that the actual return on the investment is 20 percent only if we assume that the cash inflow of $600 received at the end of Year 1 is reinvested to earn 20 percent. If this reinvestment occurs, then at the end of Year 2, the future value of $600 will be $720 [$600 $\times$ (1 + 0.2) = $720]. Adding this $720 to the $720 generated at the end of Year 2 from the original investment produces the necessary future value of $1,440.

If the cash inflows received from the project cannot be reinvested to earn the same rate as the IRR, the IRR cannot be interpreted as the actual rate of return. In this case, the actual rate of return will be a weighted average of the IRR and the reinvestment rate.

The IRR can also be defined as the rate of return being earned on the funds that remain internally invested in the project. To illustrate, again assume an investment of $1,000 with a project life of two years. The cash inflows received at the end of each year are $600 and $720. At the beginning of Year 1, $1,000 is invested in the project. At the end of Year 1, the project produces a 20 percent return on the $1,000. Since $600 is received at the end of Year 1, $200 of this represents the 20 percent return (0.2 × $1,000) on the funds invested in the project, and $400 represents a return of the capital invested. This leaves $600 of capital invested in the project ($1,000 − $400). For the second year, the return is 20 percent on the remaining funds ($600) invested in the project. Since $720 is received, $120 of it represents the return on the remaining invested funds (0.2 × $600) and the remaining $600 is the return of the rest of the original capital investment. The analysis is summarized below.

(1) Year	(2) Beginning Value of the Investment	(3) Cash Inflow	(4) 20% Return on Investment	(5)[a] Reduction in Value of the Investment	(6) Ending Value of Investment
1	$1,000	$600	$200	$400	$600
2	600	720	120	600	—

[a](3) − (4)

▪ SUMMARY OF LEARNING OBJECTIVES

1. **Explain the difference between discounting and nondiscounting models.** Managers make capital budgeting decisions by using formal models to decide whether to accept or reject proposed projects. These decision models are classified as nondiscounting and discounting, depending on whether they address the question of the time value of money. Discounting models explicitly consider the time value of money.

2. **Compute the payback period for an investment.** The payback period is the time required for a firm to recover its initial investment. For even cash flows, it is calculated by dividing the investment by the annual cash flow. For uneven cash flows, the cash flows are summed until the investment is recovered. If only a fraction of a year is needed, then it is assumed that the cash flows occur evenly within each year.

3. **Explain the role of the payback period in capital budgeting decisions.** The payback period ignores the time value of money and the profitability of projects because it does not consider the cash inflows available beyond the payback period. However, it does supply some useful information. The payback period is useful in assessing and controlling risk, minimizing the impact of an investment on a firm's liquidity, and controlling the risk of obsolescence.

4. **Compute the accounting rate of return for an investment.** This measure is computed by dividing the average income expected from an investment by either the original or average investment. Unlike the payback period, it does consider the profitability of a project; however, it ignores the time value of money.

5. **Compute the present value of future cash flows.** The present value is computed by multiplying the future cash flow by a discount factor. Exhibit 11–7 and Exhibit 11–8 provide discount factors to assist in this computation.

6. **Use NPV analysis to determine whether an investment is acceptable.** NPV is the difference between the present value of future cash flows and the initial investment outlay. To use the model, a required rate of return must be identified (usually the cost of capital). The NPV method uses the required rate of return to compute the present value of a project's cash inflows and outflows. If the present value of the inflows is greater than the present value of the outflows, the net present value is greater than zero, and the project is profitable; if the NPV is less than zero, the project is not profitable and should be rejected.

7. **Explain why the cost of capital is used as the discount rate in the NPV model.** The cost of capital is what must be paid to all sources of the capital for its use. Thus, a firm must earn at least this rate to avoid a loss. Any amount earned above this level is profit. Thus, the cost of capital represents a logical benchmark for evaluating investments and should be used as the discount rate. Using any rate below this would lead a manager to choose unprofitable investments. A rate above the cost of capital could lead to the rejection of profitable investments.

8. **Use the internal rate of return to assess the acceptability of an investment.** The IRR is computed by finding the interest rate that equates the present value of a project's cash inflows with the present value of its cash outflows. If the IRR is greater than the required rate of return (cost of capital), the project is acceptable; if the IRR is less than the required rate of return, the project should be rejected.

■ KEY TERMS

Accounting rate of return   The rate of return obtained by dividing the average accounting net income by the original investment (or by average investment). (p. 513)

Annuity   A series of future cash flows. (p. 517)

Capital budgeting   The process of planning, setting goals and priorities, arranging financing, and identifying criteria for making long-term investments. (p. 509)

Compounding of interest   Paying interest on interest. (p. 515)

Cost of capital   The cost of investment funds, usually viewed as a weighted average of the costs of funds from all sources. (p. 519)

Discount factor   The factor used to convert a future cash flow to its present value. (p. 516)

Discount rate   The rate of return used to compute the present value of future cash flows. (p. 516)

Discounted cash flows   Future cash flows expressed in present value terms. (p. 515)

Discounting   The act of finding the present value of future cash flows. (p. 516)

Discounting model   Any capital budgeting model that explicitly considers the time value of money in identifying criteria for accepting or rejecting proposed projects. (p. 511)

Future value   The value that will accumulate by the end of an investment's life if the investment earns a specified compounded return. (p. 515)

Hurdle rate   See *Required rate of return.* (p. 519)

Independent projects   Projects that, if accepted or rejected, will not affect the cash flows of another project. (p. 509)

Internal rate of return   The rate of return that equates the present value of a project's cash inflows with the present value of its cash outflows (i.e., it sets the NPV equal to zero). Also, the rate of return being earned on funds that remain internally invested in a project. (p. 522)

Mutually exclusive projects   Projects that, if accepted, preclude the acceptance of competing projects. (p. 509)

Net present value   The difference between the present value of a project's cash inflows and the present value of its cash outflows. (p. 518)

Nondiscounting model   Capital budgeting models that identify criteria for accepting or rejecting projects without considering the time value of money. (p. 511)

Payback period   The time required for a project to return its investment. (p. 511)

Present value   The current value of a future cash flow. It represents the amount that must be invested now if the future cash flow is to be received assuming compounding at a given rate of interest. (p. 516)

Required rate of return   The minimum rate of return that a project must earn in order to be acceptable. Usually corresponds to the cost of capital. (p. 519)

▪ REVIEW PROBLEM

Bill Larson is investigating the possibility of acquiring an ice-cream franchise. To acquire the franchise requires an initial outlay of $300,000 (the purchase includes building and equipment). To raise the capital, Bill will sell stock valued at $200,000 (the stock pays dividends of $18,000 per year) and borrow $100,000. The loan for $100,000 would carry an interest rate of 12 percent.

   The franchise will produce an annual cash inflow of $50,000. Bill expects to operate the business for twenty years, after which he will turn it over to one of his children.

Required:

1. Compute the payback period.

2. Assuming that depreciation is $14,000 per year, compute the accounting rate of return (on total investment).

3. Compute Bill's cost of capital.

4. Compute the NPV of the franchise.

5. Compute the IRR of the franchise.

6. Should Bill acquire the franchise?

Solution:

1. The payback period is $300,000/$50,000, or six years.

2. The accounting rate of return is ($50,000 − $14,000)/$300,000, or 12 percent.

3. The cost of capital is (⅔ × 0.09) + (⅓ × 0.12), or (0.06) + (0.04), or 10 percent. (The opportunity cost of the stock is $18,000/$200,000, or 9 percent.)

4. From Exhibit 11–8, the discount factor for an annuity with *i* at 10 percent and *n* at 20 years is 8.514. Thus, the NPV is 8.514 × 50,000 − $300,000, or $125,700.

5. The discount factor associated with the IRR is 6.00 ($300,000/$50,000). From Exhibit 11–8, the IRR is between 14 and 16 percent (using the row corresponding to period 20). The interest interval is 2 percent (0.16 − 0.14). The discount interval is 0.694 (6.623 − 5.929). The distance of the IRR discount factor into the interval is 0.623 (6.623 − 6.000), for a relative distance of 0.623/0.694 ~ 0.9. Thus, IRR ~ 0.14 + 0.9 x 0.02, or approximately 15.8 percent.

6. Since the NPV is positive and the IRR is greater than Bill's cost of capital, the franchise is a sound investment. This, of course, assumes that the cash flow projections are accurate.

APPENDIX: PRESENT VALUE TABLES

EXHIBIT 11–7
Present Value of $1[a]

Periods	2%	4%	6%	8%	10%	12%	14%	16%	18%	20%	22%	24%	26%	28%	30%	32%	40%
1	0.980	0.962	0.943	0.926	0.909	0.893	0.877	0.862	0.847	0.833	0.820	0.806	0.794	0.781	0.769	0.758	0.714
2	0.961	0.925	0.890	0.857	0.826	0.797	0.769	0.743	0.718	0.694	0.672	0.650	0.630	0.610	0.592	0.574	0.510
3	0.942	0.889	0.840	0.794	0.751	0.712	0.675	0.641	0.609	0.579	0.551	0.524	0.500	0.477	0.455	0.435	0.364
4	0.924	0.855	0.792	0.735	0.683	0.636	0.592	0.552	0.516	0.482	0.451	0.423	0.397	0.373	0.350	0.329	0.260
5	0.906	0.822	0.747	0.681	0.621	0.567	0.519	0.476	0.437	0.402	0.370	0.341	0.315	0.291	0.269	0.250	0.186
6	0.888	0.790	0.705	0.630	0.564	0.507	0.456	0.410	0.370	0.335	0.303	0.275	0.250	0.227	0.207	0.189	0.133
7	0.871	0.760	0.665	0.583	0.513	0.452	0.400	0.354	0.314	0.279	0.249	0.222	0.198	0.178	0.159	0.143	0.095
8	0.853	0.731	0.627	0.540	0.467	0.404	0.351	0.305	0.266	0.233	0.204	0.179	0.157	0.139	0.123	0.108	0.068
9	0.837	0.703	0.592	0.500	0.424	0.361	0.308	0.263	0.225	0.194	0.167	0.144	0.125	0.108	0.094	0.082	0.048
10	0.820	0.676	0.558	0.463	0.386	0.322	0.270	0.227	0.191	0.162	0.137	0.116	0.099	0.085	0.073	0.062	0.035
11	0.804	0.650	0.527	0.429	0.350	0.287	0.237	0.195	0.162	0.135	0.112	0.094	0.079	0.066	0.056	0.047	0.025
12	0.788	0.625	0.497	0.397	0.319	0.257	0.208	0.168	0.137	0.112	0.092	0.076	0.062	0.052	0.043	0.036	0.018
13	0.773	0.601	0.469	0.368	0.290	0.229	0.182	0.145	0.116	0.093	0.075	0.061	0.050	0.040	0.033	0.027	0.013
14	0.758	0.577	0.442	0.340	0.263	0.205	0.160	0.125	0.099	0.078	0.062	0.049	0.039	0.032	0.025	0.021	0.009
15	0.743	0.555	0.417	0.315	0.239	0.183	0.140	0.108	0.084	0.065	0.051	0.040	0.031	0.025	0.020	0.016	0.006
16	0.728	0.534	0.394	0.292	0.218	0.163	0.123	0.093	0.071	0.054	0.042	0.032	0.025	0.019	0.015	0.012	0.005
17	0.714	0.513	0.371	0.270	0.198	0.146	0.108	0.080	0.060	0.045	0.034	0.026	0.020	0.015	0.012	0.009	0.003
18	0.700	0.494	0.350	0.250	0.180	0.130	0.095	0.069	0.051	0.038	0.028	0.021	0.016	0.012	0.009	0.007	0.002
19	0.686	0.475	0.331	0.232	0.164	0.116	0.083	0.060	0.043	0.031	0.023	0.017	0.012	0.009	0.007	0.005	0.002
20	0.673	0.456	0.312	0.215	0.149	0.104	0.073	0.051	0.037	0.026	0.019	0.014	0.010	0.007	0.005	0.004	0.001
21	0.660	0.439	0.294	0.199	0.135	0.093	0.064	0.044	0.031	0.022	0.015	0.011	0.008	0.006	0.004	0.003	0.001
22	0.647	0.422	0.278	0.184	0.123	0.083	0.056	0.038	0.026	0.018	0.013	0.009	0.006	0.004	0.003	0.002	0.001
23	0.634	0.406	0.262	0.170	0.112	0.074	0.049	0.033	0.022	0.015	0.010	0.007	0.005	0.003	0.002	0.002	0.000
24	0.622	0.390	0.247	0.158	0.102	0.066	0.043	0.028	0.019	0.013	0.008	0.006	0.004	0.003	0.002	0.002	0.000
25	0.610	0.375	0.233	0.146	0.092	0.059	0.038	0.024	0.016	0.010	0.007	0.005	0.003	0.002	0.002	0.001	0.000
26	0.598	0.361	0.220	0.135	0.084	0.053	0.033	0.021	0.014	0.009	0.006	0.004	0.002	0.002	0.001	0.001	0.000
27	0.586	0.347	0.207	0.125	0.076	0.047	0.029	0.018	0.011	0.007	0.005	0.003	0.002	0.002	0.001	0.001	0.000
28	0.574	0.333	0.196	0.116	0.069	0.042	0.026	0.016	0.010	0.006	0.004	0.002	0.002	0.001	0.001	0.001	0.000
29	0.563	0.321	0.185	0.107	0.063	0.037	0.022	0.014	0.008	0.005	0.003	0.002	0.001	0.001	0.001	0.000	0.000
30	0.552	0.308	0.174	0.099	0.057	0.033	0.020	0.012	0.007	0.004	0.003	0.002	0.001	0.001	0.000	0.000	0.000

[a] $P_n = A/(1 + i)^n$

EXHIBIT 11–8
Present Value of an Annuity of $1 in Arrears[a]

Periods	2%	4%	6%	8%	10%	12%	14%	16%	18%	20%	22%	24%	26%	28%	30%	32%	40%
1	0.980	0.962	0.943	0.926	0.909	0.893	0.877	0.862	0.847	0.833	0.820	0.806	0.794	0.781	0.769	0.758	0.714
2	1.942	1.886	1.833	1.783	1.736	1.690	1.647	1.605	1.566	1.528	1.492	1.457	1.424	1.392	1.361	1.331	1.224
3	2.884	2.775	2.673	2.577	2.487	2.402	2.322	2.246	2.174	2.106	2.042	1.981	1.923	1.868	1.816	1.766	1.589
4	3.808	3.630	3.465	3.312	3.170	3.037	2.914	2.798	2.690	2.589	2.494	2.404	2.320	2.241	2.166	2.096	1.849
5	4.713	4.452	4.212	3.993	3.791	3.605	3.433	3.274	3.127	2.991	2.864	2.745	2.635	2.532	2.436	2.345	2.035
6	5.601	5.242	4.917	4.623	4.355	4.111	3.889	3.685	3.498	3.326	3.167	3.020	2.885	2.759	2.643	2.534	2.168
7	6.472	6.002	5.582	5.206	4.868	4.564	4.288	4.039	3.812	3.605	3.416	3.242	3.083	2.937	2.802	2.677	2.263
8	7.325	6.733	6.210	5.747	5.335	4.968	4.639	4.344	4.078	3.837	3.619	3.421	3.241	3.076	2.925	2.786	2.331
9	8.162	7.435	6.802	6.247	5.759	5.328	4.946	4.607	4.303	4.031	3.786	3.566	3.366	3.184	3.019	2.868	2.379
10	8.983	8.111	7.360	6.710	6.145	5.650	5.216	4.833	4.494	4.192	3.923	3.682	3.465	3.269	3.092	2.930	2.414
11	9.787	8.760	7.887	7.139	6.495	5.938	5.453	5.029	4.656	4.327	4.035	3.776	3.543	3.335	3.147	2.978	2.438
12	10.575	9.385	8.384	7.536	6.814	6.194	5.660	5.197	4.793	4.439	4.127	3.851	3.606	3.387	3.190	3.013	2.456
13	11.348	9.986	8.853	7.904	7.103	6.424	5.842	5.342	4.910	4.533	4.203	3.912	3.656	3.427	3.223	3.040	2.469
14	12.106	10.563	9.295	8.244	7.367	6.628	6.002	5.468	5.008	4.611	4.265	3.962	3.695	3.459	3.249	3.061	2.478
15	12.849	11.118	9.712	8.559	7.606	6.811	6.142	5.575	5.092	4.675	4.315	4.001	3.726	3.483	3.268	3.076	2.484
16	13.578	11.652	10.106	8.851	7.824	6.974	6.265	5.668	5.162	4.730	4.357	4.033	3.751	3.503	3.283	3.088	2.489
17	14.292	12.166	10.477	9.122	8.022	7.120	6.373	5.749	5.222	4.775	4.391	4.059	3.771	3.518	3.295	3.097	2.492
18	14.992	12.659	10.828	9.372	8.201	7.250	6.467	5.818	5.273	4.812	4.419	4.080	3.786	3.529	3.304	3.104	2.494
19	15.678	13.134	11.158	9.604	8.365	7.366	6.550	5.877	5.316	4.843	4.442	4.097	3.799	3.539	3.311	3.109	2.496
20	16.351	13.590	11.470	9.818	8.514	7.469	6.623	5.929	5.353	4.870	4.460	4.110	3.808	3.546	3.316	3.113	2.497
21	17.011	14.029	11.764	10.017	8.649	7.562	6.687	5.973	5.384	4.891	4.476	4.121	3.816	3.551	3.320	3.116	2.498
22	17.658	14.451	12.042	10.201	8.772	7.645	6.743	6.011	5.410	4.909	4.488	4.130	3.822	3.556	3.323	3.118	2.498
23	18.292	14.857	12.303	10.371	8.883	7.718	6.792	6.044	5.432	4.925	4.499	4.137	3.827	3.559	3.325	3.120	2.499
24	18.914	15.247	12.550	10.529	8.985	7.784	6.835	6.073	5.451	4.937	4.507	4.143	3.831	3.562	3.327	3.121	2.499
25	19.523	15.622	12.783	10.675	9.077	7.843	6.873	6.097	5.467	4.948	4.514	4.147	3.834	3.564	3.329	3.122	2.499
26	20.121	15.983	13.003	10.810	9.161	7.896	6.906	6.118	5.480	4.956	4.520	4.151	3.837	3.566	3.330	3.123	2.500
27	20.707	16.330	13.211	10.935	9.237	7.943	6.935	6.136	5.492	4.964	4.524	4.154	3.839	3.567	3.331	3.123	2.500
28	21.281	16.663	13.406	11.051	9.307	7.984	6.961	6.152	5.502	4.970	4.528	4.157	3.840	3.568	3.331	3.124	2.500
29	21.844	16.984	13.591	11.158	9.370	8.022	6.983	6.166	5.510	4.975	4.531	4.159	3.841	3.569	3.332	3.124	2.500
30	22.396	17.292	13.765	11.258	9.427	8.055	7.003	6.177	5.517	4.979	4.534	4.160	3.842	3.569	3.332	3.124	2.500

[a] $P_n = (1/i)[1 - 1/(1 + i)^n]$

■ QUESTIONS

1   Explain the difference between independent projects and mutually exclusive projects.

2   Explain why the timing and quantity of cash flows are important in capital budgeting decisions.

3   The time value of money is ignored by the payback period and the accounting rate of return. Explain why this is a major deficiency in these two models.

4   What is the payback period? Compute the payback period for an investment requiring an initial outlay of $80,000 with expected annual cash inflows of $30,000.

5   Name and discuss three possible reasons that the payback period is used to help make capital investment decisions.

6   What is the accounting rate of return? Compute the accounting rate of return for an investment that requires an initial outlay of $250,000 and promises an average net income of $75,000.

7   What is meant by the term *future value*?

8   What are discounted cash flows? Discount rate? Discount factor?

9   What is meant by the term *present value*?

10   Compute the present value of an annuity of uniform cash inflows if the discount rate is 8 percent and the annual cash inflow produced by the annuity is $32,000. The expected life of the annuity is four years.

11   The net present value is the same as the profit of a project expressed in present dollars. Do you agree? Explain.

12   What is the cost of capital? What role does it play in capital budgeting decisions?

13   What is the role that the required rate of return plays for the NPV model? For the IRR model?

14   The IRR is the true or actual rate of return being earned by the project. Do you agree or disagree? Discuss.

15   Explain how the NPV is used to determine whether a project should be accepted or rejected.

16   Explain the relationship between NPV and a firm's value.

17   Compute the IRR for a project that requires an investment of $299,100 and provides a return of $100,000 per year for four years.

18   What methods would you choose to use to make a capital investment decision? Why?

■ EXERCISES

E11–1   **Basic Concepts**   Each of the following parts is independent.

1. Harry Kingston has just invested $100,000 as a part owner of a fast-food franchise. He expects to receive an income of $30,000 per year from the investment. What is the payback period for Harry?

2. Bill Jones placed $10,000 in a three-year savings plan. The plan pays 10 percent, and he cannot withdraw the money early without a penalty. Assuming that Bill leaves the money in the plan for the full three years, how much money will he have?

3. Queens Manufacturing is considering the purchase of a robotics material handling system. The cash benefits will be $100,000 per year. The system costs $580,000 and will last ten years. Compute the NPV assuming a discount rate of 12 percent. Should the company buy the robotics system?

4. Helen Henderson has just invested $50,000 in a company. She expects to receive $8,050 per year for the next 8 years. Her cost of capital is 8 percent. Compute the internal rate of return. Did Helen make a good decision?

E11–2 **Present Value Computations** Complete the following cases, each independent of the others.

1. Two independent projects have the following cash flows:

Year	Project I	Project II
1	$10,000	$20,000
2	10,000	10,000
3	10,000	5,000
4	10,000	5,000

Compute the present value of each project, assuming a discount rate of 16 percent.

2. Suppose that two parents want to have $20,000 in a fund six years from now to provide support for their daughter's college education. How much must they invest now in order to have the desired amount if the investment can earn 8 percent? 12 percent? 16 percent?

3. Some new equipment promises to save $30,000 per year in operating expenses. The life of the machine is ten years. Assuming that the company's cost of capital is 12 percent, what is the most the company should pay for the new equipment?

4. A seller is asking $399,300 for some computer-aided manufacturing equipment, which is expected to last five years and to generate equal annual savings (because of reductions in labor costs, material waste, and so on). What is the minimum savings in operating expenses that must be earned each year to justify the acquisition? Assume the buyer's cost of capital is 14 percent.

E11–3 **Payback; Accounting Rate of Return; NPV; IRR** Palmroy Company is considering an investment in equipment that will be used to produce a new product line. The outlay required is $500,000. The equipment is expected to last five years and will have no salvage value. The expected cash flows associated with the project are given below:

Year	Cash Revenues	Cash Expenses
1	$650,000	$500,000
2	650,000	500,000
3	650,000	500,000
4	650,000	500,000
5	650,000	500,000

Required:

1. Compute the project's payback period.

2. Compute the project's accounting rate of return (a) on initial investment and (b) on average investment.

3. Compute the project's net present value, assuming a required rate of return of 10 percent.

4. Compute the project's internal rate of return.

E11–4   **Payback; Accounting Rate of Return; Present Value; NPV; IRR**   The first two parts are related; the last three are independent of all other parts.

1. Randy Willis is considering investing in one of the two following projects. Either project will require an investment of $10,000. The expected cash flows for the two projects are given below. Assume each project is depreciable.

Year	Project A	Project B
1	$ 3,000	$3,000
2	4,000	4,000
3	5,000	6,000
4	10,000	3,000
5	10,000	3,000

What is the payback period for each project? If rapid payback is important, which project should be chosen? Which would you choose?

2. Calculate the accounting rate of return for each project in Part 1. Which project should be chosen based on the accounting rate of return?

3. Wilma Golding is retiring and has the option to take her retirement as a lump sum of $225,000 or to receive $24,000 per year for twenty years. Wilma's required rate of return is 8 percent. Assuming Wilma will live for another twenty years, should she take the lump sum or the annuity?

4. David Booth is interested in investing in some tools and equipment so that he can do independent dry walling. The cost of the tools and equipment is $20,000. He estimates that the return from owning his own equipment will be $6,000 per year. The tools and equipment will last six years. Assuming a required rate of return of 8 percent, calculate the NPV of the investment. Should he invest?

5. Patsy Folson is evaluating what appears to be an attractive opportunity. She is currently the owner of a small manufacturing company and has the opportunity to acquire another small company's equipment that would provide production of a part currently purchased externally. She estimates that the savings from internal production would be $25,000 per year. She estimates that the equipment would last ten years. The owner is asking $130,400 for the equipment. Her company's cost of capital is 10 percent. Calculate the project's internal rate of return. Should she acquire the equipment?

E11–5   **NPV; Accounting Rate of Return; Payback**   The cash inflows for two independent projects are as follows:

Year	Project A	Project B
1	$50,000	$10,000
2	20,000	10,000
3	40,000	70,000
4	20,000	80,000
5	10,000	90,000

Both projects require an investment in equipment totaling $100,000. The equipment has a life of five years with no salvage value.

Required:

1. Assuming a discount rate of 12 percent, compute the net present value of each project.

2. Compute the payback period for each project. Assume that the manager of the company accepts only projects with a payback period of three years or less. Offer some reasons why this may be a rational strategy even though the NPV computed in requirement 1 may indicate otherwise.

3. Compute the accounting rate of return for each project using (a) initial investment and (b) average investment.

E11–6 **NPV: Basic Concepts** A company is considering an investment that requires an outlay of $100,000 and promises a cash inflow one year from now of $115,500. The company's cost of capital is 10 percent.

Required:

1. Break the $115,500 future cash inflow into three components: (a) the return of the original investment, (b) the cost of capital, and (c) the profit earned on the investment. Now compute the present value of the profit earned on the investment.

2. Compute the NPV of the investment. Compare this with the present value of the profit computed in requirement 1. What does this tell you about the meaning of NPV?

E11–7 **NPV; Cost of Capital; Basic Concepts** Real Company has an opportunity to invest in a new product line that will have a two-year life cycle. The investment requires a current $50,000 outlay. The capital will be raised by borrowing $10,000 and by raising $40,000 through the issue of new stock. The $10,000 loan will have net interest payments of $500 at the end of each of the two years, with the principal being repaid at the end of Year 2 (thus, the net cost of debt is 5 percent). The stock issue carries with it an expectation of a 10 percent return, expressed in the form of dividends at the end of each year ($4,000 in dividends will be paid each of the next two years). The sources of capital for this investment represent the same proportion and costs that the company typically has. Finally, the project will produce cash inflows of $30,000 per year for the next two years.

Required:

1. Compute the cost of capital for the project.

2. Compute the NPV for the project. Explain why it is not necessary to subtract the interest payments and the dividend payments from the annual inflow of $30,000 in carrying out this computation.

E11–8 **Payback; IRR Computation; Interpolation** Youngston Manufacturing is considering the installation of a new conveyor-belt system. The system will reduce the number of material handlers and increase the productivity of direct laborers by lowering the number of interruptions to production. The estimated savings of the system total $110,000 per year. The cost of the system is $510,290, and it is expected to last eight years. The company's required rate of return is 9 percent.

Required:

1. Compute the payback period for the conveyor belt.

2. Compute the IRR for the conveyor belt. Should the project be accepted?

3. Suppose that an error was found in the estimate of the annual savings that, when corrected, drops the estimate to $92,000. Recompute the IRR. Should the project be accepted?

E11–9   **IRR; Reinvestment Assumption**   Henry Johnson has invested $10,000 that is paying him 15 percent compounded interest per year. The investment will last two more years, at which time the principal of $10,000 and all interest owed will be returned. Henry can exercise an option and remove the $10,000 immediately. His investment counselor has urged Henry to remove the $10,000 and invest it in a small firm that will return $5,800 at the end of the first year and $6,728 at the end of the second. His investment counselor assures him that the project will be earning 16 percent—a better return than the 15 percent currently being earned.

Required:

1. Compute Henry's wealth at the end of two years if he leaves the $10,000 in its current investment.

2. Compute Henry's wealth at the end of two years if the $10,000 invested in the business actually earns 16 percent.

3. Compute the IRR of the investment in the small firm. Assume that any funds received at the end of Year 1 are invested to earn 10 percent. Compute Henry's wealth at the end of two years under this assumption. Repeat the computation with the assumption that any funds received at the end of Year 1 are reinvested to earn 16 percent. What does this tell you about the IRR?

4. How reasonable is it to assume that any reinvestment of funds can earn the IRR?

E11–10   **NPV; Reinvestment Assumption**   A small company is considering the acquisition of some second-hand PCs and general ledger software. The system would last two years and would then need to be replaced with newer equipment and updated software. The investment required would be $15,000 and would save $11,000 in clerical and other bookkeeping costs in the first year and $12,100 in the second. The savings realized at the end of the first year would be invested to earn the company's cost of capital, which is 10 percent.

Required:

1. Using the company's cost of capital and the reinvestment assumption, compute the total value of the savings at the end of Year 2. Now break this value into three components: (a) recovery of the initial investment, (b) recovery of the cost of capital, and (c) the profit earned by the investment. Finally, compute the present value of the profit using the cost of capital as the discount rate.

2. Compute the NPV of the investment. Compare this with the present value of the future profit computed in Requirement 1. What role did the reinvestment assumption have in the computation? How reasonable is it to assume that a firm can reinvest funds to earn its cost of capital?

E11–11   **NPV; IRR; Payback; Accounting Rate of Return**   Mercy Hospital is considering the acquisition of state-of-the-art equipment for blood analysis. The equipment costs $60,000 but will produce significant savings by reducing the number of lab technicians needed and by lowering fees paid to outside lab services due to inadequate in-house facilities. The equipment has a seven-year life with no salvage value. The estimated savings are as follows:

Year	Net Cash Savings
1	$12,000
2	18,000
3–7	25,000

The hospital requires that all investments earn 12 percent.

Required:

1. Compute the NPV of the investment.
2. Compute the IRR.
3. Compute the payback period.
4. Compute the accounting rate of return.

E11–12   **Solving for Unknowns**   Solve each of the following independent cases:

1. Thomas Company is investing $120,000 in a project that will yield a uniform series of cash inflows over the next four years. If the internal rate of return is 14 percent, how much cash inflow per year can be expected?

2. Video Repair has decided to invest in some new electronic equipment. The equipment will have a three-year life and will produce a uniform series of cash savings. The net present value of the equipment is $1,750, using a discount rate of 8 percent. The internal rate of return is 12 percent. Determine the investment and the amount of cash savings realized each year.

3. A new lathe costing $60,096 will produce savings of $12,000 per year. How many years must the lathe last if an IRR of 18 percent is realized?

4. The NPV of a project is $3,927. The project has a life of four years and produces the following cash flows:

Year 1	$10,000
Year 2	12,000
Year 3	15,000
Year 4	?

The cost of the project is two times the cash flow produced in Year 4. The discount rate is 10 percent. Find the cost of the project and the cash flow for Year 4.

E11–13   **Flexible Manufacturing System; Payback; NPV; IRR**   Gina Ripley, president of Dearing Company, is considering the purchase of a flexible manufacturing system. The benefits/savings associated with the system are described below:

Increased quality	$70,000
Decrease in operating costs	60,000
Increase in on-time deliveries	20,000

The system will cost $900,000 and will last ten years. The company's cost of capital is 12 percent.

Required:

1. Calculate the payback period for the system. Assume that the company has a policy to accept only projects with a payback of five years or less. Would the system be acquired?

2. Calculate the NPV and IRR for the project. Should the system be purchased—even if it does not meet the payback criterion?

3. The project manager reviewed the projected cash flows and pointed out that two items had been missed. First, the system would have a salvage value of $100,000 at the end of ten years. Second, the increased quality and delivery performance would allow the company to increase its market share by 20 percent. This would produce an additional annual benefit of $30,000. Recalculate the payback period, NPV, and IRR given this new information. Does the decision change?

E11–14   **Implementation of an ABC System; Payback; NPV**   Keith Young was certain that the current cost system was costing the company money. Over time, the cost system had become less useful. Products had been added and overhead had become a much greater percentage of total manufacturing costs. Keith believed that overhead costs were not being accurately assigned to products, causing distorted product costs. In harmony with these views, Keith had hired a consultant to review the company's accounting system. The consultant recommended the installation of an activity-based cost system. The justification was straightforward. The cost of errors from the current system was high. The consultant estimated the following annual cost of inaccurate cost information:

Special studies	$ 50,000
Lost bids	150,000
Suboptimal product mix	60,000
Poor marketing (mostly related to new products)	140,000
Total	$400,000

These costs can be avoided with the installation of a more accurate cost system. The consultant recommended an ABC system. The cost of implementing the system was also estimated.

Acquisition of PCs and associated software	$ 425,000
Mainframe upgrade and software development	500,000
System redesign	375,000
Training	450,000
Total investment	$1,750,000

The company's cost of capital is 14 percent. The ABC system is projected to have a life of ten years.

Required:

1. Compute the payback period for the ABC system.

2. Compute the NPV of the ABC system. Should the system be implemented?

■ PROBLEMS

Note: For all problems, assume there are no income taxes.

P11–1 **Basic NPV Analysis** Tara Anderson, marketing manager, knew that the acceptance of the new product would depend on the economic feasibility of acquiring the equipment needed to produce the product. The equipment would cost $100,000 and its cash operating expenses would total $20,000 per year. The equipment would last for seven years but would need a major overhaul costing $10,000 at the end of the fifth year. At the end of seven years, the equipment would be sold for $8,000. An increase in working capital totaling $10,000 would also be needed at the beginning of the project. This would be recovered at the end of the seven years.

   The new product (exercise equipment) would sell for $100 per unit and would cost $70 per unit to produce (in addition to the operating expenses of the equipment). Tara expects to sell 1,500 units per year. The cost of capital is 10 percent.

Required:

1. Prepare a schedule of cash flows for the proposed project.

2. Compute the NPV of the project. Should the new product be produced?

P11–2 **IRR; Interpolation; Uncertainty** A company is considering three independent projects. The cash flows associated with each project are given below:

Year	Project A	Project B	Project C
0	$(120,000)	$(85,800)	($200,000)
1	39,228	25,000	50,000
2	39,228	25,000	50,000
3	39,228	25,000	50,000
4	39,228	25,000	50,000
5	39,228	25,000	60,000

The cost of capital for the company is 12 percent.

Required:

1. Calculate the IRR for each project. Which investments should be accepted?

2. Assume that the cash flows associated with Project B are uncertain. They could actually be as low as $22,600 and as high as $27,000. Calculate the IRR for the low end. Would you now accept the project?

3. Refer to requirement 2. What annual cash flows would be needed to provide an IRR equal to 12 percent? Based on your analysis, would you accept Project B? What additional information would you like to have before making this decision?

P11–3 **NPV Analysis** Uintah Communications Company is considering the production and marketing of a communications system that will increase the efficiency of messaging for small businesses or branch offices of large companies. Each unit hooked into the system is assigned a mailbox number, which can be matched to a telephone extension number, providing access to messages twenty-four hours a day. Up to twenty units can be hooked into the system, allowing the delivery of the same message to as many as twenty people. Personal codes can be used to make messages confidential. Furthermore, messages can be reviewed, recorded, canceled, replied to, or deleted, all during the same phone call. Indicators wired to the telephone blink whenever new messages are present.

To produce this product, a $1.1 million investment in new equipment is required. The equipment would last ten years but would need major maintenance costing $100,000 at the end of its sixth year. The salvage value of the equipment at the end of ten years is estimated to be $40,000. If this new system is produced, working capital must also be increased by $50,000. This capital will be restored at the end of the product's life cycle, estimated to be ten years. Revenues from the sale of the product are estimated at $1.5 million per year; cash operating expenses are estimated at $1.26 million per year.

Required:

1. Prepare a schedule of cash flows for the proposed project.

2. Assuming that Uintah's cost of capital is 12 percent, compute the project's NPV. Should the product be produced?

P11–4   **Internal Rate of Return**   Writewell Company's Research and Development Department has developed an acoustic enclosure for printers. Based on a marketing study, it has been determined that six models would service more than 200 printer models. It also has been estimated that the annual demand for the enclosures would be 100,000 units. The enclosures would sell for $15 each. Excluding noncash expenses, the unit cost to manufacture each enclosure is $10. To produce the enclosures, the company must invest in additional equipment costing $1.75 million. The equipment will have a life of five years with no salvage value. Writewell's cost of capital is 10.5 percent.

Required:

1. Prepare a schedule of cash flows for the enclosure project.

2. Compute the IRR of the project. Should the firm produce the acoustical enclosures?

P11–5   **Payback; NPV; Managerial Incentives; Ethical Behavior**   Claude Jones, manager of an electronic components division, was pleased with his division's performance over the past three years. Each year divisional profits had increased, and he had earned a sizable bonus (bonuses are a linear function of the division's reported income). He had also received considerable attention from higher management. A vice-president had told him in confidence that if his performance over the next three years matched his first three, he would be promoted to higher management.

Determined to fulfill these expectations, Claude made sure that he personally reviewed every capital budget request. He wanted to be certain that any funds invested would provide good, solid returns (the division's cost of capital is 10 percent). At the moment, he is reviewing two independent requests. Proposal A involves automating a manufacturing operation that is currently labor intensive. Proposal B centers on developing and marketing a new relay component. A requires an initial outlay of $100,000 and B requires $125,000. Both projects could be funded given the status of the division's capital budget. Both have an expected life of six years and have the following projected cash flows after implementation:

Year	Proposal A	Proposal B
1	$60,000	$ (15,000)
2	50,000	(10,000)
3	30,000	(5,000)
4	15,000	85,000
5	10,000	110,000
6	5,000	135,000

After careful consideration of each investment, Claude approved funding of Proposal A and rejected B.

Required:

1. Compute the NPV for each proposal.
2. Compute the payback period for each proposal.
3. According to your analysis, which proposal(s) should be accepted? Explain.
4. Explain why Claude accepted only Proposal A. Considering the possible reasons for rejection, would you judge his behavior to be ethical? Explain.

P11–6   **NPV Analysis; Payback; Uncertainty**   Magic Toys is constantly developing and marketing new toys. Most toys have an expected life of five years. From past experience in forecasting the cash flows for a new toy, Magic Toys has been able to predict the cash flows for the first three years within 10 percent of what actually happens; however, the predictions for the last two years are only within 50 percent of what actually happens.

In making a decision to produce a new toy, the firm computes three NPV figures: pessimistic, optimistic, and most likely. The pessimistic computation assumes that the predicted cash flows are overestimated by 10 percent during the first three years and by 50 percent during the last two; the optimistic computation assumes that cash flows are underestimated by 10 percent during the first three years and by 50 percent during the last two; the most likely computation uses the predicted figures without adjustment. Additionally, the payback period is computed for each of the three cash-flow scenarios.

Magic Toys is considering the production of a battery-operated clown that twirls a baton. To produce the clown, $625,000 must be invested in special equipment. If the clown is produced, the Marketing Department projects the following cash flows:

Year	Projected Cash Flows
1	$200,000
2	250,000
3	200,000
4	150,000
5	100,000

The company's cost of capital is 8 percent.

Required:

1. Prepare a schedule of cash flows for each of the three scenarios described above.
2. Compute the NPV for each of the three scenarios.
3. Compute the payback period for each of the three scenarios.
4. Based on the information you developed in requirements 2 and 3, would you advise Magic Toys to make the battery-operated clown?
5. Explain why Magic Toys might be receptive to a policy not to invest in any toy that has a payback period greater than three years.

P11–7   **Basic IRR Analysis**   Timmins Company was approached by a local furnace company with the proposition of replacing its old heating system with a modern, more efficient unit. The cost of the new system was quoted at $50,000, but it would save $10,000 per year in fuel costs. The estimated life of the new system is ten years, with no salvage value expected. Excited over the possibility of saving $10,000 per year and having a more reliable unit, the president of Timmins has asked for an analysis of the project's economic viability. All capital projects are required to earn at least the firm's cost of capital, which is 12 percent.

Required:

1. Calculate the project's internal rate of return. Should the company acquire the new furnace?

2. Suppose that fuel savings are less than claimed. Calculate the minimum annual cash savings that must be realized for the project to earn a rate equal to the firm's cost of capital.

3. Suppose that the life of the furnace is overestimated by two years. Repeat requirements 1 and 2 under this assumption.

P11–8 **Basic NPV Analysis** Florence McManus has had a successful career as a dentist. However, after twenty-two years of practice, Dr. McManus has decided to retire from dentistry and pursue an alternative career. She and her husband have decided to move to Arizona. They are considering investing in a new mobile home park, which would be built to accommodate early retirees. The park would have 100 mobile-home sites, a building for social gatherings (with a special games area), and a swimming pool. It would take two years to construct. Since it would take about two years for the Mc-Manuses to wrap up their affairs, the timing of the project is ideal. The following information is available concerning the project:

a. Cost of the land, $250,000 (an up-front cost).

b. Development of the land, $100,000 (paid at the end of the first year).

c. Construction of the building and swimming pool, $100,000 (paid at the end of the second year).

d. Purchase of equipment and furniture for the building, $30,000 (paid at the end of the second year).

e. Operating expenses (pool and building maintenance, utilities, insurance, and so on), $20,000 per year, beginning at the end of the third year and continuing for each year thereafter.

f. Revenues from the rental of spaces, $120,000 per year, beginning at the end of Year 3 (rent is $1,200 per year per space).

g. The capital needed for the project will come from savings and the proceeds received from the sale of the dental practice.

h. Dr. McManus estimates that she and her husband will operate the park for sixteen years (from the date of completion) before giving the business to a son and completely retiring.

i. The McManus's cost of capital is 12 percent.

Required:

1. Develop a schedule of cash flows for the park project.

2. Compute the NPV for the park project. Should Dr. McManus and her husband acquire the park?

3. The above analysis assumes complete occupancy. Compute the minimum occupancy that must be realized for the project to be viable (assume that the occupancy rate is constant over time).

P11–9   **IRR and Interpretation**   Blaine Hampton has come to you with $100,000 in cash. He is elderly and has been told that he has an illness that will claim his life within two months. He wants to invest the $100,000 so that it provides an income of $29,109 per year over the next five years (the income can include interest as well as a return of principal), the minimum amount needed to provide living expenses for his wife.

Required:

1. Compute the internal rate of return of the proposed income stream.

2. Show that the income stream can be provided if the investment earns the rate of return computed in requirement 1 on the funds that remain internally invested (develop a table that amortizes the investment over the five-year period).

3. Suppose that Mr. Hampton has no wife and wants the $100,000 to be placed in the best possible investment for the next five years, at the end of which time the principal and interest accumulated by the investment will be donated to a local university as the Blaine Hampton Scholarship Fund. Assume that an investment is available that produces the income stream indicated above. Compute the future amount available assuming that the rate of return is equal to the internal rate of return. In all likelihood, will this future amount be the amount that is donated to the university? Explain.

P11–10   **NPV; IRR; Uncertainty**   Eden Airlines is interested in acquiring a new aircraft to service a new route. The route would be from Dallas to El Paso. The aircraft would fly one round trip daily, except for scheduled maintenance days. There are fifteen maintenance days scheduled each year. The seating capacity of the aircraft is 150. Flights are expected to be fully booked. The average revenue per passenger per flight (one-way) is $200. Annual operating costs of the aircraft are given below:

Fuel	$1,400,000
Flight personnel	500,000
Food and beverages	100,000
Maintenance	400,000
Other	100,000
Total	$2,500,000

The aircraft will cost $100,000,000 and has an expected life of twenty years. The company requires a 14 percent return.

Required:

1. Calculate the NPV for the aircraft. Should the company buy it?

2. In discussing the proposal, the marketing manager for the airline believes that the assumption of 100 percent booking is unrealistic. He believes that the booking rate will be somewhere between 70 percent and 90 percent, with the most likely rate being 80 percent. Recalculate the NPV using an 80 percent seating capacity. Should the aircraft be purchased?

3. Calculate the average seating rate that would be needed so that NPV = 0.

4. Suppose that the price per passenger could be increased by 10 percent without any effect on demand. What is the average seating rate now needed to achieve a NPV = 0? What would you now recommend?

P11–11   Review of Basic Capital Budgeting Procedures   Dr. Donna White had just returned from a conference in which she learned of a new procedure for performing root canals, which reduces the time for them by 50 percent. Given her patient-load pressures, Dr. White was anxious to try out the new technique. By decreasing the time on root canals, she could increase her total revenues by performing more services within a work period. Unfortunately, in order to implement the new procedure, some special equipment costing $20,000 was needed. The equipment had an expected life of four years, with a salvage value of $2,000. Dr. White estimated that her cash revenues would increase by the following amounts:

Year	Revenue Increases
1	$ 6,600
2	9,000
3	10,800
4	10,800

She also expected additional cash expenses amounting to $1,000 per year. The cost of capital is 12 percent.

Required:

1. Compute the payback period for the new equipment.

2. Compute the accounting rate of return using both original investment and average investment.

3. Compute the NPV and IRR for the project. Should Dr. White purchase the new equipment? Should she be concerned about payback or the accounting rate of return in making this decision?

4. Before finalizing her decision, Dr. White decided to call two dentists who had been using the new procedure for the past six months. The conversations revealed a somewhat less glowing report than she received at the conference. Nearly 25 percent of the patients receiving the procedure returned with complaints about the affected tooth. A traditional rework had to be performed on these patients. Dr. White estimated that the increase in cash revenues would be cut by 33 percent because of the extra time and cost involved in rework. Furthermore, who knew what the effect on patient goodwill would be? Using this information, recompute the NPV and the IRR of the project. What would you now recommend?

P11–12   Capital Budgeting; Ethical Considerations   Peter Hennings, manager of a cosmetics division, had asked Laura Gibson, divisional controller and CMA, to meet with him regarding a recent analysis of a capital budgeting proposal. Peter was disappointed that the proposal had not met the company's minimum guidelines. Specifically, the company requires that all proposals show a positive net present value, have an IRR that exceeds the cost of capital (which is 11 percent), and have a payback period of less than five years. Funding for any new proposal had to be approved by company headquarters. Typically, proposals are approved if they meet the minimum guidelines and if the division's allocated share of the capital budget is not exhausted. The following conversation took place at their meeting:

Peter: Laura, I asked you to meet with me to discuss Proposal 678. Reviewing your analysis, I see that the NPV is negative and that the IRR is 9 percent. The payback is 5.5 years. In my opinion, the automated material-handling system in this proposal is an absolute must for this division. My feeling is that the consulting firm has underestimated the cash savings.

Laura: I did some checking on my own because of your feelings about the matter. I called a friend who is an expert in the area and asked him to review the report on the system. After a careful review, he agreed with the report—in fact, he indicated that the savings were probably on the optimistic side.

Peter: Well, I don't agree. I know this business better than any of these so-called consulting experts. I think that the cash savings are significantly better than indicated.

Laura: Why don't you explain this to headquarters? Perhaps they will allow an exception this time and fund the project.

Peter: No, that's unlikely. They're pretty strict when it comes to those guidelines, especially with the report from an outside consulting firm. I have a better idea, but I need your help. So far, you're the only one besides me who has seen the outside report. I think it is flawed. I would like to modify it so that it reflects my knowledge of the potential of the new system. Then you can take the revised figures and prepare a new analysis for submission to headquarters. You need to tell me how much I need to revise the cash savings so that the project is viable. Although I am confident that the savings are significantly underestimated, I would prefer to revise them so that the minimum guidelines are slightly exceeded. Believe me, I will ensure that the project exceeds expectations once it's on line.

Required:

1. Evaluate the conduct of Peter Hennings. Is what he is suggesting unethical?

2. Suppose you were in Laura's position. What should you do?

3. Refer to the Appendix of Chapter 1. If Laura complies with Peter's request to modify the capital budgeting analysis, are any of the standards of ethical conduct for management accountants violated? Which ones, if any?

4. Suppose that Laura tells Peter that she will consider his request. She then meets with Jay Dixon, Peter's superior, and describes Peter's request. Upon hearing of the incident, Jay chuckles and says that he himself had pulled a couple of stunts like that when he was a divisional manager. He tells Laura not to worry about it—to go ahead and support Peter—and assures her that he will keep her visit confidential. Given this development, what should Laura do?

P11–13 **NPV; Payback** Warner Clinic, a large, for-profit medical services corporation is considering the acquisition of the practices of five physicians in Stilwell, a college town about 60 miles west of Metro. If the practices are purchased, Warner will construct a facility to house them. The facility would not only house the physicians but also would provide the means to conduct extensive laboratory work—work currently done at the local hospital. Preliminary discussions with the targeted physicians reveal strong interest provided that Warner allows the group of five to repurchase the practices and acquire the facility at the end of ten years. The purchase price would be the total amount paid by Warner at the beginning for the practices and building.

The following data have been gathered to help Warner decide whether to establish the satellite clinic:

1. Life of the investment: 10 years
2. Initial acquisition costs:

Practices	$3,500,000
Land for facility	100,000
Facility construction	1,000,000
Purchase of lab equipment	400,000

3. Annual operating costs:

Physician salaries	$ 550,000
Staff salaries	300,000
Other operating costs	250,000

4. The clinic will need to be refurbished at the end of five years and new lab equipment will need to be acquired. This will cost an additional $800,000.

5. Annual revenues:

Physician fees	$1,500,000
Laboratory fees	500,000

6. Warner's cost of capital is 16 percent.

Required:

1. Prepare a schedule of cash flows by year for the proposed project.

2. Calculate the NPV for the project. Should Warner acquire a satellite clinic in Stilwell?

3. Would the decision change if the physicians demanded a repurchase price equal to 50 percent of the original cost? What is the least Warner can sell the clinic for at the end of ten years (assuming all other financial data is the same)?

■ MANAGERIAL DECISION CASE

Payback; NPV; IRR; Effect of Differences in Sales on Project Viability Shaftel Ready Mix is a processor and supplier of concrete, aggregate, and rock products. The company operates in the intermountain Western United States. Currently, Shaftel has fourteen cement-processing plants and a labor force of more than 375 employees. With the exception of cement powder, all raw materials (e.g., aggregates and sand) are produced internally by the company. The demand for concrete and aggregates has been growing steadily nationally, and in the West, the growth rate has been above the national average. Because of this growth, Shaftel has more than tripled its gross revenues over the past ten years.

Of the intermountain states, Arizona has been experiencing the most growth. Processing plants have been added over the past several years and the company is considering the addition of yet another plant to be located in Scottsdale. A major advantage of another plant in Arizona is the ability to operate year round, a feature not found in states such as Utah and Wyoming.

In setting up the new plant, land would have to be purchased and a small building constructed. Equipment and furniture would not need to be purchased; these items would be transferred from a plant that had been opened in Wyoming during the oil-boom period and closed a few years after the end of that boom. However, the equipment needs some repair and modifications before it can be used. It has a book value of $200,000, and the furniture has a book value of $30,000. Neither has any outside market value. Other costs, such as the installation of a silo, well, electrical hookups, and so on, will be incurred. No salvage value is expected. The summary of the initial investment costs by category is as follows:

Land	$ 20,000
Building	135,000
Equipment:	
Book value	200,000
Modifications	20,000
Furniture (book value)	30,000
Silo	20,000
Well	80,000
Electrical hookups	27,000
General setup	50,000

Estimates concerning the operation of the Scottsdale plant are given below:

Life of plant and equipment	10 years
Expected annual sales (in cubic yards)	35,000
Selling price (per cubic yard)	$45.00
Variable costs (per cubic yard):	
Cement	$12.94
Sand/gravel	6.42
Fly ash	1.13
Admixture	1.53
Driver labor	3.24
Mechanics	1.43
Plant operations (batching and cleanup)	1.39
Loader operator	0.50
Truck parts	1.75
Fuel	1.48
Other	3.27
Total variable cost	$35.08
Fixed costs (annual):	
Salaries	$135,000
Insurance	75,000
Telephone	5,000
Depreciation	58,200
Utilities	25,000
Total fixed cost	$298,200

After reviewing the above data, Karl Flemming, vice-president of operations, argued against the proposed plant. Karl was concerned because the plant would earn significantly less than the normal 8.3 percent return on sales. All other plants in the company were earning between 7.5 and 8.5 percent on sales. Karl also noted that it would take more than five years to recover the total initial outlay of $582,000. In the past, the company had always insisted that payback be no more than four years. The company's cost of capital is 10 percent.

Required:

1. Prepare a variable-costing income statement for the proposed plant. Compute the ratio of net income to sales. Is Karl correct that the return on sales is significantly lower than the company average?

2. Compute the payback period for the proposed plant. Is Karl right that the payback period is greater than four years? Explain. Suppose that you were told that the equipment being transferred from Wyoming could be sold for its book value. Would this affect your answer?

3. Compute the NPV and the IRR for the proposed plant. Would your answer be affected if you were told that the furniture and equipment could be sold for their book values? If so, repeat the analysis with this effect considered.

4. Compute the cubic yards of cement that must be sold for the new plant to break even. Using this break-even volume, compute the NPV and the IRR. Would the investment be acceptable? If so, explain why an investment that promises to do nothing more than break even can be viewed as acceptable.

5. Compute the volume of cement that must be sold for the IRR to equal the firm's cost of capital. Using this volume, compute the firm's expected annual income. Explain this result.

CHAPTER 12

Capital Budgeting: Additional Considerations

■ **LEARNING OBJECTIVES**

After studying Chapter 12, you should be able to

1. Describe the role of a postaudit in capital budgeting.

2. Explain why NPV is better than IRR for capital budgeting decisions involving mutually exclusive projects.

3. Use NPV analysis to choose among competing projects.

4. Identify and explain three important factors in forecasting gross cash flows.

5. Convert gross cash flows to after-tax cash flows.

6. Choose among projects when faced with limited capital funds.

7. Describe capital budgeting in the advanced manufacturing environment.

8. Define and explain the key terms appearing at the end of the chapter.

SCENARIO

Allen Manesfield and Jenny Winters were discussing a persistent and irritating problem present in the process of producing intravenous needles (IVs). Both Allen and Jenny are employed by Honley Medical, which specializes in the production of medical products and has three divisions: the IV Products Division, the Critical Care Monitoring Division, and the Specialty Products Division. Allen and Jenny both are associated with the IV Products Division—Allen as the senior production engineer and Jenny as the marketing manager.

The IV Products Division produces needles of five different sizes. During one stage of the manufacturing process, the needle itself is inserted into a plastic hub and bonded using epoxy glue.

"Allen," Jenny complained, "using epoxy to bond the needles is causing us all kinds of problems. In many cases, the epoxy isn't bonding correctly. The rejects are high, and we are receiving a large number of complaints from our customers. It's embarrassing to have numerous reports of needles falling out when they're used. Unless we take corrective action soon, we are going to lose sales."

"I'm sensitive to the problem. Technically, there is nothing wrong with the use of epoxy for bonding. The problem is that epoxy is a two-part mix, and our operators are often not careful. They get the wrong ratio between the two parts. When the ratio is wrong, the epoxy doesn't set properly, and we get the problems you're describing."

"You're the engineer—what do you suggest that we do?"

"Jenny, I think I have the solution. Not only do we have problems getting operators to mix properly the two-part epoxy, but cleaning up at the end of the day is a hassle—the use of epoxy is messy. I am submitting a proposal suggesting that we switch from epoxy bonding to welding."

"Welding! How in the devil can you weld a needle to a plastic hub?"

"Induction welding. The needles are inserted into the plastic hub, and an RF generator is used to heat the needles. The RF generator works on the same principle as a microwave oven. Anyway, as the needles get hot, the plastic melts and the needles are bonded."

"Hmmm. Sounds clean and effective. Do you think you can get the capital to install a new system?"

"I believe so. We need to acquire the RF generators and the associated tooling; however, I think the request can be justified because of the savings associated with the new system. If we use welding, we reduce the cost of direct materials—we no longer need to buy and use epoxy. We also save considerable direct labor costs because the process is much more automated. Add to this the avoidance of our daily clean-up costs and the reduction in rejects and a strong economic argument emerges. In fact, I have already quantified the dollar savings and done a net present value analysis that compares the epoxy system with the welding system. The analysis is in favor of the welding system. I think we're home free."

One Year Later

"Allen," said Jenny Winters, "I'm quite pleased with induction welding for bonding needles. In the year since the new process was implemented, we've had virtually no complaints from our customers. The needles are firmly bonded."

"I wish that positive experience were true for all other areas as well. Unfortunately, implementing the process has uncovered some rather sticky and expensive problems that I simply didn't anticipate. The Internal Audit Department recently completed a postaudit of the project, and now my feet are being held to the fire."

"That's too bad," Jenny sympathized. "What's the problem?"

"You mean problems. Let me list a few for you. One is that the RF generators interfered with the operation of other equipment. To eliminate this interference, we had to install filtering equipment. But that's not all. We also discovered that the average maintenance person doesn't know how to maintain the new equipment. Now we are faced with the need to initiate a training program to upgrade the skills of our maintenance people. Upgrading skills also implies higher wages. Although the RF bonding process is less messy, it is also more complex. The manufacturing people complained to the internal auditors about that. They maintain that a simple process, even if messy, is to be preferred—especially now that demand for the product is increasing by leaps and bounds."

"What did the internal auditors conclude?"

"They observed that many of the predicted savings did take place, but that some significant costs were not foreseen. Because of some of the unforeseen problems, they have recommended that I look carefully at the possibility of moving back to using epoxy. They indicated that NPV analysis using actual data appears to favor that process. With production expanding, the acquisition of additional RF generators and filtering equipment plus the necessary training is simply not as attractive as returning to epoxy bonding. This conclusion is reinforced by the fact that the epoxy process is simpler and by the auditors' conclusion that the mixing of the epoxy can be automated, avoiding the quality problem we had in the first place."

"Well, Allen," Jenny observed, "you can't really blame yourself. You had a real problem and took action to solve it. It's difficult to foresee all the problems and hidden costs of a new process."

"Unfortunately, the internal auditors don't totally agree. In fact, neither do I. I probably jumped too quickly. In the future, I intend to think through new projects more carefully."

■ POSTAUDIT OF CAPITAL PROJECTS

postaudit

As the case reveals, a key element in the capital budgeting process is a follow-up analysis of a capital project once it is implemented. This analysis is called a *postaudit*. A postaudit compares the actual benefits with the estimated benefits and actual operating costs with estimated operating costs; it evaluates the overall outcome of the investment and proposes corrective action if any is needed.

In the case of the RF bonding decision, some of the estimated benefits did materialize: complaints from customers decreased, rejects were fewer, and direct labor and materials costs decreased. However, the investment was greater than expected because filtering equipment was needed, and actual operating costs were much higher because of the increased maintenance cost and the increased complexity of the process. Overall, the internal auditors concluded that the investment was a poor decision. The corrective action they recommended was to abandon the new process and return to epoxy bonding.[1]

Firms that perform postaudits of capital projects experience a number of benefits. First, by evaluating profitability, postaudits ensure that resources are used wisely. If the project is doing well, it may call for additional funds and additional attention. If the project is not doing well, corrective action may be needed to improve performance or abandon the project.

A second benefit of the postaudit is its impact on the behavior of managers. If managers are held accountable for the results of a capital investment decision, they are more likely to make such decisions in the best interests of the firm. Additionally, postaudits supply feedback to managers that should help improve future decision making. Consider Allen's reaction to the postaudit of the RF bonding process. Certainly, we would expect him to be more careful and more thorough in making future investment recommendations. In the future, Allen will probably consider more than one alternative, such as automating the mixing of the epoxy. Also, for those alternatives being considered, he will probably be especially alert to the possibility of hidden costs, such as increased training requirements for a new process.

The case also reveals that the postaudit was performed by the internal audit staff. Generally, more objective results are obtainable if the postaudit is done by an independent party. Since considerable effort is expended to ensure as much independence as possible for the internal audit staff, that group is usually the best choice for this task.

Postaudits, however, are costly. Moreover, even though they may provide significant benefits, they have other limitations. Most obvious is the fact that the assumptions driving the original analysis may often be invalidated by changes in the actual operating environment. Accountability must be qualified to some extent by the impossibility of foreseeing every possible eventuality.

---

[1] The firm whose experience is described in the case did abandon inductive welding and return to epoxy bonding, which was improved by automating the mixing. The simplicity of the epoxy process was a major qualitative factor in deciding to return to the old, but improved, process.

■ MUTUALLY EXCLUSIVE PROJECTS: NPV VERSUS IRR

The Honley Medical case raises issues above and beyond the need for a postaudit. In that case, Allen was faced with the problem of keeping the present system of epoxy bonding or switching to a welding system to bond the needles. Adoption of one system precluded the adoption of the other. The systems were mutually exclusive.

Also present in the case is the revelation that before switching to the new system, evidence in support of the change had to exist. In order to obtain the capital to invest in the new system, Allen had to show that the new system was superior economically to the current process. To do this, he used net present value analysis. Similarly, in the postaudit analysis, NPV analysis was used to show the superiority of returning to an epoxy-based process.

How NPV analysis is used to choose among competing projects is, of course, an interesting question. Although internal rate of return is not mentioned in the case, the same questions can be asked concerning IRR. An even more interesting question to consider is whether NPV and IRR differ in their ability to help managers make wealth-maximizing decisions in the presence of competing alternatives. For example, we already know that the nondiscounting models can produce erroneous choices because they ignore the time value of money. Because of this deficiency, the discounting models are judged superior. Similarly, it can be shown that the NPV model is generally preferred to the IRR model when choosing among mutually exclusive alternatives.

NPV and IRR both yield the same decision for independent projects; for example, if the NPV is greater than zero, then the IRR is also greater than the required rate of return; both models signal the correct decision. However, for competing projects, the two methods can produce different results. Intuitively, we believe that, for mutually exclusive projects, the project with the highest NPV or the highest IRR should be chosen. Since it is possible for the two methods to produce different rankings of mutually exclusive projects, the method that consistently reveals the wealth-maximizing project should be preferred. As will be shown, the NPV method is that model.

NPV differs from IRR in two major ways. First, NPV assumes that each cash inflow received is reinvested at the required rate of return, whereas the IRR method assumes that each cash inflow is reinvested at the computed IRR. Second, the NPV method measures profitability in absolute terms, whereas the IRR method measures it in relative terms. Since absolute measures often produce different rankings than relative measures, it shouldn't be too surprising that NPV and IRR can, on occasion, produce different signals regarding the attractiveness of projects. When a conflict does occur between the two methods, NPV produces the correct signal, as can be shown by a simple example.

Assume that a manager is faced with the prospect of choosing between two mutually exclusive investments whose cash flows, timing, NPV, and IRR are given in Exhibit 12–1 (a required rate of 8 percent is assumed for NPV computation). Both projects have the same life, require the same initial outlay,

EXHIBIT 12–1
NPV and IRR: Conflicting Signals

	Projects	
Year	A	B
0	$(1,000,000)	$(1,000,000)
1	—	686,342
2	1,440,000	686,342
IRR	20%	24%
NPV	$ 234,080	$ 223,748

EXHIBIT 12–2
Modified Comparison of Projects A and B

	Projects	
Year	A	Modified B
0	$(1,000,000)	$(1,000,000)
1	—	—
2	1,440,000	1,427,591[a]

[a]1.08 ($686,342) + $686,342

have positive NPVs, and have IRRs greater than the required rate of return. However, Project A has a higher NPV, whereas Project B has a higher IRR. The NPV and IRR give conflicting signals regarding which project should be chosen.

The preferred project can be identified by modifying the cash flows of one project so that the cash flows of both can be compared year by year. The modification, which appears in Exhibit 12–2, was achieved by carrying the Year 1 cash flow of Project B forward to Year 2. This can be done by assuming that the Year 1 cash flow of $686,342 is invested to earn the required rate of return. Under this assumption, the future value of $686,342 is equal to $741,249 (1.08 × $686,342). When $741,249 is added to the $686,342 received at the end of Year 2, the cash flow expected for Project B is $1,427,591.

As can be seen from Exhibit 12–2, Project A is preferable to Project B. It has the same outlay initially and a greater cash inflow in Year 2 (the difference is $12,409). Since the NPV approach originally chose Project A over Project B, it provided the correct signal for wealth maximization.

Some may object to this analysis, arguing that Project B should be preferred since it does provide at the end of Year 1 a cash inflow of $686,342,

EXHIBIT 12-3
Modified Cash Flows with Additional Opportunity

	Projects	
Year	*Modified A*	*Modified B*
0	$(1,000,000)	$(1,000,000)
1	—	—
2	1,522,361[a]	1,509,952[b]

[a]$1,440,000 + [1.20($686,342) − 1.08 ($686,342)]. This last term is what is needed to repay the capital and its cost at the end of Year 2.
[b]$686,342 + 1.20($686,342)

which can be reinvested at a much more attractive rate than the firm's required rate of return. The response is that if such an investment does exist, the firm should still invest in Project A, then borrow $686,342 at the cost of capital and invest that money in the attractive opportunity and, at the end of Year 2, repay the money borrowed plus the interest by using the combined proceeds of Project A and the other investment. For example, assume that the other investment promises a return of 20 percent. The modified cash inflows for Projects A and B are shown in Exhibit 12–3 (assuming that the additional investment at the end of Year 1 is made under either alternative). Notice that Project A is still preferable to Project B—and by the same $12,409.

NPV provides the correct signal for choosing among mutually exclusive investments. At the same time, it measures the impact competing projects have on the value of the firm. Choosing the project with the largest NPV is consistent with maximizing the wealth of shareholders. IRR, however, does not consistently result in choices that maximize wealth. IRR, as a *relative* measure of profitability, has the virtue of measuring accurately the rate of return of funds that remain internally invested. However, maximizing IRR will not necessarily maximize the wealth of firm owners because it cannot, by nature, consider the absolute dollar contributions of projects. In the final analysis, what counts are the total dollars earned—the absolute profits—not the relative profits. Accordingly, NPV, not IRR, should be used for choosing among competing, mutually exclusive projects, or competing projects when capital funds are limited.

■ NET PRESENT VALUE AND MUTUALLY EXCLUSIVE PROJECTS

An independent project is acceptable if its NPV is positive. For mutually exclusive projects, the project with the largest NPV is chosen. There are three steps in selecting the best project from several competing projects: (1) assessing the cash-flow pattern for each project, (2) computing the NPV for each project, and (3) identifying the project with the greatest NPV. To illustrate NPV analysis for competing projects, two examples will be given. The first example is concerned with a decision relating to new product lines, while the second illustrates the analysis for a lease-or-buy decision.

Example One: New Product Decision

Hintley Games Corporation has decided to market a game that will allow players to display and develop their knowledge of the geography of the United States. Given the recent interest in trivia games, the company is certain that the product will prove successful. The marketing department has selected *Travel USA* as the name of the game. Two different board designs are being considered. Design B is more elaborate than design A and will require a heavier investment and greater annual operating costs; however, it will also generate greater annual revenues. The projected annual revenues, annual costs, capital outlays, and project life for each design (in after-tax cash flows) follow:

	Design A	*Design B*
Annual revenues	$120,000	$150,000
Annual operating costs	60,000	80,000
Equipment (purchased before Year 1)	180,000	210,000
Project life	5 years	5 years

Since the games are identical except for board design, management has decided to produce and sell only one of the designs. The firm must decide which to choose. Assume that the cost of capital for the company is 12 percent.

Design A requires an initial outlay of $180,000 and has a net annual cash inflow of $60,000 (revenues of $120,000 minus costs of $60,000). Design B, with an initial outlay of $210,000, has a net annual cash inflow of $70,000 ($150,000 − $80,000). With this information, the cash-flow pattern for each project can be described and the NPV computed. These are shown in Exhibit 12–4. Based on NPV analysis, Design B is more profitable; it has the larger NPV. Accordingly, the company should select Design B over Design A.

Interestingly, Designs A and B have identical internal rates of return. Since both projects have uniform cash flows, the IRR can be found by dividing the initial investment by the annual cash flow and searching Exhibit 11–8 for the interest rate that corresponds to this discount factor. For both designs, the discount factor is 3.0 ($180,000/$60,000 and $210,000/$70,000). From Exhibit 11–8, it is easily seen that a discount factor of 3.0 and a life of five years yields an IRR of approximately 20 percent. Even though both projects have an IRR of 20 percent, the firm should not consider the two designs equally desirable.

EXHIBIT 12–4
Cash-Flow Pattern and NPV Analysis: Designs A and B

	Cash-Flow Pattern	
Year	*Design A*	*Design B*
0	$(180,000)	$(210,000)
1	60,000	70,000
2	60,000	70,000
3	60,000	70,000
4	60,000	70,000
5	60,000	70,000

Design A: NPV Analysis

Year	*Cash Flow*	*Discount Factor*[a]	*Present Value*
0	$(180,000)	1.000	$(180,000)
1–5	60,000	3.605	216,300
	Net present value		$ 36,300

Design B: NPV Analysis

Year	*Cash Flow*	*Discount Factor*[a]	*Present Value*
0	$(210,000)	1.000	$(210,000)
1–5	70,000	3.605	252,350
	Net present value		$ 42,350

[a]From Exhibit 11–8

The analysis above has just shown that Design B produces a larger NPV and, therefore, will increase the value of the firm more than Design A. Design B should be chosen.

Example Two: Equipment Purchase Decision

The Research and Development Department of a large firm needs to acquire the use of some special electronics equipment. The department is considering two options: (1) purchasing new equipment or (2) purchasing used equipment. In either case, the estimated life of the equipment is three years. If purchased new, it will cost $40,000 initially with first-year service costs of $10,000, increasing by $1,000 per year subsequently. The used equipment will cost $5,000, but service costs are $25,000 per year for the first two years and $20,000 for the third year. The cost of capital is 14 percent. Should the department buy the new or used equipment?

The cash-flow pattern for the two competing projects is shown below.

Year	New Equipment	Used Equipment
0	$(40,000)	$ (5,000)
1	(10,000)	(25,000)
2	(11,000)	(25,000)
3	(12,000)	(20,000)

The NPV for each project is shown in Exhibit 12–5.

Of the two alternatives, the one with the larger NPV should be chosen. Recall that one negative number is larger than another if it is smaller in magnitude (e.g., -3 is larger than -4). Thus, the larger NPV is that of the used equipment alternative since its negative number has the smaller magnitude. The economic interpretation is straightforward: the used equipment alternative is less costly.

As demonstrated in this example, capital budgeting decisions are often concerned with investments that do not directly involve revenue production. The electronics equipment considered here could be used in a number of research projects that might ultimately lead to new products or better designs for existing products. These results may lead to greater revenues; however, the connection of the equipment to these revenues is indirect, and it is not

EXHIBIT 12–5
NPV Analysis for the Equipment Purchase Decision

	New Equipment Alternative		
Year	Cash Flows	Discount Factor[a]	Present Value
0	$(40,000)	1.000	$(40,000)
1	(10,000)	0.877	(8,770)
2	(11,000)	0.769	(8,459)
3	(12,000)	0.675	(8,100)
Net present value			$(65,329)

	Used Equipment Alternative		
Year	Cash Flows	Discount Factor[a]	Present Value
0	$ (5,000)	1.000	$ (5,000)
1	(25,000)	0.877	(21,925)
2	(25,000)	0.769	(19,225)
3	(20,000)	0.675	(13,500)
Net present value			$(59,650)

[a]From Exhibit 11–7

possible to associate the revenue with the equipment. (Furthermore, it could be argued that because the revenues are the same across all competing alternatives, they are irrelevant.) In cases like these, the choice among competing alternatives is made on the basis of smallest cost. The alternative with the largest NPV is least costly, and thus is the one that should be chosen.

■ COMPUTATION OF CASH FLOWS

An important step in capital budgeting analysis is determining the cash-flow pattern for each project being considered. In fact, the computation of cash flows may be the most critical step in the capital budgeting process. Erroneous estimates may result in erroneous decisions, regardless of the sophistication of the decision models being used. The case presented at the beginning of the chapter illustrates this point vividly. If the cash flows associated with the inductive welding process had been more accurately forecast, a better decision could have been made.

Two steps are needed to compute cash flows: (1) forecasting revenues, expenses, and capital outlays; and (2) converting or adjusting these results to after-tax cash flows through a careful analysis of the relevant tax factors. Of the two steps, the more challenging is the first. Forecasting cash flows is demanding and difficult. Once gross cash flows are estimated, straightforward applications of tax law can be used to compute the after-tax flows.

Forecasting Gross Cash Flows: Some Factors to Consider

Since cash flows cannot be predicted with absolute certainty, the managers responsible for an investment decision should know the limitations and risks associated with using the cash-flow pattern that has been developed for the proposed project. Managers are better able to acquire this knowledge if they generate the cash-flow estimates themselves or monitor the forecasting process should they decide to use the expertise of others. In either case, managers can gain considerable insight into the limitations of a project's cash-flow projections provided they do the following:

1. Conduct a careful review of the assumptions and methods used to generate the estimates.

2. Analyze the sensitivity of the outcome (net present value) to changes in the assumptions.

3. Adjust forecasted cash flows for inflation.

Soundness of Assumptions In predicting future cash flows, managers should be confident that the assumptions used are sound and reliable. Assumptions come in two flavors: technical and planning. Technical assumptions are concerned with the statistical model (if any) that is used to forecast future cash flows. For example, a common technical assumption is that the conditions that produced the observed data will persist into the future. While this may often be true, it can easily be wrong, especially with the rapid changes that are taking place in the current manufacturing environment (e.g., adoption of JIT manufacturing, automation, and total quality control).

Planning assumptions are concerned with marketing and production strategies and dealing with random events. For example, suppose a new project using a new production strategy is based on the assumption that 90 percent of the direct labor costs can be reduced. Is this assumption reasonable? Will union pressures, community concerns, and other qualitative factors effectively prohibit or drastically reduce the expected labor savings?

Sensitivity Analysis   Even if the assumptions on which the forecast is based are judged to be reliable, they probably do not reflect exactly what will happen. It is virtually impossible to create a scenario that precisely reflects future events. Accordingly, useful insights into a project can be obtained by changing the assumptions and then assessing the impact of the changes on the cash-flow pattern. Altering the values of the variables to assess the effect on the initial outcome is referred to as *sensitivity analysis*. Sensitivity analysis is sometimes called *what-if analysis* because it addresses such questions as *what* is the effect on the decision to invest in the new project *if* the cash receipts are 5 percent less than expected? 5 percent more? 7 percent less? Although performing a sensitivity analysis would involve extensive effort if done manually, what-if questions can be rapidly and easily answered using computers and software packages such as *Lotus 1–2–3* or *IFPS*.

The following example illustrates the power and utility of sensitivity analysis. Assume that a company is considering an investment that costs $1.5 million and has an expected life of ten years. The marketing manager has estimated that the after-tax cash revenues from the new project will be $1 million per year but hedges the estimate with the observation that actual receipts could be plus or minus 20 percent of the estimated amount. The Cost Accounting and Manufacturing departments estimate that the after-tax operating costs will be $700,000 per year; they are confident that there will be little, if any, deviation from their estimate. The required rate of return is 14 percent.

If $1 million is a reasonable estimate of the expected annual cash receipts, the project's net cash inflows are projected to be $300,000 per year ($1,000,000 − $700,000). From Exhibit 11–8, the discount factor for $n = 10$ and $i = 0.14$ is 5.216. NPV analysis of the project is given below:

Year	Cash Flow	Discount Factor	Present Value
0	$(1,500,000)	1.000	$(1,500,000)
1–10	300,000	5.216	1,564,800
Net present value			$ 64,800

sensitivity analysis
what-if analysis

Since the NPV is $64,800, the project would be judged as acceptable. This decision, however, is based on the assumption that the annual cash receipts will be $1 million. The marketing manager has indicated that annual receipts could be as low as $800,000 (20 percent less) or as high as $1.2 million (20 percent more). For this example, the decision is not affected if the cash receipts are underestimated. If more cash comes in, NPV will increase, which simply reinforces the attractiveness of the investment. If cash receipts are overestimated, however, NPV decreases. If annual receipts are as low as $800,000, the net annual cash inflow drops to $100,000 ($800,000 − $700,000). This decreases the present value of the investment to $521,600 (5.216 × $100,000) and the NPV to a loss of $978,400 ($521,600 − $1,500,000). Thus, if the revenues are 20 percent less than expected, the project becomes unacceptable. In fact, if cash receipts drop below $987,576 per year, the NPV becomes negative. The decision to invest in the project is highly sensitive to errors of overestimation.

Sensitivity analysis can be used to assess the risk associated with a project and to signal the need to improve the accuracy of forecasting. In the example, sensitivity analysis revealed that the project becomes unacceptable if cash receipts are only $12,424 (1.2 percent) below the estimate. Because of the sensitivity of the project's success to cash receipts, the company may wish to expend additional resources to improve the accuracy of its forecast. Steps might include having a test market study.

Adjusting Forecasts for Inflation   In an inflationary era, financial markets react by increasing the cost of capital to reflect inflation. Thus, the cost of capital is composed of two elements:

1. The real rate.

2. The inflationary element (investors demand a premium to compensate for the loss in general purchasing power of the dollar).

Since the required rate of return used in capital budgeting analysis reflects an inflationary component at the time NPV analysis is performed, inflation must also be considered in predicting the operating cash flows. If the operating cash flows are not adjusted to account for inflation, an erroneous decision may result. In adjusting predicted cash flows, specific price change indexes should be used if possible. If that is not possible, a general price index should be used.

Note, however, that the cash inflows due to the tax effects of depreciation need *not* be adjusted for inflation. Tax law requires that depreciation be based on the *original* dollar investment. Depreciation deductions should not be increased for inflation.

To illustrate, assume that a project requires an investment of $50,000 and is expected to produce annual cash inflows of $29,000 for the coming two years. The required rate of return is 12 percent, which includes an inflationary component. The general inflation rate is expected to average 5 percent for the next two years. Net present value analysis with and without the adjustment of predicted cash flows for inflation is given in Exhibit 12–6. As the analysis shows, *not* adjusting predicted cash flows for inflation leads to a decision to reject the project, whereas adjusting for inflation leads to a decision to accept it. Thus, failure to adjust the predicted cash flows for inflationary effects can lead to an incorrect conclusion.

Conversion of Gross Cash Flows to After-Tax Cash Flows

Once gross cash flows are predicted with the desired degree of accuracy, the analyst must adjust these cash flows for taxes. To analyze tax effects, cash flows are usually broken into two categories: (1) the initial cash outflows needed to acquire the assets of the project and (2) the cash inflows produced over the life of the project. Cash outflows and cash inflows adjusted for tax effects are called *net* cash outflows and inflows. Net cash flows include provisions for revenues, operating expenses, depreciation, and relevant tax implications. They are the proper inputs for capital budgeting decisions.

Net Cash Outflows: Year 0   The net cash outflow in Year 0 (the initial out-of-pocket outlay) is simply the difference between the initial cost of the project and any cash inflows directly associated with it. The gross cost of the project

EXHIBIT 12–6
The Effects of Inflation on Capital Budgeting

	Without Inflationary Adjustment		
Year	*Cash Flow*	*Discount Factor*[a]	*Present Value*
0	$(50,000)	1.000	$(50,000)
1–2	29,000	1.690	49,010
Net present value			$ (990)

	With Inflationary Adjustment		
Year	*Cash Flow*[b]	*Discount Factor*[c]	*Present Value*
0	$(50,000)	1.000	$(50,000)
1	30,450	0.893	27,192
2	31,973	0.797	25,482
Net present value			$ 2,674

[a]From Exhibit 11–8
[b]$30,450 = 1.05 × $29,000 (adjustment for one year of inflation)
$31,973 = 1.05 × 1.05 × $29,000 (adjustment for two years of inflation)
[c]From Exhibit 11–7

includes such things as the cost of land, the cost of equipment (including transportation and installation), taxes on gains from the sale of assets, and increases in working capital. Cash inflows occurring at the time of acquisition include tax savings from the sale of assets, cash from the sale of assets, and other tax benefits such as tax credits.

Under current tax law, all costs relating to the acquisition of assets other than land must be capitalized and written off over the useful life of the assets (the write-off is achieved through depreciation). Depreciation is deducted from revenues in computing taxable income during each year of the asset's life; however, at the point of acquisition, no depreciation expense is computed. Thus, depreciation is not relevant at Year 0. The principal tax implications at the point of acquisition are related to recognition of gains and losses on the sale of existing assets and to the recognition of any investment tax credits.

Gains on the sale of assets produce additional taxes and, accordingly, reduce the cash proceeds received from the sale of old assets. Losses, on the other hand, are noncash expenses that reduce taxable income, producing tax savings; consequently, the cash proceeds from the sale of an old asset are increased by the amount of the tax savings. An investment tax credit is a direct credit against the tax liability of an organization and is usually expressed as a percentage of the net cost of the investment (e.g., 10 percent); accordingly, any appropriate investment tax credits reduce the cost of acquisition. With the Tax Reform Act of 1986, investment tax credits were repealed, but some analysts believe that because of their past popularity with the business community, they are likely to reappear.

Another consequence of the Tax Reform Act of 1986 was to restructure corporate tax rates. The current rates are given in Exhibit 12–7. Note that for income between $100,000 and $335,000, an additional 5 percent tax is imposed. The effect of this additional tax is to impose an effective flat rate of 34 percent on all income for any corporation with a taxable income over $335,000.

Let us look at an example. Currently, Jarvin Company uses two types of machines (Type A and Type B) to produce one of its products. Recent technological advances have created a single machine that can replace them. Management wants to know the net investment needed to acquire the new machine. If the new machine is acquired, the old equipment will be sold.

EXHIBIT 12–7
Corporate Income Tax Rates

Taxable Income	Tax Rate
$0 to $50,000	15%
$50,000 – $75,000	25
$75,000 – $100,000	34
$100,000 – $335,000	39
Over $335,000	34

Disposition of Old Machines

	Book Value	Sale Price
Machine A	$100,000	$130,000
Machine B	250,000	200,000

Acquisition of New Machine

Purchase cost	$1,250,000
Freight	10,000
Installation	100,000
Additional working capital	90,000
Total	$1,450,000

The net investment can be determined by computing the net proceeds from the sale of the old machines and subtracting those proceeds from the cost of the new machine. The net proceeds are determined by computing the tax consequences of the sale and adjusting the gross receipts accordingly.

The tax consequences can be assessed by subtracting the book value from the selling price. If the difference is positive, the firm has experienced a gain and will owe taxes. Money received from the sale will be reduced by the amount of taxes owed. On the other hand, if the difference is negative, a loss is experienced—a noncash loss. However, this noncash loss does have cash implications. It can be deducted from revenues and, as a consequence, can shield revenues from being taxed; accordingly, taxes will be saved. Thus, a loss produces a cash inflow equal to the taxes saved.

To illustrate, consider the tax effects of Machines A and B illustrated in Exhibit 12–8. By selling the two machines, the company receives the following net proceeds:

Sale price A	$130,000
Sale price B	200,000
Tax savings	6,800
Net proceeds	$336,800

Given these net proceeds, the net investment can be computed as follows:

Total cost of new machine	$1,450,000
Less: Net proceeds of old machines	(336,800)
Net investment (cash outflow)	$1,113,200

EXHIBIT 12–8
Tax Effects of the Sale of Two Machines

Asset	Gain (Loss)
Machine A[a]	$ 30,000
Machine B[b]	(50,000)
Net gain (loss)	$(20,000)
Tax rate	0.34
Tax savings	$ 6,800

[a]Sale price minus book value is
$130,000 − $100,000.
[b]Sale price minus book value is
$200,000 − $250,000.

Net Cash Inflows   In addition to determining the initial out-of-pocket outlay, managers must also estimate the annual after-tax cash flows expected over the life of the project. If the project generates revenue, the principal source of cash flows is from operations. Operating cash inflows can be assessed from the project's income statement. The annual after-tax cash flows are the sum of the project's after-tax profits and its noncash expenses. In terms of a simple formula, this computation can be represented as follows:

$$\text{After-tax cash flow} = \text{After-tax net income} + \text{Noncash expense}$$
$$CF = NI + NC$$

where CF = After-tax cash flow
   NI = After-tax net income
   NC = Noncash expenses

The most prominent examples of noncash expenses are depreciation and losses. At first glance, it may seem odd that after-tax cash flows are computed using noncash expenses. Noncash expenses are not cash flows but they do generate cash flows by reducing taxes. By shielding revenues from taxation, actual cash savings are created. The use of the income statement to determine after-tax cash flows is illustrated in the following example. The example is also used to show how noncash expenses can increase cash inflows by saving taxes.

Assume that a company plans to purchase a machine that costs $300,000. The machine will produce a new product that is expected to increase the firm's annual revenues by $300,000. Materials, labor, and other cash operating expenses will be $100,000 per year. The machine has a life of three years and will be depreciated on a straight-line basis. The machine will have no salvage value at the end of three years. The income statement for the project is given on the next page.

Revenues	$ 300,000
Less:	
Cash operating expenses	(100,000)
Depreciation	(100,000)
Income before taxes	100,000
Less: Taxes (@ 34%)	(34,000)
Net income	$ 66,000

Cash flow from the income statement is computed as follows:

$$CF = NI + NC$$
$$= \$66,000 + \$100,000$$
$$= \$166,000$$

The income approach to determine operating cash flows can be decomposed to assess the after-tax cash-flow effects of each individual category on the income statement. The decomposition approach calculates the operating cash flows by computing the after-tax cash flows for each item of the income statement:

$$CF = (1 - \text{Tax rate}) \times \text{Revenues} - (1 - \text{Tax rate}) \times \text{Cash expenses}$$
$$+ (\text{Tax rate}) \times \text{Noncash expenses}$$

The first term, $(1 - \text{Tax rate}) \times \text{Revenues}$, gives the after-tax cash inflows from cash revenues. For our example, the cash revenue is projected to be $300,000. The firm, therefore, can expect to keep $198,000 of the revenues received: $(1 - \text{Tax rate}) \times \text{Revenues} = 0.66 \times \$300,000 = \$198,000$. The after-tax revenue is the actual amount of after-tax cash available from the sales activity of the firm.

The second term, $- (1 - \text{Tax rate}) \times \text{Cash expenses}$, is the after-tax cash outflows from cash operating expenses. Because cash expenses can be deducted from revenues to arrive at taxable income, the effect is to shield revenues from taxation. The consequence of this shielding is to save taxes and to reduce the actual cash outflow associated with a given expenditure. In our example, the firm has cash operating expenses of $100,000. The actual cash outflow is not $100,000 but $66,000 $(0.66 \times \$100,000)$. The cash outlay for operating expenses is reduced by $34,000 because of tax savings. To see this, assume that operating expense is the only expense and that the firm has revenues of $300,000. If operating expense is *not* tax deductible, then the tax owed is $102,000 $(0.34 \times \$300,000)$. If the interest is deductible for tax purposes, then the taxable income is $200,000 ($300,000 − $100,000), and the tax owed is $68,000 $(0.34 \times \$200,000)$. Because the deductibility of operating expense saves $34,000 in taxes, the actual outlay for that expenditure is reduced by $34,000.

The third term, (Tax rate) × Noncash expenses, is the cash inflow from the tax savings produced by the noncash expenses. Noncash expenses, such as depreciation, also shield revenues from taxation. For example, assume that revenues are $300,000 and the only expense is depreciation of $100,000. If depreciation is *not* allowed as a deduction to arrive at taxable income, taxable income is $300,000, and the tax bill is $102,000 (0.34 × $300,000). If depreciation can be deducted, taxable income is $200,000 ($300,000 − $100,000), and the tax bill is $68,000 (0.34 × $200,000). The tax bill is $34,000 less because taxable income has been lowered by the $100,000 depreciation deduction. The depreciation *shields* $100,000 of revenues from being taxed and thus saves $34,000 (0.34 × $100,000) in taxes.

The sum of the three items is given below.

After-tax revenues	$198,000
After-tax cash expenses	(66,000)
Depreciation tax shield	34,000
Operating cash flow	$166,000

The decomposition approach yields the same outcome as the income approach. For convenience, the three decomposition terms are summarized in Exhibit 12–9.

One feature of decomposition is the ability to compute after-tax cash flows in a spreadsheet format. This format highlights the cash-flow effects of individual items and facilitates the use of spreadsheet software packages. The spreadsheet format is achieved by creating four columns, one for each of the three cash-flow categories and one for the total after-tax cash flow, which is the sum of the first three. This format is illustrated in Exhibit 12–10 for our example. Recall that cash revenues were $300,000 per year for three years, annual cash expenses were $100,000, and annual depreciation was $100,000.

A second feature of decomposition is the ability to compute the after-tax cash effects on an item-by-item basis. For example, suppose that a firm is considering a project and is uncertain as to which method of depreciation should be used. By computing the tax savings produced under each depreciation method, a firm can quickly assess which method is most desirable.

EXHIBIT 12–9
Computation of Operating Cash Flows: Decomposition Terms

After-tax cash revenues = (1 − Tax rate) × Cash revenues
After-tax cash expenses = (1 − Tax rate) × Cash expenses
Tax savings, noncash expenses = Tax rate × Noncash expenses

EXHIBIT 12–10

Illustration of the Spreadsheet Approach

Year	$(1-t)R^a$	$-(1-t)C^b$	tNC^c	CF
1	$198,000	$(66,000)	$34,000	$166,000
2	198,000	(66,000)	34,000	166,000
3	198,000	(66,000)	34,000	166,000

[a] R = Revenues; t = tax rate; $(1 - t)R = (1 - 0.34)\$300,000 = \$198,000$
[b] C = Cash expenses; $-(1 - t)C = -(1 - 0.34)\$100,000 = \$(66,000)$
[c] NC = Noncash expenses; $tNC = 0.34(\$100,000) = \$34,000$

In tax jargon, all depreciable business assets other than real estate are referred to as *personal property*, which is classified into one of six classes. Each class specifies the life of the assets that must be used for figuring depreciation. This life must be used even if the actual expected life is different than the class life; the class lives are set for purposes of recognizing depreciation and usually will be shorter than the actual life. Most equipment, machinery, and office furniture are classified as **seven-year assets**. Light trucks, automobiles, and computer equipment are classified as **five-year assets**. Most small tools are classified as **three-year assets**. Because the majority of personal property can be put into one of these categories, we will restrict our attention to them.

seven-year assets
five-year assets
three-year assets

modified accelerated cost recovery system (MACRS)

half-year convention

The taxpayer can use either the straight-line method or the **modified accelerated cost recovery system (MACRS)** to compute annual depreciation. Current law defines MACRS as the double-declining-balance method.[2] In computing depreciation, no consideration of salvage value is required. However, under either method, a **half-year convention** applies.[3] This convention assumes that a newly acquired asset is in service for one-half of its first taxable year of service, regardless of the date that use of it actually began. When the asset reaches the end of its life, the other half year of depreciation can be claimed in the following year. If an asset is disposed of before the end of its class life, the half-year convention allows half the depreciation for that year.

For example, assume that an asset belonging to the five-year class is purchased on March 1, 1992. The asset costs $20,000, and the firm elects the straight-line method. The annual depreciation is $4,000 for a five-year period ($20,000/5). However, using the half-year convention, the firm can deduct only $2,000 for 1992, half of the straight-line amount (0.5 × $4,000). The remaining half is deducted in the sixth year. Deductions are shown below.

[2]The tax law also allows the 150 percent declining balance method; however, we will focus on only the straight-line method and the double-declining version of MACRS.

[3]The tax law requires a mid-quarter convention if more than 40 percent of personal property is placed in service during the last three months of the year. We will not illustrate this possible scenario.

Year	Depreciation Deduction
1992	$2,000 (half-year amount)
1993	4,000
1994	4,000
1995	4,000
1996	4,000
1997	2,000 (half-year amount)

Assume that the asset is disposed of in April 1993. In this case, $2,000 of depreciation can be claimed for 1993.

If the double-declining-balance method is selected, the amount of depreciation claimed in the first year is twice that of the straight-line method. Under this method, the amount of depreciation claimed becomes progressively smaller until eventually it is exceeded by that claimed under the straight-line method. When this happens, the straight-line method is used to finish depreciating the asset. Exhibit 12–11 provides a table of depreciation rates for the double-declining-balance method for assets belonging to the three-year, five-year, and seven-year classes. The rates shown in this table incorporate the half-year convention, and therefore are the MACRS depreciation rates.

Both the straight-line method and the double-declining-balance method yield the same total amount of depreciation over the life of the asset. Both methods also produce the same total tax savings (assuming the same tax rate over the life of the asset). However, since the depreciation claimed in the early years of a project is greater using the double-declining-balance method, the tax savings are also greater during those years. Considering the time value of money, it is preferable to have the tax savings earlier than later. Thus, firms should prefer the MACRS method of depreciation over

EXHIBIT 12–11

MACRS Depreciation Rates

Year	Three-Year Assets	Five-Year Assets	Seven-Year Assets
1	33.33%	20.00%	14.29%
2	44.45	32.00	24.49
3	14.81	19.20	17.49
4	7.41	11.52	12.49
5		11.52	8.93
6		5.76	8.92
7		—	8.93
8		—	4.46

the straight-line method. This conclusion is illustrated by the following example.

A firm is considering the purchase of computer equipment for $10,000. The tax guidelines require that the cost of the equipment be depreciated over five years. However, tax guidelines also permit the depreciation to be computed using either method. Of course, the firm should choose the double-declining-balance method because it brings the greater benefit.

From decomposition, we know that the cash inflows caused by shielding can be computed by multiplying the tax rate times the amount depreciated ($t \times NC$). The cash flows produced by each depreciation method and their present value, assuming a discount rate of 10 percent, are given in Exhibit 12–12. As can be seen, the present value of the tax savings from using MACRS is greater than that using straight-line depreciation.

EXHIBIT 12–12
Value of Accelerated Methods Illustrated

		Straight-line Method			
Year	*Depreciation*	*Tax Rate*	*Tax Savings*	*Discount Factor*	*Present Value*
1	$1,000	0.34	$340.00	0.909	$ 309.06
2	2,000	0.34	680.00	0.826	561.68
3	2,000	0.34	680.00	0.751	510.68
4	2,000	0.34	680.00	0.683	464.44
5	2,000	0.34	680.00	0.621	422.28
6	1,000	0.34	340.00	0.564	191.76
	Net present value				$2,459.90

		MACRS Method			
Year	*Depreciation*[a]	*Tax Rate*	*Tax Savings*	*Discount Factor*	*Present Value*
1	$2,000	0.34	$ 680.00	0.909	$ 618.12
2	3,200	0.34	1,088.00	0.826	898.69
3	1,920	0.34	652.80	0.751	490.25
4	1,152	0.34	391.68	0.683	267.52
5	1,152	0.34	391.68	0.621	243.23
6	576	0.34	195.84	0.564	110.45
	Net present value				$2,628.26

[a]Computed by multiplying the five-year rates found in Exhibit 12–11 by $10,000. For example, depreciation for Year 1 is 0.20 × $10,000.

■ CAPITAL RATIONING

In principle, a firm should invest in all independent projects with a positive net present value. Accordingly, successful firms in the long run will raise the capital needed to invest in such projects. However, in the short run a firm may occasionally face having less funds than needed to invest in all these projects. In this case, managers must select those projects that maximize the value of the firm given the funds available. The value of the firm is maximized by selecting the combination of projects that both exhausts the available capital funds and simultaneously maximizes the summed net present values. **capital rationing** This approach, called *capital rationing*, ensures the best possible effect is achieved for the firm.

Independent Projects and Partial Investments

net present value The **net present value index** can be used to select the projects that maximize **index** total net present value provided two conditions are met: (1) projects are not mutually exclusive, and (2) partial investments are possible. The net present value index is computed by dividing a project's net present value by its initial investment[4]:

$$\text{Net present value index} = \text{NPV/Investment}$$

Thus, a project with an initial net outlay of $10,000 and an NPV of $2,000 has a net present value index of 0.20 ($2,000/$10,000).

In the presence of a limited capital budget, the NPV index can be used to select the optimal combination of projects by following two steps: (1) rank all projects in descending order using the NPV index and (2) allocate the available capital to the projects in rank order until all funds are exhausted. The second step assumes that partial investments are possible.

To illustrate, consider the five investment opportunities that follow:

Project	Investment	Net Present Value	NPV Index
A	$10,000	$2,000	0.20
B	20,000	5,600	0.28
C	8,000	2,400	0.30
D	5,000	500	0.10
E	2,000	1,000	0.50
Total	$45,000		

[4]Many use a similar index, called the profitability index, which is computed by dividing the present value of future cash flows by the investment. The same rankings will be realized using either index.

All investments have a positive NPV, making all of them desirable. To invest in all five would require total capital of $45,000. Assume, however, that only $30,000 of capital funds is available. Which projects should be selected?

Using the NPV index, the projects should be ranked in descending order and funded as follows:

Project	Investment Required	Amount Funded	Cumulative Funding
E	$ 2,000	$ 2,000	$ 2,000
C	8,000	8,000	10,000
B	20,000	20,000	30,000
A	10,000	—	30,000
D	5,000	—	30,000

Notice that Project E, with the highest NPV index, is funded first, followed by Project C and Project B. After these projects are funded, no capital funds remain and, accordingly, Projects A and D are not funded. By funding projects E, C, and B, the firm achieves a total net present value of $9,000 ($1,000 + $2,400 + $5,600).

No greater total NPV is possible given the limited funds available. Why? The NPV index gives the profit per investment dollar, and the larger the index number, the larger the return (NPV) per dollar invested.

Assume now that only $20,000 is available to invest. Assuming that partial investment is possible, the optimal solution is found the same way. In this case, $2,000 will be allocated to Project E, $8,000 to Project C, and $10,000 to Project B (representing a 50 percent investment in that project). Total net present value is now $6,200 ($1,000 + $2,400 + [0.5 × $5,600]). This amount is still the maximum total net present value possible given the funds available.

Indivisible Investments

If it is not possible to invest partially, the NPV index approach will not choose the optimal combination of projects. Assume for example, that $20,000 is the capital available, but partial investment is not allowed. Consider the following allocations of the $20,000 capital budget:

Allocation 1			
Project	Allocation	Index	NPV
E	$ 2,000	0.50	$1,000
C	8,000	0.30	2,400
A	10,000	0.20	2,000
Totals	$20,000		$5,400

Allocation 2

Project	Allocation	Index	NPV
B	$20,000	0.28	$5,600

No other allocation of the capital available will improve on the NPV achieved by either Allocation 1 or Allocation 2. Thus, the better decision is to invest in one project, B. In this particular example, the correct choice happens to be in accordance with an NPV ranking; however, this will not always be true. In general, all combinations of projects that have a total funding requirement less than or equal to the amount of capital available must be considered. Typically, integer programming models are used to model and solve problems of this nature. Discussion of these models is reserved for more advanced courses.

Mutually Exclusive Projects

When capital funds are unlimited, the project with the highest net present value is chosen from a set of mutually exclusive projects. When investment funds are limited, the NPV criterion can no longer be used because selecting any project affects the funds available for other projects. It is possible that selection of a mutually exclusive project with a lower net present value may free up additional funds that can be invested in another project that combines with the first project to produce a greater total net present value.

To illustrate, assume that a manager is evaluating projects F, G, and H. Two, F and G, are mutually exclusive. Project H is independent of either F or G. The firm has $40,000 available for investment; no other funds can be raised. The required investment and the associated net present values are as follows:

Project	Investment	NPV
F	$20,000	$12,000
G	40,000	24,000
H	20,000	14,000

In a setting of unlimited capital funds, the firm would choose Project G over Project F and would also invest in Project H. However, with only $40,000 available, the firm has two choices. It can invest all of the capital in G, with an NPV of $24,000, or it can invest in Projects F and H, which have a combined NPV of $26,000. Clearly, investing in F and H is the superior alternative.

The example emphasizes the fact that in the presence of limited capital funds, it is necessary to consider the total net present value of all projects chosen rather than focusing on the net present value of individual projects. When faced with a capital budget limitation, managers must select the combination of projects that can be funded within the budget and that yields the greatest possible total net present value.

CAPITAL BUDGETING: THE ADVANCED MANUFACTURING ENVIRONMENT

In the advanced manufacturing environment, long-term investments are generally concerned with the automation of manufacturing. Before any commitment to automation is made, however, a company should first make the most efficient use of existing technology. Many benefits can be realized by redesigning and simplifying the current manufacturing process. An example often given to support this thesis is automation of material handling. Automation of this operation can cost millions—and it is usually unnecessary because greater efficiency can be achieved by eliminating inventories and simplifying material transfers through the implementation of a JIT system.

Once the benefits from redesign and simplification are achieved, however, it becomes apparent where automation can generate additional benefits. Many companies can improve their competitive positions by adding such features as robotics, flexible manufacturing systems, and completely integrated manufacturing systems. The ultimate commitment to automation is the construction of greenfield factories. Greenfield factories are new factories designed and built from scratch; they represent a strategic decision by a company to change completely the way it manufactures.

Although discounted cash-flow analysis (using net present value and internal rate of return) remains preeminent in capital budgeting decisions, the new manufacturing environment demands that more attention be paid to the inputs used in discounted cash-flow models. How investment is defined, how operating cash flows are estimated, how salvage value is treated, and how the discount rate is chosen are all different in nature from the traditional approach.[5]

How Investment Differs

Investment in automated manufacturing processes is much more complex than investment in the standard manufacturing equipment of the past. For standard equipment, the direct costs of acquisition represent virtually the entire investment. For automated manufacturing, the direct costs can represent as little as 50 or 60 percent of the total investment; software, engineering, training, and implementation are a significant percentage of the total costs.

---

[5]Much of the information on investment in the new manufacturing environment is based on the following two sources: Robert A. Howell and Stephen R. Soucy, "Capital Investment in the New Manufacturing Environment," *Management Accounting* (November 1987), pp. 26–32; and Callie Berliner and James A. Brimson (eds.), *Cost Management for Today's Advanced Manufacturing* (Boston: Harvard Business School Press, 1988).

Thus, great care must be exercised to assess the actual cost of an automated system. It is easy to overlook the peripheral costs, which can be substantial.

How Estimates of Operating Cash Flows Differ

Estimates of operating cash flows from investments in standard equipment have typically relied on directly identifiable tangible benefits, such as direct savings from labor, power, and scrap. Intangible benefits and indirect savings were ignored because they were viewed as immaterial. In the new manufacturing environment, however, the intangible and indirect benefits can be material and critical to the viability of the project. Greater quality, more reliability, improved customer satisfaction, and an enhanced ability to maintain market share are all important intangible benefits of a JIT system. Reduction of labor in support areas such as production scheduling and stores are indirect benefits. More effort is needed to measure these intangible and indirect benefits in order to assess more accurately the potential value of investments.

An example can be used to illustrate the importance of considering intangible and indirect benefits. Consider a company that is evaluating a potential investment in a flexible manufacturing system (FMS). The choice facing the company is to continue producing with its conventional equipment, expected to last ten years, or to switch to the new system, which is also expected to have a useful life of ten years. The company's discount rate is 12 percent. The data pertaining to the investment are presented in Exhibit 12–13 (page 578). Using these data, the net present value of the proposed system can be computed as follows:

Present value ($4,000,000 × 5.65[a])	$ 22,600,000
Investment	(18,000,000)
Net present value	$ 4,600,000

[a]Discount factor for an interest rate of 12 percent and a life of ten years (see Exhibit 11–8)

The net present value is positive and large in magnitude, and it clearly signals the acceptability of the FMS. This outcome, however, is strongly dependent on explicit recognition of both intangible and indirect benefits. If those benefits are eliminated, then the direct savings total $2.2 million, and the NPV is negative.

Present value ($2,200,000 × 5.65)	$ 12,430,000
Investment	(18,000,000)
Net present value	$ (5,570,000)

EXHIBIT 12–13

Investment Data: Direct, Intangible, and Indirect Benefits

	FMS	*Status Quo*
Investment (current outlay):		
Direct costs	$10,000,000	—
Software, engineering	8,000,000	—
Total current outlay	$18,000,000	$ 0
Net after-tax cash flow	$ 5,000,000	$1,000,000
Less: After-tax cash flow		
for status quo	(1,000,000)	n/a
Incremental benefit	$ 4,000,000	n/a

Incremental Benefit Explained

Direct benefits:		
Direct labor	$1,500,000	
Scrap reduction	500,000	
Setups	200,000	$2,200,000
Intangible benefits:		
Quality savings:		
Rework	$ 200,000	
Warranties	400,000	
Maintenance of competitive		
position	1,000,000	1,600,000
Indirect benefits:		
Production scheduling	110,000	
Payroll	90,000	200,000
Total		$4,000,000

The rise of activity-based costing has made identifying indirect benefits easier with the use of cost drivers. Once they are identified, they can be included in the analysis if they are material.

Examination of Exhibit 12–13 reveals the importance of intangible benefits. One of the most important intangible benefits is maintaining or improving a firm's competitive position. A key question that needs to be asked is what will happen to the cash flows of the firm if the investment is *not* made. That is, if the company chooses to forgo an investment in technologically advanced equipment, will it be able to continue to compete with other firms on the basis of quality, delivery, and cost? (The question becomes especially relevant if competitors choose to invest in advanced equipment.) If the competitive position deteriorates, the company's current cash flows will decrease.

If cash flows will decrease if the investment is not made, this decrease should show up as an incremental benefit for the advanced technology. In Exhibit 12–13, the company estimates this competitive benefit as $1,000,000. Estimating this benefit requires some serious strategic planning and analysis, but its effect can be critical. If this benefit had been ignored or overlooked, then the net present value would have been negative, and the investment alternative rejected. This calculation is shown below.

Present value ($3,000,000 × 5.65)	$ 16,950,000
Investment	(18,000,000)
Net present value	$ (1,050,000)

Salvage Value

Terminal or salvage value has often been ignored in investment decisions. The usual reason offered is the difficulty to estimate it. Because of this un-certainty, the effect of salvage value has often been ignored or heavily dis-counted. This approach may be unwise, however, because salvage value could make the difference between investing or not investing. Given the highly competitive environment, companies cannot afford to make incorrect decisions. A much better approach to deal with uncertainty is to use sensi-tivity analysis. In the new manufacturing environment, being too conserva-tive can be fatal.

To illustrate the potential effect of terminal value, assume that the after-tax annual operating cash flow of the project shown in Exhibit 12–13 is $3.1 million instead of $4 million. The net present value without salvage value is as follows:

Present value ($3,100,000 × 5.65)	$ 17,515,000
Investment	(18,000,000)
Net present value	$ (485,000)

Without the terminal value, the project would be rejected. The net present value with salvage value of $2 million, however, is a positive result, meaning that the investment should be made.

Present value ($3,100,000 × 5.65)	$ 17,515,000
Present value ($2,000,000 × 0.322[a])	644,000
Investment	(18,000,000)
Net present value	$ 159,000

[a]Discount factor, 12 percent and ten years (Exhibit 11–7)

Discount Rates

Being overly conservative with discount rates can prove even more damaging. In theory, if future cash flows are known with certainty, the correct discount rate is a firm's cost of capital. In practice, future cash flows are uncertain, and managers often choose a discount rate higher than the cost of capital to deal with that uncertainty. If the rate chosen is excessively high, it will bias the selection process toward short-term investments.

To illustrate the effect of an excessive discount rate, consider the project in Exhibit 12–13 once again. Assume that the correct discount rate is 12 percent but that the firm uses 18 percent. The net present value using an 18 percent discount rate is calculated as follows:

Present value ($4,000,000 × 4.494[a])	$ 17,976,000
Investment	(18,000,000)
Net present value	$ (24,000)

[a]Discount rate for 18 percent and ten years (Exhibit 11–8)

The project would be rejected. With a higher discount rate, the discount factor decreases in magnitude much more rapidly than the discount factor for a lower rate (compare the discount factor for 12 percent, 5.65, with the factor for 18 percent, 4.494). The effect of a higher discount factor is to place more weight on earlier cash flows and less weight on later cash flows, which favors short-term over long-term investments. This outcome makes it more difficult for automated manufacturing systems to appear as viable projects since the cash returns required to justify the investment are received over a longer period of time.

▪ SUMMARY OF LEARNING OBJECTIVES

1. Describe the role of a postaudit in capital budgeting. Postauditing of capital projects is an important step in capital budgeting. Postaudits evaluate the actual performance of a project in relation to its expected performance. A postaudit may lead to corrective action to improve the performance of the project or to abandon it. Postaudits also serve as an incentive for managers to make capital investment decisions prudently.

2. Explain why NPV is better than IRR for mutually exclusive projects. In evaluating mutually exclusive or competing projects, managers have a choice of using NPV or IRR. When choosing among competing projects, the NPV model correctly identifies the best investment alternative. IRR, at times, may choose an inferior project. Thus, since NPV always provides the correct signal, it should be used.

3. Use NPV analysis to choose among competing projects. The net present value for each competing project should be computed. The project with the largest NPV is the one that should be selected.

4. **Identify and explain three important factors in forecasting gross cash flows.** Accurate and reliable cash-flow forecasts are absolutely critical for capital-budgeting analyses. Managers should assume responsibility for the accuracy of cash-flow projections. At a minimum, this responsibility should entail carefully reviewing the assumptions underlying the forecast, conducting a sensitivity analysis to assess the effect of changes in cash flows on the project's performance, and adjusting cash flows to reflect inflation.

5. **Convert gross cash flows to after-tax cash flows.** All cash flows in a capital-investment analysis should be after-tax cash flows. There are two different, but equivalent, ways to compute after-tax cash flows: the income method and the decomposition method. Although depreciation is not a cash flow, it does have cash-flow implications because tax laws allow depreciation to be deducted in computing taxable income. Straight-line and double-declining-balance depreciation both produce the same total depreciation deductions over the life of the depreciated asset. Because the latter method accelerates depreciation, however, it would be preferred.

6. **Choose among projects when faced with limited capital funds.** In the short run, firms may not have all the capital needed to invest in all of the available attractive opportunities. In this case, the general rule is to select the combination of investments that simultaneously exhausts the available funds and maximizes the total net present values. If we assume that partial investments are possible, the NPV index can be used to identify the optimal combination of projects.

7. **Describe capital budgeting in the advanced manufacturing environment.** Capital budgeting in the advanced manufacturing environment is affected by the way in which inputs are determined. Much greater attention must be paid to the investment outlays because peripheral items can require substantial resources. Furthermore, in assessing benefits, intangible items such as quality and maintaining competitive position can be deciding factors. Choice of the required rate of return is also critical. The tendency of firms to use hurdle rates that are much greater than the cost of capital should be discontinued. Also, since the salvage value of an automated system can be considerable, it should be estimated and included in the analysis.

■ KEY TERMS

Capital rationing The process of allocating limited capital funds to the best combination of projects when the best combination is the one that uses all available funds and maximizes the total net present values. (p. 573)

Five-year assets A group of assets that for tax purposes can be depreciated over a five-year period. (p. 570)

Half-year convention A tax rule that assumes that a newly acquired asset is in service for one-half of the taxable year regardless of when it is actually placed in service. (p. 570)

MACRS A method of accelerated depreciation permitted by tax law. The depreciation allowed is computed using a modified double-declining-balance method. (p. 570)

NPV index   An index computed by dividing NPV by the original investment. It may be used to identify the best combination of investments in a capital-rationing setting provided partial investments are possible. (p. 573)

Postaudit   A follow-up analysis of an investment decision. (p. 554)

Sensitivity analysis   The process of altering certain key variables to assess the effect on the original outcome. (p. 562)

Seven-year assets   A group of assets that for tax purposes can be depreciated over a seven-year period. (p. 570)

Three-year assets   A group of assets that for tax purposes can be depreciated over a three-year period. (p. 570)

What-if analysis   See *Sensitivity analysis*. (p. 562)

▪ REVIEW PROBLEM

Blalock Manufacturing has decided to acquire a new luxury automobile for transporting clients from the airport to its sales offices. The choice has been narrowed to two models. The following information has been gathered for each model:

	Model A	Model T
Acquisition cost	$20,000	$25,000
Annual operating costs	$3,500	$2,000
Depreciation method	MACRS	MACRS
Expected salvage value	$5,000	$8,000

Blalock's cost of capital is 14 percent. The company plans to use the car for five years and then sell it for its salvage value. Assume the tax rate is 34 percent.

Required:

1. Compute the after-tax operating cash flows for each model.
2. Compute the NPV for each model and make a recommendation.

Solution:

1. For automobiles, the MACRS guidelines allow a five-year life. Using the rates from Exhibit 12–11, depreciation is calculated for each model.

Year	Model A	Model T
1	$ 4,000	$ 5,000
2	6,400	8,000
3	3,840	4,800
4	2,304	2,880
5	1,152[a]	1,440[a]
Total	$17,696	$22,120

[a]Only half the depreciation is allowed in year of disposal.

The after-tax operating cash flows are computed using the spreadsheet format.

Model A

Year	$(1 - t)R$	$-(1 - t)C$	tNC	Other	CF
1	n/a	$(2,310)	$1,360		$ (950)
2	n/a	(2,310)	2,176		(134)
3	n/a	(2,310)	1,306		(1,004)
4	n/a	(2,310)	783		(1,527)
5	1,779[a]	(2,310)	783	$2,304[b]	2,165

[a]Salvage value ($5,000) − Book value ($20,000 − $17,696 = $2,304) = $2,696; 0.66 × $2,696 = $1,779
[b]Recovery of Capital = Book value = $2,304. Capital recovered is not taxed— only the gain on sale. Footnote a illustrates how the gain is treated.

Model T

Year	$(1 - t)R$	$-(1 - t)C$	tNC	Other	CF
1	n/a	$(1,320)	$1,700		$ 380
2	n/a	(1,320)	2,720		1,400
3	n/a	(1,320)	1,632		312
4	n/a	(1,320)	979		(341)
5	$3,379[a]	(1,320)	490	$2,880[b]	5,429

[a]Salvage value ($8,000) − Book value ($25,000 − $22,120 = $2,880) = $5,120; 0.66 × $5,120 = $3,379
[b]Recovery of Capital = Book value = $2,880. Capital recovered is not taxed— only the gain on sale of the asset. Footnote a illustrates how the gain is treated. The nontaxable item requires an additional column for the spreadsheet analysis.

2. NPV computation:

Model A

Year	Cash Flow	Discount Factor	Present Value
0	$(20,000)	1.000	$(20,000)
1	(950)	0.877	(833)
2	(134)	0.769	(103)
3	(1,004)	0.675	(678)
4	(1,527)	0.592	(904)
5	2,165	0.519	1,124
Net present value			$(21,394)

(continued on next page)

Model T

Year	Cash Flow	Discount Factor	Present Value
0	$(25,000)	1.000	$(25,000)
1	380	0.877	333
2	1,400	0.769	1,077
3	312	0.675	211
4	(341)	0.592	(202)
5	5,429	0.519	2,818
Net present value			$(20,763)

Model T should be chosen since it has the largest NPV, indicating that it is the least costly of the two cars. Note also that the net present values are negative and that we are choosing the least costly investment.

■ QUESTIONS

1   List the benefits associated with postaudits of capital investments.

2   Explain why NPV is generally preferred over IRR when choosing among competing or mutually exclusive projects. Why would managers continue to use IRR to choose among mutually exclusive projects?

3   Suppose that a firm must choose between two mutually exclusive projects, both of which have negative NPVs. Explain how a firm can legitimately choose among two such projects.

4   Why is it important to have accurate projections of cash flows for potential capital investments?

5   Describe why it is important for a manager to conduct a careful review of the assumptions and methods used in forecasting cash flows.

6   If the assumptions and the methods for forecasting cash flows are sound, why is it necessary or desirable to do a sensitivity, or what-if, analysis?

7   Why is it necessary to adjust future cash flows for inflation?

8   What are the principal tax implications that should be considered in Year 0?

9   Assume that a project's annual after-tax net income is $40,000. Annual depreciation for the project is $10,000. What is the annual after-tax operating cash inflow for the project?

10   Assume that a project has annual cash expenses of $20,000 and annual depreciation of $10,000. The tax rate is 34 percent. Using the decomposition method, compute the annual after-tax cash flow (the project has no direct revenues).

11   A new machine is to be purchased for $100,000. The old machine will be sold for $10,000 and has a book value of $5,000. Compute the after-tax cash outlay for the new machine. Assume a tax rate of 34 percent.

12   Explain why the MACRS method of recognizing depreciation is better than the straight-line method.

13 What is the half-year convention? What is the effect of this convention on the length of time it actually takes to write off the cost of a depreciable asset?

14 What are five-year assets? Seven-year assets? Why are these two categories emphasized in the text over the other four categories established by the IRS?

15 What is the net present value index? Why is it used?

16 What is capital rationing? Should capital rationing exist in the long run? Why or why not?

17 What is the correct procedure for rationing limited capital funds?

18 In a capital rationing setting, will the better of two mutually exclusive projects always be selected? Explain.

19 What is an indivisible project? What effect does indivisibility have on capital rationing?

20 Explain the important factors to consider for capital budgeting in the advanced manufacturing environment.

■ EXERCISES

E12–1 **NPV versus IRR**   A company is considering two different modifications to its current manufacturing process. The after-tax cash flows associated with the two investments are shown below.

Year	Project I	Project II
	($100,000)	($100,000)
1	—	63,857
2	135,590	63,857

The company's cost of capital is 10 percent.

Required:

1. Compute the NPV and the IRR for each investment.

2. Show that the project with the larger NPV is the correct choice for the company.

E12–2 **Computation of After-Tax Cash Flows**   The Dingle Company is considering two independent projects. The projected annual operating revenues and expenses are given below.

Project A (investment in a new product)	
Revenues	$ 60,000
Cash expenses	(30,000)
Depreciation	(10,000)
Income before taxes	$ 20,000
Taxes	(8,000)
Net income	$ 12,000

continued on next page

Project B (acquisition of two forklifts)

Cash expenses	$20,000
Depreciation	20,000

Required:

Compute the after-tax cash flows of each project. The tax rate is 40 percent and includes federal and state assessments.

E12–3   **MACRS; NPV**   A company is planning to buy a set of special tools for its manufacturing operation. The cost of the tools is $12,000. The tools have a three-year life and qualify for the use of the three-year MACRS. The tax rate is 34 percent; the cost of capital is 12 percent.

Required:

1. Calculate the present value of the tax depreciation shield, assuming that straight-line depreciation with a half-year life is used.

2. Calculate the present value of the tax depreciation shield, assuming that MACRS is used.

3. What is the benefit of using MACRS to the company?

E12–4   **Lease or Buy**   A small company has decided that it needs to have regular access to a car for local errands and occasional business trips. The owner of the company is trying to decide between buying or leasing the car. Purchase cost is $13,500. The annual operating costs are estimated at $3,000. If the car is leased, a five-year lease will be acquired. The lease requires a refundable deposit of $500 and annual lease payments of $3,500. Operating costs, in addition to the lease payment, also total $3,000 per year. The company's cost of capital is 10 percent and its tax rate is 34 percent. If the car is purchased, MACRS depreciation will be used.

Required:

Using NPV analysis, determine whether the car should be leased or purchased.

E12–5   **Inflation**   Excalibur Company is planning to introduce a new product that will have a two-year life. Producing the product requires an initial outlay of $20,000; it will generate after-tax cash inflows of $11,000 and $12,000 in the two years. The company's cost of capital is 12 percent. During the coming two years, inflation is expected to average 5 percent. The cash flows have not been adjusted for inflation. The cost of capital, however, reflects an inflationary component.

Required:

1. Compute the NPV using the unadjusted cash flows.

2. Compute the NPV using cash flows adjusted for inflationary effects.

E12–6   **Various investments**   Solve each of the following independent cases:

1. A printing company has decided to purchase a new printing press. Its old press will be sold for $10,000 (it has a book value of $25,000). The new press will cost $50,000. Assuming that the tax rate is 34 percent, compute the net after-tax cash outflow.

2. The Maintenance Department is purchasing new diagnostic equipment costing $30,000. Additional cash expenses of $2,000 per year are required to operate the equipment. MACRS depreciation will be used (five-year property qualification).

Assuming a tax rate of 34 percent, prepare a schedule of after-tax cash flows for the first four years.

3. The projected income for a project during its first year of operation is given below:

Cash revenues	$120,000
Less: Cash expenses	(50,000)
Less: Depreciation	(20,000)
Net income before taxes	$ 50,000
Less: Taxes	(17,000)
Net income	$ 33,000

Compute the following:

    a. After-tax cash flow
    b. After-tax cash flow from revenues
    c. After-tax cash expenses
    d. Cash inflow from the shielding effect of depreciation

E12–7 **Competing Investments** Jack Farmer is considering the acquisition of either a men's clothing store or a health food store. The clothing store would require an outlay of $150,000; the health food store would require an outlay of $200,000. Jack has the financial ability to acquire only one of the two stores. He would operate the store for ten years and then sell it for the original purchase price. The annual income expected over the next ten years is as follows for each store:

	Clothing Store	*Health Food Store*
Cash revenues	$100,000	$120,000
Less: Cash expenses	(80,600)	(96,333)
Less: Depreciation	(6,500)	(7,000)
Income before taxes	12,900	$ 16,667
Less: Taxes	(4,386)	(5,667)
Net income	$ 8,514	$ 11,000

Jack's cost of capital is 8 percent.

Required:

Using NPV analysis, determine which store Jack should acquire (if either).

E12–8 **Capital Rationing** Assume that a company has the opportunity to invest in the five independent projects given below:

Project	*NPV*	*Investment*
I	$ 9,000	$ 30,000
II	19,200	60,000
III	5,000	20,000
IV	8,800	10,000
V	18,000	100,000

Although the company would like to invest in all five projects, it has only $90,000 of capital available. The projects allow partial investment.

Required:

Determine the combination of projects that produces the greatest value for the company.

E12–9   **Capital Rationing**   Refer to the data in Exercise 12–6. Assume now, however, that partial investments are not possible.

Required:

Determine the combination of projects that produces the greatest value for the company.

E12–10   **Capital Rationing and Mutually Exclusive Projects**   Sweeney Manufacturing is considering three investment opportunities for the coming year. One would allow Sweeney to increase its vertical integration by acquiring a small company that would provide a reliable source of leather for its shoe division. This investment requires an initial outlay of $200,000 and has an NPV of $25,000.

      The other two investments are concerned with automation of the manufacturing process in a chemicals division. The company is evaluating two competing robotic systems. System A costs $300,000 and has an NPV of $41,000; System B costs $400,000 and has an NPV of $62,000. The capital available for investment is limited to $500,000.

Required:

1. Assume that partial investment is not possible. What investments should the company make?

2. Assume that partial investment is possible. What would be your investment decision?

3. Assume that the NPV of System B is $70,000 and that partial investments are not possible. Now what would your investment decision be?

E12–11   **Choice of Depreciation Methods; Present Value Analysis**   Suppose that the following depreciation methods are possible for an automobile acquired for business purposes: (1) straight-line with a half-year convention, (2) MACRS with a half-year convention, (3) straight-line with no half-year convention, and (4) MACRS with no half-year convention.

      Now assume that an automobile is acquired for $10,000. The automobile is classified as a five-year asset and will be depreciated accordingly. Salvage value does not need to be considered for tax purposes. The automobile is bought and placed in service at the beginning of the year. The tax rate is 34 percent. Assume that the cost of capital is 14 percent.

Required:

1. Compute the present value of the tax benefits provided by the shielding effects of each of the four depreciation methods (assume that the depreciation deduction occurs at the end of each year). Which method provides the greatest benefit? Is the half-year convention good or bad in this particular case?

2. Assume that the automobile is purchased at the beginning of the year and placed in service at the beginning of the fourth quarter. Recompute the present value of the shielding effects of the two methods that have no half-year convention. Compare this outcome with the present value of the methods using the half-year convention

computed in requirement 1. Is the half-year convention good or bad for this case? Give your overall assessment of the half-year convention.

E12–12   **Discount Rates: Advanced Manufacturing Environment**   A company is considering two competing investments. The first is for a standard piece of production equipment; the second is for some computer-aided manufacturing (CAM) equipment. The investment and after-tax operating cash flows are shown below.

Year	Standard Equipment	CAM
0	$(500,000)	$(2,000,000)
1	300,000	100,000
2	200,000	200,000
3	100,000	300,000
4	100,000	400,000
5	100,000	400,000
6	100,000	400,000
7	100,000	500,000
8	100,000	1,000,000
9	100,000	1,000,000
10	100,000	1,000,000

The company uses a discount rate of 18 percent for all of its investments. The company's cost of capital is 10 percent.

Required:

1. Calculate the net present value for each investment using a discount rate of 18 percent.

2. Calculate the net present value for each investment using a discount rate of 10 percent.

3. Which rate should the company use to compute the net present value? Explain.

E12–13   **Quality; Market Share; Advanced Manufacturing Environment**   Refer to Exercise 12–12. Assume that the company's cost of capital is 14 percent.

Required:

1. Calculate the NPV of each alternative using the 14 percent rate.

2. Now assume that if the standard equipment is purchased, the competitive position of the firm will deteriorate because of lower quality (relative to competitors who did automate). Marketing estimates that the loss in market share will decrease the projected net cash inflows by 50 percent for years 3 through 10. Recalculate the NPV of the standard equipment given this outcome. What is the decision now? Discuss the importance of assessing the effect of intangible benefits.

■ PROBLEMS

P12–1   **Replacement Decision; Basic NPV Analysis**   Morgan Manufacturing Company is considering replacing its existing mainframe computer with a new model manufactured by a different company. The old computer was acquired three years ago, has a remaining life of five years, and will have a salvage value of $10,000. The book value is $200,000. Straight-line depreciation is being used for tax purposes. The cash operating costs of the existing computer, including software, personnel, and other supplies, total $100,000 per year.

The new computer has an initial cost of $500,000 and will have cash operating costs of $50,000 per year. The new computer will have a life of five years and will have a salvage value of $100,000 at the end of the fifth year. MACRS depreciation will be used for tax purposes. If the new computer is purchased, the old one will be sold for $50,000. The company needs to decide whether to keep the old computer or buy the new one. The cost of capital is 12 percent. The tax rate is 34 percent.

Required:

Compute the NPV of each alternative. Should the company keep the old computer or buy the new one?

P12–2   **Lease versus Buy**   Trasky Company is trying to decide whether it should purchase or lease a new automated machine to be used in the production of a new product. If purchased, the new machine would cost $100,000 and would be used for ten years. The salvage value at the end of ten years is estimated at $20,000. The machine would be depreciated using MACRS over a seven-year period. The annual maintenance and operating costs would be $20,000. Annual revenues are estimated at $55,000.

If the machine is leased, the company would need to pay annual lease payments of $20,700. The first lease payment and a deposit of $5,000 are due immediately. The last lease payment is paid at the beginning of Year 10. The deposit is refundable at the end of the tenth year. In addition, under a normal contract, the company must pay for all maintenance and operating costs, although the leasing company does offer a service contract that will provide annual maintenance (on leased machines only). The contract must be paid up front and costs $30,000. Trasky estimates that the contract will reduce its annual maintenance and operating costs by $10,000. Trasky's cost of capital is 14 percent. The tax rate is 34 percent.

Required:

1. Prepare schedules showing the after-tax cash flows for each alternative. (Prepare schedules for the lease alternative with and without the service contract; assume that the service contract is amortized on a straight-line basis for the ten years.) Include all revenues and costs associated with each alternative.

2. Compute the NPV for each alternative, assuming that Trasky does not purchase the service contract. Should the machine be purchased or leased? For this analysis, was it necessary to include all of the costs and revenues for each alternative? Explain.

3. Compute the NPV for the lease alternative assuming that the service contract *is* purchased. Does this change your decision about leasing? What revenues and costs could be excluded without affecting the conclusion?

P12–3   **Competing Investments; NPV; Basic Analysis**   Harold Griggs has decided to start a dry cleaning business. As part of his service, he is planning to have a pickup and delivery service. A premium will be charged for the service, and this premium is expected to cover the extra operating costs. Harold has two options for providing the service. He can buy a delivery truck and hire a driver or he can pay an annual fee to a local agency that will provide the pickup and delivery service. Cost and other data are given below:

	Ownership Option	*Agency Option*
Initial outlay	$25,000	—
Annual premiums	20,000	$20,000
Cash expenses	12,000	8,800

The expected life of the truck is six years, and it will have a salvage value of $1,000. The truck qualifies as five-year property for MACRS purposes. Harold's tax rate is 40 percent. The cost of capital is 12 percent.

Required:

Compute the NPV of each alternative and make a recommendation to Harold.

P12–4   **Capital Budgeting; Advanced Manufacturing Environment**   "I know that it's the thing to do," insisted Pamela Kincaid, vice-president of finance for Colgate Manufacturing. "If we are going to be competitive, we need to build this completely automated plant."

"I'm not so sure," replied Bill Thomas. "The savings from labor reductions and increased productivity are only $4,000,000 per year. The price tag for this factory—and it's a small one—is $45,000,000. That gives a payback period of more than eleven years. That's a long time to put the company's money at risk."

"Yeah, but you're overlooking the savings that we'll get from the increase in quality," interjected John Simpson, production manager. "With this system, we can decrease our waste and our rework time significantly. Those savings are worth another million dollars per year."

"Another million will only cut the payback to nine years," retorted Bill. "Ron, you're the marketing manager—do you have any insights?"

"Well, there are other factors to consider, such as service quality and market share. I think that increasing our product quality and improving our delivery service will make us a lot more competitive. I know for a fact that two of our competitors have decided against automation. That'll give us a shot at their customers, provided our product is of higher quality and we can deliver it faster. I estimate that it'll increase our net cash benefits by another $6.0 million."

"Wow! Now that's impressive," Bill exclaimed, nearly convinced. "The payback is now getting down to a reasonable level."

"I agree," said Pamela, "but we do need to be sure that it's a sound investment. I know that estimates for construction of the facility have gone as high as $49.8 million. I also know that the expected residual value, after the twenty years of service we expect to get, is $5 million. Also, you're using before-tax cash flows. We need after-tax cash flows. I think I had better see if this project can cover our 14 percent cost of capital."

"Now wait a minute, Pamela," Bill demanded. "You know that I usually insist on a 20 percent rate of return, especially for a project of this magnitude."

Required:

1. Compute the NPV of the project using the original savings and investment figures. Do the calculation for discount rates of 14 percent and 20 percent. Assume straight-line depreciation with no half-year convention is used for tax purposes. The tax rate is 40 percent (includes state and federal taxes).

2. Compute the NPV of the project using the additional benefits noted by the production and marketing managers. Also use the original cost estimate of $45 million. Again do the calculation for both possible discount rates.

3. Compute the NPV of the project using all estimates of cash flows, including the possible initial outlay of $49.8 million. Do the calculation using discount rates of 14 percent and 20 percent.

4. If you were making the decision, what would you do? Explain.

P12–5   **Inflation and Capital Budgeting**   Leo Thayn, divisional manager, has been pushing headquarters to grant approval for the installation of a new flexible manufacturing system. Finally, in the last executive meeting, Leo was told that if he could show how the new system would increase the firm's value, it would be approved. Leo gathered the following information:

Year	Old System	Flexible System
Initial investment	—	$1,250,000
Annual operating costs	$300,000	$95,000
Annual depreciation	100,000	?
Tax rate	34%	34%
Cost of capital	12%	12%
Expected life	10 years	10 years
Salvage value	none	none

With the exception of the cost of capital, the above information ignores the rate of inflation, which has been 4 percent per year and is expected to continue at this level for the next decade.

Required:

1. Compute the NPV for each system.

2. Compute the NPV for each system adjusting the future cash flows for the rate of inflation.

3. Comment on the importance of adjusting cash flows for inflationary effects.

P12–6   **Sensitivity Analysis**   Applegate Enterprises is planning to introduce a new line of novelty ice-cream products. In order to produce the products in the desired shapes, Applegate was faced with an investment in new equipment that would cost $700,000. The equipment has a projected life of twelve years and an estimated salvage value of $50,000. The cash operating costs were estimated at $60,000 per year plus or minus 5 percent. The Marketing Department estimated that revenues from the new products would be $180,000, plus or minus 20 percent. The department believed that the revenues would be within the predicted range and assessed the probability of being below the expected value of $180,000 at 50 percent. The cost of capital for the company is 10 percent, and the tax rate is 34 percent.

Required:

1. Compute the NPV for the project assuming the most pessimistic outcome.

2. Compute the NPV for the project assuming the most optimistic outcome.

3. Compute the NPV for the project assuming that the expected costs and revenues are realized.

4. Assuming that the operating costs will be $63,000 per year, compute the revenues that must be realized for the project to have an NPV of zero. What is the probability that revenues will exceed this level?

5. Based on your answers in requirements 1–4 and any other analysis that you wish to make, would you recommend that Applegate produce the novelty ice-cream products? Explain.

P12–7 **Postaudit; Sensitivity Analysis** Olnack Products, Inc., is evaluating a new accounting information system. The initial cost of the system is estimated at $430,000 and includes a computer, terminals, software, and installation. There is no expected salvage value. The new system has a useful life of eight years and is projected to produce cash operating savings of $135,000 per year over the old manual system. In addition to the operating savings, the new system will produce a depreciation tax shield absent under the old system. Straight-line depreciation (with half-year convention) will be used for tax purposes. The tax rate is 34 percent and the cost of capital is 16 percent.

Required:

1. Compute the NPV of the new system. Use the proper class life for depreciation.

2. One year after implementation, the internal audit staff noted the following about the new system: (1) the cost of acquiring the system was $30,000 more than expected due to higher installation costs and (2) the annual cost savings were $10,000 less than expected because more in-house programming was needed than expected. Using the changes in expected costs and benefits, compute the NPV as if this information had been available one year ago. Did the company make the right decision?

3. Based on the assumption that it is more common to underestimate costs and overestimate benefits, the company adopts a conservative policy that requires all investments to have a positive NPV after costs are increased by 5 percent and benefits decreased by 5 percent. Would the original decision have been different if this policy had been in effect? Discuss the advantages and disadvantages of such a policy. Can you recommend a better approach?

4. Why is a postaudit beneficial to a firm?

P12–8 **Competing Investments** Florence Jackson has just purchased a building in the downtown business section for $100,000. She would like to use it to operate a business but is having difficulty in choosing between a fast-food restaurant and an office supply store. To provide more information, Florence hired a consultant, who, after some market research, prepared the following projected annual income statements:

	Fast-food Restaurant	*Office Supply*
Revenues	$ 300,000	$ 220,000
Less: Cash expenses	(150,000)	(100,000)
Less: Depreciation	(50,000)	(40,000)
Income before taxes	$ 100,000	$ 80,000
Less: Taxes	(34,000)	(27,200)
Net income	$ 66,000	$ 52,800

The fast-food restaurant requires an additional investment of $400,000 for equipment, furniture, and fixtures and $50,000 for inventory. The office supply store requires an additional investment of $300,000 for furniture and fixtures and $50,000 for inventories. Florence plans to operate either business for five years and then to sell it. The building would be sold with the business. She estimates that the fast-food res- taurant could be sold for $1 million at the end of five years and the office supply store for $800,000. In each case, inventories will be at the same level when sold as when the business was started. Florence's cost of capital is 14 percent. Assume that her effective tax rate is 34 percent.

Required:

1. Compute the NPV for each alternative and state which business investment Flo- rence should make.

2. Suppose that Florence invests in the fast-food restaurant. After the first year, she discovers that the reception to fast food by the downtown crowd is not so good as originally anticipated. Revenues and cash expenses are 10 percent less than expected. She expects this level of performance to continue indefinitely. Because of the less promising performance, the end-of-fifth-year selling price of the fast-food business is also decreased by 10 percent. Supposing that this information had been available one year ago, recompute the NPV for the restaurant alterna- tive. Is the investment still able to earn the 14 percent required rate of return? Explain why, after the fact, it would be difficult to claim that Florence should have invested in the office supply. Discuss with Florence the benefits of performing the postaudit.

P12–9   **Capital Rationing**   Cairo Medical, a for-profit hospital, has three investment oppor- tunities: (1) adding a wing for treatment of mental health patients, (2) adding a pa- thology laboratory, and (3) expanding the maternity wing. The initial investments and the net present value for the three alternatives are as follows:

	Mental Health Wing	*Laboratory*	*Maternity Wing*
Investment	$1,500,000	$500,000	$1,000,000
NPV	150,000	140,000	135,000

Although the hospital would like to invest in all three alternatives, only $1.5 million is available.

Required:

1. Rank the projects on the basis of net present value and allocate the funds in order of this ranking. What project or projects were selected? What is the total NPV realized by the hospital using this approach?

2. Compute the NPV index for each project. Rank the projects on the basis of the index and allocate the available investment funds accordingly. What project or projects were selected? What is the total NPV realized using this approach?

3. Assume that the size of the lot on which the hospital is located makes the mental health wing and the maternity wing mutually exclusive. With unlimited capital, which of those two projects would be chosen? With limited capital and the three projects being considered, which projects would be chosen?

P12–10 **Competing Projects** Ginger Davis, a local dentist, has an empty room in the building she had purchased several years ago. Initially, Ginger had offered only the basic services but since the practice had grown, she is now considering the possibility of using the empty room to offer one of two in-house services. Specifically, she is planning to add either a dental hygienist or a laboratory that could be used to prepare crowns and dentures. In either case, equipment must be purchased and skilled labor hired (a hygienist in the first case and a technician in the second). The revenues and costs associated with each alternative are shown below.

	Hygienist Office	*Laboratory*
Revenues	$120,000	$ 250,000
Less: Labor	(24,000)	(30,000)
Less: Materials	(26,000)	(100,000)
Less: Depreciation	(40,000)	(60,000)
Income before taxes	$ 30,000	$ 60,000
Less: Taxes	(12,000)	(24,000)
Net income	$ 18,000	$ 36,000

To set up the hygienist, an initial investment of $280,000 in equipment is required. The equipment investment for the laboratory is $420,000. The useful life of the equipment, in each case, is ten years, with no salvage value expected. Straight-line depreciation with a half-year convention is being used.

The tax rate used in the income statements is the sum of the federal and the state rates. The cost of capital is 16 percent.

Required:

1. Prepare a schedule of after-tax cash flows for each alternative.

2. Compute the NPV and the IRR for each alternative. Which alternative would you recommend? Do the NPV and the IRR measures recommend the same investment? Will this always be the case?

3. Someone tells Ginger that she should be using MACRS instead of straight-line depreciation. Recompute the NPV for the laboratory alternative using MACRS depreciation. By how much did NPV increase?

P12–11 **Capital Budgeting; Discount Rates; Intangible Benefits; Time Horizon; Advanced Manufacturing Environment** Mallette Manufacturing, Inc., produces washing machines, dryers, and dishwashers. Because of increasing competition, Mallette is considering making an investment in an automated manufacturing system. Since competition is most keen for dishwashers, the production process for this line has been selected for initial evaluation. The automated system for the dishwasher line would replace an existing system (purchased one year ago for $6 million). Although the existing system will be fully depreciated in nine years, it is expected to last another ten years. The automated system would also have a useful life of ten years.

The existing system is capable of producing 100,000 dishwashers per year. Sales and production data using the existing system are provided by the Accounting Department:

Sales per year (units)	100,000
Selling price	$300
Costs per unit	
Direct materials	80
Direct labor	90
Volume-related overhead	20
Direct fixed overhead	40[a]

[a]All cash expenses with the exception of depreciation, which is $6 per unit. The existing equipment is being depreciated using straight-line with no salvage value considered.

The automated system will cost $34 million to purchase, plus an estimated $20 million in software and implementation. (Assume that all investment outlays occur at the beginning of the first year.) If the automated equipment is purchased, the old equipment can be sold for $3 million.

The automated system will require fewer parts for production and will produce with less waste. Because of this, the direct materials cost per unit will be reduced by 25 percent. Automation will also require fewer support activities and, as a consequence, volume-related overhead will be reduced by $4 per unit and direct fixed overhead (other than depreciation) by $17 per unit. Direct labor is reduced by 60 percent. Assume, for simplicity, that the new investment will be depreciated on a pure straight-line basis for tax purposes with no salvage value. Ignore the half-life convention.

The firm's cost of capital is 12 percent but management chooses to use 20 percent as the required rate of return for evaluation of investments. The tax rate is 40 percent.

Required:

1. Compute the net present value for the old system and the automated system. Which system would the company choose?

2. Repeat the net present value analysis of requirement 1 using 12 percent as the discount rate.

3. Upon seeing the projected sales for the old system, the marketing manager commented: "Sales of 100,000 units per year cannot be maintained in the current competitive environment for more than one year unless we buy the automated system. The automated system will allow us to compete on the basis of quality and lead time. If we keep the old system, our sales will drop by 10,000 units per year." Repeat the net present value analysis using this new information and a 12 percent discount rate.

4. An industrial engineer for Mallette noticed that salvage value for the automated equipment had not been included in the analysis. He estimated that the equipment could be sold for $4 million at the end of ten years. He also estimated that the equipment of the old system would have no salvage value at the end of ten years. Repeat the net present value analysis using this information, the information in requirement 3, and a 12 percent discount rate.

5. Given the outcomes of the previous four requirements, comment on the importance of providing accurate inputs for assessing investments in automated manufacturing systems.

P12–12 **NPV; Make or Buy; MACRS; Basic Analysis** Jonfran Company manufactures three different models of paper shredders including the waste container, which serves as the base. While the shredder heads are different for all three models, the waste container is the same. The number of waste containers that Jonfran will need during the next five years is estimated as follows:

1992	50,000
1993	50,000
1994	52,000
1995	55,000
1996	55,000

The equipment used to manufacture the waste container must be replaced because it is broken and cannot be repaired. The new equipment would have a purchase price of $945,000 with terms of 2/10, n/30; the company's policy is to take all purchase discounts. The freight on the equipment would be $11,000, and installation costs would total $22,900. The equipment would be purchased in December 1991 and placed into service on January 1, 1992. It would have a five-year economic life and would be treated as three-year property under MACRS. This equipment is expected to have a salvage value of $12,000 at the end of its economic life in 1996. The new equipment would be more efficient than the old equipment resulting in a 25 percent reduction in both direct material and variable overhead. The savings in direct material would result in an additional one-time decrease in working capital requirements of $2,500 resulting from a reduction in direct material inventories. This working capital reduction would be recognized at the time of equipment acquisition.

The old equipment is fully depreciated and is not included in the fixed overhead. The old equipment from the plant can be sold for a salvage amount of $1,500.

Rather than replace the equipment, one of Jonfran's production managers has suggested that the waste containers be purchased. One supplier has quoted a price of $27 per container. This price is $8 less than Jonfran's current manufacturing cost, which is presented below.

Direct materials		$10
Direct labor		8
Variable overhead		6
Fixed overhead:		
Supervision	$2	
Facilities	5	
General	4	11
Total unit cost		$35

Jonfran uses a plant-wide fixed overhead rate in its operations. If the waste containers are purchased outside, the salary and the benefits of one supervisor, included in the fixed overhead at $45,000, would be eliminated. There would be no other changes in the other cash and noncash items included on fixed overhead except depreciation on the new equipment.

Jonfran is subject to a 40 percent tax rate. Management assumes that all cash flows occur at the end of the year and uses a 12 percent after-tax discount rate.

Required:

1. Prepare a schedule of cash flows for the make alternative. Calculate the NPV of the make alternative.

2. Prepare a schedule of cash flows for the buy alternative. Calculate the NPV of the buy alternative.

3. Which should Jonfran do—make or buy the containers? What qualitative factors should be considered?

(CMA adapted)

P12–13   **Capital Budgeting and Ethical Behavior**   Manny Carson, CMA and controller of the Wakeman Enterprises, had been given permission to acquire a new computer and software for the company's accounting system. The capital budgeting analysis had shown an NPV of $100,000; however, the initial estimates of acquisition and installation costs had been made on the basis of tentative costs without any formal bids. Manny now has two formal bids, one that would allow the firm to meet or beat the original projected NPV and one that would reduce the projected NPV by $50,000. The second bid involves a system that would increase both the initial cost and the operating cost.

Normally, Manny would take the first bid without hesitation. However, Todd Downing, the owner of the firm presenting the second bid, was a close friend. Manny had called Todd and explained the situation, offering Todd an opportunity to alter his bid and win the job. Todd thanked Manny and then made a counteroffer.

Todd: Listen, Manny, this job at the original price is the key to a successful year for me. The revenues will help me gain approval for the loan I need for renovation and expansion. If I don't get that loan, I see hard times ahead. The financial stats for loan approval are so marginal that reducing the bid price may blow my chances.

Manny: Losing the bid altogether would be even worse, don't you think?

Todd: True. However, I have a suggestion. If you grant me the job, I will have the capability of adding personnel. I know that your son is looking for a job, and I can offer him a good salary and a promising future. Additionally, I'll be able to take you and your wife on that vacation to Hawaii that we have been talking about.

Manny: Well, you have a point. My son is having an awful time finding a job, and he has a wife and three kids to support. My wife is tired of having them live with us. She and I could use a vacation. I doubt that the other bidder would make any fuss if we turned it down. Its offices are out of state, after all.

Todd: Out of state? All the more reason to turn it down. Given the state's economy, it seems almost criminal to take business outside. Those are the kind of business decisions that cause problems for people like your son.

Required:

Evaluate the ethical behavior of Manny. Should Manny have called Todd in the first place? What if Todd had agreed to meet the lower bid price—would there have been any problems? Identify the standards of ethical conduct (listed in the Appendix to Chapter 1) that Manny may be violating, if any.

■ MANAGERIAL DECISION CASES

Case 12–1   **Cash Flows; NPV; Choice of Discount Rate; Advanced Manufacturing Environment**
Charles Bradshaw, president and owner of Wellington Metal Works, had just returned
from a trip to Europe.[6] While there, he had toured several plants using robotic manufacturing. Seeing the efficiency and success of these companies, Charles became
convinced that robotic manufacturing is the wave of the future and that Wellington
could gain a competitive advantage by adopting the new technology.

Based on this vision, Charles requested an analysis detailing the costs and benefits of robotic manufacturing for the material handling and merchandising equipment
group. This group of products consists of such items as cooler shelving, stocking carts,
and bakery racks. The products are sold directly to supermarkets.

A committee, consisting of the controller, the marketing manager, and the production manager was given the responsibility to prepare the analysis. As a starting
point, the controller provided the following information on expected revenues and
expenses for the existing manual system:

		Percentage of Sales
Sales	$ 400,000	100%
Less: Variable expenses[a]	(228,000)	57
Contribution margin	$ 172,000	43
Less: Fixed expenses[b]	(92,000)	23
Income before taxes	$ 80,000	20

[a]Variable cost detail (as a percentage of sales):

Direct materials	16
Direct labor	20
Variable overhead	9
Variable selling	12

[b]$20,000 is depreciation; the rest are cash expenses.

Given the current competitive environment, the marketing manager thought that the
above level of profitability would likely not change for the next decade.

After some investigation into various robotic equipment, the committee settled
on an Aide 900 system, a robot that has the capability to weld stainless steel or
aluminum. It is capable of being programmed to adjust the path, angle, and speed of
the torch. The production manager was excited about the robotic system because it
would eliminate the need to hire welders, which was so attractive because the market
for welders seemed perpetually tight. By reducing the dependence on welders, better
production scheduling and fewer late deliveries would result. Moreover, the robot's
production rate is four times that of a person.

It was also discovered that robotic welding is superior in quality to manual
welding. As a consequence, some of the costs of poor quality could be reduced. By
providing better-quality products and avoiding late deliveries, the marketing manager

---

[6]This case is based, in part, on the following article: David A. Greenberg, "Robotics: One Small
Company's Experience," in *Cost Accounting for the 90s* (Montvale, N.J.: National Association of
Accountants, 1986), pp. 57–63.

was convinced that the company would have such a competitive edge that it would increase sales by 50 percent for the affected product group by the end of the fourth year. The marketing manager provided the following projections for the next ten years, the useful life of the robotic equipment:

	Year 1	Year 2	Year 3	Years 4–10
Sales	$400,000	$450,000	$500,000	$600,000

Currently, the company employs four welders, who work forty hours per week and fifty weeks per year at an average wage of $10 per hour. If the robot is acquired, it will need one operator, who will be paid $10 per hour. Because of improved quality, the robotic system will also reduce the cost of direct materials by 25 percent, the cost of variable overhead by 33.33 percent, and variable selling expenses by 10 percent. All of these reductions will take place immediately after the robotic system is in place and operating. Fixed costs will be increased by the depreciation associated with the robot. The robot will be depreciated using MACRS (the manual system uses straight-line depreciation without a half-year convention and has a current book value of $200,000). If the robotic system is acquired, the old system will be sold for $40,000.

The robotic system requires the following initial investment:

Purchase price	$380,000
Installation	70,000
Training	30,000
Engineering	40,000

At the end of ten years, the robot will have a salvage value of $20,000. Assume that the company's cost of capital is 12 percent. The tax rate is 34 percent.

Required:

1. Prepare a schedule of after-tax cash flows for the manual and robotic systems.

2. Using the schedule of cash flows computed in requirement 1, compute the NPV for each system. Should the company invest in the robotic system?

3. In practice, many financial officers tend to use a higher discount rate than is justified by what the firm's cost of capital is. For example, a firm may use a discount rate of 20 percent when its cost of capital is or could be 12 percent. Offer some reasons for this practice. Assume that the annual after-tax cash benefit of adopting the robotic system is $80,000 per year more than the manual system. The initial outlay for the robotic system is $340,000. Compute the NPV using 12 percent and 20 percent. Would the robotic system be acquired if 20 percent is used? Could this conservative approach have a negative impact on a firm's ability to stay competitive?

Case 12–2   **Capital Budgeting; Government Sector; Qualitative Factors; Postaudit**   In 1986, Utah was again faced with serious flooding. For several years, the area had experienced heavy snowfall in the surrounding mountains. Consequently, runoff from the Wasatch Mountains had also been well above average, and the Great Salt Lake was approaching a record level. As the lake expanded, commercial, residential, and public property was being inundated or threatened. Further expansion of the lake would result in losses running in the hundreds of millions of dollars. For example, a stretch of interstate highway (I-80) connecting Utah with Nevada and California was being threatened. If the lake continued to expand, the stretch would be destroyed and the highway would need to be rerouted at a cost of several hundred million dollars. Other examples of potential losses included relocating Salt Lake City International Airport, rerouting a railway, and shutting down a number of lake-shore industries.

After experiencing an extremely wet spring in 1986, the governor of Utah called a special session of the state legislature to deal specifically with the expanding lake problem. Because of the enormous cost of allowing any additional expansion of the lake, the governor decided that the state must make a significant capital investment to solve the flooding problem. Several alternative solutions were suggested, including the following:

1. Constructing a system of dikes.
2. Dredging the lake to increase its depth.
3. Constructing a system of reservoirs to collect water before it reaches the lake.
4. Diverting the runoff to the southern part of the state through the construction of a canal system.
5. Constructing pump stations to pump water from the lake into the west desert of the state where the excess water would then evaporate.

An essential requirement was that an alternative must have a reasonable chance to solve the flooding problem. Alternatives that held little promise for reversing the lake's expansion were eliminated. For example, the dredging alternative was rejected for this reason. The remaining alternatives were all assessed as being equally able to achieve the mission, meaning that only one was needed. The least costly alternative with the highest probability of immediate impact was chosen.

Required:

1. The legislature focused only on the initial outlays required by each alternative and selected the least costly alternative. Explain how this approach could be compatible with selecting the alternative with the greatest NPV.

2. A number of Utah residents complained about the state's involvement in a problem that was being faced only by businesses and residents who had chosen to build near the lake. They argued that the choice of building near the lake was a risk and that the rest of Utah's residents shouldn't have to bear the cost of the risk. Is this reasoning sound? How can the state justify spending tax revenues to arrest the expansion of the lake?

3. The legislature and the governor chose to invest in the pumping station alternative. The following two years, the snow fall was normal or below normal, and the pumping stations seemed totally unnecessary. The governor received considerable criticism for his decision to spend $60 to $70 million dollars on such a project. Some argued that the weather in Utah was cyclical—that everyone should have expected a reversal of the wet seasons given past history. Others argued that the reservoirs alternative would have provided some tangible benefits, such as recreational areas and irrigation water. Discuss the merits of the two criticisms. In general, discuss the merits and limitations of postaudits of capital budgeting decisions.

Case 12–3   Cash Flows; NPV; Ethical Considerations.[*]

Jim Edwards, the Midwest plant manager of Claire, Inc., just concluded a meeting with a salesman representing the Koch Company. Koch Company manufactures Zytec that is used in the production process at the Midwest plant.

Until now, Edwards purchased Zytec from ANG, Inc. for $0.20 per pound. The plant uses approximately 60,000 pounds of Zytec per month. The Koch Company salesman submitted a bid to supply Zytec for $0.14 per pound. The salesman told Edwards that there is no chemical difference between the products manufactured by Koch and ANG.

Claire, Inc. is a publicly traded corporation with plants in the eastern, midwestern, and southern United States. The corporation uses a decentralized organizational structure, and the plant managers have authority to make all operating decisions. Capital acquisitions over $500,000 must be approved at the corporate level.

Recently, the company's stock price has been depressed; therefore, the CEO of Claire, Inc. encouraged plant managers to cut costs in order to increase corporate income and earnings per share. Corporate and plant management performance evaluation (and bonuses) are based on profit improvement.

Edwards viewed the opportunity to buy Zytec at a lower price as a way to increase his plant's profits and make a good impression on corporate management. Therefore, he purchased 60,000 pounds of Zytec from Koch.

After using Koch Company's Zytec for less than one week, production workers began experiencing respiratory difficulties and skin irritations attributed to using Koch Company's Zytec in the production process. Edwards decided to use the remaining supply of Koch Zytec and then make all future purchases from ANG. However, the incident increased employee concern about the health effects of exposure to Zytec. Several employees in production asked to view the Occupation Safety and Health Administration (OSHA) reports regarding Zytec. The OSHA reports listed Zytec as a known carcinogen. This news spread rapidly throughout the plant.

Management had been aware of the reported adverse health effects of Zytec for some time, but there were no reported cases at any of the Claire plants. Although there is no substitute for Zytec, it was brought to Edwards' attention that one of Claire's competitors employs a production process that does not use Zytec. In order to eliminate the need for Zytec in the production process at the Midwest plant, new production equipment would have to be purchased.

Edwards collected the following information about the two alternatives available to the Midwest plant:

**Alternative 1
Continue to Use Zytec in the Production Process**

▪ The current equipment was purchased eight years ago at a cost of $500,000 and is fully depreciated for tax purposes.

▪ The equipment is estimated to have a remaining useful life of eight years with no residual value.

▪ If Zytec is used, Edwards plans to buy it from ANG for $0.20 per pound.

---

[*]*Source:* This case is provided by Donna K. Ulmer and used with her permission. © 1991 Donna K. Ulmer. All Rights Reserved.

Alternative 2
Purchase New Equipment that Eliminates Zytec
in the Production Process

▪ The new equipment costs $3 million and is estimated to have a useful life of eight years with no residual value.

▪ MACRS is used for tax purposes.

▪ If the new equipment is purchased, the old equipment would have a scrap value of $10,000.

Operating costs for the two alternatives would be the same except for maintenance costs. Maintenance costs are expected to be $30,000 per year higher for the new equipment than for the current equipment.

Cash inflows from operations from the sale of the finished product are the same under each alternative, and if included, both alternatives would have positive net present values. Both alternatives would produce a high-quality product. Claire's tax rate is 40 percent and the required rate of return on capital investments is 12 percent.

Required:

1. Calculate the annual cost savings of buying Zytec from Koch Company instead of ANG, Inc. Do you agree with the plant manager's decision to forego the cost savings and use ANG Zytec? Why or why not?

2. Calculate the net present value of alternative 1 (continue using ANG Zytec in the production process).

3. Calculate the net present value of alternative 2 (invest in new production equipment and eliminate Zytec from the production process).

4. Today Edwards learned two employees that worked at the plant for the past ten years were diagnosed with a form of cancer that reportedly is associated with exposure to Zytec. Edwards has asked you, the plant controller, for your recommendation: Should the plant continue using Zytec or should the plant purchase new equipment and discontinue the use of Zytec in the production process?

Decision Making in the New Manufacturing Environment

■ **LEARNING OBJECTIVES**

After studying Chapter 13, you should be able to

1. List the traditional reasons for carrying inventories.

2. Define *setup* and *carrying costs* and provide examples of each.

3. Compute the economic order quantity.

4. Describe the role of safety stock and identify reorder points.

5. Explain how the JIT philosophy addresses the traditional reasons for carrying inventories.

6. Describe the JIT Kanban system for controlling inventories.

7. Describe JIT purchasing.

8. Explain how activity-based costing facilitates strategic decision making.

9. Explain the impact that activity-based costing and JIT have on the following management accounting models: relevant costing, cost-volume-profit analysis, and segment analysis.

10. Define and explain the key terms appearing at the end of the chapter.

SCENARIO

Michelle Anderson, president and owner of Anderson Parts, Inc., had just finished reading the report prepared by Henry Jensen, a special consultant attached to the management advisory section of a national public accounting firm. The recommendations in the report were somewhat surprising, almost shocking, and Michelle was looking forward to her meeting with him to discuss them. She certainly had plenty of questions. If the report was realistic in its recommendations, hiring the consultant was one of the best decisions she had made since assuming control of the business over five years ago. Her thoughts were interrupted by Henry's arrival.

"Have a seat, Henry. I have to confess that your recommendations are intriguing. If you can convince me that they'll work, you'll have more than earned your fee."

"I think I can provide a lot of support for those recommendations. When we first met, you mentioned that your company had lost 20 percent of its market share over the past five years. In your industry, as in many others, much of that loss is because of the gains made by foreign competitors. Foreign producers are offering a higher-quality product at a lower price and with better delivery performance."

"I am aware of that. You remember that in our first meeting I said as much. I was certain at that time that the solution was automation and was prepared to sink millions into that approach. I was convinced that automating would improve quality, lower manufacturing costs, and cut down our lead time for production. Because so much money was involved, I hired you to tell us how to automate and exactly what type of equipment to buy. Instead you tell me that I shouldn't automate—at least not right away—but simplify our purchasing and manufacturing by installing something called a just-in-time system. You also indicate that we should adopt an activity-based costing system and that our accounting system should ultimately be integrated with other information systems within our firm. Do you really believe that this will bring the benefits I'm seeking? Are you speaking from experience or experiment?"

"Experience. You're certainly not a guinea pig for something we haven't tried before. Case after case has shown us that 80 percent of the competitive benefits from automation can be achieved by implementing JIT—and at a significantly decreased cost. First implement JIT; then you can see where automation will be of the most benefit. Complementary to this is the concurrent development of a comprehensive, integrated information system. Your information system must supply accurate cost information. Activity-based costing has helped many firms improve the accuracy of their product costing. JIT and activity-based costing are sensible solutions. The strategy we recommend is first simplify, then automate, and, finally, integrate.[1] Of course, you should realize that JIT and activity-based costing are

---

[1]For a detailed discussion of the strategy, see Stephen M. Hronec, "The Effects of Manufacturing Productivity on Cost Accounting and Management Reporting," *Cost Accounting for the 90s* (Mont-

not an easy fix to all your problems. But these measures should help. I might add that they have helped some firms more than others."

"It sounds promising. But can you be more specific? What benefits have other companies experienced?"

"Well, Michelle, your firm manufactures machine parts. Another firm in your same line of business was having a difficult time competing. It needed twenty-four weeks to produce one of its products from start to finish while a Japanese competitor produced and delivered the same part in six weeks. After installing a JIT system, the American firm was able to produce the part in only twenty days."

"Henry, that's hard to believe. Yet I know that a lot of the business we have lost is because we have such poor delivery performance compared to some of our competitors. You're telling me that we can make dramatic improvements in our lead time with our existing technology?"

"Yes—but that isn't all. Reducing lead time is only one of the benefits. A JIT purchasing and manufacturing system can reduce your inventories—raw materials, work in process, and finished goods—to much lower levels. Do you realize that U.S. industry has as much as 40 percent of its assets tied up in inventory?[2] That's a lot of nonproductive capital. The Lansing plant of GM used to carry 60,000 tons of sheet steel in inventory while consuming 900 tons a day. Now it carries 4,000 tons and consumes 1,200 tons a day. Overall, using JIT, GM has cut inventory-related costs from $8 billion to $2 billion. There are other examples. Motorola has reduced inventory by $210 million.[3] A chain saw manufacturer in Oregon has taken $15 million out of inventory through JIT."[4]

"Incredible. But what about quality?"

"JIT cannot work without adopting the concept of total quality control. Defects cannot be tolerated. JIT demands quality. For example, Hewlett-Packard's Fort Collins Division reduced scrap and rework by 60 percent. Xerox reduced its reject rate on outsourced parts from 5,000 parts-per-million one year to 1,300 parts-per-million the next."[5]

"Fascinating. Well, you've convinced me—at least about JIT. Tell me something about activity-based costing."

"Activity-based costing traces costs to activities and then to products. Products consume activities. It's a very accurate way to determine product costs. But it also provides strategic insights and should be used as a tool

vale, N.J.: National Association of Accountants, 1986), pp. 117–125. See also William G. Stoddard, Stephen G. Schaus, and Nolan W. Rhea, "New Guidelines for Factory Automation," *Material Handling Engineering* (May 1985), pp. 104–107.

[2]Ernest Raia, "Just-in-Time USA," *Purchasing* (February 13, 1986), p. 50.

[3]Raia, "Just-in-Time USA."

[4]Al Furst, "Spreading the Gospel at Fluke," *Electronic Business* (April 1, 1986), p. 82.

[5]Both examples are in Raia, "Just-in-Time USA."

for decision making. It isn't simply a replacement for your existing cost accounting system."[6]

"I'm ready to start the conversion. But before I can commit our company, we need to convince some of my key executives. The lead-time and quality issues will be easy to sell. If we can convince them that our traditional inventory management practices are outmoded, they'll buy the whole package. I need their commitment and support for all of this to work. Do you agree?"

"Absolutely. I hope that one of those key executives is your controller. JIT manufacturing and purchasing and activity-based costing affect many traditional management accounting models. I think it would be a good idea to schedule some training seminars. In these seminars, I'll review the basics of the traditional inventory management system and discuss the JIT system. In the process, I'll point out the benefits of the new system and highlight the deficiencies of the old system. I'll also discuss how activity-based costing can improve strategic decision making."

■ BASICS OF TRADITIONAL INVENTORY MANAGEMENT

Inventory Costs

In a world of certainty—a world in which the demand for a product or material is known with certainty for a given period of time (usually a year)—two major costs are associated with inventory. If the inventory is a material or good purchased from an outside source, then these inventory-related costs are known as *ordering costs* and *carrying costs*. If the material or good is produced internally, then the costs are called *setup costs* and *carrying costs*.

ordering costs
- **Ordering costs** are the costs of placing and receiving an order. Examples include the costs of processing an order (clerical costs and documents), insurance for shipment, and unloading costs.

setup costs
- **Setup costs** are the costs of preparing equipment and facilities so they can be used to produce a particular product or component. Examples are wages of idled production workers, the cost of idled production facilities (lost income), and the costs of test runs (labor, materials, and overhead).

carrying costs
- **Carrying costs** are the costs of carrying inventory. Examples include insurance, inventory taxes, obsolescence, the opportunity cost of funds tied up in inventory, handling costs, and storage space.

---

[6]Richard B. Troxel and Milan G. Weber, Jr., "The Evolution of Activity-Based Costing," *Journal of Cost Management* (Spring 1990), pp. 14–22.

Ordering costs and setup costs are similar in nature—both represent costs that must be incurred to acquire inventory. They differ only in the nature of the prerequisite activity (filling out and placing an order versus configuring equipment and facilities). Thus, in the discussion that follows, any reference to order costs can be viewed as a reference to setup costs.

stock-out costs

If demand is not known with certainty, a third category of inventory costs—called *stock-out costs*—exists. **Stock-out costs** are the costs of not having sufficient inventory. Examples are lost sales (both current and future), the costs of expediting (increased transportation charges, overtime, and so on), and the costs of interrupted production.

Inventory: Why It Is Needed

Maximizing profits requires that inventory-related costs be minimized. But minimizing carrying costs favors ordering or producing in small lot sizes, whereas minimizing ordering costs favors large, infrequent orders (minimization of setup costs favors long, infrequent production runs). Thus, minimizing carrying costs encourages small or no inventories and minimizing ordering or setup costs encourages larger inventories. The need to balance these two sets of costs so that the *total* cost of carrying and ordering can be minimized is one reason organizations choose to carry inventory.

Dealing with uncertainty in demand is a second major reason for holding inventory. Even if the ordering or setup costs were negligible, organizations would still carry inventory because of stock-out costs. If the demand for materials or products is greater than expected, inventory can serve as a buffer, giving organizations the abilities to meet delivery dates (thus keeping customers satisfied), to keep production flowing (avoiding the need to idle facilities while waiting for a part to arrive), and to continue supplying customers or processes with goods even if a process goes down because of a failed machine.

Although balancing conflicting costs and dealing with uncertainty are the two most frequently cited reasons for carrying inventories, other reasons, though perhaps not as major, do exist. For example, organizations may acquire larger inventories than normal to take advantage of quantity discounts or to avoid anticipated price increases.

Inventory Policy

In developing an inventory policy, two basic questions must be addressed.

1. How much should be ordered (or produced)?

2. When should the order be placed (or the setup done)?

The first question needs to be addressed before the second can be answered.

Order Quantity and Total Ordering and Carrying Costs Assume that demand is known. In choosing an order quantity or a lot size for production, managers need be concerned only with ordering (or setup) and carrying costs. The total ordering (or setup) and carrying cost can be described by the following equation:

$$TC = PD/Q + CQ/2 \qquad \qquad \textbf{(13.1)}$$
$$= \text{Ordering costs} + \text{Carrying cost}$$

where TC = The total ordering (or setup) and carrying cost

P = The cost of placing and receiving an order (or the cost of setting up a production run)

Q = The number of units ordered each time an order is placed (or the lot size for production)

D = The known annual demand

C = The cost of carrying one unit of stock for one year

To illustrate, assume that the following values apply for a part used in the production of refrigerators (the part is purchased from external suppliers):

D = 10,000 units
Q = 1,000 units
P = $25 per order
C = $2 per unit

Dividing D by Q produces the number of orders per year, which is 10 (10,000/1,000). Multiplying the number of orders per year by the cost of placing and receiving an order ($D/Q \times P$) yields the total ordering cost of $250 (10 × $25).

The total carrying cost for the year is given by $CQ/2$; this expression is equivalent to multiplying the average inventory on hand ($Q/2$) by the carrying cost per unit (C). For an order of 1,000 units with a carrying cost of $2 per unit, the average inventory is 500 (1,000/2) and the carrying cost for the year is $1,000 ($2 × 500). (Assuming average inventory to be $Q/2$ is equivalent to assuming that inventory is consumed uniformly.)

Applying Equation 13.1, the total cost is $1,250 ($250 + $1,000). An order quantity of 1,000 with a total cost of $1,250, however, may not be the best choice. Some other order quantity may produce a lower total cost. The objective is to find the order quantity that minimizes the total cost. This order quantity is called the *economic order quantity (EOQ)*.

economic order quantity (EOQ)

Computing the EOQ   Since the EOQ is the quantity that minimizes Equation 13.1, a formula for computing this quantity is easily derived.[7]

$$Q = EOQ = \sqrt{(2DP/C)} \qquad \qquad \textbf{(13.2)}$$

---

[7] $d(TC)/dQ = C/2 - DP/Q^2 = 0$, when $Q^2 = 2DP/C$ and $Q = \sqrt{2DP/C}$

Using the data from the example above, the EOQ can be computed using Equation 13.2:

$$EOQ = \sqrt{(2 \times 10,000 \times 25)/2}$$
$$= \sqrt{250,000}$$
$$= 500$$

Substituting 500 as the value of Q in Equation 13.1 yields a total cost of $1,000. The number of orders placed would be 20 (10,000/500); thus, the total ordering cost is $500 (20 × $25). The average inventory is 250 (500/2), with a total carrying cost of $500 (250 × $2). Notice that the carrying cost equals the ordering cost. This is always true for the simple EOQ model described by Equation 13.2. Also notice that an order quantity of 500 is less costly than an order quantity of 1,000 ($1,000 versus $1,250).

Reorder Point   The EOQ answers the question of how much to order (or produce). Knowing when to place an order (or setup for production) is also an essential part of any inventory policy. The **reorder point** is the point in time a new order should be placed (or setup started). It is a function of the EOQ, the lead time, and the rate at which inventory is depleted. **Lead time** is the time required to receive the economic order quantity once an order is placed or a setup is initiated.

To avoid stock-out costs and to minimize carrying costs, an order should be placed so that it arrives just as the last item in inventory is used. Knowing the rate of usage and lead time allows us to compute the reorder point that accomplishes these objectives:

$$\text{Reorder point} = \text{Rate of usage} \times \text{Lead time} \tag{13.3}$$

To illustrate Equation 13.3, we will continue to use the refrigerator part example. Assume that the producer uses fifty parts per day and that the lead time is four days. If so, an order should be placed when the inventory level of the refrigerator part drops to 200 units (4 × 50). Exhibit 13–1 provides a graphical illustration. Note that the inventory is depleted just as the order arrives and that the quantity on hand jumps back up to the EOQ level.

Demand Uncertainty and the Reorder Point   If the demand for the part or product is not known with certainty, the possibility of stock-out exists. For example, if the refrigerator part was used at a rate of sixty parts a day instead of fifty, the firm would use 200 parts after three and one-third days. Since the new order would not arrive until the end of the fourth day, some manufacturing facilities would be idled for two-thirds of a day. To avoid this problem, organizations often choose to carry safety stock. **Safety stock** is extra inventory carried to serve as insurance against fluctuations in demand. Safety stock is computed by multiplying the lead time by the difference between the maximum rate of usage and the average rate of usage. For example, if the

reorder point

lead time

safety stock

EXHIBIT 13–1
The Reorder Point

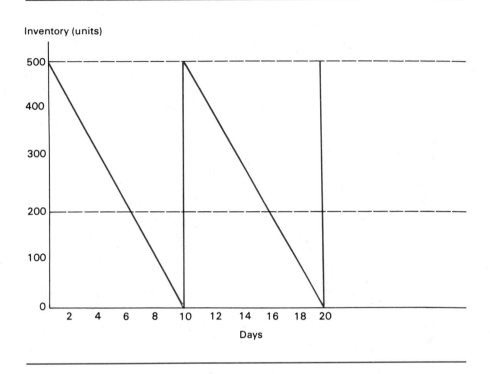

Inventory (units)

maximum usage of refrigerator parts is sixty units per day, the average usage fifty units per day, and the lead time is four days, the safety stock is computed as follows:

Maximum usage	60
Average usage	(50)
Difference	10
Lead time	×4
Safety stock	40

With the presence of safety stock, the reorder point is computed as follows:

Reorder point = (Average rate of usage × Lead time) + Safety stock

For the refrigerator example, the reorder point with safety stock is computed below:

Reorder point = 50 × 4 + 40
= 240 units

Thus, an order is automatically placed whenever the inventory level drops to 240 units.

A Comprehensive Example Peterson Cycle is a large manufacturer of motorcycles with several plants throughout the nation. Each plant produces all subassemblies necessary to assemble a particular model. The manager of the company's largest Midwestern plant is trying to determine the size of the production runs for the gas tank fabrication area. He is convinced that the current lot size is too large and wants to identify the quantity that should be produced to minimize the sum of the carrying and setup costs. He also wants to avoid stockouts since any stockout would shut down the assembly line.

To help him in his decision, the controller has supplied the following information:

- Average demand for gas tanks: 80 per day

- Maximum demand for gas tanks: 90 per day

- Annual demand for gas tanks: 20,000

- Unit carrying cost: $3

- Setup cost: $7,500

- Lead time: 20 days

Based on the above information, the economic order quantity and the reorder point are computed in Exhibit 13–2. As the computation illustrates, the gas tanks should be produced in batches of 10,000 and a new setup should be started when the supply of gas tanks drops to 1,800.

EOQ and Inventory Management

As the preceding example illustrates, the EOQ model is very useful in identifying the optimal tradeoff between inventory carrying costs and setup costs. The historical importance of the EOQ model in many American industries can be better appreciated by understanding the nature of the traditional manufacturing environment. This environment has been characterized by the mass production of a few standarized products that typically have a very high setup cost. The production of the gas tanks fits this pattern. The high setup cost encouraged a large batch size: 10,000 units. The annual demand of 20,000 units can be satisfied using only two batches. Thus, production runs for these firms tended to be quite long. Furthermore, diversity was viewed as being costly and was avoided. Producing variations of the product can be quite expensive, especially since additional, special features would usually demand even more expensive and frequent setups—the reason for the standardized products.

EXHIBIT 13–2
EOQ and Reorder Point Illustrated

$$EOQ = \sqrt{(2DP)/C}$$
$$= \sqrt{(2 \times 20,000 \times 7,500)/3}$$
$$= \sqrt{100,000,000}$$
$$= 10,000 \text{ gas tanks}$$

Safety stock:

Maximum usage	90
Average usage	80
Difference	10
Lead time	× 20
Safety stock	200

Reorder point = Average usage × Lead time + Safety stock
$$= 80 \times 20 + 200$$
$$= 1,800 \text{ units}$$

■ JIT AND INVENTORY MANAGEMENT: A DIFFERENT VIEW

The manufacturing environment for many of these traditional, large-batch, high setup cost firms has changed dramatically in the past ten to fifteen years. For one thing, the competitive markets are no longer defined by national boundaries. Advances in transportation and communication have contributed significantly to the creation of global competition. Advances in technology have contributed to shorter life cycles for products, and product diversity has increased. Foreign firms offering higher-quality, lower-cost products *with specialized features* have created tremendous pressures for our domestic large-batch, high setup cost firms to increase both quality and product diversity while simultaneously reducing total costs. These competitive pressures have led many firms to abandon the EOQ model in favor of the JIT approach. JIT offers increased cost efficiency and simultaneously has the flexibility to respond to customer demands for better quality and more variety. Quality, flexibility, and cost efficiency are foundation principles for world-class competition.

JIT manufacturing and purchasing represent the continual pursuit of productivity through the elimination of waste. Inventories, particularly, are viewed as representing waste. They tie up resources such as cash, space, and labor. They also conceal inefficiencies in production and increase the complexity of a firm's information system.

JIT, however, focuses on more than inventory management. It is a manufacturing approach that maintains that goods should be pulled through the system by demand rather than pushed through the system on a fixed schedule. In a JIT system, each operation produces only what is necessary to satisfy the demand of the succeeding operation. The material or subassembly arrives just in time for production to occur so that demand can be met.

JIT has two strategic objectives: to increase profits and to improve a firm's competitive position. These two objectives are achieved by controlling costs (enabling better price competition and increased profits), improving delivery performance, and improving quality.

One effect of JIT is to reduce inventories to very low levels. The pursuit of zero inventories is vital to the success of JIT. This idea of pursuing zero inventories, however, necessarily challenges the traditional reasons for holding inventories. These reasons are no longer viewed as valid.

Earlier, we offered the following reasons for holding inventories:

1. To balance setup and carrying costs

2. To satisfy customer demand (e.g., meet delivery dates)

3. To avoid shutting down manufacturing facilities

4. To take advantage of discounts

5. To hedge against future price increases

According to the traditional view, inventories solve some underlying problem related to each of the reasons listed above. For example, the problem of resolving the conflict between setup costs and carrying costs is solved by selecting an inventory level that minimizes the sum of these costs. Inventories prevent the failure to meet delivery dates due to changes in demand, breakdowns, and production inefficiencies. Similarly, inventories can prevent shutdowns caused by late delivery of material, defective parts, and machine failures for subassembly fabricating units. Finally, inventories are often the solution to the problem of buying the best raw materials for the least cost through the use of quantity discounts.

JIT refuses to use inventories as the solution to problems. It offers alternative solutions that do not require inventories.

Setup and Carrying Costs: The JIT Approach

JIT takes a radically different approach to minimizing total carrying and setup costs. The traditional approach accepts the existence of setup costs and then finds the order quantity that best balances the two categories of costs. JIT, on the other hand, does not accept setup costs (or ordering costs) as a given; rather, JIT attempts to drive these costs to zero. This is accomplished by reducing the time it takes to set up (for setup costs) and by developing long-term contracts with suppliers (for ordering costs). By taking these two steps, transaction costs for acquiring inventory can be driven to an insignificant level. If setup costs and ordering costs become insignificant, the only remaining cost to minimize is carrying cost, which is accomplished by reducing inventories to very low levels. This approach explains the push for zero inventories in a JIT system.

Negotiating long-term contracts for the supply of outside materials will obviously reduce the number of orders and the associated ordering costs. Reducing setup times, however, requires a company to search for new, more efficient ways to accomplish setup. Fortunately, experience has indicated that dramatic reductions in setup times can be achieved. Upon adopting a JIT system, Harley-Davidson reduced setup time by more than 75 percent on the machines evaluated.[8] In some cases, Harley-Davidson was able to reduce the setup times from hours to minutes. Other companies have experienced similar results. Generally, setup times can be reduced by at least 75 percent.[9]

Due-Date Performance: The JIT Solution

Due-date performance is a measure of a firm's ability to respond to customer needs. In the past, finished goods inventories have been used to ensure that a firm is able to meet a requested delivery date. JIT solves the problem of due-date performance not by building inventory but by dramatically reducing lead times. Shorter lead times increase a firm's ability to meet requested delivery dates and to respond quickly to the demands of the market. Thus, the firm's competitiveness is improved.

JIT cuts lead times by reducing setup times, improving quality, and using cellular manufacturing.[10]

Manufacturing cells reduce travel distance between machines and inventory; they can also have a dramatic effect on lead time. For example, in a traditional manufacturing system, one company took two months to manufacture a valve. By cutting lead times and grouping the lathes and drills used to make the valves into U-shaped cells, the lead time was reduced to two or three days. A chain-saw manufacturer was able to reduce flow distance from 2,620 feet to 173 feet and lead times from twenty-one days to three. Because of the reduced lead time and plans for even further reduction, the company will be filling orders directly from the factory rather than from finished goods warehouses.[11] These reductions in lead time are not unique—most companies experience at least a 90 percent reduction in lead times when they implement JIT.[12]

---

[8]Gene Schwind, "Man Arrives Just in Time to Save Harley-Davidson," *Material Handling Engineering* (August 1984), pp. 28–35.

[9]William J. Stoddard and Nolan W. Rhea, "Just-in-Time Manufacturing: The Relentless Pursuit of Productivity," *Material Handling Engineering* (March 1985), pp. 70–76.

[10]Cellular manufacturing is defined and discussed in detail in Chapter 6.

[11]Richard Schonberger, "Just-in-Time Production Systems: Replacing Complexity with Simplicity in Manufacturing Management," *Industrial Engineering* (October 1984), pp. 52–63.

[12]See Stoddard and Rhea, "Just-in-Time Manufacturing," p. 76.

Avoidance of Shutdown: The JIT Approach

Most shutdowns occur for one of three reasons: machine failure, defective material or subassembly, and unavailability of a raw material or subassembly. Holding inventories is one solution to all three problems.

Those espousing the JIT approach claim that inventories do not solve the problems but cover up or hide them. JIT proponents use the analogy of rocks in a lake. The rocks represent the three problems and the water represents inventories. If the lake is deep (inventories are high), then the rocks are never exposed and managers can pretend they do not exist. By reducing inventories to zero, the rocks are exposed and can no longer be ignored. JIT solves the three problems by emphasizing total preventive maintenance and total quality control and by building the right kind of relationship with suppliers.

total preventive maintenance

Total Preventive Maintenance Zero machine failures is the goal of **total preventive maintenance**. By paying more attention to preventive maintenance, most machine breakdowns can be avoided. This objective is easier to attain in a JIT environment because of the interdisciplinary labor philosophy. It is not uncommon for a cell worker to be trained in maintenance of the machines he or she operates. Because of the pull-through nature of JIT, it is also not unusual for a cell worker to have idle manufacturing time. Some of this time, then, can be used productively by having the cell workers involved in preventive maintenance.

Total Quality Control The problem of defective parts is solved by striving for zero defects. Because JIT manufacturing does not rely on inventories to replace defective parts or materials, the emphasis on quality for both internally produced and externally purchased materials increases significantly. The outcome is impressive: the number of rejected parts tends to fall by 75–90 percent.[13]

Kanban system

The Kanban System To ensure that parts or materials are available when needed, a system called the **Kanban system** is employed. This is an information system that controls production through the use of markers or cards. The Kanban system is responsible for ensuring that the necessary products (or parts) are produced (or acquired) in the necessary quantities at the necessary time. It is the heart of the JIT inventory management system.

A Kanban system uses cards or markers, which are plastic, cardboard, or metal plates measuring 4 inches by 8 inches. The Kanban is usually placed in a vinyl sack and attached to the part or a container holding the needed parts.

A basic Kanban system uses three cards: a *withdrawal Kanban*, a *production Kanban*, and a *vendor Kanban*. The first two control the movement of work among the manufacturing processes, while the third controls movement of parts between the processes and outside suppliers. A **withdrawal Kanban** specifies the quantity that a subsequent process should withdraw from the

withdrawal Kanban

---

[13]Stoddard and Rhea, "Just-in-Time Manufacturing."

preceding process. A **production Kanban** specifies the quantity that the preceding process should produce. **Vendor Kanbans** are used to notify suppliers to deliver more parts; they also specify when the parts are needed. The three Kanbans are illustrated in Exhibits 13–3, 13–4, and 13–5, respectively.

How Kanban cards are used to control the work flow can be illustrated with a simple example. Assume that two processes are needed to manufacture a product. The first process (CB Assembly) builds and tests printed circuit boards (using a U-shaped manufacturing cell). The second process (Final Assembly) puts eight circuit boards into a subassembly purchased from an outside supplier. The final product is a personal computer.

Exhibit 13–6 provides the plant layout corresponding to the manufacture of the personal computers. Refer to the exhibit as the steps involved in using Kanbans are outlined.

Consider first the movement of work between the two processing areas. Assume that eight circuit boards are placed in a container and that one such container is located in the CB stores area. Attached to this container is a production Kanban (P-Kanban). A second container with eight circuit boards is located near the Final Assembly line (the withdrawal store) with a withdrawal Kanban (W-Kanban). Now assume that the production schedule calls for the immediate assembly of a computer.

The Kanban setups can be described as follows:

1. A worker from the Final Assembly line goes to the withdrawal store, removes the eight circuit boards and places them into production. The worker also removes the withdrawal Kanban and places it on the withdrawal post.

EXHIBIT 13–3
Withdrawal Kanban

Item No. ___ 15670T07		Preceding Process ___
Item Name ___ Circuit Board		CB Assembly
Computer Type ___ TR6547 PC		
Box Capacity ___ 8		Subsequent Process ___
Box Type ___ C		Final Assembly

EXHIBIT 13–4
Production Kanban

Item No. **15670T07**	Process
Item Name **Circuit Board**	**CB Assembly**
Computer Type **TR6547 PC**	
Box Capacity **8**	
Box Type **C**	

EXHIBIT 13–5
Vendor Kanban

Item No. **15670T08**	Name of Receiving Company
Item Name **Computer Casing**	
Box Capacity **8**	**Electro PC**
Box Type **A**	Receiving Gate **75**
Time to Deliver **8:30 A.M., 12:30 P.M., 2:30 P.M.**	
Name of Supplier **Gerry Supply**	

EXHIBIT 13–6
The Kanban Process

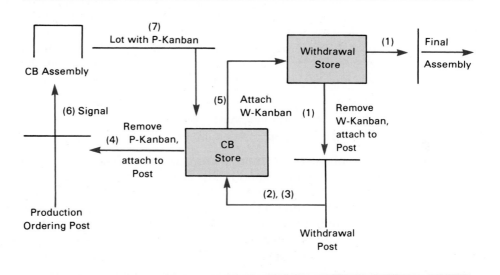

2. The withdrawal Kanban on the post signals that the Final Assembly unit needs an additional eight circuit boards.

3. A worker from Final Assembly (or a material handler called a *carrier*) removes the withdrawal Kanban from the post and carries it to CB stores.

4. At the CB stores area, the carrier removes the production Kanban from the container of eight circuit boards and places it on the production-ordering post.

5. The carrier next attaches the withdrawal Kanban to the container of parts and carries the container back to the Final Assembly area. Assembly of the next computer can begin.

6. The production Kanban on the production-ordering post signals the workers of the CB assembly to begin producing another lot of circuit boards. The production Kanban is removed and accompanies the units as they are produced.

7. When the lot of eight circuit boards is completed, the units are placed in a container in the CB stores area with the production Kanban attached. The cycle is then repeated.

The use of Kanbans ensures that the subsequent process (Final Assembly) withdraws the circuit boards from the preceding process (CB Assembly) in the necessary quantity at the appropriate time. The Kanban system also controls the preceding process by allowing it to produce only the quantities withdrawn by the subsequent process. In this way, inventories are kept at a minimum, and the components arrive just in time to be used.

Essentially the same steps are followed for a purchased subassembly. The only difference is the use of a vendor Kanban in place of a production Kanban. A vendor Kanban on a vendor post signals to the supplier that another order is needed. As with the circuit boards, the subassemblies must be delivered just in time for use. A JIT purchasing system requires the supplier to deliver small quantities on a frequent basis. These deliveries could be weekly, daily, or even several times a day. This calls for a close working relationship with suppliers.

Discounts and Price Increases: JIT Purchasing Versus Holding Inventories

Traditionally, inventories are carried so that a firm can take advantage of quantity discounts and hedge against future price increases of the items purchased. The objective is to lower the cost of inventory. JIT achieves the same objective without carrying inventories. The JIT solution is to negotiate long-term contracts with a few chosen suppliers located as close to the production facility as possible and to establish more extensive supplier involvement. Suppliers are not selected on the basis of price alone. Performance—the quality of the component and the ability to deliver as needed—and commitment to JIT purchasing are vital considerations.

Every effort is made to establish a partners-in-profits relationship with suppliers. Suppliers need to be convinced that their well-being is intimately tied to the well-being of the buyer.

To help reduce the uncertainty in demand and establish the mutual confidence and trust needed in such a relationship, JIT manufacturers emphasize long-term contracts. Other benefits of long-term contracts exist. They stipulate prices and acceptable quality levels. Long-term contracts also reduce dramatically the number of orders placed, which helps to drive down the ordering cost.

One effect of JIT purchasing is to lower the cost of purchased parts by 5 to 20 percent.[14] Another effect is to reduce the supplier base dramatically. One company decreased the number of suppliers it uses by 4,700 in one year. Another company decreased the supplier base from 820 to 180 within two years. By reducing the number of suppliers and working closely with those that remain, the quality of the incoming materials can be improved significantly—a crucial outcome for the success of JIT. As the quality of incoming materials increases, some quality-related costs can be avoided or reduced. For example, the need to inspect incoming materials disappears and rework requirements decline.

JIT: Some General Observations

JIT directly addresses such issues as plant layout, process design, quality standards, and inventories. Simplification and efficiency are the primary criteria for plant layout and process design. The JIT quality standard of zero

---

[14]Stoddard and Rhea, "Just-in-Time Manufacturing."

defects is actively pursued. Doing it right the first time is a critical feature of a system that makes no allowances for rework. Inventories are viewed as evil, and every effort is made to lower them to insignificant levels.

Implementing JIT means changing the plant layout and the traditional processing design: switching from a departmental, functional layout with a centralized stores area to a cellular manufacturing layout with materials and components located adjacent to the work area itself. It means switching from a specialized labor orientation to an interdisciplinary labor orientation. Workers in a JIT system are trained to perform a variety of tasks.

The pursuit of zero defects and zero inventories requires a commitment to continuous improvement of efficiency. The principles of continuous improvement and elimination of waste are fundamental to the JIT approach.

■ MANAGEMENT ACCOUNTING DECISION MODELS: ADVANCED MANUFACTURING ENVIRONMENT

The JIT approach to manufacturing is reshaping the manufacturing environment and also reshaping management accounting practices. JIT manufacturing and purchasing, however, are not the only forces impacting management accounting. Robotics, flexible manufacturing, computer-aided manufacturing, and activity-based costing are also changing traditional approaches. This is happening because the conventional management accounting system fails to provide the right kind of information for sound decisions in this new, advanced manufacturing environment. This is especially true for strategic decisions. Furthermore, many of the traditional control features (e.g., variance analysis) may actually encourage inappropriate behavior. Consequently, management accounting is evolving and adapting to meet the needs of the new manufacturing environment.

Traditional management accounting has three major objectives: (1) to cost out services or products, (2) to provide information for decision making, and (3) to provide information for planning and control. Product costs are needed to value inventories, to prepare financial statements, and to provide managers with the ability to plan and make decisions. Control and management of costs is essential for implementing plans and realizing the firm's objectives. All three objectives of management accounting are affected by the philosophy of continuous improvement, activity-based costing, and automation, producing significant changes in the approach required of the management accounting system.

Product costing in the advanced manufacturing environment has already been discussed (see Chapter 6). The impact on planning and control is discussed in Chapter 18. So far in this chapter, we have discussed the impact of the advanced manufacturing environment on inventory management. Other decision-making models are also affected. Decision making tends to be more broadly focused—it is more concerned with the explicit consideration of the strategic elements. Management accounting's role should be concerned with helping the firm to achieve a competitive advantage. Moreover, the value of management accounting is directly related to its ability to help an organization be successful.

Strategic Costing

strategic decision making

strategic cost analysis

Strategic decision making involves choosing among alternative strategies with the goal of selecting a strategy or strategies that provide a company with reasonable assurance of long-term growth and survival. The key to achieving this goal is to gain a competitive advantage. **Strategic cost analysis** is the use of cost data to develop and identify superior strategies that will produce a sustainable competitive advantage.[15]

Assigning a strategic role for a management accounting system requires a shift in attitude and orientation. Part of this shift has to do with switching from a short-term to a long-term focus. For example, virtually all product-related decisions are long term in focus. Yet many of the management accounting models dealing with such product-related decisions as pricing and product discontinuance (keep or drop decisions) are short term in focus. For example, in chapters 7 and 10, we learned about contribution-margin pricing—a short-term pricing strategy designed to take advantage of excess capacity and increase profits—in the short run. But there are dangers associated with short-term incremental pricing. Managers, content with the increase in profits received from special orders, may fail to search for a long-term solution to the idle capacity. They may continue the practice of accepting orders that offer short-term benefits. This pattern of short-term decisions itself becomes a strategy and has long-term consequences. In the long term, fixed costs must be covered.

Making sure that the long run is considered—even for so-called short-run decisions—is only one aspect of strategic cost analysis. Another dimension is identifying the strategic elements present in a decision. For example, selling a medium-level quality product to low-end dealers for a special, low price because of idle capacity could threaten the main channels of distribution for the product. This is true even if the dealers apply their own private labels to the product. Why? Because selling the product to low-end dealers creates a direct competitor for its regular, medium-level dealers. Potential customers of the regular retail outlets could switch to the lower-end outlets because they can buy the same quality for a lower price. And what if the regular outlets deduce what has happened?[16]

Activity-Based Costing and Strategic Decision Making

We have already learned that activity-based costing (ABC) can offer a significant contribution by producing more accurate product costs—input that is critical for firms operating in the advanced manufacturing environment. In

---

[15]As defined by John K. Shank and Vijay Govindarajan, *Strategic Cost Analysis: The Evolution from Managerial to Strategic Accounting* (Homewood, Ill.: Richard D. Irwin, 1989).

[16]A complete case study—the Baldwin Bicycle Case—concerning these kinds of strategic issues is presented and analyzed in Shank and Govindarajan, *Strategic Cost Analysis: The Evolution from Managerial to Strategic Accounting*.

fact, product profitability is itself a strategic issue and, therefore, product costs must be accurately measured. Pricing decisions, product mix, new product introduction decisions, and decisions on how to respond to competitors' products are all strategic product-related decisions. Distorted product costs can induce managers to make poor—perhaps even disastrous—decisions. For a firm with product diversity, it is common for a unit-based cost system to overcost high-volume products and undercost low-volume products. This phenomenon has been blamed for the American giveaway of high volume industries to foreign competitors such as VCRs and memory chips.[17] Another example relating to product mix is the case of the Schrader Bellows Division of Scovill Manufacturing Company. This division was producing 2,500 products, all allegedly profitable under a unit-based costing system. The use of activity-based costing, however, identified only 550 products as profitable.[18] Poor product costing contributed, in part, to a proliferation of products. It's also easy to imagine the bad pricing decisions associated with this large group of products.

Activity-based costing, however, provides benefits beyond accurate product costing. The reason is simple and compelling. Costs are caused by activities and activities are driven by strategic choices.[19] Different strategies produce different activities. For example, switching to a JIT manufacturing strategy increases quality-related activities and decreases material-handling activities. The costs of these activities are also different from the costs in a conventional environment. By identifying the activities and their associated costs, the costs of competing strategic choices can be calculated (e.g., comparing the costs of a conventional manufacturing strategy with those of a JIT strategy). This information then allows managers to make better strategic decisions—selecting the strategic choices that provide the greatest economic benefit to the organization.

Another strategic benefit of activity-based costing is its ability to include postplant, customer-level activities. Expanding cost analysis to include marketing and distribution activities can enhance strategic decision making. Suppose, for example, that a company has one customer that provides 60 percent of the business and a large number of other customers that supply 40 percent of the business. The large customer places orders twice yearly and smaller customers place frequent small orders. All customers are billed on a cost-plus basis (cost includes selling expenses). Currently, sales administration costs are allocated to customers on the basis of sales volume. Thus, the large customer receives 60 percent of this cost. Now assume that this customer complains about the magnitude of the selling costs being billed and threatens to take its business elsewhere. An investigation indicates that the number of

[17]Shank and Govindarajan, *Strategic Cost Analysis: The Evolution from Managerial to Strategic Accounting.*

[18]Robin Cooper, *Schrader Bellows Cases,* #9–186–272 (Harvard Business School, 1986).

[19]William Rotch, "Activity-Based Costing in Service Industries," *Journal of Cost Management* (Summer 1990), pp. 4–14. The discussion linking ABC with strategies is largely based on this article.

sales orders being processed is the cost driver for the sales administration activity. Using this information, it's obvious that the large customer should receive virtually none of the sales administration costs because it generates only two sales orders per year. Recognizing this, management can reassign the sales administration cost, increasing the price of the goods for the smaller customers and decreasing the price for the larger customer. Furthermore, the activity information can be used, if necessary, to explain the price changes, and price discounts can be offered for larger orders.

These postplant and customer-related benefits are particularly important for companies that have adopted a JIT approach. JIT eliminates most of the batch-related activities and locates many product-sustaining activities within the manufacturing cell. Thus, many of the benefits offered by ABC in the manufacturing area are captured by the reorganization. Postplant and customer-related activities, however, still offer significant opportunities for improvement by evaluating customers and customer segments as well as specific marketing activities associated with particular products. The example concerning the assignment of sales administration costs illustrates the potential for activity-based costing to be useful further down the value chain.[20]

Products and services, along with their characteristics, define the output strategy for an organization. This output strategy in turn defines the activities and associated activity costs. Knowledge of this process can be used to improve product-related decisions. This can be illustrated by examining the impact ABC has on some of the conventional management accounting decision models. Specifically, we will look at relevant costing, cost-volume-profit analysis, and segment analysis. As will be shown, the effect of ABC is to improve overall decision quality.

Relevant Costing: New Manufacturing Environment

The relevant costing model continues to be fully applicable in the new manufacturing environment. The utility of the model is enhanced by the strategic insights provided by activity-based costing. This enhancement is achieved by focusing and by identifying and using nonunit-based cost drivers. JIT manufacturing creates a more focused environment by redesigning and simplifying the manufacturing process. Many costs formerly common to several products are now directly traceable to specific products. This change in traceability increases managers' ability to identify costs that will change across alternatives. Add to this the ability to identify costs that respond to nonunit-based cost drivers, and managers have increased decision-making abilities. The increased decision power can be illustrated by an example comparing the analysis with a conventional cost system with that in an ABC system.

---

[20]The benefits of ABC in a JIT environment are more fully discussed in Peter B. B. Turney and James M. Reeve, "The Impact of Continuous Improvement on the Design of Activity-Based Cost Systems," *Journal of Cost Management* (Summer 1990), pp. 43–50.

Conventional Analysis   The increase in the power of relevant costing in the new manufacturing environment can best be illustrated with an example. Assume that Sweeney Manufacturing currently produces all of the components used in its line of printers (several types are produced). Sweeney is currently using a traditional, unit-based cost system. An outside supplier has offered to sell Part 678, an electro-mechanical component, for $4.75 per unit. The company normally produces 100,000 units per year. Each component requires 0.25 direct labor hours. The costs associated with the production of these 100,000 components are given below.

Direct materials	$ 50,000
Direct labor	200,000
Variable overhead[a]	80,000
Fixed overhead:	
Direct fixed:	
Supervision	50,000
Rental of special equipment	70,000
Common fixed[b]	300,000
Total	$750,000
Unit cost ($750,000/100,000)	$7.50

[a]Assigned using a variable overhead rate of $3.20 per direct labor hour
[b]Assigned used a fixed overhead rate of $12 per direct labor hour

The conventional make-or-buy analysis is shown in Exhibit 13–7. Based on the analysis, the company should continue producing the component. Notice that common fixed overhead is excluded from the analysis since it is assumed to be irrelevant. Common fixed overhead is excluded because reducing output is assumed to have no effect on this cost, which does not vary

EXHIBIT 13–7
Conventional Make-or-Buy Analysis

Cost Item	Make Alternative	Buy Alternative
Direct materials	$ 50,000	$ —
Direct labor	200,000	—
Variable overhead	80,000	—
Supervision	50,000	
Rental of equipment	70,000	—
Purchase cost	—	475,000
Total relevant cost	$450,000	$475,000

with direct labor hours. Variable overhead, however, is relevant since it varies with direct labor hours.

ABC Analysis   The conventional analysis classified all costs as variable or fixed. In reality, in a setting in which product diversity exists, much of the common fixed overhead cost pool is made up of costs driven by factors other than production volume. Many of these costs are caused by the activities that are consumed by the individual products. Thus, eliminating a product may reduce the level of some of these activities and eventually lead to additional cost savings. By using activity-based costing, the accuracy of the relevant costing analysis can be improved.

Assume, for illustrative purposes, that the activities included in variable overhead are power and labor fringe benefits, and that the activities included in common fixed overhead are inspection, engineering, material handling, setups, and plant depreciation. In an ABC framework, power and labor fringe benefits would be classified as unit-level activities; inspection, material handling, and setups would be classified as batch-level activities; engineering support as product sustaining; and plant depreciation as a facility-level activity. Of these four overhead activity categories, only the facility-level category containing plant depreciation can immediately be identified as irrelevant. Assume that the following pool rates are computed for the other three overhead categories:

Pool	Cost Driver	Rate per Unit of Cost Driver
Unit-level:		
Power and benefits	Machine hours	$ 3
Batch-level:		
Materials handling	Number of moves	20
Inspection	Inspection hours	15
Setups	Setup hours	10
Product-sustaining:		
Engineering support	Number of engineering orders	2,500

Assume that the component uses the following amounts of each cost driver:

Machine hours	30,000
Number of moves	2,000
Inspection hours	5,000
Setup hours	6,000
Engineering orders	10

Using the pool rates and the activity data for the component, the revised ABC make-or-buy analysis is given in Exhibit 13–8. The analysis now

EXHIBIT 13–8
Revised Make-or-Buy Analysis: Activity Based

Cost Item	Make Alternative	Buy Alternative
Rental of equipment	$ 70,000	$ —
Direct materials	50,000	—
Direct labor	200,000	—
Power and fringe benefits	90,000	—
Material handling	40,000	—
Inspections	75,000	—
Engineering	25,000	—
Setups	60,000	—
Purchase of parts	—	475,000
Total relevant cost	$610,000	$475,000

favors the purchase alternative. In the conventional analysis, use of a unit-based cost driver to describe the behavior of costs gave the impression that all common fixed costs were irrelevant. In reality, the production of the component was responsible for causing some of these fixed costs. By not making the component, some activities of support departments (inspection, material handling, engineering, and setups) could be reduced, creating some savings.

But is the analysis really complete? Should Sweeney buy the part instead of making it? The ABC analysis provides a more accurate picture of what it costs to make the product, but it also raises some questions. Why is the outside supplier able to offer the part for $135,000 per year less than it costs us to make it? The decision to make the part carried with it some activities and their associated costs that are hidden by conventional analysis but revealed by an ABC analysis. Will the decision to purchase the outside part also create some internal activities—activities that are costly? Changing from internal production to external sourcing is a definite strategic shift, creating a dependence that formerly didn't exist. Is this a good idea? Will the supplier deliver the part on time—in the right quantities and at the right level of quality?

Suppose that Bruce Shaver, president of Sweeney, requested his management team to address these issues and to make a recommendation. After two weeks of analysis, he received the following memo:

MEMO
TO: Bruce Shaver, President
FROM: Management Team
SUBJECT: Make or Buy: Part 678

Our recommendation is to continue internal production of Part 678. With our increased interest in providing high-quality products that will be delivered on a timely basis, we believe that maintaining control of the components used in the printer line is essential. This objective is also supported by pursuing a strategy that will allow us to lower the cost of producing Part 678 below the level that it would cost us to purchase it externally.

First, we discovered that purchasing the part carried with it costs in addition to the purchase cost. Given the work load of the Receiving Department, it would have to add an additional employee to handle the incoming parts (including inspection). This would cost an extra $30,000 per year. There would also be a material handling cost of about $5,000 per year. These additional activities reduce the benefit of buying from $135,000 to $100,000—still a very favorable outcome.

We believe, however, that we can overcome this difference. The ABC analysis revealed that this part is consuming activities that are costly—activities that can be reduced or eliminated. As you know, we plan to implement JIT on a trial basis, selecting one or two products initially so that all the bugs can be worked out before we go with the entire operation. We recommend that one of these products be Part 678. Using a manufacturing cell for Part 678, we can virtually eliminate material handling costs, saving $40,000. Setup costs can also be reduced to about $10,000, saving $50,000. Improvements in quality will decrease materials cost and inspection costs. We estimate that within a year, we can save another $20,000 to $30,000 from quality improvements—and more as we gain experience.

In total, the analysis favors internal production. It would be bad timing, given our new attitude of continual improvement and waste reduction, to go externally.

The example illustrates the power of activity-based costing for strategic analysis. The ABC analysis identified the activities that were being consumed by Part 678. By buying the part, many of the costs of these activities could be reduced or eliminated. These activity costs, however, could also be reduced or eliminated in another way—by adopting a JIT approach. And, as it turns out, the second approach is more in harmony with the company's desire to maintain full control of individual components, a desire related to the firm-wide strategy of supplying quality products on a timely basis.

CVP Analysis

Conventional cost-volume-profit (CVP) analysis assumes that all costs, manufacturing and nonmanufacturing, can be divided into two categories: those that vary with sales volume (variable costs), and those that do not (fixed costs). Further, costs are assumed to be a linear function of sales volume: $Y = F + VX$, where Y is total costs, X is units sold, F is total fixed costs, and V is the variable cost per unit sold.

In an activity-based costing system, costs are divided into unit- and nonunit-based categories. Activity-based costing admits that some costs vary with units produced and some costs do not. However, while activity-based costing acknowledges that nonunit-based costs are fixed with respect to production volume changes, it also argues that many nonunit-based costs vary with respect to other cost drivers.

The use of activity-based costing does not mean that CVP analysis is less useful. In fact, it becomes more useful since it provides more accurate insights concerning cost behavior. These insights produce better decisions. CVP analysis within an activity-based framework, however, must be modified. To illustrate, assume that a company's costs can be explained by three variables:

a unit-level cost driver, units sold; a batch-level cost driver, number of setups; and a product-sustaining cost driver, engineering hours. The ABC cost equation can then be expressed as follows:

$$Y = F_a + V_1 X_1 + V_2 X_2 + V_3 X_3 \qquad (13.4)$$
$$\text{(unit level)} \quad \text{(batch level)} \quad \text{(product sustaining)}$$

where F_a = Total fixed costs

V_1 = Variable cost per unit sold

V_2 = Variable cost per setup

V_3 = Variable cost per engineering hour

X_1 = Units sold

X_2 = Number of setups

X_3 = Number of engineering hours

Assuming that the unit selling price is P, then the profit equation is expressed as follows (I is before-tax profits):

$$I = PX_1 - V_1 X_1 - V_2 X_2 - V_3 X_3 - F_a$$

Solving for X_1 yields the units that must be sold for the company to earn a target profit, I:

$$X_1 = (I + F_a + V_2 X_2 + V_3 X_3)/(P - V_1) \qquad (13.5)$$

A comparison of Equation 13.5 with the corresponding equation in Chapter 8, $X = (I + F)/(P - V)$, reveals two significant differences. First, the fixed costs differ. Some costs previously identified as being fixed may actually vary with nonunit cost drivers. Second, the numerator of Equation 13.5 has two nonunit-variable cost terms: one for batch-related activities and one for product-sustaining activities. To make the above example more concrete, a comparison of conventional cost-volume-profit analysis with activity-based costing is useful. Let's assume that a company wants to compute the units that must be sold to earn a before-tax income of $20,000. The analysis is based on the following data:

Data about variables:		
Cost Driver	Unit Variable Cost	Level of Cost Driver
X_1 (units sold)	$ 10	—
X_2 (setups)	1,000	20
X_3 (engineering hrs)	30	1,000
Other data:		
Total fixed costs (conventional)		$100,000
Total fixed costs (ABC)		50,000
Unit selling price		20

Conventional Analysis   The units that must be sold to earn a before-tax profit of $20,000 are computed as follows:

$$X = (I + F)/(P - V)$$
$$= (\$20,000 + \$100,000)/(\$20 - \$10)$$
$$= \$120,000/\$10$$
$$= 12,000 \text{ units}$$

Activity-Based Analysis   Using Equation 13.5, the units that must be sold to earn a before-tax profit of $20,000 are computed as follows:

$$X_1 = (I + F_a + V_2X_2 + V_3X_3)/(P - V_1)$$
$$= (\$20,000 + \$50,000 + \$20,000 + \$30,000)/(\$20 - \$10)$$
$$= 12,000 \text{ units}$$

The number of units that must be sold is identical under both approaches. The reason is simple. The total fixed cost pool under conventional costing consists of nonunit-based variable costs plus costs that are fixed regardless of the cost driver. ABC breaks out the nonunit-variable costs. These costs are associated with certain levels of the associated cost drivers. For the batch-level cost driver, the level is twenty setups and for the product-sustaining variable, the level is 1,000 engineering hours. As long as the level of activity for the nonunit-based cost drivers remains the same, then the results for the conventional and ABC computations will be the same. But these levels can change and because of this, the information provided by the two approaches can be significantly different. The ABC equation for CVP analysis is a richer representation of the underlying cost behavior and can provide important strategic insights. To see this, let's use the same data provided above and look at a different application.

Strategic Implications: Conventional CVP Analysis versus ABC Analysis
Now suppose that after the conventional CVP analysis, marketing indicates that selling 12,000 units is not possible. In fact, only 10,000 units can be sold. The president of the company then directs the product design engineers to find a way to reduce the cost of making the product. The engineers also have been told that the conventional cost equation, $Y = \$100,000 + \$10X$ holds. The variable cost of $10 per unit consists of the following: direct labor, $4; direct materials, $5; and variable overhead, $1. To comply with the request to reduce the break-even point, engineering produces a new design that requires less labor. The new design reduces the direct labor cost by $2 per unit. The design would not affect materials or variable overhead. Thus, the new variable cost is $8 per unit, and the break-even point is

$$X_1 = F/(P - V)$$
$$X_1 = \$100,000/(\$20 - \$8)$$
$$X_1 = 8,333 \text{ units}$$

And the projected income if 10,000 units are sold is

Sales ($20 × 10,000)	$ 200,000
Less variable expenses ($8 × 10,000)	(80,000)
Contribution margin	$ 120,000
Fixed expenses	(100,000)
Income	$ 20,000

Excited, the president approves the new design. A year later, the president discovers that the expected increase in income did not materialize. In fact, a loss is realized. Why? The answer is provided by an ABC approach to CVP analysis.

The original ABC cost relationship for the example is given below:

$$Y = \$50,000 + \$10X_1 + \$1,000X_2 + \$30X_3$$

Suppose that the new design requires a more complex setup, increasing the cost per setup from $1,000 to $1,600. Also suppose that the new design, because of increased technical content, requires a 40 percent increase in engineering support (from 1,000 hours to 1,400 hours). The new cost equation, including the reduction in unit-level variable costs, is given below:

$$Y = \$50,000 + \$8X_1 + \$1,600X_2 + \$30X_3$$

The break-even point, setting $I = 0$, and using Equation 13.5, is calculated as follows (assume that twenty setups are still performed):

$$X_1 = [\$50,000 + (\$1,600 \times 20) + (\$30 \times 1,400)]/(\$20 - \$8)$$
$$= \$124,000/\$12$$
$$= 10,333 \text{ units}$$

And the income for 10,000 units is (recall that a maximum of 10,000 can be sold)

Sales ($20 × 10,000)		$200,000
Less unit-based variable expenses ($8 × 10,000)		(80,000)
Contribution margin		$120,000
Less nonunit-based variable expenses:		
Setups ($1,600 × 20)	$32,000	
Engineering support ($30 × 1,400)	42,000	(74,000)
Traceable margin		$ 46,000
Less fixed expenses		(50,000)
Income (Loss)		$ (4,000)

The strategic implications are now clear. The information conveyed by the conventional equation to the engineers gave the impression that any reduction in labor cost—not affecting materials or variable overhead—would reduce total costs since changes in the level of labor activity would not affect the fixed costs. The ABC equation, however, indicates that a reduction in labor input that adversely affects setup activity or engineering support might be undesirable. By providing more insight, better design decisions can be made. Providing ABC cost information to the design engineers would probably have led them down a different path—a path that would have been more advantageous to the company.

CVP Analysis and JIT   If a firm has adopted JIT, the variable cost per unit sold is reduced and fixed costs are increased. Direct labor, for example, is now viewed as fixed instead of variable. Direct materials, on the other hand, is still a unit-based variable cost. In fact, the emphasis on total quality and long-term purchasing makes materials cost even more proportional to volume changes than before (by eliminating waste and scrap and by discontinuing the use of quantity discounts). Other unit-based variable costs such as power and sales commissions also persist. Additionally, the batch-level variable is gone (in JIT the batch is one unit). Thus, the cost equation for JIT can be expressed as follows:

$$Y = F_j + V_1X_1 + V_3X_3 \qquad\qquad (13.6)$$

where F_j = Total fixed costs and the other variables are as previously defined.

Since its application is a special case of the ABC equation, no example will be given.

Segmented Reporting by Cost Behavior

In Chapter 9, we learned that a segmented report, using fixed and variable costs, offered much better information for decision making and evaluation than a functionally classified, absorption-costing statement. Similarly, segmented reporting using ABC classifications offers a significant improvement in information content over the variable-costing segmented report. JIT provides even further improvements. By localizing many costs that were formerly common to many products (e.g., maintenance, materials handling, and inspection) and by changing the behavior of some costs (e.g., direct labor), the number of traceable costs has been increased. Thus, responsibility for controlling these costs can be more readily assigned. Moreover, such decisions as whether to keep or drop a segment are facilitated by the increased traceability of costs in a JIT environment.

The benefit to decision making of the increased accuracy in segmented reporting can be illustrated with an example. Exhibit 13–9 shows a segmented income statement for a conventional manufacturing setting. More

EXHIBIT 13-9

Segmented Income Statement: Conventional Setting

	Pocket Watches	Wristwatches	Total
Sales	$ 500,000	$ 800,000	$1,300,000
Less variable costs:			
Direct materials	(150,000)	(200,000)	(350,000)
Direct labor	(105,000)	(105,000)	(210,000)
Maintenance	(45,000)	(45,000)	(90,000)
Power	(17,500)	(17,500)	(35,000)
Commissions	(15,000)	(20,000)	(35,000)
Contribution margin	$ 167,500	$ 412,500	$ 580,000
Less direct fixed costs:			
Advertising	(40,000)	(30,000)	(70,000)
Product margin	$ 127,500	$ 382,500	$ 510,000
Less common fixed expenses:			
Depreciation (machinery)			(50,000)
Depreciation (plant)			(80,000)
Setups			(100,000)
Personnel			(60,000)
General administration			(90,000)
Materials handling			(70,000)
Sales administration			(40,000)
Income before taxes			$ 20,000

detail is provided on the statement than usual so that the effects of moving to an activity-based statement can be illustrated more clearly. The statement indicates that both pocket watches and wristwatches are providing positive product margins. It is unlikely, based on the information here, that the company would drop either product line. Yet overall profitability for the company is not impressive—barely above the break-even point.

Now consider Exhibit 13-10, the segmented statement for the same company but using an activity-based costing classification. For the ABC approach, machine depreciation is converted to a unit-level cost by using the units-of-production depreciation method. Two batch level costs—setups and material handling—are assigned to products using batch-level cost drivers (number of setups and moves). There are also two product-sustaining costs—personnel and sales administration—assigned to products using the number of employees and number of sales orders. The ABC segmented statement provides a much different view of product profitability than the conventional, variable-costing segmented statement. The pocket watches are unprofitable—and are causing a significant drain on company resources. If the pocket watches were eliminated, income would increase from $20,000 to $67,500, pro-

EXHIBIT 13–10
Segmented Income Statement: Activity-Based Costing

	Pocket Watches	Wristwatches	Total
Sales	$ 500,000	$ 800,000	$1,300,000
Less variable costs:			
Direct materials	(150,000)	(200,000)	(350,000)
Direct labor	(105,000)	(105,000)	(210,000)
Machine costs[a]	(70,000)	(70,000)	(140,000)
Power	(17,500)	(17,500)	(35,000)
Commissions	(15,000)	(20,000)	(35,000)
Contribution margin	$ 142,500	$ 387,500	$ 530,000
Less traceable expenses:			
Nonunit-based variable:			
Setups	(60,000)	(40,000)	(100,000)
Material handling	(45,000)	(25,000)	(70,000)
Personnel	(20,000)	(40,000)	(60,000)
Sales administration	(25,000)	(15,000)	(40,000)
Direct fixed:			
Advertising	(40,000)	(30,000)	(70,000)
Product margin	$ (47,500)	$ 237,500	$ 190,000
Less facility-level costs:			
Plant depreciation			(80,000)
General administration			(90,000)
Income before taxes			$ 20,000

[a]Includes maintenance and depreciation. Depreciation has been changed to a unit-based approach, using machine hours to measure usage.

viding an 8 to 9 percent return on sales—a significant improvement. But should the pocket watches be eliminated?

Adopting a JIT approach may increase the profitability of both lines—to the point that keeping the pocket watches is the right decision. Assume that the segmented income statement is projected as shown in Exhibit 13–11 after the installation of a JIT system. Notice that the batch-level activities are eliminated. Also, the maintenance function is now absorbed by the cell workers (direct labor). The extra duties may cause an increase in total direct labor cost. The remaining nonunit-based costs are product-sustaining costs.

The consequences on the segmented income statement are dramatic. The number and magnitude of variable costs have decreased as direct labor, maintenance, and materials handling have become fixed. Direct fixed costs, however, have increased in number and magnitude. Because of the JIT system and activity-based costing, management now has a much better understanding of individual product performance. Both products are performing at

EXHIBIT 13–11
Segmented Income Statement: JIT and ABC Classification

	Pocket Watches	Wristwatches	Total
Sales	$ 500,000	$ 800,000	$1,300,000
Less variable costs:			
Direct materials	(150,000)	(200,000)	(350,000)
Power	(17,500)	(17,500)	(35,000)
Commissions	(15,000)	(20,000)	(35,000)
Contribution margin	$ 317,500	$ 562,500	$ 880,000
Less traceable expenses:			
Nonunit variable:			
Personnel	(30,000)	(30,000)	(60,000)
Sales administration	(25,000)	(15,000)	(40,000)
Direct fixed costs:			
Advertising	(40,000)	(30,000)	(70,000)
Direct labor	(140,000)	(140,000)	(280,000)
Machine depreciation	(20,000)	(30,000)	(50,000)
Product margin	$ 62,500	$ 317,500	$ 380,000
Less common fixed costs:			
Plant depreciation			(80,000)
General administration			(90,000)
Income before taxes			$ 210,000

a higher level. If increased profit performance is desired, management could look at the possibility of changing the selling price of one or both products.

Notice the applicability of CVP analysis in this situation. For the option to increase the selling price, the selling price needed to break even or to reach some other targeted segmented margin can be found. Thus, the increase in product-costing accuracy has enhanced the utility of some traditional management accounting decision models.

The benefits of improved traceability were achieved primarily through the JIT system. However, activity-based costing is also an important component. Personnel costs were disaggregated and assigned to each product. By treating the nonunit-based assignments as traceable costs, it is possible to continue using the variable-costing format as a useful managerial tool.

In addition to improving the usefulness of variable costing in decision making, JIT manufacturing also simplifies its use. Recall that variable and absorption costing differ in the way they treat fixed overhead. Absorption costing treats fixed overhead as a product cost, whereas variable costing treats it as a period cost. Under absorption costing, if production exceeds sales, some of the period's fixed overhead can be inventoried and is not expensed until a later period; if production is less than sales, fixed overhead attached to inventory units from prior periods is expensed in addition to the current period's fixed overhead. How fixed overhead is treated by each method, then, leads to differences in the valuation of finished goods inventory and in reported income.

In a pure JIT environment, finished goods inventories are reduced to insignificant levels. All manufacturing costs are expensed in the period. Product costs, including fixed overhead, assume the nature of period costs. No fixed overhead costs are inventoried; thus, absorption-costing income and variable-costing income would always be the same. Inventory valuation is irrelevant. The only difference between income statements using the two systems would be how expenses are presented on the income statement: absorption costing classifies costs by function, and variable costing classifies them by cost behavior.

■ SUMMARY OF LEARNING OBJECTIVES

1. List the traditional reasons for carrying inventories. In a traditional manufacturing environment, inventory management focuses on minimizing inventory-related costs to maximize total profits. Some inventory must be held to achieve this objective. For example, inventory must be held to balance ordering (or setup) and carrying costs and to minimize stock-out costs. Holding inventory helps a firm to satisfy customer demand, to keep production moving smoothly, to take advantage of quantity discounts, and to hedge against future price increases.

2. Define *setup* and *carrying costs* and provide examples of each. Setup costs are the costs of preparing equipment and facilities so that they can be used to produce a product. Examples include setup labor and the costs of test runs. Carrying costs are the costs of holding inventory. Examples include insurance, taxes, and the opportunity cost of capital (for the funds tied up in inventory).

3. Compute the economic order quantity. If demand is known with certainty, an optimal inventory policy can be developed by identifying the order (or setup) quantity that minimizes total ordering (or setup) and carrying costs and by determining when to place an order. This optimal order quantity is referred to as the *economic order quantity*. This quantity is computed using Equation 13.2.

4. Describe the role of safety stock and identify reorder points. If demand uncertainty exists, the inventory policy is altered to include provision for safety stock. Safety stock prevents significant stock-out costs such as lost sales and interrupted production. Safety stock is determined by the average rate of usage, the maximum rate of usage, the economic order quantity, and the lead time. The reorder point is when an order should be placed so that the raw materials arrive just as the inventory is depleted. The reorder point is determined by the rate of usage, the economic order quantity, and the lead time.

5. Explain how the JIT philosophy addresses the traditional reasons for carrying inventories. JIT inventory management rejects the traditional inventory model and views inventories as wasteful—as cash traps. JIT inventory management is part of an overall JIT purchasing and production system. In this system, the emphasis is on reducing waste, on finding more efficient and productive ways to do things. By reorganizing manufacturing into cells, using a demand-pull approach to production (through the use of a Kanban system), developing a partners-in-profit relationship with suppliers, and emphasizing total quality and total preventive maintenance, JIT manufacturers have reduced inventories to insignificant levels.

6. Describe the JIT Kanban system for controlling inventories. The Kanban system uses three cards: the withdrawal Kanban, the production Kanban, and the vendor Kanban. The withdrawal Kanban signals the quantity that should be taken from the preceding process. The production Kanban signals when and how much a process should produce. The vendor Kanban notifies suppliers to deliver more parts. Exhibit 13–6 illustrates how Kanban cards are used.

7. Describe JIT purchasing. JIT purchasing usually entails the development of close supplier relationships by using long-term contracts to cement the relationship. Price, delivery capabilities, and quality are all of paramount importance.

8. Explain how activity-based costing facilitates strategic decision making. Activity-based costing traces costs to activities and then to products that consume activities. Strategies cause different activities. By knowing these activities and their associated costs, the costs of different strategic choices can be assessed. This, in turn, helps a manager to select superior strategies— those that will establish a competitive advantage for the firm.

9. Explain the impact that activity-based costing and JIT have on the following management accounting models: relevant costing, cost-volume-profit analysis, and segment analysis. By identifying activities and accurately tracing costs to activities and the products that consume the activities, greater strategic insights are provided. For relevant costing, this usually means a longer-term focus with more attention paid to the strategic implications. For CVP analysis, an expanded knowledge of cost behavior allows for better planning and decision making. The improvement in segment reporting using an ABC approach can be as dramatic as moving from an absorption costing to a variable costing format—and for basically the same reason (i.e., better understanding of cost behavior).

■ KEY TERMS

Carrying costs   The costs of holding inventory. (p. 607)

Economic order quantity (EOQ)   The amount that should be ordered (or produced) to minimize the total ordering (or setup) and carrying costs. (p. 609)

Kanban system   An information system that controls production on a demand-pull basis through the use of cards or markers. (p. 616)

Lead time   For purchasing, the time to receive an order after it is placed. For manufacturing, the time to produce a product from start to finish. (p. 610)

Ordering costs   The costs of placing and receiving an order. (p. 607)

Production Kanban   A card or marker that specifies the quantity that the preceding process should produce. (p. 617)

Reorder point   The point in time at which a new order (or setup) should be initiated. (p. 610)

Safety stock   Extra inventory carried to serve as insurance against fluctuations in demand. (p. 610)

Setup costs   The costs of preparing equipment and facilities so that they can be used for production. (p. 607)

Stock-out costs   The costs of insufficient inventory. (p. 608)

Strategic cost analysis   The use of cost data to develop and identify superior strategies that will produce a sustainable competitive advantage. (p. 622)

Strategic decision making   The process of choosing among alternative strategies, with the goal of selecting a strategy or strategies that provide a company with a reasonable assurance of long-term growth and survival. (p. 622)

Total preventive maintenance   A program of preventive maintenance that has zero machine failures as its standard. (p. 616)

Vendor Kanban   A card or marker that signals to a supplier the quantity of materials that need to be delivered and the time of delivery. (p. 617)

Withdrawal Kanban A marker or card that specifies the quantity that a subsequent process should withdraw from a preceding process. (p. 616)

▪ REVIEW PROBLEM

The following unit cost information is provided for a product for three different cost systems: conventional, activity based, and JIT. The conventional system assigns overhead using unit-based cost drivers. The activity-based system assigns overhead using both unit-based and nonunit-based cost drivers. The JIT system uses a focused approach to trace costs and activity-based costing for costs not directly associated with a manufacturing cell. The company produces 1,000 units of this product each year.

	Cost System		
	Conventional	*Activity Based*	*JIT*
Direct materials	$100	$100	$100
Direct labor	20	20	30[a]
Unit-based variable overhead	40	40	10
Nonunit-based variable overhead	—	50	10
Direct fixed costs	10	10	10
Common fixed overhead	60	10	10
Total	$230	$230	$170

[a]Cell labor, including maintenance, materials handling, and packing

Required:

1. Assume that the product is a subassembly. What is the maximum amount, according to each cost system, that should be paid for the subassembly to an outside supplier? Explain why the amounts differ.

2. Assume that the product is a finished good that can be sold to a consumer for $200 per unit. For each cost system, prepare a product income statement that shows contribution margin and product margin assuming sales of 1,000 units. How do you think a manager would react to the product performance reported by the conventional system? The activity-based system? The JIT system? What are the strategic cost implications?

3. Assume that the product can be sold for $200 per unit. Compute the units of each system that must be sold to cover traceable expenses.

Solution:

1. *Conventional cost system*—For the conventional cost system, variable manufacturing costs and direct fixed costs are usually assumed to be avoidable should the company decide to buy the assembly instead of making it. Thus, the avoidable costs would be $170, which is the most the company would pay an external supplier of the subassembly.

   Activity-Based cost system—The activity-based cost system defines avoidable costs as unit-based variable costs, nonunit-based variable costs, and direct fixed expenses (such as product advertising). The traceability of the costs is improved and so the avoidable costs are more accurately specified. For this problem, the maximum price signaled by activity-based costing is $220. The difference between the conventional and the activity-based costing prices reveals some potential problems with decision making in a conventional environment.

   JIT cost system—The avoidable costs (all but common fixed overhead) signal a maximum price of $160. The JIT system produces a lower cost than activity-based costing because JIT manufacturing and purchasing reduces or eliminates many overhead costs (e.g., all batch-level costs are virtually eliminated). Because of greater efficiency, JIT makes it less likely to switch from internal production to external acquisition.

2. The income statements are as follows:

	Conventional	*Activity Based*	*JIT*
Sales	$ 200,000	$ 200,000	$ 200,000
Less: Variable expenses	(160,000)	(160,000)	(110,000)
Contribution margin	$ 40,000	$ 40,000	$ 90,000
Less: Traceable expenses			
Nonunit-based variable	—	(50,000)	(10,000)
Direct fixed expenses	(10,000)	(10,000)	(40,000)
Product margin	$ 30,000	$ (20,000)	$ 40,000

Conventional costing provides a statement indicating a profitable product. Activity-based costing gives a truer, less rosy view of the product's performance than the conventional approach. In fact, the activity-based costing statement indicates that management needs to take steps to improve profitability or drop the product. The JIT outcome reveals that one possible solution is installing a JIT system to increase efficiency. Note that JIT has converted some costs (e.g., direct labor) to direct fixed costs. Dropping a product or keeping it and improving its profitability are strategic decisions. Changing the way activities are done by using a JIT approach is a strategy that may produce a profitable product and maintain the needed competitive advantage.

3. The break-even points are as follows:

For the conventional approach
$$CM = P - V = \$200 - \$160 = \$40$$
$$X = \$10,000/\$40 = 250 \text{ units}$$

For the activity-based approach:
$$CM = P - V_1 = \$200 - \$160 = \$40$$
$$X_1 = (\$10,000 + \$50,000)/\$40$$
$$= \$60,000/\$40 = 1,500 \text{ units}$$

Note that in the absence of any other indication, the nonunit-based variable costs will remain the same as the number of units change.

For the JIT approach:
$$CM = P - V_1 = \$200 - \$110 = \$90$$
$$X_1 = \$50,000/\$90 = 556 \text{ units}$$

▪ QUESTIONS

1 What are ordering costs? Provide examples.

2 What are setup costs? Illustrate with examples.

3 What are carrying costs? Illustrate with examples.

4 Explain why, in the traditional view of inventory, carrying costs increase as ordering costs decrease.

5 Discuss the traditional reasons for carrying inventory.

6 What are stock-out costs?

7 Explain how safety stock is used to deal with demand uncertainty.

8 Suppose that a raw material has a lead time of three days and that the average usage of the material is twelve units per day. What is the reorder point? If the maximum usage is fifteen units per day, what is the safety stock?

9 What is the economic order quantity?

10 What approach does JIT take to minimize total inventory costs?

11 One reason for inventory is to prevent shutdowns. How does the JIT approach to inventory management deal with this potential problem?

12 Explain how the Kanban system helps reduce inventories.

13 Explain how long-term contractual relationships with suppliers can reduce the acquisition cost of raw materials.

14 What are the three major objectives of traditional management accounting?

15 What is strategic decision making?

16 What is strategic cost analysis?

17 Explain why activity-based costing is especially useful for strategic cost analysis.

18 How does a JIT manufacturing approach increase product-costing accuracy?

19 How are relevant-costing decisions affected by activity-based costing and JIT?

20 Explain how cost-volume-profit analysis is affected by activity-based costing. By JIT?

21 Explain why there are more directly traceable costs in a JIT manufacturing environment (or for a firm that uses activity-based costing).

22 The information supplied by ABC segmented income statements is superior to that provided by variable-costing income statements. Do you agree? Explain.

23 Segmented income statements are more meaningful in a JIT manufacturing environment. Do you agree? Explain.

■ EXERCISES

E13–1 **Ordering and Carrying Costs** Eagle Company uses 12,000 brushes each year in its production of large power generators. The cost of placing an order is $125. The cost of holding one unit of inventory for one year is $3. Currently, Eagle places six orders of 2,000 brushes per year.

Required:

1. Compute the annual ordering cost.

2. Compute the annual carrying cost.

3. Compute the cost of Eagle's current inventory policy.

E13–2 **Economic Order Quantity** Refer to the data in Exercise 13–1.

Required:

1. Compute the economic order quantity.

2. Compute the ordering cost and the carrying cost for the EOQ.

3. How much money does using the EOQ policy save the company over the policy of purchasing 2,000 brushes per order?

E13–3 **Economic Order Quantity** Golffer Chemical uses 30,000 pounds of sulphur each year. The cost of placing an order is $20, and the carrying cost for one pound of sulphur is $0.533.

Required:

1. Compute the economic order quantity for sulphur.

2. Compute the carrying cost and ordering cost for the EOQ.

E13–4 **Reorder Point** Thrig Company manufactures lawn mowers. One part it orders from an outside supplier is a specially designed carburetor. Information pertaining to this carburetor is as follows:

Economic order quantity	600 units
Average daily usage	30 units
Maximum daily usage	50 units
Lead time	5 days

Required:

1. What is the reorder point, assuming no safety stock is carried?

2. What is the reorder point assuming that safety stock is carried?

E13–5   EOQ with Setup Costs   Cross Manufacturing produces bicycles. In order to produce the frames, special equipment must be set up. The setup cost per production run is $20. The cost of carrying frames in inventory is $2 per frame per year. The company produces 20,000 bikes per year.

Required:

1. Compute the number of frames that should be produced per setup to minimize total setup and carrying costs.

2. Compute the total setup and carrying costs associated with the economic order quantity.

E13–6   Safety Stock   Pineter Manufacturing produces a component used in its production of small two-passenger airplanes. The time to set up and produce a batch of the components is five days. The average daily usage is 100 components and the maximum daily usage is 130 components.

Required:

Compute the reorder point assuming that safety stock is carried by Pineter Manufacturing. How much safety stock is carried by Pineter?

E13–7   Reasons for Carrying Inventory   The following reasons have been offered for holding inventories:

a. To balance setup (or ordering) and carrying costs

b. To meet delivery dates

c. To avoid shutting down production

d. To take advantage of discounts

e. To hedge against future price increases

Required:

Explain how the JIT approach refutes each of these reasons and, consequently, argues for zero inventories.

E13–8   Kanban Cards   Explain the use of each of the following markers or cards in the Kanban system:

1. The withdrawal Kanban

2. The production Kanban

3. The vendor Kanban

E13–9   Kanban System   Assume that two processes are needed to manufacture a product. In the first process, a subassembly is produced; in the second process, this subassembly and a subassembly purchased from outside are assembled to produce the final product.

Required:

1. Explain how Kanban cards are used to control the work flow between the two processes. How does this approach minimize inventories?

2. Explain how Kanban cards can be used to control the flow of the purchased sub-assembly. What implications does this have for supplier relationships?

E13–10 **ABC and Strategic Decision Making**   Bailey Manufacturing produces several types of potentiometers. The products are produced in batches according to customer order. Historically, the costs of order entry, sales, and marketing activities were expensed and not traced to individual products. Recently, the company decided to trace these costs to individual products using the number of customer orders as the cost driver. As a result of the tracing, the marketing manager recommended the imposition of a charge per customer order. The president of the company concurred. The outcome of the decision was an increase in the size of customer orders.

Required:

1. Consider the following claim: By expensing the marketing costs, all products were undercosted; furthermore, products ordered in small batches are significantly undercosted. Do you agree? Explain.

2. Explain why linking output (products) with activities (order entry and other marketing activities) changed the marketing strategy for Bailey Manufacturing. Do you think the change in strategy was good? Explain. If so, what does this have to say about the conventional costing system?

E13–11 **ABC and Strategic Decision Making**   NGC, Inc., has a traditional, unit-based cost system. The company produces a variety of high-tech medical products. The following cost equation is used to describe the total manufacturing costs:

$$Y = \$3,000,000 + \$20X \text{ where } X = \text{direct labor hours}$$

The variable rate of $20 is broken down as follows:

Direct labor	$7
Variable overhead	8
Direct materials	5

Because of competitive pressures, product engineering was given the charge to redesign products to reduce the total cost of manufacturing. Using the above relationships, product engineering adopted the strategy of redesigning to reduce direct labor content. As each design was completed, an engineering change order was cut, triggering a series of events such as design approval, vendor selection, bill of material update, redrawing of schematic, test runs, changes in setup procedures, development of new inspection procedures, and so on.

After one year of design change, the normal volume of direct labor was reduced from 100,000 hours to 80,000 hours, with the same number of products being produced. Fixed overhead, however, increased from $3,000,000 to $3,500,000.

Required:

1. Using normal volume, compute the manufacturing cost per labor hour before the year of design changes.

2. Using normal volume after the one year of design changes, compute the manufacturing cost per hour.

3. What do you think is the most likely explanation for the failure of the design changes to reduce manufacturing costs?

4. Explain how an ABC system could have improved the design strategy taken by product engineering.

E13–12 **ABC; Special Order** Peterson Machining was operating at 70 percent of capacity. An offer to produce 3,000 units of a specially designed tool has just been received. The customer has offered to pay $22 per tool. Peterson is currently using a conventional, unit-based cost system that allocates overhead to jobs on the basis of direct labor hours. Accounting has estimated the full cost of producing the tools:

Direct materials	$10
Direct labor	5
Variable overhead	5
Fixed overhead	16

Prior to making a decision, the president of the company commissioned a special study to see whether there would be any incremental increase in the fixed overhead costs. The results of the study revealed the following:

2 setups—$2,500 each
10 hours of inspection—$10/hr
Special engineering work: 20 hours, $15/hr
Packing: 2 orders, $400/order

Required:

1. Ignore the special study and determine whether the order should be accepted or rejected.

2. Now, using the special study data, repeat the analysis.

3. Consider this claim: The use of special cost studies is a symptom of an outmoded cost system. Comment on this observation and discuss the need for the special study if an ABC system had been in place.

E13–13 **ABC and CVP Analysis: Basic Calculations** The following cost formulas are available for a product produced by Brown Company:

Conventional: $Y = \$18,500 + \$10X_1$
ABC: $Y = \$10,000 + \$10X_1 + \$1,500X_2 + \$200X_3$

where X_1 = Units sold
X_2 = Number of batches
X_3 = Number of engineering change orders

The unit selling price is $20. The company plans to produce and sell 2,000 units. For up to 2,000 units, the company expects to issue five engineering change notices. Also, for production of 2,000 units, five batches are optimal. Thus, the company is geared to produce at a five-batch level.

Required:

1. Calculate the break-even point using the conventional cost formula.
2. Calculate the break-even point using the ABC cost formula. Explain why the two break-even points are the same.
3. Calculate the profit for sales of 2,000 units.

E13–14   **ABC and CVP Analysis: Effects of Nonunit-Based Cost Drivers**   Refer to the data of Exercise 13–13. Suppose that one week into the year, the company revises its forecast and now expects to produce and sell 3,125 units instead of 2,000. For this level, seven batches will be needed. The number of engineering change orders also will increase from five to eight. Upon hearing that sales will be 3,125 units instead of 2,000 units, Lori Milton, the president of the company, requests a revised estimate of break-even and projected profits.

James Williams, the company's accountant, responds: "That's no problem at all. Fixed costs don't change as production increases, so the break-even point is the same. The unit contribution margin is $10 —so if sales increase by 1,125 units, then profits will increase by $11,250."

Required:

Calculate the break-even point and projected profit change using the ABC cost formula. Was the accountant correct in his analysis? Explain the fallacy in his reasoning.

E13–15   **ABC and CVP Analysis: Strategic Considerations**   Refer to Exercise 13–13. The president has decided that the expected profits for sales of 2,000 units are not acceptable. She wants to lower the break-even point by decreasing costs. The Engineering Department originally proposed a new design that would reduce unit-variable cost by $2 per unit. One engineer, however, familiar with activity-based costing, suggested a more careful assessment of the proposed design's effect on activities. Based on this suggestion, the ABC formula of Exercise 13–13 was developed. This first design would have increased setup costs to $2,500 per setup and would have left the design support at the same level and cost.

This new insight into the linkage of the product with its underlying activities led to a different design. This second design lowered the unit-level cost by $2 per unit and decreased the number of design support requirements from five orders to two orders. Attention was also given to the setup activity, and engineers found a way to reduce setup time and lower setup costs from $1,500 to $1,000.

Required:

1. Calculate the break-even point and profits for the first design by appropriately modifying the ABC cost equation of Exercise *13–13*.
2. Calculate the break-even point and profits for the second design. Comment on the strategic aid provided by an ABC system.

E13–16   **JIT and CVP**   Two years ago, Carrie Company had a conventional cost system; its costs were described by the following equation:

$$Y = \$100,000 + \$12X_1 \text{ where } X_1 \text{ is units sold}$$

At the beginning of the first year, an ABC system was developed, and the cost equation now provided the following information:

$$Y = \$20{,}000 + \$12X_1 + \$1{,}000X_2 + \$40X_3$$

where X_1 = Units sold

X_2 = Number of setups = 60 planned

X_3 = Number of engineering orders = 500 planned

The insights provided by the ABC cost equation prompted the company to initiate a program to implement JIT. By the end of the second year, the JIT system was operational. The following cost equation was then developed for the JIT setting (X_1 and X_3 are defined the same as in the ABC equation):

$$Y = \$50{,}000 + \$6X_1 + \$40X_3$$

The product sells for $16 per unit. The JIT setting also plans to use 500 engineering orders.

Required:

1. Calculate the break-even points for the ABC and JIT equations.

2. Explain why the cost equation changed so dramatically when JIT was implemented.

E13–17 **Accept or Reject a Special Order; Impact of Activity-Based Costing; Strategic Considerations** Good Scent, Inc., produces two colognes, Rose and Violet. Of the two, Rose is the more popular. Data concerning the two products follow:

	Rose	*Violet*
Expected sales (in cases)	50,000	10,000
Selling price per case	$100	$80
Direct labor hours	36,000	6,000
Machine hours	10,000	3,000
Receiving orders	50	25
Packing orders	100	50
Material cost per case	$50	$43
Direct labor cost per case	$10	$7

The company uses a conventional cost system and assigns overhead costs to products using direct labor hours. Annual overhead costs are listed below. They are classified as fixed or variable with respect to direct labor hours.

	Fixed	*Variable*
Direct labor benefits	$ —	$200,000
Machine costs	200,000[a]	262,000
Receiving Department	225,000	—
Packing Department	125,000	—
Total costs	$550,000	$462,000

[a]All depreciation

The company has had excess capacity for several years. Recently, the company was approached by a prospective customer (a large retailer) who offered to buy 10,000 cases of a cologne produced according to its special formula. The customer offered $68 per case for the new cologne. The order would be filled only once and would not displace any sales of the Rose or Violet colognes. The production manager has estimated that the special cologne would have the same activity data and prime cost as that of the Violet cologne.

Required:

1. Using a conventional, unit-based analysis, calculate the incremental profit or loss that the company would receive if the special order is accepted.

2. Using activity-based costing, calculate the incremental profit or loss that the company would receive if the special order is accepted. Assume that machine hours are a better cost driver for machine costs than direct labor hours.

3. Should the order be accepted? Explain. Comment on the strategic implications.

E13–18 **Segmented Income Statements; Product Performance; Impact of Activity-Based Costing** Refer to the activity data and overhead costs presented in Exercise 13–17. Ignore the information concerning the special order.

Required:

1. Prepare a conventional segmented income statement for the two products. Assume no direct fixed costs.

2. Use activity-based costing to assign all costs to each product. With this information, revise the segmented income statement prepared in requirement 1.

3. If you were the manager of the Good Scent Company, how would you assess the performance of each product based on the information provided in the conventional statement of requirement 1? Based on the revised statement of requirement 2? Which statement do you think more accurately portrays the performance of each product? Explain.

E13–19 **Product-line Performance; Impact of JIT Manufacturing** Refer to the activity data given in Exercise 13–17. Ignore the information concerning the special order. Assume that Good Scent, Inc., installs a JIT manufacturing system. Two manufacturing cells are created, one for each cologne. Cell laborers operate the machinery, perform maintenance, and do all the packing for the cell product. The Receiving Department was abolished and replaced with just-in-time delivery adjacent to the cells themselves. Inspection of incoming materials was eliminated because of careful supplier selection—only suppliers that could produce the needed quality were retained. Because of the interdisciplinary nature of the cell labor, the company was able to reduce its packing costs by 60 percent and machine costs (specifically maintenance) by 20 percent. The direct costs (except for raw materials) of the two cells are given below.

	Rose Cell	*Violet Cell*
Cell labor[a]	$700,000	$120,000
Machine costs[b]	280,000	89,600

[a]Includes fringe benefits and packing (all fixed)
[b]90 percent fixed for each cell

Required:

1. Prepare a segmented income statement for Good Scent with segments defined as products.

2. Based on the information contained in requirement 1, evaluate the performance of each product. If you have worked Exercise 13–18, explain why the outcomes in the two exercises differ. What does this suggest concerning the potential role of JIT in improving the competitive ability of individual products?

▪ PROBLEMS

P13–1 **EOQ and Reorder Point for a Retailer**   Yummy Pizzeria is a popular pizza restaurant near a college campus. Jack Branch, an accounting student, works for Yummy Pizzeria. After several months at the restaurant, Jack began to analyze the efficiency of the business, particularly inventory practices. Jack noticed that the owner had more than fifty items regularly carried in inventory. Of these items, the most expensive to buy and carry was cheese. Cheese was ordered in blocks at $12 per block. Annual usage totals 14,000 blocks.

Upon questioning the owner, Jack discovered that the owner did not use any formal model for ordering cheese. It took five days to receive a new order when placed, which was done whenever the inventory of cheese dropped to 200 blocks. The size of the order was usually 400 blocks. The cost of carrying one block of cheese is about 10 percent of its purchase price. It costs $25 to place and receive an order.

Yummy Pizzeria stays open seven days a week and operates fifty weeks a year. The restaurant closes for the last two weeks of December.

Required:

1. Compute the total cost of ordering and carrying the cheese inventory under the current policy.

2. Compute the total cost of ordering and carrying cheese if the restaurant were to change to the economic order quantity. How much would the restaurant save per year by switching policies?

3. If the restaurant uses the economic order quantity, when should it place an order? (Assume that the amount of cheese used per day is the same throughout the year.) How does this compare with the current reorder policy?

4. Suppose that storage space allows a maximum of 600 blocks of cheese. Discuss the inventory policy that should be followed with this restriction.

5. Suppose that the maximum storage is 600 blocks of cheese and that cheese can be held for a maximum of ten days. The owner will not hold cheese any longer in order to ensure the right flavor and quality. Under these conditions, evaluate the owner's current inventory policy.

P13–2 **EOQ with Safety Stock**   Morrison Hospital uses an EOQ model to order surgical supplies. Lately, the surgeons have been complaining about the availability of surgical gloves. During the past three months, the hospital has had to place five rush orders because of stock-outs. Because of the problem, the supply officer has decided to review the current inventory policy. The following data have been gathered:

Cost of placing and receiving an order	$30
Cost of carrying one box of surgical gloves	$1.50
Average usage per day	5 boxes
Maximum usage per day	8 boxes
Lead time for an order	4 days
Annual demand	1,800 boxes

The hospital currently does not carry any safety stock.

Required:

1. Compute the economic order quantity and the reorder point. What is the total ordering and carrying cost for the hospital's current inventory policy?

2. Assume that the hospital has decided to carry safety stock. Compute how much should be carried to ensure no stock-outs. Compute the total ordering and carrying cost for this policy. Will the reorder point change? If so, what is it?

P13–3   **ABC and Strategic Costing**   Bruce Norton, owner of Wellington Works, a machining company, once again was disappointed in the year-end income statement. Profits had again dropped. The performance was particularly puzzling given that the shop was operating at 100 percent capacity and had been for two years—ever since it had landed a Fortune 500 firm as a regular customer. This firm currently supplies 40 percent of the business—a figure that had grown over the two years. Convinced that something was wrong, Bruce called Daryl Jenkins, a CPA with a large regional firm. Daryl agreed to look into the matter.

A short time later, Daryl made an appointment to meet with Bruce. Their conversation is recorded below.

Daryl: Bruce, I think I have pinpointed your problem. I think your major difficulty is bad pricing—you're undercharging your major customer. It's getting high-precision machined parts for much less than the cost to you. And I bet that you have been losing some of your smaller customers.

Bruce: You're right about losing some of our smaller customers. But their business has been replaced with more orders from our large one. But how can the large buyer be getting a great deal like you've described? It has the same markup as our regular jobs—cost plus 25 percent.

Daryl: I have prepared a report illustrating the total overhead costs for a typical quarter. This report details your major activities and their associated costs. It also provides a comparison of a typical job for your small customers and the typical job for your large customer. Given that you assign overhead costs using machine hours, I think you'll find it quite revealing.

Report
Regional CPA Firm

I. Major Activities and Their Costs	
Activity	*Costs*
Setups	$104,500
Engineering	75,600

(continued on next page)

Activity	Costs
NC programming	65,200
Machining	50,000
Rework	50,700
Inspection	11,500
Sales support	40,000

II. Job Profiles

Resources Used	Small Customer Job	Fortune 500 Job
Setup hrs	3	10
Engineering hrs	2	6
Programming hrs	1	8
Defective units	20	10
Inspection hrs	2	2
Machine hrs	2,000	200
Prime costs	$7,000	$800
Other data:		
Job size	1,000 parts	100 parts
Quarterly jobs	15	100
Overhead rate	$7.15/machine hr	$7.15/machine hr

Required:

1. Without any calculation, explain why the machining company is losing money. Discuss the strategic insights provided by knowledge of activities, their costs, and their linkage to output.

2. Compute the unit price currently being charged each customer type.

3. Compute the unit price that would be charged each customer assuming that overhead is assigned using an ABC approach. Was the CPA right? Is the large customer paying less than the cost of producing the unit? How is this conclusion affected if the sales support activity is traced to jobs? (Use orders (jobs) as the cost driver.)

4. What change in strategy would you recommend?

P13–4   **ABC and CVP Analysis; Strategic Analysis**   Payson Electronics manufactures electronic components. The components have a very short life cycle, usually lasting in the market less than a year. Design and development engineering, therefore, is a major activity within the firm. The company has established a formal procedure for developing new products. Engineering develops a proposal and, in conjunction with accounting, estimates future costs. Marketing examines the preliminary report and projects the sales volume for the most likely price. A break-even point is then computed and the expected profits are projected. Based on this information, the development of the new product is either approved or rejected.

    The company is currently using a unit-based cost system, applying overhead using direct labor hours. Recently, however, the president hired a consultant to develop an ABC system—initially independent of the existing system. To see if the new system would have any effect on new product development decisions, the president requested that the consultant prepare a cost report for the new product that had been recently approved. The data for the new product using the existing system are presented below:

Report: Conventional System
Subject: Component 22–7Z (proposed)

Cost projections:	
Advertising	$40,000
Depreciation	20,000
Unit prime costs	15
Unit variable overhead[a]	3
Commissions per unit	1

[a] Using a rate of $6 per machine hour

Marketing analysis:	
Projected selling price	$25
Break-even point (units)	10,000
Projected sales volume (units)	85,000
Volume needed for 20% return on sales	60,000
Projected income before taxes	$450,000

After reviewing the above report, the consultant wrote the following memo:

MEMO
TO: President of Payson Electronics
FROM: Consultant
SUBJECT: Cost Projections: Component 22–7Z

After reviewing the report on 22–7Z, I am convinced that you will be even more interested in an ABC system. I have detailed below some additional costs that should be considered in the analysis. .

I. *Development Costs Traceable to 22–7Z: $31,000.* Research and development costs are currently pooled and expensed each period, following GAAP. However, for managerial product costing, these costs should be traced to individual products. For CVP analysis of 22–7Z, I recommend treating these costs as direct fixed costs. They are, in effect, product-sustaining costs and could be assigned using an appropriate cost driver.

II. Common Fixed Overhead. Your conventional analysis ignores common fixed overhead, assuming it is not affected. In reality, new products consume activities and cause these costs to change. I have outlined the resource demands of 22–7Z below. The activities that 22–7Z will be consuming, the cost per unit of activity, and the projected quantities are all provided.

Activity	Cost/Unit	Quantity Consumed
Batch level:		
Inspection	$ 10	20 hours
Setups	500	10 runs
Product level:		
Programming for NC machine	$ 20	50 hrs
Rework	8	2,000 units

These "hidden costs" should have an effect on your decision concerning the development of component 22–7Z.

Required:

1. Verify the break-even point, the projected income, and the volume needed for a 20 percent return on sales using conventional break-even analysis.

2. Using the additional cost analysis provided by the consultant, calculate the break-even point, the projected income, and the sales volume needed to earn a return of 20 percent on sales. Assume that the needed amounts of the unit-based cost drivers stay the same for the production volumes being considered. Assuming that any new product must earn 20 percent on sales, should 22–7Z be developed?

3. After examining the memo from the consultant and reviewing the new projections based on the additional costs, the Engineering Department proposed an alternative design for component 22–7Z. This new design would reduce development costs by 50 percent, decrease the programming requirements for the numerically controlled machine by thirty hours, and change the setup complexity for the remaining equipment so that the cost of setting up would be reduced to $100 per run. The new design will also be easier to inspect and have fewer quality problems. As a result, rework and inspection hours are reduced by 60 percent. Calculate the new break-even point, the new income level, and the quantity needed to earn a 20 percent return on sales. Should 22–7Z be developed?

4. Based on the results of the first three requirements, comment on the effect ABC has on strategic planning and decision making.

P13–5   **Variable and Absorption Costing in a JIT Environment; CVP Analysis: Multiple Products**   Kimball Company, manufacturer of two different types of motherboards for personal computers, has installed a JIT purchasing and manufacturing system. After several years of operation, Kimball has succeeded in reducing inventories to insignificant levels. During the coming year, Kimball expects to produce 200,000 motherboards: 150,000 of Model 127X and 50,000 of Model 127Y. The boards are produced in manufacturing cells. The expected output represents 80 percent of the capacity for the 127X cell and 100 percent of capacity for the 127Y cell. (This capacity includes time for cell workers to perform maintenance and materials handling.) The selling price for Model 127X is $60; that for Model 127Y is $70.

The relevant data for next year's expected production are as follows:

	Cell 127X	Cell 127Y
Direct materials	$3,600,000	$1,050,000
Labor[a]	$900,000	$315,000
Power	$300,000	$125,000
Depreciation	$800,000	$300,000
Number of runs	100	100
Number of cell workers	20	7
Square footage	20,000	10,000

[a]Responsible for production, maintenance, and materials handling

The following overhead costs are common to each cell:

Plant depreciation	$950,000
Production scheduling	300,000
Cafeteria	100,000
Personnel	150,000

These costs are assigned to the cells using cost drivers selected from the cell activity data given above.

In addition to the overhead costs, the company expects the following nonmanufacturing costs:

Commissions (2% of sales)	$250,000
Advertising:	
Model 127X	400,000
Model 127Y	200,000
Administration (all fixed)	500,000

Required:

1. Compute the unit cost under absorption costing and under variable costing.

2. Prepare an absorption-costing income statement for the company as a whole.

3. Prepare a variable-costing income statement for the company as a whole.

4. In a JIT environment, will variable-costing income and absorption-costing income ever differ? Explain.

5. Compute the units of each product that must be sold to break even using conventional definitions. Repeat using a JIT, activity-based costing format.

P13-6 **Segmented Income Statements; Special-Order Decision; JIT and Activity-Based Costing; Strategic Considerations** Refer to Problem 13–5. The president of Kimball Company is concerned about the profit performance of each model. She wants to know the effect on the company's profitability if either model is dropped. At the same time this request was made, the company was approached by a customer in a market not normally served by the company. This customer offered to buy 30,000 units of model 127X at $30 per unit. The president summarily rejected the offer since it was half the model's normal selling price.

Required:

1. Prepare a segmented income statement for Kimball Company using products as segments. By how much will company profits be affected if either product is dropped?

2. Prepare an analysis that shows what the effect on company profitability would have been if the special order had been accepted. Was the president correct in her decision to reject the order?

3. Now assume that the motherboards are sold to companies that produce medium- to high-level quality PCs. The special-order customer will use the motherboard in a

low-end PC and plans to advertise the fact that the low-end PC can be purchased at a lower price with the same quality as a so-called higher-quality brand. Given this information and the results of Requirement 2, should the order be accepted? Explain.

P13–7   **CVP Analysis; Impact of Activity-Based Costing**   Salem Electronics currently produces two products: a programmable calculator and a tape recorder. A recent marketing study indicated that consumers would react favorably to a radio with the Salem brand name. Owner Kenneth Booth was interested in the possibility. Before any commitment was made, however, Kenneth wanted to know what the incremental fixed costs would be and how many radios must be sold to cover these costs.

In response, Betty Johnson, the marketing manager, gathered data for the current products to help in projecting overhead costs for the new product. The overhead costs follow (the high and low production volumes as measured by direct labor hours were used to assess cost behavior):

	Fixed	*Variable*
Setups	$ 60,000	$ —
Materials handling	—	18,000
Power	—	22,000
Engineering	100,000	—
Machine costs	30,000[a]	80,000
Inspection	40,000	—

[a] All depreciation

The following activity data were also gathered:

	Calculators	*Recorders*
Units produced	20,000	20,000
Direct labor hours	10,000	20,000
Machine hours	10,000	10,000
Material moves	120	120
Kilowatt hours	1,000	1,000
Engineering hours	4,000	1,000
Hours of inspection	700	1,400
Number of setups	20	40

Betty was told that a plant-wide overhead rate was used to assign overhead costs based on direct labor hours. She was also informed by engineering that if 20,000 radios were produced and sold (her projection based on her marketing study), they would have the same activity data as the recorders (use the same direct labor hours, machine hours, setups, and so on).

Engineering also provided the following additional estimates for the proposed product line:

Prime costs per unit	$ 18
Depreciation on new equipment	18,000

Upon receiving these estimates, Betty did some quick calculations and became quite excited. With a selling price of $26 and only $18,000 of additional fixed costs, only 4,500 units had to be sold to break even. Since Betty was confident that 20,000 units could be sold, she was prepared to recommend strongly the new product line.

Required:

1. Reproduce Betty's break-even calculation using conventional cost assignments. How much additional profit would be expected under this scenario, assuming that 20,000 radios are sold?

2. Use an activity-based costing approach and calculate the break-even point and the incremental profit that would be earned on sales of 20,000 units.

3. Explain why the CVP analysis done in requirement 2 is more accurate than the analysis done in requirement 1. What recommendation would you make?

P13–8 **Make-or-Buy; Conventional versus Activity-Based Costing; Impact of JIT** Pratt Company produces gas-powered generators. The manufacturing process includes five different subassemblies, which are then assembled in the final processing department. Recently, an outside supplier has offered to supply Subassembly A for $37 per unit, provided at least 80,000 units are purchased. The plant normally produces 100,000 units of A per year. The Accounting Department supplied the following information on the cost of manufacturing one unit of Subassembly A:

Direct materials	$20
Direct labor	10
Variable overhead	8
Fixed overhead	12
Total	$50

The plant uses departmental overhead rates. In the Subassembly A Department, the only direct overhead costs are the salary of the supervisor ($50,000) and equipment depreciation ($50,000). Plant depreciation accounts for $2 per unit of the subassembly's fixed overhead rate. The remaining fixed overhead assigned to the subassembly represents cost allocated from the plant's service departments using the step-down method.

Recently, an outside consultant suggested that an activity-based costing system be used. To illustrate the utility of the new system, she developed the following overhead costing system:

Overhead Cost Pool	Cost Driver	Pool Rate
Power and maintenance	Machine hours	$ 8
Materials handling	Number of moves	100
Receiving	Number of orders	40
Engineering	Number of hours	20
Setups	Number of runs	500
Plant depreciation	Square footage	200
Equipment depreciation	Machine hours	1[a]

[a] There is a cost pool for the equipment in each department. This pool is for the Subassembly A Department.

With the exception of the depreciation cost pools, the consultant claims that the costs of each pool essentially vary with the level of the cost driver.

Subassembly A uses the following amounts of each cost driver:

Machine hours	50,000
Number of material moves	200
Number of orders received	200
Number of engineering hours	2,000
Number of runs	50
Square footage	1,000

The consultant also recommended the installation of a JIT manufacturing and purchasing system. Assume that the company does so. A manufacturing cell is created to produce Subassembly A. After a short period, the company succeeds in driving setup costs to insignificant levels. Cell labor is trained to perform maintenance, making total cell labor (including maintenance) $2 million per year. Power costs, metered for each cell, total $300,000 per year for Subassembly A. By reorganizing the plant layout, materials handling costs for the subassembly are reduced by 50 percent; these costs are assigned on the basis of material moves. An engineer with a salary of $35,000 per year is assigned to the cell. Finally, receiving costs are decreased by 80 percent by having materials delivered adjacent to the cell on a just-in-time basis.

Required:

1. Using the conventional cost assignments, prepare an analysis that shows whether the company should make or buy Subassembly A.

2. Using the activity-based costing system, prepare an analysis that shows whether the company should make or buy Subassembly A.

3. Using the JIT system, prepare an analysis that shows whether the company should make or buy Subassembly A.

4. Comment on the impact that activity-based costing has on make-or-buy analysis. Also comment on the impact JIT has on make-or-buy analysis.

P13–9   **ABC and CVP Analysis: Multiple Products**   Good Scent, Inc., produces two colognes, Rose and Violet. Of the two, Rose is the more popular. Data concerning the two products follow:

	Rose	*Violet*
Expected sales (in cases)	50,000	10,000
Selling price per case	$100	$80
Direct labor hours	36,000	6,000
Machine hours	10,000	3,000
Receiving orders	50	25
Packing orders	100	50
Material cost per case	$50	$43
Direct labor cost per case	$10	$7

The company uses a conventional cost system and assigns overhead costs to products using direct labor hours. Annual overhead costs are listed below. They are classified as fixed or variable with respect to direct labor hours.

	Fixed	Variable
Direct labor benefits	$ —	$200,000
Machine costs	200,000[a]	262,000
Receiving department	225,000	—
Packing department	125,000	—
Total costs	$550,000	$462,000

[a] All depreciation

Required:

1. Using the conventional approach, compute the number of cases of Rose and the number of cases of Violet that must be sold for the company to break even.

2. Using an activity-based approach, compute the number of cases of each product that must be sold for the company to break even.

P13–10 **Ethical Issues** Martin Whitmer, controller of Cowdery Company and a CMA, was preparing a report for Bill Cowdery, the owner. The report would contain a recommendation on the make-or-buy decision for a subassembly. Martin, however, was faced with a dilemma. More than two months earlier, he had worked as a consultant for Jack Day, owner of the supplier that had offered to sell the subassembly to Cowdery Company. Martin's opportunity to work as a consultant for Jack had materialized during their weekly luncheon appointment.

Jack and Martin had been friends since high school and usually met weekly for lunch. During these luncheons, Martin discovered that Jack's company was struggling. He turned down an offer to assume the controllership of Jack's company. Financial security was too much of an issue. Jack, however, had offered to pay Martin a handsome consulting fee if he would do some basic financial analysis for his company. Martin had accepted this offer and had become involved with the company on a part-time basis. With Martin's help, Jack's company began to recover.

During his consulting activity, Martin discovered that Jack's company could produce a subassembly at a much lower cost than Cowdery Company. He then suggested to Jack that he place a bid with Cowdery Company and helped construct the bid. Since Jack's company had done business with Cowdery in the past, Martin knew that the bid would be taken seriously. Bill Cowdery had always been satisfied with the quality of the products.

Martin knew that winning the bid was important to the continued recovery of Jack's company. Martin's initial analysis had shown that Cowdery Company should definitely buy the subassembly. Based on this analysis, Martin had given some preliminary assurances to Jack that the order would be secured. However, some recent input from a consultant hired by Bill Cowdery had muddied the waters. The consultant had introduced activity-based costing, which changed the economic outcome to favor continued internal production of the subassembly. Of course, Bill Cowdery would rely on Martin's judgment, so the possibility still existed to go with the recommendation based on the current cost system. After all, the current system had worked well for years.

Required:

Evaluate the propriety of Martin Whitmer's actions (and reasoning), including his acceptance of the consulting job with Jack Day. Does Martin really have a dilemma? (In addressing the issues, consider the ethical standards for management accountants in the Appendix of Chapter 1.)

■ MANAGERIAL DECISION CASE

JIT; Creation of Manufacturing Cells; Behavioral Considerations; Impact on Costing Practices   Reddy Heaters, Inc., produces insert heaters that can be used for various applications, ranging from coffeepots to submarines. Because of the wide variety of insert heaters produced, Reddy uses a job-order cost system. Product lines are differentiated by size of heater. In the early stages of the company's history, sales were strong and profits steadily increased. In recent years, however, profits had been declining, and the company was losing market share. Alarmed by the deteriorating financial position of the company, President Doug Young requested a special study to identify the problems. Sheri Butler, the head of the internal audit department, was put in charge of the study. After two months of investigation, Sheri was ready to report her findings.

Sheri: Doug, I think we have some real concerns that need to be addressed. Production is down, employee morale is low, and the number of defective units that we have to scrap is way up. In fact, over the past several years, our scrap rate has increased from 9 percent to 15 percent of total production. And scrap is expensive. We don't detect defective units until the end of the process. By that time we lose everything. The nature of the product simply doesn't permit rework.

Doug: I have a feeling that the increased scrap rate is related to the morale problem you've encountered. Do you have any feel for why morale is low?

Sheri: I get the feeling that boredom is a factor. Many employees don't feel challenged by their work. Also, with the decline in performance, they are receiving more pressure from their supervisors, which simply aggravates the problem.

Doug: What other problems have you detected?

Sheri: Well, much of our market share has been lost to foreign competitors. The time it takes us to process an order, from time of receipt to delivery, has increased from twenty to thirty days. Some of the customers we have lost have switched to Japanese suppliers, from whom they receive heaters in less than fifteen days. Added to this delay in our delivery is an increase in the number of complaints about poorly performing heaters. Our quality has definitely taken a nosedive over the past several years.

Doug: It's amazing that it has taken us this long to spot these problems. It's incredible to me that the Japanese can deliver a part faster than we can, even in our more efficient days. I wonder what their secret is.

Sheri: I investigated that very issue. It appears that they can produce and deliver their heaters rapidly because they use a JIT purchasing and manufacturing system.

Doug: Can we use this system to increase our competitive ability?

Sheri: I think so, but we'll need to hire a consultant to tell us how to do it. Also, it might be a good idea to try it out on only one of our major product lines. I suggest the small heaters line. It is having the most problems and has been showing a loss for the past two years. If JIT can restore this line to a competitive mode, then it'll work for the other lines as well.

Under the current method of production, small heaters pass through several departments, where each department has a collection of similar machines. The first department cuts a metal pipe into one of three lengths: three, four, or five inches long. The cut pipe is then taken to the Laser Department, where the part number is printed on the pipe. In a second department, ceramic cylinders of smaller lengths than the cut pipe are wrapped with a fine wire (using a wrapping machine). The pipe and the wrapped ceramic cylinders are then taken to the Welding Department, where the wrapped ceramic cylinders are placed inside the pipe, centered, and filled with a substance that prevents electricity from reaching the metal pipe. Finally, the ends of the pipe are welded shut with two wire leads protruding from one end. This completed heater is then transferred to the Testing Department, which uses special equipment to see if it functions properly.

The various departments are scattered throughout the factory. Labor is specialized and trained to operate the machines in the respective departments. Additionally, the company has a centralized stores area that provides the raw materials for production, a centralized maintenance department that has responsibility for maintaining all production equipment, and a group of laborers responsible for moving the partially completed units from department to department.

Required:

1. One of the first actions taken by Reddy Heaters was to organize a manufacturing cell for the small heater line. Describe how you would organize the manufacturing cells. How does it differ from the traditional arrangement? Will any training costs be associated with the transition to JIT? Explain.

2. Initially, the employees resented the change to JIT. After a small period of time, however, morale improved significantly. Explain why the change to JIT increased employee morale.

3. Within a few months, Reddy was able to offer a lower price for its small heaters. Additionally, the number of complaints about the performance of the small heaters declined sharply. With improved quality, dramatically reduced lead time, and the lower price, demand for the heaters increased substantially. By the end of the second year, the product line was reporting profits greater than had ever been achieved. Discuss the JIT features that may have made the lower price and higher profits possible.

4. Within a year of the JIT installation, Reddy's controller remarked, "We have a much better idea of what it is costing us to produce these small insert heaters than ever before." Offer some justification for the controller's statement.

5. Discuss the impact that JIT has on management accounting.

PART 3

Planning and Control

Budgeting for Planning and Control

■ **LEARNING OBJECTIVES**

After studying Chapter 14, you should be able to

1. Define *budgeting* and discuss its role in planning, control, and decision making.

2. Define *responsibility accounting* and identify the three major types of responsibility centers.

3. Define the *master budget,* identify its major components, and explain the interrelationships of the various components.

4. Prepare an operating budget including the following schedules: sales budget, production budget, direct materials purchases budget, direct labor budget, overhead budget, selling and administrative budget, ending finished goods inventory budget, the cost of goods sold budget, and the budgeted income statement.

5. Prepare the following two schedules of the financial budget: cash budget and budgeted balance sheet.

6. Identify and discuss the key features that a budgetary system should have to encourage managers to engage in goal-congruent behavior.

7. Describe the difference between a static and flexible budget.

8. Use a flexible budget to prepare a performance report.

9. Define and explain the key terms appearing at the end of the chapter.

SCENARIO

By all outward appearances, Dr. Roger Jones was a successful dentist. He owned his own office building, which he leased to the professional corporation housing his dental practice. The revenues from his practice exceeded $250,000 each year, providing him with a salary of $75,000 a year. He and his family lived in a large home in a well-regarded neighborhood.

However, Dr. Jones just received a registered letter from the IRS threatening to impound his business and sell its assets for failure to pay payroll taxes for the past six months. Furthermore, the professional corporation was also having difficulty paying its suppliers. The corporation owed one supplier more than $100,000 and had made arrangements to pay interest payments on the bill but was missing even these payments. These same kinds of difficulty had been experienced repeatedly for the past five years.

In the past, Dr. Jones had solved similar problems by borrowing money on the equity in either his personal residence or his office building. Upon investigation, he discovered that sufficient equity still existed in his office building to solve the IRS problem. A visit to a local bank resulted in a refinancing agreement that produced sufficient capital to pay the back taxes and the associated penalties and interest.

This time, however, Dr. Jones was not satisfied with the short-run solution to his financial difficulties. His latest loan had exhausted his personal financial resources; further difficulties simply couldn't be tolerated. His first action was to dismiss his receptionist-bookkeeper, reasoning that a significant part of the blame was hers for failing to manage properly the financial resources of the corporation. He then called Lawson, Johnson, and Smith, a local CPA firm, and requested that a consultant determine the cause of his recurring financial difficulties.

Jeanette Smith, a partner in the CPA firm, accepted the assignment. After spending a week examining the records of the practice and extensively interviewing Dr. Jones, Jeanette delivered the following report:

Dr. Roger Jones
1091 West Apple Avenue
Reno, Nevada

Dear Dr. Jones:

The cause of your current financial difficulties is the absence of proper planning and control. Currently, many of your expenditure decisions are made in a haphazard and arbitrary manner. Affordability is seldom, if ever, considered. Because of this, resources are often committed beyond the capabilities of the practice. To meet these additional commitments, your bookkeeper has been forced to postpone payments for essential operating expenses such as payroll taxes, supplies, and laboratory services.

The following examples illustrate some of the decisions that have contributed to your financial troubles:

1. *Salary decisions.* You have been granting 5 percent increases each year whether or not the business could successfully absorb these increases. Also, your salary is 10 percent higher than dentists with comparable practices.

2. *Withdrawal decisions.* For the past five years, you have withdrawn from cash receipts approximately $500 per month. These withdrawals have been treated as a loan from the corporation to you, the president of the corporation.

3. *Equipment acquisition decisions.* During the past five years, the corporation has acquired a van, a video recorder, a refrigerator, and a microcomputer system. Some of these items were cash acquisitions, and some are being paid for on an installment basis. None of them was essential to the mission of your corporation.

Other examples could be given, but these should suffice. These decisions have had an adverse effect on both your personal financial status and the financial well-being of the corporation. The mortgage payments for your personal residence and for your office building have increased by 50 percent over the past five years. Additionally, the liabilities of the corporation have increased by 200 percent for the same period of time.

To prevent the recurrence of these financial problems, I recommend the installation of a formal budgetary system. A comprehensive financial plan is needed so that you know where you are going and what you are capable of doing. Each year you should develop a financial plan that details the expected revenues and associated expenditures necessary to support the mission of your corporation. Additionally, this financial plan can be used to control the use of the resources owned by your corporation.

My firm would be pleased to assist you in designing and implementing the recommended system. For it to be successful, you and your staff need to be introduced to the elementary principles of budgeting. As a part of implementation, we will offer three two-hour seminars on budgeting. The first will describe the basic philosophy of budgeting, the second will teach you how to prepare budgets, and the third will explore the use of budgets for planning, control, and performance evaluation.

Sincerely,

Jeanette Smith, CPA

■ DESCRIPTION OF BUDGETING

As Dr. Jones discovered, failure to plan, either formally or informally, can lead to financial disaster. Managers of businesses, whether small or large, must know their resource capabilities and have a plan that details the use of these resources. Careful planning is vital to the health of any organization.

Definition and Role of Budgeting

Jeanette Smith noted that Dr. Jones's main problem was failure to plan and exercise control over his business. Her recommendation was to install a budgetary system, but what role does budgeting play in planning and control?

budgets   Plans identify objectives and the actions needed to achieve them. **Budgets** are the quantitative expressions of these plans, stated in either physical or financial terms or both. Thus, a budget is a method for translating the goals and strategies of an organization into operational terms. As a plan of action, budgets can be used to control by comparing actual outcomes as they happen with the planned outcomes. If actual results differ significantly from the plan, actions can be taken to put the plans back on track if necessary.

Exhibit 14–1 shows the relationship between planning and control and the role that budgets play in the overall process. Before a budget is prepared,

EXHIBIT 14–1
Planning, Control, and Budgets

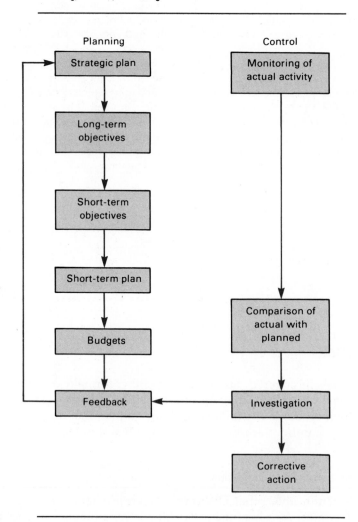

strategic plan an organization should develop a **strategic plan**. The strategic plan identifies strategies for future activities and operations generally involving at least five years.

Once an organization has developed an overall strategy, the next step is to translate this strategy into long-term and short-term objectives. From these objectives, the individual units of a company create short-term plans on which to build the budget. These short-term plans should be compatible with the overall direction of the firm itself. The management of the company should develop a tight linkage between the budget and the strategic plan. In developing this linkage, however, management should take care that all attention is not focused on the short run. This is important because budgets, as one-period plans, are short run in nature.

To illustrate the process, consider again the case of Dr. Jones. (Refer to Exhibit 14–1 as you read this illustration.) Assume that Dr. Jones's strategic plan is to increase the size and profitability of his business by building a practice that has the reputation for quality and timely service. A key element in achieving this strategy is the addition of a dental laboratory to his building so that crowns, bridges, and dentures can be made in house. This is his long-term objective. This addition would increase the quality and timeliness of his services while simultaneously increasing profitability. In order to add the laboratory, he needs additional capital. His financial status dictates that the capital must be obtained by increasing revenues. After some careful calculation, Dr. Jones concludes that annual revenues must be increased by 10 percent; this is a short-term objective.

How are these long-term and short-term objectives to be achieved? Assume that Dr. Jones discovers that his fees for fillings and crowns are below the average in his community and decides that the 10 percent increase can be achieved by increasing these fees. He now has a short-term plan. A sales budget would outline the quantity of fillings and crowns expected for the coming year, the per-unit fee reflecting the increase, and the total fees expected. Thus, the sales budget becomes the quantitative expression of the qualitative plan of action needed to achieve the objective of a 10 percent increase in revenues. As the year unfolds, Dr. Jones can compare the actual revenues being received with the budgeted revenues (monitoring and comparing). If actual revenues are falling short of planned revenues, steps should be taken to find out why (investigation). Then he can take action to remedy the shortfall, such as working longer hours or increasing fees for other dental services (corrective action). The reasons for the shortfall may also lead to an alteration of future plans (feedback).

Purposes of Budgeting

Budgets are usually prepared for areas within an organization (departments, plants, divisions, and so on) and for activities (sales, production, and so on). master budget The **master budget** is the collection of all individual area and activity budgets. It serves as the comprehensive financial plan for the organization as a whole.

A budgetary system gives an organization several advantages.

1. It forces managers to plan.

2. It provides resource information that can be used to improve decision making.

3. It aids in the use of resources and employees by setting a benchmark that can be used for subsequent evaluation of performance.

4. It improves the functions of communication and coordination.

Budgeting forces management to plan for the future. A budget or quantitative plan of action cannot be expressed unless a strategic plan exists. Budgets force managers to develop an overall direction for the organization, foresee problems, and develop future policies. If Dr. Jones had spent time planning, he would have known the capabilities of his practice and where the resources of the business should be used.

Budgets convey significant information about the resource capabilities of an organization, making better decisions possible. For example, if Dr. Jones had known the expected revenues and the costs of supplies, lab fees, utilities, salaries, and so on, he could have made more informed decisions regarding salary increases, loans, and acquisition of equipment. Knowledge of resource capabilities may have led Dr. Jones to lower the rate of salary increases, avoid borrowing money from the corporation, and limit the acquisition of nonessential equipment. These better decisions, in turn, might have prevented the financial difficulties that arose and resulted in a better financial status for both the business and Dr. Jones.

Budgets also set standards that can control the use of a company's resources and control and motivate employees. For example, if Dr. Jones knows how much amalgam should be used in a filling and what the expenditure level should be, he can evaluate his use of this resource and his own level of efficiency. If more amalgam is being used than expected, Dr. Jones may discover that he is often careless in its use and that extra care will produce savings. The same principle applies to other resources used by the corporation. In total, the savings could be significant.

Control is fundamental to the overall success of a budgetary system. **control** **Control** ensures that steps are being taken to achieve the objectives outlined in an organization's master plan. Control is achieved by comparing actual results with budgeted results on a periodic basis (e.g., monthly). If there is a significant deviation from planned results, that deviation is feedback revealing that the system is out of control. Steps should then be taken to find out why. Once the reasons are known, corrective action can be taken.

Budgets also serve the functions of communication and coordination. Budgets formally communicate the plans of the organization to each employee. Accordingly, all employees can be aware of their role in achieving those objectives. Since budgets for the various areas and activities of the organization must all work together to achieve the stated objectives of the organization, coordination is promoted. Managers are forced to view the needs of other areas and are encouraged to subordinate their individual interests to those of the organization. The role of communication and coordination becomes more significant as an organization increases in size.

Responsibility Accounting

responsibility centers

As organizations increase in size, top management typically creates areas of responsibility, which are known as **responsibility centers,** and assigns subordinate managers to those areas. There are three major types of responsibility centers.

cost center

1. **Cost center:** A responsibility center in which a manager is responsible only for incurring cost

profit center

2. **Profit center:** A responsibility center in which a manager is responsible for both revenues and costs

investment center

3. **Investment center:** A responsibility center in which a manager is responsible for revenues, costs, and investments

A production department is an example of a cost center. The manager of a production department has no ability to control pricing and marketing decisions; however, he or she does have the ability to control production costs. Plant managers, however, often are given the responsibility to price and market products. These plant managers control a profit center. Finally, divisions are often cited as examples of investment centers. In addition to having control over costs and pricing decisions, divisional managers often have the power to make investment decisions such as plant closings and openings and decisions to keep or drop a product line.

Responsibility usually entails accountability. Cost center managers are accountable for controlling costs, profit center managers are accountable for profit levels, and investment center managers are accountable for profit levels and efficient use of investment. Accountability implies performance measurement, which, in turn, implies the existence of an expected outcome or standard against which actual outcomes can be compared. Budgets are often used to set the expected outcomes for managers of responsibility centers, which become the benchmarks to evaluate actual performance and to reward the managers.

For example, consider the practice of CalBlock, a subsidiary of a large corporation located in the intermountain West. CalBlock produces concrete blocks and pipes in plants located in several Western cities. Each plant is designated as a profit center. By the beginning of the fiscal year, each plant manager must develop a budgeted income statement that is approved by higher management. At the end of the fiscal year, actual profits are compared with budgeted profits. If they exceed budgeted profits, the managers can receive a year-end bonus from 0 percent to 40 percent of salary (the maximum bonus is earned if actual profits are at least 125 percent of the budgeted profits). Additionally, promotions, salary increases, and continued employment are all affected by a plant manager's performance. Consistently poor performance can lead to dismissal or demotion. On the other hand, consistently good performance is likely to lead to promotion.

The approach described above is often referred to as **responsibility accounting** because of the key role that accounting measures and reports play in the process. The system includes five aspects. First, a responsibility center is identified with the responsibility defined in accounting terms (e.g., costs or profits). Second, an accounting standard or benchmark is set, usually through budgeting. Third, a reward system is established to encourage managers to provide good performance. Fourth, a manager's performance is measured by comparing actual performance with budgeted performance. Fifth, managers are rewarded or penalized according to the policies and discretion of higher management.

The Two Dimensions of Budgeting

The role of budgets in a responsibility accounting system reveals two dimensions to budgeting: (1) how the budget is prepared and (2) how the budget is used to implement the organization's plans. The first dimension concerns the mechanics of budget preparation.

The second involves how individuals within an organization react to a budgetary system. The use of budgets to exercise control, evaluate performance, communicate, and encourage coordination suggests that budgeting is a human activity. As such, it carries a strong behavioral dimension. Accordingly, if budgets are expected to motivate and encourage behavior consistent with organizational objectives, care must be exercised in implementing a budgetary system within an organization. In fact, the success or failure of budgeting depends on how well management considers its behavioral implications.

The remainder of this chapter is primarily concerned with these two dimensions.

■ THE MECHANICS OF BUDGETING

The Time Factor

Most of the component budgets contained in the master budget are for a one-year period usually corresponding to the fiscal year of the company. Yearly budgets are broken down into quarterly budgets and quarterly budgets are broken down into monthly budgets. The use of smaller time periods allows managers to compare actual data with budgeted data as the year unfolds and to take corrective actions whenever necessary so that overall objectives are attained as planned. Because progress can be checked more frequently with monthly budgets, problems are less likely to become too serious.

The master budget also contains a plan for acquisition of long-term assets—assets that have a time horizon much greater than the one-year operating period. Some of these assets may be purchased during the coming

capital budget

continuous budget

year; plans to purchase others may be detailed for future periods. This part of the master budget is typically referred to as the **capital budget.** Most organizations prepare the budget for the coming year during the last four or five months of the current year. However, some organizations have developed a continuous budgeting philosophy. A **continuous budget** is a moving twelve-month budget. As a month expires in the budget, an additional month in the future is added so that the company always has a twelve-month plan on hand. Proponents of continuous budgeting maintain that it forces managers to plan ahead constantly.

Directing and Coordinating

budget director

budget committee

Every organization must have someone responsible for directing and coordinating the overall budgeting process. This **budget director** is usually the controller or someone who reports to the controller. The budget director works under the direction of the budget committee. The **budget committee** has the responsibility to review the budget, provide policy guidelines and budgetary goals, resolve differences that may arise as the budget is prepared, approve the final budget, and monitor the actual performance of the organization as the year unfolds. The budget committee also has the responsibility to ensure that the budget is linked to the strategic plan of the organization. The president of the organization appoints the members of the committee, who are usually the president, vice-presidents, and the controller.

The Master Budget

operating budgets

financial budgets

The master budget is a comprehensive financial plan made up of various individual budgets. A master budget can be divided into *operating* and *financial* budgets. **Operating budgets** are concerned with the income-generating activities of a firm: sales, production, and finished goods inventories. The ultimate outcome of the operating budgets is a pro forma or budgeted income statement. **Financial budgets** are concerned with the inflows and outflows of cash and with planned expenditures for capital acquisitions. The financial statements that capture planned financing (both short and long run) are the pro forma balance sheet and the pro forma statement of cash flows. Since many of the financing activities are not known until the operating budgets are known, the preparation of the operating budget should precede the preparation of the financial budget.

Preparation of the Operating Budget

The operating budget consists of a budgeted income statement accompanied by the following supporting schedules:

1. Sales budget

2. Production budget

3. Direct material purchases budget

4. Direct labor budget

5. Overhead budget

6. Selling and administrative budget

7. Ending finished goods inventory budget

8. Cost of goods sold budget

The sales forecast is the basis for the sales budget, which, in turn, is the basis for all of the other operating budgets and most of the financial budgets. Accordingly, the accuracy of the sales forecast strongly affects the soundness of the entire master budget.

Creating the sales forecast is usually the responsibility of the marketing department. One approach to forecasting sales is the *bottom-up approach*. In this approach, the chief sales executive requests that individual salespeople submit sales predictions, which are aggregated to form a total sales forecast. The accuracy of this sales forecast may be improved by considering other factors such as the general economic climate, competition, advertising, pricing policies, and so on. Other approaches also exist. Some companies supplement the bottom-up approach with other, more formal approaches, such as time-series analysis, correlation analysis, and econometric modeling.

To illustrate an actual sales forecasting approach, we consider the practices of CalBlock. Top management has discovered that sales of its concrete blocks and pipe are highly correlated with nonresidential building activity. Therefore, in developing a forecast for the coming year, the company's first action is to obtain estimates of the coming year's nonresidential construction. These estimates are available from the state government, from reports published by local banks, and from the local university's center for economic development.

Given this estimate, the historical correlation is used to predict next year's sales for each plant. These sales estimates are submitted to each plant manager as an initial sales forecast. Because of the strong correlation between nonresidential building and sales, plant managers are required to use this initial forecast for budgeting purposes unless they can justify a departure. Most plant managers obtain sales estimates from their individual salespeople as a cross-check on the accuracy of the forecast. Occasionally, they have been successful in revising the initial sales forecast because of superior knowledge of local conditions.

Sales Budget   Once a sales forecast is generated, a sales budget is prepared. The sales budget and the sales forecast are not necessarily synonymous. The sales forecast is merely the initial estimate. The **sales budget** is the projection approved by the budget committee that describes expected sales in units and dollars.

sales budget

The sales forecast is presented to the budget committee for consideration. The budget committee may decide that the forecast is too pessimistic or too optimistic and revise it appropriately. For example, if the budget committee decides that the forecast is too pessimistic and not in harmony with the strategic plan of the organization, it may recommend specific actions to increase sales beyond the forecast level, such as increasing promotional activities and hiring additional salespeople.

Schedule 1 illustrates the sales budget for CalBlock's concrete block line. For simplicity, we assume that CalBlock has only one product: a standard block, measuring 8 × 8 × 16 inches. (For a multiple-product firm, the sales budget reflects sales for each product in units and sales dollars.)

Notice that the sales budget reveals that CalBlock's sales fluctuate seasonally. Most sales (75 percent) take place in the spring and summer quarters. Also note that the budget reflects an expected increase in selling price beginning in the summer quarter (from $0.70 to $0.80). Because of the price change within the year, an average price must be used for the column that describes the total year's activities ($0.75 = $12,000/16,000 units).

production budget **The Production Budget** The **production budget** describes how many units must be produced in order to meet sales needs and satisfy ending inventory requirements. From Schedule 1, we know how many concrete blocks are needed to satisfy sales demand for each quarter and for the year. In the absence of beginning or ending inventories, the concrete blocks to be produced would correspond exactly to the units to be sold. In the JIT firm, for example, units sold equal units produced since a customer order triggers production.

Usually, however, the production budget must consider the existence of beginning and ending inventories since traditional manufacturing firms use inventories as a buffer against demand or production line fluctuations. As-

Schedule 1 (in thousands)

CalBlock, Inc.

Sales Budget
For the Year Ended December 31, 1992

Quarter

	1	*2*	*3*	*4*	*Year*
Units	2,000	6,000	6,000	2,000	16,000
Unit selling price	×$0.70	×$0.70	×$0.80	×$0.80	×$0.75
Sales	$1,400	$4,200	$4,800	$1,600	$12,000

sume that company policy dictates that 100,000 concrete blocks be available in inventory at the beginning of the first and fourth quarters and 500,000 blocks at the beginning of the second and third quarters. The policy is equivalent to budgeting 100,000 concrete blocks as ending inventory for the third and fourth quarters and 500,000 concrete blocks as ending inventory for the first and second quarters.

To compute the units to be produced, both sales requirements and finished goods inventory information are needed.

$$\text{Units to be produced} = \text{Units, ending inventory} + \text{Expected sales} - \text{Units, beginning inventory}$$

The formula is the basis for the production budget in Schedule 2. Notice that the production budget is expressed in terms of units.

Direct Materials Budget   After the production schedule is completed, it is possible to prepare budgets for direct materials, direct labor, and overhead. The **direct materials budget** reveals the expected usage of materials in production and the purchasing needs of the firm. Expected usage is directly related to production requirements, but purchases depend on both expected usage and the inventories of direct materials.

direct materials budget

The expected usage of direct materials is determined by the technological relationship existing between direct materials and output (called the *input-output relationship*). For example, a lightweight concrete block (a single unit of output) requires approximately 26 pounds of raw materials (cement, sand, gravel, shale, pumice, and water). The relative mix of these ingredients is fixed for a specific kind of concrete block. Thus, it is relatively easy to

Schedule 2 (in thousands)

CalBlock, Inc.

Production Budget
For the Year Ended December 31, 1992

	Quarter				
	1	*2*	*3*	*4*	*Year*
Sales (Schedule 1)	2,000	6,000	6,000	2,000	16,000
Desired ending inventory	500	500	100	100	100
Total needs	2,500	6,500	6,100	2,100	16,100
Less: Beginning inventory	(100)	(500)	(500)	(100)	(100)
Unit to be produced	2,400	6,000	5,600	2,000	16,000

determine expected usage for each raw material from the production budget. It is simply a matter of multiplying the units of raw material needed per unit of output times the units of output.

Once expected usage is computed, the purchases (in units) can be computed as follows:

Purchases = Desired direct materials, ending inventory +
Expected usage − Direct materials, beginning inventory

The quantity of direct materials in inventory is determined by the firm's inventory policy. CalBlock's policy is to have 2,500 tons of raw materials (5 million pounds) in ending inventory for the third and fourth quarters and 4,000 tons of raw materials (8 million pounds) in ending inventory for the first and second quarters.

The direct materials budget for CalBlock is presented in Schedule 3. For simplicity, all raw materials are treated jointly (as if there were only one raw material input). In reality, a separate schedule would be needed for each kind of raw material.

direct labor budget   **Direct Labor Budget**   The **direct labor budget** shows the total direct labor hours needed and the associated cost for the number of units in the production budget. As with direct materials, the usage of direct labor is determined

Schedule 3 (in thousands)

	1	2	3	4	Year
CalBlock, Inc.					
Direct Materials Budget					
For the Year Ended December 31, 1992					
			Quarter		
Units to be produced (Schedule 2)	2,400	6,000	5,600	2,000	16,000
Direct materials per unit (lbs)	× 26	× 26	× 26	× 26	× 26
Production needs (lbs)	62,400	156,000	145,600	52,000	416,000
Desired ending inventory (lbs)	8,000	8,000	5,000	5,000	5,000
Total needs	70,400	164,000	150,600	57,000	421,000
Less: Beginning inventory[a]	(5,000)	(8,000)	(8,000)	(5,000)	(5,000)
Direct materials to be purchased (lbs)	65,400	156,000	142,600	52,000	416,000
Cost per pound	× $0.01	× $0.01	× $0.01	× $0.01	× $0.01
Total purchase cost	$ 654	$ 1,560	$ 1,426	$ 520	$ 4,160

[a]Follows the inventory policy of having 8 million pounds of raw materials on hand at the end of the first and second quarters and 5 million pounds on hand at the end of the third and fourth quarters

by the technological relationship between labor and output. For example, if a batch of 100 concrete blocks requires 1.5 direct labor hours, then the direct labor time per block is 0.015 hours. Assuming that the labor is used efficiently, this rate is fixed for the existing technology. The relationship will change only if a new approach to manufacturing is introduced.

Given the direct labor used per unit of output and the units to be produced from the production budget, the direct labor budget is computed as shown in Schedule 4.

In the direct labor budget, the wage rate used ($8 per hour in this example) is the *average* wage paid the direct laborers associated with the production of the concrete blocks. Since it is an average, it allows for the possibility of differing wage rates paid to individual laborers.

overhead budget   **Overhead Budget**   The **overhead budget** shows the expected cost of all indirect manufacturing items. Unlike direct materials and direct labor, there is no readily identifiable input-output relationship for overhead items. Recall, however, that overhead consists of two types of costs: costs that vary in level as activity level changes (variable overhead) and costs that remain unchanged as activity level changes (fixed overhead). These relationships can be exploited to facilitate budgeting.

Past experience can be used as a guide to determine how overhead varies with activity level. Individual items that will vary are identified (e.g., supplies and utilities), and the amount that is expected to be spent for each item per unit of activity is estimated. (These estimates are made by using the methods described in Chapter 7.) Individual rates are then totaled to obtain a variable overhead rate. For our example, assume that the variable overhead rate is $8 per direct labor hour.

Schedule 4 (in thousands)

	CalBlock, Inc.				
	Direct Labor Budget				
	For the Year Ended December 31, 1992				
	Quarter				
	1	*2*	*3*	*4*	*Year*
Units to be produced (Schedule 2)	2,400	6,000	5,600	2,000	16,000
Direct labor time per unit (hrs)	×0.015	×0.015	×0.015	×0.015	×0.015
Total hrs needed	36	90	84	30	240
Cost per hr	×$8	×$8	×$8	×$8	×$8
Total direct labor cost	$ 288	$ 720	$ 672	$ 240	$ 1,920

A similar process takes place for fixed overhead. Since fixed overhead does not vary with the activity level, however, total fixed overhead is simply the sum of all amounts budgeted. Assume that fixed overhead is budgeted at $1.28 million ($320,000 per quarter). Using this information and the budgeted direct labor hours from the direct labor budget, the overhead budget in Schedule 5 is prepared.

selling and administrative expense budget

Selling and Administrative Expense Budget The next budget to be prepared—the **selling and administrative expense budget**—outlines planned expenditures for nonmanufacturing activities. As with overhead, selling and administrative expenses can be broken into fixed and variable components. Such items as sales commissions, freight, and supplies vary with sales activity. The selling and administrative expense budget is illustrated in Schedule 6.

ending finished goods inventory budget

Ending Finished Goods Inventory Budget The **ending finished goods inventory budget** supplies information needed for the balance sheet and also serves as an important input for the preparation of the cost of goods sold budget. To prepare this budget, the unit cost of producing each concrete block must be calculated using information from Schedules 3, 4, and 5. The unit cost of a concrete block and the cost of the planned ending inventory are shown in Schedule 7.

Budgeted Cost of Goods Sold Assuming that the beginning finished goods inventory is valued at $55,000, the budgeted cost of goods sold schedule can be prepared using Schedules 3, 4, 5, and 7. The cost of goods sold schedule

Schedule 5 (in thousands)

	CalBlock, Inc.				
	Overhead Budget				
	For the Year Ended December 31, 1992				
	Quarter				
	1	*2*	*3*	*4*	*Year*
Budgeted direct labor hrs (Schedule 4)	36	90	84	30	240
Variable overhead rate	×$8	×$8	×$8	×$8	×$8
Budgeted variable overhead	$288	$720	$672	$240	$1,920
Budgeted fixed overhead[a]	320	320	320	320	1,280
Total overhead	$608	$1,040	$992	$560	$3,200

[a]Includes $200,000 of depreciation in each quarter

Schedule 6 (in thousands)

CalBlock, Inc.

Selling and Administrative Expense Budget
For the Year Ended December 31, 1992

| | Quarter | | | | |
	1	2	3	4	Year
Planned sales in units (Schedule 1)	2,000	6,000	6,000	2,000	16,000
Variable selling and administrative expense per unit	×$0.05	×$0.05	×$0.05	×$0.05	×$0.05
Total variable expense	$100	$300	$300	$100	$800
Fixed selling and administrative expense:					
Salaries	$35	$35	$35	$35	$140
Advertising	10	10	10	10	40
Depreciation	15	15	15	15	60
Insurance	—	—	15	—	15
Travel	5	5	5	5	20
Total fixed expense	$65	$65	$80	$65	$275
Total selling and administrative expense	$165	$365	$380	$165	$1,075

Schedule 7 (in thousands)

CalBlock, Inc.

Ending Inventory Budget: Finished Goods
For the Year Ended December 31, 1992

Unit cost computation:

Direct materials (26 lbs @ $0.01)	$0.26
Direct labor (0.015 hrs @ $8)	0.12
Overhead:	
Variable (0.015 hrs @ $8)	0.12
Fixed (0.015 hrs @ $5.33[a])	0.08
Total unit cost	$0.58

	Units	Unit Cost	Total Amount
Finished goods: Concrete blocks	100	$0.58	$58

[a]Budgeted fixed overhead (Schedule 5)/Budgeted direct labor hours (Schedule 4) = $1,280/240 = $5.33

Schedule 8 (in thousands)

CalBlock, Inc.	
Cost of Goods Sold Budget *For the Year Ended December 31, 1992*	
Direct materials used (Schedule 3)[a]	$4,160
Direct labor used (Schedule 4)	1,920
Overhead (Schedule 5)	3,200
Budgeted manufacturing costs	$9,280
Beginning finished goods	55
Goods available for sale	$9,335
Less: Ending finished goods (Schedule 7)	(58)
Budgeted cost of goods sold	$9,277

[a]Production needs $\times$ \$.01 = 416,000 $\times$ \$.01

Schedule 9 (in thousands)

CalBlock, Inc.	
Budgeted Income Statement *For the Year Ended December 31, 1992*	
Sales (Schedule 1)	$12,000
Less: Cost of goods sold (Schedule 8)	(9,277)
Gross margin	$ 2,723
Less: Selling and administrative expenses (Schedule 6)	(1,075)
Operating income	$ 1,648
Less: Interest expense (Schedule 10, p. 683)	(39)
Income before taxes	$ 1,609
Less: Income taxes	(650)
Net income	$ 959

is the last schedule needed before the budgeted income statement can be prepared (see Schedule 8).

Budgeted Income Statement With the completion of the budgeted cost of goods sold schedule, CalBlock has all the operating budgets needed to prepare an estimate of operating income. This budgeted income statement is shown in Schedule 9. The eight schedules already prepared, along with the budgeted operating income statement, define the operating budget for CalBlock.

Operating income is *not* equivalent to the net income of a firm. To yield net income, interest expenses and taxes must be subtracted from operating income. The interest expense deduction is taken from the cash budget shown in Schedule 10 (page 683). The taxes owed depend on the current tax laws.

merchandise purchases budget

Operating Budgets for Merchandising and Service Firms   In a merchandising firm, the production budget is replaced with a **merchandise purchases budget.** This budget identifies the quantity of each item that must be purchased for resale, the unit cost of the item, and the total purchase cost. The format is identical to that of the direct materials budget in a manufacturing firm. The only other difference between the operating budgets of manufacturing and merchandising firms is the absence of direct materials and direct labor budgets in a merchandising firm.

In a for-profit service firm, the sales budget is also the production budget. The sales budget identifies each service and the quantity of it that will be sold. Since finished goods inventories are nonexistent, the services produced will be identical to the services sold.

For a nonprofit service firm, the sales budget is replaced by a budget that identifies the levels of the various services that will be offered for the coming year and the associated funds that will be assigned to the services. The source of the funds may be tax revenues, contributions, payments by users of the services, or some combination. For example, a state university offers various services (graduate and undergraduate programs in numerous disciplines, counseling, vocational training, and so on) and receives funds to support predetermined levels of these services from state taxes, from tuition and fees, and from private contributions of alumni and friends.

Both for-profit and nonprofit service organizations lack finished goods inventory budgets. However, all the remaining operating budgets found in a manufacturing organization have counterparts in service organizations. For a nonprofit service organization, the income statement is replaced by a statement of sources and uses of funds.

Preparation of the Financial Budget

The remaining budgets found in the master budget are the financial budgets. The usual financial budgets prepared are

1. The cash budget

2. The budgeted balance sheet

3. The budgeted statement of cash flows

4. The budget for fixed asset purchases

The budget for purchases of fixed assets is referred to as the *capital budget.* Capital budgeting and the statement of cash flows are both considered in other chapters. Accordingly, only the cash budget and the budgeted balance sheet will be illustrated here.

Cash Budget Knowledge of cash flows is critical to managing a business. Often a business is successful in producing and selling a product but fails because of timing problems associated with cash inflows and outflows. By knowing when cash deficiencies and surpluses are likely to occur, a manager can plan to borrow cash when needed and repay the loans during periods of excess cash. When approaching a loan officer, the manager can use the cash budget to document the ability to repay as well as the need for cash. Because cash flow is the lifeblood of an organization, the cash budget is one of the most important budgets in the master budget. The **cash budget** is, simply, the detailed plan that shows all sources and uses of cash.

cash budget

The cash budget has the following five main sections:

1. Total cash available

2. Cash disbursements

3. Cash excess or deficiency

4. Financing

5. Cash balance

The cash available section identifies the beginning cash balance and the expected cash receipts. Expected cash receipts include all sources of cash for the period being considered. However, the principal source of cash is from sales. Because a significant proportion of sales is usually on account, a major task of an organization is to determine the pattern of collection for its accounts receivables.

The cash disbursements section lists all cash outlays for the period except for interest payments on short-term loans (these payments appear in the financing section). All expenses not resulting in a cash outlay are excluded from the list (depreciation, for example, is never included in the disbursements section).

The cash excess or deficiency section is a function of the cash needs and the cash available. Cash needs are determined by the total cash disbursements plus the minimum cash balance required by company policy. If the total cash available is less than the cash needs, a deficiency exists. In such a case, a short-term loan will be needed. On the other hand, with a cash excess (cash available is greater than the firm's cash needs), the firm has the ability to repay loans and perhaps make some temporary investments.

In the event of a deficiency, the cash budget must show the amount to be borrowed so that the cash needs are satisfied. Also, the cash budget should reveal planned repayments. Thus, the financing section discloses the planned borrowings and repayments, including interest.

The final section of the cash budget simply reveals the planned ending cash balance. Ending cash balance is the cash available plus borrowings minus cash disbursements. This ending cash balance would be at least equal to any minimum cash balance required by company policy.

To illustrate the cash budget, assume the following for CalBlock:

a. A $100,000 minimum cash balance is required for the end of each quarter.

b. Money can be borrowed and repaid in multiples of $100,000. Interest is 12 percent per year. Interest payments are made only for the amount of the principal being repaid. All borrowing takes place at the beginning of a quarter and all repayment takes place at the end of a quarter.

c. Half of all sales are for cash, 70 percent of credit sales are collected in the quarter of sale, and the remaining 30 percent are collected in the following quarter. The sales for the fourth quarter of 1991 were $2 million.

d. Purchases of raw materials are made on account; 80 percent of purchases are paid for in the quarter of purchase. The remaining 20 percent are paid in the following quarter. The purchases for the fourth quarter of 1991 were $500,000.

e. Budgeted depreciation is $200,000 per quarter for overhead and $15,000 per quarter for selling and administration (see schedules 5 and 6).

f. The capital budget for 1992 revealed plans to purchase additional equipment to handle increased demand at a small plant in Nevada. The cash outlay for the equipment, $600,000, will take place in the first quarter. The company plans to finance the acquisition of the equipment with operating cash, supplementing it with short-term loans as necessary.

g. Corporate income taxes are approximately $650,000 and will be paid at the end of the fourth quarter (Schedule 9).

Given the above information, the cash budget for CalBlock is shown in Schedule 10 (all figures are rounded to the nearest thousand).

Much of the information needed to prepare the cash budget comes from the operating budgets. In fact, Schedules 1, 3, 4, 5, and 6 all supply essential input. However, these schedules by themselves do not supply all of the needed information. The collection pattern for revenues and the payment pattern for materials must be known before the cash flow for sales and purchases on credit can be found.

Look at the revenues from credit sales for the second quarter, for example. Remember that for a given quarter, credit sales equal cash sales but that only 70 percent of credit sales are collected in that quarter. Thus, second quarter credit sales are $2.1 million (the same as cash sales), but only $1.47 million is received in the second quarter (0.70 × $2,100,000). The remaining $630,000 (0.30 × $2,100,000) is received in the following quarter. Similarly, the second quarter includes revenues from first-quarter credit sales. Total first-quarter sales of $1.4 million are multiplied by 0.5 to yield the amount of first-quarter credit sales ($700,000). This amount is multiplied by 0.3 to find the portion not collected until the second quarter, which is $210,000. As a check on the quarterly sales figures in Schedule 10, add the cash sales and the credit sales for one quarter to the credit sales collected in the next quarter that

Schedule 10 (in thousands)

			CalBlock, Inc.			
			Cash Budget			
			For the Year Ended December 31, 1992			
			Quarter			
	1	**2**	**3**	**4**	**Year**	**Source[a]**
Beginning cash balance	$ 120	$ 141	$ 102	$ 1,421	$ 120	
Collections:						
Cash sales	700	2,100	2,400	800	6,000	c, 1
Credit sales:						
Current quarter	490	1,470	1,680	560	4,200	c, 1
Prior quarter	300	210	630	720	1,860	c, 1
Total cash available	$ 1,610	$ 3,921	$ 4,812	$ 3,501	$ 12,180	
Less disbursements:						
Raw materials:						
Current quarter	$ (523)	$(1,248)	$(1,141)	$ (416)	$ (3,328)	d, 3
Prior quarter	(100)	(131)	(312)	(285)	(828)	d, 3
Direct labor	(288)	(720)	(672)	(240)	(1,920)	4
Overhead	(408)	(840)	(792)	(360)	(2,400)	e, 5
Selling and administrative	(150)	(350)	(365)	(150)	(1,015)	e, 6
Income taxes	—	—	—	(650)	(650)	g, 9
Equipment	(600)	—	—	—	(600)	f
Total disbursements	$(2,069)	$(3,289)	$(3,282)	$(2,101)	$(10,741)	
Minimum cash balance	(100)	(100)	(100)	(100)	(100)	a
Total cash needs	$(2,169)	$(3,389)	$(3,382)	$(2,201)	$(10,841)	
Excess (deficiency) of cash available over needs	(559)	532	1,430	1,300	1,339	
Financing:						
Borrowings	600	—	—	—	600	
Repayments	—	(500)	(100)	—	(600)	b
Interest[b]	—	(30)	(9)	—	(39)	b
Total financing	600	(530)	(109)	—	(39)	
Ending cash balance	$ 141	$ 102	$ 1,421	$ 1,400	$ 1,400	

[a]Letters refer to the information on page 682. Numbers refer to schedules already developed.
[b]Interest payments are 6/12 × 0.12 × $500 and 9/12 × 0.12 × $100, respectively. Since borrowings occur at the beginning of the quarter and repayments at the end of the quarter, the first principal repayment takes place after six months, and the second principal repayment takes place after nine months.

appear on the "prior quarter" line. The result is the total sales revenue for the quarter as shown in Schedule 1.

Similar computations are done for purchases. In both cases, patterns of collection and payment are needed in addition to the information supplied by the schedules.

Additionally, all noncash expenses, such as depreciation, need to be removed from the total amounts reported in the expense budgets. Thus, the budgeted expenses in schedules 5 and 6 were reduced by the budgeted depreciation for each quarter. Overhead expenses in Schedule 5 were reduced by depreciation of $200,000 per quarter. Selling and administrative expenses were reduced by $15,000 per quarter. The net amounts are what appear in the cash budget.

The cash budget shown in Schedule 10 underscores the importance of breaking the annual budget down into smaller time periods. The cash budget for the year gives the impression that sufficient operating cash will be available to finance the acquisition of the new equipment. Quarterly information, however, shows the need for short-term borrowing because of both the acquisition of the new equipment and the timing of the firm's cash flows. Breaking down the annual cash budget into quarterly time periods conveys more information. Even smaller time periods often prove to be useful. Most firms prepare monthly cash budgets, and some even prepare weekly and daily budgets.

Another significant piece of information emerges from CalBlock's cash budget. By the end of the third quarter, the firm owns a considerable amount of cash ($1,421,000). A similar amount is also owned by the end of the year. It is certainly not wise to allow this much cash to sit idly in a bank account. The management of CalBlock should consider paying dividends and making long-term investments. At the very least, the excess cash should be invested in short-term marketable securities. Once plans are finalized for use of the excess cash, the cash budget should be revised to reflect those plans. Budgeting is a dynamic process. As the budget is developed, new information becomes available and better plans can be formulated.

Budgeted Balance Sheet   The budgeted balance sheet depends on information contained in the current balance sheet and in the other budgets in the master budget. The current balance sheet for the beginning of the year is given in Exhibit 14–2.

The budgeted balance sheet for 1992 is given in Schedule 11 (page 686). Explanations for the budgeted figures follow the schedule.

As we have described the individual budgets that make up the master budget, the interdependencies of the component budgets have become apparent. A diagram displaying these interrelationships is shown in Exhibit 14–3.

▪ THE BEHAVIORAL DIMENSION OF BUDGETING

Budgets are often used to judge the actual performance of managers. Bonuses, salary increases, and promotions are all affected by a manager's ability

EXHIBIT 14–2

CalBlock, Inc.

Balance Sheet
December 31, 1991

Assets

Current assets:		
Cash	$ 120,000	
Accounts receivable	300,000	
Raw materials inventory	50,000	
Finished goods	55,000	
Total current assets		$ 525,000
Fixed assets:		
Land	$ 2,500,000	
Building and equipment	9,000,000	
Accumulated depreciation	(4,500,000)	
Total fixed assets		7,000,000
Total assets		$7,525,000

Liabilities and Owner's Equity

Current liabilities:		
Accounts payable		$ 100,000
Owner's equity:		
Common stock, no par	$ 600,000	
Retained earnings	6,825,000	
Total owner's equity		7,425,000
Total liabilities and equity		$7,525,000

to achieve or beat budgeted goals. Since a manager's financial status and career can be affected, budgets can have a significant behavioral effect. Whether that effect is positive or negative depends to a large extent on how budgets are used.

Positive behavior occurs when the goals of individual managers are aligned with the goals of the organization and the manager has the drive to achieve them. The alignment of managerial and organizational goals is often **goal congruence** referred to as *goal congruence*. In addition to goal congruence, however, a manager must also exert effort to achieve the goals of the organization.

If the budget is improperly administered, the reaction of subordinate managers may be negative. This negative behavior can be manifested in numerous ways, but the overall effect is subversion of the organization's goals.

Schedule 11 (in thousands)

CalBlock, Inc.

Budgeted Balance Sheet
December 31, 1992

Assets

Current assets:		
Cash	$ 1,400[a]	
Accounts receivable	240[b]	
Raw materials	50[c]	
Finished goods	58[d]	
Total current assets		$1,748
Fixed assets:		
Land	$ 2,500[e]	
Building and equipment	9,600[f]	
Accumulated depreciation	(5,360)[g]	
Total fixed assets		6,740
Total assets		$8,488

Liabilities and Owner's Equity

Current liabilities:		
Accounts payable		$ 104[h]
Owner's equity:		
Common stock	$ 600[i]	
Retained earnings	7,784[j]	
Total owner's equity		8,384
Total liabilities and owner's equity		$8,488

---

[a]Ending balance from Schedule 10
[b]30 percent of fourth-quarter credit sales (0.30 × $800,000)—see Schedules 1 and 10
[c]From Schedule 3
[d]From Schedule 8
[e]From the December 31, 1991, balance sheet
[f]December 31, 1991, balance ($9,000,000) plus new equipment acquisition of $600,000 (see the 1991 ending balance sheet and Schedule 10)
[g]From the December 31, 1991, balance sheet, Schedule 5, and Schedule 6 ($4,500,000 + $800,000 + $60,000)
[h]20 percent of fourth-quarter purchases (0.20 × $520,000)—see schedules 3 and 10
[i]From the December 31, 1991, balance sheet
[j]$6,825,000 + $959,000 (December 31, 1991, balance plus net income from Schedule 9)

EXHIBIT 14–3
The Master Budget and Its Interrelationships

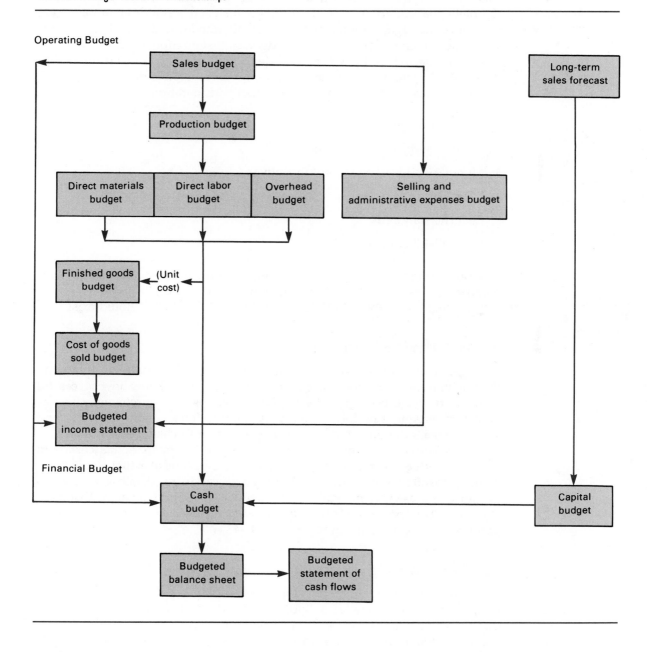

dysfunctional
behavior
ideal budgetary
system

Dysfunctional behavior is individual behavior that is in basic conflict with the goals of the organization. An **ideal budgetary system** is one that achieves complete goal congruence, and, simultaneously, creates a drive in managers to achieve the organization's goals. Currently, the level of knowledge necessary to design and operate an ideal budgetary system probably does not exist. However, research and practice have identified a number of key features that a budgetary system should have to promote a reasonable degree of positive behavior. These features emphasize human considerations.

1. Frequent feedback on performance
2. Flexible budgeting capabilities
3. Monetary and nonmonetary incentives
4. Participation
5. Realistic standards
6. Controllability of costs

One other principle is important to using a budgetary system. However important a budget is in evaluating managerial performance, it should not be the only evaluation means. Multiple measures of performance should exist.

Frequent Feedback on Performance

Managers need to know how they are doing as the year unfolds. Providing them with frequent performance reports allows them to know how successful their efforts have been, to take corrective actions, and to change plans as necessary. Frequent performance reports can reinforce positive behavior and give managers the time and opportunity to adapt to changing conditions.

In a budgetary setting, performance reports compare actual costs and revenues with budgeted costs and revenues. Deviations of actual results from planned results are computed and labeled as variances. Analysis of the significance of these variances allows managers to focus only on areas that need attention. This process is called *management by exception*. An example of a performance report is given in Exhibit 14–4.

Static Budgets Versus Flexible Budgets

Static Budgets　The budget developed for CalBlock is an example of a static budget. A **static budget** is a budget for a particular level of activity. For CalBlock, budgets were developed based on expected annual sales of 16 million units. Quarterly budgets were also developed based on particular levels of activity. Because static budgets depend on a particular level of activity, they are not very useful when it comes to preparing performance reports.

To illustrate, suppose that CalBlock has decided to provide quarterly performance reports. Further suppose that sales activity was greater than expected in the first quarter; 2.6 million concrete blocks were sold instead of

static budget

EXHIBIT 14–4
Performance Report: Quarterly Production Costs (in thousands)

	Actual	Budget	Variance	
Units produced	3,000	2,400	600.00	F[a]
Direct materials cost	$ 927.30	$ 624.00[b]	$303.30	U[c]
Direct labor cost	360.00	288.00[d]	72.00	U
Overhead:[e]				
Variable:				
Supplies	80.00	72.00	8.00	U
Indirect labor	220.00	168.00	52.00	U
Power	40.00	48.00	(8.00)	F
Fixed:				
Supervision	90.00	100.00	(10.00)	F
Depreciation	200.00	200.00	0.00	
Rent	30.00	20.00	10.00	U
Total	$1,947.30	$1,520.00	$427.30	U

[a]F means the variance is favorable.
[b]From Schedule 3 (62,400 lbs × $0.01)
[c]U means the variance is unfavorable.
[d]From Schedule 4
[e]Schedule 5 provides the aggregate amount of budgeted overhead (e.g., the aggregate variable overhead is $0.015 \times 2,400,000 \times \$8 = \$288,000$, and the total budgeted fixed overhead is $320,000). The individual budgeted amounts for each overhead item are new information (except for depreciation). Usually, this information would be detailed in an overhead budget.

the 2 million budgeted in Schedule 1. Because of increased sales activity, production was increased over the planned level. Instead of producing 2.4 million units (Schedule 2), CalBlock produced 3 million units.

A performance report comparing the actual production costs for the first quarter with the original planned production costs is given in Exhibit 14–4 (in contrast to Schedule 5, budgeted amounts for individual overhead items are provided). According to the report, unfavorable variances occur for direct materials, direct labor, all variable overhead items, and supervision. However, there is something fundamentally wrong with the report. Actual costs for production of 3 million concrete blocks are being compared with planned costs for production of 2.4 million. Because direct materials, direct labor, and variable overhead are variable costs, we would expect them to be greater at a higher activity level. Thus, even if cost control were perfect for the production of 3 million units, unfavorable variances would be produced for all variable costs.

To create a meaningful performance report, actual costs and expected costs must be compared at the *same* level of activity. Since actual output often differs from planned output, some method is needed to compute what the costs should have been for the actual output level.

Flexible Budgets   The budget that provides a firm with the capability to

flexible budget

compute expected costs for a range of activity is called a *flexible budget.* Flexible budgeting has three major uses.

1. The flexible budget can be used to prepare the budget before the fact for the expected level of activity.

2. Because flexible budgeting can determine what costs should be at various levels of activity, the budget can be used after the fact to compute what costs should have been for the actual level of activity. Once expected costs are known for the actual level of activity, a performance report that compares those expected costs to actual costs can be prepared.

3. Flexible budgeting can help managers deal with uncertainty by allowing them to see the expected outcomes for a range of activity. It can be used to generate financial results for a number of plausible scenarios.

In other words, flexible budgeting is the key to providing the frequent feedback that managers need to exercise control and effectively carry out the plans of an organization.

To compute the expected cost at different levels of activity, flexible budgeting exploits the cost behavior patterns of each item in the budget. Thus, before a flexible budget can be prepared, the cost behavior of each item in the budget must be known. This means that the cost formula $Y = F + VX$ is needed for each item in the budget. In this formula, Y is the item's total cost, X is a measure of activity level, F is the item's fixed costs, and V is the item's variable cost per unit of activity.

To illustrate the power of flexible budgeting, a flexible production budget will be developed for CalBlock. Let activity level be measured by the number of concrete blocks produced. From Schedule 7, we know the variable cost formulas for direct materials ($0.26 per unit), direct labor ($0.12 per unit), and variable overhead ($0.12 per unit). To increase the detail of the flexible budget, let us assume the variable costs per unit for supplies ($0.03), indirect labor ($0.07), and power ($0.02). The three individual formulas sum to $0.12. From Schedule 5, we also know that fixed overhead is budgeted at $320,000 per quarter. Exhibit 14–5 displays a flexible budget for production costs at three levels of activity.

Notice in Exhibit 14–5 that total budgeted production costs increase as the activity level increases. Budgeted costs change because of variable costs. Because

variable budgets

of this, flexible budgets are sometimes referred to as *variable budgets.*

Flexible budgets are powerful control tools because they allow management to compute what the costs should be for any level of activity. Exhibit 14–5 reveals what the costs should have been for the actual level of activity (3 million units). With this information, a performance report can be prepared that communicates useful information to management. A revised

EXHIBIT 14–5
Flexible Production Budget (in thousands)

	Variable Cost per Unit	Range of Production (units)		
		2,400	3,000	3,600
Production costs:				
Variable:				
Direct materials	$0.26	$ 624	$ 780	$ 936
Direct labor	0.12	$ 288	$ 360	$ 432
Variable overhead:				
Supplies	0.03	72	90	108
Indirect labor	0.07	168	210	252
Power	0.02	48	60	72
Total variable costs	$0.50	$1,200	$1,500	$1,800
Fixed overhead:				
Supervision		100	100	100
Depreciation		200	200	200
Rent		20	20	20
Total fixed costs		$ 320	$ 320	$ 320
Total production costs		$1,520	$1,820	$2,120

performance report that compares actual and budgeted costs for the actual level of activity is given in Exhibit 14–6 (page 692).

The revised performance report in Exhibit 14–6 paints a much different picture than the one in Exhibit 14–4. By comparing budgeted costs for the actual level of activity with actual costs for the same level, a problem area can be immediately identified—expenditures for direct materials are excessive. (The other unfavorable variances seem relatively small.) With this knowledge, management can search for the causes of the excess expenditures and implement corrective measures to prevent the same problems from occurring in future quarters.

Differences in the actual amount and the flexible budget amount are attributable to one of two causes: differences in the budgeted costs of the inputs, or differences in the number of inputs planned and the number actually used to produce the actual output. The first difference is referred to as a *price variance* and the second as an *efficiency variance*. The **flexible budget variance** is the sum of the price variances and the efficiency variances. (The flexible budget variance can be decomposed into price and efficiency variances; this discussion is reserved for another chapter.) Thus, the flexible budget provides the capability to assess the efficiency of a manager.

In addition to measuring the efficiency of a manager, it is often desirable to measure whether a manager accomplishes his or her goals. The static

flexible budget variance

EXHIBIT 14-6
Annual Versus Flexible Performance Report: Quarterly Production Costs (in thousands)

	Actual	*Budget*[a]	*Variance*
Units produced	3,000	3,000	—
Production costs:			
Direct materials	$ 927.30	$ 780.00	$147.30 U
Direct labor	360.00	360.00	0.00
Variable overhead:			
Supplies	80.00	90.00	(10.00) F
Indirect labor	220.00	210.00	10.00 U
Power	40.00	60.00	(20.00) F
Total variable costs	$1,627.30	$1,500.00	$127.30 U
Fixed overhead:			
Supervision	90.00	100.00	(10.00) F
Depreciation	200.00	200.00	0.00
Rent	30.00	20.00	10.00 U
Total fixed costs	$ 320.00	$ 320.00	0.00
Total costs	$1,947.30	$1,820.00	$127.30 U

[a]From Exhibit 14-5

budget represented certain goals that the firm wanted to achieve. A manager is *effective* if the goals described by the static budget are achieved or exceeded. Any differences between the flexible budget and the static budget are attributable to differences in volume. They are called *volume variances*. A five-column performance report that reveals both the flexible budget variances and the volume variances can be used. Exhibit 14-7 provides an example of this report using the CalBlock data.

As the report in Exhibit 14-7 reveals, production volume was 600,000 units greater than the original budgeted amount. Thus, the manager exceeded the original budgeted goal. This volume variance is labeled *favorable* because it exceeds the original production goal. (Recall that the *reason* for the extra production was because the demand for the product was greater than expected. Thus, the increase in production over the original amount was truly favorable.) On the other hand, the budgeted variable costs are greater than expected because of the increased production. This difference is labeled unfavorable because the costs are greater than expected; however, the increase in costs is because of an increase in production. Thus, it is totally reasonable. For this particular example, the effectiveness of the manager is not in question; thus, the main issue is how well the manager controlled costs as revealed by the flexible-budget variances.

Monetary and Nonmonetary Incentives

A sound budgetary system encourages goal-congruent behavior. The means an organization uses to influence a manager to exert effort to achieve an

EXHIBIT 14–7
Managerial Performance Report: Quarterly Production (in thousands)

	Actual Results	Flexible Budget	Flexible Budget Variances[a]	Static Budget	Volume Variances[b]
Units produced	3,000	3,000	—	2,400	600.00 F
Production costs:					
Direct materials	$ 927.30	$ 780.00	$147.30 U	$ 624.00	$156.00 U
Direct labor	360.00	360.00	0.00	288.00	72.00 U
Supplies	80.00	90.00	(10.00) F	72.00	18.00 U
Indirect labor	220.00	210.00	10.00 U	168.00	42.00 U
Power	40.00	60.00	(20.00) F	48.00	12.00 U
Supervision	90.00	100.00	(10.00) F	100.00	—
Depreciation	200.00	200.00	—	200.00	—
Rent	30.00	20.00	10.00 U	20.00	—
Total costs	$1,947.30	$1,820.00	$127.30 U	$1,520.00	$300.00 U

[a]Actual results minus flexible budget variances
[b]Flexible budget minus static budget

incentives organization's goal are called *incentives*. Incentives can be either negative or positive. Negative incentives use fear of punishment to motivate; positive incentives use the expectation of reward. What incentives should be tied into an organization's budgetary system?

Monetary Incentives Traditional organization theory assumes that individuals are primarily motivated by monetary rewards, resist work, and are inefficient and wasteful.[1] If this view is fully accepted, budgets should be imposed from above, and a manager should be held strictly accountable for each line in the budget. In this way, top management can control a subordinate manager's tendency to shirk and be wasteful. Moreover, since a manager is primarily motivated by **monetary incentives**, this control is best achieved by relating budgetary performance to salary increases, bonuses, and promotions. The threat of dismissal is the ultimate economic sanction for poor performance.

Nonmonetary Incentives The above view of human behavior is too simplistic. Individuals are motivated by more than just external or extrinsic rewards. In fact, in addition to the economic factors, individuals are motivated by a

monetary incentives

[1]An excellent discussion of traditional and modern views of organization theory and their implications for managerial accounting is given by Edwin H. Caplan, *Management Accounting and Behavioral Science* (Reading, Mass.: Addison-Wesley, 1971).

nonmonetary
incentives
complex set of intrinsic psychological and social factors. The satisfaction of a job well done, recognition, responsibility, self-esteem, and the nature of the work itself are examples of **nonmonetary incentives**. To be successful, a budgetary control system must not ignore the complex motivating forces affecting individuals. Monetary rewards, by themselves, are not sufficient to achieve the desired level of motivation in managers. In fact, overemphasis of monetary incentives may lead to frustration, anger, and rebellion. The budgetary system must also use nonmonetary incentives. Job enrichment, increased responsibility and autonomy, nonmonetary recognition programs, and so on, are all examples of nonmonetary incentives that can be used to enhance a budgetary control system. One way to enrich managers' jobs is to allow them meaningful participation in creating the budget by which they will be evaluated.

Participative Budgeting

participative
budgeting
Rather than imposing budgets on subordinate managers, **participative budgeting** allows subordinate managers considerable say in how the budgets are established. Typically, overall objectives are communicated to the manager, who helps develop a budget that will accomplish these objectives. In participative budgeting, the emphasis is on the accomplishment of the broad objectives, not on individual budget items.

The budget process described earlier for CalBlock uses participative budgeting. The company provides the sales forecast to its profit centers and requests a budget that shows planned expenditures and expected profits given that level of sales. The managers of the profit centers are fully responsible for preparing the budgets by which they will later be evaluated. Although the budgets must be approved by the president, disapproval is not common; the budgets are usually in line with the sales forecast and last year's operating results adjusted for expected changes in revenues and costs.

Participative budgeting communicates a sense of responsibility to subordinate managers and fosters creativity. Since the subordinate manager creates the budget, it is more likely that the budget's goals will become the manager's personal goals, resulting in a higher degree of goal congruence. Advocates of participative budgeting claim that the increased responsibility and challenge inherent in the process provide nonmonetary incentives that lead to a higher level of performance. They argue that individuals involved in setting their own standards will work harder to achieve them. In addition to the behavioral benefits, participative budgeting has the advantage of involving individuals whose knowledge of local conditions may enhance the entire planning process.

Participative budgeting has three potential problems that should be mentioned.

1. Setting standards that are either too high or too low

2. Building slack into the budget (often referred to as *padding the budget*)

3. Pseudoparticipation

Setting Standards Some managers may tend to set the budget either too loose or too tight. Since budgeted goals tend to become the manager's goals when participation is allowed, making this mistake in setting the budget can result in decreased performance levels. If goals are too easily achieved, a manager may lose interest and performance may actually drop. Challenge is important to aggressive and creative individuals. Similarly, if a manager sets the budget too tight, failing to achieve the standards may frustrate him or her. This frustration, too, can lead to poorer performance. The trick is to get managers in a participative setting to set high but achievable goals.

Top management needs to know their subordinate managers well to be able to guide them properly as they set their budgets. Then those top managers will know when the budgets reflect the right level of challenge. Furthermore, top management must have the ability to provide guidance without dictating the budget. A fine balance is needed. Top management must supply sufficient input to ensure a high but achievable level of performance, yet their input must be limited so that subordinate managers also have significant input. Participative budgeting means that budgets are not dictated—either from above or from below.

budgetary slack

Budgetary Slack Participative budgeting also creates the opportunity for managers to build slack into the budget. **Budgetary slack** (or *padding the budget*) exists when a manager deliberately underestimates revenues or overestimates costs. Either approach increases the likelihood that the manager will achieve the budget and consequently reduces the risk that the manager faces. Padding the budget also unnecessarily ties up resources that might be used more productively elsewhere.

Slack in budgets can be virtually eliminated by having top management dictate lower budgets, but this approach eliminates the behavioral benefits that come from participative budgeting. The benefits gained from allowing participation may far exceed the costs associated with padding the budget. Even so, top management should carefully review budgets proposed by subordinate managers and provide input, where needed, in order to decrease the effects of building slack into the budget. Again, it should be emphasized that participation is not equivalent to complete autonomy. Both top management and lower management should have input.

pseudoparticipation

Pseudoparticipation When top management assumes total control of the budgeting process and simultaneously seeks superficial participation from lower-level managers, **pseudoparticipation** exists. This participation is nothing more than endorsing the budget. Top management is simply obtaining formal acceptance of the budget from subordinate managers, not seeking real input. Accordingly, none of the behavioral benefits of participation will be realized.

Realistic Standards

Budgeted objectives are used to gauge performance; accordingly, they should be based on realistic conditions and expectations. Budgets should reflect operating realities such as actual levels of activity, seasonal variations, efficiencies, and general economic trends. Flexible budgets, for example, are used to ensure that the budgeted costs provide standards that are compatible with the actual activity level. Another factor that should be considered is that of seasonality. Some businesses receive revenues and incur costs uniformly throughout the year; thus, spreading the annual revenues and costs evenly over quarters and months is reasonable for interim performance reports. However, for businesses with seasonal variations, this practice would result in distorted performance reports.

Such factors as efficiency and general economic conditions are also important. Occasionally, top management makes arbitrary cuts in prior-year budgets with the belief that the cuts will reduce fat or inefficiencies that allegedly exist. In reality, some units may be operating efficiently and others inefficiently. An across-the-board cut without any formal evaluation may impair the ability of some units to carry out their missions. General economic conditions also need to be considered. Budgeting for a significant increase in sales when a recession is projected is not only foolish but potentially dangerous.

Controllability of Costs

controllable costs

Conventional thought maintains that managers should be held accountable only for costs over which they have control. **Controllable costs** are costs whose level a manager can influence. In this view, a manager who has no responsibility for a cost should not be held accountable for it. For example, divisional managers have no power to authorize such corporate level costs as research and development and salaries of top managers. Therefore, they should not be held accountable for the incurrence of those costs.

Many firms, however, do put noncontrollable costs in the budgets of subordinate managers. Making managers aware of the need to cover all costs is one rationale for this practice. If noncontrollable costs are included in a budget, they should be separated from controllable costs and labeled as *noncontrollable*.

Multiple Measures of Performance

myopic behavior

Often organizations make the mistake of using budgets as their only measure of managerial performance. Overemphasis on this measure can lead to a form of dysfunctional behavior called *milking the firm* or *myopia*. **Myopic behavior** occurs when a manager takes actions that improve budgetary performance in the short run but bring long-run harm to the firm.

There are numerous examples of myopic behavior. To meet budgeted cost objectives or profits, managers can reduce expenditures for preventive maintenance, for advertising, and for new product development. Managers can also fail to promote promotable employees to keep the cost of labor low and choose to use lower-quality materials to reduce the cost of raw materials. In the short run, these actions will lead to improved budgetary performance, but in the long run, productivity will fall, market share will decline, and capable employees will leave for more attractive opportunities.

Managers can engage in this kind of behavior because most have a short tenure. In most cases, managers spend three to five years before being promoted or moving to a new area of responsibility. Their successors are the ones who pay the price for their myopic behavior. The best way to prevent myopic behavior is to measure the performance of managers on several dimensions, including some long-run attributes. Market share, productivity, quality, and personnel development are examples of other areas of performance that could be evaluated. Financial measures of performance are important, but overemphasis on them can be counterproductive.

■ SUMMARY OF LEARNING OBJECTIVES

1. **Define** *budgeting* **and discuss its role in planning, control, and decision making.** Budgeting is the creation of a plan of action expressed in financial terms. Budgeting plays a key role in planning, control, and decision making. Budgets also serve to improve communication and coordination, a role that becomes increasingly important as organizations grow in size.

2. **Define** *responsibility accounting* **and identify the three major types of responsibility centers.** Responsibility accounting refers to the use of the accounting system to set standards, to measure actual outcomes, and to report the performance of responsibility centers. The three major types of responsibility centers are cost centers, profit centers, and investment centers.

3. **Define the** *master budget,* **identify its major components, and explain the interrelationships of the various components.** The master budget, the comprehensive financial plan of an organization, is made up of the operating and financial budgets. The operating budget is the budgeted income statement and all supporting schedules. The financial budget is a collection of budgets relating primarily to the balance sheet (the cash budget, the capital budget, the budgeted statement of changes in financial position).

4. **Prepare an operating budget including the following schedules: sales budget, production budget, direct materials purchases budget, direct labor budget, overhead budget, selling and administrative budget, ending finished goods inventory budget, the cost of goods sold budget, and the budgeted income statement.** The sales budget (Schedule 1) consists of the anticipated quantity and price of all products to be sold. The production budget (Schedule 2) gives the expected production in units to meet forecast sales and desired ending inventory goals; expected production is supplemented by beginning inventory. The direct materials purchases budget (Schedule 3) gives the necessary purchases during the year for every type of raw material to meet production and desired ending inventory goals. The direct labor budget (Schedule 4) and overhead budget (Schedule 5) give the amounts of these resources necessary for the coming year's production. The overhead

budget may be broken into fixed and variable components to facilitate preparation of the budget. The selling and administrative budget (Schedule 6) gives the forecast costs for these functions. The finished goods inventory budget (Schedule 7) and the cost of goods sold budget (Schedule 8) detail production costs for the expected ending inventory and the units sold, respectively. The budgeted income statement (Schedule 9) outlines the net income to be realized if budgeted plans come to fruition.

5. Prepare the following two schedules of the financial budget: cash budget and budgeted balance sheet. The cash budget (Schedule 10) is simply the beginning balance in the cash account, plus anticipated receipts, minus anticipated disbursements, plus or minus any necessary borrowing. The budgeted (or pro forma) balance sheet (Schedule 11) gives the anticipated ending balances of the asset, liability, and equity accounts if budgeted plans hold.

6. Identify and discuss the key features that a budgetary system should have to encourage managers to engage in goal-congruent behavior. The success of a budgetary system depends on how seriously human factors are considered. To discourage dysfunctional behavior, organizations should avoid overemphasizing budgets as a control mechanism. Other areas of performance should be evaluated in addition to budgets. Budgets can be improved as performance measures by the use of participative budgeting and other nonmonetary incentives, by providing frequent feedback on performance, by the use of flexible budgeting, by ensuring that the budgetary objectives reflect reality, and by holding managers accountable for only controllable costs.

7. Describe the difference between a static and flexible budget. A static budget is composed for one level of activity. The master budget is an example of a static budget. A flexible budget is prepared for a number of activity levels.

8. Use a flexible budget to prepare a performance report. A flexible budget can be prepared for the actual level of activity. In this way, the flexible budget amounts can be meaningfully compared with actual results for performance evaluation.

■ **KEY TERMS**

Base package   A decision package that describes the absolute minimum level of services a unit can offer and still be a viable unit. (p. 704)

Budget   A plan of action expressed in financial terms. (p. 666)

Budget committee   A committee responsible for setting budgetary policies and goals, reviewing and approving the budget, and resolving any differences that may arise in the budgetary process. (p. 671)

Budget director   The individual responsible for coordinating and directing the overall budgeting process. (p. 671)

Budgetary slack   The process of padding the budget by overestimating costs and underestimating revenues. (p. 695)

Capital budget   A financial plan outlining the acquisition of long-term assets. (p. 671)

Cash budget A detailed plan that outlines all sources and uses of cash. (p. 681)

Continuous budget A moving twelve-month budget with a future month added as the current month expires. (p. 671)

Control The process of setting standards, receiving feedback on actual performance, and taking corrective action whenever actual performance deviates significantly from planned performance. (p. 668)

Controllable costs Costs that managers have the power to influence. (p. 696)

Cost center A responsibility center in which a manager has responsibility for incurring cost. (p. 669)

Decision package A description of service levels with associated costs that a decision unit can or would like to offer. (p. 703)

Decision units A unit within an organization for which a budget will be prepared. (p. 703)

Direct labor budget A budget showing the total direct labor hours needed and the associated cost for the number of units in the production budget. (p. 675)

Direct materials budget A budget that outlines the expected usage of materials production and purchases of the direct materials required. (p. 674)

Dysfunctional behavior Individual behavior that conflicts with the goals of the organization. (p. 688)

Ending finished goods inventory budget A budget that describes planned ending inventory of finished goods in units and dollars. (p. 677)

Financial budget That portion of the master budget that includes the cash budget, the budgeted balance sheet, the budgeted statement of cash flows, and the capital budget. (p. 671)

Flexible budget A budget that can specify costs for a range of activity. (p. 690)

Flexible budget variance The sum of price variances and efficiency variances in a performance report comparing actual costs to expected costs predicted by a flexible budget. (p. 691)

Goal congruence The alignment of a manager's personal goals with those of the organization. (p. 685)

Ideal budgetary system A budgetary system that simultaneously achieves goal congruence and induces a manager to exert effort toward achieving the organization's goals. (p. 688)

Incentives The positive or negative measures taken by an organization to induce a manager to exert effort toward achieving the organization's goals. (p. 693)

Incremental budgeting The practice of taking the prior year's budget and adjusting it upward or downward to determine next year's budget. (p. 702)

Incremental packages Decision packages which represent additional services and costs over and above a base package. (p. 704)

Investment center A responsibility center in which a manager is responsible for revenues, costs, and investments. (p. 669)

Master budget The collection of all area and activity budgets representing a firm's comprehensive plan of action. (p. 667)

Merchandise purchases budget   A budget that details the quantity of each item that must be purchased for resale, the unit cost of each item, and the total purchase cost. (p. 680)

Milking the firm   See *Myopic behavior*. (p. 696)

Monetary incentives   The use of economic rewards to motivate managers. (p. 693)

Mutually exclusive decision packages   Packages that describe alternative ways to perform the same function. (p. 703)

Myopic behavior   Managerial actions that improve budgetary performance in the short run at the expense of the long-run welfare of the organization. (p. 696)

Nonmonetary incentives   The use of psychological and social rewards to motivate managers. (p. 694)

Operating budgets   Budgets associated with the income-producing activities of an organization. (p. 671)

Overhead budget   A budget that reveals the planned expenditures for all indirect manufacturing items. (p. 676)

Participative budgeting   An approach to budgeting that allows managers who will be held accountable for budgetary performance to participate in the budget's development. (p. 694)

Production budget   A budget that shows how many units must be produced to meet sales needs and satisfy ending inventory requirements. (p. 673)

Profit center   A responsibility center in which a manager is responsible for revenues and costs. (p. 669)

Pseudoparticipation   A budgetary system in which top management solicits inputs from lower-level managers and then ignores those inputs. Thus, in reality, budgets are dictated from above. (p. 695)

Responsibility accounting   The use of the accounting system to set standards, measure actual outcomes, and report the performance of responsibility centers. (p. 670)

Responsibility center   An area or unit within an organization over which a manager is assigned responsibility for a specific activity or set of activities. (p. 669)

Sales budget   A budget that describes expected sales in units and dollars for the coming period. (p. 672)

Selling and administrative expense budget   A budget that outlines planned expenditures for nonmanufacturing activities. (p. 677)

Static budget   A budget for a particular level of activity. (p. 688)

Strategic plan   The long-term plan for future activities and operations, usually involving at least five years. (p. 667)

Variable budget   See *Flexible budget*. (p. 690)

▪ REVIEW PROBLEM

Young Products produces coat racks. The projected sales for the first quarter of the coming year and the beginning and ending inventory data are as follows:

Sales	100,000 units
Unit price	$15
Beginning inventory	8,000 units
Targeted ending inventory	12,000 units

The coat racks are molded and then painted. Each rack requires four pounds of metal, which costs $2.50 per pound. The beginning inventory of raw materials is 4,000 pounds. Young Products wants to have 6,000 pounds of metal in inventory at the end of the quarter. Each rack produced requires thirty minutes of direct labor time, which is billed at $9 per hour.

Required:

1. Prepare a sales budget for the first quarter.
2. Prepare a production budget for the first quarter.
3. Prepare a direct materials purchases budget for the first quarter.
4. Prepare a direct labor budget for the first quarter.

Solution:

1.

Young Products

Sales Budget
For the First Quarter

Units	100,000
Unit price	× $15
Sales	$1,500,000

2.

Young Products

Production Budget
For the First Quarter

Sales (in units)	100,000
Desired ending inventory	12,000
Total needs	112,000
Less: Beginning inventory	8,000
Units to be produced	104,000

3.

Young Products	
Direct Materials *For the First Quarter*	
Units to be produced	104,000
Direct materials per unit (lbs)	×4
Production needs (lbs)	416,000
Desired ending inventory (lbs)	6,000
Total needs (lbs)	422,000
Less: Beginning inventory (lbs)	(4,000)
Materials to be purchased (lbs)	418,000
Cost per pound	×$2.50
Total purchase cost	$1,045,000

4.

Young Products	
Direct Labor Budget *For the First Quarter*	
Units to be produced	104,000
Labor: Time per unit	×0.5
Total hours needed	52,000
Cost per hour	×$9
Total direct labor cost	$468,000

▪ APPENDIX: ZERO-BASE BUDGETING

incremental
budgeting
The traditional approach to budgeting is the incremental approach. **Incremental budgeting** starts with last year's budget and adds or subtracts from that budget to reflect changing assumptions for the coming year. For example, if last year's budgeted expenditures for an agency or department were $1.2 million, the agency or department may request a 5 percent increase ($60,000) to provide the same level of service for the coming year. The typical justification for increased expenditures is the increased cost of inputs (labor, materials, and so on). The incremental approach may not entail a careful evaluation of the level of services being offered or of whether they are being offered efficiently (at least not annually).

Under the incremental approach, heads of budgeting units often strive to spend all of the year's budget so that no surplus exists at the end of the year. (This is particularly true for government agencies.) This action is taken to maintain the current level of the budget and enable the head of the unit to request additional funds. For example, at an Air Force base, a bomber wing was faced with the possibility of a surplus at the end of the fiscal year. The base commander, however, found ways to spend the extra money before the year ended. Missile officers, who normally drove to the missile command site, were flown to the sites in helicopters; several bags of lawn fertilizer were given away to all personnel with houses on base; and new furniture was acquired for the bachelor officer quarters. The waste and inefficiency portrayed in this example is often perpetuated and encouraged by incremental budgeting.

Zero-base budgeting is an alternative budgeting approach.[2] Unlike incremental budgeting, the prior year's budgeted level is not taken for granted. Existing operations are analyzed, and continuance of the activity or operation must be justified on the basis of its need or usefulness to the organization. The burden of proof is on each manager to justify why any money should be spent at all.

Translating the concepts of zero-base budgeting into practice requires four steps.

1. Identifying decision units

2. Creating decision packages for each decision unit

3. Ranking decision units in order of priority

4. Preparing the budget

decision unit

A **decision unit** is any unit (a department, an activity, a program) within an organization for which a budget is developed. For example, the Department of Accounting within the College of Business Administration is a decision unit. Other decision units would be the departments of Economics, Management, Marketing, and Finance. Alternatively, decision units could be identified as degree programs within each area (e.g., the undergraduate programs in accounting, economics, management, and so on; the master's program in accounting; the MBA program; and the doctoral programs). The organization must decide what it wishes to define as decision units.

decision packages

Decision packages are documents containing data that describe the activities within a decision unit. Each package should contain a statement of the unit's goals, programs to achieve these goals, the benefits expected, and the consequences of not approving the package. There are two main types of decision packages: mutually exclusive packages and incremental packages.

mutually exclusive decision packages

Mutually exclusive decision packages identify alternative ways to carry out the same activity. The best of the alternative packages is chosen and the others are discarded. All alternatives should be documented—including why one alternative was chosen and the others rejected. This process forces managers to take a fresh look at their operations in subsequent years and the way the operations are being executed.

---

[2]Zero-base budgeting was developed by Peter Pyhrr of Texas Instruments. For a detailed discussion of the approach, see Peter Pyhrr, *Zero-Base Budgeting* (New York: Wiley, 1973).

Incremental packages are built from a base package. Given the chosen alternative, each decision unit typically develops a minimum-level decision package or base package and then builds higher service-level packages by adding increments to this package. The **base package** describes the absolute minimum resources needed to continue a viable level of service. It describes bare bones operations.

Assume that the Department of Accounting, the decision unit, submits three incremental decision packages. (Assume that the process of identifying alternative packages has been completed and Decision Package 1 is the best alternative.)

Decision Package 1 (Base Package)

Cost of decision package:

Faculty salaries	$400,000
Secretary	12,500
Operating expense	15,000
Total	$427,500

Benefits This package provides minimal educational opportunities for accounting students. It permits employment of eight full-time, tenure-track faculty and one full-time secretary. It allows twenty-four sections of accounting to be offered each quarter. Both undergraduate and master's degrees can be offered. Because of the reduced offerings, class sizes will need to be increased. However, because of the room size limitations, the department cannot accommodate all students who want to major in accounting. If this package is approved, the department will take steps to limit enrollments. Only students with a 3.0 GPA after their first two years will be admitted to the accounting program. This package does not provide for graduate assistants, adjunct faculty, teaching assistants, faculty travel, or additional part-time secretarial help.

Consequences of Not Approving Decision Package 1 At the very least, the master's degree program would need to be eliminated. However, eliminating the master's program would likely result in losing the best students to neighboring colleges. The overall quality of the undergraduate program would drop to an unacceptable level.

Decision Package 2 (Current Level)

Cost of decision package:[a]

Faculty salaries	$ 70,000
Graduate assistants	9,000
Part-time secretary	4,000
Teaching assistants	15,000
Travel	8,000
Total	$106,000

---

[a]The costs are increments to the base package.

Benefits   Decision Package 2 provides for two additional adjunct faculty, eight graduate assistants, five teaching assistants, and one part-time secretary. Travel opportunities are restored for the faculty. This package maintains the current capability of service. However, class sizes will still be increasing because of the current trend of increasing enrollments. Some enrollment limitations will be necessary, but they will not be as severe as those in the base package. Adding back the graduate assistants and the teaching assistants maintains recruiting capability for the master's program. The package may create problems with retaining faculty because it contains no provision for salary increases for tenure-track faculty. All faculty have numerous opportunities to relocate for significant salary increases.

Consequences of Not Approving Decision Package 2   The department would be left with a minimal operating capability. This would result in a drop in program quality, a loss of faculty morale, and severe problems retaining faculty.

Decision Package 3 (Upgraded)	
Cost of decision package:[a]	
Faculty salaries	$132,000
Support services	2,500
Travel	2,000
Graduate assistants	3,500
Total	$140,000

[a]The costs are increments to Package 2.

Benefits   Two additional, full-time, tenure-track faculty are included in the budget of Decision Package 3. Support services (e.g., telephone and photocopying) and graduate assistants are increased to accommodate the addition of the two faculty. Salary increases are also provided. By adding two faculty, the expected increases in enrollment can be served without limiting enrollment. Additionally, the master's program can offer two tracks for specialization instead of a general accounting emphasis. This should increase the marketability of graduate students. This package will have the most favorable effect on the long-run health and reputation of the program. Problems retaining faculty will be minimized.

Consequences of Not Approving Decision Package 3   The department will need to limit enrollments and will have problems retaining faculty. The reputation of the master's program will not improve, and the ability to place graduate students will not be enhanced.

Notice that the decision packages above the base package simply add items to the base package and give only the incremental costs of these items. Thus, to move from Decision Package 1 (the base package) to Decision Package 2 the current-level package requires an additional $106,000. To move from the current level to the upgraded level requires another $140,000.

After developing the decision packages, the manager of the decision unit ranks them in order of priority. This priority ranking is important because the packages of lower priority are less likely to be funded. The base package is usually listed as the package of highest priority because it represents the absolute minimum level of funding required by the decision unit. The ranking provided by the chair of the Accounting Department was as follows:

Ranking	Decision Package	Total Cost
1	1	$427,500
2	3	673,500[a]
3	2	533,500[b]

[a]$427,500 + $106,000 + $140,000
[b]$427,500 + $106,000

The final step is preparing the budget for the college as a whole. The dean of the College of Business Administration receives the decision packages from all of the decision units and then develops a consolidated ranking. Next packages are funded in order of priority until the college's budget is exhausted. The information supplied by the individual departments may lead the dean to reduce or eliminate some programs in order to strengthen others. For example, the dean may decide that accounting should be a program of emphasis and consequently choose to fund Decision Package 3. If sufficient new resources are not available to accomplish this objective, the dean may have to reallocate resources internally. The dean could choose to fund another department at its minimum level and transfer the resources to the Accounting Department.

Zero-base budgeting requires extensive, in-depth analysis. Although this approach has been used successfully in industry and government (e.g., Texas Instruments and the state of Georgia), it is time consuming and costly. Advocates of the incremental approach argue that incremental budgeting also uses extensive, in-depth reviews but not as frequently because they are not justified on a cost-benefit basis. A reasonable compromise may be to use zero-base budgeting every three to five years in order to weed out waste and inefficiency.

▪ QUESTIONS

1 Define the term *budget*. How are budgets used in planning?

2 Define *control*. How are budgets used to control?

3 Explain how both small and large organizations can benefit from budgeting.

4 Discuss some of the reasons for budgeting.

5 What is the master budget? An operating budget? A financial budget?

6   Explain the role of a sales forecast in budgeting. What is the difference between a sales forecast and a sales budget?

7   All budgets depend on the sales budget. Is this true? Explain.

8   How do the master budgets differ among manufacturing, merchandising, and service organizations?

9   Why is goal congruence important?

10   Discuss the roles of monetary and nonmonetary incentives. Do you believe that non-monetary incentives are needed? Why?

11   What is participative budgeting? Discuss some of its advantages.

12   A budget too easily achieved will lead to diminished performance. Do you agree? Explain.

13   What is the role of top management in participative budgeting?

14   Explain why a manager has an incentive to build slack into the budget.

15   Discuss the differences between static and flexible budgets. Why are flexible budgets superior to static budgets for performance reporting?

16   Explain why mixed costs must be broken down into their fixed and variable components before a flexible budget can be developed.

17   Why is it important for a manager to receive frequent feedback on his or her performance?

18   Explain how a manager can milk the firm to improve budgetary performance.

19   Identify performance measures other than budgets that can be used to discourage myopic behavior. Discuss how you would use these measures.

20   How important are the behavioral aspects of a budgetary control system? Explain.

21   Explain the difference between incremental budgeting and zero-base budgeting.

22   In an era of budgetary cuts, across-the-board cuts harm good programs more than bad programs. Do you agree? What approach would you recommend? Why?

23   What is a base package? Why should it be given top priority?

■ EXERCISES

E14–1   **Sales Budget**   Milan Cereal Company produces wheat flakes and corn flakes. Both products are sold in 12-ounce boxes. Wheat flakes sell for $1.50 per box and corn flakes sell for $1.30 per box. Projected sales (in boxes) for the coming four quarters are given below.

	Wheat Flakes	Corn Flakes
First quarter	500,000	600,000
Second quarter	600,000	600,000
Third quarter	700,000	700,000
Fourth quarter	750,000	800,000

The president of the company believes that the projected sales are realistic and can be achieved by the company.

Required:

Prepare a sales budget for each quarter and for the year in total. Show sales by product and in total for each time period.

E14–2   **Production Budget**   Whiskers Products, Inc., produces a variety of products for cats. Among them is a 16-ounce can of cat food. The sales budget for the first four months of the year is presented below.

	Unit Sales	*Dollar Sales*
January	100,000	$50,000
February	120,000	60,000
March	110,000	55,000
April	100,000	50,000

Company policy requires that ending inventories for each month be 20 percent of next month's sales. At the beginning of January, the inventory of cat food is 20,000 cans.

Required:

Prepare a production budget for the first quarter of the year. Show the number of units that should be produced each month as well as for the quarter in total.

E14–3   **Direct Materials Purchases Budget**   Dulce Company produces a 6-ounce chocolate candy bar. Each 6-ounce bar contains three ounces of sugar, which costs $0.025 per ounce. Dulce has budgeted production of the chocolate bar for the next four months as follows:

	Units
October	400,000
November	800,000
December	500,000
January	600,000

Inventory policy requires that sufficient sugar be in ending monthly inventory to satisfy 15 percent of the following month's production needs. Inventory of sugar at the beginning of October equals exactly the amount needed to satisfy the inventory policy.

Required:

Prepare a direct materials purchases budget for the last quarter of the year showing purchases in units and in dollars for each month and for the quarter in total.

E14–4   **Direct Labor Budget**   Refer to the production budget in Exercise 14–3. Each chocolate bar produced requires (on average) 0.01 direct labor hours. The average cost of direct labor is $9 per hour.

Required:

Prepare a direct labor budget for the last quarter of the year showing the hours needed and the direct labor cost for each month and for the quarter in total.

E14–5 **Sales Budget** Allen, Inc., manufactures six models of molded plastic waste containers. It is now early in 1993, and Allen's budgeting team is finalizing the sales budget for 1993. Sales in units and dollars for 1992 were as follow:

Model	Number Sold	Price	Revenue
W-1	14,000	$ 9	$126,000
W-2	15,000	15	225,000
W-3	21,000	13	273,000
W-4	13,500	10	135,000
W-5	2,000	22	44,000
W-6	1,000	26	26,000
			$829,000

In looking over the 1992 sales figures, Allen's sales budgeting team recalled the following:

a. Model W-1 costs were rising faster than price could rise. Preparatory to phasing out this model, Allen, Inc., planned to slash advertising for this model and raise its price by 50 percent. The number of units of model W-1 to be sold were forecast to be 20 percent of 1992 units.

b. Models W-5 and W-6 were introduced on November 1, 1992. They are brightly colored, heavy-duty wheeled garbage containers designed for household use. Allen estimates that demand for both models will continue at the 1992 rate.

c. A competitor has announced plans to introduce an improved version of Model W-3. Allen believes that the model W-3 price must be cut 20 percent to maintain unit sales at the 1992 level.

d. It was assumed that unit sales of all other models would increase by 10 percent, prices remaining constant.

Required:

Prepare a sales forecast by product and in total for Allen, Inc. for 1993.

E14–6 **Purchases Budget** Al's Auto Supply ("You Need It—We Got It") carries a variety of auto parts including oil filters. The sales budget for oil filters for the first six months of the year is presented below.

	Unit Sales	Dollar Sales
January	200	$ 900
February	180	810
March	220	990
April	250	1,125
May	300	1,350
June	260	1,170

Al believes that ending inventories should be sufficient to cover 30 percent of the next month's projected sales. On January 1, eighty-four oil filters were in inventory.

Required:

1. Prepare a purchases budget in units of oil filters for as many months as you can.

2. If oil filters are priced at 50 percent above cost, what is the dollar cost of purchases for each month of your purchases budget?

E14–7   **Cash Receipts Budget**   CeCe's Gift Shop in Sedona, Arizona, sells a variety of t-shirts (screen printed with desert themes) and objets d'art. CeCe accepts cash, checks, and VISA, MasterCard, and American Express charges. These methods of payment have the following characteristics:

Cash	Payment is immediate; no fee is charged.
Check	Payment is immediate; the bank charges $0.25 per check; 1 percent of check revenue is from "bad" checks that CeCe cannot collect.
VISA/MasterCard	CeCe accumulates these credit card receipts throughout the month and submits them in one bundle for payment on the last day of the month. The money is credited to CeCe's account by the fifth day of the following month. A fee of 1.5 percent is charged by the credit card company.
American Express	CeCe accumulates these receipts throughout the month and mails them to American Express for payment on the last day of the month. American Express credits CeCe's account by the 6th day of the following month. A fee of 3.5 percent is charged by American Express.

During a typical month, CeCe has sales of $20,000, broken down as follows:

American Express	20%
VISA/MasterCard	50%
Check	5% (checks average $37.50 each)
Cash	25%

Required:

If CeCe estimates sales of $20,000 in April and $30,000 in May, what are her planned net cash receipts for May?

E14–8   **Production Budget; Materials Purchases Budget**   Jenna Mitchell, owner of Jenna's Jams and Jellies, produces homemade-style jellies using fruits indigenous to her local area. Jenna has estimated the following sales of 16-ounce jars of fruit jelly for the rest of the year and January of next year.

September	100
October	150
November	170
December	225
January	100

Jenna likes to have 20 percent of the next month's sales needs on hand at the end of each month. This requirement was met on August 31.

Materials needed for each jar of fruit jelly are as follows:

Fruit	1 lb
Sugar	1 lb
Pectin	3 oz
Jar set	1

The materials inventory policy is to have 5 percent of the next month's fruit needs on hand as well as 50 percent of the next month's production needs for all other materials. (The relatively low inventory amount for fruit is designed to prevent spoilage.) Materials inventory on September 1 met this company policy.

Required:

1. Prepare a production budget for September, October, November, and December for fruit jelly.

2. Prepare a purchases budget for all materials used in the production of fruit jelly for the months of September, October, and November. (Round all answers to the nearest whole unit.)

3. Why can't you prepare a purchases budget for December?

E14–9 **Overhead Budget; Flexible Budgeting** Toolson Manufacturing, Inc., has developed the following flexible budget for overhead for the coming year. Activity level is measured in direct labor hours.

	Variable Cost Formula	Activity Level (hours)		
		10,000	15,000	20,000
Variable costs:				
Maintenance	$1.50	$15,000	$22,500	$ 30,000
Supplies	0.50	5,000	7,500	10,000
Power	0.10	1,000	1,500	2,000
Total variable costs	$2.10	$21,000	$31,500	$ 42,000
Fixed costs:				
Depreciation		6,000	6,000	6,000
Salaries		60,000	60,000	60,000
Total fixed costs		$66,000	$66,000	$ 66,000
Total overhead costs		$87,000	$97,500	$108,000

Toolson produces two different hammers. The production budget for April is 12,000 units for hammer A and 15,000 units for hammer B. Hammer A requires three minutes of direct labor time and Hammer B requires two minutes. Fixed overhead costs are incurred uniformly throughout the year.

Required:

Prepare an overhead budget for April.

E14–10 **Cash Budget** The owner of a small mining supply company has requested a cash budget for June. After examining the records of the company, you find the following:

a. Cash balance on June 1 is $1,000.

b. Actual sales for April and May

	April	May
Cash sales	$10,000	$15,000
Credit sales	25,000	35,000
Total sales	$35,000	$50,000

c. Credit sales are collected over a three-month period: 50 percent in the month of sale, 30 percent in the second month, and 15 percent in the third month. The remaining sales are uncollectible.

d. Inventory purchases average 60 percent of a month's total sales. Of those purchases, 40 percent are paid for in the month of purchase. The remaining 60 percent are paid for in the following month.

e. Salaries and wages total $8,000 a month, including a $4,500 salary paid to the owner.

f. Rent is $1,000 per month.

g. Taxes to be paid in June are $5,000.

The owner also tells you that he expects cash sales of $20,000 and credit sales of $40,000 for June. There is no minimum cash balance required. The owner of the company does not have access to short-term loans.

Required:

1. Prepare a cash budget for June. Include supporting schedules for cash collections and cash payments.

2. Did the business show a negative cash balance for June? Assuming that the owner has no hope of establishing a line of credit for the business, what recommendations would you give the owner for dealing with a negative cash balance?

E14–11 **Flexible Budget** Roxanne Johnson, controller for Mix and Feed Company, has been instructed to develop a flexible budget for overhead costs. The company produces two fertilizers called *Ferone* and *Fertwo* that use common raw materials in different proportions. The company expects to produce 100,000 fifty-pound bags of each product during the coming year. Ferone requires 0.25 direct labor hours per bag and Fertwo requires 0.30. Roxanne has developed the following cost formulas for each of the four overhead items (X is measured in direct labor hours):

	Cost Formula
Maintenance	$10,000 + 0.3X$
Power	$0.5X$
Indirect labor	$24,500 + 1.5X$
Rent	$18,000$

Required:

1. Prepare an overhead budget for the expected activity level for the coming year.
2. Prepare an overhead budget that reflects production that is 10 percent higher than expected (for both products) and one for production that is 20 percent lower than expected.

E14–12 **Performance Report** Refer to the information given in Exercise 14–11. Assume that Mix and Feed actually produced 120,000 bags of Ferone and 110,000 of Fertwo. The actual overhead costs incurred were

Maintenance	$ 26,700
Power	34,000
Indirect labor	108,000
Rent	18,000

Required:

1. Prepare a performance report for the period.
2. Based on the report, would you judge any of the variances to be significant? Can you think of some possible reasons for the variances?

E14–13 **Budgeted Cash Collections; Budgeted Cash Payments** Information pertaining to Noskey Corporation's sales revenue is presented below.

	November 1993 (Actual)	December 1993 (Budget)	January 1994 (Budget)
Cash sales	$ 80,000	$100,000	$ 60,000
Credit sales	240,000	360,000	180,000
Total sales	$320,000	$460,000	$240,000

Management estimates that 5 percent of credit sales are uncollectible. Of the credit sales that are collectible, 60 percent are collected in the month of sale and the remainder in the month following the sale. Purchases of inventory each month are 70 percent of the next month's projected total sales. All purchases of inventory are on account; 25 percent are paid in the month of purchase, and the remainder are paid in the month following the purchase.

Required:

1. What are Noskey's budgeted cash collections in December 1993 from November 1993 credit sales?
2. What are total budgeted cash receipts in January 1994?
3. What is Noskey budgeting for total cash payments in December 1993 for inventory purchases?

(CMA adapted)

E14–14 **Zero-base Budgeting** Advocates of zero-base budgeting maintain that padding the budget is easier under an incremental system than under a zero-base system.

Required:

Explain why padding is less likely for a zero-base budgeting system.

E14–15   **Zero-base Budgeting**   Zero-base budgeting promises much but often delivers little. Some organizations have experienced the following difficulties:

1. Lack of agreement on what needs to be accomplished
2. Lack of credibility in the process itself
3. Resistance of middle managers (too much paperwork and perceived threat to their units)
4. Inability of top management to make tough decisions

Required:

Suppose you are a consultant retained by an organization to implement zero-base budgeting. What actions would you take to avoid some of these problems?

E14–16   **Participative versus Imposed Budgeting**   An effective budget converts the goals and objectives of an organization into data. The budget serves as a blueprint for management's plans. The budget is also the basis for control. Management performance can be evaluated by comparing actual results with the budget.

Thus, creating the budget is essential for the successful operation of an organization. Finding the resources to implement the budget—that is, getting from a starting point to the ultimate goal—requires the extensive use of human resources. How managers perceive their roles in the process of budgeting is important to the successful use of the budget as an effective tool for planning, communicating, and controlling.

Required:

1. Discuss the behavioral implications of planning and control when a company's management employs
   a. An imposed budgetary approach
   b. A participative budgetary approach
2. Communications plays an important role in the budgetary process whether a participative or imposed budgetary approach is used.
   a. Discuss the differences between communication flows in these two budgetary approaches.
   b. Discuss the behavioral implications associated with the communication process for each of the budgetary approaches.

(CMA adapted)

E14–17   **Flexible Budgeting**   Budgeted overhead costs for two different levels of activity are given below.

	Direct Labor Hours	
	1,000	*2,000*
Maintenance	$10,000	$15,000
Depreciation	5,000	5,000
Supervision	15,000	15,000
Supplies	1,300	2,600
Power	600	1,200
Other	8,100	8,200

Required:

Prepare a flexible budget for an activity level of 1,500 direct labor hours.

E14–18   **Cash Receipts Budget**   Hillerman's Department Store has found from past experience that 20 percent of its sales are for cash. The remaining 80 percent are on credit. An aging schedule for accounts receivable reveals the following pattern:

10% of credit sales are paid in the month of sale
70% of credit sales are paid in the month following sale
17% of credit sales are paid in the second month following sale
 3% of credit sales are never collected

Credit sales that have not been paid until the second month following sale are considered overdue and are subject to a 2 percent late charge.

Hillerman Department Store has developed the following sales forecast:

May	$ 76,000
June	85,000
July	68,000
August	80,000
September	100,000

Required:

Prepare a schedule of cash receipts for August and September.

E14–19   **Cash Disbursements Schedule**   Hillerman's Department Store purchases a wide variety of merchandise. Purchases are made evenly throughout the month and all are on account. On the first of every month, Hillerman's accounts payable clerk pays for all of the previous month's purchases. Terms are 2/10, n/30 (i.e., a 2 percent discount can be taken if the bill is paid within ten days; otherwise the entire amount is due within thirty days).

The forecast purchases for the months of May through September are as follows:

May	$40,000
June	50,000
July	30,000
August	60,000
September	64,000

Required:

1. Prepare a cash disbursements schedule for the months of August and September.

2. Now suppose that the store manager wants to see what difference it would make to have the accounts payable clerk pay for any purchases that have been made three times per month, on the 1st, the 11th, and the 21st. Prepare a cash disbursements schedule for the months of July and August assuming this new payment schedule.

3. Suppose that Hillerman's accounts payable clerk does not have time to make payments on two extra days per month and that a temporary employee is hired on the 11th and 21st at $22 per hour, for four hours each of those two days. Is this a good decision? Explain.

■ PROBLEMS

P14–1   **Operating Budget; Comprehensive Analysis**   The Morgan Division of Smith Manufacturing produces a handle assembly used in the production of bows. The assembly is sold to various bow manufacturers throughout the United States. Projected sales for the coming four months are given below.

January	20,000
February	25,000
March	30,000
April	30,000

The following data pertain to production policies and manufacturing specifications followed by the Morgan Division:

a. Finished goods inventory on January 1 is 16,000 units. The desired ending inventory for each month is 80 percent of the next month's sales.

b. The data on materials used are as follows:

Direct Material	Per-Unit Usage	Unit Cost
Number 325	5	$8
Number 326	3	2

Inventory policy dictates that sufficient materials be on hand at the beginning of the month to produce 50 percent of that month's estimated sales. This is exactly the amount of material on hand on January 1.

c. The direct labor used per unit of output is two hours. The average direct labor cost per hour is $9.25.

d. Overhead each month is estimated using a flexible budget formula. (Activity is measured in direct labor hours.)

	Fixed Cost Component	Variable Cost Component
Supplies	$ —	$1.00
Power	—	0.50
Maintenance	15,000	0.40
Supervision	8,000	—
Depreciation	100,000	—
Taxes	6,000	—
Other	40,000	1.50

e. Monthly selling and administrative expenses are also estimated using a flexible budgeting formula. (Activity is measured in units sold.)

	Fixed Costs	Variable Costs
Salaries	$25,000	$ —
Commissions	—	1.00
Depreciation	20,000	—
Shipping	—	0.50
Other	10,000	0.30

f. The unit selling price of the handle assembly is $90.

g. All sales and purchases are for cash. Cash balance on January 1 equals $200,000. If the firm develops a cash shortage by the end of the month, sufficient cash is borrowed to cover the shortage. Any cash borrowed is repaid one month later, as is the interest due. The interest rate is 12 percent per annum.

Required:

Prepare a monthly operating budget for the first quarter with the following schedules:

1. Sales budget
2. Production budget
3. Direct materials purchases budget
4. Direct labor budget
5. Overhead budget
6. Selling and administrative expense budget
7. Ending finished goods budget
8. Cost of goods sold budget
9. Budgeted income statement
10. Cash budget

P14–2 **Cash Budget; Pro Forma Balance Sheet** Richard Raleigh, controller for Opple Retailers, has assembled the following data to assist in the preparation of a cash budget for the third quarter of 1992:

a. Sales

May (actual)	$100,000
June (actual)	120,000
July (estimated)	90,000
August (estimated)	100,000
September (estimated)	135,000
October (estimated)	110,000

b. Each month, 30 percent of sales are for cash and 70 percent are on credit. The collection pattern for credit sales is 20 percent in the month of sale, 50 percent in the following month, and 30 percent in the second month following sale.

c. Each month the ending inventory exactly equals 50 percent of the cost of next month's sales. The markup on goods is 33.33 percent of cost.

d. Inventory purchases are paid for in the month following purchase.

e. Recurring monthly expenses are as follows:

Salaries and wages	$10,000
Depreciation on plant and equipment	4,000
Utilities	1,000
Other	1,700

f. Property taxes of $15,000 are due and payable on July 15, 1992.

g. Advertising fees of $6,000 must be paid on August 20, 1992.

h. A lease on a new storage facility is scheduled to begin on September 2. Monthly payments are $5,000.

i. The company has a policy to maintain a minimum cash balance of $10,000. If necessary, it will borrow to meet its short-term needs. All borrowing is done at the beginning of the month. All payments on principal and interest are made at the end of a month. The annual interest rate is 9 percent. The company must borrow in multiples of $1,000.

j. A partially completed balance sheet as of June 30, 1992, is given below. (Accounts payable is for inventory purchases only.)

Cash	$?		
Accounts receivable	?		
Inventory	?		
Plant and equipment	425,000		
Accounts payable		$?	
Common stock		210,000	
Retained earnings		268,750	
Total	$?	$?	

Required:

1. Complete the balance sheet given in Part *j*.

2. Prepare a cash budget for each month in the third quarter and for the quarter in total (the third quarter begins on July 1). Provide a supporting schedule of cash collections.

3. Prepare a pro forma balance sheet as of September 30, 1992.

P14–3   **Participative Budgeting; Not-for-Profit Setting**   Scott Weidner, the controller in the division of social services for the state, recognizes the importance of the budgetary process for planning, control, and motivation. He believes that a properly implemented process of participative budgeting and management by exception will motivate his subordinates to improve productivity within their particular departments. Based upon this philosophy, Scott has implemented the following budgetary procedures:

1. An appropriation target figure is given to each department manager. This amount represents the maximum funding that each department can expect to receive in the next fiscal year.

2. Department managers develop their individual budgets within the following spending constraints as directed by the controller's staff:
   a. Requests for spending cannot exceed the appropriated target.
   b. All fixed expenditures should be included in the budget. Fixed expenditures include such items as contracts and salaries at current levels.
   c. All government projects directed by higher authority should be included in the budget in their entirety.

3. The controller's staff consolidates the requests from the various departments into one budget for the entire division.

4. Upon final budget approval by the legislature, the controller's staff allocates the appropriation to the various departments on instructions from the division manager. However, a specified percentage of each department's appropriation is held back in anticipation of potential budget cuts and special funding needs. The amount and use of this contingency fund is left to the discretion of the division manager.

5. Each department is allowed to adjust its budget when necessary to operate within the reduced appropriation level. However, as stated in the original directive, specific projects authorized by higher authority must remain intact.

6. The final budget is used as the basis of control for a management-by-exception form of reporting. Excessive expenditures by account for each department are highlighted on a monthly basis. Department managers are expected to account for all expenditures over budget. Fiscal responsibility is an important factor in the overall performance evaluation of department managers.

   Scott believes his policy of allowing the department managers to participate in the budget process and then holding them accountable for the final budget is essential, especially in times of limited resources. He further believes that the department managers will be motivated to increase the efficiency and effectiveness of their departments because they have provided input into the initial budgetary process and are required to justify any unfavorable performances.

Required:

1. Discuss the advantages and limitations of participative budgeting.

2. Identify deficiencies in Scott Weidner's outline for a budgetary process. Recommend how each deficiency identified can be corrected.

(CMA adapted)

P14-4 **Cash Budgeting** The controller of Gardner Company is gathering data to prepare the cash budget for April 1993. He plans to develop the budget from the following information:

a. Of all sales, 30 percent are cash sales.

b. Of credit sales, 60 percent are collected within the month of sale. Half of the credit sales collected within the month receive a 2 percent cash discount (for accounts paid within ten days). Twenty percent of credit sales are collected in the following month; remaining credit sales are collected the month thereafter. There are virtually no bad debts.

c. Sales for the first six months of the year are given below. (The first three months are actual sales and the last three months are estimated sales.)

	Sales
January	$230,000
February	300,000
March	500,000
April	565,000
May	600,000
June	567,000

d. The company sells all that it produces each month. The cost of raw materials equals 20 percent of each sales dollar. The company requires a monthly ending inventory equal to the coming month's production requirements. Of raw materials purchases, 50 percent are paid for in the month of purchase. The remaining 50 percent is paid for in the following month.

e. Wages total $50,000 each month and are paid in the month of incurrence.

f. Budgeted monthly operating expenses total $168,000, of which $22,000 is depreciation and $3,000 is expiration of prepaid insurance (the annual premium of $36,000 is paid on January 1).

g. Dividends of $65,000, declared on March 31, will be paid on April 15.

h. Old equipment will be sold for $13,000 on April 3.

i. On April 10, new equipment will be purchased for $80,000.

j. The company maintains a minimum cash balance of $10,000.

k. The cash balance on April 1 is $12,500.

Required:

Prepare a cash budget for April. Give a supporting schedule that details the cash collections from sales.

P14–5   **Revision of Operating Budget; Pro Forma Statements for Income and Cost of Goods Sold**   Mary Dalid founded Molid Company three years ago. The company produces a modem for use with minicomputers and microcomputers. Business has expanded rapidly since the company's inception.

Bob Wells, the company's general accountant, prepared a budget for the fiscal year ending August 31, 1992. The budget was based on the prior year's sales and production activity because Mary believed that the sales growth experienced during the prior year would not continue at the same pace. The pro forma statements of income and cost of goods sold that were prepared as part of the budgetary process are presented below:

Molid Company

Pro Forma Statement of Income
For the Year Ending August 31, 1992
(in thousands)

Net sales	$ 31,248
Less: Cost of goods sold	(20,765)
Gross profit	$ 10,483
Less: Operating expenses	(5,400)
Net income before taxes	$ 5,083

Molid Company

Pro Forma Statement of Cost of Goods Sold
For the Year Ending August 31, 1992
(in thousands)

Direct materials		
Materials inventory, September 1, 1991	$ 1,360	
Materials purchased	14,476	
Available for use	15,836	
Less: Materials inventory, August 31, 1992	(1,628)	
Direct materials used		$14,208
Direct labor		1,134
Overhead:		
Indirect materials	$ 1,421	
General	3,240	$ 4,661
Cost of goods manufactured		$20,003
Finished goods, September 1, 1991		1,169
Total goods available		$21,172
Less: Finished goods, August 31, 1992		(407)
Cost of goods sold		$20,765

On December 10, 1991, Mary and Bob met to discuss the first quarter operating results. Bob believed that several changes should be made to the budget assumptions that had been used to prepare the pro forma statements. He prepared the following notes that summarized the changes, which had not become known until the first quarter results were compiled. He submitted the following data to Mary.

a. Actual first quarter production was 35,000 units. The estimated production for the fiscal year should be increased from 162,000 to 170,000, with the balance of production being scheduled in equal segments over the last nine months of the fiscal year.

b. The planned ending inventory for finished goods of 3,300 units at the end of the fiscal year remains unchanged. The finished goods inventory of 9,300 units as of September 1, 1991, had dropped to 9,000 units by November 30, 1991. The finished goods inventory at the end of the fiscal year will be valued at the average manufacturing costs for the year.

c. Direct materials sufficient to produce 16,000 units were on hand at the beginning of the fiscal year. The plan to have the equivalent of 18,500 units of production in direct materials inventory at the end of the fiscal year remains unchanged. Direct materials inventory is valued on a LIFO basis. Direct materials equivalent to 37,500 units of output were purchased for $3.3 million during the first quarter of the fiscal year. Molid's suppliers have informed the company that direct material prices will increase 5 percent on March 1, 1992. Direct materials needed for the rest of the fiscal year will be purchased evenly through the last nine months.

d. On the basis of historical data, indirect material cost is projected at 10 percent of the cost of direct materials consumed.

e. One-half of general factory overhead and all marketing and general and administrative expenses are considered fixed.

Required:

Based on the revised data presented by Bob Wells, prepare new pro forma statements for income and cost of goods sold for the year ending August 31, 1992.

(CMA adapted)

P14–6   **Performance Reporting; Behavioral Considerations**   Berwin, Inc., is a manufacturer of small industrial tools with annual sales of approximately $3.5 million. Sales growth has been steady during the year, and there is no evidence of cyclical demand. Production has increased gradually during the year and has been evenly distributed throughout each month. The company has a sequential processing system. The four manufacturing departments—Casting, Machining, Finishing, and Packaging—are all located in the same building. Fixed overhead is assigned using a plant-wide rate.

Berwin has always been able to compete with other manufacturers of small tools. However, its market has expanded only in response to product innovation. Thus, research and development is very important and has helped Berwin to expand as well as maintain demand.

Carla Viller, controller, has designed and implemented a new budget system in response to concerns voiced by George Berwin, president. Carla prepared an annual budget that has been divided into twelve equal segments; this budget can be used to assist in the timely evaluation of monthly performance. George was visibly upset upon receiving the May performance report for the Machining Department. George exclaimed, "How can they be efficient enough to produce nine extra units every working day and still miss the budget by $300 per day?" Gene Jordan, supervisor of the Machining Department, could not understand "all the red ink" when he knew that the department had operated

---

Berwin, Inc.

Machining Department Performance Report
For the Month Ended May 31, 1992

	Budget	Actual	Variance	
Volume in units	3,000	3,185	185	F
Variable manufacturing costs:				
Direct materials	$ 24,000	$ 24,843	$ 843	U
Direct labor	27,750	29,302	1,552	U
Variable overhead	33,300	35,035	1,735	U
Total variable costs	$ 85,050	$ 89,180	$4,130	U
Fixed manufacturing costs:				
Indirect labor	$ 3,300	$ 3,334	$ 34	U
Depreciation	1,500	1,500	—	
Taxes	300	300	—	
Insurance	240	240	—	
Other	930	1,027	97	U
Total fixed costs	$ 6,270	$ 6,401	$ 131	U
Corporate costs				
Research and development	$ 2,400	$ 3,728	$1,328	U
Selling and administrative	3,600	4,075	475	U
Total corporate costs	$ 6,000	$ 7,803	$1,803	U
Total costs	$ 97,320	$103,384	$6,064	U

more efficiently in May than it had in months. Gene stated, "I was expecting a pat on the back and instead the boss tore me apart. What's more, I don't even know why!"

Required:

1. Review the May performance report. Based on the information given in the report and elsewhere
   a. Discuss the strengths and weaknesses of the new budgetary system.
   b. Identify the weaknesses of the performance report and explain how it should be revised to eliminate each weakness.
2. Prepare a revised report for the Machining Department using the May data.
3. What other changes would you make to improve Berwin's budgetary system?

(CMA adapted)

P14–7 **Master Budget; Comprehensive Review**   Electra Company is a high-technology organization that produces a mass-storage system. The design of Electra's system is unique and represents a breakthrough in the industry. The units Electra produces combine positive features of both floppy and hard disks. The company is completing its fifth year of operations and is preparing to build its master budget for the coming year (1993). The budget will detail each quarter's activity and the activity for the year in total. The master budget will be based on the following information:

a. Fourth quarter sales for 1992 are 55,000 units.

b. Unit sales by quarter (for 1993) are projected as follows:

First quarter	60,000
Second quarter	65,000
Third quarter	75,000
Fourth quarter	90,000

The selling price is $400 per unit. All sales are credit sales. Electra collects 85 percent of all sales within the quarter in which they are realized; the other 15 percent are collected in the following quarter. There are no bad debts.

c. There is no beginning inventory of finished goods. Electra is planning the following ending finished goods inventories for each quarter:

First quarter	13,000 units
Second quarter	15,000 units
Third quarter	20,000 units
Fourth quarter	10,000 units

d. Each mass-storage unit uses five hours of direct labor and three units of direct materials. Laborers are paid $10 per hour, and one unit of materials costs $80.

e. There are 65,700 units of direct materials in beginning inventory as of January 1, 1993. At the end of each quarter, Electra plans to have 30 percent of the raw materials needed for next quarter's unit sales. Electra will end the year with the same level of raw materials found in this year's beginning inventory.

f. Electra buys raw materials on account. One-half of the purchases are paid for in the quarter of acquisition and the remaining half is paid for in the following quarter. Wages and salaries are paid on the fifteenth and thirtieth of each month.

g. Fixed overhead totals $1 million each quarter. Of this total, $350,000 represents depreciation. All other fixed expenses are paid for in cash in the quarter incurred. The fixed overhead rate is computed by dividing the year's total fixed overhead by the year's expected actual units produced.

h. Variable overhead is budgeted at $6 per direct labor hour. All variable overhead expenses are paid for in the quarter incurred.

i. Fixed selling and administrative expenses total $250,000 per quarter, including $50,000 depreciation.

j. Variable selling and administrative expenses are budgeted at $10 per unit sold. All selling and administrative expenses are paid for in the quarter incurred.

k. The balance sheet as of December 31, 1992, is as follows:

Assets	
Cash	$ 250,000
Inventory	5,256,000
Accounts receivable	3,300,000
Plant and equipment	33,500,000
Total assets	$42,306,000

Liabilities and Equity	
Accounts payable	$ 7,248,000[a]
Capital stock	27,000,000
Retained earnings	8,058,000
Total liabilities and equity	$42,306,000

[a] For purchase of materials only

l. Electra will pay quarterly dividends of $300,000. At the end of the fourth quarter, $2 million of equipment will be purchased.

Required:

Prepare a master budget for Electra Company for each quarter of 1993 and for the year in total. The following component budgets must be included:

a. Sales budget

b. Production budget

c. Direct materials purchases budget

d. Direct labor budget

e. Overhead budget

f. Selling and administrative expense budget

g. Ending finished goods inventory budget

h. Cost of goods sold budget

i. Cash budget

j. Pro forma income statement (using absorption costing)

k. Pro forma balance sheet

P14–8 **Flexible Budgeting** Jean Bingham, controller of Thorpe, Inc., prepared the following budget for manufacturing costs at two levels of activity for 1992:

	Direct Labor Hours	
	100,000	*120,000*
Supervision	$ 180,000	$ 180,000
Utilities	18,000	21,000
Depreciation	25,000	25,000
Supplies	25,000	30,000
Direct labor	1,000,000	1,200,000
Direct materials	220,000	264,000
Maintenance	240,000	284,000
Rent	12,000	12,000
Other	60,000	70,000
Total manufacturing cost	$1,780,000	$2,086,000

During the year, the company worked a total of 112,000 direct labor hours and incurred the following actual costs:

Supervision	$190,000
Utilities	20,500
Depreciation	25,000
Supplies	24,640
Direct labor	963,200
Direct materials	248,000
Maintenance	237,000
Rent	12,000
Other	60,500

Thorpe applies overhead on the basis of direct labor hours. Normal volume of 120,000 direct labor hours is the activity level to compute the predetermined overhead rate:

Required:

1. Prepare a performance report for Thorpe's manufacturing costs in the year 1992. Should any cost item be given special attention? Explain.

2. Assume that the product produced by Thorpe uses two direct labor hours. Calculate the normal unit manufacturing cost.

3. Compute the total applied overhead for 1992. Compute the overhead variance for the year.

P14–9 **Budgeting and Behavioral Consequences** Denny Daniels is production manager of the Alumalloy Division of WRT, Inc. Alumalloy has limited contact with outside customers and no sales staff. Most of its customers are handled by other corporate divisions. Therefore, Alumalloy is treated as a cost center rather than a profit center.

Denny perceives the Accounting Department as the unit that generates historical numbers but provides little useful information. The Accounting Department creates the budgets at the beginning of the year and then gathers the actual costs incurred by production. Denny wonders whether the accountants even understand the nature of the production process itself. It seems all they are concerned with are numbers— whether they mean anything or not. In his opinion, the whole accounting process is a negative motivational device that does not reflect how hard or efficiently he has worked as a production manager. Denny tried to discuss these perceptions and concerns with John Scott, the controller for Alumalloy. Denny told John, "I know I've had better production over a number of operating periods, but the cost report still says I have excessive costs. Look, I'm not an accountant, I'm a production manager. I know how to get a good quality product out. Over a number of years, I've even cut the raw materials used to do it. But the cost report doesn't show any of this. It's always negative no matter what I do. There is no way you can win with accounting or those people at corporate who use those reports."

John gave Denny little consolation. John stated that the accounting system and the cost reports generated by headquarters are just part of the corporate game and almost impossible for an individual to change. "Although these reports are the basis for evaluating the efficiency of your division and the means for corporate to determine whether you have done the job it wants, you shouldn't worry too much. You haven't been fired yet! Besides, these cost reports have been used by WRT for the last twenty-five years."

From talking to the production manager of the zinc division, Denny perceived that most of what John said was true. However, some minor cost reporting changes for zinc had been agreed to by corporate headquarters. He also knew from the trade grapevine that the turnover of production managers was considered high at WRT, even though relatively few managers were fired. Most seemed to end up quitting, usually in disgust, out of the belief that they were not being evaluated fairly.

A recent copy of the cost report prepared by corporate headquarters for Alumalloy is shown below. Because of an unexpected increase in demand for the final product, Alumalloy produced 10,000 units more than the 40,000 originally budgeted. Denny does not like this report because he believes that it fails to reflect the division's operations properly, thereby resulting in an unfair evaluation of performance.

Alumalloy Division

Cost Report
For the Month of April 1993
(in thousands)

	Master Budget	Actual Cost	Variance	
Aluminum	$ 400	$ 477	$ 77	U
Labor	560	675	115	U
Overhead	100	110	10	U
Total	$1,060	$1,262	$202	U

Required:

1. Comment on Denny's perception of
   a. John Scott, the controller
   b. Corporate headquarters
   c. The cost report
   d. Himself as a production manager

e. Discuss how his perception of these items affects his performance as a production manager of WRT.

2. List the deficiencies of WRT's budgetary system. Prepare a list of recommendations to improve the system so that the process and the reports produced are more useful and less threatening to the production managers.

(CMA adapted)

P14–10 **Budgetary Performance; Rewards; Ethical Behavior** Linda Ellis, manager of a division that is treated as a profit center, is evaluated and rewarded on the basis of budgetary performance. She, her assistants, and the plant managers are all eligible to receive a bonus if actual divisional profits are between budgeted profits and 120 percent of budgeted profits. The bonuses are based on a fixed percentage of actual profits. Profits above 120 percent of budgeted profits earn a bonus at the 120 percent level (in other words, there is an upper limit on possible bonus payments). If the actual profits are less than budgeted profits, no bonuses are awarded. Now consider the following actions taken by Linda:

a. Linda tends to overestimate expenses and underestimate revenues. This approach facilitates the ability of the division to attain budgeted profits. Linda believes the action is justified because it increases the likelihood of receiving bonuses and helps keep the morale of the managers high.

b. Suppose that towards the end of the fiscal year, Linda saw that the division would not achieve budgeted profits. Accordingly, she instructed the Sales Department to defer the closing of a number of sales agreements to the following fiscal year. She also decided to write off some inventory that was nearly worthless. Deferring revenues to next year and writing off the inventory in a no-bonus year increased the chances of a bonus for next year.

c. Assume that towards the end of the year, Linda saw that actual profits would likely exceed the 120 percent limit. She took actions similar to those described in part b.

Required:

1. Comment on the ethics of Linda's behavior. Are her actions right or wrong? What role does the company play in encouraging her actions?

2. Suppose that you are the marketing manager for the division and you receive instructions to defer the closing of sales until the next fiscal year. What would you do?

3. Suppose that you are a plant manager and you know that your budget has been padded by the divisional manager. Further suppose that the padding is common knowledge among the plant managers and is generally supported because it increases the ability to achieve budget and receive a bonus. What would you do?

4. Suppose that you are divisional controller and you receive instructions from the divisional manager to accelerate the recognition of some expenses that legitimately belong to a future period. What would you do?

P14–11 **Zero-base Budgeting**[3] The city of Vernal currently employs the following in its Police Department:

---

[3]The setting for this problem was suggested by an illustrative example given in Sydnee Duncombe, "Zero-Based Budgeting," in Jack Rabin, W. Bartley Hildreth, and Gerald J. Miller (eds.), *Budget Management: A Reader in Local Government Financial Management* (Carl Vinson Institute of Government, University of Georgia, 1983).

Patrol officers	7.0
Dispatchers	4.2[a]
Chief	1.0

[a]There are four full-time dispatchers and one who works one shift per week. This provides dispatching service twenty-four hours a day, seven days a week.

The cost of the current level of service is given below:

Salaries	$274,400
Personnel benefits	63,112
Supplies	12,200
Capital outlay	6,500
Total	$356,212

Supplies vary in proportion to the number of employees. Patrol officers are paid a salary of $23,000, dispatchers $17,000 (the part-time dispatcher receives $3,400 per year), and the police chief $42,000.

The city of Vernal is growing in population but its revenues are failing to keep pace; accordingly, the mayor and city council have requested each city agency to prepare a zero-base budget. All agencies are to start with a base package that represents 60–90 percent of current costs. The Police Department has been instructed to begin with a package that is 75 percent of its current costs. However, the police chief has also been told to present a package that reflects current operating costs and to prepare packages that reflect increased law enforcement capabilities.

The police chief has decided that five patrol officers and sixteen hours of dispatching per day are the absolute minimum requirements for police protection. He is convinced that even this is a risky proposition. The capital outlay of $6,500 cannot be avoided—it represents absolutely essential equipment.

Because of the growth in the city's population, the police chief sees the following needs (in order of priority):

a. Sufficient patrol officers to have two officers cover the city twenty-four hours a day, seven days a week.

b. A full-time investigator (salary $25,000). This would free the sergeants from investigation and allow them more time for supervision and patrol.

c. A full-time juvenile officer (salary $23,750). It would free patrol officers from this duty and introduce an officer with the needed skills to deal with juvenile offenders.

Required:

1. Comment on the behavioral effects of requiring the Police Department to develop a minimal-level (base) package.

2. Assume that you are the police chief. Develop five decision packages for the Vernal

police department. There should be a base package, a status quo package, and three packages that represent increased police services.

P14–12 **Flexible Budget; Purchases Budget; Direct Labor Budget; Cash Budget** Hogan's Heroes is a hole-in-the-wall sandwich shop just off the State University campus. Customers enter off the street into a small counter area to order one of ten varieties of sandwich and a soft drink. All orders must be taken out because there is no space for dining.

The owner of Hogan's Heroes, Paul Hogan, is attempting to construct a series of budgets. He has accumulated the following information:

a. The average sandwich (which sells for $4.25) requires 1 roll, 4 ounces of meat, 2 ounces of cheese, 0.05 head of lettuce, 0.25 of a tomato, and a healthy squirt (1 ounce) of secret sauce.

b. Each customer typically orders one soft drink (average price $1) consisting of a cup and twelve ounces of soda.

c. Use of paper supplies (napkins, bag, sandwich wrap, cup) varies from customer to customer but averages $350 per month.

d. Hogan's Heroes is open for two 8-hour shifts. The noon shift on Monday through Friday requires five workers earning $6 per hour (this includes fringe benefits). The evening shift is only on Friday, Saturday, and Sunday nights; the three evening shift employees also earn $6 per hour. There are 4.3 weeks in a month.

e. Rent is $75 per month. Other monthly cash expenses average $465.

f. Food costs are

Meat	$5.00/lb
Cheese	$3.50/lb
Rolls	$24/gross
Lettuce	$12/box (contains 24 heads)
Tomatoes	$1.50/box (contains approximately 20 tomatoes)
Special sauce	$6/gal
Soda (syrup and carbonated water)	$2/gal

In a normal month when school is in session, Hogan sells 5,000 sandwiches. In October, State U. holds its homecoming celebration. Therefore, Hogan figures that if he adds a noon shift on Saturday and Sunday of homecoming weekend, October sales will be 30 percent higher than normal.

Required:

Prepare flexible budgets for a normal school month and for the month of October.

P14–13 **Flexible Budgeting** Wielson Company employs flexible budgeting techniques to evaluate the performance of several of its activities. The selling expense flexible budgets for three representative monthly activity levels are shown below:

Representative Monthly Flexible Budgets for Selling Expenses

Activity measures:			
Unit sales volume	400,000	425,000	450,000
Dollar sales volume	$10,000,000	$10,625,000	$11,250,000
Number of orders	4,000	4,250	4,500
Number of salespersons	75	75	75
Monthly expenses:			
Advertising and promotion	$ 1,200,000	$ 1,200,000	$ 1,200,000
Adminstrative salaries	57,000	57,000	57,000
Sales salaries	75,000	75,000	75,000
Sales commissions	200,000	212,500	225,000
Salesperson travel	170,000	175,000	180,000
Sales office expense	490,000	498,750	507,500
Shipping expense	675,000	712,500	750,000
Total	$ 2,867,000	$ 2,930,750	$ 2,994,500

The following assumptions were used to develop the selling expense flexible budgets:

a. The average size of Wielson's salesforce during the year was planned to be seventy-five people.

b. Salespersons are paid a monthly salary plus commission on gross dollar sales.

c. The travel costs are best characterized as a step-variable cost. The fixed portion is related to the number of salespersons; the variable portion tends to fluctuate with gross dollar sales.

d. Sales office expense is a mixed cost with the variable portion related to the number of orders processed.

e. Shipping expense is a mixed cost with the variable portion related to the number of units sold.

A salesforce of eighty persons generated a total of 4,300 orders resulting in a sales volume of 420,000 units during November. The gross dollar sales amounted to $10.9 million. The selling expenses incurred for November were as follows:

Advertising and promotion	$1,350,000
Administrative salaries	57,000
Sales salaries	80,000
Sales commissions	218,000
Salesperson travel	185,000
Sales office expense	497,200
Shipping expense	730,000
Total	$3,117,200

Required:

1. Explain why the selling expense flexible budgets presented above would not be appropriate for evaluating Wielson Company's November selling expenses; indicate how the flexible budget would have to be revised.

2. Prepare a selling expense report for November that Wielson Company can use to evaluate its control over selling expenses. The report should have a line for each selling expense item showing the appropriate budgeted amount, the actual selling expense, and the monthly dollar variation.

(CMA adapted)

■ MANAGERIAL DECISION CASES

Case 14-1 **Cash Budget** According to the analysis of a local consultant, the financial difficulties facing Dr. Roger Jones have been caused by the absence of proper planning and control.[4] Budgetary control is sorely needed. To assist you in preparing a plan of action that will help his dental practice regain financial stability, Dr. Jones has made available the following financial information that describes a typical month:

	Revenues	
	Average Fee	*Quantity*
Fillings	$ 50	90
Crowns	300	19
Root canals	170	8
Bridges	500	7
Extractions	45	30
Cleaning	25	108
x-rays	15	150
	Costs	
Salaries:		
Two dental assistants	$1,900	
Receptionist/bookkeeper	1,500	
Hygienist	1,800	
Public relations (Mrs. Jones)	1,000	
Personal salary	6,500	
Total salaries		$12,700
Benefits		1,344
Building lease		1,500
Dental supplies		1,200
Janitorial		300

(continued on next page)

---

[4]Review the introduction to the chapter for a description of the financial difficulties that Dr. Jones faces on a recurring basis.

	Average Fee	*Quantity*
Utilities		400
Phone		150
Office supplies		100
Lab fees		5,000
Loan payments		570
Interest payments		500
Miscellaneous		500
Depreciation		700
Total costs		$24,964

Benefits include Dr. Jones's share of social security and a health insurance premium for all employees. Although all revenues billed in a month are not collected, the cash flowing into the business is approximately equal to the month's billings because of collections from prior months. The dental office is open Monday through Thursday from 8:30 A.M. to 4:00 P.M. and on Friday from 8:30 A.M. to 12:30 P.M. A total of thirty-two hours are worked each week. Additional hours could be worked, but Dr. Jones is reluctant to do so because of other personal endeavors that he enjoys.

Dr. Jones has noted that the two dental assistants and the receptionist are not fully utilized. He estimates that they are busy about 65–70 percent of the time. Dr. Jones's wife spends about five hours each week on a monthly newsletter that is sent to all patients; she also maintains a birthday list and sends cards to the patients on their birthdays.

Dr. Jones spends about $2,400 yearly on informational seminars. These seminars, targeted especially for dentists, teach them how to increase their revenues. It is from one of these seminars that Dr. Jones decided to invest in promotion and public relations (the newsletter and the birthday list).

Required:

1. Prepare a monthly cash budget for Dr. Jones. Does Dr. Jones have a significant cash flow problem? How would you use the budget to show Dr. Jones why he is having financial difficulties?

2. Using the cash budget prepared in Requirement 1 and the information given in the case, prepare some recommendations to solve Dr. Jones's financial problems. Prepare a cash budget that reflects these recommendations and demonstrates to Dr. Jones that the problems can be corrected. Do you think that Dr. Jones will accept your recommendations? Do any of the behavioral principles discussed in the chapter have a role in this type of setting? Explain.

Case 14–2   **Zero-base Budgeting**   Ron Bunker is the intramural director for a large Midwestern university with a student body of 23,000. Currently, intramurals offers three major programs: flag football, basketball, and softball. The cost of each program is given below:

Football	$30,000
Basketball	40,000
Softball	18,000

The costs are for salaries, wages (referees, umpires, and so on), supplies, utilities, and equipment. Ron has one full-time assistant who receives a salary of $18,000. Ron's salary is $28,000. These two salaries are allocated equally over the three programs. All other costs are direct costs of the individual programs. Before hiring the assistant, Ron was able to offer only two of the three programs.

The largest program, basketball, involves more than 1,000 students. Football is next largest; it involves around 750 students. Softball involves 150–200 students (the season is short because of the weather, and many students are reluctant to participate).

Ron has received several requests from fraternities to expand the intramural program to include swimming, track, and cross-country skiing. After some careful analysis, Ron estimates the costs of these additional programs to be as follows:

Swimming	$12,000
Track	17,000
Skiing	28,000

He also estimates that track would involve the most students (400–500), followed by swimming (150–200) and by skiing (100–150). To expand, Ron would need to hire an additional full-time assistant at $18,000. These costs are all direct except for the salary of the assistant, which would be allocated equally to each program.

The university president has asked program leaders and department heads to use zero-base budgeting for the coming year. Because of a tight budgetary situation in the state for the coming year (and for several years thereafter as the president projected), the president intends to examine every program carefully. He has indicated that some programs will be reduced in scope, some will be eliminated, and some will be expanded.

The president has given instructions to every decision unit to prepare a bare-bones operating budget for the existing program. This base package must represent no more than 75 percent of what is currently being spent by the program and must be fully justified. Any additional increments in other decision packages must also be fully justified. Once the base packages and their increments are received, the president and the vice-presidents will rank the packages and allocate the resources accordingly. The president has also indicated that the budgets must be received on a timely basis so that sufficient notice can be given to programs that will be reduced or cut. (In some cases, the new allocations may need to be implemented over a two-year period.)

Required:

1. Discuss the behavioral ramifications of the president's announcement to use zero-base budgeting.

2. Assume Ron Bunker's role and prepare a base package and several incremental packages. Discuss the consequences of nonapproval and the benefits of approval for each package. (*Note:* Several combinations are possible; choose the one that you believe has the best chance of acceptance.) Be sure to provide a ranking in terms of priority for the packages developed.

3. Assume the role of the president. What level would you fund, if any? Why?

Standard Costing: A Managerial Control Tool

■ **LEARNING OBJECTIVES**

After studying Chapter 15, you should be able to

1. Identify what standard costs are and distinguish between an actual cost system, a normal cost system, and a standard cost system.

2. Explain how standards are set and be able to define ideal and currently attainable standards.

3. Explain why standard cost systems are adopted.

4. Explain when variances should be investigated and when corrective action should be taken.

5. Compute the materials price and usage variances and explain how they are used for control.

6. Compute the labor rate and efficiency variances and explain how they are used for control.

7. Compute the fixed overhead spending and volume variances and explain their meanings.

8. Compute the variable overhead spending and efficiency variances and explain their meanings.

9. Define and explain the key terms appearing at the end of the chapter.

SCENARIO

Millie Anderson, manager of Honley Medical's IV products division, was more than satisfied with the performance of her division last year. At the beginning of the year, the division had introduced a new line of polyurethane catheters, replacing the old teflon catheters, and sales had more than tripled. The reaction of the market to the new catheter represented a virtual replay of the company's history.

Nearly thirty years ago, Lindell Honley, the founder of Honley Medical, had perceived the need for something other than a metal needle for long-term insertion into veins. Metal needles were irritating and could damage the vein. Based on this observation, Honley had developed a catheter using teflon since it was a lubricated plastic and easy to insert into the vein. The new development was well received by the medical community and produced a new and successful company, one that had expanded its activities into a variety of medical products.

For years, because of the new technology, Honley had dominated the market. Eventually, however, the patent expired and other companies entered the market with their own teflon catheters, making competition exceptionally keen. Prices had been driven down, and profit margins were eroding.

The eroding profit margins had prompted Millie and other high-level managers to examine the continued viability of the teflon catheters. After many years, the medical profession had noted that after twenty-four hours of use, an infection tended to develop around the point of insertion. Researchers at Honley Medical had discovered that the problem was one of incompatibility of the blood and tissue with the teflon. Further studies showed that different plastics produced different reactions. Research began immediately on finding a material that was more biocompatible than teflon. The outcome was polyurethane catheters. The new catheter could be left in for seventy-two hours, compared to the twenty-four hours for teflon catheters.

Once again, Honley Medical was establishing a dominant position in the IV market. Millie also knew that history would repeat itself in the later stages, as well—the time would come when other firms would produce catheters with the same degree of biocompatibility. In fact, Honley's research scientists estimated that competitors would have a competing catheter on the market within three years. This time, however, Millie was determined to protect the division's market share. And better protection required a different approach. Although further research into biocompatibility was being conducted, Millie was convinced that this approach would not be as fruitful as in the past. Most patients had little need for a catheter beyond seventy-two hours. Thus, further improvements in biocompatibility were not likely to produce the same favorable market reaction.

In the past, because of its dominant position, the division had not been too concerned with control of manufacturing costs. Only when profit margins had begun to erode had some mention of a need for better cost control been made. Unfortunately, once the opportunity for an improved catheter was identified, the focus was again on technological dominance. Millie had decided that it was time to resurrect the cost control issue. By implementing cost control measures now, she believed that the division would be better able to compete on price when the competition resurfaced within a few years. Her conversation below with Reed McCourt, divisional controller, reflects this decision.

Millie: Reed, as I see it, the only attempt we make to control manufacturing costs is our budgetary system. Is that right?

Reed: Yes. But it really isn't a very good effort. Budgets are based on last year's costs plus some allowance for inflation. At this point, we have never tried to identify what the costs *ought* to be. Nor have we really held managers responsible for cost control. Our profitability has always been good—resources have always been plentiful. My guess is that we are spending much more than necessary simply because we have been so successful.

Millie: Well, resources wouldn't be so plentiful now if we hadn't developed the polyurethane catheter. And I'm afraid that resources won't be plentiful in the future unless we take actions now to control our manufacturing costs. Besides, if we can be more profitable now by using better cost control, then we ought to do so. I want better cost control, and I want my plant and production managers to recognize their responsibilities in this area. What suggestions do you have?

Reed: We need to inject more formality into the budgetary system. First, budgets should reflect what costs should be, not what they have been. Second, we can encourage managers to be cost conscious by allowing them to help identify efficient levels of cost on which the budget will be based and by tying their bonuses and promotions into the system as well. However, I think we can gain the cost control by going one step further and establishing a standard cost system.

Millie: Doesn't that entail the specification of unit price and quantity standards for materials and labor?

Reed: That's essentially correct. Using the unit price and quantity standards, budgeted costs for labor, materials, and overhead are established for each unit produced. These unit costs are used to develop budgets and—once actual costs are in—to break down the budgetary variances into a price variance and an efficiency variance. A standard cost system provides more detailed control information than a budgetary system using normal costing. We can hold our managers responsible for meeting the standards that are established.

Millie: I think our division needs this type of system. It's about time that our managers become cost conscious. Reed, prepare a report that provides more detail on what a standard cost system is all about.

▪ BUDGETS AND UNIT STANDARDS

Millie and Reed both recognized the need to encourage operating managers to control costs. Cost control often means the difference between success and failure or between above-average profits and average or below-average profits. Millie was convinced that cost control meant that her managers had to be cost conscious and that they had to assume responsibility for this important objective. Reed suggested that the way to control costs and involve managers is through the use of a formal budgetary system.

In Chapter 14, we learned that budgets set standards that are used to control and evaluate managerial performance. However, budgets are aggregate measures of performance; they identify the revenues and costs in total that an organization should experience if plans are executed as expected. By comparing the actual costs and actual revenues with the corresponding budgeted amounts at the same level of activity, a measure of managerial efficiency emerges.

Although the process just described provides significant information for control, control can be enhanced by developing standards for *unit* amounts as well as for total amounts. In fact, the groundwork for unit standards already exists within the framework of flexible budgeting. For flexible budgeting to work, the budgeted variable cost per unit of input for each unit of output must be known for every item in the budget. The budgeted variable input cost per unit of output is a unit standard. Unit standards are the basis or foundation on which a flexible budget is built.

To determine the unit standard cost for a particular input, two decisions must be made: (1) how much of the input should be used per unit of output (the *quantity decision*) and (2) how much should be paid for the quantity of the input to be used (the *pricing decision*). The quantity decision produces **quantity standards**, and the pricing decision produces **price standards**. The unit standard cost can be computed by multiplying these two standards.

quantity standards
price standards

For example, a soft-drink bottling company may decide that five ounces of fructose should be used for every 16-ounce bottle of cola (the quantity standard) and that the price of the fructose should be $0.05 per ounce (the price standard). The standard cost of the fructose per bottle of cola is then $0.25 (5 × $0.05). The standard cost per unit of fructose can be used to predict what the total cost of fructose should be as the activity level varies; it thus becomes a flexible budget formula. Thus, if 10,000 bottles of cola are produced, the total expected cost of fructose is $2,500 ($0.25 × 10,000); if 15,000 bottles are produced, the total expected cost of fructose is $3,750 ($0.25 × 15,000).

■ THE ESTABLISHMENT OF STANDARDS

How Standards Are Developed

Historical experience, engineering studies, and input from operating personnel are three potential sources of quantitative standards. Although historical experience may provide an initial guideline for setting standards, it should not be used without caution. Often, processes are operating inefficiently; adopting input-output relationships from the past thus perpetuates these inefficiencies. The IV division of Honley Medical, for example, had never emphasized cost control and had operated in a resource-rich environment. Both the divisional manager and controller were convinced that significant inefficiencies existed. Engineering studies can determine the most efficient way to operate and can provide very rigorous guidelines; however, engineered standards are often too rigorous. They may not be achievable by operating personnel. Since operating personnel are accountable for meeting the standards, they should have significant input in setting standards. The same principles pertaining to participative budgeting pertain to setting unit standards.

Price standards are the joint responsibility of operations, purchasing, personnel, and accounting. Operations determines the quality of the inputs required; personnel and purchasing have the responsibility to acquire the input quality requested at the lowest price. Market forces, trade unions, and other external forces limit the range of choices for price standards. In setting price standards, purchasing must consider discounts, freight, and quality; personnel, on the other hand, must consider payroll taxes, fringe benefits, and qualifications. Accounting is responsible for recording the price standards and for preparing reports that compare actual performance to the standard.

Types of Standards

ideal standards

currently attainable standards

Standards are generally classified as either *ideal* or *currently attainable*. **Ideal standards** are standards that demand maximum efficiency and can be achieved only if everything operates perfectly. No machine breakdowns, slack, or lack of skill (even momentarily) are allowed. **Currently attainable standards** can be achieved under efficient operating conditions. Allowance is made for normal breakdowns, interruptions, less than perfect skill, and so on. These standards are demanding but achievable.

Of the two types, currently attainable standards offer the most behavioral benefits. If standards are too tight and never achievable, workers become frustrated and performance levels decline. However, challenging but achievable standards tend to extract higher performance levels—particularly when the individuals subject to the standards have participated in their creation.

Why Standard Cost Systems Are Adopted

Two reasons for adopting a standard cost system are frequently mentioned: to improve planning and control and to facilitate product costing.

Planning and Control   Standard costing systems enhance planning and control and improve performance measurement. Unit standards are a fundamental requirement for a flexible budgeting system, which is a key feature of a meaningful planning and control system. Budgetary control systems compare actual costs with budgeted costs by computing variances, the difference between the actual and planned costs for the actual level of activity. By developing unit price and quantity standards, an overall variance can be decomposed into a *price variance* and a *usage or efficiency variance*.

By performing this decomposition, a manager has more information. If the variance is unfavorable, a manager can tell whether it is attributable to discrepancies between planned prices and actual prices, to discrepancies between planned usage and actual usage, or to both. Since managers have more control over the usage of inputs than over their prices, efficiency variances provide specific signals regarding the need for corrective action and where that action should be focused. Thus, in principle, the use of efficiency variances enhances operational control. Additionally, by breaking out the price variance, over which managers have little control, the system provides an improved measure of managerial efficiency.

The benefits of operational control, however, may not extend to the advanced manufacturing environment. The use of a standard cost system for operational control in an advanced manufacturing environment can produce dysfunctional behavior. Thus, the detailed computation of variances—at least at the operational level—is discouraged in this new environment. Nonetheless, standards in the advanced manufacturing environment are still useful for planning, for example, in the creation of bids. Also, variances may still be computed and presented in reports to higher-level managers so that the financial dimension can be monitored.

Finally, it should be mentioned that there are many firms that are operating with conventional manufacturing systems. Standard cost systems are widely used. In a recent survey, 87 percent of the firms responding used a standard cost system.[1] Furthermore, the survey revealed that significant numbers of the respondents were calculating variances at the operational level. For example, about 40 percent of the firms using a standard costing system reported labor variances for small work crews or individual workers.

Product Costing   In a standard cost system, costs are assigned to products using quantity and price standards for all three manufacturing costs: direct materials, direct labor, and overhead. In contrast, a normal cost system predetermines overhead costs for the purpose of product costing but assigns direct materials and direct labor to products by using actual costs. Overhead is assigned using a budgeted rate and actual activity. At the other end of the cost assignment spectrum, an actual cost system assigns the actual costs of all three manufacturing inputs to products. Exhibit 15–1 summarizes these three cost assignment approaches.

Standard product costing has several advantages over normal costing and actual costing. One, of course, is the greater capacity for control. Standard cost systems also provide readily available unit cost information that can be used for pricing decisions. This is particularly helpful for companies that do a significant amount of bidding and for those paid on a cost-plus basis.[2]

---

[1]Bruce R. Gaumnitz and Felix P. Kollaritsch, "Manufacturing Variances: Current Practice and Trends," *Journal of Cost Management* (Spring 1991), pp. 58–64.

[2]For example, the concrete and pipe company (CalBlock, Inc.) mentioned in the previous chapter conducts the vast majority of its business through bidding. This company recently adopted a standard cost system primarily to facilitate the bidding process.

EXHIBIT 15-1
Cost Assignment Approaches

	Manufacturing Costs		
	Direct Materials	Direct Labor	Overhead
Actual cost system	Actual	Actual	Actual
Normal cost system	Actual	Actual	Budgeted
Standard cost system	Standard	Standard	Standard

Other simplifications are also possible. For example, if a process-costing system uses standard costing to assign product costs, there is no need to compute a unit cost for each equivalent unit-cost category. A standard unit cost would exist for each category.[3] Additionally, there is no need to distinguish between the FIFO and weighted-average methods of accounting for beginning inventory costs. Usually, a standard process costing system will follow the equivalent unit calculation of the FIFO approach. That is, *current* equivalent units of work are calculated. By calculating current equivalent work, current actual production costs can be compared with standard costs for control purposes.

■ STANDARD PRODUCT COSTS

standard cost
per unit
standard cost sheet

The most common application of standard costing is found within manufacturing organizations.[4] Standard costs are developed for materials, labor, and overhead. Using these costs, the **standard cost per unit** is computed. The **standard cost sheet** provides the detail underlying the standard unit cost.

To illustrate, let us develop a standard cost sheet for a 16-ounce bag of corn chips produced by Crunchy Chips Company. The production of corn chips begins by steaming and soaking corn kernels overnight in a lime solu-

---

[3]If you have not read the chapter on process costing, the example illustrating the simplifications made possible by standard costing will not be as meaningful. However, the point being made is still relevant. Standard costing can bring useful computational savings.

[4]Standard costs are also used in many nonmanufacturing organizations. The federal government, for example, is using a standard-costing system for purposes of reimbursement of Medicare costs. Based on several studies, illnesses have been classified into diagnostic related groups (DRGs) and the hospital costs that should be incurred for an average case identified. (The costs include patient days, food, medicine, supplies, use of equipment, and so on.) The government pays the hospital the standard cost for the DRG. If the cost of the patient's treatment is greater than the DRG allows, the hospital suffers a loss. If the cost of the patient's treatment is less than the DRG reimbursement, the hospital gains. On average, the hospital supposedly breaks even.

tion. This process softens the kernels so that they can be shaped into a sheet of dough. The dough is then cut into small triangular chips. Next, the chips are toasted in an oven and then dropped into a deep fryer. After cooking, the chips pass under a salting device and are inspected for quality. Substandard chips are sorted and discarded; the chips passing inspection are bagged by a packaging machine. The bagged chips are manually packed into boxes for shipping.

Four materials are used to process corn chips: yellow corn, cooking oil, salt, and lime. The package in which the chips are placed is also classified as a direct material. Crunchy Chips has two types of direct laborers: machine operators and inspectors (or sorters). Variable overhead is made up of three costs: gas, electricity, and water; it is applied using direct labor hours. Fixed overhead is also applied using direct labor hours. The standard cost sheet is given in Exhibit 15–2.

From Exhibit 15–2, note that it should cost $0.54 to produce a 16-ounce package of corn chips. Also notice that the company uses eighteen ounces of corn to produce a 16-ounce package of chips. There are two reasons. First, some chips are discarded during the inspection process. The company plans on a normal amount of waste. Second, the company wants to have more than sixteen ounces in each package to increase customer satisfaction with its product.

EXHIBIT 15–2
Standard Cost Sheet for Corn Chips

Description	Standard Price	Standard Usage	Standard Cost[a]	Subtotal
Direct materials:				
Yellow corn	$ 0.006	18 oz	$0.108	
Cooking oil	0.031	2 oz	0.062	
Salt	0.005	1 oz	0.005	
Lime	0.100	0.01 oz	0.001	
Bags	0.044	1 bag	0.044	
Total direct materials				$0.220
Direct labor:				
Inspection	$ 5.00	0.0070 hrs	$0.035	
Machine operators	6.50	0.0008 hrs	0.005	
Total direct labor				0.040
Overhead:				
Variable overhead	$ 3.85	0.0078 hrs	$0.030	
Fixed overhead	32.05	0.0078 hrs	0.250	
Total overhead				0.280
Total standard unit cost				$0.540

[a]Calculated by multiplying price times usage

Exhibit 15–2 also reveals other important insights. The standard usage for variable and fixed overhead is tied to the direct labor standards. For variable overhead, the rate is $3.85 per direct labor hour. Since one package of corn chips uses 0.0078 direct labor hours, the variable overhead cost assigned to a package of corn chips is $0.03 ($3.85 × 0.0078). For fixed overhead, the rate is $32.05 per direct labor hour, making the fixed overhead cost per package of corn chips $0.25 ($32.05 × 0.0078). Nearly half of the cost of production is fixed, indicating a capital-intensive production effort. Indeed, much of the operation is mechanized.

standard quantity of materials allowed

standard hours allowed

The standard cost sheet also reveals the quantity of each input that should be used to produce one unit of output. The unit quantity standards can be used to compute the total amount of inputs allowed for the actual output. This computation is an essential component in computing efficiency variances. A manager should be able to compute the **standard quantity of materials allowed** (SQ) and the **standard hours allowed** (SH) for the actual output. This computation must be done for every class of direct material and for every class of direct labor. Assume, for example, that 100,000 packages of corn chips are produced during the first week of March. How much yellow corn should have been used for the actual output of 100,000 packages? The unit quantity standard is eighteen ounces of yellow corn per package (see Exhibit 15–2). For 100,000 packages, the standard quantity of yellow corn allowed is computed as follows:

$$SQ = \text{Unit quantity standard} \times \text{Actual output}$$
$$= 18 \times 100,000$$
$$= 1,800,000 \text{ ounces}$$

The computation of standard direct labor hours allowed can be illustrated using machine operators. From Exhibit 15–2, we see that the unit quantity standard is 0.0008 hours per package produced. Thus, if 100,000 packages are produced, the standard hours allowed is as follows:

$$SH = \text{Unit quantity standard} \times \text{Actual output}$$
$$= 0.0008 \times 100,000$$
$$= 80 \text{ direct labor hours}$$

▪ VARIANCE ANALYSIS: GENERAL DESCRIPTION

A flexible budget can be used to identify the costs that should have been incurred for the actual level of activity. This figure is obtained by multiplying the amount of input allowed for the actual output by the standard unit price. Letting SP be the standard unit price of an input and SQ the standard quantity of inputs allowed for the actual output, the planned or budgeted input cost is $SP \times SQ$. The actual input cost is $AP \times AQ$, where AP is the actual price per unit of the input and AQ is the actual quantity of input used.

total budget variance

The **total budget variance** is simply the difference between the actual cost of the input and its planned cost. For simplicity, we will refer to the total budget variance as the *total variance*.

$$\text{Total variance} = (AP \times AQ) - (SP \times SQ)$$

price variance

efficiency variance

In a standard cost system, the total variance is broken down into price and usage variances. **Price variance** is the difference between the actual and standard unit price of an input multiplied by the number of inputs used. **Efficiency variance** is the difference between the actual and standard quantity of inputs multiplied by the unit price of the input. (This measure is also called the *usage variance*.) As mentioned earlier, by breaking the total budget variance down into these two components, managers can better analyze and control the total variance. They are able to identify the origin of cost increases and take appropriate corrective action.

Dividing the total variance into price and usage components is accomplished by subtracting and adding $SP \times AQ$ to the right-hand side of the total variance equation:

$$
\begin{aligned}
\text{Total variance} &= [(AP \times AQ) - (SP \times AQ)] \\
&\quad + [(SP \times AQ) - (SP \times SQ)] \\
&= (AP \times AQ - SP \times AQ) \\
&\quad + (SP \times AQ - SP \times SQ) \\
&= (AP - SP)AQ + (AQ - SQ)SP \\
&= \text{Price variance} + \text{Usage variance}
\end{aligned}
$$

Exhibit 15–3 (page 744) presents a three-pronged diagram that describes this process.

Usually, the total variance is divided into price and usage components for direct materials and direct labor. The treatment of overhead is discussed later in the chapter.

unfavorable (U) variances

favorable (F) variances

Unfavorable (U) variances occur whenever actual prices or usage of inputs is greater than standard prices or usage. When the opposite occurs, **favorable (F) variances** are obtained. Favorable and unfavorable variances are not equivalent to good and bad variances. The terms merely indicate the relationship of the actual prices or quantities to the standard prices and quantities. Whether or not the variances are good or bad depends on *why* they occurred. Determining why requires managers to do some investigation.

■ THE DECISION TO INVESTIGATE

Rarely will actual performance exactly meet the established standards nor does management expect it to. Random variations around the standard are expected. Because of this, management should have in mind an acceptable range of performance. When variances are within this range, they are assumed to be caused by random factors. When a variance falls outside this

EXHIBIT 15–3
Variance Analysis: General Description

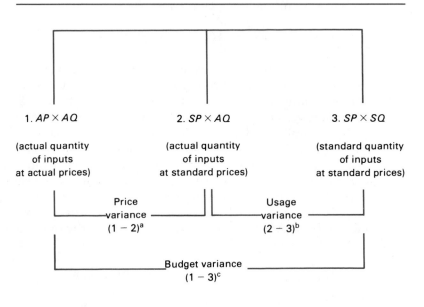

1. $AP \times AQ$ 2. $SP \times AQ$ 3. $SP \times SQ$

(actual quantity   (actual quantity   (standard quantity
of inputs   of inputs   of inputs
at actual prices)   at standard prices)   at standard prices)

Price   Usage
variance   variance
$(1 - 2)^a$ $(2 - 3)^b$

Budget variance
$(1 - 3)^c$

[a]Price variance $= (AP \times AQ) - (SP \times AQ) = (AP - SP)AQ$
[b]Usage variance $= (SP \times AQ) - (SP \times SQ) = (AQ - SQ)SP$
[c]Budget variance $= (AP \times AQ) - (SP \times SQ)$

range, the deviation is likely to be caused by nonrandom factors, either factors that managers can control or factors they cannot control. In the noncontrollable case, managers need to revise the standard.

When to investigate variances is a critical issue. Investigating the cause of variances and taking corrective action, like all activities, have a cost associated with them. As a general principle, an investigation should be undertaken only if the anticipated benefits are greater than the expected costs. Assessing the costs and benefits of a variance investigation is not an easy task, however. A manager must consider whether a variance will recur. If so, the process may be permanently out of control, meaning that periodic savings may be achieved if corrective action is taken. But how can we tell if the variance is going to recur unless an investigation is conducted? And how do we know the cost of corrective action unless the cause of the variance is known?

Because it is difficult to assess the costs and benefits of variance analysis on a case-by-case basis, many firms adopt the general guideline of investigating variances only if they fall outside an acceptable range. They are not investigated unless they are large enough to be of concern. They must be large enough to be caused by something other than random factors and large enough (on average) to justify the costs of investigating and taking corrective action.

control limits

How do managers determine whether variances are significant? How is the acceptable range established? The acceptable range is the standard plus or minus an allowable deviation. The top and bottom measures of the allowable range are called the **control limits**. The *upper control limit* is the standard plus the allowable deviation, and the *lower control limit* is the standard minus the allowable deviation. Current practice sets the control limits subjectively: based on past experience, intuition, and judgment, management determines the allowable deviation from standard.[5]

The control limits are usually expressed both as a percentage of the standard and as an absolute dollar amount. For example, the allowable deviation may be expressed as the lesser of 10 percent of the standard amount, or $10,000. In other words, management will not accept deviations of more than $10,000 even if that deviation is less than 10 percent of the standard. Alternatively, even if the dollar amount is less than $10,000, an investigation is required if the deviation is more than 10 percent of the standard amount.

Formal statistical procedures can also be used to set the control limits. In this way, less subjectivity is involved and a manager can assess the likelihood of the variance being caused by random factors. At this time, the use of such formal procedures has gained little acceptance.[6]

■ VARIANCE ANALYSIS: MATERIALS AND LABOR

The total variance measures the difference between the actual cost of materials and labor and their budgeted costs for the actual level of activity. To illustrate, consider these selected data for Crunchy Chips from the first week of March.[7]

- Actual production: 48,500 bags of corn chips

- Actual corn usage: 750,000 ounces

- Actual price paid per ounce of corn: $0.0069

- Actual hours of inspection: 360 hours

- Actual wage rate: $5.35 per hour

Using the above actual data and the unit standards from Exhibit 15–2, a performance report for the first week of March can be developed (see Exhibit 15–4). As has been mentioned, the total variance can be divided into price

---

[5]Gaumnitz and Kollaritsch, "Manufacturing Variances: Current Practice and Trends," report that about 45–47 percent of the firms use dollar or percentage control limits. Most of the remaining use judgment rather than any formal identification of limits.

[6]According to Gaumnitz and Kollaritsch, "Manufacturing Variances: Current Practice and Trends," only about 1 percent of the responding firms used formal statistical procedures.

[7]To keep the example simple, only one material (corn) and one type of labor (inspection) are illustrated. A complete analysis for the company would include all types of materials and labor categories.

EXHIBIT 15–4
Performance Report: Total Variances

	Actual Costs	Budgeted Costs[a]	Total Variance
Corn	$5,175.00	$5,238.00	$ 63.00 F
Inspection labor	1,926.00	1,697.50	228.50 U

[a]The standard quantities for materials and labor are computed as follows, using unit quantity standards from Exhibit 15–2:

Materials: 18 × 48,500 = 873,000 ounces
Labor: 0.007 × 48,500 = 339.5 hours

Multiplying these standard quantities by the unit standard prices given in Exhibit 15–2 produces the budgeted amounts appearing in this column.

and usage variances, providing more information to the manager. We will do so in the following sections.

Direct Materials Variances

The three-pronged approach illustrated in Exhibit 15–3 can be used to calculate the materials price and usage variances. This calculation for the Crunchy Chips example is illustrated in Exhibit 15–5. Only the price and usage variances for corn are shown. Many find this graphical approach to be easier than the use of variance formulas.

Materials Price Variance: Formula Approach   The materials price variance can be calculated separately. The **materials price variance** (MPV) measures the difference between what should have been paid for raw materials and what was actually paid. A simple formula for computing this variance is

materials price variance

$$MPV = AP \times AQ - SP \times AQ$$

or, factoring, we have

$$MPV = (AP - SP)AQ$$

where AP = The actual per unit price
SP = The standard per unit price
AQ = The actual quantity of material used

Computation of the Materials Price Variance   Crunchy Chips purchased and used 750,000 ounces of yellow corn for the first week of March. The purchase price was $0.0069 per ounce. Thus, AP is $0.0069, AQ is 750,000 ounces, and SP (from Exhibit 15–2) is $0.0060. Using this information, the materials price variance is computed as follows:

EXHIBIT 15–5
Price and Usage Variances: Direct Materials

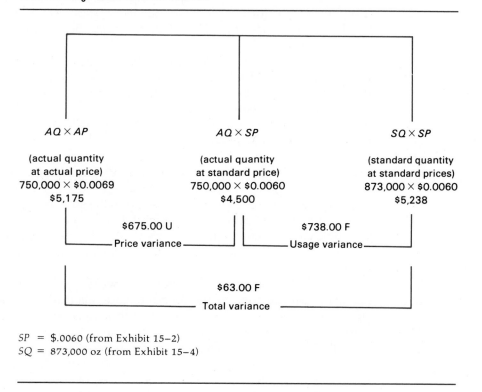

$AQ \times AP$	$AQ \times SP$	$SQ \times SP$
(actual quantity at actual price)	(actual quantity at standard price)	(standard quantity at standard prices)
750,000 × $0.0069	750,000 × $0.0060	873,000 × $0.0060
$5,175	$4,500	$5,238

$675.00 U
— Price variance —

$738.00 F
— Usage variance —

$63.00 F
— Total variance —

SP = $.0060 (from Exhibit 15–2)
SQ = 873,000 oz (from Exhibit 15–4)

$$
\begin{aligned}
MPV &= (AP - SQ)AQ \\
&= (\$0.0069 - \$0.0060)750{,}000 \\
&= \$0.0009 \times 750{,}000 \\
&= \$\ 675\ U
\end{aligned}
$$

Responsibility for the Materials Price Variance   The responsibility for controlling the materials price variance is usually the purchasing agent's. Admittedly, the price of materials is largely beyond his or her control; however, the price variance can be influenced by such factors as quality, quantity discounts, distance of the source from the plant, and so on. These factors are often under the control of the agent.

Using the price variance to evaluate the performance of purchasing has some limitations. Emphasis on meeting or beating standard can produce some undesirable outcomes. For example, if the purchasing agent feels pressured to produce favorable variances, materials of lower quality than desired may be purchased or too much inventory may be acquired to take advantage of quantity discounts.

Analysis of the Materials Price Variance The first step in variance analysis is deciding whether the variance is significant or not. If it is judged to be insignificant, no further steps are needed. Assume that an unfavorable materials price variance of $675 is judged to be significant. The next step is to find out why it occurred.

For the Crunchy Chips example, the investigation revealed that a higher-quality corn was purchased because of a shortage of the usual grade in the market. Once the reason is known, corrective action can be taken if necessary—and possible. In this case, no corrective action is needed. The firm has no control over the supply shortage; it will simply have to wait until market conditions improve.

Timing of the Price Variance Computation The materials price variance can be computed at one of two points: (1) when the raw materials are issued for use in production or (2) when they are purchased. Computing the price variance at the point of purchase is preferable. It is better to have information on variances earlier than later. The more timely the information, the more likely proper managerial action can be taken. Old information is often useless information.

Materials may sit in inventory for weeks or months before they are needed in production. By the time the materials price variance is computed, signaling a problem, it may be too late to take corrective action. Or, even if corrective action is still possible, the delay may cost the company thousands of dollars. For example, suppose a new purchasing agent is unaware of the availability of a quantity discount on a raw material. If the materials price variance that ignores the discount is computed when a new purchase is made, the resulting unfavorable signal would lead to quick corrective action. (In this case, the action would be to use the discount for future purchases.) If the materials price variance is not computed until the material is issued to production, it may be several weeks or even months before the problem is discovered.

If the materials price variance is computed at the point of purchase, then AQ needs to be redefined as the actual quantity of materials *purchased*, rather than actual materials used. Since the materials purchased may differ from the materials used, the overall materials budget variance is not necessarily the sum of the materials price variance and the materials usage variance. When the materials purchased are all used in production for the period in which the variances are calculated, the two variances will equal the total variance.

Recognizing the price variance for materials at the point of purchase also means that the raw materials inventory is carried at standard cost. The journal entry associated with the purchase of raw materials for a standard cost system is illustrated in the Appendix to this chapter.

materials usage variance (*MUV*) | **Direct Materials Usage Variance: Formula Approach** The **materials usage variance** (*MUV*) measures the difference between the direct materials actually used and the direct materials that should have been used for the actual output. The formula for computing this variance is

$$MUV = SP \times AQ - SP \times SQ$$

or, factoring,

$$MUV = (AQ - SQ)SP$$

where AQ = The actual materials used
        SQ = The standard materials allowed for the actual output
        SP = The standard unit price

Computation of the Materials Usage Variance   Crunchy Chips used 750,000 ounces of yellow corn to produce 48,500 bags of corn chips. Therefore, AQ is 750,000. From Exhibit 15–2, we see that SP is $0.006 per ounce of yellow corn. Although standard materials allowed (SQ) has already been computed in Exhibit 15–4, the details underlying the computation need to be reviewed. Recall that SQ is the product of the unit standard and the actual units produced. From Exhibit 15–2, the unit standard calls for eighteen ounces of yellow corn for every bag of corn chips. Thus, SQ is 18 × 48,500, or 873,000 ounces. Thus, the materials usage variance is computed as follows:

$$\begin{aligned} MUV &= (AQ - SQ)SP \\ &= (750,000 - 873,000)(\$0.006) \\ &= \$738 \text{ F} \end{aligned}$$

When materials are issued, the materials quantity variance can be calculated. The accounting for issuance of materials in a standard cost system is illustrated in the Appendix to this chapter.

Responsibility for the Materials Usage Variance   The production manager is generally responsible for materials usage. Minimizing scrap, waste, and rework are all ways in which the manager can ensure that the standard is met. However, at times the cause of the variance is attributable to others outside the production area, as the next section shows.

As with the price variance, using the usage variance to evaluate performance can lead to undesirable behavior. For example, a production manager feeling pressure to produce a favorable variance might allow a defective unit to be transferred to finished goods. While this avoids the problem of wasted materials, it may create customer-relations problems.

Analysis of the Variance   Investigation revealed that the favorable materials usage variance is the result of the higher-quality corn acquired by the Purchasing Department. In this case, the favorable variance is essentially assignable to Purchasing. Since the materials usage variance is favorable—and larger than the unfavorable price variance—the overall result of the change in purchasing is favorable.

If management expects the favorable usage variance to persist, the higher quality of corn should be purchased regularly and the price and quantity standards revised to reflect it. As this example reveals, standards are not static. As improvements in production take place and conditions change, standards may need to be revised to reflect the new operating environment.

Timing of the Computation of the Materials Usage Variance   The materials usage variance should be computed as materials are issued for production. To facilitate this process, many companies use three standard forms: a standard bill of materials, color-coded excessive usage forms, and color-coded

standard bill of
materials returned-materials forms. The **standard bill of materials** identifies the quantity of materials that should be used to produce a predetermined quantity of output. A standard bill of materials for Crunchy Chips is illustrated in Exhibit 15–6.

The standard bill of materials acts as a materials requisition form. The production manager presents this form to the stores area and receives the standard quantity allowed for the indicated output. If the production manager has to return to requisition more materials, the excessive usage form is used. This form, different in color from the standard bill of materials, provides immediate feedback to the production manager that excess raw materials are being used. If, on the other hand, fewer materials are used than the standard requires, the production manager can return the leftover materials, along with the returned-materials form. This form also provides immediate feedback.

Direct Labor Variances

The rate (price) and efficiency (usage) variances for labor can be calculated using either the three-pronged approach of Exhibit 15–3 or a formula approach. The three-pronged calculation is illustrated in Exhibit 15–7 (for inspection at the Crunchy Chips plant). The calculation using formulas is discussed next.

EXHIBIT 15–6
Standard Bill of Materials

Product: 16-ounce bags of corn chips		Output: 48,500 bags
Raw Material	*Unit Standard*	*Total Requirements*
Yellow corn	18 oz	873,000 oz
Cooking Oil	2 oz	97,000 oz
Salt	1 oz	48,500 oz
Lime	0.01 oz	485 oz
Bags	1 bag	48,500 bags

EXHIBIT 15–7
Rate and Efficiency Variances: Direct Labor

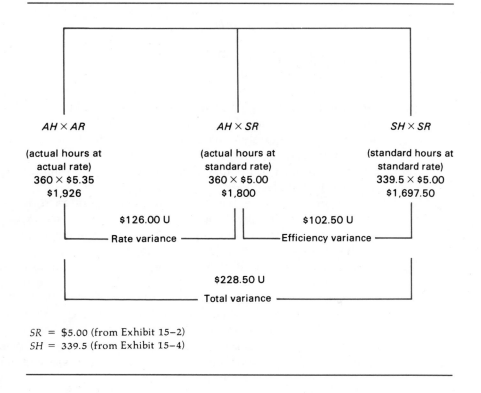

SR = \$5.00 (from Exhibit 15–2)
SH = 339.5 (from Exhibit 15–4)

labor rate variance
(LRV)

Labor Rate Variance: Formula Approach   The **labor rate variance** *(LRV)* computes the difference between what was paid to direct laborers and what should have been paid:

$$LRV = AR \times AH - SR \times AH$$

or, factoring,

$$LRV = (AR - SR)AH$$

where AR = The actual hourly wage rate
        SR = The standard hourly wage rate
        AH = The actual direct labor hours used

Computation of the Labor Rate Variance   Direct labor activity for Crunchy Chips' inspectors will be used to illustrate the computation of the labor rate variance. We know that 360 hours were used for inspection during the first week in March. The actual hourly wage paid for inspection was \$5.35. From

Exhibit 15–2, the standard wage rate is $5.00. Thus, *AH* is 360, *AR* is $5.35, and *SR* is $5.00. The labor rate variance is computed as follows:

$$
\begin{aligned}
LRV &= (AR - SR)AH \\
&= (\$5.35 - \$5.00)360 \\
&= (\$0.35) \times 360 \\
&= \$126 \text{ U}
\end{aligned}
$$

Responsibility for the Labor Rate Variance   Labor rates are largely determined by such external forces as labor markets and union contracts. The actual wage rate rarely departs from the standard rate. When labor rate variances do occur, they usually do so because an average wage rate is used for the rate standard or because more skilled and more highly paid laborers are used for less skilled tasks.

Wage rates for a particular labor activity often differ among workers because of differing levels of seniority. Rather than selecting labor rate standards reflecting those different levels, an average wage rate is often chosen. As the seniority mix changes, the average rate changes. This will give rise to a labor rate variance; it also calls for a new standard to reflect the new seniority mix. Controllability is not assignable for this cause of a labor rate variance.

However, the *use* of labor is controllable by the production manager. The use of more skilled workers to perform less skilled tasks (or vice versa) is a decision that a production manager consciously makes. For this reason, responsibility for the labor rate variance is generally assigned to the individuals who decide how labor will be used.

Analysis of the Labor Rate Variance   If the $126 unfavorable labor rate variance is judged significant, an investigation may be warranted. Assume that an investigation is conducted and that the cause is found to be the use of machine operators, more highly paid and skilled, as inspectors, which occurred because two inspectors quit without formal notice. The corrective action is to hire and train two new inspectors.

labor efficiency variance (*LEV*)   **Labor Efficiency Variance**   The **labor efficiency variance** (*LEV*) measures the difference between the labor hours that were actually used and the labor hours that should have been used:

$$
LEV = AH \times SR - SH \times SR
$$

or, factoring,

$$
LEV = (AH - SH)SR
$$

where   *AH* = The actual direct labor hours used
SH = The standard direct labor hours that should have been used
SR = The standard hourly wage rate

Computation of the Labor Efficiency Variance   Crunchy Chips used 360 direct labor hours for inspection while producing 48,500 bags of corn chips. From Exhibit 15–2, 0.007 hours per bag of chips at a cost of $5 per hour should have been used. The standard hours allowed for inspection or sorting are 339.5 (0.007 × 48,500). Thus, *AH* is 360, *SH* is 339.5, and *SR* is $5. The labor efficiency variance is computed as follows:

$$
\begin{aligned}
LEV &= (AH - SH)SR \\
&= (360 - 339.5) \times (\$5.00) \\
&= 20.5 \times \$5.00 \\
&= \$102.50 \text{ U}
\end{aligned}
$$

Responsibility for the Labor Efficiency Variance   Generally speaking, production managers are responsible for the productive use of direct labor. However, as is true of all variances, once the cause is discovered, responsibility may be assigned elsewhere. For example, frequent breakdowns of machinery may cause interruptions and nonproductive use of labor. But the responsibility for these breakdowns may be faulty maintenance. If so, the maintenance manager should be charged with the unfavorable labor efficiency variance.

Production managers may be tempted to engage in dysfunctional behavior if too much emphasis is placed on the labor efficiency variance. For example, to avoid losing hours and to avoid using additional hours because of possible rework, a production manager could deliberately transfer defective units to finished goods.

Analysis of the Labor Efficiency Variance   The $102.50 unfavorable variance was judged to be significant and its cause was investigated. The investigation revealed that more shutdowns of the process occurred because the duties of the machine operators were split between machine operations and inspection. (Recall that this reassignment was necessary because two inspectors quit unexpectedly.) This resulted in more idle time for inspection. Also, the machine operators were unable to meet the standard output per hour for inspection because of their lack of experience with the sorting process. The corrective action needed to solve the problem is the same as that recommended for the unfavorable rate variance—hire and train two new inspectors.

Sum of *LRV* and *LEV*   From Exhibit 15–7, we know that the total labor variance is $228.50 unfavorable. This total variance is the sum of the unfavorable labor rate variance and the unfavorable labor efficiency variance ($126.00 + $102.50).

■ VARIANCE ANALYSIS: OVERHEAD COSTS

For direct materials and direct labor, total variances are broken down into price and efficiency variances. The total overhead variance—the difference between applied and actual overhead—is also broken down into component variances. How many component variances are computed depends on the method of variance analysis used. We will focus on one method only. First, we will divide overhead into categories: fixed and variable. Next we look at component variances for each category. The total variable overhead variance is divided into two components: the variable overhead spending variance and the variable overhead efficiency variance. Similarly, the total fixed overhead variance is divided into two components: the fixed overhead spending variance and the fixed overhead volume variance.

Variable Overhead Variances

To illustrate the variable overhead variances, we will examine one week of activity for Crunchy Chips Company (for the first week in March). The following data were gathered for this time period:

Variable overhead rate (standard)	$ 3.85/direct labor hour
Actual variable overhead costs	1,600
Actual hours worked	400
Bags of chips produced	48,500
Hours allowed for production	378.3[a]
Applied variable overhead	$1,456.46[b]

[a].0078 × 48,500
[b]$3.85 × 378.3 (overhead is applied using hours allowed in a standard cost system).

Total Variable Overhead Variance   The total variable overhead variance is the difference between the actual and the applied variable overhead. For our example, the total variable overhead variance is computed as follows:

$$\text{Total variance} = \$1,600 - \$1,456.45$$
$$= \$143.55 \text{ U}$$

This total variance can be divided into spending and efficiency variances. This computation is illustrated using a three-pronged approach in Exhibit 15–8.

variable overhead spending variance

Variable Overhead Spending Variance   The **variable overhead spending variance** measures the aggregate effect of differences in the actual variable overhead rate ($AVOR$) and the standard variable overhead rate ($SVOR$). The actual variable overhead rate is simply actual variable overhead divided by actual hours. For our example, this rate is $4 ($1,600/400 hrs). The formula for computing the variable overhead spending variance is given below:

$$\text{Variable overhead spending variance} = (AVOR - SVOR)AH$$
$$= AVOR \times AH - SVOR \times AH$$
$$= \$4 \times 400 - \$3.85 \times 400$$
$$= \$60 \text{ U}$$

EXHIBIT 15–8
Variable Overhead Variances

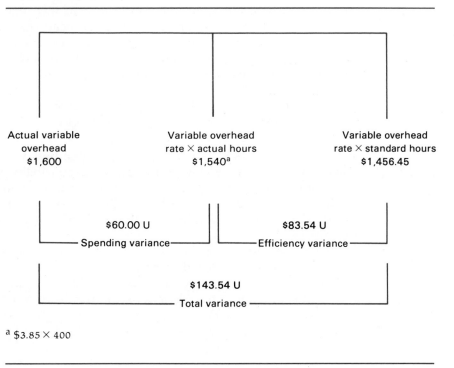

| Actual variable overhead $1,600 | Variable overhead rate × actual hours $1,540[a] | Variable overhead rate × standard hours $1,456.45 |

$60.00 U
— Spending variance —

$83.54 U
— Efficiency variance —

$143.54 U
— Total variance —

[a] $3.85 × 400

Comparison to the Price Variances of Materials and Labor   The variable overhead spending variance is similar but not identical to the price variances of materials and labor; there are some conceptual differences. Variable over-head is not a homogeneous input—it is made up of a large number of indi-vidual items such as indirect materials, indirect labor, electricity, mainte-nance, and so on. The standard variable overhead rate represents the weighted cost per direct labor hour that should be incurred for all variable overhead items. The difference between what should have been spent per hour and what actually was spent per hour is a type of price variance.

A variable overhead spending variance can arise because prices for in-dividual variable overhead items have increased or decreased. Assume, for the moment, that the price changes of individual overhead items are the only cause of the spending variance. If the spending variance is unfavorable, then price increases for individual variable overhead items are the cause; if the spending variance is favorable, then price decreases are dominating.

If the only source of the variable overhead spending variance were price changes, then it would be completely analogous to the price variances of materials and labor. Unfortunately, the spending variance also is affected by how efficiently overhead is used. Waste or inefficiency in the use of variable overhead increases the actual variable overhead cost. This increased cost, in turn, is reflected in an increased actual variable overhead rate. Thus, even if the actual prices of the individual overhead items were equal to the budgeted or standard prices, an unfavorable variable overhead spending variance could still take place. Similarly, efficiency can decrease the actual variable overhead cost and decrease the actual variable overhead rate. Efficient use of variable overhead items contributes to a favorable spending variance. If the waste effect dominates, then the net contribution will be unfavorable; if efficiency dominates, then the net contribution is favorable. Thus, the variable overhead spending variance is the result of both price and efficiency.

Responsibility for the Variable Overhead Spending Variance   Many variable overhead items are affected by several responsibility centers. For example, utilities are a joint cost.[8] To the extent that consumption of variable overhead can be traced to a responsibility center, responsibility can be assigned. Consumption of indirect materials is an example of a traceable variable overhead cost.

Controllability is a prerequisite for assigning responsibility. Price changes of variable overhead items are essentially beyond the control of supervisors. If price changes are small (as they often are), the spending variance is primarily a matter of the efficient use of overhead in production, which is controllable by production supervisors. Accordingly, responsibility for the variable overhead spending variance is generally assigned to production departments.

Analysis of the Variable Overhead Spending Variance   The $60 unfavorable variance simply reveals that, in the aggregate, Crunchy Chips spent more on variable overhead than expected. Even if the variance were insignificant, it reveals nothing about how well costs of individual variable overhead items were controlled. Control of variable overhead requires line-by-line analysis for each individual item. Exhibit 15–9 presents a performance report that supplies the line-by-line information essential for proper control of variable overhead.

From Exhibit 15–9, it is clear that two of the three items present no control problems for the firm. Electricity is the only item showing an unfavorable variance; in fact, it is the cause of the overall variable overhead spending variance. If the variance is significant, an investigation may be warranted. This investigation may reveal that the power company raised the price of electricity. If so, the cause of the variance is beyond the control of the company. The correct response is to revise the budget formula to reflect the increased cost of electricity. However, if the price of electricity has remained

---

[8]If a company installs meters to measure consumption of utilities for each responsibility center, responsibility can be assigned. However, the cost of assigning responsibility can sometimes exceed any potential benefit. The alternative is allocation. Unfortunately, allocations can be arbitrary, and it is often difficult to identify accurately the amount actually consumed.

EXHIBIT 15-9

Crunchy Chips, Inc.				
Performance Report for the Week Ended March 8, 1993				
	Cost Formula[a]	*Actual Costs*	*Budget*[b]	*Spending Variance*
Gas	$3.00	$1,190.00	$1,200.00	$10.00 F
Electricity	0.78	385.00	312.00	73.00 U
Water	0.07	25.00	28.00	3.00 F
Total cost	$3.85	$1,600.00	$1,540.00	$60.00 U

[a]Per direct labor hour
[b]The budget allowance is computed using the cost formula and an activity level of 400 actual direct labor hours.

unchanged, then the usage of electricity is greater than expected. For example, the company may find that there were more startups and shutdowns of machinery than normal, causing an increased consumption of electricity.

variable overhead efficiency variance

Variable Overhead Efficiency Variance   Variable overhead is assumed to vary as the production volume changes. Thus, variable overhead changes in proportion to changes in the direct labor hours used. The **variable overhead efficiency variance** measures the change in variable overhead consumption that occurs because of efficient (or inefficient) use of direct labor. The efficiency variance is computed using the following formula:

$$\text{Variable overhead efficiency variance} = (AH - SH)SVOR$$
$$= (400 - 378.3)\$3.85$$
$$= \$83.55 \text{ U}$$

Responsibility for the Variable Overhead Efficiency Variance   The variable overhead efficiency variance is directly related to the direct labor efficiency or usage variance. If variable overhead is truly proportional to direct labor consumption, then like the labor usage variance, the variable overhead efficiency variance is caused by efficient or inefficient use of direct labor. If more (or fewer) direct labor hours are used than the standard calls for, then the total variable overhead cost will increase (or decrease). The validity of the measure depends on the validity of the relationship between variable overhead costs and direct labor hours. In other words, do variable overhead costs *really* change in proportion to changes in direct labor hours? If so, responsibility for the variable overhead efficiency variance should be assigned to the individual who has responsibility for the use of direct labor: the production manager.

Analysis of the Variable Overhead Efficiency Variance   The reasons for the unfavorable variable overhead efficiency variance are the same as those offered for the unfavorable labor usage variance. More hours were used than the standard called for because of excessive idle time for inspectors and because the machine operators used as substitute inspectors were inexperienced in sorting.

More information concerning the effect of labor usage on variable overhead is available in a line-by-line analysis of individual variable overhead items. This can be accomplished by comparing the budget allowance for the actual hours used with the budget allowance for the standard hours allowed for each item. A performance report that makes this comparison for all variable overhead costs is shown in Exhibit 15–10.

From Exhibit 15–10, we can see that the cost of gas is affected most by inefficient use of labor. This can be explained by the need to keep the cooking oil hot (assuming gas is used for cooking) even though the cooking process is slowed down by the subsequent sorting process.

The column labeled *Budget for Standard Hours* gives the amount that should have been spent on variable overhead for the actual output. The total of all items in this column is the applied variable overhead, the amount assigned to production in a standard cost system. Note that in a standard cost system, variable overhead is applied using the hours allowed for the actual output *(SH)*, while in normal costing, variable overhead is applied using actual hours (see Chapter 3). Although not shown in Exhibit 15–10, the difference between actual costs and this column is the total variable overhead variance (underapplied by $143.55). Thus, the underapplied variable overhead variance is the sum of the spending and efficiency variances.

EXHIBIT 15–10

			Crunchy Chips, Inc.			
			Performance Report			
			For the Week Ended March 8, 1993			
			Budget for		*Budget for*	
	Cost	*Actual*	*Actual*	*Spending*	*Standard*	*Efficiency*
Cost	*Formula*[a]	*Costs*	*Hours*	*Variance*[b]	*Hours*	*Variance*[c]
Gas	$3.00	$1,190.00	$1,200.00	$10.00 F	$1,134.90	$65.10 U
Electricity	0.78	385.00	312.00	73.00 U	295.07	16.93 U
Water	0.07	25.00	28.00	3.00 F	26.48	1.52 U
Total cost	$3.85	$1,600.00	$1,540.00	$60.00 U	$1,456.45	$83.55 U

[a]Per direct labor hour
[b]Spending variance = Actual costs − Budget for actual hours
[c]Efficiency variance = Budget for actual hours − Budget for standard hours

Fixed Overhead Variances

We will again use the Crunchy Chips example to illustrate the computation of the fixed overhead variances. The data needed for the example are given below:

Budgeted/Planned Items:

Budgeted fixed overhead	$ 749,970
Expected activity	23,400 direct labor hours[a]
Standard fixed overhead rate	$32.05[b]

---

[a]Hours allowed to produce 3,000,000 bags of chips: $0.0078 \times 3,000,000$
[b]$749,970/23,400$

Actual Results:

Actual production	2,750,000 bags of chips
Actual fixed overhead cost	$749,000
Standard hours allowed for actual production	21,450[a]

---

[a]$0.0078 \times 2,750,000$

Total Fixed Overhead Variance   The total fixed overhead variance is the difference between actual fixed overhead and applied fixed overhead, when applied fixed overhead is obtained by multiplying the standard fixed overhead rate times the standard hours allowed for the actual output. Thus, the applied fixed overhead is

$$\text{Applied fixed overhead} = \text{Standard fixed overhead rate} \times \text{Standard hours}$$
$$= \$32.05 \times 21,450$$
$$= \$687,473 \text{ (rounded)}$$

The total fixed overhead variance is the difference between the actual fixed overhead and the applied fixed overhead:

$$\text{Total fixed overhead variance} = \$749,000 - \$687,473$$
$$= \$61,527 \text{ Underapplied}$$

To help managers understand why fixed overhead was underapplied by $61,527, the total variance can be broken into two variances: the fixed overhead spending variance and the fixed overhead volume variance. The calculation of the two variances is illustrated in Exhibit 15–11.

fixed overhead spending variance

The Fixed Overhead Spending Variance   The **fixed overhead spending variance** is defined as the difference between the actual fixed overhead and the budgeted fixed overhead. The spending variance is favorable because less was spent on fixed overhead items than was budgeted.

EXHIBIT 15-11
Fixed Overhead Variances

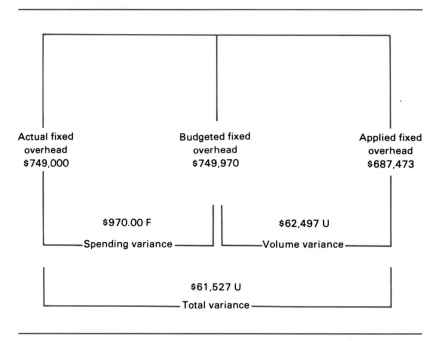

Responsibility for the Spending Variance   Fixed overhead is made up of a number of individual items such as salaries, depreciation, taxes, and insurance. Many fixed overhead items—long-run investments, for instance—are not subject to change in the short run; consequently, fixed overhead costs are often beyond the immediate control of management. Since many fixed overhead costs are affected primarily by long-run decisions, not by changes in production levels, the budget variance is usually small. For example, depreciation, salaries, taxes, and insurance costs are not likely to be much different than planned.

Analysis of the Spending Variance   Because fixed overhead is made up of many individual items, a line-by-line comparison of budgeted costs with actual costs provides more information concerning the causes of the spending variance. Exhibit 15–12 provides such a report. The report reveals that the fixed overhead spending variance is essentially in line with expectations. The fixed overhead spending variances, both on a line-item basis and in the aggregate, are relatively small.

fixed overhead volume variance   **Fixed Overhead Volume Variance**   The **fixed overhead volume variance** is the difference between budgeted fixed overhead and applied fixed overhead. The volume variance measures the effect of the actual output departing from

EXHIBIT 15–12

	Crunchy Chips, Inc.		
	Performance Report for the Year Ended 1993		
Fixed Overhead Items	*Actual Cost*	*Budgeted Cost*	*Variance*
Depreciation	$530,000.00	$530,000.00	$ —
Salaries	159,370.00	159,970.00	600.00 F
Taxes	50,500.00	50,000.00	500.00 U
Insurance	9,130.00	10,000.00	870.00 F
Total fixed	$749,000.00	$749,970.00	$970.00 F

the output used at the beginning of the year to compute the predetermined standard fixed overhead rate. To see this, let $SH(D)$ represent the standard hours allowed for the denominator volume (the volume used at the beginning of the year to compute the predetermined fixed overhead rate). The standard fixed overhead rate is computed in the following way:

$$\text{Standard fixed overhead rate} = (\text{Budgeted fixed overhead})/SH(D)$$

From this equation, we know that the budgeted fixed overhead can be computed by multiplying the standard fixed overhead rate by the denominator hours (Budgeted fixed overhead = Standard fixed overhead rate $\times$ $SH(D)$). From Exhibit 15–11, we know that the volume variance can be computed as follows:

$$
\begin{aligned}
\text{Volume variance} &= \text{Budgeted fixed overhead} - \text{Applied fixed overhead} \\
&= \text{Standard fixed overhead rate} \times SH(D) \\
&\quad - \text{Standard fixed overhead rate} \times SH \\
&= \text{Standard fixed overhead rate} \times (SH(D) - SH) \\
&= \$32.05(23,400 - 21,450) \\
&= \$62,497 \text{ U (rounded down)}
\end{aligned}
$$

Thus, for a volume variance to occur, the denominator hours, $SH(D)$, must differ from the standard hours allowed for the actual volume, SH. At the beginning of the year, Crunchy expected to produce 3,000,000 bags of chips, using 23,400 direct labor hours. The actual outcome was 2,750,000 bags produced, using 21,450 standard hours. Thus, less was produced than expected and an unfavorable volume variance arises.

But what is the meaning of this variance? The variance occurs because the actual output differs from predicted output volume. At the beginning of the year, if management had used 2.75 million bags of corn chips as the denominator volume, the volume variance would not have existed. In this view, the volume variance is seen as prediction error—a measure of the inability of management to select the correct volume over which to spread fixed overhead.

If, however, the denominator volume represented the amount that management believed *could* be produced and sold, the volume variance conveys more significant information. If the actual volume is less than the denominator volume, the volume variance signals management that a loss has occurred. That loss is not equivalent, however, to the dollar value of the volume variance. The loss is equal to the lost contribution margin on the units that were not produced and sold. However, the volume variance is positively correlated with the loss. For example, suppose that the contribution margin per standard direct labor hour is $40. By producing only 2.75 million bags of chips instead of 3 million bags, the company lost sales of 250,000 bags. This is equivalent to 1,950 hours ($0.0078 \times 250,000$). At $40 per hour, the loss is $78,000. The unfavorable volume variance of $62,497 signals this loss but understates it. In this sense, the volume variance is a measure of utilization of capacity.

Responsibility for the Volume Variance   Assuming that volume variance measures capacity utilization implies that the general responsibility for this variance should be assigned to the Production Department. At times, however, investigation into the reasons for a significant volume variance may reveal the cause to be factors beyond the control of production. In this instance, specific responsibility may be assigned elsewhere. For example, if Purchasing acquires a raw material of lower quality than usual, significant rework time may result, causing lower production and an unfavorable volume variance. In this case, responsibility for the variance rests with Purchasing, not Production.

▪ SUMMARY OF LEARNING OBJECTIVES

1. Identify what standard costs are and distinguish between an actual cost system, a normal cost system, and a standard cost system. A standard cost system budgets quantities and costs on a unit basis. These unit budgets are for labor, material, and overhead. Standard costs, therefore, are the amount that should be expended to produce a product or service. Normal cost systems, on the other hand, budget overhead costs on a unit basis. Actual labor and material costs are assigned to products, but a predetermined overhead rate is used for overhead assignment. In an actual cost system, only actual costs are assigned to products.

2. Explain how standards are set and distinguish between currently attainable and ideal standards. Standards are set using historical experience, engineering studies, and input from operating personnel, marketing, and accounting. Currently attainable standards are those that can be achieved under efficient operating conditions. Ideal standards are those achievable under maximum efficiency—under ideal operating conditions.

3. Explain why standard cost systems are adopted. Standard cost systems are adopted to improve planning and control and to facilitate product costing. By comparing actual outcomes with standards, and breaking the variance into price and quantity components, detailed feedback is provided to managers. This information allows managers to exercise a greater degree of cost control than that found in a normal or actual cost system. Decisions such as bidding are also made easier when a standard cost system is in place.

4. Explain when variances should be investigated and when corrective action should be taken. Variances should be investigated if they are material and if the benefits of corrective action are greater than the costs of investigation. Because of the difficulty to assess cost and benefits on a case-by-case basis, many firms set up formal control limits—either a dollar amount, a percentage, or both. Others use judgment to assess the need to investigate.

5. Compute the materials price and usage variances and explain how they are used for control. The materials price and usage variances are computed using either a three-pronged approach or formulas. The three-pronged approach for materials is illustrated in Exhibit 15–5. The materials price variance is the difference between what should have been paid for materials and what was paid (generally associated with the purchasing activity). The materials usage variance is the difference in the cost of the materials that should have been used and the amount that was used (generally associated with the production activity). When a significant variance is signaled, an investigation occurs to find the cause. Corrective action is taken, if possible, to put the system back in control.

6. Compute the labor rate and efficiency variances and explain how they are used for control. The labor variances are computed using either a three-pronged approach or formulas. The three-pronged approach for labor is illustrated in Exhibit 15–7. The labor rate variance is caused by the actual wage rate differing from the standard wage rate. It is the difference in the wages that were paid and those that should have been paid. The labor efficiency variance is the difference in the cost of the labor that was used and the cost of the labor that should have been used. When a significant variance is signaled, investigation is called for and corrective action should be taken, if possible, to put the system back in control.

7. Compute the fixed overhead spending and volume variances and explain their meanings. The fixed overhead spending variance is the difference between the actual fixed overhead costs and the budgeted fixed overhead costs. Therefore, it is simply a budget variance. The volume variance is the difference between the budgeted fixed overhead and the applied fixed overhead. It occurs whenever the actual production volume is different from the expected production volume and, thus, is a measure of capacity utilization.

8. **Compute the variable overhead spending and efficiency variances and explain their meanings.** The variable overhead spending variance is the difference between the actual variable overhead cost and the budgeted variable overhead cost for actual hours worked. It therefore is a budget variance, resulting from price changes and efficient or inefficient use of variable overhead inputs. The variable efficiency variance is the difference between budgeted variable overhead at actual hours and applied variable overhead. It is strictly attributable to the efficiency of labor usage and assumes that the variable overhead items are all driven by direct labor hours.

■ KEY TERMS

Control limits   The maximum allowable deviation from a standard. (p. 745)

Currently attainable standard   A standard that reflects an efficient operating state; it is rigorous but achievable. (p. 738)

Efficiency variance   The difference between standard quantities and actual quantities multiplied by standard price. (p. 743)

Favorable variance   A variance produced whenever the actual amounts are less than the budgeted or standard allowances. (p. 743)

Fixed overhead spending variance   The difference between actual fixed overhead and applied fixed overhead. (p. 759)

Fixed overhead volume variance   The difference between budgeted fixed overhead and applied fixed overhead; it is a measure of capacity utilization. (p. 760)

Ideal standard   Standards that reflect perfect operating conditions. (p. 738)

Labor efficiency variance   The difference between the actual direct labor hours used and the standard direct labor hours allowed multiplied by the standard hourly wage rate. (p. 752)

Labor rate variance   The difference between the actual hourly rate paid and the standard hourly rate multiplied by the actual hours worked. (p. 751)

Materials price variance   The difference between the actual price paid per unit of materials and the standard price allowed per unit multiplied by the actual quantity of materials purchased. (p. 746)

Materials usage variance   The difference between the direct materials actually used and the direct materials allowed for the actual output multiplied by the standard price. (p. 748)

Price standard   The price that should be paid per unit of input. (p. 737)

Price variance   The difference between standard price and actual price multiplied by the actual quantity of inputs used. (p. 743)

Quantity standard   The quantity of input allowed per unit of output. (p. 737)

Standard bill of materials   A listing of the type and quantity of materials allowed for a given level of output. (p. 750)

Standard cost per unit   The per-unit cost that should be achieved given materials, labor, and overhead standards. (p. 740)

Standard cost sheet A listing of the standard costs and standard quantities of direct materials, direct labor, and overhead that should apply to a single product. (p. 740)

Standard hours allowed The direct labor hours that should have been used to produce the actual output (Unit labor standard × Actual output). (p. 742)

Standard quantity of materials allowed The quantity of materials that should have been used to produce the actual output (Unit materials standard × Actual output). (p. 742)

Total budget variance The difference between the actual cost of an input and its planned cost. (p. 743)

Unfavorable variance A variance produced whenever the actual input amounts are greater than the budgeted or standard allowances. (p. 743)

Variable overhead efficiency variance The difference between the actual direct labor hours used and the standard hours allowed multiplied by the standard variable overhead rate. (p. 757)

Variable overhead spending variance The difference between the actual variable overhead and the budgeted variable overhead based on actual hours used to produce the actual output. (p. 754)

■ REVIEW PROBLEM

Wangsgard Manufacturing has the following standard cost sheet for one of its products:

Direct materials (2 feet @ $5)	$10
Direct labor (0.5 hrs @ $10)	5
Fixed overhead (0.5 hrs @ $2[a])	1
Variable overhead (0.5 hrs @ $4)	2
Standard unit cost	$18

[a]Rate based on expected activity of 2,500 hours

During the most recent year, the following actual results were recorded:

Production	6,000 units
Fixed overhead	$ 6,000
Variable overhead	10,500
Direct materials (11,750 ft purchased and used)	61,100
Direct labor (2,900 hrs)	29,580

Required:

Compute the following variances:

1. Materials price and usage variances
2. Labor rate and efficiency variances
3. Fixed overhead spending and volume variances
4. Variable overhead spending and efficiency variances

Solution:

1. Material variances:

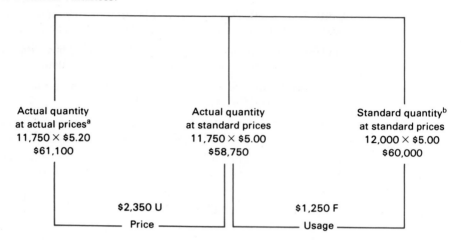

Actual quantity at actual prices[a]
11,750 × $5.20
$61,100

Actual quantity at standard prices
11,750 × $5.00
$58,750

Standard quantity[b] at standard prices
12,000 × $5.00
$60,000

$2,350 U
Price

$1,250 F
Usage

[a] $61,100/11,750 = $5.20 = Actual price
[b] 2 × 6,000

Or, using formulas

$$MPV = (AP - SP)AQ$$
$$= (\$5.20 - \$5.00)11,750$$
$$= \$2,350 \text{ U}$$

$$MUV = (AQ - SQ)SP$$
$$= (11,750 - 12,000)\$5.00$$
$$= \$1,250 \text{ F}$$

2. Labor variances:

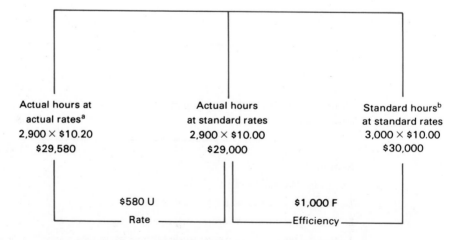

Actual hours at actual rates[a]
2,900 × $10.20
$29,580

Actual hours at standard rates
2,900 × $10.00
$29,000

Standard hours[b] at standard rates
3,000 × $10.00
$30,000

$580 U
Rate

$1,000 F
Efficiency

[a] $29,580/2,900 = $10.20 = Actual price
[b] 0.5 × 6,000 = 3,000 = Standard hours

Or, using formulas:

$$LRV = (AR - SR)AH$$
$$= (\$10.20 - \$10.00)2,900$$
$$= \$580 \text{ U}$$

$$LEV = (AH - SH)SR$$
$$= (2,900 - 3,000)\$10.00$$
$$= \$1,000 \text{ F}$$

3. Fixed overhead variances:

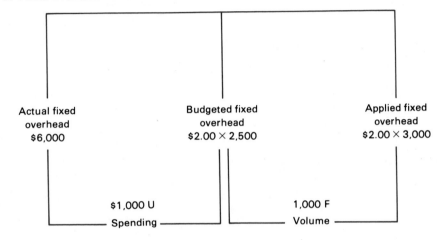

Actual fixed	Budgeted fixed	Applied fixed
overhead	overhead	overhead
$6,000	$2.00 × 2,500	$2.00 × 3,000

$1,000 U — Spending —   1,000 F — Volume —

4. Variable overhead variances:

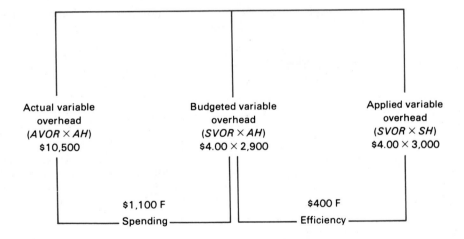

Actual variable	Budgeted variable	Applied variable
overhead	overhead	overhead
(AVOR × AH)	(SVOR × AH)	(SVOR × SH)
$10,500	$4.00 × 2,900	$4.00 × 3,000

$1,100 F — Spending — $400 F — Efficiency —

■ APPENDIX: ACCOUNTING FOR VARIANCES

To illustrate recording variances, we will assume that the materials price variance is computed at the time materials are purchased. With this assumption, we can state a general rule for a firm's inventory accounts: all inventories are carried at standard cost. Actual costs are never entered into an inventory account. In recording variances, unfavorable variances are always debits and favorable variances are always credits.

Entries for Direct Materials Variances

Materials Price Variance   The entry to record the purchase of materials is given below (assuming an unfavorable *MPV* and that *AQ* is materials purchased).

Materials	$SP \times AQ$	
Materials Price Variance	$(AP - SP)AQ$	
Accounts Payable		$AP \times AQ$

For example, if *AP* is $10, *SP* is $9.50, and 1,000 units are purchased, the entry would be

Materials	9,500.00	
Materials Price Variance	500.00	
Accounts Payable		10,000.00

Notice that the raw materials are carried in the inventory account at standard cost.

Materials Usage Variance   The general form for the entry to record the issuance and usage of materials, assuming a *favorable MUV*, is as follows:

Work in Process	$SQ \times SP$	
Materials Usage Variance		$(AQ - SQ)SP$
Materials		$AQ \times SP$

Here *AQ* is the materials issued and used, not necessarily equal to the materials purchased. Notice that only standard quantities and standard prices are used to assign costs to Work in Process; no actual costs enter this account.
    For example, if *AQ* is 875, *SQ* is 900, and *SP* is $9.50, then the entry would be

Work in Process	8,550.00	
Materials Usage Variance		237.50
Materials		8,312.50

Notice that the favorable usage variance appears as a credit entry.

Entries for Direct Labor Variances

Unlike the materials variances, the entry to record both types of labor variances is made simultaneously. The general form of this entry is given below (assuming a favorable labor rate variance and an unfavorable labor efficiency variance).

Work in Process	$SH \times SR$	
Labor Efficiency Variance	$(AH - SH)SR$	
Labor Rate Variance		$(AR - SR)AH$
Accrued Payroll		$AH \times AR$

Again notice that only standard hours and standard rates are used to assign costs to Work in Process. Actual prices or quantities are not used.

To give a specific example, assume that AH is 1,850, SH is 1,800, AR is $7.40, and SR is $7.70. The following general ledger entry would be made:

Work in Process	13,860.00	
Labor Efficiency Variance	385.00	
Labor Rate Variance		555.00
Accrued Payroll		13,690.00

Disposition of Material and Labor Variances

At the end of the year, the variances for materials and labor are usually closed to Cost of Goods Sold. (This practice is acceptable provided that variances are not material in amount.) Using the above data, the entries would take the following form:

Cost of Goods Sold	885.00	
Materials Price Variance		500.00
Labor Efficiency Variance		385.00
Materials Usage Variance	237.50	
Labor Rate Variance	555.00	
Cost of Goods Sold		792.50

If the variances are material, they must be prorated among various accounts. For the materials price variance, it is prorated among Materials Inventory, Materials Usage Variance, Work in Process, and Cost of Goods Sold. The remaining materials and labor variances are prorated among Work in Process, Finished Goods, and Cost of Goods Sold. Typically, materials variances are prorated on the basis of the materials balances in each of these accounts and the labor variances on the basis of the labor balances in the accounts.

Overhead Variances

Although overhead variances can be recorded following a pattern similar to that described for labor and materials, these variances are more generally treated as part of a periodic overhead analysis. Applied overhead is accumulated in the applied accounts, and actual overhead is accumulated in the control accounts. Periodically (e.g., monthly), performance reports that provide overhead variance information are prepared. At the end of the year, the applied accounts and control accounts are closed out and the variances isolated. The overhead variances are then disposed of by closing them to Cost of Goods Sold if they are not material, or by prorating them among Work in Process, Finished Goods, and Cost of Goods Sold if they are material.

■ QUESTIONS

1   Discuss the difference between budgets and standard costs.

2   Describe the relationship that unit standards have with flexible budgeting.

3   What is the quantity decision? The pricing decision?

4   Why is historical experience often a poor basis for establishing standards?

5   Should standards be set by engineering studies? Why or why not?

6   What are ideal standards? Currently attainable standards? Of the two, which is usually adopted? Why?

7   How does standard costing improve the control function?

8   Discuss the differences between actual costing, normal costing, and standard costing.

9   What is the purpose of a standard cost sheet?

10   The budget variance for variable production costs is broken down into quantity and price variances. Explain why the quantity variance is more useful for control purposes than the price variance.

11   Explain why the materials price variance is often computed at the point of purchase rather than at the point of issuance.

12   The materials usage variance is always the responsibility of the production supervisor. Do you agree or disagree? Why?

13   The labor rate variance is never controllable. Do you agree or disagree? Why?

14   Suggest some possible causes of an unfavorable labor efficiency variance.

15   Explain why the variable overhead spending variance is not a pure price variance.

16   The variable overhead efficiency variance has nothing to do with efficient use of variable overhead. Do you agree or disagree? Why?

17   Explain why the fixed overhead spending variance is usually very small.

18   What is the cause of an unfavorable volume variance? Does the volume variance convey any meaningful information to managers?

19   When should a standard cost variance be investigated?

20 What are control limits and how are they set?

21 Which do you think is more important for control of fixed overhead costs: the spending variance or the volume variance? Explain.

22 Explain why standard cost systems are adopted.

■ EXERCISES

E15–1 **Setting Standards and Assigning Responsibility** Associated Media Graphics (AMG) is a rapidly expanding company involved in the mass reproduction of instructional materials. Ralph Boston, owner and manager of AMG, has made a concerted effort to provide a quality product at a fair price with delivery on the promised due date. Expanding sales have been attributed to this philosophy. As the business grows, however, Boston is finding it increasingly difficult to supervise personally the operations of AMG. As a result, he is beginning to institute an organizational structure that would facilitate management control.

One recent change was to designate the operating departments as cost centers, with control over departmental operations transferred from Boston to each departmental manager. However, quality control still reports directly to Boston, as do the finance and accounting functions. A materials manager was hired to purchase all raw materials and oversee inventory handling (receiving, storage, and so on) and record-keeping. The materials manager is also responsible for maintaining an adequate inventory based upon planned production levels.

The loss of personal control over the operations of AMG caused Boston to look for a method to evaluate performance efficiently. Dave Cress, a new cost accountant, proposed the use of a standard cost system. Variances for material, labor, and overhead could then be calculated and reported directly to Boston.

Required:

1. Assume that AMG is going to implement a standard cost system and establish standards for materials, labor, and overhead.
   a. Who should be involved in setting the standards for each cost component?
   b. What factors should be considered in establishing the standards for each cost component?
2. Describe the basis for assignment of responsibility under a standard cost system.

(CMA adapted)

E15–2 **Computation of Inputs Allowed; Materials and Labor** During the year, Kindle Company produced 45,800 units of a machine tool. Kindle's material and labor standards are

Direct materials (5 lbs @ 0.80)	$4.00
Direct labor (0.2 hrs @ $10.50)	2.10

Required:

1. Compute the standard hours allowed for the production of 45,800 units.
2. Compute the standard pounds of materials allowed for the production of 45,800 units.

E15–3   **Materials and Labor Variances**   Riche Company produces a popular frozen dessert, which is sold in half gallons. Recently the company adopted the following standards for one half gallon of the frozen dessert:

Direct materials (70 oz @ $0.008)	$0.56
Direct labor (0.1 hrs @ $8.60)	0.86
Standard prime cost	$1.42

During the first week of operation, the company experienced the following actual results:

a. Half gallon units produced: 5,000.

b. Ounces of materials purchased: 370,000 ounces at $0.0085.

c. There are no beginning or ending inventories of raw materials.

d. Direct labor: 490 hours at $8.60.

Required:

1. Compute price and usage variances for direct materials.

2. Compute the rate variance and the efficiency variance for direct labor.

E15–4   **Overhead Variances**   Benson, Inc., has gathered the following data on last year's operations:

a. Units produced: 25,000

b. Direct labor: 20,000 hours @ $10

c. Actual fixed overhead: $230,000

d. Actual variable overhead: $80,000

Benson employs a standard cost system. During the year, the following rates were used: standard fixed overhead rate, $10 per hour; standard variable overhead rate, $4.05 per hour. The labor standard requires 0.75 hours per unit produced. (These rates were based on a standard normal volume of 22,500 direct labor hours.)

Required:

1. Compute the fixed overhead spending and volume variances.

2. Compute the variable overhead spending and efficiency variances.

E15–5   **Decomposition of Budget Variances; Materials and Labor**   Footewear Corporation produces leather boots. The company uses a standard cost system and has set the following standards for materials and labor (for one pair of boots):

Leather (3 strips @ $10)	$30
Direct labor (2 hrs @ $12)	24
Total prime cost	$54

During the year, Footewear produced 2,000 pairs of leather boots. The actual leather purchased was 6,200 strips at $9.96 per strip. There were no beginning or ending inventories of leather. Actual direct labor was 4,200 hours @ $12.50.

Required:

1. Compute the costs of leather and direct labor that should have been incurred for the production of 2,000 pairs of boots.
2. Compute the total budget variances for material and labor.
3. Break the total variance for materials into a price variance and a usage variance.
4. Break the total variance for labor into a rate variance and an efficiency variance.

E15–6   **Materials and Labor Variances; Journal Entries**   Inglestin Products produces instructional aids. Among the company's products are "white boards," which use colored markers instead of chalk. They are particularly popular for conference rooms in educational institutions and executive offices of large corporations. The standard cost of materials and labor for this product is given below.

Direct materials:	10 lbs @ $8.25
Direct labor:	3.5 hrs @ $9.65

During the first month of the year, 3,200 boards were produced. Information concerning actual costs and usage of materials and labor is given below.

Materials purchased:	36,000 lbs @ $8.35
Material used:	31,800 lbs
Direct labor:	11,520 hrs; total cost: $112,896

Required:

1. Compute the materials price and usage variances.
2. Compute the labor rate and efficiency variances.
3. Prepare journal entries for all activity relating to materials and labor for the month.

E15–7   **Overhead Application; Overhead Variances**   Glawson Metal Works is planning to produce 300,000 units for the coming year. Each unit requires three standard hours of labor for completion. The company uses direct labor hours to assign overhead to products. The total overhead budgeted for the coming year is $1,350,000, and the standard fixed overhead rate is $1.50 per unit produced. Actual results for the year are given below.

Actual production (units)	295,000
Actual direct labor hours	920,000
Actual variable overhead	$900,000
Actual fixed overhead	460,000

Required:

1. Compute the applied fixed overhead.
2. Compute the fixed overhead spending and volume variances.
3. Compute the applied variable overhead.
4. Compute the variable overhead spending and efficiency variances.

E15–8   **Investigation of Variances**   Underwood Company uses the following rule to determine whether material usage variances ought to be investigated. A materials usage variance will be investigated anytime the amount exceeds the lesser of $8,000 or 10 percent of the standard cost. Reports for the past five weeks provided the following information:

Week	MUV	Standard Materials Cost
1	$7,000 F	$80,000
2	7,800 U	75,000
3	6,000 F	80,000
4	9,000 U	85,000
5	7,000 U	69,000

Required:

1. Using the rule provided, identify the cases that will be investigated.

2. Suppose that investigation reveals that the cause of an unfavorable materials usage variance is the use of lower-quality materials than are usually used. Who is responsible? What corrective action would likely be taken?

3. Suppose that investigation reveals that the cause of a significant unfavorable materials usage variance is attributable to a new approach to manufacturing that takes less labor time but causes more material waste. Upon examining the labor efficiency variance, it is discovered that it is favorable and is larger than the unfavorable materials usage variance. Who is responsible? What action should be taken?

E15–9   **Overhead Application; Overhead Variances; Journal Entries**   Eureka Company uses a standard cost system. The direct labor standard indicates that four direct labor hours should be used for every unit produced. Eureka produces one product. The normal production volume is 120,000 units of this product. The budgeted overhead for the coming year (1993) is given below.

Fixed overhead	$1,286,400
Variable overhead	888,000[a]

[a]At normal volume

Eureka applies overhead on the basis of direct labor hours.

During 1993, Eureka produced 119,000 units, worked 487,900 direct labor hours, and incurred actual fixed overhead costs of $1.3 million and actual variable overhead costs of $927,010.

Required:

1. Calculate the standard fixed overhead rate and the standard variable overhead rate.

2. Compute the applied fixed overhead and the applied variable overhead. What is the total fixed overhead variance? Total variable overhead variance?

3. Break the total fixed overhead variance into a spending variance and a volume variance. Discuss the significance of each.

4. Compute the variable overhead spending and efficiency variances. Discuss the significance of each.

5. Prepare the journal entries that would be related to fixed and variable overhead at the end of the year. Assume variances are closed to Cost of Goods Sold.

E15–10 **Materials, Labor, and Overhead Variances** At the beginning of 1992, Littleman Company had the following standard cost sheet for one of its products:

Direct materials (5 lbs @ 1.60)	$ 8.00
Direct labor (1.5 hours @ $9.00)	13.50
Fixed overhead (1.5 hrs @ $2.00)	3.00
Variable overhead (1.5 hrs @ $1.50)	2.25
Standard cost per unit	$26.75

Littleman computes its overhead rates using practical volume, which is 72,000 units. The actual results for 1992 are

a. Units produced: 70,000

b. Materials purchased: 372,000 pounds at $1.50

c. Materials used: 368,000 pounds

d. Direct labor: 112,000 hours at $8.95

e. Fixed overhead: $214,000

f. Variable overhead: $175,400

Required:

1. Compute price and usage variances for materials.

2. Compute the labor rate and labor efficiency variances.

3. Compute the fixed overhead spending and volume variances.

4. Compute the variable overhead spending and efficiency variances.

E15–11 **Journal Entries** Refer to the data in Exercise 15–10. Prepare journal entries for the following:

1. The purchase of raw materials

2. The issuance of raw materials to production (Work in Process)

3. The addition of labor to Work in Process

4. The addition of overhead to Work in Process

5. Closing out of variances to Cost of Goods Sold

E15–12 **Variances, Evaluation, and Behavior** Jackie Iverson was furious. She was about ready to fire Tom Rich, her purchasing agent. Just a month ago, she had given him a salary increase and a bonus for his performance. She had been especially pleased with his ability to meet or beat the price standards. But now she finds out that it was because of a huge purchase of raw materials. It'll take months to use that inventory and there was hardly space to store it. In the meantime, where can the other materials supplies that will be ordered and processed on a regular basis be put? Additionally, she knows it was a lot of capital to tie up in inventory—money that could have been used to help finance the cash needs of the new product just coming on line.

Her interview with Tom had been frustrating. He was defensive—arguing that he thought that she wanted those standards met and that the means were not that important. He also pointed out that quantity purchases were the only way to meet the price standards. Otherwise, an unfavorable variance would have been realized.

Required:

1. Why did Tom Rich purchase the large quantity of raw materials? Do you think that this behavior was the objective of the price standard? If not, what is the objective or objectives?

2. Suppose that Tom is right and that the only way to meet the price standards is through the use of quantity discounts. Also assume that using quantity discounts is not a desirable practice for this company. What would you do to solve this dilemma?

3. Should Tom be fired? Explain.

E15–13   **Straightforward Computation of Variances: Materials and Labor**   Woodruff Company produces plastic bottles. The unit for costing purposes is a case of eighteen bottles. The following standards for producing one case of bottles have been established:

Direct material (5 lbs @ $0.80)	$ 4
Direct labor (1.5 hrs $6.00)	9
Standard prime cost	$13

During December, 52,000 pounds of material were purchased and used in production. There were 10,000 cases produced, with the following actual prime costs:

Direct materials	$40,000
Direct labor	$87,910 (for 14,900 hours)

Required:

Compute the materials and labor variances, labeling each variance as favorable or unfavorable.

E15–14   **Refer to E15–13.**   Prepare journal entries for the following:

1. The purchase of raw materials
2. The issuance of raw materials
3. The addition of labor to Work in Process
4. Closing of variances to Cost of Goods Sold

E15–15   **Incomplete Data**   Rixby Company uses a standard cost system. During the past quarter, the following variances were computed:

Variable overhead efficiency variance	$20,000 U
Labor efficiency variance	80,000 U
Labor rate variance	50,000 U

Rixby applies variable overhead using a standard rate of $2 per direct labor hour allowed. Four direct labor hours are allowed per unit produced (only one type of product is manufactured). During the quarter, Rixby used 20 percent more direct labor hours than should have been used.

Required:

1. What were the actual direct labor hours worked? The total hours allowed?
2. What is the standard hourly rate for direct labor? The actual hourly rate?
3. How many actual units were produced?

■ PROBLEMS

P15–1   **Basics of Variance Analysis: Variable Inputs**   Koco Company manufactures a plastic toy telephone. The following standards have been established for the toy's variable inputs:

	Standard Quantity	Standard Price (Rate)	Standard Cost
Direct materials	0.5 lbs	$ 1	$0.50
Direct labor	0.10 hrs	10	1.00
Variable overhead	0.10 hrs	3	0.30
			$1.80

During the first week of July, the company had the following actual results:

Units produced	40,000
Actual labor costs	$42,000
Actual labor hours	4,100
Materials purchased and used	19,500 lbs @ $1.05
Actual variable overhead costs	$13,250

Other information: The purchasing agent located a new source of slightly higher-quality plastic, and this material was used during the first week in July. Also, a new manufacturing layout was implemented on a trial basis. The new layout required a slightly higher level of skilled labor. The higher-quality material has no effect on labor utilization. Similarly, the new manufacturing approach has no effect on material usage.

Required:

1. Compute the materials price and efficiency variances. Assuming that the material variances are essentially attributable to the higher quality of material, would you recommend that the purchasing agent continue to buy this quality? Or should the usual quality be purchased? Assume that the quality of the end product is not affected significantly.

2. Compute the labor rate and efficiency variances. Assuming that the labor variances are attributable to the new manufacturing layout, should it be continued or discontinued? Explain.

3. Refer to Requirement 2. Suppose that the industrial engineer argued that the new layout should not be evaluated after only one week. His reasoning was that it would take at least a week for the workers to become efficient with the new approach. Suppose that the production is the same the second week and that the actual labor hours were 3,900 and the labor cost was $39,000. Should the new layout be adopted? Assume the variances are attributable to the new layout. If so, what would be the projected annual savings?

P15–2   **Setting Standards; Material and Labor Variances**   Osgood Company is a small manufacturer of wooden household items. Ellen Rivkin, the controller, plans to implement a standard cost system for Osgood. She has the information needed to develop standards for Osgood's products.

One of Osgood's products is a wooden cutting board. Each cutting board requires 1.25 board feet of lumber and twelve minutes of direct labor time to prepare and cut the lumber. The cutting boards are inspected after they are cut. Because the cutting boards are made of a natural material that has imperfections, one board is normally rejected for each five that are accepted (the rejected boards are totally scrapped). Four rubber foot pads are attached to each good cutting board. A total of fifteen minutes of direct labor time is required to attach all four foot pads and finish each cutting board. The lumber for the cutting boards costs $3 per board foot, and each foot pad costs $0.05. Direct labor is paid at the rate of $8 per hour.

Required:

1. Develop the standard costs for the direct cost components of the cutting board. The standard cost should identify the standard quantity, standard rate, and standard cost per unit for each direct cost component of the cutting board.

2. Identify the advantages of implementing a standard cost system.

3. Explain the role of each of the following persons in developing standards:
   a. Purchasing manager
   b. Industrial engineer
   c. Cost accountant

4. Assume that the standards have been set and that the following actual results occur during the first month under the new standard cost system:
   a. Actual good units produced: 10,000
   b. Lumber purchased: 16,000 board feet at $3.10
   c. Lumber used: 16,000 board feet
   d. Rubber foot pads purchased (and used): 51,000 at $0.048
   e. Direct labor cost: 5,550 hours at $8.05

Compute price and usage variances for materials and labor.

(CMA adapted)

P15–3   **Setting a Direct Labor Standard; Learning Effects**   Smith Company produces special metal parts for industrial equipment. A potential new customer has approached the company and requested a new part, one significantly different from the usual parts manufactured by Smith. New equipment and some new labor skills will be needed to manufacture the part. The customer is placing an initial order of 10,000 units and has indicated that if the part is satisfactory, several additional orders of the same size will be placed over the next two to three years.

Smith uses a standard cost system and wants to develop a set of standards for the new part. The usage standard for direct materials is five pounds per part; the materials price standard is $3 per pound. Management has also decided on standard rates for labor and overhead: the standard labor rate is $10 per hour, the standard variable overhead rate is $5 per hour, and the standard fixed overhead rate is $2 per hour. The only remaining decision is the standard for labor usage. To assist in developing this standard, the Production Engineering Department has estimated the following relationship between units produced and average direct labor hours used:

Units Produced	Cumulative Average Time per Unit
25	1.00 hours
50	0.80 hours
100	0.64 hours
200	0.512 hours
400	0.448 hours

As the workers learn more about the production process, they become more efficient in manufacturing the part, and the average time needed to produce one unit declines. Engineering estimates that all of the learning effects will be achieved by the time 200 units are produced. No further improvement will be realized past this level.

Required:

1. If no further improvement in labor time per unit is possible past 200 units, explain why the cumulative average time per unit at 400 is lower than the time at 200 units.

2. What standard would you set for the per-unit usage of direct labor? Explain.

3. Using the standard you set in requirement 2, prepare a standard cost sheet that details the standard cost per unit for the new part.

4. Given the standard you set in requirement 2, would you expect favorable or unfavorable labor and variable overhead efficiency variances for production of the first 200 units? Explain.

P15–4 **Basic Variance Analysis; Revision of Standards** The Emerson Division of Golding Company produces small kitchen appliances. The company uses a standard cost system for production costing and control. The standard cost sheet for its most popular product, a toaster, is given below.

Direct materials (2.5 lbs @ $4.00)	$10.00
Direct labor (0.7 hours @ $10.50)	7.35
Variable overhead (0.7 hours @ $6.00)	4.20
Fixed overhead (0.7 hours @ $3.00)	2.10
Standard unit cost	$23.65

During the year, Emerson experienced the following activity relative to the production of toasters:

a. Production of toasters totaled 50,000 units.

b. A total of 130,000 pounds of raw materials was purchased at $3.70 per pound.

c. There were 10,000 pounds of raw materials in beginning inventory (carried at $4 per pound). There was no ending inventory.

d. The company used 36,500 direct labor hours at a total cost of $392,375.

e. Actual fixed overhead totaled $95,000.

f. Actual variable overhead totaled $210,000.

Emerson produces all of its toasters in a single plant. Normal activity is 45,000 units per year. Standard overhead rates are computed based on normal activity measured in standard direct labor hours.

Required:

1. Compute the materials price and usage variances.

2. Compute the labor rate and efficiency variances.

3. Compute the fixed overhead budget and spending variances.

4. Assume that the purchasing agent for the toaster plant purchased a lower-quality raw material from a new supplier. Would you recommend that the company continue to use this cheaper raw material? If so, what standards would likely need revision to reflect this decision? Assume that the end product's quality is not significantly affected.

5. Compute the variable overhead spending and efficiency variances.

6. Prepare all possible journal entries.

P15–5   **Unit Costs; Multiple Products; Variance Analysis; Journal Entries**   Business Specialty, Inc., manufactures two staplers, small and regular. The standard quantities of labor and materials per unit for 1993 are

	Small	*Regular*
Direct materials (oz)	6	10
Direct labor (hrs)	0.1	0.15

The standard price paid per pound of direct materials is $1.60. The standard rate for labor is $8. Overhead is applied on the basis of direct labor hours. A plant-wide rate is used. Budgeted overhead for the year is given below.

Budgeted fixed overhead	$360,000
Budgeted variable overhead	480,000

The company expects to work 12,000 direct labor hours in 1993; standard overhead rates are computed using this activity level. For every small stapler produced, the company produces two regular staplers.

Actual operating data for 1993 are

a. Units produced: small staplers, 35,000; regular staplers, 70,000.

b. Direct materials purchased and used: 56,000 pounds at $1.55: 13,000 for the small stapler and 43,000 for the regular stapler. There were no beginning or ending raw materials inventories.

c. Direct labor: 14,800 hours: 3,600 hours for the small stapler, and 11,200 hours for the regular. Total cost of labor: $114,700.

d. Variable overhead: $607,500.

e. Fixed overhead: $350,000.

Required:

1. Prepare a standard cost sheet showing the unit cost for each product.

2. Compute the materials price and usage variances for each product. Prepare journal entries to record materials activity.

3. Compute the labor rate and efficiency variances. Prepare journal entries to record labor activity.

4. Compute the variances for fixed and variable overhead. Prepare journal entries to record overhead activity. All variances are closed to Cost of Goods Sold.

5. Assume that you know only the total direct materials used for both products and the total direct labor hours used for both products. Can you compute the total materials and labor usage variances? Explain.

P15–6 **Incomplete Data; Overhead Analysis** Hobbs Company produces a single product. Hobbs employs a standard cost system and uses a flexible budget to predict overhead costs at various levels of activity. For the most recent year, Hobbs used a standard overhead rate equal to $8.50 per direct labor hour. The rate was computed using normal activity. Budgeted overhead costs are $100,000 for 10,000 direct labor hours and $160,000 for 20,000 direct labor hours. During the past year, Hobbs generated the following data:

a. Actual production: 1,400 units

b. Fixed overhead volume variance: $5,000 U

c. Variable overhead efficiency variance: $3,000 F

d. Actual fixed overhead costs: $42,670

e. Actual variable overhead costs: $82,000

Required:

1. Determine the fixed overhead spending variance.

2. Determine the variable overhead spending variance.

3. Determine the standard hours allowed per unit of product.

4. If the standard labor rate is $9.25 per hour, compute the labor efficiency variance.

P15–7 **Control Limits; Variance Investigation** Demismell Company produces a well-known cologne. The standard manufacturing cost of the cologne is described by the following standard cost sheet:

Direct materials:	
Liquids (4.2 oz @ $0.25)	$1.05
Bottles (one @ $0.05)	0.05
Direct labor (0.2 hrs @ $12.50)	2.50
Variable overhead (0.2 hrs @ $4.70)	0.94
Fixed overhead (0.2 hrs @ $1.00)	0.20
Standard cost per unit	$4.74

Management has decided to investigate only those variances that exceed the lesser of 10 percent of the standard cost for each category or $20,000.

During the past quarter, 250,000 four-ounce bottles of cologne were produced. Actual activity for the quarter is described below.

a. A total of 1.15 million ounces of liquids were purchased, mixed, and processed. Evaporation was higher than expected (no inventories of liquids are maintained). The price paid per ounce averaged $0.27.

b. Exactly 250,000 bottles were used. The price paid for each bottle was $0.048.

c. Direct labor hours totaled 48,250 with a total cost of $622,425.

d. Variable overhead costs totaled $239,000.

e. Fixed overhead costs were $50,500.

Normal production volume for Demismell is 250,000 bottles per quarter. The standard overhead rates are computed using normal volume. All overhead costs are incurred uniformly throughout the year.

Required:

1. Calculate the upper and lower control limits for each manufacturing cost category.

2. Compute the total materials variance and then break it into price and usage variances. Would these variances be investigated?

3. Compute the total labor variance and break it into rate and efficiency variances. Would these variances be investigated?

4. Compute all overhead variances. Would any of them be investigated? Would you recommend a different approach to deal with overhead? Explain.

P15-8 **Flexible Budget; Standard Cost Variances; T-Accounts** Hinckley Company manufactures a line of running shoes. At the beginning of the period, the following plans for production and costs were revealed:

Units to be produced and sold	25,000
Standard cost per unit:	
Direct materials	$10
Direct labor	8
Variable overhead	4
Fixed overhead	3
Total unit cost	$25

During the year, 30,000 units were produced and sold. The following actual costs were incurred:

Direct materials	$320,000
Direct labor	220,000
Variable overhead	125,000
Fixed overhead	89,000

There were no beginning or ending inventories of raw materials. The materials price variance was $5,000 unfavorable. In producing the 30,000 units, 39,000 hours were worked, 4 percent more hours than the standard allowed for the actual output. Overhead costs are applied to production using direct labor hours.

Required:

1. Prepare a flexible budget showing the total expected costs for the actual production. Also prepare a performance report comparing expected costs with actual costs.
2. Determine the following:
   a. Materials usage variance
   b. Labor rate variance
   c. Labor usage variance
   d. Fixed overhead spending and volume variances
   e. Variable overhead spending and efficiency variances
3. Use T-accounts to show the flow of costs through the system.

P15-9 **Control Limits; Variance Investigation** The management of Troy Enterprises has determined that the cost to investigate a variance produced by its standard cost system ranges from $2,000 to $3,000. If a problem is discovered, the average benefit from taking corrective action usually outweighs the cost of investigation. Past experience from the investigation of variances has revealed that corrective action is rarely needed for deviations within 8 percent of the standard cost. Troy produces a single product, which has the following standards for materials and labor:

Direct materials (8 lbs @ $0.25)	$2
Direct labor (0.4 hours @ $7.50)	3

Actual production for the past three months with the associated actual usage and costs for materials and labor are given below. There were no beginning or ending raw material inventories.

	April	*May*	*June*
Production (units)	90,000	100,000	110,000
Direct materials			
Cost	$189,000	$218,000	$230,000
Usage (lbs)	723,000	870,000	885,000
Direct labor			
Cost	$270,000	$323,000	$360,000
Usage (hrs)	36,000	44,000	46,000

Required:

1. What upper and lower control limits would you use for materials variances? For labor variances?
2. Compute the materials and labor variances for April, May, and June. Identify those that would require investigation.
3. Let the horizontal axis be time and the vertical axis be variances measured as a percentage deviation from standard. Draw horizontal lines that identify upper and lower control limits. Plot the labor and material variances for April, May, and June. Prepare a separate graph for each type of variance. Explain how you would use these graphs (called *control charts)* to assist your analysis of variances.

P15–10   **Standard Costing and Ethical Behavior**   Pat James, the purchasing agent for a local plant of the Oakden Electronics Division, was considering the possible purchase of a component from a new supplier. The component's purchase price, $0.90, compared favorably with the standard price of $1.10. Given the quantity that would be purchased, Pat knew that the favorable price variance would help offset an unfavorable variance for another component. By offsetting the unfavorable variance, his overall performance report would be impressive and good enough to help him qualify for the annual bonus. More importantly, a good performance rating this year would help him secure a position at divisional headquarters at a significant salary increase.

Purchase of the part, however, presented Pat with a dilemma. Consistent with his past behavior, Pat made inquiries regarding the reliability of the new supplier and the part's quality. Reports were basically negative. The supplier had a reputation for making the first two or three deliveries on schedule but being unreliable from then on. Worse, the part itself was of questionable quality. The number of defective units was only slightly higher than that for other suppliers, but the life of the component was 25 percent less than what normal sources provided.

If the part were purchased, no problems with deliveries would surface for several months. The problem of shorter life would cause eventual customer dissatisfaction and perhaps some loss of sales, but the part would last at least eighteen months after the final product began to be used. If all went well, Pat expected to be at headquarters within six months. He saw very little personal risk associated with a decision to purchase the part from the new supplier. By the time any problems surfaced, they would belong to his successor. With this rationalization, Pat decided to purchase the component from the new supplier.

Required:

1. Do you agree with Pat's decision? Why or why not? How important do you think Pat's assessment of his personal risk was in the decision? Should it be a factor?

2. Do you think that the use of standards and the practice of holding individuals accountable for their achievement played major roles in Pat's decision?

3. Review the ethical standards for management accountants in the Appendix of Chapter 1. Even though Pat is not a management accountant, identify the standards that might apply to his situation. Should every company adopt a set of ethical standards that apply to their employees, regardless of their specialty?

P15–11   **Standard Costing: Planned Variances**   As part of its cost control program, Tracer Company uses a standard cost system for all manufactured items. The standard cost for each item is established at the beginning of the fiscal year, and the standards are not revised until the beginning of the next fiscal year. Changes in costs, caused during the year by changes in material or labor inputs or by changes in the manufacturing process, are recognized as they occur by the inclusion of planned variances in Tracer's monthly operating budgets.

Presented below is the labor standard that was established for one of Tracer's products effective June 1, 1992, the beginning of the fiscal year:

Assembler A labor (5 hours @ $10/hr)	$ 50
Assembler B labor (3 hours @ $11/hr)	33
Machinist labor (2 hours @ $15/hr)	30
Standard cost per 100 units	$113

The standard was based on the labor being performed by a team consisting of five persons with Assembler A skills, three persons with Assembler B skills, and two persons with machinist skills; this team represents the most efficient use of the company's skilled employees. The standard also assumed that the quality of materials that had been used in prior years would be available for the coming year.

For the first seven months of the fiscal year, actual manufacturing costs at Tracer have been within the standards established. However, the company has received a significant increase in orders, and there is an insufficient number of skilled workers to meet the increased production. Therefore, beginning in January, the production teams will consist of eight persons with Assembler A skills, one person with Assembler B skills, and one person with machinist skills. The reorganized teams will work more slowly than the normal teams; and, as a result, only 80 units will be produced in the same time period in which 100 units would normally be produced. Faulty work has never been a cause for units to be rejected in the final inspection process, and it is not expected to be a cause for rejection with the reorganized teams.

Furthermore, Tracer has been notified by its material supplier that lower quality materials will be supplied beginning January 1. Normally, one unit of raw materials is required for each good unit produced, and no units are lost due to defective material. Tracer estimates that 6 percent of the units manufactured after January 1 will be rejected in the final inspection process due to defective material.

Required:

1. Determine the number of units of lower-quality material that Tracer Company must enter into production in order to produce 47,000 good finished units.

2. How many hours of each class of labor must be used to manufacture 47,000 good finished units?

3. Determine the amount that should be included in Tracer's January operating budget for the planned labor variance caused by the reorganization of the labor teams and the lower-quality material.

(CMA adapted)

P15–12 **Incomplete Data; Variance Analysis; Standard Cost Sheet** Tina Nelson, controller of Undergate Company, was trying to decide which of two promising accountants (Bill Johnson and Sheila Myers) should be promoted to cost accounting manager. Both candidates had similar records, and the decision was difficult. To determine the depth of each candidate's knowledge of standard costing, Tina decided to administer a simple test. The candidate who performed better on the test would receive the promotion.

Each candidate was given the following data for a single-product company during its most recent year of operations:

Selected Actual Results

- Direct materials: 5,500 lbs. purchased and used, costing $22,500

- Production: 10,000 units

- Labor cost: 1,800 hours totaling $13,320

- *FOH* cost: $11,500

- *VOH* cost: $19,000

Variances	
MPV	$ 550 U
MUV	2,000 U
LEV	1,500 U
Volume variance	1,000 U
Variable overhead efficiency	2,000 U
Variable overhead spending	1,000 U
Underapplied fixed overhead	2,000 U

The overhead rates are based on expected actual activity. The company calculates two variances for variable overhead and two for fixed overhead.

Required:

1. Prepare a standard cost sheet in good form. Show fixed and variable overhead as separate items.

2. Compute the fixed overhead spending variance.

3. Compute the labor rate variance.

4. Determine the expected actual activity used to compute the predetermined fixed overhead rate.

P15–13   **Standard Costing**   Mark Wright, Inc. (MWI), is a specialty frozen-food processor located in the midwestern states. Since its founding in 1982, MWI has enjoyed a loyal clientele that is willing to pay premium prices for the high-quality frozen food it prepares from specialized recipes. In the last two years, the company has experienced rapid sales growth in its operating region and has had many inquiries about supplying its products on a national basis. To meet this growth, MWI expanded its processing capabilities, which resulted in increased production and distribution costs. Furthermore, MWI has been encountering pricing pressure from competitors outside its normal marketing region.

Because MWI desires to continue its expansion, Jim Condon, CEO, has engaged a consulting firm to assist MWI in determining its best course of action. The consulting firm recommended the institution of a standard cost system that would also facilitate a flexible budgeting system to better accommodate the changes in demand that can be expected when serving an expanding market area.

Condon met with his management team and explained the recommendations of the consulting firm. Condon then assigned the task of establishing standard costs to his management team. After discussing the situation with the respective staffs, the management team met to review the matter.

Jane Morgan, purchasing manager, advised that meeting expanded production would necessitate obtaining basic food supplies from other than MWI's traditional sources. This would entail increased raw material and shipping costs and might result in lower-quality supplies. Consequently, these increased costs would need to be made up by the Processing Department if current costs are to be maintained or reduced.

Stan Walters, processing manager, countered that the need to accelerate processing cycles to increase production, coupled with the possibility of receiving lower-grade supplies, can be expected to result in a slip in quality and a greater product rejection rate. Under these circumstances, per-unit labor utilization cannot be maintained or reduced, and forecasting future unit labor content becomes very difficult.

Tom Lopez, production engineer, advised that if the equipment is not properly maintained and thoroughly cleaned at prescribed daily intervals, it can be anticipated that the quality and unique taste of the frozen-food products will be affected. Jack Reid, vice president of sales, stated that if quality cannot be maintained, MWI cannot expect to increase sales to the levels projected.

When Condon was apprised of the problems encountered by his management team, he advised them that if agreement could not be reached on the appropriate standards, he would arrange to have them set by the consulting firm and everyone would have to live with the results.

Required:

1. List the major advantages of using a standard cost system.
2. List disadvantages that can result from the use of a standard cost system.
3. Identify those who should participate in setting standards and describe the benefits of their participation in the standard setting process.
4. What characteristics of a standard cost system make it an effective tool for cost control?
5. What could be the consequences if Jim Condon, CEO, has the standards set by the outside consulting firm?

(CMA adapted)

■ MANAGERIAL DECISION CASE

Establishment of Standards; Variance Analysis   Crunchy Chips was established in 1938 by Paul Golding and his wife Nancy (Nancy sold her piano to help raise capital to start the business). Paul assumed responsibility for buying potatoes and selling chips to local grocers; Nancy assumed responsibility for production. Since Nancy was already known for her delicious, thin potato chips, the business prospered.

Over the past forty-eight years, the company has established distribution channels in eleven western states, with production facilities in Utah, New Mexico, and Colorado. In 1980, Paul Golding died, and his son, Edward, took control of the business. By 1993, the company was facing stiff competition from national snack-food companies. Edward was advised that the company's plants needed to gain better control over production costs; to assist in achieving this objective, he hired a consultant to install a standard cost system. To help the consultant in establishing the necessary standards, Edward sent her the following memo:

To: Diana Craig, CMA
From: Edward Golding, President, Crunchy Chips
Subject: Description and Data Relating to the Production of Our Plain Potato Chips
Date: September 28, 1993

The manufacturing process for potato chips begins when the potatoes are placed into a large vat in which they are automatically washed. After washing, the potatoes flow directly to an automatic peeler. The peeled potatoes then pass by inspectors who manually cut out deep eyes or other blemishes. After inspection, the potatoes are automatically sliced and dropped into the cooking oil. The frying process is closely monitored by an employee. After they are cooked, the chips pass under a salting device and then pass by more inspectors, who sort out the unacceptable finished chips (those that are discolored or too small). The chips then continue on the conveyor belt to a bagging machine that bags them in one-pound bags. After bagging, the bags are placed in a box and shipped. The box holds fifteen bags.

The raw potato pieces (eyes and blemishes), peelings, and rejected finished chips are sold to animal feed producers for $0.16 per pound. The company uses this revenue to reduce the cost of potatoes; we would like this reflected in the price standard relating to potatoes.

Crunchy Chips purchases high-quality potatoes at a cost of $0.245 per pound. Each potato averages 4.25 ounces. Under efficient operating conditions, it takes four potatoes to produce one 16-ounce bag of plain chips. Although we label bags as containing 16 ounces, we actually place 16.3 ounces in each bag. We plan to continue this policy to ensure customer satisfaction. In addition to potatoes, other raw materials are the cooking oil, salt, bags, and boxes. Cooking oil costs $0.04 per ounce, and we use 3.3 ounces of oil per bag of chips. The cost of salt is so small that we add it to overhead. Bags cost $0.11 each, and boxes $0.52.

Our plant produces 8.8 million bags of chips per year. A recent engineering study revealed that we would need the following direct labor hours to produce this quantity if our plant operates at peak efficiency:

Raw potato inspection	3,200
Finished chip inspection	12,000
Frying monitor	6,300
Boxing	16,600
Machine operators	6,300

I'm not sure that we can achieve the level of efficiency advocated by the study. In my opinion, the plant is operating efficiently for the level of output indicated if the hours allowed are about 10 percent higher.

The hourly labor rates agreed upon with the union are

Raw potato inspectors	$7.60
Finished chip inspectors	5.15
Frying monitor	7.00
Boxing	5.50
Machine operators	6.50

Overhead is applied on the basis of direct labor dollars. We have found that variable overhead averages about 116 percent of our direct labor cost. Our fixed overhead is budgeted at $1,135,216 for the coming year.

Required:

1. Discuss the benefits of a standard cost system for Crunchy Chips.

2. Discuss the president's concern about using the result of the engineering study to set the labor standards. What standard would you recommend?

3. Develop a standard cost sheet for Crunchy Chips' plain potato chips.

4. Suppose that the level of production was 8.8 million bags of potato chips for the year as planned. If 9.5 million pounds of potatoes were used, compute the materials usage variance for potatoes.

CHAPTER 16

Quality Costs and Productivity: Measurement and Control

■ **LEARNING OBJECTIVES**

After studying Chapter 16, you should be able to

1. Explain the difference between quality of design and quality of conformance.

2. Identify and describe the four types of quality costs and prepare a quality cost report.

3. Explain the difference between the conventional view of acceptable quality level and the view espoused by total quality control.

4. Explain why quality cost information is needed and how it is used.

5. Describe and prepare four different types of quality performance reports.

6. Explain what productivity is and differentiate between partial and total measures of productivity.

7. Be able to calculate the impact of productivity changes on profits and explain why profit-linked productivity measurement is important.

8. Explain how quality and productivity are related and how they differ.

9. Define and explain the key terms appearing at the end of the chapter.

SCENARIO

Russell Walsh, president of Ladd Lighting Corporation, had just returned from a productivity seminar, excited and encouraged by what he had heard. Based on the experiences described in the seminar, he had decided to initiate some significant changes in the way Ladd Lighting operated. To lay the groundwork for these changes, he asked Sarah Burke, the company's quality manager, and Dennis Schmitt, the company's controller and financial vice-president, to meet with him.

Russell: As you both know, our profits have been declining over the past several years. The flow of imports, ranging from lamps to light bulbs, has nearly doubled from 1988 to 1992. To compete, we have cut prices, but as our prices have declined, so have our profit margins. If we are going to earn a reasonable return, we must do something to decrease our costs. After attending this productivity seminar, I'm convinced that a quality improvement program may be a big part of the solution.

Sarah: I wonder if you're right. After all, right now we spend a lot on quality-related activities. Pouring more money into quality may not be the answer.

Russell: I don't intend to spend more on quality—just the opposite. At the seminar, a representative of Tennant Company, a manufacturer of industrial floor maintenance products, related an interesting experience—one that provides an important message for our own company.[1] In the late 1970s, Tennant Company was focusing on productivity to remain competitive in the world market. Management had decided to focus on productivity because, unlike the costs of labor and materials, it offered more promise for control and higher potential for increased profitability.

At the same time that the plans for productivity improvement were unfolding, Tennant had a delivery of one of its most popular sweepers rejected by a customer. The sweeper was rejected as defective because it leaked hydraulic fluid. The problem of leaking fluid was known to Tennant, but other customers had never made a fuss over it. This was the first such reaction. The experience created a managerial awareness of the importance of quality. As a result, the company hired a consultant (Phil Crosby) and embarked on a major quality improvement program.[2]

Sarah: I think I know where you're headed now. Crosby advocates improving quality so that the costs of quality can be reduced. It costs us when

---

[1]The facts in the Tennant example are based largely on a talk given by Tim K. Shenert at the Eleventh Annual Productivity Seminar at Utah State University (April 23–24, 1986). The talk focused on the actual experiences of Tennant Company with a quality improvement program.

[2]Crosby, former quality manager for ITT, is the author of *Quality Is Free* (New York: New American Library, 1980). While he served as quality manager for ITT, ITT reduced the manufacturing cost of quality by 5 percent of sales. The savings in 1976 alone were estimated as $530 million. His book provides an excellent account of the fourteen-step quality program he developed and Tennant Company followed.

we do things wrong—in terms of rework, scrap, repairs, and so on. By controlling quality costs, profitability can be improved, and we become more competitive.

Russell: Exactly. Tennant's quality improvement efforts have been remarkable. The sweeper that was rejected averaged 1.5 hydraulic leaks per machine. Within five or six years, the average was only 0.1 leaks per machine. Other improvements were made as well. Within the first year, errors in inventory transactions were reduced from forty-one per month to twelve per month. Within three years, machines damaged in shipping dropped from 5 percent to less than 1 percent. Furthermore, since more than 65 percent of Tennant's product costs consisted of materials and parts provided by suppliers, much of the failure and rejects could be attributed to poor components purchased externally. Consequently, Tennant concentrated on working with key suppliers to improve the specifications and quality of those components. Reaction from suppliers was strongly positive; one supplier reduced its level of defects from 6.4 percent to 0.8 percent.

The most exciting thing about Tennant's experience, however, is the effect of the improved quality on its profitability. When the quality improvement program began, Tennant estimated that its cost of doing things wrong was as high as 15 percent of sales. Within a six year period, this cost had dropped to 8 percent of sales. Based on sales of $136 million, savings from improved quality totaled $9.52 million.

Dennis: I'm impressed by the potential savings through improved quality. I'm not sure, however, what role you envision for me, other than being aware of the importance of a quality improvement program.

Russell: I envision your role as being much more extensive than simple awareness. We need a solid, reliable quality cost reporting system, and I expect you to assume responsibility for its development and operation. Our company needs quality information to help our managers make quality improvement decisions. We also need to monitor and control the programs that we implement.

Dennis: I'm quite willing to do so—but in the past, Sarah's department has been responsible for issuing quality cost reports.

Russell: Well, that's changing and for good reasons. I want this quality program taken seriously by our managers, and I'm afraid that quality cost reports coming from the same department responsible for ensuring quality may be viewed as self-serving. Besides, you accountants are our experts in measuring, estimating, and allocating costs. We need good quality information so that quality-related decisions are sound. In more pragmatic terms, I think that quality costing needs to be integrated into the overall accounting system. In this way, we avoid the costs of duplication. Sarah, do you have any problems with this arrangement?

Sarah: None at all. It seems sensible that the controller's office is responsible for collecting and reporting quality costs. I know that other companies have this arrangement. The quality department should be responsible for analyzing and controlling these costs. Besides, I have a feeling that given the increased emphasis on quality, my department will have plenty to do without worrying about a cost reporting system.[3]

Russell: Good. Sarah, I would like some research done on the quality program that has worked so well for Tennant. Prepare a report that tells us what quality is and what quality costs are. Dennis, after you receive some basic guidance from Sarah on these fundamental concepts, I want to know what kind of reports you think are necessary for tracking and reporting quality costs and for monitoring the progress of our quality improvement program. We need a good reporting system if we expect to control our quality costs.

■ QUALITY AND ITS IMPACT ON PROFITABILITY

By attending a productivity seminar, Russell Walsh discovered that paying more attention to quality can produce significant savings. In a tightly competitive market, these savings can mean the difference between surviving and thriving. It should be pointed out that these savings are not confined to manufacturing firms. In 1980, the banking industry spent $435 million on rework because of faulty magnetic-ink character recognition codes; this is nearly one-half of all check processing costs. (When the recognition codes are faulty, the computer rejects the checks as unreadable, and they must be processed by hand.[4]) Imagine the savings possible if banks worked with the printers of checks to improve the reliability of their product.

As these examples illustrate, the costs of quality can be substantial and a source of significant savings. At the Eleventh Annual Conference on Productivity (at Utah State University), quality experts maintained that most American companies spend 15 to 25 percent of annual sales on costs of quality when they should be spending about 2.5 percent. The 2.5 percent benchmark is the amount quality experts estimate should be spent at the optimal quality level.

In the last two decades, U.S. firms have faced increased competition from foreign firms in both world and domestic markets. Often foreign firms have been selling higher-quality products at lower prices. Consequently, many U.S. firms have lost market share. In an effort to combat this stiff

---

[3]North American Phillips Consumer Electronics Corporation, ITT, and Xerox are examples of companies that have assigned responsibility for quality cost reporting to the accounting or financial departments. See Chapters 6 and 9 in Wayne J. Morse, Harold P. Roth, and Kay M. Poston, *Measuring, Planning, and Controlling Quality Costs* (Montvale, N.J.: National Association of Accountants, 1987).

[4] William J. Latzko, ''Quality Control for Banks,'' *The Banker's Magazine* (Autumn 1981), pp. 64–70.

competition, U.S. firms have begun to pay increasing attention to quality and productivity, especially because of the potential to reduce costs and improve product quality simultaneously.

Who should be responsible for measuring and reporting quality costs? As the introductory case indicates, the accounting department is ideally suited for this task. By having the accounting department measure and report quality costs, the performance of the quality department can be assessed more objectively. Moreover, it seems eminently reasonable that the department responsible for cost systems ought to be responsible for developing and operating the quality cost system.

■ MEASURING THE COSTS OF QUALITY

Managers must be able to monitor their firms' progress in achieving objectives for quality improvement and in maintaining quality levels. Reporting and measuring quality performance is absolutely essential to the success of an ongoing quality improvement program. A fundamental prerequisite for this reporting is measuring the costs of quality. But to measure those costs, an operational definition of quality itself is needed.

Quality Defined

The typical dictionary definition of *quality* is the degree or grade of excellence; in this sense, quality is a relative measure of goodness. But how does this translate into day-to-day business realities? Operationally, a *quality product* is a product that conforms to customer expectations. Generally, two types of quality are recognized: quality of design and quality of conformance.

quality of design   **Quality of design** is a function of a product's specifications. For example, the function of watches is to allow an individual to tell what time it is. Yet one watch may have a steel casing, require winding, have a leather strap, and be engineered to lose no more than two minutes per month; another may have a gold-plated casing, be battery operated, have a gold-plated back, and be engineered to lose no more than one minute per year. Obviously, the design qualities are different. Most would agree that the gold watch is the higher quality of the two: Higher design quality is usually reflected in higher manufacturing costs and in higher selling prices.

quality of   **Quality of conformance** is a measure of how a product meets its re-
conformance   quirements or specifications. If the product meets all of the designed specifications, it is fit for use. For example, a customer buying a steel-plated watch expects that the watch will function for a reasonable period of time. Suppose that the first time the customer winds the watch, the stem breaks off, or suppose that the watch consistently loses twenty minutes per day. What type of quality assessment will the customer make? On the other hand, a competitor's watch at the *same* design level may rarely experience problems with the stem or with keeping time. What is the quality assessment of this watch?

Of the two types of quality, quality of conformance should receive the most emphasis. It is nonconformance to requirements that creates the most problems for companies. When quality experts speak of improving quality, they mean reducing the incidence of nonconformance. To them, the word *quality* is synonymous with conformance to requirements—with doing it right the first time. The product should be produced as the design specifies it; requirements should be followed. If the product is not good, then the design needs to be changed. Throughout the remainder of this chapter, whenever you see the word *quality*, think of it as quality of conformance.

Costs of Quality Defined

costs of quality The **costs of quality** are the costs that exist because poor quality may or does exist.[5] Thus, quality costs are the costs associated with the creation, identification, repair, and prevention of defects. These costs can be classified into four categories: prevention costs, appraisal costs, internal failure costs, and external failure costs. Because things may go wrong, a company incurs prevention and appraisal costs. When things do go wrong, a company experiences failure costs.

prevention costs **Prevention costs** are incurred to prevent defects in the products or services being produced. As prevention costs increase, we would expect the costs of failure to decrease; thus, prevention costs are incurred in order to decrease the number of nonconforming units. Examples of prevention costs are quality engineering, quality training programs, quality planning, quality reporting, supplier evaluations, quality audits, quality circles, and design reviews.

appraisal costs **Appraisal costs** are incurred to determine whether products and services are conforming to their requirements. Examples include inspecting and testing raw materials, packaging inspection, supervising appraisal activities, product acceptance, process acceptance, supplier verification, and field testing. Two of these terms require further explanation.

Product acceptance involves sampling from batches of finished goods to determine whether they meet an acceptable quality level; if so, the goods are accepted. *Process acceptance* involves sampling goods while in process to see if the process is in control and producing nondefective goods; if not, the process is shut down until corrective action can be taken. The main objective of the appraisal function is to prevent nonconforming goods from being shipped to customers.

internal failure costs **Internal failure costs** are incurred because nonconforming products and services are detected prior to being shipped to outside parties. These are the failures detected by appraisal activities. Examples of internal failure costs are scrap, rework, downtime (due to defects), reinspection, retesting, and design changes. These costs disappear if no defects exist.

---

[5]This is the definition in Morse, Roth, and Poston, *Measuring, Planning, and Controlling*, p. 19.

external failure costs   **External failure costs** are incurred because products and services fail to conform to requirements after being delivered to customers. Of all the costs of quality, this category can be the most devastating. For example, Firestone spent approximately $135 million in a 1977 recall of 7.5 million steel-belted radial tires.[6] Other examples include lost sales because of poor product performance, returns and allowances because of poor quality, warranties, repair, product liability, and complaint adjustment. External failure costs, like internal failure costs, disappear if no defects exist.

Exhibit 16–1 summarizes the four quality cost categories and lists specific examples of costs within each category.

■ REPORTING AND USING QUALITY COST INFORMATION

A quality cost reporting system is essential if an organization is serious about improving and controlling quality costs. The first and simplest step in creating such a system is an assessment of current actual quality costs. A detailed listing of actual quality costs by category can provide two important insights. First, it reveals the magnitude of the quality costs in each category, allowing managers to assess their financial impact. Second, it shows the distribution of quality costs by category, allowing managers to assess the relative cost of each category.

EXHIBIT 16–1

Prevention Costs	*Appraisal Costs*
Quality engineering	Inspection of raw materials
Quality training	Packaging inspection
Quality planning	Product acceptance
Quality audits	Process acceptance
Design reviews	Field testing
Quality circles	Supplier verification
Internal Failure Costs	*External Failure Costs*
Scrap	Lost sales (performance related)
Rework	Returns/allowances
Downtime (defect related)	Warranties
Reinspection	Repair
Retesting	Product liability
Design changes	Complaint adjustment

[6]Robert M. Reece, ''QC as an Inflation Fighter,'' *Quality Progress* (August 1980), pp. 24–25.

Quality Cost Reports

The financial significance of quality costs can be assessed more easily by expressing these costs as a percentage of actual sales. Exhibit 16–2, for example, reports the quality costs of Jensen Products for fiscal 1992.[7] According to the report, quality costs represent almost 12 percent of sales. Given the rule of thumb that quality costs should be no more than about 2.5 percent, Jensen Products has ample opportunity to improve profits by decreasing quality costs. Understand, however, that reduction in costs should come through improvement of quality. Reduction of quality costs without any effort to improve quality could prove to be a disastrous strategy.

Additional insight concerning the relative distribution of quality costs can be realized by constructing a pie chart. Exhibit 16–3 provides such a chart,

EXHIBIT 16–2

Jensen Products		

Quality Cost Report *For the Year Ended March 31, 1992* Quality Costs		Percentage of Sales[a]
Prevention costs:		
Quality training	$35,000	
Reliability engineering	80,000	$115,000 4.11%
Appraisal costs:		
Materials inspection	$20,000	
Product acceptance	10,000	
Process acceptance	38,000	68,000 2.43
Internal failure costs:		
Scrap	$50,000	
Rework	35,000	85,000 3.04
External failure costs:		
Customer complaints	$25,000	
Warranty	25,000	
Repair	15,000	65,000 2.32
Total quality costs		$333,000 11.90%[b]

[a]Actual sales of $2,800,000
[b]$333,000/$2,800,000 = 11.89 percent. Difference is rounding error.

---

[7]The quality cost report given in Exhibit 16–2 parallels the format used by ITT except for several minor differences. First, the ITT report combines the internal and external categories into one failure category. Second, the ITT report has a third column allowing the reporting unit to express quality costs as a percentage of a measure other than sales. For more detail, see Morse, Roth, and Poston, *Measuring, Planning, and Controlling*, pp. 78–81.

EXHIBIT 16-3
Pie Chart: Quality Costs

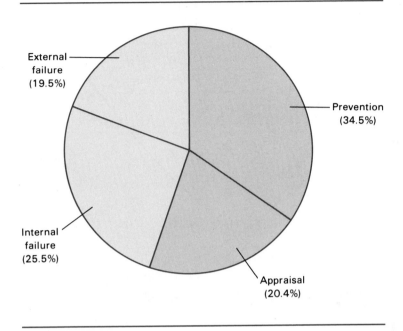

using the quality costs reported in Exhibit 16–2. Managers, of course, have the responsibility to assess the optimal level of quality and to determine the relative amount that should be spent in each category. There are two views concerning optimal quality costs: the traditional view, calling for an *acceptable quality level,* and the view being adopted by world-class firms referred to as *total quality control.* Each view offers managers insights about how quality costs ought to be managed.

Optimal Distribution of Quality Costs: Traditional View   Many quality experts believe that an optimal balance exists between prevention and appraisal costs and the internal and external failure costs. As prevention and appraisal costs increase, failure costs should decrease. As long as the decrease in failure costs is greater than the corresponding increase in prevention and appraisal costs, a company should continue increasing its efforts to prevent or detect nonconforming units. Eventually a point is reached at which any additional increase in this effort costs more than the corresponding reduction in failure costs. Without any change in technology, this point represents the minimum level of total quality costs. It is the optimal balance between prevention and appraisal costs and failure costs. This theoretical relationship is illustrated in Exhibit 16–4.

In Exhibit 16–4, two cost functions are assumed: one for prevention and appraisal costs and one for failure costs. It is also assumed that the percentage

EXHIBIT 16–4
Traditional Quality Cost Graph

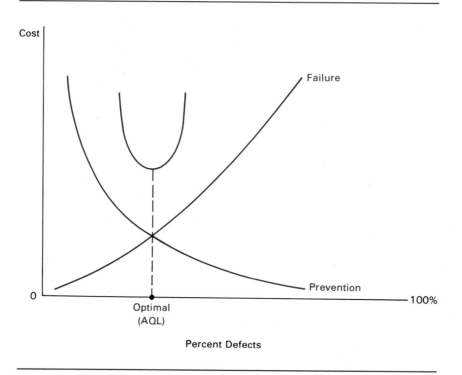

of defective units increases as the amount spent on prevention and appraisal activities decreases; failure costs, on the other hand, increase as the number of defective units increases. From the total quality cost function, we see that total quality costs decrease as quality improves up to a point. After that, no further improvement is possible. An optimal level of defective units is identified and the company works to achieve this level. This level of allowable defective units is defined as the **acceptable quality level (AQL).**

acceptable quality level (AQL)

Optimal Distribution of Quality Costs: World-Class View   For firms operating in an advanced manufacturing environment, competition is intense and quality can offer an important competitive advantage. If the conventional view is wrong, then firms that recognize this error can capitalize on it by decreasing the number of defective units while simultaneously decreasing their total quality costs. This is exactly what has happened, and it is changing the approach to quality cost management. The optimal level for quality costs is where zero defects are produced. Exhibit 16–5 illustrates the zero-defect view of the total quality cost function.

The discovery that tradeoffs among quality cost categories can be managed differently than what is implied by the relationships portrayed in Exhibit

EXHIBIT 16–5
Zero-Defect Graph

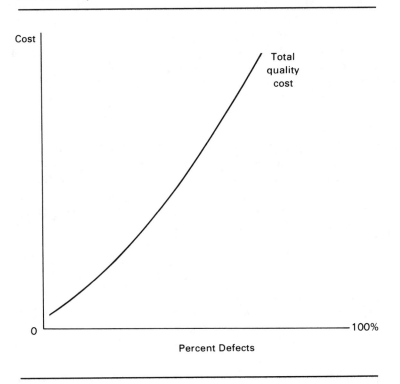

16–4 is analogous to the discovery that inventory cost tradeoffs can be managed differently than the traditional inventory model (EOQ) implied. Essentially, what happens is that as firms increase their prevention and appraisal costs and reduce their failure costs, they discover that they can then cut back on the prevention and appraisal costs. What initially appears to be a tradeoff turns out to be a permanent reduction in costs for all quality cost categories.

Suppose, for example, that a firm has decided to improve the quality of its raw material inputs through the implementation of a supplier selection program. The objective is to identify and use suppliers who are willing to meet certain quality standards. As the firm works to implement this program, additional costs may be incurred (e.g., review of suppliers, communication with suppliers, contract negotiations, and so on). And, initially, other prevention and appraisal costs may continue at their current levels. However, once the program is fully implemented and evidence is surfacing that the failure costs are being reduced (for example, less rework, fewer customer complaints, and fewer repairs), then the company may decide to cut back on inspections of incoming raw materials, reduce the level of product acceptance activities, and so on. The net effect is a reduction in *all* quality cost categories. And quality has increased!

Using Quality Cost Information

The principal objective of reporting quality costs is to improve and facilitate managerial planning, control, and decision making. For example, to decide to implement a supplier selection program to improve the quality of material inputs, a manager will need an assessment of current quality costs by item and by category, an assessment of the additional costs associated with the program, and an assessment of the projected savings by item and by category. When the costs and savings will occur must also be projected. Once these cash effects are projected, then a capital budgeting analysis can be done to assess the merits of the proposed program. If the outcome is favorable and the program is initiated, then it becomes important to monitor the program through fairly standard performance reporting.

Using quality cost information for quality program implementation decisions and for evaluating the effectiveness of these programs, once implemented, is only one potential use of a quality cost system. Other important uses can also be identified. The following two scenarios illustrate the utility of quality cost information. The first scenario reveals the value of quality cost information for a strategic pricing decision. The second scenario reveals the value of quality costs for cost-volume-profit analysis.

Scenario A: Strategic Pricing   Leola May Wise, marketing manager, muttered to herself as she reviewed the latest market share data for the company's low-priced electronic measurement instruments. Once again the share had dropped! Anticipating this outcome, Leola had begun preparing a brief to support a significant price decrease for this line of products. The new price, however, would not quite cover the costs of making and selling the instruments. Yet if something were not done, the Japanese firms would continue to expand their market share. One possibility was simply to drop the low-level line and concentrate on instruments in the medium and high-level quality categories. Leola knew, however, that this was a short-term solution. It wouldn't be long until the same Japanese firms would be competing at the higher quality levels.

In the last executive meeting, the discussion focused on what strategic position the firm ought to take. Leola had suggested that the company should adopt a total quality control position and work to reduce the cost of the lower-level instruments by decreasing quality costs. If costs could be reduced to sustain a price decrease of about 15 percent, then Leola was confident that the company could increase its market share to its former level and restore the profitability of the line. She suggested that the same actions be taken for the other lines but that the first step should focus on the one being threatened. She then asked Earl Simpson, the controller, what the quality costs were for the lower-level instruments. Earl had responded with an admission that the costs were not tracked separately. For example, the cost of scrap was buried in the Work in Process account. He did promise, however, to have some estimates of the costs—perhaps not complete—by the end of the month. The report for the low-level instruments (in the form of a memo from Earl Simpson) arrived a week ago and is given below.

Memo

To: Leola Wise
From: Earl Simpson
Subject: Quality Costs

Lee, I have assembled some data that may be useful to you. First, I have provided an income statement for the low-quality instruments (for the most recent year). Second, I have provided some estimates of the quality costs associated with this line. I have not included any costs of lost sales due to nonconforming products. You are probably in a better position to assess this effect.

Instrument Line: Low-level	
Revenues (1,000,000 @ $20)	$ 20,000,000
Cost of goods sold:	(15,000,000)
Operating expenses:	(3,000,000)
Product-line income	$ 2,000,000
Quality costs (estimated)	
Inspection of raw materials	$ 200,000
Scrap	800,000
Rejects	500,000
Rework	400,000
Product inspection	300,000
Warranty work	1,000,000
Total estimate	$ 3,200,000

Upon receiving the memo, Leola had immediately called the Quality Control Department and arranged a meeting with Art Smith, manager of the department. Art had recently attended several seminars on total quality control and was excited about the prospects of improving quality performance. After meeting with Leola and reviewing the memo, Art was confident that the quality costs could be reduced by 50 percent within eighteen months. He had already begun planning the implementation of a new quality program.

With this information, Leola calculated that a 50 percent reduction in the quality costs associated with the low-quality instruments would reduce costs by about $1.60 per unit ($1,600,000/1,000,000)—which would make up slightly more than half of the $3 reduction in selling price that would be needed (the reduction is 15 percent of $20). Based on this outcome, Leola decided to implement the price reduction in three phases: a $1 reduction immediately, a $1 reduction in six months, and the final reduction of $1 in twelve months. This phased reduction would likely prevent any further erosion of market share and would start increasing it sometime into the second phase. By phasing in the price reductions, it would give the quality department time to reduce costs so that any big losses could be avoided.

Scenario A illustrates that both quality cost information and the implementation of a total quality control program contributed to a significant strategic decision. It also illustrates that improving quality was not a panacea. The reductions were not as large as needed to bear the full price reduction. Other productivity gains will be needed to ensure the long-range viability of the product line. Implementing JIT manufacturing, for example, might reduce inventories and decrease costs of material handling and maintenance.

Scenario B: Cost-Volume-Profit Analysis   Tara Anderson, the marketing manager, and Britany Fox, the design engineer, were both unhappy. They had been certain that a proposal for the new product was going to be approved. Instead, they received the following report from the controller's office.

Report: New Product Analysis, Project #675

Projected sales potential: 44,000 units

Production capacity: 45,000 units

Unit selling price: $60

Unit variable costs: $40

Fixed Costs:

Product development:	$ 500,000
Manufacturing:	200,000
Selling:	300,000
Total	$1,000,000

Projected breakeven: 50,000 units

Decision: Reject

Reason(s): The break-even point is greater than the production capacity as well as the projected sales volume.

"You know," Tara remarked, "I can't quite believe this report. Why don't we ask Bob how he came up with these figures?"

"I agree, " responded Britany. "I'll arrange a meeting for tomorrow. I'll ask him to provide more detail than just aggregate figures shown on the report."

The next day, the following conversation was recorded. Tara and Britany had just completed a review of the detailed cost projections supplied by Bob Brown, the assistant controller.

Britany: Bob, I would like to know why there is a $3 per-unit scrap cost. Can you explain it?

Bob: Sure. It's based on the scrap cost that we track for existing, similar products.

Britany: Well, I think you have overlooked the new design features of this new product. Its design virtually eliminates any waste—especially when you consider that the product will be made on a numerically controlled machine.

Tara: Also this $2 per-unit charge for repair work should be eliminated. The new design that Britany is proposing solves the failure problems we have had with related products. It also means that the $100,000 of fixed costs associated with the repair center can be eliminated.

Bob: Britany, how certain are you that this new design will eliminate some of these quality problems?

Britany: I'm absolutely positive. The early prototypes did exactly as we expected. The results of those tests are included in the proposal.

Bob: Right. Reducing the variable cost by $5 per unit and the fixed costs by $100,000 produces a break-even point of 36,000 units. These changes alone make the project viable. I'll change the report to reflect a positive recommendation.

Scenario B illustrates the importance of further classifying quality costs by behavior. Although only unit-based behavior is assumed, activity-based classification is also possible and could enhance the decision usefulness of quality costs. The scenario also reinforces the importance of identifying and reporting quality costs separately. The new product was designed to reduce its quality costs and only by knowing the quality costs assigned could Britany and Tara have discovered the error in the break-even analysis.

Reporting quality costs so that they can be used for decision making is only one objective of a good quality costing system. Another objective is controlling quality costs—a factor critical in helping expected outcomes of decisions come to fruition. The pricing decision of Scenario A, for example, depended on the plan to reduce quality costs.

■ CONTROLLING QUALITY COSTS

Reporting quality costs is not sufficient to ensure that they are controlled. Proper control requires standards and a measure of actual outcomes so that performance can be gauged and corrective actions taken when necessary. Quality cost performance reports have two essential elements: actual outcomes and standard or expected outcomes. Any deviations of actual outcomes from the expected outcomes are used to evaluate managerial performance and provide signals concerning possible problems. Performance reports provide essential feedback so that managers can evaluate their own behavior and take corrective action when needed.

Performance reports are essential to quality improvement programs. A report like the one shown in Exhibit 16–2 forces managers to identify the various costs that should appear in a performance report, to identify the current quality performance level of the organization, and to begin thinking about the level of quality performance that should be achieved. Identifying the quality standard is a key element in a quality performance report.

Choosing the Quality Standard

The Traditional Approach In the traditional approach, the appropriate quality standard is an acceptable quality level (AQL). An AQL is simply an admission that a certain number of defective products will be produced and sold. For example, the AQL may be set at 3 percent. In this case, any lot of products (or production run) that has no more than 3 percent defective units will be shipped to customers. Typically, the AQL reflects the current operating status, not what is possible if a firm has an excellent quality program. As the basis for a quality standard, AQL has the same problems as historical experience does for materials and labor usage standards: it may perpetuate past operating mistakes.

Unfortunately, AQL has additional problems. Setting a 3 percent AQL is a commitment to deliver defective products to customers. Out of every 1 million units sold, 30,000 will yield dissatisfied customers. Why plan to make a certain number of defective units? Why not plan instead to make the product according to its specifications? Is there not a matter of integrity involved here? How many customers would accept a product if they knew that it was defective? How many people would consult a surgeon if they knew that the surgeon planned to botch three of every one hundred operations?

The Zero-Defects Approach   These questions reflect a new attitude towards quality being popularized by a number of quality experts. These experts suggest that a more sensible standard is to produce products as they were intended to be. This standard is often referred to as the *zero-defects concept.* **Zero defects** is a performance standard that calls for products and services to be produced and delivered according to requirements. It reflects a philosophy of total quality control. Recall that the need for total quality control is inherent in a JIT manufacturing approach. Thus, the movement towards total quality control is being sustained by the firms adopting JIT. JIT, however, is not a prerequisite for moving towards total quality control. This philosophy can stand by itself.

Admittedly, the zero defects standard is one that may not be completely attainable; however, evidence exists that it can be closely approximated. Defects are caused either by lack of knowledge or by lack of attention. Lack of knowledge can be corrected by proper training, lack of attention by effective leadership. Note also that the zero-defects concept implies the ultimate elimination of failure costs. Those believing in zero defects will continue to search for new ways to improve quality costs. Thus, implicit in the standard is the capability to move down the total cost curve shown in Exhibit 16–5.

Some may wonder whether zero defects is a realistic standard. Consider the following anecdote. An American firm placed an order for a particular component with a Japanese firm. In the order, the American firm specified that 1,000 components should be delivered with an AQL of 5 percent defects. When the order arrived, it came in two boxes—one large and one small. A note explained that the large box contained 950 good components and the small one fifty defective components; the note also asked why the firm wanted fifty defective parts (implying the capability of delivering no defective parts).

Consider another case. A firm engaged in a significant volume of business through mailings. On average, 15 percent of the mailings were sent to the wrong address. Returned merchandise, late payments, and lost sales all resulted from this error rate. In one case, a tax payment was sent to the wrong

zero defects

address. By the time the payment arrived, it was late, causing a penalty of $300,000. Why not spend the resources (surely less than $300,000) to get the mailing list right and have no errors? Is a mailing list that is 100 percent accurate really impossible to achieve? Why not do it right the first time?

Quantifying the Quality Standard

Quality can be measured by its costs; as the costs of quality decrease, higher quality results—at least up to a point. Even if the standard of zero defects is achieved, a company must still have prevention and appraisal costs. A company with a well-run quality management program can get by with quality costs that are no more than 2.5 percent of sales. (If zero defects are achieved, this cost is for prevention and appraisal.) This 2.5 percent standard is accepted by many quality control experts and many firms that are adopting aggressive quality improvement programs.

The 2.5 percent standard is for total costs of quality. Costs of individual quality factors, such as quality training or materials inspection, will be less. Each organization must determine the appropriate standard for each individual factor. Budgets can be used to set spending for each standard so that the total budgeted cost meets the 2.5 percent goal.

Behavior of Quality Costs   To make the 2.5 percent standard work, the cost behavior of individual quality factors must be identified. Some quality costs vary with sales; others do not. For performance reports to be useful, quality costs must be classified as variable or fixed with respect to sales. For variable quality costs, improvements in quality are reflected by reductions in the variable cost ratios. The beginning and ending variable cost ratios for a period can be used to compute the actual dollar savings (or actual increased costs). Budgeted and actual ratios can also be used to gauge the progress towards the period's goals. For fixed costs, quality improvements are best reflected by absolute dollar changes.

If maintaining a zero-defects standard requires a 1.5 percent variable cost ratio, meeting the overall goal of costs at 2.5 percent of sales limits fixed quality costs to 1 percent of sales. This budget for fixed quality costs would be set at the beginning of the year.

Fixed quality costs are evaluated by comparing actual costs with the budgeted costs. The dollars actually spent on these costs are what is compared. Comparing these costs using a percentage of sales, rather than actual dollars spent, is not useful. Since budgeted sales may not equal actual sales, the actual percentage could be greater or less than the budgeted percentage even if the actual fixed costs were exactly equal to the budgeted fixed costs.

Variable quality costs, on the other hand, can be compared using either percentages of sales or actual dollars or both. Since managers are accustomed to dealing with dollar amounts, the best approach is comparing absolute dollars and supplementing that measure with percentages. Furthermore, computing the overall percentage, using both variable and fixed costs, is also recommended. This will provide management with an idea of how well the overall 2.5 percent standard is being met.

Physical Standards   For line managers and operating personnel, physical measures of quality—such as number of defects per unit, the percentage of external failures, billing errors, contract errors, and other physical measures— may be more meaningful. For physical measures, the quality standard is zero defects or errors. The objective is to get everyone to do it right the first time.

Use of Interim Standards   For most firms, the standard of zero defects is a long-range goal. The ability to achieve this standard is strongly tied to supplier quality. For most companies, materials and services purchased from outside parties make up a significant part of the cost of the product. For example, more than 65 percent of the product cost for Tennant Company was from materials and parts purchased from more than 500 different suppliers. To achieve the desired quality level, Tennant had to launch a major campaign to involve its suppliers in similar quality improvement programs. Developing the relationships and securing the needed cooperation from suppliers takes time—in fact, it takes years. Similarly, getting people within the company itself to understand the need for quality improvement and to have confidence in the program can take several years.

interim quality
standards

   Because improving quality to the zero-defect level can take years, yearly quality improvement standards should be developed so that managers can use performance reports to assess the progress made on an interim basis. These **interim quality standards** express quality goals for the year. Progress should be reported to managers and employees in order to gain the confidence needed to achieve the ultimate standard of zero defects. Even though reaching the zero-defect level is a long-range project, management should expect significant progress on a yearly basis. For example, Tennant cut its quality costs from 15 percent of sales to 8 percent of sales in six years—an average reduction of more than 1 percent per year. Furthermore, Tennant is still actively pursuing the goal of reducing its quality costs to 2.5 percent of sales. Once the 2.5 percent goal is reached, efforts must be expended continuously to maintain it. Performance reports, at this stage, assume a strict control role.

Types of Quality Performance Reports

Quality performance reports should measure the progress realized by an organization's quality improvement program. Four types of progress can be measured and reported:

1. Progress with respect to a current-period standard or goal (an interim standard report)

2. Progress with respect to last year's quality performance (a one-period trend report)

3. The progress trend since the inception of the quality improvement program (a multiple-period trend report)

4. Progress with respect to the long-range standard or goal (a long-range report)

Interim Standard Report   As noted above, the organization must establish an interim quality standard each year and make plans to achieve this targeted level. Since quality costs are a measure of quality, the targeted level can be expressed in dollars budgeted for each category of quality costs and for each cost item within the category. At the end of the period, the **interim quality performance report** compares the actual quality costs for the period against the budgeted costs. This report measures the progress achieved within the period relative to the planned level of progress for that period.

interim quality performance report

Exhibit 16–6 (p. 808) illustrates such a report. For variable costs, the budgeted figures are based on actual sales using variable cost ratios, which were obtained by dividing budgeted variable costs by budgeted sales. The original budgeted amounts are used for fixed costs.

The interim report reveals the within-period quality improvement relative to specific objectives as reflected by the budgeted figures. For Jensen Products, the overall performance is close to what was planned: total actual quality costs differ by only $2,000 from total budgeted quality costs and the actual costs, a mere 0.07 percent as a percentage of sales.

One-Year Trend   Additional insight can be realized by comparing the current year's performance with what the cost of quality would have been using the prior year's quality costs. The vehicle for doing so is a **one-year quality performance report**. To make this comparison, the prior year's actual variable cost ratio is used to compute the variable quality costs expected under the prior year's cost structure by multiplying the ratio by this year's actual sales. For example, if the prior year's actual variable cost ratio for materials inspection was 1.2 percent, then $33,600 (0.012 × $2,800,000) would have been spent for materials inspection this year. The prior year's actual fixed quality costs are compared directly with this year's fixed quality costs. This report allows managers to assess the short-run trend of its quality improvement program.

one-year quality performance report

The one-year performance report in Exhibit 16–7 (p. 809) shows that Jensen Products made significant progress in reducing its quality costs from 1991 to 1992. Overall, quality costs are $73,000 less than what they would have been had Jensen continued to spend at the 1991 level (2.61 percent less as a percentage of sales). The report also provides detailed information concerning the areas in which the gains have been made. For example, the cost of reliability engineering has dropped by $40,000. This drop could be explained by a reduction in staff—one engineer was released because of quality gains made in prior years. Similarly, the drop in the cost of product acceptance could be explained by a gradual phaseout of this activity as management gains assurance that product defects are decreasing.

EXHIBIT 16-6

Jensen Products			
Interim Standard Performance Report: Quality Costs *For the Year Ended March 31, 1992*			
	Actual *Costs*	*Budgeted* *Costs*[a]	*Variance*
Prevention costs:			
Fixed:			
Quality training	$ 35,000	$ 30,000	$ 5,000 U
Reliability engineering	80,000	80,000	0
Total prevention	$115,000	$110,000	$ 5,000 U
Appraisal costs:			
Variable:			
Materials inspection	$ 20,000	$ 28,000	$ 8,000 F
Product acceptance	10,000	15,000	5,000 F
Process acceptance	38,000	35,000	3,000 U
Total appraisal	$ 68,000	$ 78,000	$10,000 F
Internal failure costs:			
Variable:			
Scrap	$ 50,000	$ 44,000	$ 6,000 U
Rework	35,000	36,500	1,500 F
Total internal failure	$ 85,000	$ 80,500	$ 4,500 U
External failure costs:			
Fixed:			
Customer complaints	$ 25,000	$ 25,000	$ 0
Variable:			
Warranty	25,000	20,000	5,000 U
Repair	15,000	17,500	2,500 F
Total external failure	$ 65,000	$ 62,500	$ 2,500 U
Total quality costs	$333,000	$331,000	$ 2,000 U
Percentage of actual sales[b]	11.89%	11.82%	0.07% U

[a]Based on actual sales
[b]Actual sales of $2,800,000

Multiple-period Trend   The report in Exhibit 16–7 provides management with information concerning the change in quality costs relative to the most recent period. Also useful is a picture of how the quality improvement program has been doing since its inception. Is the multiple-period trend—the overall change in quality costs—in the right direction? Are significant quality gains being made each period? Answers to these questions can be given by providing a chart or graph that tracks the change in quality from the begin-

EXHIBIT 16–7

Jensen Products			

Performance Report: Quality Cost, One-year Trend
For the Year Ended March 31, 1992

	Actual Costs[a] 1992	Actual Costs 1991	Variance
Prevention costs:			
Fixed:			
Quality training	$ 35,000	$ 36,000	$ 1,000 F
Reliability engineering	80,000	120,000	40,000 F
Total prevention	$115,000	$156,000	$41,000 F
Appraisal costs:			
Variable:			
Materials inspection	$ 20,000	$ 33,600	$13,600 F
Product acceptance	10,000	16,800	6,800 F
Process acceptance	38,000	39,200	1,200 F
Total appraisal	$ 68,000	$ 89,600	$21,600 F
Internal failure costs:			
Variable:			
Scrap	$ 50,000	$ 48,000	$ 2,000 U
Rework	35,000	40,000	5,000 F
Total internal failure	$ 85,000	$ 88,000	$ 3,000 F
External failure costs:			
Fixed:			
Customer complaints	$ 25,000	$ 33,000	$ 8,000 F
Variable:			
Warranty	25,000	23,000	2,000 U
Repair	15,000	16,400	1,400 F
Total external failure	$ 65,000	$ 72,400	$ 7,400 F
Total quality costs	$333,000	$406,000	$73,000 F
Percentage of actual sales			
(current year)	11.89%	14.5%	2.61% F

[a]Based on actual current sales of $2,800,000

multiple-period
quality trend report ning of the program to the present. Such a graph is called a **multiple-period quality trend report**. By plotting quality costs as a percentage of sales against time, the overall trend in the quality program can be assessed. The first year plotted is the year prior to the implementation of the quality improvement program. Assume that Jensen Products has experienced the following:

	Quality Costs	Actual Sales	Costs as a Percentage of Sales
1988	$462,000	$2,200,000	21.0
1989	423,000	2,350,000	18.0
1990	412,500	2,750,000	15.0
1991	406,000	2,800,000	14.5
1992	333,000	2,800,000	11.9

Letting 1988 be Year 0, 1989 be Year 1, and so on, the trend graph is shown in Exhibit 16–8. Periods of time are plotted on the horizontal axis and percentages on the vertical. The ultimate quality cost objective of 2.5 percent, the target percentage, is represented as a horizontal line on the graph.

The graph reveals that there has been a steady downward trend in quality costs expressed as a percentage of sales. The most dramatic decreases were experienced in the first two years. The graph also reveals that there is still ample room for improvement towards the long-run target percentage.

EXHIBIT 16–8
Multiple-period Trend Graph:
Total Quality Costs

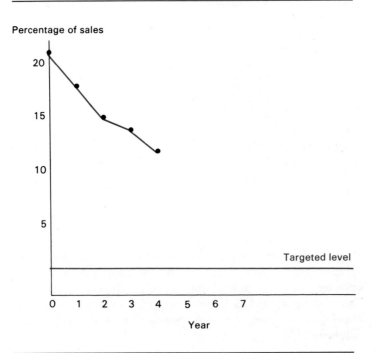

Additional insight can be provided by plotting the trend for each individual quality category. Assume that each category is expressed as a percentage of sales for the same period of time.

	Prevention	*Appraisal*	*Internal Failure*	*External Failure*
1988	6.0%	4.5%	4.5%	6.0%
1989	6.0	4.0	3.5	4.5
1990	5.4	3.6	3.0	3.0
1991	5.6	3.2	3.1	2.6
1992	4.1	2.4	3.0	2.3

The graph showing the trend for each category is displayed in Exhibit 16–9. From Exhibit 16–9, we can see that Jensen Products has had dramatic success in reducing external failures. In fact, all four categories have shown

EXHIBIT 16–9
Multiple-period Trend Graph:
Individual Quality Costs

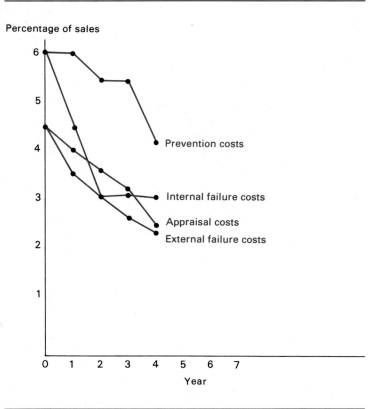

significant reductions in costs expressed as a percentage of sales. Furthermore, the reductions apparently reflect actual improvements in quality since the cost of failures is declining.

Long-range Standard   At the end of each period, a report that compares the period's actual quality costs with the costs that the firm eventually hopes to achieve should be prepared. This report forces management to keep the ultimate quality goal in mind, reveals the room left for improvement, and facilitates planning for the coming period. Under a zero-defects philosophy, the costs of failure should be virtually nonexistent. Reducing the costs of failure increases a firm's competitive ability. Tennant Company, for example, is now able to offer warranties that last two to four times longer than those of its competitors because of improved quality resulting in lower external failure rates. Thus, not only have quality costs been reduced by almost 50 percent, but because of improved quality, sales performance has increased.

Remember that achieving higher quality will not totally eliminate prevention and appraisal costs. In fact, increased emphasis on zero defects may actually increase the cost of prevention, depending on what kind of efficiencies can be realized in this area. Generally, we would expect appraisal costs to decrease. Product acceptance, for example, may be phased out entirely as product quality increases; however, increased emphasis on process acceptance is likely. The firm must have assurance that the process is operating in a zero-defect mode. Exhibit 16–10 illustrates a **long-range quality performance report**. It compares the current period's actual costs with the costs that would be allowed if the zero-defect standard were being met (assuming a sales level equal to that of the current period). The report emphasizes the fact that the company is still spending too much money on quality—too much money for not doing things right the first time. As quality improves, savings can be realized by having fewer workers to correct the mistakes made initially. Rework people, for example, will disappear when there is no more rework, warranty costs will stop when there are no failures in the field, and so on.

By spending less money on defects, a company can use the money to expand—and employ additional people to support this expansion. Increased quality may naturally cause expansion by increasing the competitive position of a firm. By having fewer problems with existing products, a firm can focus more attention on growth. Thus, although improved quality may mean fewer jobs in some areas, it also means that additional jobs will be created through expanded business activity. In fact, more jobs will probably be added than are lost.

long-range quality performance report

Incentives for Quality Improvement

Most organizations provide both monetary and nonmonetary recognition for significant contributions to quality improvement. Of the two types of incentives, most quality experts believe that the nonmonetary are more useful.

As with budgets, participation helps employees internalize quality im-

EXHIBIT 16-10

	Jensen Products		
	Long-range Performance Report *For the Year Ended March 31, 1992*		
	Actual *Costs*	*Target* *Costs*[a]	*Variance*
Prevention costs:			
Fixed:			
Quality training	$ 35,000	$15,000	$ 20,000 U
Reliability engineering	80,000	40,000	40,000 U
Total prevention	$115,000	$55,000	$ 60,000 U
Appraisal costs:			
Variable:			
Materials inspection	$ 20,000	$ 5,000	$ 15,000 U
Product acceptance	10,000	—	10,000 U
Process acceptance	38,000	10,000	28,000 U
Total appraisal	$ 68,000	$15,000	$ 53,000 U
Internal failure costs:			
Variable:			
Scrap	$ 50,000	$ —	$ 50,000 U
Rework	35,000	—	35,000 U
Total internal failure	$ 85,000	$ —	$ 85,000 U
External failure costs:			
Fixed:			
Customer complaints	$ 25,000	$ —	$ 25,000 U
Variable:			
Warranty	25,000	—	25,000 U
Repair	15,000	—	15,000 U
Total external failure	$ 65,000	$ 0	$ 65,000 U
Total quality costs	333,000	70,000	$263,000 U
Percentage of actual sales	11.89%	2.5%	9.39% U

[a]Based on actual sales of $2,800,000

error cause identification

provement goals as their own. One approach used by many companies in their efforts to involve employees is the use of error cause identification forms. **Error cause identification** is a program in which employees describe problems that interfere with their ability to do the job right the first time. The error-cause-removal approach is one of the fourteen steps in Phillip Crosby's quality improvement program. To ensure the success of the program, each employee submitting an entry should receive a note of appreciation from management. Additional recognition should be given to those who submit particularly beneficial information. Tennant Company, for example, gives 20 percent of the first year's savings from submissions that are adopted to the employees who made them.

Other nonfinancial awards can also be given to recognize employees for their efforts. One company, for example, gives an award of excellence to, at most, 2 percent of its work force for outstanding quality contributions. The award, given at a special dinner, consists of a specially designed gold and diamond ring. This same company use two other awards: one individual and one group. Outstanding individual work can earn the Koala T. Bear Award. Groups can also earn excellence awards.

The important thing is not the award itself but the public recognition of outstanding achievement. By publicly recognizing significant quality contributions, management underscores its commitment to quality improvement. Also, the individuals and groups so recognized feel the benefits of that recognition, which include pride, job satisfaction, and a further commitment to quality.

▪ PRODUCTIVITY: MEASUREMENT AND CONTROL

While quality improvements offer significant economic benefits, a firm can increase its financial well-being even more by simultaneously focusing on improving productivity. Quality and productivity improvements are compatible and, in fact, are critical strategic issues for the advanced manufacturing environment. Continual striving for improvement in both quality and productivity is mandated.

Productivity Measurement Defined

productivity

total productive efficiency

technical efficiency
price efficiency

Productivity concerns producing output efficiently and specifically addresses the relationship of output and the inputs used to produce the output. Usually, different combinations or mixes of inputs can be used to produce a given level of output. **Total productive efficiency** is the point at which two conditions are satisfied: (1) for any mix of inputs that will produce a given output, no more of any one input is used than necessary to produce the output and (2) given the mixes that satisfy the first condition, the least costly mix is chosen. The first condition is driven by technical relationships and, therefore, is referred to as **technical efficiency.** The second condition is driven by relative input price relationships and, therefore, is referred to as **price efficiency**. Productivity improvement programs involve moving towards a state of total productive efficiency. Productivity improvement, for example, can be achieved by using fewer of all inputs to produce the same output or by producing more output using the same inputs. Exhibit 16–11, Part A, illustrates these two ways to achieve an improvement in technical efficiency. Productivity improvement can also be achieved by trading off more costly inputs for less costly inputs. Exhibit 16–11, Part B, illustrates the possibility of improving productivity by increasing price efficiency.

EXHIBIT 16–11
Illustration of Productivity Improvement

A. Technical Efficiency Improvement

Current Productivity:

Inputs   Output

Same output, fewer inputs

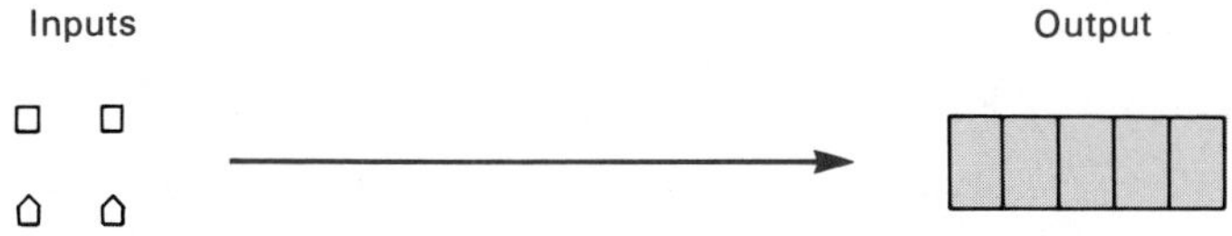

Inputs   Output

More output, same inputs:

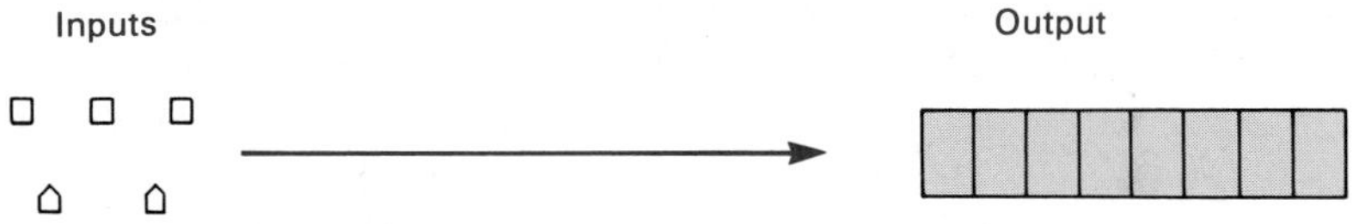

Inputs   Output

B. Price Efficiency Improvement

Combination I: Total Cost of Inputs = $28

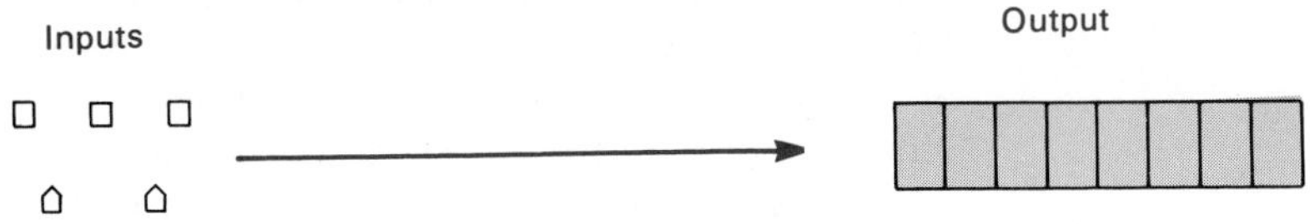

Inputs   Output

Combination II: Total Cost of Inputs = $27

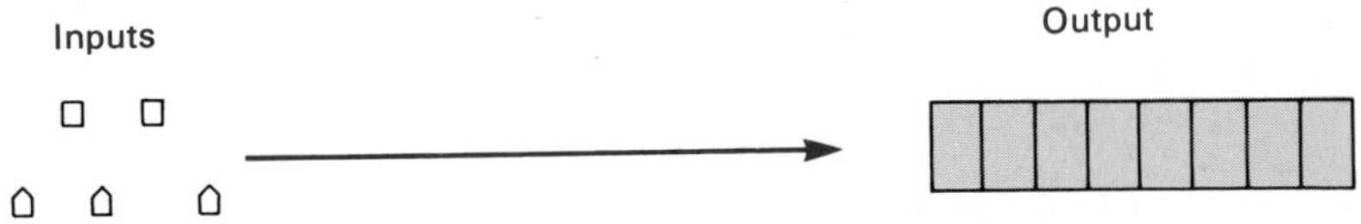

Inputs   Output

Of the two combinations that produce the same output, the least costly combination would be chosen.

Productivity measurement concerns measuring productivity changes so that efforts to improve productivity can be evaluated. Measurement can also be prospective and serve as input for strategic decision making. Productivity measures can be developed for each input separately or for all inputs jointly.

Measuring productivity for one input at a time is called **partial productivity measurement**. Measuring productivity for all inputs at once is called **total productivity measurement**.

Partial Productivity Measurement

Definition of a Partial Productivity Measure Productivity of a single input is typically measured by calculating the ratio of the output to the input:

$$\text{Productivity ratio} = \text{Output/Input}$$

Because the productivity of only one input is being measured, the measure is called a *partial productivity measure*. If both output and input are measured in physical quantities, then we have an **operational productivity measure**. If output or input is expressed in dollars, then we have a **financial productivity measure**.

Assume, for example, that in 1991, Hotkumfurt Company produced 11,000 space heaters and used 1,100 hours of labor. The labor productivity ratio is ten space heaters per hour (11,000/1,100). This is an operational measure since the units are expressed in physical terms. If the selling price of each heater is $25 and the cost of labor is $10 per hour, then output and input can be expressed in dollars. The labor productivity ratio, expressed in financial terms, is $25 of revenue per dollar of labor cost ($275,000/$11,000).

Partial Measures and Measuring Productivity Changes The labor productivity ratio of ten heaters per hour measures the 1991 productivity experience of Hotkumfurt. By itself the ratio conveys little information about productive efficiency or whether the company has improving or declining productivity. It is possible, however, to make a statement about increasing or decreasing productivity efficiency by measuring *changes* in productivity. To do so, the actual current productivity measure is compared with the productivity measure of a prior period. This prior period is referred to as the *base period* and

serves to set the benchmark or standard for measuring changes in productive efficiency. The prior period can be any period desired. It could, for example, be the preceding year, the preceding week, or even the period during which the last batch of products was produced. For strategic evaluations, the base period is usually chosen as an earlier year.

To illustrate, assume that 1991 is the base period and the labor productivity standard, therefore, is ten heaters per hour. Further assume that late in 1991, Hotkumfurt decided to try a new procedure for assembling the heaters with the expectation that the new procedure would use labor more efficiently. In 1992, 110,000 heaters were produced, using 10,000 hours of labor. The labor productivity ratio for 1992 is eleven heaters per hour (110,000/10,000). The *change* in productivity is a one-unit per hour *increase* in productivity (from ten units per hour in 1991 to eleven units per hour in 1992). The change is a significant improvement in labor productivity and provides evidence supporting the efficacy of the new assembly process.

Advantages of Partial Measures   Partial measures allow managers to focus on the use of a particular input. Furthermore, partial operational measures are easy to use for assessing productivity performance of operating personnel. Laborers, for instance, can relate to units produced per hour or units produced per pound of material. Thus, partial operational measures provide feedback that operating personnel can relate to and understand—measures that deal with the specific inputs over which they have control. Furthermore, for operational control, the standards for performance are often very short-run in nature. For example, standards can be the productivity ratios of prior batches of goods. Using this standard, productivity trends within the year itself can be tracked.

Disadvantages of Partial Measures   Partial measures, used in isolation, can be misleading. A decline in the productivity of one input may be necessary to increase the productivity of another. Such a tradeoff is desirable if overall costs decline, but the effect would be missed by using either partial measure. For example, changing a process so that direct laborers take less time to assemble a product may increase scrap and waste while leaving total output unchanged. Labor productivity has increased but productive use of materials has declined. If the increase in the cost of waste and scrap outweighs the savings of the decreased labor, overall productivity has declined.

   Two important conclusions can be drawn from this example. First, the possible existence of tradeoffs mandates a total measure of productivity for assessing the merits of productivity decisions. Only by looking at the total productivity effect of all inputs can managers accurately draw any conclusions about productivity performance. Second, because of the possibility of tradeoffs, a total measure of productivity must assess the aggregate financial consequences, and, therefore, should be a financial measure.

Total Productivity Measurement

Productivity Changes with No Tradeoffs   Producing a product involves numerous inputs such as labor, materials, capital, and energy. A total measure would assess the effect of all inputs. For simplicity, our discussion of total measurement will use only two inputs: labor and materials. Let's return to the Hotkumfurt Company example. As before, Hotkumfurt implements a new assembly process in 1992. Only now let's assume that the new assembly process affects both labor and materials. Initially, let's look at the case for which the productivity of both inputs moves in the same direction. The following data for 1991 and 1992 are available:

	1991	1992
Number of heaters produced	110,000	110,000
Labor hours used	11,000	10,000
Materials used (lbs)	110,000	88,000
Unit selling price (heaters)	$25	$25
Wages per labor hour	$10	$10
Cost per pound of material	$5	$5

Exhibit 16–12 provides a summary of the productivity ratios for each input for each year. Notice that productivity increased for both labor and materials (from 10 to 11 for labor and from 1.00 to 1.25 for materials). The two ratios provide enough information so that a manager can conclude that the new assembly process has definitely improved overall productivity. The *value* of this improvement, however, is not revealed by the ratios. Knowing the value of the productivity change is important for assessing the economic impact of the decision to change the assembly process. Furthermore, by valuing the productivity change, we obtain a total measure of productivity.

profit-linked productivity measurement   Assessing the effects of productivity changes on current profits is one way to value productivity changes. Profits change from the base period to the current period. Some of that profit change is attributable to productivity changes. Assessing the amount of profit change attributable to productivity change is defined as **profit-linked productivity measurement**.[8]

Profit-Linked Productivity Measurement   A direct way to value the productivity changes is to assess their effect on current-period profits. Knowing this effect will help managers understand the economic importance of productivity changes. Linking productivity changes to profits is described by the following rule:

Profit-Linkage Rule

For the current period, calculate the cost of the inputs that would have been used in the absence of any productivity change and compare this cost with the cost of

---

[8]Several profit-linked productivity measures have been developed and used by firms. The American Productivity Center has developed a profit-linked measure described in J. G. Belcher Jr., *The Productivity Management Process* (Houston: The American Productivity Center, 1984). D. M. Miller developed and used a profit-linked measure while working for Ethyl Corporation. It is described in D. M. Miller, "Profitability = Productivity + Price Recovery," *Harvard Business Review* (May–June 1984), pp. 145–153. A third profit-linked measure is described in R. D. Banker, S. M. Datar, and R. S. Kaplan, "Productivity Measurement and Management Accounting," *Journal of Accounting, Auditing, and Finance* (1989). The profit-linked measure described in this text is essentially a modification of the three measures above. The modification increases the accuracy of profit-linked measurement and allows a connection to the operational and partial measures of productivity. It also establishes an equivalency among the three measures. See Don R. Hansen, Maryanne Mowen, and Lawrence Hammer, "Profit-Linked Productivity Measurement," *Journal of Management Accounting Research* (forthcoming 1992).

EXHIBIT 16–12
Total Productivity Measurement:
No Input Tradeoffs

A. Operational Productivity Ratios		
	1991[a]	1992[b]
Labor productivity ratio	10.00	11.00
Material productivity ratio	1.00	1.25

[a]Labor: 110,000/11,000; Materials: 110,000/110,000
[b]Labor: 110,000/10,000; Materials: 110,000/88,000

the inputs actually used. The difference in costs is the amount by which profits changed because of productivity changes.

To apply the linkage rule, the inputs that would have been used for the current period in the absence of a productivity change must be calculated. Let PQ represent this productivity-neutral quantity of input. To determine the productivity-neutral quantity for a particular input, divide the current-period output by the input's base-period productivity ratio:

PQ = Current output/Base-period productivity ratio

For our example, current output is 110,000 heaters. The productivity-neutral quantity for each input is computed below.

PQ (labor) = 110,000/10 = 11,000 hrs
PQ (materials) = 110,000/1 = 110,000 lbs

Since output quantity did not change from 1991 to 1992, the inputs that would have been used in 1992, assuming no productivity change, would have been the inputs used in 1991, which is what we obtained. What the cost would have been for these productivity-neutral quantities in 1991 is computed by multiplying each individual input quantity (PQ) by its current price (P) and adding:[9]

Cost of labor: $PQ \times P$ = 11,000 × \$10 =	\$110,000
Cost of materials: $PQ \times P$ = 110,000 × \$5 =	550,000
Total PQ cost	\$660,000

[9]Base-period input prices are frequently used to value productivity changes. It has been shown, however, that current input prices should be used for accurate profit-linked productivity measurement. See Hansen, Mowen, and Hammer, "Profit-Linked Productivity Measurement."

The actual cost of inputs is obtained by multiplying the actual quantity (AQ) by current input price (P) for each input and adding:

Cost of labor: $AQ \times P = 10,000 \times \$10 =$	$100,000
Cost of materials: $AQ \times P = 88,000 \times \$5 =$	440,000
Total current cost	$540,000

Finally, the productivity effect on profits is computed by subtracting the total current cost from the total PQ cost.

$$\text{Profit-linked effect} = \text{Total } PQ \text{ cost} - \text{Total current cost}$$
$$= \$660,000 - \$540,000$$
$$= \$120,000 \text{ increase in profits}$$

The calculation of the profit-linked effect is summarized in Exhibit 16–13.

The summary in Exhibit 16–13 reveals that the profit-linked productivity effects can be assigned to individual inputs. Labor, for example, accounts for only $10,000 of the total improvement. Most of the improvement, $110,000, came from a reduction in materials usage. Thus, the profit-linked measure provides partial measurement effects as well as a total measurement effect. The total profit-linked productivity measure is the sum of the individual partial measures. This property makes the profit-linked measure ideal for assessing tradeoffs.

Total Productivity Measurement: Tradeoffs Considered   The value of profit-linked productivity measurement is more fully appreciated when the trade-offs among inputs are caused by the implementation of a new productivity program. In this case, looking at the change in productivity ratios will not provide any clear indication of whether the change is good or bad. The profit-linked measure, however, provides the overall effect and reveals the value of

EXHIBIT 16–13
Profit-Linked Productivity Measurement:
No Tradeoffs

	(1)	(2)	(3)	(4)	(2) − (4)
Input	PQ[a]	$PQ \times P$	AQ	$AQ \times P$	$PQ \times P - AQ \times P$
Labor	11,000	$110,000	10,000	$100,000	$ 10,000
Materials	110,000	550,000	88,000	440,000	110,000
		$660,000		$540,000	$120,000

[a]Labor: 110,000/10; Materials: 110,000/1

the tradeoffs among inputs. To illustrate this, let's revise the Hotkumfurt data to allow for tradeoffs.

	1991	1992
Number of heaters produced	110,000	120,000
Labor hours used	11,000	10,000
Materials used (lbs)	110,000	126,000
Unit selling price (heaters)	$25	$25
Wages per labor hour	10	10
Cost per pound of material	5	5

The productivity ratios for each input are calculated in Exhibit 16–14. For this scenario, notice that labor productivity has increased (from 10 to 12) but that material productivity has decreased (from 1.00 to 0.95). The partial operational measures provide mixed signals about the new assembly process. The profit-linked productivity measure, however, is a total measure of productivity—one that assesses the overall effect and values the tradeoffs of the individual inputs. The computation of the profit-linked measure is illustrated in Exhibit 16–15.

EXHIBIT 16–14
Operational Productivity Ratios:
Tradeoffs Present

	1991[a]	1992[b]
Labor	10.00	12.00
Materials	1.00	0.95

[a]Labor: 110,000/11,000; Materials: 110,000/110,000
[b]Labor: 120,000/10,000; Materials: 120,000/126,000

EXHIBIT 16–15
Profit-Linked Productivity Measurement

Input	(1) PQ[a]	(2) PQ × P	(3) AQ	(4) AQ × P	(2) − (4) PQ × P − AQ × P
Labor	12,000	$120,000	10,000	$100,000	$ 20,000
Materials	120,000	600,000	126,000	630,000	(30,000)
		$720,000		$730,000	$(10,000)

[a]Labor: 120,000/10 = 12,000; Materials: 120,000/1 = 120,000

From Exhibit 16–15, we obtain a clear picture of the productivity consequences of the new assembly process. Under this scenario, labor is reduced, saving $20,000, but waste and scrap apparently increase, causing materials cost to jump by $30,000. The net effect is a $10,000 drop in profits. Unless the scrap and waste can be brought under better control, the company ought to return to the old assembly process.

Price-Recovery Component   The profit-linked measure computes the amount of profit change from the base period to the current period attributable to productivity changes. This generally will not be equal to the total profit change between the two periods. The difference between the total profit change and the profit-linked productivity change is called the **price-recovery component**. This component is the change in revenue less a change in the cost of inputs, *assuming no productivity changes*. It therefore measures the ability of revenue changes to cover changes in the cost of inputs, assuming no productivity change. The second review problem at the end of the chapter allows you to compute this factor.

price-recovery component

Quality and Productivity

Improving quality may improve productivity and vice versa. For example, if rework is reduced by producing fewer defective units, less labor and fewer materials are used to produce the same output. Reducing the number of defective units improves quality; reducing the amount of inputs used improves productivity.

Since most quality improvements reduce the amount of resources used to produce and sell an organization's output, most quality improvements will improve productivity. Thus, quality improvements generally will be reflected in productivity measures. However, there are other ways to improve productivity other than through quality improvement. A firm may produce a good with little or no defects but still have an inefficient process.

For example, consider a good that passes through two 5-minute processes. (Assume the good is produced free of defects.) One unit, then, requires ten minutes to pass through both processes. Currently, units are produced in batches of 1,200. Process 1 produces 1,200 units; then the batch is conveyed by forklift to another location, where the units pass through Process 2. Thus, for each process, a total of 6,000 minutes, or 100 hours, are needed to produce a batch. The 1,200 finished units, then, require a total of 200 hours (100 hours for each process) plus conveyance time; assume that to be fifteen minutes.

By redesigning the manufacturing process, efficiency can be improved. Suppose that the second process is located close enough to the first process so that as soon as a unit is completed by the first process, it is passed to the second process. In this way, the first and second processes can be working at the same time. The second process no longer has to wait for the production of 1,200 units plus conveyance time before it can begin operation. The total time to produce 1,200 units now is 6,000 minutes plus the waiting time for the first unit (five minutes). Thus, production of 1,200 units has been reduced from 200 hours, 15 minutes to 100 hours, 5 minutes. More output can be produced with fewer inputs (time).

■ SUMMARY OF LEARNING OBJECTIVES

1. Explain the difference between quality of design and quality of conformance. Quality of design concerns quality differences that arise for products with the same function but different specifications. Quality of conformance, on the other hand, concerns meeting the specifications required by the product.

2. Identify and describe the four types of quality costs and prepare a quality cost report. There are four categories of quality costs: prevention, appraisal, internal failure, and external failure. Prevention costs are those incurred to prevent poor quality. Appraisal costs are those incurred to detect poor quality. Internal failure costs are those incurred because products fail to conform to requirements and this lack of conformity is discovered before an external sale. External failure costs are those incurred because products fail to conform to requirements after an external sale is made. A quality cost report is prepared by listing costs for each item within each of the four major quality cost categories. See Exhibit 16–2.

3. Explain the difference between the conventional view of acceptable quality level and the view espoused by total quality control. The conventional view holds that there is a tradeoff between costs of failure and prevention and appraisal costs. This tradeoff produces an optimal level of performance called the *acceptable quality level*. AQL is the level at which the number of defects allowed minimizes total quality costs. Total quality control maintains that the conflict between failure and appraisal and prevention costs is more conjecture than real. The actual optimal level of defects is the zero-defect level; companies should be striving to achieve this level of quality. Although quality costs do not vanish at this level, they are much lower than the optimal envisioned by the conventional view.

4. Explain why quality cost information is needed and how it is used. Quality cost information is needed to help managers control quality performance and to serve as input for decision making. It can be used to evaluate the overall performance of quality improvement programs. It can also be used to help improve a variety of managerial decisions, for example, strategic pricing and cost-volume-profit analysis.

5. Describe four different types of quality performance reports. Four reports are mentioned in the chapter: (1) the interim report, (2) the one-period trend report, (3) the multiple-period trend report, and (4) the long-range report. The interim report is used to evaluate the firm's ability to meet its budgeted quality costs. Managers use the report to compare the actual quality costs with those that were targeted for the period. The one-period trend report is used to compare the actual quality costs with those of the prior period, adjusting for differences in activity (a flexible-budget adjustment). This report allows managers to evaluate the progress made relative to the previous year. The multiple-period trend report is a trend graph for several years. The graph allows managers to assess the direction and magnitude of change since the inception of a total quality program. Finally, the long-range report compares actual costs with the ideal, zero-defect level.

6. **Explain what productivity is and differentiate between partial and total measures of productivity.** Productivity concerns how efficiently inputs are used to produce the output. Partial measures of productivity evaluate the efficient use of single inputs. Total measures of productivity assess efficiency for all inputs.

7. **Be able to calculate the impact of productivity changes on profits and explain why profit-linked productivity measurement is important.** Profit-linked productivity effects are calculated by using the linkage rule. Essentially, the profit effect is computed by taking the difference between the cost of the inputs that would have been used without any productivity change and the cost of the actual inputs used. Because of the possibility of input tradeoffs, it is essential to value productivity changes. Only in this way can the effect of productivity changes be properly assessed.

8. **Explain how quality and productivity are related and how they differ.** Quality improvement programs seek to achieve a zero-defect state. As success is realized, there are fewer inputs used—less waste, less inspection, and so on. Thus, the same output can be produced with fewer inputs, and productivity is improved. Quality improvements generally lead to an improved productivity measure. Quality improvement, however, is only one way to improve productivity. Productivity gains can be realized by other means.

■ KEY TERMS

Acceptable quality level (AQL)   A predetermined level of defective products that a company permits to be sold. (p. 798)

Appraisal costs   Costs incurred to determine whether products and services are conforming to requirements. (p. 794)

Base period   A prior period used to set the benchmark for measuring productivity changes. (p. 816)

Costs of quality   Costs incurred because poor quality may exist or because poor quality does exist. (p. 794)

Error cause identification   A program in which employees describe problems that prevent them from doing their jobs right the first time. (p. 813)

External failure costs   Costs incurred because products fail to conform to requirements after being sold to outside parties. (p. 795)

Financial productivity measure   A productivity measure in which inputs and outputs are expressed in dollars. (p. 816)

Interim quality performance report   A comparison of current actual quality costs with short-run budgeted quality targets. (p. 807)

Interim quality standard   A standard based on short-run quality goals. (p. 806)

Internal failure costs   Costs incurred because products and services fail to conform to requirements where lack of conformity is discovered prior to external sale. (p. 794)

Long-range quality performance report   A performance report that compares current actual quality costs with long-range budgeted quality costs. (p. 812)

Multiple-period quality trend report   A graph that plots quality costs (as a percentage of sales) against time. (p. 809)

One-year quality performance report   A report that compares current-year quality costs with prior-year quality costs based on current-year sales. (p. 807)

Operational productivity measures   Measures that are expressed in physical terms. (p. 816)

Partial productivity measurement   A ratio that measures productive efficiency for one input. (p. 816)

Prevention costs   Cost incurred to prevent defects in products or services being produced. (p. 794)

Price efficiency   The least-cost, technically efficient mix of inputs. (p. 814)

Price recovery component   The difference between the total profit change and the profit-linked productivity change. (p. 822)

Productivity   Producing output efficiently, using the least quantity of inputs possible. (p. 814)

Productivity measurement   Assessment of productivity changes. (p. 816)

Profit-linked productivity measurement   An assessment of the amount of profit change—from the base period to the current period—attributable to productivity changes. (p. 818)

Quality of conformance   Conforming to the design requirements of the product. (p. 793)

Quality of design   Quality differences that arise for products with the same function but different specifications. (p. 793)

Technical efficiency   Point at which for any mix of inputs that will produce a given output, no more of any one input is used than is absolutely necessary. (p. 814)

Total productive efficiency   The point at which technical and price efficiency are achieved. (p. 814)

Total productivity measurement   An assessment of productive efficiency for all inputs combined. (p. 816)

Zero defects   A quality performance standard that requires all products and services to be produced and delivered according to specifications. (p. 804)

■ REVIEW PROBLEMS

I.   **Quality**   At the beginning of the year, Kare Company initiated a quality improvement program. Considerable effort was expended to reduce the number of defective units produced. By the end of the year, reports from the production manager revealed that scrap and rework had both decreased. The president of the company was pleased to hear of the success but wanted some assessment of the financial impact of the improvements. To make this assessment, the following financial data were collected for the current and preceding year:

	Preceding Year (1991)	Current Year (1992)
Sales	$10,000,000	$10,000,000
Scrap	400,000	300,000
Rework	600,000	400,000
Product inspection	100,000	125,000
Product warranty	800,000	600,000
Quality training	40,000	80,000
Materials inspection	60,000	40,000

Required:

1. Classify the costs as preventive, appraisal, internal failure, and external failure.

2. Compute quality cost as a percentage of sales for each of the two years. By how much has profit increased because of quality improvements? Assuming that quality costs can be reduced to 2.5 percent of sales, how much additional profit is available through quality improvements (assume that sales revenues will remain the same)?

3. Prepare a one-year trend performance report.

Solution:

1. Appraisal costs: quality training and materials inspection; prevention costs: product inspection; internal failure costs: scrap and rework; external failure costs: warranty.

2. *Preceding year*—Total quality costs: $2,000,000; percentage of sales: 20 percent ($2,000,000/$10,000,000). *Current year*—Total quality costs: $1,545,000; percentage of sales: 15.45 percent ($1,545,000/$10,000,000). Profit has increased by $455,000. If quality costs drop to 2.5 percent of sales, another $1,295,000 of profit improvement is possible ($1,545,000 − $250,000).

3.

Kare Company

Interim Quality Performance Report
For the Year Ended 1992

	Actual Costs	Budgeted Costs[a]	Variance
Prevention costs:			
Quality training	$ 80,000	$ 40,000	$ 40,000 U
Appraisal costs:			
Product inspection	$125,000	$ 100,000	$ 25,000 U
Materials inspection	40,000	60,000	20,000 F
Total prevention	$165,000	$ 160,000	$ 5,000 U
Internal failure costs:			
Scrap	$300,000	$ 400,000	$100,000 F
Rework	400,000	600,000	200,000 F
Total internal failure	$700,000	$1,000,000	$300,000 F

	Actual Costs	Budgeted Costs[a]	Variance
External failure costs:			
Product warranty	$ 600,000	$ 800,000	$200,000 F
Total quality costs	$1,545,000	$2,000,000	$455,000 F
Percentage of sales	15.45%	20%	4.55% F

[a]Based on actual results for 1991.

II. **Productivity** Bearing Company made some changes at the end of 1991 that it hoped would favorably affect the efficiency of the input usage. Now, at the end of 1992, the president of the company wants an assessment of the changes on the company's productivity. The data needed for the assessment are given below.

	1991	1992
Output	5,000	6,000
Output prices	$10	$10
Materials (lbs)	4,000	4,200
Materials unit price	$3	$4
Labor (hrs)	2,500	2,400
Labor rate per hour	$8	$8
Power (kwh)	1,000	1,500
Price per kwh	$2	$3

Required:

1. Compute the partial operational measures for each input for both 1991 and 1992. What can be said about productivity improvement?

2. Prepare an income statement for each year and calculate the total change in profits.

3. Calculate the profit-linked productivity measure for 1992. What can be said about the productivity program?

4. Calculate the price-recovery component. What does this tell you?

Solution:

1. Partial Measures:

	1991	1992
Material	5,000/4,000 = 1.25	6,000/4,200 = 1.43
Labor	5,000/2,500 = 2.00	6,000/2,400 = 2.50
Power	5,000/1,000 = 5.00	6,000/1,500 = 4.00

Productive efficiency has increased for materials and labor and decreased for power. The outcome is mixed and no statement about overall productivity improvement can be made without valuing the tradeoff.

2. Income statements:

	1991	*1992*
Sales	$50,000	$60,000
Cost of inputs	34,000	40,500
Income	$16,000	$19,500

Total change in profits: $19,500 − $16,000 = $3,500 increase

3. Profit-linked measurement:

	(1)	*(2)*	*(3)*	*(4)*	*(2) − (4)*
Input	PQ^a	$PQ \times P$	AQ	$AQ \times P$	$PQ \times P - AQ \times P$
Materials	4,800	$19,200	4,200	$16,800	$2,400
Labor	3,000	24,000	2,400	19,200	4,800
Power	1,200	3,600	1,500	4,500	(900)
		$46,800		$40,500	$6,300

[a]Materials: 6,000/1.25; Labor: 6,000/2; Power: 6,000/5

The value of the increases in efficiency for materials and labor more than offsets the increased usage of power. Thus, the productivity program should be labeled successful.

4. Price recovery:

$$\text{Price recovery component} = \text{Total profit change} - \text{Profit-linked productivity change}$$

$$\text{Price recovery component} = \$3,500 - \$6,300 = \$(2,800)$$

This says that without the productivity improvement, profits would have declined by $2,800. The $10,000 increase in revenues would not have offset the increase in the cost of inputs. From the solution to Requirement 3, the cost of inputs without a productivity increase would have been $46,800 (column (2)). The increase in the input cost without productivity would have been $46,800 − $34,000 = $12,800. This is $2,800 more than the increase in revenues. Only because of the productivity increase did the firm show an increase in profitability.

▪ QUESTIONS

1 What is the difference between quality of design and quality of conformance?

2 Why are quality costs the costs of doing things wrong?

3 Identify and discuss the four kinds of quality costs.

4 Explain why external failure costs can be more devastating to a firm than internal failure costs.

5 What is the difference between an AQL standard and a zero-defects standard?

6   Many quality experts maintain that quality is free. Do you agree? Why or why not?

7   What is the purpose of interim quality standards?

8   Describe the four types of quality performance reporting. How can managers use each report to help evaluate their quality improvement programs?

9   Discuss the different kinds of incentives that can be used to motivate employees to become involved in quality improvement programs.

10 If a firm's annual sales are $200 million, what percentage of sales should be spent on quality costs? Suppose that the firm is spending 18 percent of sales on quality costs. What is the potential savings from quality improvement?

11 Define *total productive efficiency.*

12 Explain why it is important for a manager to assess the relative distribution of quality costs among the four categories.

13 Discuss the benefits of quality cost reports that simply list the quality costs for each category.

14 Explain the difference between partial and total measures of productivity.

15 Discuss the advantages and disadvantages of partial measures of productivity.

16 How can a manager measure productivity improvement?

17 What is profit-linked productivity measurement?

18 Explain why profit-linked productivity measurement is important.

19 What is the price-recovery component?

20 Can productivity improvements be achieved without improving quality? Explain.

21 Why is it important for managers to be concerned with both productivity and quality?

22 Explain why the accounting department should be responsible for producing quality cost reports. Also discuss the role accounting has in productivity measurement.

23 What are the differences between quality and productivity? The similarities?

■ EXERCISES

E16–1   **Quality Cost Classification**   Classify the following quality costs as prevention costs, appraisal costs, internal failure costs, or external failure costs:

1. Scrap
2. Inspection labor
3. Extra raw materials for rework
4. Warranty work
5. Goods returned because they failed to meet customer specifications
6. Goods returned because they were damaged in transit
7. Training program for new personnel
8. Work stoppage to correct process malfunction (discovered using statistical process control procedures)
9. Settlement of a product liability suit

10. Extra overhead and labor for rework

11. Lost sales because of incorrect product labeling

12. Internal audit

13. Engineering design changes

14. Purchase order changes

15. Replacement of defective product

16. Test labor

17. Field service personnel

18. Software correction

19. Supplier evaluations

20. Packaging inspection

21. Consumer complaint department

22. Prototype inspection and testing

23. Retest work

E16-2   **Quality Improvement and Profitability**   Reading, Inc., reported the following sales and quality costs for the past four years. Assume that all quality costs are variable and that all changes in the quality cost ratios are due to a quality improvement program.

Year	Sales Revenues	Quality Costs as Percent of Revenues
1	$10,000,000	0.21
2	11,000,000	0.18
3	11,000,000	0.14
4	12,000,000	0.10

Required:

1. Compute the quality costs for all four years. By how much did net income increase from Year 1 to Year 2 because of quality improvements? From Year 2 to Year 3? From Year 3 to Year 4?

2. Assume that Reading produces one type of product, which is sold on a bid basis. In years 1 and 2, the average bid was $200. In Year 1, total variable costs were $125 per unit. In Year 3, competition forced the bid to drop to $190. Compute the total contribution margin in Year 3 assuming the same quality costs as in Year 1. Now compute the total contribution margin in Year 3 using the actual quality costs for Year 3. What is the increase in profitability resulting from the quality improvements made from Year 1 to Year 3?

3. Assume that the quality standard is 2.5 percent of sales. What is the remaining profit potential facing Reading at the end of Year 4?

E16-3   **Quality Costs: Profit Improvement and Distribution Across Categories**   Sandoval Company had sales of $10,000,000 in 1992. During the year, Sandoval completed an analysis of its quality costs.

Internal failure costs	$ 700,000
External failure costs	900,000
Appraisal costs	300,000
Prevention costs	150,000
Total quality costs	$2,050,000

Required:

1. Compute the quality cost-to-sales ratio.

2. Compute the improvement in profits possible if quality costs are reduced to the following levels: (a) 10 percent of sales, (b) 8 percent of sales, and (c) 2.5 percent of sales.

3. Prepare a pie chart showing the relative distribution of costs by category. What do you think of the way costs are distributed? How do you think they will be distributed as the company approaches a zero-defects state?

E16–4 **Tradeoffs Among Quality Cost Categories** Progressive Company has sales of $1 million and quality costs of $200,000. The company is embarking on a major quality improvement program. During the next three years, Progressive intends to increase its appraisal and prevention costs in order to reduce the failure costs. The appraisal and prevention costs will result from adding five specific activities: sorting, process control, quality training, supplier evaluation, and engineering redesign of two major products. Current quality costs and the costs of these five activities are given in the following table. Each activity is added sequentially so that its effect on the cost categories can be assessed. For example, after sorting is added, the appraisal and prevention costs increase to $40,000 and the cost of failures drops to $130,000. Even though the activities are presented sequentially, they are totally independent of each other.

	Appraisal and Prevention Costs	Failure Costs
Current quality costs	$ 20,000	$180,000
Sorting	40,000	130,000
Process control	65,000	90,000
Quality training	75,000	82,000
Supplier evaluation	90,000	25,000
Engineering redesign	120,000	15,000

Upon seeing the effect of the quality improvement program, the president of Progressive was pleased—especially with the fact that total failure costs would be reduced to only $15,000 after all five activities are implemented.

Required:

1. Should all five quality improvement activities be implemented? If not, identify the ones that should be. Calculate the total quality costs for the activities selected. By how much were current costs reduced?

2. What does the outcome in requirement 1 suggest about the relationship between the two failure categories and appraisal and prevention? Do you think that quality costs can be reduced to zero? Explain.

E16–5   **One-year Trend Report**   In 1992, Karmon Microwave Foods, Inc., instituted a quality improvement program. At the end of 1993, the management of the corporation requested a report to show the amount saved by the measures taken during the year. The actual sales and actual quality costs for 1992 and 1993 are

	1992	1993
Sales	$500,000	$600,000
Scrap	15,000	15,000
Rework	20,000	10,000
Training program	5,000	6,000
Consumer complaints	10,000	5,000
Lost sales, incorrect labeling	8,000	—
Test labor	12,000	8,000
Inspection labor	25,000	24,000
Supplier evaluation	15,000	13,000

Required:

1. Classify each cost as variable or fixed and compute the variable cost ratio. Be careful—costs may change because of quality improvement, not cost behavior.

2. Prepare the one-year trend report that corporate management requested. How much did profits increase by because of quality improvements made in 1993 (assume that all reductions in quality costs are attributable to quality improvements)?

E16–6   **Long-range Performance Report**   Refer to the data in Exercise 16–5. Karmon's management believes that quality costs can be reduced to 2.5 percent of sales within the next five years. At the end of Year 5, Karmon's sales are projected to have grown to $750,000. The relative distribution of quality costs at the end of Year 5 is as follows:

Scrap	15%
Training	20
Supplier evaluation	25
Test labor	25
Inspection	15
Total quality costs	100%

Required:

Prepare a long-range performance report that compares the quality costs incurred at the end of 1993 with the quality-cost structure expected at the end of 1998. What would be the increase in profits in 1998 if the 2.5 percent performance standards had been met in that year?

E16–7   **Multiple-year Trend Reports**   The controller of Golden Company has computed quality costs as a percentage of sales for the past five years (1989 was the first year the company implemented a quality improvement program). This information is presented below:

	Prevention	Appraisal	Internal	External	Total
1988	2%	3%	8%	12%	25%
1989	3	4	8	10	25
1990	4	4	5	7	20
1991	5	3	3	5	16
1992	6	4	1	2	13

Required:

1. Prepare a trend graph for total quality costs. Comment on what the graph has to say about the success of the quality improvement program.

2. Prepare a graph that shows the trend for each quality cost category. What does the graph have to say about the success of the quality improvement program? Does this graph supply more insight than the total cost trend graph? What does the graph have to say about the distribution of quality costs in 1988?

E16–8 **Productivity Measurement; Partial Measures**   Pinson Company produces a product that uses two inputs, X and Y. During the past month, twenty units of the product were produced, requiring fifteen units of Input X and twenty-four units of Input Y. An engineering study revealed that Pinson can produce the same output of twenty units using either of the following two combinations of inputs:

	Input X	Input Y
Combination A	10	20
Combination B	15	16

The cost of Input X is $5 per unit; the cost of Input Y is $10 per unit.

Required:

1. Compute the output-input ratio for each input of Combination A. Does this represent a productivity improvement over the current use of inputs? What is the total dollar value of the improvement?

2. Calculate output-input ratios for each input of Combination B. Does this represent a productivity improvement over the current use of inputs? Now compare these ratios to those of Combination A. What has happened?

3. Compute the cost of producing the twenty units of output using Combination B. Compare this cost to the cost using Combination A. Does moving from Combination A to Combination B represent a productivity improvement? Explain.

E16–9 **Interperiod Measurement of Productivity; Basic Computations**   The following data pertain to the last two years of operation of Handley, Inc.:

	1991	1992
Output	8,000	10,000
Power (quantity used)	2,000	2,000

continued on next page

	1991	*1992*
Materials (quantity used)	4,000	4,500
Unit price (Power)	$1	$2
Unit price (Materials)	$3	$4
Unit selling price	$8	$8

Required:

1. Compute the partial operational productivity ratios for each year. Did productivity improve? Explain.

2. Compute the profit-linked productivity measure. By how much did profits increase due to productivity?

3. Calculate the price-recovery component for 1992. Explain its meaning.

E16–10   Productivity Measurement: Tradeoffs   Liddy Company decided to install an automated manufacturing system. After one year of operation, management wants to evaluate the productivity change. The president is particularly interested in knowing whether the tradeoff between capital and labor was favorable. Data concerning output, labor, and capital are provided for the year before implementation and the year after.

	Year Before	*Year After*
Output	100,000	120,000
Input quantities:		
Labor (hours)	10,000	4,000
Capital (dollars)	10,000	300,000
Input prices:		
Labor	$5	$5
Capital	15%	15%

Required:

1. Compute the partial measures for labor and capital for each year. What caused the change in labor productivity?

2. Calculate the change in profits attributable to the change in productivity of the two inputs. Assuming that these are the only two inputs, evaluate the decision to automate.

E16–11   Productivity Measurement: Technical and Price Efficiency Illustrated   The manager of Dowson Company was reviewing two competing proposals for the Machining Department. The fiscal year was coming to a close and the manager wanted to make a decision concerning the proposed process changes so that they could be used, if beneficial, during the coming year. The process changes would affect the department's input usage. For the year just ending, the Accounting Department provided the following information about the inputs used to produce 50,000 units of output:

	Quantity	*Unit Prices*
Materials	90,000 lbs	$ 8
Labor	40,000 hrs	10
Energy	20,000 kwh	2

Each proposal offers a different process design than the one currently used. And neither proposal would cost anything to implement. Both proposals project input usage for producing 60,000 units (the expected output for the coming year).

	Proposal A	*Proposal B*
Materials	90,000 lbs	100,000 lbs
Labor	40,000 hrs	30,000 hrs
Energy	20,000 kwh	20,000 kwh

Input prices are expected to remain the same for the coming year.

Required:

1. Compute the operational partial productivity measures for the most recently completed year and each proposal. Does either proposal improve technical efficiency? Explain. Can you make a recommendation about either proposal using only the physical measures?

2. Calculate the profit-linked productivity measure for each proposal. Which proposal offers the best outcome for the company? How does this relate to the concept of price efficiency? Explain.

E16–12 **Productivity and Quality** Rington Company is considering the acquisition of an automated system that would decrease the number of units scrapped because of poor quality. (This proposal is part of an ongoing effort to improve quality.) The production manager is pushing for the acquisition because he believes that productivity will be greatly enhanced—particularly when it comes to labor and material inputs. Output and input data are given below. The after-acquisition data are projections.

	Current	*After Acquisition*
Output (units)	10,000	10,000
Output selling price	$40	$40
Input quantities:		
Materials	40,000	35,000
Labor	20,000	15,000
Capital (dollars)	20,000	100,000
Energy	10,000	25,000
Input prices:		
Materials	$4.00	$4.00
Labor	$9.00	$9.00
Capital (percent)	10.00%	10.00%
Energy	$2.00	$2.50

Required:

1. Compute the partial operational ratios for labor and materials under each alternative. Is the production manager right in thinking that labor and materials productivity increases with the automated system?

2. Compute the partial ratios for all four inputs. Does the system improve productivity?

3. Determine the amount by which profits will change if the system is adopted. Are the tradeoffs among the inputs favorable? Comment on the system's ability to improve productivity.

E16–13   **Basics of Productivity Measurement**   Roberts Company gathered the following data for the past two years:

	Base Year	Current Year
Output	100,000	120,000
Output prices	$20	$20
Input quantities:		
Input X	200,000	180,000
Input Y	50,000	90,000
Input prices:		
Input X	$5	$6
Input Y	$8	8

Required:

1. Calculate the partial operational measures for each year.

2. Prepare income statements for each year. Calculate the total change in income.

3. Calculate the change in profits attributable to productivity changes.

4. Calculate the price recovery component. Explain its meaning.

▪ PROBLEMS

P16–1   **Classification of Quality Costs**   Classify the following quality costs as prevention, appraisal, internal failure, or external failure. Also label each cost as variable or fixed with respect to sales volume.

1. Quality engineering

2. Scrap

3. Product recalls

4. Returns and allowances because of quality problems

5. Data reentered because of keypunching errors

6. Supervision of in-process inspection

7. Quality circles

8. Component inspection and testing

9. Quality training

10. Reinspection of reworked product

11. Product liability

12. Internal audit assessing the effectiveness of quality system

13. Disposal of defective product

14. Downtime attributable to quality problems

15. Quality reporting

16. Proofreading

17. Correction of typing errors

18. In-process inspection

19. Process controls

20. Pilot studies

P16–2 **Quality Cost Summary** The president of Cooper Company is convinced that her firm's profitability can increase significantly by improving quality. Before committing the company to a quality improvement program, however, she wants a preliminary estimate of the total quality costs currently being incurred. She also wants the costs classified as prevention, appraisal, and failure costs. She has asked you to prepare a summary of quality costs and to compare the total costs to sales and profits. To assist you in this task, the following information has been prepared from the past year, 1993:

a. Sales revenue: $5,000,000; net income: $500,000.

b. During the year, customers returned 30,000 units needing rework. Rework cost averages $1 per unit.

c. Four inspectors are employed, each earning an annual salary of $20,000. The inspectors are involved only with final inspection (product acceptance).

d. Total scrap is 50,000 units. Of this total, 60 percent is quality related. The cost of scrap is about $5 per unit.

e. Each year, approximately 150,000 units are rejected in final inspection. Of these units, 80 percent can be recovered through rework. The costs of rework is $0.75 per unit.

f. A large customer canceled an order that would have increased profits by $50,000. The customer's reason for cancellation was poor product performance.

g. The company employs three full-time employees in its complaint department. Each earns $13,500 a year.

h. The company gave sales allowances totaling $15,000 due to substandard products being sent to the customer.

i. The company requires all new employees to take its three-hour quality training program. The estimated annual cost of the program is $10,000.

Required:

1. Prepare a simple quality cost report classifying costs by category.

2. Compute the quality cost-sales ratio. Also compare the total quality costs with total profits. Should the president of the company be concerned with the level of quality costs?

3. Prepare a pie chart for the quality costs. Discuss the distribution of quality costs among the four categories. Are they properly distributed? Explain.

4. Discuss how the company can improve its overall quality and at the same time reduce total quality costs.

5. By how much will profits increase if quality costs are reduced to 2.5 percent of sales?

P16–3 **Quality Costs; Pricing Decisions; Market Share** Tannert Company manufactures furniture. One of its product lines is an economy-line kitchen table. During the last year, Tannert produced and sold 100,000 units for $100 per unit. Sales of the table are on a bid basis, but Tannert has always been able to win sufficient bids using the $100 price. This year, however, Tannert was losing more than its share of bids. Concerned, Larry Franklin, owner and president of the company, called a meeting of his executive committee (Megan Johnson, marketing manager; Fred Davis, quality manager; Kevin Jones, production manager; and Helen Jackson, controller).

Larry: I don't understand why we're losing bids. Megan, do you have an explanation?

Megan: Yes, as a matter of fact. Two competitors have lowered their price to $92 per unit. That's too big a difference for most of our buyers to ignore. If we want to keep selling our 100,000 units per year, we will need to lower our price to $92. Otherwise, our sales will drop to about 20,000 to 25,000 per year.

Helen: The unit contribution margin on the table is $10. Lowering the price to $92 will cost us $8 per unit. Based on a sales volume of 100,000, we'd make $200,000 in contribution margin. If we keep the price at $100, our contribution margin would be $200,000 to $250,000. If we have to lose, let's just take the lower market share. It's better than lowering our prices.

Megan: Perhaps. But the same thing could happen to some of our other product lines. My sources tell me that these two companies are on the tail-end of a major quality improvement program—one that allows them significant savings. We need to rethink our whole competitive strategy—at least if we want to stay in business. Ideally, we should match the price reduction and work to reduce the costs to recapture the lost contribution margin.

Fred: I think I have something to offer. We are about to embark on a new quality improvement program of our own. I have brought the following estimates of the current quality costs for this economy line. As you can see on the overhead, these costs run about 16 percent of current sales. That's excessive, and we believe that they can be reduced to about 4 percent of sales over time.

Scrap	$ 700,000
Rework	300,000
Rejects (sold as seconds to discount houses)	250,000
Returns (due to poor workmanship)	350,000
	$1,600,000

Larry: This sounds good. Fred, how long will it take you to achieve this reduction?

Fred: All these costs vary with sales level, so I'll express their reduction rate in those terms. Our best guess is that we can reduce these costs by about 1 percent of sales per quarter. So it should take about twelve quarters, or three years, to achieve the full benefit. Keep in mind that this is with an improvement in quality.

Megan: This offers us some hope. If we meet the price immediately, we can maintain our market share. Furthermore, if we can ever reach the point of reducing the price beyond the $92 level, then we can increase our market share. I estimate that we can increase sales by about 10,000 units for every $1 of price reduction beyond the $92 level. Kevin, how much extra capacity for this line do we have?

Kevin: We can handle an extra 30,000 or 40,000 tables per year.

Required:

1. Assume that Tannert immediately reduces the bid price to $92. How long will it be before the unit contribution margin is restored to $10, assuming that quality costs

are reduced as expected and that sales are maintained at 100,000 units per year (25,000 per quarter)?

2. Assume that Tannert holds the price at $92 until the 4 percent target is achieved. At this new level of quality costs, should the price be reduced? If so, by how much should price be reduced and what is the increase in contribution margin? Assume that price can be reduced only in $1 increments.

3. Assume that Tannert immediately reduces the price to $92 and begins the quality improvement program. Now suppose that Tannert does not wait until the end of the three-year period before reducing prices. Instead, prices will be reduced when profitable to do so. Assume that prices can be reduced only by $1 increments. Identify when the first future price change should occur (if any).

4. Discuss the differences in viewpoints concerning the decision to decrease prices and the short-run contribution margin analysis done by Helen, the controller. Did quality cost information play an important role in the strategic decision making illustrated by the problem?

P16–4 **Quality Costs; Profitability Analysis**   In 1989, Ralph Keating had been hired to manage a troubled division of Henderson Company, a large electronics firm. Ralph had the reputation of turning around businesses that were having difficulty. In 1989, the division had sales of $25,000,000, a variable cost ratio of 0.8, and total fixed costs of $6,000,000. The division produced only one product and sales were all to external customers. At the beginning of 1989, the quality costs totaled $10,000,000 and were distributed as follows:

	Fixed	*Variable*
Prevention	$ 200,000	—
Appraisal	300,000	$1,000,000
Internal failure	500,000	2,000,000
External failure	1,000,000	5,000,000
Total	$2,000,000	$8,000,000

Ralph was astounded at the level of expenditure on quality costs and immediately implemented a program to improve conformance quality. By the end of 1990, the following quality costs were reported:

	Fixed	*Variable*
Prevention	$1,000,000	—
Appraisal	1,000,000	$1,000,000
Internal failure	500,000	1,000,000
External failure	1,000,000	3,500,000
Total	$3,500,000	$5,500,000

Revenues and other costs were unchanged for 1990.

Ralph projects that by 1994 the defective rate will be 0.1 percent, compared to the AQL rate of 2 percent of 1989. He also projects that quality costs will be reduced to $500,000, distributed as follows:

	Fixed	Variable
Prevention	$200,000	—
Appraisal	200,000	—
Internal failure	—	$ 20,000
External failure	—	80,000
Total	$400,000	$100,000

Required:

1. Calculate the break-even point in revenues for 1989. How much was the division losing?
2. Calculate the break-even point in 1990. Explain the change.
3. Calculate the break-even point in 1994, assuming that revenues and other costs have remained the same. Is it possible to reduce quality costs as dramatically as portrayed?
4. Assume that from 1991 to 1994, the division was forced to cut selling prices so that total revenues dropped to $15,000,000. Calculate the income (loss) that would be reported under a 1989 cost structure. Now calculate the income (loss) that would be reported under the 1994 quality-cost structure (assuming all other costs remain unchanged). Discuss the strategic significance of quality cost management.

P16–5   **Interim Quality Cost Performance Report**   Taylor Company recently evaluated its quality costs and discovered that they total about 21 percent of its sales revenues. Somewhat shocked by the magnitude of the costs, Ryan Carson, president of Taylor Company, launched a major quality improvement program. For the coming year, it was decided to reduce quality costs to 17 percent of sales revenues. Although the amount of reduction was ambitious, most company officials believed that the goal could be realized. To help monitor the progress of the quality improvement program, Ryan directed the controller to prepare monthly performance reports comparing budgeted and actual quality costs. Budgeted costs and sales for the first two months of the year are as follows:

	January	February
Sales	$500,000	$600,000
Quality costs:		
Warranty	15,000	18,000
Scrap	10,000	12,000
Incoming materials inspection	2,500	2,500
Product acceptance	13,000	15,000
Quality planning	2,000	2,000
Field inspection	12,000	14,000
Retesting	6,000	7,200
Allowances	7,500	9,000
New product review	500	500
Rework	9,000	10,800
Complaint adjustment	2,500	2,500
Downtime (defective parts)	5,000	6,000
Quality training	1,000	1,000
Total budgeted costs	$ 86,000	$100,500
Quality costs-sales ratio	17.2%	16.75%

Actual sales and actual quality costs for January are

Sales	$550,000
Quality costs:	
Warranty	17,500
Scrap	12,500
Incoming materials inspection	2,500
Product acceptance	14,000
Quality planning	2,500
Field inspection	14,000
Retesting	7,000
Allowances	8,500
New product review	700
Rework	11,000
Complaint adjustment	2,500
Downtime	5,500
Quality training	1,000

Required:

1. Reorganize the monthly budgets so that quality costs are grouped in one of four categories: appraisal, prevention, internal failure, and external failure. Also identify each cost as variable or fixed. (Assume that none are mixed costs.)

2. Prepare a performance report for January that compares actual costs with budgeted costs. Use a flexible budget to make the comparison. Comment on the company's progress in improving quality and reducing its quality costs.

P16–6 **Quality Cost Performance Reporting: One-year Trend; Long-range Analysis** In 1992, Randall Company initiated a full-scale quality improvement program. At the end of the year, the president noted with some satisfaction that the defects per unit of product had dropped significantly compared to the prior year. She was also pleased that relationships with suppliers had improved and defective raw materials had declined. The new quality training program was also well accepted by employees. Of most interest to the president, however, was the impact of the quality improvements on profitability. To help assess the dollar impact of the quality improvements, the actual sales and the actual quality costs for 1991 and 1992 are given below by quality category:

	1991	1992
Sales	$20,000,000	$25,000,000
Appraisal costs:		
Product inspection	800,000	750,000
Raw material inspection	100,000	70,000
Prevention costs:		
Quality training	10,000	100,000
Quality reporting	5,000	50,000
Quality improvement projects	5,000	250,000

continued on next page

	1991	1992
Internal failure costs:		
Scrap	700,000	600,000
Rework	900,000	800,000
Yield losses	400,000	250,000
Retesting	500,000	400,000
External failure costs:		
Returned materials	400,000	400,000
Allowances	300,000	350,000
Warranty	1,000,000	1,100,000

All prevention costs are fixed (by discretion). All other quality costs are variable.

Required:

1. Compute the relative distribution of quality costs for each year (pie charts may be helpful). Do you believe that the company is moving in the right direction in terms of the balance among the quality-cost categories? Explain.

2. Prepare a one-year trend performance report for 1992. How much have profits increased because of the quality improvements made by Randall Company?

3. Estimate the additional improvement in profits if Randall Company ultimately reduces its quality costs to 2.5 percent of sales revenues (assume sales of $25 million).

P16–7   **Distribution of Quality Costs**   Paper Products Division produces paper diapers, napkins, and paper towels. The divisional manager has decided that quality costs can be minimized by distributing quality costs evenly among the four quality categories and reducing them to no more than 5 percent of sales. He has just received the following quality cost report:

Paper Products Division			
Quality Cost Report *For the Year Ending December 31, 1992*			
	Diapers	*Napkins*	*Towels*	*Total*
--------------------------	----------:	----------:	---------:	--------:
Prevention:				
Quality training	$ 3,000	$2,500	$2,000	$ 7,500
Quality engineering	3,500	1,000	2,500	7,000
Quality audits	—	500	1,000	1,500
Quality reporting	2,500	2,000	1,000	5,500
Total	$ 9,000	$6,000	$6,500	$21,500
Appraisal:				
Inspection, materials	$ 2,000	$3,000	$3,000	$ 8,000
Process acceptance	4,000	2,800	1,200	8,000
Product acceptance	2,000	1,200	2,300	5,500
Total	$ 8,000	$7,000	$6,500	$21,500
Internal failure:				
Scrap	$10,000	$3,000	$2,500	$15,500

	Diapers	Napkins	Towels	Total
Disposal costs	7,000	2,000	1,500	10,500
Downtime	1,000	1,500	2,500	5,000
Total	$18,000	$ 6,500	$ 6,500	$ 31,000
External failure:				
Allowances	$10,000	$ 3,000	$ 2,750	$ 15,750
Customer complaints	4,000	1,500	3,750	9,250
Product liability	1,000	—	—	1,000
Total	$15,000	$ 4,500	$ 6,500	$ 26,000
Total quality costs	$50,000	24,000	$26,000	$100,000

Assume that all prevention costs are fixed and that the remaining quality costs are variable.

Required:

1. Assume that the sales revenue for the year totaled $2 million, with sales for each product as follows: diapers, $1 million; napkins, $600,000; towels, $400,000. Evaluate the distribution of costs for the division as a whole and for each product line. What recommendations do you have for the divisional manager?

2. Now assume that total sales of $1 million have this breakdown: diapers, $500,000; napkins, $300,000; towels, $200,000. Evaluate the distribution of costs for the division as a whole and for each product line in this case. Do you think it is possible to reduce the quality costs to 5 percent of sales for each product line and for the division as a whole and, simultaneously, achieve an equal distribution of the quality costs? What recommendations do you have?

3. Assume total sales of $1 million with this breakdown: diapers, $500,000; napkins, $180,000; towels, $320,000. Evaluate the distribution of quality costs. What recommendations for the divisional manager do you have?

4. Discuss the value of having quality costs reported by segment.

P16–8 **Trend Analysis; Quality Costs** In 1989, Jack Donaldson, president of Thayn Electronics, received a report indicating that quality costs were 23 percent of sales. Faced with increasing pressures from imported goods, Jack resolved to take measures to improve the overall quality of the company's products. After hiring a consultant, the company began, in 1990, an aggressive program of total quality control. At the end of 1993, Jack requested an analysis of the progress the company had made in reducing and controlling quality costs. The Accounting Department assembled the following data:

	Sales	Prevention	Appraisal	Internal Failure	External Failure
1989	$500,000	$ 5,000	$10,000	$40,000	$50,000
1990	600,000	20,000	20,000	50,000	60,000
1991	700,000	30,000	25,000	30,000	40,000
1992	600,000	35,000	35,000	20,000	25,000
1993	500,000	35,000	15,000	8,000	12,000

Required:

1. Compute the quality costs as a percentage of sales by category and in total for each year.

2. Explain why quality costs increased in total and as a percentage of sales in 1990, the first year of the quality improvement program.

3. Prepare a multiple-year trend graph for quality costs, both by total costs and by category. Using the graph, assess the progress made in reducing and controlling quality costs. Does the graph provide evidence that quality has improved? Explain.

4. Using the 1989 quality cost relationships (assume all costs are variable), calculate the quality costs that would have prevailed in 1991. By how much did profits increase in 1991 because of the quality improvement program? Repeat for 1993.

P16–9   **Quality Performance and Ethical Behavior**   Reece Manufacturing rewards its plant managers for their ability to meet budgeted quality cost reductions. The bonus is increased if the productivity goal is met or exceeded. The productivity goal is computed by multiplying the units produced by the prevailing market price and dividing this measure of output by the total cost of the inputs used. Additionally, if the plant as a whole met the budgeted targets, the production supervisors and workers receive salary and wage increases. Matt Rasmussen, the manager of a plant in Nebraska, felt obligated to do everything he could to provide this increase to his employees. Accordingly, he has decided to take the following actions during the last quarter of the year to meet the plant's budgeted targets and increase the productivity ratio:

a. Decrease inspections of the process and final product by 50 percent and transfer inspectors temporarily to quality training programs. Matt believes this move will increase the inspectors' awareness of the importance of quality; also, decreasing inspection will produce significantly less downtime and less rework. By increasing the output and decreasing the costs of internal failure, the plant can meet the budgeted reductions for internal failure costs and, simultaneously, increase its productivity measure. Also, by showing an increase in the costs of quality training, the budgeted level for prevention costs can be met.

b. Delay replacing and repairing defective products until the beginning of the following year. While this may increase customer dissatisfaction somewhat, Matt believes that most customers expect some inconvenience. Besides, the policy of promptly dealing with dissatisfied customers could be reinstated in three months. In the meantime, the action would significantly reduce the costs of external failure, allowing the plant to meet its budgeted target.

Required:

1. Evaluate Matt's ethical behavior. In this evaluation, consider his concern for his employees. Was he justified in taking the actions described in the problem? If not, what should he have done?

2. Assume that the company views Matt's behavior as undesirable. What can it do to discourage it?

3. Assume that Matt is a CMA and a member of the NAA. Refer to the ethical code for management accountants in the Appendix of Chapter 1. Are any of these ethical standards violated?

P16–10   **Productivity Measurement; Basics**   Dixon Company has just completed the first year of its productivity improvement program, and the president of the company wants to know how much profits have increased from the prior year because of the program. In order to provide this information to the president, the following data have been gathered:

	1991	1992
Unit selling price	$16	$16
Output produced and sold	10,000	12,000
Materials used	20,000	22,000
Labor used	5,000	5,000
Unit price of materials	$4	$5
Unit price of labor	$9	$10

Required:

1. Compute the partial productivity ratios for each year. Comment on the effectiveness of the productivity improvement program.
2. Compute the increase in profits attributable to increased productivity.
3. Calculate the price-recovery component and comment on its meaning.

P16–11 **Productivity Measurement** In 1991, Weber products, Inc., used the following input combination to produce 1,000 units of output:

Materials	500 lbs
Labor	1,600 hrs

The following combination is optimal for an output of 1,000 units (but unknown to Weber Products):

Materials	300 lbs
Labor	1,750 hrs

The cost of materials is $30 per pound, and the cost of labor is $10 per hour. These input prices hold for 1991 and 1992. In 1992, Weber Products again produced 1,000 units, with the following input combination:

Materials	350 lbs
Labor	1,800 hrs

Required:

1. Compute the partial productivity ratios for each of the following:
   a. The actual inputs used in 1991
   b. The actual inputs used in 1992
   c. The optimal input combination
   Did productivity increase in 1992—as measured by the partial ratios?
2. Compute the cost of 1991's productive inefficiency relative to the optimal input combination.
3. By how much did profits increase because of improvements in productive efficiency from 1991 to 1992?

4. How much additional improvement in profits is possible after 1992 (assuming input costs remain the same and that output doesn't change)?

P16–12　**Productivity Measurement: Partial and Total Measures; Price Recovery**　The small motor division of Backley Company has recently engaged in a vigorous effort to increase productivity. Over the past several years, competition has become very intense, and the divisional manager knew that a significant price decrease for its small motors was in order. Otherwise, the division would lose at least 50 percent of its market share.

　　To maintain its market share, Backley had to decrease its per-unit price by $5 by the end of 1992. Decreasing the price by $5, however, absolutely required a similar increase in cost efficiency. If divisional profits dropped by $5 per unit, the continued existence of the division would be in question. To assess the outcome of the productivity improvement program the following data were gathered:

	1991	1992
Output	200,000	250,000
Input quantities:		
Materials	100,000	100,000
Labor	400,000	200,000
Capital	4,000,000	$10,000,000
Energy	100,000	300,000
Input prices:		
Materials	$2.00	$ 2.00
Labor	8.00	10.00
Capital	0.15	0.10
Energy	1.50	1.50

Required:

1. Calculate the partial productivity ratios for each year. Can you say that productivity has improved? Explain.

2. Calculate the profit change attributable to productivity changes.

3. Calculate the cost per unit for 1991 and 1992. Was the division able to decrease its per-unit cost by at least $5? Comment on the relationship of competitive advantage and productive efficiency.

P16–13　**Quality and Productivity; Interaction; Use of Operational Measures**　Daryl Anderson, production-line manager, had arranged a visit with Dick Anderson, plant manager. He had some questions about the new operational measures that were being used.

　　Daryl:　Dick, my questions are more to satisfy my curiosity than anything else. At the beginning of the year, we began some new procedures that require us to work towards increasing our output per pound of material and decreasing our output per labor hour. As instructed, I've been tracking these operational measures for each batch we've produced so far this year. Here's a copy of a trend report for the first five batches of the year. Each batch had 10,000 units in it.

Batches	Material Usage	Ratio	Labor Usage	Ratio
1	3,000 lbs	3.33	2,000 hrs	5.00
2	2,970 lbs	3.37	2,020 hrs	4.95
3	2,800 lbs	3.57	2,150 hrs	4.65
4	2,700 lbs	3.70	2,200 hrs	4.55
5	2,650 lbs	3.77	2,250 lbs	4.44

Dick: Daryl, this report is very encouraging. The trend is exactly what we hoped for. I'll bet we meet our goal of getting the batch productivity measures. Let's see, those goals were 4.00 units per pound for materials and 4.00 units per hour for labor. Last year's figures were 5.00 for labor and 3.33 for materials. Things are looking good. I guess tying bonuses and raises to improving these productivity stats was a good idea.

Daryl: Maybe so—but I don't understand why you want to make these trade-offs between labor and materials. Labor costs $10 per hour and the materials cost only $5 per pound. It seems like you're simply increasing the cost of making this product.

Dick: Actually, it may seem that way, but it's not so. There are other factors to consider. You know we've been talking quality improvement. Well, the new procedures you are implementing are producing products that conform to the product's specification. More labor time is needed to achieve this and as we take more time, we do waste fewer materials. But the real benefit is the reduction in our external failure costs. Every defect in a batch of 1,000 units costs us $1,000—warranty work, lost sales, a customer service department, and so on. If we can reach the labor and material productivity goals, our defects will drop from twenty per batch to five per batch.

Required:

1. Discuss the advantages of using only operational measures of productivity for controlling shop-level activities.

2. Assume that the batch productivity statistics are met by the end of the year. Calculate the change in a batch's profits from the beginning of the year to the end attributable to changes in labor and materials productivity.

3. Now assume that three inputs are to be evaluated: materials, labor, and quality. Quality is measured by the number of defects per batch. Calculate the change in a batch's profits from the beginning of the year to the end attributable to changes in productivity of all three inputs. Do you agree that quality is an input? Explain.

P16–14 **Productivity; Tradeoffs; Price Recovery** Connie Baker, president of Fleming Chemicals, had just concluded a meeting with two of her plant managers. She had told each that the product being produced was going to have a 50 percent increase in demand—next year—over this year's output (which is expected to be 10,000 gallons). A major foreign source of the raw material had been shut down because of civil war. It would be years before the source would be available again. The result was two-fold. First, the price of the raw material was expected to quadruple. Second, many of the less efficient competitors would leave the business, creating more demand and higher output prices—in fact, output prices would double.

In discussing the situation with her plant managers, she had reminded them that the automated process now allowed them to increase the productivity of the raw material. By using more machine hours, evaporation could be decreased significantly (this was a recent development and would be operational by the beginning of the new fiscal year). There were, however, only two other feasible settings beyond the current setting. The current usage of inputs for the 10,000 gallon output (current setting) and the input usage for the other two settings are given below. The input usage for the remaining two settings is for an output of 15,000 gallons. Inputs are measured in gallons for the material and in machine hours for the equipment.

	Current	Setting A	Setting B
Input quantities:			
Material	25,000	15,000	30,000
Equipment	6,000	15,000	7,500

The current prices for this year's inputs are $3 per gallon for materials and $12 per machine hour for the equipment. The materials price will change for next year as explained, but the $12 rate for machine hours will remain the same. The chemical is currently selling for $20 per gallon. Based on separate productivity analyses, one plant manager chose setting A and the other chose setting B.

The manager who chose setting B justified his decision by noting that it was the only setting that clearly signaled an increase in both partial measures of productivity. The other manager agreed that setting B was an improvement but that setting A was even better.

Required:

1. Calculate the partial measures of productivity for the current year and for the two settings. Which of the two settings signals an increase in productivity for both inputs?

2. Calculate the profits that will be realized under each setting for the coming year. Which setting provides the greatest profit increase?

3. Calculate the profit change for each setting attributable to productivity changes. Which setting offers the greatest productivity improvement? By how much? Explain why this happened. (*Hint:* Look at tradeoffs.)

■ MANAGERIAL DECISION CASE

Quality Cost Performance Reports   Nickles Company, a large printing company, is in its fourth year of a five-year quality improvement program. The program began in 1989 with an internal study that revealed the quality costs being incurred. In that year, a five-year plan was developed to lower quality costs to 10 percent of sales by the end of 1993. Sales and quality costs for each year are as follows:

	Sales Revenues	Quality Costs
1989	$10,000,000	$2,000,000
1990	10,000,000	1,800,000
1991	11,000,000	1,815,000
1992	12,000,000	1,680,000
1993[a]	12,000,000	1,320,000

[a]Budgeted figures

Quality costs by category are expressed as a percentage of sales as follows:

	Prevention	Appraisal	Internal Failure	External Failure
1989	1.0%	3.0%	7.0%	9.0%
1990	2.0	4.0	6.0	6.0
1991	2.5	4.0	5.0	5.0
1992	3.0	3.5	4.5	3.0
1993	3.5	3.5	2.0	2.0

The detail of the 1993 budget for quality costs is also provided.

Prevention costs:	
Quality planning	$ 150,000
Quality training	20,000
Quality improvement (special project)	80,000
Quality reporting	10,000
Appraisal costs:	
Proofreading	$ 500,000
Other inspection	50,000
Failure costs:	
Correction of typos	$ 150,000
Rework (because of customer complaints)	75,000
Plate revisions	55,000
Press downtime	100,000
Waste (because of poor work)	130,000
Total quality costs	$1,320,000

All prevention costs are fixed; all other quality costs are variable.

During 1993, the company had $12 million in sales. Actual quality costs for 1992 and 1993 are as follows:

	1993	1992
Quality planning	$150,000	$140,000
Quality training	20,000	20,000
Special project	100,000	120,000
Quality reporting	12,000	12,000
Proofreading	520,000	580,000
Other inspection	60,000	80,000
Correction of typos	165,000	200,000
Rework	76,000	131,000
Plate revisions	58,000	83,000
Press downtime	102,000	123,000
Waste	136,000	191,000

Required:

1. Prepare an interim quality cost performance report for 1993. Comment on the firm's ability to achieve its quality goals for the year.

2. Prepare a one-period quality performance report for 1993. How much did profits change because of improved quality?

3. Prepare a graph that shows the trend in total quality costs as a percentage of sales since the inception of the quality improvement program.

4. Prepare a graph that shows the trend for all four quality-cost categories for 1989 through 1993. How does this graph help management know that the reduction in total quality costs is attributable to quality improvements?

5. Assume that the company is preparing a second five-year plan to reduce quality costs to 2.5 percent of sales. Prepare a long-range quality cost performance report assuming sales of $15 million dollars at the end of five years. Assume that the final planned relative distribution of quality costs is as follows: proofreading, 50 percent; other inspection, 13 percent; quality training, 30 percent; and quality reporting, 7 percent.

Decentralization, Performance Evaluation, and Transfer Pricing

■ **LEARNING OBJECTIVES**

After studying Chapter 17, you should be able to

1. Explain why firms choose to decentralize.

2. Compute return on investment (ROI) and residual income (RI).

3. List the advantages and disadvantages of using ROI and RI to measure managerial performance.

4. Explain how environmental factors can affect performance evaluation in the multinational firm.

5. Explain the role of transfer pricing in a decentralized firm.

6. Define and discuss the transfer pricing problem.

7. Use the opportunity costing approach to determine when internal transfers should take place and to define the negotiation set.

8. Explain why negotiated transfer prices are preferred in the absence of perfectly competitive markets for the intermediate product.

9. Discuss the merits and propriety of various transfer-pricing schemes.

10. Discuss the impact of tax rates on transfer-pricing decisions in the multinational firm.

11. Define and explain the key terms appearing at the end of the chapter.

SCENARIO

Paterson Company is a U.S.–based company that manufactures and sells electronic components worldwide. Virtually all of the manufacturing takes place in the United States. The company has marketing divisions located throughout Europe, including one in France. Debbie Kishimoto is manager of this division; she had been hired away from a competitor three years ago. Debbie, recently informed of a price increase in one of the major product lines, had requested a meeting with Jeff Phillips, the marketing vice-president.

"Jeff, I simply don't understand why the price of our main product has increased from $5 to $5.50 per unit. We negotiated an agreement earlier in the year with our manufacturing division in Philadelphia for a price of $5 for the entire year. I called the manager of that division, and he indicated that the original price was still acceptable—he said that the increase was a directive from headquarters. That's why I requested a meeting with you. I need some explanations. When I was hired, I was told that pricing decisions were made at the divisional level—that divisions were given a lot of decision-making latitude. This directive not only interferes with this decentralized philosophy but also will lower my division's profits. Given current market conditions, there is no way that we can pass on the cost increase. Profits for my division will drop at least $600,000 if this price is maintained. I think a mid-year increase of this magnitude is unfair to my division."

"Debbie, under normal operating conditions, headquarters will *not* interfere with divisional decisions. As a company, however, we are having some problems. What you just told me is exactly why the price of your product has been increased. We want the profits of all of our European marketing divisions to drop."

"Wait a minute. What do you mean that you want the profits to drop? That doesn't make any sense. Aren't we in business to make money?"

"Debbie, what you lack is corporate perspective. We *are* in business to make money, and that's why we want European profits to decrease. Let me explain. Our divisions in the United States are not doing well this year. Projections show significant losses. At the same time, projections for European operations show good profitability. By increasing the cost of key products transferred to Europe—to your division, for example—we increase revenues and profits in the United States. By decreasing your profits we avoid paying taxes in France; with losses on other U.S. operations to offset the corresponding increase in domestic profits, we avoid paying taxes in the United States as well. The net effect is a much-needed increase in our cash inflow. Besides, you know how difficult it is in some of these European countries to transfer out capital. This is a clean way of doing it."

"I'm not so sure that it's clean. It doesn't seem right to me. I can't imagine the tax laws permitting this type of scheme. There is another problem as well. You know that the company's bonus plans are tied to a division's profitability. This plan could cost all the European managers a lot of money."

"Debbie, you have no reason to worry about the effect on your bonus—or on our evaluation of your performance, for that matter. Corporate management has already taken steps to ensure no loss of compensation. The plan is to compute what income would have been if the old price had prevailed and base bonuses on that figure. I plan to meet with the other divisional managers and explain the situation to them as well."

"The bonus adjustment seems fair, although I wonder if the reasons for the drop in profits will be remembered in a couple of years when I'm being considered for promotion. Anyway, I still have some strong concerns about the propriety of all this. How does this scheme relate to the tax laws?"

"We will be in technical compliance with the tax laws. In the United States, Section 482 of the Internal Revenue Code governs this type of transaction. The key to this law, as well as most European laws, is evidence of an arm's-length price. Since you're a distributor, we can use the resale price method to determine such a price. Essentially, the arm's-length price for the transferred good is backed into by starting with the price at which you sell the product and then adjusting that price for the markup and other legitimate differences, such as tariffs and transportation."

"If I were a French tax auditor, I would wonder why the markup dropped from last year to this year. I also wonder if we are being good citizens and meeting the fiscal responsibilities imposed on us by each country in which we operate."

"Well, a French tax auditor might wonder about the drop in markup. The markup, however, is still within reason, and we can make a good argument for increased costs. In fact, we have already instructed the managers of our manufacturing divisions to find as many costs as they can that can be legitimately reassigned to the European product lines affected by this increase. So far they have been very successful. I think our records will support the increase that you are receiving. Debbie, you really do not need to be concerned with the tax authorities. Our Tax Department assures me that this has been carefully researched and planned—it's unlikely that a tax audit will create any difficulties. It'll all be legal and above board. We've done this several times in the past with total success. We have some good people in that department."

THE DIVISIONAL SETTING: AN OVERVIEW OF THE MAJOR ISSUES

Debbie Kishimoto's meeting with Jeff Phillips brought out three issues and problems common to an organization with a divisional structure:

1. The degree of decentralization

2. Performance measurement

3. The setting of transfer prices

Discussion of these three issues is the major thrust of this chapter.

Of course, this case also raises the question of the ethics of the tax-avoidance scheme. While this question is not necessarily common to all divisional structures, evaluating the ethical content of divisional decisions is common. This matter is addressed in a problem at the end of the chapter.

The Issue of Decentralization

At the beginning of the conversation, Debbie complained about corporate headquarters interfering with a pricing arrangement she had negotiated with the manager of the manufacturing division. She complained because Paterson Company had been espousing decentralization. This was her first experience with any interference by headquarters.

centralized decision making **decentralized decision making** **decentralization** Organizations usually choose one of two approaches to manage their diverse and complex activities: centralized decision making or decentralized decision making. In **centralized decision making,** decisions are made at the very top level and lower-level managers are charged with implementing these decisions. On the other hand, **decentralized decision making** allows managers at lower levels to make and implement key decisions pertaining to their areas of responsibility. **Decentralization** is the practice of delegating or decentralizing decision-making authority to the lower levels.

Given that Paterson Company followed a decentralized structure, one can appreciate Debbie's frustration when corporate headquarters reversed a pricing decision that had been made earlier. This frustration was not totally alleviated even when it was made clear that it was necessary to maximize profits for the firm as a whole. Thus, one major issue facing a firm with a divisional structure is the degree of decentralization and when interference should and should not take place.

The Issue of Performance Evaluation

Another of Debbie's concerns was the effect of this centrally dictated price change on performance measures and the reward structure. By increasing the price of the product, she expected divisional profits to decrease significantly. As a result, she feared a less favorable evaluation and lower rewards.

When companies decentralize decision making, they do not relinquish control over the managers of the subunits. Control is maintained by organizing decentralized units as responsibility centers, developing performance measures for each, and basing rewards on an individual's performance at controlling the responsibility center. The major types of responsibility centers are cost centers, profit centers, and investment centers.

Performance measures are developed to provide some direction for managers of decentralized units and to evaluate their performance. The development of performance measures and the specification of a reward structure are major issues for a decentralized organization. Because performance measures can affect the behavior of managers, the measures chosen should encourage a high degree of goal congruence. In other words, they should influence managers to pursue the company's objectives.

Furthermore, as Debbie's situation illustrates, performance measurement and reward must be consistent and fair. Even with the adjustment for bonus payments, Debbie was skeptical about how her future opportunities would be affected. Consistent application of the guidelines governing performance measurement is important for instilling confidence in the performance evaluation system.

The Issue of Transfer Pricing

transfer prices

A related issue that is intertwined with performance measurement is transfer pricing. **Transfer prices** are the prices charged for goods produced by one division and transferred to another. Often the output of one division can be used as input for another division. For example, integrated circuits produced by one division can be used by a second division to make video recorders. The price charged affects the revenues of the transferring division and the costs of the receiving division. As a result, the profitability of both divisions is affected.

■ DECENTRALIZATION

Organizations range from highly centralized to strongly decentralized. Although some firms lie at either end of the continuum, most fall somewhere between the two extremes; most companies cluster on the decentralized side of the center. Decentralization appears to be a more popular form of organizational design than centralization. A number of reasons have been offered as to why decentralization is so popular.

Reasons for Decentralization

Access to Local Information   The quality of decisions is affected by the quality of information available. As a firm grows in size and operates in different markets and regions, central management can have difficulty accessing information that is locally available. Lower-level managers, however, who are in contact with immediate operating conditions (e.g., the strength and nature of local competition, the nature of the local labor force, and so on) do have access to this information. This is particularly true in multinational corporations (MNCs), where far-flung divisions may be operating in a number of different countries, subject to various legal systems and customs. As a result, local managers are often in a position to make better decisions. Decentralization allows an organization to take advantage of this specialized knowledge.

Cognitive Limitations   Even if local information somehow were made available to central management, those managers would face another problem. In a large, complex organization that operates in diverse markets with hundreds or thousands of different products, it is virtually impossible for any single individual to possess all of the expertise and training needed to process and use the information. Individuals with specialized skills would still be needed. Rather than having different individuals at headquarters for every specialized area, why not let these individuals have direct responsibility in the field itself? In this way, the firm can avoid the cost and bother of collecting and transmitting local information to headquarters.

Timely Response Possible   Furthermore, by placing managers at the scene, a more timely response is possible. The manager making the decision is also responsible for implementing it. In a centralized setting, time is needed to transmit the local information to headquarters and to transmit the decision back to the local unit. The delay caused by the two transmissions may decrease the effectiveness of the response. A local manager with decision-making power can act more quickly.

Another plus for decentralization is related to the need, in centralization, to transmit instructions. The manager responsible for implementing the decision might misinterpret the instructions. This decreases the effectiveness of the response. In a decentralized organization, where the local manager both makes and implements the decision, this problem does not arise.

Focusing of Central Management   By decentralizing the operating decisions, central management is free to engage in strategic planning and decision making. The long-run survival of the organization should be of more importance to central management than day-to-day operations.

Training and Evaluation   An organization always has a need for highly trained managers who can replace the higher-level managers as they retire or move to take advantage of other opportunities. By decentralizing, lower-level managers are given the opportunity to make decisions as well as implement them. What better way to prepare a future generation of higher-level managers than providing them the opportunity to make significant decisions? These opportunities also give top managers the occasion to evaluate the local manager's capabilities. Those who make the best decisions are the ones who can be selected for promotion to central management.

Motivation   By giving local managers freedom to make decisions, some of their higher-level needs (self-esteem and self-actualization) are being met. Greater responsibility can produce more job satisfaction and motivate the local manager to exert greater effort. More initiative and more creativity can be expected. Of course, the extent to which the behavioral benefits can be realized depends to a large degree on how managers are evaluated and rewarded for their performance.

The Units of Decentralization

Decentralization is usually achieved by creating decentralized units called *divisions*. One way in which divisions are differentiated is by the types of goods or services produced. For example, a company may have a small appliance division, a large appliance division, a small parts division, and a large parts division. These divisions are organized on the basis of product lines. Notice that some interdependencies between divisions exist. The output of the parts divisions can be used as inputs for the appliance divisions. In a decentralized setting, some interdependencies usually exist; otherwise, a company would merely be a collection of totally separate entities. The presence of these interdependencies creates the need for transfer pricing.

Divisions may also be created along geographic lines. IBM, for example, has divisional boundaries that organize production and sales for Asia and the Far East (AFE), North America, Latin and South America, and Europe and Africa. The presence of divisions spanning more than one country creates the need for performance evaluation that can take into account differences in divisional environments.

A third way divisions differ is by the type of responsibility given to the divisional manager. Recall the three major types of responsibility centers: cost centers, profit centers, and investment centers. Managers of cost centers have responsibility for controlling costs, managers of profit centers for controlling revenues and costs, and managers of investment centers for revenues, costs, and investments. Notice that investment centers represent the greatest degree of decentralization (followed by profit centers and finally by cost centers) because their managers have the freedom to make the greatest variety of decisions.

Organizing divisions as responsibility centers not only differentiates them on the degree of decentralization but also creates the opportunity for control of the divisions through the use of responsibility accounting. Control of cost centers is achieved by evaluating the efficiency and the effectiveness of divisional managers. Performance reports are the typical instruments used in this evaluation. Profit centers, on the other hand, are evaluated by assessing the unit's profit contribution, measured on income statements. Since performance reports and contribution income statements have been discussed elsewhere, this chapter will not go into the evaluation of managers of cost centers or profit centers. The focus will be on the evaluation of managers of investment centers.

■ MEASURING THE PERFORMANCE OF INVESTMENT CENTER MANAGERS

If managers are responsible for investment decisions as well as decisions regarding sales and costs, the use of contribution income statements may provide misleading information regarding their performance. For example, suppose that two divisional managers report profit contributions of $100,000 and $200,000, respectively. Can we say that the second manager is doing a better job than the first? What if the first manager used an investment of $500,000 to produce the contribution of $100,000 while the second manager used an investment of $2 million to produce the $200,000 contribution? Does your response change? Clearly, relating the reported operating profits to the assets used to produce them is a more meaningful measure of performance.

One way to relate operating profits to assets employed is to compute the profit earned per dollar of investment. For example, the first division earned $0.20 per dollar invested ($100,000/$500,000); the second division earned only $0.10 per dollar invested ($200,000/$2,000,000). In percentage terms, the first division is providing a 20 percent rate of return and the second division 10 percent. This method of computing the relative profitability of investments is known as the *return on investment*.

Return on Investment Defined

return on investment (ROI)   **Return on investment (ROI)** is the most common measure of performance for an investment center. It can be defined in the following three ways:

$$\begin{aligned} \text{ROI} &= \text{Net operating income/Average operating assets} \\ &= (\text{Net operating income/Sales}) \times (\text{Sales/Operating assets}) \\ &= \text{Operating income margin} \times \text{Operating asset turnover} \end{aligned}$$

net operating income   In this formulation, **net operating income** refers to earnings before interest and **operating assets**   taxes. **Operating assets** are all assets acquired to generate operating income. They usually include cash, receivables, inventories, land, buildings, and equipment. The figure for average operating assets is computed as follows:

$$\begin{aligned} \text{Average operating assets} = \,&(\text{Beginning net book value} \\ &+ \text{Ending net book value})/2 \end{aligned}$$

Opinions vary regarding how long-term assets (plant and equipment) should be valued (e.g., gross book value versus net book value or historical cost versus current cost). Most firms use historical cost net book value, however.[1]

Margin and Turnover

margin   The initial ROI formula is decomposed into two component ratios: *margin* and *turnover*. **Margin** is simply the ratio of net operating income to sales. It expresses the portion of sales that is available for interest, taxes, and profit. **turnover**   **Turnover** is a different measure; it is found by dividing sales by average operating assets. The result shows how productively assets are being used to generate sales.

Both measures can affect ROI. By decomposing the total ROI into these two measures, more information about the performance of the manager becomes available. To illustrate this additional information, consider the data

---

[1]For a discussion of the relative merits of gross book value, see James S. Reese and William R. Cool, "Measuring Investment Center Performance," *Harvard Business Review* (May–June 1978), pp. 28–46, 174–176.

presented in Exhibit 17–1. The Electronics Division improved its ROI from 18 percent to 20 percent from 1991 to 1992. The Medical Supplies Division's ROI, however, dropped from 18 percent to 15 percent. A better picture of what caused the change in rates is revealed by computing the margin and turnover ratios for each division. These ratios are also presented in Exhibit 17–1.

Notice that the margins for both divisions dropped from 1991 to 1992. In fact, the divisions experienced the *same* percentage of decline (16.67 percent). A declining margin could be explained by increasing expenses, by competitive pressures (forcing a decrease in selling prices), or both.

In spite of the declining margin, the manager of the Electronics Division was able to increase the division's rate of return. This increase resulted from an increase in the turnover rate that more than compensated for the decline in margin. The increase in turnover could be explained by a deliberate policy to reduce inventories. (Notice that the average assets employed remained the same for the Electronics Division even though sales increased by $10 million.)

EXHIBIT 17–1
Comparison of Divisional Performance

Comparison of ROI		
	Electronics Division	*Medical Supplies Division*
1991:		
Sales	$30,000,000	$117,000,000
Net operating income	1,800,000	3,510,000
Average operating assets	10,000,000	19,500,000
ROI[a]	18%	18%
1992:		
Sales	$40,000,000	$117,000,000
Net operating income	2,000,000	2,925,000
Average operating assets	10,000,000	19,500,000
ROI[a]	20%	15%

	Margin and Turnover Comparisons			
	Electronics Division		*Medical Supplies Division*	
	1991	*1992*	*1991*	*1992*
Margin[b]	6.0%	5.0%	3.0%	2.5%
Turnover[c]	3.0	4.0	6.0	6.0
ROI	18.0%	20.0%	18.0%	15.0%

[a] Net operating income divided by average operating assets
[b] Net operating income divided by sales
[c] Sales divided by average operating assets

The experience of the other division was less favorable. Because its turnover rate remained unchanged, its ROI dropped. The manager of this division, unlike the other manager, was unable to overcome the decline in margin. Although more information is needed before any definitive conclusion is reached, the different responses to similar difficulties may say something about the relative skills of the two managers.

Advantages of the ROI Measure

At least three positive results stem from the use of ROI:

1. It encourages managers to pay careful attention to the relationship among sales, expenses, and investment, as should be the case for a manager of an investment center.

2. It encourages cost efficiency.

3. It discourages excessive investment in operating assets.

Each of these three advantages is illustrated by the following three scenarios.

Scenario A   A division manager is faced with the suggestion from her marketing vice-president that the advertising budget be increased by $100,000. The marketing vice-president is confident that this increase will boost sales by $200,000 and raise the contribution margin by $110,000. To support the anticipated increase in sales, an additional $50,000 of operating assets will be needed. Currently, the division has sales of $2 million, operating income of $150,000, and operating assets of $1 million.

If advertising increased by $100,000 and the contribution margin by $110,000, net income would increase by $10,000 ($110,000 − $100,000). Investment in operating assets must also increase by $50,000. The ROI without the additional advertising is 15 percent ($150,000/$1,000,000). With the additional advertising, the ROI is 15.24 percent ($160,000/$1,050,000). Since the ROI is increased by the proposal, the divisional manager should increase advertising.

Scenario B   Kyle Chugg, manager of Turner's Battery Division, groaned as he reviewed the projections for the last half of the current fiscal year. The recession was hurting his division's performance. Adding the projected earnings of $200,000 to the actual earnings of the first half produced expected annual earnings of $425,000. Kyle then divided the expected operating income by the division's operating assets to obtain an expected ROI of 12.15 percent. "This is awful," muttered Kyle. "Last year our ROI was 16 percent. And I'm looking at a couple more bad years before business returns to normal. Something has to be done to improve our performance."

Kyle directed all operating managers to cut costs by specified amounts without impairing the company's ability to maintain expected sales. Lower-level managers found ways to reduce costs by $150,000 for the remaining half of the year. This reduction increased the annual operating income from $425,000 to $575,000, increasing ROI from 12.15 percent to 16.43 percent as a result. Interestingly, Kyle found that some of the reductions could be maintained after business returned to normal.

Scenario C The Electronic Storage Division prospered during its early years. In the beginning, the division developed a new technology for mass storage of data; sales and returns were extraordinarily high. However, during the past several years, competitors had developed competing technology, and the division's ROI had plunged from 30 percent during the golden years to 15 percent during the past two years. Cost cutting had helped initially, but the fat had all been removed, and further improvement from cost reductions could not be expected. Moreover, any increase in sales was unlikely— competition was too stiff. The divisional manager was searching for some way to increase the ROI by at least 3 to 5 percent. Only by raising the ROI so that it compared favorably to that of other divisions could the division expect to receive additional capital for research and development.

The divisional manager initiated an intensive program to reduce operating assets. Most of the gains were made in the area of inventory reductions; however, one plant was closed because of a long-term reduction in market share. By installing a just-in-time purchasing and manufacturing system, the division was able to reduce its asset base without threatening its remaining market share. Furthermore, by looking at possible reductions in operating assets, the division was able to reduce its operating costs further. The end result was a 50 percent increase in the division's ROI, from 15 percent to more than 22 percent.

Disadvantages of the ROI Measure

Two negative aspects associated with ROI are frequently mentioned.

1. It discourages managers from investing in projects that would decrease the divisional ROI but would increase the profitability of the company as a whole (generally, projects with an ROI less than a division's current ROI would be rejected).

2. It encourages managers to focus on the short run at the expense of the long run (myopic behavior).

These disadvantages are illustrated by the following two scenarios.

Scenario D A cleaning products division has the opportunity to invest in two projects for the coming year. The outlay required for each investment, the dollar returns, and the ROI are as follows:

	Project I	*Project II*
Investment	$10,000,000	$4,000,000
Operating income	1,300,000	640,000
ROI	13%	16%

The division is currently earning an ROI of 15 percent, using operating assets of $50 million; operating income on current investment is $7.5 million. The division has approval to request up to $15 million in new investment capital. Corporate headquarters requires that all investments earn at least 10 percent (this rate represents how much the corporation must earn to cover the cost of acquiring the capital). Any capital not used by a division is invested by headquarters so that it earns exactly 10 percent.

The divisional manager has four alternatives: (a) invest in Project I; (b) invest in Project II; (c) invest in both Projects I and II; and (d) invest in neither project. The divisional ROI was computed for each alternative.

	Alternatives			
	A	*B*	*C*	*D*
Operating income	$ 8,800,000	$ 8,140,000	$ 9,440,000	$ 7,500,000
Operating assets	60,000,000	54,000,000	64,000,000	50,000,000
ROI	14.67%	15.07%	14.75%	15.00%

The divisional manager chose to invest only in Project II (alternative B) since it would have a favorable effect on the division's ROI (15.07 percent is greater than 15.00 percent).

Assuming that any capital not used by the division is invested at 10 percent, the manager's choice produced a lower profit for the company than could have been realized. If Project I had been selected, the company would have earned $1.3 million. By not selecting Project I, the $10 million in capital is invested at 10 percent, earning only $1 million (0.10 × $10,000,000). By maximizing the division's ROI, then, the divisional manager cost the company $300,000 in profits ($1,300,000 − $1,000,000).

Scenario E   Ruth Lunsford, manager of a small tools division, was displeased with her division's performance during the first three quarters. Given the expected income for the fourth quarter, the ROI for the year would be 13 percent, at least two percentage points below where she had hoped to be. Such an ROI might not be strong enough to justify the early promotion she was seeking. With only three months left, some drastic action was needed. Increasing sales for the last quarter was unlikely. Most sales were booked at least two to three months in advance. Emphasizing extra sales activity would benefit next year's performance. What was needed were some ways to improve this year's performance.

After careful thought, Ruth decided to take the following actions:

1. Lay off five of the highest paid salespeople.

2. Cut the advertising budget for the fourth quarter by 50 percent.

3. Delay all promotions within the division for three months.

4. Reduce the preventive maintenance budget by 75 percent.

5. Use cheaper raw materials for fourth-quarter production.

In the aggregate, these steps would reduce expenses, increase income, and raise the ROI to about 15.2 percent.

While Ruth's actions increase the profits and ROI in the short run, they have some long-run negative consequences. Laying off the highest paid salespeople (who are, quite possibly, the best salespeople) may adversely affect the division's future sales-generating capabilities. Future sales could also be harmed by cutting back on advertising and using cheaper raw materials. By delaying promotions, employee morale would be affected, which could, in turn, lower productivity and future sales. Finally, reducing preventive maintenance will likely cut into the productive capability of the division by increasing downtime and decreasing the life of the productive equipment.

Residual Income

residual income

In an effort to overcome the tendency to use ROI to turn down investments that are profitable for the company but that lower a division's ROI, some companies have adopted an alternative performance measure known as *residual income*. **Residual income** is the difference between operating income and the minimum dollar return required on a company's operating assets:

Residual income = Operating income − (r × Operating assets)

where r = The minimum rate of return

To illustrate the use of residual income, consider Scenario D again. In that scenario, the division manager rejected Project I because it would have reduced divisional ROI, which cost the company $300,000 in profits. The use of residual income as the performance measure would have prevented this loss. The residual income for each project is computed below.

Project I
Residual income = Operating income − (r × Operating assets)
= $1,300,000 − (0.10 × $10,000,000)
= $1,300,000 − $1,000,000
= $300,000

Project II

Residual income = $640,000 − (0.10 × $4,000,000)
              = $640,000 − $400,000
              = $240,000

Notice that both projects increase residual income; in fact, Project I increases divisional residual income more than does Project II. Thus, both would be selected by the divisional manager. For comparative purposes, the divisional residual income for each of the four alternatives identified in Scenario D follows:

	Alternatives			
	A	B	C	D
Operating assets	$60,000,000	$54,000,000	$64,000,000	$50,000,000
Operating income	8,800,000	8,140,000	9,440,000	7,500,000
Minimum return[a]	6,000,000	5,400,000	6,400,000	5,000,000
Residual income	$ 2,800,000	$ 2,740,000	$ 3,040,000	$ 2,500,000

[a]0.10 × Operating assets

As indicated, selecting both projects produces the greatest increase in residual income. Alternative C is now the preferred alternative. With this new measure employed, managers are encouraged to accept any project that earns above the minimum rate.

Disadvantages of Residual Income   Residual income, like ROI, can encourage a short-run orientation. If the manager in Scenario E were being evaluated on the basis of residual income, she could have taken the same actions. The problem of myopic behavior is not solved by switching to this measure.

Another problem with residual income is that it, unlike ROI, is an absolute measure of profitability. Thus, direct comparisons of the performance of two different investment centers become unfair, since the level of investment may differ. For example, consider the residual income computations for Division A and Division B, where the minimum required rate of return is 8 percent.

	Division A	Division B
Average operating assets	$15,000,000	$2,500,000
Operating income	1,500,000	300,000
Minimum return[a]	(1,200,000)	(200,000)
Residual Income	$ 300,000	$ 100,000
Residual return[b]	2%	4%

[a]0.08 × Operating assets
[b]Residual income divided by operating assets

At first glance, it is tempting to claim that Division A is outperforming Division B since its residual income is three times higher. Notice, however, that Division A used six times as many assets to produce this difference. If anything, Division B is more efficient.

One possible way to correct this disadvantage is to compute a residual return on investment by dividing residual income by average operating assets. This measure indicates that Division B earned 4 percent while Division A earned only 2 percent. Another possibility is to compute both return on investment and residual income and use both measures for performance evaluation. ROI could then be used for interdivisional comparisons.[2]

Measuring Performance in the Multinational Firm

A multinational corporation (MNC) is one that "does business in more than one country in such a volume that its well-being and growth rest in more than one country."[3] The MNC may be a large decentralized firm consisting of corporate headquarters and a series of divisions. Alternatively, the MNC may consist of a parent company and a number of subsidiaries.

It is important for the MNC to separate the evaluation of the *manager* of a subsidiary from the evaluation of the *subsidiary*. The manager's evaluation should not include factors over which he or she exercises no control, such as transfer prices, currency fluctuations, taxes, and so on. Instead, managers should be evaluated on the basis of revenues and costs incurred. It is particularly difficult to compare the performance of a manager of a subsidiary in one country with the performance of a manager of a subsidiary in another country. Even subsidiaries that appear to be similar in terms of production may face very different economic, social, or political forces. The manager should be evaluated on the basis of the performance he or she can control. Once a manager is evaluated, then the subsidiary financial statements can be restated to the home currency and uncontrollable costs can be allocated.[4]

International environmental conditions may be very different from, and more complex than, domestic conditions.[5] Environmental variables facing local managers of subsidiaries include economic, legal, political, social, and educational factors. Some important economic variables are inflation, foreign exchange rates, taxes, and transfer prices. Legal and political actions also have differing impacts. For example, a country may not allow cash outflows,

---

[2]In their study, Reese and Cool found that only 2 percent of the companies surveyed used residual income by itself whereas 28 percent used both residual income and return on investment. See Reese and Cool, "Measuring Investment Center Performance."

[3]Yair Aharoni, "On the Definition of a Multinational Corporation," in A. Kapoor and Phillip D. Grub (eds.), *The Multinational Enterprise in Transition* (Princeton, N.J.: Darwin Press, 1972), p. 4.

[4]Gerhard G. Mueller, Helen Gernon, and Gary Meek, *Accounting: An International Perspective* (Homewood, Ill.: Richard D. Irwin, 1987).

[5]Wagdy M. Abdallah, "Change the Environment or Change the System," *Management Accounting* (October 1986), pp. 33–36.

forcing the corporation to find ways to trade for the host country's output.[6] Educational variables vary from country to country as does the sophistication of the accounting system. Sociological and cultural variables affect how the multinational firm is treated by the subsidiary's country.

The existence of differing environmental factors makes interdivisional comparison of ROI potentially misleading. Suppose a U.S.–based MNC has three subsidiaries located in Canada, Brazil, and Spain with the following information:

	Assets	Revenues	Net Income	Margin	Turnover	ROI[a]
Brazil	15	10	6	0.60	0.67	0.40
Canada	10	6	3	0.50	0.60	0.30
Spain	18	13	10	0.77	0.72	0.55

[a]Rounded to two decimal places

On the basis of ROI, it appears that the manager of the Spanish subsidiary did the best job while the manager of the Canadian subsidiary did the worst job. But is this a fair comparison? Spain and Canada face very different legal, political, educational, and economic conditions. For example, a minimum wage law in one country will restrict the manager's ability to affect labor costs. Another country, in South America for example, may be very familiar with the effects of inflation. Companies there routinely write up the value of assets to accord with general price-level changes. Therefore, the corporation must be aware of and control for these differing environmental factors when assessing managerial performance. Exhibit 17–2 lists some environmental factors that may make interdivisional comparisons misleading.

Foreign Currency Revaluation   Often the parent company restates all subsidiaries' income into the home currency. This restatement can result in gain and loss opportunities on the revaluation of foreign currencies and can impact a subsidiary's financial statements and the related ROI and residual income computations. Suppose you are a division manager based in Mexico. Your division earned 320 million pesos this year, up from 200 million pesos the year before, a hefty 60 percent increase. Now suppose that your income is translated into dollars. If the exchange rate last year was 1,500 pesos per dollar and the exchange rate this year is 3,000 pesos per dollar, your net income figures translate into $133,333 net income last year and $106,667 net income this year. Suddenly, there is a 20 percent decrease in net income. Similar nasty surprises await ROI and net worth computations. The potential for gain or loss on

---

[6]One MNC faced with Philippine prohibitions on taking cash out of the country decided to hold its annual meeting in Manila. All corporate costs of the meeting (e.g., hotel, meals) could then be paid in pesos earned by the MNC's Philippine subsidiary. Example taken from Jeff Madura, *International Financial Management*, 2nd ed. (St. Paul, Minn.: West Publishing Company, 1989), p. 382.

EXHIBIT 17–2
Environmental Factors Affecting Performance Evaluation
in the Multinational Firm[a]

Economic factors:
  Organization of central banking system
  Economic stability
  Existence of capital markets
  Currency restrictions
Political and legal factors:
  Quality, efficiency, and effectiveness of legal structure
  Effect of defense policy
  Impact of foreign policy
  Level of political unrest
  Degree of governmental control of business
Educational factors:
  Literacy rate
  Extent and degree of formal education and training systems
  Extent and degree of technical training
  Extent and quality of management development programs
Sociological factors:
  Social attitude toward industry and business
  Cultural attitude toward authority and persons in subordinate positions
  Cultural attitude toward productivity and achievement (work ethic)
  Social attitude toward material gain
  Cultural and racial diversity

[a]Adapted from Wagdy M. Abdallah, "Change the Environment or Change the System," *Management Accounting* (October 1986), pp. 33–36. Used with the permission of the Institute of Management Accountants.

currency revaluation is particularly relevant for countries whose currencies are volatile—and depreciating vis-à-vis the home company's currency.

Multiple Measures of Performance

Both residual income and ROI are important measures of managerial performance. However, they are both short-run measures. As such, the temptation exists for managers to trade off short-run benefits at the expense of the long-run well-being of the company. One way to discourage this myopic behavior is to use additional measures of performance that relate more closely to the long-run health of the division. For example, in addition to ROI and residual income, top management could look at such factors as market share, customer complaints, personnel turnover ratios, and personnel development. By letting lower-level managers know that attention to long-run factors is also vital, the tendency to overemphasize ROI or residual income should diminish.

Additionally, the use of ROI and RI in the evaluation of managerial performance in divisions of a MNC is subject to problems beyond those faced by a decentralized company that operates in only one country. It is particularly important, then, to take a responsibility accounting approach. That is, managers should be evaluated on the basis of factors under their control. This can be facilitated by using multiple measures of performance.

▪ TRANSFER PRICING: GENERAL CONCERNS

intermediate product
final product

In most decentralized organizations, interdependencies exist among divisions. In a major form of this interdependency, the output of one division is used as the input of another. The product of the first division (the selling or transferring division) is referred to as the **intermediate product.** The product of the receiving division is called the **final product.**

Treating divisions as responsibility centers requires that the intermediate good be priced as it is transferred from one division to the next. The need for transfer pricing within a decentralized setting creates a number of interrelated and complex issues.

Overview of the Major Issues

Impact on Performance Measures The price charged for the intermediate good impacts the costs of the buying division and the revenues of the selling division. Thus, the profits of both divisions are affected by the transfer price. Since profit-based performance measures of the two divisions are affected (e.g., ROI and residual income), transfer pricing can often be a very emotionally charged issue. Exhibit 17–3 illustrates the effect of the transfer price on two divisions of ABC, Inc.

Impact on Firm-wide Profits While the actual transfer price nets out for the company as a whole, transfer pricing can affect the level of profits earned by the company as a whole if it affects divisional behavior. Divisions, acting independently, may set transfer prices that maximize divisional profits but adversely affect firm-wide profits. For example, the price set by the selling division can affect the output decision of the buying division. The quantity of final goods that the buying division's manager decides to produce and sell may not be the output level that maximizes firm-wide profits. Alternatively, the buying division may decide to purchase the good from an outside party because the outside price appears to be lower when, in reality, the cost of producing the good internally is much lower. For example, suppose that Division A in Exhibit 17–3 sets a transfer price of $30 for a component that costs $24 to produce. If Division C can obtain the component from an outside supplier for $28, it will refuse to buy from Division A. Division C will realize a savings of $2 per component ($30 internal transfer price − $28 external

EXHIBIT 17–3
Impact of Transfer Price on Transferring Divisions
and the Company as a Whole

ABC, Inc.	
A Division	*C Division*
Produces component and transfers it to C for transfer price of $30/unit	Purchases component from A at transfer price of $30/unit and uses it in production of final product.
Transfer price = $30/unit	Transfer price = $30/unit
Revenue to A	Cost to C
Increases net income	Decreases net income
Increases ROI	Decreases ROI

Transfer price revenue = Transfer price cost
Zero impact on ABC, Inc.

price). However, assuming that Division A cannot replace the internal sales with external sales, the company as a whole will be worse off by $4 per component ($28 external cost − $24 internal cost). This outcome would increase the total cost to the firm as a whole. Thus, how transfer prices are set can be critical for profits of the business as a whole.

Impact on Autonomy   Because transfer pricing decisions can affect firm-wide profitability, top management is often tempted to intervene and dictate desirable transfer prices. If such intervention becomes a frequent practice, however, the organization has effectively abandoned decentralization and all of its advantages. In fact, if the reasons for decentralization are valid, intervention may cause more harm than the perceived immediate benefits. Organizations decentralize because the benefits are greater than any associated costs. One of the costs of decentralization is occasional suboptimal behavior on the part of divisional managers. Thus, intervention by central management to reduce this cost may actually prove to be more costly in the long run than nonintervention.

The Transfer Pricing Problem

A transfer pricing system should satisfy three objectives: accurate performance evaluation, goal congruence, and preservation of divisional autonomy.[7] Accurate performance evaluation means that no one divisional manager should benefit at the expense of another (in the sense that one division is made better off while the other is made worse off). Goal congruence means that divisional managers select actions that maximize firm-wide profits. Autonomy means that central management should not interfere with the decision-making freedom of divisional managers. The **transfer pricing problem** concerns finding a system that simultaneously satisfies all three objectives.

transfer pricing problem

■ SETTING TRANSFER PRICES

Although direct intervention by central management to set specific transfer prices may not be advisable, the development of some general guidelines or policies may be entirely appropriate. One general guideline, called the *opportunity cost approach,* can be used to describe a wide variety of transfer pricing practices. Under certain conditions, this approach is compatible with the objectives of performance evaluation, goal congruence, and autonomy.

A Guide for Transfer Pricing

opportunity cost approach

In establishing a transfer pricing policy, the views of both the selling division and the buying division must be considered. The **opportunity cost approach** achieves this goal. It identifies the minimum price that a selling division would be willing to accept and the maximum price that the buying division would be willing to pay. These minimum and maximum prices correspond to the opportunity costs of transferring internally. They are defined for each division as follows:

minimum transfer price

1. The **minimum transfer price** is the transfer price that would leave the selling division no worse off if the good is sold to an internal division.

maximum transfer price

2. The **maximum transfer price** is the transfer price that would leave the buying division no worse off if an input is purchased from an internal division.

The opportunity cost rule signals when it is possible to increase firm-wide profits through internal transfers. Specifically, the intermediate good should be transferred internally whenever the opportunity cost (minimum price) of the selling division is less than the opportunity cost (maximum price) of the buying division. By its very definition, this approach ensures that the divisional manager of either division is no worse off by transferring internally.

---

[7]Joshua Ronen and George McKinney, "Transfer Pricing for Divisional Autonomy," *Journal of Accounting Research* (Spring 1970), pp. 100–101.

But what is meant by indifferent or no worse off? In practical terms, this means that total divisional profits are not decreased by the internal transfer.

Market Price

If there is an outside market for the intermediate product and that outside market is perfectly competitive, the correct transfer price is the market price.[8] In such a case, divisional managers' actions will simultaneously optimize divisional profits and firm-wide profits. Furthermore, no division can benefit at the expense of another division. In this setting, central management will not be tempted to intervene.

The opportunity cost approach also signals that the correct transfer price is the market price. Since the selling division can sell all that it produces at the market price, transferring internally at a lower price would make the division worse off. Similarly, the buying division can always acquire the intermediate good at the market price, so it would be unwilling to pay more for an internally transferred good. Since the minimum transfer price for the selling division is the market price and the maximum price for the buying division is also the market price, the only possible transfer price is the market price.

In fact, moving away from the market price will decrease the overall profitability of the firm. This principle can be used to resolve divisional conflicts that may occur, as the following example illustrates.

Tyson Manufacturers is a large, privately held corporation that produces small appliances. The company has adopted a decentralized organizational structure. The Small Parts Division, managed by Ned Kimberly, produces parts that are used by the Small Motor Division managed by Andrea Ferguson. The parts can also be sold to other manufacturers and to wholesalers. For all practical purposes, the market for the parts is perfectly competitive. Frank Johnston, a vice-president at corporate headquarters and the immediate supervisor of Ned and Andrea, had just received the following memo from Andrea:

Memorandum

To: Frank Johnston, Vice-President
From: Andrea Ferguson
Subject: Transfer Price of Component No. 14
Date: October 15, 1992

Frank, as you know, our division is operating at 70 percent capacity. Last week we received a request for 100,000 units of Model 1267. The offering price was $30. Listed below are the detailed costs we incur to produce that particular motor (because of the special arrangements, we avoid any costs of distribution). The full cost includes the component that we usually buy from Ned's division.

---

[8] A perfectly competitive market for the intermediate product requires four conditions: (1) the division producing the intermediate product is small relative to the market as a whole and cannot influence the price of the product; (2) the intermediate product is indistinguishable from the same product of other sellers; (3) firms can easily enter and exit the market; and (4) consumers, producers, and resource owners have perfect knowledge of the market.

Direct materials	$10
Transferred-in component	8
Direct labor	2
Variable overhead	1
Fixed overhead	10
Total cost	$31

As you can see, if we accept the order we will lose $1 per unit. The purpose of this memo is to register a complaint about the Small Parts Division. I must confess that I am somewhat irritated with Ned. I know the full cost of the component supplied by his division is $5. Well, I asked for a more favorable transfer price— $6.50 instead of the $8 we normally pay. He absolutely refused and seemed somewhat put out by my request. I believed the concession was needed so that I could accept the order and show a small profit. The benefits of this order are appealing. My capacity utilization jumps to 85 percent and I avoid the need to lay off some skilled workers. Avoiding the layoff will save the company at least $50,000 in training costs next year. Also, the special order may open up some new markets for the company within a year.

Can't you persuade Ned to make this small concession for the good of the company? In my opinion, more teamwork is needed. After all, I have been a faithful customer of Ned's for several years.

If you were Frank Johnston, how would you react to the memo? Should Frank intervene and dictate a lower transfer price? Is the market price guideline for transfer pricing invalid for this particular case? To answer these questions, let's turn to the opportunity cost approach. Since Ned can sell all he produces, the minimum transfer price for his division is the market price of $8. Any lower price would make his division worse off. For Andrea's division, identifying the maximum transfer price that can be paid so that her division is no worse off requires a more complex analysis.

Since the Small Motor Division is under capacity, the fixed overhead portion of Model 1267's cost is not relevant. Whether the order is accepted or rejected, the division will incur those costs. The relevant costs are those additional costs that will be incurred if the order is accepted. These costs, excluding for the moment the cost of the transferred-in component, are as follows:

Direct materials	$10
Direct labor	2
Variable overhead	1
Total	$13

Thus, the contribution to profits before considering the cost of the transferred-in component is $17 ($30 − $13). The division could actually pay $17 for the component and still break even on the special order; however, since the component can always be purchased from an outside supplier for $8, the maximum price that the division should pay internally is $8. If the buying division pays $8, the transferring division is no worse off. Furthermore, relative to the status quo, the buying division is better off by $9 ($17 − $8). Thus, the transfer price of $8 should be paid and the special order accepted.

In this setting, central management should not intervene and force a lower transfer price. Market price is the correct transfer price. At worst, the vice-president could point out the benefits of the special order to Andrea. The need to do so, however, raises some questions about Andrea's managerial abilities or her training in the use of accounting information.

Negotiated Transfer Prices

In reality, perfectly competitive markets exist in few settings. In most cases, producers can take actions that have a perceptible influence on price (e.g., by being large enough to influence demand by dropping the price of the product or by selling closely related but differentiated products). When imperfections exist in the market for the intermediate product, market price may no longer be suitable. In this case, negotiated transfer prices may be a practical alternative. Opportunity costs can be used to define the boundaries of the negotiation set.

Negotiated outcomes should be guided by the opportunity costs facing each division. A negotiated price should be agreed to only if the opportunity cost of the selling division is less than the opportunity cost of the buying division.

Example 1: Avoidable Distribution Costs To illustrate, assume that a division produces a circuit board that can be sold in the outside market for $22. The division can sell all that it produces at $22; however, the division incurs a distribution cost of $2 per unit. Currently, the division is selling 1,000 units per day, with a variable manufacturing cost of $12 per unit. Alternatively, the board can be sold internally to the company's Electronic Games Division. The distribution cost is avoidable if the board is sold internally. (The presence of the distribution cost is the only imperfection in the market for the circuit board.)

The Electronic Games Division is also producing at capacity. The division produces and sells 350 games per day. These games sell for $45 per unit and have a variable manufacturing cost of $32 per unit. Variable selling expenses of $3 per unit are also incurred. Sales and production data for each division are summarized in Exhibit 17–4.

Since the Electronic Games Division was recently acquired, no transfers between the two divisions have yet taken place. Susan Swift, the manager of the circuit board division, requested a meeting with Randy Schrude, manager of the games division, to discuss the possibility of internal transfers. The following is their conversation:

EXHIBIT 17-4
Summary of Sales and Production Data

	Board Division	Games Division
Units sold:		
Per day	1,000	350
Per year[a]	260,000	91,000
Unit data:		
Selling price	$22	$45
Variable costs:		
Manufacturing	$12	$32
Selling	$ 2	$ 3
Annual fixed costs	$1,480,000	$610,000

[a]There are 260 selling days in a year.

Susan: Randy, I'm excited about the possibility of supplying your division with circuit boards. What is your current demand for the type of board we produce? And how much are you paying for the boards?

Randy: We would use one in each of our video games, and our production is about 350 games per day. We pay $22 for each board.

Susan: We can supply that amount simply by displacing external sales. Furthermore, we would be willing to sell them at the same price—that's the price we charge outside customers. We can at least meet your price—that way you are no worse off.

Randy: Actually, I was hoping for a better price than $22. The circuit board is by far our most expensive input. By transferring internally, you can avoid some selling, transportation, and collection expenses. I called corporate headquarters, which estimated these costs at approximately $2 per unit. I'd be willing to pay $20 each for your units. You'd be no worse off, and, with a less expensive component, I can make about $700 per day more profit. This deal would make the company $182,000 more during the coming year.

Susan: Your information about avoiding $2 per unit is accurate. I also understand how the cheaper component can allow you to increase your profits. However, if you were to purchase the board at $22, I could increase my division's profits, and the corporation's for that matter, by $700 per day— just by selling you the 350 units and saving the $2 per unit I must spend to sell externally. You would be no worse off, and my division and the corporation would be better off by the $182,000 per year that you mentioned. It seems to me that most of the benefits to the corporation come from avoiding the distribution costs incurred when we sell externally. Nonetheless, I'll sweeten the deal. Since we're both members of the same family, I'll let you have the 350 boards for $21.50 each. That price allows you to increase your profits by $175 per day and reflects the fact that most of the savings are generated by my division.

Randy: I don't agree that most of the savings are generated by your division. You can't achieve those savings unless I buy from you. I'm willing to buy internally, but only if there is a fair sharing of the joint benefits. I think a reasonable arrangement is to split the benefits equally; however, I will grant a small concession. I'll buy 350 units at $21.10 each—that will increase your divisional profits by $385 per day and mine by $315 per day. Deal?

Susan: Sounds reasonable. Let's have a contract drawn up.

This dialogue illustrates how the minimum transfer price ($20) and the maximum transfer price ($22) set the limits of the negotiation set. The example also demonstrates how negotiation can lead to improved profitability for each division and for the firm as a whole. Exhibit 17–5 provides income statements for each division before and after the agreement. Notice how total profits of the firm increase by $182,000 as claimed; notice, too, how that profit increase is split between the two divisions.

EXHIBIT 17–5
Comparative Income Statements

	Board Division	Games Division	Total
Before Negotiation: All Sales External			
Sales	$ 5,720,000	$ 4,095,000	$ 9,815,000
Less variable expenses:			
Cost of goods sold	(3,120,000)	(2,912,000)	(6,032,000)
Variable selling	(520,000)	(273,000)	(793,000)
Contribution margin	$ 2,080,000	$ 910,000	$ 2,990,000
Less: Fixed expenses	(1,480,000)	(610,000)	(2,090,000)
Net income	$ 600,000	$ 300,000	$ 900,000

	Board Division	Games Division	Total
After Negotiation: Internal Transfers @ $21.10			
Sales	$ 5,638,100	$ 4,095,000	$ 9,733,100
Less variable expenses:			
Cost of goods sold	(3,120,000)	(2,830,100)	(5,950,100)
Variable selling	(338,000)	(273,000)	(611,000)
Contribution margin	$ 2,180,100	$ 991,900	$ 3,172,000
Less: Fixed expenses	(1,480,000)	(610,000)	(2,090,000)
Net income	$ 700,100	$ 381,900	$ 1,082,000
Change in net income	$ 100,100	$ 81,900	$ 182,000

Example 2: Excess Capacity   In perfectly competitive markets, the selling division can sell all that it wishes at the prevailing market price. In a less ideal setting, a selling division may be unable to sell all that it produces; accordingly, the division may reduce its output and, as a consequence, have excess capacity.[9]

To illustrate the role of transfer pricing and negotiation in this setting, consider the dialogue between Sharon Bunker, manager of a plastics division, and Carlos Rivera, manager of a pharmaceutical division:

Carlos: Sharon, my division has shown a loss for the past three years. When I took over the division at the beginning of the year, I set a goal with headquarters to break even. At this point, projections show a loss of $5,000 — but I think I have a way to reach my goal, if I can get your cooperation.

Sharon: If I can help, I certainly will. What do you have in mind?

Carlos: I need a special deal on your plastic bottle Model 3. I have the opportunity to place our aspirins with a large retail chain on the West Coast—a totally new market for our product. But we have to give it a real break on price. The chain has offered to pay $0.85 per bottle for an order of 250,000 bottles. My variable cost per unit is $0.60, not including the cost of the plastic bottle. I normally pay $0.40 for your bottle, but if I do that the order will lose me $37,500. I cannot afford that kind of loss. I know that you have excess capacity. I'll place an order for 250,000 bottles, and I'll pay your variable cost per unit, provided it is no more than $0.25. Are you interested? Do you have sufficient excess capacity to handle a special order of 250,000 bottles?

Sharon: I have enough excess capacity to handle the order easily. The variable cost per bottle is $0.15. Transferring at that price would make me no worse off; my fixed costs will be there whether I make the bottles or not. However, I would like to have some contribution from an order like this. I'll tell you what I'll do. I'll let you have the order for $0.20. That way we both make $0.05 contribution per bottle, for a total contribution of $12,500. That'll put you in the black and help me get closer to my budgeted profit goal.

Carlos: Great. This is better than I expected. If this West Coast chain provides more orders in the future—as I expect it will—and at better prices, I'll make sure you get our business.

Notice again the role that opportunity costs play in the negotiation. In this case, the minimum transfer price is the plastic division's variable cost ($0.15), representing the incremental outlay if the order is accepted. Since the division has excess capacity, only variable costs are relevant to the decision. By covering the variable costs, the order does not affect the division's total profits. For the buying division, the maximum transfer price is the purchase

---

[9]Output can be increased by decreasing selling price. Of course, decreasing selling price to increase sales volume may not increase profits—in fact, profits could easily decline. We assume in this example that the divisional manager has chosen the most advantageous selling price and that the division is still left with excess capacity.

price that would allow the division to cover its incremental costs on the special order ($0.25). Adding the $0.25 to the other costs of processing ($0.60), the total incremental costs incurred are $0.85 per unit; since the selling price is also $0.85 per unit, the division is made no worse off. Both divisions, however, can be better off if the transfer price is between the minimum price of $0.15 and the maximum price of $0.25.

Comparative statements showing the contribution margin earned by each division and the firm as a whole are shown in Exhibit 17–6 for each of the four transfer prices discussed. These statements show that the firm earns the same profit for all four transfer prices; however, different prices do affect the individual divisions' profits differently. Because of the autonomy of each division, however, there is no guarantee that the firm will earn the maximum profit. For example, if Sharon had insisted on maintaining the price of $0.40, no transfer would have taken place, and the $25,000 increase in profits would have been lost.

Disadvantages of Negotiated Transfer Prices Negotiated transfer prices have three disadvantages or limitations that are commonly mentioned.

EXHIBIT 17–6
Comparative Statements

	Transfer Price of $0.40		
	Pharmaceuticals	*Plastics*	*Total*
Sales	$ 212,500	$100,000	$ 312,500
Less: Variable expenses	(250,000)	(37,500)	(287,500)
Contribution margin	$ (37,500)	$ 62,500	$ 25,000
	Transfer Price of $0.25		
Sales	$ 212,500	$ 62,500	$ 275,000
Less: Variable expenses	(212,500)	(37,500)	(250,000)
Contribution margin	$ 0	$ 25,000	$ 25,000
	Transfer Price of $0.20		
Sales	$ 212,500	$ 50,000	$ 262,500
Less: Variable expenses	(200,000)	(37,500)	(237,500)
Contribution margin	$ 12,500	$ 12,500	$ 25,000
	Transfer Price of $0.15		
Sales	$ 212,500	$ 37,500	$ 250,000
Less: Variable expenses	(187,500)	(37,500)	(225,000)
Contribution margin	$ 25,000	$ 0	$ 25,000

1. One divisional manager, possessing private information, may take advantage of another divisional manager.

2. Performance measures may be distorted by the negotiating skills of managers.

3. Negotiation can consume considerable time and resources.

It is interesting to observe that Carlos, the manager of the pharmaceutical division, did not know the variable cost of producing the plastic bottle. Yet that cost was a key to the negotiation. This lack of knowledge gave Sharon, the other divisional manager, the opportunity to exploit the situation. For example, she could have claimed that the variable cost was $0.27 and offered to sell for $0.25 per unit as a favor to Carlos, saying that she would be willing to absorb a $5,000 loss in exchange for a promise of future business. In this case, she would capture the full $25,000 benefit of the transfer. Alternatively, she could have misrepresented the figure and used it to turn down the request, thus preventing Carlos from achieving his budgetary goal; after all, she is in competition with Carlos for promotions, bonuses, salary increases, and so on.

Fortunately, Sharon displayed sound judgment and acted with integrity. For negotiation to work, managers must be willing to share relevant information. How can this requirement be satisfied? The answer lies in the use of good internal control procedures.

Perhaps the best preventive course of action—the best internal control—is to hire managers with integrity, managers who have a commitment to ethical behavior. Additionally, top management can take other actions to discourage the use of private information for exploitive purposes. For example, corporate headquarters could give divisional managers access to relevant accounting information of other divisions. This step would minimize the possibility of exploitive behavior because of differences in information.

The second disadvantage of negotiated transfer prices is that the practice distorts the measurement of managerial performance. According to this view, divisional profitability may be affected too strongly by the negotiating skills of managers, masking the actual management of resources entrusted to each manager. Although this argument may have some merit, it ignores the fact that negotiating skill is also a desirable managerial skill. Perhaps divisional profitability *should* reflect differences in negotiating skills.

The third criticism of this technique is that negotiating can be very time consuming. The time spent in negotiation by divisional managers could be spent managing other activities, which may have a bearing on the success of the division. Occasionally, negotiations may reach an impasse, forcing top management to spend time mediating the process. The involvement of top management also has attached to it a very high opportunity cost.[10] Although

---

[10]The involvement of top management may be very cursory, however. In the case of a very large oil company that negotiates virtually all transfer prices, two divisional managers could not come to an agreement after several weeks of effort and appealed to their superior. His response: "Either come to an agreement within twenty-four hours, or you are both fired." Needless to say, an agreement was reached within the allotted time.

the use of managerial time may be costly, it may prove to be far more costly if this interaction is not allowed to take place. A mutually satisfactory negotiated outcome can produce increased profits for the firm that easily exceed the cost of the managerial time involved. Furthermore, negotiation does not have to be repeated each time for similar transactions.

Advantages of Negotiated Transfer Prices Although time consuming, negotiated transfer prices offer some hope of complying with the three criteria of goal congruence, autonomy, and accurate performance evaluation. As previously mentioned, for many organizations, decentralization is essential to organizational success. Also essential, however, is the process of ensuring that the efforts of appropriately differentiated units are sufficiently integrated to attain the overall goals of the organization. Negotiated transfer prices have been identified as an important integrating mechanism, a means by which goal congruence can be achieved.[11] If negotiation helps ensure goal congruence, the temptation for central management to intervene is diminished considerably. There is, quite simply, no need to intervene. Finally, if negotiating skills of divisional managers are comparable, or if the firm views these skills as an important managerial skill, concerns about motivation and accurate performance measures are avoided.

Cost-Based Transfer Prices

Three forms of cost-based transfer pricing will be considered: full cost, full cost plus markup, and variable cost plus fixed fee. In all three cases, to avoid passing on the inefficiencies of one division to another, standard costs should be used to determine the transfer price. A more important issue, however, is the propriety of cost-based transfer prices. Should they be used? If so, under what circumstances?

Full-Cost Transfer Pricing Perhaps the least desirable aspect of any transfer-pricing approach is that of full cost. Its only real virtue is simplicity. Its disadvantages are considerable. Full-cost transfer pricing can provide perverse incentives and distort performance measures. As we have seen, the opportunity costs of both the buying and selling division are essential for determining the propriety of internal transfers; at the same time, they provide useful reference points for determining a mutually satisfactory transfer price. Only rarely will full cost provide accurate information about opportunity costs.

A full-cost transfer price would have shut down the negotiated prices described earlier. In the first example, the manager would never have considered transferring internally if the price had to be full cost. Yet by transferring at selling price less some distribution expenses, both divisions—and the firm

---

[11]For an excellent discussion of the role of negotiated transfer prices in a decentralized organization, see David Watson and John Baumler, "Transfer Pricing: A Behavorial Context," *The Accounting Review* (July 1975), pp. 466–474.

as a whole—were better off. In the second example, the manager of the pharmaceutical division would never have placed the special order with the West Coast chain. Both divisions and the company would have been worse off, both in the short run and in the long run.

Full Cost Plus Markup   Full cost plus markup suffers from virtually the same problems as full cost. It is somewhat less perverse, however, if the markup can be negotiated. For example, a full cost plus formula could have been used to represent the negotiated transfer price of the first example. In some cases, a full-cost markup formula may be the outcome of negotiation; if so, it is simply another example of negotiated transfer pricing. In these cases, the use of this method is fully justified. Using full cost plus to represent all negotiated prices, however, is not possible (e.g., it could not be used to represent the negotiated price of the second example). The superior approach is negotiation since more cases can be represented and full consideration of opportunity costs is possible.

Variable Cost Plus Fixed Fee   Like full cost plus, variable cost plus fixed fee can be a viable transfer pricing approach provided that the fixed fee is negotiable. This method has one advantage over full cost plus markup: if the selling division is operating below capacity, variable cost is its opportunity cost. Assuming that the fixed fee is negotiable, the variable-cost approach can be equivalent to negotiated transfer pricing. Negotiation with full consideration of opportunity costs is preferred.

Propriety of Use   In spite of the disadvantages of cost-based transfer prices, companies actively use these methods, especially full cost and full cost plus markup.[12] There must be some compelling reasons for their use—reasons that outweigh the benefits associated with negotiated transfer prices and the disadvantages of these methods. The methods do have the virtue of being simple and objective. These qualities, by themselves, cannot justify their use, however. Some possible explanations for the use of these methods can be given.

In many cases, transfers between divisions have a small impact on the profitability of either division. For this situation, it may be cost beneficial to use an easy-to-identify cost-based formula rather than spending valuable time and resources on negotiation.

In other cases, the use of full cost plus markup may simply be the formula agreed upon in negotiations. That is, the full cost plus formula is the outcome of negotiation, but the transfer pricing method being used is reported as full cost plus. Once established, this formula could be used until the original conditions change to the point where renegotiation is necessary. In

---

[12]In a survey of profit centers, Umapathy found that 42 percent used full cost and full cost plus markup. Over 50 percent used either market price or negotiated prices. See Srinivasan Umapathy, "Transfers Between Profit Centers," in Richard F. Vancil (ed.), *Decentralization: Managerial Ambiguity by Design* (Homewood, Ill.: Dow Jones-Irwin, 1978).

this way, the time and resources of negotiation can be minimized. For example, the goods transferred may be custom-made, and the managers may have little ability to identify an outside market price. In this case, reimbursement of full costs plus a reasonable rate of return may be a good surrogate for the transferring division's opportunity costs.

Transfer Pricing and the Multinational Firm

For the multinational firm, transfer pricing must accomplish two objectives, performance evaluation and optimal determination of income taxes.

Performance Evaluation   Subsidiaries are frequently evaluated on the basis of net income and return on investment.[13] As is the case for any transfer price, the selling subsidiary wants a high transfer price that will raise its net income, and the buying subsidiary wants a low transfer price that will raise its net income. A problem arises in that transfer prices in MNCs are frequently set by the parent company (as in the opening scenario). Therefore, the use of mandated transfer prices makes the use of ROI and net income suspect. That is, they are not under the control of division managers and no longer serve as indicators of management performance.

Income Taxes and Transfer Pricing   If all countries had the same tax structure, then transfer prices would be set independently of taxes. However, as the opening scenario illustrated, this does not happen. Instead, there are high-tax countries (like the United States) and low-tax countries (such as the Cayman Islands). As a result, MNCs may use transfer pricing to shift costs to high-tax countries and shift revenues to low-tax countries. Exhibit 17–7 illustrates this concept, as two transfer prices are set. The first transfer price is $100 as title for the goods passes from the Belgian subsidiary to the reinvoicing center. Because the first transfer price is equal to full cost, profit is zero and taxes on zero profit also equal zero. The second transfer price is set at $200 by the reinvoicing center in Puerto Rico. The transfer from Puerto Rico to the United States does result in profit, but this profit does not result in any tax because Puerto Rico has no corporate income taxes. Finally, the U.S. subsidiary sells the product to an external party at the $200 transfer price. Again, price equals cost so there is no profit on which to pay income taxes. Consider what would have happened without the reinvoicing center. The goods would have gone directly from Belgium to the United States. If the transfer price was set at $200, the profit in Belgium would have been $100, subject to the 42 percent tax rate. Alternatively, if the transfer price set was $100, no Belgian tax would have been paid, but the U.S. subsidiary would

---

[13]A study of seventy multinationals revealed that 80 percent used these measures. See Helen Gernon Morsicato, *Currency Translation and Performance Evaluation in Multinationals* (Ann Arbor: UMI Research Press, 1982).

EXHIBIT 17–7
Use of Transfer Pricing to Affect Taxes Paid

Action	*Tax Impact*
Belgian subsidiary of Parent Company produces a component at a cost of $100 per unit. Title to the component is transferred to a Reinvoicing Center[a] in Puerto Rico at a transfer price of $100/unit.	42% tax rate $100 revenue − $100 cost = $0 Taxes paid = $0
Reinvoicing Center in Puerto Rico, also a subsidiary of Parent Company, transfers title of component to U.S. subsidiary of Parent Company at a transfer price of $200/unit.	0% tax rate $200 revenue − $100 cost = $100 Taxes paid = $0
U.S. subsidiary sells component to external company at $200 each.	35% tax rate $200 revenue − $200 cost = $0 Taxes paid = $0

[a]A reinvoicing center takes title to the goods but does not physically receive them. The primary objective of a reinvoicing center is to shift profits to subsidiaries in low-tax countries.

have realized a profit of $100 and that would have been subject to the U.S. corporate income tax rate of 35 percent.

U.S.–based multinationals are subject to Internal Revenue Code Section 482 on the pricing of intercompany transactions. This section gives the IRS the authority to reallocate income and deductions among subsidiaries if it believes that such reallocation will reduce potential tax evasion. Basically, Section 482 requires that sales be made at "arm's length." That is, the transfer price set should match the price that would be set if the transfer were being made by unrelated parties. The IRS allows three pricing methods that approximate arm's-length pricing. In order of preference, these are the comparable uncontrolled price method, the resale price method, and the cost-plus method. The **comparable uncontrolled price method** is essentially market price. The **resale price method** is equal to the sales price received by the reseller less an appropriate markup. That is, the subsidiary purchasing a good for resale sets a transfer price equal to the resale price less a gross profit percentage. The **cost-plus method** is simply the cost-based transfer price.

The determination of an arm's-length price is a difficult one. Many times, the transfer pricing situation facing a company does not "fit" any of the three preferred methods outlined above. Then the IRS will permit a fourth method—a transfer price negotiated between the company and the IRS. The IRS, taxpayers, and the Tax Court have struggled with negotiated transfer

comparable
uncontrolled price
method
resale price method
cost-plus method

prices for years. However, this type of negotiation occurs after the fact—after income tax returns have been submitted and the company is being audited. Recently, the IRS has authorized the issuance of **advance pricing agreements** (APAs) to assist tax-paying firms to determine whether or not a proposed transfer price is acceptable to the IRS in advance of tax filing. "An APA is an agreement between the IRS and a taxpayer on the pricing method to be applied in an international transaction. It can cover transfers of intangibles (such as royalties on licenses), sales of property, provision of services and other items. An APA is binding on both the IRS and the taxpayer for the years specified in the APA and is not made public."[14] Since the APA procedure is so new, neither the IRS nor the firms are sure of the informational requirements.

(margin note: **advance pricing agreements**)

Transfer-pricing abuses are illegal—if they can be proved to be abuses. Many examples of both foreign and U.S. firms charging unusual transfer prices exist. The IRS successfully showed that Toyota had been overcharging its U.S. subsidiary for cars, trucks, and parts sold in the United States. The effect was to lower Toyota's reported income substantially in the United States and increase income reported in Japan. The settlement reportedly approached $1 billion.[15]

Of course, MNCs are also subject to taxation by other countries as well as the United States. Since income taxes are virtually universal, consideration of income tax effects pervades management decision making. Managers may legally avoid taxes; they may not evade them. The distinction is important. Unfortunately, the difference between avoidance and evasion is less a line than a blurry gray area. While the situation depicted in Exhibit 17–7 is clearly abusive, other tax-motivated actions are not. For example, an MNC may decide to establish a needed research and development center within an existing subsidiary in a high-tax country since the costs are deductible. MNCs may have tax-planning information systems that attempt to accomplish global tax minimization. This is not an easy task.

■ SUMMARY OF LEARNING OBJECTIVES

1. Explain why firms choose to decentralize. In order to increase overall efficiency, many companies choose to decentralize. The essence of decentralization is decision-making freedom. In a decentralized organization, lower-level managers make and implement decisions, whereas in a centralized organization, lower-level managers are responsible only for implementing decisions.

Reasons for decentralization are numerous. Companies decentralize because local managers can make better decisions using local information. Local managers can also provide a more timely response to changing conditions.

---

[14]"New Intercompany Pricing Rulings Create and Eliminate Tax Uncertainty," *Deloitte & Touche Review* (March 25, 1991), p. 6.

[15]"The Corporate Shell Game," *Newsweek* (April 15, 1991), pp. 48–49.

Additionally, decentralization for large, diversified companies is necessary because of cognitive limitations—it is impossible for any one central manager to be fully knowledgeable of all products and markets. Other reasons include training and motivating local managers and freeing up top management from day-to-day operating conditions so that they can spend time on more long-range activities, such as strategic planning.

2. Compute return on investment (ROI) and residual income (RI). ROI is the ratio of net operating income to operating assets. This ratio can be broken down into two components: margin (the ratio of net operating income to sales) and turnover (the ratio of sales to operating assets). Residual income is the difference between operating income and the minimum required dollar return on a company's operating assets.

3. List the advantages and disadvantages of using ROI and RI to measure managerial performance. Return on investment is the most common measure of performance for managers of decentralized units. Return on investment encourages managers to focus on improving their divisions' profitability by improving sales, controlling costs, and using assets efficiently. Unfortunately, the measure can also encourage managers to forego investments that are profitable for the firm but that would lower the divisional ROI. The measure can also encourage managers to increase ROI by sacrificing the long-run for short-run benefits.

Residual income is an alternative performance measure that overcomes managers' tendency to pass up investments that are profitable for the company as a whole. Unfortunately, residual income also can encourage myopic behavior. Additionally, it is a measure expressed in absolute terms and, consequently, is difficult to use for interdivisional comparisons.

4. Explain how environmental factors can affect performance evaluation in the multinational firm. Environmental factors are those social, economic, political, legal, and cultural factors that differ from country to country and that managers cannot affect. These factors, however, do affect profits and ROI. Therefore, evaluation of the divisional manager should be separated from evaluation of the subsidiary.

5. Explain the role of transfer pricing in a decentralized firm. When one division of a company produces a product that can be used in production by another division, transfer pricing exists. The transfer price is revenue to the selling division and cost to the buying division.

6. Define and discuss the transfer pricing problem. When one division produces a product that can be used as the input for another division's product, a potential transfer pricing problem exists. The price charged for the intermediate good affects the revenues of both divisions. Since both divisions are evaluated on their profitability, the price charged for the intermediate good can be a point of serious contention.

The transfer pricing problem involves finding a mutually satisfactory transfer price that is compatible with the company's goals of accurate performance evaluation, divisional autonomy, and goal congruence.

7. **Use the opportunity costing approach to determine when internal transfers should take place and to define the negotiation set.** An opportunity cost approach is recommended as a guide in setting transfer prices. If a perfectly competitive market exists for the intermediate product, the optimal transfer price is the market price.

8. **Explain why negotiated transfer prices are preferred in the absence of perfectly competitive markets for the intermediate product.** If a perfectly competitive market for the intermediate product does not exist, the recommended transfer price is achieved through the process of negotiation, using opportunity costs to establish the upper and lower limits.

9. **Discuss the merits and propriety of various transfer-pricing schemes.** If a perfectly competitive market exists for the intermediate product, market price is the best transfer price. In this case, the market price reflects the opportunity costs of both the buying and selling divisions. If no perfectly competitive market exists, a negotiated transfer price is preferred. In this case, opportunity costs for the buying and selling divisions differ and they form the upper and lower boundaries for the transfer price. The use of cost-based transfer prices is not generally recommended; however, if the transfers have little effect on either division's profitability, such an approach is acceptable. Additionally, cost-based pricing formulas may be appropriate if they are set through the process of negotiation.

10. **Discuss the impact of tax rates on transfer-pricing decisions in the MNC.** MNCs with subsidiaries in both high-tax and low-tax countries may use transfer pricing to shift costs to the high-tax countries (where their deductibility will lower tax payments) and to shift revenues to low-tax countries.

■ KEY TERMS

Advance pricing agreement   An agreement between the Internal Revenue Service and a taxpayer on the acceptability of a transfer price. The agreement is private and is binding on both parties for a specified period of time. (p. 883)

Centralized decision making   A system in which decisions are made at the top level of an organization and local managers are given the charge to implement them. (p. 854)

Comparable uncontrolled price method   The transfer price most preferred by the Internal Revenue Service under Section 482. The comparable uncontrolled price is essentially equal to the market price. (p. 882)

Cost-plus method   A transfer price acceptable to the Internal Revenue Service under Section 482. The cost-plus method is simply a cost-based transfer price. (p. 882)

Decentralization   The granting of decision-making freedom to lower operating levels. (p. 854)

Decentralized decision making   A system in which decisions are made and implemented by lower-level managers. (p. 854)

Final product   The finished output of a buying division that uses an intermediate product as one of its inputs. (p. 868)

Intermediate product   The output of one division that can be used as input in another division. (p. 868)

Margin   The ratio of net operating income to sales. (p. 858)

Maximum transfer price   The transfer price that will make the buying division no worse off if an input is acquired internally. (p. 870)

Minimum transfer price   The transfer price that will make the selling division no worse off if the intermediate product is sold internally. (p. 870)

Net operating income   Earnings before interest and taxes. (p. 858)

Operating assets   Those assets used to generate operating income, consisting usually of cash, inventories, receivables, property, plant, and equipment. (p. 858)

Opportunity cost approach   A transfer pricing system that identifies the minimum price that a selling division would be willing to accept and the maximum price that a buying division would be willing to pay. (p. 870)

Resale price method   A transfer price acceptable to the Internal Revenue Service under Section 482. The resale price method computes a transfer price equal to the sales price received by the reseller less an appropriate markup. (p. 882)

Residual income   The difference between operating income and the minimum required dollar return on a company's operating assets. (p. 863)

Return on investment (ROI)   The ratio of operating net income to operating assets. (p. 858)

Transfer price   The price charged for goods transferred from one division to another. (p. 855)

Transfer pricing problem   The problem of finding a transfer pricing system that simultaneously satisfies the three objectives of accurate performance evaluation, goal congruence, and autonomy. (p. 870)

Turnover   The ratio of sales to average operating assets. (p. 858)

■ REVIEW PROBLEM

The Components Division produces a part that is used by the Goods Division. The cost of manufacturing the part is given below:

Direct materials	$10
Direct labor	2
Variable overhead	3
Fixed overhead[a]	5
Total cost	$20

[a]Based on a practical volume of 200,000 parts

Other costs incurred by the Components Division are as follows:

Fixed selling and administrative	$500,000
Variable selling	$1/unit

The part usually sells for between $28 and $30 in the external market. Currently, the Components Division is selling it to external customers for $29. The division is capable of producing 200,000 units of the part per year; however, because of a weak economy, only 150,000 parts are expected to be sold during the coming year. The variable selling expenses are avoidable if the part is sold internally.

The Goods Division has been buying the same part from an external supplier for $28. It expects to use 50,000 units of the part during the coming year. The manager of the Goods Division has offered to buy 50,000 units from the Components Division for $18 per unit.

Required:

1. Determine the minimum transfer price that the Components Division would accept.

2. Determine the maximum transfer price that the manager of the Goods Division would pay.

3. Should an internal transfer take place? Why? If you were the manager of the Components Division, would you sell the 50,000 components for $18 each? Explain.

4. Suppose that the average operating assets of the Components Division total $10 million. Compute the ROI for the coming year, assuming that the 50,000 units are transferred to the Goods Division for $21 each.

Solution:

1. The minimum transfer price is $15. The Components Division has idle capacity and so must cover only its incremental costs, which are the variable manufacturing costs. (Fixed costs are the same whether or not the internal transfer occurs; the variable selling expenses are avoidable.)

2. The maximum transfer price is $28. The Goods Division would not pay more for the part than what it has to pay an external supplier.

3. Yes, an internal transfer ought to occur; the opportunity cost of the transferring division is less than the opportunity cost of the buying division. The Components Division would earn an additional $150,000 profit ($3 × 50,000). The total joint benefit, however, is $650,000 ($13 × 50,000). As the manager of the Components Division, I would attempt to negotiate a more favorable outcome for my division.

4. Income statement:

Sales ([$29 × 150,000] + [$21 × 50,000])	$ 5,400,000
Less: Variable cost of goods sold ($15 × 200,000)	(3,000,000)
Less: Variable selling expenses ($1 × 150,000)	(150,000)
Contribution margin	$ 2,250,000
Less: Fixed overhead ($5 × 200,000)	(1,000,000)
Less: Fixed selling and administration	(500,000)
Net income	$ 750,000

ROI = Net income/Average operating assets
  = $750,000/$10,000,000
  = 0.075

■ QUESTIONS

1   Discuss the differences between centralized and decentralized decision making.

2   What is decentralization?

3   Explain why firms choose to decentralize.

4   Explain how access to local information can improve decision making.

5   One division had operating profits of $500,000, and a second division had operating profits of $3 million. Which divisional manager did the best job? Explain.

6   Assume that a division earned operating profits of $500,000 on average operating assets of $2 million. What is the division's return on investment? Suppose that a second division had operating profits of $3 million and average operating assets of $30 million. Compute this division's ROI. Which division did the better job? Explain.

7   What are margin and turnover? Explain how these concepts can improve the evaluation of an investment center.

8   What are the three benefits of ROI? Explain how each can lead to improved profitability.

9   What are two disadvantages of ROI? Explain how each can lead to decreased profitability.

10   What is residual income? Explain how residual income overcomes one of ROI's disadvantages.

11   What disadvantage is shared by ROI and residual income? What can be done to overcome this problem?

12   What is a transfer price?

13   Explain how transfer prices can impact performance measures, firm-wide profits, and the decision to decentralize decision making.

14   What is the transfer pricing problem?

15   Explain the opportunity cost approach to transfer pricing.

16   If the minimum transfer price of the selling division is less than the maximum transfer price of the buying division, the intermediate product should be transferred internally. Do you agree? Why?

17   If an outside, perfectly competitive market exists for the intermediate product, what should the transfer price be? Why?

18   Suppose that a selling division can sell all that it produces for $50 per unit. Of that $50, however, $3 represents the costs of distribution (commissions, freight, collections, and so on). Assuming the distribution costs are avoidable if the product is sold internally, what is the minimum transfer price? The maximum transfer price?

19   Discuss the advantages of negotiated transfer prices.

20   Discuss the disadvantages of negotiated transfer prices.

21   Identify three cost-based transfer prices. What are the disadvantages of cost-based transfer prices? When might it be appropriate to use cost-based transfer prices?

22   The performance of the subsidiary manager is equivalent to the performance of a subsidiary. Do you agree? Explain.

23 What environmental factors may affect divisional performance in a multinational firm?

24 What is the purpose of Internal Revenue Code Section 482? What four methods of transfer pricing are acceptable under this section?

■ EXERCISES

E17–1 **ROI; Margin; Turnover** The following data have been collected for the past two years for one of the larger divisions of Foley Company:

	1991	*1992*
Sales	$40,000,000	$50,000,000
Net operating income	3,000,000	3,200,000
Average operating assets	20,000,000	20,000,000

Required:

1. Compute the ROI for each year.

2. Compute the margin and turnover ratios for each year.

3. Explain how the division managed to increase its ROI from 1991 to 1992 in spite of a declining margin.

E17–2 **ROI; Margin; Turnover** Data are provided below for a second division of Foley Company (see Exercise 17–1).

	1991	*1992*
Sales	$25,000,000	$25,000,000
Net operating income	1,500,000	1,400,000
Average operating assets	10,000,000	10,000,000

Required:

1. Compute the ROI for the second division for each year.

2. Compute the margin and turnover ratios for each year.

3. How does the performance of the manager of the second division compare with the performance of the manager of the first division (refer to Exercise 17–1)?

E17–3 **ROI and Investment Decisions** The manager of a division that produces sleeping bags, tents, and other camping gear is faced with the opportunity to invest in two independent projects. The first will provide the capability to produce a new type of camp stove; the second will provide the opportunity to produce a backpack, a product the division does not currently offer. Without the investments, the division will have average assets for the coming year of $15 million and expected operating income of $2.4 million. The outlay required for each investment and the expected operating incomes are as follows:

	Camp Stove	*Backpack*
Outlay	$1,000,000	$500,000
Operating income	140,000	67,500

Corporate headquarters has made available $2 million of capital for the camping goods division. Any funds not invested by the division will be retained by headquarters and invested to earn the company's minimum required rate, 12 percent.

Required:

1. Compute the ROI for each investment.

2. Compute the divisional ROI for each of the following four alternatives:
   a. No investment is made.
   b. The camp stove investment is made.
   c. The backpack investment is made.
   d. Both investments are made.
   Assuming that divisional managers are evaluated and rewarded on the basis of ROI performance, which alternative do you think the divisional manager will choose?

3. Compute the profit gained or lost for the company as a whole, based on your answer given for requirement 2. Was the correct decision made?

E17–4   **Residual Income and Investment Decisions**   Refer to the data given in Exercise 17–3.

Required:

1. Compute the residual income for each of the opportunities.

2. Compute the divisional residual income for each of the following four alternatives:
   a. No investment is made.
   b. The camp stove investment is made.
   c. The backpack investment is made.
   d. Both investments are made.
   Assuming that divisional managers are evaluated and rewarded on the basis of residual income, which alternative do you think the divisional manager will choose?

3. Based on your answer in requirement 2, compute the gain or loss from the divisional manager's investment decision. Was the correct decision made?

E17–5   **Transfer Pricing; Outside Market with Full Capacity**   Jacox Company's Can Division produces a variety of cans that are used for food processing. The Nut Division of Jacox buys nuts, deshells, roasts, and salts them, and places them in cans. It sells the cans of roasted nuts to various retailers. The most frequently used can is the 12-ounce size. In the past, the Nut Division has purchased these cans from external suppliers for $0.60 each. The manager of the Nut Division has approached the manager of the Can Division and has offered to buy 200,000 12-ounce cans each year. The Can Division currently is producing at capacity and produces and sells 300,000 12-ounce cans to outside customers for $0.60 each.

Required:

1. What is the minimum transfer price for the Can Division? What is the maximum transfer price for the Nut Division? Is it important that transfers take place internally? If transfers do take place, what should the transfer price be?

2. Now assume that the Can Division incurs selling costs of $0.04 per can that could be avoided if the cans are sold internally. Identify the minimum transfer price for the Can Division and the maximum transfer price for the Nut Division. Should internal transfers take place? If so, what is the benefit to the firm as a whole?

3. Suppose you are the manager of the Can Division. Selling costs of $0.04 per can are avoidable if the cans are sold internally. Would you accept an offer of $0.58 from the

manager of the other division? How much better off (or worse off) would the Can Division be if this price is accepted?

E17-6 **Transfer Pricing; Idle Capacity** The Box Division of Mano Enterprises produces boxes that can be sold externally or internally to Mano's candy division. Sales and cost data on the most popular box are given below:

Unit selling price	$0.95
Unit variable cost	0.60
Unit fixed cost[a]	0.15
Practical capacity	500,000 units

[a]$75,000/500,000

During the coming year, the Box Division expects to sell 350,000 units of this box. The Candy Division currently plans to buy 150,000 units of the box on the outside market for $0.95 each. Neil Hansen, manager of the Box Division, has approached Martha Rasmussen, manager of the Candy Division, and offered to sell the 150,000 boxes for $0.94 each. Neil explained to Martha that he can avoid selling costs of $0.02 per box and that he would split the savings by offering a $0.01 discount on the usual price.

Required:

1. What is the minimum transfer price that the Box Division would be willing to accept? What is the maximum transfer price that the Candy Division would be willing to pay? Should an internal transfer take place? What would be the benefit (or loss) to the firm as a whole if the internal transfer takes place?

2. Suppose Martha knows that the Box Division has idle capacity. Do you think that she would agree to the transfer price of $0.94? Suppose she counters with an offer to pay $0.85. If you were Neil, would you be interested in this price? Explain with supporting computations.

E17-7 **ROI; Margin; Turnover** Ready Electronics is facing stiff competition from imported goods. Its operating income margin has been declining steadily for the past several years; the company has been forced to lower prices so that it can maintain its market share. The operating results for the past three years are as follows:

	1990	1991	1992
Sales	$10,000,000	$ 9,500,000	$ 9,000,000
Net operating income	1,200,000	1,045,000	945,000
Average assets	15,000,000	15,000,000	15,000,000

For the coming year, Ready's president plans to install a JIT purchasing and manufacturing system. She estimates that inventories will be reduced by 70 percent during the first year of operations, producing a 20 percent reduction in the average operating assets of the company, which would remain unchanged without the JIT system. She also estimates that sales and operating income will be restored to the 1990 level because of simultaneous reductions in operating expenses and selling prices. Lower selling prices will allow Ready to expand its market share.

Required:

1. Compute the ROI, margin, and turnover for 1990, 1991, and 1992.

2. Suppose that in 1993 the sales and operating income were achieved as expected but inventories remained at the same level as in 1992. Compute the expected ROI, margin, and turnover. Explain why the ROI increased over the 1992 level.

3. Suppose that the sales and operating net income for 1993 remained the same as in 1992 but inventory reductions were achieved as projected. Compute the ROI, margin, and turnover. Explain why the ROI exceeded the 1992 level.

4. Assume that all expectations for 1993 were realized. Compute the expected ROI, margin, and turnover. Explain why the ROI increased over the 1992 level.

E17–8   **ROI and Residual Income**   Consider the following data for two divisions of the same company:

	Paper Products	**Plastic Products**
Sales	$3,000,000	$10,000,000
Average operating assets	1,000,000	3,000,000
Net operating income	120,000	330,000
Minimum required return	8%	8%

Required:

1. Compute residual income for each division. By comparing residual income, is it possible to make a useful comparison of divisional performance? Explain.

2. Compute the residual rate of return by dividing the residual income by the average operating assets. Is it possible now to say that one division outperformed the other? Explain.

3. Compute the return on investment for each division. Can we make meaningful comparisons of divisional performance? Explain.

4. Add the residual rate of return computed in requirement 2 to the required rate of return. Compare these rates with the ROI computed in requirement 3. Will this relationship always be the same?

E17–9   **Transfer Pricing and Autonomy**   The Parts Division supplies Part 678 to the Medical Products Division, which uses it in manufacturing a heart monitor. The Medical Products Division is currently operating below capacity (by 10,000 units), while the Parts Division is operating at capacity. Part 678 sells externally for $50. The cost of producing the heart monitor is given below:

Part 678	$ 50
Direct materials	100
Direct labor	20
Variable overhead	30
Fixed overhead	40
Total unit cost	$240

The Medical Products Division has received an order for 1,000 heart monitors from a wholesaler, with an offering price of $230. Since company policy prohibits selling any product below full cost, the division manager requested a price concession from the Parts Division. When that manager refused the request, the manager of the Medical Products Division filed an appeal with higher-level management, arguing that a transfer price of full cost should be used so that pricing decisions in his division would not be distorted.

Required:

1. Assume that the full cost of Part 678 is $30. Will the firm as a whole benefit if the part is transferred at $30? Should top management intervene?

2. Is anything wrong with the company policy that a division's selling price cannot be below full cost?

3. Compute the minimum and maximum transfer prices. Is an internal transfer indicated? If a transfer were to take place, what should the transfer price be?

E17–10 **Divisional Performance Evaluation in the MNC** Bianca Phillips, vice-president for Electronics for Consolidated, Inc., was reviewing the latest results for two divisions. The first, located in Baja California, Mexico, had posted net income of $150,000 on assets of $1,500,000. The second, in Punt-on-Thames, England, showed net income of $230,000 on assets of $2,000,000.

Required:

1. Calculate the ROI for each division.

2. Can a meaningful comparison be made of the British division's ROI to the Mexican division's ROI? Explain.

E17–11 **Transfer Pricing in the MNC** Carnover, Inc., manufactures a broad line of industrial and consumer products. One of its plants is located in Madrid, Spain, and another in Singapore. The Madrid plant is operating at 85 percent capacity. Softness in the market for its main product, electric motors, has led to predictions of further softening of the market, leading perhaps to production at 65 percent capacity. If that happens, workers will have to be laid off and one wing of the factory closed. The Singapore plant manufactures heavy duty industrial mixers that use the motors manufactured by the Madrid plant as an integral component. Demand for the mixers is strong. Price and cost information for the mixers is as follows:

Price	$2,200
Direct materials	630
Direct labor	125
Variable overhead	250
Fixed overhead	100

Fixed overhead is based on an annual budgeted amount of $3,500,000 and budgeted production of 35,000 mixers. The direct materials cost includes the cost of the motor at $200 (market price).

The Madrid plant capacity is 20,000 motors per year. Cost data are as follows:

Direct materials	$ 75
Direct labor	60
Variable overhead	60
Fixed overhead	100

Fixed overhead is based on budgeted fixed overhead of $2,000,000.

Required:

1. What is the maximum transfer price the Singapore plant would accept?
2. What is the minimum transfer price the Madrid plant would accept?
3. Consider the following environmental factors.

Madrid Plant	*Singapore Plant*
Full employment is very important.	Cheap labor is plentiful.
Local government prohibits layoffs without permission (which is rarely granted).	Accounting is based on British-American model, oriented toward decision-making needs of creditors and investors.
Accounting is legalistic and conservative, designed to ensure compliance with government objectives.	

How might these environmental factors impact on the transfer pricing decision?

E17–12   **Margin; Turnover; ROI**   Calculate the missing data for each of the four independent companies below.

	A	*B*	*C*	*D*
Revenue	$10,000	$30,000	$192,000	—
Expenses	8,000	—	180,000	—
Net income	2,000	12,000	—	—
Assets	20,000	—	96,000	9,600
Margin	—%	40%	—%	6.25%
Turnover	—	0.3125	—	2.00
ROI	—	—	—	—

E17–13   **Residual Income**   Refer to Exercise 17–12. Assume that the cost of capital is 12 percent for each of the four firms.

Required:

Compute the residual income for each of the four firms.

E17–14   **Transfer Pricing** Adler Industries is a vertically integrated firm with several divisions that operate as decentralized profit centers. Adler's Systems Division manufactures scientific instruments and uses the products of two of Adler's other divisions. The Board Division manufactures printed circuit boards (PCBs). One PCB model is made exclusively for the Systems Division using proprietary designs, while less complex models are sold in outside markets. The products of the Transistor Division are sold in a well-developed competitive market; however, one transistor model is also used by the Systems Division. The costs per unit of the products used by the Systems Division are presented below:

	PCB	Transistor
Direct material	$2.50	$0.80
Direct labor	4.50	1.00
Variable overhead	2.00	0.50
Fixed overhead	0.80	0.75
Total cost	$9.80	$3.05

The Board Division sells its commercial product at full cost plus a 25 percent markup and believes the proprietary board made for the Systems Division would sell for $12.25 per unit on the open market. The market price of the transistor used by the Systems Division is $3.70 per unit.

Required:

1. What is the minimum transfer price for the Transistor Division? What is the maximum transfer price of the transistor for the Systems Division?

2. Assume the Systems Division is able to purchase a large quantity of transistors from an outside source at $2.90 per unit. Further assume that the Transistor Division has excess capacity. Can the Transistor Division meet this price?

3. The Board and Systems divisions have negotiated a transfer price of $11 per printed circuit board. Discuss the impact this transfer price will have on each division.

(CMA adapted)

E17–15   **ROI, Residual Income** Raddington Industries produces tool and die machinery for manufacturers. The company expanded vertically in 1984 by acquiring one of its suppliers of alloy steel plates, Reigis Steel Company. To manage the two separate businesses, the operations of Reigis are reported separately as an investment center.

Raddington monitors its divisions on the basis of both unit contribution and return on average investment (ROI), with investment defined as average operating assets employed. Management bonuses are determined on ROI. All investments in operating assets are expected to earn a minimum return of 11 percent before income taxes.

Reigis's cost of goods sold is considered to be entirely variable while the division's administrative expenses are not dependent on volume. Selling expenses are a mixed cost with 40 percent attributed to sales volume. Reigis contemplated a capital acquisition with an estimated ROI of 11.5 percent; however, division management decided against the investment because it believed that the investment would decrease Reigis's overall ROI.

The 1992 operating statement for Reigis is presented below. The division's operating assets employed were $15,750,000 at November 30, 1992, a 5 percent increase over the 1991 year-end balance.

Reigis Steel Division

Operating Statement
For the Year Ended November 30, 1992
($000 omitted)

Sales revenue		$25,000
Less expenses		
Cost of goods sold	$16,500	
Administrative expenses	3,955	
Selling expenses	2,700	23,155
Income from operations before income taxes		$ 1,845

Required:

1. Calculate the unit contribution for Reigis Steel Division if 1,484,000 units were produced and sold during the year ended November 30, 1992.

2. Calculate the following performance measures for 1992 for the Reigis Steel Division:
   a. Pretax return on average investment in operating assets employed (ROI)
   b. Residual income calculated on the basis of average operating assets employed

3. Explain why the management of the Reigis Steel Division would have been more likely to accept the contemplated capital acquisition if residual income rather than ROI were used as a performance measure.

4. The Reigis Steel Division is a separate investment center within Raddington Industries. Identify several items that Reigis should control if it is to be evaluated fairly by either the ROI or residual income performance measures.

(CMA adapted)

▪ PROBLEMS

P17–1   **ROI and Residual Income; Ethical Considerations**   Grate Care Company specializes in producing products for personal grooming. The company operates six divisions, including the Hair Products Division. Each division is treated as an investment center. Managers are evaluated and rewarded on the basis of ROI performance. Only those managers who produce the best ROIs are selected to receive bonuses and to fill higher-level managerial positions. Fred Olsen, manager of the Hair Products Division, has always been one of the top performers. For the past two years, Fred's division has produced the largest ROI; last year, the division earned a net operating income of $2.56 million and employed average operating assets valued at $16 million. Fred was pleased with his division's performance and had been told that if the division does well this year, he would be in line for a headquarters position.

For the coming year, Fred's division has been promised new capital totaling $1.5 million dollars. Any of the capital not invested by the division will be invested to earn the company's required rate of return (9 percent). After some careful investigation, the marketing and engineering staff recommended that the division invest in equipment that could be used to produce a crimping and waving iron, a product currently not produced by the division. The cost of the equipment was estimated at $1.2 million. The division's marketing manager estimated operating earnings from the new line to be $156,000 per year.

After receiving the proposal and reviewing the potential effects, Fred turned it down. He then wrote a memo to corporate headquarters, indicating that his division would not be able to employ the capital in any new projects within the next eight to ten months. He did note, however, that he was confident that his marketing and engineering staff would have a project ready by the end of the year. At that time, he would like to have access to the capital.

Required:

1. Explain why Fred Olsen turned down the proposal to add the capability of producing a crimping and waving iron. Provide computations to support your reasoning.

2. Compute the effect that the new product line would have on the profitability of the firm as a whole. Should the division have produced the crimping and waving iron?

3. Suppose that the firm used residual income as a measure of divisional performance. Do you think Fred's decision might have been different? Why?

4. Explain why a firm like Grate Care might decide to use both residual income and return on investment as measures of performance.

5. Did Fred display ethical behavior when he turned down the investment? In discussing this issue, consider why he refused to allow the investment.

P17–2 **Market Price versus Full Cost** Hyrum Products manufactures radios, televisions, and VCRs in its four divisions: Radio, TV, VCR, and Components. The Components Division produces electronic components that can be used by the other three. All the components this division produces can be sold to outside customers; however, from the beginning, about 70 percent of its output has been used internally. The current policy requires that all internal transfers of components be transferred at full cost.

Recently, Jason Arnold, the new chief executive officer of Hyrum, decided to investigate the transfer pricing policy. He was concerned that the current method of pricing internal transfers might force decisions by divisional managers that would be suboptimal for the firm. As part of his inquiry, he gathered some information concerning Component 12F, used by the Radio Division in its production of a clock radio, Model 357K.

The Radio Division sells 100,000 units of Model 357K each year at a unit price of $21. Given current market conditions, this is the maximum price that the division can charge for Model 357K. The cost of manufacturing the radio is

Component 12F	$ 7
Direct materials	6
Direct labor	3
Variable overhead	1
Fixed overhead	2
Total unit cost	$19

The radio is produced efficiently and no further reduction in manufacturing costs is possible.

The manager of the Components Division indicated that she could sell 100,000 units (the division's capacity for this part) of Component 12F to outside buyers at $12 per unit. The Radio Division could also buy the part for $12 from external suppliers. She supplied the following detail on the manufacturing cost of the component:

Direct materials	$3.00
Direct labor	0.50
Variable overhead	1.50
Fixed overhead	2.00
Total unit cost	$7.00

Required:

1. Compute the firm-wide contribution margin associated with Component 12F and Model 357K. Also, compute the contribution margin earned by each division.

2. Suppose that Jason Arnold abolishes the current transfer pricing policy and gives divisions autonomy in setting transfer prices. Can you predict what transfer price the manager of the Components Division will set? What should the minimum transfer price for this part be? The maximum?

3. Given the new transfer pricing policy, predict how this will affect the production decision for Model 357K of the manager of the Radio Division. How many units of Component 12F will the manager of the Radio Division purchase, either internally or externally?

4. Given the new transfer price set by the Components Division and your answer to Requirement 3, how many units of 12F will be sold externally?

5. Given your answers to requirements 3 and 4, compute the firm-wide contribution margin. What has happened? Was Jason's decision to grant additional decentralization good or bad?

P17–3   **Transfer Pricing with Idle Capacity**   Dormir Company produces mattresses, chairs, and couches in its two divisions: the Mattress Division and the Couch Division. The Couch Division produces a hideaway bed. All of the components for the bed are produced internally with the exception of the mattress, which is purchased from the Mattress Division. Company policy, however, permits each manager freedom to decide whether to buy or sell internally. Each divisional manager is evaluated on the basis of return on investment and residual income.

Recently, an outside supplier has offered to sell the mattress to the Couch Division for $68. Since the current price paid to the Mattress Division is $70, Gina Fuller, the manager of the Couch Division, was interested in the offer. However, before making the decision to switch to the outside supplier, Gina decided to approach Juan Ortega, manager of the Mattress Division, to see if he wanted to offer an even better price. If not, then Gina would buy from the outside supplier.

Upon receiving the information from Gina about the outside offer, Juan gathered the following information about the mattress:

Direct materials	$20
Direct labor	10
Variable overhead	10
Fixed overhead	10
Total unit cost	$50
Selling price	$70
Production capacity	20,000
Internal sales	10,000

Required:

1. Suppose that the Mattress Division is producing at capacity and can sell all that it produces to outside customers. How should Juan respond to Gina's request for a lower transfer price? What will be the effect on firm-wide profits? Compute the effect of this response on each division's profits.

2. Now assume that the Mattress Division is currently selling 18,000 units. If no units are sold internally, the total sales of the hideaway mattress will drop to 16,000 units. Suppose that Juan refuses to lower the transfer price from $70. Compute the effect on firm-wide profits and on each division's profits.

3. Refer to requirement 2. What are the minimum and maximum transfer prices? Suppose that the transfer price is the maximum price less $1. Compute the effect on the firm's profits and on each division's profits. Who has benefitted from the outside bid?

P17–4   **ROI Calculations with Varying Assumptions**   Frozen Products is a division of Hyly Foods Company. During the coming year, it expects to earn a net operating income of $276,000 based on sales of $3.45 million; without any new investments, the division will have average net operating assets of $3 million. The division is considering a capital investment project—adding novelty ice cream products—that requires an additional investment of $600,000 and increases net operating income by $57,500 (sales would increase by $575,000). If made, the investment would increase beginning net operating assets by $600,000 and ending net operating assets by $400,000. Assume that the minimum rate of return required by the company is 7 percent.

Required:

1. Compute the ROI for the division without the investment.

2. Compute the margin and turnover ratios without the investment. Show that the product of the margin and turnover ratios equals the ROI computed in requirement 1.

3. Compute the ROI for the division with the new investment. Do you think the divisional manager will approve the investment?

4. Compute the margin and turnover ratios for the division with the new investment. Compare these with the old ratios.

5. Assume that a JIT purchasing and manufacturing system is installed, reducing average operating assets by $800,000. Compute the ROI with and without the investment under this new scenario. Now do you think the divisional manager will accept the new investment? Should he accept it? Explain your answer.

6. Refer to Requirement 5. Compute the margin and turnover ratios without the investment. Use these ratios to explain why the ROI increases.

P17–5   **Market Price versus Full Cost Plus**   Nashmen Manufacturing Corporation produces lawn mowers, snow blowers, and tillers. The company has six divisions, each set up as investment centers. Managers of the divisions are evaluated and rewarded on the basis of return on investment and residual income. Company policy dictates that internal transfers must take place whenever possible and that the transfer price will be full cost plus 10 percent. Ken Booth, vice-president of operations, is reevaluating the company's current internal transfer policy in light of a recent memo received from Dana Lemmons, manager of the Parts Division. The memo is presented below.

Memorandum

To: Ken Booth, Vice-President of Operations
From: Dana Lemmons, Manager of Parts Division
Subject: Transfer Pricing Policy

Ken, I must register serious concern about our current transfer pricing policy of full cost plus 10 percent. First, I believe this policy creates a significant understatement of my division's ROI. Second, it creates a disincentive for my division to decrease our costs of manufacturing.

For example, consider our production of Part 34 (small carburetors). Currently, we are capable of producing 300,000 of these units each year. Of these 300,000 carburetors, 200,000 are transferred to the Small Motor Division at a price of $16.50 per unit; 100,000 are sold to external customers at $20 each. I know that we can sell every carburetor we make to external customers. By forcing us to transfer internally, we are losing income and showing a much smaller ROI than we could otherwise.

But the problem is even greater. My engineers have created a new design that will allow us to decrease our fixed manufacturing costs for carburetors by $5 per unit. However, if we implement this design, our transfer price will drop to $11, and the revenues we receive from internal sales will drop significantly. All the savings and more are transferred to the buying division.

In my opinion, all of these problems can be resolved by allowing each divisional manager to set transfer prices and allowing each of us to buy or sell our products as we see fit.

After reading the memo, Ken also gathered the following information:

Manufacturing cost of carburetor	
Direct materials	$ 6.00
Direct labor	1.25
Variable overhead	1.50
Fixed overhead	6.25
Total cost	$15.00
Manufacturing cost of small motor	
Carburetor	$16.50
Direct materials	23.50
Direct labor	8.75
Variable overhead	3.25
Fixed overhead	8.40
Total cost	$60.40

Production and sales of small motor

Production	200,000
Sales	200,000
Unit price	$75

Required:

1. Assume that the Parts Division implements the new design change. Assume also that the internal demand for the carburetors remains constant. Compute the change in profits for the firm as a whole from this decision. Now compute the change in profits for the Parts Division and the Small Motor Division. Was Dana's concern valid? Were all the benefits of the improved design captured by the Small Motor Division?

2. Refer to requirement 1. Now assume that the reduced cost of the carburetor increases the internal demand from 200,000 to 300,000 units. Evaluate the impact on firm-wide profits and on each division's profits. If Dana anticipated this effect, do you think she would implement the cost-reducing design?

3. Refer to the original data. Ken Booth wants to know the effect of decentralizing the internal pricing decisions. Assuming that the Small Motor Division can buy carburetors of equal quality for $20 from outside suppliers, provide Dana with a complete assessment of the effect. In your assessment, include the change in firm-wide and divisional profits. Also comment on the incentives that Dana would have for implementing the cost-reducing design.

P17–6 **Full Cost Plus Pricing and Negotiation**   Entertainment Products Corporation has two divisions: Auxiliary Components and Stereo and Radio. Divisional managers are encouraged to maximize return on investment and residual income. Managers are essentially free to determine whether goods will be transferred internally and what internal transfer prices will be. Headquarters has directed that all internal prices be expressed on a full cost plus basis. The markup in the full-cost pricing arrangement, however, is left to the discretion of the divisional managers.

Recently, the two division managers met to discuss a pricing agreement for a headset that would be sold with a portable stereo unit. Production of the headsets is at capacity. Headsets can be sold for $29 to outside customers. The Stereo and Radio Division can also buy the headset from external sources for the same price; however, the manager of this division is hoping to obtain a price concession by buying internally. The full cost of manufacturing the headset is $20. If the manager of the Auxiliary Components Division sells the headset internally, $3 of selling and distribution costs can be avoided. The volume of business would be 250,000 units per year, well within the capacity of the producing division.

After some discussion, the two managers agreed on a full cost-plus pricing scheme that would be reviewed annually. Any increase in the outside selling price would be added to the transfer price by simply increasing the markup by an appropriate amount. Any major changes in the factors that led to the agreement could initiate a new round of negotiation; otherwise, the full cost plus arrangement would continue in force for subsequent years.

Required:

1. Calculate the minimum and maximum transfer prices.

2. Assume that the transfer price agreed upon between the two managers is halfway between the minimum and maximum transfer prices. Calculate the full cost plus transfer price that would represent this transfer price.

3. Refer to requirement 2. Assume that in the following year the outside price of headsets increases to $30. What is the new full cost plus transfer price?

4. Assume that two years after the initial agreement, the market for headsets has softened considerably, causing excess capacity for the Auxiliary Components Division. Would you expect a renegotiation of the full cost-plus pricing arrangement for the coming year? Explain.

P17–7   Transfer Pricing and Ethical Issues   Reread the introductory case at the beginning of the chapter.

Required:

1. Do you think that the tax minimization scheme described to Debbie Kishimoto is in harmony with the ethical behavior that should be displayed by top corporate executives? Why or why not? What would you do if you were Debbie?

2. Apparently, the Tax Department of Paterson Company has been strongly involved in developing the tax-minimization scheme. Assume that the accountants responsible for the decision are CMAs and members of the IMA, subject to the IMA standards of ethical conduct. Review the IMA standards for ethical conduct in the Appendix to Chapter 1. Are any of these standards being violated by the accountants in Paterson's Tax Department? If so, identify them. What should these tax accountants do if requested to develop a questionable tax-minimization scheme?

P17–8   Transfer Pricing: Various Computations   Blalock Company has a decentralized organization with a divisional structure. Each divisional manager is evaluated on the basis of ROI.

The Plastics Division produces a plastic container that the Chemical Division can use. Plastics can produce up to 100,000 of these containers per year. The variable costs of manufacturing the plastic containers are $4. The Chemical Division labels the plastic containers and uses them to store an important industrial chemical, which is sold to outside customers for $50 per container. The division's capacity is 20,000 units. The variable costs of processing the chemical (in addition to the cost of the container itself) are $26.

Required:

(Assume each part is independent, unless otherwise indicated.)

1. Assume that all of the plastic containers produced can be sold to external customers for $10 each. The Chemical Division wants to buy 20,000 containers per year. What should the transfer price be?

2. Refer to requirement 1. Assume $1 of avoidable distribution costs. Identify the maximum and minimum transfer prices. Identify the actual transfer price, assuming that negotiation splits the difference.

3. Assume that the Plastics Division is operating at 75 percent of capacity. The Chemical Division is currently buying 20,000 containers from an outside supplier for $7.50 each. Assume that any joint benefit will be split evenly between the two divisions. What is the expected transfer price? How much will the profits of the firm increase under this arrangement? How much will the profits of the Plastics Division increase, assuming that it sells the extra 20,000 containers internally?

4. Assume that both divisions have excess capacity. Currently, 15,000 containers are being transferred between divisions at a price of $8. The Chemical Division has an opportunity to take a special order for 5,000 containers of chemical at a price of $33.75 per container. The manager of the Chemical Division approached the manager of the Plastics Division and offered to buy an additional 5,000 plastic contain-

ers for $5 each. Assuming that the Plastics Division has excess capacity totaling at least 5,000 units, should the manager take the offer? What is the minimum transfer price? The maximum? Assume that the manager of the plastics division counters with a price of $5.50. Would the manager of the Chemical Division be interested?

P17–9 **Transfer Pricing: Custom-made Subassembly** The Industrial Machine Division has requested a specially designed subassembly from the Metal Fabricating Division. Because the subassembly is specially designed, there is no outside market price that can serve as a reference point for establishing an internal transfer price. The estimated cost of manufacturing the subassembly is given below:

Direct materials	$100
Direct labor	25
Variable overhead	50
Fixed overhead[a]	30
Total unit cost	$205

[a]Representing an allocation of existing fixed overhead. The total fixed overhead is the same regardless of whether the Metal Fabricating Division produces the subassembly.

The industrial machine division will use 10,000 of the subassemblies per year.

Required:

1. Assume that producing the special subassembly displaces other potential jobs. How should the manager of the Metal Fabricating Division set the transfer price for the custom-made subassembly?

2. Assume that two potential jobs will be displaced by the special subassembly. The expected revenues and the total expected costs of these jobs are as follows:

	Job 1	Job 2
Revenues	$2,600,000	$1,500,000
Variable manufacturing	1,950,000	1,050,000
Fixed overhead	200,000	300,000

Compute the minimum price the Metal Fabricating Division should charge.

3. Now assume that the Metal Fabricating Division can produce the special subassembly without displacing any work for outside customers. What is the minimum transfer price that should be charged for the subassembly?

4. Refer to requirement 3. The manager of the Metal Fabricating Division has offered to supply the subassembly for full cost plus the division's average markup. Assuming that average markup is 35 percent, compute the offered transfer price. What do you think of the pricing scheme suggested by the manager of the selling division?

5. Refer to requirement 4. The manager of the Industrial Machine Division refuses to pay the average markup. He indicates that an outside supplier has offered to produce the subassembly for $200 per unit. He offers to pay variable costs plus a

lump sum of $125,000 to help cover fixed costs and provide some profit. Do you think the manager of the Metal Fabricating Division should accept this last offer? Would she be tempted to do so? Explain.

P17-10   **Transfer Pricing and ROI: Various Computations**   Rockwell Company has two divisions: the Milk Division and the Dairy Products Division. Divisional managers are evaluated on the basis of return on investment. The Milk Division has the capability to produce 500,000 gallons of milk per year. The Dairy Products Division uses milk to produce ice cream, cheese, and cottage cheese. The following data are available for the Milk Division:

Selling price per gallon	$2.25
Variable production cost	0.50
Fixed production cost[a]	1.00

[a]Based on 500,000 gallons of output

The Dairy Products Division uses 600,000 gallons of milk per year when it is operating at capacity.

Required:

(Unless otherwise indicated, assume that the parts are independent of each other.)

1. Assume that the Milk Division can sell all that it produces. The Dairy Products Division is operating at 90 percent of capacity. It can buy all the milk that it needs for $2.35 per gallon from outside suppliers. What are the minimum and maximum transfer prices? What transfer price would you recommend? How many gallons of milk will the Dairy Products Division buy internally, assuming that it is operating at 90 percent of capacity?

2. Refer to requirement 1. How would your answers differ if the Milk Division can avoid distribution costs of $0.15 per gallon if the milk is sold internally?

3. The manager of the Milk Division realizes that excess capacity will exist for the last six months of the current year. He is reluctant to sell any of the milk cows to reduce production because he expects the market to rebound in the coming year. Accordingly, the cows will continue to be milked, creating excess production of 40,000 gallons. Unless a market for the excess milk can be found, it will simply be dumped. Discouraged with the possibility of finding any new outside customers, the manager of the Milk Division approaches the manager of the Dairy Products Division to see if a deal for internal sales can be arranged. The Dairy Products Division has been buying all of its milk from outside suppliers at $2 per gallon. Assume that production of milk is spread evenly over the year and that milk sold externally is sold for the normal price. Under these conditions, identify the minimum and maximum transfer prices. Assume that the managers split the difference between the two prices. How many gallons will be transferred internally? By how much will the profits of the firm and each division increase?

4. Refer to requirement 3. Now assume that the Milk Division has an offer to sell the 40,000 gallons of extra milk to a government agency for conversion into powdered milk. The offering price is $1 per gallon. How does this change your answers to requirement 3?

P17-11   **Transfer Pricing**   PortCo Products is a divisionalized furniture manufacturer. The divisions are autonomous segments with each division being responsible for its own sales, costs of operations, working capital management, and equipment acquisition. Each division serves a different market in the furniture industry. Because the markets and products of the divisions are so different, there have never been any transfers between divisions.

The Commercial Division manufactures equipment and furniture that is purchased by the restaurant industry. The division plans to introduce a new line of counter and chair units that feature a cushioned seat for the counter chairs. John Kline, the division manager, has discussed the manufacture of the cushioned seat with Russ Fiegel of the Office Division. They both believe a cushioned seat currently made by the Office Division for use on its deluxe office stool could be modified for use on the new counter chair. Consequently, Kline has asked Russ Fiegel for a price for 100 unit lots of the cushioned seat. The following conversation took place about the price to be charged for the cushioned seats.

Russ: John, we can make the necessary modifications to the cushioned seat easily. The raw materials used in your seat are slightly different and should cost about 10 percent more than those used in our deluxe office stool. However, the labor time (0.5 DLH) should be the same because the seat fabrication operation basically is the same. I would price the seat at our regular rate—full cost plus 30 percent markup.

John: That's higher than I expected, Russ. I was thinking that a good price would be your variable manufacturing costs. After all, your capacity costs will be incurred regardless of this job.

Russ: John, I'm at capacity. By making the cushion seats for you, I'll have to cut my production of deluxe office stools. Of course, I can increase my production of economy office stools. The labor time freed by not having to fabricate the frame or assemble the deluxe stool can be shifted to the frame fabrication and assembly of the economy office stool. Fortunately, I can switch my labor force between these two models of stools without any loss of efficiency. As you know, overtime is not a feasible alternative in our community. I'd like to sell it to you at variable cost, but I have excess demand for both products. I don't mind changing my product mix to the economy model if I get a good return on the seats I make for you. Here are my standard costs for the two stools and a schedule of my manufacturing overhead.

	Office Division	
Standard Costs and Prices	*Deluxe Office Stool*	*Economy Office Stool*
Raw materials		
Framing	$ 8.15	$ 9.76
Cushioned seat		
Padding	2.40	—
Vinyl	4.00	—
Molded seat (purchased)	—	6.00
Direct labor		
1.5 DLH @ $7.50	11.25	
0.8 DLH @ $7.50		6.00
Manufacturing Overhead		
1.5 DLH @ $12.80	19.20	
0.8 DLH @ $12.80		10.24
Total standard cost	$45.00	$32.00
Selling price (30% markup)	$58.50	$41.60

Office Division

Manufacturing Overhead Budget

Overhead Item	Nature	Amount
Supplies	Variable—at current market prices	$ 420,000
Indirect labor	Variable	375,000
Supervision	Nonvariable	250,000
Power	Use varies with activity; rates are fixed	180,000
Heat and light	Nonvariable—light is fixed regardless of production while heat/air conditioning varies with fuel charges	140,000
Property taxes and insurance	Nonvariable—any change in amounts/rates is independent of production	200,000
Depreciation	Fixed dollar total	1,700,000
Employee benefits	20% of supervision, direct and indirect labor	575,000
Total overhead		$3,840,000
Capacity in DLH		300,000
Overhead rate/DLH		$ 12.80

John: I guess I see your point, Russ, but I don't want to price myself out of the market. Maybe we should talk to corporate to see if it can give us any guidance.

Required:

1. John Kline and Russ Fiegel did ask PortCo corporate management for guidance on an appropriate transfer price. Corporate management suggested they consider using a transfer price based upon variable manufacturing cost plus opportunity cost. Calculate a transfer price for the cushioned seat based upon variable manufacturing cost plus opportunity cost.

2. Which alternative transfer price system—full cost, variable manufacturing cost, or variable manufacturing cost plus opportunity cost—would be better as the underlying concept for an intracompany transfer price policy? Explain your answer.

(CMA adapted)

▪ MANAGERIAL DECISION CASE

Transfer Pricing; International Setting; Tax Implications Valley Electronics Corporation is a large multinational firm involved in the manufacture and marketing of various electronic components. Recently, Rhonda Cooper, president of Valley Electronics, received some complaints from divisional managers about the company's international transfer pricing practices. Essentially, the managers believed that they had less control over how prices were set than they wished. After reviewing some of the practices, Rhonda found that three different methods were being used: (1) the comparable uncontrolled price method, (2) the resale price method, and (3) the cost-plus method. Unable to determine why there were three methods and exactly how each worked, Rhonda had requested a meeting with Wayne Sill, vice-president of finance.

Rhonda: Wayne, I need to respond to our divisional managers' concerns about the transfer pricing policies that we apply to goods shipped internationally. It appears that three methods are being used and that they differ across divisions.

Wayne: The three methods used are the ones allowed by Section 482 of the Internal Revenue Code. Which method is applicable depends on the operating circumstances surrounding the transfer of a particular component.

Rhonda: So the way we price these internal transfers is driven to some degree, at least, by tax laws. Interesting. Perhaps you can describe for me how each method works and what conditions dictate that we use that method.

Wayne: The basic concept underlying any transfer price we use is the notion of an arm's-length price. Ideally, an arm's-length price is the price that an unrelated party would pay for the good being transferred. The IRS allows four methods to determine the arm's-length price. We use three of those methods. The comparable uncontrolled method is based on market price. If the good being transferred has an external market, then the transfer price should be the price paid by an unrelated party, adjusted for differences that have a measurable effect on the price.

Rhonda: What kind of differences? Give me some examples.

Wayne: Well, the market price can be adjusted for differences such as landing costs (freight, insurance, customs duties, and special taxes) and marketing costs (commissions and advertising can be avoided with internal transfers). Adding landing costs and subtracting avoidable marketing costs are allowable adjustments to the market price.

Rhonda: I see. What happens if we sell the product to a related buyer who then resells it without any further processing? Or if the transferred good has no outside market at all?

Wayne: For the resale scenario, we use the resale price method. We take the resale price realized by our marketing divisions and adjust that price for the markup percentage and any differences like the ones we mentioned for the comparable uncontrolled method. We work back from the third-party selling price to obtain an allowable transfer price.

Rhonda: How is the markup determined?

Wayne: It corresponds to the percentage of gross profit earned by the reseller or the gross profit percentage earned by other parties who buy and resell similar products.

Rhonda: I'm beginning to understand why we have three different methods. We have divisions that fit both of the first two types. We also have some transfers that have no outside market, nor do they have any potential for resale. These goods are simply used as components of other products that are sold. Is this where cost-plus pricing is used?

Wayne: Absolutely. In this case, the transfer price is defined as the costs of production plus an appropriate gross profit percentage, with adjustments for differences such as landing costs.

Rhonda: How do we define the appropriate gross profit percentage?

Wayne: Well, it could be the gross profit percentage earned by the seller on the sale of the final product. Or if we can obtain the information, it could be the gross profit percentage earned by another party on a similar product.

Rhonda: Seems to me that the cost-plus method could be used for all three settings. Why don't we do that so that we have some uniformity in the way we compute transfer prices?

Wayne: There is a problem. If the requirements are met for any one of the methods, then it must be used—unless we can show that another method is more appropriate. The burden of proof is on us. I doubt that uniformity would be an acceptable justification. If the IRS audits us and determines that the transfer price does not fairly reflect profits recognized in the United States, it can reallocate corporate income for purposes of taxation.

Required:

1. Assume that Valley Electronics transfers a component from a U.S. division to a German division for $11.70. The landing costs are $2.50 per unit and the avoidable commissions and advertising total $0.50 per unit. The component has a market price within the United States of $10. Is the company complying with the comparable uncontrolled price method? Would the IRS be concerned if the transfer price is greater than the market price after adjustments? Why or why not?

2. Assume that a manufacturing division in the United States transfers a component to a marketing division for resale. The resale price is $8, the gross profit percentage (gross profit divided by sales) is 25 percent, and landing costs total $1.20 per unit. Suppose that the actual transfer price (excluding landing costs) is $4.50. Should the company continue transferring at $4.50?

3. Suppose that a U.S. division has excess capacity. A European division has offered to buy a component that would increase the U.S. division's utilization of its capacity. The component has an outside market in the United States with a unit selling price of $12. The variable costs of production for the component are $6. Landing costs total $2 per unit, and an internal transfer avoids $1.25 per unit of marketing costs. The European division can purchase the component locally for $12. Ignoring income taxes, what is the minimum price that the European division should pay for the component (including landing costs)? The maximum price? Assuming that the joint benefit is split equally, what is the transfer price? Now discuss the impact of the Section 482 regulations on this decision. (*Hint:* Consider Wayne's closing statement.)

CHAPTER 18

Planning and Control: The Advanced Manufacturing Environment

9. Discuss how control at the operational level in a JIT environment differs from that in a conventional environment.

10. Explain why time-based performance measures are increasing in importance.

11. Define and explain the key terms appearing at the end of the chapter.

SCENARIO

Michelle Anderson, president and owner of Anderson Parts, Inc., was not totally satisfied with the results of the company's new JIT purchasing and manufacturing system. True, inventories had been reduced, but they were still well above the levels that had been predicted by Henry Jensen, the consultant from a national public accounting firm who recommended the JIT system. Furthermore, although lead times had been reduced, they, too, were still higher than projected. Significant problems with quality, delivery, excessive scrap, and machine performance were persisting. Before she became too concerned, however, she wanted to hear what Jensen had to say. He had come to provide a progress report and additional recommendations for changes.

"Glad to see you again, Henry. I'm anxious to hear what you have to say about our new system and what can be done to continue improving our efficiency. It appears that we still haven't realized many of the benefits you predicted six months ago."

"Well, that's certainly true. Change does take time, but actually your company is making the transition from conventional manufacturing to JIT much more easily than other firms I've had as clients. You've already shown some significant improvement—more so than usual for this stage of development."

"That's encouraging. How much longer will it take to realize the full benefits? What else do we need to do?"

"You have to realize that JIT is more than just a technique. It is a philosophy of continuous improvement. Still, the levels of improvement that I predicted should be achieved within a year. After that, I would expect to see additional improvement each year. However, in order to achieve the short-term and long-term goals possible with JIT, you must have a system of performance measurement in place. Good evaluation and control are critical to the success of continuous-flow manufacturing."

"Henry, we do have a good system for evaluating and controlling our operations. We have a standard costing system and budgetary control of all our major responsibility centers. We also have good incentive pay schemes in place to encourage both labor and managerial productivity."

"Michelle, key factors in implementing JIT purchasing and manufacturing are measuring and controlling performance. But performance measurement must be compatible with the concept of continuous improvement. Otherwise, the measures used can actually limit the efficiency made possible by JIT. Unfortunately, some of the traditional control measures you mentioned are no longer suitable for your new manufacturing environment."

"Explain. I don't see why our performance measures are so bad."

"The traditional approach concerns managing costs, but costs can't be managed—only the activities that cause the costs can be. The typical accounting report produces variances and these variances are supposed to signal problems, if any exist. This approach encourages reactive decision making and is essentially backward-looking management. After all, the events that caused the costs are past, and we can't change those events.[1]

"True, but an investigation may reveal that the event that caused the problem persists and can be corrected to avoid future problems."

"I agree, but it seems more sensible to have your information system structured so that the cause of the costs is revealed without extensive investigation. This underscores the philosophy of activity management—an essential part of control in an advanced manufacturing environment. Managing activities is fundamental to continual improvement. Implementing an activity-based responsibility accounting system is recommended. There are other problems as well. Using variance analysis at the operational level can create some perverse incentives—encouraging behavior that is contrary to achieving continual improvement."

"Interesting. I really need more information about all this. Henry, prepare a report that outlines the performance and control issues for the new system. Once I fully understand what needs to be done, I'll see that the necessary changes are put into place."

▪ LIMITATIONS OF TRADITIONAL PERFORMANCE MEASURES

As the dialogue between Michelle and Henry indicates, many traditional measures used to evaluate and control workers and managers are no longer suitable for the new manufacturing environment. Managing activities and using an activity-based responsibility system provide a better approach for achieving continual improvement. Furthermore, continued use of conventional cost-based performance measures actually interferes with the efficient operation of a JIT system.

The traditional control mechanism of management accounting has been to compare actual costs with standard or budgeted costs. If actual costs exceed budgeted or standard costs by a material amount, managers conclude that the process is not operating as intended—that significant inefficiencies are present in the system. They then investigate the cause and take corrective actions. Furthermore, the ability to meet cost standards has been viewed as an important performance measure for managers and workers alike. Bonuses and other incentives are tied to reports that compare actual to budgeted performance.

Firms that advocate continual improvement usually alter the role of standard costing as a managerial control tool. The JIT approach emphasizes

---

[1]C. J. McNair, "Interdependence and Control: Traditional vs. Activity-Based Responsibility," *Journal of Cost Management* (Summer 1990), pp. 15–24.

total quality control, continual improvement, and zero inventories. Those espousing JIT strongly object to the incentives present in a conventional standard cost system. They view efficiency reporting, the attendant variance analysis, and the accompanying mindset as impediments to continual improvement.[2]

Standard costing encourages those responsible for the achievement of standards to produce favorable variances. But the pressure to meet standards may create dysfunctional behavior. For example, purchasing agents may acquire materials of low quality or in large lots in order to produce a favorable materials price variance. As a consequence, scrap, the number of defective units, and the amount of rework activity may increase, or raw materials inventories may be excessive. These outcomes run contrary to the JIT objectives of total quality control and zero inventories.

In the new manufacturing environment, efficiency reporting receives considerably less emphasis. Labor efficiency variances computed at the cell level may encourage workers to produce more than needed to achieve targeted efficiency levels or to avoid an unfavorable volume variance. For example, including setup labor as part of the labor standard (as is often done) encourages large production runs and, thus, excess production; by using fewer setup hours, the actual hours reported move closer to standard. But producing more product than needed is diametrically opposed to the JIT goal of zero inventories. In a JIT environment, idle workers (in the short run) are not necessarily viewed as bad—keeping workers active by overproducing can be much more costly than the labor services lost. Furthermore, labor becomes multidisciplinary—workers are trained to do what was formerly classified as indirect labor. In a JIT environment, production labor standards are less meaningful.

The computation of materials usage variances can also pose problems for JIT manufacturing. Workers may pass on poor quality components to avoid an unfavorable materials usage variance. Unfortunately, defective parts disrupt production in a JIT environment. Because there are no inventories to serve as a buffer for interruptions in production, incentives that encourage defective components are not desirable. Thus, the conventional approach to control operations through efficiency reporting and variance analysis is not compatible with a JIT environment.

Emphasis on individual overhead variances can also be detrimental to the JIT firm. Avoiding preventive maintenance to ensure a favorable budget variance may result in equipment being unavailable for production. This behavior, however, runs counter to the JIT objective of total preventive maintenance and creates an incentive for buffer inventories.

---

[2]Robert S. Kaplan, "Limitations of Cost Accounting in Advanced Manufacturing Environments," in Robert S. Kaplan (ed.), *Measures for Manufacturing Excellence* (Boston: Harvard Business School Press, 1990); McNair, "Interdependence and Control," pp. 15–23; Henry J. Johansson, Thomas Volmann, and Vivian Wright, "The Effect of Zero Inventories on Cost (Just-in-Time)," *Cost Accounting for the 90s* (Montvale, N.J.: National Association of Accountants, 1986), pp. 141–164. See also Robert A. Howell and Stephen R. Soucy, "Cost Accounting in the New Manufacturing Environment," *Management Accounting* (July 1987), pp. 21–31.

The concept of currently attainable standards is also opposed to the JIT philosophy of continual improvement. Currently attainable standards allow for a certain level of inefficiency. All too often, in a standard costing system, those who achieve the standard believe that they have arrived and that no further efforts are needed to improve efficiency. Of course, this is possible because the standard allows for inefficiency and is viewed as somewhat static in nature. Yet JIT demands that efforts be continually exerted to improve quality, to improve efficiency, to find better ways to do the same task. Innovation and simplicity are encouraged and rewarded. A dynamic view of efficiency, not a static one, is characteristic of JIT.

The conventional control measures, their limitations, and the objectives of JIT that are violated by these measures are summarized in Exhibit 18–1 for easy reference. Keep in mind that the exhibit provides only selected examples and is in no way exhaustive. Other examples could be given. However, the selected examples are sufficient to illustrate why Henry Jensen was unimpressed with Anderson's existing control system and why he recommended that a new system that is more compatible with the new manufacturing system be devised.

▪ ACTIVITY-BASED RESPONSIBILITY ACCOUNTING

Conventional responsibility accounting is characterized by four essential elements. First, a responsibility center must be identified. This center is typi-

EXHIBIT 18–1
Limitations of Conventional Control Methods:
Selected Examples

Control Measure	Limitation	JIT Objective Violated
Materials price variance	Encourages low quality and large lot purchases	Total quality control and zero inventories
Labor efficiency variance	Encourages over-production	Zero inventories
Materials usage variance	Provides incentive for low quality	Total quality control
Budget variance Maintenance	Provides incentive for downtime	Total preventive maintenance
Currently attainable standards	Encourages inefficiency	Continual improvement, zero inventories, total quality control, and total preventive maintenance

cally an organizational unit such as a department or production line, or it can even be a work team or an individual. Whatever the unit is, responsibility is assigned to the individual in charge. Responsibility is defined in financial terms (e.g., costs). Second, standards are set to serve as benchmarks for performance measurement. Budgeting and standard costing are the cornerstones of the benchmark activity. Third, performance is measured by comparing actual outcomes with budgeted outcomes. In principle, individuals are held accountable only for those items over which they have control. Fourth, individuals are rewarded or penalized according to the policies and discretion of higher management. Of course, the reward system is designed to encourage individuals to manage costs—to achieve or beat budgetary standards.

Controllability implies that costs are traced to individuals—individuals responsible for the incurrence of the costs. The emphasis of the conventional responsibility accounting system is on managing costs—not activities. The emerging consensus, however, is that management of activities—not costs—is the key to successful control in the advanced manufacturing environment.[3] To become a global competitor, managers must know what the customers want and when they want it and must be able to produce the product or service with the lowest cost possible—and do so rapidly. Only by knowing how activities contribute value to customers and by eliminating waste can a company be successful in achieving these objectives. This, in turn, requires, a new form of responsibility accounting: *activity-based responsibility accounting.*

Activity-based responsibility accounting requires accountability for activities rather than costs; it is a system-wide, integrated approach that focuses management's attention on activities.[4] Costs are caused by activities and so it makes sense to change the focus to the underlying causes of costs rather than the costs themselves. Since activities cut across functional and departmental lines, they are system wide in focus and require a global approach to control. Thus, activity-based responsibility accounting does not require individual maximization of performance but concerns maximizing system-wide performance; essentially, this form of control admits that maximizing the efficiency of individual subunits does not necessarily lead to maximum efficiency for the system as a whole. Thus, the possibility of direct laborers not continuously producing is allowed—provided that the system-wide effect is beneficial.

Marginal note: **Activity-based responsibility accounting**

---

[3]The following all support this view: McNair, "Interdependence and Control"; Kaplan, "Limitations of Cost Accounting"; Alfred J. Nanni, Jr., J. Robb Dixon, and Thomas E. Volmann, "Strategic Control and Measurement," *Journal of Cost Management* (Summer 1990), pp. 33–42; and H. Thomas Johnson, "Professors, Customers, and Value: Bringing a Global Perspective to Management Accounting Education," in Peter B. B. Turney (ed.), *Performance Excellence in Manufacturing and Service Organizations* (Proceedings of the Third Annual Management Accounting Symposium, March 1989), pp. 8–20.

[4]The definition and subsequent discussion is taken from McNair, "Interdependence and Control."

Activity Management

activity management

The heart of activity-based responsibility accounting is *activity management*. **Activity management** is the process of identifying activities an organization performs, assessing their value to the organization, and selecting and keeping only those that add value.[5] Because of increased competition, many firms are paying more attention to activities that add unnecessary cost and impede performance.

nonvalue-added activities

nonvalue-added costs

These activities, referred to as *nonvalue-added activities*, are either unnecessary or are necessary but inefficient and improvable.[6] **Nonvalue-added costs** are the costs caused by these activities. Activity management attempts to identify and eventually eliminate all unnecessary activities and, simultaneously, increase the efficiency of necessary activities. Activity management also involves adding new activities—activities that increase value.

The theme of activity management is waste elimination. As waste is eliminated, costs are reduced. The cost reduction *follows* the elimination of waste. Note the value of managing the *causes* of the costs rather than the costs themselves. Managing costs may increase the efficiency of an activity—but if the activity is unnecessary, what does it matter if it's performed efficiently? An unnecessary activity is wasteful and should be eliminated. For example, moving raw materials and partially finished goods is often cited as a nonvalue-added activity. Installing an automated materials handling system may increase the efficiency of this activity, but changing to cellular manufacturing with on-site, just-in-time delivery of raw materials could virtually eliminate the activity. It's easy to see which is preferable.

Examples of Nonvalue-Added Activities   The effort spent to produce accounting reports that have no utility and are not used by anyone is an example of an unnecessary activity. All too often, managers are flooded with reams of computer paper containing reports totally useless for running the company. The costs associated with producing these reports are nonvalue-added costs. By eliminating the unnecessary reports, personnel in the accounting department could be reduced and savings realized.

The activity of creating unnecessary accounting reports illustrates the important point that nonvalue-added activities can exist anywhere in the organization. In the manufacturing operation, five major activities are often cited as wasteful and unnecessary. These activities are listed and defined below.

1. Scheduling: an activity that uses time and resources to determine when different products have access to processes (or when and how many setups must be done) and how much will be produced

---

[5]This definition and much of the discussion of activity management are derived from Johnson, "Professors, Customers, and Value."

[6]This definition is found in James A. Brimson, "Improvement and Elimination of Non-Value-Added Costs," *Journal of Cost Management for the Manufacturing Industry* (Summer 1988), pp. 62–65.

2. Moving: an activity that uses time and resources to move raw materials, work in process, and finished goods from one department to another

3. Waiting: an activity in which raw materials or work in process use time and resources by waiting on the next process

4. Inspecting: an activity in which time and resources are spent on ensuring that the product meets specifications

5. Storing: an activity that uses time and resources while a good or raw material is held in inventory

None of these activities adds any value for the customer. Thus, the challenge of activity management is to find ways to produce the good without using any of these activities.

Cost Reduction Continuous improvement carries with it the objective of cost reduction. World-class competitors must deliver products the customers want, on time, and at the lowest possible cost. This means that an organization must continually strive for cost improvement. Activity management is the key to achieving cost reduction objectives. Activity management can reduce costs in four ways:[7]

1. Activity elimination

2. Activity selection

3. Activity reduction

4. Activity sharing

activity elimination

     Activity elimination focuses on nonvalue-added activities. Once activities that fail to add value are identified, measures must be taken to rid the organization of these activities. For example, the activity of inspecting incoming parts seems necessary to ensure that the product using the parts functions according to specifications. Use of a bad part can produce a bad final product. Yet this activity is necessary only because of the poor quality performance of the supplying firms. Selecting suppliers that are able to supply high-quality parts or who are willing to improve their quality performance to achieve this objective eventually will allow the elimination of incoming inspection. Cost reduction then follows.

activity selection

     Activity selection involves choosing among different sets of activities that are caused by competing strategies. Different strategies cause different activities. Different product design strategies, for example, can require significantly different activities. Activities, in turn, cause costs. Each product

---

[7]This classification and its discussion are based on Peter B. B. Turney, "How Activity-Based Costing Helps Reduce Cost," *Journal of Cost Management* (Winter 1991), pp. 29–35.

design strategy has its own set of activities and associated costs. All other things equal, the lowest-cost design strategy should be chosen. Thus, activity selection can have a significant effect on cost reduction.

activity reduction

    Activity reduction decreases the time and resources required by an activity. This approach to cost reduction should be primarily aimed at improving the efficiency of necessary activities or a short-term strategy for improving nonvalue-added activities until they can be eliminated. Setup activity, for example, is a necessary activity that is often cited as an example for which less time and fewer resources need to be used. Upon adopting a JIT system, Harley-Davidson reduced setup times by more than 75 percent.[8] This usually means that costs are being reduced.

activity sharing

    Activity sharing increases the efficiency of necessary activities by using economies of scale. Specifically, the quantity of the cost driver is increased without increasing the total cost of the activity itself. This lowers the per-unit cost of the cost driver and the amount of cost that is traceable to the products that consume the activity. For example, a new product can be designed to use components already being used by other products. By using existing components, the activities associated with these components already exist and the company avoids the creation of a whole new set of activities.

Cost Reporting: Value-Added and Nonvalue-Added Costs

A company's accounting system should distinguish between value-added costs and nonvalue-added costs.[9] The distinction is necessary so that management can focus on reducing and eventually eliminating nonvalue-added costs. Highlighting nonvalue-added costs also reveals the magnitude of the waste the company is currently experiencing. Reporting nonvalue-added costs separately encourages managers to place more emphasis on controlling nonvalue-added activities. Furthermore, tracking these costs over time permits managers to assess the effectiveness of their activity-management programs. Cost reduction should follow and knowing the amount of costs saved is important for strategic purposes. For example, if an activity is eliminated, then the costs saved should be traceable to individual products. These savings can produce price reductions for customers and make the firm more competitive. Changing the pricing strategy, however, requires knowledge of the cost reductions created by activity management. A cost reporting system, therefore, is an important ingredient in an activity-based responsibility accounting system. The activity-based cost report should include both value-added and nonvalue-added costs.

---

[8]Gene Schwind, "Man Arrives Just In Time To Save Harley-Davidson," *Material Handling Engineering* (August 1984), pp. 28–35.

[9]Expanding cost reporting to provide visibility for nonvalue-added costs was recommended by CAM-I. See Callie Berliner and James A. Brimson (eds.), *Cost Management for Today's Advanced Manufacturing* (Boston: Harvard Business School Press, 1988).

value-added activities
value-added costs

Value-added activities are necessary activities that are carried out with perfect efficiency. **Value-added costs** are the costs caused by value-added activities. These are the only costs that should be incurred in producing a product. The value-added standard would call for the complete elimination of nonvalue-added activities; the ideal would be a zero cost for these activities. This standard also calls for the complete elimination of the inefficiency of activities that are necessary but inefficiently carried out.

Ideal Standards   Value-added costs sound suspiciously like standard costs based on ideal standards; indeed, that is exactly what they are. When ideal standards were first discussed, they were criticized because they were assessed as being difficult, if not impossible, to attain and would be frustrating to those workers and supervisors held responsible for achieving them. This view conflicts with the JIT goal of continual improvement and can create an attitude of complacency. Complacency, in turn, may prove disastrous for a firm whose competitors are pursuing a goal of continual improvement.

Achieving an ideal standard is frustrating only if workers are required to achieve the standard immediately. The idea of continual improvement is to move toward the ideal, not to achieve it immediately. Workers can be rewarded for improvement. Moreover, operational performance measures, nonfinancial in nature, can be used to supplement and support the goal of eliminating nonvalue-added costs. Finally, measuring the efficiency of individual workers and supervisors is not the way to eliminate nonvalue-added activities. Remember, activities cut across departmental boundaries and are interdependent. Focusing on the activities and providing incentives to find better, more efficient ways to produce are more productive approaches.

By comparing actual costs with ideal standards, management can assess the level of nonproductive costs incurred and know the potential remaining for improvement. For unnecessary activities, the difference between actual costs and the absolute standard (which would be zero) is a direct measure of the nonvalue-added costs. For activities that are necessary but inefficient, the difference between actual and absolute standard costs can include price differences as well as differences attributable to inefficiency. In this case, price variances could be excluded, if desired.

Fundamental to identifying and calculating value- and nonvalue-added costs is the identification of cost drivers for each activity. Once cost drivers are identified, then ideal levels, or optimal standards, for each cost driver can be defined. Value-added costs can be computed by multiplying the ideal standards by the price standard. Nonvalue-added costs can be calculated as the difference between the actual level of the cost driver and the standard level, multiplied by the unit standard cost. These formulas are presented in Exhibit 18–2.

To illustrate the power of the above concepts, let's focus on the following four activities for a product manufactured in a JIT environment: material usage, power, setups, and inspection of incoming parts (raw materials). Of

EXHIBIT 18–2

Computational Formulas for Value- and Nonvalue-Added Costs

Value-added costs = $SQ \times SP$

Nonvalue-added costs = $(AQ - SQ)SP$

where SQ = The ideal quantity level of a cost driver
           SP = The standard price per unit of cost driver
           AQ = The actual quantity of cost driver used

the four activities, three are viewed as necessary: material usage, power, and setups; inspections are unnecessary (in an ideal sense, working with suppliers should eliminate it). The following data pertain to the four activities:

	Cost Driver	SQ	AQ	SP
Material usage	Pounds	20,000	22,000	$20.00
Power	Kilowatt hours	40,000	44,000	3.00
Setups	Setup time	—	3,000	30.00
Inspections	Inspection hours	—	2,000	25.00

Notice that the ideal standard for inspection calls for its elimination; the ideal standard for setups calls for a zero setup time. As pointed out earlier, by selecting the right suppliers and working with them on quality issues, inspections of incoming parts can soon be eliminated. Setups are necessary, but in a JIT environment, efforts are made to drive setup times to zero.

Exhibit 18–3 classifies the costs for the four activities as value-added or nonvalue-added. For simplicity, and to show the relationship to actual costs, the actual price per unit of the cost driver is assumed to be equal to the standard price. In this case, the value-added cost plus the nonvalue-added cost equals actual cost. In reality, this is always true for unnecessary activities, but not always true for necessary but inefficient activities. Normally, it might be necessary to add a price variance column. However, it can be argued that actual costs ought to be used as they reflect the total nonvalue-added cost. Our approach is always to assume that actual prices equal standard prices.

The cost report in Exhibit 18–3 allows managers to see the nonvalue-added costs; as a consequence, it emphasizes the opportunity for improvement. By decreasing scrap, waste, and rework, management can reduce its material cost. By reducing rework and improving labor efficiency, management can reduce kilowatt hours (the machines would be used more efficiently) and power costs. Reducing setup time and increasing the quality of incoming parts are also areas in which improvement can be realized and costs reduced.

EXHIBIT 18-3
Value- and Nonvalue-Added Cost Report
for the Year Ending December 31, 1991

	Costs		
Activity	Value Added	Nonvalue Added	Actual
Material usage	$400,000	$ 40,000	$440,000
Power	120,000	12,000	132,000
Setups	—	90,000	90,000
Inspections	—	50,000	50,000
Total	$520,000	$192,000	$712,000

Thus, reporting value- and nonvalue-added costs at a point in time may trigger managerial actions to manage activities more effectively. Seeing the amount of waste may induce managers to search for ways to reduce, select, share, and eliminate activities to bring about cost reductions. Reporting these costs may also help managers improve planning, budgeting, and pricing decisions. For example, lowering the selling price to meet a competitor's price may be seen as possible if a manager can see the potential for reducing nonvalue-added costs to absorb the effect of the price reduction.

Trend Reporting As managers take actions to reduce, eliminate, select, and share activities, do the cost reductions follow as expected? One way to answer this question is to compare the costs for each activity over time. The goal is cost reduction, and so we should see a decline in nonvalue-added costs from one period to the next—provided activity management is effective. Assume, for example that at the beginning of 1992, the following actions are taken to manage the four activities in Exhibit 18-3:

1. Material usage activity: Statistical process control is implemented. Scrap and waste are expected to decrease.

2. Setups: The product is redesigned creating a requirement for a simpler die. The simpler die should reduce setup time.

3. Power: The product redesign also is expected to reduce the rework and lower power consumption.

4. Inspections: A supplier selection program is implemented. The program focuses on selecting suppliers that can deliver high-quality parts. Inspections of incoming parts will eventually be eliminated.

Three major activity-management decisions were made: the use of statistical process control, product redesign, and supplier selection. How effective were these decisions? Did a cost reduction occur as expected? Exhibit 18–4 provides a cost report that compares the nonvalue-added costs of 1991 with those that occurred in 1992 (after implementing the changes described above). The 1992 costs are assumed but would be computed the same way as shown for 1991. We assume that SQ is the same for both years. Comparing 1992 nonvalue-added costs directly with 1991 value-added costs of 1991 requires SQ to be the same for both years. If SQ changes, prior-year nonvalue-added costs are adjusted by simply assuming the same percentage deviation from standard in the current year as was realized in the prior year.

The trend report reveals that cost reductions followed, as expected. Half of the nonvalue-added costs have been eliminated. There is still ample room for improvement, but activity management so far has been successful. As a note of interest, comparison of the actual costs of the two periods would have revealed the same reduction. Reporting nonvalue-added costs, however, not only reveals the reduction but also provides managers with information on how much potential for cost reduction remains. There is an important qualification, however.

Ideal standards, like any standard, are not cast in stone. New technology, new designs, and other innovations can change them. As standards change, new ways for improvement may surface. Managers should not become content even with absolute standards but should continually seek higher levels of efficiency.

The Role of Currently Attainable Standards

Although ideal standards are preeminent in the advanced manufacturing environment, the use of currently attainable standards can be retained in a modified form; however, detailed reporting of deviations from these standards should not be done at the operational level. Doing so may encourage behavior that is not compatible with the objectives of JIT manufacturing. The reporting of variance analysis using currently attainable standards should be at the plant level (or higher). In the JIT system, these reports have the primary

EXHIBIT 18–4
Trend Report: Nonvalue-Added Costs

	Nonvalue-Added Costs		
Activity	*1991*	*1992*	*Change*
Material usage	$ 40,000	$10,000	$30,000 F
Power	12,000	6,000	6,000 F
Setups	90,000	45,000	45,000 F
Inspections	50,000	35,000	15,000 F
Totals	$192,000	$96,000	$96,000 F

purpose of assessing performance under existing conditions and evaluating progress towards goals. With these purposes, the definition of what is meant by a currently attainable standard is changed.

If a company is emphasizing the reduction of nonvalue-added costs, the currently attainable standards should reflect the increased efficiency expected for the year. Comparing actual costs with the currently attainable standards would then provide a measure of how well the current year's goals for improvement have been met.

This use of currently attainable standards is equivalent to emphasizing actual costs and trends in actual costs. Cost reduction targets are set; evaluations concern how well managers meet these targets. Of course, comparison of actual costs with cost reduction targets is equivalent to comparing them to a currently attainable standard provided that the currently attainable standard is defined as last year's actual costs less the targeted reduction.

For example, the absolute standard may call for 3 pounds of raw material priced at $12 each, or an ideal materials cost of $36 per unit. Assume that in the prior year, the $12 price was achieved, but 3.5 pounds of material were used per unit produced, yielding an actual cost of materials per unit of $42 (a nonvalue-added cost of $6 per unit). For the current year, the company has a goal to reduce the nonvalue-added cost by $1.80 per unit. This goal is to be achieved by reducing material usage by 0.15 pounds per unit (the price of materials is assumed to be the same). Thus, the currently attainable quantity standard is defined as 3.35 pounds per unit. The currently attainable standard cost of materials per unit is $40.20, the actual cost less the targeted reduction ($42.00 − $1.80). For the following year, additional improvements would be sought and a new currently attainable standard defined.

Target Costing A related, but conceptually distinct, approach being used by many companies is target costs. A **target cost** is the difference between the sales price needed to capture a predetermined market share and the desired profit per unit.[10] If the target cost is less than what is currently achievable, then management budgets cost reductions that move the actual cost toward the target cost. Progress is measured by comparing actual costs with target costs.

target cost

For example, suppose that the current sales price of a product is $10 and that the market share is 12 percent. The marketing manager indicates that reducing the sales price to $8.50 will increase market share from 12 percent to 20 percent. The president of the company indicates that the desired profit per unit is $2. The target cost is computed as follows:

Target cost = $8.50 − $2.00 = $6.50

Suppose that it currently costs $7.75 per unit to produce the product. Thus, the cost reduction needed to achieve the target cost and desired profit is $1.25

[10]Berliner and Brimson, *Cost Management for Today's Advanced Manufacturing,* pp. 9 and 221.

($7.75 − $6.50). To realize the target cost, management must build in cost reductions by judicious activity management. The idea is to achieve the reduction needed over time. Variances are computed periodically by comparing actual costs with targeted costs.

Target costs are a type of currently attainable standard. But they are conceptually different from the modified standards discussed above. What makes them different is the motivating force. The initial modified definition of currently attainable standards was motivated by the objective of moving towards an ideal standard generated internally by industrial engineers and production managers. Target costs, on the other hand, are externally driven, generated by an analysis of markets and competitors. Regardless of motivation, the two standards generally share the common goal of cost reduction or continual improvement.

Selection of Cost Drivers: Behavioral Effects

As indicated, identifying cost drivers is a critical part of controlling nonvalue-added costs. If an individual's performance is affected by his or her ability to control nonvalue-added costs, then the selection of cost drivers, and how they are used, can affect an individual's behavior. For example, if the cost driver for setup costs is chosen as setup time, an incentive is created for workers to reduce setup time. Since the ideal standard for setup costs calls for their complete elimination, then the incentive to drive setup time to zero is compatible with the company's objectives, and the induced behavior is beneficial.

Suppose, however, that the objective is to reduce the number of unique parts a company processes, to simplify activities such as incoming inspection, bill of materials, and vendor selection.[11] If the costs of these activities are assigned to products based on the number of parts, the incentive created is to reduce the number of parts in a product. While this behavior may be desirable to a point, it can also have negative consequences. Designers may actually reduce the marketability of the product by reducing the number of parts too greatly and adversely affecting its functionality.

This type of behavior can be discouraged by the proper use of standard costing. First, if the number of parts truly drives the costs of incoming inspection, bill of materials, and vendor selection, then a budgeted cost per unit of cost driver can be computed (i.e., a standard price per unit). Next, the ideal number of parts for each product should be identified (the standard quantity). The value-added costs are then simply the product of the standard price and standard quantity $(SP \times SQ)$. As before, nonvalue-added costs are the difference between the actual parts used and the standard parts allowed, multiplied by the standard price $[(AQ - SQ)SP]$.

---

[11]This example is taken from the discussion concerning behavioral effects of cost drivers found in Robin Cooper, "The Rise of Activity-Based Costing—Part Three: How Many Cost Drivers Do You Need, and How Do You Select Them?" *Journal of Cost Management for the Manufacturing Industry* (Winter 1989), pp. 34–46.

For example, assume that a company has two products: a hand stapler and a hair setter. The company has determined that activities driven by parts should cost $4,000 per part *(SP)*. The ideal and actual parts for each product are given below.

	Hand Stapler	*Hair Setter*
Ideal number *(SQ)*	5	10
Actual number *(AQ)*	10	15

The value-added and nonvalue-added costs for each product are presented below.

	Hand Stapler	*Hair Setter*
Value-added costs	$20,000	$40,000
Nonvalue-added costs	20,000	20,000

Designers should be encouraged to reduce the nonvalue-added costs by reaching the ideal level, but indiscriminate use of cost drivers can produce dysfunctional behavior. This example illustrates the importance of setting standards. The absence of any standard can lead designers to reduce parts in order to reduce costs, without any sense of direction or purpose. However, by identifying, before the fact, the number of parts each product *should* have, using the number of parts as a cost driver can encourage reduction of only nonvalue-added costs. The standard has provided a concrete objective and defined the kind of behavior that the incentive allows.

Life-Cycle Costing and Management

product life cycle
life-cycle costs

life-cycle management

The example just given illustrates the impact design can have on costs. In fact, 90 percent or more of the costs associated with a product are *committed* during the development stage of the product's life cycle.[12] **Product life cycle** is simply the time a product exists—from conception to abandonment. **Life-cycle costs** are all costs associated with the product for its entire life cycle. These costs include development (planning, design, and testing), production (conversion activities), and logistics support (advertising, distribution, warranty, and so on). The product life cycle and the associated cost commitment curve are illustrated in Exhibit 18–5. **Life-cycle management** involves activity management during the development stage to ensure the lowest total life-cycle

[12]See John P. Campi, "Corporate Mindset: Strategic Advantage or Fatal Vision," *Journal of Cost Management* (Spring 1991), pp. 53–57. Also see Berliner and Brimson, *Cost Management for Today's Advanced Manufacturing.* The section on life-cycle costing is based on these two sources, with particular emphasis on the second source.

EXHIBIT 18-5

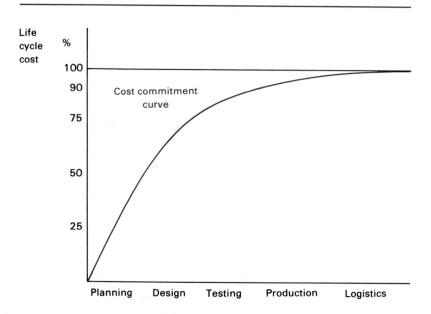

By the end of the development stage, at least 90 percent of the life-cycle costs are *committed (but not incurred).*

cost. Since 90 percent or more of a product's costs are committed during the development stage, it makes sense to focus on managing activities during this phase of a product's existence.

Yet in spite of this observation, the traditional emphasis has been on controlling costs during the production stage (when much less can be done to influence them). Furthermore, product cost has been narrowly defined as production costs; development and logistics costs have been treated as period costs and have been virtually ignored when computing product profitability. While this practice may be acceptable for external reporting, it is not acceptable for managerial product costing. In the highly competitive environment of today, world-class competitors need comprehensive product cost information.

From a life-cycle point of view, product cost is made up of three major elements: (1) nonrecurring costs (planning, designing, and testing), (2) manufacturing costs, and (3) logistic costs. Measuring, accumulating, and reporting all of a product's life-cycle costs allows managers to better assess the effectiveness of life-cycle planning (by comparing actual life-cycle costs with budgeted life-cycle costs). Life-cycle costing also increases their ability to make good pricing decisions and to improve the assessment of product profitability.

Short Life Cycles Although life-cycle costing and management are important for all manufacturing firms, it is particularly important for firms that have products with short life cycles. Products must recover all life-cycle costs and provide an acceptable profit. If a firm's products have long life cycles, profit performance can be increased by changing prices and by altering the product mix. In contrast, firms that have products with short life cycles usually do not have time to react in this way and so their approach must be proactive. Thus, for short life cycles, good life-cycle planning is critical and prices must be set properly to recover all the life-cycle costs and provide a good return. Activity-based costing can be used to encourage good life-cycle planning. By careful selection of cost drivers, design engineers can be motivated to choose cost-minimizing designs.[13] (This is a proactive strategy—how this can be done was discussed in the previous section on behavioral effects.)

Life-Cycle Costing: An Example Murphy Company produces electronic products that typically have about a twenty-seven–month life cycle. At the beginning of the last quarter of 1991, a new component was proposed. Design engineering believed that the product would be ready to produce by the beginning of 1992. To produce this and other similar products, resistors had to be inserted into a circuit board. Management had discovered that the cost of the circuit board was driven by the number of insertions. Knowing this, design engineering produced the new component using fewer insertions than the products in the past had employed.

The budgeted costs and profits for the product over its two-year life cycle are illustrated in Exhibit 18–6. Notice that the life-cycle unit cost is $10 per unit compared with the conventional definition of $6 (which includes only the production costs). To be viable, of course, the product must cover all of its costs and produce an acceptable profit. The $15 price was set with this objective in mind. Focusing only on the $6 cost could have led to a suboptimal pricing decision. Changing the focus requires managers to move away from the traditional, financially driven definition of product cost. Conventional cost systems do not directly identify development costs with the product being developed.

Feedback on the effectiveness of life-cycle planning is also helpful. This information can help future new product planning as well as be useful for assessing how design decisions affect operational and support costs. Comparing actual costs with the budgeted costs can provide useful insights. Exhibit 18–7 illustrates a simple life-cycle cost performance report. As can be seen, production costs were greater than expected. Investigation revealed that costs are driven by total number of insertions, not just insertions of resistors. Thus, future design work can benefit by the assessment.

---

[13]Robin Cooper and Peter B. B. Turney, "Internally Focused Activity-Based Cost Systems," in Kaplan (ed.), *Measures for Manufacturing Excellence*, pp. 291–305.

EXHIBIT 18-6
Life-Cycle Costing: Budgeted Costs

Item	1991	1992	1993	Item Total
Development costs	$200,000	$ —	$ —	$200,000
Production costs	—	240,000	360,000	600,000
Logistics costs	—	80,000	120,000	200,000
Annual total	$200,000	$320,000	$ 480,000	$1,000,000
Cumulative total	$200,000	$520,000	$1,000,000	
Units produced		40,000	60,000	
Budgeted unit cost			$10	
Budgeted unit price			$15	

Budgeted Product Income Statements

Year	Revenues	Costs	Annual Income	Cumulative Income
1991	$ —	$(200,000)	$(200,000)	$(200,000)
1992	600,000	(320,000)	280,000	80,000
1993	900,000	(480,000)	420,000	500,000

EXHIBIT 18-7
Performance Report: Life-Cycle Costs

Year	Item	Actual Costs	Budgeted Costs	Variance
1991	Development	$190,000	$200,000	$10,000 F
1992	Production	300,000	240,000	60,000 U
	Logistics	750,000	80,000	5,000 F
1993	Production	435,000	360,000	75,000 U
	Logistics	110,000	120,000	10,000 F

Analysis: Production costs were higher than expected because insertions of diodes and integrated circuits also drive costs. The design of future products should try to minimize total insertions.

▪ FLEXIBLE BUDGETING: A NEW APPROACH

In both the conventional and new manufacturing environments, static budgets are used for planning. Similarly, the comparison of actual and budgeted costs can be used in either environment to evaluate performance. For example, trend analysis is an important part of performance assessment in the advanced manufacturing environment. Yet comparing costs over time may require an adjustment for changes in activity levels. This possibility was mentioned when the trend report for nonvalue-added costs was developed. Typically, however, reports showing these comparisons are restricted to levels higher than the operating level for JIT firms. For meaningful comparisons in either a conventional or JIT setting, actual costs must be compared with budgeted costs for the actual level of activity (we define *prior actual costs* as budgeted costs when preparing trend reports; this definition is especially relevant if prior costs must be adjusted for changes in activity levels).

In a conventional setting, budgeted costs for the actual level of activity are obtained by assuming that all costs are driven by a single unit-based cost driver (usually direct labor hours). A cost formula is developed for each cost item as a function of direct labor hours. This formula is then used to predict what the costs ought to be for any level of activity. If, however, costs vary with respect to more than one cost driver, and the cost drivers are not highly correlated with direct labor hours, then comparisons with actual costs can be misleading.

The solution, of course, is to build flexible budget formulas for more than one cost driver. Cost estimation procedures (high-low method, the method of least squares, and so on) can be used to estimate the cost formulas for each cost driver. This multiple-formula approach allows managers to predict more accurately what costs ought to be for different levels of the cost drivers. These costs can then be compared with the actual costs for control purposes.

To illustrate, assume that a company used only direct labor hours as the driver for flexible budgeting. A flexible budget is created with two different levels of activity (see Exhibit 18–8). The budgeted costs associated with 10,000 hours are compared with the actual costs for that level in Exhibit 18–9.

Now assume that the company discovers that the costs driven by direct labor hours are materials, supplies, and labor. Maintenance costs are driven by machine hours, setup costs by number of setups, and receiving costs by the number of orders placed. Using this information, flexible budget formulas

EXHIBIT 18–8
Conventional Flexible Budget

	Formula		Direct Labor Hours	
	Fixed	*Variable*	*10,000*	*20,000*
Direct materials	$ —	$10	$100,000	$200,000
Direct labor	—	8	80,000	160,000
Supplies	—	2	20,000	40,000
Maintenance	20,000	3	50,000	80,000
Setups	16,000	—	16,000	16,000
Receiving	20,000	—	20,000	20,000
Total	$56,000	$23	$286,000	$516,000

EXHIBIT 18–9
Conventional Performance Report[a]

	Actual Costs	Budgeted Costs	Budget Variance
Direct materials	$101,000	$100,000	$ 1,000 U
Direct labor	80,000	80,000	—
Supplies	23,500	20,000	3,500 U
Maintenance	52,000	50,000	2,000 U
Setups	20,000	16,000	4,000 U
Receiving	24,000	20,000	4,000 U
Total	$300,500	$286,000	$14,500 U

[a]Level of actual activity is 10,000 direct labor hours.

are developed for each item using its associated cost driver. The flexible budget for two different levels of each cost driver is shown in Exhibit 18–10. (The respective levels of each cost driver are assumed to occur at the same time; these simultaneous values define an overall activity level.)

From Exhibit 18–10, we see that the budgeted amounts for materials, labor, and supplies are the same as before; they use the same cost driver. Notice, however, that the budgeted amounts for the other items differ significantly from the conventional amounts.

Exhibit 18–11 compares the budgeted costs for the first level of cost drivers with the actual costs. The actual costs are the same as those reported in Exhibit 18–9; the only difference in the two performance reports is the method used to compute the budgeted costs. Notice, however, the difference in the signals of the two reports. The report in Exhibit 18–9, using a single cost driver, shows all unfavorable variances, with a total unfavorable variance of $14,500. The activity-based report in Exhibit 18–11 provides a different (and more accurate) view of budgetary performance. Three items are on target, and the other three items are mixed. The net outcome is a favorable variance of $3,500. Activity-based costing increases the soundness and reliability of performance evaluation.

In a JIT environment, activity-based flexible budgets are also appropriate. However, the behavior and traceability of some costs change. For example, direct labor and maintenance become more fixed in nature. Even with this change, the principle of using cost formulas based on multiple cost drivers remains a valid, useful tool.

▪ CONTROL AT THE OPERATING LEVEL

Other differences in the approach to control under a JIT system need to be mentioned. In a JIT environment, operational control becomes more before the fact than after the fact. In a traditional environment, actual results are

EXHIBIT 18-10
Flexible Budget: Activity-Based Approach

Cost Driver: Direct Labor Hours

	Formula		Level of Activity	
	Fixed	*Variable*	*10,000*	*20,000*
Direct materials	$—	$10	$100,000	$200,000
Direct labor	—	8	80,000	160,000
Supplies	—	2	20,000	40,000
Subtotal	$ 0	$20	$200,000	$400,000

Cost Driver: Machine Hours

	Fixed	*Variable*	*8,000*	*16,000*
Maintenance	$20,000	$5	$60,000	$100,000

Cost Driver: Number of Setups

Setups	*Fixed*	*Variable*	*25*	*30*
	—	$800	$20,000	$24,000

Cost Driver: Number of Orders

	Fixed	*Variable*	*120*	*150*
Receiving	$6,000	$150	$ 24,000	$ 28,500
Total			$304,000	$552,500

EXHIBIT 18-11
Activity-Based Performance Report

	Actual Costs	*Budgeted Costs*	*Budget Variance*
Direct materials	$101,000	$100,000	$1,000 U
Direct labor	80,000	80,000	—
Supplies	23,500	20,000	3,500 U
Maintenance	52,000	60,000	8,000 F
Setups	20,000	20,000	—
Receiving	24,000	24,000	—
Total	$300,500	$304,000	$3,500 F

periodically compared with standards. While the comparison may be made as often as weekly or monthly, there is often a delay from the time actual performance is achieved and when it is reported to managers. Control in a JIT system tends to be much more timely. To achieve this change in orientation, worker involvement in the control process increases. Up front, workers are encouraged to reduce scrap, minimize the number of units reworked, and, generally, to find ways to improve the productive process and the overall quality of the goods being manufactured. In effect, operating results are reported on a real-time basis, as it happens, rather than on a delayed basis. Immediate feedback allows a quicker reaction time and increases in efficiency.[14]

operational measures

Since workers relate to operational measures more readily than financial measures, such things as scrap and rework are reported on an operating as well as a financial basis. Thus, managerial accountants should now be involved in measuring and reporting many physical and nontraditional gauges of operational performance. **Operational measures** concern physical measures of input and output. For example, pounds of scrap divided by pounds issued provides an operational manager and workers an idea of the amount of waste being produced. Five major areas of operating control have been identified: quality, inventory, materials cost, delivery, and machine performance.[15] To these five, productivity probably should be added.

Quality

Control of quality costs was discussed extensively in Chapter 16. The importance of control of quality cannot be overemphasized. Significant savings are available to firms if they increase the quality of their products. Operational measures of quality include defects per unit, number of defective units/total units produced, percentage of external failures, pounds of scrap per total pounds of material issued, and so on. These operational measures, as well as the costs of quality, are reported and used for control purposes.

Inventory

Control of work-in-process and finished-goods inventories also presents a firm with exceptional opportunities for savings. These savings and how they can be achieved were discussed in Chapter 13. The key to controlling these inventories is the use of JIT manufacturing and the Kanban information network. Operational measures such as inventory turnover rates, days of inven-

---

[14]For additional discussion on cost control in the JIT environment, see George Foster and Charles Horngren, "JIT: Cost Accounting and Cost Management Issues," *Management Accounting* (June 1987), pp. 19–25; and Robert McIlhattan, "How Cost Management Systems Can Support the JIT Philosophy," *Management Accounting* (September 1987), pp. 20–26.

[15]Robert A Howell and Stephen R. Soucy, "Operating Controls in the New Manufacturing Environment," *Management Accounting* (October 1987), pp. 25–31.

tory, and number of inventoried items can be used to assess how successfully the firm is reducing inventories to reasonable levels. For example, trends in days of inventory can be assessed; if the number of days of inventory is decreasing, the trend is favorable.

Materials Cost

Materials cost presents another example of before-the-fact control. Rather than emphasizing materials price variance, the JIT firm emphasizes quality and availability. Price reductions are achieved by negotiating long-term contracts with suppliers. By becoming a regular and reliable purchaser, the JIT firm can extract price concessions and, at the same time, choose suppliers that are most reliable and willing (as well as able) to supply quality raw materials. Developing close relationships with suppliers is a key requisite for this form of control.

Productivity

Productivity concerns how efficiently inputs are used in producing output. This topic was covered thoroughly in Chapter 16. Both operational and financial measures of productivity were developed and presented. Operational measures of productivity include output/materials, output/labor hours, output/kilowatt hours, and output/persons employed.

Delivery Performance

As competition has increased, delivery performance has become more important. One measure of delivery performance is on-time delivery. To measure on-time delivery, a firm sets delivery dates, then finds on-time delivery performance by dividing the orders delivered on time by the total number of orders delivered. The goal, of course, is to achieve a ratio of 100 percent.

cycle time

velocity

Cycle Time and Velocity Delivering on time is an important measure of delivery performance but perhaps not the most important. Cycle time and velocity are even more essential measures since they directly impact the ability of a company to deliver on time. **Cycle time** is the length of time it takes to manufacture a product (time divided by units produced). **Velocity** is the number of units that can be produced in a given period of time. Both velocity and cycle time are used to measure the time it takes a product to move through a cell.

Velocity and cycle time have become important operational measures of performance because of the increased emphasis on time-based capabilities. In fact, time-based capabilities may be one of the more critical competitive dimensions for firms in the 1990s. If this is true, then these time-based measures and others may receive increased attention.

Incentives can be used to encourage operational managers to reduce cycle time or increase velocity and thus improve delivery performance. A natural way to accomplish this objective is to tie product costs to cycle time and reward operational managers for reducing product costs. For example, cell conversion costs can be assigned to products on the basis of the time that it takes a product to move through the cell. Using the theoretical productive time available for a period (in minutes), an ideal standard cost per minute can be computed.

Standard cost per minute = Cell conversion costs/Minutes available

To obtain the conversion cost per unit, this standard cost per minute is multiplied by the actual cycle time used to produce the units during the period. By comparing the unit cost computed using the actual cycle time with the unit cost possible using the theoretical or optimal cycle time, a manager can assess the potential for improvement. Note that the more time it takes a product to move through the cell, the greater the unit product cost. With incentives to reduce product cost, this approach to product costing encourages operational managers and cell workers to find ways to decrease cycle time or increase velocity.

An example can be used to illustrate the concepts. Assume that a company has the following data for one of its manufacturing cells:

Theoretical velocity: 12 units per hour
Productive minutes available (per year): 400,000
Annual conversion costs: $1,600,000
Actual velocity: 10 units per hour

The actual and theoretical conversion costs per unit are shown in Exhibit 18–12.

Notice from Exhibit 18–12 that the per-unit conversion cost can be reduced from $24 to $20 by decreasing cycle time from six minutes per unit to five minutes per unit (or increasing velocity from ten units per hour to twelve units per hour). At the same time, the objective of improving delivery performance is achieved.

Manufacturing Cycle Efficiency   Another time-based operational measure calculates manufacturing cycle efficiency (MCE) as follows:

MCE = Processing time/(Processing time + Move time
        + Inspection time + Waiting time)

where processing time is the time it takes to convert raw materials into a finished good. The other activities have been defined earlier in the chapter and were identified as nonvalue-added activities. Processing, on the other hand, is a value-added activity. Thus, the ideal is to eliminate the nonvalue-added activities by reducing to zero the time spent on them. If this is accom-

EXHIBIT 18–12
Conversion Cost Computations

Actual Conversion Cost per Unit	
Standard cost per minute	= \$1,600,000/400,000
	= \$4 per minute
Actual cycle time	= 60 minutes/10 units
	= 6 minutes per unit
Actual conversion cost	= \$4 × 6
	= \$24 per unit
Theoretical (Ideal) Conversion Cost per Unit	
Theoretical cycle time	= 60 minutes/12 units
	= 5 minutes per unit
Ideal conversion cost	= \$4 × 5
	= \$20 per unit

plished, the value of MCE would be 1.0. As MCE improves (moves toward 1.0), cycle time decreases. Furthermore, since the only way MCE can improve is by decreasing the nonvalue-added activities, cost reduction must also follow.[16]

To illustrate MCE, let's use the data from Exhibit 18–12. The actual cycle time is 6.0 minutes and the theoretical cycle time is 5.0 minutes. Thus, the time attributable to nonvalue-adding activities is 1.0 minute (6.0 − 5.0), and MCE is computed as follows:

$$MCE = 5.0/6.0$$
$$= 0.83$$

Actually, this is a fairly efficient process, as measured by MCE. Many manufacturing companies have MCEs less than 0.10.[17]

Machine Performance

In a JIT environment, machine performance receives increased attention. Equipment can be placed into one of two categories: *nonbottleneck equipment*

---

[16]The source for this measure is Berliner and Brimson, *Cost Management for Today's Advanced Manufacturing*.

[17]Berliner and Brimson, *Cost Management for Today's Advanced Manufacturing*, p. 4.

and *bottleneck equipment*. Bottleneck equipment is critical for production, and the demand for its services is the greatest (often more than it can handle, thus the label *bottleneck*). When equipment in this category is down, it usually means an interruption in production. For a JIT firm, this downtime can be costly since there are no inventories to buffer interruptions in production. Thus, great efforts are made to ensure that machinery in this category is available and utilized. When available, one would expect bottleneck equipment to be utilized 100 percent of the time.

For nonbottleneck equipment, machine availability is the relevant performance measure, not machine utilization. This equipment is not needed all the time and thus should not be used constantly. Using machine utilization as the measure encourages unnecessary production and, thus, the buildup of inventories. However, when needed, the equipment should be available; thus, availability is important for all equipment.

Machine utilization and machine availability are both operational, nonfinancial measures. In addition to these measures, detailed maintenance records can help managers monitor the care that equipment is receiving.

Operational Measures: A Qualification

Operational measures can be of tremendous value. They can be produced quickly and can be expressed in terms that operational personnel can readily understand. These measures, if used in isolation, can be detrimental to the firm's overall objectives. Operational measures may actually conflict—for instance, increasing material productivity may cause a decline in labor productivity. Yet encouraging this outcome may be much better than increasing both partial operational measures. It depends on the value of the tradeoffs. For operational measures to work, there must be a tight linkage between the operational control system and the overall objectives of the business.[18] Since the overall success of the firm is defined in financial terms, there must be a linkage between operational performance and financial performance. The profit-linked productivity measure described in Chapter 16 is an example of how these linkages ought to exist. By knowing the linkages, operational measures can be used to foster the achievement of the firm's strategic objectives.

For convenience, the operational measures are summarized in Exhibit 18–13. You should realize that this listing is simply a sample of possible measures and is not exhaustive by any means.

▪ SUMMARY OF LEARNING OBJECTIVES

1. Explain why many traditional control measures are not suitable for a JIT manufacturing environment. The control procedures used in conventional manufacturing environments are not directly transferable to a JIT environ-

---

[18]Kelvin Cross and Richard Lynch, "Accounting for Competitive Performance," *Journal of Cost Management* (Spring 1989), pp. 20–28.

EXHIBIT 18-13
Summary of Operational Measures

Quality:
  Defects/units
  Number of defective units/total units
  Percentage of external failures
  Pounds of scrap/Pounds of materials issued

Inventory:
  Inventory turnover
  Days of inventory
  Number of inventoried items
  Trends in days of inventory

Time based:
  Cycle time
  Velocity
  MCE

Productivity:
  Output/pounds of material
  Output/hours of labor
  Output/kilowatt hrs
  Output/person employed

Machine performance:
  Machine availability
  Machine utilization

ment. Detailed variance analysis, based on currently attainable standards, can provide incentives that are not compatible with the operating objectives found in a JIT environment. Using materials price variances as a measure, for example, can encourage purchase of larger lots than desirable in order to take advantage of quantity discounts or lesser quality. This behavior encourages inventories of raw materials and low-quality materials, both of which are in opposition to the JIT objectives of zero inventories and total quality control.

2. Explain what activity-based responsibility accounting is and how it differs from traditional responsibility accounting. Activity-based responsibility accounting is a system-wide, integrated approach that focuses on activity management rather than the cost management approach of traditional responsibility accounting. It recognizes that activities cause costs and that management of activities will produce more efficient outcomes.

3. Explain what activity management is and how it is compatible with the philosophy of continuous improvement. Activity management is the process of identifying a firm's activities, assessing their value to the organization, and selecting only those that are of value. Activity management can bring about cost reduction by decreasing, eliminating, selecting, and sharing activities.

4. Distinguish between value-added and nonvalue-added costs. In the new manufacturing environment, emphasis is placed on identifying nonvalue-added costs and eliminating them. These costs are the result of unnecessary activities and inefficiencies found in necessary activities. Value-added costs are those that are incurred by carrying out necessary activities with perfect efficiency.

5. Describe the role of ideal and currently attainable standards in identifying, calculating, and controlling nonvalue-added costs. Setting ideal quantity standards and prices for cost drivers allows managers to compute value-added and nonvalue-added costs. Ideal standards also can be used to limit and define the kind of behavior induced by cost drivers. Reports highlighting value-added and nonvalue-added costs should be prepared so that managers are encouraged to focus on the elimination of nonvalue-added costs. Currently attainable standards, in a modified form, can still be useful. The difference between last year's costs and the targeted reduction can be defined as the currently attainable standard. This standard changes each year as continuous improvement is sought.

6. Discuss the behavioral effects associated with the choice of cost drivers. Different cost drivers will induce different behaviors. Using number of setups, for example, may induce longer runs and larger inventories—an undesirable outcome—but using setup hours may induce shorter setup times—a desirable outcome. Choosing the right cost drivers can help an organization achieve its strategic objectives.

7. Explain what life-cycle costing and management are and why they are important for the advanced manufacturing environment. Life-cycle costing is accumulating costs for a product over its entire life cycle. Life-cycle management is activity management during the development stage in which more than 90 percent of the life-cycle costs are committed. Life-cycle costing is important because of the ability to assess the effectiveness of life-cycle planning and to identify product profitability more accurately. It is especially important for firms that have products with short life cycles.

8. Describe the difference between traditional flexible budgeting and activity-based flexible budgeting. Traditional flexible budgeting assumes that costs change in direct proportion to unit-based cost drivers. If true, then costs at different production levels can be computed. Activity-based budgeting calculates costs for different levels of activities, using multiple cost drivers. The outcome is more accurate budgeting.

9. Discuss how control at the operational level in a JIT environment differs from that in a conventional environment. Operational measures are increasing in importance in the new manufacturing environment. At this level, there is an increased emphasis on real-time feedback and the use of operational measures. More worker involvement in the day-to-day control process is being encouraged. This involvement impacts quality, inventories, materials cost, delivery performance, productivity, and machine performance.

10. Explain why time-based performance measures are increasing in importance. Firms are increasing their ability to compete by decreasing the time it takes to produce and deliver a product. Time-based measures such as cycle time and MCE provide barometers of a firm's time-based capabilities.

■ KEY TERMS

Activity-based responsibility accounting   Accountability for activities rather than costs; it is a system-wide, integrated approach that focuses management's attention on activities. (p. 915)

Activity elimination   The process of eliminating nonvalue-added activities. (p. 917)

Activity management   The process of identifying activities performed by an organization, assessing their value to the organization, and selecting and keeping only those that are value adding. (p. 916)

Activity reduction   Decreasing the time and resources required by an activity. (p. 918)

Activity selection   The process of choosing among sets of activities caused by competing strategies. (p. 917)

Activity sharing   Increasing the efficiency of necessary activities by using economies of scale. (p. 918)

Cycle time   The length of time required to produce one unit of a product. (p. 933)

Life-cycle costs   Costs associated with the product for its entire life cycle. (p. 925)

Life-cycle management   Activity management during the development stage to ensure the lowest possible total life-cycle cost. (p. 925)

Nonvalue-added activities   Any activities that are either unnecessary or necessary but inefficient and improvable. (p. 916)

Nonvalue-added costs   Costs caused by nonvalue-added activities. (p. 916)

Operational measures   Physical or nonfinancial measures of performance. (p. 932)

Product life cycle   The time a product exists—from conception to abandonment. (p. 925)

Target cost   The difference between the sales price needed to achieve a projected market share and the desired per-unit profit. (p. 923)

Value-added activities   Necessary, perfectly efficient activities. (p. 919)

Value-added costs   Costs caused by value-added activities. (p. 919)

Velocity   The number of units that can be produced in a given period of time (e.g., output per hour). (p. 933)

■ REVIEW PROBLEMS

1.   The labor standard for a company is 2.0 hours per unit produced, which includes setup time. At the beginning of the last quarter, 20,000 units had been produced and 44,000 hours used. The production manager was concerned about the prospect of reporting an unfavorable labor efficiency variance at the end of the year. Any unfavorable variance over 9 to 10 percent of the standard usually meant a negative performance rating. Accordingly, for the last quarter, the production manager had decided to reduce the number of setups and use longer production runs. He knew that his production workers usually were within 5 percent of standard. The real problem was with setup times. By reducing the setups, the actual hours used would be within 7 to 8 percent of the standard hours allowed.

Required:

Explain why the behavior of the production manager is unacceptable for a JIT environment.

Solution:

In a JIT environment, efforts are made to reduce inventories and eliminate nonvalue-added costs. The production manager is focusing on meeting the labor usage standard and is ignoring the impact on inventories that longer production runs may have. Furthermore, instead of avoiding setups to save time, the manager and workers should be provided incentives to find ways to reduce setup time, which is a nonvalue-added activity.

2. Ludlow Manufacturing has developed optimal standards for labor usage, receiving, and packing. The optimal levels of the inputs for each of the activities, their actual levels achieved, and the standard prices are as follows:

	Cost Driver	*SQ*	*AQ*	*SP*
Labor usage	Labor hours	12,000	15,000	$ 8
Receiving	Purchase orders	400	500	100
Packing	Sales orders	600	800	80

The actual prices paid for the inputs equal the standard prices.

Required:

1. Prepare a cost report that details value- and nonvalue-added costs.

2. Suppose that the company wants to reduce nonvalue-added costs by 30 percent in the coming year. Prepare currently attainable standards that can be used to evaluate the company's progress towards this goal.

Solution:

1.

	Costs		
	Value Added	*Nonvalue Added*	*Total*
Labor usage	$ 96,000	$24,000	$120,000
Receiving	40,000	10,000	50,000
Packing	48,000	16,000	64,000
Totals	$184,000	$50,000	$234,000

2.

	Currently Attainable Standard	
	Quantity	*Cost*
Labor usage	14,100	$112,800
Receiving	470	47,000
Packing	740	59,200

■ QUESTIONS

1   Explain how materials price variances can work against the JIT objectives of zero inventories and total quality control.

2   Explain how materials usage variances can impede JIT manufacturing.

3   Currently attainable standards are not compatible with the JIT philosophy of continual improvement. Do you agree? Explain your reasoning.

4   What is activity-based responsibility accounting? How does it differ from traditional responsibility accounting?

5   What is activity management? Why is this approach compatible with a goal of continual improvement?

6   Identify and define four different ways to manage activities. Explain how each can reduce costs.

7   What are nonvalue-added activities? Nonvalue-added costs? Give an example of each.

8   What are value-added costs?

9   Explain how ideal standards can be used to identify value-added and nonvalue-added costs.

10 What is the standard cost allowed for nonvalue-added activities that are unnecessary? Explain why.

11 Explain how trend reports of nonvalue-added cost can be used.

12 Explain why the selection of cost drivers is an important step in the control of nonvalue-added costs.

13 Suppose that the ideal standard quantity allowed for a cost driver is 100 units and that the actual quantity achieved is 120 units. If the standard price allowed per unit of cost driver is $5, calculate the value-added cost and the nonvalue-added cost.

14 In controlling nonvalue-added costs, explain how cost drivers can induce behavior that is either beneficial or harmful. How can ideal standards be used to reduce the possibility of dysfunctional behavior?

15 What are target costs?

16 What is a product life cycle?

17 What is life-cycle costing? Life-cycle management?

18 Explain why life-cycle costing is especially important for firms with products that have short life cycles.

19 Explain how the use of multiple cost drivers can improve performance reports that compare actual costs with budgeted costs.

20 Why are nonfinancial measures of performance used more at the operating level?

21 In a non–JIT company, price reductions for raw materials are often obtained through the use of quantity discounts. In a JIT company, how are price reductions obtained?

22 Identify and define two operational measures of delivery performance.

23 What is cycle time? Velocity?

24   If the velocity of a product is twenty units per hour, what is its cycle time?

25   What is manufacturing cycle efficiency?

26   Explain why time-based performance measures are becoming more important.

27   Identify two operational measures of machine performance.

28   Machine performance is more important in a JIT environment than in a non–JIT environment. Do you agree? Explain.

▪ EXERCISES

E18–1   **Materials Usage Variance; Ethical Issues; Incentives**   Tom Waters, production supervisor, was given the charge to produce 1,000 units of a subassembly used in the manufacture of the company's main product. He had two weeks to produce the units. The job took priority over several other jobs that were less urgent. Each subassembly required three pounds of raw material. After producing a unit, the subassembly was inspected and rejected if defective. Defective units had no salvage value; because of the nature of the process, rework was not possible.

At the end of the first week, Tom had produced 500 units and used 1,640 pounds of material, 100 pounds more than the standard allowed. Tom knew that a performance report would be prepared when the batch of 1,000 subassemblies was completed. This report would compare the materials used with the materials allowed. He also knew that any variance in excess of 5 percent of standard would be investigated, possibly resulting in a poor performance rating for him. Accordingly, at the beginning of the second week, Tom directed that no inspections be done because production had to be accelerated so that the other jobs could be completed on time. He temporarily assigned his inspector to the production line.

Required:

1. Explain why Tom stopped inspections on the current job and reassigned his inspector to production. Was his behavior ethical?

2. What likely effect would Tom's actions have on the quality of the final product? On the ability of subsequent processes to meet its production schedule?

3. What implications does Tom's behavior have for a firm using JIT manufacturing? Explain.

E18–2   **Currently Attainable Standards and JIT**   Proponents of currently attainable standards argue that they should be adopted because workers can achieve them. Some go on to say that continual failure to achieve a standard can be frustrating and lead to a decision by workers to give less effort (why bother if it's not possible to achieve the standard, they wonder). In this view, a realistic standard should include an expectation of a normal level of inefficiency. That is, machines will break down, workers will make mistakes, some components will be defective, and so on.

Required:
Explain why this view of standards is incompatible with JIT.

E18–3   **Conventional Control Measures and JIT**   For each action below, describe which JIT objective is being violated (more than one may be involved).

1. To reduce setup costs so that the budgetary goal can be met, the number of setups is decreased.

2. A large lot of raw materials is purchased to take advantage of a quantity discount.

3. Production is increased so that idle time for direct laborers is minimized.

4. The maintenance supervisor lays off one of the workers in order to meet budget. With fewer personnel, the Maintenance Department focuses only on repair and less on preventive care.

E18-4 **Activity Versus Traditional Responsibility Accounting** For each of the following situations, identify which characteristic is descriptive of activity-based responsibility accounting and which is descriptive of traditional responsibility accounting. Provide a brief commentary on the differences between the two systems for each situation, addressing the advantages of the ABC view over the traditional view. Characteristics of each situation are labeled *A* and *B*.

Situation 1:

A: Assumes that activities can be collected into independent subgroups

B: Assumes that activities are linked

Situation 2:

A: The focus is the organization

B: The focus is individuals

Situation 3:

A: The control emphasis is costs

B: The control emphasis is activities

Situation 4:

A: Standards are engineered and tend to be static

B: Standards are ideal/historical trends

Situation 5:

A: The goal is continuous improvement

B: The goal is to meet standard

Situation 6:

A: Control is financial

B: Control is financial and operational

E18-5 **Activity-Based Responsibility Accounting** The following comment is the heart of an activity-based responsibility system: "Costs cannot be managed—only activities can."

Required:

Comment on the validity of this statement, giving examples to support your position.

E18-6 **Identification of Nonvalue-Added Activities and Costs** Identify the nonvalue-added activities from those listed below and provide an estimate of the nonvalue-added cost caused by each activity.

1. It takes twenty minutes to produce a product. A time and motion study revealed that it should take fifteen minutes. The cost per labor hour is $10.

2. With its original design, a product requires forty minutes of direct labor. Redesigning the product could reduce the labor needed to an absolute minimum of twenty-five minutes. The cost per direct labor hour is $10.

3. The time required to move components of a product from one department to another is three hours. By redesigning the manufacturing layout, this move time can be reduced to twenty minutes. The labor cost per move hour is $10.

4. Setup time for a product is eight hours. A Japanese firm producing the same product has reduced the setup time to ten minutes. The cost of setup labor is $12 per hour.

5. Each unit of a product requires 4 components. The average number of components is 4.2 due to component failure, requiring rework and extra components. By developing relations with the right suppliers and increasing the quality of the purchased component, the average number of components can be reduced to 4 components per unit. The cost per component is $30.

E18–7   **Calculation of Value-Added and Nonvalue-Added Costs**   Hinckley Medical Products produces a variety of medical supplies. The company uses a conventional, departmental structure. After a careful study, the company decided that machine hours were a good cost driver for maintenance costs. In addition to a fixed base of $40,000, maintenance costs $2 per machine hour. For the production level expected for the coming year (essentially the same year after year), management decided that the optimal number of machine hours is 18,000 (an absolute standard). If a certain amount of inefficiency is allowed, the number of machine hours expected would be 19,000 hours (a currently attainable standard). Assume that the actual machine hours used were 19,100. Also assume that the cost formula above is a perfect predictor of maintenance costs.

Required:

1. Calculate the value-added and nonvalue-added costs for maintenance.

2. Prepare a report that presents value-added, nonvalue-added, and actual costs. Explain why highlighting the nonvalue-added costs is important.

E18–8   **Cost Report; Value-Added and Nonvalue-Added Costs**   Blount Company has developed absolute standards for four activities: labor, materials, maintenance, and receiving. The activities, the cost driver, the standard and actual quantities, and the price standards are given below for 1991.

Activities	Cost Driver	SQ	AQ	SP
Labor	Hours	7,500	8,000	$ 9
Materials	Pounds	40,000	45,000	6
Maintenance	Machine hours	20,000	25,000	5
Receiving	Orders	100	120	600

The actual prices paid per unit of each cost driver were equal to the standard prices.

Required:

Prepare a cost report that lists the value-added costs, nonvalue-added costs, and actual costs for each activity.

E18–9   **Trend Report: Nonvalue-Added Costs**   Refer to Exercise 18–8. Suppose that Blount Company used an activity management program during 1992 in an effort to reduce nonvalue-added costs. The absolute standards, actual quantities, and prices for 1992 are given below.

	Cost Driver	SQ	AQ	SP
Labor	Hours	7,500	7,800	$ 9
Materials	Pounds	40,000	42,000	6
Maintenance	Machine hours	20,000	26,000	5
Receiving	Orders	100	110	600

Required:

1. Prepare a report that compares the nonvalue-added costs for 1991 with those of 1992.

2. Comment on the value of a trend report.

E18–10   **Trend Report with Flexible-Budgeting Adjustment**   Refer to Exercise 18–9. In 1993, additional efforts were made to reduce activities with the following financial results:

	Cost Driver	SQ	AQ	SP
Labor	Hours	8,250	7,800	$ 9
Materials	Pounds	48,000	50,000	6
Maintenance	Machine hours	24,000	28,000	5
Receiving	Orders	100	110	600

Required:

Prepare a trend report, comparing nonvalue-added costs for 1993 and 1992. Adjust the 1992 historical standard for changes in the activity level as reflected by the changes in SQ. (*Hint:* Assume the same percentage deviation from standard for the new level as was experienced in 1992). Comment on the changes.

E18–11   **Cost Drivers and Behavioral Effects; Activity Management**   Betty Underwood, controller of Keystone Company, was responsible for implementing a new activity-based costing system (the company had also recently installed a JIT manufacturing system). For the past two weeks, she has been identifying cost pools and selecting cost drivers to assign these costs to individual products. At the moment, she is trying to decide which cost drivers should be selected for assigning the following costs: setup costs, scrap (mostly from rejects), and incoming parts inspection. The alternatives for each activity are listed below:

- Setups: setup time or number of setups
- Scrap: pounds of scrap or number of defective units
- Incoming inspection: hours of inspection or number of defective parts

Because the existing cost system already produces information on both cost drivers, there is no incremental cost of measurement. Additionally, the method of least squares was used to estimate the variable and fixed cost components. In all three cases, costs were strictly variable and highly correlated with the individual cost driver. The only remaining issue Betty has to resolve is the effect each cost driver might have on the behavior of operating managers. Assume that operating managers are evaluated on their ability to control product costs.

Required:

1. For each activity, decide whether it should be eliminated or reduced and explain why.

2. Describe the behavior that each cost driver will encourage and evaluate the suitability of that behavior for a JIT environment.

E18–12 **Ideal and Currently Attainable Standards** Winter Company has adopted an activity-based costing system and identified ideal standards for its set of cost drivers. For raw materials, the ideal standard calls for 4.1 quarts per gallon of output. The standard price of materials is $10 per quart. For engineering, the standard is 2,000 engineering hours for each product group that has been on the market or in development for five years or less, and 800 hours per product group of more than five years. The standard price per hour of engineering is $25. Four product groups have fewer than five years' experience and ten product groups have more.

   Current actual material usage and engineering are 20 percent above the levels called for by the ideal standards. The target for the coming year (1992) is to reduce this deviation by 30 percent. Selected actual results achieved for 1992 are as follows:

Gallons produced	20,000
Materials used	93,000
Engineering hours	18,800

The actual prices paid for materials and engineering hours are identical to the standard or budgeted prices.

Required:

1. Using the targeted reduction, establish the currently attainable standards for materials and engineering.

2. Using the currently attainable standards prepared in requirement 1, compute the quantity variances (expressed in both physical and financial measures) for materials and labor. Comment on the company's ability to achieve its targeted reductions.

3. For 1993, management set a target of reducing the 1992 deviations from optimal standards by 30 percent. Compute the currently attainable standards for 1993 for materials and engineering.

E18–13 **Target Costing and Nonvalue-Added Costs** Healthcare Products manufactures a line of wheelchairs. The regular model sells for $340. Sales volume averages 10,000 units per year. Recently, its largest competitor reduced the price of a similar model to $300. Healthcare's marketing manager indicated that the price must be matched or sales will drop dramatically. The president of Healthcare indicated that the current profit per unit must be maintained and wants to know what the cost per unit must be to achieve this goal. He also wants to know how the company can achieve the cost reduction. The controller has assembled the following data for the most recent year. The actual cost of inputs, their ideal quantity levels, and the actual quantity levels are provided (for production of 10,000 units).

	SQ	AQ	*Actual Cost*
Materials (lbs)	237,500	250,000	$1,500,000
Labor (hrs)	57,000	60,000	750,000
Setups (hrs)	—	4,000	150,000

	SQ	AQ	Actual Cost
Material handling (moves)	—	10,000	100,000
Warranties (no. repaired)	—	10,000	500,000
Total			3,000,000

Required:

1. Calculate the target cost for maintaining current market share and profitability.

2. Calculate the nonvalue-added cost per unit. Assuming that nonvalue-added costs can be reduced to zero, can the target cost be achieved?

E18–14 **Life-Cycle Costing** Randy Thompson, president of Short Cycle, Inc., had just completed examining the two-year profit summary for two products that had completed their life cycle. Both had been conceived, developed, produced, and sold at the same time. Each product's life cycle was two years. The profit performance of the two items produced a return on sales of 10 percent—less than the 16 percent rate set by company standards. From the statements below, it appeared to Randy that the culprit was Component 12B—its gross profit percentage was much lower than that of Component 12A. Component 12B simply did not contribute enough to help cover the period costs.

	Component 12A	Component 12B	Total
Sales	$1,000,000	$1,000,000	$ 2,000,000
Cost of goods sold	(500,000)	(700,000)	(1,200,000)
Gross profit	$ 500,000	$ 300,000	$ 800,000
Research and development expenses			(500,000)
Selling expenses			(100,000)
Profit before taxes			$ 200,000

Required:

1. Explain why Randy Thompson may be wrong in his assessment of the relative performances of the two products. What change in the company's management accounting system would you suggest?

2. Suppose that the 80 percent of the R & D and selling expenses are traceable to Component 12A. Prepare life-cycle income statements for each product and calculate the return on sales. What does this tell you about the importance of accurate life-cycle costing? Managerial product costing?

E18–15 **Flexible Budgeting with Multiple Cost Drivers** The following costs and cost drivers have been identified:

Cost	Cost Driver
Labor	Direct labor hours
Materials handling	Number of moves
Cafeteria	Number of people served

Using the method of least squares, the following cost formulas have been developed:

Labor cost = 9X
Materials handling cost = 200Y
Cafeteria cost = $15,000 + 150P

The variables in each equation correspond to the value chosen for the appropriate cost driver.

For the coming month, the company has estimated three possible levels of activity.

	Level 1	Level 2	Level 3
Labor hours	40,000	60,000	80,000
Number of moves	100	120	150
Number of persons	30	40	45

Required:

Prepare a flexible budget for the three levels of activity using the cost formulas.

E18–16 **Cycle Time and Conversion Cost per Unit**   The theoretical cycle time for a product is ten minutes per unit. The budgeted conversion costs for the manufacturing cell are $600,000 per year. The total labor minutes available are 200,000. During the year, the cell was able to produce five units of the product per hour.

Required:

1. Compute the theoretical conversion cost per unit.

2. Compute the applied conversion cost per minute (the amount of conversion cost actually assigned to the product).

3. Discuss how this approach to assigning conversion cost can improve delivery time performance.

E18–17 **Cycle Time and Velocity; MCE**   A manufacturing cell has the theoretical capability to produce 30,000 stereo speakers per quarter. The conversion cost per quarter is $60,000. There are 5,000 production hours available within the cell per quarter.

Required:

1. Compute the theoretical velocity (per hour) and the theoretical cycle time (minutes per unit produced).

2. Compute the ideal amount of conversion cost that will be assigned per speaker.

3. Suppose the actual time required to produce a stereo is fifteen minutes. Compute the amount of conversion cost actually assigned to each speaker. Now calculate MCE.

4. Based on your analysis in requirements 2 and 3, how much nonvalue-added time is being used? How much is it costing per speaker?

E18–18 **MCE** A company makes a product that experiences the following activities (and times):

Processing (two departments):	10 hrs
Moving (three moves):	3 hrs
Waiting (for the second process)	12 hrs
Storage (before delivery to customer)	25 hrs

Required:

1. Compute the MCE for this product.
2. Discuss how activity management can help improve this efficiency measure.

■ PROBLEMS

P18–1 **JIT; Control and Performance Measurement** Richardson Manufacturing is installing a JIT purchasing and manufacturing system; management wants to use performance measures that are compatible with the objectives of its new system. The following is a list of measures being considered for use:

a. Materials price variances

b. Cycle time

c. Comparison of actual product costs with target costs

d. Materials quantity or efficiency variances

e. Comparison of actual product costs over time (trend reports)

f. Comparison of actual overhead costs, item by item, with the corresponding budgeted costs

g. Comparison of product costs with competitors' product costs

h. Percentage of on-time deliveries

i. Quality reports

j. Reports of value-added and nonvalue-added costs

k. Labor efficiency variances

l. Machine utilization rates

m. Days of inventory

n. Downtime

o. Manufacturing cycle efficiency (MCE)

Required:

1. Describe how each of the above measures would impact the objectives associated with JIT manufacturing and purchasing.
2. Classify the measures into operational and financial categories. Explain why operational measures are better for control at the shop level (production floor) than financial measures. Should any financial measures be used at the operational level?

P18–2 **JIT; Performance Measurement** At the beginning of 1992, Pratt Company installed a JIT purchasing and manufacturing system. Now, after two years of operation, the president of Pratt wants some assessment of the system's achievements. To help provide this assessment, the following information on one product has been gathered:

	1992	1993
Theoretical annual capacity	50,000	50,000
Actual production	40,000	46,000
Production hours available	2,000	2,000
On-time deliveries	3,000	4,000
Total deliveries	4,000	4,600
Scrap (pounds)	10,000	8,000
Materials used (pounds)	90,000	100,000
Actual cost per unit	$100	$96
Days of inventory	5	3
Number of defective units	4,000	4,700

Required:

1. Compute the following measures for 1992 and 1993:
   a. Theoretical velocity and cycle time
   b. Actual velocity and cycle time
   c. On-time delivery percentage
   d. Scrap as a percentage of total material issued
   e. Percentage change in actual product cost
   f. Percentage change in days of inventory
   g. Defective units as a percentage of total units produced

2. Based on your computations in requirement 1, evaluate the progress that Pratt Company is making with its JIT system. As part of this evaluation, indicate the ultimate goals that the company is striving for and how each performance measure helps achieve these goals.

P18–3   **Activity Management; Nonvalue-Added Costs; Target Costs**   Jennifer Harget, president of Wagner Electronics, was concerned about the latest marketing report. According to Larry Barton, marketing manager, a price decrease was again needed to maintain the market share of the company's integrated circuit boards (CBs). This would make a bad situation worse. The current selling price of $16 per unit was producing a $1 per-unit profit—much less than the customary $3 per-unit profit. Foreign competitors kept reducing their prices. To match the latest reduction would reduce the price from $16 to $13. This would put the price below the cost to produce and sell it. How could these firms sell for such a low price?

Determined to find out if there were problems with the company's operations, Jennifer decided to hire a consultant to evaluate the way in which the CBs were produced and sold. After two weeks, the consultant had identified the following activities and costs:

Batch-level activities:	
Setups	$ 50,000
Material handling	150,000
Inspection	100,000
Product-sustaining activities:	
Engineering support	$ 90,000

Customer complaints	85,000
Warranties	125,000
Unit-level activities:	
Material usage	$500,000
Power	50,000
Manual insertion labor[a]	200,000
Other direct labor	150,000

[a]Diodes, resistors, and integrated circuits are inserted manually into the circuit board.

The consultant indicated that some preliminary activity analysis indicates that per-unit costs can be reduced by at least $5. Since the marketing manager had indicated that the market share for the boards could be increased by 50 percent if the price could be reduced to $11, Jennifer became quite excited.

Required:

1. What is activity management? What phases of activity management were provided by the consultant? What else remains to be done?

2. Identify as many nonvalue-added activities as possible. Compute the cost savings per unit that would be realized if these activities were eliminated. Was the consultant correct in his preliminary cost reduction assessment? Discuss actions that the company can take to reduce/eliminate the nonvalue-added activities.

3. Compute the target cost required to maintain current market share, while earning a profit of $3 per unit. Now compute the target cost required to expand sales by 50 percent. How much cost reduction would be required to achieve each target?

4. Assume that further activity analysis revealed the following: switching to automated insertion would save $40,000 of engineering support and $150,000 of direct labor. Now what is the total potential cost reduction per unit available from activity management? With these additional reductions, can Wagner achieve the target cost to maintain current sales? To increase it by 50 percent?

5. Calculate income based on current sales, prices, and costs. Now calculate the income using a $13 price and an $11 price, assuming that the maximum cost reduction possible is achieved. What price should be selected?

P18–4 **Life-Cycle Costing and Management** Gordon Productions manufactures products with life cycles that average thirty months. Six of the thirty months involve product development, and the remaining two years concern production and sales. A budgeted life-cycle income statement has been developed for two proposed products and is presented below. Each product will sell 100,000 units. The price has been set to yield a 50 percent gross margin ratio.

	Product A	Product B	Total
Sales	$ 2,000,000	$ 3,000,000	$ 5,000,000
Cost of goods sold	(1,000,000)	(1,500,000)	(2,500,000)
Gross margin	$ 1,000,000	$ 1,500,000	$ 2,500,000
Period expenses:			
Research and development			(1,000,000)
Marketing			(800,000)
Life cycle income			$ 700,000

Upon seeing the budget, Aaron Boyce, president of Gordon Products, called in Wilma Johnson, marketing manager, and Tom Meek, design engineer.

Aaron: These two products are earning only a 14 percent return on sales. We need 20 percent to earn an acceptable return on our investment. Can't we raise prices?

Wilma: I doubt the market would bear any increase in prices. However, I will do some additional research and see what's possible. The gross-profit ratio is already high. The problem appears to be with R & D. Those expenses seem higher than normal.

Tom: These products are more complex than usual and we need to have the extra resources—at least if you want to have a product that functions as we are claiming it will. Also, we are charting some new waters with the features these products are offering. In the future, we can probably get by on less—after we gain some experience. But it wouldn't be much less—perhaps $50,000.

Aaron: That would still allow us to earn only about 15 percent—even after you get more proficient. Maybe we ought to stay with our more standard features.

Wilma: Before we abandon these new lines, perhaps we ought to look at each product individually. Maybe one could be retained. These new features will give us an edge in the market. Also, I'll bet Tom could redesign the product so that production costs could be lowered—if he knew what was driving those costs. I'm concerned that our competitors will beat us to the punch if we're not careful.

Required:

1. What specific improvements would suggest to Aaron to improve Gordon's life-cycle costing and management system?

2. Assume that the "period" expenses are traceable to each product. Product A is responsible for 50 percent of the costs in each category. Prepare a revised income statement for each product. Based on this analysis, should either product be produced?

3. Based on the revised income statements (of requirement 2), how much must production costs be reduced to make each product acceptable? Discuss how activity management can help achieve this outcome. Explain why this should occur now, not after the products are in production.

P18–5 **Cost Report; Value-Added and Nonvalue-Added Costs; Target Costs; Activity-Based Responsibility Accounting** For 1992, Hearye Company is expecting to produce 200,000 hearing aids: 150,000 units of its budget model and 50,000 units of its luxury model. This expected output is identical to the output of the year just completed. The actual quantities of inputs and actual costs associated with the production of the 50,000 luxury models in 1991 are as follows:

	Actual Quantity	*Actual Cost*
Plastic components	55,000	$ 440,000
Electronic components	57,000	5,700,000
Labor (hours)	30,000	300,000
Power (kilowatt hours)	10,000	30,000
Receiving (orders)	1,000	150,000
Setups (setup time)	2,000	30,000
Materials handling (moves)	500	100,000
Maintenance (machine hours)	5,000	150,000
Warranty (number of defectives)	2,500	300,000

The actual price paid per unit of input in 1991 is equal to the standard price for that year. The ideal quantities of each input that should have been used in producing the 50,000 luxury models are also known.

Ideal Quantities	
Plastic components	50,000
Electronic components	50,000
Labor (hours)	25,000
Power (kilowatt hours)	9,000
Receiving (orders)	500
Setups (setup time)	—
Materials handling (moves)	50
Maintenance (machine hours)	4,000
Warranty (defectives)	—

The selling price per unit of the luxury model is $216. The largest competitor sells a comparable unit for $190. The marketing manager for Hearye has estimated that the company could increase its current sales from 50,000 to 75,000 units (increasing its share of the market by 5 percent) by dropping its price to $180. The president is willing to drop the price if the company can increase the total profits it currently is earning on the luxury model by 10 percent.

Required:

1. Prepare a cost report that details the value- and nonvalue-added costs for 1991.

2. Compute the value-added cost per unit and the nonvalue-added cost per unit.

3. Compute the operating profit in total and per unit for the luxury model in 1991.

4. Suppose that the president of the company agrees to implement the price reduction if the desired operating profit can be reached by the end of 1993. Assume also that any cost reductions necessary to achieve the desired profit will be split evenly over 1992 and 1993. Compute the target cost for each year.

5. Refer to requirement 4. Suppose that all cost reductions will come by eliminating nonvalue-added costs. Is it possible for the company to reach the targeted cost? Explain how an activity-based responsibility accounting system would be helpful in achieving this target.

P18–6 **Flexible Budgeting; Multiple Cost Drivers** Jerry Erickson, controller for Atwood, Inc., prepared the following budget for manufacturing costs at two different levels of activity for 1992:

	Direct Labor Hours	
	Level of Activity	
	50,000	*100,000*
Direct materials	$200,000	$ 400,000
Direct labor	330,000	650,000
Depreciation	200,000	200,000
Subtotal	$730,000	$1,250,000

continued on next page

Machine Hours

	Level of Activity	
	200,000	**300,000**
Maintenance	$ 700,000	$1,000,000
Power	220,000	320,000
Subtotal	$ 920,000	$1,320,000

Number of Setups

	Level of Activity	
	100	**200**
Setups	$ 150,000	$ 300,000
Inspections	250,000	450,000
Subtotal	$ 400,000	$ 750,000
Total	$2,050,000	$3,320,000

During 1992, the company worked a total of 80,000 direct labor hours, used 250,000 machine hours, and performed 120 setups. The following actual costs were incurred:

Direct materials	$170,000
Direct labor	560,000
Depreciation	200,000
Maintenance	850,000
Power	280,000
Setups	220,000
Inspections	320,000

Atwood applies overhead using pool rates based on direct labor hours, machine hours, and number of setups. The second level of activity (the right column in the preceding table) is the normal level of activity and is used to compute predetermined overhead pool rates.

Required:

1. Prepare a performance report for Atwood's manufacturing costs in 1992.

2. Assume that one of the products produced by Atwood uses two direct labor hours, three machine hours, and five setups. A total of 10,000 units was produced during the year. Calculate the normal unit manufacturing cost.

P18–7 **Identifying Nonvalue-Added Activities and Costs**   For each of the following activities, estimate the nonvalue-added costs:

1. A company currently purchases a component used in production for $25 per unit. If the component is produced internally, the cost would be $20. There are 10,000 components used annually.

2. A company has five days of finished-goods inventories on hand. Carrying costs of the inventories average $200,000 per day.

3. Machine-operator error produces one defective unit of every thirty produced. There is no possibility for rework; the defective unit has no market value. The cost per unit is $100. The company produces 300,000 units per year.

4. Design engineers produce a bill of materials as part of the design process. Later, manufacturing engineers, during process planning, produce their own bill of materials for the same product. The time required to prepare a bill of materials is two hours. Design engineers earn an average of $25 per hour. Manufacturing engineers average $22 per hour. The company is a job operation and averages 500 product designs per year.

5. A company spends $5 million per year on repair and warranty work.

6. Inspection costs for incoming raw materials are $135,000.

7. A time and motion study revealed that packing should ideally take thirty minutes per case. The actual time averages forty-five minutes per case. Labor cost is $12 per hour.

8. Downtime for critical machinery (bottleneck category) averages 1,000 hours per year (involving ten machines). The cost of lost sales is approximately $400,000.

9. Cell workers average 200 hours per year of idle time. Workers are paid $11 per hour.

P18–8 **Flexible Budgeting; Single Cost Driver versus Multiple Cost Drivers** Mark Nelson, production manager, was upset with the latest performance report, which indicated that he was $90,000 over budget. Given the efforts that he and his workers had made, he was confident that they had met or beat the budget. Now he was not only upset but also genuinely puzzled over the results. Three items—supplies, power, and setups— were over budget. The actual costs for these three items only are given below.

	Actual Costs
Supplies	$205,000
Power	120,000
Setups	110,000
Total	$435,000

Mark knew that his operation had produced more units than originally had been budgeted, so that more power and supplies had naturally been used. He also knew that the uncertainty in scheduling had led to more setups than planned. When he pointed this out to Stacy Winter, the controller, she assured him that the budgeted costs had been adjusted for the increase in productive activity. Curious, Mark questioned Stacy about the methods used to make the adjustment.

Stacy: If the actual level of activity differs from the original planned level, we adjust the budget by using budget formulas—formulas that allow us to predict what the costs will be for different levels of activity.

Mark: The approach sounds reasonable. However, I'm sure something is wrong here. Tell me exactly how you adjusted the costs of supplies, power, and setups.

Stacy: First we obtain formulas for the individual items in the budget by using the method of least squares. We assume that cost variations can be explained by variations in productive activity where activity is measured by direct labor hours. Here is a list of the cost formulas for the three items you mentioned. The variable X is the number of direct labor hours.

Cost of supplies = $5X$
         Power cost = $5,000 + $2X$
                Setups = $100,000

Mark: I think I see the problem. Power costs don't have a lot to do with direct labor hours. They have more to do with machine hours. As production increases, machine hours increase more rapidly than direct labor hours. Also, . . .

Stacy: You know, you have a point. The coefficient of determination for power cost is only about 50 percent. That leaves a lot of unexplained cost variation. The coefficient for supplies, however, is much better—it explains about 96 percent of the cost variation. Setup costs, of course, are fixed.

Mark: Well, as I was about to say, setup costs also have very little to do with direct labor hours. And I might add that they certainly are not fixed. We had to do more setups than our original plan called for because of the scheduling changes. And we have to pay our people when they work extra hours. Did you build this increased activity into your budget?

Stacy: No, we assumed that setup costs were fixed. I see now that they could vary as the number of setups increases. Mark, let me see if I can develop some cost formulas based on better explanatory variables. I'll get back with you in a few days.

Assume that after a few days work, Stacy developed the following cost formulas, all with a coefficient of determination greater than 95 percent:

Supplies cost = $5X$, where X = Direct labor hours
Power cost = $35,000 + Y, where Y = Machine hours
Setup cost = $1,000Z$, where Z = Number of setups

The actual measures of each of the cost drivers are as follows:

Direct labor hours	40,000
Machine hours	90,000
Number of setups	110

Required:

1. Prepare a performance report for supplies, power, and setups using the direct-labor based formulas.

2. Prepare a performance report for supplies, power, and setups using the multiple cost driver formulas that Stacy developed.

3. Of the two approaches, which provides the most accurate picture of Mark Nelson's performance? Why?

P18–9 **Value-Added Costs; Nonvalue-Added Costs; Currently Attainable Standards; Activity-Based Responsibility Accounting** Rexburn Company produces 400,000 units of a cordless telephone each year. At the beginning of 1991, Rexburn developed optimal standards for the inputs used to produce the phone. At the end of the year, the optimal quantities of these inputs, the actual quantities, and the standard prices were made available.

Activity	Cost Driver	SQ	AQ	SP
Materials usage	Components	800,000	880,000	$ 50
Labor usage	Labor hours	125,000	160,000	10
Engineering	Engineering hours	25,000	30,000	25
Maintenance	Machine hours	60,000	70,000	20
Warranties	Number of defectives	—	6,000	110
Materials handling	Number of moves	400,000	800,000	4
Setups	Setup time	—	4,000	15
Other	Machine hours	60,000	70,000	12

Assume that the actual prices paid for the inputs are equal to the standard prices.

Required:

1. Calculate the actual cost per phone for 1991, including warranty costs.

2. Calculate the standard cost per phone for 1991.

3. Prepare a cost report that presents value-added, nonvalue-added, and actual costs for each of the inputs. Explain why setup costs and warranty are both classified as nonvalue-added costs.

4. For 1992, the company again expects to produce 400,000 units of the phone. Management has set a goal of reducing nonvalue-added costs by 25 percent (for each input). Prepare currently attainable standards for 1992. Explain how these standards would be used and discuss why they would be compatible with activity-based responsibility accounting.

5. Assume that the reductions envisioned for 1992 were achieved. Assume the same production of 400,000 phones for 1993. Management sets a goal of reducing nonvalue-added costs by another 20 percent for each input. Prepare currently attainable standards for 1993. How do currently attainable standards, as defined in this chapter, differ from the conventional definition? How does their use differ?

P18–10 **Cycle Time; Velocity; Product Costing** Silverman Company has a JIT system in place. Each manufacturing cell is dedicated to the production of a single product or major subassembly. One cell, dedicated to the production of guns, has four operations: machining, finishing, assembly, and qualifying (testing). The machining process is automated, using computers. In this process, the gun's frame, slide, and barrel are constructed. In finishing, sandblasting, buffing, and bluing are done. In assembly, the three parts of the gun are assembled along with the grip, the sight, the label, the magazine, and the clip. Finally, each firearm is tested using twenty rounds of ammunition.

For the coming year, the firearm cell has the following budgeted costs and cell time (both at theoretical capacity):

Budgeted conversion costs	$1,250,000
Budgeted raw materials	1,500,000
Cell time	2,000 hours
Theoretical output	30,000 guns

During the year, the following actual results were obtained:

Actual conversion costs	$1,250,000
Actual materials	1,300,000
Actual cell time	2,000 hours
Actual output	25,000 guns

Required:

1. Compute the velocity (number of guns per hour) that the cell can theoretically achieve. Now compute the theoretical cycle time (number of hours or minutes per gun) that it takes to produce one gun.

2. Compute the actual velocity and the actual cycle time.

3. Compute MCE. Comment on the efficiency of the operation.

4. Compute the budgeted conversion cost per minute. Using this rate, compute the conversion cost per gun if theoretical output is achieved. Using this measure, compute the conversion cost per gun for actual output. Does this product-costing approach provide an incentive for the cell manager to reduce cycle time? Explain.

P18–11   **Selection of Cost Drivers; Behavioral Considerations**   Assume that managers are rewarded according to their ability to control product costs and that cost drivers are used to assign costs to individual products. Listed below are a number of costs and some potential cost drivers:

	Cost Driver
Inspections	Inspection hours
	Number of inspections
	Direct labor hours
Setups	Number of setups
	Setup time
	Direct labor hours
Engineering	Engineering hours
	Direct labor hours
	Machine hours
Maintenance	Maintenance hours
	Direct labor hours
	Machine hours
Materials handling	Number of moves
	Number of subassemblies
	Machine hours
	Direct labor hours

Required:

1. For each cost category, identify the negative and positive behavioral consequences of the suggested cost drivers.

2. Indicate which cost driver you would choose for each cost category. Justify your choice.

P18–12 **Ethical Considerations** One of the standards of ethical conduct for management accountants is objectivity. Management accountants have a responsibility "to fully disclose all relevant information that could reasonably be expected to influence an intended user's understanding of reports, comments, and recommendations presented."[19] They are also required to communicate information fairly and objectively.

Required:

1. In view of the objectivity standard, are management accountants obligated ethically to prepare flexible budgets using multiple cost drivers?

2. Are management accountants obligated to spearhead the development and use of accounting-based performance reporting that reflects the objectives sought in a JIT environment?

3. Refer to the competence standard presented in the Appendix of Chapter 1. Does this standard have any bearing on the first two requirements?

---

[19]"Standards of Ethical Conduct for Management Accountants," SMA1C, National Association of Accountants, 10 Paragon Drive, Montvale, N.J., 1983.

PART 4

Special Topics

CHAPTER 19

Financial Statement Analysis

■ **LEARNING OBJECTIVES**

After reading Chapter 19, you should be able to

1. Explain why financial statement analysis is important.

2. Analyze financial statements using two forms of common-size analysis: horizontal analysis and vertical analysis.

3. Explain why historical standards and industrial averages are important for ratio analysis.

4. Calculate and use liquidity ratios to assess the ability of a company to meet its current obligations.

5. Calculate and use leverage ratios to assess the ability of a company to meet its long-term and short-term obligations.

6. Calculate and use profitability ratios to assess the extent to which a company's resources are being used efficiently.

7. Define and explain the key terms appearing at the end of the chapter.

SCENARIO

Patricia Benson, the new commercial loan officer, had requested a meeting with Doug Litster, the president of National Bank. Patricia had gained significant experience in the commercial loan business with a large, successful bank in a neighboring city. Doug had hired Patricia by offering her a large salary increase and the promise of an opportunity to become a vice-president within two to three years. Doug was concerned about the bank's performance in commercial loans and wanted someone to revamp the commercial loan department. Patricia requested the meeting to brief Doug on the problems she had encountered during her first month and to make some tentative recommendations for improvements.

"Doug, after examining the bank's portfolio of loans, I'm appalled at the sloppy procedures used to process commercial loan applications."

"I suppose this shouldn't surprise me," Doug remarked, "but can you give me some examples?"

"For every commercial loan application, our bank faces two major issues. First, should it grant the loan or not? Second, if the loan is granted, what specific controls can we build into the agreement? In the past, the first decisions were made on some very vague, informal criteria. Furthermore, none of our agreements has any financial controls."

"Patricia, I don't quite understand. We've always required our loan applicants to submit a current financial statement so that we could assess their financial capabilities, and we always have the standard late penalties and default provisions built into our agreements."

"It's not the submission of the financial statements that's the issue. It's the analysis of those statements. Currently, there are no guidelines for their analyses. It's essentially a seat-of-the-pants approach with a touch of favoritism. Loans are often approved because someone on the loan committee knows the applicant. More attention must be given to what the statements are saying and less to favoritism. I might also mention that what the applicant does after the loan is approved is critical. We do have the right to specify what default means, and, in my opinion, it should be more than just missing a payment. More control over the loans we make is needed. Our loan losses are excessive."

"I know that. That's why I hired you. I'm hoping for some major improvements. What do you have in mind?"

"Before any loan is approved, we must make a serious evaluation of the applicant's financial capabilities. Some specific financial ratios and other indicators need to be computed and used as aids in making a loan decision. Furthermore, we need to include certain ratios as part of the loan agreement. Falling below the ratio's specified minimum value or exceeding its specified maximum value is then used to define default. More careful screening and better control of the loans we make should decrease the loan losses we have been experiencing."

"Sounds good. After you identify the ratios and work with our contract people to refine the loan agreements, I want you to schedule some training seminars. I want all commercial loan officers in our branches trained to use this more formal approach."

TECHNIQUES FOR STATEMENT ANALYSIS

As the introductory scenario illustrates, the formal analysis of financial statements can provide important input for commercial loan managers in making loan decisions. By using ratio analysis, common-size analysis, and other techniques, loan managers can assess the creditworthiness of potential customers. The formal analysis of financial statements can also provide a means to exercise control over outstanding loans.

Managers of commercial loan departments, however, are not the only persons who can benefit from analysis of financial statements. Individuals interested in investing in a company and managers of the company to whom the financial statements belong need this skill as well. Investors need to analyze financial statements to assess the attractiveness of a company as a potential investment. Managers need to analyze their own financial statements so as to assess profitability, liquidity, debt position, and progress towards organizational objectives.

The analysis of financial statements is designed to reveal relationships among items on the financial statements and trends of individual items over time. By knowing these relationships and trends, users are in a better position to make sound judgments regarding the current or future performance of a company. The two major techniques for financial analysis are common-size analysis and ratio analysis.

COMMON-SIZE ANALYSIS

common-size analysis

horizontal analysis

vertical analysis

Common-size analysis expresses line items or accounts in the financial statements as percentages. The two major forms of common-size analysis are horizontal analysis and vertical analysis. **Horizontal analysis** expresses line items as a percentage of some prior-period amount; this approach allows the trend over time to be assessed. **Vertical analysis** expresses the line item as a percentage of some other line item for the same period. With this approach, within-period relationships can be assessed.

Horizontal Analysis

There are two major types of horizontal analysis. In the first, line items are expressed as a percentage of a base period amount. In the second, line items are expressed as a percentage of an amount from the immediately preceding period. Exhibits 19–1 and 19–2 illustrate these two types.

EXHIBIT 19–1
Base Period Horizontal Analysis: Simpson Company

	1990		1991		1992	
	Dollars	*Percent*	*Dollars*	*Percent*	*Dollars*	*Percent*
Net sales	$100,000	100%	$120,000	120.0%	$132,000	132.0%
Less: Cost of goods sold	(60,000)	100	(75,000)	125.0	(81,000)	135.0
Gross margin	$ 40,000	100	$ 45,000	112.5	$ 51,000	127.5
Less: Operating expenses	(20,000)	100	(24,000)	120.0	(29,000)	145.0
Less: Income taxes	(8,000)	100	(9,000)	112.5	(10,000)	125.0
Net income	$ 12,000	100	$ 12,000	100.0	$ 12,000	100.0

EXHIBIT 19–2
Preceding Year Horizontal Analysis: Simpson Company

	1990		1991		1992	
	Dollars	*Percent*	*Dollars*	*Percent*	*Dollars*	*Percent*
Net sales	$100,000	100%	$120,000	120.0%	$132,000	110.0%
Less: Cost of goods sold	(60,000)	100	(75,000)	125.0	(81,000)	108.0
Gross margin	$ 40,000	100	$ 45,000	112.5	$ 51,000	113.3
Less: Operating expenses	(20,000)	100	(24,000)	120.0	(29,000)	120.8
Less: Income taxes	(8,000)	100	(9,000)	112.5	(10,000)	111.1
Net income	$ 12,000	100	$ 12,000	100.0	$ 12,000	100.0

Notice that the base year in Exhibit 19–1 is 1990. All line amounts in subsequent years are compared to the amount in the base year. For example, 1992 sales are expressed as a percentage of 1990 sales. By comparing each subsequent amount to the base period, trends can be seen. The data reveal that sales have increased by 32 percent over the three years. With such a large increase in sales, many would expect net income likewise to experience a significant increase. The percentage analysis, however, shows that net income has shown no change from the base period. Net income has stayed flat because expenses and taxes have also increased; cost of goods sold has increased by 35 percent, operating expenses by 45 percent, and taxes by 25 percent. As a result of the percentage analysis, the manager of the company may decide to focus more attention on controlling costs.

Exhibit 19–2 provides the percentage changes on a year-to-year basis. This approach allows users of financial statements to assess the rate of change in line items. For example, the year-to-year analysis for Simpson Company reveals that cost of goods sold increased significantly from 1990 to 1991 (25 percent), but the rate of increase slowed considerably for the following year (only 8 percent). Finding out why the rates of increase differ may provide valuable information for future cost control. Both types of horizontal analysis can provide useful information for managerial purposes.

Vertical Analysis

While horizontal analysis involves relationships among items over time, vertical analysis is concerned with relationships among items within a particular time period. Vertical relationships are obtained by expressing an item within a financial statement as a percentage of some other item. Line items on income statements are often expressed as percentages of net sales; items on the balance sheet are often expressed as a percentage of total assets. Exhibit 19–3 illustrates vertical analysis with the same example used in Exhibits 19–1 and 19–2. Net sales is used as the base for computing percentages.

Although the main purpose of vertical analysis is to highlight relationships among components of a company's financial statements, changes in these relationships over time can also be informative. For example, even though Exhibits 19–1 and 19–2 reveal large increases of operating expenses over time, Exhibit 19–3 reveals that the relative amount of these expenses is actually very small. In 1990, operating expenses represented 20 percent of sales, whereas in 1992 they represented only 22 percent of sales.

Percentages and Size Effects

The use of common-size analysis makes comparisons more meaningful because percentages eliminate the effects of size. For example, if one company

EXHIBIT 19–3
Vertical Analysis Using Net Sales as the Base:
Simpson Company

	1990		1991		1992	
	Dollars	*Percent*	*Dollars*	*Percent*	*Dollars*	*Percent*
Net sales	$100,000	100%	$120,000	100.0%	$132,000	100.0%
Less: Cost of goods sold	(60,000)	60	(75,000)	62.5	(81,000)	61.4
Gross margin	$ 40,000	40	$ 45,000	37.5	$ 51,000	38.6
Less: Operating expenses	(20,000)	20	(24,000)	20.0	(29,000)	22.0
Less: Income taxes	(8,000)	8	(9,000)	7.5	(10,000)	7.6
Net income	$ 12,000	12	$ 12,000	10.0	$ 12,000	9.1

earns $100,000 and another company earns $1 million, which is the more profitable? The answer depends to a large extent on the assets employed to earn the profits. If the first company used an investment of $1 million to earn the $100,000, then the return expressed as a percentage of dollars invested is 10 percent ($100,000/$1,000,000). If the second company used an investment of $20 million to earn its $1 million, the percentage return is only 5 percent ($1,000,000/$20,000,000). By using percentages, it is easy to see that the first firm is relatively more profitable than the second.

A Cautionary Note   Because percentages abstract from size, a user must exercise caution in their interpretation, particularly when the numbers involved are small. If the base is small, small changes in line items can produce large percentage changes. For example, assume that a company's net income is $1,000 one year and $1,500 the following year. The percentage increase in net income is 50 percent. The rate of increase sounds impressive, but the company increased its total earnings by only $500.

▪ RATIO ANALYSIS

Ratio analysis is the second major technique for financial statement analysis. Ratios are fractions or percentages computed by dividing one account or line-item amount by another. For example, net income divided by net sales produces a ratio that measures the profit margin on sales.

Standards for Comparison

Ratios by themselves tell little about the financial well-being of a company. For meaningful analysis, the ratios should be compared with a standard. Only through comparison can someone using a financial statement assess the financial health of a company. Two standards are commonly used: the past history of the company and industrial averages.

Past History   One way to detect progress—or problems—is to compare the value of a ratio over time. Doing so allows trends to be assessed. Ratios measuring liquidity, for example, may be dropping over time, signaling a deteriorating financial condition. The company's management can use this information to take corrective action. Investors and creditors, on the other hand, may use this information to decide whether or not to invest money in the company.

Industrial Averages   Additional insight can be gained by comparing a company's ratios with the same ratios for other companies in the same business. To facilitate this comparison, a number of annual publications provide industrial figures. Dun and Bradstreet, for example, reports the median, upper quartile, and lower quartile for fourteen commonly used ratios for more than 900 lines of business. The title and publisher of some of the more common sources of industrial ratios are listed below.

1. *Key Business Ratios,* Dun and Bradstreet
2. *Standard and Poor's Industry Survey,* Standard and Poor's
3. *Annual Statement Studies,* Robert Morris Associates
4. *The Almanac of Business and Industrial Financial Ratios,* Prentice-Hall
5. *Dow Jones-Irwin Business and Investment Almanac,* Dow Jones-Irwin

Even though the industrial figures provide a useful reference point, they should be used with care. Companies within the same industry may use different accounting methods, which diminishes the validity of the average. Other problems such as small sample sizes for the industrial report, different labor markets, the impact of extreme values, and terms of sale can produce variations among companies within the same industry. The industrial statistics should not be taken as absolute norms but rather as general guidelines for purposes of making comparisons.

Classification of Ratios

liquidity ratios
leverage ratios

profitability ratios

Ratios can be classified into one of three general categories: liquidity, borrowing capacity or leverage, and profitability. **Liquidity ratios** measure the ability of a company to meet its current obligations. **Leverage ratios** measure the ability of a company to meet its long-term and short-term obligations. These ratios provide a measure of the degree of protection provided to a company's creditors. **Profitability ratios** measure the earning ability of a company. These ratios allow investors, creditors, and managers to evaluate the extent to which invested funds are being used efficiently.

Some of the more common and popular ratios for each category will be defined and illustrated. Exhibits 19–4 and 19–5 provide an income statement, a statement of retained earnings, and comparative balance sheets for Payne Company, a manufacturer of glassware. These financial statements provide the basis for subsequent analyses.

Liquidity Ratios

Liquidity ratios are used to assess the short-term debt-paying ability of a company. If a company does not have the short-term financial strength to meet its current obligations, it is likely to have difficulty meeting its long-term obligations. Accordingly, evaluation of the short-term financial strength of a company is a good starting point in financial analysis. Although there are numerous liquidity ratios, only the most common ones will be discussed in this section.

EXHIBIT 19–4

Payne Company

Income Statement
For the Year Ended December 31, 1992
(dollars in thousands)

	Amount	Percent
Net sales	$ 50,000	100.0%
Less: Cost of goods sold	(35,000)	70.0
Gross margin	$ 15,000	30.0
Less: Operating expenses	(10,000)	20.0
Operating income	$ 5,000	10.0
Less: Interest expense	(400)	0.8
Net income before taxes	$ 4,600	9.2
Less: Taxes (50%)[a]	(2,300)	4.6
Net income	$ 2,300	4.6

Payne Company

Statement of Retained Earnings
For the Year Ended December 31, 1992

Balance, beginning of period	$ 5,324
Net income	2,300
Total	$ 7,624
Less: Preferred dividends	(224)
Less: Dividends to common stockholders	(1,000)
Balance, end of period	$ 6,400

[a]Includes both state and federal taxes

current ratio **Current Ratio**   The **current ratio** is computed by dividing the current assets by the current liabilities:

$$\text{Current ratio} = \text{Current assets/Current liabilities}$$

Since current liabilities must be paid within an operating cycle (usually within a year) and current assets can be converted to cash within an operating cycle, the current ratio provides a direct measure of the ability of a company to meet its short-term obligations. Payne Company's current ratio for 1992 is computed below, using data from Exhibit 19–5.

$$\text{Current ratio} = \$22,000,000/\$12,000,000$$
$$= 1.83$$

EXHIBIT 19-5

Payne Company		

Comparative Balance Sheets
For the Years Ended December 31, 1991 and 1992
(dollars in thousands)

Assets

	1992	1991
Current assets:		
Cash	$ 1,600	$ 2,500
Marketable securities	1,600	2,000
Accounts receivable (net)	8,000	10,000
Inventories	10,000	3,000
Other	800	1,500
Total current assets	$22,000	$19,000
Property and equipment:		
Land	$ 4,000	$ 6,000
Building and equipment (net)	6,000	5,000
Total long-term assets	$10,000	$11,000
Total assets	$32,000	$30,000

Liabilities and Stockholders' Equity

	1992	1991
Current liabilities:		
Notes payable, short term	$ 3,200	$ 3,000
Accounts payable	6,400	5,800
Current maturity of long-term debt	400	400
Accrued payables	2,000	1,876
Total current liabilities	$12,000	$11,076
Long-term liabilities:		
Bonds payable, 10%	4,000	4,000
Total liabilities	$16,000	$15,076
Stockholder's equity:		
Preferred stock, $25 par, 7%	$ 3,200	$ 3,200
Common stock, $2 par	1,600	1,600
Additional paid-in capital[a]	4,800	4,800
Retained earnings	6,400	5,324
Total equity	$16,000	$14,924
Total liabilities and stockholders' equity	$32,000	$30,000

[a] For common stock only

To interpret Payne's current ratio, we need additional information. Does the ratio of 1.83 signal good or poor debt-paying ability? Many creditors use the rule of thumb that a 2.0 ratio is needed to provide good debt-paying ability. Based on this assessment, Payne does not have sufficient liquidity; however, this rule has many exceptions. For example, the industrial norm might be less than 2.0. Information on the ratio's trend is also helpful.

Suppose that the upper quartile, median, and lower quartile values of the current ratio for the glassware industry are 2.2, 1.7, and 1.3, respectively.[1] Payne's current ratio of 1.83 is above the median ratio for its industry, suggesting that Payne does not have liquidity problems. More than half of the firms in its industry have lower current ratios.

It is possible, however, that Payne's current ratio for 1992 is not representative of what usually happens. By comparing this year's ratio with ratios for prior years, some judgment about whether it is representative or not can be made. For example, if the ratio in prior years has been reasonably stable with values in the 1.7 to 1.9 range, this year's ratio is representative. If the ratio has been declining for the past several years, the company's financial position could be deteriorating.

A declining current ratio is not necessarily bad, particularly if it is falling from a high value. A high current ratio may signal excessive investment in current resources. Some of these current resources may be more productively employed by reducing long-term debt, paying dividends, or investing in long-term assets. Thus, a declining current ratio may signal a move toward more efficient utilization of resources. But a declining current ratio coupled with a current ratio lower than that of other firms in the industry supports the judgment that a company is having liquidity problems.

Quick or Acid-test Ratio   For many companies, inventory represents 50 percent or more of total current assets. (Payne Company's inventory represents 45 percent of its total current assets.) The liquidity of inventory is often less than that of receivables, marketable securities, and cash. Inventory may be slow moving, nearly obsolete, or even pledged in part to creditors. Because including inventory may produce a misleading measure of liquidity, it is often excluded in computing liquidity ratios. For similar reasons, other current assets, such as miscellaneous assets, are excluded.

quick or acid-test ratio   The **quick or acid-test ratio** excludes these nonliquid assets. It is computed by dividing only the most liquid assets (cash, marketable securities, and receivables) by current liabilities:

$$\text{Quick ratio} = (\text{Cash} + \text{Marketable securities} + \text{Receivables})/\text{Current liabilities}$$

---

[1]Although these ratios are assumed, they are, in fact, representative of what has occurred in the glassware industry in the past as reported by the Robert Morris Associates Annual Statement Studies.

For Payne Company, the quick ratio is calculated as follows (using data from Exhibit 19–5):

Quick ratio = ($1,600,000 + $1,600,000 + $8,000,000)/$12,000,000
= $11,200,000/$12,000,000
= 0.93

Payne's quick ratio reveals that it does not have the capability to meet its current obligations with its most liquid assets; a ratio of 1.0 is the usual standard. But half of the companies in the glassware industry have quick ratios below the value of 1.1. Moreover, the lower quartile value is 0.6. This suggests that Payne's quick ratio is at a reasonable level, with perhaps some attention needed to raise it somewhat.

Accounts Receivable Turnover Ratio The extent of Payne's liquidity problem can be further investigated by examining the liquidity of its receivables. If the liquidity of receivables is low, this would signal more difficulty since the quick ratio would be overstated. The liquidity of receivables is measured by the **accounts receivable turnover ratio.** This ratio is computed by dividing net sales by average accounts receivable.

accounts receivable turnover ratio

Accounts receivable turnover ratio = Net sales/Average accounts receivable

Average accounts receivable is defined as follows:

Average accounts receivables = (Beginning receivables
+ Ending receivables)/2

The accounts receivable turnover ratio can be taken further to determine the number of days the average balance of accounts receivable is outstanding before being converted into cash. This is found by dividing the days in a year by the receivables turnover ratio:

Turnover in days = 365/Receivables turnover ratio

Payne Company's accounts receivable turnover is computed as follows (using data from Exhibits 19–4 and 19–5):

Accounts receivable turnover = $50,000,000/$9,000,000[a]
= 5.56 times per year, or every
65.6 days (365/5.56)

[a]Average receivables = ($10,000,000 + $8,000,000)/2

Payne's receivables are held for almost 66 days before being converted to cash. Whether this is good or bad depends to some extent on what other companies in the industry are experiencing.

For glassware, assume the upper quartile, median, and lower quartile turnover ratios for 1992 to be 11, 7.5, and 5.3, placing Payne in the lower quartile for its industry. The low turnover ratio suggests a need for Payne's managers to modify credit and collection policies to speed up the conversion of receivables to cash. This need is particularly acute if a historical analysis shows a persistent problem or a trend downward.

Note that net sales were used to compute the turnover ratio. Technically, credit sales should be used; however, external financial reports do not usually break net sales into credit and cash components. Consequently, if a turnover ratio is to be computed by external users, net sales must be used. For many firms, most sales are credit sales and the computation is a good approximation. If sales are mostly for cash, liquidity is not an issue. In that case, the ratio provides a measure of the company's operating cycle.

Inventory Turnover Ratio Inventory turnover is also an important liquidity measure. The **inventory turnover ratio** is computed by dividing the cost of goods sold by the average inventory.

inventory turnover ratio

Inventory turnover ratio = Cost of goods sold/Average inventory

Average inventory is found as follows:

Average inventory = (Beginning inventory + Ending inventory)/2

The ratio tells an analyst how many times the inventory turns over during the year. The number of days inventory is held before being sold can be computed by dividing the number of days in a year by the turnover ratio:

Turnover in days = 365/Inventory turnover ratio

The inventory turnover ratio for Payne Company is computed below, using data from Exhibits 19–4 and 19–5.

Inventory turnover = $35,000,000/$6,500,000[a]
= 5.38 times per year, or every 67.8 days (365/5.38)

[a]Average inventory = ($3,000,000 + $10,000,000)/2

For the glassware industry in 1992, assume the upper quartile, median, and lower quartile turnover figures in days to be thirty-four, fifty-seven, and seventy-nine, respectively. Payne's turnover ratio is midway between the median and the lower quartile. The evidence seems to indicate that the turnover ratio is lower than it should be. A low turnover ratio may signal the presence of too much inventory or sluggish sales. More attention to inventory policies and marketing activities may be in order.

Leverage Ratios

When a company incurs debt, it has the obligation to repay the principal and the interest. Holding debt increases the riskiness of a company. Unlike other sources of capital (e.g., retained earnings or proceeds from the sale of capital stock), debt carries with it the threat of default, foreclosure, and bankruptcy if income does not meet projections. Both potential investors and creditors need to evaluate a company's debt position. A potential creditor may find that the amount of debt and debt-servicing requirements of a company make it too risky to grant further credit. Similarly, the company may be too risky for some potential investors. Leverage ratios can help an individual evaluate a company's debt-carrying ability.

times-interest-earned ratio

Times-Interest-Earned Ratio   The first leverage ratio uses the income statement to assess a company's ability to service its debt. This ratio, called the *times-interest-earned ratio,* is computed by dividing net income before taxes and interest by interest expense:

$$\text{Times-interest-earned} = (\text{Income before taxes} + \text{Interest expense})/\text{Interest expense}$$

Income before taxes must be *recurring* income; thus, unusual or infrequent items appearing on the income statement should be excluded in order to compute the ratio. Recurring income is used because it is the income that is available each year to cover interest payments.

The times-interest-earned ratio for Payne Company is computed below, using data from Exhibit 19–4.

$$\begin{aligned}\text{Times-interest-earned ratio} &= (\$4,600,000 + 400,000)/\$400,000 \\ &= \$5,000,000/\$400,000 \\ &= 12.5\end{aligned}$$

Since the assumed upper quartile for the glassware industry is 10.0 for 1992, Payne's time-interest-earned ratio is among the highest in its industry. Payne does not have a significant interest expense burden.

debt ratio

Debt Ratio   Investors and creditors are the two major sources of capital. As the percentage of assets financed by creditors increases, the riskiness of the company increases. The **debt ratio** measures this percentage. It is computed by dividing a company's total liabilities by its total assets:

$$\text{Debt ratio} = \text{Total liabilities}/\text{Total assets}$$

Since total liabilities are compared with total assets, the ratio measures the degree of protection afforded creditors in case of insolvency. Creditors often impose restrictions on the percentage of liabilities allowed. If this percentage is exceeded, the company is in default and foreclosure can take place.

The debt ratio for Payne Company is calculated as follows:

$$\text{Debt ratio} = \$16,000,000/\$32,000,000$$
$$= 0.50$$

Payne's debt ratio indicates that 50 percent of its assets are financed by creditors. Is this good or bad? How much risk will the stockholders allow? Will creditors be willing to provide more capital?

For guidance, we again turn to industrial figures. The upper quartile, median, and lower quartile figures for 1992 are 0.47, 0.55, and 0.69, respectively. With respect to industrial performance, Payne's debt ratio is not out of line. In fact, Payne is close to the upper quartile figure of 0.47. This may indicate that Payne still has the capability to use additional credit.

Profitability Ratios

Investors earn a return through the receipt of dividends and appreciation of the market value of their stock. Dividends and market price of shares are both related to the profits generated by companies. Since they are the source of debt-servicing payments, profits are also of concern to creditors. Managers also have a vested interest in profits. Bonuses, promotions, and salary increases are often tied to reported profits. Profitability ratios, therefore, are given particular attention by both internal and external users of financial statements.

Return on Sales   Return on sales is the profit margin on sales. It tells what
return on sales   percentage of each sales dollar is earned as net income. **Return on sales** is one measure of the efficiency of the firm, and it is computed by dividing net income by sales.

$$\text{Return on sales} = \text{Net income/Sales}$$

Payne Company's return on sales for 1992 can be calculated from data in Exhibit 19–4.

$$\text{Return on sales} = 2,300/50,000$$
$$= 0.046, \text{ or } 4.6\%$$

For the glassware industry, Payne's return on sales of 4.6 percent is somewhat below the median. However, other measures of profitability must be checked before Payne's managers can determine the reasons for the lower profit margin.

Return on Total Assets Return on assets measures how efficiently assets are used to generate profits. **Return on total assets** is computed by dividing net income plus the after-tax cost of interest by the average total assets:

$$\begin{aligned}\text{Return on total assets} &= \text{Operating income after taxes/Average} \\ &\qquad \text{total assets} \\ &= [\text{Net income} + \text{Interest expense } (1 - \text{Tax} \\ &\qquad \text{rate})]/\text{Average total assets}\end{aligned}$$

Average total assets is found as follows:

$$\text{Average total assets} = (\text{Beginning total assets} + \text{Ending total assets})/2$$

By adding back the after-tax cost of interest, this measure reflects only how the assets were employed; it does not consider the manner in which they were financed (interest expense is a cost of *obtaining* the assets, not a cost of *using* them).

For Payne Company, the return on assets for 1992 is computed using data from Exhibits 19–4 and 19–5.

$$\begin{aligned}\text{Return on total assets} &= [\$2,300,000 + (0.5 \times \$400,000)]/\$31,000,000^{a} \\ &= (\$2,300,000 + \$200,000)/\$31,000,000 \\ &= \$2,500,000/\$31,000,000 \\ &= 8.06\%\end{aligned}$$

[a] Average assets = ($30,000,000 + $32,000,000)/2

For the glassware industry, Payne's 8.06 percent return on total assets is about halfway between the lower quartile and the median return. This suggests that Payne's managers need to be more effective in using the company's assets.

Return on Common Stockholders' Equity Return on total assets is measured without regard to the source of invested funds. For common stockholders, however, the return they receive on their investment is of paramount importance. Of especial interest to common stockholders is how they are being treated relative to other suppliers of capital funds. The **return on stockholders' equity** provides a measure that can be used to compare against other return measures (e.g., preferred dividend rates and bond rates). This return is computed by dividing net income less preferred dividends by the average common stockholders' equity:

$$\begin{aligned}\text{Return on stockholders' equity} &= (\text{Net income} \\ &\qquad - \text{Preferred dividends})/\text{Average} \\ &\qquad \text{common stockholders' equity}\end{aligned}$$

Average equity is computed as follows:

Average common stockholders' equity = (Beginning common stockholders' equity + Ending common stockholders' equity)/2

Payne Company's return on common stockholders' equity is computed below, using data from Exhibits 19–4 and 19–5.

$$\text{Return on stockholders' equity} = (\$2,300,000 - \$224,000)/\$12,262,000^a$$
$$= \$2,076,000/\$12,262,000$$
$$= 16.93\%$$

[a]Average stockholders' equity = ($11,724,000 + $12,800,000)/2; this assumes that additional paid-in capital is all from common shareholders.

Compared with the bond return of 10 percent and the preferred dividend rate of 7 percent, common stockholders are faring quite well. Furthermore, since the industrial average is about 14 percent, the rate of return provided common stockholders is above average.

Earnings per Share   Investors also pay considerable attention to a company's profitability on a per-share basis. **Earnings per share** is computed by dividing net income less preferred dividends by the average number of shares of common stock outstanding during the period.

earnings per share

$$\text{Earnings per share} = (\text{Net income} - \text{Preferred dividends})/\text{Average common shares}$$

Average common shares outstanding is computed by taking a weighted average of the common shares for the period under study. For example, assume that a company has 8,000 common shares at the beginning of the year. At the end of the first quarter, 4,000 additional shares are issued. No other transactions take place during the period. The weighted average is computed as follows:

Outstanding Shares		*Weight*	*Weighted Shares*
First quarter	8,000	3/12	2,000
Last three quarters	12,000	9/12	9,000
Average common shares outstanding			11,000

For Payne Company, earnings per share is computed as follows (using data from Exhibits 19–4 and 19–5):

$$\text{Earnings per share} = (\$2,300,000 - \$224,000)/800,000$$
$$= \$2,076,000/800,000$$
$$= \$2.60$$

The 800,000 common shares are computed by dividing the total par value of common stock in Exhibit 19–5 by the $2 per-share figure. Since no stock was issued during 1992, the weighted average is simply the shares outstanding for the year. Since the median value for the industry is about $3.47 per share, Payne's earnings per share is somewhat low and may signal a need for management to focus on increasing earnings.

Although in principle the computation of earnings per share is straightforward, it can be complicated by the presence of convertible securities. If there are securities that can be converted to common stock, such as convertible preferred stock, convertible bonds, stock warrants, stock purchase rights, and contingent shares, then computing earnings per share using only outstanding common stock may be overly optimistic. By converting or exercising these securities, the number of common shares outstanding could reduce or dilute the earnings per share of common stock.

For example, assume that the preferred stock reported on Payne's balance sheet can be converted into common stock share for share. With 128,000 shares of preferred stock (Exhibit 19–5) converted, the earnings per share would be computed as follows:

$$\text{Earnings per share} = \$2,300,000/928,000$$
$$= \$2.48$$

Notice that both the denominator and the numerator increased. The denominator increased because the number of common shares outstanding increased with the conversion. The numerator increased because if the conversion took place, there would be no need to pay preferred dividends. Notice also that the earnings per share is diluted by $0.12, or 4.6 percent if the conversion were to occur.

According to Accounting Principles Board Opinion No. 15, companies with securities that dilute earnings per share by less than 3 percent have a simple capital structure. Companies with securities that dilute this measure by 3 percent or greater have a complex capital structure. A company with a simple capital structure can report earnings per share using only the common shares outstanding. If, however, a company has a complex capital structure, it must report two earnings per share figures: primary earnings per share and fully diluted earnings per share. **Primary earnings per share** includes common stock outstanding and common stock equivalents.[2] **Fully diluted earnings per share** includes common stock, common stock equivalents, and other potentially dilutive securities.

primary earnings per share

fully diluted earnings per share

The rules and detail associated with computing earnings per share for companies with complex capital structures are too involved for a meaningful discussion at an introductory level. The important thing to realize at this point

---

[2]According to APB Opinion No. 15, common stock equivalents are those securities that are in substance equivalent to common stock. Stock options and warrants are examples.

is that earnings per share can be affected by convertible securities. Users of financial statements should factor this into their evaluations of profitability.

price-earnings ratio

Price-Earnings Ratio   The **price-earnings ratio** is found by dividing the price per share by the earnings per share:

$$\text{Price-earnings ratio} = \text{Market price per share/Earnings per share}$$

Price-earnings ratios are viewed by many investors as important indicators of stock values. If investors believe that a company has good growth prospects, then the price-earnings ratio should be high. If investors believe that the current price-earnings ratio is low based on their view of future growth opportunities, the market price of the stock may be bid up.

Assume that the price per common share for Payne Company is $15. With this assumption, the price-earnings ratio can be computed.

$$\begin{aligned} \text{Price-earnings ratio} &= \$15/\$2.60 \\ &= 5.77 \end{aligned}$$

Thus, Payne's stock is selling for 5.77 times its current earnings per share. This ratio compares with an industrial median value of 6.3. Thus, Payne's price earnings ratio is lower than more than half of the firms in the industry.

dividend yield

Dividend Yield and Payout Ratios   The profitability measure called **dividend yield** is computed by dividing the dividends received per unit of common share by the market price per common share.

$$\text{Dividend yield} = \text{Dividends per share/Price per share}$$

By adding the dividend yield to the percentage change in stock price, a reasonable approximation of the total return accruing to an investor can be obtained.

For Payne Company, the dividend yield is computed below. This computation assumes that the market price per common share is $15, as before; the dividends per share can be computed from Exhibits 19–4 and 19–5.

$$\begin{aligned} \text{Dividend yield} &= \$1.25^{a}/\$15 \\ &= 8.33\% \end{aligned}$$

[a]Dividends per share = $1,000,000/800,000

dividend payout ratio

The **dividend payout ratio** is computed by dividing the total common dividends by the earnings available to common stockholders, as follows:

$$\begin{aligned} \text{Dividend payout ratio} = \text{Dividends/(Net income} \\ - \text{Preferred dividends)} \end{aligned}$$

The payout ratio tells an investor the proportion of earnings that a company pays in dividends. Investors who prefer regular cash payments instead of returns through price appreciation will want to invest in companies with a high payout ratio; investors who prefer gains through appreciation will generally prefer a lower payout ratio.

The dividend payout ratio for Payne Company is computed as follows:

$$\text{Dividend payout ratio} = \$1,000,000/(\$2,300,000 - \$224,000)$$
$$= \$1,000,000/\$2,076,000$$
$$= 0.48$$

The industrial median for the payout ratio is approximately 0.62. This reveals that Payne has a low payout ratio relative to other firms in the industry.

■ IMPACT OF THE JIT MANUFACTURING ENVIRONMENT

In the new manufacturing environment, reducing inventories and increasing quality are critical activities. Both activities are essential for many companies to retain their competitive ability. Accordingly, users of financial statements should have a special interest in ratios that measure a company's progress in achieving the goals of zero inventories and total quality.

As a company reduces its inventory, the inventory turnover ratio should increase dramatically. For example, one company increased its inventory turnover within eighteen months from 5.9 turns to 20 turns.[3] Traditionally, high inventory turnovers have had a negative connotation. It was argued that a high inventory turnover ratio might signal such problems as stockouts and disgruntled customers. In the new manufacturing environment, however, a high turnover ratio is viewed positively. High turnover is interpreted as a signal of success—of achieving the goal of zero inventories with all of the efficiency associated with that state (see Chapter 13).

As inventory levels drop, the current ratio is also affected. Without significant inventories, the current ratio will drop; in fact, it will approach the value of the quick ratio. Since many lenders require a 2.0 current ratio to grant and control a loan, some reevaluation of the use of this ratio is needed for customers with a JIT system. It may be necessary to rely more on the quick ratio or other alternative ratios (such as cash flow divided by current maturities of long-term debt).

A ratio that says something about quality is also desirable for JIT firms. The usual approach is to express quality costs as a percentage of sales. External users, however, may not have access to quality costs as a separate category. Warranty costs, returns and allowances, unfavorable material quantity variances, and other quality costs that are readily identifiable from the

---

[3]Gene Schwind, "Man Arrives Just in Time to Save Harley Davidson," *Material Handling Engineering* (August 1984), p. 28.

financial statement can be added. This sum can then be divided by sales to give the external users some idea of the company's capability in this important area. Tracking this ratio over time will reveal the progress that the company is making. As quality improves, quality costs as a percentage of sales should decline. (For a discussion of quality cost control, see Chapter 16.)

■ SUMMARY OF LEARNING OBJECTIVES

1. **Explain why financial statement analysis is important.** Financial statement analysis is an important activity for managers, creditors, and investors. Managers can identify both strengths and weaknesses and reveal areas for which particular attention is needed. Creditors need to evaluate carefully the financial statements of a company to make sound loan decisions and control outstanding loans. Investors can assess the risk and profitability associated with investing in a company.

2. **Analyze financial statements using two forms of common-size analysis: horizontal analysis and vertical analysis.** Common-size analysis expresses accounts or line items in financial statements as percentages, either horizontally, over time, or vertically, as compared to some other line item. Horizontal analysis allows an analyst to assess trends. Vertical analysis allows an analyst to assess relationships among financial statement items.

3. **Explain why historical standards and industrial averages are important for ratio analysis.** When using ratios for evaluation, it is important to have a standard against which the ratios can be compared. The most common standards are historical values and industrial values. By comparing ratio values against prior-period values or the values of other companies in the same industry, meaningful analysis becomes possible.

4. **Calculate and use liquidity ratios to assess the ability of a company to meet its current obligations.** Liquidity ratios are used to assess the short-term debt-paying ability of a company. Frequently used liquidity ratios include the current ratio, the quick or acid-test ratio, accounts receivable turnover, and inventory turnover. The computation of these ratios is summarized in Exhibit 19–6.

5. **Calculate and use leverage ratios to assess the ability of a company to meet its long-term and short-term obligations.** Leverage ratios measure the ability of a company to meet its long-term debt obligations. Frequently used leverage ratios include the times-interest-earned ratio and the debt ratio. The calculation of these ratios is given in Exhibit 19–6.

6. **Calculate and use profitability ratios to assess the extent to which a company's resources are being used efficiently.** Profitability ratios relate the firm's earnings to the resources used to create those earnings. Profitability ratios include return on sales, return on total assets, earnings per share, price-earnings ratio, dividend yield, and dividend payout. The formulas used to calculate these ratios can be found in Exhibit 19–6.

EXHIBIT 19–6
Summary of Ratios

	Formula
Liquidity ratios:	
Current ratio	Current assets/Current liabilities
Quick ratio	(Cash + Marketable securities + Receivables)/Current liabilities
Accounts receivable turnover	Net sales/Average receivables
Inventory turnover	Cost of goods sold/Average inventory
Leverage ratios:	
Times-interest-earned	(Income before taxes + Interest expense)/Interest expense
Debt ratio	Total liabilities/Total assets
Profitability ratios:	
Return on sales	Net income/Sales
Return on total assets	[Net income + Interest expense (1 − tax rate)]/Average total assets
Return on stockholders' equity	(Net income − Preferred dividends)/Average stockholders' equity
Earnings per share	(Net income − Preferred dividends)/Average common shares
Price-earnings ratio	Market price per share/Earnings per share
Dividend yield	Dividends per common share/Market price per common share
Dividend payout	Common dividends/(Net income − Preferred dividends)

■ KEY TERMS

Accounts receivable turnover ratio   A liquidity ratio found by dividing net sales by average accounts receivable; a measure of the liquidity of receivables. (p. 973)

Common-size analysis   Expressing accounts or line items in financial statements as percentages. (p. 965)

Current ratio   A liquidity ratio found by dividing current assets by current liabilities; a measure of a company's ability to meet short-term obligations. (p. 970)

Debt ratio   A leverage ratio found by dividing a company's total liabilities by its total assets; a measure of the percentage of assets financed by creditors. (p. 975)

Dividend payout ratio   A profitability ratio found by dividing the total common stock dividends by the earnings available to common stockholders. (p. 980)

Dividend yield   A profitability ratio found by dividing the dividends received per unit share by the market price per common share. (p. 980)

Earnings per share   A profitability measure found by dividing the difference of net income minus preferred dividends by the average number of shares of common stock outstanding during the period. (p. 978)

Fully diluted earnings per share One of two earnings per share figures required of a company with complex capital structure, which includes common stock, common stock equivalents, and other dilutive securities. (p. 979)

Horizontal analysis A type of common-size analysis that expresses line items or accounts as percentages of a prior-period amount so that trends over time can be assessed. (p. 965)

Inventory turnover ratio A liquidity ratio found by dividing cost of goods sold by average inventory. (p. 974)

Leverage ratios Ratios that measure the ability of a company to meet its short-term and long-term obligations. (p. 969)

Liquidity ratios Ratios that measure the ability of a company to meet its current obligations. (p. 969)

Price-earnings ratio A profitability ratio found by dividing the price per share by the earnings per share; a signal of a stock's value. (p. 980)

Primary earnings per share One of two earnings per share figures required of a company with a complex capital structure, which includes common stock and common stock equivalents. (p. 979)

Profitability ratios Ratios that measure the earning ability of a company. (p. 969)

Quick or acid-test ratio A liquidity ratio found by dividing the most liquid current assets by current liabilities. (p. 972)

Return on sales A profitability measure found by dividing the firm's net income by sales. Return on sales is also called the *profit margin*. (p. 976)

Return on stockholders' equity A profitability measure found by dividing the difference of net income minus preferred dividends by the average stockholders' equity. (p. 977)

Return on total assets A profitability measure found by dividing the sum of net income and the after-tax cost of interest by average total assets; a measure of how efficiently assets are used to generate profits. (p. 977)

Times-interest-earned ratio A leverage ratio found by dividing the sum of net income before taxes and interest expense by interest expense; an indication of a company's ability to meet interest payments. (p. 975)

Vertical analysis A type of common-size analysis that expresses a line item as a percentage of another line item for the same period so that within-period relationships can be assessed. (p. 965)

■ REVIEW PROBLEM

Manzle Manufacturing has just completed its second year of operations. The comparative income statements for these years are as follows:

	1991	1992
Sales revenue	$ 500,000	$ 800,000
Less cost of goods sold	(300,000)	(464,000)
Gross profit	$ 200,000	$ 336,000

	1991	*1992*
Operating expenses	(80,000)	(164,000)
Interest expense	(20,000)	(20,000)
Income before taxes	$100,000	$ 152,000
Taxes	(34,000)	(51,680)
Net income	$ 66,000	$ 100,320

Selected information from the balance sheet for 1992 is also given.

Current assets	$100,000
Long-term assets	400,000
Total assets	$500,000
Current liabilities	$ 80,000
Long-term liabilities	220,000
Total liabilities	$300,000
Common stock	$100,000
Retained earnings	100,000
Total equity	$200,000

The company had 100,000 shares of stock outstanding. At the end of 1992, a share had a market value of $1.80. The shares outstanding have not changed since the original issue. Dividends of $30,000 were paid in 1992. Total assets have not changed during 1992.

Required:

1. Using 1991 as a base period, express all line items of the income statements as a percentage of the corresponding base period item.

2. Express each line item of the two income statements as a percentage of sales.

3. Comment on the trends revealed by the computations in requirements 1 and 2.

4. Compute the following ratios for 1992:
   a. Current ratio
   b. Debt ratio
   c. Return on total assets
   d. Times-interest-earned
   e. Earnings per share
   f. Dividend yield

Solution:

1. Horizontal analysis:

	1991	*Percent*	*1992*	*Percent*
Sales	$ 500,000	100	$ 800,000	160.0
Cost of goods sold	(300,000)	100	(464,000)	154.7
Gross margin	$ 200,000	100	$ 336,000	168.0

continued on next page

	1991	Percent	1992	Percent
Operating expenses	(80,000)	100	(164,000)	205.0
Interest expense	(20,000)	100	(20,000)	100.0
Income before taxes	$100,000	100	$ 152,000	152.0
Taxes	(34,000)	100	(51,680)	152.0
Net income	$ 66,000	100	$ 100,320	152.0

2. Vertical analysis:

	1991	Percent	1992	Percent
Sales	$ 500,000	100.0	$ 800,000	100.0
Cost of goods sold	(300,000)	60.0	(464,000)	58.0
Gross margin	$ 200,000	40.0	$ 336,000	42.0
Operating expenses	(80,000)	16.0	(164,000)	20.6
Interest expense	(20,000)	4.0	(20,000)	2.5
Income before taxes	$ 100,000	20.0	$ 152,000	19.0
Taxes	(34,000)	6.8	(51,680)	6.5
Net income	$ 66,000	13.2	$ 100,320	12.5

3. The trends reflected by both the horizontal and vertical analyses are basically favorable. Sales have increased and, with the notable exception of operating expenses, expenses have not increased as rapidly as sales and have declined as a percentage of sales. Operating expenses, however, have more than doubled from 1991 to 1992 and have also increased as a percentage of sales.

4. Ratio computation:
   a. Current ratio = $100,000/$80,000 = 1.25
   b. Debt ratio = $300,000/$500,000 = 0.60
   c. Return on total assets = [$100,320 + $20,000(0.66)]/$500,000 = 22.7%
   d. Times-interest-earned ratio = $172,000/$20,000 = 8.6
   e. Earnings per share = $100,320/100,000 = $1.003 per share
   f. Dividend yield = $0.30/$1.80 = 16.7%

▪ QUESTIONS

1 Name the two major types of financial statement analysis discussed in this chapter.

2 What is horizontal analysis? Vertical analysis? Should both horizontal and vertical analyses be done? Why?

3 Explain how creditors, investors, and managers can use common-size analysis as aids in decision making.

4 What are liquidity ratios? Leverage ratios? Profitability ratios?

5 Why are standards needed in ratio analysis?

6 Identify two types of standards used in ratio analysis. Explain why it is desirable to use both types.

7   What are some of the limitations associated with the use of industrial standards for ratio analysis?

8   What information does the quick ratio supply that the current ratio does not?

9   Suppose that the accounts receivable turnover ratio of a company is low when compared to other firms within its industry. How would this information be useful to the managers of this company?

10 A high inventory turnover ratio provides evidence that a company is having problems with stockouts and disgruntled customers. Do you agree? Explain.

11 A loan agreement between a bank and a customer specified that the debt ratio could not exceed 60 percent. Explain the purpose of this restrictive agreement.

12 A bank has the policy not to grant loans to any manufacturing company that does not have a 2.0 current ratio. Should this policy be applied to all companies? Explain.

13 A manager decided to acquire some expensive equipment through the use of an operating lease even though a capital budgeting analysis showed that it was more profitable to buy than to lease. However, the purchase alternative would have required the issuance of some bonds. Offer some reasons that would explain the manager's choice.

14 Explain why an investor would be interested in a company's debt ratio.

15 Assume that you have been given the responsibility to invest some funds in the stock market to provide an annuity to an individual who has just retired. Explain how you might use the dividend yield and payout ratios to help you with this investment decision.

16 Explain how an investor might use the price-earnings ratio to value the stock of a company.

17 Why would investors and creditors be interested in knowing the dilutive effects of convertible securities on earnings per share?

18 Explain the significance of the inventory turnover ratio in a JIT manufacturing environment.

19 In a JIT manufacturing environment, the current ratio and the quick ratio are virtually the same. Do you agree? Why?

■ EXERCISES

E9–1   **Horizontal Analysis**   Fogel Company's income statements for the last three years are given below:

Fogel Company			

Income Statements
For the Years Ended December 31, 1990, 1991, and 1992

	1990	1991	1992
Sales	$ 2,000,000	$ 1,800,000	$ 1,700,000
Less: Cost of goods sold	(1,400,000)	(1,200,000)	(1,000,000)
Gross margin	$ 600,000	600,000	700,000

continued on next page

	1990	1991	1992
Less operating expenses:			
Selling expenses	(300,000)	(300,000)	(250,000)
Administrative expenses	(100,000)	(110,000)	(120,000)
Total operating expenses	$(400,000)	$(410,000)	$(370,000)
Net operating income	$ 200,000	$ 190,000	330,000
Less: Interest expense	(50,000)	(40,000)	(40,000)
Income before taxes	$ 150,000	$ 150,000	$ 290,000

Required:

1. Using 1990 as a base period, express all line items as percentages of the corresponding base period line item.

2. Express each line item as a percentage of the prior-period line item (except for 1990).

3. Comment on the trends revealed by the computations in requirements 1 and 2.

E19–2 **Vertical Analysis** Refer to the income statements in Exercise 19–1.

Required:

1. For each year, express each line item as a percentage of sales revenue.

2. Comment on the information conveyed by this analysis.

E19–3 **Liquidity Analysis** The following selected information is taken from the financial statements of Riflen Company for its most recent year of operations:

Beginning balances:	
Inventory	$200,000
Accounts receivable	300,000
Ending balances:	
Inventory	$250,000
Accounts receivable	400,000
Cash	100,000
Marketable securities (short term)	200,000
Prepaid expenses	50,000
Accounts payable	175,000
Taxes payable	85,000
Wages payable	90,000
Short-term loans payable	50,000

During the year, Riflen Company had net sales of $2.45 million. The cost of goods sold was $1.3 million.

Required:

1. Compute the following ratios:
   a. Current ratio
   b. Quick or acid-test ratio

    c. Accounts receivable turnover ratio (compute turnover in times per year as well as in days)

    d. Inventory turnover ratio (times per year and days)

2. Assume that the lower quartile, median, and upper quartiles for Riflen's industry are as follows for the ratios computed in requirement 1:

Current ratio: 1.4, 1.9, 3.3
Quick ratio: 0.6, 1.0, 1.9
Accounts receivable turnover: 5.3, 7.4, 11.0 times per year
Inventory turnover: 3.7, 6.2, 9.8 times per year

Assess the performance of Riflen relative to its industry.

E19–4   Leverage Ratios Timmins Company has just completed its third year of operations. The income statement is presented below.

Sales revenue	$ 2,460,000
Less: Cost of goods sold	(1,410,000)
Gross profit	$ 1,050,000
Less: Selling and administrative expenses	(710,000)
Operating income	$ 340,000
Less: Interest expense	(140,000)
Income before taxes	$ 200,000
Less: Income taxes	(68,000)
Net income	$ 132,000

Selected information from the balance sheet is also given below.

Current liabilities	$1,000,000
Long-term liabilities	1,500,000
Total liabilities	2,500,000
Common stock	$4,000,000
Retained earnings	750,000
Total equity	$4,750,000

Required:

1. Compute the following for Timmins Company:
    a. The times-interest-earned ratio
    b. The debt ratio

2. Assume that the lower quartile, median, and upper quartile values for debt and times-interest-earned ratios in Timmins' industry are as follows:

Times-interest-earned: 2.3, 5.4, 16.1
Debt: 2.4, 0.8, 0.5

How does Timmins compare to the industrial norms? Does it have too much debt?

E19-5   **Profitability Ratios**   The following information has been gathered for Leatroy Manufacturing:

Net income	$5,000,000
Interest expense	$400,000
Average total assets	$60,000,000
Preferred dividends	$400,000
Common dividends	$1,200,000
Average common shares outstanding	800,000
Average common stockholders' equity	$20,000,000
Market price per common share	$40

Assume that the firm has no common stock equivalents. The tax rate is 34%.

Required:

Compute the following for Leatroy Manufacturing:

1. Return on total assets
2. Return on common stockholders' equity
3. Earnings per share
4. Price-earnings ratio
5. Dividend yield
6. Dividend payout ratio

E19-6   **Horizontal Analysis**   Mike Sanders is considering the purchase of Kepler Company, a firm specializing in the manufacture of office supplies. To be able to assess the financial capabilities of the company, Mike has been given the company's financial statements for the two most recent years.

Kepler Company		
Comparative Balance Sheets		
Assets		
	This Year	*Last Year*
Current assets:		
Cash	$ 50,000	$100,000
Accounts receivable, net	300,000	150,000
Inventory	600,000	400,000
Prepaid expenses	25,000	30,000
Total current assets	$ 975,000	$680,000
Property and equipment, net	125,000	150,000
Total assets	$1,100,000	$830,000

Liabilities and Stockholders' Equity

	This Year	Last Year
Liabilities:		
Accounts payable	$ 400,000	$290,000
Short-term notes payable	200,000	60,000
Total current liabilities	$ 600,000	$350,000
Long-term bonds payable, 12%	100,000	150,000
Total liabilities	$ 700,000	$500,000
Stockholders' equity:		
Common stock (100,000 shares)	$ 200,000	$200,000
Retained earnings	200,000	130,000
Total stockholders' equity	$ 400,000	$330,000
Total liabilities and equity	$1,100,000	$830,000

Kepler Company

Comparative Income Statements

	This Year	Last Year
Sales	$ 950,000	$ 900,000
Less: Cost of goods sold	(500,000)	(490,000)
Gross margin	$ 450,000	$ 410,000
Less: Selling and administrative expenses	(275,000)	(260,000)
Operating income	$ 175,000	$ 150,000
Less: Interest expense	(12,000)	(18,000)
Income before taxes	$ 163,000	$ 132,000
Less: Taxes	(65,200)	(52,800)
Net income	$ 97,800	$ 79,200
Less: Dividends	(27,800)	(19,200)
Net income retained	$ 70,000	$ 60,000

Required:

Compute the percentage change for each item in the balance sheet and income statement. Comment on any significant trends.

E19–7 **Vertical Analysis** Refer to the financial statements for Kepler Company in Exercise 19–6.

Required:

1. Express each item in the asset section of the balance sheet as a percentage of total assets for each year.

2. Express each item in the liabilities and equity section as a percentage of total liabilities and equity for each year.

3. Express each item in the income statement as a percentage of sales for each year.

E19–8 **Liquidity Ratios** Refer to the financial statements for Kepler Company in Exercise 19–6.

Required:

1. Compute the following ratios for each year:
   a. Current ratio
   b. Quick ratio
   c. Receivables turnover (in days)
   d. Inventory turnover (in days)

2. Has the liquidity of Kepler improved over the past year?

3. Explain why industrial liquidity performance would be useful information in assessing Kepler's liquidity performance.

E19–9   **Leverage Ratios**   Refer to the financial statements for Kepler Company in Exercise 19–6.

Required:

1. Compute the following for each year:
   a. The times-interest-earned ratio
   b. The debt ratio

2. Does Kepler have too much debt? What other information would help in answering this question?

E19–10   **Profitability Ratios**   Refer to the financial statements for Kepler Company in Exercise 19–6. For the current year, the market price per share of common stock is $2.98. For last year, assets and equity were the same at the beginning and end of the year.

Required:

1. Compute the following for each year:
   a. Return on total assets
   b. Return on stockholders' equity
   c. Earnings per share
   d. Price-earnings ratio
   e. Dividend yield
   f. Dividend payout

2. Based on the analysis in requirement 1, would you invest in the common stock of Kepler Company?

E19–11   **Profitability Analysis**   Albion, Inc., provided the following information for its most recent year of operation: The tax rate is 40 percent.

Revenue	$100,000
Cost of goods sold	$ 45,000
Net income	$ 10,500
Interest expense	$ 350
Assets—beginning balance	$120,000
Assets—ending balance	$126,000
Preferred dividends	$ 300
Common dividends (paid December 31)	$ 8,000
Common shares outstanding—January 1	30,000
Common shares outstanding—December 31	40,000
Average common stockholders' equity	$ 55,000
Market price per common share	$ 12

Required:

1. Compute the following:
   a. Return on sales
   b. Return on assets
   c. Return on common stockholders' equity
   d. Earnings per share
   e. Price-earnings ratio
   f. Dividend yield
   g. Dividend payout ratio

2. If you were considering purchasing stock in Albion, Inc., which of the above ratios would be of most interest to you? Explain.

E19–12 Leverage Ratios Barrett, Inc., has been in business for five years and has provided the following data:

Income Statement	
Sales	$224,000
Cost of goods sold	(78,400)
Marketing and administrative expenses	(89,600)
Interest expense	(7,500)
Income taxes	(17,000)
Net Income	$ 31,500

Selected balance sheet information is as follows:

Current liabilities	$ 90,000
Long-term liabilities	110,000
Total liabilities	$200,000
Common stock	500,000
Retained earnings	450,000
Total equity	$950,000

Required:

1. Compute the times-interest-earned ratio.

2. Compute the debt ratio.

E19–13 Liquidity Analysis Refer only to the income statement for Barrett, Inc., in Exercise 19–12. Additional information is as follows:

	Beginning Balance	Ending Balance
Cash	$ 36,000	$ 41,000
Marketable securities	15,000	18,000
Accounts receivable	56,000	70,000
Inventory	110,000	150,000
Total current assets	$217,000	$279,000

continued on next page

	Beginning Balance	Ending Balance
Accounts payable	$15,000	$22,000
Wages payable	—	3,000
Short-term notes payable	80,000	65,000
Total current liabilities	$95,000	$90,000

Required:

Compute the following ratios using end-of-the-year data:

1. Current ratio
2. Quick ratio
3. Accounts receivable turnover ratio in times per year
4. Accounts receivable turnover ratio in days
5. Inventory turnover ratio in times per year
6. Inventory turnover ratio in days

▪ PROBLEMS

P19–1   **Comprehensive Ratio Analysis**   Roberta Chesser, commercial loan officer for First Family Bank, has been approached by Finley Manufacturing with a request for a large loan. Since Roberta is somewhat unfamiliar with the company and its industry, she has requested the most recent income statement and balance sheets for the past two years. In addition, she collected the following industrial statistics for some key ratios that she intends to calculate for Finley Company:

	Lower Quartile	Median	Upper Quartile
Current ratio	1.3	2.0	2.6
Quick ratio	0.9	1.2	1.5
Receivables turnover (days)	63.0	41.0	28.0
Inventory turnover (days)	101.0	63.0	29.0
Times-interest-earned	1.7	7.1	29.5
Debt ratio	0.7	0.4	0.2
Return on total assets	3.4	7.8	12.6
Return on common equity	7.8	15.8	23.9
Price-earnings ratio	4.2	6.2	11.7
Dividend payout	30.4	42.0	61.2

The financial statements submitted by Finley Manufacturing are as follows:

Finley Manufacturing

Income Statement
For the Year Ended December 31, 1991

Sales revenue	$ 650,000
Less: Cost of goods sold	(400,000)
Gross profit	$ 250,000

Less: Selling and administrative expenses	(80,000)
Operating income	$170,000
Less: Interest expense	(50,000)
Income before taxes	$120,000
Less: Income taxes	(48,000)
Net income	$ 72,000
Retained earnings, January 1, 1991	228,000
	$300,000
Less dividends:	
Preferred stock	(20,000)
Common stock	(30,000)
Retained earnings, December 31, 1991	$250,000

Finley Manufacturing

Comparative Statements of Financial Position

Assets

	1991	1990
Current assets:		
Cash	$ 50,000	$ 90,000
Marketable securities	100,000	50,000
Accounts receivable (net)	115,000	125,000
Inventories	95,000	85,000
Prepaid items	10,000	10,000
Total current assets	$ 370,000	$ 360,000
Property, plant, and equipment	1,230,000	1,340,000
Total assets	$1,600,000	$1,700,000

Liabilities and Equity

Current liabilities:		
Accounts payable	$ 143,000	$ 140,021
Short-term notes	80,000	140,000
Wages payable	20,421	35,000
Total current liabilities	$ 243,421	$ 315,021
Long-term bonds payable	900,000	950,400
Total liabilities	$1,143,421	$1,265,421
Equity:		
Preferred stock	40,000	40,000
Common stock (110,000 shares)	166,579	166,579
Retained earnings	250,000	228,000
Total equity	$ 456,579	$ 434,579
Total liabilities and equity	$1,600,000	$1,700,000

At the end of 1991, the price per common share of Finley's stock was $12.50.

Required:

1. Compute all of the ratios for Finley Manufacturing that appear in Roberta's list.

2. Using the ratios computed in requirement 1 and the industrial values, evaluate Finley's financial capabilities.

3. Suppose that Finley is requesting a five-year loan of $150,000. Would you grant the loan if you were Roberta? If you would agree to grant the loan, what restrictions would you build into the loan agreement?

P19–2   **Analysis of Accounts Receivable and Credit Policy**   Based on customer feedback, Ted Pendleton, manager of a company that produces photo supplies, decided to grant more liberal credit terms. Ted decided to allow customers to have sixty days before full payment of the account was required. From 1987 through 1989, the company's credit policy for sales on account was 2/10, n/30. In 1990, the policy of 2/10, n/60 became effective. By the end of 1992, Ted's company was beginning to experience cash-flow problems. Although sales were strong, collections were sluggish, and the company was having a difficult time meeting its short-term obligations.

Ted noted that the cash-flow problems materialized after the credit policy was changed and wondered if there was a connection. To help assess the situation, he gathered the following data pertaining to the collection of accounts receivable (balances are end-of-year balances; the 1987 balance was the same as that in 1986):

	1987	1988	1989	1990	1991
Accounts receivable	$100,000	$120,000	$100,000	$150,000	$190,000
Net credit sales	500,000	600,000	510,000	510,000	520,000

Required:

1. Compute the number of times receivables turned over per year for each of the five years. Also express the turnover in days instead of times per year.

2. Based on your computation in requirement 1, evaluate the effect of the new credit policy. Include in this assessment the impact on the company's cash inflows.

3. Assume that the industry has an average receivables turnover of six times per year. If this knowledge had been available in 1989, along with knowledge of the company's receivable turnover rate, do you think that Ted Pendleton would have liberalized his company's credit policy?

P19–3   **Restrictive Covenants and Managerial Choice of Accounting Procedures**   Treegreen Company, a manufacturer of paper products, borrowed $10 million from a bank in order to expand its production facilities. As part of the loan agreement, the company agreed to abide by the following restrictive covenants:

a. The debt ratio will not exceed 0.60.

b. The times-interest-earned ratio will be at least 5.0.

c. The dividend payout ratio will not exceed 0.30.

d. The current ratio will be at least 2.0.

If the company violates any of these covenants, the loan will be considered in technical default and the bank can take action.

Subsequent to the loan, the company issued some long-term bonds, which pushed the debt ratio to 0.57. In the year following the loan, economists projected a recession for the coming year. Planners for Treegreen factored the anticipated recession into the budget for the coming year and produced lower income figures. Because of this revision downward, the projected times-interest-earned ratio at the end of the year was 4.0, which would push the company into technical default. Additionally, decreased sales would force the company to make greater use of short-term credit, increasing current liabilities. Although this would not cause problems with the current ratio, it would force the debt ratio above 0.60, again creating a technical default on the bank loan.

Upon consulting the controller, the president of Treegreen discovered that accelerated depreciation and LIFO were used for external financial reporting. After further consultation, the president of Treegreen authorized the controller to switch to straight-line depreciation and to use FIFO for inventory valuation. Based on this decision to switch to alternative accounting procedures, the president was assured that technical default could be avoided.

Required:

1. Explain why the president's decision to switch from accelerated to straight-line depreciation and from LIFO to FIFO could solve Treegreen's potential problem of technical default. Specifically, identify the effect that the changes will have on the debt ratio and the times-interest-earned ratio.

2. Suppose that the Financial Accounting Standards Board issues a memorandum on a proposed new procedure that would force Treegreen to expense some costs that are currently being capitalized, thus lowering reported net income. What effect would this have on the company's debt ratio and its times-interest-earned ratio? Would you expect management to support or oppose the new standard?

3. Suppose that Treegreen is considering installing a JIT purchasing and manufacturing system. The company expects to reduce inventories to insignificant levels within one year. Unfortunately, if the other current assets and current liabilities are maintained at approximately the same level, this new system will drive the current ratio below the 2.0 default level. What would you advise the company to do in this situation?

P19–4 **Profitability Analysis for an Investment Decision** Suppose that you are considering investing in one of two companies, each in the same industry. The most recent income statements for each company and other relevant information are given below:

Income Statements (in thousands)		
	Company A	*Company B*
Sales	$ 50,000	$ 40,000
Less: Cost of goods sold	(30,000)	(26,000)
Gross margin	$ 20,000	$ 14,000
Less: Selling and administrative expenses	(15,000)	(7,000)
Operating income	$ 5,000	$ 7,000
Less: Interest expense	(1,000)	(3,000)
Income before taxes	$ 4,000	$ 4,000
Less: Taxes	(1,360)	(1,360)
Net income	$ 2,640	$ 2,640
Retained earnings	8,000	6,000
	$ 10,640	$ 8,640
Less: Dividends	(840)	(1,040)
Ending retained earnings	$ 9,800	$ 7,600

continued on next page

	Company A	Company B
Average total assets	$20,000,000	$22,000,000
Average common equity	10,000,000	13,000,000
Average common shares	1,000,000	1,200,000
Average preferred shares[a]	300,000	100,000
Market price per common share	5.00	9.80

[a]For both Company A and Company B, the preferred dividend is $1 per share. Company A's preferred stock is convertible to common stock at a rate of two common shares for one share of preferred. The preferred stock of Company B is not convertible.

Required:

1. Compute the following for each company:
   a. Primary earnings per share
   b. Fully diluted earnings per share
   c. Dividend yield ratio
   d. Dividend payout ratio
   e. Price-earnings ratio
   f. Return on total assets
   g. Return on common equity

2. In which of the two companies would you invest? Explain.

P19–5 **Common-Size Analysis; Horizontal and Vertical Approaches; Ratio Analysis** Harrison Company has the following financial statements for the past three years:

Harrison Company

Comparative Income Statements
For the Years Ended June 30, 1991, 1990, and 1989
(in thousands)

	1991	1990	1989
Sales	$ 5,000	$ 4,500	$ 4,000
Less: Cost of goods sold	(2,500)	(2,500)	(2,700)
Gross margin	$ 2,500	$ 2,000	$ 1,300
Less: Selling and administrative	(750)	(800)	(750)
Income before taxes	$ 1,750	$ 1,200	$ 550

Harrison Company

Comparative Balance Sheets
June 30, 1991, 1990, and 1989
(in thousands)

Assets

	1991	1990	1989
Current assets:			
Cash	$ 50	$ 100	$110
Accounts receivable	1,200	1,000	800

Assets

	1991	1990	1989
Inventory	100	700	1,300
Total current assets	$1,350	$1,800	$2,210
Plant and equipment, net	1,650	1,200	1,000
Total assets	$3,000	$3,000	$3,210

Liabilities and Equity

	1991	1990	1989
Liabilities:			
Current liabilities	$ 900	$ 800	$ 800
Long-term liabilities	200	600	1,200
Total liabilities	$1,100	$1,400	$2,000
Stockholders' equity:			
Common stock	$ 500	$ 500	$ 500
Retained earnings	1,400	1,100	710
Total equity	$1,900	$1,600	$1,210
Total liabilities and equity	$3,000	$3,000	$3,210

At the end of 1989, Harrison installed a JIT purchasing and manufacturing system. Upon examining the performance of the company over the three-year period, the president of the company was generally pleased. He was especially impressed with the increase in net income. Since the installation of the JIT system, the company had identified areas for automation, but the major investment was yet to come. To finance it, the company planned to borrow $2 million from a local bank. The president was somewhat nervous about the upcoming meeting with the loan officer and requested that the controller develop an analysis of the financial statements that would help convince the loan officer of the company's creditworthiness.

Required:

1. Favorable trends in financial performance can be useful in presenting a loan request. Prepare a report that shows the trends for the line items in both the income statements and the balance sheets. Use vertical and horizontal relationships in developing the report. As part of the report, prepare arguments that support the company's loan request.

2. In addition to common-size analysis, ratio analysis can be used to support a loan application. Using the financial statements, prepare all of the ratios possible that may bear on the loan application. As part of the analysis, prepare arguments that support the loan application.

3. Upon reviewing the loan application, the loan officer is generally pleased with the financial position of the firm. However, she does express some concern about the current ratio and its trend and the high inventory turnover ratio. How would you respond to these observations?

P19–6 **Utilities; Return on Assets; Choice of Accounting Procedures** Regulatory bodies set rates of return that utilities are allowed to earn. These regulated rates determine the prices the utility can charge for its services. Typically the revenues that regulated utilities are allowed to earn are set according to the following formula:

$$\text{Revenues} = (\text{Operating expenses} + \text{Depreciation} + \text{Taxes})$$
$$+ (\text{Rate of return} \times \text{Total assets})$$

The price per unit of service is computed by dividing the total service units (e.g., kilowatt hours) into the expected revenues.

The rate of return, which is multiplied by total assets to produce the allowed net income, is set by the regulatory commission. Once the rate is set, the commission can be pressured to change it for two reasons: evidence that the utility company is making excessive profits and evidence that the utility company is incurring additional expenses, reducing the allowed net income. Consumer groups are typically behind any movement to reduce utility rates; the company is typically behind any movement to increase rates.

The revenue formula is usually set using generally accepted accounting procedures. Changes in accepted accounting procedures can work for or against the utility company.

Required:

1. A number of years ago, the tax law allowed an investment tax credit for new investments. Essentially, when a new asset was purchased, a percentage of its price (usually about 10 percent) could be used to reduce the acquiring firm's tax liability. In accounting for the tax credit, two positions emerged: the flow-through method and the amortization method. Under the flow-through method, the entire amount of the credit would be recognized immediately on the firm's income statement. Under the amortization method, the credit would be capitalized and amortized over the life of the asset. Which method would utility companies be likely to support? Consumer groups? Explain.

2. Assume that one utility company acquires another. Suppose that the accounting profession is debating two methods to account for business combinations. Under one method (the purchase method), the purchase price of the acquired company can be used to revalue the acquired company's assets by allocating the purchase price across its tangible assets. Under the second method (the pooling method), the assets of an acquired company are simply pooled with those of the acquiring company, using the book value of the assets of each company. Which method would utility companies likely support? Consumer groups? Explain.

P19–7 **Manipulation of Ratios and Ethical Behavior**   Pete Donaldson, president and owner of Donaldson Mining Supplies, was concerned about the firm's liquidity. He had an easy time selling supplies to the local coal mines but had a difficult time collecting the receivables. He had even tried offering discounts for prompt payment. The outcome wasn't as expected. The coal mines still took as long to pay as before but took the discount as well. Although he had complained about the practice, he was told that other suppliers would provide the supplies for the same terms. Collections were so slow that he was unable to pay his own payables on time and was receiving considerable pressure from his own creditors.

The solution was a line of credit that could be used to smooth his payment patterns. Getting the line of credit was another matter, however. One bank had turned him down, indicating that he already had too much debt and that his short-term liquidity ratios were marginal. Pete had begun the business with $5,000 of his own capital and a $30,000 loan from his father-in-law. He was making interest payments of $3,000 per year to his father-in-law with a promise to pay the principal back in five years (three years from now).

While mulling over his problem, Pete suddenly saw the solution. By changing accountants, he could tell the next accountant that the $30,000 had been donated to the business and therefore would be reclassified into the equity section. This would dramatically improve the debt ratio. He would simply not disclose the $3,000 annual payment—or he could call it a dividend. Additionally, he would not tell the next accountant about the $6,000 of safety gear that was now obsolete. That gear could be added back and the current ratio would also improve. With an improved financial statement, the next bank would be more likely to grant the needed line of credit.

Required:

1. Evaluate Pete Donaldson's ethical behavior.

2. Suppose that you have been hired as a part-time accountant for Donaldson's. You possess a CMA and belong to the IMA. You have been told that the $30,000 has been donated to the company. During the second week of your employment, the father-in-law drops in unexpectedly and introduces himself. He then asks you how the company is doing and wants to know if his $30,000 loan is still likely to be repaid in three years. Suppose also that same day you overhear an employee mention that the safety equipment is no longer usable because regulations now require a newer and different model.

   a. Assume that you have yet to prepare the financial statements for the loan application. What should you do? What standards of ethical conduct (listed in the Appendix of Chapter 1) apply to this situation?

   b. Suppose that the financial statements have been prepared and have been submitted to the bank. In fact, that morning, you received a call from the bank indicating that a decision was imminent and that the line of credit would likely be approved. What should you do under these circumstances?

3. Suppose that Pete invites you in as a consultant. He describes his problem to you. Can you think of a better solution?

P19–8   **Analysis of Ratios**   In 1989, Tesoro Company installed a JIT purchasing and manufacturing system. The new system revealed where robotics could be used effectively. However, before investing in robotics, the president of Tesoro wanted some assessment of the impact of the new system. The controller computed a number of financial and performance ratios for two years before and two years after the implementation of JIT.

	1987	1988	1989	1990	1991	Industrial Average
Current ratio	3.3	3.4	2.7	2.1	1.95	2.7
Quick ratio	2.0	1.9	1.9	1.9	1.9	1.2
Receivables turnover	12	12	13	14	16	10.7
Inventory turnover (days)	56	58	35	20	10	52.0
Debt ratio	0.3	0.4	0.4	0.5	0.55	0.50
Return on total assets	8%	8.2%	9.5%	10%	12%	8%
On-time deliveries	50%	51%	60%	70%	90%	—
Quality costs/sales	23%	24%	18%	16%	14%	—

Required:

1. Explain why the current ratio decreased significantly while the quick ratio remained constant.

2. Based on the ratios, do you think that Tesoro can afford to borrow the capital needed to finance the acquisition of robotics? Suppose that a potential creditor questions the decline of the current ratio. How can this be justified?

3. Why did the controller include such nontraditional ratios as on-time deliveries and quality as a percentage of sales?

4. Offer some explanations for the dramatic increase in return on total assets.

5. Do you think the JIT system may have had anything to do with the increase in the receivables turnover ratio? Explain.

6. Based on the ratios given on page 1001, what is your overall evaluation of the progress made by Tesoro?

P19–9 **Ratio and Trend Analysis**   Tierra Chemicals is involved in the production of agricultural chemicals. At the beginning of 1991, Linda Dees, owner and president of Tierra, set the following goals for the year:

Earnings per share	$3
Debt ratio	35%
Current ratio	2.5
Receivables turnover in days	36 days
Return on total assets	14%
Increase in sales	25%
Increase in net income	40%
Dividend payout ratio	40%

At the end of 1991, Linda assembled the following comparative financial statements in order to assess the progress made toward these goals:

Tierra Chemicals

Comparative Income Statements
For the Years Ended December 31, 1991 and 1990
(in thousands)

	1991	1990
Sales	$ 49,000	$ 40,000
Less: Cost of goods sold	(32,000)	(26,000)
Gross margin	$ 17,000	$ 14,000
Less: Selling and administrative expenses	(6,000)	(5,000)
Operating income	$ 11,000	$ 9,000
Less: Interest expense	(1,000)	(1,000)
Income before taxes	$ 10,000	$ 8,000
Less: Income taxes	(5,000)	(4,000)
Net income	$ 5,000	$ 4,000
Retained earnings (beginning)	6,000	4,000
	$ 11,000	$ 8,000
Less: Dividends	(2,000)	(1,000)
Retained earnings	$ 9,000	$ 7,000

Tierra Chemicals

Comparative Balance Sheets
December 31, 1991 and 1990
(in thousands)
Assets

	1991	1990
Current assets:		
Cash	$ 400	$ 800
Accounts receivable (net)	5,500	6,500
Inventory	6,000	3,000
Prepaid expenses	200	300
Total current assets	$12,100	$10,600
Plant and equipment, net	18,900	16,400
Total assets	$31,000	$27,000

Liabilities and Stockholders' Equity

	1991	1990
Liabilities:		
Current liabilities	$ 5,000	$ 3,000
Bonds payable	10,000	10,000
Total liabilities	$15,000	$13,000
Stockholders' equity:		
Common stock (2 million shares)	7,000	7,000
Retained earnings	9,000	7,000
Total equity	$16,000	$14,000
Total liabilities and equity	$31,000	$27,000

Required:

Compare the actual values achieved with the targeted values set by Linda at the beginning of 1991. Did Linda achieve most of her goals? Based on the data contained in the 1990 statements, were all of her goals realistic? Explain.

P19–10 **Loan Analysis**   Refer to the financial statements in Problem 19–9. Assume that Linda has approached a local bank with a request for a $5 million loan. To support her application, the financial statements for 1990 and 1991 were submitted. The following industrial median values have been gathered by the loan officer for the agricultural chemical industry:

Current ratio	1.9
Quick ratio	1.0
Debt ratio	45%
Times-interest-earned ratio	7.0
Receivables turnover (days)	45
Return on total assets	9%
Dividend payout ratio	23%
Return on common equity	16%

Required:

1. Prepare an analysis of Tierra Chemicals' request for a $5 million loan. Would you grant the loan?

2. Assume that you would grant the $5 million loan. What restrictions, if any, would you build into the loan agreement?

P19–11   **Horizontal Analysis**   Anna Teubner has just graduated from college and is working as a financial analyst for Big Blue, Inc. Anna is considering investing in Big Blue stock through the company's payroll deduction plan. First, however, she wants to learn as much about the company's financial health as possible. She has gotten the last few annual reports together and compiled the following data: All numbers are expressed in 1,000's.

Comparative Income Statements

	1990	1991	1992
Sales	$ 59,680	$ 62,710	$ 69,000
Cost of goods sold	(25,600)	(27,700)	(30,700)
Gross profit	34,080	35,010	38,300
Operating expenses	(25,200)	(28,100)	(27,200)
Interest expense	(700)	(1,000)	(1,300)
Earnings before taxes	8,180	5,910	9,800
Income taxes	(3,500)	(2,900)	(4,200)
Net income	$ 4,680	$ 3,010	$ 5,600

Balance Sheet Information

	1990	1991	1992
Assets:			
Current assets:			
Cash	$ 1,000	$ 1,740	$ 2,200
Marketable securities	4,000	6,000	6,300
Accounts receivable	20,000	21,000	26,490
Other accounts receivable	1,000	2,300	1,660
Inventory	9,000	10,450	10,100
Prepaid expenses	1,000	2,850	1,600
Long-term assets:			
Property, plant, and equipment	46,000	48,400	53,700
Less: Accumulated depreciation	(22,000)	(23,070)	(26,450)
Total assets	$ 60,000	$ 69,670	$ 75,600
Liabilities and equity:			
Current liabilities:			
Taxes	$ 2,500	$ 2,700	$ 3,200
Short-term debt	$ 9,500	10,900	13,200
Accounts payable	2,500	3,170	3,300
Compensation and benefits	2,500	2,800	3,000
Deferred income	—	1,390	2,475
Long-term debt:	8,000	11,900	10,800

	1990	*1991*	*1992*
Stockholders' equity:			
Capital stock	6,300	6,300	6,400
Retained earnings	28,700	30,510	33,225
Total liabilities and equity	$60,000	$69,670	$75,600

Required:

Express each item in the balance sheet and income statement as a percentage of 1990 items. Round calculations to two decimal places. Comment on any significant trends.

P19–12 Vertical Analysis   Refer to the financial statements for Big Blue in Problem 19–11.

Required:

1. Express each item in the asset section of the balance sheet as a percentage of total assets for each year. Round all computations to two decimal places.
2. Express each item in the liabilities and equity section as a percentage of total liabilities and equity for each year. Round all computations to two decimal places.
3. Express each item in the income statement as a percentage of sales for each year. Round all computations to two decimal places.

P19–13 Liquidity Ratios   Refer to the financial statements for Big Blue in Problem 19–11.

Required:

1. Compute the following ratios for each year (assume that the average receivables and average inventory for 1990 correspond to the reported amounts):
   a. Current ratio
   b. Quick ratio
   c. Receivables turnover in days
   d. Inventory turnover in days
2. Has Big Blue's liquidity improved over time?

P19–14 Leverage Ratios   Refer to the financial statements for Big Blue in Problem 19–11.

Required:

1. Compute the times-interest-earned ratio and the debt ratio for 1991 and 1992.
2. Assess Big Blue's ability to handle increased debt.

■ MANAGERIAL DECISION CASE

Ratio Analysis   (This case requires library research.) In 1978, the airline industry was deregulated. Airlines were free to choose their own routes and set their own fares. Additionally, entry into the industry by new airlines became much easier. Subsequent to deregulation, competition among the airlines intensified, and many less efficient airlines were driven out of business. With the intensified competition, concern about the attention to safety increased. Those concerned with safety argued that cost cutting by the airlines might extend to safety-related expenditures. Many believed that managers of airlines would be more concerned about increasing income and avoiding technical default on loan agreements than with safety.

As an example, critics could point to a March 1988 FAA report citing a prominent airline for deferring maintenance and flying aircraft in an unairworthy condition (a memo was discovered that actually told employees of the airline how to skirt time limits for repairs). By cutting back on maintenance expenses, airline managers could increase net income and decrease cash outflows. By increasing net income, assets and equity could be increased, reducing the possibility of violating debt ratio covenants. Or the freed-up cash could be used to reduce liabilities, also reducing the debt ratio.

Required:

1. Use information in *Moody's Transportation Manual* to compute the maintenance expense of any two airlines as a percentage of sales for the three years before and three years after deregulation. Plot the trend for the years examined. Based on the trend for these two airlines, is there any evidence that supports the critics' view that airline safety is being adversely affected by deregulation?

2. Compute the profitability and liquidity measures discussed in the chapter for the same two airlines before and after deregulation. Is there evidence that the financial position of either airline is deteriorating? Would you expect a correlation between deteriorating financial position and a tendency to decrease maintenance expenditures?

CHAPTER 20

Statement of Cash Flows

■ **LEARNING OBJECTIVES**

After studying Chapter 20, you should be able to

1. Explain why a statement of cash flows is important.

2. Describe the activity format for a statement of cash flows.

3. Compute the change in cash for a period.

4. Compute the cash flows from operating activities using either the indirect method or the direct method.

5. Identify the cash flows from investing activities.

6. Identify the cash flows from financing activities.

7. Prepare a statement of cash flows.

8. Prepare a statement of cash flows using a worksheet approach.

9. Define and explain the key terms appearing at the end of the chapter.

SCENARIO

The president of Golding Company, a manufacturer of large machinery, has called a meeting of the company's executive team to consider the purchase of a small company that produces one of the critical components used in the production of Golding's main product line. The following is the discussion that took place.

President: We have the opportunity to acquire Flemington, Inc., for the same offer we made two years ago. It appears to be a good buy and will contribute to our long-run objective of vertical integration. As you know, we've been trying for years to acquire a company that manufactures this particular component. I have a nagging suspicion, however, that there's a catch somewhere in this deal. I don't understand why the owner is so eager to sell now when a few years ago he was strongly opposed to any deal whatsoever. I wonder if the company is having cash-flow problems.

Vice-president of Operations: That's hard to believe. The income statements for the past several years show stable profits. The most recent balance sheet shows a small but positive cash balance. Furthermore, the financial statements also indicate that the working capital provided by operations has been fairly stable.[1]

Vice-president of Finance: The positive cash balance on the balance sheet really doesn't say much about the firm's cash flows—we know nothing about the sources and uses of cash during the reporting period. We need to be very cautious in our interpretation of stable profits and working capital. W. T. Grant, a national retail chain, reported stable profits and working capital from 1970 through 1973 yet during the same period was a net user rather than a provider of cash. It went bankrupt shortly thereafter.[2]

President: Flemington may or may not be in the same category as W. T. Grant, but I want to know more about its cash flows before we commit formally to any acquisition. I want to evaluate Flemington's current cash flows and assess its future cash-flow potential. If the firm is in a cash crisis, acquiring it will cost us more than the purchase price. We still may be able to work out a deal if a cash crisis exists but on much more favorable terms. I want a statement of cash flows from Flemington for each of the past five years of operations. In that statement, I want the cash flows from operations detailed as well as the cash flows from the firm's financing and investing activities.

---

[1]Working capital is the difference between current assets and current liabilities.

[2]James Largay and Clyde Stickney, "Cash Flows, Ratio Analysis, and the W. T. Grant Company Bankruptcy," *Financial Analysts Journal* (July-August 1980), pp. 51–55.

■ STATEMENT OF CASH FLOWS

As the dialogue reveals, cash-flow performance is an important input for the decision concerning the acquisition of Flemington, Inc. While the cash-flow performance of Flemington was the focus of the discussion, the cash-flow performance of Golding Company is also important. Golding's management needs to know the sources and uses of cash within its own company to assess its financing capabilities. Golding's management might raise a number of questions. Can Golding purchase Flemington using cash generated from operations? Will Golding need to borrow all or some of the needed cash? If borrowing is necessary, can the debt be serviced? Can some or all of the cash be raised by issuing additional capital stock?

statement of cash flows
Answers to these questions and others like them are not available in a company's income statement or balance sheet. A third financial statement— the **statement of cash flows**—does provide this information. All SEC– registered firms must issue a statement of cash flows.

Overview of the Statement

The statement of cash flows provides information regarding the sources and uses of a firm's cash. Activities that increase cash are sources of cash; they are referred to as *cash inflows.* Activities that decrease cash are uses of cash, referred to as *cash outflows.* The statement provides additional information by classifying cash flows into three categories.

cash inflows
cash outflows

1. Cash flows from operating activities
2. Cash flows from investing activities
3. Cash flows from financing activities

activity format
This classification, referred to as the *activity format,* is the format that should be followed in preparing a statement of cash flows.

operating activities
Operating activities are the ongoing, day-to-day, revenue-generating activities of an organization. These activities are the major source of internally generated cash. Cash inflows from operating activities come from the collection of sales revenues. Cash outflows are caused by payment for operating costs. The difference between the two produces the net cash inflow (or outflow) from operations.

investing activities
Investing activities are those activities that involve the acquisition or sale of long-term assets. Long-term assets may be productive assets or long-term activities.

financing activities
Financing activities are those activities that raise cash from outside sources (e.g., borrowing or issuing capital stock). These activities not only provide a source of cash but also involve a cash outflow. External parties who provide the resources for the company expect to receive the return *of* their

investment and a return *on* their investment. Thus, payment of dividends and retirement of debt and capital stock are examples of cash outflows. (Although interest payments could be seen as financing outflows, the statement includes these payments in the operating section.)

Major sources and uses of cash and the statement category in which they are reported are identified as follows:

Sources of Cash

1. Profitable operations (operating section)

2. Sales of long-term assets, for example, plant, equipment, and securities (investing section)

3. Long-term debt (financing section)

4. Capital stock (financing section)

Uses of Cash

1. Unprofitable operations (operating section)

2. Cash dividends (financing section)

3. Purchase of long-term assets, for example, plant, equipment, and securities (investing section)

4. Reduction of long-term debt (financing section)

5. Retirement of capital stock (financing section)

Occasionally, investing and financing activities take place without affecting cash. For example, land may be exchanged for common stock. These noncash transactions must also be disclosed, either as a part of the statement of cash flows itself or as a supplementary schedule. (The requirement to report noncash financing and investing activity is essentially an "all-financial-resources approach.") Since the major purpose of the statement is to provide cash-flow information, the noncash nature of these transactions should be identified and highlighted. The best way to do so is to report them not in the main statement but in a supplementary schedule.

Preparation of the Statement

Five basic steps are followed in preparing a statement of cash flows.

1. *Compute the change in cash for the period.* This figure is the difference between the ending and beginning cash balances shown on the balance sheets. It must equal the net cash inflow or outflow shown on the statement of cash flows.

2. *Compute the cash flows from operating activities.* Use the period's beginning and ending balance sheets and information about other events and trans-

actions to adjust the period's income statement to an operating cash-flow basis.

3. *Identify the cash flows from investing activities.* Use the period's beginning and ending balance sheets and information about other events and transactions to identify the cash flows associated with the sale and purchase of long-term assets.

4. *Identify the cash flows from financing activities.* Use the period's beginning and ending balance sheets to identify the cash flows associated with long-term debt and capital stock.

5. *Prepare the statement of cash flows based on the previous four steps.*

An example is needed to illustrate the specific details underlying the application of the five steps.

The comparative balance sheets and the income statement for Lemmons Company, a merchandising firm, are shown in Exhibit 20–1. Other information that will be needed follows:

1. Equipment with a book value of $50,000 was sold for $70,000. (The original cost of the equipment was $90,000.)

2. Dividends of $90,000 were declared and paid.

Step One: Compute the Change in Cash Flow From Exhibit 20–1, we see that cash increased by $95,000 in 1992. This number serves as a control figure for the statement of cash flows. The sum of the operating, investing, and financing cash flows must equal $95,000.

Step Two: Compute Operating Cash Flows Income statements are prepared on an accrual basis. Thus, revenues and expenses that involve no cash inflows and outflows may be recognized. Also, cash inflows and outflows that are not recognized on the income statement may occur. The accrual income statement can be converted to an operating cash-flow basis by making four adjustments to net income.

1. Add to net income any increases in current liabilities and decreases in noncash current assets.

2. Deduct from net income any decreases in current liabilities and increases in noncash current assets.

3. Add to or deduct from net income the remaining net income items that do not affect cash flows.

4. Eliminate any income items that belong in either the investing or financing section.

EXHIBIT 20–1

Lemmons Company

Comparative Balance Sheets
For the Years Ended December 31, 1991 and 1992

			Net Changes	
	1991	*1992*	*Debit*	*Credit*
Assets				
Cash	$ 45,000	$ 140,000	$ 95,000	
Accounts receivable	140,000	112,500		$ 27,500
Inventories	50,000	60,000	10,000	
Plant and equipment	400,000	410,000	10,000	
Accumulated depreciation	(200,000)	(210,000)		10,000
Land	200,000	287,500	87,500	
Total assets	$ 635,000	$ 800,000		
Liabilities and stockholders' equity				
Accounts payable	$ 120,000	$ 95,000	25,000	
Mortgage payable	—	100,000		100,000
Common stock	50,000	50,000		
Contributed capital in excess of par	100,000	100,000		
Retained earnings	365,000	455,000		90,000
Total liabilities and stockholders' equity	$ 635,000	$ 800,000	$227,500	$227,500

Lemmons Company

Income Statement
For the Year Ended December 31, 1992

Revenues	$ 480,000
Gain on sale of equipment	20,000
Less: Cost of goods sold	(260,000)
Less: Depreciation expense	(50,000)
Less: Interest expense	(10,000)
Net income	$ 180,000

Making these adjustments yields the cash flows from operating activities shown below:

Operating net income	$180,000
Add (deduct) adjusting items:	
Decrease in accounts receivable	27,500
Decrease in accounts payable	(25,000)

Increase in inventories	(10,000)
Depreciation expense	50,000
Gain on sale of equipment	(20,000)
Net cash from operating activities	$202,500

Five adjusting items are shown to compute operating cash flows for Lemmons Company. These five entries exhibit each of the four types of adjustments.

Decrease in Accounts Receivable A decrease in accounts receivable represents a decrease in a noncash current asset. It indicates that cash collections from customers were greater than the revenues reported on the income statement by the amount of the decrease. Thus, to compute the operating cash flow, the decrease must be added to net income. To understand fully why this amount is added back to net income, we can review the cash collection activity of Lemmons.

At the beginning of the year, the company reported accounts receivable of $140,000 (see Exhibit 20–1). This beginning balance represents revenues recognized during 1991 but not collected. During 1992, additional operating revenues of $480,000 were earned and recognized on the income statement (Exhibit 20–1). Lemmons Company, therefore, had a total cash collection potential of $620,000 ($140,000 + $480,000). Since the ending balance of accounts receivable was $112,500, the company collected cash totaling $507,500 ($620,000 − $112,500). The cash collected from operations was $27,500 greater than the amount recognized on the income statement ($507,500 versus $480,000)—an amount exactly equal to the decrease in accounts receivable. Thus, the change in accounts receivable can be used to adjust revenues from an accrual to a cash basis.

Decrease in Accounts Payable and Increase in Inventories The second adjusting item in the operating section reflects a decrease in accounts payable and the third an increase in inventories. Taken together, these two items adjust the cost of goods sold to a cash basis. A decrease in accounts payable means that cash payments to creditors were larger than the purchases made during the period; the difference is the amount that accounts payable decreased. The total cash payment made to creditors, therefore, is equal to the purchases plus the decrease in accounts payable. Since inventories increased, purchases are larger than the cost of goods sold by the amount that inventories increased. Thus, by deducting both the decrease in accounts payable and the increase in inventories, the cost of goods sold figure is increased to reflect the cash outflow for goods during the period.

The effect of the above adjustments is best illustrated with the actual figures from the Lemmons Company example. From Exhibit 20–1, the following statement of costs of goods sold can be prepared. (In this statement, goods available for sale and purchases are obtained by working backwards from cost of goods sold.)

Beginning inventory	$ 50,000
Purchases	270,000
Goods available for sale	$320,000
Less: Ending inventory	(60,000)
Cost of goods sold	$260,000

Adding purchases to the beginning balance in accounts payable (from Exhibit 20–1) yields the total potential payments to creditors: $390,000 ($270,000 + $120,000). Subtracting the ending balance of accounts payable (see Exhibit 20–1) from the total potential payments gives the total cash payments for the year: $295,000 ($390,000 − $95,000). By deducting the decrease in accounts payable ($25,000) and the increase in inventories ($10,000), an additional $35,000 is deducted, bringing the cost of goods sold figure from $260,000 to $295,000. This is the total cash payment for goods during 1992.

Depreciation Expense   While depreciation expense is a legitimate deduction from revenues to arrive at net income, it does not require any cash outlay. As a noncash expense, it should be added back to net income as part of the adjustment needed to produce operating cash flow.

Gain on the Sale of Equipment   The sale of long-term assets is a nonoperating activity and should be classified in the section that reveals the firm's investing activities. Furthermore, the gain on the sale of the equipment does not reveal the total cash received—it gives only the cash received in excess of the equipment's book value. The correct procedure is to deduct the gain and report the full cash inflow from the sale in the investing section of the statement of cash flows.

Step Three: Compute Investing Cash Flows   Investing activities include the purchase and sale of long-term assets (plant and equipment, land, and long-term securities). Lemmons Company had three investing transactions in 1992. These are summarized in the investing section below. An analysis of each transaction follows the section.

Sale of equipment	$ 70,000
Purchase of equipment	(100,000)
Purchase of land	(87,500)
Net cash from investing activities	$(117,500)

Sale of Equipment   As part of the other information relating to transactions and events during 1992, we learned that equipment with an original cost of $90,000 was sold for $70,000; its book value at the time of sale was $50,000. The receipt of the $70,000 should be reported in the investing section.

Purchase of Equipment   There is no explicit information concerning the purchase of equipment. The purchase is inferred from the comparative balance sheets shown in Exhibit 20–1, and the information pertaining to the sale of equipment (the fact that equipment originally costing $90,000 was sold and removed from the books). The purchase price of the new equipment can be computed by the following procedure:

Beginning plant and equipment	$400,000
Purchases of equipment	100,000
Less: Sale of equipment	(90,000)
Ending balance, plant, and equipment	$410,000

Thus, a cash purchase of equipment totaling $100,000 should be reported in the investing section. (*Note:* $40,000 of accumulated depreciation was deducted from the books, removing the accumulated depreciation associated with the equipment that was sold, and $50,000 was added to reflect the depreciation expense for 1992, giving a net increase of $10,000.)

Purchase of Land   The comparative balance sheets in Exhibit 20–1 reveal that land was purchased for $87,500. This transaction also should appear in the investing section.

Step Four: Cash Flows from Financing   Issuance of long-term debt or capital stock can produce cash inflows; retirement of debt or stock and payment of dividends produce cash outflows. The cash flows associated with the financing activities of Lemmons Company are listed below.

Issuance of mortgage	$100,000
Payment of dividends	(90,000)
Net cash flow from financing	$ 10,000

Issuance of Mortgage   The comparative balance sheets show that the only change in long-term debt and capital stock accounts is the apparent issue of a mortgage during 1992. The proceeds from this mortgage should be shown as a source of cash in the financing section.

Payment of Dividends   From information given on other transactions and events, we know that $90,000 in dividends were paid to stockholders. Since dividends represent a return on the funds provided by stockholders, this amount should be shown in the financing section.

Step Five: Prepare the Statement of Cash Flows   The outcomes of Steps 2, 3, and 4 correspond to the individual sections needed for the statement of cash flows. This statement is presented in Exhibit 20–2. Notice that the change in cash flow computed in Step 1 from the comparative balance sheets corresponds to the net increase in cash identified in the statement of cash flows. The computation produced by Step 1 serves as a control on the accuracy of Steps 2 through 4.

The Direct Method: An Alternative Approach

indirect method

direct method

The section of operating cash flows in Exhibit 20–2 computes cash flows by adjusting net income for items that do not affect cash flows. This approach is known as the **indirect method.** Some prefer to show operating cash flows as the difference between cash receipts and cash payments. To do so, each item on the accrual income statement is adjusted to reflect cash flows. The same adjustments and the same reasoning behind the indirect method are used to produce the operating cash flows; however, the presentation of the information is different. This approach, known as the **direct method,** is illustrated in Exhibit 20–3 using the Lemmons Company example. Either approach to computing and presenting operating cash flows may be used; which to use is a matter of preference.

EXHIBIT 20–2

Statement of Cash Flows
For the Year Ended December 31, 1992

Cash flows from operating activities:		
Net income	$ 180,000	
Add (deduct) adjusting items:		
Decrease in accounts receivable	27,500	
Decrease in accounts payable	(25,000)	
Increase in inventories	(10,000)	
Depreciation expense	50,000	
Gain on sale of equipment	(20,000)	
Net operating cash		$ 202,500
Cash flows from investing activities:		
Sale of equipment	$ 70,000	
Purchase of equipment	(100,000)	
Purchase of land	(87,500)	
Net cash from investing activities		(117,500)
Cash flows from financing activities:		
Issuance of mortgage	$ 100,000	
Payment of dividends	(90,000)	
Net cash from financing activities		10,000
Net increase in cash		$ 95,000

EXHIBIT 20-3
Alternative Presentation of Operating Cash Flows

	Income Statement	Adjustments	Cash Flows
Revenues	$ 480,000	$ 27,500[a]	$ 507,500
Gain on sale of equipment	20,000	(20,000)	—
Less: Cost of goods sold	(260,000)	(25,000)[b]	
		(10,000)[c]	(295,000)
Less: Depreciation expense	(50,000)	50,000	—
Less: Interest expense	(10,000)	—	(10,000)
Net income	$ 180,000		
Net operating cash			$ 202,500

[a]Decrease in accounts receivable
[b]Decrease in accounts payable
[c]Increase in inventories

Cash Equivalents

cash equivalents **Cash equivalents** are highly liquid investments such as Treasury bills, money market funds, and commercial paper. Many firms, as part of their cash management programs, invest their excess cash in these short-term securities. Because of their high liquidity, these short-term investments are treated as cash for the statement of cash flows. They should not be placed in the investing section; items targeted for that section must have a long-term orientation.

For example, suppose that a company has $100,000 of cash and $200,000 of marketable securities on its beginning balance sheet and $120,000 of cash and $310,000 of marketable securities on its ending balance sheet. The change in cash computed in Step 1 would not be $20,000 ($120,000 − $100,000). Marketable securities would also be viewed as cash and the change in cash for the period would include any change in the dollar value of marketable securities. Thus, the change in cash is $130,000 ([$120,000 − $100,000] + [$310,000 − $200,000]). Interest earned on marketable securities would be classified as revenues and would appear in the operating section as part of the net income figure.

■ A WORKING PAPER APPROACH TO THE STATEMENT OF CASH FLOWS

As transactions increase in number and complexity, a worksheet becomes a useful and almost necessary aid in preparing the statement of cash flows. One advantage of a worksheet is the fact that it uses a spreadsheet format, allowing the preparer to use a PC and spreadsheet software. Furthermore, a worksheet offers the user an efficient, logical means to organize the data needed to prepare a statement of cash flows. Although the worksheet itself is not the statement of cash flows, the statement can be easily extracted from the worksheet.

The use of a worksheet is best illustrated with an example. The comparative balance sheets of Portermart Company are presented in Exhibit 20–4. Other information pertaining to cash flows for Portermart in 1992 is given below.

1. Cash dividends of $10,000 were paid.

2. Equipment was sold for $8,000. It had an original cost of $30,000 and a book value of $15,000. The loss is included in operating expenses.

3. Land with a fair market value of $40,000 was acquired by issuing common stock with a par value of $10,000.

EXHIBIT 20–4

			Net Changes	
Portermart Company				
Comparative Balance Sheets *For the Years Ended December 31, 1991 and 1992*				
	1991	*1992*	*Debit*	*Credit*
Assets:				
Cash	$ 20,000	$ 20,000		
Marketable securities	70,000	163,000	$ 93,000	
Accounts receivable	55,000	60,000	5,000	
Inventory	80,000	55,000		$ 25,000
Plant and equipment	130,000	100,000		30,000
Accumulated depreciation	(65,000)	(60,000)	5,000	
Land	25,000	65,000	40,000	
Total assets	$315,000	$403,000		
Liabilities and stockholders' equity:				
Accounts payable	$ 40,000	$ 60,000		20,000
Wages payable	5,000	3,000	2,000	
Bonds payable	30,000	20,000	10,000	
Preferred stock (no par)	5,000	15,000		10,000
Common stock	50,000	60,000		10,000
Paid-in capital in excess of par	50,000	80,000		30,000
Retained earnings	135,000	165,000		30,000
Total liabilities and stockholders' equity	$315,000	$403,000	$155,000	$155,000

4. One thousand shares of preferred stock (no par) were sold for $10 per share.

5. The income statement for 1992 is as follows:

Sales	$ 400,000
Less: Cost of goods sold	(250,000)
Gross margin	$ 150,000
Less: Operating expenses	(110,000)
Net income	$ 40,000

The worksheet for preparing Portermart's statement of cash flows is shown in Exhibit 20–5. Notice that the worksheet is divided into two major sections, one corresponding to the balance sheet classifications and one corresponding to the classifications of the statement of cash flows. Four columns are needed: two for the beginning and ending balances of the balance sheet and two to analyze the transactions that produced the changes in cash flows. The columns for the analysis of transactions are the focus of the worksheet approach. Generally, a debit or credit in a balance-sheet column produces a corresponding credit or debit in a cash-flow column. Once all changes are accounted for, the statement of cash can be prepared.

Analysis of Transactions

The summary transactions on the worksheet will be explained by examining the items on the worksheet in order of their appearance (essentially equivalent to the numerical order of the entries). The entries are developed by considering each balance sheet item and the associated supplementary information.

Change in Cash   Entry 1 identifies the total change in cash during 1992.

(1)	Marketable securities	93,000	
	Net increase in cash		93,000

The actual cash balance remained the same from the beginning to the end of the year; however, the company increased its investment in short-term securities by $93,000. Since short-term securities are cash equivalents, the change is counted as a change in cash.

Change in Accounts Receivable   Entry 2 reflects the increase in accounts receivable.

(2)	Accounts receivable	5,000	
	Operating cash		5,000

EXHIBIT 20-5
Worksheet: Portermart Company

	1991	Debit		Credit		1992
		Transactions				
Assets:						
Cash	$ 20,000					$ 20,000
Marketable securities	70,000	(1)	$93,000			163,000
Accounts receivable	55,000	(2)	5,000			60,000
Inventory	80,000			(3)	$25,000	55,000
Plant and equipment	130,000			(4)	30,000	100,000
Accumulated depreciation	(65,000)	(4)	15,000	(5)	10,000	(60,000)
Land	25,000	(6)	40,000			65,000
Total assets	$315,000					$403,000
Liabilities and stockholders' equity:						
Accounts payable	$ 40,000			(7)	20,000	$ 60,000
Wages payable	5,000	(8)	2,000			3,000
Bonds payable	30,000	(9)	10,000			20,000
Preferred stock (no par)	5,000			(10)	10,000	15,000
Common stock	50,000			(11)	10,000	60,000
Paid-in capital in excess of par	50,000			(11)	30,000	80,000
Retained earnings	135,000	(13)	10,000	(12)	40,000	165,000
Total liabilities and stockholders' equity	$315,000					$403,000
Operating cash flows:						
Net income		(12)	40,000			
Depreciation expense		(5)	10,000			
Loss on sale of equipment		(4)	7,000			
Decrease in inventory		(3)	25,000			
Increase in accounts payable		(7)	20,000			
Increase in accounts receivable				(2)	5,000	
Decrease in wages payable				(8)	2,000	
Cash flows from investing:						
Sale of equipment		(4)	8,000			
Cash flows from financing:						
Reduction in bonds payable				(9)	10,000	
Payment of dividends				(13)	10,000	
Issuance of preferred stock		(10)	10,000			
Net increase in cash				(1)	93,000	
Noncash investing and financing activities:						
Land acquired with common stock		(11)	40,000	(6)	40,000	

Increasing accounts receivable means that revenues were recognized on the income statement but not collected. Thus, net income must be adjusted to show that cash inflows from revenues were less by this amount.

Decrease in Inventory   Entry 3 reflects the effect of a decrease of inventory on operating cash flow.

(3)	Operating cash	25,000	
	Inventory		25,000

Operating cash should be increased since a decrease in inventory would be included in the cost of goods sold but would not represent a cash outflow.

Sale of Equipment   The sale of equipment affects two balance sheet accounts and two cash-flow accounts. The effect is captured in Entry 4.

(4)	Operating cash	7,000	
	Cash from investing activities	8,000	
	Accumulated depreciation	15,000	
	Plant and equipment		30,000

Operating cash shows an increase because the loss on the sale is a noncash expense and should be added back to net income to arrive at the correct cash provided by operating activities. The equipment is sold for $8,000. This produces a cash inflow that is recognized as a cash flow from investing activities. The other two entries reflect the fact that the original cost of the equipment and the accumulated depreciation have been removed from the company's books.

Depreciation Expense   Entry 5 shows an increase in operating cash flow because depreciation expense, a noncash expense, is added back to net income.

(5)	Operating cash	10,000	
	Accumulated depreciation		10,000

Although the amount of depreciation expense is not explicitly given, it can be easily computed. The net decrease in the Accumulated Depreciation account is $5,000 (see Exhibit 20–4 or compare the beginning and ending amounts in Exhibit 20–5). The sale of the equipment decreased accumulated depreciation by $15,000 (accumulated depreciation removed is equal to original cost minus book value, or $30,000 − $15,000). Thus, the amount of depreciation expense recognized for the period must be $10,000. Depreciation expense increases accumulated depreciation—an increase of $10,000 and a decrease of $15,000 produces a net decrease of $5,000.

Land for Common Stock   In the noncash transaction that acquires land in exchange for common stock, three balance sheet accounts are affected. To balance the transactions columns, two separate entries are needed.

(6)	Land	40,000	
	Noncash investing activities		40,000
(11)	Noncash investing activities	40,000	
	Common stock		10,000
	Paid-in capital in excess of par		30,000

Accounts Payable   Entry 7 provides the adjusting entry for an increase in accounts payable.

(7)	Operating cash	20,000	
	Accounts payable		20,000

An increase in accounts payable means that some of the purchases were not acquired through the use of cash. Accordingly, the amount of the increase needs to be added back to net income.

Wages Payable   Wages payable decreased by $2,000 during 1992. This means that the company had a cash outflow $2,000 larger than the wage expense recognized on the income statement. Entry 8 reflects this $2,000 decrease.

(8)	Wages payable	2,000	
	Operating cash		2,000

Bonds Payable   Bonds payable decreased by $10,000, indicating a cash outflow belonging to the financing section. Entry 9 recognizes the reduction of debt and the associated cash outflow.

(9)	Bonds payable	10,000	
	Cash flow from financing activities		10,000

Preferred Stock   Entry 10 reflects the cash inflow that resulted from the issuance of preferred stock.

(10)	Cash flow from financing activities	10,000	
	Preferred stock		10,000

Net Income   Net income is assigned to the operating cash-flow section by Entry 12.

(12)	Operating cash	40,000	
	Retained earnings		40,000

Payment of Dividends   The payment of dividends is given in Entry 13.

(13)	Retained earnings	10,000	
	Cash flow from financing activities		10,000

The Final Step

Once the worksheet is completed, the final step in preparing the statement of cash flows is relatively straightforward. The lower half of the worksheet contains all of the sections needed. The debit column provides the cash inflows and the credit column the cash outflows. The noncash section is an exception; either column may be used to provide the information. The only additional effort needed is to compute subtotals for each section. The statement of cash flows for Portermart Company is shown in Exhibit 20–6 (p. 1024).

■ SUMMARY OF LEARNING OBJECTIVES

1. Explain why a statement of cash flows is important. Knowing a company's cash flows enables managers, investors, creditors, and others to assess more fully the economic strength and viability of the company by allowing the evaluation of the company's current cash flows and by assessing future cash-flow potential. Cash management is a particularly critical activity for any organization. The FASB, recognizing the need for cash-flow information, has recommended that all firms prepare a statement of cash flows. Public companies must prepare this statement as part of their required financial reporting.

2. Describe the activity format for a statement of cash flows. The activity format for a statement of cash flows has three sections: cash flows from operating activities, cash flows from investing activities, and cash flows from financing activities. It also reports noncash financing and investing activities.

3. Compute the change in cash for a period. The change in cash for a period is the difference between the beginning and ending balances of the cash account. The change in cash equivalents is also included in the change in cash.

4. Compute the cash flows from operating activities using either the indirect method or the direct method. Operating activities are the main revenue-generating activities engaged in by the organization. Operating cash flows are computed by adjusting the period's net income for noncash expenses, accrual effects, and nonoperating revenues or expenses.

EXHIBIT 20-6

Portermart Company

Statement of Cash Flows
For the Year Ended December 31, 1992

Operating cash flows:		
Net income	$40,000	
Add (deduct) adjusting items:		
Depreciation expense	10,000	
Loss on sale of equipment	7,000	
Decrease in inventory	25,000	
Increase in accounts payable	20,000	
Increase in accounts receivable	(5,000)	
Decrease in wages payable	(2,000)	
Net operating cash		$ 95,000
Cash flows from investing activities:		
Sale of equipment		8,000
Cash flows from financing activities:		
Reduction in bonds payable		$(10,000)
Payment of dividends		(10,000)
Issuance of preferred stock		10,000
Total cash flow from financing		(10,000)
Net increase in cash		$ 93,000
Investing and financing activities not affecting cash:		
Acquisition of land by issuing common stock		$ 40,000

---

5. Identify the cash flows from investing activities. Investing activities involve the acquisition and sale of long-term assets.

6. Identify the cash flows from financing activities. Financing activities involve raising outside capital through the issuance of debt and capital stock. Financing activities also involve the retirement of debt and capital stock.

7. Prepare a statement of cash flows. Preparing the statement of cash flows includes five basic steps: (1) computing the change in cash flows, (2) computing operating cash flows, (3) identifying investing cash flows, (4) identifying financing cash flows, and (5) assembling the data into a statement of cash flows. Preparation of the statement relies on the beginning and ending balance sheets and information regarding other activities and events that may not be fully apparent from the balance sheets themselves.

8. Prepare a statement of cash flows using a worksheet approach. Worksheets can be used to organize the preparation of the statement of cash flows. In addition to increased efficiency in form, worksheets offer the increased efficiency of the PC and spreadsheet software packages.

■ KEY TERMS

Activity format   A format for the statement of cash flows that reports cash flows for three categories: (1) cash flows from operating activities, (2) cash flows from investing activities, and (3) cash flows from financing activities. (p. 1009)

Cash equivalents   Highly liquid investments that are treated as cash. (p. 1017)

Cash inflows   Sources of cash. (p. 1009)

Cash outflows   Uses of cash. (p. 1009)

Direct method   A method for computing cash flows for operations that converts the accrual income statement to a cash income statement. (p. 1016)

Financing activities   Those activities that raise cash from outside sources and promise providers a return of their investment plus a return on their investment. (p. 1009)

Indirect method   A method for computing cash flows from operations by adjusting net income for items that do not affect cash flows. (p. 1016)

Investing activities   Those activities that involve the sale or purchase of long-term assets. (p. 1009)

Operating activities   The ongoing, day-to-day, revenue-generating activities of an organization. (p. 1009)

Statement of cash flows   A financial statement that lists the sources and uses of cash for a given period of time. The cash flows are organized in an activity format. (p. 1009)

■ REVIEW PROBLEM

The following balance sheets are taken from the records of Golding, Inc.:

Assets:	*1991*	*1992*
Cash	$130,000	$150,000
Accounts receivable	25,000	20,000
Plant and equipment	50,000	60,000
Accumulated depreciation	(20,000)	(25,000)
Land	10,000	10,000
Total assets	$195,000	$215,000
Liabilities and equity:		
Accounts payable	$ 10,000	$ 5,000
Bonds payable	8,000	18,000
Common stock	120,000	120,000
Retained earnings	57,000	72,000
Total liabilities and equity	$195,000	$215,000

Additional information is as follows:

a. Equipment costing $10,000 was purchased at year-end. No equipment was sold.

b. Net income for the year was $25,000; $10,000 in dividends were paid.

Required:

Prepare a statement of cash flows using the indirect method.

Solution:

1. Cash flow change: $150,000 − $130,000 = $20,000

2. Operating cash flows

Operating net income	$25,000
Add (deduct):	
Decrease in accounts receivable	5,000
Depreciation expense	5,000
Decrease in accounts payable	(5,000)
Net cash from operations	$30,000

3. Cash from investing activities for purchase of equipment is $(10,000).

4. Cash from financing activities

Payment of dividends	$(10,000)
Issuance of bonds	10,000
Net cash from financing	$ 0

5.

Golding, Inc.

Statement of Cash Flows
For the Year Ended 1992

Cash flows from operating activities:		
Net income	$ 25,000	
Add (deduct) adjusting items:		
Decrease in accounts receivable	5,000	
Depreciation expense	5,000	
Decrease in accounts payable	(5,000)	
Net operating cash		$ 30,000
Cash flows from investing activities:		
Purchase of equipment		(10,000)
Cash flows from financing activities:		
Payment of dividends	$(10,000)	
Issuance of bonds	10,000	
Net cash from financing		0
Net increase in cash		$ 20,000

QUESTIONS

1   Explain why the president of Golding in the scenario at the beginning of the chapter wanted information on Flemington's cash-flow performance.

2   The activity format calls for three categories on the statement of cash flows. Define each category.

3   Of the three categories on the statement of cash flows, which do you think provides the most useful information? Explain.

4   Explain what is meant by the all-financial-resources approach to reporting financing and investing activities.

5   Why is it better to report the noncash investing and financing activities in a supplementary schedule rather than to include these activities in the body of the statement of cash flows?

6   What are the five steps for preparing the statement of cash flows? What is the purpose of the first step?

7   What are cash equivalents? How are cash equivalents treated in preparing a statement of cash flows?

8   What are the advantages in using worksheets when preparing a statement of cash flows?

9   Explain how a company can report a positive net income and yet still have a negative net operating cash flow.

10   Explain how a company can report a loss and still have a positive net operating cash flow.

11   In computing the period's net operating cash flows, why are increases in current liabilities and decreases in current assets added back to net income?

12   In computing the period's net operating cash flows, why are decreases in liabilities and increases in current assets deducted from net income?

13   In computing the period's net operating cash flows, why are noncash expenses added back to net income?

14   If a machine costing $50,000 with a book value of $20,000 is sold for $30,000, describe the impact this transaction has on the operating and financing sections of the statement of cash flows.

15   Explain the reasoning for including the payment of dividends in the financing section of the statement of cash flows.

16   During the year, accounts receivable decreased from $120,000 to $100,000. Explain why this decrease is added to net income.

17   During the year, inventories increased by $25,000 and accounts payable decreased by $10,000. In computing net operating cash flows, what adjustments to net income will these changes cause? Explain.

18   During the year, a company issued $70,000 of preferred stock for equipment that had a fair market value of $70,000. Should this transaction be reported as part of the statement of cash flows? Explain.

19   The beginning and ending balances of wages payable are $38,000 and $52,000, respectively. Give the worksheet entry associated with this transaction.

20   Explain how the statement of cash flows can be prepared using the worksheet approach.

▪ EXERCISES

E20–1   **Activity Classification**   Classify each of the following transactions as an operating activity, an investing activity, or a financing activity. Also indicate whether the activity is a source of cash or a use of cash.

    a. A plant was sold for $750,000.

    b. A profit of $100,000 was reported.

    c. Long-term bonds were retired.

    d. Cash dividends of $350,000 were paid.

    e. Five hundred thousand shares of preferred stock were sold.

    f. A new robotic system was purchased.

    g. A long-term note payable was issued.

    h. A 40 percent interest in a company was purchased.

    i. A loss for the year was reported.

    j. Additional common stock was sold.

E20–2   **Adjustments to Net Income**   Indicate whether each of the events described below will be added to or deducted from net income in order to compute cash flow from operations.

    a. Amortization of a patent

    b. Increase in accounts receivable

    c. Decrease in prepaid insurance

    d. Depreciation expense

    e. Increase in accounts payable

    f. Uncollectible accounts expense

    g. Decrease in wages payable

    h. Increase in inventory

    i. Gain on sale of an asset

E20–3   **Adjustment for Prepaid Rent**   Jenkins Company showed $12,000 in Prepaid Rent on December 31, 1992. On December 31, 1993, the balance in the Prepaid Rent account was $14,400. Rent expense for 1993 was $30,000.

Required:

1. What was the amount of cash paid for rent in 1993?

2. What adjustment in prepaid expenses is needed if the indirect method is used to prepare Jenkins Company's statement of cash flows?

E20–4   **Operating Cash Flows**   The income statement for the Riobamba Merchandising Corporation appears below.

Sales		$375,000
Less: Cost of goods sold		
Beginning inventory	$100,000	
Purchases	200,000	
Ending inventory	(50,000)	(250,000)

Less: Depreciation expense	(25,000)
Less: Amortization of patent	(5,000)
Less: Wages expense	(20,000)
Less: Insurance expense	(10,000)
Income before taxes	$ 65,000
Less: Income taxes (all current)	(26,000)
Net income	$ 39,000

Other information is as follows:

a. Accounts payable decreased by $5,000 during the year.

b. Accounts receivable increased by $5,000.

c. All wages were paid at the beginning of the year; at the end of the year, wages payable had a balance of $3,000.

d. Prepaid insurance increased by $6,000 during the year.

Required:

Prepare a schedule that provides the operating cash flows for the year using the indirect method.

E20–5 **Operating Cash Flows; Direct Method**   Refer to the data given in Exercise 20–4.

Required:

Prepare a schedule of operating cash flows using the direct method.

E20–6 **Statement of Cash Flows**   Richmoon Corporation has the following comparative financial statements:

Richmoon Corporation		
Comparative Balance Sheets		
For the Years Ended December 31, 1992 and 1993		
	1993	1992
Assets:		
Cash	$ 9,000	$ 5,500
Accounts receivable, net	12,000	15,000
Inventory	6,000	3,000
Plant and equipment	20,000	20,000
Accumulated depreciation	(5,000)	(4,000)
Total assets	$42,000	$39,500
Liabilities and equity:		
Accounts payable	$ 2,000	$ 6,400
Common stock	23,000	21,200
Retained earnings	17,000	11,900
Total liabilities and equity	$42,000	$39,500

Richmoon Corporation	

Income Statement
For the Year Ended December 31, 1993

Sales	$ 33,000
Less: Cost of goods sold	(19,500)
Gross margin	$ 13,500
Less: Operating expenses	(6,500)
Net income	$ 7,000

Dividends of $1,900 were paid. No equipment was purchased or retired during the current year.

Required:

Using the indirect method, prepare a statement of cash flows.

E20–7   **Statement of Cash Flows**   Refer to the financial statements and other data in Exercise 20–6.

Required:

Using the direct method, prepare a statement of cash flows.

E20–8   **Operating Cash Flows**   During the year, Inmac Company earned a net income of $12,050. Beginning and ending balances for the year for selected accounts are given below:

	Account Balance	
	Beginning	*Ending*
Cash	$24,000	$30,000
Accounts receivable	15,000	21,500
Inventory	8,000	11,300
Prepaid expenses	6,000	4,000
Accumulated depreciation	18,000	19,500
Accounts payable	10,000	12,250
Wages payable	6,000	4,000

There were no financing or investing activities for the year. The above balances reflect all of the adjustments needed to adjust net income to operating cash flows.

Required:

Prepare a schedule of operating cash flows using the indirect method.

E20–9   **Statement of Cash Flows**   The financial statements given below were furnished by Betten Company.

Betten Company

Balance Sheets
For the Years Ended September 30, 1992 and 1993

	1992	1993
Assets:		
Cash	$11,000	$ 2,000
Marketable securities	500	1,500
Accounts receivable	3,800	4,800
Inventory	10,400	9,000
Plant and equipment	20,000	30,000
Accumulated depreciation	(5,000)	(8,000)
Total assets	$40,700	$39,300
Liabilities and equity:		
Accounts payable	2,400	1,600
Accrued wages	600	400
Common stock	25,000	25,000
Retained earnings	12,700	12,300
Total liabilities and equity	$40,700	$39,300

Betten Company

Income Statement
For the Year Ended September 30, 1993

Sales		$ 20,000
Less: Cost of goods sold		
Beginning inventory	$10,400	
Purchases	13,000	
Ending inventory	(9,000)	(14,400)
Less: Wages expense		(2,000)
Less: Advertising		(1,000)
Less: Depreciation expense		(3,000)
Net income (loss)		$ (400)

At the end of 1993, Betten purchased some additional equipment for $10,000.

Required:

Prepare a statement of cash flows using the indirect method.

E20–10 **Statement of Cash Flows; Direct Method** Refer to the data for the Betten Company in Exercise 20–9.

Required:

Prepare a statement of cash flows using the direct method.

E20-11 **Statement of Cash Flows** Parvis Company provided the following comparative financial statements:

Parvis Company

Balance Sheets
For the Years Ended December 31, 1991 and 1992

	1991	1992
Assets:		
Cash	$ 8,600	$ 1,700
Accounts receivable	26,900	25,200
Inventory	32,700	34,800
Plant and equipment	68,000	78,000
Accumulated depreciation	(30,000)	(34,000)
Total assets	$106,200	$105,700
Liabilities and equity:		
Accounts payable	23,150	22,150
Wages payable	15,000	10,000
Common stock	20,000	20,000
Retained earnings	48,050	53,550
Total liabilities and equity	$106,200	$105,700

Parvis Company

Income Statement
For the Year Ended December 31, 1992

Sales		$ 98,700
Less: Cost of goods sold		
Beginning inventory	$ 32,700	
Purchases	58,700	
Ending inventory	(34,800)	(56,600)
Less: Operating expenses		(36,600)
Net income (loss)		$ 5,500

Operating expense includes depreciation. During 1992, Parvis purchased equipment but did not sell any property, plant, or equipment.

Required:

Prepare a statement of cash flows using the indirect method.

E20-12 **Statement of Cash Flows; Direct Method** Refer to the data for the Parvis Company in Exercise 20-11.

Required:

Prepare a statement of cash flows using the direct method.

E20–13 **Cash Flow from Investing** During 1992, Danforth Company had the following transactions:

a. Purchased $50,000 of ten-year bonds issued by Martin, Inc.

b. Acquired land valued at $14,000 in exchange for machinery

c. Sold equipment with original cost of $90,000 for $55,000 and accumulated depreciation taken on the equipment to the point of sale was $30,000

d. Purchased new machinery for $40,000

e. Purchased common stock in Lemmons Company for $19,000

Required:

Prepare the net cash flow from investing activities of the statement of cash flows.

E20–14 **Cash Flow from Financing Activities** Hobart Company experienced the following during 1992:

a. Sold preferred stock for $98,000

b. Declared dividends of $50,000 payable on March 1, 1993

c. Borrowed $120,000 from bank on a two-year note

d. Purchased $25,000 of its own common stock to hold as treasury stock

e. Repaid five-year bonds issued in 1987 for $250,000 due in December

Required:

Prepare the net cash flow from financing activities of the statement of cash flows.

E20–15 **Operating Cash Flows** Daniels Company revealed the following information for the years 1992 and 1993:

Daniels Company

Income Statement
For the Year Ended December 31, 1993

Sales	$ 45,000
Cost of goods sold	(20,000)
Depreciation expense	(2,000)
Other expenses	(13,000)
Net income	$ 10,000

Daniels Company

Comparative Balance Sheets
As of December 31, 1992 and 1993

	1992	1993
Assets:		
Cash	12,000	29,800
Accounts receivable	3,700	4,600
Inventory	2,500	3,000

continued on next page

	1992	1993
Property, plant, and equipment	80,000	80,000
Accumulated depreciation	(8,000)	(10,000)
Land	10,000	23,500
Total assets	$100,200	$130,900
Liabilities and equity:		
Accounts payable	4,300	5,000
Mortgage payable	—	20,000
Stockholders' equity	95,900	105,900
Total liabilities and equity	$100,200	$130,900

Required:

Prepare a schedule that provides operating cash flows for the year 1993 using the indirect method.

E20–16 Operating Cash Flows   Refer to the data for the Daniels Company in Exercise 20–15.

Required:

Prepare a schedule that provides operating cash flows for the year 1993 using the direct method.

▪ PROBLEMS

P20–1 Statement of Cash Flows: Indirect Method   Booth Manufacturing has provided the following financial statements:

Booth Manufacturing

Comparative Balance Sheets
For the Years Ended December 31, 1992 and 1993

	1992	1993
Assets:		
Cash	$ 112,500	$ 350,000
Accounts receivable	350,000	281,250
Inventories	125,000	150,000
Plant and equipment	1,000,000	1,025,000
Accumulated depreciation	(500,000)	(525,000)
Land	500,000	718,750
Total assets	$1,587,500	$2,000,000
Liabilities and equity:		
Accounts payable	$ 300,000	$ 237,500
Mortgage payable	—	250,000
Common stock	75,000	75,000
Contributed capital in excess of par	300,000	300,000
Retained earnings	912,500	1,137,500
Total liabilities and equity	$1,587,500	$2,000,000

Booth Manufacturing

Income Statement
For the Year Ended December 31, 1993

Revenues	$1,200,000
Gain on sale of equipment	50,000
Less: Cost of goods sold	(640,000)
Less: Depreciation expense	(125,000)
Less: Interest expense	(35,000)
Net income	$ 450,000

Other information:

a. Equipment with a book value of $125,000 was sold for $175,000 (original cost was $225,000).

b. Dividends of $225,000 were declared and paid.

Required:

1. Calculate the cash flows from operations using the indirect method.

2. Prepare a statement of cash flows.

P20–2 **Statement of Cash Flows: Direct Method**   Refer to the information in Problem 20–1. Assume that all data are the same except that during 1993, common stock was exchanged for land with a fair market value of $60,000. This transaction changes the balance sheet for 1993 by increasing the Land account by $60,000 and the capital stock accounts by $60,000.

Required:

1. Calculate the operating cash flows using the direct method.

2. Prepare a statement of cash flows.

P20–3 **Statement of Cash Flows: Indirect Method**   The comparative balance sheets and income statement of Piura Company are as follows:

Piura Company

Comparative Balance Sheets
For the Years Ended June 30, 1991 and 1992

	1991	1992
Assets:		
Cash	$ 15,000	$ 16,000
Marketable securities	57,000	130,400
Accounts receivable	44,000	48,000
Inventory	64,000	44,000
Plant and equipment	104,000	112,000
Accumulated depreciation	(52,000)	(48,000)
Land	20,000	20,000
Total assets	$252,000	$322,400

continued on next page

	1991	1992
Liabilities and equity:		
Accounts payable	$ 32,000	$ 48,000
Wages payable	4,000	2,400
Bonds payable	24,000	16,000
Preferred stock (no par)	4,000	12,000
Common stock	30,000	36,000
Paid-in capital in excess of par	50,000	76,000
Retained earnings	108,000	132,000
Total liabilities and equity	$252,000	$322,400

Piura Company

Income Statement
For the Year Ended June 30, 1992

Sales	$ 320,000
Less: Cost of goods sold	(200,000)
Gross margin	$ 120,000
Less: Operating expenses	(88,000)
Net income	$ 32,000

Additional information for 1992 follows:

a. Cash dividends paid were $8,000.

b. Equipment was acquired by issuing common stock with a par value of $6,000. The fair market value of the equipment is $32,000.

c. Equipment with a book value of $12,000 was sold for $6,000. The original cost of the equipment was $24,000. The loss is included in operating expenses.

d. Two thousand shares of preferred stock were sold for $4 per share.

Required:

1. Prepare a schedule of operating cash flows using the following:
   a. The indirect method
   b. The direct method
2. Prepare a statement of cash flows using the indirect method.

P20–4   **Statement of Cash Flows; Worksheet**   Refer to the financial statements and other information pertaining to Piura Company in Problem 20–3.

Required:

Using a worksheet similar to the one shown in Exhibit 20–5, prepare a statement of cash flows.

P20–5   **Statement of Cash Flows: Indirect Method**   Balance sheets for Brierwold Corporation follow:

	Beginning Balances	Ending Balances
Assets:		
Cash	$ 100,000	$ 150,000
Accounts receivable	200,000	180,000
Inventory	400,000	410,000
Plant and equipment	700,000	690,000
Accumulated depreciation	(200,000)	(245,000)
Land	100,000	150,000
Total assets	$1,300,000	$1,335,000
Liabilities and equity:		
Accounts payable	$ 300,000	$ 250,000
Mortgage payable	—	110,000
Preferred stock	60,000	—
Common stock	240,000	280,000
Contributed capital in excess of par:		
Preferred stock	40,000	—
Common stock	360,000	420,000
Retained earnings	300,000	275,000
Total liabilities and equity	$1,300,000	$1,335,000

Additional information is given below.

a. Equipment costing $50,000 was purchased.

b. Equipment costing $60,000 with a book value of $25,000 was sold for $40,000.

c. Preferred stock was retired at a cost of $110,000. The premium is debited to retained earnings.

d. The company issued 10,000 shares of its common stock (par value, $4) for $10 per share.

e. The company reported a loss of $15,000 for the year.

f. Land was purchased for $50,000.

Required:

Prepare a statement of cash flows using the indirect method.

P20–6   **Statement of Cash Flows; Worksheet**   Refer to the financial statements and additional information concerning Brierwold Corporation in Problem 20–5.

Required:

Prepare a statement of cash flows using the worksheet approach.

P20–7   **Schedule of Operating Cash Flows: Direct Method**   The income statement for the Mendelin Corporation is as follows:

Revenues		$ 380,000
Less: Cost of goods sold		
Beginning inventory	$ 50,000	
Purchases	200,000	
Ending inventory	(34,000)	(216,000)
Less: Patent amortization		(20,000)
Less: Advertising		(12,000)
Less: Depreciation expense		(60,000)
Less: Wages expense		(30,000)
Less: Insurance expense		(10,500)
Less: Bad debt expense		(6,400)
Less: Interest expense		(7,600)
Net income		$ 17,500

Additional information is given.

a. Interest expense includes $1,800 of discount amortization.

b. The Prepaid Insurance expense account decreased by $2,000 during the year.

c. Accrued wages decreased by $3,000 during the year.

d. Accounts Payable increased by $7,500 (this account is for purchase of merchandise only).

e. Accounts receivable increased by $10,000 (net of allowance for doubtful accounts).

Required:

Prepare a schedule of operating cash flows using the indirect method.

P20–8   **Classification of Transactions**   Classify the following transactions as operating activities, investing activities, financing activities, or financing-investing activities not affecting cash. If an activity is an operating activity, indicate whether it will be added to or deducted from net income to compute cash from operations.

a. Payment of a cash dividend

b. Amortization of goodwill

c. Gain on disposal of equipment

d. Exchange of common stock for land

e. Increase in accrued wages

f. Retirement of preferred stock

g. Purchase of a new plant

h. Depreciation expense

i. Decrease in accounts payable

j. Increase in accounts receivable

k. Proceeds from the sale of land

l. Increase in prepaid expenses

m. Retirement of a bond

n. Purchase of a 60 percent interest in another company

P20-9 **Statement of Cash Flows** The following balance sheets are taken from the records of Blalock Company:

	1992	1993
Assets:		
Cash	$150,000	$185,000
Accounts receivable	70,000	80,000
Investments	—	30,000
Plant and equipment	100,000	105,000
Accumulated depreciation	(30,000)	(32,000)
Land	20,000	30,000
Total assets	$310,000	$398,000
Liabilities and equity:		
Accounts payable	$ 40,000	$ 50,000
Bonds payable	60,000	—
Mortgage payable	—	50,000
Preferred stock	20,000	—
Common stock	100,000	160,000
Retained earnings	90,000	138,000
Total	$310,000	$398,000

Additional information is as follows:

a. Equipment costing $12,000 with accumulated depreciation of $9,000 was sold for $2,000.

b. On December 31, bonds were retired at a price of $60,000.

c. Net income for the year was $68,000; cash dividends of $20,000 were paid.

Required:

Prepare a statement of cash flows using the indirect method.

P20-10 **Statement of Cash Flows; Worksheet** Refer to the balance sheets and other information given in Problem 20-9 concerning Blalock Company.

Required:

Prepare a statement of cash flows using the worksheet approach.

P20-11 **Statement of Cash Flows** Logan, Inc., provided the following information pertaining to the years 1991 and 1992:

Logan, Inc.

Comparative Statements of Financial Position
For the Years Ended December 31, 1991 and 1992

	1991	1992
Assets:		
Cash	$ 14,000	$ 85,300
Marketable securities	15,000	25,000
Accounts receivable	26,000	20,000
Inventory	13,000	15,700
Prepaid expenses	10,000	7,000
Property, plant, and equipment	150,000	100,000
Accumulated depreciation	(50,000)	(37,500)
Land	40,000	30,000
Total assets	$218,000	$245,500
Liabilities and equity:		
Accounts payable	19,000	15,000
Taxes payable	5,000	6,000
Bonds payable	45,000	25,000
Common stock	60,000	60,000
Retained earnings	89,000	139,500
Total liabilities and equity	$218,000	$245,500

Logan, Inc.

Income Statement
For the Year Ended December 31, 1992

Revenue	$130,000
Less: Cost of goods sold	(40,000)
Less: Loss on sale of equipment	(10,000)
Less: Operating expense	(17,500)*
Net Income	$ 62,500

*Includes depreciation

During 1992, Logan, Inc., sold equipment with an original cost of $60,000 and accumulated depreciation of $20,000 for $30,000. Logan acquired new equipment valued at $10,000 in exchange for a parcel of land costing $10,000. In addition, Logan paid off $20,000 of five-year bonds, and declared and paid dividends of $12,000.

Required:

Prepare a statement of cash flows for 1992 using the indirect method.

P20–12   **Operating Cash Flows**   Refer to the data provided for Logan, Inc., in Problem 20–11.

Required:

Prepare a statement of cash flows for 1992 using the direct method.

■ MANAGERIAL DECISION CASE

Management of Statement of Cash Flows; Ethical Issues   Fred Jackson, president of Bailey Company, was concerned about the company's ability to obtain a loan from a major bank. The loan was a key factor in the firm's plan to expand its operations. Demand for the firm's product was high, too high for the current production capacity to handle. Fred was convinced that a new plant was needed. To build the new plant, however, required an infusion of new capital. Fred called a meeting with Karla Jones, financial vice-president.

Fred: Karla, give us the status of our loan application. Do you think that the bank will approve?

Karla: Perhaps, but at this point, there is a real risk. The loan officer has requested a complete set of financials for this year and the past two years. He has indicated that he is particularly interested in the statement of cash flows. As you know, our income statement looks great for all three years, but the statement of cash flows will show a significant increase in receivables, especially for this year. It will also show a significant increase in inventory, and I'm sure that he'll want to know why inventory is increasing if demand is so great that we need another plant. Both of these effects show decreasing cash flows from operating activities.

Fred: Well, it is certainly true that cash flows have been decreasing. One major problem is the lack of operating cash. This loan will solve that problem. Bill Lawson has agreed to build the plant for the amount of the loan but will actually charge me for only 95 percent of the stated cost. We get 5 percent of the loan for operating cash. Bill is willing to pay 5 percent to get the contract.

Karla: The loan may help with operating cash flows, but we can't get the loan without showing some evidence of cash strength. We need to do something about the increases in inventory and receivables that we expect for this year.

Fred: The increased inventory is easy to explain. We had to work overtime and use subcontractors to take care of one of our biggest customers. That inventory will be gone by the first of next year.

Karla: The problem isn't explaining the inventory. The problem is that the increase in inventory decreases our operating cash flows and this shows up on the statement of cash flows. This effect coupled with the increase in receivables reveals us as being cash poor. It'll definitely hurt our chances.

Fred: I see. Well, this can be solved. The inventory is for a customer that I know well. She'll do me a favor. I'll simply get her to take delivery of the inventory early, before the end of our fiscal year. She can pay me next year as originally planned.

Karla: Fred, all that will do is shift the increase from inventory to receivables. It'll still report the same cash position.

Fred: No problem. We'll report the delivery as a cash sale and I'll have Bill Lawson advance me the cash as a temporary loan. He'll do that to get the contract to build our new plant. In fact, we can do the same with some of our other receivables. We'll report them as collected and I'll get Bill to cover. If he understands that this is what it takes to get the loan, he'll cooperate. He stands to make a lot of money on the deal.

Karla: Fred, this is getting complicated. The bank will have us audited each year if this loan is approved. If an audit were to reveal some of this manipulation, we could be in big trouble, particularly if the company has any trouble in repaying the loan.

Fred: The company won't have any trouble. Sales are strong and the problem of collecting receivables can be solved, especially given the extra time that the 5 percent of the loan proceeds will provide.

Required:

1. Discuss the propriety of the arrangement that Fred has with Bill Lawson concerning the disbursement of the proceeds from the loan.

2. Discuss the propriety of the actions that Fred is proposing to improve the firm's statement of cash flows. Suppose that there is very little risk that the loan will not be repaid. Does this information affect your assessment?

3. Assume that Karla is subject to the IMA code of ethics, described in the Appendix to Chapter 1. Identify the standards of ethical conduct that would be violated, if any, by Karla should she agree to cooperate with Fred's scheme.

4. If you were in Karla's position, what would you do (suppose that Fred insists on implementing his plan)? Now answer the question assuming that Fred is willing to consider alternative ways to solve the company's problems.

INDEX